www.wadsworth.com

www.wadsworth.com is the World Wide Web site for Wadsworth and is your direct source to dozens of online resources.

At *www.wadsworth.com* you can find out about supplements, demonstration software, and student resources. You can also send email to many of our authors and preview new publications and exciting new technologies.

www.wadsworth.com
Changing the way the world learns®

Abnormal Child Psychology

THIRD EDITION

Eric J. Mash
University of Calgary

David A. Wolfe
University of Toronto

Australia · Canada · Mexico · Singapore · Spain · United Kingdom · United States

THOMSON

WADSWORTH

Publisher: Vicki Knight
Psychology Editor: Marianne Taflinger
Assistant Editor: Dan Moneypenny
Editorial Assistant: Justin Courts
Technology Project Manager: Darin Derstine
Marketing Managers: Lori Grebe Cook, Chris Caldeira
Marketing Assistant: Laurel Anderson
Advertising Project Manager: Brian Chaffee
Senior Project Manager, Editorial Production: Paul Wells
Creative Director: Vernon Boes
Print/Media Buyer: Barbara Britton

Permissions Editor: Joohee Lee
Production: The Book Company
Text: Lisa Buckley Design
Photo Researcher: Myrna Engler
Copy Editor: Cathy Baehler
Illustrations: G&S Typesetters
Cover Designer: Tani Hasegawa
Cover Image: Timothy Shonnard/Getty Images
Cover Printer: Quebecor World/Taunton
Compositor: G&S Typesetters
Printer: Quebecor World/Taunton

Printed in the United States of America
1 2 3 4 5 6 7 08 07 06 05 04

For more information about our products, contact us at:
Thomson Learning Academic Resource Center
1-800-423-0563
For permission to use material from this text or product, submit a request online at http://www.thomsonrights.com. Any additional questions about permissions can be submitted by email to thomsonrights@thomson.com.

Library of Congress Control Number: 2004107966

Student Edition: ISBN 0-534-55419-9

Instructor's Edition: ISBN 0-534-55420-2

International Instructor's Edition: ISBN 0-534-55435-0

Thomson Wadsworth
10 Davis Drive
Belmont, CA 94002-3098
USA

Asia
Thomson Learning
5 Shenton Way #01-01
UIC Building
Singapore 068808

Australia/New Zealand
Thomson Learning
102 Dodds Street
Southbank, Victoria 3006
Australia

Canada
Nelson
1120 Birchmount Road
Toronto, Ontario M1K 5G4
Canada

Europe/Middle East/Africa
Thomson Learning
High Holborn House
50/51 Bedford Row
London WC1R 4LR
United Kingdom

Latin America
Thomson Learning
Seneca, 53
Colonia Polanco
11560 Mexico D.F.
Mexico

Spain/Portugal
Paraninfo
Calle Magallanes, 25
28015 Madrid, Spain

In loving memory of my parents,
Abe and Mary Mash
E.J.M.

To my father, Darrell Kenneth Wolfe,
for inspiring my desire to write;
and to my mother, Eleanor Gray Wolfe,
for her gift of compassion.
D.A.W.

About the Authors

Eric J. Mash completed his undergraduate studies at City University of New York, and his graduate work in Philadelphia and Florida. He earned his Ph.D. in clinical psychology at Florida State University in 1970. After completing his residency in clinical child psychology at the Oregon Health Sciences University in Portland, Oregon, he joined the faculty at the University of Calgary where he is currently a Professor in the Department of Psychology. He is a Fellow of the American and Canadian Psychological Associations and has served as an editorial board member and consultant for numerous scientific and professional journals and grant agencies at the local and federal levels. Eric's research interests are in abnormal child psychology, child and family assessment, child psychotherapy, and child development, and he has published many books and journal articles on these topics. He has studied interaction patterns in families with children with attention-deficit disorder and conduct problems, and in families in which children have been physically abused. Eric enjoys teaching undergraduate courses in abnormal child psychology, behavior modification, and child development, and graduate courses in clinical psychology including child psychopathology, child assessment, and child psychotherapy. When he is not working, Eric enjoys exploring the Canadian Rockies and walking on the beaches of Oregon with his wife, Heather, and dog, Sadie.

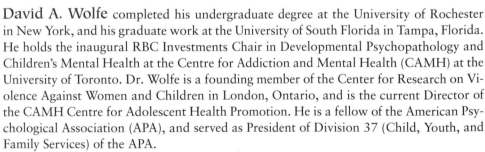

David A. Wolfe completed his undergraduate degree at the University of Rochester in New York, and his graduate work at the University of South Florida in Tampa, Florida. He holds the inaugural RBC Investments Chair in Developmental Psychopathology and Children's Mental Health at the Centre for Addiction and Mental Health (CAMH) at the University of Toronto. Dr. Wolfe is a founding member of the Center for Research on Violence Against Women and Children in London, Ontario, and is the current Director of the CAMH Centre for Adolescent Health Promotion. He is a fellow of the American Psychological Association (APA), and served as President of Division 37 (Child, Youth, and Family Services) of the APA.

David has broad research and clinical interests in abnormal child psychology, with a special focus on child abuse, domestic violence, and developmental psychopathology. He has authored numerous articles on these topics, especially in relation to the impact of early childhood trauma on later development in childhood, adolescence, and early adulthood. He is currently studying ways to prevent violence in relationships with adolescents. He enjoys teaching undergraduate courses in abnormal child psychology, child assessment and psychotherapy, and community psychology.

For joy and recreation, David spends his time with his wife and three children at their cottage on Georgian Bay, where they enjoy skiing, hiking, and boating.

Contents in Brief

Contents

PART V
Problems Related to Physical and Mental Health

Case Examples

Preface

Keeping up with the many exciting new developments in the rapidly growing field of abnormal child psychology is a challenging, yet rewarding, task, which has brought us to our third edition in only six years! We are extremely gratified by the positive reception to the previous editions of our book in the short time since they were released. We are fortunate in receiving helpful feedback from professors and students throughout this time, resulting in a comprehensive yet student friendly textbook. The third edition maintains its focus on the child, not just the disorders, while continuing to keep the text on the cutting edge of scholarly and practical advancements in the field.

We have completely updated this third edition to include important new developments such as recent findings on causes, subtypes, comorbidity, developmental pathways, risk and protective factors, gender, ethnicity, evidence-based treatments, and early intervention. At the same time, the text retains the hallmark features that make it one of the most successful texts in courses on child psychopathology, abnormal child psychology, developmental psychopathology, atypical development, and behavior disorders of childhood. Among these features are engaging first-person accounts and case histories designed to create powerful links between key topics and the experiences of individual children and their families.

Advances in Abnormal Child Psychology

The past few years have continued to produce extraordinary advances in understanding the special issues pertaining to abnormal child psychology. Today we have a much better ability to distinguish among different disorders of children and adolescents, which has given rise to increased recognition of poorly understood or undetected problems such as learning disorders, childhood depression and bipolar disorder, teen suicide and substance abuse, eating disorders, conduct disorders, and problems stemming from chronic health problems, abuse, and neglect. Similarly, the field is more aware of the ways children's and adolescents' psychological disorders are distinguishable from those of adults, and how important it is to maintain a strong developmental perspective.

In a relatively short time, the study of abnormal child psychology has moved well beyond the individual child and family to consider the roles of community, social, and cultural influences in an integrative and developmentally sensitive manner. Similarly, those of us working in this field are more attuned to the many struggles faced by children with psychological disorders and their families, as well as the demands and costs such problems place on the mental health, education, medical, and juvenile justice systems.

A Focus on the Child, Not Just the Disorders

We believe that one of the best ways to introduce students to a particular problem of childhood or adolescence is to describe a real child. Clinical descriptions, written in an accessible, engaging fashion, help students understand a child's problem in context, and provide a framework from which to explore the complete nature of the disorder. We introduce case examples of children with disorders in each chapter from our own clinical files and from those of colleagues. We then refer to these children when describing the course of the disorder, which provides the student with a well-rounded picture of the child in the context of his or her family, peers, and community.

In addition to clinical case material, we use extracts, quotes, and photos throughout each chapter to help the student remain focused on the real challenges faced by children with disorders and their families. First person accounts and case descriptions enrich the reader's understanding of the daily lives of children and adolescents with problems, and allow for a more realistic portrayal of individual strengths and limitations.

A Comprehensive and Integrative Approach

To reflect the expansion of this field, causes and effects of various childhood disorders are explained from an integrative perspective that acknowledges biological, psychological, social, and emotional influences and their interdependence. This strategy was further guided by a consideration of developmental processes that shape and are shaped by the expression of each disorder. The broader context of family, peers, school, community, culture, and society that effect development are also important considerations for understanding child and adolescent disorders, and are a critical feature of this text.

We use both categorical and dimensional approaches in describing disorders, because each method offers unique and important definitions and viewpoints. Each topic area is defined using DSM-IV-TR criteria, accompanied by clinical descriptions, examples, and empirically derived dimensions. The clinical features of each disorder are described in a manner that allows students to gain a firm grasp of the basic dimensions and expression of the disorder across the life span. Since children referred for psychological services typically show symptoms that overlap into more than one diagnostic category, each chapter discusses common comorbidities and developmental norms that help inform diagnostic decisions.

Developmental Pathways and Adult Outcomes

To provide balance we approach each disorder from the perspective of the whole child. Diagnostic criteria, therefore, are accompanied by an added emphasis on the strengths of the individual and environmental circumstances that influence the developmental course. Moreover, the developmental course of each disorder is followed from its early beginnings in infancy and childhood through adolescence and into early adulthood, highlighting the special issues pertaining to younger and older age groups and the risk and protective factors affecting developmental pathways. In this regard we examine developmental continuities and discontinuities, and attempt to understand why some children with problems continue to experience difficulties as adolescents and adults, whereas others do not.

Child Maltreatment and Relationship-Based Disorders

A distinguishing feature of this textbook is its expansion and emphasis on several of the more recent and important areas of developmental psychopathology that do not easily fit into a deficits model or a categorical approach. These problems are sometimes referred to as relationship-based disorders, because they illustrate the transactional nature of children's behavior in the context of significant relationships. Along with recognition of the importance of biological dispositions in guiding development and behavior, we discuss the strong connection between children's behavior patterns and the availability of a suitable child-rearing environment. Students are made aware of how children's overt symptoms can sometimes be adaptive in particular settings or with care-giving relationships that are atypical or abusive, and how traditional diagnostic labels may not be helpful.

Integration of Treatment and Prevention

Treatment and prevention approaches are integral parts of understanding a particular disorder. Applying knowledge of the clinical features and developmental courses of childhood disorders to benefit children with these problems and their families always intrigues students and helps them make greater sense of the material. Therefore, we emphasize current approaches to treatment and prevention in each chapter, where such information can be tailored to the particular childhood problem. Consistent with current health system demands for accountability, we emphasize interventions for which there is some empirical support.

Easy-to-Understand Organization

The book is organized into a five-part logical framework to facilitate an understanding of the disorders and mastery of the material. Following the introductory chapters, the contents can be readily assigned to the students in any order that suits the goals and preferences of the instructor:

I. Understanding Abnormal Child Psychology (definitions, theories, clinical description, research, assessment, and treatment issues);

II. Behavioral Disorders (attention-deficit/hyperactivity disorders and conduct problems);

III. Emotional Disorders (anxiety and mood disorders);

IV. Developmental and Learning Disorders (mental retardation, autism, childhood-onset schizophrenia, and communication and learning disorders);

V. Problems Related to Physical and Mental Health (health-related and substance use disorders, eating disorders, and child maltreatment and nonaccidental trauma).

Flexible, User-Friendly Chapters

Several important refinements have been incorporated into the text. Chapters are organized to allow instructors to consistently reduce the assignment of particular sections of each chapter (e.g., biological causes) that may not appeal to the level of their students, or eliminate particular sub-topics in a chapter (e.g., childhood-onset schizophrenia or pediatric bipolar disorder). For instructors wanting a more detailed presentation of research findings, *supplementary readings* can be drawn from the many up-to-date citations of original research.

We identify additional, but less critical, information that enhances each topic with the notation "*A Closer Look.*" In this manner, students can easily recognize that the material is presented to add further interest or examples to the major content areas of the chapter.

The chapter structure and organization provide many useful features: *key terms* are defined where they appear in the text, listed at the chapter's end, and defined in a separate glossary to help students grasp important terminology; *bulleted points* guide students to key concepts; and *chapter outlines* at the beginning of each chapter and *interim summaries* at the end of each section help students consolidate a chapter's key concepts.

DSM-IV-TR criteria have been shortened to their most essential elements.

The design and length of the text is completely student-centered and manageable, yet does not sacrifice academic standards of content and coverage.

Key Content Changes and Updates

Highlights of some of the key content changes and updates to this edition include:

The most current information concerning prevalence, age of onset, and gender distribution for each disorder.

Enriched coverage of gender and culture appears in each chapter, for example, exciting new findings related to sex differences in the expression and development of ADHD, conduct problems, and anxiety and mood disorders.

The most recent theories about developmental pathways for different disorders including the childhood precursors of eating disorders.

Integrative developmental frameworks for ADHD, conduct problems, anxiety disorders, and depression.

Exciting new findings on the interplay between early experience and brain development, for example, how early stressors, such as abuse, alter the brain systems associated with regulating stress and place the child at risk for developing later problems, such as anxiety or mood disorders.

New genetic discoveries for autism, ADHD, learning and communication disorders.

Findings from neuroimaging studies that illuminate neurobiological causes.

New information on family factors in externalizing and internalizing disorders, and developmental disabilities.

New findings on subtypes for disorders such as ADHD and conduct disorders.

Recent findings on the development of precursors of psychopathy.

Recent findings on patterns of use and misuse of medications for treating ADHD and childhood depression.

Most recent follow-up findings from groundbreaking early intervention and prevention programs such as Fast Track and the Multimodal Treatment Study for Children with ADHD.

A focus on evidence-based treatments helps students' overall comprehension. Treatment examples include:

- Behavior therapy and psychopharmacological treatments for ADHD in Chapter 5
- Parent management training, problem-solving skills training, and multi-systemic therapy for oppositional and conduct disorders in Chapter 6
- Cognitive behavior therapy, exposure, and modeling for anxiety disorders in Chapter 7
- Cognitive behavior therapy for depression in Chapter 8
- New treatments for autistic spectrum disorders in Chapter 10
- Treatment for child and adolescence substance abuse problems in Chapter 12
- Treatment outcome studies with anorexia and bulimia in Chapter 13

Added coverage on important, contemporary topics includes:

- Subtypes of disorders (for example, the predominantly inattentive subtype of ADHD)
- Temperament and personality disorders
- Parenting styles
- The stigma of mental illness
- Cases in prevention

Coverage of many significant reports from the surgeon general, the President's Freedom Commission, and others that will shape the future of research and practice in children's mental health.

Support organizations for parents and children are now listed in the instructor's manual.

A new chart in Chapter 4 stresses the dramatic increase in psychopharmacological agents with children since the late 1980s.

Key Features

"A Closer Look" boxes found throughout the book, draw students into the material and enrich each topic with engaging information. Some examples include: "What Are the Long-Term Criminal Consequences of Child Maltreatment" "Common Fears in Infancy, Childhood, and Adolescence," and "Did Darwin Have a Panic Disorder?"

Visual learning aids—including a variety of artistic cartoons, cases, extracts, and quotes help illustrate key points throughout the text and complement student understanding.

The authors' in-depth coverage of the role of the normal developmental process in understanding each disorder, as well as their close attention to important sex differences in the expression, determinants, and outcomes of child and adolescent disorders, promote greater understanding.

Current findings regarding the reliability and validity of DSM diagnostic criteria for specific disorders.

A Comprehensive Teaching and Learning Package

Also available with the third edition is a completely revised *Instructor's Manual with Test Bank* (Welder, Mash, and Wolfe, 2005) that is closely matched to our main points in each chapter and guides the students to additional sources of learning. For each chapter, the instructor's manual portion includes learning objectives, lecture outlines and notes, video recommendations, and relevant web sites, ideas for student activities, and "warning signs" transparency masters for various disorders. The supplement also contains new and expanded test items. The teaching package also includes ExamView® testing software.

The InfoTrac™ College Edition edge brings professors and students an online database of hundreds of scholarly and popular publications, and is now automatically packaged *free* with this text. InfoTrac is fully integrated into the text with relevant InfoTrac search terms included at the end of each chapter. Using InfoTrac, students can access full-text articles from key journals in the field including the *Journal of Abnormal Child Psychology*, the *Journal of the American Academy of Child and Adolescent Psychiatry, Brown University Child and Adolescent Behavior,* and the *Journal of Child and Adolescent Psychiatric Nursing*. The Instructor's Manual contains Ideas for activities to help students fully utilize Infotrac.

In addition, the text now offers the Multimedia Manager Instructor's Resource CD-ROM which includes advanced Microsoft® PowerPoint®-based lecture outlines and art, video clips for *Abnormal Child Psychology* that include attention-deficit/hyperactivity disorder, autism, preventing bullying, life skills, and Down's syndrome, and a direct link to the Wadsworth Psychology Study Center web site (http://psychology.wadsworth.com), all of which enhances classroom presentation capabilities. In addition, the CD contains Microsoft Word files of the instructor's manual and test bank to allow instructors to easily modify and customize these resources to suit their needs. All this material is packaged in a sleek user-friendly interface.

An updated book companion web site available at http://psychology.wadsworth.com includes text-specific content for students and instructors. It contains tutorial quizzing, flashcards, glossaries, web links, chapter outlines, crossword puzzles, and more.

Acknowledgments

One of the most rewarding aspects of this project has been the willingness and commitment on the part of many to share their knowledge and abilities. With great pleasure and appreciation we wish to acknowledge individuals who have in one way or another contributed to its completion, while recognizing that any shortcomings of this book are our responsibility alone.

In Calgary, Alison and Megan Wiigs, as creative and talented a mother and daughter team as there is, contributed enormously to every phase of this project. For their devotion to the project, they have our special gratitude. Dayna Lee-Baggley provided invaluable feedback from a student's perspective, and Jennifer Wilkie provided generous help in locating resource material. In London, Vivien Lee and Alex McIntyre-Smith deserve rich praise for their skilled efforts at locating resource material, and Joy Lang for her help in preparing the materials. Andrea Welder managed to offer advice and feedback about clarity of content, and to make our new and expanded Instructor's Manual a strong asset of the text.

Generous feedback and suggestions for individual chapters were also provided by other valued colleagues, including Sally During, Sharon Foster, Greg Fouts, Charlotte Johnston, and John Weisz. We are also grateful to colleagues who generously provided us with case materials and other information, including Thomas Achenbach, Ann Marie Albano, Russell Barkley, David Dozois, Alan Kazdin, Philip Kendall, David Kolko, Ivar Lovaas, Margaret McKim, Robert McMahon, Gerald Patterson, John Pearce, William Pelham, John Piacentini, Phyl and Rachel Prout, Jerry Sattler, David Shaffer, and Rosemary Tannock. We extend our special thanks to the many students in our courses and those from other universities, who provided us with helpful feedback on this edition, particularly those at the University of Utah and UCLA.

The production of a textbook involves many behind-the-scenes individuals who deserve special thanks. Marianne Taflinger, our Senior Editor at Wadsworth, contributed creative ideas, valuable assistance, and friendly reality checks from start to finish. The devoted and talented staff at Wadsworth including Justin Courts, Nicole Root, Chris Caldeira, Brian Chaffee, Dan Moneypenny, Paul Wells, Vernon Boes, Joohee Lee, and our production manager Dusty Friedman, and copy editor, Cathy Baehler, all deserve our thankful recognition for their contribution toward making the third edition of this text top quality.

Last but not least, we wish to thank our families, whose steadfast support and tolerance for the demands and excesses that go into a project such as this were critically important and exceedingly strong. The preparation of this textbook placed a heavy burden on our time away from them, and we are grateful for their unyielding support and encouragement. Eric Mash thanks his wife and soul mate of 35 years for her tolerance of the time that a project like this takes away from family life, and her wise advice on many matters relating to this book. David Wolfe thanks his three children, Amy, Anne, and Alex, and his wife, Barbara Legate, who were incredible sources of inspiration, information, humor, and photographs.

Reviewers

A critical part of writing this textbook involved feedback from teachers and experts. We would like to thank several dedicated reviewers and scholars who read most of the chapters for this book and provided us with detailed comments and suggestions that were enormously helpful in shaping the final manuscript.

Third edition reviewers:

Paul Florsheim
University of Utah

Jill Norvilitis
Buffalo State College

Clark McKown
University of California–Berkeley

Laura Freberg
California Polytechnic State University–San Luis Obispo

Kristin Christodulu
University at Albany, State University of New York

Stacy Overstreet
Tulane University

Second edition reviewers:

Robert Emery
University of Virginia

Virginia E. Fee
Mississippi State University

Yo Jackson
University of Kansas

Narina Nunez
University of Wyoming

Donald T. Saposnek, Ph.D.
University of California, Santa Cruz

Dana Schneider, M.A., MFT
Sonoma State University

Eric A. Youngstrom, Ph.D.
Case Western Reserve University

Carol K. Whalen
University of California, Irvine

First edition reviewers:

Debora Bell-Dolan
University of Missouri-Columbia

June Madsen Clausen
University of San Francisco

Richard Clements
Indiana University Northwest

Nancy Eldred
San Jose State University

Gary Harper
DePaul University

Christopher Kearney
University of Nevada-Las Vegas

Janet Kistner
Florida State University

Marvin Kumler
Bowling Green State University

Patrick McGrath
Dalhousie's University

Kay McIntyre
University of Missouri-St. Louis

Robert McMahon
University of Washington

Richard Milich
University of Kentucky

Martin Murphy
University of Akron

Michael Roberts
University of Kansas

Michael Vasey
Ohio State University

Student Reviewers:

Thanks to Paul Florsheim's students at the University of Utah: Josh Brown, Heather Woodhouse, Kristen Yancey, Michael Lambert, Jaime Fletcher, Julie Blundell, Matthew Warthen, Regina Hiraoka, Monica Stauffer, Trisha Jorgensen, Trisha Aberton, Matthew Zollinger, Jeff Ford, Nick Gilson, and Kimbery Downing.

We offer a special thanks to Nancy Eldred of San Jose State University for pilot-testing the second edition with her students. The comments were quite helpful in sharpening the student focus of this edition, and we are grateful to her for volunteering for this mission! Gabriela Beas, Maria Brown, Sara Carriere, Gina Costanza, Gera-Lyne Delfin, Julene Donovan, Brieann Durose, Shelly Gillan, Rochelle Hernandez, Keri Kennedy, Doris Lan, Maggie Lau, Christine McAfee-Ward, Deisy Muñoz, Shirat Negev, Kristi Pimentel, Veronica Rauch, Sandra Ronquillo, Becky Schripsema, Dianalin Stratton, Loyen Yabut, Melissa Zahradnik.

Thanks to John Weisz' students at UCLA: Chris Link and Natalia Nikolova.

Eric J. Mash   David A. Wolfe

Introduction to Normal and Abnormal Behavior in Children and Adolescents

When I was a boy of fourteen, my father was so ignorant I could hardly stand to have the old man around. But when I got to be twenty-one, I was astonished at how much he had learned in seven years.

—Mark Twain (1835–1910)

After centuries of silence, misunderstanding, and outright abuse, children's mental health problems and needs now receive greater attention, which corresponds to society's recent concern about children's well-being (President's New Freedom Commission, 2003). Fortunately, today more people like yourself want to understand and address the needs of children and adolescents. Perhaps you have begun to recognize that children's mental health problems differ in many ways from those of adults, so you

Georgina

Counting for Safety

At age 10, Georgina's strange symptoms had reached the point where her mother needed answers—and fast. Her behavior first became a concern about two years ago, when she started talking about harm befalling herself or her family. Her mother recalled how Georgina would come home from the third grade and complain that "I need to finish stuff but I can't seem to," and "I know I'm gonna forget something so I have to keep thinking about it." Her mother expressed her own frustration and worry: "As early as age 5, I remember Georgina would touch and arrange things a certain way, such as brushing her teeth in a certain sequence and rearranging folders in her backpack for several minutes. Sometimes I'd notice that she would walk through doorways over and over, and she seemed to need to check and arrange things her way before she could leave a room." Georgina's mother had spoken to their family doctor about it back then and was told "it's probably a phase she's going through, like stepping on cracks will break your mother's back. Ignore it and it'll stop."

But it didn't stop. Georgina developed more elaborate rituals for counting words and objects, primarily in groups of four. She told her mom "I need to count things out and group them a certain way—only I know the rules how to do it." When she came to my office, Georgina told me "when someone says something to me or I read something, I have to count the words in groups of four and then organize these groups into larger and larger groups of four." She looked at the pile of magazines in my office and the books on my shelf and explained, matter-of-factly, that she was counting and grouping these things while we talked! Georgina was constantly terrified of forgetting a passage or objects or being interrupted. She believed that if she could not complete her counting, some horrible tragedy would befall her parents or herself. Nighttime was the worst, she explained, because "I can't go to sleep until my counting is complete, and this can take a long time." (In fact, it took up to several hours, her mother acknowledged.) Understandably, her daytime counting rituals had led to decline in her schoolwork and friendships. Her mother showed me her report cards: Georgina's grades had gone from above average to near failing in several subjects. (Based on Piacentini & Graae, 1997)

Georgina's strange counting ritual was a symptom of her obsessive-compulsive disorder

have chosen to take a closer look. Maybe you are planning a career in teaching, counseling, medicine, law, rehabilitation, or psychology—all of which rely somewhat on knowledge of children's special needs to shape their focus and practice. Whatever your reason is for reading this book, we are pleased to welcome you to an exciting and very active field of study, which we believe will expose you to concepts and issues that will have a profound and lasting influence. Children's mental health issues are becoming very relevant to many of us in our current and future roles as professionals, community members, and parents, and the needs for trained personnel are increasing (President's New Freedom Commission, 2003).

Let's begin by considering Georgina's problems, which raise several fundamental questions that guide our current understanding of children's psychological disorders. Ask yourself: Does Georgina's behavior seem abnormal, or are aspects of her behavior normal under certain circumstances?

How would you describe Georgina's problem? Is it an emotional problem? A learning problem? A developmental disability? Could something in her environment cause these strange rituals, or is she more likely responding to internal cues we do not know? Will she continue to display these behaviors and, if so, what can we do to help?

When seeking assistance or advice, parents often ask questions similar to these about their child's behavior, and understandably need to know the probable course and outcome. These questions also exemplify the following issues that research studies in abnormal child psychology seek to address:

- Defining what constitutes normal and abnormal behavior for children of different ages and sexes

- Identifying the causes and correlates of abnormal child behavior
- Making predictions about long-term outcomes
- Developing and evaluating methods for treatment and/or prevention

How you choose to describe the problems children show, and what harm or impairments such problems may lead to is often the first step toward understanding the nature of their problems. As we will learn in Chapter 7, Georgina's symptoms fit the diagnostic criteria for obsessive-compulsive disorder. This diagnostic label, although far from perfect, tells a great deal about the nature of her disorder, the course it may follow, and the possible treatments.

Georgina's problems also illustrate important features that distinguish most child and adolescent disorders:

- *When adults seek services for children, it is not often clear whose "problem" it is.* Children usually enter the mental health system as a result of concerns raised by adults—parents, pediatricians, teachers, or school counselors—and the children themselves may have little choice in the matter. Children do not refer themselves for treatment. This has important implications for how we detect children's problems and how we respond to them.
- *Many child and adolescent problems involve failure to show expected developmental progress.* The problem may be transitory, like most types of bedwetting, or it may be an initial indication of more severe problems ahead, like we see in Georgina's case. Determining the problem requires familiarity with normal as well as abnormal development.
- *Many problem behaviors shown by children and youth are not entirely abnormal.* To some extent the behaviors are shown by most children and youth. For instance, worrying from time to time about forgetting things or losing track of thoughts is common; Georgina's behavior, however, seems to involve more than these normal concerns. Thus, decisions about what to do also require familiarity with known psychological disorders and troublesome problem behaviors.
- *Interventions for children and adolescents often are intended to promote further development, rather than merely to restore a previous level of functioning.* Unlike interventions for most adult disorders, the goal for many children is to boost their abilities and skills, not only to eliminate distress.

Before we look at today's definitions of abnormal behavior in children and adolescents, it is valuable to discover how society's interest and approaches to these problems during previous generations have improved the quality of life and mental health for children and youths. Many children, especially those with special needs, fared poorly in the past because they were forced to work as coal miners, field hands, or beggars. Concern for children's needs, rights, and care requires a prominent and consistent social sensitivity and awareness that simply did not exist prior to the 20th century (Aries, 1962). As you read the following historical synopsis, note how the relatively short history of abnormal child psychology has been strongly influenced by philosophical and societal changes in how adults view and treat children in general (Borstelmann, 1983; V. French, 1977).

Historical Views and Breakthroughs

These were feverish, melancholy times; I cannot remember to have raised my head or seen the moon or any of the heavenly bodies; my eyes were turned downward to the broad lamplit streets and to where the trees of the garden rustled together all night in undecipherable blackness; . . .

—*(Robert Louis Stevenson, describing memories of childhood illness and depression [quoted in Calder, 1980, p. 36])*

The ability of a society to help children develop normal lives and competencies requires not only medical, educational, and psychological resources, but also a social philosophy that recognizes children as persons with a value independent of any other purpose. Although this view of children should seem self-evident to us today, valuing children as persons in their own right has not been a priority of previous societies. Early writings suggest that children were considered servants of the state in the city–states of early Greece. Ancient Greek and Roman societies believed any person—young or old—with a physical or mental handicap, disability, or deformity was an economic burden and a social embarrassment, and thus was to be scorned, abandoned, or put to death (V. French, 1977).

Prior to the 18th century, children's mental health problems, unlike adult disorders, were seldom mentioned in professional or other forms of communication. Some of the earliest historical interest in abnormal child behavior surfaced near the end of the 18th century. The church used its strong influence to attribute children's unusual or disturbing behaviors to their inherently uncivilized and provocative nature (Kanner, 1962). In fact, during this period nonreligious explanations for disordered behavior in children were rarely given serious consideration because possession by the devil and similar forces of evil was the only explanation anyone needed (Rie, 1971). No one was eager to challenge this view, given that they too could be seen as possessed and dealt with accordingly.

Sadly, during the 17th and 18th centuries as many as two-thirds of children died before their fifth birthday, often because there were no antibiotics or similar medications to treat deadly diseases (Zelizer, 1994). Many children were also subjected to harsh treatment or indifference by their parents. Cruel acts ranging from extreme parental indifference and neglect to physical and sexual abuse of children went unnoticed or were considered an adult's right for educating or disciplining a child (Radbill, 1968). For many generations, the implied view of society that children are the exclusive property and responsibility of their parents was unchallenged by any countermovement to seek more humane treatment for children. A parent's prerogative to enforce child obedience, for example, was formalized by the Massachusetts' Stubborn Child Act of 1654, which permitted parents to put "stubborn" children to death for noncompliance. (Fortunately, no one met this ultimate fate.) Into the mid-1800s, the law allowed children with severe developmental disabilities to be kept in cages and cellars (Donohue, Hersen, & Ammerman, 2000).

The Emergence of Social Conscience

If the children and youth of a nation are afforded the opportunity to develop their capacities to the fullest, if they are given the knowledge to understand the world and the wisdom to change it, then the prospects for the future are bright. In contrast, a society which neglects its children, however well it may function in other respects, risks eventual disorganization and demise.

—Urie Bronfenbrenner (1977)

Fortunately, the situation gradually improved for children and youth's throughout the 19th century, and progressed significantly during the latter part of the 20th century. However, until very recent changes in laws and attitudes, children (along with women, members of minority groups, and persons with special needs) were often the last to benefit from society's prosperity and were the primary victims of its shortcomings. With the acuity of hindsight, we know that before any real change occurs it requires a philosophy of humane understanding in how society recognizes and addresses the special needs of some of its members. In addition to humane beliefs, each society must develop ways and means to recognize and protect the rights of individuals, especially children, in the broadest sense (U.N. Convention on the Rights of the Child, 1989). An overview of some of these major developments provides important background for understanding today's approaches to children's mental health issues.

In Western society, an inkling of the necessary prerequisites for a social conscience first occurred during the 17th century when both a philosophy of humane care and institutions of social protection began to take root. One individual at the forefront of these changes was John Locke (1632–1704), a noted English philosopher and physician who influenced the beginnings of present-day attitudes and practices of childbirth and child-rearing. Locke believed in individual rights, and he expressed the novel opinion that children should be raised with thought and care instead of indifference and harsh treatment. Rather than see children as uncivilized tyrants, he saw them as emotionally sensitive beings who should be treated with kindness and understanding, and given proper educational opportunities (Illick, 1974). In his words, "the only fence [archaic use, meaning "defense"] against the world is a thorough knowledge of it."

Then, at the turn of the 19th century, one of the first documented efforts to work with a special child was undertaken by Jean-Marc Itard (1775–1838). Box 1.1 explains how Itard treated Victor (discovered living in the woods outside Paris) for his severe developmental delays rather than sending him to an asylum. Symbolically, this undertaking launched a new era of a helping orientation toward special children, which initially focused on the care, treatment, and training of what were then termed "mental defectives."

As the influence of Locke and others fostered the expansion of universal education throughout Europe and North America during the latter half of the 19th century, children unable to handle the demands of school became a visible and troubling group. Psychologists, such as Leta Hollingworth (1886–1939), argued that many mentally defective children were actually suffering from emotional and behavioral problems primarily due to inept treatment by adults and lack of appropriate intellectual challenge (Benjamin & Shields, 1990). This view led to an important and basic distinction between persons with mental retardation ("imbeciles") and those with psychiatric or mental disorders ("lunatics"), although this distinction was far from clear at the time (Costello & Angold, 1995). Essentially, local governments needed to know who was responsible for helping children with cognitive development that appeared normal, but showed serious emotional or behavioral problems. The only previous guidance they had in distinguishing children with intellectual deficits from children with behavioral and emotional problems was derived from religious views of immoral behavior: Children with normal cognitive abilities, but who were disturbing, were thought to suffer from moral insanity, which implied a disturbance in personality or character (Pritchard, 1837). Benjamin Rush (1745–1813), a pioneer in psychiatry, argued that children were incapable of true adultlike insan-

BOX 1.1 Victor of Aveyron

Victor, often referred to as the "wild boy of Aveyron," was discovered in France by hunters when he was about 11 or 12 years old, having lived alone in the woods presumably all of his life. Jean-Marc Itard, a young physician at the time, believed the boy was "mentally arrested" because of social and educational neglect, and set about to demonstrate whether such retardation could be reversed. Victor—who initially was mute, walked on all fours, drank water while lying flat on the ground, and bit and scratched—became the object of popular attention as rumors spread that he had been raised by animals. He was dirty, nonverbal, incapable of attention, and insensitive to basic sensations of hot and cold. Despite the child's appearance and behavior, Itard believed that environmental stimulation could humanize him. Itard's account of his efforts poignantly reveals the optimism, frustration, anger, hope, and despair that he experienced in working with this special child. His experiences are familiar to those of us who have undertaken a similar responsibility.

Itard used a variety of methods to bring Victor to an awareness of his sensory experiences: hot baths, massages,

tickling, emotional excitement, even electric shocks. After five years of training by Dr. Itard, Victor had learned to identify objects, identify letters of the alphabet, comprehend many words, and apply names to objects and parts of objects. Victor also showed a preference for social life over the isolation of the wild. Despite his achievements, Itard felt his efforts had failed, because his goals of socializing the boy to make him normal were never reached. Nevertheless, the case of Victor was a landmark in the effort to assist children with special needs. For the first time an adult had tried to really understand—feel and know— the mind and emotions of a special child, and had proved that a child with severe impairments could improve through appropriate training. This deep investment on the part of an individual in the needs and feelings of another person's child remains a key aspect of the helping orientation to this day.

Source: From *A History of the Care and Study of the Mentally Retarded,* by L. Kanner, 1964, p. 15. Courtesy of Charles C. Thomas, Publisher, Springfield, Illinois.

---

ity, because the immaturity of their developing brains prevented them from retaining the mental events that caused insanity (Rie, 1971). Consequently, the term *moral insanity* grew in acceptance as a means of accounting for non-intellectual forms of abnormal child behavior.

The implications of this basic distinction created a brief, yet significant, burst of optimism among professionals (Achenbach, 1982). Concern for the plight and welfare of children with mental and behavioral disturbances began to rise in conjunction with two important influences. First, with advances in general medicine, physiology, and

neurology the moral insanity view of psychological disorders was replaced by the organic disease model that emphasized more humane forms of treatment. This advancement was furthered by advocates such as Dorothea Dix (1802–1887), who in the mid-19th century established 32 humane mental hospitals for the treatment of troubled youth previously relegated to cellars and cages (Achenbach, 1982). Second, the growing influence of the philosophies of Locke and others led to the view that children needed moral guidance and support. With these changing views came an increased concern for moral education, compulsory education, and improved health practices. These early efforts to assist children provided the foundation for evolving views of abnormal child behavior that resulted from combinations of biological, environmental, and psychological influences.

Early Biological Attributions

The successful treatment of infectious diseases during the latter part of the 19th century strengthened the emerging belief that illness and disease, including mental illness, were biological problems. However, early attempts at biological explanations for deviant or abnormal behavior were highly biased in favor of locating the cause within the individual child or adult. The public generally distrusted and scorned anyone who appeared "mad" or "possessed by the devil" and similar evil forces. Box 1.2 describes masturbatory insanity, a good illustration of how such thinking can lead to an explanation of abnormal behavior without consideration of objective scientific findings and the base rate of masturbation in the general population. The notion of masturbatory insanity also illustrates how the prevailing political and social climates influence definitions of child psychopathology, as true today as in the past. Views on masturbation evolved from the moral judgment that it was a sin of the flesh, to the medical opinion that it was harmful to one's physical health, to the psychiatric assertion that sexual overindulgence caused insanity.

In contrast to the public's general ignorance and avoidance of issues concerning persons with mental disorders that remained during the late 19th century, the mental hygiene movement provides a benchmark of changing attitudes toward children and adults with mental disorders. In 1909, Clifford Beers, a layperson who had recovered from a severe psychosis, spearheaded efforts to change the plight of others also afflicted. Believing that mental disorders were a form of disease, he criticized society's ignorance and indifference and sought to prevent mental disease by raising the standards of care and disseminating reliable information (M. Levine & Levine, 1992). As a result, detection and intervention methods began to flourish, based on a more tempered, yet still quite frightened and ill-informed, view of afflicted individuals.

Unfortunately, because this paradigm was based on a biological disease model, intervention was limited to persons with the most visible and prominent disorders, such as psychoses or severe mental retardation. Although developmental explanations were a part of this early view of psychopathology, they were quite narrow. The development of the disease was progressive and irreversible, tied to the development of the child only in that it manifested itself differently as the child grew, but remained impervious to other influences such as treatment or learning. All one could do was to prevent the most extreme manifestations by strict punishment and to protect those not affected.

Sadly, this early educational and humane model for assisting persons with mental disorders soon returned to a custodial model during the early part of the 20th century. Once again, attitudes toward anyone with mental or intellectual disabilities turned from cautious optimism to dire pessimism, hostility, and disdain. Particularly children, youths, and adults with mental retardation were blamed for crimes and social ills during the ensuing alarmist period (Achenbach, 1982). Rather than viewing knowledge as a form of protection, as Locke had argued, society returned to the view that mental illness and retardation were diseases that could spread if left unchecked.

For the next two decades, many communities chose to prevent the procreation of the insane through eugenics (sterilization) and segregation (institutionalization). We will return to these important developments in our discussion of the history of mental retardation in Chapter 9.

Early Psychological Attributions

Today, many of us take for granted the idea that biological influences must be balanced with important developmental and environmental factors, including the family, peer group, and school, in the attempt to conceptualize and understand abnormal child psychology (Mash & Dozois, 2003). Of course, this perception was not always the case. The long-standing, medically based view that abnormal behavior is a disorder or disease residing within the person unfortunately led to neglect of the essential role of a person's surroundings, context, and relations, and of the interactions among these variables.

The roots of psychological influences emerged early in the 20th century, when attention was drawn to the importance of recognizing major psychological disorders and formulating a taxonomy of illnesses. Such recognition allowed researchers to organize and categorize ways of differentiating among various psychological problems, resulting in some semblance of understanding and control. At the same time, there was concern that attempts to recognize the wide range of mental health needs of children and adults could easily backfire and lead to the neglect of persons with more severe disorders. This shift in perspective and increase in knowledge also prompted the development of diagnostic categories and new criminal offenses, expanded descriptions of deviant behavior, and added more comprehensive monitoring procedures for identified individuals (Costello & Angold, 1995). Two major theoretical paradigms helped shape these emerging psychological and environmental influences—psychoanalytic theory and behaviorism. We'll limit our discussion here to their historical importance, but additional content concerning their contemporary influences appears in the Chapter 2 discussion of theories and causes.

Psychoanalytic Theory In Sigmund Freud's day, near the beginning of the 20th century, many child psychiatrists and psychologists had grown pessimistic about their ability to treat children's mental disorders in a fashion other than custodial or palliative. Freud was one of the first to reject such pessimism and raise new possibilities for treatment as the roots of these disorders were traced to early childhood (Fonagy & Target, 2000). Although he believed that individuals have innate drives and predispositions that strongly affect their development, he also believed that experiences play a necessary role in psychopathology. For perhaps the first time, the course of mental disorders was not viewed as inevitable; children

and adults could be helped if provided with the proper environment, therapy, or both.

Psychoanalytic theory significantly influenced advances in our ways of thinking about causes and treatment of mental disorders. Perhaps most important from the perspective of abnormal child psychology was that Freud was the first to give meaning to mental disorder by linking it to childhood experiences (Rilling, 2000). His radical theory incorporated developmental concepts into an understanding of psychopathology at a time when early childhood development was virtually ignored by mainstream child psychiatry and psychology. Rather than focusing on singular, specific causes (a hallmark of the disease model in vogue at the time), psychoanalytic theory emphasized that personality and mental health outcomes had multiple roots. Outcomes depended to a large degree on the interaction of developmental and situational processes that change over time in unique ways (Fonagy & Target, 2000). In effect, Freud's writings shifted the view of children as innocent or insignificant to that of human beings in turmoil, struggling to achieve control over biological needs and to make themselves acceptable to society through the microcosm of the family (Freud, 1909/1953).

Contributions based on Freud's theory continued to expand throughout the early part of the 20th century, as clinicians and theorists broke from some of his earlier teachings and brought new insights to the field. His daughter, Anna Freud (1895–1984), was instrumental in expanding his ideas to children, in particular by noting how children's symptoms were related more to developmental stages than those of adults. Anna's Freud's contemporary, Melanie Klein (1882–1960), also took an interest in the meaning of children's play, arguing that all actions could be interpreted in terms of unconscious fantasy. The work of both women made possible the analysis of younger children and the recognition of nonverbal communication for patients of all ages (Mason, 2003).

In recent years, psychoanalytic theory's approach to abnormal child psychology has had less influence on clinical practice and teaching, largely because of the popularity of the phenomenological (descriptive) approach to psychopathology (Costello & Angold, 1995). Nevertheless, it is important to remember that current **nosologies** (the efforts to classify psychiatric disorders into descriptive categories) are essentially nondevelopmental in their approaches. Rather than attempting, as the Freudian approach does, to describe the development of the disease in the context of the development of the individual, nosologies such as those in the Diagnostic and Statistical Manual (DSM-IV-TR [Text Revision]; American Psychiatric Association, 2000) attempt to find common denominators that describe the manifestations of a disorder at every age (Achenbach, 2000). Despite valid criticism and a lack of empirical validation of the content of psychoanalytic theory and its many derivatives, the idea of emphasizing the interconnection between children's normal and abnor-

BOX 1.3 Little Albert, Big Fears, and Sex in Advertising

Most of us are familiar with the story of little Albert and his fear of white rats and other white furry objects, thanks to the work of John Watson and his graduate assistant (soon to become wife) Rosalie Rayner. However, understanding the times and background of John Watson helps put these pioneering efforts into a broader historical perspective, and highlights the limited concern for ethics in research that existed in his day.

Watson's fascination and life dedication to the study of fears may have stemmed from his own acknowledged fear of the dark, which afflicted him throughout his adult life. His career break arrived when he was given an opportunity to create a research laboratory at Johns Hopkins University for the study of child development. Instead of conditioning rats, he could now use humans to test his emerging theories of fear conditioning. However, then the only source of human subjects was persons whose rights were considered insignificant or who had less than adequate powers to protect themselves, such as orphans, mental patients, and prisoners. Just as he had studied rats in their cages, Watson now studied babies in their cribs.

Clearly, his method of obtaining research subjects and experimenting with them would be highly unethical today. To demonstrate how fear might be conditioned in a baby, Watson and Rayner set out to condition fear in an 11-month-old orphan baby they named Albert B. who was given a small white rat to touch, to which he showed no fear. After this warm-up, every time the infant would reach to touch the rat, Watson would strike a steel bar with a hammer. After repeated attempts to touch the rat brought on the same shocking sounds, "the infant jumped violently, fell forward and began to whimper." The process was repeated intermittently, enough times so that eventually Albert B. would break down and cry, desperately trying to crawl away, whenever he saw the rat. Watson and Rayner had successfully conditioned the child to fear rats. They then conditioned him to fear rabbits, dogs, fur coats and—believe it or not—Santa Claus masks.

John Watson and his wife Rosalie at the Longshore Yacht Club in Westport, Connecticut.

It is disconcerting that Albert B. was adopted and moved away before any deconditioning was attempted, destined to go through life with a strange set of fears he would never understand. It is ironic, moreover, that Watson went on to develop a career in advertising after he was ousted from the university as a result of concerns over his extramarital relationship with his graduate student. His brand of behaviorism, with its emphasis on the prediction and control of human behavior, met with unqualified success on Madison Avenue. As he explained, "No matter what it is, like the good naturalist you are, you must never lose sight of your experimental animal—the consumer." We can thank John B. Watson for advertising's dramatic shift in the 1930s toward creating images around any given product that exploited the sexual desires of both men and women whenever possible.

Source: Based on Karier, 1986.

---

mal development retains considerable attraction as a model for abnormal child psychology.

Behaviorism The development of evidence-based treatments for children, youths, and families (Kazdin & Weisz, 2003) can be traced to the rise of behaviorism in the early 1900s, as reflected in Pavlov's experimental research that established the foundations for classical conditioning, and the classic studies on the conditioning and elimination of children's fears (Jones, 1924b; J. B. Watson & Rayner, 1920). Initially John Watson (1878–1958), the "Father of Behaviorism," intended to explain Freud's concepts in

more scientific terms, based on the new learning theory of classical conditioning.

Ironically, Watson was perhaps more psychoanalytically inspired by Freud's theories than he intended. As he attempted to explain terms such as *unconscious* and *transference* using the language of conditioned emotional responses (and thereby discredit Freud's theory of emotions), he in fact pioneered the scientific investigation of some of Freud's ideas (Rilling, 2000). Box 1.3 highlights some of Watson's scientific ambitions and his famous study with Little Albert, which you will see went well beyond the scientific laboratory.

Watson is known for his theory of emotions, which he extrapolated from normal to abnormal behavior. His infamous words exemplify the faith some early researchers—and the public—placed in laboratory-based research on learning and behavior:

"Give me a dozen healthy infants . . . and I'll guarantee to take any one at random and train him to become any type of specialist I might select—doctor, lawyer, artist, merchant-chief and, yes, even beggar-man and thief, regardless of his talents, penchants, tendencies, abilities, vocations, and race of his ancestors." (J. B. Watson, 1925, p. 82)

Beyond the work in their lab, the Watson household must have been an interesting place. Consider the following contrasting views and advice on raising children from one of America's first "child experts" and his wife:

From John Watson:

> *Never hug and kiss them, never let them sit*
> *in your lap. If you must, kiss them once on*
> *the forehead when they say goodnight.*
> *Shake hands with them in the morning.*

—(J. B. Watson, 1925)

From Rosalie Rayner Watson:

> *I cannot restrain my affection for the chil-*
> *dren completely. . . . I like being merry and*
> *gay and having the giggles. The behavior-*
> *ists think giggling is a sign of maladjust-*
> *ment, so when the children want to giggle*
> *I have to keep a straight face or rush them*
> *off to their rooms.*

—(R. R. Watson, 1930/1996)

This example and the study of Little Albert illustrate the importance of keeping a perspective on any new advancements and insights that at first may seem like panaceas for age-old problems. As any soiled veteran of parenting would attest, no child-rearing shortcuts or uniform solutions guide us in dealing with children's problems—raising children is part skill, part wisdom, and part luck. Nonetheless, families, communities, and societal values play a strong role in determining how successful current child-rearing philosophies are at benefiting children.

Evolving Forms of Treatment

Compared with the times that followed, the period from 1930 to 1950 was a quiet time for research and treatment in abnormal child psychology. A few reports in the 1930s described the behavioral treatment of isolated problems such as bed-wetting (O. H. Mowrer & Mowrer, 1938), stuttering (Dunlap, 1932), and fears (F. B. Holmes, 1936). Other than these reports, however, psychodynamic approaches were the dominant form of treatment during this period. As a carryover from the 1800s, most children with intellectual or mental disorders were still institutionalized. This practice came under mounting criticism by the late 1940s, however, when studies by Rene Spitz raised serious questions about the harmful impact of institutional life on children's growth and development (R. Spitz, 1945). He discovered that infants raised in institutions without adult physical contact and stimulation developed severe physical and emotional problems. Efforts were undertaken to close institutions and place dependent and difficult children in foster family homes or group homes. Within a 20-year period, from 1945 to 1965, there was a rapid decline in the number of children in institutions, while the number of children in foster family homes and group homes increased.

During the 1950s and early 1960s, behavior therapy emerged as a systematic approach to the treatment of child and family disorders. The therapy was originally based on operant and classical conditioning principles established through laboratory work with animals. In their early form, these laboratory-based techniques to modify undesirable behaviors and shape adaptive abilities stood in stark contrast to the dominant psychoanalytic approaches, which stressed resolution of internal conflicts and unconscious motives. Behavior therapy focused initially on children with mental retardation or severe disturbances. Psychoanalytic practices for these children were perceived as ineffective or inappropriate. Much of this early work took place in institutions or classroom settings that were thought to provide the kind of environmental control needed to change behavior effectively. Since that time behavior therapy has continued to expand in scope and has emerged as a prominent form of therapy for a wide range of children's disorders (Kazdin & Weisz, 2003).

Progressive Legislation

Just how far some countries have advanced in the humane and egalitarian treatment of children and youths is exemplified by the various laws enacted in the past few decades to protect the rights of those with special needs. In the United States, the Individuals with Disabilities Education Act (IDEA; Public Law 101-476) mandates free and appropriate public education for children with special needs in the least restrictive environment for that child. Each child, regardless of age, must be assessed with culturally appropriate tests. Each child must have an individualized education program (IEP) tailored to his or her needs, and must be continually re-assessed. Similar legislation for testing exists in Canada and other Western nations.

SECTION SUMMARY

- Early biological explanations for abnormal child behavior favored locating the cause of the problem within the individual, which sometimes led to simplistic or inaccurate beliefs about causes of the behavior.

- Early psychological approaches attempted to integrate basic knowledge of innate processes with environmental conditions that shape behavior, emotions, and cognitions.

- Greater attention to the problems of children and youths in recent years has improved their quality of life and mental health. This improvement resulted from greater societal recognition and sensitivity to children's special status and needs since the turn of the 20th century.

What Is Abnormal Behavior in Children and Adolescents?

Lee

Early Troubles

I felt sorry for him. I asked him why he didn't go to school: "Oh," he said, "school is just a waste of time. I'm not learning anything there. I got other things to do. Besides, the kids all make fun of me. I wear jeans and they laugh at me. I talk with a Southern drawl and they laugh at me. They don't like me. I don't like them." Although he had hobbies, "most of all, I like to be by myself and do things by myself." And that's what he did a good part of those 18 months in New York. He'd get up at 9 A.M., watch television till 2 or 3 in the afternoon. There was no one else at home. His mother was out working. I asked him what he thought about his mother. He answered: "Well, I've got to live with her, so I guess I love her." But he showed no real relationship to her nor did she to him.

— (Sites, 1967)

These comments were made by a probation officer, reflecting on his involvement with a 13-year-old boy named Lee Harvey Oswald, who was under probation for chronic truancy. Note that the presenting complaint—truancy—was linked to dislike of school, embarrassment by peers, social isolation and alienation, and even his lack of emotional closeness to his mother. This illustration reveals how a relatively discrete problem can be difficult to classify into its causes, expression, and contributing factors. It also raises several key questions: First, how do we judge what is normal? A lot of kids skip school during adolescence. Second, when does an issue become a problem? In this instance, did anyone sense that Oswald's truancy might lead to or be due to potentially serious social problems? Finally, why are some children's abnormal patterns of behavior relatively continuous from early childhood through adolescence and into adulthood, whereas other children show more variable (discontinuous) patterns of development and adaptation? Was there anything about Oswald's behavior in childhood that

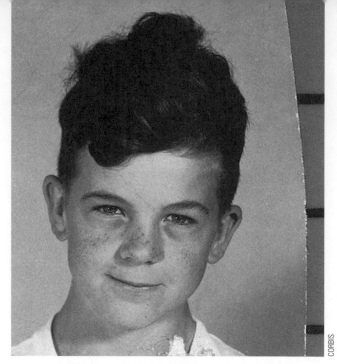

CORBIS

Were there any clues in Lee Harvey Oswald's childhood that might suggest his violent behavior later on?

could have possibly indicated that he would assassinate President John F. Kennedy years later?

Although these questions are central to defining and understanding abnormal child behavior and warrant thoughtful consideration, no simple, straightforward answers exist. (This should be familiar ground to those of you who are psychology majors.) More often than not, childhood disorders are accompanied by various layers of abnormal behavior or development, ranging from the more visible and alarming (such as truancy or physical assault), to the more subtle yet critical (such as teasing and peer rejection), to the more hidden and systemic (such as depression or parental rejection).

Moreover, mental health professionals, while attempting to understand children's weaknesses, too often unintentionally overlook their strengths. Yet, many children cope effectively in other areas of their lives despite the limitations posed by specific psychological disorders. An understanding of children's unique strengths and abilities can lead to ways to assist them in healthy adaptation. Also, some children may show less extreme forms of difficulty, or only the early signs of an emerging problem rather than a full-blown disorder. Therefore, to judge what is abnormal we need to be sensitive to each child's stage of development, and consider each child's unique methods of coping and ways of compensating for difficulties (Compas, Connor-Smith, Saltzman, Thomsen, & Wadsworth, 2001).

Childhood disorders, like adult disorders, have commonly been viewed in terms of deviancies from normal, yet disagreement remains as to what constitutes normal and abnormal. While reading the following discussion, keep in mind that attempting to establish boundaries between abnormal versus normal functioning is an arbitrary process at best, and current guidelines are constantly being reviewed for their accuracy, completeness, and usefulness.

Defining Psychological Disorders

The study of abnormal behavior often makes us more sensitive to and wary of the ways used to describe the behavior of others. Whose standard of "normal" do we adopt, and who decides if this arbitrary standard has been breached? Does abnormal behavior or performance in one area, such as mood or behavior, have implications for the whole person?

Although there are no easy answers to these questions, Georgina's real-life problems require an agreement on how to define a psychological (or mental) disorder. A **psychological disorder** traditionally has been defined as a pattern of behavioral, cognitive, emotional, or physical symptoms shown by an individual. Such a pattern is associated with one or more of the following three prominent features:

- The person shows some degree of distress, such as fear or sadness.
- His or her behavior indicates some degree of disability, such as impairment that substantially interferes with or limits activity in one or more important areas of functioning, including physical, emotional, cognitive, and behavioral.
- Such distress and disability increase the risk of further suffering or harm, such as death, pain, disability, or an important loss of freedom. (American Psychiatric Association [APA], 2000).

To account for the fact that we sometimes show transitory signs of distress, disability, or risk under unusual circumstances (such as the loss of a loved one), this defini-

tion of a psychological disorder excludes circumstances where such reactions are expected and appropriate as defined by our culture. Furthermore, these three primary features of psychological disorders only describe what a person does or does not do in certain circumstances. The features do not attempt to attribute causes or reasons for abnormal behavior to the individual alone. To the contrary, the understanding of particular impairments should be balanced with a recognition of developmental strengths and weaknesses. A child's behavior, thinking, and physical status are all important considerations in determining the degree of success or failure in adapting to the demands of the environment.

The Importance of Relationships Although abnormality is often defined as a pattern displayed by individuals, a child's dependency on other people means that many childhood problems are better depicted in terms of relationships than as problems contained in the individual. Many of these relationships, (such as with family members) involve critical aspects of dependency, caring, and trust. Other relationships involve the larger social network of peers and other adults who help shape a child's behavior. Children of all ages are active, vibrant beings who act on and are acted upon by their environment, so their psychological profiles are almost always a reflection of such interactions. Even in cases of pervasive developmental disorders such as autism, children's responses to their environment emerge from the interplay of inherent learning abilities and available environmental opportunities.

Labels Describe Behavior, Not People It is very important to keep in mind that terms used to describe abnormal behavior do not describe people; they only describe patterns of behavior that may or may not occur in certain circumstances. We must be careful to avoid the common

Calvin and Hobbes   by Bill Watterson

mistake of identifying the person with the disorder, as reflected in expressions such as "retarded child" or "autistic child." The field of child and adult mental health is often challenged by **stigma,** which refers to a cluster of negative attitudes and beliefs that motivates fear, rejection, avoidance, and discrimination against people with mental illnesses (Hinshaw & Cicchetti, 2000). Due to stigma, persons with mental disorders may also suffer from low self-esteem, isolation, and hopelessness, and may become so embarrassed or ashamed that they conceal symptoms and fail to seek treatment (President's New Freedom Commission, 2003). Accordingly, throughout this text we separate the child from the disorder by using language such as "Ramon is a child with mental retardation," rather than "Ramon is mentally retarded." Children like Ramon have many other attributes that should not be overshadowed by global descriptives or negative labels.

In addition, the problems shown by some children may be the result of their attempts to adapt to abnormal or unusual circumstances. Children with chronic health problems must adapt to their medical regimens and to negative reactions from peers; children raised in abusive or neglectful environments must learn how to relate to others adaptively and to regulate emotions that may, at times, be overwhelming. Therefore, the primary purpose of using terms such as *disorder* and *abnormal behavior* for describing the psychological status of children and adolescents is to aid clinicians and researchers in describing, organizing, and expressing the complex features often associated with various patterns of behavior. By no means do the terms imply a common cause, since the causes of abnormal behavior are almost always multifaceted and interactive.

This approach to defining abnormal behavior is similar to the one most often used to classify and diagnose mental disorders, according to the guidelines in the DSM-IV-TR (APA, 2000). We use the approach in guiding the thinking and structure of this book because of its clinical and descriptive utility. Yet, despite advances in defining abnormality and vast improvements in the diagnostic and classification systems, ambiguity still remains, especially in defining a particular child's maladaptive dysfunction (Pickles & Angold, 2003). Boundaries between what constitutes normal and abnormal conditions, or distinctions among different abnormal conditions are not easily drawn. At present, the DSM-IV-TR approach has achieved some consensus supporting its value in facilitating greater communication and increased standardization of research and clinical knowledge concerning abnormal child psychology. We will consider the DSM-IV-TR and current alternatives to classification of childhood disorders in Chapter 4.

Competence

Definitions of abnormal child behavior must take into account the child's **competence**—that is, the ability to successfully adapt in the environment. Developmental competence is reflected in the child's ability to use internal and external resources to achieve a successful adaptation (Masten & Curtis, 2000). Of course, this begs the question of what is successful? Successful adaptation varies across culture and ethnicity, so it is important that the traditions, beliefs, languages, and value systems of a particular culture also be taken into account when defining a child's competence. Judgments of deviancy also require knowledge of a child's performance relative to that of same-age peers as well as an individual course of development and cultural context. In effect, the study of abnormal child psychology considers not only the degree of maladaptive behavior children show, but also the extent to which they achieve normal developmental milestones. As with deviancy, the criteria for defining competence can be very specific and narrow in focus, or as plentiful and broad as we wish (Masten & Coatsworth, 1998).

How do we know if a particular child is doing well, and how do we, as parents, teachers, or professionals, guide our expectations? **Developmental tasks,** which include broad domains of competence such as conduct and academic achievement, tell how children typically progress within each domain as they grow. Knowledge of the developmental tasks provides an important backdrop for considering a child or adolescent's developmental progress and impairments. Examples of several important developmental tasks are shown in Table 1.1.

Conduct is one of the fundamental domains in Table 1.1 and it indicates how well a person follows the rules of a particular society. From a young age, children are expected to begin controlling their behavior and to comply with their parents' requests (this doesn't mean they always do so . . .). By the time children enter school, they are expected to follow the rules for classroom conduct and to restrain from harming others. Then, by adolescence, they are expected to follow the rules set by school, home, and society without direct supervision (Masten & Coatsworth, 1998). Similar developmental progression occurs in the self domain where children initially learn to differentiate themselves from the environment, and to gradually develop self-identity and autonomy. In the discussion of disorders in the chapters to follow, we attempt whenever possible to balance the information on abnormal behavior with the growing awareness of children's competencies and strengths.

Developmental Pathways

Why don't children with similar early experiences have similar problems later in life? Conversely, why do children and adolescents with the same disorder sometimes have very different early experiences or family characteristics? Another aspect of judging deviancy involves deciding when a concern or issue about a child's behavior starts to become a more recognizable pattern, especially since be-

Table 1.1
Examples of Developmental Tasks

AGE PERIOD	TASK
Infancy to preschool	Attachment to caregiver(s)
	Language
	Differentiation of self from environment
	Self-control and compliance
Middle childhood	School adjustment (attendance, appropriate conduct)
	Academic achievement (e.g., learning to read, do arithmetic)
	Getting along with peers (acceptance, making friends)
	Rule-governed conduct (following rules of society for moral behavior and prosocial conduct)
Adolescence	Successful transition to secondary schooling
	Academic achievement (learning skills needed for higher education or work)
	Involvement in extracurricular activities (e.g., athletics, clubs)
	Forming close friendships within and across gender
	Forming a cohesive sense of self-identity

Source: From "The Development of Competence in Favorable and Unfavorable Environments: Lessons From Research on Successful Children," by A. S. Masten and J. D. Coatsworth, 1998, *American Psychologist, 53,* 205–220. Copyright © 1998 by the American Psychological Association. Reprinted by permission of the author and the publisher.

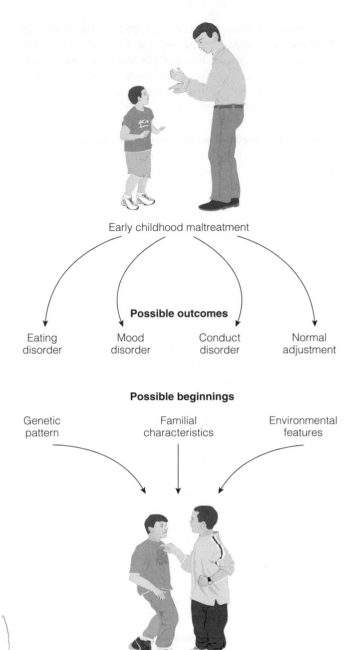

Figure 1.1. (a) Multifinality: Similar early experiences lead to different outcomes; (b) Equifinality: Different factors lead to a similar outcome

havior fluctuates and changes considerably as a child develops. Therefore, in addition to distinguishing between normal and abnormal adaptation, we must consider the temporal relationship between emerging concerns, for disorders in early childhood, and later. A **developmental pathway** refers to the sequence and timing of particular behaviors and possible relationships between behaviors over time. The concept allows us to visualize development as an active, dynamic process that can account for very different beginnings and outcomes (Cicchetti & Rogosch, 1996; 2002). It helps us to understand the course and nature of normal and abnormal development.

Let's look at two examples of developmental pathways, shown in Figure 1.1. The child at the top of the figure has experienced maltreatment at a young age. Maltreatment can significantly alter the child's initial course of development, resulting in very diverse and often unpredictable outcomes, such as eating, mood, or conduct disorders. This example illustrates **multifinality,** the concept that various outcomes may stem from similar beginnings (in this case, child maltreatment).

In contrast, other children might set out on their developmental journeys with very different strengths and weaknesses, but later have a similar disorder. As illustrated in the bottom example of Figure 1.1, genetic patterns, familial characteristics, and features of the child's environment represent different pathways leading to a similar outcome (conduct disorder). This example illustrates **equifinality,** the concept that similar outcomes stem from different early experiences and developmental pathways. As we will learn in Chapter 6, children with conduct problems may have very diverse early experiences and risk factors, but later show similar patterns of behavior. By looking at possible developmental pathways, we gain a better understanding of the ways in which children's problems may change or remain the same over time (Sameroff, 2000).

In summary, diversity in how children acquire psychological strengths and weaknesses is a hallmark of abnormal child psychology. Because no clear cause-and-effect relationship exists for each child and adolescent disorder, the following assumptions need to be kept firmly in mind (Mash & Dozois, 2003):

- There are many contributors to disordered outcomes in each individual.
- Contributors vary among individuals who have the disorder.
- Individuals with the same specific disorder express the features of their disturbance in different ways (for example, some children with a conduct disorder are aggressive, whereas others may be destructive to property or engage in theft or deceit).
- The pathways leading to any particular disorder are numerous and interactive, as opposed to unidimensional and static.

SECTION SUMMARY

- Defining a psychological disorder involves agreement on particular patterns of behavioral, cognitive, and physical symptoms shown by an individual.
- Because of children's dependency on others, their psychological problems need to be considered in terms of relationships, rather than as problems contained solely within the child.
- Terms used to describe abnormal behavior are meant to define behavior, not to be used as labels to describe individuals.
- Defining abnormal behavior requires judgment concerning the degree to which a person's behavior is maladaptive or harmful, as well as dysfunctional or impaired.
- Diversity in how children acquire psychological strengths and weaknesses is a hallmark of abnormal child psychology. The many contributors to abnormal behavior may vary within and between individuals with similar disorders.
- The study of psychological disorders involves attempts to describe the presenting problems and abilities, to understand contributing causes, and to treat or prevent them.
- Developmental pathways help to describe the course and nature of normal and abnormal development; multifinality means that various outcomes may stem from similar beginnings, whereas equifinality means that similar outcomes stem from different early experiences.

Risk and Resilience

I am convinced that, except in a few extraordinary cases, one form or another of an unhappy childhood is essential to the formation of exceptional gifts.

—*Thornton Wilder (1897–1975)*

Raoul and Jesse
Why the Differences?

Raoul and Jesse were childhood friends who grew up in the same run-down housing project, in a neighborhood plagued by drugs and crime. By the time they were 10 years old they were both familiar with domestic and community violence, and each lived with his mother and an older sibling after his parents divorced. The boys rarely saw their fathers, and when they did it usually wasn't a pleasant experience. By the time they reached grade 6 they were falling behind at school, and started to get into trouble with the police for staying out too late, hassling kids at school, and breaking into cars. Despite these problems and a struggle to keep up, Raoul finished high school and received two years of training in a local trade school. He is now 30 years old, works at a local factory, and lives with his wife and two children. Raoul sums up his life thus far as "dodging bullets to reach where I want to go," but he's happy to be living in a safe neighborhood and to have the hope of sending his children to college.

His friend Jesse, however, never graduated from high school. He dropped out after being expelled for bringing a weapon to school, and has been in and out of prison several times. At age 30, Jesse drinks too much and has a poor record of finding and keeping a job. He had several short-term relationships that produced two children, but he rarely visits them and never married either mother. Jesse has lived in several locations over the years, mostly in his old, unchanged neighborhood. (Based on Zimmerman & Arunkumar, 1994)

These brief life histories illustrate two very different developmental paths that started out at the same place. Jesse's troubles might have been predicted based on present knowledge of abnormal development, but it is more difficult to explain how some children, like Raoul, seem to escape harm despite stress and adversity (Luthar, 2003). Perhaps you are familiar with someone—from a novel, movie, or personal friendships—who seems to come out on top, despite adversity and limited resources. How do you suppose individuals, such as Oprah Winfrey (see Box 1.4), escape the odds and achieve their life goals?

The answer to this complicated question is coming into focus, thanks to studies that look at risk as well as resilience factors affecting children's courses of develop-

BOX 1.4 **Finding One's Strength**

Sometimes we can learn a lot from the personal stories of individuals who are famous or well known for their talent or achievements. In some cases, like that of Oprah Winfrey, the popular talk show host, publisher, actor, and entertainer, her stories reveal early experiences of adversity or loss that they remember as being instrumental in setting them on a life course.

Her grandparents raised Oprah for the first six years of her life. Despite living in poverty and being subjected to harsh physical discipline, she was grateful for her grandmother's influence: "I am what I am because of my grandmother. My strength. My sense of reasoning. Everything. All that was set by the time I was six." While moving back and forth between her two parents' homes in her later child and adolescent years, Oprah was sexually abused by several people, and as a result gave birth to a stillborn baby at 14 years old. This traumatic experience renewed her resolve to make something of herself. Oprah credits her father and various teachers for helping her navigate those troubled years and giving her the confidence to succeed: "Since my childhood, [my father] has set excellent standards that helped me succeed. For every one of us that succeeds, it's because there's somebody there to show you the way out. The light doesn't necessarily have to be in your family; for me it was teachers and school." Throughout her career, Oprah has channelled these hardships into a driving ambition to succeed, and is currently one of the most successful and influential women in entertainment

© Mitchell Gerber/Corbis

Oprah Winfrey's life exemplifies one of strength in the face of adversity.

and the popular culture. Oprah's life showcases her resilient adaptation to unfavorable life circumstances, and is a source of her attitude toward life: ". . . I believe that you tend to create your own blessings. You have to prepare yourself so that when opportunity comes, you're ready."

Source: Lowe, 1998.

---

ment. A **risk factor** is a variable that precedes a negative outcome of interest, and increases the chances that the outcome will occur. In contrast, a **resilience factor** is a variable that increases one's ability to avoid negative outcomes, despite being at risk for psychopathology. As you might suspect, children like Raoul and Jesse, who face many known risk factors, such as community violence and parental divorce, are vulnerable to abnormal development. Acute, stressful situations as well as chronic adversity put children's successful development at risk. Chronic poverty, serious care-giving deficits, parental mental illness, death of a parent, community disasters, homelessness, family breakup, and pregnancy and birth complications are known risk factors that increase children's vulnerability to psychopathology—especially in the absence of compensatory strengths and resources (Brooks-Gunn & Duncan, 1997).

Yet, like Raoul, some vulnerable children do not develop later problems. Instead, they seem resilient to their stress-filled environments, managing to achieve positive outcomes, despite being at significant risk for psychopathology (Luthar, Cicchetti, & Becker, 2000). Children

who survive risky environments by using their strong self-confidence, coping skills, and abilities to avoid risk situations may be considered resilient—they seem able to fight off or recover from their misfortune (Wyman, Sandler, Wolchik, & Nelson, 2000). These children are also most likely to show sustained competence while under stress, or to rebound to a previously healthy level of competence following traumatic or stressful experiences (Werner & Smith, 2001). Resilience is not a universal, categorical, or fixed attribute of the child. It varies according to the type of stress, its context, and similar factors. Individual children may be resilient to some specific stressors but not to others, and resilience may vary over time and across situations (Luthar et al., 2000). Despite the extraordinary circumstances that children have overcome, resilience is actually the result of ordinary adaptive processes (Masten, 2001).

The concept of resilience suggests a direct causal pathway rarely leads to a particular outcome. Ongoing interactions exist between protective and risk factors within the child, between the child and his or her surroundings, and among risk factors themselves. Protective factors are personal or situational variables that reduce the chances

Introduction to Normal and Abnormal Behavior in Children and Adolescents **15**

Chronic poverty is one of several factors that can put children at higher risk for the development of psychopathology.

for a child to develop a disorder. Risk factors do the exact opposite—they increase the child's likelihood of developing a problem. Risk factors and protective factors should be thought of as processes rather than absolutes, since the same event or condition can function as either factor depending on the overall context in which it occurs (Rutter, 2000b). For example, placing young children with another family may serve to protect them if they were being severely mistreated. For some children, however, out-of-home placement could increase their vulnerability if it creates more stress due to being removed from their mother or father. Throughout each chapter, we offer similar examples of children's vulnerability and resilience in relation to particular circumstances and disorders.

Figure 1.2 illustrates some of the better-known characteristics of children and adolescents who display resilience, which are sometimes overlooked in attempts to explain abnormal development. These characteristics constitute a protective triad of resources and health-promoting events: strengths of the individual, the family, and the school and community (Garmezy, 1991). Protective factors vary tremendously in magnitude and scope, however, and not all three sources are necessary. For some children, merely the availability of a supportive grandparent or teacher, can effectively change the course and direction of their development. Other children may need additional or different protective factors, such as a better learning environment, community safety, or sufficient family resources (Masten et al., 1999).

SECTION SUMMARY

- Children's normal development may be put in jeopardy due to risk factors, which can include acute, stressful situations and chronic adversity.

Source	Characteristics
Individual	Good intellectual functioning
	Appealing, sociable, easygoing disposition
	Self-efficacy, self-confidence, high self-esteem
	Talents
	Faith
Family	Close relationship to caring parent figure
	Authoritative parenting, warmth, structure, high expectations
	Socioeconomic advantages
	Connections to extended supportive family networks
School and community	Adults outside the family who take an interest in promoting the child's welfare
	Connections to social organizations
	Attendance at effective schools

Figure 1.2. Characteristics of children and adolescents who display resilience in the face of adversity (Based on Masten & Coatsworth, 1998)

- Some children seem to be more resilient to risk factors. Resiliency is related to strong self-confidence, coping skills, and ability to avoid risk situations, as well as ability to fight off or recover from misfortune.
- Children's resiliency is connected to a protective triad of resources and health-promoting events that include individual opportunities, close family ties, and opportunities for individual and family support from community resources.

The Significance of Mental Health Problems Among Children and Youth

Mankind owes to the child the best it has to give.

—*U.N. Convention on the Rights of the Child (1989)*

Until very recently, children's mental health problems were the domain of folklore and unsubstantiated theories in both the popular and scientific literatures. Only a few generations ago, in the mid-19th century, overstimulation in the schools was seen as a cause of insanity (Makari, 1993), and only one generation ago, in the mid-20th century, autism was believed to be caused by inadequate, uncaring parents (Bettelheim, 1967). We now recognize that mental health problems of children and adolescents are a frequently occurring and significant societal concern worldwide (National Advisory Mental Health Council, 2001).

Surveys conducted in North America and elsewhere find that about one child in five has a mental health problem that significantly impairs functioning (U.S. Public Health Service, 2000), and 10–20 percent meet diagnostic criteria for a specific psychological disorder (Angold et al., 2002; Waddell & Shepherd, 2002). Many other children have emerging problems that place them at risk for the later development of a psychological disorder (McDermott & Weiss, 1995). Some children have difficulties adapting to school or to family circumstances, so they behave in ways that are developmentally or situationally inappropriate. Others, however, show more pronounced patterns of poor development and maladjustment that suggest one or more specific disorders of childhood or adolescence. The process of deciding which problems merit professional attention and which ones might be outgrown involves a good understanding of both normal and abnormal child development and behavior.

To gain an immediate sense of the magnitude of children's mental health needs today, consider that the annual cost of treating children and adolescents for mental health problems in the United States is almost $12 billion (Ringel & Sturm, 2001). This cost represents only the tip of the iceberg, however, because very few children needing mental health services actually receive them. Of those youth who require mental health services, three-quarters of them do not receive it (Costello, Messer, Bird, Cohen, & Reinherz, 1998; Kataoka, Zhang, & Wells, 2002). Moreover, the U.S. Bureau of Health Professions (APA, 2003) projects that by 2020 the demand for children's mental health services will double, since the number of child and adolescent mental health professionals is not expected to increase at the required rate. A career in children's mental health anyone?

The chapters that follow explain that a significant proportion of children do not grow out of their childhood difficulties, although the ways in which children express difficulties are likely to change in both form and severity over time. Children's developmental impairments may have a lasting negative impact on later family, occupations, and social adjustment, even when they no longer have the disorder.

The Changing Picture of Children's Mental Health

If all children and adolescents with known psychological disorders could be captured in a photograph, the current picture would be much clearer than that of only a genera-

www.comstock.com

Surveys estimate that about one child in five has a mental health problem that interferes with his or her development, and one in ten has a specific psychological disorder.

tion ago. The improved focus and detail are the result of efforts to increase recognition and assessment of children's psychological disorders. In the past, children with various mental health and educational needs were too often described in global terms, such as *maladjusted*, because assessment devices were not sensitive to different syndromes and diagnostic clusters of symptoms (Achenbach, 1995). Today, we have a better ability to distinguish among the various disorders. This has given rise to increased and earlier recognition of previously poorly understood or undetected problems—learning disorders, depression, teen suicide, eating disorders, conduct disorders, and problems stemming from chronic health conditions and from abuse and neglect.

Another difference in today's portrait would be the group's composition. Younger children (Zeanah, 2000) and teens (American Psychological Association, 2002; Wolfe & Mash, in press) would appear more often in the photo, reflecting greater awareness of their unique mental health issues. Specific communication and learning disorders, for example, have only recently been recognized as significant concerns among preschoolers and young school-age children. Similarly, emotional problems, such as anxiety and depression, which increase dramatically during adolescence (Rudolph, Hammen, & Daley, in press) were previously overlooked because the symptoms are often less visible or disturbing to others than are the symptoms of behavior or learning problems.

What would not have changed in our photo is the proportion of children who are receiving proper services. Today less than 10 percent of children with mental health problems receive proper services to address impairments related to personal, family, or situational factors. This figure has remained unchanged for over 30 years (Costello & Angold, 2000). Limited and fragmented resources mean that children do not receive appropriate mental health services at the appropriate time. Fortunately, this situation is beginning to change, with greater attention paid to empirically supported prevention and treatment programs for many childhood disorders (Kazdin & Weisz, 2003; B. Weiss, Catron, Harris, & Phung, 1999), and integrated services for children within the school system (President's New Freedom Commission, 2003).

The children and teens in the picture would not reflect a random cross section of all children, because mental health problems are unevenly distributed. Those disproportionately afflicted with mental health problems are:

- Children from disadvantaged families and neighborhoods (Leventhal & Brooks-Gunn, 2000; McLoyd, 1998)
- Children from abusive or neglectful families (Emery & Laumann-Billings, 1998)
- Children receiving inadequate child care (Love et al., 2003)
- Children born with very low birth weight due to maternal smoking, diet, or abuse of alcohol and drugs (Korkman, Kettunen, & Autti-Raemoe, 2003; Singer, Hawkins, Huang, Davillier, & Baley, 2001)
- Children born to parents with criminal histories (Gabel & Schindledecker, 1993) or severe mental illness (Resnick, Harris, & Blum, 1993).

Also, the children in the picture could not easily be grouped according to these categories, because children often face combinations of environmental stressors and psychosocial deprivations. Such children are especially at risk of having their healthy development compromised to the degree that they are said to show abnormal behavior or to suffer from a mental disorder (Steinhauer, 1998).

What Affects Rates and Expression of Mental Disorders? A Look at Some Key Factors

Diverse voices make sweet music; as diverse conditions in our life render sweet harmony.

—*Dante, Paradiso IV: 124–126*

New pressures and social changes may place children at increasingly greater risk for the development of disorders at younger ages (Caspi, Taylor, Moffitt, & Plomin, 2000). Many stressors today are quite different from those faced by our parents and grandparents. Some have been around for generations: chronic poverty, inequality,

family breakup, single parenting, and so on. Others are now more recent or more visible: homelessness, adjustment problems of children in immigrant families, inadequate child care for working parents, and conditions associated with the impact of prematurity, HIV, cocaine, and alcohol on children's growth and development (McCall & Groark, 2000). Even welcome medical advances can have a negative effect. Higher rates of fetal survival have contributed to a greater number of children with behavior and learning difficulties who require specialized services at a younger age.

It is important to remember that the manner in which one's circumstances affect the course (for example, progression) of a disorder should be distinguished from how they may initially contribute to the problem. That is, environmental stressors, such as poverty, child abuse, or lack of safety, may act as nonspecific stressors that bring about poor adaptation or even the onset of a disorder in some vulnerable children. In contrast, these same environmental influences may affect the course of the disorder in other children by affecting the extent to which a child's problems are attenuated or exacerbated (Steinberg & Avenevoli, 2000). Examples of major factors in the development and expression of child psychopathology are noted next, and resurface throughout our subsequent discussions of each disorder.

Poverty and Socioeconomic Disadvantage

If you looked beyond the faces of the children in our photo, you would note that in many cases, the background and circumstances of children and youth with mental health problems provide obvious clues to their origins. Some of the most telling clues are the experiences of poverty, disadvantage, and violence faced by many, which can have a cumulative effect on their mental health. (Luthar, 1999)

Childhood poverty is a daily reality for about 1 in 6 children in both the United States (U.S. Bureau of the Census, 2003) and Canada (Statistics Canada, 2003). Disturbingly, about one in three American children will be poor at some point in childhood (Children's Defense Fund, 2002). Growing up with poverty has a substantial effect on the well-being of children and adolescents, especially in terms of impairments in learning ability and school achievement (Duncan & Brooks-Gunn, 2000). Moreover, low income is tied to many other forms of disadvantage: less education, low-paying jobs, inadequate health care, single-parent status, limited resources, poor nutrition, and greater exposure to violence. Any one disadvantage can impair children's developmental progress significantly (Brooks-Gunn & Duncan, 1997).

The impact of childhood poverty is telling. Children from poor and disadvantaged families show almost three times the conduct disorders, twice the chronic illness, and more than twice the rate of school problems, hyperactivity, and emotional disorders than children who are not poor (D. P. Ross, Shillington, & Lochhead, 1994). Moreover, the deeper the level of poverty, the higher the incidence of children's violence: three times greater in girls, five times greater in boys (Tremblay, Pihl, Vitaro, & Dobkin, 1994). Economic deprivation alone is not responsible for these higher rates, however, because many children do succeed under harsh circumstances. Nevertheless, the greater the degree of inequity, powerlessness, and lack of control over their lives, the more children's physical and mental health are undermined (United States Public Health Service, 2001a).

Poverty has a significant, yet indirect, effect on children's adjustment, most likely because of its association with such negative influences, particularly harsh, inconsistent parenting and elevated exposure to acute and chronic stressors, that define the day-to-day experiences of children in poverty (McLoyd, 1998). For example, youth who live in inner-city areas and witness community violence are most likely to develop post–traumatic stress disorder (PTSD), depression, and aggression (Buka, Stichick, Birdthistle, & Earls, 2001).

Sex Differences

We have known for some time that boys and girls express their problems in different ways (Crick & Zahn-Waxler, 2003). For example, hyperactivity, autism, childhood disruptive behavior disorders, and learning and communication disorders are more common in boys than girls; the opposite is true for most anxiety disorders, adolescent depression, and eating disorders (Hartung & Widiger, 1998). What we don't understand, however, is whether these differences are caused by definitions, reporting biases (more "disturbing" problems are most likely to come to the attention of mental health agencies), or differences in the expression of the disorder. For example, aggressive behavior may be expressed more directly by boys (fighting) and more indirectly by girls (spreading rumors). Although mental health problems for girls have been understudied, this situation is changing (Bell, Foster, & Mash, in press), and therefore we consider the expression of problems for boys and girls in each chapter.

Sex differences in problem behaviors are negligible in children under the age of 3 (Gadow, Sprafkin, & Nolan, 2001), but increase with age. Boys show higher rates of early onset disorders that involve some form of neurodevelopmental impairment, and girls show more emotional disorders with a peak age of onset in adolescence (Rutter, Caspi, & Moffitt, in press). For example, boys generally have higher rates of reading disorders, autism spectrum disorders, attention deficit disorder, and early onset persistent conduct problems, whereas girls have

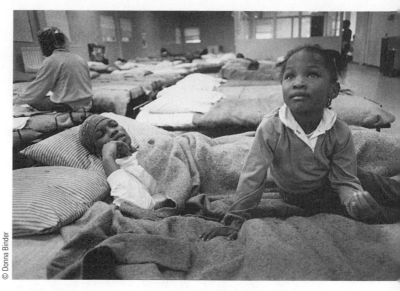

Mother and child at a shelter in Brooklyn, New York; 88% of homeless families in the United States are headed by women.

higher rates of depression and eating disorders (Rutter et al., in press).

Figure 1.3 depicts the normal developmental trajectories for girls and boys across the two major dimensions of internalizing and externalizing behaviors. **Internalizing problems** include anxiety, depression, somatic complaints, and withdrawn behavior; **externalizing problems** encompass more acting-out behaviors such as aggression and delinquent behavior. You'll notice from Figure 1.3 (top) that externalizing problems for boys start out higher than for girls in preschool and early elementary years, and that these problems decrease gradually for both boys and girls until they almost converge by age 18. The opposite pattern emerges for internalizing problems. Parents report similar rates of internalizing problems for boys and girls in early childhood, but girls outpace boys in these problems over time (Bongers, Koot, van der Ende, & Verhulst, 2003). These developmental trajectories of problem behaviors provide a useful basis against which deviations from the normal course can be identified, although these overall trends need to be considered in relation to a number of additional factors that we discuss throughout the text.

Finally, it is interesting to note that the types of childrearing environments predicting resilience to adversity also differ for boys and girls. Resilience in boys is associated with households in which there is a male role model (such as a father, grandfather, older brother), structure, rules, and some encouragement of emotional expressiveness. In contrast, girls who display resiliency come from households that combine risk taking and independence with support from a female caregiver (such as a mother, grandmother, older sister) (Werner, 1995).

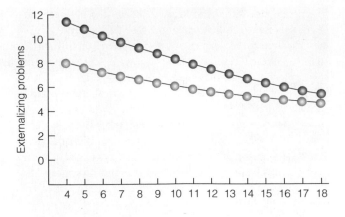

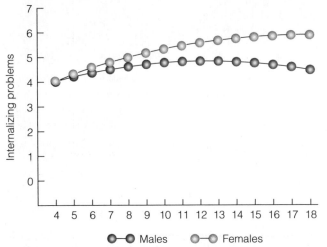

● — ● Males   ○ — ○ Females

Figure 1.3. Normative developmental trajectories of Externalizing problems (top graph) and Internalizing problems (bottom graph) from the Child Behavior Checklist. Ages are shown on the *x* axis. The *y* axis represents the raw scores (higher score means more problems). *Source:* Bongers, Koot, van der Ende, & Verhulst, 2003

Race and Ethnicity

Racial and ethnic minority persons comprise a substantial and vibrant segment of many countries, enriching each society with many unique strengths, cultural traditions, and important contributions. In the United States. these groups are growing rapidly, with current population projections showing that by 2025 they will account for more than 40 percent of all Americans (President's New Freedom Commission, 2003). Minority children in the United States are overrepresented in rates of some disorders, such as substance abuse, delinquency, and teen suicide (McLoyd, 1998). However, once the effects of socioeconomic status (SES), sex, age, and referral status are controlled (that is, the unique contributions of these factors are removed or accounted for), very few differences in

the rate of children's psychological disorders emerge in relation to race or ethnicity (Achenbach, Howell, Quay, & Conners, 1991; U.S. Public Health Service, 2000). Some minority groups, in fact, show less psychopathology after controlling for SES (Samaan, 2000).

Even though rates of problems are similar, significant barriers remain in access, quality, and outcomes of care for minority children. As a result, American Indians, Alaska Natives, African Americans, Asian Americans, Pacific Islanders, and Hispanic Americans bear a disproportionately high burden of disability from mental disorders (U.S. Public Health Service, 2001b). Specifically, the majority culture has neglected to incorporate respect or understanding of the histories, traditions, beliefs, languages, and value systems of culturally diverse groups. Misunderstanding and misinterpreting behaviors have led to tragic consequences, including inappropriately placing minorities in the criminal and juvenile justice systems (President's New Freedom Commission, 2003).

Minority children and youth face multiple disadvantages, such as poverty and exclusion from society's benefits. This exclusion is often referred to as marginalization and can result in a sense of alienation, loss of social cohesion, and rejection of the norms of the larger society (Steinhauer, 1996). Resisting the combined effects of poverty and marginalization takes unusual personal strength and family support. Since there is an overrepresentation of minority-status children in low SES groups (U.S. Public Health Service, 2000), we must interpret with caution the relationships among SES, ethnicity, and behavior problems that often emerge while discussing childhood disorders.

We also have to keep in mind that, despite the growing ethnic diversity of the North American population, ethnic representation in research studies and the study of ethnicity-related issues are most likely to receive relatively little attention in studies of child psychopathology (García Coll, Akerman, & Cicchetti, 2000; U.S. Public Health Service, 2001b). Research into child psychopathology has generally been insensitive to the possible differences in prevalence, age of onset, developmental course, and risk factors related to ethnicity (Kazdin & Kagan, 1994), and to the considerable heterogeneity that exists within specific ethnic and racial groups (Murry, Bynum, Brody, Willert, & Stephens, 2001).

As was the case for SES and sex differences, global comparisons of the prevalence of different types of problems for different ethnic groups are not likely to be very revealing. On the other hand, studies into the processes affecting the form, associated factors, and outcomes of different disorders for various ethnic groups hold promise for increasing our understanding of the relationship between ethnicity and abnormal child behavior (Bradley, Corwyn, McAdoo, & Garcia Coll, 2001).

Culture

The values, beliefs, and practices that characterize a particular ethno-cultural group contribute to the development and expression of children's disorders, and affect how people and institutions react to a child's problem (Wang & Ollendick, 2001). Because the meaning of children's social behavior is influenced by cultural beliefs and values, it is not surprising that children express their problems differently across cultures (Weisz, Weiss, Suwanlert, & Chaiyasit, 2003). For example, shyness and oversensitivity in children have been found to be associated with peer rejection and social maladjustment in Western cultures, but associated with leadership, school competence, and academic achievement in Chinese children in Shanghai (Chen, Rubin, & Li, 1995).

Because of cultural influences, it is important that research on abnormal child behavior not be generalized from one culture to another unless there is support for doing so. Some underlying processes, such as regulating emotion and its relationship to social competence, may be similar across diverse cultures (Eisenberg, Pidada, & Liew, 2001). Similarly, some disorders, particularly those with a strong neurobiological basis (for example, ADHD, autistic disorder), may be less susceptible to cultural influences. Nonetheless, social and cultural beliefs and values are likely to influence the meaning given to these behaviors, the ways in which they are responded to, their forms of expression, and their outcomes. We caution throughout this text that few studies have compared the attitudes, behaviors, and biological and psychological processes of children with mental disorders across different cultures, and we indicate places where this situation is beginning to change.

Child Maltreatment and Non-Accidental Trauma

Children and adolescents are being neglected and abused at an epidemic rate worldwide (Krug et al., 2002). Each year nearly one million verified cases of child abuse and neglect occur in the United States (U. S. Department of Health and Human Services, 2003), and over 60,000 in Canada (Trocmé & Wolfe, 2001). U. S. phone surveys of children and youths between 10 and 16 years old estimate that over one-third (6 million) experience physical and/or sexual assaults during these ages, not only by family members, but also by persons they may know from their communities and schools (Boney-McCoy & Finkelhor, 1995).

These related forms of non-accidental trauma—being the victim of violence at school or being exposed to violent acts in their homes or neighborhoods—lead to signficant mental health problems in children and youth.

In a telephone survey of over 4,000 youths between 12–17 years of age, 16 percent of boys and 19 percent of girls met the criteria for either post–traumatic stress disorder, major depressive episode, or substance abuse/dependence in relation to acts of violence (Kilpatrick et al., 2003). Tragically, these acts of abuse and trauma are estimated to cost $94 billion per year in the United States as a result of direct and indirect harm to the lives of these children (Fromm, 2001). Due to its increasing significance, more attention is being given to developing ways to prevent and help youngsters exposed to maltreatment and trauma. We acknowledge this concern by devoting Chapter 14 to this issue.

Special Issues Concerning Adolescents

Early- to mid-adolescence is a particularly important transitional period for healthy versus problematic adjustment (Cicchetti & Rogosch, 2002; D. A. Wolfe & Mash, in press). Substance use, risky sexual behavior, violence, accidental injuries, and mental health problems are only a few of the major issues that make adolescence a particularly vulnerable period (Kilpatrick et al., 2000; Leitenberg & Saltzman, 2000). Disturbingly, mortality rates more than double between early adolescence (ages 10 to 14) and later adolescence (ages 15 to 19), primarily due to risk-taking behaviors (Irwin and Duncan, 2002).

In response to these mounting concerns, special needs and problems for adolescents are receiving greater attention, especially because serious consequences are preventable. Health promotion efforts to reduce harm from normal risk taking and experimentation in adolescence, for example, are being implemented in primary health care settings, schools, and community programs (Irwin & Duncan, 2002). Because adolescent problems have been neglected relative to those of children, throughout this text we look at the expression of each disorder in both childhood and adolescence as much as possible.

Lifespan Implications

Over the long term, the impact of children's mental health problems is most severe when the problems continue untreated for months or years. The developmental tasks of childhood are challenging enough without the added burden of emotional or behavioral disturbances that interfere with the progress and course of development. About 20 percent of the children with the most chronic and serious disorders face sizable difficulties throughout their lives (Costello & Angold, 1995). They are least likely to finish school and most likely to have social problems or psychiatric disorders that affect many aspects of their lives throughout adulthood.

BOX 1.5. Current Reports on Mental Health Issues Pertaining to Children and Youth

From the U.S. Surgeon General's Report on Mental Health in 1999 to the President's New Freedom Commission's Report on Mental Health in 2003 there have been many important national and international initiatives and reports about understanding and helping children and adolescents with mental health problems. The wonders of the information age provide free access to this wealth of information (as if reading your textbook was not enough!). For those of you who are interested in obtaining more . . . we are providing a listing of some (by no means all) of the more important documents that are shaping the field.

Mental Health

United States Public Health Service Office of the Surgeon General (1999). *Mental health: A report of the Surgeon General.* Rockville, MD: Department of Health and Human Services, U.S. Public Health Service.
http://www.surgeongeneral.gov/Library/MentalHealth/home.html

Development and Psychopathology

Institute of Medicine (2000). *From neurons to neighborhoods: The science of early childhood development.* Washington, DC: National Academies Press.
http://www.nap.edu/books/0309069882/html/

Culture, Race, and Ethnicity

United States Public Health Service Office of the Surgeon General (2001). Mental health: *Culture, race, and ethnicity: A supplement to Mental health: A report of the Surgeon General.* Rockville, MD: Department of Health and Human Services, U.S. Public Health Service.
http://www.surgeongeneral.gov/library/mentalhealth/cre/

Children's Mental Health

United States Public Health Service Office of the Surgeon General (2001). *Report of the Surgeon General's Conference on Children's Mental Health: A National Action Agenda.* Rockville, MD: Department of Health and Human Services, U.S. Public Health Service.
http://www.surgeongeneral.gov/topics/cmh/childreport.htm

Research on Children's Mental Health

National Advisory Mental Health Council (NAMHC) Workgroup on Child and Adolescent Mental Health Intervention Development and Deployment (2001). A blueprint for change: Research on child and adolescent mental health. Washington, DC: U.S. Government Printing Office.
http://www.nimh.nih.gov/child/blueprint.cfm

Mental Health: International Perspective

World Health Organization. (2001). *The world health report 2001—Mental health: New understanding, new hope.* Geneva: World Health Organization.
http://www.who.int/whr2001/2001/main/en/index.htm

Transforming Mental Health Care

The President's New Freedom Commission on Mental Health (2003). *Achieving the promise: Transforming mental health care in America.* Rockville, MD: Substance Abuse and Mental Health Services Administration (SAMHSA).
http://www.mentalhealthcommission.gov/reports/reports.htm

Substance Abuse

Department of Health and Human Services: Substance Abuse and Mental Health Services Administration (2002). National household survey on drug abuse: Volume I. Summary of national findings: Prevalence and treatment of mental health problems.
http://www.samhsa.gov/oas/nhsda.htm#NHSDAinfo

Suicide Prevention

U.S. Department of Health and Human Services (2001). *National strategy for suicide prevention: Goals and objectives for action.* Rockville, MD: Department of Health and Human Services, U.S. Public Health Service.
http://www.mentalhealth.org/publications/allpubs/SMA01-3517/

Youth Violence

United States Public Health Service Office of the Surgeon General (2001). *Youth violence: A report of the Surgeon General.* Rockville, MD: Department of Health and Human Services, U.S. Public Health Service.
http://www.surgeongeneral.gov/library/youthviolence/

Reducing Suicide

Institute of Medicine (2002). *Reducing suicide: A national imperative.* Washington, DC: National Academies Press.
http://books.nap.edu/books/0309083214/html/index.html

Reducing Health Risks

World Health Organization. (2002). *The world health report 2002—Reducing risks, promoting healthy life.* Geneva: World Health Organization.
http://www.who.int/whr/2002/en/

Violence and Health

World Health Organization (2002). *World report on violence and health.* Geneva: World Health Organization.
http://www.who.int/violence_injury_prevention/violence/world_report/wrvh1/en/

The lifelong consequences associated with child psychopathology are exceedingly costly in terms of economic impact and human suffering. The costs are enormous with respect to demands on community resources such as health, education, mental health, and criminal justice systems; loss in productivity; the need for repeated and long-term interventions; and the human suffering of both the afflicted children and the family and community members they encounter. Fortunately, children and youths can overcome major impediments when circumstances and opportunities promote healthy adaptation and competence.

The growing recognition of the concerns presented in this chapter has led to a number of major initiatives to achieve the goals of prevention and help. These initiatives are summarized in a number of government reports that include recommendations as to how these goals can be achieved. Many of these important reports are available on the internet (see Box 1.5) and we recommend that you familiarize yourself with these developments.

SECTION SUMMARY

- A clear understanding of both normal and abnormal child development and behavior is needed to decide which problems are likely to continue and which might be outgrown.

- About one child in five has a mental health problem that significantly impairs functioning, and about one child in ten meets criteria for a specific psychological disorder.

- A significant proportion of children do not grow out of their childhood difficulties, although the ways in which these difficulties are expressed are likely to change in both form and severity over time.

- Mental health problems are unevenly distributed. Children who experience more social and economic disadvantage or inequality and children exposed to more violent, inadequate, or toxic environments are disproportionately afflicted with mental health problems.

- A child's biological sex, ethnic background, and cultural surroundings are all important contributors to the manner in which their behavioral and emotional problems are expressed to and recognized by others.

- Many childhood problems can have lifelong consequences for the child and for society.

LOOKING AHEAD

The significance of children's mental health problems emerge over and over again throughout this text, as we consider the many different individual, family, social, and cultural influences that define abnormal child psychology. Because children cannot advocate on their own behalf, and their mental health needs and developmental issues differ markedly from those of adults, it is important that we keep these concerns in mind. Moreover, children's problems don't come in neat packages. Many disorders discussed in the text overlap with other disorders in terms of symptoms, characteristics, and treatment needs. Once again the importance of viewing the whole child in relation to his or her difficulties emerges as the best strategy in understanding abnormal child and adolescent psychology, using diagnostic criteria as guideposts rather than firm rules.

The next three chapters discuss theories, causes, research, and clinical issues. Chapter 2 looks at current ways of viewing child and adolescent disorders. It includes the exciting advances made possible by new discoveries about the brain, and notes how these discoveries have become more integrated with knowledge of the biological and psychological processes affecting children's development and disorders. Chapter 3 reviews research methods with children, youths, and families that help us understand features, causes, course, and treatment methods. Chapter 4 discusses clinical issues pertaining to children's mental health, especially current approaches to assessment, diagnosis, and treatment. Because psychological interventions vary considerably in relation to each disorder, we will describe the most recent and effective treatments for specific disorders in the context of the chapters to which they apply. This allows information on treatments and their effectiveness to be woven into our knowledge about the description and causes of the disorder.

Chapters 5 through 13 examine specific disorders and conditions affecting children and adolescents. We examine four general types of disorders, and the impact of child abuse and neglect:

- *Behavioral disorders.* Chapters 5 and 6 deal with attention-deficit/hyperactivity disorder and oppositional and conduct problems, which are sometimes referred to as externalizing problems because they involve conflicts with the environment.

- *Emotional disorders.* Chapters 7 and 8 discuss anxiety and mood disorders, which are sometimes referred to as internalizing problems because they involve conflicts within the child, which are less visible to others.

- *Developmental and learning disorders.* Chapters 9 through 11 examine a broad range of disorders affecting children's ability to learn or perform normally, including mental retardation, pervasive developmental disorders such as autistic disorder, specific problems related to reading and mathematics, and communication difficulties. Many of these disorders constitute chronic conditions that affect children's ongoing development.

- *Problems related to physical and mental health.* Chapters 12 and 13 discuss child and adolescent disorders stemming from medical or physical conditions that may affect children's overall psychological functioning, and vice versa, such as chronic illness, substance abuse, and eating disorders and related conditions.

- *Child maltreatment and non-accidental trauma.* Chapter 14 is unique because it considers conditions that may be a focus of clinical attention during childhood but are not mental disorders. This chapter, with its particular focus on children at risk, deals with the significance of child abuse and other forms of non-accidental trauma on children's developmental progress and course.

Far greater attention has been devoted to the description and classification of abnormality in children than to healthy child functioning and how children adapt to the challenges of growing up. In light of this imbalance, throughout this text we introduce each disorder with a discussion of normal developmental processes, such as children's normal intellectual development (in relation to mental retardation) and the normal range of misbehavior and acting-out (in reference to conduct problems). We also consider children's strengths and adaptive abilities, regard-

less of the presence of a particular disorder, and factors that are believed to encourage healthy adaptation regardless of other impairments. We then present the core features of each disorder (such as hyperactivity-impulsivity, sad mood, or antisocial behavior), followed by significant associated features, (such as problems in self-esteem, peer relations, or substance abuse).

As you begin your journey into the field of abnormal child psychology, keep in mind that the threats facing children today—child poverty, chronic illness, maltreatment, and indifference—are no less significant than those of the past, although they sometimes fail to arouse the indignation of society to the extent that major changes are implemented and maintained. Even in a country that has outlawed child labor, child abuse, and many other forms of actual and potential harm, we have only recently begun to recognize the profound importance of the quality of the early childhood environment on children's health, well-being, and competence. Fortunately, it is unlikely that children and youths will ever again be seen as insignificant, costly burdens on society in the mainstream of North American culture. As each chapter in this text indicates, efforts aimed at change in policies and programs directed toward children and youths are gaining momentum.

Key Terms

competence, p. 12
developmental pathway, p. 13
developmental tasks, p. 12
equifinality, p. 13
externalizing problems, p. 19
internalizing problems, p. 19
multifinality, p. 13
nosologies, p. 7
protective factors, p. 16
psychological disorder, p. 11
resilience factor, p. 15
risk factor, p. 15
risk factors, p. 15
stigma, p. 12

 InfoTrac College Edition

To research recent articles on the subject, go to: www.infotrac-college/thomsonlearning.com

Enter search terms: CHILD DEVELOPMENT, CHILD PSYCHOLOGY, DIAGNOSIS OF MENTAL ILLNESS, ADJUSTMENT IN CHILDREN, RESILIENCE, PSYCHOLOGICAL ASPECTS OF POVERTY, CHILDREN'S RIGHTS

Theories and Causes

*To be a real philosopher all that is necessary
is to hate someone else's type of thinking.*

—William James (1842–1910)

At the risk of sounding vague, we must acknowledge that nearly all child and family disturbances result from multiple, interacting risk factors and processes (Pennington, 2002; Steinberg & Avenevoli, 2000). As we noted in the discussion of risk and resilience in Chapter 1, contextual events in the family or school environment exert considerable influence over an individual's course of development (Kagan, 2003; Rutter & Maughan, 2002). Therefore, a given child's problems must be considered in relation to multiple levels of influence—individual, family, community, and culture—rather than attributed to any one factor. Since the causes of psychological disorders are significant, we devote this chapter to a description of the primary contributions derived from biological, cognitive, and environmental influences.

In this chapter we consider theories and findings on influences that shape the child's ongoing development in many different ways. Some influences (such as biological and environmental factors) are contained within the child, whereas many others (such as family patterns and cultural norms) lie at various distances from the child's immediate surroundings. We will see how these various causal influences contribute to a better understanding of

abnormal child development and how they are conceptually related to one another. Let's begin by considering Jake's situation:

25

Jake

Not Keeping Up

Jake was almost 12 years old when he was referred to me because of his academic problems. Since grade 4 he had been performing well below average in his classes, had difficulty concentrating, and was considered to be "too quiet and nervous." For the last four summers he took extra classes to improve his reading, but was currently reading at the third-grade level. As a result, his parents received a letter from the school saying he likely would not be promoted to the next grade if his work didn't improve. Everyone seemed angry at Jake for not keeping up.

When I met with Jake, his version of his school problems was short and to the point: "It's the teachers," he said, as he looked at the floor and squirmed in his seat. "How am I expected to learn anything when they yell at you? When I told my English teacher that I hadn't finished reading my book for class, he said I take too long 'cuz my mind wanders too much. How am I expected to learn when they think I'm dumb?" After further discussion, Jake summed up his view of the problem in a quiet, sullen voice: "I know I'll never get anywhere with the brain I've got. I can't figure stuff out very fast, and the teachers aren't much help. Just thinking about school makes me jittery. I'm afraid I'll say something stupid in class and everyone will laugh at me."

Jake's mother and father met with me separately and were quick to add their own opinions about why their son didn't do well in school. His mother admitted that she becomes aggravated and starts to yell when Jake says he doesn't want to go to school or can't do his schoolwork, but she didn't think this was an issue. She quickly added, "I've read about learning disabilities and I think he's got one. He can't control his mind enough to center on anything. He's scared to go to school, and avoids homework as if his life depended on it." By the end of the interview it was evident that Jake's parents were angry at him. They felt Jake blamed his teachers for his own lack of effort, and that he should be in a special classroom and maybe given medications to calm him down so he wouldn't worry so much about school.

Jake's situation and his parents' complaints raise important issues. Could Jake have mild mental retardation that impairs his learning? Is Jake's mother right about his having a learning disability? Does Jake have a specific communication or learning problem unrelated to mental retardation that affects his schoolwork? Perhaps his school and family environments have contributed to his learning difficulties and fear of school. Have his parents and teachers expected him to fail? Has he been given much assistance? Has he been abused or neglected at home?

What Caused Jake's Problems?

Suppose you were asked to interview Jake, his teachers, and his parents to find out why the schoolwork was difficult for him. How would you go about this task? What information do you feel would be essential to know, and what plan might you follow to organize and explore the many possible reasons for his problem? Most likely, you would form a working theory in your mind that would assist you in determining what to ask and why. At first, your theory might be very basic and unrefined. Jake's problem in school might be connected to the negative comments and pressure he is getting from his parents and teacher. As you proceed, your theory about Jake's problem would likely expand and become more detailed, allowing you to probe particular questions with greater precision.

Let's briefly consider possible causes of Jake's behavior:

1. *Biological influences.* Because we know little about Jake's early development, we might ask his mother about her prenatal history, including major illnesses, injuries, or perhaps marital problems or undue stress that might have affected her pregnancy. Jake's problems also reflect a tendency toward behavioral inhibition; he may approach new or challenging situations with greater apprehension and fear than other children (Kagan, Snidman, Zentner, & Peterson, 1999).

   Children with fears and anxiety, which are affected by levels of stress hormones circulating in the body, are more likely to have parents who had similar problems during childhood (Biederman et al., 1993a). Jake may have inherited a tendency to respond to his environment with heightened arousal or sensitivity. Alternatively, his early neurological development and the patterns of connections established within his brain may have been influenced by the child-rearing styles his parents used when he was an infant. These early patterns, in turn, can influence how Jake approaches new tasks, reacts to criticism, or relates to others. Another possibility is that Jake may have inherited one or more genes that influence his phonological awareness. He may not be able to recognize and process all the phonemes (individual sounds) of his native language.

2. *Emotional influences.* Children like Jake not only think and behave in ways that provide clues to their distress, but also show various emotional signals that at first are not obvious. Emotional expression offers another unique window for viewing Jake's inner world, especially his emotional reactions to challenges like reading. Consider this possibility: As Jake approaches his reading assignment or thinks about returning to school the next morning, he is overwhelmed by fear, bordering on panic. His heart

races, his breathing quickens, and his thoughts turn to ways to escape from this dreaded situation as quickly as possible. Preoccupied by such feelings and worry, his concentration further declines.

Jake's inability to regulate his feelings of arousal, distress, or agitation that may surface without warning is a key element in describing his problem, but we still have not determined how it might have originated. Emotional reactivity and expression are the ways infants and young children first communicate with the world around them, and their ability to regulate these emotions as they adapt is a critical aspect of their early relationships with caregivers (Emde & Spicer, 2000). Emotions can be powerful events, demanding that the child find ways to reduce or regulate their force. The most adaptive way is to seek comfort from a caregiver, which gradually helps the child learn ways of self-regulation. By extension, Jake's school refusal or phobia could have emerged at a younger age from his anxiety about his mother's availability that grew to a more pronounced and generalized insecurity (Bowlby, 1973).

3. *Behavioral and cognitive influences.* Jake had been performing below average in reading for some time. Using our knowledge of learning principles, we might investigate Jake's current situation from the perspective of events that elicit fear or avoidance, and events that maintain such avoidance by reducing unpleasant reactions. Jake's lack of progress may be a function of punitive events when he is criticized by his parents or singled out by his teacher.

A behavioral approach to Jake's problem might be to try to change aspects of his environment, such as the attention from his teacher or parents for his gradual efforts to do his schoolwork, to see what effect this approach has on his school performance and avoidance. We might also consider the teasing or rejection by peers in his school environment that may make him fearful. By observing Jake at school and narrowing the list of possible events that may contribute to his fears, we can begin to develop hypotheses about Jake's learning history and, most importantly, possible ways to remediate the problem. One possibility might be to increase the likelihood of reinforcement that is contingent on Jake's efforts to complete his schoolwork.

Cognitive influences, such as a person's interpretation of events, are also important to consider. How does Jake view the situation, and does his view accurately reflect the situation? Children with fears and worries sometimes develop a belief system that can be self-defeating, leading them to believe that they will fail at anything they try (Greenberg, Lengua, Coie, & Pinderhughes, 1999). Jake has experienced failure in reading and other events at school, and it is plausible

that he anticipates further struggles with schoolwork and other children. His own words are quite clear in this respect: "How am I expected to learn when they think I'm dumb?" "I know I'll never get anywhere with the brain I've got." "Just thinking about school makes me jittery." Such thoughts only tend to make him more anxious and more likely to avoid school as much as possible. In short, his expectations about his performance at school could be

Everyone seemed to be angry with Jake.

heavily laden with fear of failure or ridicule, issues that certainly warrant attention. Children's self-expressions and other cognitions offer a unique window on their inner world, which may provide clues that we miss when observing their actions.

4. *Family and cultural influences.* An understanding of the possible causes of Jake's difficulties would be incomplete without consideration of his family and peer relationships, and his larger social and cultural network (S. B. Campbell, Shaw, & Gilliom, 2000). Although his early relationship with his parents may have contributed to a lessened ability to regulate his emotions adaptively, his current relationships with his teachers, peers, and family members offer further clues. At the family level, how sensitive are his parents to recognizing his special limitations, and how willing are they to teach him alternative strategies? His mother has high hopes and expectations for her child, as well as a life and problems of her own (including a job). Even though she wants only what's best for Jake, her behavior is understandable but may still be a problem. Her pointed statement, "I've read about learning disabilities and I think he's got one," suggests that she dismisses the problem by labelling it as "his" problem. Neither parent appeared to be open to considering other possible explanations. Furthermore, his mother admitted to becoming exasperated and yelling at Jake. What effect might this have on his tenuous self-concept and his attempts to regulate his fear and arousal?

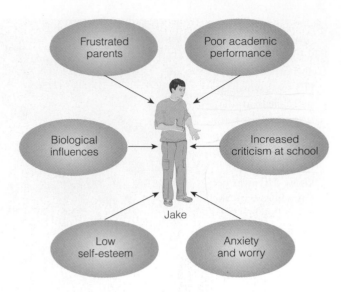

Figure 2.1. Jake's Concerns: Where do we intervene?

All children, not only those with problems, require a parenting style that is sensitive to their unique needs and abilities, and that places appropriate limits on them to help them develop self-control (McGroder, 2000). Significant adults both within Jake's family and at school were not responding to him with sensitivity so it's not surprising that Jake's behavior grew worse over time. Finally, for proper development, children require a basic quality of life that includes a safe community, good schools, proper health and nutrition, access to friends their own age, and opportunities to develop close relationships with extended family and members of their community. These opportunities and necessities are in the background of every child's developmental profile and can emerge as very significant issues for children undergoing parental divorce or living in poverty (Shaw, Winslow, & Flanagan, 1999; Rutter, 2003c).

Several important factors that need to be considered in addressing Jake's problems are shown in Figure 2.1. Although there are many "strikes against Jake" that need to be considered, clinicians and researchers often attempt to visualize the multiple causes to allow assessment and intervention to address them properly.

SECTION SUMMARY

- Jake's case exemplifies many interconnected factors that cause or contribute to psychological problems in children.
- The study of causes of abnormal child behavior involves theory and findings on biological, psychological, social, and cultural factors.
- Biological factors include genetic and neurobiological contributors, among others.

- Psychological influences include the role of behavioral and cognitive processes, as well as emotional and relationship influences.
- Major social contributors to child problems involve family patterns, peer relations, community factors, and cultural norms.
- Factors in any one of these areas impact and interact with the other areas.

Theoretical Foundations

Defining what is abnormal within the context of children's ongoing adaptation and development, and sorting out the most probable causes of identified problems is a complicated process. Very few simple or direct cause-and-effect relationships exist. The study of abnormal child behavior requires an appreciation of developmental processes, as well as individual and situational events that can have a major bearing on the course and direction of a particular child. Studying normal development informs our theories of abnormal development, and vice versa.

Most clinical and research activity begins with a theoretical formulation for guidance and information. Theory is essentially a language of science that allows us to assemble and communicate existing knowledge more comprehensively. A theory permits us to make educated guesses and predictions about behavior based on samples of knowledge, moving us forward to explore possible explanations. Like a treasure map that provides clues and signposts, a theory offers guidance for our pursuit of causal explanations. Knowledge, skill, and evidence must be added to bring these theoretical clues to life.

The study of the causes of childhood disorders is **etiology,** which considers how biological, psychological, and environmental processes interact to produce the outcomes that are observed over time. Research into biological determinants has focused on possible causes such as structural brain damage or dysfunction, neurotransmitter imbalances, and genetic influences. Psychological and environmental models emphasize the role of environmental toxins, early experiences, learning opportunities, disciplinary practices, family systems, and sociocultural contexts. Although these factors are often described as possible "causes," they are in fact primarily risk factors and correlates associated with certain disorders—their causal role is not always clear.

Numerous theoretical models have been proposed to explain and treat children's psychological disorders, although many of the theories have not been substantiated or even tested (Kazdin, 2000). Until recently, most models focused on single explanations that failed to consider other influences and their interactions. One-dimensional models do not capture the complexities of abnormal child behavior that are increasingly evident from research

(Kazdin & Kagan, 1994; Lahey, Waldman, & McBurnett, 1999). The alternative to single-factor explanations is much more complex and informative. It involves consideration of multiple causes that can interact in various ways over time to affect normal and abnormal development. Keeping in mind this central theme of multiple, interactive causes will help you grasp the complexity of each disorder discussed throughout this text.

Underlying Assumptions

The value of theory lies not only in providing answers, but also in raising new questions and looking at familiar problems in different ways. Theory, research, and practice in abnormal child psychology all require an understanding of the assumptions underlying work in this area. Let's look at three prominent assumptions and how they have shaped our approach to abnormal child psychology.

Abnormal Development Is Multiply Determined Our first underlying assumption is that abnormal child behavior is *multiply determined*. Thus we have to look beyond the child's current symptoms and consider developmental pathways and interacting events that, over time, contribute to the expression of a particular disorder.

Let's return to Jake's problems to illustrate this assumption. One way to look at Jake's problems is to say that he lacks motivation. Although it is a reasonable explanation, this one-dimensional causal model, which attempts to trace the origins of Jake's reading difficulty to a single underlying cause, is probably too simplistic. Scientific method emphasizes the need to simplify variables to those of most importance, but focusing on one primary explanation rather than identifying and allowing for several possible explanations (for genetic factors, reinforcement history, and peer problems) fails to consider the concept of developmental pathways (discussed in Chapter 1). A particular problem or disorder may stem from a variety of causes, and similar risk factors may lead to very different outcomes.

Another way to view Jake's difficulties—the way we emphasize here—takes into account multiple influences, including his developmental profile and abilities, his home and school environment, and the ongoing, dynamic interactions between these factors. To address Jake's reading problem from a multidimensional perspective, we would first assess his current abilities by using multiple sources of data on his ability to function in different settings. Even if we were interested only in his reading ability, we would consider a wide range of characteristics besides those we initially believe to be signs of reading problems. Otherwise, our assumptions about the nature of reading problems might prevent us from considering other explanations. Could criticism and yelling from Jake's mother affect his concentration or self-esteem? Is Jake different

Children's comfort with the environment is shown by their actions.

from other children in terms of his ability to recognize language sounds from written words? These are some of the questions we would want to answer through careful observation and assessment, using a theoretically guided decision-making strategy.

Child and Environment Are Interdependent Our second assumption extends the influence of multiple causes by stressing how the child and environment are **interdependent**—how they influence each other. This concept departs from the tradition of viewing the environment as acting on the child to cause changes in development, and instead argues that children also influence their own environment. In simple terms, the concept of interdependence appreciates how nature and nurture work together and are, in fact, interconnected (Rutter, 2002d; Sameroff, 1995). Thus, children elicit different reactions from the same environment; different environments, such as home or school, elicit different reactions from the same child.

The dynamic interaction of child and environment is referred to as a **transaction** (Gottlieb & Halpern, 2002; Sameroff & MacKenzie, 2003). The child and the environment both contribute to the expression of a disorder, and one cannot be separated from the other. A transactional view regards both children and the environment as *active contributors* to adaptive and maladaptive behavior. Most persons who know children best—parents, teachers, child care workers, and others—would probably agree this view makes the most sense: Children act on their environment, and their environment acts on them, like in the example of Jake. According to this trans-

Theories and Causes **29**

"The title of my science project is 'My Little Brother: Nature or Nurture.'"

actional perspective, children's psychological disorders do not reside within the child, nor are they due solely to environmental causes. They most often emerge from a combination of factors, which interact in ways that follow general laws of organized development. Box 2.1 shows an example of this transactional process.

Although a transactional view considers general principles of development that apply to all children, it is also sensitive to unique individual circumstances—in the child's family or biological makeup—that influence or alter typical outcomes. Learning about such deviations from the norm is what this textbook is all about.

Abnormal Development Involves Continuities and Discontinuities   Think for a moment about how Jake's various problems might have begun and how they might change or even disappear over time. Might his current problems of avoiding school and homework be connected to his earlier difficulties in reading? Are these qualitatively different problems or different manifestations of the same one? Are his current problems qualitatively different from those he had at a younger age, since today his problems include avoiding school and homework?

Few psychological disorders or impairments suddenly emerge without at least some warning signs or connections to earlier developmental issues. This connection is apparent, for example, in early-onset and persistent conduct disorders, where parents and other adults often see troublesome behaviors at a young age that continue in some form into childhood and adolescence (Loeber et al., 2000). However, it is a critical issue if some forms of abnormal child development are continuous or discontinuous across childhood, adolescence, and adulthood, in either a consistent or transformed manner (S. B. Campbell et al., 2000).

Continuity implies that developmental changes are gradual and quantitative, and future behavior patterns can be predicted from earlier patterns. **Discontinuity**, in contrast, implies that developmental changes are abrupt and qualitative, and future behavior is poorly predicted by earlier patterns. As an example, consider a preschool child who uses physical aggression with peers. What would you expect that child to be like 10 years later? According to the notion of continuity, he or she would be more likely to engage in antisocial and delinquent behavior as an adolescent and adult. That is, the pattern of problem behavior (in this case, physical aggression) is continuous across developmental periods, although it gradually changes in form and intensity. Pushing a peer may turn into striking someone with a fist or object. Importantly, continuity refers to patterns of behavior, rather than specific symptoms, that remain over time. Continuity is well supported for early-onset and persistent conduct disorders, which have a significant likelihood of later evolving into serious antisocial acts (Moffitt & Caspi, 2001; Nagin & Tremblay, 1999).

Other problem behaviors, such as eating disorders, seem to follow a more discontinuous pattern; they occur more suddenly and without much prior warning. In these cases, there are few good behavioral predictors from early childhood as to why a particular child begins to restrict eating or purge food during early adolescence, as discussed in Chapter 13. Sometimes discontinuity can refer to an unexpected or atypical outcome, like a child who shows normal development until about 18 months of age, and then displays loss of language and reduced social engagement (characteristics of autism). In such circumstances the connection between early and later patterns seems abrupt and discontinuous, which is very baffling to parents.

As we will see throughout our discussion of each disorder, positive factors such as individual competence or social intervention (Masten & Curtis, 2000) as well as negative factors such as poverty or discrimination (Rutter, 2000b) can influence the continuity or discontinuity of development over time. Returning to Jake, can you think about which of his behavior patterns (if any) were continuous, and which seemed to be more discontinuous? Like many problems in abnormal child psychology, Jake's current behavior pattern involves *both* continuities and discontinuities. Some of his troubles, like school and homework avoidance, seem qualitatively different (discontinuity) from his reading disorder. His other behaviors, like slow reading and comprehension, seem to follow (continuity) from his earlier academic problems.

Remember that the concepts of continuity and discontinuity apply to the understanding of abnormal and normal development. However, even with wide fluctuations in the way problems are expressed over time, children show some degree of consistency in organizing their experiences and interacting with their environment, whether it be adaptive or maladaptive (Rutter & Sroufe, 2000; Waters, Weinfield, & Hamilton, 2000). The degree of continuity or discontinuity will vary as a function of changing environmental circumstances, and transactions

BOX 2.1 Explaining Causation: It's Not That Simple

Consider how a child's language delay may result from the interplay of child and environment over time, as shown in the figure here. Complicated childbirth may have caused an otherwise calm mother to worry about her new role and her child's health. The mother's anxiety during the child's first few months of life may cause her to be less sensitive and nurturing toward her infant. In response to inconsistent or insensitive child care, the infant may develop some irregularities in sleeping and feeding patterns, which give the appearance of a difficult temperament. This difficult temperament decreases the mother's pleasure and enjoyment of her infant, so she tends to spend less time with her child. If care-givers do not actively interact with their child and, especially, if they don't speak clearly and appropriately, the youngster falls behind in language development, resulting in a diagnosis of language delay.

What caused the child's language delay? A complicated childbirth, the mother's anxiety, the child's difficult temperament, or the mother's avoidance of social interaction? Too often we select the cause that is closer in time to when the disorder was discovered (in this case, the mother's avoidance of her child), but this clearly oversimplifies a complex developmental sequence. From a prevention and early-intervention standpoint, efforts to assist this mother and child can be applied at any point

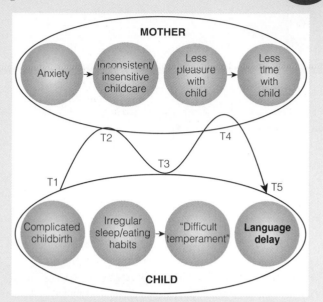

along this sequence, although greater benefit is seen with interventions that begin as early as possible.

Source: From "General System Theories and Developmental Psychopathology," by A. J. Sameroff, 1995. In D. Cicchetti and D. J. Cohen (eds.), *Developmental Psychopathology, Volume 1: Theory and Methods,* pp. 659–695. Copyright © 1995 by John Wiley & Sons. Reprinted by permission of John Wiley & Sons, Inc.

---

between the child and environment. These continual changes, in turn, will affect the child's developmental course and direction.

In sum, a central theme of our basic assumptions is that the study of abnormal child psychology must consider abnormality in relation to multiple, interdependent causes, and major developmental changes that typically occur across the life cycle. Until recently, developmental aspects of abnormal child behavior were often overlooked in relation to children's behavioral and emotional problems (Achenbach, 2000). To redress this imbalance, throughout this text we discuss developmental issues pertaining to the nature, symptoms, and course of each disorder.

Changes, Typical and Atypical   Figure 2.2 presents an overview of developmental periods by age. It gives examples of normal achievements for each period, as well as behavior problems most often reported in general population samples and the clinical disorders that typically become evident at each period. Guidelines for the typical sequence of development across several important dimensions are helpful, but we must keep in mind that age in years is an arbitrary way to segment continuous sequences of development. You may find yourself turning back to

this table to reorient yourself to children's normal and abnormal development.

An Integrative Approach

How do we attempt to make sense of the many environmental and individual factors that influence child behavior? Since no single theoretical orientation can explain various behaviors or disorders, we must be familiar with many theories and conceptual models—each contributes important insights into normal and abnormal development.

Even models that consider more than one primary cause can be limited by the boundaries of their discipline or orientation. Biological explanations, for instance, emphasize genetic mutations, neuroanatomy, and neurobiological mechanisms as factors contributing to psychopathology. Similarly, psychological explanations emphasize causal factors such as excessive, inadequate, or maladaptive reinforcement and/or learning histories. Biological and psychological models are both multicausal and distinctive in terms of the relative importance each attaches to certain events and processes. Each model is restricted in its ability to explain abnormal behavior to the extent that it fails to incorporate important components of

APPROXIMATE AGE	NORMAL ACHIEVEMENTS	COMMON BEHAVIOR PROBLEMS	CLINICAL DISORDERS
0–2	Eating, sleeping, attachment	Stubbornness, temper, toileting difficulties	Mental retardation, feeding disorders, autistic disorder
2–5	Language, toileting, self-care skills, self-control, peer relationships	Arguing, demanding attention, disobedience, fears, overactivity, resisting bedtime	Speech and language disorders, problems stemming from child abuse and neglect, some anxiety disorders, such as phobias
6–11	Academic skills and rules, rule-governed games, simple responsibilities	Arguing, inability to concentrate, self-consciousness, showing off	ADHD, learning disorders, school refusal behavior, conduct problems
12–20	Relations with opposite sex, personal identity, separation from family, increased responsibilities	Arguing, bragging	Anorexia, bulimia, delinquency, suicide attempts, drug and alcohol abuse, schizophrenia, depression

Figure 2.2. A developmental overview (Based on Achenbach, 1982)

other models. Fortunately, such disciplinary boundaries are gradually diminishing, as different perspectives take into account important variables derived from other models. For example, biological influences are often taken into account when explaining how psychological factors, like behavior or cognition, interact over time and result in a psychological disorder (Curtis & Cicchetti, 2003).

Over time, major theories of abnormal child psychology have become compatible with one another. Rather than offering contradictory views, each theory contributes one or more pieces of the puzzle of atypical development. As all the available pieces are assembled, the picture of a particular child or adolescent disorder becomes more and more distinct. Psychological theories are merely tools to study human behavior; the more you learn what these tools can and cannot do and which tool to use for which purpose, the more knowledgeable and skilled you will become. Remember that no single integrative theory fully captures the diversity of perspectives and findings represented by current research in abnormal child psychology.

SECTION SUMMARY

- A theory allows us to make educated guesses and predictions about behavior based on existing knowledge, and to explore these possible explanations empirically.

- A central theme of the text is the importance of considering multiple, interactive causes for abnormal behavior, in conjunction with major developmental changes that typically occur.

- Three underlying assumptions about abnormal development are stressed: It is multiply determined, the child and the environment are interdependent, and it involves continuities and discontinuities of behavior patterns over time.

- The complexity of abnormal child behavior requires consideration of the full range of biological, psychological, and sociocultural factors that influence children's development.

Developmental Considerations

Even though children's psychological disorders have very different symptoms and causes, they share a common ground: They are an indication of adaptational failure in one or more areas of development (Rutter & Sroufe, 2000). **Adaptational failure** is the failure to master or progress in accomplishing developmental milestones. In other words, at the broadest level, children with psychological disorders deviate from children their own age on some as-

Digital Stock/Corbis

Children's development follows an organized pattern, which is nurtured through positive experiences with their caregivers.

pect of normal development. Again, such failure or deviation is rarely due to a single cause, but typically results from an ongoing interaction between individual development and environmental conditions.

The causes and outcomes of abnormal child behavior operate in dynamic and interactive ways over time, making them a challenge to disentangle. Designating a specific factor, like Jake's reading problem, as a cause or an outcome of a particular disorder usually reflects the point at which we take note of the problem. His reading problem, for example, may be viewed as a disorder in its own right (such as a learning disorder in reading), the cause of his other difficulties (such as poor study habits and oppositional behavior), or the outcome of some other condition or disorder, (such as a communication disorder).

Organization of Development

Change and reorganization are fundamental aspects of biological and behavioral systems (Rutter & Sroufe, 2000). An organizational viewpoint looks closely at the psychological processes that may explain how these systems influence each other. In an attempt to understand abnormal development, we may choose to focus on any or all aspects of this organizational process. In **organization of development,** early patterns of adaptation, such as infant eye contact and speech sounds, evolve over time with structure and transform into higher-order functions, like speech and language. Prior patterns of adaptation are incorporated into successive reorganizations at subsequent periods of development, much like how toddlers learn to make certain speech sounds before they develop the ability to use language.

An organizational view of development implies an active, dynamic process of continual change and transformation. As the child's biological abilities unfold during each new stage of development, they interact with environmental factors to direct and redirect the course of development (Emde & Spicer, 2000). Because development is organized, sensitive periods play a meaningful role in any discussion of normal and abnormal behavior. **Sensitive periods** are windows of time during which environmental influences on development, both good and bad, are enhanced (Bruer, 2001). Infants, for example, are highly sensitive to emotional cues and proximity to their caregivers, which assists them in developing secure attachments (R.A. Thompson, 2001). Toddlers are sensitive to the basic sounds of language, which helps them distinguish and combine sounds to form words (Bruer, 2001). Sensitive periods can be enhanced opportunities for learning but are not the only opportunities; change can take place at other times. For example, children adopted from orphanages show a number of negative developmental outcomes as a result of their early institutional deprivation. However, their outcome is also affected by later experiences in the post-institutional environment (Maclean, 2003). Human development is a process of increasing differentiation and integration, more like a network of interconnecting pathways than one straight line.

The attempt to understand the seemingly endless possible causes that influence children's normal and abnormal development is made easier by the fact that it generally proceeds in an organized, hierarchical manner (Sameroff, 2000). Simply stated, a child's current abilities or limitations are influenced by prior accomplishments, similar to your progress through trigonometry or calculus depends on the command of arithmetic you acquired in elementary school. As children develop greater abilities or show signs of adaptational failure, these changes influence their further developmental success or failure. Studying abnormal child behavior within a developmental psychopathology perspective, as described next, fosters an understanding of the interactive, progressive nature of children's abilities and difficulties.

Developmental Psychopathology Perspective

Developmental psychopathology is an approach to describing and studying disorders of childhood, adolescence, and beyond in a manner that emphasizes the importance of developmental processes and tasks. This approach uses abnormal development to inform normal development and vice versa (Lewis, 2000; Rutter & Sroufe, 2000). It also provides a useful framework for organizing the study of abnormal child psychology around milestones and sequences in physical, cognitive, social-emotional, and educational development. Simply stated, developmental psychopathology emphasizes the role of developmental processes, the importance of context, and the influence of multiple and interacting events in shaping adaptive and maladaptive development. We adopt this perspective as an organizing framework to describe this dynamic, multi-

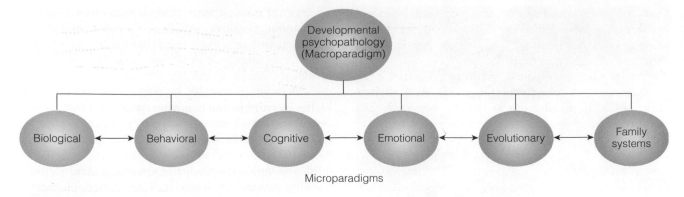

Figure 2.3. Developmental psychopathology as a macroparadigm. (Based on Achenbach, 1990).

dimensional process leading to abnormal outcomes in development (Mash & Dozois, 2003).

The developmental psychopathology perspective is a way to integrate different approaches around a common core of phenomena and questions. For this reason, it is viewed as a **macroparadigm** (*macro,* broad or global; *paradigm,* philosophical approach or framework for studying phenomena), which means it serves to coordinate other paradigms that deal with particular subsets of variables, methods, and explanations (Luthar, Burack, & Cicchetti, 1997). Figure 2.3 illustrates relations between developmental psychopathology viewed as a macroparadigm and relevant microparadigms and theories. A developmental psychopathology perspective does not replace particular theories; it is intended to sharpen our awareness of connections among phenomena that might otherwise seem unrelated (Achenbach, 1990).

A central belief of developmental psychopathology is that to understand maladaptive behavior adequately, one must view it in relation to what is normative for a given period of development (Cicchetti & Sroufe, 2000). The main focus is to highlight developmental processes, such as language and peer relations, and how they function by looking at extremes and variations in developmental outcome (Cicchetti & Richters, 1993). In so doing, it emphasizes the importance and complexity of biological, family, and sociocultural factors in predicting and understanding developmental changes. It draws on knowledge from several disciplines, including psychology, psychiatry, sociology, and neuroscience, and integrates this knowledge within a developmental framework (Pennington, 2002). Throughout this book, the developmental psychopathology perspective adds developmental relevance and richness to categorically based DSM-IV-TR disorders.

SECTION SUMMARY

- Children's development is organized, which means that early patterns of adaptation evolve over time and transform into higher-order functions in a structured, predictable manner.

- Developmental psychopathology provides a useful framework for organizing the study of abnormal child psychology around milestones and sequences in physical, cognitive, social-emotional, and educational development.

We turn now to three major perspectives on abnormal child development: (1) biological perspectives, which include both genetic and neurobiological factors that are often established (but by no means fixed) at birth or soon thereafter; (2) psychological perspectives, such as emotions, relationships, and thought processes; and (3) family, social, and cultural influences, which set additional parameters on normal and abnormal development.

Biological Perspectives

Broadly speaking, a neurobiological perspective considers brain and nervous system functions as underlying causes of psychological disorders in children and adults. Biological influences on the very young child's brain development include genetic and constitutional factors, neuroanatomy, and rates of maturation. Regions of the brain are highly influenced by the availability of various biochemicals and neurohormones, which interact differently to affect an individual's psychological experiences (Cicchetti & Cannon, 1999). This process depends on environmental factors that serve to direct or reroute ongoing brain processes. Remember that a neurobiological perspective acknowledges and recognizes the need to incorporate environmental influences in accounting for disorders.

The developing brain has long been a mystery, but its secrets are gradually being revealed. The examination of biological influences begins with the amazing process of neuronal growth and differentiation. During pregnancy, the fetal brain develops from a few all-purpose cells into a complex organ made up of billions of specialized, interconnected neurons (Nowakowski & Hayes, 1999). The speed and distance these emerging neurons travel are astonishing as they multiply to form various brain structures and functions. The brain stem commands heartbeat and breathing, the cerebellum controls and coordinates sensory-motor integration, and the cortex is where thought and perception originate.

Embryonic development generates an initial over-abundance of neurons (Innocenti, 1982). At first these cells are largely undifferentiated, but as they reach their destinations, they become neurons with axons that carry electrical signals to other parts of the brain. These axonal connections, or synapses, form the brain's circuits and lay the foundation for further growth and differentiation. Notably, genes determine the main highways along which axons travel to make their connection, but to reach particular target cells, axons follow chemical cues strewn along their path that tell them the direction to various destinations.

By the fifth month of prenatal development, most axons have reached their general destination, although there are far more axons than the target cells can accommodate. Thus, during early childhood, synapses multiply, then selective *pruning* reduces the number of connections in a way that gradually shapes and differentiates important brain functions (Derryberry & Reed, 1994). The nervous system seems to prepare itself for new growth and demands by sending in reinforcements, and then cutting back once the environment has signaled it has everything it needs. Throughout life we undergo cycles that narrow the gap between structure and function. At the level of the nervous system, the microanatomy of the brain is constantly redefined to meet the demands and requirements of an adult world (C. A. Nelson & Bloom, 1997). Like the pruning of a tree, this process fosters healthy growth of different areas of the brain according to individual needs and environmental demands, and eliminates connections that serve to restrict healthy growth.

How permanent are the early connections formed as brain development proceeds in an organized, predictable fashion? This question has provoked different theories and agonized many parents concerned about the significance of children's early development. For instance, if early brain functions are unlikely to change, this implies that early experiences set the course for lifetime development. Freud's similar contention implied that an individual's core personality is formed from an early age, which sets the pace and boundaries for further personality formation. To the contrary, scientists now believe that brain functions undergo continual changes as they adapt to environmental demands.

Neural Plasticity and the Role of Experience

Many early neural connections are not stable; some are strengthened and become more established due to use, while many others regress or disappear. Thus, the answer

". . . It now appears that virtually any manipulation that produces an enduring change in behavior leaves an anatomical footprint in the brain." (Kolb, Gibb, & Robinson, 2003, p. 4).

to the question about the permanence of early connections is that the brain shows neural plasticity throughout the course of development (Reiss & Neiderhiser, 2000). **Neural plasticity,** or malleability, means the brain's anatomical differentiation is use-dependent: Nature provides the basic processes, whereas nurture provides the experiences needed to select the most adaptive network of connections, based on the use and function of each (Cicchetti & Cannon, 1999). It is truly fascinating how nature and nurture work together to create such highly specific, extremely adaptive central nervous system functions.

Think of the developing brain as a work in progress, one in which the environment plays an essential role as supervisor of this dynamic rewiring project (Thatcher, 1994). In fact, environmental experience is now recognized to be critical to the differentiation of brain tissue itself. Although nature has a plan for creating the human brain and central nervous system, environmental opportunities and limitations significantly influence this plan from the beginning. Thus, a transactional model is needed to explain normal and abnormal development. Because the structure of a child's brain remains surprisingly malleable for months and even years after birth, transaction occurs between ongoing brain development and environmental experiences; neither nature nor nurture is sufficient to explain the complexity of the developing brain (Grossman et al., 2003).

Experience, of course, comes in all shapes and sizes. The prenatal environment and childhood illness and diet count as experience, as do maltreatment and inadequate stimulation. Children's early caregiving experiences play an especially important role in designing the parts of the brain involved in emotion, personality, and behavior (Sameroff & Fiese, 2000a). Attachment with their caregivers, for instance, may increase children's ability to learn and cope with stress (E. Waters, Merrick, Treboux, Crowell, & Albersheim, 2000). Abuse and neglect can prime the brain for a lifetime of struggle with handling stress or forming healthy relationships (Scott, Wolfe, & Wekerle, 2003).

The maturation of the brain is an organized, hierarchical process that builds on earlier function, with brain structures restructuring and growing throughout the life span (Plomin & Rutter, 1998). Primitive areas of the brain mature first, during the first 3 years of life; these brain regions, which govern basic sensory and motor skills, undergo the most dramatic restructuring early in life. Moreover, these perceptual centers, along with instinctive centers, such as the limbic system, are strongly affected by early childhood experiences and set the foundation for further development (Thatcher, 1994). The frontal cortex, which governs planning and decision-making, and the cerebellum, a center for motor skills, are not rewired until a person is 5 to 7 years old. Major restructuring of the brain occurs between ages 9 and 11 in relation to pubertal development, and then throughout adolescence the brain once again prunes unnecessary synaptic connections. Thus, the brain certainly does not stop changing after three years. For some functions, the windows of influence are only beginning to close at that age, while for others they are only beginning to open (C.A. Nelson, 1999). Our brain functions undergo lifelong renovation, with restructuring being a natural by-product of maturity.

Because the brain is intrinsically shaped by the effects of early experience, the consequences of inadequate or traumatic experience may be enduring and extremely difficulty to change (Teicher, Andersen, Polcari, Anderson, & Navalta, 2002). During this evolution of brain growth and differentiation many things can go wrong, thereby altering how neurons form or interconnect. Typically, problems or disruptions occurring at a younger age are generally associated with more severe organic disorders and central nervous system complications. Safeguards such as proper prenatal care, proper nutrition, and avoidance of tobacco or alcohol during pregnancy can go a long way in reducing the risk of such complications and lifelong disabilities.

Genetic Contributions

"Genetics explains why you look like your father, and if you don't, why you should."

—Tammy, age 8

To address the important role of genetic influences, we first must understand the nature of genes, bearing in mind that virtually any trait a child possesses results from the interaction of environmental and genetic factors (Rende & Plomin, 1995; Rutter & Silberg, 2002). A review of genetics terminology and function may assist our understanding of some causes of abnormal child behavior.

Each person's unique genome is established at conception, which consists of approximately 30,000 genes. Genes contain genetic information from each parent, and they are distributed on 22 matched pairs of chromosomes and a single pair of sex chromosomes. In males, the sex chromosome pair consists of an X and a Y chromosome (XY), and in females the sex chromosome pair consists of two X chromosomes (XX).

Genetic factors are implicated in all of the childhood disorders discussed in this text. Some genetic influences are expressed early in development, such as behavioral inhibition or shyness (Nigg, 2000), whereas others show up years later, such as a depressive cognitive style (Garber & Flynn, 1998). Moreover, the expression of genetic influences is malleable and responsive to the social environment (Reiss & Neiderhiser, 2000). Positive environmental circumstances can help a child "beat the odds" of developing a significant disorder, despite genetic predisposition (C. A. Nelson, 2000).

Many genes have been implicated in childhood disorders, but very rarely is one gene a single cause of a disorder (State, Lombroso, Pauls, & Leckman, 2000). Therefore, rather than ask whether a specific disorder is due to genetic makeup or environmental influences, we should be concerned with this question: To what extent are given behaviors due to variations in genetic endowment and the environment, and the interaction between these two factors? An understanding of the nature of genes sheds light on this question.

The Nature of Genes　A gene is basically a stretch of DNA, and by itself, it does not produce a behavior, an emotion, or even a passing thought. Rather, it produces a

Calvin and Hobbes　　　　　　by Bill Watterson

Calvin and Hobbes. © Watterson. Reprinted with permission of Universal Press Syndicate. All rights reserved.

protein. Although these proteins are vital for the brain to function, very rarely do they cause a behavior to happen. Instead, they produce tendencies to respond to the environment in certain ways (Sapolsky, 1997). Each of us may have different genetic vulnerabilities, tendencies, and predispositions, but rarely are the outcomes inevitable (Fox, Calkins, & Bell, 1994). The lesson in all of this is simple, yet important: The false notion that genes determine behavior should be replaced with the more accurate statement: Genes influence how we respond to the environment.

Behavioral Genetics　Sorting out the interactive influences of nature and nurture is the not-so-easy task of **behavioral genetics,** a branch of genetics that investigates possible connections between a genetic predisposition and observed behavior, taking into account environmental and genetic influences. Behavioral genetics researchers often begin their investigation by conducting familial aggregation studies. They look for nonrandom clustering of disorders or characteristics within a given family, and compare these results with the random distribution of the disorders or characteristics in the general population (Cleveland, Wiebe, van den Oord, & Rowe, 2000). For example, parents of children with childhood-onset schizophrenia tend to have higher rates of schizophrenia spectrum disorders relative to normative prevalence rates.

Family aggregation studies cannot control for environmental variables that may also contribute to a particular outcome. For example, a child may be anxious because of his parents' child-rearing methods rather than their genetic contributions. To increase scientific rigor following suggestive familial aggregation studies, researchers may conduct twin studies to control for the contribution of genetic factors (Rutter, 2000b). Twin studies may involve identical, or monozygotic (MZ), twins, who have the same set of genes, as well as fraternal, or dizygotic (DZ), twins, who share about half of each other's genes (the same as all first-degree relatives). The crucial scientific question is whether identical twins share the same trait—say, reading difficulties—more than fraternal twins. Studies on twins provide a powerful research strategy for examining the role of genetic influences in both psychiatric and nonpsychiatric disorders. For example, the common or shared environment presents a potential confound in any twin study, unless the twins are reared apart (Deutsch & Kinsbourne, 1990).

"Behind every crooked thought there is a crooked molecule."

—*Anonymous*

Molecular Genetics　In contrast to the methods of behavioral genetics, methods of molecular genetics offer more direct support for genetic influences on child psychopathology. **Molecular genetics** methods directly assess the association between variations in DNA sequences and variations in particular trait(s). More than an association, variations in genetic sequences are thought to cause the variations in the trait(s) (Pennington, 2002). As we shall discuss throughout this book, molecular genetic methods have been used to identify specific genes for many childhood disorders including autism, attention-deficit/hyperactivity disorder, and learning disability. However, discovering that mutations in one gene or another causally influence a particular form of child psychopathology is only the beginning. The longer-term goal is to determine how genetic mutations alter how the genes function in the development of the brain and behavior for different psychopathologies (Pennington, 2002).

The identification of specific genes has the potential to greatly enhance our understanding of a disorder, and its specific components (Stodgell, Ingram, & Hyman, 2000). However, identifying a specific gene for any disorder addresses only a small part of genetic risk. Similar and multiple interactive genes are a far more likely cause than a single gene (Rutter, 2000a). Moreover, genetic influences are probabilistic rather than deterministic; environmental and genetic factors generally have equal importance (Plomin & Rutter, 1998). Most forms of abnormal child behavior are polygenic, involving a number of susceptibility genes that interact with one another, and with environmental influences to result in observed levels of impairment (State et al., 2000).

In summary, it is fair to say that many genes influence much of our development and most of our behavior, personality, and even intelligence. However, individual genes cannot account for the major psychological disorders presented in this text. Specific genes are sometimes associated with certain psychological disorders such as some forms of mental retardation. The behavioral geneticists conclude that genetic contributions to psychological disorders come from many genes, and each makes a relatively small contribution (Rende & Plomin, 1995).

Neurobiological Contributions

The study of abnormal child psychology requires a working familiarity with brain structures, as shown in Figures 2.4, 2.5, and 2.6. This section provides an overview of major structures mentioned later in the context of specific disorders. Once you are familiar with the various areas and functions of the brain, you will have the basic vocabulary needed to understand the remarkable discoveries being made.

Brain Structure and Function　The brain is often divided into the *brain stem* and the *forebrain* (telencephalon) because of their unique functions. The brain stem, located at the base of the brain, handles most of the autonomic functions necessary to stay alive. The lowest part of the brain

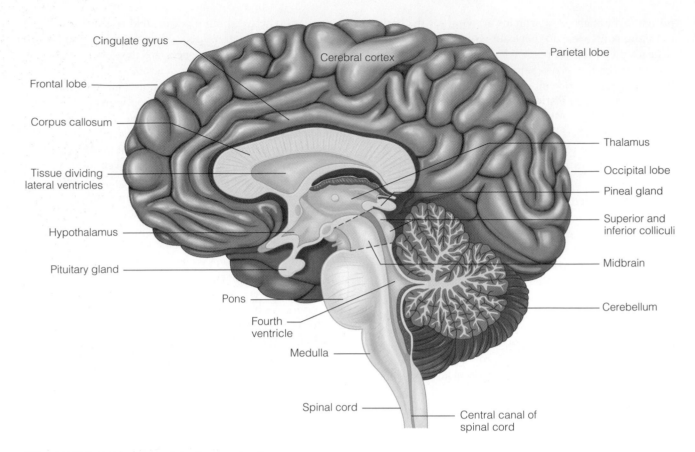

Figure 2.4. Structures of the human brain

Source: Adapted from *Brain and Behavior,* by Bob Garrett.

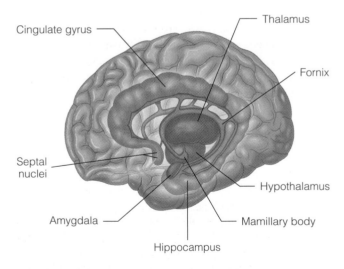

Figure 2.5. Structures of the limbic system

Source: Adapted from *Brain and Behavior,* by Bob Garrett.

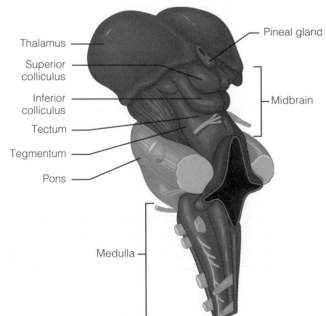

Figure 2.6. The brain stem (cerebellum removed to reveal other structures)

Source: Adapted from *Brain and Behavior,* by Bob Garrett.

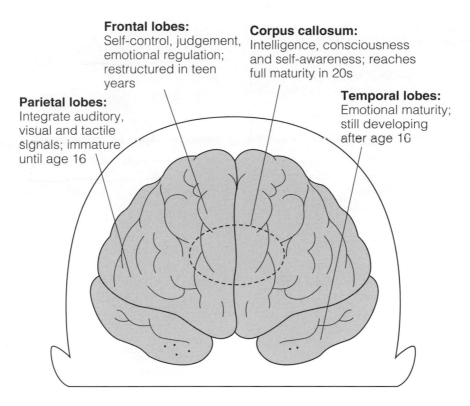

Frontal lobes:
Self-control, judgement, emotional regulation; restructured in teen years

Corpus callosum:
Intelligence, consciousness and self-awareness; reaches full maturity in 20s

Parietal lobes:
Integrate auditory, visual and tactile signals; immature until age 16

Temporal lobes:
Emotional maturity; still developing after age 16

Figure 2.7. The lobes of the brain and their functions

stem, called the *hindbrain*, contains the *medulla*, the *pons*, and the *cerebellum*. The hindbrain provides essential regulation of autonomic activities such as breathing, heartbeat, and digestion, and the cerebellum controls motor coordination. The brain stem also contains the *midbrain*, which coordinates movement with sensory input. The midbrain houses the *reticular activating system* (RAS), which contributes to processes of arousal and tension.

At the very top of the brain stem is the diencephalon, located just below the forebrain. The diencephalon contains the *thalamus* and *hypothalamus*, which are both essential to the regulation of behavior and emotion. The diencephalon functions primarily as a relay between the forebrain and the remaining lower areas of the brain stem.

Next is the forebrain, which has evolved in humans into highly specialized functions. At the base of the forebrain is an area known as the *limbic*, or border, *system*. It contains a number of structures that are suspected causes of psychopathology, such as the *hippocampus, cingulate gyrus, septum,* and *amygdala*. These important structures regulate emotional experiences and expressions and play a significant role in learning and impulse control. The limbic system also regulates the basic drives of sex, aggression, hunger, and thirst.

Also at the base of the forebrain lies the basal ganglia, which includes the *caudate nucleus*. Researchers are discovering that this area regulates, organizes, and filters information related to cognition, emotions, mood and motor function, and has been implicated in attention-deficit/hyperactivity disorder (ADHD; discussed in Chapter 5), disorders affecting motor behavior, such as tics and tremors and obsessive-compulsive disorder (discussed in Chapter 7).

The cerebral cortex, the largest part of the forebrain, gives us our distinctly human qualities and allows us to look to the future and plan, to reason, and to create. The cerebral cortex is divided into two hemispheres that look very much alike, but have unique specialties, or functions. The left hemisphere (dominant in right-handed persons) plays a chief role in verbal and other cognitive processes. The right hemisphere (dominant in left-handed persons) is better at social perception and creativity. (This is why we left-handed persons are considered the only ones in our right minds.) Researchers believe that each hemisphere plays a different role in certain psychological disorders, such as communication and learning disorders.

Around puberty, the brain develops new brain cells and neural connections, and then once again begins to reorganize and consolidate (P. M. Thompson et al., 2000). This new growth and restructuring results in further maturation of the lobes of the brain. Figure 2.7 shows the *temporal, parietal,* and *frontal lobes* of the brain and their important functions of each area. The frontal lobes show up most often in subsequent chapters on disorders and are worth special attention. The **frontal lobes** contain the functions underlying most of our thinking and reasoning abilities, including memory. These functions enable us to make sense of social relationships and customs and to relate to the world and the people around us, which is why they have considerable relevance in the study of abnormal child psychology. Fortunately, all of these functions continue to mature well into late adolescence and early adulthood. By implication, the brain you have when you reach adolescence is not the one you have now.

Remarkably, these critical brain areas perform their functions in an integrated, harmonious fashion, aided by important regulatory systems and neurotransmitters, which permits the whole to be much larger than the sum of its parts. However, for many disorders defined in this text one or more of these brain areas are not performing their functions as they should, either as a result of other problems, or as a primary cause of the disorder.

The Endocrine System   The endocrine system is an important regulatory system that has been linked to specific psychological disorders, such as anxiety and mood disorders, in both children and adults. There are several endocrine glands, and each produces a particular hormone that it releases into the bloodstream. The *adrenal* glands (located on top of the kidneys) are most familiar because they produce **epinephrine** (also known as adrenaline) in response to stress. Epinephrine energizes us and prepares our bodies ready for possible threat or challenge.

The *thyroid* gland produces a hormone, thyroxine, that is needed for proper energy metabolism and growth and is implicated in certain eating disorders of children and youth (discussed in Chapter 13). Finally, the *pituitary* gland, located deep within the brain, orchestrates the body's regulatory functions by producing a variety of regulatory hormones, including estrogen and testosterone. Because the endocrine system is closely related to the immune system, which protects us from disease and many other biological threats, it is not surprising that it is implicated in a variety of disorders, particularly health- and stress-related disorders (discussed in Chapter 12).

One brain connection that is implicated in some psychological disorders involves the hypothalamus and the endocrine system. The *hypothalamus* carries out the commands it receives from the adjacent pituitary gland and other hormones, such as those regulating hunger and thirst. The pituitary gland in turn stimulates the adrenal glands to produce epinephrine and the stress hormone known as **cortisol**. The hypothalamus control center, coupled with the pituitary and adrenal glands, that produce cortisol, make up a regulatory system in the brain known as the **hypothalamic-pituitary-adrenal (HPA) axis.** Box 2.2 explains how this axis has been implicated in several psychological disorders, especially those connected to a person's response to stress and ability to regulate emotions, such as anxiety and mood disorders.

Neurotransmitters   Neurotransmitters are similar to biochemical currents in the brain. These currents develop in an organized fashion to make meaningful connections

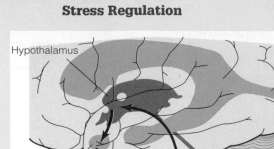

BOX 2.2. **The HPA Axis and Stress Regulation**

The HPA axis is a central component of the brain's neuroendocrine response to stress. The hypothalamus, when stimulated, secretes the corticotropin-releasing hormone (CRH), which stimulates the pituitary gland to secrete the andrenocorticotropic hormone (ACTH) into the bloodstream. ACTH then causes the adrenal glands to release cortisol, the familiar stress hormone that arouses the body to meet a challenging situation. This system, like many others, works on a feedback loop: Cortisol modulates the stress response by acting on the hypothalamus to inhibit the continued release of CRH (Sternberg & Gold, 1997). Researchers are discovering that this important feedback loop, which regulates our level of arousal and apprehension, can be seriously disrupted or damaged by various traumatic and uncontrollable events. These events can cause a child or adolescent to maintain a state of fear or alertness that becomes toxic over prolonged periods of time (Bremner & Vermetten, 2001; DeBellis, Burke, Trickett, & Putnam, 1996).

that serve larger functions, like thinking and feeling. Neurons that are more sensitive to one type of neurotransmitter, such as serotonin, tend to cluster together and form **brain circuits**, which are paths from one part of the brain to another (R. R. Dean, Kelsey, Heller, & Ciaranello, 1993). Tens of thousands of these circuits operate in our brains. Their connective pathways and function have been revealed in recent years in ways that were inconceivable over a decade ago.

Brain circuits and neurotransmitters have been tied to particular psychological disorders, but they also offer pos-

Table 2.1

Major Neurotransmitters and Their Implicated Roles in Psychopathology

NEUROTRANSMITTER	NORMAL FUNCTIONS	IMPLICATED ROLE IN PSYCHOPATHOLOGY
Benzodiazepine-GABA	Reduces arousal and moderates emotional responses, such as anger, hostility, and aggression Is linked to feelings of anxiety and discomfort	Anxiety disorder
Dopamine	May act as a *switch* that turns on various brain circuits, allowing other neurotransmitters to inhibit or facilitate emotions or behavior Is involved in exploratory, extroverted, and pleasure-seeking activity	Schizophrenia Mood disorders Attention-deficit/hyperactivity disorder (ADHD)
Norepinephrine	Facilitates or controls emergency reactions and alarm responses Plays a role in emotional and behavioral regulation	Not *directly* involved in specific disorders (acts generally to regulate or modulate behavioral tendencies)
Serotonin	Plays a role in information processing and motor coordination Inhibits children's tendency to explore their surroundings Moderates and regulates a number of critical behaviors, such as eating, sleeping, and expressing anger	Regulatory problems, such as eating and sleep disorders Obsessive-compulsive disorder Schizophrenia and mood disorders

sible avenues for treatment. Psychoactive drugs work by either increasing or decreasing the flow of various neurotransmitters, for example, increasing dopamine in the case of stimulant medications for ADHD. However, like the influence of genetics, changes in neurotransmitter activity may make people *more or less likely* to exhibit certain kinds of behavior in certain situations, but they do not cause the behavior directly. Table 2.1 summarizes the four neurotransmitter systems most often mentioned in connection with psychological disorders, and is a useful guide to discussions of etiology in later chapters.

SECTION SUMMARY

- Brain functions undergo continual changes, described as neural plasticity, as they adapt to environmental demands.

- Genetic influences depend on the environment. Genetic endowment influences behavior, emotions, and thoughts; environmental events are necessary for this influence to be expressed.

- Neurobiological contributions to abnormal child behavior include knowledge of brain structures, the endocrine system, and neurotransmitters, which perform their functions in an integrated, harmonious fashion.

Psychological Perspectives

Each major psychological perspective described in this section has value in explaining the development of psychopathology. At the same time, each perspective has certain limitations, and may be more or less applicable to any particular disorder or situation. Again, bear in mind that abnormal behavior results from transactions between environmental and individual influences. Children's inherited characteristics coupled with the experiences and influences in their environment make them the way they are today. Also, some seemingly maladaptive behaviors, like excessive fearfulness or watchfulness, may in fact be understandable when considered in the context of the child's environment that involves parental abuse or school violence.

Our interest in psychological bases for abnormal behavior begins with a focus on the role of emotions in establishing an infant's ability to adapt to her new surroundings. To an infant who has limited means of expression and interpretation, emotions provide the initial filter for organizing so much new information and avoiding potential harm. Similarly, early relationships with one or more caregivers provide structure and regulation to these emotional responses. As the child develops, cognitive pro-

The ability to infer another's emotional state by reading facial, gestural, postural, and vocal cues has an important adaptive function, especially for infants and toddlers.

cesses like self-efficacy and subjective values play a larger role in assisting the young child to make sense of her world, and to reorganize earlier functions that may be unnecessary or even maladaptive as she faces new challenges involving language development, peer interactions, and similar skills. As with brain development, things can go wrong at any point along this continuum of emotional and cognitive development as a function of the child's interaction with her environment.

Emotional Influences

Emotions and affective expression are core elements of human psychological experience. From birth, they are a central feature of infant activity and regulation (Sroufe, 1997). Throughout our lives, emotional reactions assist us in our fight-or-flight response—to alert us to danger and to ensure our safety. From an evolutionary perspective, emotions give special value to events and make particular actions most likely to occur. In effect, emotions tell us what to pay attention to and what to ignore, what to approach and what to avoid. Given their important job, backed up by powerful stress-regulating hormones like cortisol, emotions are critical to healthy adaptation.

Interest in emotional processes and their relation to abnormal child behavior has grown considerably in recent years (Lemerise & Arsenio, 2000). Children's emotional experiences, expressions, and regulation affect the quality of their social interactions and relationships, and thus are at the foundation of early personality development. Researchers are discovering a wealth of information demonstrating the influential role of emotion in children's lives. Emotions serve not only as important internal monitoring and guidance systems designed to appraise events as being beneficial or dangerous, but also provide motivation for action (Zahn-Waxler, Klimes-Dougan, & Slattery, 2000).

Children have a natural tendency to attend to emotional cues from others, which helps them learn to interpret and regulate their own emotions. They learn, from a very young age, through the emotional expressions of others (Bretherton, 1995). Within their first year of life, they learn the importance of emotions for communication and regulation; by their second year, they have some ability to attribute cause to emotional expression. Of particular interest to abnormal child psychology is the finding that children look to the emotional expression and cues of their caregivers to provide them with the information needed to formulate a basic understanding of what's going on. To young children, emotions are a primary form of communication that permits them to explore their world with increasing independence (LaFreniere, 1999).

Emotion Reactivity and Regulation   We can divide emotional processes into two dimensions: emotion reactivity and emotion regulation. **Emotion reactivity** refers to individual differences in the threshold and intensity of emotional experience, which provide clues to an individual's level of distress and sensitivity to the environment. **Emotion regulation,** on the other hand, involves enhancing, maintaining, or inhibiting emotional arousal, which is usually done for a specific purpose or goal (Southam-Gerow & Kendall, 2002). Jake, for example, was emotionally reactive to certain academic tasks, and became upset and couldn't concentrate. This emotional reaction may lead to poor regulation, resulting in Jake becoming very distraught and difficult to manage at times. Once again, a transactional process is at work, whereby emotional reactions prompt the need for regulation, which influences further emotional expression.

A further distinction can be made between problems in *regulation* and problems in *dysregulation*. Regulation problems involve weak or absent control structures, such as Jake's trouble concentrating in class; dysregulation means that existing control structures operate maladaptively (Keenan, 2000). For example, a child may be fearful even when there is no reason in the environment to be fearful or anxious.

Children's emotion regulation abilities, as often shown by their emotion reactivity and expression, are important signals of normal and abnormal development. Emotions also help young children learn more about themselves and their surroundings, as part of the process of learning to identify and monitor their feelings and behavior. The child–caregiver relationship plays a critical role in this process because it provides the basic setting for children to express emotions and to have caring guidance and limits placed on them. Authoritative parents establish limits for the child that are both sensitive to the child's individual development and needs, and demanding of the child to foster self-control and healthy regulation (Maccoby & Martin, 1983). Because of its vital role in emotional development, the child–caregiver relationship surfaces again and again in discussing childhood disorders.

Some forms of emotion dysregulation may be adaptive in one environment or at one time but maladaptive in other situations. Children who have been emotionally and sexually abused may show shallow emotions, known as numbing, which is a symptom of a post-traumatic stress reaction that serves to protect the child from overwhelming pain and trauma (described in Chapter 14). If numbing becomes a characteristic way of coping with stressors later in life, however, it may interfere with adaptive functioning and long-term goals.

Temperament and Early Personality Styles You hear it all the time: "She was an easy baby, right from the first day I brought her home from the hospital," or "Sleep? What's that? Since little Freddy was born, we are up all hours of the night, feeding, changing, and trying to soothe him." Unmistakably, some infants are more placid than others, some are more active, and some are more high-strung, and these differences are often recognizable in the first few days or weeks of life (Thomas & Chess, 1977). What relevance does this have to abnormal development?

The development of emotion regulation or dysregulation is thought to derive from both socialization and innate predispositions, or temperament. **Temperament** refers to the child's organized style of behavior that appears early in development, such as fussiness or fearfulness, which shapes the child's approach to his or her environment and vice versa (Emde & Spicer, 2000; Rothbart & Bates, 1998). Temperament is a subset of the broader domain of personality, so it is often considered an early building block of personality (Shiner & Caspi, 2003).

Such constitutional predispositions do not imply a certain destiny leading to a psychological disorder; a particular outcome appears to be based on a series of reciprocal interactions between innate predispositions (debilitative or protective) and situational circumstances, such as a supportive or stressful environment.

Three primary dimensions of temperament have relevance to risk of abnormal child development (Rothbart & Mauro, 1990):

1. *Positive affect and approach*. This dimension describes the "easy child," who is generally approachable and adaptive to his or her environment, and possesses the ability to regulate basic functions of eating, sleeping, and elimination relatively smoothly.

2. *Fearful or inhibited*. This dimension describes the "slow-to-warm-up child," who is cautious in his or her approach to novel or challenging situations. These children are more variable in self-regulation and adaptability, and may show distress or negativity toward some situations.

3. *Negative affect or irritability*. This dimension describes the "difficult child," who is predominantly negative or intense in mood, not very adaptable, and arrhythmic. Some children with this temperament show distress when faced with novel or challenging situations, and others are prone to general distress or irritability, including when limitations are placed on them.

These temperament dimensions, or early self-regulatory styles, may be linked to the development of psychopathology or risk conditions in several ways. In some instances, a temperamental style may be highly related to a particular disorder. In other instances, the condition may develop from the features closely related to temperament, but the condition itself may appear unrelated (Rothbart & Bates, 1998). For example, an infant's extreme sensitivity to emotional stimuli may contribute to a tendency to withdraw from others as a toddler or preschooler; over time, this tendency may transform into an interpersonal style characterized by a self-reported lack of feeling toward others and, consequently, peer rejection or other risk conditions. Also, infant negative affect can contribute to maternal withdrawal or indifference, leading to insecure attachment and its associated risk conditions. There is growing empirical evidence linking early behavioral styles to adult personality characteristics, as described in Box 2.3.

To recap, emotion reactivity and regulation processes begin at birth, and form recognizable patterns of infant temperament and later personality. Emotion regulation involves a variety of increasingly complex developmental tasks aided by the formation of healthy relationships and other environmental resources. The degree of interference

BOX 2.3 Similarities in Children's Early Behavioral Styles and Adult Personality

Caspi et al. (2003) conducted a landmark study of the connection between early temperament style in children and their later personality traits as adults. These researchers observed 1000 children at age 3 and evaluated their temperament along five dimensions: Undercontrolled, Inhibited, Confident, Reserved, and Well-adjusted. Twenty-three years later they conducted an assessment of these same individuals as adults, and found some interesting consistencies in "personality style" over this length of time.

When observed at age 3, children classified as Undercontrolled (10% of the sample) were rated as irritable, impulsive, and restless. At age 26, these same individuals scored high on personality traits linked to "negative emotionality." They were easily upset, most likely to overreact to minor events, and reported feeling mistreated, deceived, and betrayed by others. Children classified as Inhibited (8% of the sample) were considered a bit fearful and easily upset, and by age 26 they were described as unassertive and took little pleasure in life. The researchers found that the remaining three temperament groups did not display such dramatic personality profiles as adults, but a considerable amount of continuity in style did occur over time. Confident children (28% of the sample) were seen as friendly and eager to explore, and they were the least conventional and most extroverted as adults. Reserved children (15% of the sample) were described as timid and somewhat uncomfortable, and by adulthood they described themselves as unassertive and were seen by others as being introverted. Finally, the Well-adjusted children (40% of the sample), who behaved in an age- and situation-appropriate manner at age 3, showed adult personality traits that closely resembled the average, well-adjusted adult.

These findings provide the longest and strongest evidence to date that children's early behavioral styles can forecast how they will typically behave, think, and feel as adults, supporting the assumption that the foundations of the human personality begin in the early years of life.

Source: Caspi et al., 2003

Behavioral and Cognitive Influences

Behavioral and cognitive explanations for abnormal child behavior emphasize principles of learning and cognition, which shape children's behavior and their interpretation of things around them. Behavioral and cognitive approaches differ essentially in the extent to which they apply cognitive concepts and procedures to the understanding of behavior (Wilson, 1995). Applied behavior analysis, at one end of this continuum, focuses primarily on observable behavior and rejects the notion that cognitive mediation is a necessary consideration for explaining behavior. At the other end is social learning theory, which relies more broadly on cognitive processes and explanations.

Most behavioral explanations assume that the child is best understood and described by behavior in a particular situation rather than in terms of stable traits. Although a child's particular learning history is of interest, behavioral methods focus on the most pragmatic, parsimonious explanation for a particular problem behavior. By the same reasoning, this approach recognizes that success in changing a problem behavior does not imply knowledge about its origin, but rather emphasizes contemporaneous causes, referred to as controlling variables. Cognitive theorists, on the other hand, are interested in how certain thought patterns develop over time and how they relate to particular behavioral strategies, such as problem solving. Following is a refresher of some of the major behavioral and cognitive theories.

Applied Behavior Analysis (ABA)   Based on B. F. Skinner's classical studies, ABA takes a functional approach to behavior, especially the relationships between behavior and its antecedents and consequences. No implicit assumptions are made about underlying needs or motives that contribute to abnormal behavior; ABA describes and tests functional relationships between stimuli, responses, and consequences. ABA is based on four primary operant learning principles, which explain how behaviors are acquired or changed as a result of particular consequences. These four principles are probably familiar to you: *Positive* and *negative reinforcement* are any actions that increase the target response; *extinction* and *punishment* have the effect of decreasing a response. Children are quite accomplished at learning the contingencies between their behavior and its consequences, and have an uncanny ability to apply some of their own! These principles of operant conditioning remain influential across a variety of applied areas—from basic experimental research to clinical treatment (DeGrandpre, 2000).

Classical Conditioning   Based on extension of Pavlov's famous learning trials and Watson's experiments with Little Albert, classical conditioning explains the acquisition of deviant behavior on the basis of paired associations between previously neutral stimuli (such as math

with these tasks depends on the fit between the child, her or his environment, and the interaction between the child and the environment. Emotion dysregulation is believed to be the result of interference in the associated developmental processes.

Children's increasing cognitive abilities play a role in both normal and abnormal development.

problems) and unconditioned stimuli, (such as food or criticism). Any neutral event can become a *conditioned stimulus* if it is paired enough times with an event that already elicits a certain response. Paired associations can help explain many adjustment problems in children and adolescents, although we do not typically know what the original association may have been. Additionally, more than one learning paradigm may occur at the same time. For this reason, dual learning explanations for undesirable behavior are common (that is, combinations of features of both operant and classical conditioning).

Returning to Jake's problem, imagine that he associates reading (a neutral event) with humiliation or anxiety (unconditioned stimuli), which prompts him to escape or avoid the activity. His avoidance, in turn, is negatively reinforced by its consequences: His anxiety decreases and he avoids feelings of humiliation. This analysis considers both instrumental (operant) and respondent (classical) conditioning as part of his learning history. Can you think of possible environmental changes or contingencies that might modify Jake's behavior in a desirable fashion?

Social Learning and Cognition **Social learning** explanations consider not only overt behaviors like Jake's school problems, but also the role of possible *cognitive mediators* that may influence the behaviors directly or indirectly. According to Albert Bandura's (1977, 1986) social learning explanation, behavior may be learned not only by operant and classical conditioning, but also indirectly through *observational* (vicarious) learning. Children can learn a new behavior merely by watching another person model the behavior, without apparent reinforcement or practice.

Social learning also incorporates the role of social cognition in acquiring desirable and undesirable behavior. **Social cognition** relates to how children think about themselves and others, resulting in the formation of mental representations of themselves, their relationships, and their social world. These representations are not fixed, but are continuously updated on the basis of maturation and social interaction (Noam, Chandler, & LaLonde, 1995). Children's ongoing cognitive development in reasoning, problem solving, and making attributions helps them make sense of who they are and how they relate to their surroundings. Moreover, social learning and social-cognitive

viewpoints also consider the role of affect and the importance of contextual variables, such as family and peers, in both the origins and maintenance of problem behaviors (Lemerise & Arsenio, 2000).

Like individual differences in temperament and emotion regulation, crucial differences exist in how children process information and make sense of their social worlds. Like adults, children have a natural desire to evaluate their behavior in various circumstances, especially those involving some element of possible failure, harm, or personal risk. For some children, teens, and adults, these self-appraisals of performance may be based on faulty beliefs or distortions; for others, an *attributional bias* about their ability or the intention of others leads them to reinterpret the event in a way that fits their preexisting belief about themselves or others. ("I got a good grade in math because the exam was too easy"; "He's a jerk, so who cares if I tease him?") (Dodge et al., 2003).

Since the first description of observational learning in the early 1960s, cognitive models have grown in both richness and complexity, and their constructs appear quite often throughout this text. The role of cognitive distortions, insufficient cognitive mediation, and attributional styles and expectations are important determinants in the development treatment of behavioral and emotional problems in children and adolescents (Crick & Dodge, 1994; Kendall, 2000).

SECTION SUMMARY

- Emotion reactivity and regulation are critical aspects of early and subsequent development, affecting the quality of children's social interactions and relationships throughout the life span.

- Three major approaches to abnormal behavior, based on principles of learning, are applied behavior analysis, principles of classical conditioning, and social learning and social cognition theories. The latter theories place more significance on cognitive processes and overt behavior.

Family, Social, and Cultural Influences

In addition to biological and psychological influences, children's normal and abnormal development depends on its social and environmental contexts. Understanding context requires a consideration of both *proximal* (close-by) and *distal* (further-removed) events, as well as those that impinge directly on the child in a particular situation at a particular time. We consider these wide-ranging environmental conditions and learning experiences in relation to the family and peer context and the social and cultural context.

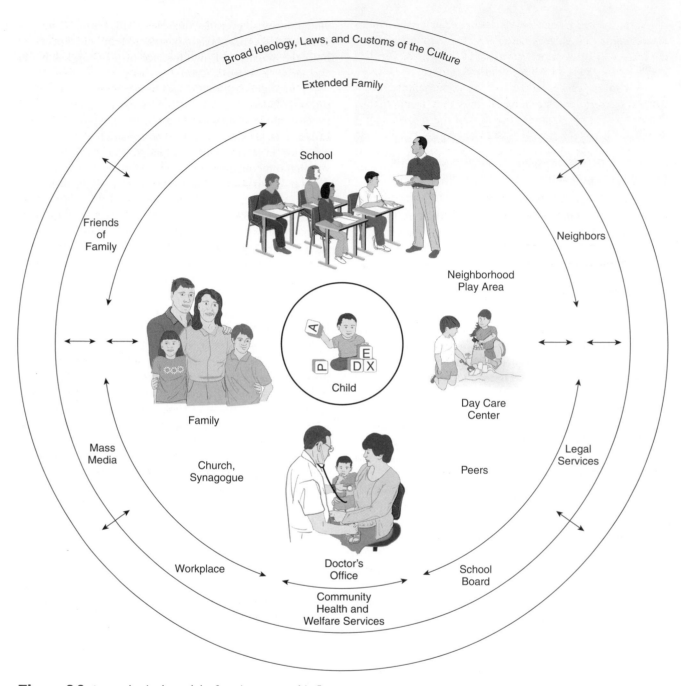

Figure 2.8 An ecological model of environmental influences

What exactly do we mean when we refer to a child's environment? Family? Peer groups? Clean air? To appreciate the complex network that constitutes a child's world and contributes to maladjustment, we need to go beyond the traditional view of the environment as being unidimensional or narrowly defined. A child's environment is constantly changing in relation to its many components, much like a lake or stream is affected by a proximal event, such as a rainstorm, as well as more distal events, such as the seasons.

Environmental influences are then further subdivided into shared and nonshared types. **Shared environment** re-fers to those environmental factors that produce similarities in developmental outcomes among siblings in the same family. For example, if siblings are more similar than expected from only their shared genetics, this implies an effect of the environment both siblings share, such as being exposed to marital conflict or poverty, or being parented in a similar manner. In the example of the twins, shared environmental influence is estimated indirectly from correlations among twins by subtracting the heritability estimate from the MZ twin correlation. **Nonshared environment,** which refers to environmental factors that produce behavioral differences among siblings in the same family, can then be estimated. Nonshared environmental influence is calculated by then subtracting the MZ twin correlation from 1.0 (O'Connor & Plomin, 2000; Pike & Plomin, 1996; Rende & Plomin, 1995).

Interestingly, it is nonshared, environmental factors that create differences among siblings that seem to contribute to a large portion of the variation. Environmental factors that have been postulated as nonshared include differential treatment by parents, peer influences, and school environment (O'Connor & Plomin, 2000; Pike & Plomin, 1996).

Figure 2.8 depicts Bronfenbrenner's (1977) ecological model, which shows the richness and depth of the various layers of a child's environment by portraying it as a series of nested and interconnected structures. Note that the child is at the center of this sphere of influence, which contains various levels interconnected in meaningful ways. The child's immediate environment begins with family members and home surroundings, but it quickly grows more complex as children enter preschool, visit neighborhood parks, and make friends.

Social settings also affect the child, even when the child does not directly experience these influences. Parents' friends and jobs, the availability of family support services such as health and welfare programs, and similar community resources and activities that are positive and negative make up the child's larger social framework (Burton & Jarrett, 2000; Sameroff & Fiese, 2000b). Finally, though far removed from the child's day-to-day activities, cultural ideology or identity governs how children should be treated (the sanctioning of corporal punishment), what they should be taught, and what goals are important to achieve (Garcia Coll, Akerman, & Cicchetti, 2000). These levels of environmental influences and their reciprocal connections (they affect the child, and the child affects them) are key elements in understanding the nature of child abuse and neglect, eating disorders, and many other disorders.

Evolution and Attachment

The study of abnormal development has profited from extensive work on child–caregiver relationships, which has painted a dramatic picture of the importance of early caregiver attachment to a child's emotional health (Cassidy & Shaver, 2002). Bowlby (1973, 1988) integrated aspects of evolutionary biology with existing psychodynamic conceptions of early experiences to derive his theory of attachment. **Attachment** refers to the process of establishing and maintaining an emotional bond with parents or other significant individuals. This process is ongoing, typically beginning between 6 and 12 months of age, and provides infants with a secure, consistent base from which to explore and learn about their worlds (Waters, Merrick, et al., 2000).

In attachment theory, instinctive behaviors are not rigidly predetermined but rather become organized into flexible, goal-oriented systems through learning and goal-corrected feedback. Bowlby reasoned that infants are "preadapted" to engage in relationship-enhancing behaviors, such as orienting, smiling, crying, clinging, signaling, and, as they learn to move about, proximity seeking. In order to survive, however, infants must become attached to a specific person(s) who is available and responsive to their needs. Adults are similarly equipped with attachment-promoting behaviors to respond to an infant's needs, which are complementary to the needs of the infant—smiling, touching, holding, and rocking.

The evolving infant–caregiver relationship helps the infant regulate her or his behavior and emotions, especially under conditions of threat or stress. Accordingly, attachment serves an important stress-reduction function. The infant is motivated to maintain a balance between the desire to preserve the familiar and the desire to seek and explore new information. Self-reliance develops when the attachment figure provides a secure base for the exploration (Bretherton, 1995). Moreover, a child's *internal working model* of relationships—what he or she expects from others and how he or she relates to others—emerges from this first crucial relationship and is carried forward into later relationships. The three major organized patterns of attachment (and one disorganized pattern) are summarized in Table 2.2, along with their theoretical and empirical links to various forms of psychopathology. Keep in mind, however, that attachment features constitute only one aspect of human relationships. Insecure attachments have been implicated in a number of childhood disorders, but no one-to-one correspondence exists between specific patterns of attachment and particular disorders (Rutter & Sroufe, 2000).

The Family and Peer Context

Child psychopathology research has increasingly focused on the role of the family system, the complex relationships within families, and the reciprocal influences among various family subsystems. There is a need to consider the processes occurring within disturbed families, and the common and unique ways these processes affect both individual family members and subsystems. Within the family, the roles of the mother–child (O'Connor, 2002) and marital (Cummings & Davies, 2002) subsystems have received the most research attention, with less attention given to the role of siblings (Hetherington, Reiss, & Plomin, 1994) or fathers (Cabrera, Tamis-LeMonda, Bradley, Hofferth, & Lamb, 2000).

Family systems theorists argue that it is difficult to understand or predict the behavior of a particular family member, such as a child, in isolation from other family members (B. M. Wagner & Reiss, 1995). This view is in line with our earlier discussion of underlying assumptions about children's abnormal development—*relationships*, not individual children or teens, are very often the crucial focus. This view, however, is often at odds with main-

Table 2.2
Types of Attachment and Their Relation to Disordered Outcomes

TYPE OF ATTACHMENT	DESCRIPTION DURING STRANGE SITUATION [1]	POSSIBLE INFLUENCE ON RELATIONSHIPS	POSSIBLE DISORDERED OUTCOMES
Secure	Infant readily separates from care-giver and likes to explore. When wary of a stranger or distressed by separation, the infant seeks contact and proximity with care-giver; then returns to exploration and play after contact.	Individuals with secure attachment histories tend to seek out and make effective use of supportive relationships.	Although individuals with secure attachments may suffer psychological distress, their relationship strategy serves a protective function against disordered outcomes.
Insecure *Anxious, avoidant type*	Infant engages in exploration, but with little affective interaction with care-giver. Infant shows little wariness of strangers, and generally is upset only if left alone. As stress increases, avoidance increases.	As children and adults, individuals with an *insecure, avoidant* pattern of early attachment tend to mask emotional expression. They often believe they are invulnerable to hurt, and others are not to be trusted.	Conduct disorders; aggressive behavior; depressive symptoms (usually as a result of failure of self-reliant image).
Insecure *Anxious, resistant type*	Infant shows disinterest or resistance to exploration and play, and is wary of novel situations or strangers. Infant has difficulty settling when reunited with care-giver, and may mix active contact-seeking with crying and fussiness.	As children and adults, individuals with an *insecure, resistant* pattern of early attachment have difficulties managing anxiety. They tend to exaggerate emotions and maintain negative beliefs about the self.	Phobias; anxiety; psychosomatic symptoms; depression.
Disorganized, disoriented type (not an organized strategy)	Infant lacks a coherent strategy of attachment. Appears disorganized when faced with a novel situation and has no consistent pattern of regulating emotions.	Individuals with disorganized, disoriented style show an inability to form close attachments to others; may show an indiscriminate friendliness (little selective attachment).	No consensus, but generally a wide range of personality disorders (van Ijzendoorn, Schuengel, & Bakermans-Kranenburg, 1999)

[1] *The Strange Situation is a method of assessing infant–caregiver attachment. It involves a series of increasingly stressful separations and reunions that resemble typical daily occurrences, such as meeting strangers and being left alone (Ainsworth, Blehar, Waters, & Wall, 1978).*

Note: *The relationships between attachment styles and abnormal development are based on both theoretical and empirical findings, summarized in E. A. Carlson and Sroufe (1995).*

stream psychological and psychiatric approaches to psychopathology, yet it is compatible with developmental processes.

More and more, the study of individual factors and the study of the child's context are being seen as mutually compatible and beneficial to both theory and intervention. Furthermore, the manner in which the family, as a unit, deals with typical and atypical stresses plays an instrumental role in children's adjustment and adaptation. Stress brings about change, growth, and reorganization of families (P.A. Cowan & C. P. Cowan, 2003). The outcome of the events depends in part on the nature and severity of the stress, the level of family functioning prior to the stress, and the family's coping skills and resources (Rutter, 2000b). Some of the more influential family-related issues involved in discussions of childhood disorders are parental depression, child abuse, parental alcoholism, parental divorce, marital violence, and parental criminality.

Although quite distinct, these major family and individual issues share a common thread in terms of their impact on child development: They disrupt, disturb, or interfere with consistent and predictable child care and basic necessities. Such disruption or impairment, in turn, affects the child's ability to form satisfactory relationships with peers, teachers, and other adults (Sameroff, 1995).

SECTION SUMMARY

- Evolutionary approaches to abnormal child behavior emphasize the evolving infant–caregiver relationship, which helps the infant regulate behavior and emotions, especially under conditions of threat or stress.
- Children's normal and abnormal development depends on a variety of social and environmental settings, including the child's family and peer system, and the larger social and cultural context.

LOOKING AHEAD

Society's understanding of children's healthy, normal development has been gradually evolving toward a more holistic, health-promoting orientation, which is impacting the definitions and services related to children's mental health (McClure, 2000). This emerging dynamic, interactive view of health recognizes the importance of both individual and environmental factors in achieving positive development. The neuroscience and ecological perspectives on human health and behavior add momentum to this growing view, because they consider human adaptation within its normal context.

Children's health and successful adaptation are today seen as worthy and appropriate aspects of the study of abnormal child psychology. Along with an increased emphasis on health promotion, today's research and thinking accepts the notion that various childhood disorders share many clinical features and causes. **Health promotion** encourages changes, opportunities, and competence to achieve one's health potential (R. M. Kaplan, 2000). When applied to children, this view recognizes the multicausal and interactive nature of many child and adolescent psychological disorders and the importance of contextual factors. It also speaks to the importance of balancing the abilities of individuals with the challenges and risks of their environments (Masten & Curtis, 2000). Throughout the text we return to the many ways abnormal child psychology can be studied in a developmentally sensitive, systems-oriented manner.

These conceptual shifts are gradually changing the face of mental health and educational services for children and youths, with important implications for pediatrics, psychology, psychiatry, social work, nursing, education, and child development. How individuals think about health, how daily life is organized and experienced, how social policy is developed, how social resources are allocated, and how people are trained to implement these policies have reached their greatest potential in history for achieving a major impact on improved services to assist younger populations that cannot speak for themselves (President's New Freedom Report, 2003). Although this tremendous impact on the field of mental health, and on children and youths in particular, has not yet become reality (Cicchetti et al., 2000), we are encouraged by how society has progressed in addressing the needs of children.

Key Terms

 InfoTrac College Edition

To research recent articles on the subject, go to:
www.infotrac-college/thomsonlearning.com

Enter search terms: DEVELOPMENTAL PSYCHOPATHOLOGY, NATURE AND NURTURE, BRAIN DEVELOPMENT, BEHAVIOR GENETICS, NEUROTRANSMITTER, TEMPERAMENT, ATTACHMENT BEHAVIOR IN CHILDREN, FAMILY (PSYCHOLOGICAL ASPECTS SUBDIVISION)

Research

All who drink this remedy recover in a short time except those whom it does not help, who all die. Therefore, it is obvious that it only fails in incurable cases.

—Attributed to Galen (second century A.D.)

In this chapter, we look at the process of research and the many challenges faced by those who study disturbed children and their families. Although people differ on the specifics, **research** is generally viewed as a systematic way of asking questions—a method of inquiry that follows certain rules.

A Scientific Approach

Scientific research strategies investigate claims in systematic ways that improve on casual observations. Science requires that a claim like the one attributed to Galen be based on theories backed up by data from controlled studies, and that observations be checked and repeated before conclusions are drawn. A scientific approach is especially important in abnormal child psychology. Although relationships between variables of interest may seem obvious when observed casually—a child consumes too much sugar and becomes hyperactive—these relationships are often obscured by complex interactions and combinations of variables. Parents and professionals who work with children have a tendency to associate variables that they observe, and to integrate them with their own belief systems. These relationships can become firmly established, independent of how they are supported by facts (Kazdin, 2003c).

Considerable folklore and numerous home remedies and fad treatments characterize the field of abnormal child psychology. Simple explanations, such as "sugar causes hyperactivity," or simple solutions, such as "spare the rod and spoil the child," appeal to parents or teachers because they promise an easy answer or quick remedy for a complex problem. Folklore and fad treatments, unintentionally or otherwise, play to the vulnerabilities of parents of children with problems, parents who desperately want the best for their children. More often than not, these answers or remedies don't work, and sometimes bring unfortunate consequences and costs for disturbed children and their families. People have always shown some skepticism about scientific research leading to new knowledge. Consider the following comments:

Recent research in abnormal child psychology has led to important new discoveries.

"After a few more flashes in the pan, we shall hear very little more of Edison and his electric lamp. Every claim he makes has been tested and proved impracticable." (*New York Times,* January 16, 1880)

"Louis Pasteur's theory of germs is ridiculous fiction." (Pachet, professor of physiology, Toulouse, 1872)

Fortunately, the lightbulb, pasteurization, and many other ideas once viewed with skepticism have clearly caught on. Nevertheless, good reasons exist for skepticism of research in abnormal child psychology (Kazdin, 2003c). First, experts on childhood disorders frequently disagree. Newspapers, magazines, and TV talk shows provide a steady diet of conflicting opinions. The answers we get to questions—Does violence on TV make children more aggressive? Does day care have a harmful effect on children's emotional adjustment?—often depend on whom we ask. Second, research findings in abnormal child psychology are often in conflict with one another. For example, most studies find that school-age girls are more prone to depression than boys, but some report higher rates of depression in boys and other studies report no differences. How do we make sense out of inconsistent and sometimes contradictory findings?

A third reason for skepticism is that research has led to different recommendations regarding how children with problems should be helped. In some cases, the same treatment has been shown to be helpful, to have no effects, and to be harmful. As one practitioner put it after hearing about an effective new treatment method at a conference, "I'd better hurry home and use it quickly before a study is published to show that it doesn't work!" Many conclusions from research with children are qualified—rarely are there black-and-white answers. A moderate amount of discipline is good; too little or too much discipline is bad. Certain treatments may work for some children but not for others, for boys but not for girls, for younger but not for older children, and in some situations but not in others.

Finally, even when scientific evidence is relatively clear and produces a consensus, many parents and professionals may dismiss the findings because they have encountered an exception, usually one drawn from personal experience. For example, despite the voluminous research showing that the habitual use of harsh physical punishment by parents can have extremely negative effects on children, a parent may still say, "My father used his belt on me when I was a kid and it sure taught me how to behave properly!"

Because no single study is perfect, it is important to be an informed consumer and to keep in mind that it is the accumulation of findings—not a single study—that advances the field. Recent research in abnormal child psychology has led to enormous and exciting advances in understanding children with problems and how they can best be helped. The next section provides an example of some of the lessons to be learned when scientific methods and evidence are ignored or dismissed.

Facilitated Communication

A Case Example

Facilitated communication provides an example of how the general public and, unfortunately, some professionals may fail to recognize the need for scientific evidence (Gorman, 1999; Jacobson, Mulick, & Schwartz, 1995). *Facilitated communication* (FC) is a seemingly well-meant but highly controversial and misused procedure for teaching communication skills to children with autism and other impairments. Using this method, a facilitator provides manual assistance by lightly holding a child's hand, wrist, or arm, while the child supposedly communicates by typing on a keyboard or by pointing to letters on an alphabet board. The alleged purpose of the manual assistance by the facilitator is to help the child press the keys that she or he wants to press—not to influence key selection. However, because the assistance is continued indefinitely, the possibility of direct influence by the facilitator exists.

FC was widely publicized when it was reported that children who received FC showed feats of literacy and intellectual competence far exceeding their presumed abilities (Biklen, 1990). The results were considered remarkable because the typical youngster using FC had a lifelong history of autism, profound mental retardation, or both, and had never talked (Jacobson et al., 1995). Proponents of FC claim that with this method, children with autism can generate phrases and sentences describing complex memories and feelings, and demonstrate other advanced language skills (Biklen & Cardinal, 1997).

Hand placement, with facilitator (participant) below and communicator (confederate) above.

Courtesy David M. Wegner

A Closer Look

BOX 3.1 Faciliated Communication: Who's Doing the Communicating?

FC is of special interest to our discussion of a scientific approach because it meets many of the criteria of pseudoscience: Demonstrations of benefit are based on anecdotes or testimonials, the child's baseline abilities and the possibility of spontaneous improvement are ignored, and related scientific procedures are disavowed (Jacobson et al., 1995). Facilitated communication also illustrates the potentially damaging effects of using practices not based on scientific evidence. Parents who want the best for their children and overburdened staff are particularly vulnerable to the false promise of questionable interventions, especially when the recognized authorities misrepresent or misinterpret treatment effects while introducing the approach to parents. The negative impact of FC on families is apparent in the following comments by the father of a young boy with autism:

"Professionals are very quick to dismiss the abilities of autistics. . . . So when Facilitated Communication (FC) proponents say they have found a way around the wall, parents are quick to believe. FC confirms our faith in our children. But . . . the workshops can cost $250. The equipment $800 more. And what do we get for our money? Parents themselves "can't facilitate," they tell us. Our children will require FC for life, they say, and will never communicate on their own. . . . In short, the price we are asked to pay in an effort to communicate with our children is to allow strangers into our families to mediate our relationships with our own kids and to accept everything the stranger tells us on blind faith." Mark S. Painter, Sr. (Dillon, 1993, p. 286)

FC received widespread exposure in the media, and continues to be used each day with thousands of handicapped youngsters throughout the world. However, critics of FC view the method as quackery—no different from using a Ouija board. Are the extraordinary outcomes attributed to FC fact, or are they fiction? Scientific research would indicate fiction—objective demonstrations and controlled studies have consistently found that the child's supposed communication is being controlled by the facilitator (Wegner, Fuller, & Sparrow, 2003) (see Box 3.1).

SECTION SUMMARY

- A scientific approach to abnormal child psychology is a way of thinking about how to best understand and answer questions of interest, not just an accumulation of specific methods, practices, or procedures.

- Science requires that theories be backed up by evidence from controlled studies, and that observations be checked and repeated before conclusions are drawn.
- Facilitated communication meets many of the criteria of pseudoscience because typical scientific procedures are ignored.

In the sections that follow, we consider the research process in abnormal child psychology. We first discuss the ideas and questions that researchers who study childhood disorders typically seek to address. Next, we consider the methods, general approaches, and research designs used to study developmental psychopathology. In the last section, we discuss important ethical and pragmatic issues.

The Research Process

There is something fascinating about science. One gets such wholesale returns of conjecture out of such a trifling investment of fact.

—*Mark Twain (1835–1910)*

Research in abnormal child psychology is best characterized as a multistage process involving key decisions at various points. The process typically begins with developing hypotheses on the basis of theory and previous findings, then deciding on a general approach to research. The next stage is selecting or developing data-collection measures, identifying the population to be studied, then developing a plan for sampling from that population. The research design and procedures must balance the practicalities of implementation with the adequacy of the research to address the hypotheses under investigation. The final stage consists of gathering and analyzing the data, and interpreting the results in relation to theory and previous findings. During an ongoing process, findings and interpretations from the study can then be used to generate future research questions and stimulate further research.

The main stages of the research process are summarized in Figure 3.1. Keep in mind that ethical considerations in conducting research with children and families must be considered at every stage of this process.

In practice, most problems in abnormal child psychology are best studied by using multiple methods and strategies. Since there is no one correct approach, research is best conceptualized within a decision-making framework. This framework requires an understanding of the theoretical, methodological, and practical considerations that permit the researcher to make informed decisions about when certain research methods and strategies are appropriate, and when they are not. To study developmental psychopathology, researchers must include research designs and methods of data analysis that can distinguish direct and indirect effects, and that can identify, compare, and evaluate different causal pathways for vari-

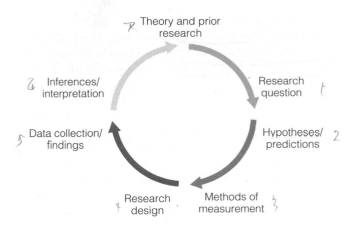

Figure 3.1. The research process in abnormal child psychology.

ous disorders (Cicchetti & Hinshaw, 2003). We next consider some specific issues encountered at different stages of the research process.

Sample Research Questions

Whitney
Always Sad

I don't understand why Whitney is so sad all the time. She's continually arguing with her brother, hates school, and has no friends. She's always been a moody child, but became much worse after my husband and I divorced. Is her sadness due to her moody personality, the divorce, or is something at home or at school making her feel this way?

Tito
Constantly Fighting

Tito is constantly fighting with other kids at school. He never does what we ask him to do. When things don't go his way, he has a full-blown tantrum and throws and breaks things. My husband thinks Tito's just a tough kid, and that all he needs is firm discipline. He uses his belt a lot with Tito, but it doesn't seem to make a difference. I'm really worried. Will Tito outgrow his behavior? Is my husband being too strict? What can I do about it?

These are typical questions that parents ask about their children's problem behavior and development. They are also questions that spawn research into abnormal child behavior. Research typically begins with a hypothesis, which predicts behavior that follows from a theory. Hypotheses for research are often based on the theories of atypical development and behavior that we discussed in Chapter 2. Some research studies attempt to compare hypotheses based on one theory versus another, whereas other studies attempt to test predictions drawn from a single theory. When little or no theory is available, investigators may also develop a research question without an explicit prediction. For example, what impact does growing up in a single-parent family have for children's psychological adjustment? Are more children depressed these days than a generation ago? Is child abuse more prevalent in our society than in other parts of the world?

Common Research Topics

Research hypotheses guide the researcher's choice of methods and the research designs most appropriate for answering certain questions. We discuss common research topics in abnormal child psychology in the sections that follow.

Nature and Distribution of Childhood Disorders

These questions are concerned with how disorders are defined, diagnosed, and expressed at different ages and in different settings, patterns of symptoms, base rates for various problems and competencies, and natural progressions of problems and competencies over time. Such questions are frequently addressed through **epidemiological research,** which is the study of the incidence, prevalence, and co-occurrence of childhood disorders and competencies in clinic-referred and community samples (Costello, 1990). **Incidence rates** reflect the extent to which new cases of a disorder appear over a specified period (for example, the number of children who develop a mood disorder during the school year). **Prevalence rates** refer to all cases, whether new or previously existing, that are observed during a specified period of time (for example, the number of teens with conduct disorder in the general population during 2003–2004). Estimates of incidence and prevalence can be obtained over a limited period such as 6 months, or over a longer period. *Lifetime prevalence* indicates whether children in the sample have had the disorder at any time.

Knowledge about the risk for, and expression of, individual disorders over the life course helps us understand the nature of the disorder and use this understanding as the basis for prevention and treatment (Costello & Angold, 1995). For example, studies of teens over time have found depression to be a recurrent disorder with poor long-term outcomes for many youngsters. This knowledge about the course of depression has resulted in promising new approaches to treating and preventing depression in young people, which we present in Chapter 8 on mood disorders.

As noted in Chapter 1, about 10% of children have a clinically diagnosable disorder, and many more exhibit specific symptoms or subclinical problems. However, over-

Children's cultural differences play an important role in a proper understanding of their behavior and customs

all rates obscure the enormous variability in reported rates from study to study. It can be very confusing when one study reports a prevalence rate of 1% and another reports a rate of 20% for the same disorder and at roughly the same point in time. Similarly, rates of reported problems in children have been found to vary from 6% to 20% when reported by teachers and from 10% to 40% when reported by parents (Costello & Angold, 1995). Some studies would lead you to conclude that almost every child you encounter has a problem; for others, the problem is so rare you wonder whether it even exists. Which conclusion is accurate? To answer this question we must know something about epidemiological research and how estimates are obtained.

An important question in epidemiological research is, "What constitutes a case?" Cases may be defined in terms of single symptoms, multiple symptoms, or patterns of symptoms with known causes and associated characteristics. Estimates of prevalence vary widely depending on which definition we use. Case definition in abnormal child psychology is complex because children don't refer themselves for treatment. Therefore, equating illness with seeking treatment can be misleading. The factors that lead to referral sometimes have more to do with the child's parents, teachers, or doctor than with the child's behavior.

BOX 3.2 Cross-Cultural Epidemiological Research: Behavior Problems Reported by Parents of Children in Seven Cultures

Widespread movements of refugees and immigrants are placing millions of children into new and unfamiliar environments. Evaluating the mental health of these children can be difficult because of cultural variations in what constitutes abnormal behavior, how to identify such behavior, and what to do about it. Crijnen, Achenbach, and Verhulst (1997) examined the 6-month prevalence rates of child problems as reported by parents or parent surrogates in studies carried out in seven cultures, using the same measurement instrument—the Child Behavior Checklist (CBCL) (Achenbach, 1991). As shown in the figure, the total problem scores of children in Puerto Rico and China were above the overall cultural mean. In contrast, the total problem scores of children in Israel, Germany, and Australia were below the overall mean. These epidemiological studies indicate that parents in different cultures report different rates of problem behavior in their children. However, the studies do not indicate why these differences occur. Other kinds of studies are needed to answer that question.

Source: Adapted from "Comparisons of Problems Reported by Parents of Children in 12 Cultures: Total Problems, Externalizing, and Internalizing," by A. A. M. Crijnen, T. M. Achenbach and F. C. Verhulst, 1997, *Journal of the American Academy of Child and Adolescent Psyshiatry, 36*, 1269–1277. Adapted by permission.

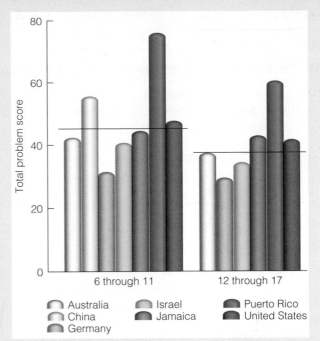

Total problem scores for children in seven different cultures. Overall mean Child Behavior Checklist (CBCL) problem scores and mean CBCL problem scores for each culture at ages 6 through 11, and 12 through 17. Overall mean scores at different ages are indicated by *solid lines.* China did not provide enough 12- through 17-year-olds. Key to cultures: 1. Australia; 2. China; 3. Germany; 4. Israel; 5. Jamaica; 6. Puerto Rico; 7. United States.

Therefore, it is important that we study developmental psychopathology in children who are *not* referred to clinics for treatment as well as those who are. Throughout this book you will see many examples of striking differences in research findings depending on whether children from clinics versus community samples are the focus of study.

The rate and expression of childhood symptoms and disorders often vary in relation to demographic and situational factors, such as socioeconomic status (SES), parent's marital status, and the child's age, gender, race, and ethnicity (Crick & Zahn-Waxler, 2003; Swanson et al., 2003) to name but a few. Consequently, these variables must be assessed and controlled for in most studies. Many inconsistent findings in abnormal child psychology are the direct result of research designs and/or interpretations of findings that fail to take these important variables into account.

Physically abused children, for example, display more parent-rated problem symptoms than nonabused children. However, this difference may not be found when groups of abused and nonabused children are well matched with respect to SES (D. A. Wolfe & Mosk, 1983). Similarly, although conduct problems are reported to be more frequent in African American than Caucasian youngsters, this finding is likely an artifact related to SES. That is, conduct problems are more prevalent in low-SES families, and since African American children are overrepresented in such families in North America, it is likely that the link between race and conduct problems is accounted for by stressful conditions associated with growing up in a poor family (Bird et al., 2001). The importance of cultural differences is highlighted in Box 3.2, which shows an example of an epidemiological research study into the types of behavior problems reported by parents in seven cultures.

Correlates, Risks, and Causes Whitney, described at the beginning of this section, displays persistent sadness that seems to be related to several variables: her history of being a moody child, her parents' divorce, her problems at school, and her lack of friends. Do any of these variables, alone or in combination, account for her sadness? If so, in what ways? Variables of interest in abnormal child psychology can be correlates, risk or protective factors, or causes of other variables. Most research in abnormal child psychology is designed to answer questions about the relation between the three general variables and childhood disorders. Because most childhood disorders are the result of multiple variables interacting with one another over time, answers to these questions are rarely straightforward.

Correlated variables are associated at a particular point in time with no clear proof that one precedes the other. For example, Whitney's having no friends is associated with her sadness. Is she sad because she has no friends, or has her sadness prevented her from making friends? Since we don't know which variables came first, her lack of friends and sadness are correlated variables.

As discussed in Chapter 1, a risk factor is a variable that precedes an outcome of interest and increases the chances of a negative outcome. For example, Whitney's mood got worse following her parents' divorce. Do you think parental divorce constitutes a risk factor for the development of depression or other problems in children? Remember that a risk factor increases the chances for a certain outcome. It does not mean that it will occur; this will depend on other factors. Obviously, most children of parents who divorce do not become depressed. Divorce is not a cause of depression and low self-esteem, but it can be a risk factor (Hetherington, Bridges, & Insabella, 1998). A protective factor is a positive variable that precedes an outcome of interest and decreases the chances that the outcome will occur. The close relationship enjoyed by Whitney and her mother may serve as a protective factor against future episodes of depression.

Research into risk and protective factors often requires that large samples of children be studied and that multiple areas of child functioning—physical, intellectual, psychosocial—be assessed over long periods of time. This is necessary because (1) only a small proportion of children at risk for a problem will actually develop the disorder; (2) the areas of child functioning that will be affected, and how they will be affected, are not known in advance; and (3) the points in development when a disorder may occur or reoccur are also not known in advance. Sometimes the effects of exposure to a risk factor during infancy or early childhood may not be visible until adolescence or adulthood. The possibility that delayed, or *sleeper*, effects will occur complicates the study of risk and protective factors, since children must be studied for many years if delayed effects are to be detected.

Finally, other variables are causes. They influence, either directly or indirectly through other variables, the occurrence of a behavior or disorder of interest. Tito's father uses severe punishment when his son misbehaves. Is this

punishment the cause of Tito's aggressive behavior? Is Tito learning how to be aggressive from his father? Questions about causes are complicated because what qualifies as a cause will vary according to the variables of interest, and how far back in time a causal chain can be traced. Where in this chain of events does the cause begin? The determinants of childhood disorders rarely involve simple one-to-one, cause-and-effect relations (Kazdin & Kagan, 1994). Because childhood disorders are almost always the result of multiple causes, a challenge for researchers is to identify the relative contributions of each factor and determine how they combine and interact over time to produce specific outcomes (Dodge & Pettit, 2003).

Moderating and Mediating Variables   Factors that influence the *direction* or *strength* of the relationship of variables of interest are called **moderator variables**. The association between two variables depends on or is different as a function of moderating variables, such as the child's sex, age, SES, ethnicity, or family characteristics. For example, in a study examining the relation between adolescents' self-reported history of physical abuse and their self-reports of internalizing problems such as anxiety and depression, McGee, Wolfe, and Wilson (1997) found that the correlation between the severity of abuse history and internalizing problems was greater for females than males. The child's sex was a moderator variable, that is, the relationship between two of the variables (in this case, abuse and internalizing problems) differed, depending on the third (if the adolescent was a boy or a girl) (see Figure 3.2).

Mediator variables refer to the process, mechanism, or means through which a variable produces a particular outcome. They describe what happens at the psychological or neurobiological level to explain how one variable results from another. In one study, J. Snyder (1991) found that on days when mothers of 4- to 5-year-old children experienced negative moods and frequent hassles, they were

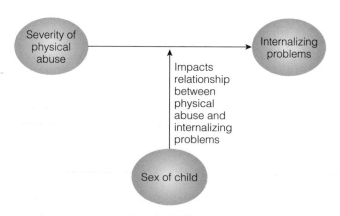

Figure 3.2. Example of a moderator variable. Sex of the child moderates the relationship between abuse and internalizing problems.

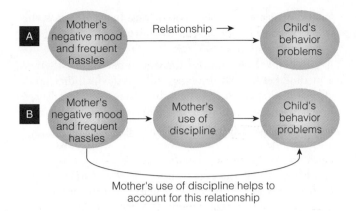

Figure 3.3. Mediating variables: The type of discipline used by mothers on days they are feeling distressed mediates the relationship between maternal distress and child behavior problems.

most likely to respond negatively to their children's misbehavior and to reinforce their children's coercive tactics during mother–child conflicts. In turn, the use of this maternal discipline was related to an increase in same-day child behavior problems. As shown in Figure 3.3, these findings indicate that the relationship between maternal distress and child conduct problems is partly mediated by the disciplinary strategies used by mothers on days they feel distressed. Mothers' disciplinary strategies help explain the relationship between maternal distress and child conduct problems. The key difference between the two variables is that mediators *account for* some or all of the apparent relationship between two variables, while moderators have an *independent effect* on the existing relationship between the two variables.

Outcomes What are the long-term outcomes for children who experience problems? Many childhood problems decrease or go away as children mature, but we need to know at approximately what age such improvements may be expected. Similarly, will other problems emerge, such as the child developing a low opinion of himself or herself due to trouble with, say, wetting the bed or worrying too much about school? Returning to Tito's oppositional and aggressive behaviors, will we expect problems to decrease or go away as he gets older, or do they forecast continued conflict with peers, future school problems, and later difficulties in social adjustment?

Interventions How effective are our methods for treating or preventing child problems? Are some types of intervention more effective than others? Questions about treatment and prevention are concerned with evaluating the immediate and long-term effects of psychological, environmental, and biological treatments; comparing the relative effectiveness of differing forms and combinations

of treatment; and identifying the reasons that a particular treatment works. The questions are also concerned with identifying factors that influence the referral and treatment process; understanding how intermediate therapy processes contribute to treatment outcomes, and assessing the acceptability of equivalent forms of treatment to children and significant adults (Kazdin, 2003b).

Many treatments for children and adolescents have not been evaluated although this situation is steadily improving (Kazdin & Weisz, 2003). As we discuss in Chapter 4, controlled research studies suggest that children who receive treatment are generally better off than children who do not. However, an important distinction needs to be made between treatment efficacy and treatment effectiveness. **Treatment efficacy** refers to whether the treatment can produce changes under well-controlled conditions. In efficacy research, careful control is exercised over the selection of cases, therapists, and delivery and monitoring of treatment. In contrast, **treatment effectiveness** refers to whether the treatment can be shown to work in clinical practice rather than well-controlled laboratory conditions. In research on effectiveness, treatment is evaluated in clinical settings, clients are usually referred rather than selected, and therapists provide services without many of the rigorous controls used in research. The benefits of treatment for children with problems have generally been found to be greater in controlled research settings (efficacy trials) than in clinical practice (effectiveness trials) (Weisz, 1998; Weiss, Catron, & Harris, 2000).

SECTION SUMMARY

- Research is a multistage process that involves generating hypotheses, devising an overall plan, selecting measures, developing a research design and procedures, gathering and analyzing the data, and interpreting the results.
- A researcher's theory of abnormal child behavior will determine the variables studied, the choice of research methods, and the interpretation of research findings.
- Common questions in abnormal child psychology focus on correlates, risk and protective factors, causes, moderating and mediating variables, outcomes, and interventions for childhood disorders.

Methods of Studying Behavior

The study of behavioral and emotional problems of children requires that the ways we measure these problems are reliable, valid, and capable of being statistically tested. This is no easy task. Children's problems must be evaluated, based on samples of behavior in situations that often reflect differing perspectives of adults. These evaluations are likely affected by the child's age, sex, cultural background, and the assessors' personal values. As a result, no single measurement can provide an adequate picture of children's problems, and multiple measures and sources of information are needed.

Standardization, Reliability, and Validity

The measures and methods that we use to study child and family behavior must undergo careful study to determine how well they measure constructs, such as depression, anxiety, or mental retardation. The use of well-standardized, reliable, and valid measures and procedures is essential to scientifically sound research, as depicted in Figure 3.4.

Standardization is a process that specifies a set of standards or norms for a measurement procedure to be used consistently across different assessments of the construct of interest. These standards and norms relate to the procedures that must be followed during administration, scoring, and evaluation of findings. In some cases, the measure may be given to many children who vary in age, gender, race, SES, or diagnosis. The scores are then used for comparison purposes. For example, the test scores of an 8-year-old boy from a low-SES background should be compared with the scores of other children like him, not with the scores of a 16-year-old girl from an upper-SES background.

Reliability refers to the consistency, or repeatability, of measures. To be reliable, measures must not depend on a single observer or clinician; various people must agree on what they see. This is known as *interrater agreement*. Imagine how you might react if you took your child to see three different psychologists and received three different diagnoses and three different treatment recommendations. How would you know which one was correct? In this case, the diagnoses would not be reliable because two or more of the psychologists did not agree. Similarly, tests or interviews repeated within a short time interval should yield similar results on both occasions. In other words, the results need to be stable over time, which is referred to as *test-retest reliability*.

Reliability alone isn't sufficient to determine whether a method reflects the investigator's goals—validity must also be demonstrated. The **validity** of a method is reflected in the extent to which it actually measures the dimension or construct that the researcher sets out to measure. Validity can be assessed many ways. First, the measure can be examined for its *face validity*, or the extent to which it appears to assess the construct of interest. *Construct validity* refers to whether scores on a measure behave as predicted by theory or past research—the meaning ascribed to scores. *Convergent validity* reflects the correlation between measures that are expected to be related—an indication of the extent to which the two measures assess similar or related constructs. This is in contrast to *discriminant validity*, which refers to the degree of correlation between measures that are not expected to be related to one another.

Finally, *criterion-related validity* refers to how well a measure predicts behavior in settings where we would expect it to do so—at the same time (concurrent validity), or in the future (predictive validity). For example, a child's high scores on a measure of social anxiety should predict that the child will display anxiety or avoidance in current social situations, and perhaps have difficulties making friends in the future. Criterion-related validity tells whether scores on a measure can be used for their intended purpose—to determine if the measure has *utility*.

Measurement

A variety of measurement methods are available to assess important dimensions of children's cognitive, behavioral, and emotional functioning (Mash & Terdal, 1997a; Sattler, 2001, 2002). These methods are explicit plans to observe and assess children and their surroundings in ways that will reveal relatively clear relations among variables of interest. An important question regarding methods of measurement relates to who will make inferences about behaviors—the participants through self-report methods or the researcher using observational methods?

Among the methods used in abnormal child psychology are interviews, questionnaires, checklists and rating scales, psychophysiological recordings, and direct observations of behavior (Bellack & Hersen, 1998; Kamphaus & Frick, 1996; Mash & Terdal, 1997b). A variety of intellectual, academic, and neuropsychological tests are also used. In this chapter we focus primarily on how these methods are used in research. We will talk more about their use in clinical practice and about tests and testing in Chapter 4.

As presented in Table 3.1, a comparison of three of the most commonly used methods of gathering data—

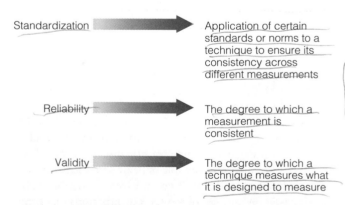

Figure 3.4. Concepts that determine the value of our methods of measurement and assessment.

Table 3.1
Interview, Questionnaire, and Observation

	INTERVIEW	QUESTIONNAIRE	OBSERVATION
Structure of situation	Semistructured or structured.	Highly structured.	Structured or naturalistic.
Structure of responses	Can probe, expand, and clarify.	Highly structured; no opportunity for probes or clarification.	Data can vary from very inclusive to highly selective.
Resource requirements	Considerable time needed for interviewing and coding responses.	Little experimenter time needed.	Extensive time needed for observing and coding observations.
Sources of bias	Relies on participants' perception and willingness to report. Responses may be influenced by interviewer characteristics and mannerisms.	Relies on participants' perception and willingness to report.	Does not rely on participants' disclosure, but may be influenced by reactivity.
Data reduction	Requires analysis or recoding of narrative responses.	Little data reduction needed.	Highly influenced by the observational coding system.

interviews, questionnaires, and observations—shows how they differ on important dimensions. Because the information we obtain from children and families often varies as a function of the methods used, researchers frequently rely on a *multimethod* approach to define and assess the constructs of interest.

Reporting

Reporting methods assess the perceptions, thoughts, abilities, attitudes, beliefs, feelings, and past experiences of the child, parents, and teachers. These instruments include relatively unstructured clinical interviews, highly structured diagnostic interviews, and questionnaires. A concern with all reporting methods is how accurately children and parents report their own thoughts, feelings, and behaviors. Inaccuracies may occur because of a failure to recall important events, selective recall or bias, and, in some cases, intentional distortions. Some informants may try to make themselves or others look better or worse than they are. Furthermore, reporting methods require a certain level of verbal ability and may not accurately assess individuals who have difficulty expressing themselves. Obviously, young children would fall into this category—children under the age of 7 or 8 are usually not reliable informants.

Psychophysiology and Neuroimaging

Psychophysiological methods assess the relationship between physiological processes and behavior to identify which nervous system structures and processes contribute to children's atypical development and behavior. Among the most common measures are autonomic nervous system activity, such as heart rate, blood pressure, respira-

tion, pupil dilation, and electrical conductance of the skin. Changes in heart rate, for example, may be related to emotional responses. In addition, specific patterns of autonomic arousal may be associated with differences in children's temperament—their degree of shyness with people or responses to novel events (discussed in Chapter 7).

There are many limitations associated with psychophysiological measures, especially with young children. Sometimes findings for these measures are inconsistent from one study to the next, and researchers may have to infer how the child may have processed a particular event or stimulus. Also, the child's physiological response can be influenced easily by other factors, such as a child's reaction to the recording equipment or to hunger, fatigue, or boredom. These extraneous influences must be minimized if conclusions are to be based on psychophysiological measures.

Many studies have used an *electrophysiological measure* of brain functioning, the **electroencephalogram (EEG),** to link the brain's measurable electrical activity with ongoing thinking, emotion, or states of arousal. The EEG records electrical brain activity using electrodes taped to the surface of the child's scalp. Because different EEG waves are related to states of arousal, differential patterns of EEG activation may suggest sleep disturbances or various emotional states. For example, fearful or inhibited children have been found to show more electrical activity in the right frontal lobe of the brain relative to the left frontal lobe, when compared with nonfearful children (McManis, Kagan, Snidman, & Woodward, 2002). The same pattern has been found in girls with externalizing behavior problems (Baving, Laucht, & Schmidt, 2003).

Finally, new ways of studying the living brain using neuroimaging procedures make it possible to test neurobiologic theories for many childhood disorders (Posner,

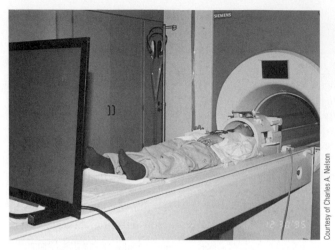

A 10-year-old child about to be tested using functional magnetic resonance imaging (fMRI)

2001; Zametkin, Ernst, & Silver, 1998). **Neuroimaging** refers to techniques used to examine the structure and/or function of the brain (C. A. Nelson & Bloom, 1997). *Structural* brain imaging procedures include *magnetic resonance imaging* (MRI) and *coaxial tomographic* (CT) scan. MRI uses radio signals generated in a strong magnetic field and passed through brain tissue to produce fine-grained analyses of brain structures. CT scans reveal the various structures of the brain. As we will see, findings from CT and MRI studies have led to the formulation of pathophysiological models, such as the cerebellar model in autism (Chapter 10) and the hypothesis of abnormal neural maturation in ADHD (Chapter 5).

A variety of *functional* imaging techniques have also been used. Two of the more common techniques are *positron emission tomography* (PET) and *functional magnetic resonance imaging* (fMRI). PET scans assess cerebral glucose metabolism. Glucose is the brain's main source of energy, so measuring how much is used is a good way to determine the brain's activity level. Changes in blood flow within brain tissue in response to specific stimulus events are detected magnetically, with extremely clear computerized pictures of activated brain areas. Functional imaging procedures provide three-dimensional images of brain activity, and supply the most precise information regarding which regions of the brain are specialized for certain functions, or are functioning abnormally in cases of certain disorders.

Neuroimaging studies tell us that children with a particular disorder have structural differences or less activity in certain areas of the brain, but they do not tell us why. Although remarkable advances have been made in the use of brain-imaging procedures with children during the past two decades, their promise for advancing our understanding of developmental disorders is just beginning (Peterson, 2003).

Observation

*It was six men of Indostan
To learning much inclined,
Who went to see the Elephant
(Though all of them were blind),
That each by observation
Might satisfy his mind.*

John Godfrey Saxe (1816–1887)

Using systematic *observational methods,* a researcher can directly observe the behavior of the child and others under conditions that range from unstructured observations in the child's natural environment, referred to as **naturalistic observation,** to highly structured situations involving specific tasks or instructions usually carried out in the clinic or laboratory, referred to as **structured observation.** When using naturalistic observation, the researcher goes into the child's home, classroom, or day care center to observe and record the behaviors of interest of the child, and often parents, teachers, siblings, and peers with whom the child interacts. Alternatively, the researcher may videotape behavior in the natural environment, which can be coded at a later time.

A researcher who uses structured observations in the laboratory or clinic sets up a situation or provides instructions to elicit behaviors of particular interest (Roberts & Hope, 2001). For example, numerous studies of attachment have assessed young children's reactions to increasingly stressful episodes of separation from and reunion with their care-givers in the laboratory, using the Ainsworth Strange Situation (Ainsworth, Blehar, Waters, & Wall, 1978). By structuring the situation to elicit specific attachment behaviors, the strange situation permits researchers to assess the security of children's attachment by noting how effectively they can use their caregivers as a source of comfort during times of distress.

Structured laboratory- or clinic-based observations are cost-effective and offer the advantage of focusing observations on the phenomena of interest. The method is especially useful for studying child behaviors that occur infrequently in everyday life. Structured observations give the researcher greater control over the situation than do naturalistic observations, and permit the use of other assessment procedures. For example, when a problem-solving discussion is videotaped, replays of the interaction can be used to ask family members what they were thinking during the discussion (Sanders & Dadds, 1992). One negative aspect is questions arise as to whether observations in the laboratory or clinic provide a representative sample of the behaviors of interest (Mash & Foster, 2001). Being videotaped or observed through a one-way mirror is a bit like being in a fishbowl; children and parents may not behave in the laboratory as they do in real-life settings. In general, samples of behavior obtained us-

A 7-year-old child with a behavior disorder is observed while playing in a natural setting.

© David Young-Wolff/PhotoEdit

ing observational methods—laboratory or in real-world settings—should be regarded as "behavior in the presence of an observer."

SECTION SUMMARY

- The measures and methods used to study child and family behavior must be standardized, reliable, and valid.

- Self-report methods include unstructured interviews, questionnaires, and formal tests.

- Psychophysiological methods are used to assess the relationship between physiological processes and behavior, and include measures of heart rate, blood pressure, respiration, pupil dilation, and electrical conductance of the skin.

- Electrophysiological measures, such as the EEG, link electrical brain activity with ongoing thinking, emotion, or states of arousal.

- Neuroimaging procedures are used to examine the structure and/or function of the brain.

- Observational methods are used to directly observe the behavior of the child and others in unstructured situations such as the home or classroom, and in structured task situations in the laboratory or clinic.

Research Strategies

The research strategies used to study children with problems ultimately contribute to the overall accuracy of research findings and conclusions. If a researcher uses bias in selecting participants, or chooses a research task that does not represent the problem of interest, then the validity of the results may be on shaky grounds—the study may not be a fair test of the research question.

Research studies may be examined with respect to their internal and external validity. **Internal validity** reflects how much a particular variable, rather than extraneous influences, accounts for the results, changes, or group differences. Threats to internal validity include maturation, the effects of testing, and subject selection biases. For example, let's suppose you found that providing relaxation training over several months to a group of 5-year-old children decreased their nighttime fears. It's possible that the observed decrease may be due to the extraneous influences of maturation or testing—the children's fears decrease because they are getting older or are being assessed repeatedly, rather than as a result of the relaxation training.

The reduction in fears could also be due to *subject selection biases,* which are factors that operate in selecting subjects or in the selective loss or retention of subjects during the study. For example, if children with only mild fears are selected for our study, a high likelihood exists that their fears will decrease over time, even in the absence of treatment, relative to children with more severe fears. Also, if children with more severe fears, or who do not benefit from relaxation training, dropped out of the study prematurely, the observed decrease in fears may be the result of this selective loss of subjects rather than treatment. Threats to internal validity must be addressed in our research design and interpretation of findings.

External validity refers to the degree to which findings can be generalized, or extended to people, settings, times, measures, and characteristics other than the ones in a particular study. Threats to external validity may include characteristics of the subjects that apply to some people but not others, the reactivity of subjects to participating in the research, the setting in which the research is carried out, or the time when measurements are made (Kazdin, 2003c). For example, children or parents may not behave naturally in an unfamiliar laboratory setting. If findings from a study in the laboratory are quite different from what is found in real-life settings, our study would have low external validity.

Identifying the Sample

Careful thought must be given to how samples of children are identified and selected. First, the validity of any research study in abnormal child psychology ultimately depends on the classification systems used to identify the samples of children who participate in the research (Pickles & Angold, 2003). A careful definition of the sample is critical for comparability of findings across studies and clear communication among researchers. Without such uniform standards, wide differences may result in esti-

Comorbidity: Seven-year-old boy with multiple handicaps of autism, epilepsy, ADHD, and mental retardation

mated base rates for various childhood disorders and many other findings.

In addition to our sample definition, a second issue is the need to consider possible comorbidities among our sample. **Comorbidity** is the simultaneous occurrence of two or more childhood disorders that is far more common than would be predicted from the general population base rates of the individual disorders. Such comorbidity has direct implications for the selection of research participants and for the interpretation of results. Research samples drawn from clinical populations will have a disproportionately high rate of comorbidity because referral for treatment is most likely based on the combined symptomatology of all disorders.

To deal with comorbidity in research samples, some researchers may select only participants with single, or pure, disorders. This strategy may yield small, atypical samples whose findings do not generalize to other populations. Alternatively, a failure to consider comorbidity may result in an interpretation of findings in relation to one disorder, when these findings are more validly attributed to a second disorder or to a combination of disorders. Research strategies that compare children showing single disorders with children showing comorbid

disorders are needed to help disentangle the effects of comorbidity.

Third, we must be sensitive to the setting and source of referral of children for research. *Random selection* is the way subjects are drawn from a population that gives each individual in that population an equal chance of being selected for the study. This is rare in studies of child psychopathology. At the other end of the spectrum are studies that use *samples of convenience,* in which subjects are selected for a study merely because of their availability, regardless of whether they provide a suitable test of the questions or conditions of interest. Research samples in abnormal child psychology have been selected from numerous settings, including outpatient psychology and psychiatry clinics, schools, hospitals, day care centers, and the community. Effects related to different settings are often confounded with effects related to different referral sources, since referral sources also differ across settings.

General Approaches

There are several different, yet complementary, approaches to research design that offer various advantages and disadvantages. The choice of approach frequently depends on the research questions being addressed, the nature of the childhood disorder under investigation, and the availability of resources.

Nonexperimental and Experimental Research One goal of scientific research is to simplify and isolate variables in order to study them more closely. This goal is met by varying or manipulating values of the variable(s) of interest while trying to control or hold constant other factors that could influence the results. Doing this makes it possible to study the association between the particular variables of interest (Kazdin, 2003c). The basic distinction between nonexperimental versus experimental research reflects the degree to which the investigator can manipulate the experimental variable or, alternatively, must rely on examining the natural covariation of several variables of interest. The *independent variable* is manipulated by the researcher. Based on a research hypothesis, the independent variable is anticipated to cause a change in another variable. The variable expected to be influenced by the independent variable is called the *dependent variable.* The greater the degree of control that the researcher has over the independent variable(s), the more the study approximates a true experiment.

In a **true experiment** the researcher has maximum control over the independent variable or conditions of interest, and can use random assignment of subjects to groups, include needed control conditions, and control possible sources of bias. Conversely, the less control the researcher has in determining which participants will and will not be exposed to the independent variable(s), the more nonexperimental the research will be. Most variables of interest in child psychopathology cannot be manipulated directly, including the nature or severity of the child's disorder, parenting practices, or genetic influences. As a result, much of the research conducted with disturbed children and their families relies on nonexperimental, correlational approaches.

In *correlational studies,* researchers often examine relationships among variables by using a **correlation coefficient,** a number that describes the degree of association between two variables. A correlation coefficient can range from -1.00 to $+1.00$. The size of the correlation indicates the strength of the association between two variables. A zero correlation indicates no relationship; the closer the value gets to -1.00 or $+1.00$, the stronger is the relationship. The sign of the correlation coefficient (plus or minus) indicates the direction of the relationship. A positive sign ($+$) indicates that as one variable increases in value, so does the other, whereas a negative sign ($-$) indicates that as one variable increases, the other decreases.

For example, a positive correlation of $+.70$ between symptoms of anxiety and depression indicates that children who show many symptoms of anxiety are also likely to display symptoms of depression. Alternatively, children who show few symptoms of anxiety are likely to display few symptoms of depression. However, a negative correlation of $-.70$ between symptoms of depression and social skills, for example, indicates that children who show many symptoms of depression have fewer social skills.

The primary limitation of correlational studies is that interpretations of causality cannot be made. A correlation between two variables does not imply that one variable causes the other. If we find a relationship between depression in children and their parents, it could mean that being around a child who is depressed may lead to depression in parents, or that parental depression may lead to depression in the child, or that depression in the child and parent may both be due to another more fundamental variable, such as a shared genetic disposition for depression.

In experimental investigations, researchers must take steps to control for the characteristics of participants that could decrease the accuracy of the findings. For example, if two groups of children differ with respect to education, intelligence, SES, or the presence of related disorders, it would be impossible to determine whether the independent variable or the other characteristics led to the results. **Random assignment** of participants to treatment conditions protects against this problem, because the probability of a subject's appearing in any of the groups is equal. By assigning participants to groups on the basis of the flip of a coin, numbers drawn from a hat, or a table of random numbers, the chance is increased that characteristics other than the independent variable will be equally distributed across treatment groups.

As we have noted, many hypotheses in abnormal

© Thinkstock

Children's symptoms of anxiety and depression are often positively correlated.

child psychology cannot be tested by randomly assigning participants to conditions and manipulating conditions in the real world. A compromise involves the use of natural experiments, also called *quasi-experimental designs* or *known-group comparisons*. In **natural experiments,** comparisons are made between conditions or treatments that already exist. The experiments may involve children with different disorders, parents with different problems, or different family environments, for example, children who have been abused versus children who have not. These studies are essentially correlational, but the subjects are selected to ensure that their characteristics are as comparable as possible with the exception of the independent variable. Despite the extreme care exercised by researchers to equate existing groups, natural experiments cannot achieve the same level of precision and rigor as true experimental research. Nevertheless, for many important questions in abnormal child psychology, natural experiments are the only option.

Prospective and Retrospective Research   Research designs that address questions about the causes and long-term outcomes of childhood disorders may differ with respect to the time the sample is identified and the time data are collected. In a **retrospective design,** a sample of people is identified at the current time, and asked for information relating to an earlier time. Cases are identified who already show the outcome of interest, and they are compared with controls who do not show the outcome. Assessments focus on characteristics in the past, and inferences are made about past characteristics and the current outcome. For example, a sample of young adults with a substance use disorder might be asked to provide retrospective ratings and descriptions of their early family experiences.

Although data are immediately available in retrospective studies, they are also highly susceptible to bias and distortion in recall. Parents of teenagers diagnosed with schizophrenia may reinterpret their views of the teen's childhood, distorting their recollection of the teen's prior behavior or friendships. Moreover, retrospective designs fail to identify the individuals who were exposed to certain earlier experiences but do not develop the problem. Young adults with a substance use disorder may report more negative early experiences. However, this finding could not serve as the basis for a conclusion that negative early experiences were specific precursors of adult substance abuse. The retrospective study fails to identify those children whose early experiences were negative, but who did not develop substance use disorders as young adults.

In **real-time prospective designs,** the research sample is identified and then followed over time, with data collected at specified time intervals. The same youngsters are followed or assessed over time in order to understand the course of change or differences that may develop over time or during important developmental transitions such as middle-school entry or adolescence. For example, infants who are fearful in response to novel events may be followed over time to determine if they develop later anxiety disorders or other problems when compared with infants who are not fearful.

Prospective designs correct for several of the problems associated with retrospective research. By following a sample over time we can identify children who develop a disorder as well as those who do not. Since information is collected at the time it occurs, problems relating to bias and distortion in recall are minimized. Disadvantages of prospective designs include loss of participants over time and the extended length of time needed to collect data.

Analogue Research **Analogue research** evaluates a specific variable of interest under conditions that only resemble or approximate the situation to which one wishes to generalize. Analogue studies focus on a circumscribed research question under well-controlled conditions. Often, the purpose of the research is to illuminate a specific process that would otherwise be difficult to study.

For example, Lang, Pelham, Johnston, and Gelernter (1989) were interested in whether the higher-than-normal rates of alcohol consumption observed in fathers of boys with attention-deficit disorder (ADD)/conduct disorder (CD) might be partly due to the distress associated with interacting with their difficult children (these researchers must have been parents, too!). Male and female single college students who were social drinkers were randomly assigned to interact with boys who were trained to perform behaviors characteristic of either normal children (friendly

and cooperative) or children with ADD/CD (overactive and disruptive). Participants also rated their own mood before and after interactions with the child. Following the interaction, participants were given a 20-minute break while they anticipated another interaction with the same child. During the break, beer was freely available for their consumption. Both male and female participants reported comparable levels of elevated distressed mood after interacting with children enacting the ADD/CD role. However, only men who had interacted with these children drank enough to increase blood alcohol levels.

The findings suggest that interacting with a child with ADD/CD may increase alcohol consumption in fathers. However, an analogue study only resembles the conditions of interest—the study participants were single college students not parents of children with ADD/CD, the children did not really have ADD/CD, drinking was confined to an artificial laboratory setting, only beer was available. Therefore, it is difficult to know if similar effects would occur in real-life circumstances (despite anecdotal reports by some parents that their kids drive them to drink!). These conditions raise the question of external validity, or the generalizability of research findings.

Research Designs

Case Study The **case study,** which involves an intensive, usually anecdotal, observation and analysis of an individual child, has a long tradition in the study of abnormal development and behavior. Itard's description of Victor, the Wild Boy of Aveyron, Freud's treatment of a phobia in Little Hans, John Watson's conditioning of a phobic reaction in Albert B., and many other similar case studies have played an influential role in shaping the way we think about children's problems. The case study, especially as used in the clinical context, brings together a wide range of information about an individual child from various sources, including interviews, observations, and test results. The goal is to get as complete a picture as possible of the child's psychological functioning, current environment, and developmental history. Sometimes the goal is to describe the effects of treatment on the child.

Case studies yield narratives that are rich in detail and provide valuable insights into factors associated with a child's disorder. Nevertheless, they also have drawbacks. They are typically viewed as unscientific and flawed because they are characterized by the uncontrolled methods and selective biases, the inherent difficulties associated with integrating diverse observations, drawing valid inferences among the variables of interest, and generalizing from the particular child of interest to other children. Hence, case studies have been viewed primarily as rich sources of descriptive information that provide a basis for subsequent testing of hypotheses in research using larger samples and more controlled methods. They also provide a source for developing and trying out treatment techniques.

Despite their unscientific nature, systematically conducted case studies are likely to continue to play a useful role in research on childhood disorders. First, some childhood disorders such as childhood-onset schizophrenia are rare, making it difficult to generate large samples of children for research. Second, the analyses of individual cases may contribute to the understanding of many striking symptoms of childhood disorders that either occur infrequently or that are hidden and therefore difficult to observe directly. Third, significant childhood disturbances such as post–traumatic stress disorder (Chapter 7) often develop as the result of natural disaster, severe trauma, or abuse. These extreme events and circumstances are not easily studied using controlled methods. Nevertheless, generalization remains a problem with case studies, as does the time-consuming nature of the intensive analyses of single cases.

Single-Case Experimental Designs **Single-case experimental designs** have most frequently been used to evaluate the impact of a clinical treatment, such as reinforcement or stimulant medication, on a child's problem. The central features of single-case experimental designs that distinguish these from uncontrolled case studies include systematic repeated assessment of behavior over time, the replication of treatment effects within the same subject over time, and the participant's serving as his or her own control by experiencing all treatment conditions (Barlow & Hersen, 1984; Kazdin, 1982). Many single-subject designs exist, the most common being the A-B-A-B (reversal) design, and the multiple-baseline design carried out across behaviors, situations, or individuals.

Findings from a study using a *reversal design* are presented in Figure 3.5. In this example, a behavioral intervention was used to reduce self-injurious behavior (SIB) in Ann, a 5-year-old girl with profound mental retardation and multiple handicaps. Ann's SIB consisted of biting her hand and wrists during grooming activities, such as brushing her teeth. These behaviors were getting progressively worse and causing open wounds. During the initial baseline phase, the percentage of intervals in which Ann engaged in SIB during three brief sessions of tooth brushing ranged from 20% to 60%.

Intervention consisted of a negative reinforcement procedure in which Ann was permitted to escape from the grooming activity when she performed an appropriate competing behavior. She was also physically guided by a trainer to brush her teeth whenever she engaged in SIB (guided compliance). When these procedures were implemented during the intervention phase, an immediate reduction of SIB to 10% resulted, with no SIB occurring in the next two sessions. During the reversal, or return-to-baseline, phase, Ann's SIB increased to previous baseline levels. When treatment was reinstituted, SIB decreased

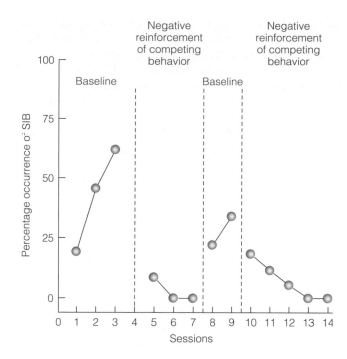

Figure 3.5. A-B-A-B (reversal) design: treatment of Ann's self-injurious behavior.

Source: Adapted from "Use of Negative Reinforcement in the Treatment of Self-Injurious Behavior," by M. W. Steege, D. P. Wacker, K. C. Cigrand, W. K. Berg, C. C. Novak, T. M. Reimers, G. M. Sasso, and A. DeRaad, 1990, Journal of Applied Behavior Analysis, 23, 459–467. Copyright © 1990 by the Society for the Experimental Analysis of Behavior, Inc. Adapted by permission of the author.

again, with no biting observed during the final two sessions. The finding that Ann's levels of SIB decreased only during the intervention phases, and not during the baseline or return-to-baseline phases, suggests that the reductions in Ann's SIB resulted from the intervention procedures.

The reversal design is applicable for use with a wide range of behaviors, however, there are limitations. One limitation is that if a treatment really works, the behavior may not reverse. Do you see any other limitations of this design? Once Ann stopped engaging in SIB following intervention, do you think there was sufficient justification for reinstituting her harmful behavior for experimental purposes? We intentionally selected this example to illustrate a major limitation of the A-B-A-B design, which is the ethical concerns surrounding the return-to-baseline condition following effective treatment for dangerous or even undesirable behaviors. The multiple-baseline design that we describe next gets around this concern, because no reversal is needed once intervention is introduced.

In a **multiple-baseline design** across behaviors, different responses of the same individual are identified and measured over time to provide a baseline against which changes may be evaluated. Each behavior is then successively modified in turn. If each behavior changes only

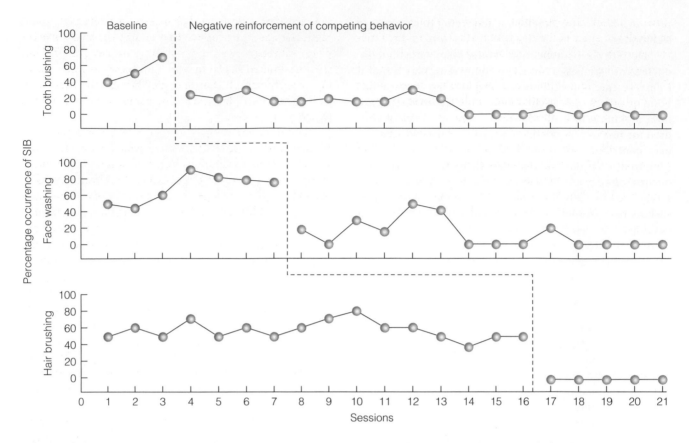

Figure 3.6. Multiple-baseline design across situations: treatment of Dennis's self-injurious behavior.

Source: Adapted from "Use of Negative Reinforcement in the Treatment of Self-Injurious Behavior," by M. W. Steege, D. P. Wacker, K. C. Cigrand, W. K. Berg, G. C. Novak, T. M. Reimers, G. M. Sasso & A. DeRaad, 1990, *Journal of Applied Behavior Analysis, 23,* 459–467. Copyright © 1990 by the Society for the Experimental Analysis of Behavior, Inc. Adapted by permission of the author.

when it is specifically treated, the inference of a cause-and-effect relationship between the treatment and the behavior change is made. Other common varieties of multiple-baseline designs involve successive introductions of treatment for the same behavior in the same individual across different situations, or for the same behavior across several individuals in the same situation. The critical feature of the multiple-baseline approach is that change must occur only when treatment is instituted, and only for the behavior, situation, or individual that is the target of treatment. Simultaneous changes must not occur for untreated behaviors, situations, or individuals until the time that each is, in turn, targeted for treatment.

Findings from a study using a multiple-baseline design across situations are presented in Figure 3.6. In this example, the same intervention procedures used with Ann were used to reduce self-injurious behavior (SIB) in Dennis, a 6-year-old boy, also with profound mental retardation and multiple handicaps. Dennis's SIB consisted of biting his hands, wrists, or arms during grooming activities such as tooth brushing, face washing, and hair brushing. His SIB was getting worse and causing open wounds. During the initial baseline phase, the percentage of intervals

in which Dennis engaged in SIB averaged 54% during tooth brushing, 70% during face washing, and 58% during hair brushing. When intervention was implemented during tooth brushing, an immediate decrease in Dennis's SIB resulted, with consistently low rates of SIB maintained throughout treatment. Moreover, no changes in Dennis's SIB were observed during face washing or hair brushing until the intervention was introduced during those situations.

When intervention was introduced during face washing, an immediate reduction in SIB occurred, with SIB occurring once during the final eight sessions. During the hair-brushing situation, no SIB occurred after intervention was introduced. Because changes in Dennis's SIB occurred only when intervention was introduced during each of the specific situations, there is support for the hypothesis that intervention led to those changes. A multiple-baseline design avoids the problem associated with the reversal design of having to return to baseline when treating dangerous or unwanted behaviors.

Several advantages and limitations are associated with the use of single-case designs. These designs preserve the personal quality of the case study, and offer some degree of control for potential alternative explanations of the findings, such as the effects of maturation and reactivity to observation. Single-case designs also provide an objective evaluation of treatment for individual cases, permit the study of rare disorders, and facilitate the development and evaluation of alternative and combined forms of treatment. The negative aspects of the design are the possibilities that specific treatments will interact with unique characteristics of a particular child, the limited generality of findings to other cases, and the subjectivity involved when visual inspection is used as the primary means for evaluating the data. The findings in the examples of Ann and Dennis were fairly clear-cut. Difficulties in interpretation arise when baseline data or observed changes are often highly variable.

Between-Group Comparison Designs Many research designs are based on comparisons between one group of children assigned to one or more conditions, and other groups of children assigned to one or more different conditions. When participants are randomly assigned to groups, and groups are presumed to be equivalent in all other respects, one group typically serves as the *experimental group* and the other serves as the *control group*. Any differences observed between groups are then attributed to the experimental condition.

The choice of an appropriate control or comparison group often depends on what we know prior to the study and the questions we wish to answer. For example, if an established and effective treatment for adolescent depression exists, testing a new approach against a no-treatment control group will likely answer the wrong question, not to mention raising ethical concerns about withholding a proven effective treatment. We don't want to know if the new approach is better than nothing; we want to know if it is better than the best available alternative treatment.

Cross-Sectional and Longitudinal Studies Researchers interested in developmental psychopathology need information about the ways in which children and adolescents change over time. To obtain this information, researchers extend correlational and experimental approaches to include measurements taken at different ages. Both cross-sectional and longitudinal designs are research strategies in which a comparison of children of different ages serves as the basis for research.

In **cross-sectional research,** different youngsters at different ages or periods of development are studied at the same point in time, whereas in **longitudinal research,** the same children are studied at different ages or periods of development. In cross-sectional studies, researchers don't have to worry about the many problems associated with studying the same group of children over a long period. When participants are measured only once, researchers need not be concerned about selective loss of participants,

practice effects, or general changes in the field that would make the findings obsolete by the time the study is complete. Although cross-sectional approaches are efficient, they are limited in the information they generate regarding developmental changes. Evidence about individual change is not available. Rather, comparisons are limited to age-group averages.

Longitudinal designs are conducted prospectively. Data collection occurs at specified points in time from the same individuals initially selected because of their membership in one or more populations of interest. In studies of child psychopathology, the populations of interest often consist of children at risk for developmental problems due to exposure to any one of a number of factors, for example, having a mother who uses drugs or alcohol during pregnancy or who has a mental disorder, or living in an abusive family situation.

The prospective longitudinal design allows the researcher to identify patterns that are common to all youngsters, and to track differences in developmental paths that children follow. For example, a longitudinal study can tell that certain fears may decrease with age for all children, but that some children may have an anxious disposition and show less of a reduction in specific fears with age. Because data are collected on the same individuals at time 1 and time 2, causal inferences between earlier events and later events and behavior based on temporal ordering can be made. Such inferences of causality cannot be made in cross-sectional designs, where different individuals are assessed at the two time points. Longitudinal designs also allow for identification of individual developmental trends that would be masked by aggregating over individuals. The prepubertal growth spurt exemplifies this, where rapid accelerations in growth occurring at different ages across the population are not reflected in growth measures aggregated across adolescents. An example of a longitudinal study is presented in Box 3.3.

Despite their advantages, longitudinal designs have many practical and design difficulties. Practical concerns include obtaining and maintaining research funding and resources over many years and the long wait for meaningful data. Design difficulties relate to aging effects and cohort effects. *Aging effects* are general changes that occur because as participants age there are increases in physical prowess, impulse control, or social opportunity. *Cohort effects* are influences related to being a member of a specific **cohort,** which is a group of individuals who are followed during the same time, and experience the same cultural or historical events. For example, the cohort of teens who lived in war-torn Yugoslavia in the early 1990s differ in many respects from North American teenagers living through the technological boom of the early 1990s.

The experience of being repeatedly studied, observed, interviewed, and tested may also threaten the validity of a longitudinal study. Children and adults may become more sensitized to the thoughts, feelings, and behaviors under

BOX 3.3 Does Child Maltreatment Lead to More Peer Rejection Over Time?

Dodge, Pettit, and Bates (1994a) assessed a representative sample of 585 boys and girls for physical maltreatment in the first 5 years of life and then followed them for 5 consecutive years from kindergarten through the fourth grade. Twelve percent of the sample was identified as having experienced maltreatment. The children's peers, teachers, and mothers independently rated the maltreated children as being more disliked, less popular, and more socially withdrawn than the nonmaltreated children in every year of evaluation—and the magnitude of the difference increased over time. As shown in Figure 3.7, by grade 4 more than twice as many maltreated as nonmaltreated children were rejected by their peer group. The results suggest that early maltreatment may disrupt relationships with adults, which in turn impairs a child's ability to form effective relationships with other children.

Source: Adapted from "Effects of Physical Maltreatment on the Development of Peer Relations," by K. A. Dodge, G. S. Pettit, and J. E. Bates, 1994, *Development and Psychopathology, 6,* 43–55. Copyright © 1994 by Cambridge University Press. Adapted with permission of Cambridge University Press and K. A. Dodge.

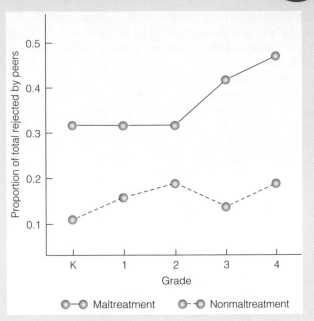

Proportions of maltreated and nonmaltreated children rejected by their peer group. (Adapted from Dodge et al., 1994a)

---

investigation, thus thinking about them and revising them in ways that have nothing to do with age-related change. Furthermore, with repeated testing, participants may improve as the result of practice effects, including greater familiarity with test items and better test-taking skills. Finally, changes within the field of abnormal child psychology may create problems for longitudinal studies that cover an extended period. Theories and methods are constantly changing, and those that first led to the longitudinal study may become outdated.

Qualitative Research

Qualitative research focuses on narrative accounts, description, interpretation, context, and meaning (Berg, 1998; Fiese & Bickham, 1998). The purpose of qualitative research is to describe, interpret, and understand the phenomenon of interest in the context in which it is experienced (Patton, 1990). This approach can be contrasted with a quantitative approach, which emphasizes operational definitions, careful control of the subject matter, attempts to isolate variables of interest, quantification of dimensions of interest, and statistical analysis. Rather than beginning with already developed observational systems or assessment tools, qualitative researchers strive to understand the phenomenon from the participant's perspective. Qualitative data are typically collected through observations or open-ended interviewing and recorded narratively as case study notes, for example. The observations and narrative accounts obtained are examined to build general categories and patterns. Table 3.2 describes some of the key characteristics of qualitative research.

To get a feel for qualitative methods, consider the study described in Box 3.4. This study looks at some ways that parents of children with mental retardation and child psychology professionals may arrive at a consensus during a diagnostic feedback session.

Proponents of qualitative research believe that it provides an intensive and intimate understanding of a situation that is rarely achieved in quantitative research (Denzin & Lincoln, 1994; L. B. Murphy, 1992). Qualitative methods, such as the use of vignettes, may be more engaging to children and enable the discussion of sensitive topics, while allowing the children a sense of control over the research situation (Barter & Renold, 2000). On the other hand, qualitative methods may be biased by the researcher's values and preferences, and the findings cannot easily be generalized to individuals and situations other than the ones studied. Nonetheless, quantitative and qualitative research methods can be used in complementary ways (Camic, Rhodes, & Yardley, 2003). The methods

Table 3.2

Key Characteristics of Qualitative Research

- Qualitative research is conducted through an intense and/or prolonged contact with a "field," or life, situation, which are typically reflective of the everyday life of individuals, groups, societies, and organizations.
- Data: perceptions of local actors from the inside, through a process of deep attentiveness, empathic understanding, and suspension of preconceptions.
- Isolate certain themes and expressions that can be reviewed with informants but that should be maintained in their original forms throughout the study.
- A main task is to explicate the ways people in particular settings come to understand, account for, take action on, and otherwise manage their day-to-day situations.
- Relatively little standardized instrumentation is used at the outset. The researcher is essentially the main measurement device in the study.
- Most analysis is done with words. The words can be assembled, subclustered, and broken into segments. They can be organized to permit the researcher to contrast, compare, analyze, and bestow patterns on them.

Source: From *Qualitative Data Analysis: An Expanded Sourcebook,* by M. B. Miles and A. M. Huberman, 1994, pp. 6–7. Copyright © 1994 by Sage Publications, Inc. Reprinted by permission.

can be combined in a qualitative approach to identify important dimensions, which are then developed into a theoretical model that can be tested quantitatively, or tested in qualitative case studies to illuminate the meaning of quantitatively derived findings. Additionally, if qualitative data have been reduced to numbers through word counts or frequency counts of themes, the data can be analyzed using quantitative methods.

SECTION SUMMARY

- Careful attention must be given to the way in which samples are identified for research in abnormal child psychology, including issues such as how the disorder of interest is defined, criteria for inclusion in the study, comorbidity, the setting from which subjects are drawn, and sample size.

- We can distinguish between nonexperimental versus experimental research strategies on the basis of the degree to which the investigator can manipulate the experimental variable or, alternatively, must rely on examining the covariation of variables of interest.

- In prospective research, a sample is followed over time with data collected at specified intervals. In retrospective research, a sample is identified at the current time and asked for information relating to an earlier time.

BOX 3.4 Professionals and Parents Negotiate Bad News

In a study using qualitative research methods, Abrams and Goodman (1998) were interested in what transpires between parents of children with developmental delays and professionals during a diagnostic feedback session. In particular, they wanted to learn more about negotiation—a process that describes the socially constructed nature of encounters in which participants come to a mutual understanding through the natural use of language. Parents were told that the purpose of the study was to examine how professionals communicate information to parents, and signed a release form so that the feedback sessions could be audiotaped. Tapes from 10 feedback sessions with different parents were then transcribed in complete detail, resulting in over 700 pages of transcription. Analysis of the discourse identified negotiation over the diagnostic label in 8 of the 10 cases. As a form of negotiation, some parents engaged in "bargaining," in which they tried to circumscribe the label and limit its impact. Here's an example of bargaining in the case of a child who received a diagnosis of mental retardation:

PROFESSIONAL: This degree of delay means that he's mentally retarded.

FATHER: Is there anything that can be done for him?

PROFESSIONAL: There are always things that can be done. [Mother weeps]

MOTHER: But he's not severely retarded?

PROFESSIONAL: No.

FATHER: More moderate.

PSYCHOLOGIST: Our best guess is that he will continue to be slow and probably in the mildly retarded range—which would mean that he would be—let's call him "educable."

At first, the mother found the diagnosis of mental retardation emotionally difficult to accept. However, after regaining her composure, she actively engaged in a cognitive adjustment of the diagnostic label to make it less overwhelming. By doing this, she was able to locate her son's label in the mildly retarded range and in so doing, limited her sense of loss. In reality, her son had an IQ score of 54, which placed him on the borderline between moderate and mild retardation. On the basis of their analysis of this and many other samples of discourse, the researchers concluded that interpretations made during a diagnostic feedback session are arrived at through a process of negotiation and are not simply "given" by professionals.

Source: Abrams and Goodman, 1998, p. 94.

- Analogue research evaluates a specific variable under conditions that only resemble the situation to which the researcher wishes to generalize.

- The case study involves an intensive, usually anecdotal, observation and analysis of an individual child.

- Single-case designs involve repeated assessments of the same subject over time, the replication of treatment effects within the same subject, and the subject's serving as his or her own control. Two common examples are the A-B-A-B (reversal) design and multiple-baseline design across behaviors, situations, or individuals.

- Between-group designs compare the behavior of groups of individuals assigned to different conditions, such as an experimental group, or a comparison group and a control group.

- In cross-sectional research, different individuals at different ages or stages of development are studied at the same point in time. In longitudinal research, the same individuals are studied at different ages or stages of development.

- Qualitative research focuses on narrative accounts, description, interpretation, context, and meaning, and strives to understand the phenomenon from the participant's perspective and in the context in which it is experienced.

Ethical and Pragmatic Issues

The image of overzealous scientists using children as guinea pigs for their experiments is a far cry from current research practices in abnormal child psychology. Researchers have become increasingly sensitive to the possible ethical misuses of research procedures, and are correspondingly more aware of the need for standards to regulate research practices (Hoagwood, 2003).

Research in abnormal child psychology must meet certain standards that protect children and families from stressful procedures. Any study must undergo careful ethical review before it can be conducted. Current ethical guidelines for research with children are provided through institutional review boards, federal funding agencies, and professional organizations such as the American Psychological Association (2002) and the Society for Research in Child Development (1996).

Ethical standards for research with children attempt to strike a balance between supporting freedom of scientific inquiry and protecting the rights of privacy and the overall welfare of the research participants. Finding this balance is not always easy, especially with children. Although researchers are obligated to use nonharmful procedures, exposing the child to mildly stressful conditions may be necessary in some instances if therapeutic benefits

associated with the research are to be realized. Children are more vulnerable than adults to physical and psychological harm, and their immaturity may make it difficult or impossible for them to evaluate exactly what research participation means. In view of these realities, precautions must be taken to protect children's rights during the course of a study.

Informed Consent and Assent

The individual's fully informed consent to participate, obtained without coercion, serves as the single most protective regulation for research participants. **Informed consent** requires that all participants be fully informed of the nature of the research, as well as the risks, benefits, expected outcomes, and alternatives, before they agree to participate. Informed consent also includes informing participants of the option to withdraw from the study at any time, and of the fact that participation or nonparticipation in the research does not affect eligibility for other services.

Regarding research with children, protection is extended to obtaining the informed consent of the parents or other legal guardian acting for the child and the assent of the child. **Assent** means that the child shows some form of agreement to participate without necessarily understanding the full significance of the research, which may be beyond younger children's cognitive capabilities. Guidelines for obtaining assent of the child call for doing so when the child is around the age of 7 or older. Researchers must provide school-age children with a complete explanation of the research activities in language they can understand. Factors that require particular attention when seeking children's assent include age, developmental maturity, psychological state, role constraints, family factors, and the influence of the investigator seeking assent (Meaux & Bell, 2001). In addition to parents and children, consent must be obtained from other individuals who act on behalf of children, such as institutional officials when research is carried out in schools, day care centers, or medical settings.

Voluntary Participation

Participation in research is to be voluntary, yet some individuals may be more susceptible to subtle pressure and coercion than others. Protection for vulnerable populations, including children, has received considerable attention. Fisher (1991) identifies families of high-risk infants and children as potentially more vulnerable, related in part to the families' distress over their children's high-risk status. Although instructed otherwise, parents recruited from social service agencies or medical settings may still feel that their treatment or quality of care will be threatened if they do not participate in the research. Maltreating parents may feel that their failure to participate in research could result in the loss of their child, a jail sentence, or failure to receive services.

The role of the researcher requires balancing successful recruiting and not placing pressure on potential participants (Grisso et al., 1991). Volunteerism is itself a biasing factor in research. Individuals who agree to participate in research obviously differ from individuals who are approached but refuse. The question of whether volunteerism significantly biases findings on the variables of interest remains unanswered.

Confidentiality and Anonymity

Information revealed by individuals through participation in research is to be safeguarded. Most institutions require that individuals be informed that any information they disclose will be kept confidential, and that they be advised regarding any exceptions to confidentiality. Adult informants must be told about the limits of confidentiality prior to their participation in research. In research with children, one of the most frequently encountered challenges to confidentiality occurs when the child or parent reveals past abuse or information that would suggest the possibility of future abuse of the child. Procedures for handling this situation vary across studies. They depend on the circumstances of the disclosure (for example, by an adult within the context of therapy) and the reporting requirements of the state or province. The quality of research data that are collected may vary with the degree to which the confidentiality of information is emphasized (Blanck, Bellack, Rosnow, Rotheram-Borus, & Schooler, 1992).

Nonharmful Procedures

No research procedures should be used that may harm the child either physically or psychologically. Whenever possible, the researcher is also obligated to use procedures that are the least stressful to the child and family. In some instances, psychological harm may be difficult to define, but when doubt is present, the researcher has the responsibility to seek consultation from others. If harm seems inevitable, alternative methods must be found or the research must be abandoned. In cases where exposure of the child to stressful conditions may be necessary if therapeutic benefits associated with the research are to be realized, careful deliberation and analysis of the risks and benefits by an institutional review board are needed.

Other Ethical and Pragmatic Concerns

Sensitivity to ethical concerns is especially important when the research involves potentially invasive procedures, deception, the use of punishment, the use of participant pay-

ment or other incentives, or possible coercion. In longitudinal research, investigators must be particularly sensitive to the occurrence of unexpected crises, unforeseen consequences of research, and issues surrounding the continuation of the research when findings suggest that another course of action is required to ensure the child's well-being.

Many research problems typically addressed through standardized instructions and procedures, and through a reliance on the prior experiences and expectations of the participants, are compounded by children's generally limited experience and understanding of novel research tasks, and by the particular characteristics of disturbed children and families. Children with psychiatric conditions and developmental disorders may present research challenges, such as motivating the children; keeping within time limitations; ensuring that instructions are well understood; and coping with possible boredom, distraction, and fatigue. Similarly, the families of children with problems often exhibit characteristics that may compromise their research participation and involvement. These characteristics include high levels of stress, marital discord, parental psychiatric disorders, substance use disorders, restricted resources and/or time for research, and limited verbal abilities.

The final responsibility for the ethical integrity of any research project is with the investigator. Researchers are advised or, in the case of research funded by the federal government, required to seek advice from colleagues. Special committees exist in hospitals, universities, school systems, and other institutions to evaluate research studies on the basis of risks and benefits. This evaluation involves weighing the participant's costs of the research in terms of inconvenience and possible psychological or physical harm, against the value of the study for advancing knowledge and improving the child's life situation. If there are any risks to the safety and welfare of the child or family that the research does not warrant, priority is always given to the participants.

SECTION SUMMARY

- Research in abnormal child psychology must meet certain standards that protect children and families from stressful procedures, including informed consent and assent, voluntary participation, confidentiality and anonymity, and nonharmful procedures.

- To ensure that research meets ethical standards, researchers seek advice from colleagues and have their research evaluated by institutional ethics review committees. The final responsibility for the ethical integrity of any research project is with the investigator.

Key Terms

 InfoTrac College Edition

To research recent articles on the subject, go to:
www.infotrac-college/thomsonlearning.com

Enter search terms: EXPERIMENTAL DESIGN, NEUROIMAGING, RESEARCH METHODS, ETHICS

Assessment, Diagnosis, and Treatment

If there is anything that we wish to change in the child, we should first examine it and see whether it is not something that could better be changed in ourselves.

—C. G. Jung

Clinical Issues

Most youngsters referred for assessment and treatment have multiple problems. More often than not, the accumulation of these problems over time results in a referral. We have emphasized that most childhood disorders involve breakdowns in normal development. Felicia, for example, is having difficulty coping with the demands of adolescence—gaining autonomy from her parents, getting along with peers, performing well in school, establishing her self-identity, and regulating her emotions. Felicia also experienced the added stress of her mother's hospitalization for pneumonia.

The clinician who sees Felicia will need to evaluate how well she can cope with events in her life in relation to the nature of the events; her appraisal of the events; her physical status, cognitive abilities, and personality; and support from her parents or teachers. To sort out the importance of these complex and interacting forces, we must devise an effective plan of assessment that leads to diagnostic and treatment decisions. We will be revisiting Felicia's case throughout the chapter to see how we address these issues.

In this chapter we emphasize the clinical strategies and methods used to assess children with psychological and behavioral problems, and the various approaches to the classification and diagnosis of childhood disorders. We also provide a brief introduction to treatment—a topic that we will discuss in detail for the individual disorders in the chapters that follow. We begin this important overview of clinical issues with a look at the decision-making process that surrounds assessment, diagnosis, and treatment.

Felicia
Multiple Problems

Felicia, age 13, was referred because of depression, school refusal, social withdrawal at home and school, and sleep disturbance. Her parents first noticed her recent difficulties about a year ago, just after her mother was hospitalized for pneumonia. Felicia was in a regular eigth-grade class and began to refuse to attend school. She complained of frequent stomach pains before school as a reason not to attend. Her social behavior also got worse at this time. She wanted to be close to her mother at all times and frequently requested her mother's help with homework or chores. Felicia became extremely quiet, appeared sad and unhappy, and withdrew from social activities. Not long after, she began to complain of sleep problems and a loss of appetite. At about this time her grades in school dropped from mostly Bs to Cs and Ds. She reported that no one liked her, that she couldn't do anything well, and that her life was hopeless. (Adapted from "Depression," by D. J. Kolko, 1987. In M. Hersen and V. B. Van Hasselt (Eds.), *Behavior Therapy with Children and Adolescents: A Clinical Approach*, pp. 137–182. Copyright © 1987 by John Wiley & Sons, Inc. Reprinted by permission of John Wiley & Sons, Inc.)

Felicia seemed unhappy and withdrawn at home and at school.

The Decision-Making Process

How do we determine whether Felicia has a psychological disorder that requires professional attention, or whether she will simply outgrow or overcome her problems on her own? Mental health clinicians have to consider many important questions systematically to understand a child's basic problem(s), and to make diagnoses and devise treatment plans. In many ways this process is like good detective work. It requires sorting through the many factors that bring a youngster to the attention of professionals, and checking out alternative hypotheses and plans. This ongoing decision-making process is aimed at finding answers to both immediate and long-term questions about the nature and course of the child's disorder and its optimum treatment (Mash, 1998; Schroeder & Gordon, 2002).

The decision-making process typically begins with a clinical assessment. **Clinical assessments** involve the use of deliberate problem-solving strategies to understand children with disturbances and their environment of family, school, and peer relationships (Mash & Terdal, 1997a). Strategies typically include an assessment of the child's emotional, behavioral, and cognitive functioning, as well as the role of environmental circumstance and influence (Sattler, 2002). These strategies form the basis of a flexible and ongoing process of hypothesis testing regarding the nature of the problem, its causes, and the likely outcomes if the problem is treated or left untreated.

Clinical assessment is much broader than interviewing or testing alone. The ultimate goal of assessment is to achieve effective solutions to the problems being faced by children and their families, and to promote and enhance their well-being. *Assessments are meaningful to the extent that they result in practical and effective interventions.* In other words, a close and continuing partnership between assessment and intervention is vital; they should not be viewed as separate processes (Mash & Hunsley, in press).

Although general knowledge about specific disorders can provide guidelines for the important variables to assess in all children referred for a certain problem, clinical assessment must focus on these variables in relation to the individual child and family. Detailed understanding of the individual child or family as a unique entity is an **idiographic** case formulation. This is in contrast to a **nomothetic** formulation, which emphasizes broad general inferences that apply to large groups of individuals (e.g., children with ADHD). A clinician's nomothetic knowledge about general principles of psychological assessment, normal and abnormal child and family development, and specific childhood disorders is likely to result in better hypotheses to test at the idiographic level (Kazdin, 2000).

As you can imagine, the process of decision making is similar to studying for several exams at the same time. You must be familiar with fundamental information such as childhood depression or learning disorders, and then be

© Photodisc

Clinical assessment is like good detective work.

able to integrate this knowledge in new ways to make it applicable to help solve a particular problem. Like studying for exams, this process at first seems like you are trying to cram everything into a funnel to distill what is most important. Unlike studying for exams, however, working with children and families and applying your training and experience to new situations is often very enjoyable!

Clinicians begin their decision making with an assessment, which can range from a clinical interview with the child and parents to more structured behavioral assessments and psychological testing. Keep in mind that assessment is not something done *to* a child or family; it is a collaborative process in which the child, family, and teacher all play active roles. Because adults play a critical role in defining the child's problem and providing information, it is particularly important to establish a rapport and active family and teacher involvement are particularly important.

Developmental Considerations

Age, Gender, and Culture   A recognition of differences in the growing array of children's developmental functions and capacities at various ages is a crucial building block for assessment and treatment (Achenbach, 1997). Does Felicia's age, gender, or cultural background have a bearing on our approach to assessment, diagnosis, and treatment?

School refusal in a 13-year-old like Felicia is significant because it results in missed academic and social opportunities. In contrast, a 13-year-old's refusal to travel by airplane may be inconvenient or distressing, but in most cases would not have the same serious consequences as missing school. A child's age has implications not only for judgments about deviancy, but also for selecting the most appropriate assessment and treatment methods. For example, how old does a child need to be before he or she can provide reliable information in an interview? With respect to treatment, how might the use of time-out for mis-

behavior for a 3-year-old be different from a school-age child?

Like age, the child's sex also has implications for assessment and treatment. Numerous studies have reported sex differences in the rates and expression of childhood disorders (Bell, Foster, & Mash, in press; Crick & Zahn-Waxler, 2003). As shown in Table 4.1, some childhood disorders and conditions are more common in males than females, others are more common in females than males, and others are equally common (Hartung & Widiger, 1998; Rutter, Caspi, & Moffitt, in press).

As we have emphasized, most childhood disorders are defined by adults, usually because adults find the child's symptoms particularly salient or troublesome. In general, overt displays of overactivity and aggression are more common in boys than girls, who tend to express their problems in less observable ways (Keenan & Shaw, 1997). Thus, boys may receive an excess of referrals, and girls may be overlooked due to their less visible forms of suffering. Our assessments and interventions must be sensitive to possible referral biases related to gender and gender differences. The difficulty in distinguishing between true gender differences and differences in reporting is illustrated by the finding that the rate of ADHD diagnoses during the early- to mid-1990s, increased approximately three-fold among girls, compared with two-fold for boys (Robison, Skaer, Sclar, & Galin, 2002). Could the rate of ADHD in girls possibly increase three-fold

---

Table 4.1

Gender Patterns for Selected Disorders of Childhood and Adolescence

MORE COMMONLY REPORTED AMONG MALES

Attention-deficit/ hyperactivity disorder	Autistic disorder
	Language disorder
Childhood conduct disorder	Reading disorder
Mental retardation	Enuresis

MORE COMMONLY REPORTED AMONG FEMALES

Anxiety disorders	Eating disorders
Adolescent depression	Sexual abuse

EQUALLY REPORTED AMONG MALES AND FEMALES

Adolescent conduct disorder	Feeding disorder
Childhood depression	Physical abuse and neglect

Source: Adapted from "Gender Differences in Diagnosis of Mental Disorders. Conclusions and Controversies of DSM-IV," by C. M. Hartung and T. A. Widiger, 1998, *Psychological Bulletin, 123,* 260–278. Copyright © 1998 by the American Psychological Association. Adapted by permission of the author and the publisher.

Biological influences and socialization practices likely interact to create different interests and behavior profiles of girls and boys.

during one decade? It is more likely that increasing recognition of the disorder and its various forms of expression contributed to the dramatic increase in these ADHD diagnoses (Hinshaw & Blachman, in press).

One other gender-related difference is noteworthy. Girls are more likely than boys to be emotionally upset by aggressive social exchanges. When girls are angry, they are more likely than boys to indirectly show aggression with verbal insults, gossip, ostracism, getting even, or third-party retaliation (Crick & Rose, 2000). As girls move into adolescence, the function of their aggressive behavior increasingly centers on group acceptance and affiliation, whereas for boys, aggression remains confrontational. Thus, the targets for change in treatments for socially aggressive girls versus boys may be quite different. In addition, children who engage in forms of social aggression that are not typical of their sex (overtly aggressive girls and relationally aggressive boys) are significantly more maladjusted than children who engage in gender-normative forms of aggression (Crick, 1997).

Finally, cultural factors must be carefully considered during assessment and treatment for ethnic minority children and their families. Cultural information is necessary to establish a relationship with the child and family, obtain valid information, arrive at an accurate diagnosis, and develop meaningful recommendations for treatment. Similarly, what is considered abnormal may vary from one

culture to the next (Draguns & Tanaka-Matsumi, 2003; Mesquita & Walker, 2003). Children's shyness and oversensitivity are likely to lead to peer rejection and social maladjustment in Western cultures, but the same qualities are associated with leadership, school competence, and academic achievement in Chinese children (Chen, Rubin, Li, & Li, 1999). In addition, it may be difficult to engage parents from some cultures if mental health issues are seen as particularly taboo (Kim, Kim, & Rue, 1997), if intervention into personal family matters by strangers is viewed quite negatively (Canino & Spurlock, 1994), or if the causes of the illness in that culture are seen as physical or spiritual (Walker, 2002).

A clinician must recognize the diversity that exists across and within ethnic groups in lifestyle and patterns of acculturation (i.e., level of adaptation to dominant culture versus background culture. Generalizations about cultural practices frequently fail to capture these regional, generational, SES, and lifestyle differences. For example, SES level is a major confound in findings of differences in rates of psychopathology between various cultures, because ethnic minority cultures are frequently overrepresented in low SES populations (Glover & Pumariega, 1998). An individual's acculturation level can also significantly impact assessment and subsequent interventions. The lower the level of one's acculturation, the higher one scores on measures of psychopathology, particularly in

Recognizing diversity across and within ethnic groups is an important role of the clinician.

conjunction with low SES and education level (Cuéllar, 2000). Awareness of the cultural customs and values that can affect behaviors, perceptions, and reactions to assessment and treatment, as well as recognizing the major confound of SES with these factors, puts the clinician in a better position to develop a meaningful strategy (Cohen & Kasen, 1999).

Normative Information   Felicia's school refusal and sad mood began to occur following her mother's hospitalization. Is Felicia showing a normal reaction to a stressful life event? How common are these symptoms in girls her age after a brief period of separation from a parent? Felicia also withdrew from social contact and experienced sleep disturbances. Adolescence is a time of biological and social upheaval for many youngsters, therefore, how do we know if Felicia is different from other girls her age with respect to these problems, and if so, when do we become concerned and take action?

Knowledge, experience, and basic information about norms of child development and behavior problems are the crucial beginning to understanding how children's problems or needs come to the attention of professionals. As many parents discover, figuring out what to expect of their children at various ages can be very challenging. Parents are faced with determining what difficulties are likely to be chronic versus common and transient, deciding when to seek advice of others, and determining what treatment is best for their child. Immigrant parents can have even more difficulty with these tasks when trying to assess their second-generation child's behavior as the child attempts to navigate at least two different cultures (Falicov, 2003).

Isolated symptoms of behavioral and emotional problems generally show little correspondence with children's overall adjustment. This is also true for symptoms once thought to be significant indicators of psychological dis-

turbances in children, such as thumb sucking after 4 years of age (Friman, Larzelere, & Finney, 1994). Usually, the *age inappropriateness* and *pattern* of symptoms, rather than individual symptoms, define childhood disorders. Nevertheless, certain symptoms do occur more frequently in children referred for assessment and treatment.

Examples of parent-reported symptoms that best distinguish referred and nonreferred children ages 4 to 16 are shown in Table 4.2. As you can see, these symptoms are relatively common behaviors that occur to some extent in all children—poor schoolwork and a lack of concentration top the list. In fact, most individual symptoms do not, by themselves, discriminate between referred and nonreferred children (Achenbach, Howell, Quay, & Conners, 1991). Primarily, the problems displayed by children referred for treatment are similar to problems that occur in less extreme forms in the general population or young children.

Purposes of Assessment

Description and Diagnosis   The first step in understanding a child's particular problem is to provide a **clinical description,** which summarizes the unique behaviors, thoughts, and feelings that together make up the features of the child's psychological disorder. A clinical description attempts to establish basic information about children's (and usually the parents') presenting complaints, especially

---

Table 4.2
Individual Parent-Rated Problems That Best Discriminate Between Referred and Nonreferred Children

· Poor schoolwork
· Can't concentrate or pay attention for long
· Lacks self-confidence
· Behavior doesn't change after punishment
· Disobedient at home
· Has trouble following directions
· Sad or depressed
· Uncooperative
· Nervous, high-strung, or tense
· Feels worthless or inferior
· Disobedient at school
· Looks unhappy without good reason

Source: Adapted from "National Survey of Problems and Competences Among Four-to-Sixteen-Year-Olds," by T. M. Achenbach, C. T. Howell, H. C. Quay, and C. K. Conners, 1991, *Monographs of the Society for Research in Child Development,* 107–115, 56 (3), Serial No. 225. Copyright © 1991 by The Society for Research in Child Development. Reprinted by permission of The Society for Research in Child Development and T. M. Achenbach.

how their behavior or emotions are different or similar to those of other children the same age and sex.

If you conducted an evaluation of Felicia, what information would be most important to include in your clinical description? You would start by describing how her behavior differs from normal behavior of girls her age. First, assessing and describing the *intensity, frequency,* and *severity* of her problem would communicate a sense of how excessive or deficient her behavior is, under what circumstances it may be a problem, how often it does or does not occur, and how severe the occurrences are. Second, you would need to describe the *age of onset* and *duration* of her difficulties. Some problems are transient and will spontaneously remit, while others persist over time. Like frequency and intensity, age of onset and duration of the problem behavior must be appraised with respect to what is considered normative for a given age. Finally, you would want to convey a full picture of her *different symptoms and their configuration.* Although Felicia needed help because of particular problems at school and with her peers, you need to know the full range, or profile, of her strengths and weaknesses to make informed choices about the likely course, outcome, and treatment of her disorder.

After establishing an initial picture of Felicia's presenting complaints, you would next determine whether this description meets criteria for diagnosis of one or more psychological disorders. **Diagnosis** means analyzing information and drawing conclusions about the nature or cause of the problem, or assigning a formal diagnosis. Does Felicia meet standard diagnostic criteria for a depressive disorder, and if so, what might be the cause?

Diagnosis has acquired two separate meanings, which can be confusing. The first meaning is *taxonomic diagnosis,* which focuses on the formal assignment of cases to specific categories drawn from a system of classification such as the DSM-IV-TR (APA, 2000) or from empirically derived categories (discussed later in this chapter) (Achenbach, 1998; Pickles & Angold, 2003). The second, much broader meaning of diagnosis, *problem-solving analysis,* is similar to assessment and views diagnosis as a process of gathering information, used to understand the nature of an individual's problem, its possible causes, treatment options, and outcomes.

Thus, Felicia's assessment will involve a complete diagnostic (problem-solving analysis) to get the most comprehensive picture possible. In addition, Felicia may receive a formal diagnosis of major depressive disorder (discussed in Chapter 8), which means that she possesses characteristics that link her to similar youngsters presumed to have the same disorder (taxonomic diagnosis). A secondary diagnosis of an anxiety disorder, such as separation anxiety disorder or school phobia, may be necessary for Felicia since comorbidity of depression and anxiety is very common among girls her age. As we discussed in Chapter 3, comorbidity exists when certain disorders among children and adolescents are likely to co-occur within the same individual, especially disorders that share many common symptoms. Awareness of one disorder alerts us to the increased possibility of another disorder. Some of the more common comorbid disorders are conduct disorder (CD) and attention-deficit/hyperactivity disorder (ADHD), autistic disorder and mental retardation, and childhood depression and anxiety.

Prognosis and Treatment Planning **Prognosis** is the formulation of predictions concerning future behavior under specified conditions. If Felicia does not receive help for her problem, what will likely happen to her in the future? Will her problems diminish as she gets older or will they get worse?

Naturally, parents and others immediately want to know the possible short- and long-term outcomes for their child, and what events might alter such projections. Remember that many childhood concerns, such as fears, worries, and bed-wetting, are common at certain ages, so any decision to treat a child's particular problem must be based on an informed prognosis. Clinicians must weigh the probability that circumstances will remain the same, improve, or deteriorate with or without treatment, as well as what course of treatment should be followed.

In addition, treatments for children and adolescents often focus on enhancing the child's development rather than merely removing symptoms or restoring a previous level of functioning. In Felicia's case, for example, an assessment might reveal that she has poor social skills, so intervention plans might focus on efforts to teach her these skills in a concerted fashion to reduce the chances of continuing social relationship difficulties. A prognosis based on careful assessment can also serve to inform parents and others about the importance of doing something now that may reduce the likelihood of major problems later.

Treatment planning means using assessment information to generate a plan to address the child's problem and evaluate its effectiveness. Felicia's mother keeps her daughter home from school when Felicia complains of stomach pains. She also does Felicia's homework. Does this information suggest a possible course of action? Felicia thinks she can't do anything well. Will helping her to change this and other irrational beliefs make a difference in her depression? When action is taken, how can we evaluate whether it is having the desired effect?

Treatment planning and evaluation may involve further specification and measurement of possible contributors to the problem, determination of resources and motivation for change, and recommendations for the treatments likely to be the most acceptable and effective for the child and family. For example, are Felicia's parents unintentionally rewarding her physical complaints and school refusal by giving her extra attention when she doesn't go to school? Is Felicia willing to discuss with a therapist why she refuses to go to school? Are her parents willing to set limits on her behavior despite a history of struggle and failure with previous attempts?

SECTION SUMMARY

- Clinical assessment is directed at differentiating, defining, and measuring the child's behaviors, cognitions, and emotions of concern, as well as the environmental circumstances that may contribute to these problems.

- Assessments are meaningful to the extent that they result in effective interventions; a close and continuing partnership must exist between assessment and intervention.

- Age, gender, and culture influence how children's symptoms and behavior may be expressed and recognized, and have implications for selecting the most appropriate methods of assessment and treatment.

- The age inappropriateness and pattern of symptoms, rather than individual symptoms, usually define childhood disorders.

- Three purposes of assessment are (1) description and diagnosis that determine the nature and causes of the child's problem, formal diagnosis, (2) prognosis that predicts future behavior under specified conditions, and (3) treatment planning and evaluation.

Assessing Disorders

If something exists, it exists in some amount. If it exists in some amount, then it is capable of being measured.

—*Rene Descartes*

Not everything important can be measured, and not everything that can be measured is important.

—*Albert Einstein*

If you were planning to assess Felicia's problems, where would you begin and what might you include in your assessment? Should you interview both parents, Felicia, and her teacher? Do you need to observe Felicia at home? At school? Are there psychological tests or questionnaires to help you pinpoint Felicia's strengths and weaknesses, such as intelligence, emotion, concentration, social skills, and learning ability?

You'll soon recognize how quickly the decision-making process can seem massive. In view of this complexity, many clinical settings use a multidisciplinary team approach to assessment. Individuals with specific expertise in psychological test administration and interpretation work with others to generate the most complete picture of a child's mental health needs. Multidisciplinary teams may include a psychologist, a physician, an educational specialist, a speech pathologist, and a social worker.

Some children may need to be referred for a medical exam as part of a comprehensive assessment to investigate if a physical problem is related to their disorder. For example, a physiological problem may be causing a particular child's bed-wetting or sleep disorder. A thorough medical assessment by a physician could evaluate Felicia's stomach pains, sleep disturbances, and weight loss and be used to determine whether Felicia's depression was related to drug use or a general medical condition such as hypothyroidism (low levels of thyroid hormones).

Ideally, the clinical assessment of children experiencing difficulties relies on a **multimethod assessment approach,** which emphasizes the importance of obtaining information from different informants, in a variety of settings, using a variety of procedures that include interviews, observations, questionnaires, and tests. Decisions regarding which available assessment method will be useful in a specific case are based on whether the assessment is for diagnosis, treatment planning, or treatment evaluation, whether the problem is observable like aggression, or internal like anxiety, and the child's and family's characteristics and abilities. In addition, it is critical to use methods that have high reliability, validity, utility for treatment, and cost-effectiveness.

Clinical assessment consists of many strategies and procedures designed to help understand the child's thoughts, feelings, and behaviors as they occur in specific situations. Clinical interviews are usually conducted with the parents and child separately or in a family interview, and help establish a good working relationship with the child and family. They are also extremely useful in obtaining basic information about existing concerns as viewed by the child and family members and in pinpointing directions for further inquiry. Behavioral assessments, checklists and rating scales, and psychological tests are then used in accordance with a decision-making approach. Information is also obtained from teachers and other significant individuals who interact with the child in various settings. The purpose is to obtain the most complete picture necessary to develop and implement an appropriate treatment plan, within the limits of available resources.

A comprehensive assessment requires that some consideration be given to evaluating the child's strengths and weaknesses in areas ranging from basic language and self-care skills to coping and leadership abilities. If our detective work suggests that a particular area of functioning deserves closer scrutiny, then a more in-depth assessment of this area is warranted. However, if initial assessments indicate that certain areas of functioning are not a problem, then the assessments may not be necessary. For example, for a child performing poorly in school, an assessment of intellectual functioning and academic performance is essential. On the other hand, for a child experiencing difficulties at home but is doing fine at school, assessment of intellectual and academic functioning may be unnecessary.

Clinical Interviews

Children and adolescents don't usually refer themselves for treatment. Typically, they are referred because of the impact of their behavior on others. Thus, they often do not understand why they are seeing someone, and in fact they may not even experience any distress or recognize any cause for concern. (To be fair, some adults are like this too!) The initial clinical interview can be very important not only in obtaining information, but also in setting the stage for collaboration and cooperation between the child, family members, and other concerned parties.

The clinical interview continues to be the assessment procedure most universally used with parents and children (Sattler, 1998). Interviews may vary considerably in terms of the kinds of information obtained and the meaning assigned to that information, based on interviewers' theoretical orientations, styles, and purposes (Sattler & Mash, 1998). Interviews allow professionals to gather information in a flexible manner over many sessions. The findings can then be integrated with more time-consuming assessments, such as family observations or psychological testing.

Children's initial reactions to seeing a mental health professional are often ones of fear and resistance.

Clinical interviews use a flexible, conversational style that helps the child or parent to present the most complete picture possible. Interviewees will be encouraged to tell their stories with minimal guidance, which permits the children and parents to convey their thoughts and feelings in ways that approximate how they think in everyday life. During the clinical interview, the interviewer may observe nonverbal communications by the child and parent, such as facial expressions, body posture, vocal behaviors, gestures, mannerisms, and motor behavior. These informal observations can provide the clinician with additional insights into the parent/child relationship that may be relevant in determining the presenting problem and the direction for treatment planning.

Clinical interviews can provide a large amount of information during a brief period. For example, during an hour-long interview with a parent, much detail about the child's developmental history, likes and dislikes, behavioral strengths and deficits, response to discipline, relationships with others, and school performance can be obtained—far more than would be learned by observing the parent and child interacting for the same amount of time (Sattler, 1998).

Many clinicians develop their own style for engaging school-age children and adolescents in discussing their situation. We often use video games, crafts, and similar enticements to help the child feel more comfortable. When younger children are referred, it may be more appropriate to involve one parent in a joint game or activity. Younger children are more likely to "be themselves" around their parents than a stranger. (For this age group, drawing, coloring, and similar fun activities are almost always successful at initiating a new relationship.) Also, because of their developmental level, younger children or children with mental retardation may be capable of providing only general impressions of their internal states, behavior, and circumstances.

Depending on the child's age, you may want to adopt a child-friendly approach for the interview that fits with the child's developmental status, the nature of the problem, and the interview purpose. The interview typically will attempt to elicit information about the child's self-perceptions and perceptions of others, and to obtain samples of how the child responds in a social situation with an adult. Children's views of the circumstances that brought them to the clinic, their expectations for improvement, and their understanding of the assessment situation are all important to consider, along with the manner in which they interpret significant events such as divorce or family violence. Engaging unwilling children can be difficult. Since other people typically seek help on behalf of the child, some children and adolescents may not feel they have a problem and see no need to be interviewed.

What questions would you ask Felicia's parents? Perhaps you want to know how long Felicia's reluctance to separate from her parents has been a concern, and whether prior help has been sought. You might also want to discuss the exact nature of the problems they are concerned about, and to provide her parents with some indication of the next steps in the assessment and treatment process.

Developmental and Family History   Initial assessments often include a **developmental history** or **family history**, in which information is obtained from the parents regarding potentially significant developmental milestones and historical events that might have a bearing on the child's current difficulties. This information can be gained using a background questionnaire or interview that typically covers the following areas (Sattler, 1998):

- *The child's birth and related events*, such as pregnancy and birth complications or a mother's use of drugs, alcohol, or cigarettes during pregnancy

- *The child's developmental milestones,* such as age of walking, use of language, bladder and bowel control, and self-help skills
- *The child's medical history,* including injuries, accidents, operations, illnesses, and prescribed medications
- *Family characteristics and family history,* including age, occupation, marital status of family members, and medical, educational, and mental health history of parents and siblings
- *The child's interpersonal skills,* including relations with adults and other children, and play and social activities
- *The child's educational history,* including schools attended, academic performance, attitudes toward school, relations with teachers and peers, and special services
- *The adolescents', occupational information and relationships,* including others of the same sex and the opposite sex
- *A description of the presenting problem,* including a detailed description of the problem and surrounding events, and how parents have attempted to deal with the problem in the past
- *The parents' expectations* for assessment and treatment of their child and themselves

Here is part of the developmental and family history given by Felicia's parents:

Felicia
History

Her parents reported that Felicia was the result of an unplanned pregnancy following an initial miscarriage, the adoption of a son, and birth of a sister. The pregnancy and Felicia's early life were described as uncomplicated and generally happy. Felicia reached developmental milestones late, required extra assistance with tasks, was quite reserved and uncommunicative, and experienced speech articulation problems. Her parents said they tended to "baby" Felicia since she was seen as "slow." She was similarly described as developmentally immature by her teachers, although her attendance and academic performance were consistently good ever after repeating the first grade.

Felicia's adopted brother, age 23, attended a local college and lived at home. Her sister, age 16, also lived at home and attended high school. Felicia's mother had trained to become a registered nurse; her father held a Ph.D. in chemistry and managed the research department of a large company. No significant problems were reported for the other children, with the exception of some difficulty by the brother in establishing independence.

Felicia's mother described experiencing a significant depression after each of her pregnancies and following her own father's death the previous year, a loss that was reported to have been very painful for Felicia also. Felicia's father reported no difficulties and was considered a stable and dependable person. (Adapted from "Depression," by D. J. Kolko, 1987. In M. Hersen and V. B. Van Hasselt (Eds.), *Behavior Therapy with Children and Adolescents: A Clinical Approach,* pp. 159–160. Copyright © 1987 by John Wiley & Sons, Inc. Reprinted by permission of John Wiley & Sons, Inc.)

Many events presented in this developmental and family history may be relevant to the assessment of Felicia's current problems and must be explored as the assessment proceeds. For example, the babying described by Felicia's parents may reflect a more general pattern of overdependency on her parents that is contributing to her school refusal. The significant depression experienced by Felicia's mother following her pregnancies may suggest a family risk for depression. The death of Felicia's grandfather a year earlier may have been a triggering event, leading to a mood disturbance in both Felicia and her mother. During the early stages of assessment, these are hypotheses; as evidence accumulates with ongoing detective work, hypotheses can be supported or rejected as indicated by new data.

As part of an initial interview, a clinician may sometimes conduct a mental status exam to assess the child's general mental functioning. During a **mental status exam,** which is usually carried out during the course of an interview, the clinician asks questions and observes the child in five general areas: appearance and behavior, thought processes, mood and affect, intellectual functioning, and sensorium (e.g., the child's awareness of his or her surroundings).

Here are the findings from a brief mental status exam that was carried out during an initial interview with Felicia:

Felicia
Mental Status

Felicia presented herself as a quiet, uncommunicative, and resistant girl who used only a few basic social skills. She rarely made eye contact, spoke in an inaudible tone, used few words, infrequently initiated a conversation, and was unable to report anything positive about herself. She admitted to feeling depressed and denied any positive attributes, giving few details regarding her experiences. She also acknowledged sleep difficulties, but denied any anxiety or panic attacks. She denied suicidal or homicidal thoughts, intent, or plan; gave no evidence for perceptual or thought disturbance; and was oriented to person, time, and place (i.e., she knows who she is, the time and day, and where she is). (Adapted from "Depression," by D. J. Kolko, 1987. In M. Hersen and V. B. Van Hasselt (Eds.), *Behavior Therapy with Children and Adolescents: A Clinical Approach*, p. 160. Copyright © 1987 by John Wiley & Sons, Inc. Reprinted by permission of John Wiley & Sons, Inc.)

Informal observations from a mental status exam allow the clinician to zoom in on aspects of the child's behavior and condition that must be assessed in greater depth using more focused behavioral assessments or formal psychological tests. What can we learn from Felicia's mental status exam? The flow of her speech was slow and the content limited. She made little eye contact, did not initiate any social interaction, and reported sleep difficulties. These observations are consistent with Felicia's report of depression and suggest a depressive disorder. However, additional information, obtained perhaps via structured interviews or questionnaires, will be necessary to confirm or disconfirm this possibility, and other areas related to her social anxiety and social skills deficits will need to be assessed.

Semistructured Interviews   Most interviews with children and parents are unstructured. Clinicians use their preferred interview style and format, as well as their knowledge of the disorder, to pursue various questions in an informal and flexible manner. Unstructured clinical interviews provide a rich source of clinical hypotheses. However, their lack of standardization may result in low reliability and selective or biased gathering of information. To address this problem, clinicians sometimes use **semistructured interviews** that include specific questions designed to elicit information in a relatively consistent manner regardless of who is doing the interview. The format of the interview usually ensures that the most important aspects of a particular disorder are covered. An appealing feature of semistructured interviews, especially for older children and youths, is that they can be administered by computer, something many children find entertaining and often less threatening at first than a face-to-face interview. The format also permits the clinician to follow up on issues of importance that may emerge during the interview.

The consistency and coverage of semistructured interviews may be offset by a loss of spontaneity between the child and clinician, especially if the interview is conducted too rigidly. Under such circumstances, children and adolescents may be reluctant to volunteer important information not directly relevant to the interviewer's questions. With appropriate modifications that make the interview

Table 4.3
Semistructured Interview Questions for a Child or Adolescent with an Eating Problem

Current Eating Patterns
· Do your eating habits vary from day to day?
· Do you feel that the way you eat is different from the way others eat?

Specific Eating Problems
· Do you avoid eating foods you like?
· Do you ever eat in secret?

Attitudes toward Eating and Food
· Do you ever feel guilty after eating?
· Do you think you can control your eating?

Body Image
· Do you always think about wanting to be thinner?
· Are you scared of being overweight?

Weight
· Has your weight changed in the last 3 months? [If yes] By how much?
· Are you now trying to lose weight or are you on a diet to lose weight?

Binge Eating
· Have you ever been unable to control the amount or type of food you ate?
· How do you feel after you eat lots of food quickly?

Purging Behavior
· Do you deliberately try to vomit after you eat?
· [If yes] How do you go about getting yourself to vomit?

Other Methods Used to Control Weight
· Do you take laxatives, diet pills, or anything else to control your weight?
· How often do you take [cite substance]?

Exercise and Activity Patterns
· What kind of exercise do you do?
· Is your exercising connected with your eating in any way?

Health Status
· How are your teeth? (Tooth decay can accompany purging because regurgitated stomach acid erodes the enamel that protects teeth.)
· Tell me about your menstrual periods [for female adolescents].

Source: Adapted from *Clinical and Forensic Interviewing of Children and Families: Guidelines for the Mental Health, Education, Pediatric, and Child Maltreatment Fields*, by J. M. Sattler, pp. 938–940. Copyright © 1998 by Jerome M. Sattler, Publisher. Adapted by permission.

process easier to follow, however, semistructured interviews are reliable and very useful at assessing a wide range of children's symptoms (Edelbrock, Crnic, & Bohnert, 1999). Sample questions from a semistructured interview for youngsters with an eating problem are presented in Table 4.3.

Behavioral Assessment

The clinical interviews described in this chapter are valuable in eliciting information from parents and school-age children. They provide an initial look at how the child and family think, feel, and behave, and the factors that might be contributing to the child's problems. However, it is often necessary to obtain a firsthand look at the child's behavior in everyday life situations at home or at school, or to ask someone who sees the child on a regular basis to the child's behavior.

Behavioral assessment is a strategy for evaluating the child's thoughts, feelings, and behaviors in specific settings, and then using this information to formulate hypotheses about the nature of the problem and what can be done about it (Francis & Chorpita, 2004; Mash & Terdal, 1997a). In general, behavioral assessment frequently involves observing the child's behavior directly, rather than inferring how children think, behave, or feel on the basis of their descriptions of inkblots or the pictures they draw.

Using behavioral assessment, the clinician or another person who sees the child regularly identifies **target behaviors,** which are the primary problems of concern, with the goal of then determining what specific factors may be controlling or influencing these behaviors. Sometimes this is a straightforward task, as with a child who complains of illness every Monday morning and, as a result, is kept out of school for the day (sound familiar?). In other cases, the child displays multiple problems at home or school. Felicia's school refusal appears to be part of a larger pattern of difficulties that includes social withdrawal, depression, and possible separation anxiety.

Even the seemingly simple task of identifying what is bothering a child can be a challenge. Remember that an adult usually decides the child has a problem and whether the child should be referred for an assessment. Adults frequently disagree about the nature of the problem, especially when they observe children in different settings (Achenbach, McConaughy, & Howell, 1987; Bingham, Fitzgerald, & Zucker, 2003). Severity ratings by various people may be influenced by the differences between their cultures and that of the child. For example, when teachers rate youths from another cultural background, they are more likely to rate them higher on behavioral and emotional problems than are the teachers of a similar background, the parents, or the children themselves (Dion, Gotowiec, & Beiser, 1998; Skiba, Knesting, & Bush, 2002). Further, a child's presenting problem can often be very different from the one eventually identified as the target for intervention.

A commonly used and simple framework for organizing findings in behavioral assessment has been dubbed the "ABCs of assessment":

A = Antecedents, or events that immediately precede a behavior

B = Behavior(s) of interest

C = Consequences, or the events that follow a behavior

In Felicia's case we might observe the following sequence: (A) Whenever Felicia's mother asks her to go to school (antecedent), (B) Felicia complains that she has stomach pains and refuses to go (behaviors), and (C) her mother lets Felicia stay home (consequence). This antecedent-behavior-consequence sequence might suggest that Felicia is being reinforced for her physical complaints and school refusal by not having to go to school. In addition, because there are no positive consequences for going to school and no negative ones for staying at home, Felicia might act this way on future school days. The ABCs of assessment can be used to organize information in specific contexts, as just described, or as an overall framework for assessment (Beck, 2000).

Behavior analysis or **functional analysis of behavior** is the more general approach to organizing and using assessment information in terms of antecedents, behaviors, and consequences across many levels (Hanley, Iwata, & McCord, 2003). As shown in Figure 4.1, functional analysis can be used to identify a wide range of antecedents and consequences that might be contributing to Felicia's school refusal and depression. The antecedents and consequences for Felicia's behavior include events in the immediate situation (a reduction in anxiety), more remote occurrences (being teased at school), events in the external environment, and Felicia's inner thoughts and feelings.

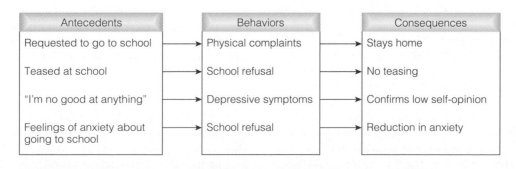

Figure 4.1. Functional analysis: antecedents, behaviors, consequences.

The goal of functional analysis is to identify as many factors as possible that could be contributing to a child's problem behaviors, thoughts, and feelings, and to develop hypotheses for the factors that are most important and/or most easily changed. In some cases, hypotheses can be confirmed or rejected by changing the antecedents and consequences to see if the behavior changes. For example, we might teach Felicia to relax when thinking about going to school (changing an antecedent) to see if this decreases her school refusal. Or she could be instructed to substitute more positive self-statements ("I can succeed in school") for her negative ones ("I'm no good at anything") to see if this decreases her depressive symptoms and raises her self-esteem. In these examples, you can see a close interplay between assessment and intervention when carrying out a functional analysis.

The process of gathering information about the child's behavior in specific settings takes many different forms. Often it involves either asking the parent, teacher, or child about what goes on in specific situations, or observing the child. Clinicians develop their initial hypotheses based on information provided by the parents and the child during the interview. They pursue the hypotheses further using behavioral assessments, such as behavior checklists and rating scales, and observations of behavior in real life or in role-play simulations. In general, functional analysis can be viewed as an approach to organizing assessment information for an individual child and developing hypotheses for treatment (Evans, 1999).

Checklists and Rating Scales   Reports concerning child behavior and adjustment can be obtained using global checklists and problem-focused rating scales. Global behavior checklists ask parents, teachers, and sometimes the youngsters themselves to rate the presence or absence of a wide variety of child behaviors, or the frequency and intensity of these behaviors.

Unlike a clinical interview, the use of a well-developed checklist is strengthened by its known degree of standardization, and by the opportunities to compare an individual child's score with a known reference group of children of a similar age and the same gender (Fernandez-Ballesteros, 2004). Checklists are also economical to administer and score. They provide a rich source of information about parents' or teachers' perceptions of children's behavior, including possible differences in the perceptions of parents in the same family, and the differences between parent and teacher perceptions. Keep in mind, however, that informants may differ in their views of the child's strengths and weaknesses, since they interact with the child in different surroundings and circumstances. These discrepancies are not necessarily bad, however, because they inform the clinician of the possible range of behavior the child engages in, possible circumstances that increase or decrease target behaviors, and possible demands or expectations placed on the child that may be unrealistic.

The Child Behavior Checklist/4-18 (CBCL) developed by Thomas Achenbach (1991a; 1999) and his colleagues is a leading checklist for assessing behavioral problems in children and adolescents. The reliability and validity of the CBCL has been documented in many studies, and it is widely used in treatment settings and schools. The parent-completed form of the CBCL is part of a set of scales for children, ages 4 to 18, that also includes a teacher and youth self-report, a classroom observation measure, and an interview.

The scales of the CBCL can be used to form a profile that gives the clinician an overall picture of the variety and degree of the child's behavioral problems. A CBCL profile derived from a checklist completed by Felicia's mother is shown in Figure 4.2. The profile shows that her major areas of concern about her daughter are with respect to symptoms of social withdrawal, somatic complaints, anxiety/depression, and other social problems. Felicia's scores on the first three of these dimensions are extreme, and place her in the upper 5% or higher when compared with girls of a similar age.

In addition to checklists that cover a wide range of behavior problems, other rating scales focus on specific disorders—depression, anxiety, autism, ADHD, and antisocial behavior, or on particular areas of functioning—social competence, adaptive behavior, or school performance (Mash & Terdal, 1997b; Merrell, 2003). Ratings of the child are usually provided by parents and teachers, older children, and the adolescents themselves. Many of these scales provide the clinician with a more focused look at specific problems than a global behavior checklist provides. You will see many examples of rating scales used to assess specific problems in the chapters to follow.

Clinicians may opt to administer self-report checklists in an engaging, child-friendly manner that increases the child's interest in the material. We like to administer questionnaires to adolescents by computer, simply because they find this approach more interesting. With younger children, we like to hand them a card showing the range of responses they may have, using happy or sad faces and similar icons that appeal to that age group.

Behavioral Observation and Recording   Since some children are not old enough or skilled enough to report on their own behavior parents, teachers, or clinicians may keep careful records of specific target behaviors. Parents or other observers typically record *baseline* (prior to intervention) data on one or two problems that they wish to change, for example, how often their child complies with their requests or how often he or she throws a temper tantrum (Dishion & Granic, 2004).

Recordings by parents have the advantage of providing ongoing information about behaviors of interest in life settings that might not otherwise be accessible to observation by the clinician. Parental monitoring may also provide secondary benefits that are not directly related to

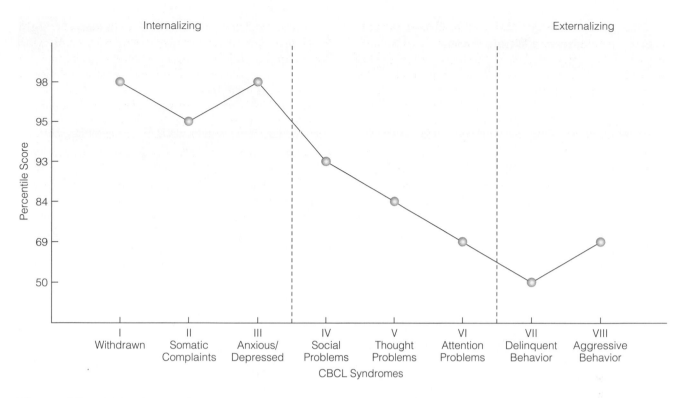

Figure 4.2. Child Behavior Checklist (CBCL) profile for Felicia. (Based on Achenbach, 1993a)

assessment—teaching parents better observation skills, assessing parental motivation, and providing parents with more realistic estimates of their children's rate of responding and feedback regarding the effects of treatment. However, many practical problems may arise in getting parents to keep accurate records. Children often know when they are being watched and may react differently. As well, it is important to consider the role of culture in determining and defining social interaction (Dishion & Granic, 2004). Box 4.1 illustrates why observing behavior can be a useful part of any clinical assessment.

The clinician may also set up a *role-play simulation* in the clinic to see how the child and family might behave in daily situations encountered at home or school, or a problem-solving situation, like figuring out how to play a game together (Roberts, 2001). When observing families who have physically abused their preschool-age child, for example, we choose activities most likely to elicit both parent–child cooperation and conflict: We first ask parents to play with their child so that we can observe their teaching style, and then ask them to have the child put away her or his favorite toys, which often results in noncompliance and conflict (D. A. Wolfe, 1991).

In Felicia's case, role-play simulations were used to assess her social skills. The clinician first described the situation to Felicia as follows: "You're sitting in the school cafeteria eating lunch by yourself when Janet, a girl from your math class, comes over to your table and sits across from you." Next, the clinician takes the role of Janet and

says, "Hi Felicia. How's your lunch?" Felicia then responds, and the interaction continues, giving the clinician a chance to directly observe Felicia's social skills in a situation that might come up in everyday life (Kolko, 1987).

Remember, direct observation is not foolproof. Clinicians must take into account the informant, the child, the nature of the problem, and the family and cultural context because any of these issues can distort the findings. Despite its limitations, direct observation is a valid and beneficial step in the decision-making process for most families who voluntarily seek assistance and understand what may be required to conduct a thorough assessment and treatment plan, and can be quite helpful to less motivated families as well.

Psychological Testing

A **test** is a task or set of tasks given under standard conditions with the purpose of assessing some aspect of the child's knowledge, skill, or personality. Most tests are standardized on a clearly defined reference group, for example, children of a certain age, sex, or SES, referred to as a *norm group*. An individual child's scores can then be compared with the scores of a comparable group of children to determine the extent to which that child's scores deviate from the norm. The prevalence and visibility of test use in our culture have led some people to adopt the mistaken view that testing and psychological assessment are one and the same. Although tests play an important

BOX 4.1 **Seeing the Whole Picture**

Sometimes observations of a child with his or her parent can be extremely illuminating. Recently, the mother of Sammy, a 4-year-old child with severe behavior problems, came to one of our clinics for assistance. During the interview she told the clinician that her son was "impossible to get dressed," and "doesn't listen to a thing I say to him." She had been told by a family member that Sammy seemed "hyperactive," and her family doctor had requested a psychological assessment as a result of her insistence on this diagnosis.

A note from his preschool teacher painted a very different picture of this young boy. His teacher spoke frankly of Sammy's undeveloped skills at following directions or concentrating on a task for any length of time, but pointed out how he settled down much like the other children once he found something to do that he enjoyed. This boy seemed calm during our visit with him at the clinic, so we decided to get a clearer picture of the situation by visiting his home and school.

When we visited the home, the problem stood out within minutes. His home was littered with his toys and games, which his mother let him rummage through and toss around the room freely. Attempts to get her to provide some structure to his play and other activities resulted in an immediate confrontation between the two—he simply turned away and grabbed the toys he wanted, and she became upset and started to chase after him, yelling at him to put his toys away. "See," she said, turning to the observer, "he doesn't do a thing I ask him to do." The boy clutched his toys and quieted down at this point, turned on the TV, and plunked himself in front of it. Similar attempts on Sammy's part to avoid doing what his teacher asked were observed during our school visit, although his teacher was more successful at getting him back to the activity at hand by using praise and other positive rewards.

Observing behavior directly assists in obtaining an accurate picture of the child's behavior under certain circumstances.

Obviously, the description this mother gave us of her son's behavior lacked a few of the details that make an accurate diagnosis possible. Her description also failed to mention how upset she got when Sammy "didn't listen," and that the home environment was rather chaotic and unstructured for a child his age. Without this home observation visit, our assessment of the problem and recommendations for treatment might have been quite different if we attributed his misbehavior primarily to hyperactivity, as the mother initially led us to assume. We developed strategies to teach the mother how to structure her home in a child-friendly manner, how to spend time playing with her son, and how to encourage his compliance by starting with simple requests and using the positive rewards of praise, attention, and activities he enjoyed.

---

role in a child's assessment, they represent only one part of the overall decision-making process.

Clinicians commonly use developmental scales, intelligence and educational tests, projective tests, personality tests, and neuropsychological tests to assess children's disorders of development, learning, and behavior (Sattler, 2001, 2002). In fact, tests (particularly intelligence tests) are among the most frequently used assessment methods with children (Halperin & McKay, 1998). Remember that test scores should always be interpreted in the context of other assessment information. Often, observations of a child's behavior during the test situation can tell us as much or more about the child as his or her test scores.

Developmental tests are used to assess infants and young children, and are generally carried out for the pur-

poses of screening, diagnosis, and evaluation of early development. **Screening** refers to the identification of children at risk, who are then referred for a more thorough evaluation. The assessment of infants and young children at risk for developing later problems has increased in frequency as new laws direct public attention and action to the importance of early assessment in developing effective strategies for early intervention and prevention (Osofsky, 1998). Because screening tests are brief, a more thorough assessment of a young child's development is needed.

Intelligence Testing   Evaluating a child's intellectual and educational functioning is a key ingredient in clinical assessments for a wide range of childhood disorders (Sattler, 2001). For some children, impairments in thinking and learning may result from their behavioral or emotional problems. The drop in Felicia's grades from Bs to Cs and Ds was likely a function of the impact of her school refusal and depression on her school performance. For other children, particularly those with mental retardation or learning and language disorders, problems in thinking and learning may be part of the disorder itself.

In many other cases, the nature of the relationship between the child's disorder and disturbances in thinking and learning is less clear. For example, children with ADHD score lower on standard tests of intelligence and do more poorly in school than other children. Is this lowered performance related to their inattentiveness in the test situation or classroom, or to some other more basic deficit in how they process information (Glutting, Youngstrom, Ward, Ward, & Hale, 1997)? Intellectual and educational assessments can help answer some of these questions.

How would you define intelligence? Most people think intelligence involves problem-solving ability, verbal ability, and social intelligence. David Wechsler, whose test has come to be the one most frequently used to assess intelligence in children, defined intelligence as "the overall capacity of an individual to understand and cope with the world around him" (Wechsler, 1974, p. 5). This definition is consistent with theories on which commonly used intelligence tests are based. Although debate remains about how intelligence should be defined, intelligence tests are used primarily for answering practical questions, such as identifying children who would not succeed in a regular classroom.

Numerous tests for assessing intelligence in children exist, each with unique strengths and weaknesses. The most popular intelligence scale used with children today is the Wechsler Intelligence Scale for Children (WISC-IV) (Wechsler, 2003). It is the most recent version of a test that was introduced over 50 years ago. The WISC-IV is made up of ten mandatory and five supplementary subtests that all span the age range of 6 to 16 years. According to Wechsler, these subtests assess the child's global capacity in different ways, but do not represent different types of intelligence. Most recent changes from the third to fourth edition of the WISC include more emphasis on fluid reasoning abilities, higher order reasoning, and information processing speed, and less emphasis on possible externally or culturally influenced factors, including performance speed, motor skills, and dependence on arithmetic knowledge (Williams, Weiss, & Rolfhus, 2003). Other tests assess intelligence in younger children, including the Wechsler Preschool and Primary Scale of Intelligence—III (WPPSI-R) (Wechsler, 2002), Stanford-Binet-5 (SB5) (Roid, 2003), and the Kaufman Assessment Battery for Children (K-ABC-II) (A. S. Kaufman & N. L. Kaufman, 2004).

Examples of questions and items included on each WISC-IV subtest are shown in Box 4.2. The WISC-IV is individually administered to the child by a highly trained examiner who follows specific procedures. Previous editions of the WISC yielded a Verbal IQ score, a Performance IQ score, and a combined Full Scale IQ score. The newer WISC-IV produces a Full Scale IQ, but this is derived from four indices: Verbal Comprehension Index, Perceptual Reasoning Index, Working Memory Index, and Processing Speed Index (see Box 4.2 for descriptions of these indices). The first two scores can be compared with Verbal and Performance scores from previous versions of the WISC (Williams et al., 2003). The profile of these four abilities represents key indicators of the cognitive strengths and weaknesses considered important to the assessment of learning disabilities, executive functions, attention disorders, traumatic brain injuries, mental retardation, lead poisoning, giftedness, and various other medical and neurological concerns (Williams et al., 2003). True to tradition, IQ scores on the WISC-IV are good predictors of academic achievement.

Felicia obtained a Verbal Comprehension IQ score of 107, a Perceptual Reasoning Index of 105, and a Full Scale IQ score of 106 on the WISC-IV, which means that her intelligence is in the average range. With this information, the clinician must next consider how her test scores relate to each other, and if there is a pattern to the results that might clarify her relative strengths and weaknesses. He or she must also consider any circumstances in the testing situation that might have affected her performance—anxiety, personality factors, motivation, or medication—and how her scores compare with those of other girls of comparable age, grade, ethnic group, and/or disability. Finally, and most important, the clinician must consider how the test scores will be used in treatment and educational planning.

Projective Testing **Projective tests** present the child with ambiguous stimuli, such as inkblots or pictures of people and the child is asked to describe what she or he sees. The hypothesis is that the child will "project" his or her own personality—unconscious fears, needs, and inner conflicts—on the ambiguous stimuli of other people and things. Without being aware, the child discloses his or her unconscious thoughts and feelings to the clinician, thus revealing information that would not be shared in response to direct questioning (Chandler & Johnson, 1991). Many "junior-sized" versions of projective tests have been developed for younger children, in which the ambiguous stimuli have been made child-friendly by incorporating family scenes or pictures of animals (E. E. Levitt & French, 1992).

Projective testing has generated more controversy over the past 50 years than any other clinical assessment method. Most clinicians have strong views about projective testing, either pro or con. You may very well have your own strong opinions about the Rorschach inkblot and similar methods. Some clinicians believe that projective tests provide a rich source of information about the

BOX 4.2 Items Similar to Those Included in WISC-IV

Similarities (23 items)

In what way are a pencil and a piece of chalk alike?
In what way are tea and coffee alike?
In what way are an inch and a mile alike?
In what way are binoculars and a microscope alike?

Vocabulary (36 items)

What is a ball?
What does *running* mean?
What is a poem?
What does *obstreperous* mean?

Comprehension (21 items)

Why do we wear shoes?
What is the thing to do if you see someone dropping a package?
In what two ways is a lamp better than a candle?
In the United States, why are we tried by a jury of our peers?

Information (33 items)

How many legs do you have?
What must you do to make water freeze?
Who developed the theory of relativity?
What is the capital of France?

Word Reasoning (24 items)

The task is to identify the common concept being described with a series of clues.
Clue 1: This has a motor . . .
Clue 2: . . . and it is used to cut grass.

Block Design (14 items)

The task is to reproduce stimulus designs using four or nine blocks (see below).

Picture Concepts (28 items)

The task is to choose one picture from each of two or three rows of pictures in such a way that all the pictures selected have a characteristic in common (see below).

Matrix Reasoning (35 items)

The task is to examine an incomplete matrix and select whichever of the five choices best completes the matrix (see below).

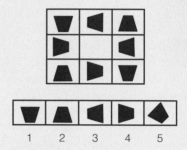

1   2   3   4   5

Picture Completion (38 items)

The task is to look at a picture—such as that of a car without a wheel, a scissors without a handle, or a telephone without numbers on the dial—and identify the essential missing part (see below).

(continued)

child's coping styles, affect, self-concept, interpersonal functioning, and ways of processing information (Verma, 2000). Other clinicians see them as inadequate with respect to minimum standards for reliability and validity (Seitz, 2001; Wood, Lilienfeld, Garb, & Nezworski, 2000).

Despite the controversy surrounding their use, projective tests continue to be one of the most frequently used clinical assessment methods (Merrell, 2003; Watkins, Campbell, Nieberding, & Hallmark, 1995). Representative of the many projective techniques that continue to be used with children and adolescents are human figure drawings, the Rorschach inkblot test, and thematic picture tests such as the Roberts Apperception Test for Children (RATC) (McArthur & Roberts, 1982). Clinicians may also attempt to assess children's inner life through

play, for example, the use of puppets, storytelling, or other material (Chethik, 1989). Although not formal projective tests, for some clinicians play and figure drawings are presumed to function in much the same way as projectives—as a window into the child's unconscious processes.

Personality Testing   Personality is usually considered an enduring trait or pattern of traits that characterize the individual and determine how he or she interacts with the environment (B. W. Roberts & DelVecchio, 2000). For example, children who withdraw from social contact may be characterized by their parents as shy; others who are socially busy are characterized as outgoing. In a sense, a child's early temperament, (discussed in Chapter 2) provides the foundation on which personality is built.

Several dimensions of personality have been identified, including whether a child or adolescent is timid or

"You must be Mary's parents. I recognized you from her drawings!"

Assessment, Diagnosis, and Treatment   **89**

Table 4.4
Self-Report of Personality Scale Definitions

CONSTRUCT	DEFINITION
Anxiety	Feelings of nervousness, worry, and fear; the tendency to be overwhelmed by problems
Attitude toward school	Feelings of alienation, hostility, and dissatisfaction regarding school
Attitude toward teachers	Feelings of resentment and dislike of teachers; the belief that teachers are unfair, uncaring, or overly demanding
Atypicality	The tendency toward gross mood swings, bizarre thoughts, subjective experiences, or obsessive-compulsive thoughts and behaviors
Depression	Feelings of unhappiness, sadness, and dejection; the belief that nothing goes right
Interpersonal relations	The perception of having good social relationships and friendships with peers
Locus of control	The belief that rewards and punishments are controlled by external events or other people
Relations with parents	A positive regard for parents and a feeling of being esteemed by them
Self-esteem	Feelings of self-esteem, self-respect, and self-acceptance

Source: From *Clinical Assessment of Child and Adolescent Personality and Behavior,* by R. W. Kamphaus and P. J. Frick, 1996, p. 89. Copyright © 1996 by Allyn & Bacon. Reprinted by permission.

bold, agreeable or disagreeable, dependable or undependable, tense or relaxed, reflective or unreflective (L. R. Goldberg, 1992). These central dimensions of personality have been dubbed the "Big 5" factors. It remains unclear, however, whether personality traits are the most appropriate way to describe individual differences in children (Mervielde & Fruyt, 2002). A recent longitudinal investigation of adolescents developing from 12 to 18 years of age showed modest changes for some factors over time, although the factor levels remained relatively stable (McCrae et al., 2002).

Many of the methods already discussed, such as interviews, projective techniques, and behavioral measures, provide some information about the child's personality. However, many objective inventories focus specifically on personality, using either the child or parent as informants. Two of the more frequently used personality inventories with children are the Minnesota Multiphasic Personality Inventory—Adolescent (MMPI-A) (Butcher et al., 1992) and the Personality Inventory for Children, Second Edition (PIC-2) (Lachar, 1999). Examples of the content that may be included in personality inventories are shown in Table 4.4.

Neuropsychological Testing In the clinical context, **neuropsychological assessment** attempts to link brain functioning with objective measures of behavior known to depend on an intact central nervous system. For example, try closing your eyes and then touching the tip of your nose with your ring finger, first with your right hand and then with your left. How do you think you would do on this task if you were sleep-deprived? Even a simple task like this one depends on many psychological functions and an intact nervous system. For children with certain

brain injuries or dysfunctions, carrying out this or other tasks may prove difficult.

The premise underlying neuropsychological assessments is that behavioral measures can be used to make inferences about central nervous system dysfunction and, more important, the consequences of this dysfunction for the child. Neuropsychological assessments use this information clinically for determining a diagnosis, planning treatment, documenting the course of recovery, measuring subtle but significant improvements, and following up on children with neurological impairments or learning disorders (Farmer & Muhlenbruck, 2000).

Neuropsychological assessments frequently consist of comprehensive batteries that assess a full range of psychological functions: verbal and nonverbal *cognitive functions* such as language, abstract reasoning, and problem solving; *perceptual functions* including visual, auditory, and tactile-kinesthetic; *motor functions* relating to strength, speed of performance, coordination, and dexterity; and *emotional/executive control* functions such as attention, concentration, frustration tolerance, and emotional functioning.

Although neuropsychological assessments were originally used to identify an underlying brain injury or process, this is no longer their primary purpose. The routine use of neuroimaging procedures (Chapter 3), combined with mixed or inconsistent neuropsychological findings, has led the focus away from diagnosis to obtaining information about deficits in functioning. The information will lead to effective treatment and rehabilitation for children with neurological disorders and learning problems (Hoon & Melhem, 2000). The assessments were conducted for the neurological disorders in children including: traumatic brain injury (e.g., head injury due to a fall); brain malformations (e.g., spina bifida, hydrocephalus); genetic, metabolic, or degenerative disorders; tumors; infectious disorders; cerebrovascular disease; and epilepsy (J. M. Fletcher & Taylor, 1997; Reitan & Wolfson, 2003).

SECTION SUMMARY

- Clinical assessment relies on a multimethod assessment approach, which emphasizes obtaining information from different informants in a variety of settings, using a variety of procedures.

- The clinical interview continues to be the most universally used assessment procedure with parents and children.

- In unstructured interviews, interviewers use their preferred style and format to pursue various questions in an informal and flexible manner. In contrast, semistructured interviews include specific questions designed to elicit information in a relatively consistent manner regardless of who is doing the interview.

- Behavioral assessment evaluates the child's thoughts, feelings, and behaviors in specific settings, and uses this information to formulate hypotheses about the nature of the problem and what can be done about it.

- Reports concerning child behavior and adjustment can be obtained using global checklists and problem-focused rating scales. An individual child's score can be compared with a known reference group of children of similar age and same gender.

- Tests are tasks given under standard conditions with the purpose of assessing some aspect of the child's knowledge, skill, or personality.

- Evaluating a child's intellectual functioning is a key ingredient in clinical assessments for a wide range of childhood disorders.

- Projective tests present children with ambiguous stimuli to assess their inner thoughts and feelings that reflect aspects of their personality.

- Objective personality tests assess whether a child is timid or bold, agreeable or disagreeable, dependable or undependable, tense or relaxed, reflective or unreflective.

- Neuropsychological assessment attempts to link brain functioning with objective measures of behavior that are known to depend on central nervous system functioning.

Classification and Diagnosis

Over the past two decades, major changes have occurred in the classification of childhood disorders (Achenbach, 1999). By **classification**, we mean a system for representing the major categories or dimensions of child psychopathology, and the boundaries and relations among them.

As you may recall, one definition of diagnosis refers to the assignment of cases to categories of the classification system.

We begin our discussion of this important topic by considering some of the reasons for classification and diagnosis with children and adolescents, and go into some detail about the current strategies available. Because diagnosis is not without criticism, we also raise awareness of the impact of labeling children. Until now, we have looked at Felicia's problems on a very individual basis. We looked at her depression, school refusal, and social skills deficits, and assessed her mental status, general intellectual functioning, and behavior. This information tells us what is unique about Felicia and how she differs from others her age. Isn't this enough, you might ask? Why do we need to pigeonhole Felicia by tagging her with a diagnostic label such as "major depressive disorder"? Can't we just find a way to help her with her problems based on what we have learned about her unique characteristics?

The limitation of this approach is that if we treated every child as unique, research into the causes and treatment of childhood disorders would be impossible to conduct, and we would have little direction in how to proceed in treating an individual case (Waldman & Lilienfeld, 1995). For this reason, we also need to consider what Felicia has in common with others who present with similar problems or symptoms, and whether there are general principles that apply to many children. In effect, we do this throughout this text, as we learn about the core symptoms of child and adolescent disorders, their prevalence and course, their prognosis, and their treatment. Without such information to use for comparison, making the best decisions concerning Felicia's problem and course of action would be difficult.

As you may recall from our earlier discussion, clinical assessment and diagnosis involve two related strategies for determining the best plan for a given individual. We use an idiographic strategy when we want to highlight a child's unique circumstances, personality, cultural background, and similar features that pertain to his or her particular situation. Each child who comes in for an assessment has unique strengths and challenges that make his or her problem seem a little different than the "textbook" case description.

In addition, we use a nomothetic strategy as part of our assessment, to benefit from all the information accumulated on a given problem or disorder, and to attempt to determine the general class or grouping of problems to which the presenting problem belongs. That is, we attempt to name or classify the problem using an existing system of diagnosis, such as DSM-IV-TR (APA, 2000). Classifying the problem leads to the existing body of knowledge from which we can draw to understand the child and family, and to choose an intervention, preferably one shown through treatment-outcome studies to be effective for children with similar difficulties.

Although most of us recognize the advantages of a system of classification for medical and psychological problems, developing a classification system that is simple and concise enough to be of practical benefit is not an easy task. In fact, despite years of effort, there is no single, agreed-upon, reliable and valid, worldwide classification system for childhood disorders. Although the DSM-IV-TR has become the standard in North America (Mash & Terdal, 1997a), concerns continue to be raised that current classification systems are inadequate in their coverage of childhood disorders, and insensitive to the developmental complexities that characterize these problems (Achenbach, 1999; Scotti et al., 1996).

Categories and Dimensions

The first approach for diagnosis and classification of child psychopathology involves the use of categorical classification systems. **Categorical classification** systems have been based primarily on informed professional consensus, an approach that has dominated and continues to dominate the field of child (and adult) psychopathology (APA, 2000). A *classical* (or pure) categorical approach assumes that every diagnosis has a clear underlying cause, like an infection or a malfunction of the nervous system, and that each disorder is fundamentally different from other disorders. Therefore, individual cases can be placed into distinctive categories.

We might say, for example, that Felicia meets criteria for a major depressive disorder but not for separation anxiety disorder. The disadvantage to this approach, of course, is that children's behavior seldom falls neatly into established categories, so a certain degree of confusion remains. Moreover, categories of behavior (as opposed to some medical diseases) do not typically share the same underlying causes; thus, the mental health field has had to modify the classical categorical approach to accommodate the current state of knowledge. Children given the same diagnosis don't necessarily have disturbances that share the same etiology, nor do they respond to the same treatment. It is therefore crucial to understand that current diagnostic categories represent only our current knowledge about how symptoms cluster together.

The second approach to describing abnormal child behavior involves empirically based dimensional classification. **Dimensional classification** approaches assume that many independent dimensions or traits of behavior exist, and that all children possess them to varying degrees. For example, rather than saying that Felicia's symptoms fit the category of major depressive disorder, we might say that she is significantly above average (often referred to as being within the clinical range) on the dimension of depression, and that she is somewhat above average on the dimension of anxiety. These and other traits or dimensions

are typically derived using statistical methods from samples drawn from both clinically referred and nonreferred child populations, to establish ranges along each dimension (Achenbach, 1998).

Although empirically derived schemes are more objective and potentially more reliable than clinically derived classification systems, they too have limitations. First and foremost, the derived dimensions are dependent on sampling, method, and informant characteristics, as well as the age and sex of the child (Mash & Terdal, 1997a). Consequently, integrating information obtained from different methods and various informants, over time or across situations, can be difficult. Dimensional approaches may also be insensitive to contextual influences. For example, suppose you were a parent and were asked to describe whether your child "acts too young" using the scale "never, sometimes, a lot." You might want to clarify the circumstances or context under which he sometimes acts too young ("whenever I take him grocery shopping" or "when he is playing with other children"). Dimensions provide a useful estimate of the degree to which a child displays certain traits and not others, yet they often have to be tailored to the child's unique circumstances and developmental opportunities.

Many general and more specific dimensions of child psychopathology have been identified through research. These include the externalizing and internalizing dimensions and the subdimensions or syndromes that we talked about earlier in our discussion of behavior rating scales. Some of the most common syndromes in children and adolescents are presented in Table 4.5, along with selected examples of specific problem behaviors.

The category versus continuum distinction will ultimately be decided based on research (Meehl, 1999). Although the debate has not been resolved as to which approach is "best," there is agreement that each approach has value in classifying childhood disorders, and that a combined approach may be needed (Beauchaine, 2003; Maser & Patterson, 2002; Pickles & Angold, 2003). Some severe forms of mental retardation may be best conceptualized as qualitatively distinct conditions (categories), whereas others, such as depression or anxiety, may be best described as extreme points on one or more continuous dimensions.

Also, whether the purpose is clinical diagnosis or research, one approach may be more useful than the other (Kazdin & Kagan, 1994). A dimensional approach to conceptualizing psychological factors, such as behavior, affect, and cognitive abilities, among children is compatible with research methods that determine the degree of association among two or more variables. Therefore, the dimensional approach is often preferred by those conducting psychological research. A categorical approach, on the other hand, is often more compatible for clinical purposes, where the objective is to incorporate the whole pat-

Table 4.5
Commonly Identified Dimensions of Child Psychopathology and Examples of Items That Reflect Each Dimension

WITHDRAWN/DEPRESSED	SOCIAL PROBLEMS	ANXIOUS/DEPRESSED
Would rather be alone	Too dependent	Cries a lot
Refuses to talk	Doesn't get along with peers	Worries
Secretive	Gets teased	Feels worthless
Shy, timid	Not liked	Nervous, tense
SOMATIC COMPLAINTS	**THOUGHT PROBLEMS**	**AGGRESSIVE BEHAVIOR**
Feels dizzy	Hears things	Argues
Overtired	Sees things	Mean to others
Aches, pains	Strange behavior	Attacks people
Headaches	Strange ideas	Destroys others' things
ATTENTION PROBLEMS	**RULE-BREAKING BEHAVIOR**	
Inattentive	Lacks guilt	
Can't concentrate	Bad companions	
Can't sit still	Lies	
Confused	Runs away from home	

Source: Achenbach, T. M., & Rescorla, L. A. (2001) Manual for the ASEBA School-Age Forms and Profiles. Burlington, VT: University of Vermont, Research Center for Children, Youth, and Families. Reprinted with permission.

tern of the child's behavior into a meaningful diagnosis and treatment plan. In addition, categories are useful for communicating among clinicians (Mead, Hohenshil, & Singh, 1997), and categorical diagnoses are often required to determine a child's eligibility for services.

The Diagnostic and Statistical Manual (DSM)

A synopsis of the evolution of current systems is shown in Box 4.3, which provides a perspective on how far we have come in recognizing mental disorders in children and adolescents. The terminology and focus of prior systems reflected the major theoretical views of mental illness at the time; a shift to a more objective, informed approach occurred by the 1980s.

DSM-IV-TR (the "TR" stands for "text revision") (APA, 2000) includes the same diagnostic criteria as DSM-IV (APA, 1994) and updates the text information and wording to reflect new information and findings about prevalence and associated features since the DSM-IV was originally introduced in 1994. The DSM-IV-TR is a multiaxial system consisting of five axes. A **multiaxial system** is a classification system consisting of several axes (domains) of information about the child or adolescent that may assist a clinician in planning the treatment of a disorder. In other words, the axes serve to add further context and detail to the description of an individual's particular circum-

stances by organizing and communicating clinical information, capturing the complexity of clinical situations, and describing the diversity of individuals with the same diagnosis. The five axes of the DSM-IV-TR are as follows:

Axis I   Clinical disorders
          Other conditions that may be a focus of clinical attention
Axis II   Personality disorders
          Mental retardation
Axis III General medical conditions
Axis IV   Psychosocial and environmental problems
Axis V   Global assessment of functioning

Source: Adapted with permission from *Diagnostic and Statistical Manual of Mental Disorders, Fourth Edition,* Text Revision, pp. 29, 31. Copyright 2000 by the American Psychiatric Association.

Axis I is where the various clinical disorders or conditions are reported, except for mental retardation and personality disorders that are reported on Axis II because they are presumed to be stable. Axis I diagnostic categories that apply to infants, children, and adolescents are shown in Table 4.6, and will be discussed in detail in the chapters to follow. The disorders in Table 4.6 traditionally have been thought of as first occurring in childhood or as exclusive to childhood, so they require operational criteria that differ from those used to define disorders in adults.

BOX 4.3 The Evolution of Current Classification

The slow process of formal recognition of the prevalence and significance of mental disorders began in 1948, when the sixth edition of the *World Health Organization's International Classification of Diseases* (ICD) added a section on mental disorders (APA, 1994; Clementz & Iacono, 1993). Because this early attempt of the ICD system to classify mental disorders was felt to be inadequate, the American Psychiatric Association developed its own *Diagnostic and Statistical Manual* (DSM-I) in 1952 (APA, 1952) and revised it in 1968 (DSM-II) (APA, 1968). These first attempts by the APA were not a huge success, but they launched a sustained effort to improve the classification of mental disorders, an effort that continues today. Unfortunately, children and adolescents were virtually neglected in the early versions of DSM; most childhood disorders were relegated to the adult categories, with the exception of mental retardation and schizophrenia—childhood type (Cass & Thomas, 1979).

As a formal classification system, the DSM-III (APA, 1980) was a significant advance over the earlier editions. Clinical descriptions were replaced by explicit criteria that, in turn, enhanced diagnostic reliability (Achenbach, 1985; APA, 1980). In addition, DSM-III included more child categories, adopted a multiaxial system, and placed a greater emphasis on empirical data (Achenbach, 1985). These changes reflected the beginnings of a conceptual shift in both diagnostic systems and etiological models away from an isolated focus on a disorder as existing within the child alone, toward an increased emphasis on also considering the surrounding context in which the problem occurred.

The DSM-III was revised in 1987 (DSM-III-R) to help clarify the numerous inconsistencies and ambiguities that were noted in its use. The DSM-III-R was also developed to be a prototypical classification system by which a child could be diagnosed with a certain subset of symptoms without having to meet all criteria. This was an important change, especially in view of the heterogeneity associated with most childhood disorders (Mash & Terdal, 1997a). On the other hand, it also means that individuals with the same diagnosis can and often do show very different patterns of symptoms. To make this point stick, consider that there were nearly 150 million different ways for an individual to meet the DSM-III-R criteria for an antisocial personality disorder (Widiger, 1993).

Table 4.6

DSM-IV-TR Categories That Apply to Children

I. Disorders Usually First Diagnosed in Infancy, Childhood, or Adolescence

Mental Retardation (mild, moderate, severe, profound)

Learning Disorders (in reading, mathematics, and written expression)

Communication Disorders (expressive, mixed receptive-expressive, phonological, and stuttering)

Pervasive Developmental Disorders (autistic disorder, Rett's disorder, Asperger's disorder)

Attention Deficit and Disruptive Behavior Disorders (attention-deficit/hyperactivity disorder, conduct disorder, oppositional defiant disorder)

Feeding and Eating Disorders of Infancy or Early Childhood (pica, rumination, feeding disorder of infancy or early childhood)

Elimination Disorders (encopresis, enuresis)

Other Disorders of Infancy, Childhood, or Adolescence (separation anxiety, selective mutism, reactive attachment disorder of infancy or early childhood, stereotypic movement disorder)

II. Selected Categories for Disorders of Childhood or Adolescence That Are Not Listed Separately for Children in DSM-IV-TR

Mood Disorders (depressive disorders, bipolar disorders)

Anxiety Disorders (specific phobia, social phobia, obsessive-compulsive disorder, posttraumatic stress disorder, acute stress disorder, generalized anxiety disorder, anxiety disorder due to a general medical condition)

Eating Disorders (anorexia nervosa, bulimia nervosa)

Sleep Disorders (dyssomnias, parasomnias)

Source: Based on DSM-IV-TR Copyright © 2000 by APA.

The second section in Table 4.6 lists other major disorders that are not listed separately for children in DSM-IV-TR. Under the current DSM-IV-TR guidelines, diagnostic criteria for mood, anxiety, eating, and sleep disorders can apply to children as well as adults, with minor modifications. A child can receive more than one Axis I diagnosis, with the principal diagnosis listed first (e.g., attention-deficit/hyperactivity disorder; reading disorder). You should not try to memorize all of these terms right now, but simply get a feel for the organization and coverage to follow.

Axis II is used to report personality disorders and mental retardation. The purpose for using a separate axis for these two disorders is to ensure they are given consideration, especially when a more visible or acute Axis I disorder is present. Axis II is often used for diagnosing children with mental retardation. However, personality disorders are rarely diagnosed until late adolescence, by which time it is evident that the person's pattern of behavior or inner experience is enduring and problematic (Johnson, Bromley, & Bornstein, in press). Personality Disorders (PDs) include: antisocial, avoidant, borderline, dependent, depressive, histrionic, narcissistic, obsessive-compulsive, paranoid, passive-aggressive, schizoid, and schizotypal.

As described in the DSM-IV-TR (APA, 2000), PDs share a common set of criteria:

- An enduring pattern of inner experience and behavior that deviates markedly from the expectations of the individual's culture. For example, one individual may show very different ways of thinking, feeling, and behaving compared to others in his or her culture.

- This pattern of unusual thinking, feeling, or behaving is enduring, inflexible, and pervasive across a broad range of personal and social situations, and leads to clinically significant distress or impairment in social, occupational, or other important areas of functioning.

In addition to the general diagnostic criteria noted above, the DSM-IV-TR stipulates that additional diagnostic considerations should be used in describing PDs among children and adolescents:

- Personality Disorder categories may be applied to children or adolescents in those relatively unusual instances when the individual's particular maladaptive personality traits appear to be pervasive, persistent, and unlikely to be limited to a particular developmental stage or an episode of an Axis I disorder (APA, 2000; p. 687).

- To diagnose a Personality Disorder in an individual under age 18, the features must have been present for at least 1 year (APA, 2000; p. 687). (The one exception to this is Antisocial Personality Disorder, which cannot be diagnosed in individuals under the age of 18 years.)

Remember, some personality traits that may be regarded as pathological during adulthood are considered relatively normal during adolescence (such as mood swings and impulsivity)! For this reason the diagnostic criteria emphasize that a personality trait must *deviate markedly* from cultural expectations to be considered symptomatic of a personality disorder. As well, PDs may be applied to children or adolescents in those *relatively unusual instances* in which the individual's particular maladaptive personality traits appear to be pervasive, persistent, and unlikely to be limited to a particular developmental stage or an episode of an Axis I disorder (APA, 2000; p. 687; italics added).

Axis III is used to report current general medical conditions that may be relevant to the understanding or management of the individual's mental disorder. Because the DSM-IV-TR assumes that mental disorders are closely related to physical and biological factors, the purpose of distinguishing general medical conditions is to encourage thoroughness in evaluation and to enhance communication among health care providers.

General medical conditions can be related to mental disorders in a variety of ways. In some cases, the medical condition may play a direct causal role in the development of behavioral or psychological problems, such as a disruption in sleep due to depression. Most commonly with children, however, an Axis I disorder, such as anxiety, may be a psychological reaction to a medical condition, such as being diagnosed with childhood cancer or diabetes. Clearly, it is important to document the co-occurrence and temporal order of problems to gain an overall understanding and to develop an appropriate treatment plan for an individual.

Axis IV describes any psychosocial and environmental problems that may affect the diagnosis, treatment, and prognosis of disorders listed on Axes I and II. Such problems include negative life events, environmental disruptions or deficiencies, family or other interpersonal stress, and lack of social support or personal resources (APA, 2000). Typically, clinicians note only those problems that have been present over the past year, unless prior events— for example, an automobile accident—have likely contributed to the mental disorder. Contextual factors, such as child abuse or parental unemployment, are potentially important for understanding an individual's behavior and emotions. We remind you of this important consideration throughout our discussion of various disorders of childhood and adolescence because a child's presenting problem is often better understood if we can see the whole picture.

Finally, Axis V is used to report the clinician's ratings of the individual's overall level of functioning, primarily for planning treatment and monitoring its impact. A Global Assessment of Functioning (GAF) rating scale, ranging from 1 to 100, provides a hypothetical continuum of mental health and mental illness with respect to psychological, social, and occupational functioning. A low score indicates greater impairment in social functioning or personal care, whereas a higher score reflects mild or transient symptoms or the absence of symptoms.

Based on our clinical assessment, Felicia was given the following DSM-IV-TR diagnosis and multiaxial evaluation:

Axis I   Major depressive disorder, single episode
Axis II   No diagnosis
Axis III None

Axis IV   Death of a family member; disruption of family by separation; academic problems

Axis V   GAF = 60 (this score indicates moderate symptoms and moderate difficulties in social and school functioning as the highest level of functioning in the past year)

A diagnosis of Major Depressive Disorder (MDD), which you will learn more about in Chapter 8, was made because Felicia showed symptoms of depressed mood, loss of interest in almost all activities, significant weight loss, insomnia nearly every day, and feelings of worthlessness that persisted for more than 2 weeks and represented a change from her previous functioning. These symptoms were causing significant distress and impairment in Felicia's social and school functioning. Although the loss of her grandfather may have been a factor in Felicia's depression, it did not seem to be the major factor accounting for her symptoms.

Criticisms of DSM-IV-TR   Although DSM-IV-TR includes numerous improvements over previous versions, with its greater emphasis on empirical research and more explicit diagnostic criteria sets, it is not faultless. Because DSM-IV-TR focuses on superficial descriptions of symptoms as the basis for generating categories, it has been criticized for failing to capture the complex adaptations, transactions, and setting influences that we have identified as crucial to understanding and treating psychopathology in children (Beauchaine, 2003; Mash & Terdal, 1997a). DSM-IV-TR also gives relatively less attention to disorders of infancy and childhood than adulthood, and fails to capture the interrelationships and overlap known to exist among many childhood disorders.

A further difficulty with DSM-IV-TR diagnostic criteria for children is the relative lack of emphasis on the situational and contextual factors surrounding and contributing to various disorders in making a clinical diagnosis (Beauchaine, 2003). This reflects the fact that DSM-IV-TR views mental disorder as individual psychopathology or risk for psychopathology, rather than in terms of problems in psychosocial adjustment or adaptation. However, DSM-IV-TR does consider factors, such as culture, age, and gender, associated with the expression of each disorder, and has increased its recognition of the importance of family problems and extrafamilial relational difficulties. In all likelihood, this awareness of the context for childhood disorders will increase in sophistication and depth with future revisions.

A final criticism deals with how DSM-IV-TR is used rather than with the classification system itself. In some cases, DSM-IV-TR categorical diagnoses can be an impediment to gaining proper services to address children's needs. For example, to qualify for a special education class, a child may be required to meet specific diagnostic criteria for a learning disorder. In the "typical" case such requirements are usually met. However, some children may not have developed problems to the degree that they meet specific diagnostic criteria, or their problems may relate to more than one DSM category. These children may not qualify for services that otherwise could prove beneficial. In this context, it would be difficult to access programs to *prevent* future problems from developing in at-risk children.

Pros and Cons of Diagnostic Labels   Despite every attempt to the contrary, the history of classification of mental disorders has been fraught with negative connotations that become attached to the terms used to describe them (Hinshaw & Cicchetti, 2000). The word *moron*, for instance, was originally chosen as a neutral term to describe a lower range of intellectual functioning, but quickly became an insult when it began to be used in common language. Much has been written about the positive and negative aspects of assigning diagnostic labels to children.

On the positive side, labels help clinicians summarize and order observations. This can facilitate communication among professionals and sometimes aid parents by providing more recognition and understanding of their child's problem. Moreover, descriptive labels are consistent with the natural tendency to think in terms of categories. That is, we tend to talk about ourselves, our friends, and our children as being happy, angry, depressed, or fearful, rather than use a number on a scale that signifies a range of emotion, even if a number might give a more accurate account. Finally, the use of descriptive terms or labels assists clinicians in locating a relevant body of detailed research and clinical data, and facilitates research on the causes, epidemiology, and treatment of specific disorders.

On the negative side are criticisms as to whether current diagnostic labels are effective in achieving any of the aforementioned purposes. There are also concerns about negative effects and stigmatization associated with the assignment of labels to children. Once labeled, others may perceive and react to children differently ("he's a hyperactive boy—you'll never get him to listen") (Bromfield, Weisz, & Messer, 1986). Classmates pick up on the use of labels, especially labels associated with visible treatment requirements such as taking medication. A note sent by a classmate to a boy with ADHD reflects this: "Jack was ill, he took his pill, let's hope it makes him sit still." Standing out and being teased by other children may exacerbate the problem. Equally disturbing is the finding that labels can influence children's views of themselves and their behavior (Guskin, Bartel, & MacMillan, 1975). In general, the reactions of others to persons who seem different or who have been diagnosed with a mental illness reveal a ten-

Table 4.7
DSM-IV multiaxial diagnosis of conditions demonstrated by the inhabitants of the Hundred Acre Wood

Inhabitant	AXIS I Clinical disorders	AXIS II Personality disorders/ mental retardation	AXIS III General medical conditions	AXIS IV Psychosocial/ environmental problems
Winnie-the-Pooh	ADHD, inattentive subtype; OCD (provisional diagnosis)	Borderline intellectual functioning (Very Little Brain)	Poor diet, obesity, binge eating	—
Piglet	Generalized anxiety disorder	—	Failure to thrive	—
Eeyore	Dysthymic disorder	—	Traumatic amputation of tail	Housing problems
Rabbit	—	Narcissistic personality disorder	—	—
Owl	Reading disorder	—	—	Housing problems
Tigger	ADHD, hyperactivity- impulsivity subtype	—	—	—
Kanga	—	—	—	Single parent, unemployed, overprotective of child
Roo	—	—	—	Single parenthood, undesirable peer group, victim of unusual feeding practices (extract of malt)
Christopher Robin	Gender identity disorder of childhood (provisional diagnosis)	—	—	Lack of parental super- vision, possible educational problems

Note: ADHD = attention deficit hyperactivity disorder, OCD = obsessive compulsive disorder.

*The Axis V (global assessment of functioning) scale was deferred.

Source: Shea, S. E., Gordon, K., Hawkins, A., Kawchuk, J., & Smith, D. (2000). Pathology in the Hundred Acre Wood: A neurodevelopmental perspective on A.A. Milne. Canadian Medical Association Journal, 163(12), 1557–1559. (p. 1558.)

dency to generalize inappropriately from the labels (Corrigan, 2000). See Table 4.7 for a tongue-in-cheek look at the inhabitants of the Hundred Acre Wood.

SECTION SUMMARY

- Classification refers to a system for representing the major categories of child psychopathology and the relations among them.
- Diagnosis refers to the assignment of cases to categories of the classification system.
- Childhood disorders have been classified using categories and dimensions.
- Categorical classification systems have been based primarily on informed professional consensus.
- Dimensional classification approaches assume that many independent dimensions or traits of behavior exist and that all children possess these to varying degrees.

- The DSM-IV-TR is a multiaxial system consisting of five axes: clinical disorders, personality disorders and mental retardation, general medical conditions, psychosocial and environmental problems, and global assessment of functioning.
- The DSM-IV-TR has been criticized for failing to capture the complexity of child psychopathology, for giving less attention to disorders of infancy and childhood than to those of adulthood, and for its relative lack of emphasis on situational and contextual factors.

I have found the best way to give advice to your children is to find out what they want and then advise them to do it.

—Harry S. Truman

Treatment

Over the last two decades, treatment approaches based on expanding research and clinical knowledge of children's behavioral, cognitive, emotional, and physical development have grown tremendously in their sophistication and their breadth (Kazdin & Weisz, 2003; Mash & Barkley, 1998). Interventions today are often planned by combining the most effective approaches to particular problems in an ongoing, developmentally sensitive manner (Kazdin, 2000). Behavioral methods, for example, may be very useful for teaching parents of a young, difficult child ways to encourage desirable behavior. Once the child is a bit older he or she may profit from cognitive-behavioral methods that address how the child thinks about social situations, such as making friends and avoiding conflicts.

A thorough clinical assessment and diagnosis constitute a critical first step in helping Felicia and other children who have psychological problems and their families. However, assessment and diagnosis are only the beginning of an ongoing helping process. We next must ask: "How can we help Felicia reduce her feelings of depression and hopelessness, eliminate her sleep disturbances and other somatic complaints, increase her school attendance and performance, and improve her social skills and relationships with other children and her parents?" This is where intervention comes into play.

How do we determine the best type of intervention for children like Felicia and for children with other problems? We will consider this question in some detail for each disorder discussed in the chapters that follow; thus, the coverage of treatment and prevention in this section is intended to be brief. Our discussion of intervention in the context of specific disorders follows from our general conviction that the most useful treatments are likely based on what we know about the nature, course, associated characteristics, and causes of a particular childhood disorder. However, this is not enough. We also need to have empirical support for the effectiveness and efficacy of our interventions (Kazdin & Weisz, 2003). Interventions that zoom in on a specific problem with clear guidelines for treatment appear to be the most effective (Weisz & Weiss, 1993). Thus, our chapter-by-chapter coverage of intervention strategies will be selective, focusing primarily on those interventions that are tailored to what we know about individual disorders and that have shown promising results in controlled outcome studies.

In this section, we provide an overview of what we mean by intervention, discuss special considerations in intervention such as different models of treatment, highlight some of the main approaches and strategies used to help children with problems and their families, and take stock of what we know about the general effectiveness of interventions for children. The overall goal is to introduce you to the important foundational issues associated with interventions for children.

Intervention

Intervention is a broad concept that encompasses many different theories and methods with a range of problem-solving strategies directed at helping the child and family adapt more effectively to their current and future circumstances. There is no single approach to working with children and families—multiple problems require multiple solutions. Clinical assessment and diagnosis are usually followed by efforts to select and implement the most promising approach to intervention (Mash, 1998). Since psychological disorders represent failures in adaptation on the part of the child and/or his or her social environment, problem-solving strategies are part of a spectrum of activities for treatment, maintenance, and prevention (Adelman, 1995).

Figure 4.3 illustrates an intervention spectrum for childhood disorders. Note that intervention efforts cover a wide range of actions, from prevention to maintenance. **Prevention** efforts are directed at decreasing the chances that undesired future outcomes will occur; **treatment** refers to corrective actions that will permit successful adaptation by eliminating or reducing the impact of an undesired outcome that has already occurred; **maintenance** refers to efforts to increase adherence with treatment over time to prevent relapse or recurrence of a problem.

Interventions are best depicted as part of the ongoing decision-making approach that we have been discussing throughout this chapter (Mash, 1998). Our assessments should help us answer many questions that are essential for intervention. In Felicia's case, our answers to some of the following questions will guide us in determining which, if any, of the numerous available treatment options will be used:

- Should Felicia's difficulties be treated? If so, which ones? Depression? School refusal? Social skills deficits? Relations with family members? All of them?
- What are the projected outcomes for Felicia in the absence of treatment?
- What treatments are likely to be most effective, efficient, and cost effective for Felicia's depression, school refusal, and social skills deficits?
- When should treatment for Felicia begin? When should treatment be terminated?
- Is the intervention having the desired impact on Felicia's behavior? Are the changes meaningful for Felicia and her family? Do they make a real difference in their lives?

The ultimate goal of addressing these questions should be to achieve effective solutions to the problems

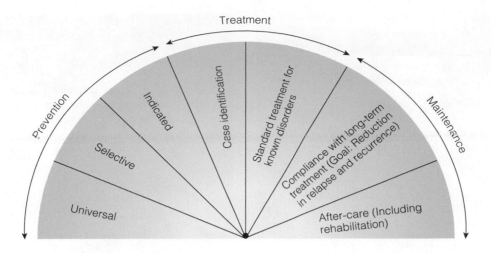

Figure 4.3. The intervention spectrum for childhood disorders.

Source: Adapted from *Reducing Risks for Mental Disorders: Frontiers for Preventive Intervention,* by P. J. Mrazek and R. J. Haggerty (Eds.), 1994. Copyright © 1994 National Academy of Sciences. Adapted by permission of the National Academy Press.

faced by Felicia, her family, and other children like her, then promote and enhance long-term adjustments.

Cultural Considerations

As interventions have developed, so has a growing awareness of the need to give greater attention to the cultural context of children and families receiving psychological interventions. Parenting values and child-rearing methods vary among ethnic minority groups, and more interventions involving parent education and training are becoming sensitive to cultural variations (McNeil, Capage, & Bennett, 2002; Schwab-Stone, Ruchkin, Vermeiren, & Leckman, 2001).

Treatment services for children, therefore, must not only attend to the presenting symptoms, but also consider the specific values, norms, and expectations held by many social classes and within many cultures; the various religious beliefs and practices of each family; and other circumstances that might make a successful treatment for one family a failure for another (Cohen & Kasen, 1999; Schwoeri, Sholevar, & Combs, 2003). Cultural values and common parenting practices and beliefs in four ethnic minority groups are shown in Table 4.8.

Can you think of how these cultural differences might lead us to different treatments? One issue might be the different parenting styles cross-culturally. African American families place greater emphasis on strict discipline,

Table 4.8
Cultural Values and Parenting Practices and Beliefs

	AFRICAN AMERICAN	ASIAN AMERICAN	LATINO	NATIVE AMERICAN
Cultural values	Independence Respect for authority Obedience Racial identity	Self-control Social courtesy Emotional maturity Respect for elders	Family loyalty Interpersonal connectedness Mutual respect Self-respect	Centrality of family Sharing Harmony Humility
Common parenting practices and beliefs	Strict discipline Communal parenting	Parental control Strict discipline Negotiation of conflict Parent as teacher	Permissive discipline Communal parenting Freedom	Permissive discipline Communal parenting Shame as discipline

Source: From "Cultural Diversity: A Wake-Up Call for Parent Training," by R. L. Forehand and B. A. Kotchick, 1996, *Behavior Therapy, 27,* 171–186. Copyright © by the Association for Advancement of Behavior Therapy. Reprinted by permission.

Cultural background is an important consideration in understanding the child's uniqueness and expectations.

whereas Latino and Native American parents are generally more permissive. In helping families establish effective rules and forms of discipline for their children the clinician must be aware of these important differences and find methods that each parent is comfortable using. As we emphasized earlier, generalizations about cultural practices and beliefs may fail to capture the diversity that exists within and across ethnic groups, so we must be extremely careful not to stereotype individuals of any cultural group.

Treatment Goals

What are the typical goals of treatment—reducing symptoms (problems), producing more substantial changes that will enhance the child's long-term functioning—or both? Because children's symptoms are often an expression of their unsuccessful attempts to adapt to their social environment more emphasis is placed today on the child's family and peers than on the child alone (Cummings, Davies, & Campbell, 2000; Fiese, Wilder, & Bickham, 2000). Accordingly, treatment goals often focus on building children's skills for adapting to facilitate long-term adjustment, rather than focus on merely eliminating problem behaviors or briefly reducing subjective distress. Other treatment goals and outcomes are also of crucial importance to the child, family, and society (Jensen, Hoagwood, & Petti, 1996), and are summarized here (Kazdin, 1997a):

- **Outcomes Related to Child Functioning:** Reduction or elimination of symptoms, reduced degree of impairment in functioning, enhanced social competence, improved academic performance
- **Outcomes Related to Family Functioning:** Reduction in level of family dysfunction, improved marital and sibling relationships, reduction in stress, improvement in quality of life, reduction in burden of care, enhanced family support
- **Outcomes of Societal Importance:** Improvement in child's participation in school-related activities (increased attendance, reduced truancy, reduction in school dropout rates), decreased involvement in the juvenile justice system, reduced need for special services, reduction in accidental injuries or substance abuse, enhancement of physical and mental health

The interlocking network of physical, behavioral, social, and learning difficulties that characterizes most childhood disorders requires a multidisciplinary approach to attain these treatment and prevention goals. In many instances, children require medication or medical intervention that must be coordinated with psychosocial interventions, such as in connection with ADHD, autism, eating disorders, depression, and chronic medical conditions. Thus, the use of combined interventions is common (Kazdin, 1996a). In addition, psychological interventions for children and adolescents often require integration with effective teaching strategies, as illustrated in later chapters on learning disorders, communication disorders, and mental retardation. Finally, some children require the integration of community and social services that aid in their protection and basic needs, which we discuss in Chapter 14 on child abuse and neglect.

Models of Delivery

When we think of psychological treatment, most of us picture someone going to see a therapist whenever he or she has "symptoms" or is struggling with situational problems at home or school. In this *conventional* model of treatment for abnormal child behavior, a child is seen individually by a therapist for a limited number of treatment sessions in the clinic. However, as we have seen, many other options are in use today that involve various treatment agents, such as parents and teachers, and take place in settings where the problems are most likely to emerge.

The growing emphasis on a systems perspective toward abnormal child behavior translates into the need for a variety of intervention activities and treatment delivery models. These models range from universal (primary) prevention programs available to all, to selective preschool and early school interventions aimed at children with particular risk signs, to standard treatments that focus on the current needs of children with known disorders (Offord, Kraemer, Kazdin, Jensen, & Harrington, 1998). The conventional model of delivering treatment services for children, youths, and families is driven primarily by symptoms or problems that prompt a referral. Although this method is still widely used and well matched to some childhood problems, such as bed-wetting, certain fears, and problems adjusting to new circumstances, two *continuing care* models have emerged as alternatives to the conventional care model of treatment in some cases (Kazdin, 2000).

The first alternative is a *chronic care* model, in which treatment is maintained and adjusted in the same way that it would be for a child with a chronic illness such as diabetes mellitus or asthma. Ongoing treatment is provided to ensure that the benefits of treatment are maintained. Autism and life-course-persistent conduct disorder are two long-term continuing problems in which a chronic care model of treatment may be the best strategy for establishing basic competencies at each developmental level.

The second approach to continuing care is a *dental care* model, in which ongoing follow-ups are carried out on a regular basis following initial treatment, in much the same way that regular dental checkups are recommended at 6-month intervals. Follow-ups may be conducted periodically at prescribed intervals, or on an as-needed basis related to emergent issues in development and adjustment. Several childhood disorders described in this text would be well served by ongoing checkups.

Ethical and Legal Considerations

As we have seen, many children referred for assessment and treatment experience multiple disadvantages and arguably need special help and protection. Both ethically and legally, clinicians who work with children are required to think not only about the impact that their actions will have on the children they see, but also on the responsibilities, rights, and relationships that connect children and parents (Melton, 1996).

Minimum ethical standards for practice include: (a) selecting treatment goals and procedures that are in the best interests of the client; (b) making sure that client participation is active and voluntary; (c) keeping records that document the effectiveness of treatment in achieving its objectives; (d) protecting the confidentiality of the therapeutic relationship; and (e) ensuring the qualifications and competencies of the therapist (Melton & Ehrenreich, 1992). There is also a growing emphasis on involving children, depending on their developmental level, as active partners in decision making regarding their own psychological or medical treatment (McCabe, 1996).

Ethical issues with children are complex because of ongoing changes in the legal status of children and a trend toward recognition of minors' constitutional rights, including self-determination and privacy (Melton, 2000). However, a more basic issue is determining when a minor is competent to make his or her own decisions, rather than only determining whether he or she has the legal right to do so. Some of the challenging issues faced by clinicians working with children involve deciding when a minor can provide informed consent or refuse treatment and balancing the rights of the child to confidentiality against those of the parents and the integrity of the family.

In addition to these ethical and legal concerns, much larger ethical questions concern the provision of services for children and families. Many interventions currently used to treat children with complex problems are known to be limited in scope—for example, one hour per week of therapy—and cannot realistically be expected to have a meaningful or lasting impact on children experiencing severe problems. Furthermore, many currently used interventions are intrusive, expensive, and not supported by data (Kazdin, 2000). A more fundamental and thorny ethical question in some cases is whether we should provide any treatment when we know that the treatment may not make a difference or, even worse, have harmful effects.

Clinicians who work with children and their parents need to be aware of federal, state, and local laws that affect both the assessment and treatment of children with special needs. Many of these laws apply to children with mental and physical disabilities and handicaps, and are based on the recognition that disability is a natural part of the human experience, and that all citizens (children included) are entitled to equal treatment and education.

One law that has had a profound influence on services for children with disabilities is the Education for All Handicapped Children Act (Public Law 94-142, 1975) and its amendment, the Individuals with Disabilities Education Act (Public Law 101-476). Following are two of the many purposes of these laws:

- To ensure that all children with disabilities have available to them a free, appropriate public education that emphasizes special education and related services designed to meet their unique needs and prepare them for employment and independent living
- To ensure that the rights of children with disabilities and parents of such children are protected

General Approaches

The number and diversity of treatments for children have grown tremendously, to the point where more than 550 treatments are currently in use to help children (Kazdin, 2000)! While we will (thankfully) not attempt to cover them all, in the remainder of this chapter we provide an overview of several of the major approaches. More than 70% of practicing clinicians who work with children and families identify their approach as **eclectic** (Kazdin, Siegel, & Bass, 1990), which means that they use different approaches for children with different problems and circumstances, and they see most of these approaches as having value. Let's now turn to a description of some of the general approaches to treatment and see how they might apply to Felicia.

Psychodynamic Treatments Psychodynamic approaches view child psychopathology as determined by underlying unconscious and conscious conflicts (Lesser, 1972). Therefore, the focus is on helping the child develop an awareness of unconscious factors that may be contributing to his or her problems (Galatzer-Levy, Bachrach, Skolnikoff, & Waldron, 2000). With younger children, this awareness can occur through play therapy (Campbell, Baker, & Bratton, 2000; Chethik, 2000); with older children, it occurs through verbal interactions with the therapist. As underlying conflicts are revealed the therapist helps the child resolve the conflicts and develop more adaptive ways of coping.

In Felicia's case, a therapist would help her gain insight into her problem through an intensive process of psychotherapy, perhaps lasting months or even years. The therapist might explore her earliest memories of her relationship with her parents by having her recall positive and negative memories, and exploring how she constructs her childhood memories and relationships. The assumption is that once she resolves the underlying problems, such as insecure attachment to her mother, Felicia's overt symptoms of depression, social withdrawal, school refusal, and

physical complaints will be alleviated (Muratori, Picchi, Bruni, Patarnello, & Romagnoli, 2003).

Behavioral Treatments Behavioral approaches assume that many abnormal child behaviors are learned. Therefore, the focus of treatment is on re-educating the child, using procedures derived from theories of learning or from research (Krasner, 1991). Such procedures include positive reinforcement or time-out, modeling, and systematic desensitization (Morris & Kratochwill, 1998). Behavioral treatments often focus on changing the child's environment by working with parents and teachers.

In Felicia's case, a therapist might try to decrease her school refusal by instructing her parents to not let her stay at home when she protests, and by rewarding her for going to school with praise or a preferred activity. In addition, the therapist might use modeling and practice to help Felicia learn more effective social skills.

Cognitive Treatments Cognitive approaches view abnormal child behavior as the result of deficits and/or distortions in the child's thinking, including perceptual biases, irrational beliefs, and faulty interpretations (Kendall, 2000). For example, for an attractive girl who gets A grades but thinks she is ugly and is going to fail in school, the emphasis in treatment is on changing these faulty cognitions. As cognitions change, the child's behaviors and feelings are also expected to change.

In Felicia's case, she may be convinced that she can't do well in school, or that if she goes to school, then harm will befall her mother, or that children at school will think she's stupid. Changing these negative views by challenging them, and by helping Felicia develop more rational and more adaptive forms of thinking, should lead to changes in her behavior.

Cognitive-Behavioral Treatments Cognitive-behavioral approaches view psychological disturbances as partly the result of faulty thought patterns, and partly the result of faulty learning and environmental experiences. These approaches begin with the basic premise that the way children and parents think about their environment determines how they will react to it (Meichenbaum, 1977). Combining elements of both the behavioral and cognitive models, the cognitive-behavioral approach grew rapidly as behavior therapists began to focus on the important role of cognition in treatment for both the child (Kendall, 2000) and the family (Foster & Robin, 1998).

Faulty thought patterns that are the targets of change include deficiencies in cognitive mediators, and distortions in both cognitive content (e.g., erroneous beliefs) and cognitive process (e.g., irrational thinking and faulty problem solving). As you will learn, cognitive distortions and attributional biases have been identified in children with a variety of problems, including depression, conduct disorder, and anxiety disorders.

The major goals of cognitive-behavioral treatment are to identify maladaptive cognitions and replace them with more adaptive ones, to teach the child to use both cognitive and behavioral coping strategies in specific situations, and to help the child learn to regulate his or her own behavior. Treatment may also involve how others respond to the child's maladaptive behavior. Using a cognitive-behavioral approach, a therapist would help Felicia learn to think more positively and use more effective social skills and coping strategies.

Client-Centered Treatments   Client-centered approaches view child psychopathology as the result of social or environmental circumstances that are imposed on the child and interfere with his or her basic capacity for personal growth and adaptive functioning. The interference causes the child to experience a loss or impairment in self-esteem and emotional well-being, resulting in even further problems. The therapist relates to the child in an empathic way, providing unconditional, nonjudgmental, and genuine acceptance of the child as an individual, often through the use of play activities with younger children and verbal interaction with older youngsters (Axline, 1947; Ellinwood & Raskin, 1993). The therapist respects the child's capacity to achieve his or her goals without the therapist's serving as a major adviser, analyst, coach, or provocateur— the therapist respects the child's self-directing abilities.

In Felicia's case, being babied by her parents who viewed her as slow may have led to interference in her adaptive functioning and to low self-esteem. In treatment, a therapist would comment on what Felicia is saying and feeling to help her understand her feelings, and to increase the congruence between her feelings and behavior. In therapy, Felicia would lead the way as the clinician follows.

Family Treatments   Family models challenge the view of psychopathology as residing only within the individual child and, instead, view child psychopathology as determined by variables operating in the larger family system (Gurman & Kniskern, 1991). Like the other approaches, many varieties of family therapy differ widely in their underlying assumptions and approach to treatment (Szapocznik, 2000). However, all of the approaches view individual child disorders as manifestations of disturbances in family relations.

Treatment involves a therapist and sometimes a cotherapist, who interact with the entire family or a select subset of family members, such as the parents and child or the husband and wife. Therapy typically focuses on the family issues underlying problem behaviors. Depending on the approach, the therapist may focus on family inter-

action, communication, dynamics, contingencies, boundaries, or alliances. It is also essential to adapt family interventions to the cultural context of the family (Kumpfer, Alvarado, Smith, & Bellamy, 2002).

In Felicia's case, her overall helplessness and physical symptoms may be serving to maintain her role as the baby in the family, or may be serving as the parents' way of avoiding their own marital difficulties by focusing the problem on Felicia. A therapist would assist Felicia and her family in identifying and changing this and other dysfunctional ways in which family members relate to one another.

Biological Treatments   Medical models view child psychopathology as resulting from biological impairment or dysfunction, and rely primarily on pharmacological and other biological approaches to treatment. Examples include the use of stimulant medications for the treatment of ADHD (Althoff, Rettew, & Hudziak, 2003), antipsychotic medications for the treatment of schizophrenia or serious aggressive and destructive behavior (Birmaher, 2003), and selective serotonin reuptake inhibitors (SSRIs) such as fluoxetine (Prozac) for treatment of depression and other disorders (Wagner, 2003). Table 4.9 provides a convenient summary of medications and their typical uses with children and adolescents, which you may find helpful when reviewing treatment for specific disorders in subsequent chapters.

Other much more controversial forms of biological intervention include electroconvulsive therapy (ECT) for severe depression, the administration of large doses of vitamins or minerals to children with ADHD or autism, and the scrupulous elimination of food additives and preservatives from the diets of children with ADHD. In Felicia's case, a psychiatrist might consider using SSRIs or other medications to treat her depressive symptoms. As shown in Figure 4.4, the use of medications for children's mental health problems increased significantly from the late 1980s to the mid 1990s, which is attributed to increasing public acceptance of these medications as part of the treatment of mental health problems among children and youths (Olfson, Marcus, Weissman, & Jensen, 2002).

Combined Treatments   Combined treatments refer to the use of two or more interventions, each of which can stand on its own as a treatment strategy (Kazdin, 1996a). In some instances, combinations of stand-alone interventions may cross conceptual approaches—using cognitive-behavioral and pharmacological treatments for children with ADHD (Arnold, Abikoff, & Wells, 1997; Barkley, 1998) or children with obsessive-compulsive disorder (Piacentini & Graae, 1997), or using cognitive-behavioral treatment and family therapy (Fauber & Kendall, 1992) or family education (Asarnow, Scott, & Mintz, 2002) in

Table 4.9
Description of Common Medications for Children and Youths[a]

TYPE OF MEDICATION	TREATMENT USES	EXAMPLES
Stimulant Medications	Attention deficit hyperactive disorder (ADHD).	Dextroamphetamine (*Dexedrine, Adderall*), Methylphenidate (*Ritalin*), and Pemoline (*Cylert*)
Antidepressant Medications	Depression, school phobias, panic attacks, and other anxiety disorders, bedwetting, eating disorders, obsessive-compulsive disorder, personality disorders, posttraumatic stress disorder, and ADHD.	**1. Tricyclic antidepressants:** Amitriptyline (*Elavil*), Clomipramine (*Anafranil*), Imipramine (*Tofranil*). **2. Selective serotonin reuptake inhibitors** (SSRI's): Fluoxetine (*Prozac*), Sertraline (*Zoloft*), Paroxetine (*Paxil*), Fluvoxamine (*Luvox*), Venlafaxine (*Effexor*), and Citalopram (*Celexa*). **3. Monoamine oxidase inhibitors** (*MAOI's*): Phenelzine (*Nardil*), and Tranylcypromine (*Parnate*).
Antipsychotic Medications	Controlling psychotic symptoms (delusions, hallucinations) or disorganized thinking. They are occasionally used to treat severe anxiety and may help in reducing very aggressive behaviour.	Chlorpromazine (*Thorazine*), Thioridazine (*Mellaril*), Fluphenazine (*Prolixin*), Trifluoperazine (*Stelazine*), Thiothixene (*Navane*), and Haloperidol (*Haldol*). Newer antipsychotic medications (also known as atypical or novel) include: Clozapine (*Clozaril*), Risperidone (*Risperdal*), Quetiapine (*Seroquel*), Olanzapine (*Zyprexa*), and Ziprasidone (*Zeldox*).
Mood Stabilizers and Anticonvulsant Medications	manic-depressive episodes, excessive mood swings, aggressive behavior, impulse control disorders and severe mood symptoms in schizoaffective disorder and schizophrenia.	Mood stabilizer: Lithium (lithium carbonate, *Eskalith*). Some anticonvulsant medications can also help control severe mood changes. Examples include: Valproic Acid (*Depakote, Depakene*), Carbamazepine (*Tegretol*), Gabapentin (*Neurontin*), and Lamotrigine (*Lamictil*).
Anti-anxiety Medications	severe anxiety	**Benzodiazepines:** Alprazolam (*Xanax*), lorazepam (*Ativan*), Diazepam (*Valium*), and Clonazepam (*Klonopin*).

[a] these medications are often used in association with other forms of intervention such as psychotherapy, parent training, etc.
Source: American Academy of Child and Adolescent Psychiatry (1999). Psychiatric medication for children and adolescents part II: Types of medications. *Available:* http://www.aacap.org/publications/factsfam/29.htm

combination. Other examples include social skills training, cognitive-behavior therapy (CBT), and parental involvement for children with social phobia (Spence, Donovan, & Brechman-Toussaint, 2000), or group CBT and family intervention for various childhood anxiety disorders (Barrett, 1998). In other instances, combined treatments may be derived from the same overall conceptual approach—using social skills training and cognitive restructuring in a group treatment program for adolescents with a social phobia (Marten, Albano, & Holt, 1991), or using individual behavior management and family behavior therapy in the treatment of children with oppositional disorders (Fauber & Long, 1991).

More communities are now implementing comprehensive mental health programs for children, often delivered through schools to reach the most children and their families. Box 4.4 describes an innovative school-based program that pays particular attention to the cultural diversity of families in their community.

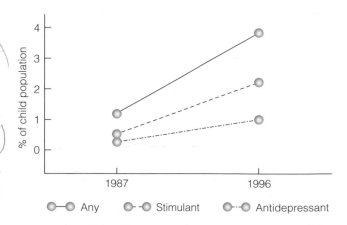

Figure 4.4. Psychiatric medication usage by children in the US since 1987
Source: Olfson, M., Marcus, S. C., Weissman, M. M., & Jensen, P. S. (2002). National trends in the use of psychotropic medications by children. *Journal of the American Academy of Child and Adolescent Psychiatry, 41,* 514–521. Adapted from p. 516.

BOX 4.4 Model Program: A Culturally Competent School-Based Mental Health Program

Program	Dallas School-Based Youth and Family Centers
Goal	To establish the first comprehensive, culturally competent, school-based program in mental health care in the 12th largest school system in the nation. The program overcomes stigma and inadequate access to care for underserved minority populations.
Features	Annually serves the physical and mental health care needs of 3,000 low-income children and their families. The mental health component features partnerships with parents and families, treatment (typically six sessions), and follow-up with teachers. The well-qualified staff, who reflect the racial and ethnic composition of the population they serve (more than 70% Latino and African American), train school nurses, counselors, and principals to identify problems and create solutions tailored to meet each child's needs.
Outcomes	Improvements in attendance, discipline referrals, and teacher evaluation of child performance. Preliminary findings reveal improvement in children's standardized test scores in relation to national and local norms.
Biggest challenge	To sustain financial and organizational support of collaborative partners despite resistance to change or jurisdictional barriers. Program's $3.5 million funding comes from the school district and an additional $1.5 million from Parkland Hospital.
How other organizations can adopt	Recognize the importance of mental health for the school success of all children, regardless of race or ethnicity. Rethink how school systems can more efficiently partner with and use State and Federal funds to deliver culturally competent school-based mental health services.
Sites	Dallas and Fort Worth, Texas

Source: President's New Freedom Commission on Mental Health (2003). Achieving the promise: Transforming mental health care in America. Available http://www.mentalhealthcommission.gov. Accessed February 16, 2004.

In Felicia's case, we used a combined treatment approach that included cognitive-behavioral treatment for depression, behavioral treatment for school refusal, and social skills training:

Felicia
Multiple Solutions

Our clinical assessment of Felicia suggested a combined treatment approach to treat three significant problems: school refusal, depression, and social difficulties.

To treat Felicia's school refusal, a behavioral program was implemented that required her to attend class daily. Felicia earned points for her attendance, class participation, and completion of class assignments, which could later be traded in for the opportunity to engage in preferred activities such as a movie, or for money that could be used to purchase CDs and other things that Felicia had previously selected. When Felicia refused to go to school, she lost points and was given a brief period of time-out from positive reinforcement. She had to sit in the kitchen by herself and was not permitted to read or watch TV. This behavioral program resulted in consistent school attendance and much improved academic performance.

To treat Felicia's depressive symptoms, we used a cognitive-behavioral approach. Felicia learned that depression can occur for many reasons—the loss of her grandfather, thinking lots of negative thoughts, and not having any friends. We next taught Felicia how to relax to give her some immediate relief and provide her with a successful experience. Felicia then learned to monitor and rate her mood daily, and to identify thoughts and events that accompanied both her positive and negative moods. Felicia increased her positive thinking by learning to identify, challenge, and change her negative cognitions. After several weeks of treatment, Felicia began to feel less depressed, as reflected in her positive daily mood ratings and reports by her parents.

Both Felicia's teacher and parents felt that her feelings of depression might be the result of her social interaction difficulties at home and school, and thought that she might become less depressed if these problems could be decreased. Therefore, a social-cognitive skills training program was also implemented to simultaneously address her depressive symptoms and interpersonal difficulties. This program consisted of three parts. First, Felicia was given behavioral social skills training that consisted of instruction, modeling of appropriate and inappropriate social behaviors, role playing and rehearsal, coaching, feedback, and a final role play. This training focused on the social skills such as making eye contact and speaking clearly that our initial assessment identified as lacking. Training was conducted in the situations that Felicia and her therapist identified as being problematic, for example, the role-play simulation we described earlier in which another youngster sits at Felicia's table in the school cafeteria.

The second part of the treatment focused on cognitive skills including general problem-solving skills, self-evaluation, and self-reinforcement. Felicia was taught to use certain cues that would prompt the correct use of her individual social skills in different situations—"What do I want to accomplish?" or "How do I do this now?" She also learned to evaluate the adequacy of her social behavior and whether she had improved on each social skill. To support Felicia's use of these strategies, a third behavioral component was included whereby Felicia could earn points for the accuracy of her judgments and the effectiveness of her social skills during the role plays. The results of the behavioral role-playing intervention for Felicia are shown in Figure 4.5.

Following treatment, Felicia began to show increased emotional expressiveness and social responsiveness at home. She smiled more and argued less with her parents. She also began to assert herself more appropriately. Attempts by her teacher to have her speak up in class were met with considerable success. Gradually, she began to engage in more interactions with other youngsters and to participate in activities. Her mood also began to brighten as she made efforts to initiate conversations and engage in more reciprocal interactions with other children, her teacher, and parents. At the end of the treatment program Felicia was more interactive and assertive and had learned to be more socially appropriate during interactions. She was less depressed and more animated.

One year following her treatment, Felicia reported no symptoms of depression and few feelings of hopelessness. She was attending school regularly, showed improved academic performance, and was participating in activities and interacting more with other children. In this example, a combined approach of cognitive-behavioral therapy, behavioral social skills training, and cognitive problem-solving training was successful in helping Felicia and her family. (Adapted from "Depression," by D. J. Kolko, 1987. In M. Hersen and V. B. Van Hasselt (Eds.), *Behavior Therapy with Children and Adolescents: A Clinical Approach*, pp. 163–164. Copyright © 1987 by John Wiley & Sons, Inc. Reprinted by permission of John Wiley & Sons, Inc.)

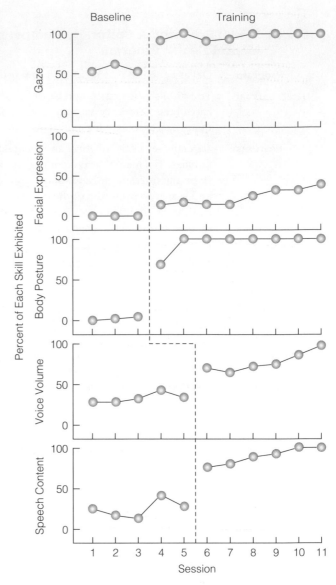

Figure 4.5. Results of behavioral role-play intervention (Kolko, 1987).

Source: From "Depression," by D. J. Kolko, 1987. In M. Hersen and V. B. Van Hasselt (Eds.), *Behavior Therapy with Children and Adolescents: A Clinical Approach*, p. 164. Copyright © 1987 by John Wiley & Sons, Inc. Reprinted by permission of John Wiley & Sons, Inc.

Treatment Effectiveness

Efforts to evaluate treatments for childhood disorders have intensified (Kazdin & Weisz, 2003; Weisz, Donenberg, Han, & Weiss, 1995), which allow us to take a closer look at the effectiveness of commonly used treatment methods.

Let's begin with the good news:

- Changes achieved by children receiving psychotherapy are consistently greater than changes for children not receiving therapy.

- The average child who is treated is better off at the end of therapy than at least 75% of those children who did not receive treatment.

- Treatments have been shown to be equally effective for children with internalizing and externalizing disorders.

- Treatment effects tend to be lasting, with the effects at follow-up (usually around 6 months after treatment) similar to those found immediately following treatment.

- Effects are about twice as large for problems that are specifically targeted in treatment as they are for changes in nonspecific areas of functioning. This result suggests that treatments are producing focused changes in targeted areas such as anxiety, rather than producing nonspecific or global effects such as changes in how the child feels (Kazdin, 1996b; Weisz, 1998; Weisz & Weiss, 1993).

- The more outpatient therapy sessions children receive, the more improvement is seen in their symptoms (Angold, Costello, Burns, Erkanli, & Farmer, 2000).

So what's the bad news? Although research findings present a generally positive picture of psychotherapy with children, and of behavioral and cognitive-behavioral approaches in particular, there are a number of important caveats.

First, we must be aware of the difference between research therapy that is carried out in laboratory outcome studies, and therapy that it is carried out in community-based clinics (Wagner, Swenson, & Henggeler, 2000). Most of the treatment outcome studies for specific disorders that we will discuss in this text fall into the category of research therapy. However, compared with research therapy, clinic therapy is typically conducted with more severe cases, directed at a heterogeneous set of problems and children, and carried out in clinic or hospital settings by professional career therapists with large caseloads (Weisz & Weiss, 1993). In general, clinic therapy is less structured and more flexible than research therapy, and uses proportionately more nonbehavioral methods, such as psychodynamic and eclectic approaches. In contrast to the findings for research therapy, similar analyses for studies of clinic therapy have resulted in minimal or no effects (Andrade, Lambert, & Bickman, 2000; Weiss, Catron, Harris, & Phung, 1999; Weisz, Donenberg, et al., 1995; for exceptions, see the study by Angold et al., 2000; and the meta-analytic review by Shadish, Matt, Navarro, & Phillips, 2000).

These findings suggest that conventional services for children may have limited effectiveness, and that integrating these commonly used interventions into more coordinated systems of care also shows minimal support for the beneficial effects of treatment (Weisz, 1998). However, few studies exist of child therapy outcomes in settings where it is typically conducted. Thus, it is premature to draw any conclusions from the findings from clinic and community studies until more empirical data about therapy in practice are available (Shadish et al., 1997).

SECTION SUMMARY

- Interventions for childhood disorders cover a wide range of strategies related to prevention, treatment, and maintenance.

- Treatment goals now include outcomes related to child and family functioning as well as those of societal importance.

- Both ethically and legally, clinicians who work with children are required to think not only about the impact that their actions will have on the children they see, but also on the responsibilities, rights, and relationships that connect children to their parents.

- A tremendous number and diversity of treatments for children and families now exist, including psychodynamic, behavioral, cognitive, cognitive-behavioral, client-centered, family, medical, and combined approaches.

- Integrative reviews of controlled treatment outcome studies have found that the changes achieved by children receiving therapy are consistently greater than changes for children not receiving therapy. However, these differences are not consistently found in studies of treatment outcomes based on clinic samples.

Key Terms

 InfoTrac College Edition

To research recent articles on the subject, go to:
www.infotrac-college/thomsonlearning.com

Enter search terms: BEHAVIORAL ASSESSMENT, BEHAVIOR THERAPY FOR CHILDREN, DIAGNOSIS OF MENTAL ILLNESS, PSYCHOLOGICAL TESTS FOR CHILDREN, CLINICAL INTERVIEWS, DIAGNOSTIC AND STATISTICAL MANUAL.

Attention-Deficit/ Hyperactivity Disorder (ADHD)

ADHD is not a problem with knowing what to do; it is a problem with doing what you know.

—Russell A. Barkley

John

Inattentive, Hyperactive, Impulsive

John is a 7-year-old whose mother is desperate for help. "He walked at 10 months and has kept me running ever since. As a child he was always bouncing around the house and crashing into things. He's in constant motion, impulsive, and never listens. When I ask him to put his shirt in the hamper, I find him playing, his shirt still on the floor. John has no routines and seldom sleeps. Discipline doesn't work, nor do the techniques that work for my other boys. He's oblivious to his behavior. He never finishes anything, and except for sitting down to play a video game, rarely watches TV except on the run."

John's teacher says his main problems in school are staying on task and keeping track of what's happening. "He blurts things out in class and is constantly fidgeting or out of his chair," she says. Although John can complete his assignments, he forgets to bring home the book he needs to do his homework. When he does complete his homework, he forgets to put it in his backpack or to hand it in. John has great difficulty waiting his turn or following rules with other children. Other kids think he's weird and don't want to play with him.

John's mother sought help after he gave his 2-year-old brother a book of matches and showed him how to strike them. Both parents are demoralized and don't know what to do. (Copyright © 1993 by Patricia Kennedy, Leif Terdal, and Lydia Fusetti. From *The Hyperactive Child Book*, by Patricia Kennedy, Leif Terdal, and Lydia Fusetti, pp. 8–9. Reprinted by permission of St. Martin's Press, Incorporated.)

Fidgety Phil, 1845

Dusty N., 1994

Mealtimes are an especially trying time for children with ADHD and their parents.

- *BEWARE LABELS FOR KIDS DOING BADLY IN SCHOOL, DOCTOR WARNS*
- *ATTENTION DEFICIT DISORDER LINKED TO GENE*
- *ESTABLISHMENT EDUCATORS PUSH DRUGS ON DISRUPTIVE FUSSY KIDS*

The above headlines reflect the enormous attention from media and science that ADHD has generated. They also preview the controversies, hopes, and disappointments about questions such as: What is ADHD? What causes it? How can we help these children?

Description and History

Description

Attention-deficit/hyperactivity disorder, or **ADHD,** describes children who display persistent age-inappropriate symptoms of inattention, hyperactivity, and impulsivity that are sufficient to cause impairment in major life activities (American Psychiatric Association [APA], 2000).

The term *ADHD* may be new, but children who display overactive and unrestrained behaviors have been around for some time. In 1845, Heinrich Hoffmann, a German neurologist, wrote in a child's storybook one of the first known accounts of hyperactivity. His humorous poem described the mealtime antics of a child aptly named "Fidgety Phil," who "won't sit still; / He wriggles, / And jiggles," and "Swings backwards and forwards, / And tilts up his chair." When his chair falls, Philip screams and grabs the tablecloth, and "Down upon the ground they fall, / Glasses, plates, knives, forks, and all" (Hoffmann, 1845).

In 1994, a compelling article about ADHD titled "Life in Overdrive" described the recent behavior of Dusty N.:

Dusty awoke at 5:00 one recent morning in his Chicago home. Every muscle in his 50-pound body flew in furious motion as he headed downstairs for breakfast. After pulling a box of cereal from the cupboard, Dusty started grabbing cereal with his hands and kicking the box, scattering the cereal across the room. Next he began peeling the decorative paper covering off the TV table. Then he started stomping the spilled cereal to bits. After dismantling the plastic dustpan he had gotten to clean up the cereal, he moved on to his next project: grabbing three rolls of toilet paper from the bathroom and unraveling them around the house (Adapted from *Time*, July 18, 1994, p. 43.)

Although Phil and Dusty are separated by more than 150 years, the mealtime behaviors of both boys typify the primary symptoms of ADHD. The boys are **inattentive**, by not focusing on demands and behaving carelessly, **hyperactive** by constantly being in motion, and **impulsive**, by acting without thinking.

ADHD has no distinct physical symptoms that can be seen in an X ray or a lab test. It can only be identified by characteristic behaviors that vary considerably from child to child. ADHD has become a blanket term used to describe several different patterns of behavior that differ slightly, and one day may prove to have different causes.

The behavior of youngsters with ADHD is puzzling and full of contradictions. Rash and disorganized behaviors are a constant source of stress for the child, and for parents, siblings, teachers, and classmates. Why can't he sit still? Why can't she ever get anything done? Why does he make so many careless mistakes? However, at certain times or in some situations, the child with ADHD seems fine. Such inconsistencies may cause others to think the child could do better if only she tried harder or if her parents or teachers would set firmer limits. However, increased effort and stricter rules usually don't help, because most children with ADHD are already trying hard. They want to do well but are constantly thwarted by their limited self-control. As a result, they experience the hurt, confusion, and sadness of being blamed for not paying attention, or being called names like "space cadet." They may be scolded, put down, or even spanked for failing to complete homework or chores. Unfortunately, they may not know why things went wrong or how they might have done things differently.

Feelings of frustration and hopelessness may overwhelm a child with ADHD. For example, David says: "I got no friends cause I don't play good and when they call me Dope Freak and David Dopey I cry, I just can't help it" (D. M. Ross & Ross, 1982). Such comments leave little doubt that ADHD can severely disrupt a child's life, consume vast amounts of energy, produce emotional pain, damage self-esteem, and seriously disrupt relationships.

History

Over the past 100 years, there have been numerous explanations for the troublesome behaviors of ADHD. In the early 1900s, compulsory education demanded self-controlled behavior in a group setting, and focused attention on children with the symptoms of ADHD (Hinshaw, 1994a). Symptoms of overactivity were first described as a disorder in 1902 by the English physician George Still (what a coincidence!), who believed the symptoms arose out of poor "inhibitory volition" and "defective moral control" (see Figure 5.1).

Another view of ADHD arose from the worldwide epidemic of encephalitis (inflammation of the brain) from

THE LANCET, APRIL 19, 1902.

The Goulstonian Lectures

ON

SOME ABNORMAL PSYCHICAL CONDITIONS IN CHILDREN.

Delivered before the Royal College of Physicians of London on March 4th, 6th, and 11th, 1902,

BY GEORGE F. STILL, M.A., M.D. CANTAB., F.R.C.P. LOND.,

ASSISTANT PHYSICIAN FOR DISEASES OF CHILDREN, KING'S COLLEGE HOSPITAL; ASSISTANT PHYSICIAN TO THE HOSPITAL FOR SICK CHILDREN, GREAT ORMOND-STREET.

———

LECTURE II.

Delivered on March 6th.

MR. PRESIDENT AND GENTLEMEN, — In my first lecture I drew your attention to some points in the psychology and development of moral control in the normal child and then considered the occurrence of defective moral control in association with general impairment of intellect; before going further it may be well to review briefly the points which have been raised. Moral control, we saw, is dependent upon three psychical factors, a cognitive relation to environment, moral consciousness, and volition, which in this connexion might be regarded as inhibitory volition. Moral control, therefore, is not present at birth, but under normal psychical conditions is gradually developed as the child grows older. The variation in the degree of moral control which is shown by different children at the same age and under apparently similar conditions of training and environment suggested that the innate capacity for the development of such control might also vary in different individuals.

Figure 5.1. The symptoms of ADHD were first described by the English physician George Still. (*Lancet,* April 19, 1902)

1917–26. For many child survivors, it caused multiple behavior problems, including irritability, impaired attention, and hyperactivity. These children and others who had suffered birth trauma, head injury, or exposure to toxins displayed behavior problems that were labeled *brain injured child syndrome*, which was associated with mental retardation. In the 1940s and 1950s this label was then applied to children displaying similar behaviors, but with no evidence of brain damage or retardation, and led to the terms *minimal brain damage* and *minimal brain dysfunction (MBD)* (A. A. Strauss & Lehtinen, 1947). These terms provided a convenient way to attribute behavior problems to a physical cause (Schachar, 1986). Although certain head injuries can explain some cases of ADHD, the brain damage theory was eventually rejected because it could explain only a few cases (Rie, 1980).

In the late 1950s, ADHD was referred to as *hyperkinesis*, which was attributed to the poor filtering of stimuli entering the brain (Laufer, Denhoff, & Solomons, 1957). This view led to the definition of the *hyperactive child syndrome*, in which motor overactivity was considered the main feature of ADHD (Chess, 1960). However, it was soon realized that hyperactivity was not the only problem, it was the child's failure to regulate motor activity in relation to situational demands.

In the 1970s, it was argued that in addition to hyperactivity, deficits in attention and impulse control were also primary symptoms of ADHD (Douglas, 1972). This theory was widely accepted and has had a lasting influence on the DSM criteria for defining ADHD. More recently, the symptoms of poor self-regulation and difficulty in inhibiting behavior have been emphasized as central impairments of the disorder (Barkley, 1997a; Douglas, 1999; Nigg, 2001). Although there is growing agreement about the nature of ADHD, views continue to evolve with new findings and discoveries (Barkley et al., 2002; Nigg, 2003).

SECTION SUMMARY

- Attention-deficit/hyperactivity disorder (ADHD) describes children who display persistent age-inappropriate symptoms of inattention and hyperactivity-impulsivity that cause impairment in major life activities.

- ADHD can only be identified by characteristic patterns of behavior, which vary quite a bit from child to child.

- The behavior of children with ADHD is a constant source of stress and frustration for the child, and for parents, siblings, teachers, and classmates.

- Over the past 100 years, numerous explanations have been used to explain the troublesome behaviors of ADHD.

- The disorder that we now call ADHD has had many different names, primary symptoms, and presumed causes, and views of the disorder are still evolving.

Core Characteristics

Experts developed the DSM-IV-TR criteria for ADHD after reviewing research and conducting field trials with children throughout North America (APA, 2000). Table 5.1 shows two lists of key symptoms were identified for defining ADHD and distinguishing it from related problems. The first list includes symptoms of inattention; the second list includes symptoms of hyperactivity-impulsivity. These two dimensions have now been well documented in research across various ethnic and cultural groups in North America and throughout the world (Burns, Boe, Walsh, Sommers-Flannagan, & Teegarden, 2001). However, to define the two dimensions of ADHD as inattention and hyperactivity-impulsivity oversimplifies the disorder. Each dimension includes many distinct processes that have been defined and measured in various ways.

Inattention (IA)

Lisa
Just Can't Focus

At age 17, Lisa still struggles to pay attention and act appropriately. But this has always been hard for her. She still gets embarrassed thinking about the time that her parents took her to a restaurant to celebrate her 10th birthday. She was so distracted by the waitress's bright red hair that her father had to call her name three times before she remembered to order. Then, before she could stop herself, she blurted, "Your hair dye looks awful!"

In school, Lisa was quiet and cooperative but often seemed to be daydreaming. She was smart, yet couldn't improve her grades no matter how hard she tried. Several times she failed exams. She knew the answers, but couldn't keep her mind on the test. Her parents responded to her low grades by taking away privileges and scolding her, "You're just lazy. You could get better grades if you only tried."

Lisa found it agonizing to do homework. Often, she forgot to plan ahead by writing down the assignment or bringing home the right books. And when trying to work, every few minutes she found her mind drifting to something else. As a result, she rarely finished and her work was full of errors. One day, after Lisa had failed yet another exam, her teacher found her sobbing, "What's wrong with me?" (Adapted from National Institute of Mental Health [NIMH], 1994a).

Children who are inattentive find it difficult, during work or play, to focus on one task or follow through on requests or instructions. While playing soccer, as the rest of the

Either (1) or (2):

(1) Six (or more) of the following symptoms of **inattention** have persisted for at least 6 months to a degree that is maladaptive and inconsistent with developmental level:

Inattention

(a) Often fails to give close attention to details or makes careless mistakes in schoolwork, work, or other activities

(b) Often has difficulty sustaining attention in tasks or play activities

(c) Often does not seem to listen when spoken to directly

(d) Often does not follow through on instructions and fails to finish schoolwork, chores, or duties in the workplace (not due to oppositional behavior or failure to understand instructions)

(e) Often has difficulty organizing tasks and activities

(f) Often avoids, dislikes, or is reluctant to engage in tasks that require sustained mental effort (e.g., schoolwork or homework)

(g) Often loses things necessary for tasks or activities (e.g., toys, school assignments, pencils, books, or tools)

(h) Is often easily distracted by extraneous stimuli

(i) Is often forgetful in daily activities

(2) Six (or more) of the following symptoms of **hyperactivity-impulsivity** have persisted for at least 6 months to a degree that is maladaptive and inconsistent with developmental level:

Hyperactivity

(a) Often fidgets with hands or feet or squirms in seat

(b) Often leaves seat in classroom or in other situations in which remaining seated is expected

(c) Often runs about or climbs excessively in situations in which it is inappropriate (in adolescents or adults, may be limited to subjective feelings of restlessness)

(d) Often has difficulty playing or engaging in leisure activities quietly

(e) Is often "on the go" or often acts as if "driven by a motor"

(f) Often talks excessively

Impulsivity

(g) Often blurts out answers before questions have been completed

(h) Often has difficulty awaiting turn

(i) Often interrupts or intrudes on others (e.g., butts into conversations or games)

Source: Reprinted with permission from *Diagnostic and Statistical Manual of Mental Disorders, DSM-IV-TR, Fourth Edition Text Revision.* Copyright 2000 by the American Psychiatric Association.

team heads downfield with the ball, the child with ADHD may get sidetracked by playing in a mud puddle. The child may attend automatically to enjoyable things, but have great difficulty focusing on new or less enjoyable tasks. Common complaints about inattention (IA) are that the child doesn't or won't listen, follow instructions, or finish chores or assignments (Barkley, 1998b). It is not sufficient to say that a child has an attention deficit when there are so many different types of attention (E. Taylor, 1995). The child could have a deficit in only one type or more than one type (Bjorklund, 1995).

Attentional capacity is the amount of information we can remember and attend to for a short time. When someone gives you directions or a phone number, how much information can you attend to and remember briefly? Children with ADHD do not have a deficit in their attentional capacity. They can remember the same amount of information for a short time as other children (E. Taylor, 1995).

Selective attention is the ability to concentrate on relevant stimuli and not be distracted by noise in the environment. When you're studying for a test (relevant stimuli), how easily are you distracted by voices in another room? **Distractibility** is a common term for a deficit in selective attention. Distractions can be disruptive to all children including those with ADHD. However, children with ADHD are much more likely than others to be distracted by stimuli that are *highly salient and appealing* (Milich & Lorch, 1994).

Sustained attention is the ability to maintain a persistent focus over time or when fatigued. When you're tired and have to study for a test, can you still pay attention until you've reviewed all the required material? The primary attention deficit in ADHD seems to be sustained attention (Douglas, 1972). When children with ADHD are assigned an uninteresting or repetitive task, their performance deteriorates over time compared to other children. Although no one likes to work on uninteresting tasks, most of us will when we have to. Children with ADHD may not be able to persist at a task even when they want to. They work best on self-paced tasks they have chosen—playing a computer game or building a model airplane—and on tasks they find especially interesting that do not require them to sustain their attention. Most situations, though, require sustained attention for successful performance, and many situations are not particularly interesting. As described in Box 5.1, a continuous performance test (CPT) can be used to assess sustained attention (and impulsivity).

Although findings may vary with the definitions and tasks used to assess sustained attention (Hinshaw, 1994a), deficits in this area remain one of the core symptoms of ADHD (Newcorn et al., 2001).

Hyperactivity-Impulsivity (HI)

Mark
Junior Wild Man

Mark, age 14, has more energy than most boys his age. But then, he's always been overactive. At age 3 he was a human tornado, dashing around and disrupting everything in his path. At home, he darted from one activity to the next, leaving a trail of toys behind him. At meals, he upset dishes and talked nonstop. He was reckless and impulsive, running into the street despite oncoming cars, no matter how often his mother explained the danger or scolded him. At the playground, his tendency to overreact—like socking playmates simply for bumping into him—had already gotten him into trouble several times. His parents didn't know what to do. Mark's doting grandparents reassured them, "Boys will be boys. Don't worry, he'll grow out of it." But he didn't. (Adapted from NIMH, 1994a)

Although the symptoms of hyperactivity and impulsivity are distinct in DSM, when children display one symptom they usually display another. These symptoms are best viewed as a single dimension of behavior called hyperactivity-impulsivity (HI) (Lahey, Pelham, et al., 1988). The strong link between hyperactivity and impulsivity suggests that both are part of a fundamental deficit in regulating behavior (Barkley, 1997a; Quay, 1997). There are also different types of HI (Nigg, 2000). For example, a child may be constantly out of his seat in the classroom because he can't control his motor behavior, because he wants to look outdoors, or because he is anxious about completing an assigned task. The main prob-

BOX 5.1 A Continuous Performance Test

In a continuous performance test (CPT), the child is presented with a series of stimuli, such as letters, that appear one at a time on a computer screen. The child is seated in front of the computer screen, and is instructed to press a button only when a certain letter follows another. In the following sequence, the child is instructed to press the button only when the letter *Z* immediately follows the letter *A* and not at any other time. If the child fails to press the button when *Z* follows *A*, this is an **error of omission (O)**, and a sign of inattention. If the child presses the button when *Z* does not follow *A*, this is an **error of commission (C)**, and a sign of impulsivity.

A A C Z A A A Z A A A A B Z A A A Z A B Z A A A Z
        O   O   O
   C   C   C

Children with ADHD typically make more errors of omission and commission than other children when performing on continuous performance tests.

lem in ADHD seems to be one of regulating motor behavior (Barkley, 2003; Nigg, 2001).

Hyperactivity   The image of a motor-driven ball of speed is the stereotype of a child with ADHD. Hyperactivity, or overactive behavior, takes many forms. Sitting still through a class lesson can be impossible for children with ADHD. They may fidget, squirm, climb, run about the room aimlessly, touch everything in sight, or noisily tap a pencil. Parents and teachers describe them as always on the go and talking incessantly. The activity is excessively energetic, intense, inappropriate, and not goal-directed. The children are extremely active, but unlike other children with a high energy level, they accomplish very little. Sophisticated recordings of body movements indicate that even when they sleep children with ADHD display more motor activity than other children (Teicher, Ito, Glod, & Barber, 1996). However, the largest differences are found in situations requiring the child to inhibit motor activity—to slow down or sit still in response to the structured task demands of the classroom.

Impulsivity   Children who are impulsive seem unable to bridle their immediate reactions or think before they act. They may take apart an expensive clock with little thought about how to put it back together. It's very hard for them to stop an ongoing behavior, or to regulate their behavior in accordance with demands of the situation or the wishes

Sitting through a class lesson is hard for a child with ADHD.

of others. As a result, they may blurt out inappropriate comments or give quick, incorrect answers to questions that are not yet completed. Because it is difficult to wait or take turns, they interrupt conversations, intrude on others' activities, and lash out in frustration when upset. They may also experience difficulty resisting immediate temptations and delaying gratification (Solanto et al., 2001). Minor mishaps are common, such as spilling drinks or knocking things over, but more serious accidents and injuries can result from reckless behavior, such as running into the street without looking.

Impulsivity may take different forms (Milich & Kramer, 1984):

- *Cognitive impulsivity:* Symptoms reflect disorganization, hurried thinking, and the need for supervision. Remember John not handing in his homework even though it was done?

- *Behavioral impulsivity:* Symptoms include calling out in class or acting without considering the consequences. Children who are behaviorally impulsive have difficulty inhibiting their response when the situation requires it. A child may touch a stove to see if it is hot when she is old enough to know better.

Cognitive and behavioral impulsivity (and inattention) predict problems with academic achievement, particularly in reading (Rabiner, Coie, & The Conduct Problem Prevention Research Group, 2000). However, only behavioral impulsivity predicts antisocial behavior, and thus may be a specific sign of increased risk for conduct problems (J. L. White et al., 1994; Willoughby, Curran, Costello, & Angold, 2000).

Methods have been developed that permit a precise assessment of the cognitive processes underlying ADHD. For example, the Stop Task, as described in Box 5.2, has

A Closer Look

BOX 5.2 **The Stop Task**

The Stop Task is a laboratory measure designed to simulate real-life activities that require quick and precise decision-making processes regarding the execution or inhibition of selected actions. The Stop Task consists of two components: a *go* response and a *stop* response.

Go trials: The subject is asked to focus on a computer-generated letter stimulus. Each letter is paired with a response button located on a response box that the subject holds. When either an *X* or *O* appears on the screen, the subject is asked to push the corresponding button on the response box.

Stop trials: At given times during the presentation of the letters, a tone known as a stop-signal will sound. The subject is instructed to withhold responding when the tone sounds.

Stop-signals are presented on one-quarter of all trials. Compared to children without ADHD, children with ADHD have more difficulty inhibiting their responses on the Stop trials. The task thus gives an accurate measure of the time required for a child to inhibit responses, and provides other measures such as processing speed and variability in response times.

Youngster performing on a Stop Task.

been developed to assess children's impulsivity. Further research will be needed to clarify whether performance deficits on this task are unique to children with ADHD (Oosterlaan, Logan, & Sergeant, 1998), and which elements of performance on the Stop Task best predict ADHD symptoms (Rucklidge & Tannock, 2002).

In summary, the core features of ADHD—IA and HI—are made up of many processes. Children with ADHD display a unique constellation and severity of symptoms but may not differ from comparison children on all types and measures of IA and HI. The primary attention deficit in ADHD is an inability to sustain attention and to follow through on directions or rules while resist-

Attention-Deficit/Hyperactivity Disorder (ADHD) **115**

ing salient distractions. The primary impairment in HI is an inability to voluntarily inhibit dominant or ongoing behavior. These specific types of deficits in IA and HI distinguish children with ADHD from normal children and from children with different disorders, and are not due to other psychiatric disorders or learning problems that may co-occur with ADHD (Barkley, 2003).

Subtypes

Since children with ADHD differ in many ways, investigators have become increasingly interested in identifying subtypes (Milich, Balentine, & Lynam, 2001). A subtype is a group of individuals with something in common—symptoms, etiology, problem severity, or likely outcome—something that makes them distinct from other groupings. DSM specifies three subtypes of ADHD based on primary symptoms.

- **Predominantly inattentive type (ADHD-PI)** describes children who primarily have symptoms of IA.
- **Predominantly hyperactive-impulsive type (ADHD-HI)** describes children who have primarily symptoms of HI.
- **Combined type (ADHD-C)** describes children who have symptoms of IA and HI.

Children with ADHD-PI ("pure" attention deficit) are described as inattentive and drowsy, daydreamy, spacey, in a fog, or easily confused. They may have a learning disability, process information slowly, and find it hard to remember things. They are often rated as anxious and apprehensive and may display mood disorders. Socially, they may be withdrawn, shy, or neglected (Barkley, 2003; Maedgen & Carlson, 2000).

Controversy.   There is vigorous debate on the inattentive subtype (PI) within the larger category of ADHD. Some argue that at least some children with ADHD-PI constitute a distinct subgroup, or perhaps have a completely different disorder than children with the ADHD-HI or ADHD-C (Barkley, 2001; Milich et al., 2001). These children appear to display different symptoms, patterns of stimulus processing, and associated conditions, with various family histories, outcomes, and responses to treatment (Barkley, 1998b; Johnstone, Barry, & Dimoska, 2003). Others contend that a distinction of subtypes is not yet warranted or useful (Hinshaw, 2001; Pelham, 2001). Despite these differences of opinion, there is some agreement that a subgroup of children *displaying only high levels of inattention associated with cognitive sluggishness and behavioral passivity* likely have an attention problem that differs from children with ADHD (Carlson & Mann, 2002; McBurnett, Pfiffner, & Frick, 2001). Thus, the ADHD-PI diagnosis as currently applied includes a di-

verse mix of children, some of whom may have a different attentional and cognitive problem.

In contrast to children who are predominantly IA, children in the ADHD-HI and ADHD-C subtypes are more likely to display problems in inhibiting behavior and in behavioral persistence (Nigg, Blaskey, Huang-Pollack, & Rappley, 2002). They are also most likely to be aggressive, defiant, rejected by peers, and suspended from school or placed in special education classes (Milich et al., 2001). Children with ADHD-C are the ones most often referred for treatment.

The ADHD-HI subtype is the rarest group. It is possible that the expression, impairment, and etiology for HI may be different when severe symptoms of IA are not also present (Chhabildas, Pennington, & Willcutt, 2001; Willcutt, Pennington, & DeFries, 2000). The ADHD-HI subtype primarily includes preschoolers and may have limited validity for older children. Since this group is usually younger than children with ADHD-C, it is not yet known whether they are actually two distinct subtypes, or the same children at different ages (Barkley, 2003).

The subtypes may differ in the components of ADHD that are affected. Preliminary findings suggest that children with ADHD-PI may have greater difficulty than children with ADHD-C with selective attention, retrieving verbal information from memory, and visual spatial deficits. In contrast, those with ADHD-C may experience greater difficulty with motor inhibition, sequencing, and planning (Barkley, 2003). However, different profiles for the two groups are not always found (Chhabildas et al., 2001), indicating that our knowledge of the different subtypes is still "under construction."

Most previous research has studied mixed groups of children with ADHD not broken out by subtype. It is extremely important to keep this in mind, since inconsistencies in the literature are often due to samples that mix together findings from different subtypes.

Additional DSM Criteria

Not every youngster who displays IA or HI behavior has ADHD. Most children blurt out things they didn't mean to say, jump from one activity to another, make careless mistakes, or become forgetful and disorganized at times. This doesn't mean they will have a lifelong disorder. To diagnose ADHD using DSM the behaviors must also:

- appear before age 7.
- occur more often and with greater severity than in other children of the same age and sex.
- be a persistent problem (for at least 6 months).
- occur across several settings and not only in one location (e.g., home and school).
- produce significant impairments in the child's social or academic performance.

Illnesses, accidents, middle ear infections, mild seizures, chronic abuse, or stressful life events such as a major move can mimic the symptoms of ADHD. A normally agreeable 9-year-old boy who becomes inattentive or argumentative immediately after the separation of his parents is likely having an adjustment reaction, not experiencing ADHD. The disruptive behaviors of children with mild mental retardation, learning disorders, or conduct problems may be mistaken for ADHD, as can the inattentive or restless behaviors of children with anxiety disorders. Before a diagnosis of ADHD is made, it is essential to carry out a thorough assessment that includes a developmental history, parent and teacher reports, normed assessment instruments, and behavioral observations. It is also important to investigate other possible reasons for the child's symptoms (American Academy of Pediatrics, 2000; Barkley, 1997b; Hechtman, 2000).

What DSM Criteria Don't Tell Us

The DSM criteria for ADHD have a number of limitations (Barkley, 2003):

- *Developmentally insensitive.* Although clinical judgment may be used to assess whether symptoms are "inconsistent with developmental level," DSM applies the same symptoms to individuals of all ages, even though some symptoms, particularly for HI (running and climbing), apply more to young children (Steinhausen, Dreschler, Foldenyi, Imhof, & Brandeis, 2003). Similarly, the number of symptoms needed to make a diagnosis is not adjusted for age or level of maturity, even though many children with HI show a general decline in symptoms with age.

- *Categorical view of ADHD.* According to DSM, ADHD is a disorder that a child either has or doesn't have. However, because the number and severity of symptoms are also calculated on a scale, children who fall just below the cutoff for ADHD are not necessarily different from children just above the cutoff. In fact, over time, some children may move in and out of the DSM category as a result of fluctuations in their behavior. Research supports the idea that ADHD is a dimensional rather than a categorical disorder, representing an extreme or delay in normal traits that all children possess to a degree (Levy & Hay, 2001). However, it may still be useful to talk about categories even when a disorder is of a continuous or changing nature. For example, there is no "magic" cutoff for high blood pressure, but most of us would agree that people with high blood pressure are at greater risk for certain negative outcomes.

- *Requirement of an onset before age 7 is uncertain.* Some studies find little difference between children with an onset of ADHD before or after age 7 (Barkley & Biederman, 1997), and about one-half of the children with ADHD-PI do not manifest the disorder until after age 7 (Applegate et al., 1997). It may be that the DSM requirement for age of onset may be useful for ADHD-C but not for ADHD-IA. Symptoms of IA typically show a later age of onset than those of HI (Willoughby et al., 2000).

- *Requirement of persistence for 6 months may be too brief for young children.* Many preschoolers display symptoms for 6 months that then go away.

- *Requirement that symptoms must be demonstrated across at least two environments confounds settings (home, school) with informants (parent, teacher).* The requirement that ADHD symptoms occur in at least two settings provides useful information about the pervasiveness of symptoms. However, it may unfairly limit diagnosis for some children as the result of differences of opinion between informants. At times, differences between parents and teachers may contribute more strongly to ratings of ADHD than do the child's actual symptoms (Gomez, Burns, Walsh, & Alvez de Moura, 2003). The most accurate identification of children with ADHD is best achieved by using multiple sources of information and blending parent and teacher reports, rather than requiring agreement (Crystal, Ostrander, Chen, & August, 2001; DuPaul, 2003).

SECTION SUMMARY

- DSM-IV-TR uses two lists of symptoms to define ADHD. The first list includes symptoms of inattention, poor concentration, and disorganization. The second list includes symptoms of hyperactivity-impulsivity.

- Children who are inattentive find it difficult to sustain mental effort during work or play, and to resist salient distractions while doing so.

- Children with ADHD are extremely active, but unlike other children with a high energy level, they accomplish very little.

- Children with ADHD are impulsive, which means they seem unable to bridle their immediate reactions or think before they act.

- DSM specifies three subtypes of ADHD based on primary symptoms of inattention, hyperactivity-impulsivity, or a combination of both.

- A diagnosis of ADHD requires the appearance of symptoms before age 7, a greater frequency and severity of symptoms than in other children of the same age and gender, persistence of symptoms, occurrence of symptoms in several settings, and impairments in functioning.

- Although useful, the DSM criteria have several limitations; an important one is developmental insensitivity.

Associated Characteristics

In addition to their primary difficulties, children with ADHD often display other problems. For example, Lisa was failing in school and Mark was getting into fights. In the sections that follow, we consider the characteristics and problems commonly associated with ADHD, including cognitive deficits, speech and language impairments, medical and physical concerns, and social problems.

Cognitive Deficits

Executive functions The control processes in the brain that activate, integrate, and manage other brain functions are called **executive functions** (Welsh & Pennington, 1988). They underlie the child's capacity for self-regulation, such as self-awareness, planning, self-monitoring, and self-evaluation (Pennington & Ozonoff, 1996). Like a symphony conductor whose artistic direction enables an orchestra to produce complex music, executive functions allow the brain to perform both routine and complex tasks (Brown, 2000). Executive functions are varied and include the following (Eslinger, 1996):

- *Cognitive processes*, such as working memory (holding facts in mind while manipulating information), mental computation, planning and anticipation, flexibility of thinking, and the use of organizational strategies
- *Language processes*, such as verbal fluency, communication, and the use of self-directed speech
- *Motor processes*, such as allocation of effort, following prohibitive instructions, response inhibition, and motor coordination and sequencing
- *Emotional processes*, such as self-regulation of arousal level, tolerating frustration, and mature moral reasoning

Children with ADHD consistently show deficits in one or more executive function (Pennington & Ozonoff, 1996). In fact, many of their symptoms of IA and HI seem to reflect impairments in the executive functions of working memory and response inhibition respectively.

Intellectual Deficits Most children with ADHD are of at least normal overall intelligence, and many are quite bright. Their difficulty is not in a lack of intelligence, but rather in applying their intelligence to everyday life situations (Barkley, 2003). As a result, the children never quite live up to their potential. They do score about 5 to 8 points lower on IQ tests than both control children and their own siblings (remember that most still have total IQ scores within the average or above-average range). Since IQ tests, like the WISC-IV, include subtests related to specific deficits of children with ADHD (e.g., working memory) their lower test scores are not surprising (Barkley,

1997d). In addition, lower IQ scores can be the direct result of ADHD symptoms on test-taking behavior. For example, children with ADHD do poorly on tests that require sustained attention (Anastopoulos, Spisto, & Maher, 1994). However, a child who scores lower on an IQ test because he or she is not paying attention to instructions is not necessarily less intelligent.

> **Ian**
> **School Misery**
>
> The days are overcast, cold, steel gray. I don't know what's going on at school. I'm failing everything. Throughout grade school some teachers made sincere efforts to help, others opted to pass me over, demanding little, expecting even less, and hoping for my eventual classroom conformity. Rote phrases I hear throughout my childhood are "Slow down Ian," or "Now remember Ian, you are fooling nobody but yourself." They were wrong. I never wanted to fool myself and I did not know how to slow down. Often I am sent out of the class for disruptive behavior . . . I knew that I had fallen so far behind the others that no amount of catching up would change the perceptions or expectations that others had of me. (From "Looking Back: Reminiscences from Childhood and Adolescence," by I. Murray, 1993, pp. 301–325. In G. Weiss and L. T. Hechtman (Eds.), *Hyperactive Children Grown Up: ADHD in Children, Adolescents and Adults*, 2nd ed. Copyright © 1993 Guilford Publications. Reprinted by permission.)

Impaired Academic Functioning Most children with ADHD experience severe difficulties in school, regardless of whether they have a specific learning disorder. They frequently have lower productivity, grades, and scores on achievement tests. They may also fail to advance in grade, or be placed more frequently in special education classes. Finally, they may be expelled or fail to finish high school (Fischer, Barkley, Edelbrock, & Smallish, 1990; G. Weiss & Hechtman, 1993). Particularly disturbing are findings that the academic skills of children with ADHD are impaired before they enter the first grade (Barkley, Shelton et al., 2002).

Learning Disorders Many children with ADHD have a specific learning disorder (see Chapter 11); that is, they have trouble with language or certain academic skills, typically reading, spelling, and math (Aaron, Joshi, Palmer, Smith, & Kirby, 2002; Cutting & Denckla, 2003; Tannock & Brown, 2000). When learning disorders are broadly defined as performance below expected grade level, nearly 80% of children with ADHD qualify for a learning disorder by late childhood (Cantwell & Baker, 1992). However, when defined more narrowly as a significant delay in reading, arithmetic, or spelling that is relative to the child's

The structured demands of the classroom can be painful for children with ADHD.

general intellectual functioning or low achievement in a specific academic subject(s), the number drops to 25% or less (Barkley, 1998b; Semrud-Clikeman et al., 1992).

Different pathways may underlie the association between ADHD and learning disorders. For example, the child's cognitive and intellectual deficits may directly lead to learning problems. ADHD may also predispose the child to conduct problems in school that may in turn result in poor academic performance (Rapport, Scanlan, & Denney, 1999). The association could also be due to a common genetic link, although findings suggest that the two disorders are transmitted independently (Doyle, Faraone, DuPre, & Biederman, 2001).

Distorted Self-Perceptions The many failures experienced by children with ADHD has led to the common belief that the children must suffer from low self-esteem—and there is some support for this (Treuting & Hinshaw, 2001). However, many children with ADHD report a higher self-esteem than is warranted by their behavior (Hoza, Perlham, Dobbs, Owen, & Pillow, 2002). For example, they may perceive their relationships with their parents no differently than do control children, even though their parents see things in a more negative light (Gerdes, Hoza, & Pelham, 2003). This exaggeration of one's competence is referred to as a **positive illusory bias.** Recent findings suggest that self-esteem in children with ADHD may vary with the subtype of ADHD, the accompanying disorders, and the area of performance being assessed (e.g., conduct, scholastic). Children with ADHD who display inattentive and depressive/anxious symptoms tend to report lower self-esteem, whereas children with symptoms

of hyperactivity-impulsivity and conduct problems appear to exaggerate their self-worth (Owens & Hoza, 2003). The bias in the latter group is most dramatic in the areas of performance that the child is most severely impaired.

Several explanations for the positive illusory bias in children with hyperactivity-impulsivity have been proposed—it serves a self-protective function that allows the child to cope every day despite frequent failures; it reflects a diminished self-awareness as a result of impairments in executive functions; or is a result of not knowing what constitutes successful or unsuccessful performance (Ohan & Johnston, 2002). One or more explanations will likely play a role.

Speech and Language Impairments

About 30% to 60% of children with ADHD also have impairments in their speech and language (N. J. Cohen et al., 2000; Tannock, 2000). In addition to a higher prevalence of formal speech and language disorders (see Chapter 11), they may have difficulties comprehending others' speech and using appropriate language in everyday situations (McInnes, Humphries, Hogg-Johnson, & Tannock, 2003). Excessive and loud talking, frequent shifts and interruptions in conversation, inability to listen, and inappropriate conversation are a few common examples of impairments.

Children with ADHD not only ramble on but also use fewer pronouns and conjunctions, making it difficult for the listener to understand who and what the child is talking about (Tannock, Purvis, & Schachar, 1993). They may also use unclear links in their conversation, requiring the listener to use information from another part of the conversation or from the surrounding context to understand. Can you understand the following statement by a boy with ADHD? (Words in capital letters indicate unclear links.)

And all of a sudden the soldiers—and all of a sudden HE gets faint and you know when HE says "Good doctors, I want to talk with you" and all of a sudden HE goes in THE DOOR and inside they come off IT from THE THING. So HE puts—I think THIS SOMETHING on THE DOORKNOB.   (Tannock, Fine, Heintz, & Schachar, 1995)

When links are unclear, as they are in this example, the listener must either make an inference about what the child means, or be left with an inadequate understanding. Unfortunately, miscommunication is all too common in children with ADHD.

Medical and Physical Concerns

Health Related Problems The association between ADHD and general health is not clear at this time (Barkley, 1998b; Daly et al., 1996). In terms of specific problems, some studies have reported higher rates of bed-wetting and related problems (Duel, Steinberg-Epstein, Hill, & Lerner, 2003). Sleep disturbances are also common in children with ADHD (Gruber, Sadeh, & Raviv, 2000; Prince et al., 1996). Resistance to going to bed, fewer total hours asleep, and involuntary sleep movements such as teeth grinding or restless sleep may be the most significant disturbances (Corkum, Tannock, & Moldofsky, 1998). Some of the sleep problems in children with ADHD may be related to their use of stimulant medications and/or co-occurring psychiatric disorders, rather than to only their ADHD (Mick, Biederman, Jetton, & Faraone, 2000).

Children with ADHD may display slight growth deficits in height through mid-adolescence, which appear unrelated to medication use, and seem to normalize by late adolescence suggesting a delay in development (Spencer et al., 1996). Thus, neither ADHD nor its treatment with stimulant medication are associated with harmful long-term effects on a child's growth (Biederman et al., 2003).

These children often display motor coordination difficulties, such as clumsiness, poor performance in sports, or poor handwriting, especially when they attempt to execute complex motor sequences (Gillberg, 2003a). An overlap exists between ADHD and **developmental coordination disorder (DCD)**, a condition characterized by marked motor incoordination (e.g., clumsiness and delays in achieving motor milestones) (Gillberg, 2003b). Some children with ADHD also have **tic disorders**—sudden, repetitive, nonrhythmic motor movements or phonic productions, such as eye blinking, facial grimacing, throat clearing, and grunting or other sounds. However, ADHD does not appear to increase the risk of a diagnosis of tic disorders in childhood. When they are present in a child, tic disorders decline to low rates by adolescence and do not significantly affect psychosocial functioning (Peterson, Pine, Cohen, & Brook, 2001; Spencer et al., 1999).

Accident-Proneness and Risk Taking   Given their problems with impulsivity, motor inhibition, and lack of planning and forethought, it is not surprising that over 50% of children with ADHD are described by their parents as accident-prone. These children are about three times more likely to experience serious accidental injuries, such as broken bones, lacerations, severe bruises, poisonings, or head injuries (Barkley, 1998b; Brehaut, Miller, Raina, & McGrail, 2003). The impulsivity and dangerous behaviors of children with ADHD may also place them at higher risk than others for experiencing trauma and subsequent post-traumatic stress disorder (Cuffe, McCullough, & Pumariega, 1994). Young adult drivers with ADHD are at higher risk than others for traffic accidents (Barkley, Murphy, DuPaul, & Bush, 2002; Nada-Raja et al., 1997).

ADHD is a significant risk factor for the early initiation of cigarette smoking (Burke, Loeber, & Lahey, 2001), substance abuse (Flory & Lynam, 2003; Molina & Pelham, 2003), and risky sexual behaviors such as mul-

tiple partners and unprotected sex (Barkley, Fisher, & Fletcher, 1997). These findings suggest a progression of hyperactive-impulsive behaviors during childhood to a pattern of irresponsible and risky adult behavior. (Some of these excesses may be due to co-occurring conduct problems.)

One longitudinal study spanning over a half century found that impulsive behavior was the most significant childhood characteristic that predicted reduced life expectancy (an average of 8 years less) (H. S. Friedman et al., 1995). A lifelong pattern of accident-proneness, auto accidents, and risk taking, combined with a reduced concern for health-promoting behaviors, such as exercise, proper diet, safe sex, and moderate use of tobacco, alcohol, and caffeine, may very well predict a reduced life expectancy for individuals with ADHD (Barkley, 1998b).

The need for further research into health-related problems in youngsters with ADHD is accentuated by recent findings that show they have significantly higher rates of inpatient and outpatient hospitalizations and emergency room visits. Average medical costs for youngsters with ADHD are more than double the costs for youngsters without ADHD (Leibson, Katusic, Barbaresi, Ransom, & O'Brien, 2001) and at least comparable to the costs for children with asthma (Chan, Zhan, & Homer, 2002). In the United States alone, the costs of health care for children with ADHD are estimated to be more than 2 billion dollars annually (Burd, Klug, Coumbe, & Kerbeshian, 2003).

Social Problems

> ### Dennis
> **Nothing Sticks**
>
> With my other children, I could tell them one time, "Don't do that," and they would stop. But Dennis, my child with ADHD, I could tell him a hundred times, "Dennis, don't carve soap with my potato peeler," "Don't paint the house with used motor oil," or "Don't walk on Grandma's white sofa in your muddy shoes," but he still does it. It's like every day is a brand new day and yesterday's rules are long forgotten . . . I just cannot stay one step ahead of him. He does things my other kids never thought of. (Copyright © 1993 by Patricia Kennedy, Leif Terdal, and Lydia Fusetti. From *The Hyperactive Child Book*, by Patricia Kennedy, Leif Terdal, and Lydia Fusetti, p. 80. Reprinted by permission of St. Martin's Press, Incorporated.)

Social problems in family life and at school are common in children with ADHD. Those who experience the most severe social disability are at greatest risk for poor adolescent outcomes and other disorders such as depression and conduct disorder (Greene et al., 1996). Children with ADHD don't listen and are often hostile, argumentative, unpredictable, and explosive. As a result, they are in frequent conflict with adults and other children. It is common for a child with ADHD to be removed from swimming lessons because of disruptive behavior, or to be kicked out of gymnastics. For one child taking dance lessons, the teachers offered to buy back her shoes if only her parents would take her out!

To get along with others you must follow social rules and respect conventions. Children with ADHD do not play by the same rules as others and don't seem to learn from past mistakes, despite their awareness of expected social behaviors and a desire to conform to them. Many social blunders by children with ADHD appear more thoughtless than intentional. Even with good intentions, their behaviors have an annoying quality and are a source of great distress for their parents, siblings, teachers, and classmates. In the words of one mother: *Our grade one parent interview was highly traumatic; her teacher cried!*

Ian

Sibling Conflict

Ian talks about his siblings: "When I see Andrea and David talking seriously to each other, or sharing secrets or activities, I feel left out and cheated. Sometimes, Andrea bellows out that someone has been in her room because things are not as she left them. She says, 'Look, even my drawers have been gone through. Ian, it's you. Who else could it be? Stay out of my g_ddam room, do you understand? I can't keep anything without you getting your grubby little fingers on it.' I refuse to admit my culpability and adamantly swear up and down that I wasn't in her room. Besides, it could have been someone else." (From "Looking Back: Reminiscences from Childhood and Adolescence," by I. Murray, 1993, pp. 301–325. In G. Weiss and L. T. Hechtman (Eds.), *Hyperactive Children Grown Up: ADHD in Children, Adolescents and Adults,* 2nd ed. Copyright © 1993 Guilford Publications. Reprinted by permission.)

Family Problems Families of children with ADHD experience many difficulties, including interactions characterized by negativity, child noncompliance, high parental control, and sibling conflict (Mash & Johnston, 1982; Whalen & Henker, 1999). Parents may experience high levels of distress and related problems, which are most commonly depression in mothers and antisocial behavior, such as substance abuse, in fathers. Further stress on family life stems from the fact that parents of children with ADHD may themselves have ADHD and other associated conditions (C. Johnston & Mash, 2001). This can also be a barrier to effective treatment (Sonuga-Barke, Daley, & Thompson, 2002).

Conflict between these children and their mothers is severe during the preschool years and continues into childhood and adolescence (DuPaul, McGoey, Eckert, & VanBrakle, 2001). Conflict with fathers is less frequent, but still greater than between other children and fathers (Edwards, Barkley, Laneri, Fletcher, & Matevia, 2001). Mother–child conflict during early childhood is a significant predictor of parent–adolescent conflict 8 to 10 years later (Barkley, Fischer, Edelbrock, & Smallish, 1991). It also predicts child noncompliance in play settings, stealing outside of the home, and disobedience in the classroom (Whalen & Henker, 1999).

Interestingly, mothers tend to interact similarly with their children without ADHD as they do with their child with ADHD (Tarver-Behring, Barkley, & Karlsson, 1985). These findings suggest that problems in the family are not restricted to situations that directly involve the child with ADHD, but may spill over into other family interactions. When interviewed, siblings of children with ADHD report that they feel victimized by their ADHD sibling, and that this experience is often minimized or overlooked by the family (J. Kendall, 1999).

Families of children with ADHD also report more maternal mental health problems (Lesesne, Visser, & White, 2003), greater parenting stress and less parenting competence (Mash & Johnston, 1983), fewer contacts with extended family members, greater caregiver strain (Bussing et al., 2003), less instrumental support, and slightly higher rates of marital conflict, separation, and divorce (Barkley, 1998b; C. Johnston & Mash, 2001). Parents of these children also show increased alcohol consumption that in some instances could be a direct result of stressful interactions with their children (Pelham & Lang, 1999).

It is important to note that high levels of family conflict, and the links between ADHD and parental psychopathology and marital discord in many cases are due to the child's co-occurring conduct problems rather than to ADHD alone (C. Johnston & Mash, 2001; see Chapter 6).

Things I've learned from my ADHD Child (honest and no kidding)

"If you hook a dog leash over a ceiling fan, the motor is not strong enough to rotate a 42 pound boy wearing a Batman underwear and a Superman cape."

"It is strong enough, however, if tied to a paint can, to spread paint on all four walls of a 20 × 20 foot room."

(An anonymous mother in Austin, Texas)

Peer Problems Children and adolescents with ADHD display little of the give-and-take that characterizes other children (Henker & Whalen, 1999). Although there is much variation in how difficulties with peers are expressed, we also find some common features (Whalen & Henker, 1992). Children with ADHD can be bothersome, stubborn, socially awkward, and socially insensitive. Others describe them as socially conspicuous, loud, intense, and quick to react. They are socially active, but usually "off the mark" with respect to the style, content, or timing of their behavior, which often has an annoying quality that brings out the worst in other children. Children with ADHD seem to get into trouble even when trying to be helpful, and although their behavior seems thoughtless, it is often unintentional. They rate their own behavior more favorably than it is perceived by others, and may be puzzled by others' negative reactions.

In light of these characteristics, it is not surprising that children with ADHD are disliked and uniformly rejected by peers, have few friends, are often unhappy, and report receiving low social support from peers (Demaray & Elliot, 2001; Gresham, MacMillan, Bocian, Ward, & Forness, 1998). Their difficulties in regulating emotions (Melnick & Hinshaw, 2000) and the aggressiveness that frequently accompanies ADHD lead to conflict and a negative reputation (Erhardt & Hinshaw, 1994). However, even nonaggressive children with ADHD experience disapproval by peers (Milich & Landau, 1989). Stimulant medications that decrease the negative behaviors of children with ADHD may not improve social behavior or acceptance, because medication alone does not increase the child's social competence or change a bad reputation.

Interestingly, children with ADHD are not deficient in social reasoning or understanding (Whalen & Henker, 1992). They simply don't apply their knowledge during social exchanges, and continue to be dominant or assertive even after the situation changes and requires accommodation, negotiation, or submission (Landau & Milich, 1988). Their social agenda may also differ from the agenda of their peers, especially when ADHD is accompanied by aggression. They may actually value and prefer troublemaking, sensation seeking, and fun at the expense of following rules and getting along with others (Melnick & Hinshaw, 1996).

SECTION SUMMARY

- Besides their primary difficulties, children with ADHD display other problems such as cognitive deficits, speech and language impairments, medical and physical concerns, and social problems.

- Children with ADHD display deficits in executive functions, the higher-order mental processes that underlie the child's capacity for planning and self-regulation.

- Children with ADHD score slightly lower on IQ tests, but most are of normal intelligence. Their difficulty is in applying their intelligence to certain everyday life situations.

- Children with ADHD experience school performance difficulties including lower grades, a failure to advance in grade, and more frequent placements in special education classes.

- Many children with ADHD have a specific learning disorder, typically in reading, spelling, or math.

- Some children with ADHD report a higher self-esteem than is warranted by their behavior, referred to as a positive illusory bias.

- They often have speech and language impairments, and have difficulty using language in everyday situations.

- They may experience health-related problems, especially sleep disturbances, and are accident-prone.

- They experience numerous social problems with family members, teachers, and peers.

Accompanying Psychological Disorders and Symptoms

One reason that ADHD is so challenging is that as many as 80% of children with ADHD have a co-occurring psychological disorder (Kadesjo & Gillberg, 2001; Pliszka, 2000), such as oppositional and conduct disorders (particularly for children with ADHD-C), anxiety, and mood disorders. As we noted previously, learning disorders and motor coordination problems are also quite common.

Oppositional Defiant Disorder and Conduct Disorder

Shawn
Bad Boy

Shawn, an energetic and talkative 29-year-old, recalls his childhood as a total disaster: "I did really bad in school. My parents and teachers were always on my back. They bugged me about being a bully—too aggressive, too explosive, too loud, and too defiant. I had no friends. Then I began to use drugs: marijuana, and later, cocaine. I barely managed to squeak through high school. I couldn't concentrate at all. I'd study for hours and then forget everything I'd read. I had to cheat my way through high school."

About one-half of all children with ADHD—mostly boys—meet criteria for oppositional defiant disorder (ODD) by age 7 or later (Biederman, Faraone, & Lapey, 1992). Children with ODD overreact by lashing out at adults and other kids. They are stubborn, short-tempered, and combative. About 30% to 50% of children with ADHD eventually develop conduct disorder (CD) (Waschbusch, 2002), a condition that is more severe than ODD. Children with CD violate societal rules and are at high risk for getting into serious trouble at school or with the police. They may fight, cheat, steal, set fires, destroy property, or use illegal drugs. Early occurring ADHD, particularly when severe symptoms of hyperactivity-impulsivity are present, is one of the most reliable predictors of ODD and CD (Burns & Walsh, 2002; Connor et al., 2003).

ADHD, ODD, and CD run in families, which suggests a common predisposing cause (Biederman et al., 1992). In support of this, there is a substantial common genetic contribution for the three disorders, especially between ADHD and ODD (Coolidge, Thede, & Young, 2000). There is also evidence for contribution from a shared environment, perhaps related to family adversity and deficits in parenting (Burt, Krueger, McGue, & Iacono, 2001; Patterson, Degarmo, & Knutson, 2000).

The frequent co-occurrence of ADHD and ODD/CD has led some to suggest an aggressive subtype of ADHD (Faraone, Biederman, & Monuteaux, 2000). The rationale for this subtype is that the presence of accompanying ODD/CD fundamentally alters the clinical expression, course, outcome, and response to treatment of ADHD. In support of this idea, children with ADHD and ODD/CD display specific brain correlates, have more severe deficits in verbal ability and memory, and worse outcomes in terms of substance abuse and driving-related accidents. They also respond more poorly to stimulant medication than children with only one disorder (P. S. Jensen, Martin, & Cantwell, 1997). A comprehensive review of the evidence to date suggests that co-occurring ADHD and CD is an additive combination of the two disorders, rather than a qualitatively different subtype (Waschbusch, 2002). This issue is yet to be resolved (Banaschewski et al., 2003).

"Sam, neither your father nor I consider your response appropriate."

Anxiety Disorders

T. J.

Overactive and Anxious

T. J. was first referred for help at age 6. He had been very active and impulsive since he was a toddler. His parents reported that he had trouble sleeping and would wake up several times each night. They also said that he showed great anxiety during even brief separations from them and seemed to be worrying about something the whole time. T. J. confirmed that he had "terrible bad dreams" and felt that no one liked him. (Adapted from Tannock, 2000)

About 25% of clinic-referred children with ADHD—usually younger boys—experience excessive anxiety (Tannock, 2000). These children worry about being separated from their parents, trying something new, taking tests, making social contacts, or visiting the doctor. They may feel tense or uneasy and constantly seek reassurance that they are safe and protected. Because their anxieties are unrealistic, more frequent, and more intense than normal, they have a negative impact on the child's thinking and behavior.

Interestingly, the overall relationship between ADHD and anxiety disorders is reduced or eliminated during adolescence. It is possible that the co-occurrence of an anxiety disorder may inhibit the adolescent with ADHD from engaging in the impulsive behaviors that characterize other youngsters with ADHD (Pliszka, 1992). The link between ADHD and anxiety disorders appears to be strongest for the predominantly inattentive subtype, ADHD-PI (Milich et al., 2001). Consistent with this, children having a later age of ADHD onset display more symptoms of anxiety than children having an earlier age of onset (Conner et al., 2003). Studies are needed that examine ADHD in relation to specific types of anxiety disorders (e.g., social phobia, obsessive-compulsive disorder; see Chapter 7).

Mood Disorders

As many as 20–30% of children with ADHD experience depression (Spencer, Wilens, Biederman, Wozniak, & Harding-Crawford, 2000). Even more will develop depression or another mood disorder by early adulthood, especially when ADHD is accompanied by a conduct disorder (Fischer, Barkley, Smallish, & Fletcher, 2002). These youngsters feel so hopeless and overwhelmed that they are unable to cope with everyday life. Depression lowers self-esteem, increases irritability, and disrupts sleep, appetite and the ability to think (Mick, Santangelo, Wypij, & Biederman, 2000). The association between ADHD and depression may be a function of family risk for one disorder increasing risk for the other (Faraone & Biederman, 1997). This suggests that depression in a child with ADHD is not due solely to the child's demoralization as a result of their symptoms (Biederman, Mick, & Faraone, 1998). Similarly, depression in mothers of these children is not due entirely to the cumulative stress of raising a child with ADHD (Faraone & Biederman, 1997).

Controversy abounds regarding the association between ADHD and bipolar (BP) [manic-depressive] mood disorder (Geller & Luby, 1997; Kent & Craddock, 2003). Although findings are mixed, the relationship between the two disorders seems to go in one direction—a diagnosis of childhood BP sharply increases the child's risk for previous or co-occurring ADHD, but a diagnosis of ADHD does not appear to increase the child's risk for BP (Barkley, 2003; Spencer, Wilens et al., 2000). Children with both ADHD and BP have an increased prevalence of BP in their biological relatives, and an earlier age of BP onset than children with BP alone (Faraone, Biederman, & Manuteaux, 2001). Thus, children with both disorders may represent a distinct subgroup of children with ADHD with a genetic risk for BP (Faraone, Glatt, & Tsuang, 2003). It is also possible that some of the overlap between ADHD and BP is an artifact of using similar symptoms in making both DSM diagnoses, such as hyperactivity and distractibility.

SECTION SUMMARY

- A factor that makes ADHD so challenging is that children with the disorder have much higher than expected rates of other psychiatric disorders, particularly conduct problems, anxiety, and mood disorders.

- Many children with ADHD also meet criteria for oppositional defiant disorder and conduct disorder.

- About 25% of children with ADHD experience excessive anxiety. The presence of anxiety may inhibit impulsive behaviors that characterize other youngsters with ADHD.

- Many children with ADHD experience depression. Although depression may be partly related to their demoralization as a result of their symptoms, it also can result from an elevated risk for depressive disorders in families of children with ADHD.

- The relation between ADHD and bipolar disorder (BP) is controversial. A diagnosis of childhood BP appears to sharply increase the child's risk for previous or co-occurring ADHD, but a diagnosis of ADHD does not appear to increase the child's risk for BP.

Prevalence and Course

ADHD affects millions of children throughout the world and across all socioeconomic levels. Although rates vary widely with sampling methods, the best estimate is that about 3% to 5% of all school-age children in North America have ADHD, about one child in every classroom (Briggs-Gowan, Horwitz, Schwab-Stone, Leventhal, & Leaf, 2000). As many as one-half of all children referred to clinics display ADHD symptoms either alone or in combination with other disorders, making ADHD one of the most common referral problems in North America and elsewhere (Barkley, 1998b).

Reports of parents, teachers, and doctors are all used to identify children with ADHD. However, these people don't always agree, because the child's behavior may differ from setting to setting. Also, different adults may emphasize different symptoms when making a judgment. Teachers, for example, are most likely to rate a child as inattentive when oppositional symptoms are also present (Abikoff, Courtney, Pelham, & Koplewicz, 1993). Their ratings of ADHD are better predictors of later antisocial outcomes than are ratings by parents (Mannuzza, Klein, & Moulton, 2002). Prevalence rates and patterns of comorbidity also differ when teacher reports are compared with parent's reports (Gadow & Nolan, 2002). Since adults may disagree, prevalence estimates are much higher when based on one person's opinion rather than based on a consensus (N. M. Lambert, Sandoval, & Sassone, 1978).

Gender

ADHD occurs more frequently in boys than in girls, with estimates ranging from 2% to 4% for girls and 6% to 9% for boys 6 to 12 years of age (Breton et al., 1999). In adolescence, overall rates of ADHD drop for both boys and girls, but boys still outnumber girls by the same ratio of about 3:1. This ratio is even higher in clinic samples, where boys outnumber girls by 6:1 or higher (Lahey, Miller, Gordon, & Riley, 1999). Boys with ADHD are probably referred more often than girls, because of their defiance and aggression. Interestingly, when girls with ADHD also display oppositional symptoms, they are referred at a younger age than boys, a finding that implies lower tolerance by adults or a greater concern for these behaviors when they occur in girls (Silverthorn, Frick, Kuper, & Ott, 1996).

It is possible that ADHD in girls may go unrecognized and unreported because teachers may fail to recognize and report inattentive behavior unless it is accompanied by the disruptive symptoms normally associated with boys (McGee & Feehan, 1991). In addition, the symptoms used to diagnose ADHD may also contribute to the sex difference in prevalence. DSM criteria were developed and tested mostly with boys with ADHD, and many of the specified symptoms, such as excessive running around, climbing, and blurting out answers in class, are generally more common in boys than girls. Thus, the specified cut-offs and symptoms may be more appropriate to boys than girls, because girls with ADHD may have to display not only extreme behavior but also uncharacteristic behavior of their same-sex peers before they will be referred (Barkley, 2003).

Girls with ADHD may be more likely than boys to display inattentive/disorganized symptoms characteristic of a sluggish cognitive tempo including: forgetfulness, sluggishness, drowsiness, tendency to daydream, (McBurnett et al., 2001), anxiety, depression (Rucklidge & Tannock, 2001), and hyperverbal rather than hyperactive motor behavior (Nadeau, Littman, & Quinn, 1999). Thus, current DSM criteria may be insensitive to the problems that are especially relevant to girls. Although it may be premature to expand the current symptom lists for ADHD to include additional items appropriate to girls, it is clear that sampling, referral, and definition biases may all contribute to reports of the prevalence of ADHD as higher in boys than girls. The extent to which they can *explain* this difference is not known at this time.

Compared to girls without ADHD, those with the disorder are more likely to have conduct, mood, and anxiety disorders; higher rates of verbal aggression; lower IQ and school achievement scores; and greater impairment on measures of social, school, and family functioning (Abikoff et al., 2002; Gaub & Carlson, 1997b; Hartung et al., 2002). Girls who meet criteria for ADHD in community samples tend to be less impaired than boys with ADHD with respect to their core symptoms and accompanying academic and social difficulties (Gershon, 2002). Girls are also less likely to receive treatment with stimulant medication (Angold, Erkanli, Egger, & Costello, 2000), perhaps due to sociocultural attitudes that during childhood medications are a less appropriate treatment for girls than boys (Hinshaw & Blachman, in press).

However, among clinic-referred school-age children with ADHD, boys and girls have been found to be quite similar with respect to their expression and severity of symptoms, brain abnormalities, deficits in response inhibition, level of impairment, family correlates, and response to treatment (Gershon, 2002; Hill et al., 2003; E. B. Owens, et al., 2003; Rucklidge & Tannock, 2002). When sex differences are found in clinic samples, boys show more hyperactivity, aggression, and antisocial behavior, whereas girls show more symptoms of inattention, anxiety, depression, stress, poorer verbal abilities, and lower IQ scores (Gaub & Carlson, 1997b; Rucklidge & Tannock, 2001). Notwithstanding these differences, ADHD

Girls with ADHD may be described by their teachers as "spacey" or "in a fog." Without hyperactivity and disruptive behavior, ADHD in girls may go unrecognized or be ignored.

in girls is a significant disorder with most of the same features seen in boys with ADHD (Biederman et al., 2002; Hinshaw & Blachman, in press).

Differences in findings for community versus clinic samples suggest that girls who are referred for treatment may be the most severely affected and may not represent the larger group of girls with ADHD. Consistent with this, clinic-referred girls with ADHD appear to have a poorer adult outcome than boys with ADHD (Dalsgaard, Mortensen, Frydenberg, & Thomson, 2002). It is possible that a substantial number of girls with ADHD who are not referred as children may develop more severe problems as adolescents or adults as they encounter more stress, or as their symptoms of inattention become more salient (Nadeau et al., 1999). Prospective studies of girls using community samples that consider subtypes of ADHD (particularly the inattentive type) are needed to address these issues.

Culture and Ethnicity

ADHD affects children from all social classes, although there are slightly more children with ADHD in lower SES groups than in higher groups (Szatmari, 1992). Such differences are best accounted for by the presence of co-occurring conduct problems in children with ADHD (Szatmari, Offord, & Boyle, 1989). Conduct problems are known to be associated with the conditions that often accompany low SES—for example, family adversity and stress.

ADHD has been identified in every country around the world where it has been studied. Estimates of the prevalence of ADHD across countries and cultures vary: 2% in Japan, 5% in China, 15% in the United Arab Emirates, 20% in Italy and the Ukraine, and over 29% in India (Barkley, 2003). These variations clearly reflect differences in the ages and sex of the children studied and the different ways ADHD has been defined across many countries. For example, the prevalence of ADHD is extremely low in England because the label has been narrowly used to describe children who display excessive motor overactivity that is pervasive across situations and excludes children who display conduct disorders (Pendergrast et al., 1988).

Differences across cultures may also reflect varying cultural norms and tolerance for the symptoms of ADHD (Weisz, Weiss, Suwanlert, & Chaiyasit, 2003). In cultures that value reserved and inhibited patterns of child behavior, such as Thailand, symptoms of ADHD are less common than in the United States. Moreover, when ADHD symptoms do occur, teachers in Thailand view them as more problematic—likely due to their culture-linked values and expectations (Weisz, Chayasit, Weiss, Eastman, & Jackson, 1995). Clearly, ADHD is a universal phenomenon that is reported to occur more frequently in boys than girls in all cultures.

Course and Outcome

In the sections that follow, we describe how symptoms of ADHD change with development (Campbell, 2000a; Willoughby, 2003). These symptoms are illustrated with Alan, now age 35, diagnosed with ADHD in grade 1.

> **Alan**
>
> **Off and Running**
>
> Our baby-sitter swears I was sitting up watching TV by 4 months. Then from a crawling position I ran, and we were off . . . I was all over the house, into everything, and Mom soon realized I could not be left alone. Darting here, there, and anywhere, I didn't like playing with my toys, preferring to explore on my own. (From a chapter by R. A. Barkley and L. J. Pfiffner in *Taking Charge of ADHD: The Complete, Authorized Guide for Parents*, by R. A. Barkley, 1995, p. 208. Copyright © 1995 by Guilford Publications.)

Infancy It is likely that ADHD is present at birth (one mother reported her child was so overactive in the womb that the kicking nearly knocked her over!). However, we don't know the precise form it takes during infancy because there are no reliable and valid methods to identify ADHD prior to age 3. When parents of an older child with ADHD describe what their child was like as a baby, they often say the infant had a difficult temperament—extremely active, unpredictable, over- or undersensitive to stimulation, and irritable with erratic sleep patterns or feeding difficulties. Although these reports suggest the early presence of ADHD, there are two problems with the interpretation. First, parents' recollections may be colored by their child's later difficulties. Second, most infants with a difficult temperament do not develop ADHD. Although a difficult temperament in infancy may indicate something amiss in development, and in some cases may be a risk factor for later ADHD, it cannot by itself be taken as an early sign of ADHD. For example, one study reported an association between persistent crying during infancy and a ten-fold higher risk for hyperactivity at 8 to 10 years of age (Wolke, Rizzo, & Woods, 2002). However, most infants who cry persistently do not go on to develop ADHD.

> **Alan**
>
> **Preschool Outcast**
>
> I often wondered why I wasn't in group time in preschool. The teacher sent me in the corner to play with a toy by myself. Because of being singled out I didn't have many friends. I was different, but I didn't know why or what it was. (From a chapter by R. A. Barkley and L. J. Pfiffner in *Taking Charge of ADHD: The Complete, Authorized Guide for Parents*, by R. A. Barkley, 1995, p. 208. Copyright © 1995 by Guilford Publications.)

Preschool With the appearance of hyperactive-impulsive symptoms at 3 to 4 years of age, ADHD becomes increasingly visible (Hart, Lakey, Loeber, Applegate, & Frick, 1996). Preschoolers with ADHD act suddenly without thinking, dashing from activity to activity, grabbing at immediate rewards; they are easily bored and react strongly and negatively to routine events (Barkley, DuPaul, & McMurray, 1990; S. B. Campbell, 2002). Parents find it very difficult to manage the hyperactivity and noncompliance of their child, who may also be defiant and aggressive (Mash & Johnston, 1982; Gadow & Nolan, 2002). Preschoolers with ADHD often roam about the classroom, talking excessively and disrupting other children's activities. Those who display a persistent pattern of hyperactive-impulsive and oppositional behavior for at least 1 year are likely to continue on to difficulties into middle childhood and adolescence (Olson, Bates, Sandy, & Lanthier, 2000). At this age the combination of severe ADHD-related symptoms and disruptions in the parent–child relationship are especially predictive of continuing ADHD behavior patterns (S. B. Campbell, Shaw, & Gilliom, 2000).

Toward the middle half of first grade the teacher called my Mom in for a conference. She was telling my Mom, "I'm always having to call on Alan. 'Alan, be still. Please. Yes, you can sharpen your pencil for the third time. You have to go to the bathroom again?'" By the time I got to third grade things were getting off track. I felt like nothing I did was right. I would try to do good work. My teacher would write on my papers, "Needs to concentrate more on answers," "Needs to turn in all work," "Needs to follow directions." I really didn't think my teacher liked me. She was very stern, never seemed to smile, and was always watching me. (From a chapter by R. A. Barkley and L. J. Pfiffner in *Taking Charge of ADHD: The Complete, Authorized Guide for Parents,* by R. A. Barkley, 1995, p. 208. Copyright © 1995 by Guilford Publications.)

Elementary School   Symptoms of inattention emerge at 5 to 7 years of age, becoming especially evident when the child starts school (Hart et al., 1996). Classroom demands for sustained attention and goal-directed persistence are formidable challenges for these children. Not surprisingly, this is when they are usually identified as having ADHD and referred for special assistance. Symptoms of inattention continue through grade school, resulting in low academic productivity, distractibility, poor organization, trouble meeting deadlines, and an inability to follow through on social promises or commitments to peers (Barkley, 2003). The hyperactive-impulsive behaviors that were present in preschool continue, with some decline, from 6 to 12 years of age.

During elementary school, oppositional defiant behaviors may increase or develop (Barkley, 1998b). By 8 to 12 years of age, defiance and hostility may take the form of serious problems, such as lying or aggression. During the school years, ADHD increasingly takes its toll as children experience problems with self-care, personal responsibility, chores, trustworthiness, independence, social relationships, and academic performance (Koplowicz & Barkley, 1995; Stein, Szumoski, Blondis, & Roizen, 1995).

It wasn't until Alan was 13 that I understood that ADHD was a lifelong condition. His inability to block out the high level of activity in junior high caused him to become a frequent visitor to the principal's office. And he began to do poorly in math, the subject he had always done well at, because he couldn't concentrate on all the steps involved. I had him thoroughly evaluated for ADHD again and discovered he wasn't outgrowing it. In fact, it was causing him more trouble, not less. It was then that I realized how ADHD shapes personality, torments the victims, and fragments relationships. (Adapted from L. Weiss, 1992)

Adolescence   Many children with ADHD do not outgrow their problems when they reach adolescence, and sometimes their problems can get much worse. Although hyperactive-impulsive behaviors decline significantly by adolescence, they still occur at a level higher than in 95% of same-age peers who don't have ADHD (Barkley, in press). The disorder continues into adolescence for at least 50% or more of clinic-referred elementary school children (Barkley, Fisher, Edelbrock, & Smallish, 1990). Childhood symptoms of hyperactivity-impulsivity (more so than those of inattention) are generally related to poor adolescent outcomes (Barkley, 1998b).

My file cabinet symbolizes my inadequacy for me. Ten years ago I was going to straighten it out. Now, ten years later, the file cabinet still isn't straightened out . . . It makes me feel ashamed and inadequate. It makes me feel frustrated and helpless. How big a deal is it to organize a file cabinet? We're not talking about brain surgery . . . I feel like I'm not a grownup yet. (L. Weiss, 1992)

Adulthood   Although difficult to confirm, many well-known and highly successful adults, from Thomas Edison to Robin Williams, have been suspected of having ADHD as children. Some youngsters with ADHD either outgrow their disorder or learn to cope with it. However, most children will continue to experience problems, leading to a lifelong pattern of suffering and disappointment (Barkley, 2003). Adults with ADHD are restless and easily bored, constantly seeking novelty and excitement; they may experience work difficulties, impaired social relations, and suffer from depression, low self-concept, substance abuse, and personality disorder (Rasmussen & Gillberg, 2001). Although the situation may be changing, many adults with ADHD have never been diagnosed, particularly those without accompanying behavior problems. As a result they may feel that something is wrong with them, but they don't know what it is. Since many adults with ADHD are bright and creative individuals, they often feel frustrated about not living up to potential (Wender, 2000).

A few words of caution are in order regarding the developmental course and outcomes for ADHD. First, age of onset, course, and outcomes may differ depending on the samples, measures used, accompanying disorders, and the subtype of ADHD. For example, negative outcomes are much greater in clinic versus community samples and for those children with accompanying conduct problems. Little information is currently available regarding outcomes for the ADHD-PI subtype. Interestingly, ADHD symptoms and impairments in adulthood are more severe when reported by other adults than by the person with ADHD. By relying on self-reports of those with ADHD, findings from past follow-up studies may underestimate the persistence of ADHD into adulthood (Barkley, Fischer, Smallish, & Fletcher, 2002). Thus, the developmental course and outcomes we have presented describe an overall pattern, but additional follow-up studies are needed to fill in important details.

SECTION SUMMARY

- The best estimate is that ADHD affects about 3% to 5% of all school-age children.

- The diagnosis of ADHD is about three times more common in boys than girls.

- Girls with ADHD have a significant disorder; clinic-referred girls with ADHD display many of the same features as boys with ADHD; girls with ADHD in community samples appear to be less impaired than boys with ADHD.

- ADHD occurs across all socioeconomic levels and has been identified in every country where it has been studied.

- Symptoms of ADHD change with development. A difficult infant temperament may be followed by hyperactive-impulsive symptoms at 3 to 4 years of age, which are followed, in turn, by the emergence of symptoms of inattention around the time that the child begins school.

- Although some symptoms of ADHD may decline in prevalence and intensity as children grow older, for many individuals ADHD is a lifelong and painful disorder.

Theories and Causes

"The word cause is an altar to an unknown god."

—*William James (1842–1910)*

Many explanations for ADHD have been advanced, some highly controversial. For example, it has been argued (without much support) that ADHD is a trait left over from our evolutionary past as hunters (Hartmann, 1993)

(see Box 5.3). Others contend that ADHD is a myth, a disorder that has been fabricated because as a society we need it (T. Armstrong, 1995; Breggin, 1998).

Despite much attention to the nature and causes of ADHD, clear answers have been elusive because diagnostic practices are not standardized and research is challenging. Nevertheless, research into the basic nature of ADHD leads to fascinating theories about possible mechanisms and causes (Sergeant, 2000). As summarized in Box 5.4, interrelated theories emphasize deficits in motivation, arousal level, self-regulation, and response inhibition. Separating the influences of the processes emphasized by each theory will help increase our understanding of ADHD (Crone, Jennings, van der Molen, 2003).

Numerous causes for ADHD have been proposed. However, many have not been adequately tested, or have fallen by the wayside in the face of weak, inconsistent, or

BOX 5.4 Interrelated Theories of ADHD

Motivation Deficits   Children with ADHD display disturbances in their sensitivity to rewards and punishments, usually with a heightened sensitivity to rewards (Barkley, 1998b). As a result, they perform well when rewards are frequent but otherwise become frustrated and do poorly (Carlson & Tamm, 2000; Douglas & Parry, 1994). Findings in support of this theory are mixed, with results depending on the specific procedures and rewards used (Barber, Milich, & Welsh, 1996).

Arousal Level Deficits   Children with ADHD have an abnormal level of arousal, either too high or, more commonly, too low. Hyperactivity reflects an underaroused child's effort to maintain an optimal level of arousal by excessive self-stimulation (Zentall, 1985). Although this theory has received some support (Antrop, Roeyers, Van Oost, & Buysse, 2000), it has not yet been presented as a comprehensive model to account for the full range of problems found in children with ADHD.

Self-Regulation Deficits   Children with ADHD have a higher-order deficit in their ability to self-regulate—to using thought and language to direct behavior. Deficient self-regulation leads to impulsivity, poor maintenance of effort, deficient modulation of arousal level, and attraction to immediate rewards (Douglas, 1988, 1999). Some children with ADHD have been found to display decreased functioning in the parts of the brain that mediate self-regulation (Barkley, Grodzinsky, & DuPaul, 1992; Zametkin et al., 1990).

Response Inhibition Deficits   Children with ADHD (excluding those who are predominantly inattentive) have response inhibition deficits, a fundamental inability to delay their initial reactions to events, or to stop their behavior once it gets going. This has been likened to a ballistic missile—once fired, there's no turning back (Logan, 1994). This core deficit in behavioral inhibition leads to many cognitive, language, and motor difficulties (Barkley, 1997d, 2000). Evidence continues to accumulate for behavioral inhibition deficits in children with ADHD (Barkley, 2003; Nigg, 2001), although many specific aspects of this theory still must be tested.

While many factors may lead to ADHD, current research strongly suggests that ADHD is a disorder for which genetic and neurobiological factors play a central role (Barkley, 2003; Biederman & Spencer, 1999). Biological and environmental risk factors together shape the expression of ADHD symptoms over time following several different pathways (Hinshaw, 1994a; E. Taylor, 1999). Since ADHD is a complex and chronic disorder of brain, behavior, and development, any explanation that focuses on one cause is likely to be inadequate (Rapport & Chung, 2000). Although data do not yet permit a comprehensive causal model, Figure 5.2 shows a possible developmental pathway for ADHD that highlights several known causal influences and outcomes. We discuss these causal influences in the sections that follow.

Most of what we know about the causes of ADHD pertains to children with the combined subtype, ADHD-C, or what was previously called hyperactivity. We know far

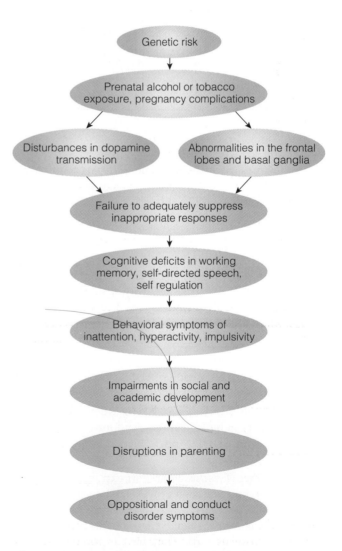

Figure 5.2. A possible developmental pathway for ADHD

nonexistent support. Among these are that ADHD is caused by too much sugar intake, food allergies, yeast, fluorescent lighting, motion sickness, bad parenting, poor school environment, urban living, or too much TV.

less about causes for the predominantly inattentive subtype, ADHD-I, particularly the subgroup with a sluggish cognitive tempo.

Genetic Influences

Several lines of evidence point to genetic influences as important causal factors in ADHD (Kuntsi & Stevenson, 2000; Tannock, 1998).

- *ADHD runs in families.* About one-third of the biological relatives of children with ADHD also have the disorder (Faraone et al., 2000; Smalley et al., 2000). Remarkably, if a parent has ADHD, the risk to their child is nearly 60% (Biederman et al., 1995).

- *Adoption studies.* Rates of ADHD are nearly three times higher in biological versus adoptive parents of children with ADHD (Sprich, Biederman, Crawford, Mundy, & Faraone, 2000).

- *Twin studies.* Twin studies report extraordinarily high heritability estimates for ADHD, averaging about 70% to 80% (Levy & Hay, 2001; Thapar, 2003). In contrast, shared environmental factors are things that twins and siblings have in common by virtue of growing up in the same family, and seem to play a very small role of less than 5% of the variance in accounting for ADHD. Nonshared environ-

mental factors are things in the social and biological environment of a nongenetic origin that affect only one twin or sibling, such as different treatment by parents or an accidental injury, and account for 10% to 20% of the variance. They are somewhat larger than shared environment influences, but are still substantially less than the genetic contribution. Further, ADHD concordance rates for identical twins average 65%, about twice that of fraternal twins (Levy & Hay, 2001).

- *Specific gene studies.* Molecular genetic analysis suggests that specific genes may account for the expression of ADHD in some children (Faraone et al., 1992). The focus has been on genes within the dopaminergic and adrenergic system, for two primary reasons. First, brain structures implicated in ADHD are rich with dopamine innervation. Second, primary medications that reduce ADHD symptoms act primarily by blocking the dopamine transporter (DAT1), a receptor on the presynaptic neuron involved in the reuptake of dopamine, thereby increasing the availability of dopamine in the synapse. Since receptors are coded for by genes, a gene for the dopamine transporter or other dopamine receptors are logical candidates. To date, findings for the association between the dopamine transporter gene (DAT1) and ADHD have been mixed (E. H. Cook et al., 1995;

Gill, Daly, Heron, Hawi, & Fitzgerald, 1997). More consistent (but not yet conclusive) support has been found for the association between ADHD and a variant of one of the dopamine receptor genes, DRD4 (seven-repeat form) (Mill et al., 2002). Interestingly, this gene has previously been linked to the personality trait of sensation seeking (high levels of thrill-seeking, impulsive, exploratory, and excitable behavior) (Benjamin et al., 1996; Ebstein et al., 1996), affects responsiveness to medication, and impacts on parts of the brain associated with executive functions and attention.

Findings that implicate specific genes within the dopamine system in ADHD are intriguing, and are consistent with a model suggesting that reduced dopaminergic activity may be related to the behavioral symptoms of ADHD. Keep in mind, however, that in the vast majority of cases the heritable components of ADHD are likely to be the result of multiple genes interacting on several different chromosomes—it is highly unlikely that ADHD is caused by only one gene.

Taken together, the findings from family, adoption, twin, and specific gene studies strongly suggest that ADHD is inherited, although the precise mechanisms are not yet known (Levy & Hay, 2001). In addition, as we saw with prevalence, findings from genetic studies may vary depending on the subtype and whether ratings of ADHD are made by parents or teachers (Martin, Scourfield, McGuffin, 2002).

Pregnancy, Birth, and Early Development

Many factors that compromise the development of the nervous system before and after birth may be related to ADHD symptoms including: pregnancy and birth complications, low birth weight, malnutrition, early neurological insult or trauma, and diseases of infancy (Linnet et al., 2003; Mick, Biederman, Prince, Fischer, & Faraone, 2002). Although these early factors predict later symptoms of ADHD, they may not be specific to ADHD; they may elevate the risk of developing many later problems, not only ADHD. Also, keep in mind that exposure to these risk factors is not randomly assigned and therefore could be related to ADHD in the parent or child.

A mother's use of cigarettes, alcohol, or other drugs during pregnancy can have damaging effects on her unborn child. Consistent support has been found for an association between maternal cigarette smoking during pregnancy and ADHD (Kotimaa et al., 2003; Linnet et al., 2003). Exposure to alcohol before birth may also lead to inattention, hyperactivity, impulsivity, and associated impairments in learning and behavior (Mick, Biederman, Faraone, Sayer, & Kleinman, 2002).

Evidence suggests that mothers of children with ADHD use more alcohol, tobacco, and drugs than do control parents, even when they are not pregnant (Mick et al., 2002). Since parental substance use is often associated with a chaotic home environment both before and after birth, it is difficult to disentangle the influence of substance abuse and other factors that occur prior to birth from the cumulative impact of a negative family environment that occurs during later development. Other substances used during pregnancy, such as cocaine and crack can adversely affect the normal development of the brain and lead to higher than normal rates of ADHD and other psychiatric disorders (Weissman et al., 1999). To summarize, although pregnancy and birth complications are not the cause of most cases of ADHD, they may be important contributing factors for some children.

Neurobiological Factors

ADHD is far from well understood, but there is substantial indirect and direct support for neurobiological causal factors (Barkley, 2003; Faraone & Biederman, 1998). Indirect support is evidence that does not include direct measures of brain structure or function and is derived from known associations between events or conditions related to neurological status and symptoms of ADHD. Among these are:

- Peri- and postnatal events such as birth complications and diseases
- Environmental toxins such as lead
- Language and learning disorders
- Signs of neurological immaturity such as clumsiness, poor balance and coordination, and abnormal reflexes
- Improvement in ADHD symptoms produced by stimulant medications known to affect the central nervous system
- Similarity between symptoms of ADHD and symptoms associated with lesions to the prefrontal cortex (Fuster, 1989; Grattan & Eslinger, 1991)
- Performance deficits of children with ADHD on neuropsychological tests associated with prefrontal lobe functions (Barkley, Grodzinsky, & DuPaul, 1992)

Although none of the indirect observations or findings are conclusive, their cumulative weight provides strong support to neurobiological factors as possible causes for ADHD.

Direct evidence for a connection between ADHD and neurobiological causal influences comes from research showing differences between children with and without ADHD on measures of brain function, including (Barkley, 2003):

- Differences on psychophysiological measures (e.g., EEG, galvanic skin response, and heart rate deceleration), suggesting diminished arousal or arousability (Beaucheine, Katkin, Strassberg, & Snarr, 2001; Monastra, Lubar, & Linden, 2001).

- Differences on measures of brain activity during vigilance tests (Frank, Lazar, & Seiden, 1992), suggesting under-responsiveness to stimuli and deficits in response inhibition (Pliszka, Liotti, & Woldorff, 2000).
- Differences in blood flow to the prefrontal regions of the brain and the pathways connecting these regions to the limbic system, suggesting decreased blood flow to these regions (Hendren, De Backer, & Pandina, 2000).

Brain Abnormalities   Neuroimaging studies make it possible to test neurobiological theories about the causes of ADHD. MRI findings suggest abnormalities primarily in the **frontostriatal circuitry of the brain.** This region consists of the prefrontal cortex and interconnected areas of gray matter located deep below the cerebral cortex collectively known as the *basal ganglia* (basement structures). These areas of the brain are associated with attention, executive functions, delayed responding, and response organization. Lesions in this region result in symptoms similar to those of ADHD. Children with ADHD have a smaller right prefrontal cortex than children without ADHD (Filipek et al., 1997) and show structural abnormalities in several parts of the basal ganglia (Semrud-Clikeman et al., 2000). Interestingly, in identical twins who are discordant for ADHD, it is only the twin with ADHD who displays abnormalities in these brain structures (Castellanos et al., 2003).

However, brain structure differences may not be restricted exclusively to the prefrontal cortex and parts of the basal ganglia. Recent MRI findings indicate that youngsters with ADHD have smaller total cerebral volumes (by 3% to 4%) and a smaller cerebellum (Castellanos et al., 2002). It is of interest to note that growth curves for nearly all brain regions of youngsters with ADHD mirror those of controls, but on a lower track. Also, smaller brain size in children with ADHD is not a result of drug treatment. Although simple and direct relations cannot be assumed between brain size and abnormal function, smaller brain volumes in children with ADHD are associated with more severe symptoms (Castellanos et al., 2002). Anatomic measures of frontostriatal circuitry are related to the performance of children with ADHD on response inhibition and attention tasks (B. J. Casey et al., 1997; Semrud-Clikeman et al., 2000).

Neuroimaging studies indicate the importance of the frontostriatal region of the brain in ADHD and the pathways connecting this region with the limbic system (via the striatum) and the cerebellum (Barkley, 2003). However, further research is required to determine whether these regions are primary, and to reliably identify more localized anatomical abnormalities. Furthermore, although

neuroimaging studies can tell us that children with ADHD have a structural difference or less activity in certain regions of the brain, they don't tell us why. Finally, it is of interest that growth curve trajectories for nearly all brain structures in youngsters with ADHD and controls seem to parallel one another. This suggests that influences on brain development in ADHD during childhood and adolescence may be fixed, not progressive, and unrelated to drug treatment (Castellanos et al., 2002).

Neurophysiological and Neurochemical Findings   Precise neurophysiological and neurochemical abnormalities underlying ADHD have been extremely difficult to document. No consistent differences have been found in the biochemistry of urine, plasma, blood, and cerebrospinal fluid of children with and without ADHD (Barkley, 1998b). At a neurochemical level, the known action of effective medications for ADHD suggests that the neurotransmitters dopamine, norepinephrine, epinephrine, and serotonin may be involved (Pliszka, McCracken, & Maas, 1996; Swanson, Castellanos, Murias, LaHoste, & Kennedy, 1998), with most evidence suggesting a selective deficiency in the availability of both dopamine and norepinephrine. However, we must be cautious in drawing conclusions from the effects of medications alone. Using medication for effective treatment of ADHD symptoms does not prove that deficits in the drug or its action are the cause of the symptoms, any more than the elimination of a headache by aspirin implies that the headache was caused by aspirin deficiency. Medications may operate at levels of neuroanatomy and neurochemistry that are far removed from primary causal influences (Hinshaw, 1994a).

Diet, Allergy, and Lead

The relationship of sugar to hyperactivity achieved epic significance when "What is sugar?" was the correct response to "The major cause of hyperactivity in North America" on the popular TV show *Jeopardy* (Barkley, 1995). However, study after study has conclusively shown that sugar is not the cause of hyperactivity (Milich, Wolraich, & Lindgren, 1986). So why do nearly one-half of the parents and teachers who are asked think that children are sugar sensitive? It may be the power of suggestion.

In one study, mothers who believed their children were sugar sensitive were told their children would be given a drink of Kool-Aid containing either sugar or, as a placebo, the sugar substitute aspartame. After the children drank their Kool-Aid, they and their mothers spent time playing and working together. In fact, none of the children was given sugar—they all received Kool-Aid with aspartame. But the mothers who thought their children had received sugar rated them as more hyperactive than the mothers who believed their children had received aspartame. Perhaps even more telling was that during play and work interactions, mothers who thought their children had received sugar were more critical of them, hovered more, and talked to them more frequently (Hoover & Milich, 1994). These findings suggest that what parents believe about the causes of their children's ADHD can affect their views of their children and how they treat them (Johnston & Leung, 2001).

There has been much controversy about the possibility that allergic reactions and diet are causes of ADHD. This connection has not received much support (McGee, Stanton, & Sears, 1993). A popular view in the 1970s and 1980s was that food additives caused children to be hyperactive and inattentive. Parents were encouraged to withhold foods containing artificial flavorings, preservatives, and sugars. However, research does not support the role of food additives as a primary cause of ADHD (Conners, 1980; Kavale & Forness, 1983). Restricted diets may help a small subgroup of children with ADHD, mostly the very young and those with specific food allergies (Arnold, 1999).

Exposure to low levels of lead that are found in dust, soil, and flaking paint in areas where leaded gasoline and paint were once used may be associated with ADHD symptoms in the classroom (Fergusson, Horwood, & Lynskey, 1993). However, most children with ADHD do not have significantly elevated lead levels in their teeth or blood (Kahn, Kelly, & Walker, 1995). Thus, the relationship between lead and ADHD is weak (Barkley, 1998b). In summary, although diet, allergy, and lead have received much attention as possible causes of ADHD, their role as a primary cause is minimal to nonexistent.

Family Influences

As we have discussed, twin studies find that psychosocial factors in the family account for only a small amount of the variance in ADHD symptoms, and explanations of ADHD based exclusively on negative family influences have received little support. Nevertheless, family influences are important in understanding ADHD for several reasons (C. Johnston & Mash, 2001; Whalen & Henker, 1999).

- *Family influences may lead to ADHD symptoms or to a greater severity of symptoms.* In some cases, ADHD symptoms may be the result of interfering and insensitive early care-giving practices (Jacobvitz & Sroufe, 1987). In addition, for children at risk for ADHD, family conflict may raise the severity of their hyperactive-impulsive symptoms to a clinical level (Barkley, 2003). Especially important is the **goodness of fit,** or the match between the child's early temperament and the parent's style of interaction (Chess & Thomas, 1984). An overactive child with an overstimulating parent is a seemingly poor fit. As we have

seen, many parents of children with ADHD also have the disorder, which means that the parents' ADHD symptoms may disrupt early parent–child interactions.

- *Family problems may result from interacting with a child who is impulsive and difficult to manage* (Mash & Johnston, 1990). The clearest support for this child-to-parent direction of effect comes from double-blind placebo control drug studies in which children's ADHD symptoms were decreased using stimulant medications. Decreases in children's ADHD symptoms produced a corresponding reduction in the negative and controlling behaviors that parents had previously displayed when their children were unmedicated (Barkley, 1988).

- *Family conflict is likely related to the presence, maintenance, and later emergence of associated oppositional and conduct disorder symptoms.* Many interventions for ADHD try to change patterns of family interaction to head off an escalating cycle of oppositional behavior and conflict. Family influences may play a major role in determining the outcome of ADHD and its associated problems, even if the influences are not the primary cause of ADHD (S. B. Campbell, March, Pierce, Ewing, & Szumowski, 1991; Hinshaw et al., 2000).

In sum, ADHD has a strong biological basis and is an inherited condition for many children. Although evidence is converging on specific brain areas, most findings are correlational, and we do not yet know the specific causes of the disorder. ADHD is likely the result of a complex pattern of interacting influences perhaps giving rise to the disorder through a final common pathway in the nervous system. We are just beginning to understand the complex ways in which biological risk factors, family relationships, and broader system influences interact to shape the development and outcome of ADHD (E. Taylor, 1999).

SECTION SUMMARY

- Theories about possible mechanisms and causes for ADHD have emphasized deficits in motivation, arousal level, self-regulation, and response inhibition.

- There is strong evidence that ADHD is a neurobiological disorder; however, biological and environmental risk factors together shape its expression.

- Findings from family, adoption, twin, and specific gene studies suggest that ADHD is inherited, although the precise mechanisms are not yet known.

- Many factors that compromise the development of the nervous system before and after birth may be related to ADHD symptoms, such as pregnancy and birth complications, maternal smoking during pregnancy, low birth weight, malnutrition, maternal alcohol or drug use, early neurological insult or trauma, and diseases of infancy.

- ADHD appears to be related to abnormalities in the frontostriatal circuitry of the brain and the pathways connecting this region with the limbic system and the cerebellum. Neuroimaging studies tell us that in children with ADHD there is a structural difference or less activity in certain regions of the brain, but they don't tell us why.

- The known action of effective medications for ADHD suggests that several neurotransmitters are involved, with most evidence suggesting a selective deficiency in the availability of both dopamine and norepinephrine.

- Psychosocial factors in the family do not typically cause ADHD, although they are important in understanding the disorder. Family problems may lead to a greater severity of symptoms and relate to the emergence of associated conduct problems.

Treatment

Mark

Medication and Behavior Therapy

In third grade, Mark's teacher threw up her hands and said, "Enough!" In one morning, Mark had jumped out of his seat six times to sharpen his pencil, each time accidentally charging into other children's desks and toppling books and papers. He was finally sent to the principal's office when he began kicking a desk he had overturned. In sheer frustration, his teacher called a meeting with his parents and the school psychologist.

But even after they developed a plan for managing his behavior in class, Mark showed little improvement. Finally, after an extensive assessment, they found that he had an attention deficit that included hyperactivity. He was put on Ritalin™, a stimulant medication to control the hyperactivity during school hours. With a psychologist's help, his parents learned to reward desirable behaviors and to have Mark take time out when he became too disruptive. Soon Mark was able to sit still and focus on learning. (Adapted from NIMH, 1994a)

Lisa

Behavior Therapy and Counseling

Because Lisa wasn't disruptive in class, it took a long time for teachers to notice her problem. Lisa was first referred to the school evaluation team when her teacher realized that she was a bright girl with failing grades. The team ruled out a learning disability but determined that she had an attention deficit, ADHD without hyperactiv-

ity. The school psychologist recognized that Lisa was also dealing with depression.

Lisa's teachers and the school psychologist developed a treatment plan that included a program to increase her attention span and develop her social skills. They also recommended that Lisa receive counseling to help her recognize her strengths and overcome her depression. (Adapted from NIMH, 1994a)

More and more children are receiving help for their ADHD, with rates of outpatient treatment for ADHD more than tripling from 1987 to 1997, from .9 to 3.4 per 100 children (Olfson, Gameroff, Marcus, & Jensen, 2003). Although there is no known cure for ADHD, a variety of treatments can be used to help children like Mark and Lisa cope with their symptoms and any secondary problems that may arise (Barkley, 1998b; Hinshaw, 2000). An overview of these treatments is presented in Table 5.2.

The primary approach (recommended by *Consumer Reports* and the U.S. Surgeon General) combines stimulant medication, parent management training, and educational intervention (Pelham, Wheeler, & Chronis, 1998). Interventions that use elements of all approaches have also been provided in intensive summer treatment programs. Additional treatments, for which there is less evidence, include family counseling and support groups, and child-focused treatments, such as social skills training, cognitive-behavioral self-control training, and individual counseling (Barkley, 1998a).

Although somewhat similar treatments are used for children and adolescents with ADHD, research with teens has been extremely limited (Barkley, in press; Smith, Waschbusch, Willoughby, & Evans, 2000). Similarly, there are few studies that have looked at treatment efficacy for specific ADHD subtypes. Therefore, most of our discussion centers on treatments for school-age children with ADHD who display symptoms of both inattention and hyperactivity-impulsivity.

Several key considerations underlie any treatment program for a child with ADHD:

- The most effective interventions overall, are intensive, ongoing, and use a combination of treatments.
- Treatment should provide the child with an external structure that will compensate for his or her lack of internal structuring and organizational skills.
- Treatment must be directed at the behaviors of concern as they occur in the child's typical life settings—for example, the classroom or home (Barkley, 1998a).
- To be effective, an intervention must be sensitive to the child's level of development and the individual strengths and needs of the child and family (Waschbusch, Kipp, & Pelham, 1998).

Table 5.2
Treatments for Children with ADHD

PRIMARY TREATMENTS	FOCUS OF TREATMENT
Stimulant medication	Managing ADHD symptoms at school and home
Parent management training	Managing disruptive child behavior at home, reducing parent–child conflict, and promoting prosocial and self-regulating behaviors
Educational intervention	Managing disruptive classroom behavior, improving academic performance, teaching pro-social and self-regulating behaviors

INTENSIVE TREATMENT	FOCUS OF TREATMENT
Summer treatment programs	Enhancing present adjustment at home and future success at school by combining many of the primary and additional treatments in an intensive program

ADDITIONAL TREATMENTS	FOCUS OF TREATMENT
Family counseling	Coping with individual and family stresses associated with ADHD, including mood disturbance and marital strain
Support groups	Connecting adults with other parents of children with ADHD, sharing information and experiences about common concerns and providing emotional support
Individual counseling	Providing a supportive relationship in which the child can discuss personal concerns and feelings

Medication: The Great Debate

Pete (age 6) says: It makes us not 'hyper-phrenalicky.' (sic)

—(Henker & Whalen, 1980)

The use of stimulants and other medications to treat the symptoms of ADHD in children has been the subject of considerable debate (Jacobvitz, Sroufe, Stewart, & Leffert, 1990). Most of you likely have opinions about stimulants for ADHD—perhaps that they are overprescribed, used as a quick fix, do not let kids be kids, and lead to overdiagnosis. Let's look at the role of stimulant medications and the controversy that surrounds them.

Stimulants Since the chance discovery of their effectiveness in the 1930s (see Box 5.5), stimulant medications have been used to treat the symptoms of ADHD. Several other medications have also been used, including noradrenergic drugs, tricyclic antidepressants, and antihypertensives. We focus our discussion on stimulants, which come in a variety of forms, because they are the most studied, most effective, and most commonly used treatment for the management of symptoms of ADHD and its associated impairments (Spencer, Biederman, & Wilens, 2000; Wolraich, 2003). Nevertheless, it is important to keep in mind that many other potentially effective medication options are available for children with ADHD, including the newest *drug-du-jour*, the non-stimulant drug atomoxetine [Strattera™] (Barkley, in press).

The two most effective stimulants in treating children with ADHD are dextroamphetamine (Dexedrine or Dextrostat™) and **methylphenidate** (Ritalin™) the most commonly used drug by far. These medications alter ac-

BOX 5.5 The Discovery of Math Pills

The use of stimulant medication for children with learning and behavior problems was first reported in 1937 by Charles Bradley, the medical director of a small hospital for children with major difficulties in learning or behavior. Dr. Bradley described dramatic improvements in some of the children he treated with Benzedrine. Why did Dr. Bradley decide to use stimulants to treat these problems in the first place?

Dr. Bradley was a very conscientious physician, and all patients were given careful work-ups. These work-ups included a spinal tap, which naturally led to headaches afterward that frequently were lasting, severe, or both, and were presumed to be due to the loss of spinal fluid. Dr. Bradley speculated that if he could stimulate the choroid plexus to secrete spinal fluid at a faster rate, the headaches would be relieved more quickly. He decided to proceed along these lines and chose the most potent stimulant available at the time, Benzedrine. (*Note:* This type of powerful stimulant is no longer used.) The effect on the headaches was negligible, but to his astonishment, the teachers reported major improvements in learning and behavior in many children that lasted until the Benzedrine regimen was withdrawn. The children themselves noted the greater ease of learning and called the medication "math pills," presumably because mathematics was the hardest subject for them, and their improved ability to learn was most noticeable in that subject.

Source: Adapted from Gross, 1995.

tivity in the frontostriatal region of the brain by affecting neurotransmitters (dopamine) important to this region (Volkow et al., 1997). For about 80% of children with ADHD, stimulants produce dramatic increases in sustained attention, impulse control, persistence of work effort, and decreases in task-irrelevant activity and noisy and disruptive behaviors (Swanson, McBurnett, Christian, & Wigal, 1995).

Stimulants may also improve the child's social interactions and cooperation with parents, teachers, and peers (Danforth, Barkley, & Stokes, 1991) and, occasionally, physical coordination such as handwriting or sports ability (Lerer, Lerer, & Artner, 1977). Stimulants can help children with ADHD control their noncompliant, destructive, or aggressive behaviors (D. A. Murphy, Pelham, & Lang, 1992). Stimulants also improve academic productivity, which is defined as the number and accuracy of completed problems (Rapport & Kelly, 1993).

Stimulant medications, used appropriately and with proper supervision are usually quite safe. Some children may experience side effects such as weight loss, reduced appetite, temporary growth suppression, or problems falling asleep. However, the potential side effects are typically benign and can be carefully monitored and often eliminated by reducing the dose. Although stimulants can be addictive if misused or abused (one recreational name for Ritalin is Vitamin R!), they are not addictive for most children who take them, nor do they lead to an increased risk for later substance abuse (Wilens, Faraone, Biederman, & Gunawardene, 2003). Stimulants seldom make children "high," nervous, or jumpy, or turn them into nonfeeling zombies.

The short-term benefits of medication are well documented (Spencer, Biederman, et al., 2000). Unfortunately, follow-up studies suggest limited long-term benefits of stimulants on school achievement, peer relationships, behavior problems in adolescence, or adult adjustment (Pelham, 1993). The effects of stimulants are temporary and occur only while the child is taking medication. In this sense, the use of stimulants is similar to other important treatments for chronic conditions, such as insulin used for diabetes; however, they are not a cure. Many young people receiving stimulants for severe behavior problems remain impaired, despite many years of medication treatment. The limited long-term benefit of stimulants raises important issues about their clinical use that are yet to be resolved (Safer, 2000b).

Controversy   Controversy about the potential misuse of medication is evidenced by the recent introductions of legislation in the U.S. Congress whose express purpose is "to protect children and their parents from being coerced into administering psychotropic medication in order to attend school, and for other purposes" (Child Medication Safety Act of 2003). Why the concern? Community and physician surveys, increased production of Ritalin, and pharmacy

audits all indicate that stimulant consumption has more than doubled since 1990 in North America (Olfson et al., 2003). It is estimated that about 1.3 million children regularly take stimulants, which is approximately 3% of school-age children (Zito et al., 2003). Moreover, the use of Ritalin is at least 5 times higher in North America than in the rest of the world, although use worldwide is increasing (Bramble, 2003). This increase may stem from a widening of the diagnostic criteria for ADHD and greater use of stimulants among girls and older individuals. Also, as changes in public policy and laws increase eligibility for special education and other services for individuals with ADHD (DuPaul & Stoner, 2003), more individuals may receive this diagnosis and subsequently be placed on medication.

Given this increase and the consumption of stimulants to treat ADHD in North America, we need to ask if ADHD is overdiagnosed and if stimulants are overprescribed (Safer, 2000a). Because of the wide variability in diagnostic practices, treatment decisions, and rates of stimulant use in various schools, communities, geographic regions, and populations it is not surprising that research findings concerning diagnosis and medication use are inconsistent (Angold et al., 2000; P. S. Jensen et al., 1999). Perhaps the best overall conclusion to be drawn from the research is that in many cases stimulants are currently being used inappropriately, underprescribed in some cases and overprescribed in others. We need a better understanding of the factors leading to the diagnosis of ADHD and stimulant use so that further steps can be taken to increase appropriate use—for example, improved screening and diagnosis, and better education of service providers (P. S. Jensen, 2000).

"When all is said and done, we stand in the middle on the issue of medication—not dramatically opposed, but not wildly enthusiastic either. Ideally, stimulants should be prescribed, monitored carefully, and there should be ongoing communication with parents and school personnel. However, the world being what it is, a lot of people seem to be falling short of the ideal a lot of the time." (Ken and Andrea McClusky, 2000, p. 11)

Despite their limitations, stimulants, when properly used, remain the most effective treatment for managing symptoms of ADHD. Nevertheless, since stimulants are often not used during the entire day and do not address all the associated problems of children with ADHD, other primary interventions such as parent management training and educational interventions are needed.

Parent Management Training (PMT)

Being the parent of a child who is overactive, disorganized, irritable, and does not listen or follow directions is difficult and exhausting. Usual discipline tactics like reasoning, warning, or scolding often don't work. Thus, parents may feel powerless and at a loss as to what to do. Out of frustration, they may spank, ridicule, or yell at their child, even though they know it is not effective. These reactions leave everyone in the family feeling more upset than ever. **Parent management training (PMT)** provides parents with a variety of skills to help them

- manage their child's oppositional and noncompliant behaviors.
- cope with the emotional difficulties of raising a child with ADHD.
- contain the problem so that it does not worsen.
- keep the problem from adversely affecting other family members.

Parents are first taught about ADHD so they understand the biological basis of the disorder. This helps to remove the burden of guilt from parents who may think they have caused the problem. Parents are also given a set of guiding principles for raising a child with ADHD, such as using more immediate, frequent, and powerful consequences; striving for consistency; planning ahead; not personalizing the child's problems; and practicing forgiveness (Barkley, 1995).

Parents are next taught behavior management principles and techniques, such as identifying behaviors they wish to encourage or discourage, using rewards and sanctions to achieve specified goals, establishing a home token program, noticing what their child does well, and praising their child's strengths and accomplishments. For disruptive behavior, parents also learn to use penalties, such as loss of privileges or time-out and how to manage noncompliance in public places. Parents may also learn to use a school–home-based reward program where teachers evaluate the child on a daily report card. This card serves as a means for rewards or punishments (usually tokens) that will be administered at home for classroom conduct. Parents also learn how to manage future misconduct and are given follow-up sessions (Barkley, 1998a).

Parents are encouraged to spend time each day sharing an enjoyable activity with their child. They learn to structure situations in ways that will maximize the child's success and minimize failures. For example, if the child has difficulty completing tasks, it may be necessary to break the task into smaller steps and then praise the completion of each step. In PMT, parents also learn to reduce their own levels of arousal through relaxation, meditation, or exercise. Reduced arousal or anger allows parents to respond more calmly to their child's behavior.

Numerous studies support the effectiveness of PMT in decreasing oppositional and defiant child behaviors (McMahon & Forehand, 2003); however, its relative advantages and long-term benefits for the treatment of children with ADHD have yet to be documented. As we will discuss, the effects of stimulants appear to be as strong as or stronger than the effects of PMT in treating the primary symptoms of ADHD. PMT may produce additional therapeutic benefits by treating the associated problems, improving family functioning, and increasing consumer satisfaction (Anastopoulos & Farley, 2003; Barkley, 1998a; P. S. Jensen, 1999).

Educational Intervention

Alan
Boxed in at School

My teacher wanted to make me concentrate better, so one day she put my desk in the far corner, separated from the rest of the class. A few days had passed. I still wasn't finishing my work on time, but I was trying. My teacher didn't care; it wasn't finished. She then put a refrigerator box around my desk so I couldn't see anyone. I could hear, as other kids in class would make fun of me. It really hurt; I was ashamed of myself and mad at my teacher. I couldn't tell my Mom because I might get into trouble. I hated school, didn't like my teacher, and started not liking myself. . . . It was hard to face the next day. A week had passed, and I poked holes in the cardboard so I could see who was making fun of me. I started peeping through the holes, making the other kids laugh. The teacher would get so annoyed. So I became the class clown. I was expelled for two days. When my Mom found out what was going on, boy, did she get angry; she was mad that the teacher would do this and mad that the principal allowed it and no one could see what this was doing to me. (From a chapter by R. A. Barkley and L. J. Pfiffner in *Taking Charge of ADHD: The Complete, Authorized Guide for Parents,* by R. A. Barkley, 1995, p. 209. Copyright © 1995 by Guilford Publications. Reprinted by permission.)

Classroom requirements to sit still, pay attention, listen to instructions, wait your turn, complete assignments, and get along with classmates are not easily met by children with ADHD. Their inattention and hyperactivity-impulsivity make learning very difficult, at times even painful. Although some children with ADHD are placed in a special education class for all or part of the day, most remain in the regular classroom. Whenever possible, it is preferable to keep children with ADHD in class with their peers.

Educational interventions focus on managing inattentive and hyperactive-impulsive behaviors that interfere with learning, and providing a classroom environment that capitalizes on the child's strengths (DuPaul & Stoner, 2003). Techniques for managing classroom behavior are similar to those recommended to parents. The teacher and child set realistic goals and objectives, set up a mutually

Children with ADHD participating in the Summer Treatment Program.

ADHD may require other accommodations to help them learn. For example, the teacher may seat the child near his or her own desk, provide a designated area in which the child can move about, establish a clearly posted system of rules, and give the child frequent cues for expected behaviors. A card or a picture on the child's desk can provide a visual reminder for acceptable behavior such as raising a hand instead of shouting out. Repeating instructions, providing extra time, writing assignments on the board, and listing all of the books and materials needed for a task may increase the likelihood that children with ADHD will complete their work (DuPaul & Stoner, 2003; Pfiffner & Barkley, 1998).

School-based interventions for ADHD have received considerable support. An integrative review found that contingency management procedures aimed at improving behavior, and interventions directed at increasing academic performance both had substantial positive effects (DuPaul & Eckert, 1997).

Intensive Interventions

Summer Treatment Program   There are no quick cures for ADHD. More intensive (and ongoing) treatments than previously used might be required to produce meaningful changes in long-term outcomes. An exemplary intensive summer program has been developed by William Pelham and his colleagues (Pelham et al., 1996: Pelham & Hoza, 1996). In this program, treatment is provided to children with ADHD ages 5 to 15 in a camp-like setting where they engage in classroom and recreational activities with other children. Summer treatment has two major advantages over other interventions: It maximizes opportunities to build effective peer relations in normal settings, and it provides continuity to academic work to ensure gains made during the school year are not lost. These programs are coordinated with stimulant medication trials, PMT, and educational interventions in an all-out treatment effort (Pelham et al., 1996).

The Summer Treatment Program packs 360 hours of treatment into a period of 8 weeks, the equivalent of 7 years of weekly therapy. Ratings by parents and counselors suggest that children who participate show overall improvements in behavior, decreases in problem severity, and improvements in social skills and academic performance. Children also rate themselves as doing better, and parents report higher levels self-efficacy. Dropout rates are low and consumer satisfaction is high. The program is also cost-effective compared to more traditional treatments. Preliminary findings from controlled studies of outcomes are promising (Pelham et al., 2000); however, it's still too early to tell whether this kind of intensive program will make a long-term difference for these children.

The MTA Study   The Multimodal Treatment Study of Children with ADHD (MTA Study) is a landmark multi-

agreed upon reward system, carefully monitor performance, and reward the child for meeting goals. Disruptive or off-task classroom behaviors may be punished with **response-cost procedures** that involve the loss of privileges, activities, points, or tokens contingent upon inappropriate behavior, or brief periods of time-out. These procedures have proved to be effective in reducing disruptive classroom behavior and enhancing academic productivity (DuPaul, Guevremont, & Barkley, 1992; Pfiffner & Barkley, 1998).

Many strategies for instructing children with ADHD are simply good teaching methods. Letting children know what is expected of them, using visual aids, providing cues for expected behavior, and giving written as well as oral instructions all help children focus their attention and remember important points. In addition, children with site study sponsored by the U.S. National Institute of Mental Health (NIMH) and Department of Education (Arnold, Abikoff, Cantwell, et al., 1997; Richters et al., 1995). It represents the first large randomized clinical trial for children with ADHD. The study seeks to answer three questions: How do long-term medication and behavioral treatments compare with one another? Are there additional benefits when they are used together? What is the effectiveness of systematic carefully delivered treatments versus routine community care? (MTA Cooperative Group, 1999a).

A carefully diagnosed sample of children 7 to 9 years of age with ADHD were randomly assigned to one of four treatments, followed by major assessments at periodic intervals during and after treatment.

- *Behavioral treatment:* Thirty-five sessions of parent management training, up to 10 teacher and school visits per year, a 12-week classroom aide, and participation in a summer treatment program
- *Medication:* Psychostimulant medication 7 days a week
- *Combined behavioral treatment and medication:* Both behavioral treatment and medication as described earlier are used.
- *Routine community care:* Treatment as it was routinely delivered in community care (comparison control group)

The major finding from the MTA study was that all groups showed reductions in ADHD symptoms over time, but there were significant variations in the amount of change. First, stimulant medication was superior to behavioral treatment and to routine community care in treating the symptoms of ADHD. Second, adding behavioral treatments to medication resulted in no additional benefits for the core symptoms of ADHD, but did provide modest benefits for non-ADHD symptoms and other outcomes related to positive functioning (MTA Cooperative Group, 1999b). Three years following the end of the intensive treatment, only the medication management group continued to benefit, so long as medications were sustained.

One major criticism of this research is that outcomes of behavioral treatment were measured 4 to 6 months after the most intensive phase, whereas outcomes for medication treatment were measured during its most intensive phase (Pelham, 1999). Other issues now being addressed are concerned with what treatments work best for which children (e.g., boys versus girls, children with or without comorbid conditions), and which areas of functioning (home, school, peers) (S. B. Campbell, 2000b; Jensen, 2001; E. B. Owens et al., 2003; Swanson et al., 2002). It is likely that the findings from the MTA study will be reported and debated for a long time (Cunningham, 1999). Whatever the final verdict, the study should answer many

more real-world questions of clinical importance for children with ADHD and their families (Boyle & Jadad, 1999).

Additional Interventions

Other interventions have been used to provide support to children with ADHD and their families. Among these interventions are family counseling and support groups and individual counseling for the child. (A brief overview of these and other additional interventions can be found in Table 5.2.)

Family Counseling and Support Groups   Many families of children with ADHD experience frustration, blame, and anger for some time. As we have discussed, siblings may feel neglected or resent the time their parents spend with the child with ADHD. Family members may require special assistance not only in managing behavior but also in dealing with their own thoughts and feelings. Counseling the family helps everyone develop new skills, attitudes, and how to relate more effectively.

Support groups for people who are coping with ADHD in various ways can be very helpful to members. There are many local and national support groups for parents of children with ADHD. Members share information, emotional support, personal frustrations and successes, referrals to qualified professionals, discoveries about what works, and their aspirations for their children and themselves. There are also on-line bulletin boards and discussion groups. Sharing experiences with others that have similar concerns helps parents feel that they are not alone.

Ian
Masking the Pain

So if that's it, if I am just plain stupid, there was no way that I would let on to anyone that this was the case. I promised myself never to cry in front of others again. If only I could just make a couple of friends, I'd be alright. I know that none of the kids would dare tease me about my stupidness for fear of being punched . . . My dignity and self-esteem rested on my ability to conceal from anyone that there was something wrong with me. This strange dishonesty had stuck with me since my early years . . . (From "Looking Back: Reminiscences from Childhood and Adolescence," by I. Murray, 1993, pp. 301–325. In G. Weiss and L. T. Hechtman (Eds.), *Hyperactive Children Grown Up: ADHD in Children, Adolescents and Adults,* 2nd ed. Copyright © 1993 Guilford Publications. Reprinted by permission.)

Individual Counseling   Life can be very hard for children with ADHD. They have few successes on which to build their sense of self-competence. Perhaps as a result,

BOX 5.6 Questions Asked by Children and Adolescents with ADHD

CHILDREN (AGES 4 TO 10)

I just found out I have ADD. How can I keep this secret from my brother?

I heard ADD means you're weird. Is that right?

Is it true that if you have ADD you can think faster than other people?

Will the medicine make me smarter?

ADOLESCENTS (AGES 11 TO 17)

How do you know the medicine isn't dangerous?

Any advice on how to deal with the fact that I feel like a reject because I have ADD?

How long am I going to have ADD?

How can I convince [my teacher] that ADD exists and that it affects my performance?

Source: Adapted from Hallowell & Ratey, 1994.

even when they succeed they attribute their success to uncontrollable factors such as task ease or luck (Hoza, Waschbusch, Pelham, Molina, & Milich, 2000). Being punished or told they are stupid or bad is often their main form of attention. They have few friends and are constantly in trouble. The cumulative impact can leave them feeling isolated and believing that they are abnormal, stupid, and doomed to failure. Individual counseling attempts to address these concerns, although evidence for its effectiveness in treating children with ADHD is limited. Children usually come into counseling with many questions about ADHD and treatment that are addressed at the outset and in later sessions (see Box 5.6).

With counseling, children learn to identify and build on their strengths. They eventually understand that having ADHD does not mean they are bad people. They discuss upsetting thoughts and feelings, explore self-defeating patterns of behavior, and learn adaptive ways to handle their emotions. Through discussion and practice, children understand that they can change and lead happier, more productive lives.

A Comment on Controversial Treatments

Understandably, parents want to explore all possible ways to help their children with ADHD. Over the years, many treatments that sound plausible have been proposed. Some are enthusiastically endorsed by professionals, and individual patient reports claim dramatic success; others are pure charlatanism. Treatments proposed for children with ADHD that have not been scientifically substantiated

include: restricted diets, allergy treatments, medication to correct inner ear problems, vestibular stimulation, running, treatment for yeast infection, megavitamins, sensory integration training, chiropractic adjustment, eye training, special colored glasses, metronome therapy, EMG biofeedback and relaxation training, and EEG biofeedback or neurofeedback. Fad treatments may prove to be expensive, provide false hope for a quick cure, and delay the use of evidence-based treatments that are known to be of some benefit (Waschbush & Hill, 2003).

Keeping Things in Perspective

Mark

Good Support System

Through my years so far, I've been through a lot. My Mom says I have a good heart; I care about those in need. I'm not dumb. You can't always measure smartness by tests. I feel I'm doing better now. It helps to talk to people who understand. What I'm trying to say is: no matter what comes my way, I can survive. I have those who really care, and from that I draw my strength. (R. A. Barkley and L. J. Pfiffner in *Taking Charge of ADHD: The Complete, Authorized Guide for Parents,* by R. A. Barkley, 1995, p. 211. Copyright © 1995 by Guilford Publications. Reprinted by permission.)

Young people with ADHD have problems that should not be minimized, especially if doing so prevents youngsters with ADHD and their families from receiving help. However, as Mark's comments illustrate, in helping those with ADHD and their families, it is important not to lose sight of the fact that each youngster is unique and has many strengths and resources that need to be recognized and supported.

SECTION SUMMARY

- There is no cure for ADHD, but a variety of treatments can be used to help children cope with their symptoms and any secondary problems that may arise over the years.

- The primary approach to treatment combines stimulant medication, parent management training, and educational intervention.

- Stimulants are the most effective treatment for managing symptoms of ADHD; however, their limited long-term benefit raises important issues about their clinical use that are yet to be resolved.

- Parent management training (PMT) provides parents with a variety of skills to help them manage their child's oppositional and defiant behaviors and cope with the difficulties of raising a child with ADHD.

- Educational interventions focus on managing inattentive and hyperactive-impulsive behaviors that interfere with learning, and providing a classroom environment that capitalizes on the child's strengths.
- The MTA Study, a landmark controlled comparison of intensive treatments for ADHD, found that all groups showed reductions in ADHD symptoms over time, but there were significant differences among them in the amount of change; stimulants appeared to be the most effective form of treatment.
- Additional interventions for ADHD include family counseling and support groups, and individual counseling for the child.

Key Terms

attentional capacity, p. 113
attention-deficit/hyperactivity disorder (ADHD), p. 110
combined type (ADHD-C), p. 116
developmental coordination disorder, p. 120
distractibility, p. 113
executive functions, p. 118
frontostriatal circuitry of the brain, p. 132
goodness of fit, p. 133
hyperactive, p. 111
impulsive, p. 111
inattentive, p. 111
methylphenidate, p. 135
parent management training (PMT), p. 137
positive illusory bias, p. 119
predominantly hyperactive-impulsive type (ADHD-HI), p. 116

predominantly inattentive type (ADHD-PI), p. 116
response-cost procedures, p. 138
selective attention, p. 113
stimulant medications, p. 135
subtype, p. 116
sustained attention, p. 113
tic disorders, p. 120

 InfoTrac College Edition

To research recent articles on the subject, go to:
www.infotrac-college/thomsonlearning.com

Enter search terms: ATTENTION DEFICIT HYPERACTIVITY DISORDER, HYPERACTIVE CHILDREN, INATTENTION

Conduct Problems

Our youth now love luxury. They have bad manners, contempt for authority and disrespect for their elders. Children nowadays are tyrants.

—Socrates, 470–399 B.C.

Children's conduct problems have long been a societal concern, and considered to be forerunners of juvenile delinquency and adult criminality. However, despite enormous public and professional attention, substantial numbers of youths continue to display antisocial, destructive, and violent behaviors, many of which are hidden from the public. Although the most lethal forms of youth violence in the United States have been steadily decreasing since 1994, the prevalence of aggravated assault in particular, remains alarmingly high (H. N. Snyder & Sickmund, 1999). A nationally representative survey of U.S. high school students found that 36% reported being in a physical fight in the past year, and 26% reported carrying a weapon in the last month (Brener, Simon, Krug, & Lowry, 1999).

The high prevalence of youths with conduct problems and the harm inflicted on their victims create an urgent need to offer them understanding and assistance (Reese, Vera, Simon, & Ikeda, 2000). Tragic school shootings by youths provide stark reminders of the societal impact of youth violence. There are more gun dealers than teachers in California, and bulletproof vests now come in children's sizes (Toch, 1993). Unfortunately, school shootings and media portrayals of extreme antisocial acts by young people fuel popular beliefs that aggression is inherent in humans, that some children are born bad, or that youth violence is symptomatic of a decaying society. In fact, although youth violence is an ongoing and extremely serious problem, much progress has been made in understanding, reducing, and preventing it, as well as less harmful but still serious forms of antisocial conduct (U.S. Department of Health and Human Services, 2001).

Description

Andy
Young Rage

"Andy threw his booster seat in my face and hit my jaw. He thought it was funny. He was acting up, and I think he had already had one time-out for yelling and screaming and interrupting us at the table. And I said, "Fine, you are not having dessert." He flew into a rage. He picked up a metal fork and threw it at me with all his force, and hit me—barely missed my eye. There was blood on my forehead. I was hysterical. I was terrified to see that type of rage in a 4-year-old." (Adapted from *Troubled Families—Problem Children: Working with Parents: A Collaborative Process,* by C. Webster-Stratton and M. Herbert, 1994, pp. 44–45. Copyright © 1994 by John Wiley & Sons, Ltd. Reprinted by permission of John Wiley & Sons, Ltd.)

Marvelle
Defiant

"She just drives me up the wall. She's irritable all the time and never does anything I ask her to do. When she doesn't get her way she throws a full-blown tantrum. Her behavior is also a problem at school. Her teacher can't get her to do schoolwork—she simply refuses. She's also defiant, won't stay in her seat, and talks constantly. She's disrupting the entire class. I'm worried that she's headed for serious problems if she doesn't shape up soon."

Nick
Not Like Other Kids

Outwardly, Nick is a normal 10-year-old. He loves sports, especially football. He has a talent for drawing and an aptitude for math . . . but Nick isn't like other kids. At age 2, he put a can of cat food on the stove, and lit the burner—it exploded. In one 5-day period last March, he threw a rock at a girl at the YMCA, hitting her in the head and drawing blood; set fire to his room; pushed his sister down the stairs; whipped the family dog with a chain; and stole $20 from his mother's wallet. (Adapted from Colapinto, 1993, p. 122)

Bulletproof vests now come in children's sizes.

Conduct problem(s) (CPs) and antisocial behavior(s) (ASBs) are age-inappropriate actions and attitudes of a child that violate family expectations, societal norms, and the personal or property rights of others (McMahon & Estes, 1997). Like the children in our examples, youngsters with CPs display a wide range of disruptive and rule-violating behaviors from whining, swearing, and temper tantrums to vandalism, theft, and assault. Given this diversity, we consider many types, pathways, causes, and outcomes of ASB.

Although we may be shocked by their actions, children with CPs frequently (not always) grow up in extremely unfortunate family and neighborhood circumstances where they experience physical abuse, neglect, poverty, or exposure to criminal activity (Lahey, Miller, Gordon, & Riley, 1999). These circumstances do not excuse their behavior but rather provide an important backdrop for understanding and preventing CPs.

Steve's tragic family situation may evoke sympathy and concern. Children with CPs are often seriously disturbed and need help. At the same time, the callousness of their deeds may evoke outrage, concern for innocent victims, and a desire to severely punish or confine them (Kazdin, 1995). As they grow older, these children walk a fine line between pleas from the mental health and juvenile justice systems for understanding and rehabilitation, and demands from the general public and the criminal justice system to punish the offenders and protect the victims. Most people have opinions about the nature of youth violence and what can be done about it. To examine some of your own views, consider the statements in Box 6.1.

Policies and practices that place youth with conduct problems together in therapy or other settings can increase their antisocial and delinquent behavior.

SECTION SUMMARY

- Conduct problems (CPs) or antisocial behavior(s) (ASBs) are age-inappropriate actions and attitudes of a child that violate family expectations, societal norms, and the personal or property rights of others.

- The nature, causes, and outcomes of CPs in children are wide-ranging, requiring that we consider several different types and pathways.

- Many children with CPs grow up in extremely unfortunate family and neighborhood circumstances.

Context, Costs, and Perspectives

Context

Most young people break the rules from time to time. Did you ever defy authority, lie, fight, skip school, run away, break curfew, destroy property, steal, or drive under the influence of alcohol? If so, welcome to the club—many young people admit to these antisocial acts. In fact, about 80% of high school students have consumed alcohol, 60% have smoked cigarettes, and 50% have smoked marijuana (Johnston, O'Malley, & Bachman, 2002). Very few adolescents (about 6%) refrain from ASBs entirely, and those adolescents tend to be excessively conventional, trusting, anxious, and socially incompetent—not well-adjusted (Moffitt, Caspi, Dickson, Silva, & Stanton, 1996).

ASBs appear and then decline during normal development (Tremblay et al., 1999). Most toddlers hit, kick, intentionally break things, tell lies, and resist adult authority, but most also learn to control these behaviors by the time they enter school. About 50% of parents report that

their preschoolers steal, lie, disobey, or destroy property, in contrast to 10% of parents who report the same about young adolescents (Achenbach, 1991a). This decline partially reflects the parents' lack of awareness of the trouble their teens may be getting into. However, teens also report that their own ASBs decrease with age (Achenbach, 1991b). Common ASBs for clinic-referred and nonreferred boys and girls, as reported by their parents, are shown in Figure 6.1.

The graphs in Figure 6.1 illustrate several important features of ASBs in the context of normal development:

- ASBs vary in severity, from minor disobedience to fighting.
- Some ASBs decrease with age (e.g., disobeying at home), whereas others increase with age and opportunity (e.g., hanging around kids who get into trouble).
- ASBs are more common in boys than girls during childhood but this difference narrows in adolescence.

Even though ASB often decreases with age, children who are the most physically aggressive in early childhood maintain their relative standing over time (Broidy et al., 2003). Longitudinal studies find aggressive acts such as persistent physical fighting to be highly stable, with an average correlation of about .70 for measures of these behaviors taken at different times (Loeber, Green, Lahey, & Kalb, 2000). This makes aggressive behavior about as stable as IQ scores!

Social and Economic Costs

The world remains a threatening, often dangerous place for children and youths. And in our country today, the greatest threat to the lives of children and adolescents is not disease or starvation or abandonment, but the terrible reality of violence.

—Donna E. Shalala, U.S. Surgeon General's Report on Youth Violence, 2001

The staggering costs borne by the educational, health, criminal justice, social service, and mental health systems that deal with youngsters with CPs make ASB the most costly mental health problem in North America (M. A. Cohen, Miller, & Rossman, 1994). Although antisocial acts are universal in young people, an early, persistent, and extreme pattern of ASB occurs in only about 5% of children (Hinshaw & Lee, 2003). These children cause considerable and disproportionate amounts of harm, accounting for over 50% of all crime in the United States, and about 30% to 50% of clinic referrals (Loeber, Burke, Lahey, Winters, & Zera, 2000).

More than 2,000 juveniles were arrested for murder and nonnegligent manslaughter in 1997, and more than

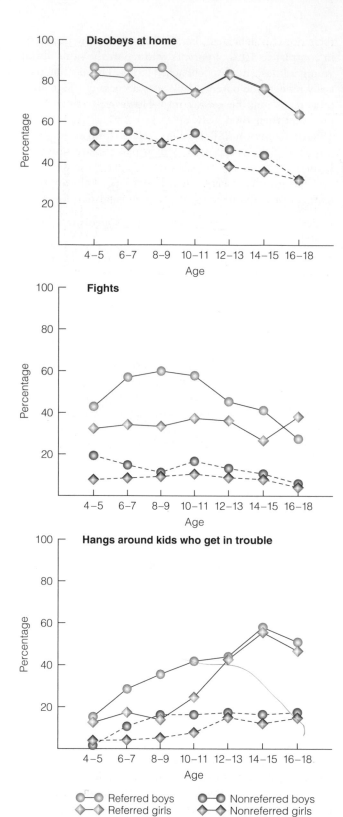

Figure 6.1. Parent-reported frequencies for common ASB in clinic and nonreferred boys and girls ages 4–18

Source: From Manual for the Child Behavior Checklist/4–18 and 1991 Profile, by T. M. Achenbach, 1991, pp. 131, 134, 138, 145. University of Vermont. Copyright by T. M. Achenbach. Reproduced by permission.

100,000 for other violent crimes (Maguire & Pastore, 1998). More teenagers in the United States die from firearm injuries than from all diseases combined, and are more than twice as likely as adults to be victims of violence, most often commited by other teens (H. N. Snyder & Sickmund, 1999). Each school day, thousands of students stay home—not because of illness, but because they are afraid of being stabbed, shot, or beaten.

The costs of ASB can be understood not only in terms of lives but also in dollars. As much as 20% of all mental health expenditures in the United States are attributable to crime (National Institute of Justice, 1996). As shown in Figure 6.2, it has been estimated that allowing just one youth to leave high school for a life of crime and drug abuse costs society about $2 million (M. Cohen, 1998).

Perspectives

CPs have been viewed from several perspectives, each using different terms and definitions to describe similar patterns of behavior. These include the legal, psychological, psychiatric, and public health perspectives.

Legal   Legally, CPs are defined as delinquent or criminal acts. Legal definitions depend on laws that change over time or differ across locations. Since delinquent acts result from apprehension and court contact, legal definitions exclude the ASBs of very young children that usually occur at home or school. It is also important to distinguish official delinquency from self-reported delinquency. Youths who display ASB and are apprehended by police may differ from youths who display the same patterns but are not apprehended because of their intelligence or resourcefulness. Debate is ongoing about the age at which children should be held responsible for their delinquent behavior. The minimum age of responsibility is 12 in most states and provinces, but this has fluctuated over the years in relation to society's tolerance or intolerance of ASB.

Given the large numbers of youths involved in criminal activities, we must ask whether these behaviors are understandable (albeit objectionable) adaptations to a hostile environment—the most common reason that youngsters give for carrying a weapon is self-defense (Simon, Dent, & Sussman, 1997). Unfortunately, no clear boundaries exist between delinquent acts that are a reaction to environmental conditions, such as a high-crime neighborhood, and those that result from factors within the child, such as impulsivity. Some criminal behaviors, such as arson and truancy, are arbitrarily included in current mental health definitions, whereas selling drugs and prostitution are not. A legal definition of delinquency may result from one or two isolated acts, whereas a mental health definition usually requires the child to display a persistent pattern of ASBs. Thus, only a subgroup of chil-

INVOICE

To: American public
For: One lost youth

DESCRIPTION	COST
Crime:	
Juvenile career (4 years @ 1–4 crimes/ year)	
Victim costs	$62,000–$250,000
Criminal justice costs	$21,000–$84,000
Adult career (6 years @ 10.6 crimes/year)	
Victim costs	$1,000,000
Criminal justice costs	$335,000
Offender productivity loss	$64,000
Total crime cost	**$1.5–$1.8 million**
Present value*	**$1.3–$1.5 million**
Drug abuse:	
Resources devoted to drug market	$84,000–$168,000
Reduced productivity loss	$27,600
Drug treatment costs	$10,200
Medical treatment of drug-related	
illnesses	$11,000
Premature death	$31,800–$223,000
Criminal justice costs associated with	
drug crimes	$40,500
Total drug abuse cost	**$200,000–$480,000**
Present value*	**$150,000–$360,000**
Costs imposed by high school dropout:	
Lost wage productivity	$300,000
Fringe benefits	$75,000
Nonmarket losses	$95,000–$375,000
Total dropout cost	**$470,000–$750,000**
Present value*	**$243,000–$388,000**
Total loss	**$2.2–$3 million**
Present value*	**$1.7–$2.3 million**

* Present value is the amount of money that would need to be invested today to cover the future costs of the youth's behavior.
Source: Authors' adaptation of Cohen's The monetary value of saving a high-risk youth, *Journal of Quantitative Criminology, 14*(1) From H. N. Snyder & M. Sickmund (1999), p. 82.

Figure 6.2. The cost of one lost youth: About $2 million

dren who meet a legal definition of delinquency will also meet the definition for a mental disorder (Cicchetti & Richters, 1993).

Psychological From a psychological perspective, CPs fall along a continuous dimension of **externalizing behavior,** which includes a mix of impulsive, overactive, aggressive, and delinquent acts (Burns et al., 1997). Children at the upper extreme, usually one or more standard deviations above the mean, are considered to have CPs. The

externalizing dimension itself consists of two related but independent subdimensions labeled "delinquent" and "aggressive" (Achenbach, 1991a). **Delinquent** behaviors include rule violations such as running away, setting fires, stealing, skipping school, using alcohol and drugs, and committing acts of vandalism. Aggressive behaviors include fighting, destructiveness, disobedience, showing off, being defiant, threatening others, and being disruptive at school (Achenbach, 1993a).

Two additional independent dimensions of ASB have

been identified: overt-covert and destructive-nondestructive (Frick et al., 1993). The **overt-covert dimension** ranges from overt visible acts such as fighting to covert hidden acts such as lying or stealing. Children who display overt ASB tend to be negative, irritable, and resentful in their reactions to hostile situations, and to experience higher levels of family conflict (Kazdin, 1992). In contrast, those displaying covert ASB are less social, more anxious, and more suspicious of others, and come from homes that provide little family support. Most children with CPs display both overt and covert ASBs. These children are in frequent conflict with authority, show the most severe family dysfunction, and have the poorest long-term outcomes (Loeber, Lahey, & Thomas, 1991). The **destructive-nondestructive dimension** ranges from acts such as cruelty to animals or physical assault to nondestructive behaviors such as arguing or irritability.

As shown in Figure 6.3, crossing the overt-covert with the destructive-nondestructive dimension results in four categories of CPs: (A) covert-destructive, or property violations; (B) overt-destructive, or aggression; (C) covert-nondestructive, or status violations; and (D) overt-nondestructive, or oppositional behavior. Children who display overt-destructive behaviors, particularly persistent physical fighting, are at high risk for later psychiatric problems and impairment in functioning (Broidy et al., 2003).

Psychiatric   From a psychiatric perspective, CPs are defined as distinct mental disorders based on DSM symptoms (APA, 2000). In DSM-IV-TR, **disruptive behavior disorders** are persistent patterns of ASB, represented by the categories of oppositional defiant disorder (ODD) and conduct disorder (CD) (Loeber, Green, Lahey, & Kalb, 2000). Also relevant to understanding CPs in children and their adult outcomes is the diagnosis of antisocial personality disorder (APD). In the next section on features of the DSM we define each of these disorders.

Public Health   This perspective blends the legal, psychological, and psychiatric perspectives with public health concepts of prevention and intervention (U.S. Department of Health and Human Services, 2001). The goal is to reduce the number of injuries, deaths, personal suffering, and economic costs associated with youth violence, in the same way that other health concerns such as automobile accidents or tobacco use are addressed. The public health approach cuts across disciplines and brings together policy makers, scientists, professionals, communities, families, and individuals to understand CPs in youths and determine how they can be treated and prevented (Pettit & Dodge, 2003).

Two sides of the externalizing dimension: overt and covert

© Elizabeth Crews

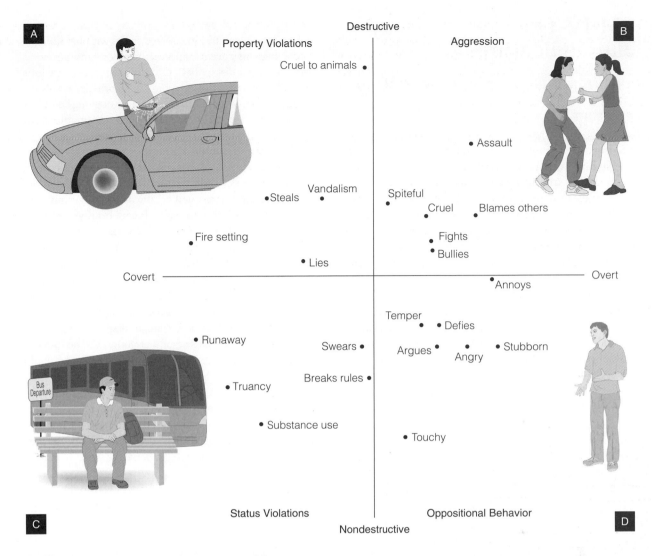

Destructive

Property Violations   Aggression

Cruel to animals •

• Assault

Steals •   Vandalism •   Spiteful •   Cruel •   Blames others •

Fire setting •   • Fights
                 • Bullies
        • Lies

Covert ————————————————————————— Overt
                                    • Annoys

                    Temper •   • Defies
Runaway •   Swears •   Argues •   • Stubborn
                              Angry •
Truancy •   Breaks rules •

Substance use •

                    • Touchy

Status Violations   Oppositional Behavior

Nondestructive

Figure 6.3. Four categories of conduct problems

Source: Adapted from "Oppositional Defiant Disorder and Conduct Disorder: A Meta-Analytic Review of Factor Analyses and Cross-Validation in a Clinic Sample," by P. J. Frick, Y. Van Horn, B. B. Lahey, M. A. G. Christ, R. Loeber, E. A. Hart, L. Tannenbaum, and K. Hanson, *Clinical Psychology Review, 13,* 319–340. Copyright © 1993 Elsevier Science, Ltd. Reprinted with permission from Elsevier Science.

SECTION SUMMARY

- For most children, ASBs appear and then decline during normal development, although children who are most aggressive maintain their relative standing over time.

- Costs to the educational, health, social service, criminal justice, and mental health systems that deal with youth with CPs make ASB the most costly mental health problem in North America.

- From a legal perspective, CPs are defined as delinquent or criminal acts that result in apprehension and court contact.

- From a psychological perspective, CPs fall along a continuous dimension of externalizing behavior, which includes a mix of impulsive, overactive, aggressive, and delinquent acts.

- From a psychiatric perspective, CPs are viewed as distinct mental disorders based on DSM symptoms. These are called disruptive behavior disorders, and include oppositional defiant disorder and conduct disorder.

- A public health perspective cuts across disciplines and blends the legal, psychological, and psychiatric perspectives with public health concepts of prevention and intervention.

DSM-IV-TR: Defining Features

Oppositional Defiant Disorder (ODD)

> ### Gordon
> **Enjoying His Power**
>
> He just digs his heels in, "That's it, I am not wearing these socks! Forget it, I'm not going!" And he is right. He's gone to school in his pajamas, without lunch, in the pouring rain without a coat . . . He will explain to me, "Mom, we are done with this discussion." . . . He doesn't have an easy-going bone in his body. He is not ever going to say, "Okay, I'll put that turtleneck on." It's going to be, "I will do something but only on my terms . . . I will do nothing that you want me to do and furthermore I'll throw such a tantrum and throw this cereal bowl all over the wall, so you will be late, and mad at me when you clean it up." . . . He enjoys that power. (Adapted from *Troubled Families—Problem Children: Working with Parents: A Collaborative Process*, by C. Webster-Stratton and M. Herbert, 1994, p. 47. Copyright © 1994 by John Wiley & Sons, Ltd. Reprinted by permission of John Wiley & Sons, Ltd.)

Children with **oppositional defiant disorder (ODD)** display an age-inappropriate recurrent pattern of stubborn, hostile, and defiant behaviors (see Table 6.1 for DSM diagnostic criteria). ODD was included in DSM to capture early displays of antisocial and aggressive behavior by preschool and school-age children. Because many of these behaviors, such as temper tantrums or arguing, are extremely common in young children, there are doubts about the viability of this category (Angold & Costello, 1996; Kirk & Hutchins, 1994). However, evidence for an independent cluster of nondestructive-overt behaviors, such as defying and arguing, supports ODD as a distinct disorder (see quadrant D of Figure 6.3). ODD behaviors have also been found to have extremely negative effects on parent–child interactions (Greene & Doyle, 1999). In fact, 75% of clinic-referred preschoolers from low-income environments meet DSM criteria for ODD (Keenan & Wakschlag, 2000).

Conduct Disorder (CD)

> ### Greg
> **Dangerous Distress**
>
> Greg, age 10, was referred because of his excessive fighting, hyperactivity, temper tantrums, and disruptive behavior at home and at school. At home, Greg argued with his mother, started fights with his siblings, stole from his parents, and constantly threatened to set fires when disciplined. On three separate occasions, he actually had set fires to rugs, bedspreads, and trash in his home. One fire led to several thousand dollars in damages. Greg also lied frequently; at school his lying got others into trouble, precipitating frequent fights with peers and denials of any wrongdoing.
>
> Greg was brought to the clinic because his parents felt that he was becoming totally unmanageable. A few incidents were mentioned as unusually dangerous—for example, Greg's attempt to suffocate his 2-year-old brother by holding a pillow over his face. Also, Greg had recently wandered the streets at night and had broken windows of parked cars.
>
> Greg's parents occasionally resorted to severe punishment, using paddles and belts, or locking him in his room for 2 to 3 days. His father has been employed only sporadically for the last 2 years, and spends much of his time at home sleeping or watching TV. The loss of income led to increased stress. Greg said that he could not stand to be with his dad because his dad got mad all the time over little things. Greg's mother worked full-time and was not at home very much. She had a history of depression with two suicide attempts in the last 3 years. She was hospitalized on each occasion for approximately 2 months. Greg's behavior became even worse during these periods.
>
> Although Greg's intelligence was within the normal range, his academic performance was behind grade level, and he was in a special class because of his overactive and disruptive behavior. His parents were told that unless they got help, Greg could not return to the school the next year. His parents did not know where to turn. They talked about giving Greg up or putting him in a special boarding school where more discipline might make him "shape up." (Adapted from *Conduct Disorders in Childhood and Adolescence,* by A. E. Kazdin, pp. 2–3. Copyright © 1995 by Sage Publications. Adapted by permission.)

Conduct disorder (CD) describes children who display a repetitive and persistent pattern of severe aggressive and antisocial acts that involve inflicting pain on others or interfering with rights of others through physical and verbal aggression, stealing, or committing acts of vandalism (see Table 6.2 for DSM diagnostic criteria).

Greg's case illustrates several key features of CD (Adapted from *Conduct Disorders in Childhood and Adolescence,* by A. E. Kazdin, pp. 2–3. Copyright © 1995 by Sage Publications. Adapted by permission.):

- Children with CD engage in severe behaviors. Greg set fires and tried to suffocate his 2-year-old brother.

He also displayed less severe problems, such as noncompliance and temper tantrums, but these weren't the primary reasons for referral.

- They often experience accompanying problems such as ADHD, academic deficiencies, and poor relations with peers.

- Their families often display child-rearing practices that contribute to the problem, such as the use of harsh punishment, and have their own problems and stresses, such as marital discord, psychiatric problems, and unemployment. Greg's mother had a history of depression.

- Their parents feel these children are out of control, and feel helpless to do anything about it. Greg's parents want to give him up or put him in a boarding school.

At age 6 he was known to have started fights, including punching an older boy because he wouldn't give him a pickle. He was made to stay after school almost every day for saying "the F word," flipping people off, pinching and hitting. He had stabbed a girl with a pencil. And one day he shot and killed a classmate, 6-year-old Kayla. He had attacked her before and, on the day before the killing, tried to kiss her and was rebuffed. (Rosenblatt, 2000).

CD and Age of Onset   Should we attach any special significance to the age at which symptoms of CD first occur?

DSM makes the distinction between youngsters with an early or late onset of CD. Those with **childhood-onset CD** display at least one symptom of the disorder before age 10, whereas those with **adolescent-onset CD** do not. Increasing evidence points to the importance of age of onset in diagnosing and treating children with CD (Lahey &

Waldman, 2003). Children with childhood-onset CD are more likely to be boys, show more aggressive symptoms, account for a disproportionate amount of illegal activity, and persist in their ASB over time (Lahey, Goodman, et al., 1999). In contrast, children with adolescent-onset CD are as likely to be girls as boys, and do not display the severity or psychopathology that characterizes the childhood-onset group. They are also less likely to commit violent offenses or to persist in their ASB as they get older. Age of onset does make a difference.

CD and ODD There is much overlap between the symptoms of CD and ODD (Nottelman & Jensen, 1995). A hotly debated issue is whether ODD is a separate disorder from CD, a milder, earlier version, or a reflection of the same underlying temperament and deficits (Lahey & Waldman, 2003; Patterson, DeGarmo, & Knutson, 2000). Symptoms of ODD typically emerge 2 to 3 years before CD symptoms, at about age 6 years for ODD versus age 9 years for CD (Loeber, Green, Lahey, Christ, & Frick, 1992). Since ODD symptoms emerge first, it is possible that they are precursors of CD for some children. However, most children who display ODD do not progress to more severe CD—at least 50% maintain their ODD diagnosis without progressing, and another 25% cease to display ODD problems entirely (Hinshaw, Lahey, & Hart, 1993). Thus for most children, ODD is an extreme developmental variation, but not one that necessarily signals an escalation to more serious CPs (Speltz, McClellan, DeKlyen, & Jones, 1999). In contrast, new cases of CD are almost always preceded by ODD, and nearly all children with CD continue to display ODD symptoms (Biederman et al., 1996).

Lower rates of CD in young children may also result from the nature of the DSM criteria. DSM prescribes the same symptoms for diagnosing CD at all ages, even though many don't apply to young children (e.g., breaking into houses, skipping school). Thus, lower rates of CD in young children could reflect the use of an insensitive diagnostic system that is unadjusted for the child's age.

Jason

No Conscience

Jason, age 13, had been involved in serious crime—including breaking and entering, thefts, and assaults on younger children—by age 6. Listening to Jason talk was frightening. Asked why he committed crimes, this product of a stable, professional family replied, "I like it. My f___ parents really freak out when I get in trouble, but I don't give a sh_ as long as I'm having a good time. Yeah, I've always been wild." About other people, including his victims, Jason had this to say: "You want the truth? They'd screw me if they could, only I get my shots in first." He liked to rob

homeless people, especially "f_gots," "bag ladies," and street kids, because, "They're used to it. They don't whine to the police . . . One guy I got into a fight with pulled a knife and I took it and rammed it in his eye. He ran around screaming like a baby. What a jerk!" (Adapted from Hare, 1993, p. 162)

CD and Antisocial Personality Disorder (APD) Persistent aggressive behavior and ASB in childhood may be a precursor of adult **antisocial personality disorder (APD)**, a pervasive pattern of disregard for, and violation of, the rights of others, as well as involvement in multiple illegal behaviors (APA, 2000). As many as 40% of children with CD develop APD as adults (Hinshaw, 1994). In addition to their early ASB, adults with APD may also display **psychopathy,** which is defined as a pattern of callous, manipulative, deceitful, and remorseless behavior (Sutker, 1994).

Far less is known about psychopathy in children than in adults. However, signs of a lack of conscience occur in some children as young as 3 to 5 years (Kochanska, De Vet, Goldman, Murray, & Putnam, 1994). Other youngsters, like Jason, began commiting brutal acts of violence at age 6 with little remorse. A subgroup of preschoolers with behavior problems show a worrisome increase in their lack of concern for others as they begin to enter middle childhood (Hastings, Zahn-Waxler, Robinson, Usher, & Bridges, 2000). Finally, adolescents with CD are less likely than peers to show embarrassment, which suggests a failure to inhibit emotions and actions in accordance with social conventions (Keltner, Moffitt, & Stouthamer-Loeber, 1995).

These and other findings point to a subgroup of children with CPs whose lack of concern for others may place them at especially high risk for extreme antisocial and aggressive acts. They display a **callous and unemotional interpersonal style (CU)** characterized by traits such as lacking in guilt, not showing empathy, not showing emotions, and related traits of narcissism and impulsivity (Frick & Ellis, 1999). The behaviors and characteristics making up these traits are shown in Table 6.3. Children who display a CU style also display a lack of *behavioral inhibition* as reflected in their preference for novel and perilous activities, and a diminished sensitivity to cues for danger and punishment when seeking rewards (Frick et al., 2003).

Despite their higher intelligence, children with a CU style display a greater number and variety of CPs, have more frequent contact with police, and a stronger parental history of APD than other children with CPs (Christian, Frick, Hill, Tyler, & Frazer, 1997). Research suggests that different developmental mechanisms may underlie the behavioral and emotional problems seen in children with CD who also display the CU style (Frick et al., 2003).

Table 6.3
Callous and Unemotional Traits and Related Dimensions in Children

CALLOUS AND UNEMOTIONAL TRAITS	NARCISSISTIC TRAITS	IMPULSIVITY
Is unconcerned about the feelings of others.	Thinks he or she is more important than others.	Acts without thinking of the consequences.
Does not feel bad or guilty over misdeeds.	Brags excessively about abilities, accomplishments, or possessions.	Does not plan ahead or leaves things until the last minute.
Is unconcerned about how well he/she does at school or work.	Uses or "cons" others to get what he/she wants.	Engages in risky and dangerous activities.
Is not good at keeping promises.	Can be charming at times, but in ways that seem insincere or superficial.	Blames others for mistakes.
Does not show feelings or emotions.	Teases or makes fun of others.	Gets bored easily.
Does not keep the same friends.	Becomes angry when corrected or punished.	

From "A Comprehensive and Individualized Treatment Approach for Children and Adolescents with Conduct Disorders." By P. J. Frick, 2000, *Cognitive and Behavioral Practice, 7,* pp. 30–37. Copyright © 2000 by the Association for Advancement of Behavior Therapy. Reprinted by permission of the publisher.

It is also possible that the CU style in childhood may be related to adult forms of psychopathy, although a link is yet to be established.

At this point you might want to look at Box 6.2 to sharpen your knowledge of DSM criteria by considering whether or not TV cartoon personality Bart Simpson qualifies for a diagnosis of ODD or CD.

SECTION SUMMARY

- Children with oppositional defiant disorder (ODD) display an age-inappropriate pattern of stubborn, hostile, and defiant behaviors.

- Conduct disorder (CD) describes children who display severe aggressive and antisocial acts involving inflicting pain upon others or interfering with rights of others through physical and verbal aggression, stealing, or committing acts of vandalism.

- Children who display childhood-onset CD (before age 10) are more likely to be boys, show more aggressive symptoms, account for a disproportionate amount of illegal activity, and persist in their ASB over time.

- Children with adolescent-onset CD are as likely to be girls as boys, and do not display the severity or psychopathology that characterizes the childhood-onset group.

- There is much overlap between CD and ODD. However, most children who display ODD do not progress to more severe CD.

- Persistent aggressive behavior and ASB in childhood may be a precursor of adult antisocial personality disorder (APD), a pervasive pattern of disregard for, and violation of, the rights of others, as well as involvement in multiple illegal behaviors.

A Closer Look

BOX 6.2 Bart Simpson: ODD or CD?

Sharpen your knowledge of DSM-IV-TR criteria for ODD and CD by considering whether TV cartoon personality Bart Simpson qualifies for a diagnosis of one of these disorders. Here is a list of antisocial acts displayed by Bart:

- Flushes a cherry bomb down the toilet
- Rearranges party snacks to say "Boy our party sucks"
- Loosens the top on Milhouse's salt shaker
- Lights Homer's tie on fire
- Tricks Flanders kids into giving cookies away
- Pretends to be Timmy (trapped in a well)
- Pulls carpet up, writes "Bart" on carpet
- Plays with and later breaks grandpa Abe's false teeth
- Flushes Homer's wallet and keys down toilet
- Cuts all of baby Maggie's hair off
- Paints extra lines on parking lot
- Leaves box factory tour
- Pops heads off Mr. Burns' statues/floods his car
- Smashes Mr. Burns' windows
- Recounts throwing mail in sewer with Milhouse
- Phones 911 to get babysitter into trouble

Comment: Based on Bart's symptoms of aggression, destruction of property, deceitfulness, and serious violation of rules, he easily qualifies for a DSM diagnosis of CD. Like most children with CD, Bart also displays behaviors of ODD, but this diagnosis is not made when criteria for CD are met.

- A subgroup of children with CPs display a callous and unemotional interpersonal style (CU) characterized by traits such as lacking in guilt, not showing empathy, and not displaying feelings or emotions. These children display a preference for novel and perilous activities and a diminished sensitivity to cues for danger and punishment when seeking rewards.

Associated Characteristics

Many child, family, peer, school, and community factors are associated with CPs in youths. Some factors co-occur with CPs, others increase the likelihood of CPs, and still others are the result of CPs. To fully understand this behavior, we must examine these various factors and how they interact over time.

Cognitive and Verbal Deficits

Although most children with CPs have normal intelligence, they score nearly 8 points lower than their peers on IQ tests (Hogan, 1999). This IQ deficit may be greater (more than 15 points) for children with childhood-onset CD, and cannot be accounted for solely by socioeconomic disadvantage, race, or detection by the police (Lynam, Moffitt, & Stouthamer-Loeber, 1993). Lower IQ scores in children with CPs may be related to the co-occurrence of ADHD (Waschbusch, 2002). When ADHD is also present, the association between a lower IQ and an increased risk for ASB is clear. It is less clear how a lower IQ mediates this risk (Rutter, 2003a).

Verbal IQ is consistently lower than performance IQ in children with CPs, suggesting a specific and pervasive deficit in language (Lynam & Henry, 2001). This deficit may affect the child's receptive listening, reading, problem solving (Jafee & D'Zurilla, 2003), expressive speech and writing, and memory for verbal material (Brennan, Hall, Bor, Najman, & Williams, 2003; Dionne, Tremblay, Boivin, Laplante, & Perusse, 2003). It has been suggested that verbal and language deficits may contribute to ASB by interfering with the development of self-control, emotion regulation, or the labeling of emotions in others, which may lead to a lack of empathy (Caspi & Moffitt, 1995; Hastings et al., 2000).

Lower IQ and verbal intelligence are present early in a child's development, long before the emergence of CPs and delinquent behavior. However, their presence alone does not predict future aggression—family factors are also important. Children with both verbal impairments and family adversity display 4 times as much aggressive behavior as children with only one factor (Moffitt, 1990). Thus, verbal deficits may increase the child's vulnerability to the effects of a hostile family environment. How this

occurs is not known, but one possibility is that a child's verbal deficits may make it more difficult for parents to understand their child's needs, which leads to parents' frustration, fewer positive interactions, more punishment, and greater difficulties in teaching social skills (Patterson, 1996).

Children with CPs rarely consider the future implications of their behavior or its impact on others. They fail to inhibit their impulsive behavior, keep social values or future rewards in mind, or adapt their actions to changing circumstances. This pattern suggests deficits in executive functions similar to those of children with ADHD (Toupin, Dery, Pauze, Mercier, & Fortin, 2000). Because ODD/CD and ADHD frequently co-occur, the observed deficits in executive functions in these children could be due to the presence of co-occurring ADHD (Pennington & Ozonoff, 1996).

School and Learning Problems

Every time you stop a school, you will have to build a jail.

—Mark Twain, 1900

Youngsters with CPs display many school difficulties including academic underachievement, grade retention, special education placement, dropout, suspension, and expulsion (Roeser & Eccles, 2000). Although the frustration and demoralization associated with school failure can lead to ASB in some children (Maughan, Gray, & Rutter, 1985), there is little evidence that academic failure is the primary cause of ASB, particularly in early childhood. Since many young children display patterns of ASB long before they enter school, it is more likely that a common factor, such as a neuropsychological or language deficit or socioeconomic disadvantage, underlies both CPs and school difficulties (Lahey & Waldman, 2003).

Children with CPs are most likely to experience academic underachievement in language and reading (Moffitt 1993b). However, as with their cognitive and verbal deficits, this relationship may be best accounted for by the co-occurrence of ADHD. When ADHD is not present, children with CPs are no more likely to underachieve than other children (Frick et al., 1991; Hinshaw, 1992a). Thus, CP is related to academic underachievement, but ADHD is a crucial mediating factor (Rapport, Scanlan, & Denney, 1999).

Underachievement and CP are also likely to influence one another over time. Subtle early language deficits may lead to reading and communication difficulties, which in turn may heighten ASB in elementary school. Youngsters with poor academic skills are increasingly likely to lose interest in school and to associate with delinquent peers. By adolescence, the relationship between ASB and underachievement is firmly established.

Self-Esteem Deficits

Although many children with CPs have low self-esteem, there is little support for the view that low self-esteem is the primary cause of ASB. Rather, ASB seems to be related to an inflated, unstable, and/or tentative view of self (R. F. Baumeister, Bushman, & Campbell, 2000). For example, aggressive children may overestimate their acceptance by other children (David & Kistner, 2000). Any perceived threat to their biased view of self may lead to violence, which provides a way to avoid a lowering of self-concept (R. F. Baumeister, Smart, & Boden, 1996). Consistent with this view, self-esteem among youth gang members seems to conform to a pattern in which any increment in status, respect, or prestige in self-esteem for one group member takes away from what is available for others (E. Anderson, 1994). Thus, although low self-esteem is not the primary concern, youngsters with CPs may experience other disturbances in self-concept that contribute to their ASB.

Peer Problems

He is so aggressive around other children. We can't really trust him not to walk up and wallop the smaller ones. He pokes them in the eyes or pushes them down . . . It's almost like he seeks out other children to hurt them.

(Adapted from *Troubled Families—Problem Children: Working with Parents: A Collaborative Process,* by C. Webster-Stratton and M. Herbert, 1994, p. 46. Copyright © 1994 by John Wiley & Sons, Ltd. Reprinted by permission of John Wiley & Sons, Ltd.)

Young children with CPs display verbal and physical aggression toward other children and poor social skills (Miller & Olson, 2000). As they grow older, most are rejected by their peers although some may remain quite popular (Rodkin, Farmer, Van Acker, & Van Acker, 2000). Social rejection by elementary school peers is a strong risk factor for adolescent CPs (Laird, Jordan, Dodge, Pettit, & Bates, 2001). For example, children rejected for a period of 2 or 3 years by grade 2, are about 5 times more likely than others to display CPs later in adolescence. As they enter school, some children with CPs become bullies, a particularly offensive pattern associated with continuing ASB into adolescence and adulthood (see Box 6.3).

Children with CPs are able to make friends. Unfortunately, their friendships are often based on a mutual attraction of like-minded antisocial individuals (Poulin, Dishion, & Haas, 1999; Vitaro, Brendgen, & Tremblay, 2000). Notably, the combination of early ASB and associating with deviant peers is the single most powerful predictor of CPs during adolescence (Moffitt, 1993a). Involvement with antisocial peers becomes increasingly stable during childhood, and supports the transition to adolescent criminal acts such as stealing, truancy, or substance abuse (Patterson, 1996). In fact, about two-thirds of all recorded youth offenses are committed in the company of two to three peers (Dishion, Andrews, & Crosby, 1995). Involvement with deviant peers is also one of the strongest predictors of accelerated autonomy and early sexual activity in adolescence (French & Dishion, 2003).

Tom and Matthew
Murderous Meeting of Minds

On February 16, 1995, in the small Minnesota town of Delano, 14-year-old Tom and his best friend Matthew ambushed and killed Tom's mother . . . These boys spent much time together. They admitted to planning the ambush (one saying they had planned it for weeks, the other, for a few hours). They were armed and waiting when Tom's mother came home from work. One conclusion seems relatively certain: This murder was an unlikely event until these antisocial friends reached consensus about doing it. (Adapted from Hartup, 1996, p. 1)

Friendships between antisocial boys are abrasive, unstable, of short duration, and not very productive (Dishion, Andrews, & Crosby, 1995). Positive exchanges, when they do occur, are compromised by the bossy and coercive behaviors that accompany them. Antisocial friends may engage in "deviant talk," selectively rewarding one another for discussions of rule breaking, but having little to say about prosocial behavior. As a result of this differential reinforcement, they may become more alike in their antisocial tendencies over time, leading to a further escalation in the frequency and variety of their antisocial activities (Granic & Dishion, 2003).

The fact that deviant peer involvement is an especially strong predictor of substance use, delinquent behavior, and violence makes intervention in this area a high priority. Unfortunately, many well-intentioned programs such as group therapy, summer programs, or boot camps, tend to create groups for youth with CPs—the very situation that may produce the most damage (Dishion, Bullock, & Granic, 2002).

Aggressive children also show deficits in how they think about social situations. They underestimate their own aggressiveness and its negative impact, and they overestimate the amount of aggression directed at them. Subgroups of aggressive children may think about social situations in different ways. For example, *reactive-aggressive*

BOX 6.3 Bullies and Their Victims

For two years, Johnny, a quiet 13-year-old, was a human plaything for some of his classmates. The teenagers badgered Johnny for money, forced him to swallow weeds and drink milk mixed with detergent, beat him up in the rest room and tied a string around his neck, leading him around as a "pet." (Olweus, 1995, p. 196)

Bullying among school children is a very old, familiar, and particularly offensive form of ASB. **Bullying** occurs when one or more children repeatedly expose another child to negative actions. Such actions may take the form of physical contact, offensive words, making faces or dirty gestures, and intentional exclusion from a group. Bullying usually involves an imbalance of power so that the victim has difficulty defending herself or himself (Olweus, 1995). The scope of this problem is large, with 7% or more of school-age children bullying other kids. Boys are much more likely than girls to bully other children, and are also somewhat more likely to be the victims of bullying.

A child's status as a victim or a bully is likely to be stable over time, and victims and bullies display certain typical characteristics. Typical victims are characterized by anxious and submissive patterns of behavior and, in the case of boys, by physical weakness. These children send a signal to others that if they are attacked or insulted, they won't retaliate. Typical bullies are distinguished by their aggressiveness toward both peers and adults. They are often impulsive, need to dominate other people, are stronger than other boys, show little empathy for their victims, and derive satisfaction, and, often, material gain from inflicting injury and suffering on their victims. One study found that nearly 40% of boys who were bullies in school were later convicted of three or more criminal offenses by the time they were 24 years old (Olweus, 1995). Thus, bullying in school appears to be part of a more general pattern of ASB.

The high prevalence of bullying and its impact on victims (sadly, some may commit suicide) make it a significant social problem. To combat this problem, school-wide interventions and policies that increase awareness of the problem, develop clear rules against bullying, and provide support and protection for victims, have been developed and successfully used in countries throughout the world (Olweus, 2003; Smith et al., 1999).

---

children (those showing an angry, defensive response to frustration or provocation) display a **hostile attributional bias,** which means they are more likely to attribute negative intent to other children, especially when the intentions of others are unclear (e.g., when a child accidentally bumps into a child, they are likely to think the other child did it on purpose). In contrast, *proactive-aggressive* children (those who use aggressive behavior deliberately to obtain a desired goal) are more likely to view their aggressive actions as positive, and to value social goals of dominance and revenge rather than affiliation (Crick & Dodge, 1996). Aggressive children display a lack of concern for others (Hastings et al., 2000), and their solutions to social problems are few in number, mostly aggressive, and inappropriate (McFadyen-Ketchum & Dodge, 1998).

It is important to keep in mind that many children with CPs live in highly aggressive and threatening circumstances. In some cases, their bias toward seeing threat and aggression in others may be an accurate reflection of the realities of living in a hostile social world, and their aggressive style of responding may be an adaptive reaction to that world.

Family Problems

Family problems are among the strongest and most consistent correlates of ASB (C. L. Carlson, Tamm, & Hogan, 1999; Reid, Patterson, & Snyder, 2002). Two types of family disturbances are related to CPs in children. *General family disturbances* are parental psychopathology, a family history of ASB, marital discord, family instability, limited resources, and antisocial family values. *Specific disturbances in parenting practices and family functioning* are excessive use of harsh discipline, lack of supervision, lack of emotional support and involvement, and parental disagreement about discipline.

The two types are interrelated, since general family disturbances such as maternal depression often lead to poor parenting practices that can lead to ASB and feelings

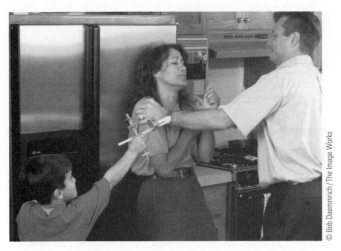

Conflict in families of children with conduct problems is common.

of parental incompetence that may lead to increased maternal depression, which completes the circle.

High levels of conflict are common in families of children with CPs. So too are poor parenting practices such as ineffective discipline, negative control, inappropriate use of punishment and rewards, failure to follow through on commands, and a lack of involvement in child rearing (Dishion & Bullock, 2002; Winsler, Diaz, McCarthy, Atencio, & Chabay, 1999). Parents may also exhibit social-cognitive deficits similar to those of their children, which suggests that the tendency of antisocial children to infer hostile intent may mirror the social perceptions of their parents (Bickett, Milich, & Brown, 1996). Finally, there is often a lack of family cohesion that is reflected in emotional detachment, poor communication and problem solving, low support, and family disorganization (Henggeler, Melton, & Smith, 1992).

"He is so violent with his sister. He split her lip a couple of times. And he almost knocked her out once when he hit her over the head with a 5-pound brass pitcher. He's put plastic bags over her head."

(Adapted from Troubled Families—Problem Children: Working with Parents: A Collaborative Process, by C. Webster-Stratton and M. Herbert, 1994, p. 45. Copyright © 1994 by John Wiley & Sons, Ltd. Reprinted by permission of John Wiley & Sons, Ltd.)

From Cain and Abel to TV's Bart and Lisa Simpson, conflict between siblings has generated much attention (C. Johnston & Freeman, 1998). Conflict is especially high between children with CPs and their siblings, and nonreferred siblings sometimes display as much negative behavior as their referred siblings, (L. M. Lewin, Hops, Davis, & Dishion, 1993), even when their sibling with CPs is not present. This suggests that their difficulties are not simply reactions to the annoying behaviors of their

antisocial brother or sister. There are many possible reasons for the similarities in the ASB of siblings, including poor parenting practices, the effects of modeling, direct influence of the other sibling, marital discord, parent psychopathology, and shared hereditary influences. Whatever the reasons, the collaboration of siblings in one another's deviant behavior can heighten their risk for developing later ASB (Bullock & Dishion, 2002).

In this section we have described many common problems in families of children with CPs. Later in this chapter we consider how these family problems might combine with other factors to cause ASB.

Health-Related Problems

Young people with CPs engage in many behaviors that place them at high risk for personal injuries, illnesses, overdoses from drug abuse, sexually transmitted diseases, and substance abuse. Rates of premature death (before age 30) due to various causes (e.g., homicide, suicide, accidental poisoning, traffic accident, drug overdose) are 3 to 4 times higher in boys with CPs than in boys without CPs (contrary to popular belief, it's not the good that die young!) (Kratzer & Hodgins, 1997). ASB is also associated with an early onset and persistence of sexual activity (Capaldi, Crosby, & Stoolmiller, 1996; Paul, Fitzjohn, Herbison, & Dickson, 2000). This exposes young people to more years at risk for contracting AIDS, which is heightened by high-risk sexual behaviors such as multiple partners and a failure to use contraceptives (Biglan et al., 1990).

Illicit drug use and adolescent ASB are strongly associated (H. R. White, Loeber, Stouthamer-Loeber, & Farrington, 1999). For example, youths who have used or sold drugs are more likely than non-users to carry a handgun, belong to a gang, use alcohol, or engage in a host of other ASBs (H. N. Snyder & Sickmund, 1999). Adolescent substance abuse is related to the imminent dangers of accidents, violence, school dropout, family difficulties, and risky sexual behavior (Gilvarry, 2000). For some youngsters, persistent drug use is also related to delinquency, early sexual behavior, and pregnancy (Weinberg, Rahdert, Colliver, & Glantz, 1998).

Early ASB is a known risk factor for adolescent substance use throughout the world (Rutter, 2002c). The prevalence of delinquent behavior varies with substance use severity, with about 10% of adolescent multiple drug users committing more than 50% of all felony assaults, felony thefts, and index offenses (O'Malley, Johnston, & Bachman, 1999). One distinguishing feature of adult criminal offenders is their use of tobacco, alcohol, and marijuana prior to age 15 (Farrington, 1991a). Thus, the evidence indicates that CPs during childhood are a risk factor for adult substance abuse, and this relationship is mediated by drug use and delinquency during early and late adolescence (Brook, Whiteman, Finch, & Cohen,

1996; Gilvarry, 2000). We talk more about substance use problems in Chapter 12, when we discuss health-related disorders.

SECTION SUMMARY

- Many children with CPs show verbal and language deficits, despite their normal intelligence.

- These children experience a variety of school difficulties, including academic underachievement in language and reading, which may result from co-occurring ADHD.

- ASB may be related to an inflated, unstable, and/or tentative view of self.

- Children with CPs have interpersonal difficulties with peers, including rejection and bullying. Their friendships are often with other antisocial children.

- General family disturbances, and disturbances in parenting practices and family functioning, are among the strongest and most consistent correlates of ASB.

- Youngsters with CPs engage in many behaviors that place them at high risk for health-related problems including personal injuries, illnesses, sexually transmitted diseases, and substance abuse.

Accompanying Disorders and Symptoms

Most youngsters with CPs suffer from one or more additional disorders, most commonly ADHD, depression, and anxiety (Angold & Costello, 2001; Speltz, McClellan, et al., 1999).

Attention-Deficit/Hyperactivity Disorder (ADHD)

About 50% of children with CD also have ADHD (Nottelman & Jensen, 1995). There are several possible reasons for this overlap:

- A common underlying factor such as impulsivity, poor self-regulation, or temperament may lead to both ADHD and CD (Lahey & Waldman, 2003)

- ADHD may be a catalyst for CD by contributing to its persistence and escalation to more serious CPs (Loeber, Stouthamer-Loeber, & Green, 1991)

- ADHD may lead to childhood-onset of CD, which is a strong predictor of continuing problems (Robins, 1991).

Despite the large overlap, two lines of research suggest that ADHD and CD are distinct disorders. First, a model that includes both ADHD and CD consistently provides a better fit to the data than a model based on only a single disruptive behavior disorder (Fergusson, Horwood, & Lloyd, 1991; Hinshaw, 1987). Second, ADHD is more likely than CD to be associated with cognitive impairments, neurodevelopmental abnormalities, inattentiveness in the classroom, and higher rates of accidental injuries (Hinshaw & Lee, 2003).

Youngsters with CD and ADHD also differ with respect to parental characteristics. CD by itself and CD with ADHD are associated with high rates of parental antisocial personality disorder (APD) and a parental history of aggressive behavior, whereas ADHD by itself is not (Hinshaw, 1987). Children with both CD and ADHD usually display more severe behavioral, academic, and social impairments than children with only one of these disorders (Hinshaw, Lahey, & Hart, 1993; Moffitt, 1990).

Depression and Anxiety

Depression and anxiety occur more frequently than expected in youngsters with CPs (Hops, Lewinsohn, Andrews, & Roberts, 1990; Zoccolillo, 1992). About one-third are diagnosed with depression or a co-occurring anxiety disorder (Dishion, French, & Patterson, 1995). Most girls with CD develop a depressive or anxiety disorder by early adulthood, and for both sexes, the increasing severity of ASB is associated with the increasing severity of depression and anxiety (Zoccolillo, Pickles, Quinton, & Rutter, 1992; Zoccolillo & Rogers, 1991, 1992). The strong connection between CPs and depression and anxiety is evident when we consider that young adolescents with externalizing disorders are also likely to experience internalizing and externalizing problems later in adolescence (Nottelman & Jensen, 1995). This is especially true of adolescent girls whose antisocial symptoms are a better predictor of later depression and anxiety than of later externalizing problems (Robins & Rutter, 1990). Adolescent CD is also a risk factor for completed suicide in youngsters with co-occurring problems of substance abuse and a family history of depression (Renaud, Brent, Birmaher, Chiappetta, & Bridge, 1999).

Findings regarding the relation between anxiety disorders and antisocial outcomes for children with CPs have been puzzling but quite interesting. In some studies, co-occurring anxiety has been found to be a protective factor that may inhibit aggressive behavior (Pine, Cohen, Cohen, & Brook, 2000). However, other studies have found that anxiety may increase the risk for later ASB (Rutter, Giller, & Hagell, 1998). In support of anxiety as a protective factor, boys with CD and anxiety disorder show a higher level of salivary cortisol—associated with a greater degree of behavioral inhibition (McBurnett et al., 1991). In boys with CD only, lower levels of salivary cortisol are directly associated with more aggressive and disruptive behaviors (McBurnett, Lahey, Rathouz, & Loeber, 2000). It has been hypothesized that the relation between anxiety and

CP outcomes may depend on the type of anxiety. In this formulation, anxiety related to shyness, inhibition, and fear may protect against CPs, whereas anxiety associated with negative emotionality and social avoidance/withdrawal based on a lack of caring about others may increase the child's risk for CP (Lahey & Waldman, 2003). Consistent with this view, children with a callous-unemotional interpersonal style (CU) show less anxiety than other children with CPs (Frick, Lilienfeld, Ellis, Loney, & Silverthorn, 1999).

SECTION SUMMARY

- About 50% of children with CD also have ADHD. Despite the overlap, ADHD and CD appear to be distinct disorders.
- About one-third of children with CP are diagnosed with depression or a co-occurring anxiety disorder.
- Anxiety related to shyness, inhibition, and fear may protect against CPs, whereas anxiety associated with negative emotionality and social avoidance/withdrawal based on a lack of caring about others may increase the child's risk for CPs.

Prevalence, Gender, and Course

Prevalence

The prevalence of clinically diagnosed CD is substantial, ranging from 2% to 6% of all children, or about 1 to 4 million children in North America (Angold & Costello, 2001; Hinshaw & Lee, 2003). Rates of ODD are about twice those of CD, averaging about 12% of all children (Nottelman & Jensen, 1995). Keep in mind, however, that prevalence varies widely with how CPs are defined and the child's gender, age, and SES.

Gender

Ann

Runaway

Until recently, Ann, age 13, lived with her mother, stepfather, and younger brother. For the last 6 months, she has been living in a youth shelter under the custody of the courts, because of repeatedly running away from home. Ann was described by her parents as defiant and argumentative, and often lied and stole. She often stole clothes and jewelry from the homes of relatives and friends, as well as from her parents. . . . Over the past 3 years, Ann had run away from home on four occa-

sions. Each time, the police had to be called. Running away was precipitated by being grounded for stealing or smoking cigarettes. . . . One time, Ann was gone for 3 nights. The police found her wandering the streets late at night on the other side of town (about 10 miles from her home). Ann would not tell them who she was or where she lived . . . (Adapted from *Conduct Disorders in Childhood and Adolescence,* by A. E. Kazdin, pp. 3–5. Copyright © 1995 by Sage Publications. Adapted by permission.)

Clear gender differences in the frequency and severity of ASB are evident by 4 years of age (Keenan & Shaw, 1997; Lahey et al., 2000). Rates of ASB are about 3 or 4 times higher for boys than girls during childhood, with boys showing an earlier age of onset and greater persistence (Keenan, Loeber, & Green, 1999; Zoccolillo, 1993). Nevertheless, many girls also display severe CPs, with lifetime prevalence estimates averaging 3% of all girls (Eme & Kavanagh, 1995; Webster-Stratton, 1996).

The gender disparity in CPs increases through middle childhood, narrows greatly in early adolescence, due mainly to a rise in covert nonaggressive ASB in girls (McDermott, 1996), and then increases again in late adolescence and beyond (Moffitt, Caspi, Rutter, & Silva, 2001). Ann steals, lies, and runs away from home, but she is not physically aggressive. In contrast to boys, whose

Girls will be girls.

early symptoms of CD are aggression and theft, early symptoms for girls are usually sexual misbehaviors (Offord, Alder, & Boyle, 1986). Antisocial girls are more likely than others to develop relationships with antisocial boys (Caspi, Elder, & Bem, 1987), then become pregnant at an earlier age (Woodward & Fergusson, 1999), and display a wide spectrum of later problems including anxiety, depression, and poor parenting (Serbin, Moskowitz, Schwartzman, & Ledingham, 1991).

Although gender differences in the overall amount of ASB decrease in early adolescence, boys remain more violence-prone than girls throughout their life span, and are more likely to engage in repeated acts of physical violence (Broidy et al., 2003; Odgers & Moretti, 2002). For conduct disorders (CDs) that are chronic from early childhood to adulthood, the male-to-female ratio is marked, about 10:1. In contrast, more transient forms of ASB in adolescence show a male-to-female ratio of about 2:1 (Moffitt et al., 2001).

In addition, physical aggression by girls during childhood, when it does occur, does not seem to forecast continued physical violence and other forms of delinquency in adolescence as it does for boys (Broidy et al., 2003). This does not mean that girls are nonviolent—about 45% of girls commit at least one violent act (compared with 65% of boys). Interestingly, the sex difference in ASB has decreased by more than 50% over the past 50 years, suggesting that females may be more susceptible to or affected by contemporary risk factors, such as family discord (Rutter, Giller, & Hagell, 1998). Unfortunately, ASB is increasingly becoming an equal opportunity affliction.

Explaining Gender Differences   The precise reasons for gender differences in ASB are not known, although differences in both genetic, neurobiological, and environmental risk factors likely play a role (Eley, Lichtenstein, & Stevenson, 1999). Genetic factors have been found to be predominant in girls' substance use whereas boys' substance use appears to be mediated more by environmental factors, such as family dysfunction and deviant peers (Silberg, Rutter, D'Onofrio, & Eaves, 2003). Neurobiologically, steep declines in testosterone production throughout the day is related to higher levels of disruptive behavior problems in girls than boys, depending on level of pubertal development (Granger et al., 2003). From the standpoint of environmental risk, girls may be easier to socialize than boys because girls display advanced communication skills and higher levels of empathy and inhibitory control at a younger age (Keenan & Shaw, 1997; Kochanska, Murray, & Coy, 1997). Consistent with this, girls may be less likely than boys to attribute hostile intentions to the behavior of others (Frick et al., 2003).

Gender differences may also result from definitions of CPs that place a strong emphasis on physical aggression, and minimal emphasis on the less physically aggressive forms of ASB that characterize girls (Crick, Bigbee,

A Closer Look

BOX 6.4 Social Aggression in Girls: "I Hurt Her Through the Grapevine" [1]

© Photodisc

Girls are more likely than boys to use indirect forms of social aggression such as gossip and spreading rumors.   = relational

Over the course of a school day, Rachel Simmons (2002) met with eight groups of 9th grade girls and began each meeting with the same question:

"What are some of the differences between the ways guys and gals are mean?"

From periods one through eight she heard the same responses (pp. 15–16): "Girls can turn on you for anything." "Girls whisper." "They glare at you." "They destroy you from the inside." "Girls are manipulative." "There's an aspect of evil in girls that there isn't in boys." "Girls target you when they know you're weakest." "Girls do a lot behind each other's backs." "Girls plan and premeditate."

"In bold, matter-of-fact voices, girls described themselves . . . as disloyal, untrustworthy, and sneaky. They claimed girls use intimacy to manipulate and overpower others. They said girls are fake, using each other to move up the social hierarchy. They described girls as unforgiving and crafty, lying in wait for a moment of revenge that will catch the unwitting victim off guard, and with an almost savage eye-for-an-eye mentality."

[1] Crick et al. (2001, p. 15)

& Howes, 1996). When girls are angry they are more likely to use indirect and relational forms of aggression (see Box 6.4), such as verbal insults, gossip, tattling, ostracism, threatening to withdraw one's friendship, getting even, or third-party retaliation (Crick & Nelson, 2002; Underwood, 2003). In addition, girls are more likely than boys to become emotionally upset by aggressive social exchanges (Crick, 1995). As girls move into adolescence, the function of their aggressive behavior increasingly revolves around group acceptance and affiliation, whereas for boys, aggression remains confrontational (Crick & Rose, 2000).

Fewer differences in ASB exist between boys and girls referred for treatment than for children in community samples. Although clinically referred boys and girls with CPs display comparable amounts of externalizing behavior (Dishion & Andrews, 1995), referred girls are more deviant than boys in relation to their same-age, same-sex peers (Webster-Stratton, 1996; Zoccolillo, 1993). Girls' behavior is considered more covert because boys typically engage in more rough and tumble play, bullying, fighting, and noncompliance than girls (Achenbach, 1991a; Maccoby, 1986). With overt ASB more common in boys, their symptoms are more noticeable at a younger age, which could account for the reported earlier age of onset of CPs in boys. Since early displays of ASB are less visible in girls, lower thresholds or different diagnostic criteria may be needed to detect girls with CD at a young age (Zoccolillo, 1993).

Girls may also display different patterns of adjustment problems and different pathways to ASB than boys (Wangby, Bergman, & Magnusson, 1999). One pathway, the early onset pathway, describes girls who exhibit ASB during childhood, associate with deviant peers, and exhibit delinquent behavior and drug use during adolescence. A second, referred to as the delayed onset pathway, describes girls who, despite having many of the risk factors for ASB during childhood (e.g., cognitive and neuropsychological deficits, dysfunctional family environments), do not begin to display ASB until adolescence (Silverthorn & Frick, 1999).

Some girls have an early menarche, which indirectly heightens their CPs through increasing their involvement with deviant peers (Caspi, Lynam, Moffitt, & Silva, 1993). Interestingly, early onset of menarche predicts increased delinquency primarily for girls who attend mixed-gender schools rather than all-girl schools. In mixed-gender schools, girls' exposure to boys who model ASB and pressure girls for early sexual relations may interact with early physical maturation. Such exposure may lead to ASB in these girls, who are more likely to find rewards and opportunities for antisocial activities in the company of boys than girls (Moffitt, Caspi, Belsky, & Silva, 1992).

Course

Longitudinal studies have greatly advanced our understanding of antisocial patterns, by revealing both a general developmental progression and important variations on this theme (Loeber, Green, Lahey, Frick, & McBurnett, 2000).

General Progression An approximate ordering of the different forms of disruptive behavior and ASB from early childhood through adolescence is shown in Figure 6.4.

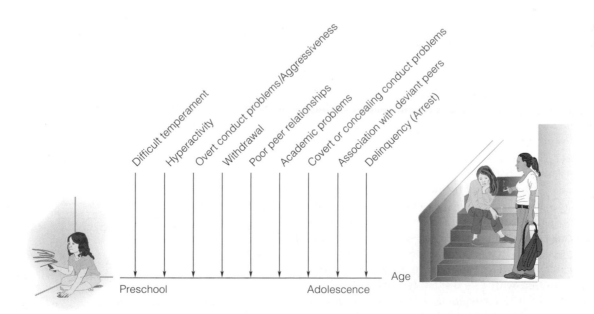

Figure 6.4. Approximate ordering of the different forms of disruptive and antisocial behavior from childhood through adolescence

Source: From "Development and Risk Factors of Juvenile Antisocial Behavior and Delinquency," by R. Loeber, 1990, *Clinical Psychology Review, 10* 1–41. Copyright © 1990 Elsevier Science Ltd. Reprinted with permission of Elsevier Science.

Although there are isolated reports, such as that of a 9-month-old infant being expelled from day care for punching other children, early signs of CPs are usually not so obvious (Kazdin, 1995, p. 27). The earliest indications of ASB may be considered a *difficult temperament* in the first few years of life, expressed as fussiness, irritability, irregular sleeping and eating patterns, or frustration in response to novel events. However, as we discussed for ADHD, these behaviors often precede later CPs, but they are not specific to CPs.

During the pre- and early school years, possible neurodevelopmental impairments may lead to noticeable *hyperactivity* as the child gains mobility, with a heightened risk for simple forms of *oppositional and aggressive behaviors* that peak during the preschool years (Tremblay, 2000). Preschoolers with ODD display stubbornness, temper tantrums, irritability, and spitefulness—problems that remain stable from 2 to 5 years of age (S. B. Campbell, 2002). Discipline problems and poor self-control during early childhood, especially when accompanied by negative parenting and high levels of stress, are strong indicators that the child will continue to experience behavior problems (S. B. Campbell, Shaw, & Gilliom, 2000).

Most children with CPs show *diversification*—they add new forms of ASB over time rather than simply replacing old behaviors. Poor social skills and social–cognitive deficits often accompany early oppositional and aggressive behaviors, predisposing the child to poor peer relationships, rejection by peers, and social isolation and withdrawal. When the child enters school, impulsivity and attention problems may result in reading difficulties and academic failure. Covert CPs, such as truancy or substance abuse, also begin to appear during the elementary school years and increase into early adolescence. From ages 8 to 12, behaviors such as fighting, bullying, fire setting, vandalism, cruelty to animals and people, and stealing begin to emerge.

Across cultures, major CPs become more frequent during adolescence. Delinquent behavior shows a dramatic rise in middle adolescence that peaks around the age of 17, followed by an equally dramatic drop in late adolescence and young adulthood (Hirschi & Gottfredson, 1983). Adolescence is characterized by a growing association with deviant peers, and by increasing rates of arrest, re-arrest, and conviction as the age of criminal responsibility is met. From ages 12 to 14, property destruction, running away from home, truancy, mugging, breaking and entering, use of a weapon, and forced sex occur with increasing frequency (Lahey & Waldman, 2003). By age 18, many children with CPs display behaviors that portend an antisocial future, including substance dependence, unsafe sex, dangerous driving habits, delinquent friends, and unemployment (Moffitt et al., 1996).

Does this developmental progression mean that every young child with CPs goes on to become a delinquent adolescent? Definitely not. The sequence in Figure 6.4 shows a maximum progression that begins early in life and persists through adolescence. Although some children display this maximum progression, others will desist from their ASB at a young age. About 50% of children with early CPs do improve. Those who desist tend to display less extreme levels of early CPs, have higher intelligence and SES, fewer delinquent friends, mothers that are not teenagers, and parents who have more social skills and with fewer mental health problems (Lahey, Loeber, Burke, & Rathouz, 2002; Nagin & Tremblay, 2001). It is important to note, however, that even among children who desist from ASB at a young age, problems may emerge in young adulthood, suggesting that their recovery is far from complete (Moffitt, Caspi, Harrington, & Milne, 2002). Other children may not display problems until adolescence, and not all children display the full range of difficulties described. Still others may display a chronic low-level of persistent ASB from childhood or adolescence through adulthood (Fergusson & Horwood, 2002). These differences lead us to consider important variations on the general progression.

Two Pathways   There are likely as many unique pathways to the development of ASB as there are children who display these problems. However, evidence across cultures and nations supports two common pathways (Moffitt & Caspi, 2001)—the life-course-persistent path and the adolescent-limited path. As shown in Figure 6.5, a small

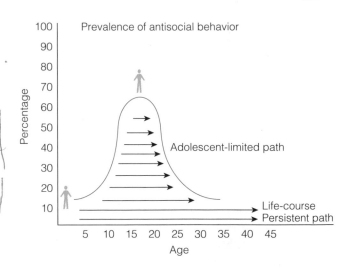

Figure 6.5. The changing prevalence of participation in ASB across the life span

Source: From "Adolescence-Limited and Life-Course-Persistent Antisocial Behavior: A Developmental Taxonomy," by T. E. Moffitt, 1993, *Psychological Review, 100,* 674–701. Copyright © 1993 by the American Psychological Association. Reprinted by permission of the author and the publisher.

number of children show a persistent pattern of ASB throughout their lives, whereas a majority display ASB that occurs mainly during adolescence.

The **life-course-persistent (LCP) path** describes children who engage in aggression and ASB at an early age and continue to do so into adulthood (Moffitt et al., 1996). They may display "biting and hitting at age 4, shoplifting and truancy at age 10, selling drugs and stealing cars at age 16, robbery and rape at age 22, and fraud and child abuse at age 30" (Moffitt, 1993a, p. 679). Their underlying disposition remains, but the way it is expressed changes with new "opportunities" at different points in development. For these children, ASB begins early because of subtle neuropsychological deficits that may interfere with their development of language, memory, and self-control, resulting in cognitive delays and a difficult temperament by age 3 or younger. These deficits heighten the child's vulnerability to antisocial elements in the social environment, such as abuse or poor parenting, which in turn lead to oppositional and conduct problems (Lansford et al., 2002; Moffitt, 1993a).

About one-half of the children who display high levels of childhood-onset ASB continue on the LCP path by engaging in less serious forms of nonaggressive ASB (e.g., stealing and truancy) during middle childhood, followed by more serious delinquent activities during adolescence (Brame, Nagin, & Tremblay, 2001). They are the subgroup of teens most likely to commit violent crimes and to drop out of school. LCP youths display consistency in their behavior across situations, for example, by lying at home, stealing from stores, and cheating at school. As young adults, they have difficulty forming lasting relationships and may display a hostile mistrust of others, aggressive dominance, impulsivity, and psychopathy. Complete spontaneous recovery is rare after adolescence. The LCP path is often perpetuated by the progressive accumulation of its own consequences. For example, poor self-control and diminished verbal intellect may lead to irreversible decisions, such as dropping out of school or abusing drugs, which further limit opportunities (Caspi & Moffitt, 1995).

The **adolescent-limited (AL) path** describes youngsters whose ASB begins around puberty and continues into adolescence, but who later desist from these behaviors during young adulthood (Farrington, 1986). This path includes most juvenile offenders whose ASB is limited primarily to their teen years (Hamalainen & Pulkkinen, 1996). Youngsters on the AL path display less extreme ASB than those on the LCP path, are less likely to drop out of school, and have stronger family ties. Their delinquent activity is often related to temporary situational factors, especially peer influences. The behavior of AL youngsters is not consistent across situations; they may use drugs or shoplift with their friends while continuing to follow rules and to do well in school.

Marcus

Call of the Wild

"I grew up in a real poor family. My mom was on welfare all my life—we never had much. As soon as I got to the age of 11, I was interested in other kids who were breaking the rules. I used to see what they used to do—and what they had."

Marcus joined a gang when he turned 13. Two years later, after a number of arrests and four detentions in a juvenile facility, he became disillusioned with gang life and managed to turn his life around. He is now 17 and works as a youth minister for a church dedicated to helping other young people like himself. (Adapted from Goldentyer, 1994)

The attraction of still-forbidden adult privileges, such as drinking alcohol, driving a car, and having sex, may motivate some youths with few previous risk signs to engage in ASB as they enter adolescence. These youngsters may observe their LCP peers obtaining desired adult privileges via illicit means and mimic their delinquent activities. Eventually, when access to adult privileges becomes available, AL youngsters cease their law-breaking, relying instead on the more adaptive and prosocial behaviors and values they learned prior to adolescence (Moffitt, Lynam, & Silva, 1994).

Contrary to expectations, some youngsters on the "adolescent-limited" path continue to display ASB well into their twenties before they eventually stop. Others do not desist in their twenties at all but continue to display higher than normal levels of impulsivity, substance abuse and dependence, property crimes, and mental health problems (Moffitt et al., 2002). Persistence in early adulthood is often the result of *snares*, or outcomes of ASB that close the door to getting a good job, pursuing higher education, or attracting a supportive partner. Common snares include: unplanned parenthood, school dropout, addiction to drugs or alcohol, disabling injuries, unemployment or erratic work history, severed family connections, imprisonment, bad reputation, and a delinquent self-image (Moffitt et al., 1994). Thus, despite their potential, some individuals with no history of childhood ASB who initiate delinquent activity in adolescence continue to experience problems well into adulthood (Moffitt et al., 2002). Therefore, referring to these individuals as "adolescent-limited" is somewhat misleading.

The identification of the LCP and AL pathways (and their variations) helps us understand why adult ASB is almost always preceded by ASB during childhood (Brame et al., 2001). Nevertheless, most antisocial adolescents do not go on to become antisocial adults (Robins, 1978). At the crossroads of early adulthood, LCP and most AL teens go different ways. ASB is stable for youngsters on the LCP path, who continue on the same road, but unstable for those on the AL path.

Adult Outcomes

By their early twenties, the number of active offenders decreases by about 50%, and by their late twenties, almost 85% of former delinquents desist from offending. This general relationship between age and crime applies to males and females, for most types of crimes, and in numerous Western nations (Caspi & Moffitt, 1995). Clearly, looking forward, most children with CPs do not grow up to be antisocial adults (Maughan & Rutter, 2001). However, adult outcomes depend not only on the type and variety of CPs developed during childhood and adolescence, but also on the number and combination of risk and protective factors in the child, family, and community (Kokko & Pulkkinen, 2000). Also, even when ASB decreases in adulthood, coercive interpersonal styles may sometimes persist, along with family, health, and work difficulties.

A significant number of children with CPs, particularly those on the LCP path, do go on as adults to display criminal behavior, psychiatric problems, social maladjustment, health problems, lost productivity, and poor parenting of their own children. As adults, they are more likely to be downwardly socially mobile and to display an erratic work history, perhaps due to lower skill attainment and difficulties in getting along with co-workers and supervisors. They also have more violent marriages and cohabitations, higher rates of divorce, and are more likely than others to select partners with similar antisocial characteristics, providing the next generation with a double dose of both genetic and environmental risk (Moffitt et al., 2002). One follow-up study of adult women who displayed severe CPs in adolescence found that most continued to display CPs. A majority had depressive and anxiety disorders, 6% died a violent death, many had dropped out of school, one-third were pregnant before the age of 17 years, one-half were re-arrested, and many had suffered traumatic physical injuries (Zoccolillo & Rogers, 1991, 1992).

SECTION SUMMARY

- The estimated prevalence of CD is about 2% to 6% of all children. The prevalence of ODD is at least twice as high, averaging about 12%.
- During childhood, CPs are about 3 or 4 times more common in boys than girls. This difference narrows greatly in early adolescence, due mainly to a rise in covert nonaggressive ASB in girls, and then increases again in late adolescence and beyond.
- Girls are more likely than boys to use indirect and relational forms of aggression, for example, verbal insults, gossip, or third-party retaliation.

- There is a general progression of ASB from difficult early temperament and hyperactivity, to oppositional and aggressive behavior, to social difficulties, to school problems, to delinquent behavior in adolescence, to criminal behavior in adulthood.
- The life-course-persistent (LCP) path describes children who display ASB at an early age and who continue to do so into adulthood.
- The adolescent-limited (AL) path describes youngsters whose ASB begins around puberty and continues into adolescence, and who later desist from these behaviors in young adulthood.
- A significant number of children with CPs continue to experience difficulties as adults, including criminal behavior, psychiatric problems, social maladjustment, health and employment problems, and poor parenting of their own children.

Causes

When it comes to CPs, there are no simple or single causes. Consider two brothers—one, John Edgar, is an award-winning author (*Brothers and Keepers*), while his brother Robbie is in prison for murder. How do we account for such striking differences between brothers raised in the same family? Are they due to differences in genetic makeup, neurobiological functioning, birth complications, temperament, intelligence, family experiences, peer influences, difficulties in school, or some combination of these factors?

Previous approaches to CPs focused mainly on the child's aggression and invoked one primary cause, such as an aggressive drive, frustration, poor role models, reinforcement, or deficits in social cognition as an explanation. However, most of these "smoking gun" explanations can be challenged on one point or another. For example, not all children behave aggressively as would be predicted by the aggressive-drive theory, and frustration sometimes leads to cooperation rather than aggression. In addition, single-cause theories do not effectively predict why the amount and type of aggressive behavior changes with the child's age and situation (Patterson, 1996). Although each single-cause theory highlights a potentially important determinant, no single theory can explain all forms of ASB (Tremblay, 2000).

In the next section we consider several proposed causes of CP. Although we examine them separately for conceptual simplicity, recall that CPs in children are best accounted for by multiple causes, or risk and protective factors, that operate in a transactional fashion over time (Hinshaw & Lee, 2003). CPs result from the interplay among predisposing child, family, community, and cultural factors (Dodge & Pettit, 2003; Hill, 2002; Lahey,

Child

Genetic risk, prenatal and birth complications, exposure to lead, low arousal and reactivity, functional and structural deficits in pre-frontal cortex, difficult temperament, attention-deficit/hyperactivity (ADHD), insecure attachments, childhood-onset of aggression, social avoidance and withdrawal, social-cognitive deficits, lowered verbal intelligence and verbal deficits.

Family

Antisocial family values, parental antisocial or criminal behavior, paternal antisocial personality disorder, maternal depression, parental substance abuse, marital discord, teen motherhood, single parenthood, large family, low socioeconomic status of family, low education of mother, family carelessness in permitting access to weapons.

Ineffective Parenting

Poor supervision and monitoring, inconsistent discipline, harsh discipline and maltreatment, discordant parent-child interactions, poor communication and problem solving, parental neglect, low parental warmth.

Peers

Rejection by peers, association with deviant siblings, association with deviant peers.

School

Poor academic performance, weak bonding to school, low educational aspirations, low school motivation, poorly organized and functioning schools.

Neighborhood and Community

Neighborhood disadvantage and poverty, disorganized neighborhoods, gang membership, availability of weapons.

Sociocultural

Media portrayal of violence, cultural attitudes encouraging use of aggression, socialization of children for aggression.

Source: Adapted from Loeber and Farrington (2000, p. 749).

Moffitt, & Caspi, 2003; Raine, 2002a). These factors are summarized in Table 6.4.

Genetic Influences

The universality of aggressive behavior and ASB in humans, and the fact that such behaviors run in families within and across generations, suggests the importance of genetic influences. Although CPs are not inherited, many biologically based traits, such as a difficult temperament, hyperactivity-impulsivity, lack of fear in the face of dan-

ger, and a tendency for addiction may predispose children at birth to develop ASB. For example, some children seem predisposed to impulsivity, a variable mood, lack of persistence in problem solving, restlessness, negativity, and sensitivity to stress (Caspi, Henry, McGee, Moffitt, & Silva, 1995). Several studies have found a link between a difficult early temperament and risk for the development of later CPs (Sanson & Prior, 1999). Difficult temperament at 6 months has been shown to predict externalizing problems in middle childhood (Bates, Bayles, Bennett, Ridge, & Brown, 1991), and restless, impulsive, risk-taking, and emotionally labile behaviors at age 3 have been shown to differentiate adolescents with antisocial disorders from those displaying other disorders or no disorders at all (Caspi et al., 1995). Other studies have found that a difficult temperament during childhood is specifically associated with convictions for violent offenses in late adolescence and adulthood (B. Henry, Caspi, Moffitt, & Silva, 1996).

Adoption and twin studies indicate that about 50% of the population variance in ASB is attributable to heredity (Nuffield Council on Bioethics, 2002; Simonoff, 2001; Taylor, Iacono, & McGue, 2000). Children who display the LCP pattern show twice the genetic risk for ASB as those displaying the AL pattern (Frick & Jackson, 1993). The strength and nature of the genetic contribution to ASB differs somewhat depending on the type of ASB and the child's age, as genes may be expressed in different ways during different periods of development (Jacobson, Prescott, & Kendler, 2002). In childhood, aggressive ASB has been found to be highly heritable compared to nonaggressive ASB, which is influenced by genes and by shared environment (Edelbrock, Rende, Plomin, & Thompson, 1995). However, during adolescence, genes and shared environment are equally influential for both aggressive and nonaggressive forms of ASB. The continuity in aggressive ASB from childhood to adolescence appears to be mediated predominantly by genetic influences, whereas continuities in nonaggressive ASB are mediated by both shared environment and genetics (Eley, Lichtenstein, & Moffitt, 2003).

Overall, adoption and twin studies suggest that genetic and environmental factors contribute to ASB across development. The studies do not, however, specify the mechanisms by which the factors operate. It is likely that genetic risks for ASB operate via several pathways (Rutter, 2003a). First, genetic factors may be related to difficult temperament, impulsivity, a tendency to seek rewards, or an insensitivity to punishment that combine to create an antisocial "propensity" or "personality" (Lahey & Waldman, 2003; Miller, Lynam, & Leukefeld, 2003). Second, genetic factors may increase the likelihood that a child will be exposed to environmental risk factors, such as parental divorce, maltreatment, or other negative life events that are associated with an increased risk of ASB. Third, children's genotype may moderate their susceptibility to these environmental insults in determining whether they develop later ASB. Maltreated children with a genotype related to high levels of expression of the neurotransmitter-metabolizing enzyme monoamine oxidase-A (MAOA) were less likely to develop ASB than maltreated children not having this genotype (Caspi et al., 2002). These and other pathways reflecting the interplay between genetic and environmental risk and protective factors, will need to be addressed if the causes of ASB are to be understood (Rutter, 2003b).

Prenatal Factors and Birth Complications

Malnutrition during pregnancy is associated with later ASB, which may be mediated by protein deficiency (Raine, 2002b). Lead poisoning before birth and mother's use of nicotine, alcohol, marijuana, and other substances during pregnancy may also lead to later CPs (Day, Richardson, Goldschmidt, & Cornelius, 2000; Needleman, Reiss, Tobin, Biesecker, & Greenhouse, 1996). However, evidence that proves prenatal and birth complications as direct biological causes of ASB is lacking (Hodgins, Kratzer, & McNeil, 2001). For example, it has been found that the relation between mothers' smoking during pregnancy and children's CPs in adolescence is best accounted for by the transmission of an underlying antisocial tendency from mother to child, rather than exposure to cigarette byproducts during pregnancy (Silberg et al., 2003).

Neurobiological Factors

Gray (1987) proposed that people's behavioral patterns are related to two subsystems of the brain, each having distinct neuroanatomical regions and neurotransmitter pathways (McBurnett, 1992; Quay, 1993). The **behavioral activation system (BAS)** stimulates behavior in response to signals of reward or nonpunishment. In contrast, the **behavioral inhibition system (BIS)** produces anxiety and inhibits ongoing behavior in the presence of novel events, innate fear stimuli, and signals of nonreward or punishment. Other behavioral patterns may result from the relative balance or imbalance of activity in these two neural systems. Think of the BAS as similar to the gas pedal and the BIS as similar to the brakes—some individuals ride one more heavily than the other.

It has been proposed that antisocial patterns of behavior result from an overactive BAS and an underactive BIS—a pattern determined primarily by genetic predisposition. Consistent with an overactive BAS, children with CPs show a heightened sensitivity to rewards (Frick et al., 2003). In addition, they fail to respond to punishment and continue to respond under conditions of no reward—patterns that are consistent with an underactive BIS (Fowles, 2001).

Youngsters with CD who show an early onset of aggressive symptoms also display low psychophysiological and/or cortical arousal (Magnusson, 1988), and low autonomic reactivity (Pennington & Ozonoff, 1996; Raine, 2002b). Low arousal and autonomic reactivity may lead to diminished avoidance learning in response to warnings or reprimands, a poor response to punishment, and a fearless, stimulus-seeking temperament. In turn, this may lead to ASB, a failure to develop the anticipatory fear needed to avoid such behavior, and a lack of conscience. Most children respond to discipline and punishment by reducing their ASB. Often, the opposite occurs with children with CPs—when disciplined or punished they may increase their ASB and become even more defiant.

Other findings also suggest the role of neurobiological factors in CP (McBurnett & Lahey, 1994):

- Children with CPs have somewhat higher rates of neurodevelopmental risk factors, such as birth complications and closed head injuries.
- Children with CPs display neuropsychological deficits as suggested by lower verbal IQ and deficits in verbal reasoning and executive functions (Moffitt & Lynam, 1994).
- Findings from neuropsychological, neurological, and brain imaging studies suggest that structural and functional deficits in the prefrontal cortex of the brain are related to ASB (Raine, 2000b).
- Findings for a relationship between testosterone and aggression are inconsistent, with testosterone levels more highly correlated with reactive than with unprovoked forms of aggression (McBurnett & Lahey, 1994).

In general, low levels of cortical arousal and autonomic reactivity seem to play a central role in ASB, particularly for early-onset and persistent CPs. Many neural, endocrine, and psychophysiological influences have been implicated in ASB. However, the evidence is strong that it is the interaction between these neurobiological risks and negative environmental circumstances that leads to the development and maintenance of ASB (Raine, 2002a).

Social-Cognitive Factors

The connections between children's thinking and their aggressive behavior has been looked at in several ways. Some approaches focus on immature forms of thinking, such as egocentrism and a lack of social perspective taking (Selman, Beardslee, Schultz, Krupa, & Podorefsky, 1986). Others emphasize cognitive deficiencies, such as the child's failure to use verbal mediators to regulate behavior (Meichenbaum, 1977), or cognitive distortions,

Table 6.5

Steps in the Thinking and Behavior of Aggressive Children in Social Situations

Step 1: Encoding Socially aggressive children use fewer cues before making a decision. When defining and resolving an interpersonal situation, they seek less information about the event before acting.

Step 2: Interpretation Socially aggressive children attribute hostile intentions to ambiguous events.

Step 3: Response Search Socially aggressive children generate fewer and more aggressive responses and have less knowledge about social problem solving.

Step 4: Response Decision Socially aggressive children are more likely to choose aggressive solutions.

Step 5: Enactment Socially aggressive children use poor verbal communication and strike out physically.

Sources: From "A Review and Reformulation of Social Information Processing Mechanisms in Children's Social Adjustment," by N. R. Crick and K. A. Dodge, 1994, *Psychological Bulletin, 115,* 74–101. Copyright © 1994 by the American Psychological Association. Reprinted by permission of the author and the publisher.

Physical abuse is a strong risk factor for later aggressive behavior.

such as interpreting a neutral event as an intentionally hostile act (Crick & Dodge, 1994).

Crick and Dodge (1994) and Dodge and Pettit (2003) have presented a comprehensive social-cognitive framework to account for aggressive behavior and ASB in children. In this model, cognitive and emotional processes play a central mediating role. Children are presumed to develop social knowledge about their world based on a unique set of predispositions, life experiences, and sociocultural contexts. In specific social situations, children then use this social knowledge to guide their processing of social information in ways that lead directly to certain behaviors. For example, when teased in the schoolyard by peers, does the child laugh with the crowd, walk away, or strike back aggressively? A set of emotional and thought processes are presumed to occur between the social stimulus of being teased and the child's reaction. The thinking and behavior of antisocial/aggressive children in social situations are often characterized by deficits in one or more of these steps, as outlined in Table 6.5.

Family Factors

> *I am convinced that increasing rates of delinquency are due to parents who are either too careless or too busy with their own pleasure to give sufficient time, companionship, and interest to their children.*
>
> —Former FBI director J. Edgar Hoover,
> *The New York Times,* December 6, 1947

Many family factors have been implicated as possible causes of children's ASB, including poor disciplinary practices, harsh discipline, a lack of parental supervision, a lack of affection, marital conflict, family isolation, and violence in the home (Benjet & Kazdin, 2003; Lansford et al., 2002; Reese et al., 2000). Although the association between family factors and CPs is well established, the nature of this association and the possible causal role of family factors continues to be debated (Deater-Deckard & Dodge, 1997).

Family difficulties are related to the development of both CD and ODD, with a stronger association for CD than for ODD, and for children on the LCP versus the AL path (Lahey, Loeber, Quay, Frick, & Grimm, 1992). A combination of individual child risk factors (e.g., difficult temperament) and extreme deficits in family management skills most likely accounts for the more persistent and severe forms of ASB (Caspi & Moffitt, 1995).

Family factors are related to children's ASB in complex ways, and are understood by also considering factors in the environment and in the child. For example, physical abuse is a strong risk factor for later aggressive behavior. One reason for this link between factors appears to be deficits in the child's social information processing that result from the physical abuse (Dodge, Pettit, Bates, & Valente, 1995). As we have seen, the child's genotype can also moderate the link between maltreatment and later ASB, a possible reason that all children who have been abused do not grow up to victimize others (Caspi et al., 2002).

The effect of marital conflict on children's aggressive behavior may be affected by several factors including: the parents' unavailability, the use of inconsistent or harsh discipline, lax monitoring, how the child interprets conflict between parents (Cummings & Davies, 2002), and/or individual and demographic factors (Emery, Waldron, Kitzmann, & Aaron, 1999). Other conditions associated with marital conflict or divorce such as stress, depression, loss of contact with one parent, financial hardship, and greater responsibility at home may also contribute to ASB (Emery, 1999). Interestingly, contact with an absent father following marital break-up can be either a risk or a protective factor for ASB, depending on whether the father is antisocial (Jaffee, Moffitt, Caspi, & Taylor, 2003).

Nick's mother says: "Nick hit a neighborhood kid on the head with a two-by-four; the injured child required 16 stitches. Then he killed another kitten by jumping on it from his bunk bed. I lost control. I told him I hated him, I grabbed him by the cheek, I pinched it a little too hard. I didn't know what to do." (Colapinto, 1993, p. 150)

Cruel and aggressive behaviors can evoke strong reactions, like the anger and overly harsh response by Nick's mother. An important concept for understanding family influences on ASB is **reciprocal influence,** which means that the child's behavior is both influenced by and influences the behavior of others. Negative parenting practices may lead to ASB, but they may also be a reaction to the oppositional and aggressive behaviors of their children (Lytton, 1990).

In an interesting study of reciprocal influence, mothers of boys with and without CD were asked to interact with three boys—their own son, a boy with CD, and a boy without CD (K. E. Anderson, Lytton, & Romney, 1986). All mothers were more demanding and negative when interacting with a child with CD, which supports a child-to-parent effect. However, mothers of boys with CD responded most negatively to their own sons, suggesting that previous negative interactions with their child also had an effect. Reciprocal influence is a useful way to think of the interplay between family influences and ASB over the course of development. However, it is also possible that some aspects of the family environment are related to ASB as a result of a shared genetic predisposition that leads both parent and child to display similar behavior patterns (Frick & Jackson, 1993).

BOX 6.5 Coercive Parent–Child Interaction: Four-Step Escape Conditioning Sequence

Step 1: Raising her voice, Paul's mother scolds, "Why are you sitting in front of the TV when you should be doing your homework?"

Step 2: Paul snaps back, "School is boring, my teachers are stupid, and I don't have any homework to do." Paul's arguing has the immediate effect of punishing his mother for her scolding and, over time, may reduce her efforts to do something about his homework and school problems.

Step 3: Paul's mother withdraws her demand for him to complete his homework, allowing herself to be satisfied that he does not have any homework to do. She lowers her voice and says, "Does Mrs. Smith still put everyone to sleep in her English class?" The mother's withdrawal of her demand for homework negatively reinforces Paul's arguing and increases the chances that the next time she makes an issue of homework, he will argue with her. Over time, Paul may also turn up the volume of his negative reactions by shouting or throwing things.

Step 4: As soon as Paul's mother withdraws her demand, Paul stops arguing and engages in neutral or even positive behavior. He says "You're sure right about Mrs. Smith, Mom. It's tough to keep your eyes open in her class." Paul, by ceasing his noxious behavior, negatively reinforces his mother for giving in and increases the likelihood that she will do so again in response to his arguing and protests.

Source: From *Antisocial Boys,* by G. R. Patterson, J. B. Reid, and T. J. Dishion, 1992, p. 41. Copyright © 1992 by Castalia Publishing. Reprinted by permission.

Coercion Theory Gerald Patterson's **coercion theory** contends that parent–child interactions provide a training ground for the development of ASB (Patterson, 1982; Patterson, Reid, & Dishion, 1992). This occurs through a four-step, escape-conditioning sequence in which the child learns to use increasingly intense forms of noxious behavior to escape and avoid unwanted parental demands. The coercive parent–child interaction described in Box 6.5 begins when a mother finds her son Paul, who is failing in school, watching TV rather than doing his homework. Coercive parent–child interactions are made up of well-practiced actions and reactions, which may occur with little awareness. This process is called a **reinforcement trap** because, over time, all family members become trapped by the consequences of their own behaviors. For example, mothers of antisocial children are eight times less likely to enforce demands than are mothers of nonproblem children (Patterson et al., 1992).

The relationship between parenting and CPs also appears to be moderated by a child's callous-unemotional traits. In one report, ineffective parenting was related to CPs, but only in children low on callous-unemotional traits (Wootton, Frick, Shelton, & Silverthorn, 1997). Children with a callous and unemotional interpersonal style (CU) displayed significant CPs regardless of the quality of parenting they received. The relationship between parental discipline and CPs may also be affected by the amount of discipline—too much or too little can both have adverse effects. The relationship between parental discipline and ASB may also vary with the family's cultural background, the emotional climate in which discipline is used, and the gender of the parent–child pair. For example, discipline may be most effective in same-gender parent–child pairs—discipline of daughters by mothers and sons by fathers (Deater-Deckard & Dodge, 1997).

Attachment Theories   Attachment theories emphasize that the quality of children's attachment to parents will determine their eventual identification with parental values, beliefs, and standards. Secure bonds with parents promote a sense of closeness, shared values, and identification with the social world. Attachment theories contend that children refrain from ASB because they have a stake in conformity.

Children with CPs often show little internalization of parent and societal standards. Even when they comply with parental requests, they do so because of perceived threats to their freedom or physical safety (Shaw & Bell, 1993). When these threats are not present, such as when the child is unsupervised, ABS is likely to occur. Weak bonds with parents may lead the child to associate with deviant peers, which in turn may lead to delinquency and substance abuse (Elliott, Huizinga, & Ageton, 1985; Elliott, Huizinga, & Menard, 1989).

Research findings support a relationship between insecure attachments and ASB during childhood and adolescence (M. T. Greenberg, DeKlyen, Speltz, & Endriga, 1997; Rosenstein & Horowitz, 1996). However, it is unclear whether quality of attachment by itself can predict current or future variation in the severity of CPs (Speltz, DeKlyen, & Greenberg, 1999). It is likely that the relationship between attachment and ASB is affected by many factors, including the child's gender, temperament, and family management practices (Burgess, Marshall, Rubin, & Fox, 2003).

Other Family Problems

Jake and Reggie
All Odds Against Them

Linda M., single mother of 2-year-old Jake and 4-year-old Reggie, sought treatment because Reggie was engaging in severe and uncontrollable aggressive behaviors, including hitting, kicking, and biting Jake. She was depressed and at risk for suicide. Her boyfriend Hank is the father of the two children. He lives nearby and demands that she come over so he can see the children. During these visits, he engages her in what she refers to as "forced sex" (i.e., rape), and he demands that Jake and Reggie remain with them and watch. In principle, Linda could have refused the visits. However, Hank threatened that if she did not comply, he would stop paying child support, take Jake and Reggie away in a custody battle, kill himself, or come over to the house and kill her and the two boys. These threats of violence were to be taken seriously because Hank had a prior arrest record for assault and brandished a gun. (Adapted from *Conduct Disorders in Childhood and Adolescence,* by A. E. Kazdin, p. 17. Copyright © 1995 by Sage Publications. Adapted by permission.)

Family Instability and Stress   Families of children with CPs are often characterized by an unstable family structure with frequent transitions, including changes in parents and changes in residence (Dishion, French, & Patterson, 1995). Family instability is related to a child's heightened risk for ASB, academic problems, anxiety and depression, association with deviant peers, and criminal conviction (Kasen, Cohen, Brook, & Hartmark, 1996). In most cases, the impact of divorce on a child's ASB is related to the family disruption and conflict that accompany it (Emery, 1999). In some cases, a child's ASB may contribute to family instability by increasing the chances of divorce (Block, Block, & Gjerde, 1986).

High family stress is associated with negative child behavior in the home, and may be both a cause and an outcome of ASB. Unemployment, low SES, and multiple family transitions are related specifically to childhood-onset CD, but not adolescent-onset CD. Among family stressors, poverty is one of the strongest predictors of CD and high rates of crime (Pagani, Boulerice, Vitaro, & Tremblay, 1999). But what constitutes the "active ingredient" in the link between poverty and ASB? In this regard, instability, residential mobility, and disruptions in parenting practices have all been found to be important (Dodge, Pettit, & Bates, 1994b; Elder, Robertson, & Ardelt, 1994). The **amplifier hypothesis** states that stress amplifies the maladaptive predispositions of parents (e.g., poor mental health), thereby disrupting family management practices and compromising parents' ability to be supportive of their children (Conger, Ge, Elder, Lorenz, & Simons, 1994).

Parental Criminality and Psychopathology Aggressive and antisocial tendencies run in families, within and across generations (Capaldi, Conger, Hops, & Thornberry, 2003). In fact, children's aggression is correlated with their parents' childhood aggression at the same age (Huesmann, Eron, Lefkowitz, & Walder, 1984). Parents of antisocial children have higher rates of arrests, motor vehicle violations, license suspensions, and substance abuse (Patterson, 1996). Antisocial individuals are likely to be ineffective parents, especially during discipline confrontations when they display an irritable, explosive style of interaction. Certain types of parental psychopathology, such as antisocial personality disorder (APD), are strongly and specifically related to CD in their children (Faraone, Biederman, Keenan, & Tsuang, 1991a). This relationship is particularly clear for fathers (Frick et al., 1992), as is the link between paternal criminal behavior and substance abuse and child antisocial patterns (Lahey, Piacentini, et al., 1988). The strong association between paternal APD and child ASB is independent of whether the father lives in the home, or of the degree of contact between father and child (Tapscott, Frick, Wootton, & Kruh, 1996). For mothers, both *histrionic personality* (excessive emotionality and attention seeking) and depression are related to children's ASB, although these findings are not as consistent (Patterson, 1996).

To illustrate antisocial family values, Mrs. Jones, who was referred by her son's school because of his frequent fighting and repeated suspensions, explained why she had missed a first appointment several months ago:

> **Jones Family**
> **You Never Shoot Someone in Public**
>
> Mrs. Jones apologized for not showing up for her prior appointment, saying that she was unable to come in because she "broke a family rule." She said that she and her husband, and a number of their relatives, would often shoot each other (with guns). However, they had one family rule: "You never shoot someone in public." Mrs. Jones said she broke this rule; some neighbors saw her shoot her husband, and she spent 3 months in prison. Now that she is out of prison, she said, she is ready for her son to begin treatment. (Adapted from *Conduct Disorders in Childhood and Adolescence,* by A. E. Kazdin, pp. 16–17. Copyright © 1995 by Sage Publications. Adapted by permission.)

Societal Factors

Causes of ASB at the level of the individual and family tell only part of the story, since they interact with the larger societal and cultural context in determining CPs (Sampson, 1992). There is little doubt that poverty, neighborhood crime, family disruption, and residential mobility are related to crime and delinquency in young people (Caspi & Moffitt, 1995; Sampson, Raudenbush, & Earls, 1997). However, the specific mechanisms by which these conditions lead to crime and delinquency are not known. Theories of social disorganization propose that community structures impact the family processes that then affect the child's adjustment (Sampson, 1992; Sampson & Laub, 1994).

Adverse contextual factors (e.g., low SES) are associated with poor parenting, particularly coercive and inconsistent discipline and poor parental monitoring. In turn, these factors are associated with an early onset of ASB, early arrest, and chronic offending during adolescence (Capaldi & Patterson, 1994; Shaw & Vondra, 1994). A vicious cycle of adaptational failure and added stress places downward pressure on both the parent and the child. The antisocial individual is more vulnerable and at greater risk of entering a class of divorced, unemployed, and disadvantaged people (Patterson, 1996). For example, social disadvantage, increased motility, divorce, early sexual activity, and working-mother status may lead to an increase in mothers who are at greater risk for antisocial parenting practices. Also, less skilled antisocial mothers may drift into areas of large cities that isolate them from family and neighbors, and lead them to func-

"Like grandfather, like father, like son..."

Source: Cartoon by Cheryl Reed from *Antisocial Boys,* by G. R. Patterson, J. B. Reid and T. J. Dishion, 1992, p. 41. Copyright © 1992 by Castalia Publishing. Reprinted by permission.

tion in an atmosphere of mistrust and minimal communication. When these women become pregnant again, they may have reduced access to public health services. Poor diet and drugs may result in a higher incidence of low birth weight, prematurity, and birth defects in their offspring, which in turn make their infants and toddlers more difficult to parent. The combination of a difficult infant and an unskilled parent increases the likelihood of ASB and subsequent onset of arrest (Patterson, 1996). In this way, the generation of CP cycles again and again.

Neighborhood and School   ASB in youth is disproportionately concentrated in poor neighborhoods characterized by a criminal subculture that supports drug dealing and prostitution, peer group violence, delinquent gang membership, frequent transitions and mobility, and low social support from neighbors or religious groups (Leventhal & Brooks-Gunn, 2000, 2003; Tolan, Gorman-Smith, & Henry, 2003). In addition, antisocial people tend to select neighborhoods with other people like them. The **social selection hypothesis** states that people who move into different neighborhoods differ before they arrive, and those who remain, differ from those who leave. This creates a community organization that minimizes productive social relations and effective social norms, and the ASB becomes stabilized (Caspi & Moffitt, 1995; Sampson et al., 1997). The effects of community characteristics on crime and delinquency are likely to be reinforced by neighborhood social disorganization characterized by few local friendship and acquaintance networks, low participation in local community organizations, and an inability to supervise and control teenage peer groups (Sampson & Groves, 1989). In fact, the main influence of effective parents in high risk neighborhoods seems to be in countering gang membership (Tolan et al., 2003).

Weapons signs such as this one in the Los Angeles area are routinely posted outside schools.

In high-risk neighborhoods, enrollment in a poor school is associated with antisocial and delinquent behavior, whereas a positive school experience can be a protective factor for the development of these behaviors (Rutter, 1989b). A good school environment characterized by clear requirements for homework completion, high academic expectations, clear and consistent discipline policies, and incentives for appropriate school behavior and achievement may partially compensate for poor family circumstances. Systematic interventions to promote these school characteristics have resulted in school-wide reductions in children's CP (Gottfredson, Gottfredson, & Hybel, 1993).

Media

I believe that this kind of vicarious adventure, escape, excitement, even blood and thunder is necessary and important to most children as outlets for their own emotions, particularly their feelings of aggression.

—Josette Frank, Media Consultant

Programs interestingly depicting antisocial conduct, crime, murder, influence children to antisocial attitudes and lead to aggression.

—Judge Jacob Panken, New York City Children's Court

These contrasting expert opinions were presented nearly 60 years ago (*The New York Times*, April 14, 1946)— in reference to the influence of radio on children. The controversy regarding media influences on aggression in young people rages on today. At one extreme, some researchers claim that TV violence verges on child maltreatment and that we can reduce murders by unplugging the TV; others argue that there is little evidence for a causal relation between TV violence and aggressive behavior.

By the time a child in the United States reaches grade 6, he or she has witnessed 8,000 or more murders on TV and well over 100,000 other acts of violence (Leland, 1995). The concern is that this steady diet of violence leads children to think violence is normal, to become desensitized to the suffering of real people, or to become aroused by images they see and want to mimic these violent acts. For example, one 5-year-old boy, after watching his favorite cartoon characters pull one of their famous arson stunts, set his house ablaze. His younger sister was killed in the fire. Thus, exposure to media violence can be both: (1) a short term *precipitating* factor for aggressive and violent behavior that results from priming, excitation, or imitation of specific behaviors, and (2) a long-term *predisposing* factor for aggressive behavior acquired via desensitization to violence and observational learning of an aggression-supporting belief system (i.e., "the world is a hostile place," "aggression is acceptable," "aggression can be used to solve social problems") (Huesmann, Moise-Titus, Podolski, & Eron, 2003).

Exposure to media violence may reinforce preexisting antisocial tendencies in some children. For example, in a series of studies spanning a decade, children with CPs were found to view relatively large amounts of violent material, prefer aggressive characters, and believe fictional content to be true (Gadow & Sprafkin, 1993). However, it is not only children with preexisting violent tendencies who are likely to be affected. Long-term studies have found that childhood exposure to media violence between ages 6 and 9, identification with aggressive TV characters, and perceived realism of TV violence predict serious aggressive and criminal behavior 15 years later (Huesmann et al., 2003).

The correlation between TV violence and aggression is indisputable—but does TV violence cause aggression, and if so, how? Although research suggests a causal relation (Anderson & Bushman, 2002; Johnson, Cohen, Smailes, Kasen, & Brook, 2002), answers to these questions remain elusive despite decades of research and a pressing concern to act on research findings through social policies. For example, require manufacturers to equip new TVs with the V-chip and require networks to implement a TV ratings system (Zoglin, 1996). It is unlikely that media influences alone can account for the substantial amount of ASB in young people (Rutter & Smith, 1995). Like other risk factors, media influences interact with child, family, community, and cultural factors in contributing to CPs. But clearly they are an important and unique contributing factor. Exposure to media violence won't turn an otherwise well-adjusted child into a violent criminal. However, "just as every cigarette one smokes increases a little bit the likelihood of a lung tumor some day . . . every violent TV show increases a little bit the likelihood of a child growing up to behave more aggressively in some situation" (Huesmann et al., 2003, p. 218).

Cultural Factors

Cultural differences in the expression of aggressive behavior are dramatic. Across cultures, socialization of children for aggression has been found to be one of the strongest predictors of aggressive acts, such as homicide and assault. As the following examples of contrasting socialization practices illustrate, aggression may be an inadvertent consequence of a culture's emphasis on training "warriors":

The Kapauku of Western New Guinea

"At about 7 years of age, a Kapauku boy begins to be under the father's control, gradually sleeping and eating only with the men and away from his mother. . . . His training [to be a brave warrior] begins when the father engages his son in mock stick fights. Gradually the fights become more serious and possibly lethal when the father and son shoot real war arrows at each other. Groups of boys play at target shooting; they also play at hitting each other over the head with sticks." (C. R. Ember & Ember, 1994, p. 639–640)

The homicide rate among the Kapauku from 1953 to 1954 was estimated at 200 per 100,000, approximately 20 times current murder rates in the United States.

Calvin and Hobbes   by Bill Watterson

Source: Calvin & Hobbes. © Watterson. Reprinted with permission of Universal Press Syndicate. All rights reserved.

The Lepcha of the Indian Himalayas

The Lepcha are very clear about what they expect from their children. "Good children help out with the work, tell the truth, listen to teaching from elders, help old people, and are peaceable. Bad children quarrel with and insult people, tell lies, draw their knives in anger when reprimanded, and do not do their share of the work." (C. R. Ember & Ember, 1994, p. 641)

Interviews with the Lepcha people revealed that the only authenticated murder in their culture had occurred about 200 years ago (C. R. Ember & Ember, 1994).

Rates of ASB vary widely across cultures, and not necessarily in relation to technological gains, material wealth, or population density. For example, some third world countries that value interdependence are characterized by high rates of prosocial behavior, and some places with high population density, such as Singapore, have very low rates of violence. The United States is by far the most violent of all industrialized nations, with homicide rates that are many times the rates in Europe.

"We live in a culture that is permissive toward violence. We live in a context in which we glorify heroes who kill and maim. We are not suffering from racial violence—it's cultural violence. The horror of people being intentionally injured or killed because of their affiliation with a group is with us every day. Killings within families, violence inside schools, attacks on people who are gay, or who profess a certain religion, or belong to a particular ethnic group are in the news daily." (Reverend Jesse Jackson, 2000, p. 328)

Minority status is associated with ASB in the United States, with elevated rates of ASB in African American, Hispanic American, and Native American youths (D. S. Elliott et al., 1985). However, studies of national samples have reported either no or very small differences in ASB related to race or ethnicity when SES, gender, age, and referral status are controlled for (Achenbach, Howell, Quay, & Conners, 1991; Lahey et al., 1995). Thus, although externalizing problems are reported to be more frequent among minority-status children, this finding is likely related to economic hardship, limited employment opportunities, residence in high-risk urban neighborhoods, and membership in antisocial gangs (Lahey & Waldron, 2003).

SECTION SUMMARY

- CPs in children are best accounted for by multiple causes or risk and protective factors that operate in a transactional fashion over time.
- Adoption and twin studies indicate that genetic influences account for about 50% of the variance in ASB.

Genetic contributions to overt forms of ASB, such as aggression, are stronger than for covert acts such as stealing or lying.

- ASB may result from an overactive behavioral activation system (BAS) and an underactive behavioral inhibition system (BIS). Low levels of cortical arousal and autonomic reactivity and deficits in the prefrontal cortex seem to play an important role, particularly for childhood onset/persistent CD.
- Many family factors have been implicated as possible causes of children's ASB, including marital conflict, family isolation, violence in the home, poor disciplinary practices, a lack of parental supervision, and insecure attachments.
- Family instability and stress, parental criminality and antisocial personality, and antisocial family values are risk factors for CPs.
- The structural characteristics of the community provide a backdrop for the emergence of CP by giving rise to community conditions that interfere with the adoption of social norms and the development of productive social relations.
- School, neighborhood, and media influences are all potential risk factors for ASB, as are cultural factors, such as minority group status and ethnicity.

Treatment and Prevention

Scott

Salvageable?

Scott, age 10, was referred after setting a fire in the schoolyard. While his therapist saw Scott as "potentially salvageable," his parents were not willing to pursue therapy. As a result, Scott was placed in a boarding school for "troubled boys" . . . After 3 weeks at this school, he was expelled for burning down the dorm . . . Charges were pressed and he was sent to a group home for delinquent boys. He remained there for 3 months before he and two older boys ran away. They were caught a few days later when they attacked a homeless man, stealing his money ($4.85) and beating him. As a result of this crime, Scott was sent to a detention facility until he turned 18. His therapist heard nothing further. (Adapted from R. K. Morgan, 1999)

Many forms of treatment will be tried throughout the life of a youngster with severe CPs (McMahon & Wells, 1998). Treatment may begin during the preschool years or, more typically, as was the case with Scott, when severe ASB at school leads to referral. Ongoing contacts with the educational, mental health, and judicial systems may result in referral for one or more of a wide range of treatments (Tolan & Guerra, 1994). The most promising treatments use a combination of approaches, which are applied across individual, family, school, and community settings. In addition, treatment frequently requires that related family problems, such as maternal depression, marital discord, abuse, and other stressors must be addressed if gains are to be generalized and maintained (Kazdin & Whitley, 2003).

Most people understand that abuse, family dysfunction, school expulsion, association with drug-using peers, residence in a high-crime area, and minimal parental supervision contribute to serious CPs (Henggeler, 1996). However, despite this recognition, typical and often court-mandated treatments, such as psychotherapy, group therapy, tutoring, punishment, wilderness programs, or boot camps fail to meaningfully address these determinants, and thus are among the least effective approaches (Henggeler, Schoenwald, & Pickrel, 1995; Lipsey, 1995). Despite their lack of effectiveness in treating serious ASB, office-based individual counseling and family therapy are often provided because they can be relatively inexpensive (Tate, Reppucci, & Mulvey, 1995). Group treatments that bring together antisocial adolescents may make the problem worse, since associating with like-minded individuals often encourages ASB (Dishion, McCord, & Poulin, 1999).

As we saw for Scott, restrictive approaches, such as residential treatment, inpatient psychiatric hospitalization, and incarceration, also show little effectiveness and have the additional disadvantage of being extremely expensive (Henggeler & Santos, 1997). Unfortunately, a significant proportion of mental health dollars for youths is still spent on restrictive out-of-home placements that may cause more harm than good (Sondheimer, Schoenwald, & Rowland, 1994). Incarceration may not even serve a community protection function, since youths who are incarcerated and then released often commit more crimes than youths kept at home and given treatment (Henggeler, 1996).

Since children's CPs are known to show a developmental progression, diversification, and escalation over time, treatments must be sensitive to where a child is in this trajectory. Treatment methods and goals will differ for preschoolers, school-age children, and adolescents, and differ according to the type and severity of the child's CPs. In general, the further along a child is in the progression of ASB, the greater is the need for intensive interventions and, unfortunately, for children like Scott, the poorer is the prognosis. In fact, if ASB is not changed by the end of grade 3, it might best be treated as a chronic condition, much like diabetes, which cannot be cured but can be managed or contained through ongoing interventions and supports (Kazdin, 1995). This troubling situation of high treatment effort and cost with less return for older children has led to a re-evaluation of priorities and a growing emphasis on early intervention and prevention (Conduct Problems Prevention Research Group, 2002a). A comprehensive two-pronged approach to the treatment of CPs is needed that includes (Frick, 2000):

- *Ongoing interventions* to help older youths and their families cope with the many associated social, emotional, and academic problems

- *Early intervention/prevention* programs for young children just starting to display problem behaviors

To illustrate the many treatments for children and adolescents with CPs (McMahon & Wells, 1998), in the next section we highlight three treatment approaches with some proven success (Brestan & Eyberg, 1998)—parent management training (PMT), problem-solving skills training (PSST), and multisystemic treatment (MST) (See Table 6.6). We also discuss promising new preventive interventions for young children. Almost all forms of treatment attempt to provide corrective interpersonal ex-

---

Table 6.6
Effective Treatments for Children with Conduct Problems

TREATMENT	OVERVIEW
Parent Management Training (PMT)	Teaches parents to change their child's behavior in the home using contingency management techniques. The focus is on improving parent–child interactions and enhancing other parenting skills (e.g., parent–child communication, monitoring, and supervision).
Problem-Solving Skills Training (PSST)	Identifies the child's cognitive deficiencies and distortions in social situations and provides instruction, practice, and feedback to teach new ways of handling social situations. The child learns to appraise the situation, change his or her attributions about other children's motivations, be more sensitive to how other children feel, and generate alternative and more appropriate solutions.
Multisystemic Treatment (MST)	An intensive approach that draws on other techniques such as PMT, PSST, and marital therapy, as well as specialized interventions such as special education, and referral to substance abuse treatment programs or legal services.

periences with parents, siblings, and peers, because most antisocial acts, including violence, occur between the child and family members or peers. In addition, given the pervasiveness of CPs across settings, nearly all treatments have come to include components designed to change the child's behavior at home, at school, and in the community.

Parent Management Training (PMT)

Parent management training (PMT) teaches parents to change their child's behavior at home (Brinkmeyer & Eyberg, 2003; McMahon & Forehand, 2003; Webster-Stratton & Reid, 2003). Its underlying assumption is that maladaptive parent–child interactions are at least partly responsible for producing and sustaining the child's ASB. Changing the way parents interact with their child will lead to improvements in the child's behavior (Dishion & Kavanagh, 2003; Ducharme, Atkinson, & Poulton, 2000). Although coercive exchanges are seen as the joint outcome of parent and child behavior, the easiest and most desirable point of entry in modifying these interactions is by changing parent behavior. The goal of PMT is for the parent to learn specific new skills. Many of the variations of PMT, can be individual versus group training, training in the clinic versus in the home, or the use of live versus videotaped training materials, and all share several features (see Table 6.7).

PMT has a number of strengths and some limitations (McMahon & Wells, 1998). Many excellent treatment manuals and training materials have been developed that facilitate its widespread use (e.g., Barkley, 1997e; McMahon & Forehand, 2003). In addition, PMT has been evaluated more than any other treatment for CPs (Brestan & Eyberg, 1998). These evaluations have repeatedly demonstrated the short-term effectiveness in producing changes in parent and child behavior. The average child whose parents participate in PMT shows better adjustment after treatment than 80% of children whose parents do not participate (Serketich & Dumas, 1996). In addition to changes in the referred child, PMT has also been associated with reductions in the problem behaviors of siblings and reduced stress and depression in the parents.

PMT has been most effective with parents of children younger than 12 years of age and less so with adolescents (Dishion & Patterson, 1992). Although PMT can produce short-term gains, its long-term effectiveness is less clear (Kazdin, 1997b; McMahon & Wells, 1998). In addition, PMT makes numerous demands on parents to master and implement procedures in the home, attend meetings, and maintain phone contacts with the therapist. For families under stress with few resources, these demands may be too great to continue in treatment (Armbruster & Kazdin, 1994; C. E. Cunningham et al., 2000).

The application of PMT is rarely straightforward. The use of coercion may not be recognized by parents who believe that difficulties occur because their child is stubborn,

Table 6.7
Key Features of Parent Management Training (PMT)

- There is minimal or no direct intervention of the therapist with the child.
- Parents learn procedures to change parent–child interactions, promote positive child behavior, and decrease ASB.
- Parents learn new ways to identify, define, and observe their child's problem behaviors.
- Treatment sessions cover the effective use of commands; ways to set clear rules; use of praise, tangible rewards, or tokens for desired behavior; use of mild punishment such as time-out from reinforcement or loss of privileges; negotiation; and contingency contracting.
- Sessions allow parents to see how new techniques are implemented, to practice using them, and to review progress in the home.
- Homework assignments are used to promote generalization of the skills learned in treatment to the home.
- Progress in treatment is carefully monitored, and ongoing adjustments are made as needed.

Source: Adapted from *Conduct Disorders in Childhood and Adolescence,* by A. E. Kazdin, pp. 83–84. Copyright © 1995 by Sage Publications. Adapted by permission.

their marriage is bad, work is interfering with the time they spend together, or school personnel are unfair. In fact, parents of children with CP frequently believe they use good parenting practices but their child fails to respond. It is important to address these parental beliefs and concerns if treatment is to be successful (C. Johnston, 1996; Morrisey-Kane & Prinz, 1999). In addition, PMT has increasingly come to recognize the importance of marital and social support, therapy style and engagement, and ethnic and cultural factors in treatment (McMahon & Wells, 1998).

Problem-Solving Skills Training (PSST)

Problem-solving skills training (PSST) focuses on the cognitive deficiencies and distortions displayed by children and adolescents with CPs in interpersonal situations (Kazdin, 1996c; Kazdin, 2003a). PSST is used both alone and in combination with PMT, as required by the family's circumstances. The underlying assumption of PSST is that the child's perceptions and appraisals of environmental events will trigger aggressive and antisocial responses, and that changes in faulty thinking will lead to changes in behavior. As described in Box 6.6, the child is taught to use five problem-solving steps to identify thoughts, feelings, and behaviors in problem social situations.

BOX 6.6 Cognitive Problem-Solving Steps

Problem situation: Jason, one of the kids in your class has taken your Nintendo game. You want to get it back. What do you do?

Step 1: What am I supposed to do?
I want to get my Nintendo game back from Jason.

Step 2: I have to look at all my possibilities.
I can beat him up and take it back, ask him to give it back, or tell my teacher.

Step 3: I had better concentrate and focus.
If I beat him up, I would get into trouble. If I asked him, he might give it back.

Step 4: I need to make a choice.
I'll try asking him, and if that doesn't work, I will tell my teacher.

Step 5: I did a good job or I made a mistake.
I made a good choice. I won't get into trouble. Jason and I can still be friends if he returns my Nintendo game. If not, I did my best to get it back before asking my teacher for help. I did a good job!

Source: Adapted from "Problem Solving and Parent Management Training in Treating Aggressive and Antisocial Behavior," by A. E. Kazdin, 1996, pp. 377–408 (383). In E. D. Hibbs and P. S. Jensen (Eds.), *Psychosocial Treatments for Child and Adolescent Disorders: Empirically Based Strategies for Clinical Practice.* Copyright © 1996 by the American Psychological Association. Reprinted by permission of the author.

Table 6.8

Key Features of Problem-Solving Skills Training (PSST)

- Emphasizes the child's thinking, although the behaviors that result from thinking are also viewed as important.
- Self-statements are used to direct attention to aspects of the problem that lead to effective solutions.
- Treatment uses structured tasks, which include games, school activities, or stories.
- The child learns to apply cognitive problem-solving skills to real-life situations.
- The therapist plays an active role in treatment, giving examples of the cognitive processes and providing feedback and praise.
- Treatment combines modeling, practice, role playing, behavioral contracts, reinforcement, and mild punishments, such as the loss of points or tokens.
- Treatment emphasizes the extension of problem solving to the child's everyday life through the use of homework assignments and parent involvement.

Source: Adapted from *Conduct Disorders in Childhood and Adolescence,* by A. E. Kazdin, pp. 81–82. Copyright © 1995 by Sage Publications. Adapted by permission.

During PSST, the therapist uses instruction, practice, and feedback to help the child discover different ways to handle social situations. To accomplish this, children learn to appraise the situation, identify self-statements and reactions, and alter their attributions about other children's motivations. They also learn to be more sensitive to how other children feel, to anticipate others' reactions, and to generate appropriate solutions to social problems. The key features of PSST are outlined in Table 6.8.

PSST is effective with children and youths who are clinically referred for CPs, with benefits extending to parent and family functioning (Kazdin, 2003a; Kazdin & Wassell, 2000). Research supports the relationship between maladaptive cognitions and aggressive behavior on which PSST is based, and PSST procedures are carefully specified in treatment manuals. However, it is not yet clear whether changes in maladaptive cognitions are responsible for behavioral improvements. Indeed, the alteration of cognitive processes may not necessarily lead to changes in behavior (Dodge, 1989). Finally, although most children improve as a result of PSST, some may continue to display more problems than their nondeviant peers. Thus,

more enduring PSST interventions are being developed to meet the needs of families of children with CPs whose problems are particularly severe.

Multisystemic Treatment (MST)

Multisystemic treatment (MST) is an intensive family- and community-based approach for adolescents with severe CPs that place them at risk for out-of-home placements (Henggeler & Lee, 2003). MST views the child with CPs as functioning within interconnected social systems, including the family, school, neighborhood, and court and juvenile services (Henggeler, Schoenwald, Borduin, Rowland, & Cunningham, 1998). ASB results from, or can be maintained by, transactions within or between any of those systems. MST seeks to empower caregivers to improve youth and family functioning (Cunningham, Henggeler, Brondino, & Pickrel, 1999). Thus, treatment is carried out with all family members, school personnel, peers, juvenile justice staff, and other individuals in the child's life. MST is an intensive approach that also draws on PMT, PSST, and marital therapy, as well as specialized interventions, such as special education and referral to substance abuse treatment programs or legal services. In effect, MST attempts to address the many determinants of severe ASB (Rowland et al., 2000). The guiding principles of MST are outlined in Table 6.9.

Outcome studies of MST with extremely antisocial and violent youths have found this approach to be superior to usual services, individual counseling, community

Table 6.9
Guiding Principles of Multisystemic Treatment

Principle 1: Assessment focuses on understanding the 'fit' between the identified problems and their broader context.

Principle 2: Interventions are present-focused and action-oriented, targeting specific and well-defined problems.

Principle 3: Interventions focus on behavioral transactions within or between multiple systems.

Principle 4: Interventions are developmentally appropriate and fit the needs of the youth.

Principle 5: Interventions require daily and weekly effort by family members.

Principle 6: Interventions are evaluated continuously from multiple perspectives.

Principle 7: Interventions are designed to promote generalization and long-term maintenance.

Principle 8: Interventions emphasize the positive, and use systemic strengths as levers for change.

Principle 9: Interventions are designed to promote responsible behavior and decrease irresponsible behavior.

Source: Adapted from *Treating Conduct Problems in Children and Adolescents: An Overview of the Multisystemic Approach with Guidelines for Intervention Design and Implementation* by S. W. Henggeler, 1991, Division of Children, Adolescents and Their Families, South Carolina Department of Mental Health, Charleston, SC. Reprinted by permission of the author.

services, and psychiatric hospitalization. In addition, studies have found decreases in delinquency and aggression with peers, and improved family relations. Importantly, MST has been found to reduce long-term rates of criminal behavior for periods as long as 5 years after treatment. MST is also cost-effective, with costs estimated at one-fifth of the costs for more conventional interventions (Henggeler & Lee, 2003).

Since studies of MST have not yet differentiated between adolescents who show LCP and adolescents with AL patterns of ASB, it is difficult to know whether successful outcomes reported for this approach apply equally to both groups. It is possible that part of the success of MST may be in helping AL adolescents decrease their association with deviant peers and, by doing so, lowering the age at which they desist from delinquent behavior.

Preventive Interventions

Until recently, treatments for older children with CPs were given far greater attention than programs of early intervention and prevention. Fortunately, this situation is changing, with a growing recognition of the need for intensive home- and school-based interventions that can compete with the child's negative developmental history, poor family and community environment, and deviant peer associations (Sanders, 1999; Tolan, Guerra, & Kendall, 1995). The main assumptions of preventive interventions are (Webster-Stratton, 1996):

- CPs can be treated more easily and more effectively in younger than older children.
- By counteracting risk factors and strengthening protective factors at a young age, it is possible to limit or prevent the escalating developmental trajectory of increased aggression, peer rejection, self-esteem deficits, conduct disorder, and academic failure that is commonly observed in children with childhood-onset CPs.
- In the long run, preventive interventions will reduce the substantial costs to the educational, criminal justice, health, and mental health systems that are associated with CPs.

Carolyn Webster-Stratton has developed an intensive and increasingly multifaceted effective early-intervention program for parents and teachers of 2- to 8-year-old children with or at risk for CPs (Webster-Stratton & Reid, 2003). This program uses interactive videotapes as a foundation for training, which permits widespread use at a relatively low cost. In addition to teaching child management skills, the program also addresses the associated individual, family, and school difficulties that accompany CPs. Parents are taught personal self-control strategies for managing anger, depression, and blame. As a result, they learn effective communication skills, strategies for coping with conflict at home and at work, and ways to strengthen social supports. Teachers are taught ways to strengthen positive relationships with students, effective classroom discipline, strategies for teaching social skills, anger management, problem solving skills, and how to increase collaboration with parents. A number of studies have provided support for the effectiveness of these early interventions in reducing later CPs for two-thirds or more of children whose parents are involved (Webster-Stratton, 1996). This early intervention/prevention program is now more frequently based in schools, with a growing emphasis on matching the type, timing, and amount of intervention to the level of risk and specific needs of the child and family (Webster-Stratton & Reid, 2003).

An innovative program designed to prevent chronic ASB is FAST Track (Conduct Problems Prevention Research Group, 1992, 2000). This early intervention is an excellent example of the comprehensive effort needed to treat children with serious CPs. FAST Track is directed at high-risk kindergarten children who are identified in terms of their disruptive behavior and poor peer relations. The goals of FAST Track are to reduce disruptive and aggressive behaviors at home and school and to improve the quality of the child's relationships with parents, teachers, and peers. Children are taught the social-cognitive skills needed for effective interpersonal problem solving and emotion regulation. Other important goals are to strengthen academic skills, especially reading, and to improve the quality of the relationship between family members and school personnel.

Five integrated treatment components are used to achieve these goals: (1) parent management training; (2) home visiting/case management; (3) cognitive-behavioral social skills training; (4) academic tutoring; and (5) teacher-based classroom intervention. FAST Track interventions are implemented with close collaboration among parents, teachers, and project staff. The strengths of the program are that they target the deficits and determinants that research has shown to be important in children with CPs and uses treatment procedures for which there is already some empirical support.

Initial reports of outcomes at the end of grade 1 indicated moderate improvements in peer relations, academic performance, and classroom climate; decreases in CPs and use of special education resources; and enhanced parenting attitudes and values (Coie, 1997; Conduct Problems Prevention Research Group, 1999a, 1999b). By the end of grade 3, 37% of children in the intervention group were free of serious CPs, compared with 27% of the control children. Parent and teacher ratings provided further support for the prevention of CPs at home and school, and many, but not all (peer relations and academic performance were two important exceptions) of the outcomes at the end of grade 1 were maintained at the end of grade 3 (Conduct Problems Prevention Research Group, 2002b). Although these findings are promising, only time will tell whether this all-out effort will achieve its intended long-term goal to prevent serious chronic ASB and to enhance psychosocial and academic outcomes. Future assessments when these high-risk children enter adolescence will be critical since this is the time when most early starting delinquency occurs.

Although tremendous advances have been made in the treatment and prevention of CPs, much work remains to be done. The main conclusion to be drawn from intervention and prevention efforts over the past 100 years is that *the degree of success or failure in treating ASB*

depends on the type and severity of the child's conduct problem and related risk and protective factors (Kazdin & Wassell, 1999). Children from mostly middle-class healthy families with mild CPs are likely to benefit from individual, parent, family, and school-based interventions— those from highly dysfunctional homes and poor neighborhoods who display severe and persistent problems are likely to benefit very little, if at all. If interventions are to succeed, it will also be necessary to find effective ways to help families persevere with interventions that could prove to have real benefits (Rutter, 2003a). Although small but significant short-term gains for children with severe CPs have been achieved using intensive interventions, the degree of normalization and long-term impact of these approaches is yet to be determined (Kazdin, 1995).

SECTION SUMMARY

- Despite considerable efforts to help children and adolescents with CPs, there is an absence of clearly effective interventions. However, several approaches have some proven success.

- The focus of parent management training (PMT) is on teaching parents to change their child's behavior in the home.

- The underlying assumption of problem-solving skills training (PSST) is that faulty perceptions and appraisals of interpersonal events trigger antisocial responses. The focus is on changing behavior by changing the way the child thinks in social situations.

- Multisystemic treatment (MST) is an intensive approach that is carried out with all family members, school personnel, peers, juvenile justice staff, and other individuals in the child's life.

- Recent efforts have focused on trying to prevent CPs through intensive programs of early intervention/ prevention.

- The degree of success or failure in treating ASB depends on the type and severity of the child's conduct problem and related risk and protective factors.

Key Terms

 InfoTrac College Edition

To research recent articles on the subject, go to:
www.infotrac-college/thomsonlearning.com

Enter search terms: ANTISOCIAL BEHAVIOR, CONDUCT PROBLEMS, DEVIANT BEHAVIOR, BULLYING, BEHAVIOR DISORDERS IN CHILDREN, AGGRESSIVENESS IN CHILDREN, PSYCHOPATHY, JUVENILE DELINQUENCY

Anxiety Disorders

"It is hard to be brave, when you're only a Very Small Animal."

—Piglet (*Pooh's Little Instruction Book, 1995*).

Separation Anxiety: Brad is terrified of being separated from his mother. He follows her around the house constantly, always needing to know where she is.

Generalized Anxiety: Alesha "worries about everything"—how she is doing in school, events in the news, and family finances.

Social Anxiety: Dante is very preoccupied with what others think of him. He doesn't interact with anyone at school, and feels completely isolated.

Obsessive-Compulsive Disorder: Wayman can't stop thinking about not being able to sleep. Every night before bedtime he goes through the same routine of opening and closing the closet door and making and remaking his bed.

Panic Attack: Claudia describes her sudden attack of overwhelming anxiety. "My heart started pumping so fast I thought it would explode. I thought I was going to die."

All children experience fear, worry, or anxiety as a normal part of growing up, but each child in our examples suffers from an anxiety disorder that is excessive and debilitating. An anxiety disorder is one of the most common mental health problems in young people (Essau, Conradt, & Petermann, 2000b). Despite their high frequency and associated problems, anxiety disorders in children often go unnoticed and untreated (Silverman & Treffers, 2001; Vasey & Dadds, 2001). This may be due to the frequent occurrence of fears and anxiety during normal development, the invisible nature of many symptoms (e.g., a knot in the stomach), and the fact that anxiety is not nearly as damaging to other people or property as are conduct problems (Albano, Chorpita, & Barlow, 2003).

For a long time, anxiety in children was thought to be a mild and transitory disturbance that would fade over time with normal life experiences. However, we now know that many children who experience anxiety continue to have problems during adolescence and adulthood (Roza, Hofstra, van der Ende, & Verhulst, 2003). Although isolated symptoms of fear and anxiety are usually short-lived, anxiety disorders have a more chronic course (Woodward & Fergusson, 2001). In fact, nearly one-half of those affected have an illness duration of 8 years or longer (Keller et al., 1992).

Description

Anxiety is a mood state characterized by strong negative emotion and bodily symptoms of tension in which an individual apprehensively anticipates future danger or misfortune (Barlow, 2002). This definition captures two key features of anxiety—strong negative emotion and an element of fear. Children who experience excessive and debilitating anxieties are said to have **anxiety disorders**. These disorders occur in many forms. Some children, like Brad, feel anxious whenever they are separated from their mother or are away from home. Others, like Alesha, worry about almost everything and feel anxious most of the time for no apparent reason. Some children feel anxious only in certain situations, such as when they have to travel by airplane or, like Dante, when they have to give a talk in class. Others, like Wayman, experience repeated, intrusive, and unwanted thoughts that produce anxiety, and they spend hours in ritualized behavior in an effort to alleviate that anxiety. Some children, like Claudia, have unpredictable bouts of such sudden and intense anxiety that they become terrified and immobilized. Still others have persistent and frightening thoughts after a traumatic event, such as a flood, sexual abuse, or exposure to war.

Many youngsters with anxiety disorders suffer from more than one type, either simultaneously or at separate times during their development (Eisen, Kearney, & Schaefer, 1995). In view of the substantial overlap among these disorders, we begin this chapter by discussing the general features and mechanisms of anxiety that apply across all types. The common occurrence of fears and anxieties in childhood and adolescence requires that we also consider the role of these emotions in normal development. We then examine each anxiety disorder and what makes it unique.

Experiencing Anxiety

When Matt saw a dog running loose in front of his house, he became "pale, sweaty, cold, and trembly." His "thoughts raced so fast that he couldn't think. He froze. His heart pounded, he felt tense, and he found it difficult to breathe."

Matt is experiencing anxiety in response to an event he sees as potentially threatening or dangerous. As humans we are programmed to detect and react to signs of anxiety in ourselves and in others. In fact, anxiety is both expected and normal at certain ages and in certain situations. One-year-old infants become distressed when separated from their mothers, and almost all young children have short-lived specific fears—of the dark, for example. The child's world can be a strange and menacing place, full of unknown dangers—some real, others imagined. Although no one likes to feel anxious, the alternative of not feeling anxious when the situation calls for it is far worse.

Anxiety often hits us when we do something important, and in moderate doses it helps us think and act more effectively. You will probably be better prepared for your next exam if you're just a little bit nervous about taking it.

Table 7.1
The Many Symptoms of Anxiety

PHYSICAL

Increased heart rate	Dizziness	Blushing
Fatigue	Blurred vision	Vomiting
Increased respiration	Dry mouth	Numbness
Nausea	Muscle tension	Sweating
Stomach upset	Heart palpitation	

COGNITIVE

Thoughts of being scared or hurt	Thoughts of incompetence or inadequacy	Thoughts of bodily injury
Thoughts or images of monsters or wild animals	Difficulty concentrating	Images of harm to loved ones
	Blanking out or forgetfulness	Thoughts of going crazy
Self-deprecatory or self-critical thoughts	Thoughts of appearing foolish	Thoughts of contamination

BEHAVIORAL

Avoidance	Trembling lip	Avoidance of eye contact
Crying or screaming	Swallowing	Physical proximity
Nail biting	Immobility	Clenched jaw
Trembling voice	Twitching	Fidgeting
Stuttering	Thumb sucking	

Source: Adapted from "Fears and Anxieties," by B. A. Barrios and D. P. Hartmann, 1997, p. 235. In E. J. Mash and L. G. Terdal (Eds.), *Assessment of Childhood Disorders,* 3rd ed. Copyright © 1997 by Guilford Publications. Reprinted by permission.

Similarly, some anxiety may help a child prepare harder for an upcoming oral report or athletic event. In this sense, anxiety is an adaptive emotion that readies children both physically and psychologically for coping with people, objects, or events that could be dangerous to their safety or well-being (Barlow, 2002).

Although some anxiety is good, too much is not. Excessive, uncontrollable anxiety can be debilitating. A child may fail a test because she spends too much time thinking about how awful it would be to fail, making it nearly impossible to think about anything else (for example, how to solve a math problem). In children with anxiety disorders, this normally useful emotion works against them.

When children experience fears beyond a certain age, in situations that pose no real threat or danger, to an extent that seriously interferes with daily activities, anxiety is a serious problem. Even if the child knows there is little to be afraid of, he or she is still terrified and does everything possible to escape or avoid the situation. This pattern of self-defeating behavior, known as the **neurotic paradox** (Mowrer, 1950), can become self-perpetuating—much like Sisyphus repeatedly pushing the rock up the hill, only to have it roll back down on him each time.

First and foremost, anxiety is an immediate reaction to perceived danger or threat—a reaction known as the **fight/flight response.** All of its effects are aimed at escaping potential harm, either by confronting the source of danger (fight), or by evading it (flight). If you look up to see a grand piano about to fall in your direction and experience no anxiety whatsoever, you will pay serious consequences. To avoid such a fate, your fight/flight response would kick in to overdrive and you would jump out of harm's way.

Think of a recent situation that made you anxious. What was it about the situation that made you anxious? What physical symptoms did you notice? What were you thinking? What did you do? Describing what it's like to be anxious isn't easy because anxiety is a complex reaction with many symptoms, as shown in Table 7.1. How many of these symptoms did you experience? What do these many symptoms have in common?

The symptoms of anxiety are expressed through three interrelated response systems: the *physical system,* the *cognitive system,* and the *behavioral system* (Rapee, Craske, & Barlow, 1996). It is essential to know how the three sets of symptoms work, since more than one may be evident in different children with the same anxiety disorder. Also, as we will discuss, different response systems are dominant in certain anxiety disorders. Let's take a closer look at how each response system works.

Physical System　When a person perceives or anticipates danger, the brain sends messages to the sympathetic nervous system, which produces the fight/flight response. The activation of this system produces many important chemical and physical effects that mobilize the body for action:

- *Chemical effects.* Adrenaline and noradrenaline are released from the adrenal glands.
- *Cardiovascular effects.* Heart rate and strength of the heart beat increase, readying the body for action by speeding up blood flow and improving delivery of oxygen to the tissues.
- *Respiratory effects.* Speed and depth of breathing increase, which brings oxygen to the tissues and removes waste. This may produce feelings of breathlessness, choking or smothering, or chest pains.
- *Sweat gland effects.* Sweating increases, which cools the body and makes the skin slippery.
- *Other physical effects.* The pupils widen to let in more light, which may lead to blurred vision or spots in front of the eyes. Salivation decreases, resulting in a dry mouth. Decreased activity in the digestive system may lead to nausea and a heavy feeling in the stomach. Muscles tense in readiness for fight or flight, leading to subjective feelings of tension, aches and pains, and trembling.

These physical symptoms are familiar signs of anxiety. Overall, the fight/flight response produces general activation of the entire metabolism. As a result, the individual may feel hot and flushed and, because this activation takes a lot of energy, he or she feels tired and drained afterward.

Cognitive System   Since the main purpose of the fight/flight system is to signal possible danger, its activation produces an immediate search for potential threat. For children with anxiety disorders it is difficult to focus on everyday tasks because their attention is consumed by a constant search for threat or danger. When these children can't find proof of danger, they may turn their search inward: "If nothing is out there to make me feel anxious, then something must be wrong with me." Or they may distort the situation: "Even though I can't find it, I know there's something to be afraid of." Or they may do both. Children with anxiety disorders will invent explanations for their anxiety: "I must be a real jerk." "Everyone will think I'm a dummy if I say something." "Even though I can't see them, there are germs all over the place." Activation of the cognitive system often leads to subjective feelings of apprehension, nervousness, difficulty concentrating, and panic.

Behavioral System   The overwhelming urges that accompany the fight/flight response are aggression and a desire to escape the threatening situation, but social constraints may prevent fulfilling either impulse. For example, just before a final exam you may feel like attacking your professor or not showing up at all, but fortunately for your professor and your need to pass the course, you are likely to inhibit these urges! However, they may show up as foot tapping, fidgeting, or irritability (consider the number of teeth marks in pencils), or as escape or avoidance by getting a doctor's note, requesting a deferral, or even faking illness. Unfortunately, avoidance is the very thing that perpetuates anxiety despite the temporary feeling of relief. Avoidance behaviors are negatively reinforced; that is, they are strengthened when they are followed by a rapid reduction in anxiety. As a result, each time a child is confronted with an anxiety-producing situation, she or he tries to get out of it more quickly, the anxiety drops off more quickly, and the more the child avoids such situations. As children with anxiety disorders engage in more and more avoidance, carrying out everyday activities becomes exceedingly difficult.

Chantelle
The Terror of Being Home Alone

When Chantelle, age 14, realized she was at home alone, she was terrified. Her thoughts raced so fast it was impossible to think clearly. She forgot all the right things to do. Her heart pounded and she tensed up. She felt like she couldn't breathe, and she began to sob. She wanted to run but felt completely immobilized.

Chantelle's reactions show how the three response systems of anxiety interact and feed off one another. Physically, Chantelle's heart pounded, she tensed, and she had difficulty breathing. Cognitively, she could not think clearly. Behaviorally, she was completely immobilized.

Anxiety Versus Fear and Panic

It is important to distinguish anxiety from two closely related emotions—fear and panic. **Fear** is an immediate alarm reaction to current danger or life-threatening emergencies. Although fear and anxiety have much in common, the fear reaction differs both psychologically and biologically from the emotion of anxiety. Fear is a *present-oriented* emotional reaction to current danger, marked by strong escape tendencies and an all-out surge in the sympathetic nervous system. The overriding message is alarm: "If I don't do something right now, I might not make it at all." In contrast, anxiety is a *future-oriented* emotion characterized by feelings of apprehension and lack of control over upcoming events that might be threatening. Fear and anxiety both warn of danger or distress. However, only anxiety is frequently felt when no danger is actually present (Barlow, 2002).

Panic is a group of physical symptoms of the fight/flight response that unexpectedly occur in the absence of any obvious threat or danger. With no explanation for physical symptoms such as a pounding heart, the individual may invent one: "I'm dying." The sensations themselves can feel threatening and may trigger further fear, apprehension, anxiety, and panic (Barlow, 2002).

Normal Fears, Anxieties, Worries, and Rituals

Since fear and anxiety in moderate doses are adaptive, it is not surprising that emotions and rituals that increase feelings of control are common during childhood and adolescence. It is only when the emotions and rituals become excessive, or occur in a developmentally inappropriate context, that they are of concern.

Normal Fears Since children and their environments constantly change, fears that are normal at one age can be debilitating a few years later. For example, fear of strangers may serve a protective function for infants and young children, but when it persists beyond a certain age it can seriously interfere with the development of peer relations. Whether or not a specific fear is normal also depends on its effect on the child and how long it lasts. If a fear has little impact on the child's daily life or lasts only a few weeks, it is likely a part of normal development.

The number and type of fears change over time with a general age-related decline in number (Barrios & Hartmann, 1997; Gullone, 1999). Even so, specific fears are common in older children, and many teens report that their fears cause them considerable distress and significantly interfere with daily activities (Ollendick & King, 1994b). Girls tend to have more fears than boys at almost every age; they also rate themselves as more fearful and report fears that are more intense and disabling than do boys (Ollendick, Yang, Dong, Xia,

All children experience some fear, anxiety, and worry as a normal part of growing up.

© Jeff Greenberg/The Image Works

Table 7.2
Common Fears in Infancy, Childhood, and Adolescence

AGE	OBJECTS OF FEAR
0–6 months	Loss of physical support, loud noises
7–12 months	Strangers; sudden, unexpected, or looming objects
1 year	Separation from parent, injury, toilet, strangers
2 years	Loud noises, animals, dark room, separation from parent, large objects or machines, change in personal environment
3 years	Masks, dark, animals, separation from parent
4 years	Separation from parent, animals, dark, noises
5 years	Animals, "bad" people, dark, separation from parent, bodily injuries
6 years	Supernatural beings (e.g., ghosts or witches), bodily injuries, thunder and lightning, dark, sleeping or staying alone, separation from parent
7–8 years	Supernatural beings, dark, media events, staying alone, bodily injuries
9–12 years	Tests and examinations in school, school performance, bodily injuries, physical appearance, thunder and lightning, death
Adolescence	Personal relations, personal appearance, school, political issues, future, animals, supernatural phenomena, natural disasters, safety

Source: Adapted from _Anxiety Disorders in Children_, by R. G. Klein and C. G. Last, 1989, pp. 100–101. Copyright © by Sage Publications. Reprinted by permission.

& Lin, 1995). Although fears show a general decline with age, some, such as school-related fears, remain stable, and others, such as social fears, may increase. The most common fears of infants, children, and adolescents are shown in Table 7.2.

Normal Anxieties Like fears, anxieties are very common during childhood and adolescence. Various types of anxiety are evident by age 4 (Eley et al., 2003), and about 25% of parents report that their child is too nervous, fearful, or anxious (Achenbach, 1991a). The most frequent symptoms of anxiety in normal samples are separation anxiety, test anxiety, overconcern about competence, excessive need for reassurance, and anxiety about harm to a parent (Barrios & Hartmann, 1997).

Younger children generally experience more anxiety

symptoms than do older children, primarily about separation from parents (Beidel, Silverman, & Hammond-Laurence, 1996; Bell-Dolan, Last, & Strauss, 1990). Girls display more anxiety than boys, but generally the types of symptoms they experience are quite similar. Although some specific anxieties, such as separation anxiety, decrease with age, nervous and anxious symptoms do not show the age-related decline observed for many specific fears. Anxious symptoms may reflect a stable trait that predisposes children to develop excessive fears related to their stage of development. Thus, the disposition to be anxious may remain stable over time, even though the objects of children's fears change (W. K. Silverman & Nelles, 1989).

Normal Worries   If worrying about the future is so unproductive, why do we do so much of it? Part of the reason seems to be that the process of worry, thinking about all possible negative outcomes, serves an extremely useful function in normal development. In moderate doses, worry can help children prepare for the future, for example, by checking their homework before they hand it in or by rehearsing for an upcoming class play. Worry is a central feature of anxiety, and anxiety is related to the number of children's worries and to their intensity (W. K. Silverman, La Greca, & Wasserstein, 1995; Vasey, 1993). Children of all ages worry, but the forms and expressions change. Older children report a greater variety and complexity of worries, and are better able to describe them than are younger children (Chorpita, Tracey, Brown, Collica, & Barlow, 1997; Vasey & Daleiden, 1994).

Children with anxiety disorders do not necessarily worry more than other children, but they seem to worry more intensely (S. Perrin & Last, 1997; Weems, Silverman, & La Greca, 2000). Intense worries about being around strangers, going to school, or having bad things happen to the child or parents occur frequently in children with anxiety disorders and rarely in other children. Other intense worries over personal safety, doing a good job, and being embarrassed occur in both groups, but more often in children with anxiety disorders. Still other intense worries about schoolwork, aches and pains, or performance in sports, are equally common in all children.

Normal Rituals and Repetitive Behavior   Ritualistic, repetitive activity is extremely common in young children (Peleg-Popko & Dar, 2003). A familiar example is the bedtime ritual of saying good night—addressing people in a certain order or giving a certain number of hugs and kisses. Ritualistic behaviors in young children include preferences for sameness in the environment (e.g., watching the same video over and over again), rigid likes and dislikes, preferences for symmetry (e.g., carrying a toy in each hand), awareness of minute details or imperfections in toys or clothes (e.g., being bothered by a minuscule

thread on a jacket sleeve), and arranging things so they are "just right" (e.g., insisting that different foods not touch each other on the plate). Rituals help young children gain control and mastery over their social and physical environments, and make their world more predictable and safer (D. W. Evans et al., 1997). Any parent who has violated these rituals and paid the price can appreciate how important they are to the young child.

Many common routines of young children fall into two distinct categories: repetitive behaviors and doing things "just right." These categories are strikingly similar to those found for older individuals with obsessive-compulsive disorder (OCD), which is discussed in detail later in the chapter (Carter, Pauls, & Leckman, 1995). However, it is not known whether OCD is an extreme point on a continuum of normal developmental rituals or an entirely different problem (D. W. Evans, Gray, & Leckman, 1999).

Anxiety Disorders According to DSM-IV-TR

Anxiety disorders in DSM-IV-TR are divided into nine categories that closely define the varieties of reaction and avoidance. These nine categories are briefly described in Box 7.1. In the sections that follow, we discuss the characteristic features of each anxiety disorder, including its prevalence, comorbidity, and developmental course. Then we examine the associated characteristics and causes of anxiety disorders, and the treatments used to help children with these problems.

SECTION SUMMARY

- Anxiety disorders are among the most common mental health problems in children and adolescents, but they often go unnoticed and untreated.

- Anxiety is an adaptive emotion that prepares youngsters to cope with potentially threatening people, objects, or events. Strong negative emotions, physical tension, and apprehensive anticipation of future danger or misfortune characterize it.

- The symptoms of anxiety are expressed through three interrelated response systems: physical, cognitive, and behavioral.

- Fear is a present-oriented emotional reaction to current danger. In contrast, anxiety is a future-oriented emotion characterized by feelings of apprehension and a lack of control over upcoming events that might be threatening.

- Fears, anxieties, worries, and rituals in children are common, change with age, and follow a predictable developmental pattern with respect to type.

- DSM-IV-TR specifies nine anxiety disorders based on types of reaction and avoidance.

BOX 7.1 Main Features of Nine DSM-IV-TR Anxiety Disorders

Separation Anxiety Disorder (SAD)

Age-inappropriate, excessive, and disabling anxiety about being apart from parents or away from home.

Generalized Anxiety Disorder (GAD)

Chronic or exaggerated worry and tension; almost constant anticipation of disaster even though nothing seems to provoke it (apprehensive expectation). Worrying is often accompanied by physical symptoms such as trembling, muscle tension, headache, and nausea.

Specific Phobia

Extreme and disabling fear of specific objects or situations that pose little or no danger. Fears may include animals, heights, or injections.

Social Phobia

Fear of being the focus of attention, or scrutiny, or of doing something that will be intensely humiliating.

Obsessive-Compulsive Disorder (OCD)

Repeated, intrusive, and unwanted thoughts that cause anxiety, often accompanied by ritualized behavior to relieve this anxiety.

Panic Disorder (PD)

Characterized by panic attacks, sudden feelings of terror that strike repeatedly and without warning. Physical symptoms include chest pain, heart palpitations, shortness of breath, dizziness, or abdominal stress. Persistent concern about having another attack and the possible implications and consequences.

Panic Disorder with Agoraphobia

In the context of a panic disorder, anxiety about being in places or situations from which escape might be difficult (or embarrassing), or in which help might not be available in the event of having a panic attack or panic-like symptoms. Common situations include being outside the home or in a crowd of people.

Post–traumatic Stress Disorder (PTSD)

Persistent, frightening thoughts that occur after undergoing a frightening and traumatic event.

Acute Stress Disorder

Anxiety and other symptoms develop after exposure to an extreme traumatic stressor; symptoms do not persist for more than 4 weeks after the trauma.

Source: Based on DSM-IV-TR, 2000 by APA.

Separation Anxiety Disorder

Brad

"Don't Leave Me!"

Brad, age 9, is unable to enter any situation that requires separation from his parents—playing in the backyard, going to other children's homes, or staying with a babysitter. When forcibly separated from his parents, Brad cries or throws a full-blown tantrum. When his mother plans to leave the house, he runs through all the horrible things that might happen to her, in an endless series of what-if questions. When she becomes frustrated and angry, Brad becomes even more anxious. The more anxious he gets, the more he argues with his mother, and the angrier she gets. Brad has also threatened to hurt himself if forced to go to school.

Brad's separation problems began about a year ago, when his father was drinking too much and was frequently absent for long periods. Brad's problem gradually worsened over the course of the year, until he completely refused to go to school. Help was sought but Brad continued to get worse. He developed significant depressive symptoms, including sadness, guilt about his problems, and occasional wishes to die. (Adapted from C. G. Last, 1988)

Separation anxiety is important for the young child's survival and is normal at certain ages. From about age 7 months through the preschool years, almost all children fuss when they are separated from their parents or others to whom they are close. In fact, a lack of separation anxiety at this age may suggest insecure attachment or other problems. Unfortunately, like Brad, some children continue to display such anxiety long after the age when it is typical or expected. When anxiety persists for at least 4 weeks and is severe enough to interfere with normal daily routines such as going to school or participating in recreational activities, the child may have a separation anxiety disorder. The DSM-IV-TR criteria are presented in Table 7.3.

Children with **separation anxiety disorder (SAD)** display age-inappropriate, excessive, and disabling anxiety about being apart from their parents or away from home. Young children may have vague feelings of anxiety or repeated nightmares about being kidnapped or killed, or about the death of a parent. Older children may have specific fantasies of illness, accidents, kidnapping, or physical harm. For example, one 10-year-old girl with SAD feared that someone would sneak into her house at night, take her to the basement, and keep her tied up with a stream of water slowly dripping down her forehead.

Table 7.3

Main Features of Diagnostic Criteria for
Separation Anxiety Disorder (SAD)

Developmentally inappropriate and excessive anxiety concerning separation from home or from those to whom the individual is attached, as evidenced by three (or more) of the following:

(1) Recurrent excessive distress when separation from home or major attachment figures occurs or is anticipated

(2) Persistent and excessive worry about losing, or possible harm befalling, major attachment figures

(3) Persistent and excessive worry that an untoward event will lead to separation from a major attachment figure (e.g., getting lost or being kidnapped)

(4) Persistent reluctance or refusal to go to school or elsewhere because of fear of separation

(5) Persistently and excessively fearful or reluctant to be alone or without major attachment figures at home or without significant adults in other settings

(6) Persistent reluctance or refusal to go to sleep without being near a major attachment figure or to sleep away from home

(7) Repeated nightmares involving the theme of separation

(8) Repeated complaints of physical symptoms (such as headaches, stomachaches, nausea, or vomiting) when separation from major attachment figures occurs or is anticipated

Source: Reprinted with permission from *Diagnostic and Statistical Manual of Mental Disorders, DSM-IV-TR, Text Revision, Fourth Edition.* Copyright 2000 by the American Psychiatric Association.

Young children with SAD frequently display excessive demands for parental attention by clinging to their parents and shadowing their every move, trying to climb into their parents' bed at night, or sleeping on the floor just outside their parents' bedroom door. Older children may have difficulty being alone in a room during the day, sleeping alone even at home, running errands, going to school, or going to camp.

Children with SAD fear new situations and may display physical complaints. To avoid separation, they may fuss, cry, scream, or threaten suicide if their parent leaves (although serious symptoms of suicide are rare); physical complaints may include rapid heart beat, dizziness, headaches, stomachaches, and nausea. Not surprisingly, parents, especially mothers, become highly distressed. Over time, as we saw with Brad, children with SAD may become increasingly withdrawn, apathetic, and depressed (Albano, Miller, Zarate, Cote, & Barlow, 1997), and are at risk for developing a variety of other anxiety disorders

during adolescence (Aschenbrand, Kendall, Webb, Safford, & Flannery-Schroeder, 2003).

Prevalence and Comorbidity

Separation anxiety disorder is the most common anxiety disorder that occurs during childhood, and is found in about 10% of all children. It seems to be equally common in boys and girls, although when sex differences are found, they tend to be more prevalent in girls (C. G. Last, Perrin, Hersen, & Kazdin, 1992).

Most children with SAD have another anxiety, which is most commonly generalized anxiety disorder (GAD) (C. G. Last, Perrin, Hersen, & Kazdin, 1996). About one-third develop a depressive disorder within several months of the onset of SAD. They may also display specific fears of getting lost, or of the dark. School reluctance or refusal is also quite common in older children with SAD (Albano et al., 2003).

Onset, Course, and Outcome

Of children referred for anxiety disorders, SAD has the earliest reported age of onset (7 to 8 years), and the youngest age of referral (10 to 11 years) (Keller et al., 1992). The early age of onset for SAD is consistent with the early occurrence of separation fears in normal development (G. Francis, Last, & Strauss, 1987).

SAD generally progresses from mild to severe. It may begin with harmless requests or complaints, such as restless sleep or nightmares, that progress to the child sleeping nightly in his or her parents' bed. Similarly, school mornings may evoke physical complaints and an occasional absence from school, which escalates into daily tantrums about leaving for school and outright refusal. The child may become increasingly concerned about the parents' daily routine and whereabouts (Albano et al., 2003).

Often, SAD occurs after a child has experienced major stress, such as moving to a new neighborhood, entering a new school, death or illness in the family, or an extended vacation. Brad's SAD emerged after his father developed a problem with alcohol and subsequently left home. The symptoms of SAD may also fluctuate over the years as a function of stress and transitions in the child's life. Although they may lose friends as a result of their repeated refusal to participate in activities away from home, children with SAD are reasonably socially skilled, get along with others, and are not disliked by their peers. However, their school performance may suffer as a result of frequent school absences. The child may require special assignments just to keep up, and in extreme cases may have to repeat the school year or be ordered to attend (Albano et al., 2003).

Since school reluctance and refusal are quite common in children with SAD, this is an opportune time to consider these problems. However, as we discuss next, it is critical to recognize they can occur for many different reasons, not only as a result of separation anxiety. We also discuss test anxiety, another problem related to school that is common in children and adolescents but does not fit easily into the DSM categories for anxiety disorders.

School Reluctance and Refusal

Eric

Won't Go to School

Eric, age 12, was referred by a school psychologist and his parents for his intense school refusal behavior. On entering seventh grade and a new school, he began to experience a variety of negative symptoms, such as hyperventilation, anxiety, sad mood, and somatic complaints. Although attendance was not a problem at first, by mid-September Eric began to report severe headaches on school mornings. School attendance then became intermittent. By late September, his aversion to school had worsened and he was staying at home on most days. (Adapted from Kearney, 1995)

Although starting school is exciting and enjoyable for most children, many are reluctant to go to school and, for a few, school may create so much fear and anxiety that they will not go. These children can become literally sick with worry, let minor physical complaints keep them at home, or pretend to be ill. **School refusal behavior** is defined as the refusal to attend classes or difficulty remaining in school for an entire day. It includes youngsters who resist going to school in the morning but eventually attend, those who go to school but leave at some point during the day, those who attend with great dread that leads to future pleas for nonattendance, and those who miss the entire day (Kearney, 1995, 2001).

School refusal is equally common in boys and girls, and occurs most often between the ages of 5 and 11 years. Excessive and unreasonable fears of school usually first occur during preschool, kindergarten, or first grade, and peak during the second grade. However, school refusal can occur at any time and may have a sudden onset at a later age, as happened with Eric. Children who refuse school may complain of a headache, upset stomach, or sore throat just before it's time to leave for school, then begin to "feel better" when permitted to stay at home, only to feel "sick" again the next morning. As the time for school draws near, the child may plead, cry, and refuse to leave the house, and even have a full-blown panic reac-

tion. School refusal often follows a period at home during which the child has spent more time than usual with a parent (e.g., brief illness, holiday break, or summer vacation). At other times, school refusal may follow a stressful event such as a change of schools (as happened with Eric), an accident, or the death of a relative or family pet.

For many children, fear of school is really a fear of leaving their parents—separation anxiety. However, school reluctance and refusal can occur for many reasons (Kearney & Albano, 2004). Most children who refuse to go to school have average or above average intelligence, suggesting it is not a difficulty with academics that leads to this problem. A fear of school may be associated with submitting for the first time to authority and rules outside the home, being compared with unfamiliar children, and experiencing the threat of failure. Some children fear school because they are afraid of being ridiculed, teased, or bullied by other children, or being criticized or disciplined by their teachers. In other cases the child's fear may result from an excessive or irrational fear of being socially evaluated or embarrassed when having to recite in class or undress in front of unfamiliar people in a gym class. Eric was extremely anxious about meeting new people, being late for class, moving from class to class, taking classes involving public speaking, and participating in gym class. He refused to attend school mainly to escape being socially evaluated and, to a lesser extent, to gain attention from his parents (Kearney & Silverman, 1996).

The possible long-term consequences are serious for a child who displays a persistent pattern of school refusal behavior and does not receive help. Academic or social problems may develop as a result of missed instruction and peer interaction. Treatment usually emphasizes an immediate return to school and other routines, and must take into account the specific functions being served by school refusal behaviors (Kearney, 2001; C. G. Last, Hansen, & Franco, 1998). Cognitive-behavioral treatment, by itself and in combination with antidepressant medication, has also shown some success (Bernstein et al., 2000; King, Tonge, Heyne, & Ollendick, 2000).

Test Anxiety   Most of us have experienced some degree of **test anxiety**, which is defined as the experience of intense somatic, cognitive, and behavioral symptoms of anxiety during test-taking situations that usually interferes with test performance. Imagine that you are halfway through an important exam when another student stands up and confidently walks to the front of the room and hands in her paper. How do you react? You might think, "She couldn't possibly write good answers to these questions so quickly," and simply continue writing your exam. If you reacted in this way, you're probably not test-anxious. However, you might think, "Oh no. She's al-

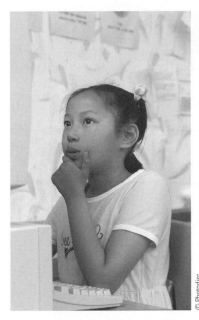

Test anxiety is a common problem in children and adolescents.

ready done and I've barely begun. I must be really stupid for taking so long. I'll never finish in time." You may be so rattled that your heart beats fast, your hands sweat, and your mind goes blank. It's very hard to think, much less continue the test. If you respond in this way, you may be test-anxious.

Test anxiety is a common problem that occurs in as many as 50% of all children and adolescents (N. J. King, Ollendick, & Gullone, 1991b). Since test anxiety usually interferes with test performance, it is not surprising that the academic achievement of children who are test-anxious is significantly lower than that of other children. In addition, youngsters with test anxiety view themselves as less cognitively and socially competent, have lower self-esteem, and report significantly more general worries and non-test-related fears than other children (King, Mietz, Tinney, & Ollendick, 1995; B. G. Turner, Beidel, Hughes, & Turner, 1993).

Children and adolescents with test anxiety frequently report fears of being negatively evaluated when taking a test (e.g., "My teacher will think I'm stupid"). For many, this fear is not confined to the test situation but also occurs in nonacademic settings. For example, about 50% of children with test anxiety also suffer from generalized worries or fear of being scrutinized by others. For a much smaller group, test anxiety may reflect a specific phobia of test situations, or an anxiety reaction to being separated from their parents. Thus, although test anxiety is not a DSM disorder, many children who are test-anxious do meet DSM criteria for an anxiety disorder. However, since many children do not meet criteria for any DSM diagnosis, test anxiety is likely a complex problem with a variety of expressions, severities, and causes (Beidel & Turner, 1988). A combination of approaches has been used to help children and adolescents overcome their test anxiety, including systematic desensitization, cognitive restructuring, and educational approaches such as study skills training and modeling (Beidel, Turner, & Taylor-Ferreira, 1999; Ergene, 2003).

SECTION SUMMARY

- Children with separation anxiety disorder (SAD) display age-inappropriate, excessive, and disabling anxiety about being apart from parents or away from home.
- SAD is the most common anxiety disorder that occurs during childhood, and is found in about 10% of all children. Of children referred for anxiety disorders, SAD has the earliest reported age of onset and the youngest age of referral.
- School refusal behavior is defined as the refusal to attend classes or difficulty remaining in school for an entire day.
- Test anxiety is defined as the experience of intense somatic, cognitive, and behavioral symptoms of anxiety during test-taking situations that usually interferes with test performance.

Generalized Anxiety Disorder

Alesha
Perpetual Worrywart

Alesha, age 10, was referred because of her excessive anxiety, worry, and somatic complaints—her mother describes her as overly concerned about everything. Alesha says she worries about most things, but especially about not being good enough for her parents, being teased by other kids, not doing well at school, making mistakes, and being in an accident in which she or her parents are injured. Alesha ruminates for days about things that have already occurred, such as what she said in class the previous day or how she did on last week's test. Once she begins to worry, she says, "I just can't stop, no matter how hard I try." Alesha reports that when she is worrying about the past or anticipating an upcoming event she has headaches, stomachaches, and a rapid heartbeat. Her mother (who also worries a lot, but not nearly as much as Alesha) says that Alesha is extremely self-critical and needs constant reassurance.

Some worrying is a part of normal development. However, children like Alesha with a **generalized anxiety disorder (GAD)** experience excessive and uncontrollable anxiety and worry about many events or activities on most days. They worry when there's nothing obvious to provoke the worry. The technical term for this type of exaggerated worry and tension in the absence of conditions that would normally provoke such a reaction is **appre-**

hensive expectation. For children with GAD, worrying can be episodic or almost continuous. Often the worrier is unable to relax and has physical symptoms such as muscle tension, headaches, or nausea. Other symptoms may include irritability, a lack of energy, difficulty falling asleep, and restless sleep. The DSM criteria for GAD are presented in Table 7.4.

In other anxiety disorders, anxiety converges on specific situations or objects, such as separation, social performance, animals or insects, or bodily sensations. In contrast, the anxiety experienced by children with GAD is widespread and focuses on a variety of everyday life events. It was once thought that children who were generally anxious did not focus their anxiety on one specific thing, which is referred to as "free-floating anxiety." However, these children do in fact focus their anxiety, but on many different things. Hence, the term *generalized anxiety* is more accurate.

Children with GAD are likely to pick up on every frightening event in a book, in a movie, or on TV and relate it to themselves. If they see a news report on TV about a car accident, they may begin to worry about being in a car accident themselves. They always expect the worst possible outcome and underestimate their ability to cope with situations or events that are less than ideal. They don't seem to realize that the events they worry about have an extremely low likelihood of actually happening. Thus, their thinking often consists of what-if statements: "What if the school bus breaks down?" "What if I get hit by lightning?" Children with GAD do not restrict their worries to frightening or catastrophic events; they also worry excessively about minor everyday occurrences, such as what to wear or what to watch on TV. This generalized worry about minor events distinguishes children with GAD from those with other anxiety disorders (Albano et al., 2003).

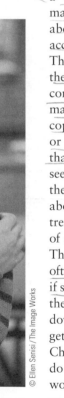

Youngsters with a generalized anxiety disorder worry about almost everything.

Table 7.4

Main Features of Diagnostic Criteria for Generalized Anxiety Disorder (GAD)

A. Excessive anxiety and worry (apprehensive expectation), occurring more days than not for at least 6 months, about a number of events or activities (such as work or school performance).

B. The person finds it difficult to control the worry.

C. The anxiety and worry are associated with three (or more) of the following six symptoms (with at least some symptoms present for more days than not for the past 6 months).

Note: Only one item is required in children.

(1) Restlessness or feeling keyed up or on edge

(2) Being easily fatigued

(3) Difficulty concentrating or mind going blank

(4) Irritability

(5) Muscle tension

(6) Sleep disturbance (difficulty falling or staying asleep, or restless unsatisfying sleep)

Source: Reprinted with permission from *Diagnostic and Statistical Manual of Mental Disorders, DSM-IV-TR, Text Revision, Fourth Edition.* Copyright 2000 by the American Psychiatric Association.

Like Alesha, children with GAD are often self-conscious, self-doubting, and worried about meeting others' expectations. Their worry may lead to significant interpersonal problems, especially those involving a tendency to be overly nurturing to others. Children with GAD seek constant approval and reassurance from adults and fear people whom they perceive as unpleasant, critical, or unfair. They tend to set extremely high standards for their own performance and, when they fall short, they are highly self-critical. Moreover, they continue to worry even when evidence contradicts their concern. For example, a child with GAD who received a grade of A on every previous class assignment may worry about failing on the next assignment (W. K. Silverman & Ginsburg, 1995).

Children with GAD can't seem to stop worrying even when they recognize how unhappy they are making themselves and others. This characteristic is what makes their anxiety abnormal. A normal child who is worried about an upcoming sport competition can still concentrate on other tasks and will stop worrying once the competition is over. However, for children with GAD one "crisis" is followed by another in a never-ending cycle. The uncontrollable nature of the worry is an important clinical feature of GAD (Chorpita et al., 1997).

A diagnosis of GAD in children requires at least one somatic symptom. In fact, GAD is frequently identified by a doctor as a result of a child's physical complaints, which involve muscle tension and agitation rather than the heart rate increases and sweating that characterize other anxiety disorders. Headaches, stomachaches, muscle tension, and trembling are among the most commonly reported symptoms (Eisen & Engler, 1995; C. G. Last, 1991).

Chronic worry may function as a type of cognitive avoidance that inhibits emotional processing (T. D. Borkovec, Ray, & Stoeber, 1998). Because children with GAD are so busy thinking about upcoming problems they may not produce images of threat that elicit intense negative emotion and autonomic activity. Although they don't experience most of the unpleasantness that accompanies negative imagery, they never have a chance to confront their problems and find solutions. For children with GAD, chronic worry may serve the same dysfunctional purpose as behavioral avoidance does in children with specific phobias (T. M. Borkovec, 1994; T. M. Borkovec & Inz, 1990).

Prevalence and Comorbidity

Along with SAD, GAD is one of the most common anxiety disorders that occurs during childhood, found in 3% to 6% of all children (Albano et al., 2003). In general, the disorder is equally common in boys and girls, with perhaps a slightly higher prevalence in older adolescent females (C. C. Strauss, Lease, Last, & Francis, 1988). Children with GAD present with a high rate of other anxiety disorders and depression. For younger children, co-occurring SAD and ADHD are most common; older children with GAD tend to have specific phobias and major depression, impaired social adjustment, low self-esteem, and an increased risk for suicide (Keller et al., 1992; C. C. Strauss, Last, Hersen, & Kazdin, 1988).

About one-half of the children referred for treatment for anxiety disorders have GAD. This proportion is higher than for adults, with whom the disorder is more common, but fewer adults seek treatment. Parents may recognize their children's problems and bring them to treatment. It is also possible that children are more likely to be referred than adults because of associated impairments such as depression or suicidal ideation (Keller et al., 1992). It may also be that excessive worry is viewed as a normal part of being an adult that does not require treatment. Alternatively, adults have more control over their lives than children; they have more options for coping with anxiety-arousing situations, in contrast to children, who have to go to school "regardless" (Albano et al., 2003).

Onset, Course, and Outcome

The average age of onset for GAD is 10–14 years (Albano et al., 2003). Older children present with a higher total number of symptoms, and report higher levels of anxiety and depression than younger children, but these symptoms may diminish with age (C. C. Strauss, Last et al., 1988). In a community sample of adolescents with GAD, the likelihood of their having GAD at follow-up was higher if symptoms at the time of initial assessment were severe (P. Cohen, Cohen, & Brook, 1993). Nearly one-half of severe cases were rediagnosed after 2 years, suggesting that severe generalized anxiety symptoms persist over time, even in youngsters who have not been referred for treatment.

SECTION SUMMARY

- Youngsters with a generalized anxiety disorder (GAD) experience chronic or exaggerated worry and tension often accompanied by physical symptoms.

- For children with GAD, worry may serve the same dysfunctional purpose as behavioral avoidance does in children with specific phobias.

- GAD is one of the most common anxiety disorders that occur during childhood, found in 3% to 6% of all children, with an onset in late childhood or early adolescence.

Specific Phobia

Charlotte
Arachnophobia

For two years, Charlotte, age 8, has complained of an intense fear of spiders. "Spiders are disgusting," she says. "I'm scared to death that one will crawl on me, especially when I'm sleeping. When I see a spider, even a little one, my heart pounds, my hands feel cold and sweaty, and I start to shake." Charlotte's mother says that her daughter goes completely pale when she sees a spider, even at a distance, and tries to avoid any situation where she thinks there might be one. Charlotte's fear is beginning to interfere with her daily activities. For example, she won't play in the backyard and refuses to go on class or family outings where she might encounter a spider. She is afraid to go to sleep at night because she thinks a spider might crawl on her.

As we have seen, many children have specific fears that are mildly troubling, come and go rapidly until about age 10, and rarely require special attention. However, if the child's fear occurs at an inappropriate age, persists, is irrational or exaggerated, leads to avoidance of the object or event, and causes impairment in normal routines, it is called a **phobia.** Like Charlotte, children with a **specific**

Table 7.5
Main Features of Diagnostic Criteria for Specific Phobia

A. Marked and persistent fear that is excessive or unreasonable, cued by the presence or anticipation of a specific object or situation (e.g., flying, heights, animals, receiving an injection, seeing blood).

B. Exposure to the phobic stimulus almost invariably provokes an immediate anxiety response, which may take the form of a situationally bound or situationally predisposed panic attack.

Note: In children, the anxiety may be expressed by crying, tantrums, freezing, or clinging.

C. The person recognizes that the fear is excessive or unreasonable.

Note: In children, this feature may be absent.

D. The phobic situation(s) is avoided or else is endured with intense anxiety or distress.

Source: Reprinted with permission from *Diagnostic and Statistical Manual of Mental Disorders, DSM-IV-TR, Text Revision, Fourth Edition.* Copyright 2000 by the American Psychiatric Association.

phobia display a marked fear of clearly discernible objects or situations for at least 6 months. The DSM-IV-TR criteria for specific phobia are shown in Table 7.5.

Children with a specific phobia show an extreme and disabling fear of objects or situations that in reality pose little or no danger or threat, and children go to great lengths to avoid them. Like Charlotte, they experience extreme fear or dread, physiological arousal to the feared stimulus, and fearful anticipation and avoidance when confronted with the object of their fear. Their thinking usually focuses on threats to their personal safety, such as being stung by a bee or struck by lightning. Anticipatory anxiety is also common. For example, a child with a phobia of dogs may think: "What if a big dog is running loose on my way to school and I get attacked and bitten in the face?" These worries cause distress severe enough to disrupt everyday activities. The children are constantly on the lookout for the feared stimulus and, as we saw with Charlotte, go to great lengths to avoid contact (Albano et al., 2003).

Children's beliefs regarding the danger of the feared stimulus are likely to persist despite evidence no danger exists or efforts to reason with them. Unlike most adults with a specific phobia, children often do not recognize that their fears are extreme and unreasonable. If the feared object is rarely encountered, the phobia may not lead to serious impairment. However, if it is encountered regularly or if the fear seriously interferes with important life events, the child's phobia can become a serious problem (Albano et al., 2003).

The phobias that can develop in children and adolescents seem limitless, and include fears of telephones, water, menstruation, newspapers, mathematics, haircuts, and bowel movements, to name just a few. Although it is possible to develop a phobia of almost any object, situation, or event that is named from A (apiphobia, a fear of bees) to Z (zemmiphobia, a fear of the great mole rat), certain fears are more likely than others to develop in children.

According to evolutionary theory, human infants are biologically predisposed as a result of natural selection to learn certain fears rather than others (M. E. P. Seligman, 1971). Most children's phobias have sources of natural danger during human evolution—snakes, the dark, predators, heights, blood, loud noises, and unfamiliar places. These fears are adaptive in an evolutionary sense because they alert the individual to possible sources of danger, thereby increasing the likelihood of survival. It's not only by chance that the most common and most heritable specific phobia in children is a fear of animals, particularly dogs, snakes, insects, and mice (Essau, Conradt, & Petermann, 2000a). Although evolutionary theory explains a readiness to acquire specific types of fears, it doesn't explain why children differ in their fearfulness or why some children develop pathological anxiety.

DSM categorizes specific phobias into five subtypes based on the focus of the phobic reaction and avoidance. These subtypes and the focus of fear of each are as follows:

- *Animal.* Animals or insects.
- *Natural environment.* Objects in the natural environment, such as heights, darkness, storms, or water.
- *Blood-injection-injury.* Seeing blood or an injury, or receiving an injection or other invasive medical procedure.
- *Situational.* A specific situation, such as flying in airplanes, riding in elevators, going through tunnels or over bridges, driving, or being in enclosed places.
- *Other.* Phobic avoidance of loud sounds or costumed characters, or of situations that may lead to choking, vomiting, or contracting an illness.

(Reprinted with permission from *Diagnostic and Statistical Manual of Mental Disorders, DSM-IV-TR, Text Revision, Fourth Edition.* Copyright 2000 by the American Psychiatric Association.)

Prevalence and Comorbidity

About 2% to 4% of all children experience specific phobias at some time in their lives (Essau et al., 2000a), with some studies reporting a much higher prevalence (Muris & Merckelbach, 2000). However, only very few of these children are referred for treatment, suggesting that most parents do not view specific phobias as significantly harmful. Specific phobias, particularly blood phobia, are more common in girls than boys (Essau et al., 2000a). The most common co-occurring disorder for children with a specific phobia is another anxiety disorder. Although comorbidity is frequent for children with specific phobias, it tends to be lower than for other anxiety disorders (C. C. Strauss & Last, 1993).

Onset, Course, and Outcome

Phobias involving animals, darkness, insects, blood, and injury typically have their onset at 7 to 9 years of age, which is similar to normal development. However, clinical phobias are more likely to persist over time than are normal fears, even though both decline with age. Specific phobias can occur at any age but seem to peak between 10 and 13 years of age (C. C. Strauss & Last, 1993).

SECTION SUMMARY

- Children with a specific phobia exhibit an extreme and disabling fear of particular objects or situations that in reality pose little or no danger.

- Evolutionary theory contends that human infants are biologically predisposed to learn certain fears that alert them to possible sources of danger. This may explain why the most common specific phobia in children is a fear of animals such as dogs, snakes, and insects.

- DSM categorizes specific phobias into five subtypes based on the focus of the phobic reaction and avoidance: animal, natural environment, blood-injection-injury, situational, and other.

- About 2% to 4% of children experience specific phobias, but only very few are referred for treatment. Specific phobias can occur at any age but seem to peak between 10 and 13 years of age.

Social Phobia (Social Anxiety)

To understand the world one must not be worrying about one's self.

—*Albert Einstein (1879–1955)*

- Dante is terrified to use the phone because, he says, he doesn't know how to have a conversation and would be embarrassed by the long periods of silence.
- Gene is too embarrassed to use a public rest room.
- Kaylie is terrified of speaking in front of her class—she's afraid of being humiliated.

Each of these youngsters has **social anxiety** or a **social phobia**—a marked and persistent fear of social or perfor-

---

Table 7.6

Main Features of Diagnostic Criteria for **Social Phobia**

A. A marked and persistent fear of one or more social or performance situations in which the person is exposed to unfamiliar people or to possible scrutiny by others. The individual fears that he or she will act in a way (or show anxiety symptoms) that will be humiliating or embarrassing.
   Note: In children, there must be evidence of the capacity for age-appropriate social relationships with familiar people, and the anxiety must occur in peer settings, not only in interactions with adults.

B. Exposure to the feared social situation almost invariably provokes anxiety, which may take the form of a situationally bound or situationally predisposed panic attack.
   Note: In children, the anxiety may be expressed by crying, tantrums, freezing, or shrinking from social situations with unfamiliar people.

C. The person recognizes that the fear is excessive or unreasonable.
   Note: In children, this feature may be absent.

D. The feared social or performance situations are avoided or else are endured with intense anxiety or distress.

Source: Reprinted with permission from *Diagnostic and Statistical Manual of Mental Disorders, DSM-IV-TR, Text Revision, Fourth Edition.* Copyright 2000 by the American Psychiatric Association.

---

mance requirements that expose them to scrutiny and possible embarrassment (Ollendick & Hirshfeld-Becker, 2002). They go to great lengths to avoid these situations, or they may face the challenge with great effort, wearing a mask of fearlessness. Long after the age at which a fear of strangers is considered normal, children with social phobias continue to shrink from people they don't know. When in the presence of other children or adults, they may blush, fall silent, cling to their parents, or try to hide. The DSM criteria for social phobia are shown in Table 7.6.

In addition to their extreme anxiety in social situations that make many people anxious, youngsters with social phobias may feel anxious about the most mundane activities—handing out papers in class, buttoning their coat in front of others, or ordering a Big Mac and fries at McDonalds. Their most common fear is doing something in front of other people. They fear that if they speak in public, they may stumble over their words; if they ask a question they may sound stupid; if they enter a room, they may trip and look awkward. One teenage girl was so fearful of being the focus of attention during meals that she spent every lunch period during her first year in high school sitting in a bathroom stall (Albano et al., 2003,

"Look. If you're so self-conscious about it, get yourself a gorilla mask."

p. 287). Not surprisingly, children with a social phobia become especially anxious in the presence of people in authority or peers with high social status (Vasey, 1995).

Youngsters with social phobias are more likely than other children to be highly emotional, socially fearful and inhibited, sad, and lonely. They frequently experience socially distressing events with which they are unable to cope effectively, in part related to a lack of social skills (Beidel, Turner, & Morris, 1999). These children want to be liked by other people. However, their fear of acting in a way that may invite humiliation is so intense and pervasive that it often leads to loneliness and suffering because they cannot form the relationships they desire (G. S. Ginsburg, La Greca, & Silverman, 1998; La Greca & Lopez, 1998). If other people attempt to push them into social situations they may cry, have a tantrum, freeze, or withdraw even further. In the most severe cases, children develop a **generalized social phobia.** They fear most social situations, are afraid to meet or talk with new people, avoid contact with anyone outside their family, and find it extremely difficult to attend school, participate in recreational activities, or socialize (Hofmann et al., 1999).

The anxiety associated with social phobia can be so severe that it produces stammering, sweating, upset stomach, rapid heartbeat, or a full-scale panic attack. Adolescents with a social phobia frequently believe that their visible physical reactions will expose their hidden feelings of inadequacy, which makes them more anxious. In repeating cycle, children with a social phobia anticipate their awkwardness and poor performance, which triggers further anxiety as they approach the feared situation, and further increases their nervousness and physical symptoms. As a result, they avoid social activities such as calling a classmate for missed homework, asking the teacher to explain something, answering the telephone, or dating (Albano, 1995).

Although transitory social anxiety and self-consciousness are part of normal development, adolescents with a social phobia experience persistent anxiety. Consider the painful interchange in Box 7.2, which is typical of the social anxiety and self-focused and self-critical thinking of adolescents with a social phobia.

Prevalence, Comorbidity, and Course

Social phobia occurs in 1% to 3% of children, affecting slightly more girls than boys (Essau, Conradt, & Petermann, 1999). Girls may experience more social anxiety because they are more concerned with social competence than are boys, and attach greater importance to interpersonal relationships (Inderbitzen-Nolan & Walters, 2000). Among children referred for treatment for anxiety disorders, as many as 20% have social phobia as their primary diagnosis. It is the most common secondary diagnosis for children referred for other anxiety disorders (Albano et al., 2003). Even so, many cases of social phobia are overlooked because shyness is common in our society and because these children are not likely to call attention to their problem even when they are severely distressed (Essau et al., 1999).

Two-thirds of children and adolescents with a social phobia have another anxiety disorder—most commonly, a specific phobia or panic disorder (Beidel et al., 1999). About 20% of adolescents with a social phobia suffer from major depression. They may also use alcohol and other drugs as a form of self-medication to reduce their anxiety in social situations (Albano et al., 2003).

Social phobias are extremely rare in children under the age of 10, and generally develop after puberty, with the most common age of onset in early to mid-adolescence (Wittchen, Stein, & Kessler, 1999). This is a time when teens experience heightened self-consciousness, doubts, and worries about their appearance, social prowess, and what others may think of them. How to walk, what to say, and how to dress are ever present in the minds of most teens, a fact often exploited by advertisers. Common

BOX 7.2 Adolescent Social Phobia: Self-Focused and Self-Critical Thinking

It's the first day of school. In the school yard Kristin and Jennifer, two students with social phobias, happen to be sitting near each other. They've never met before today.

KRISTIN: To herself: I can't just sit here and look stupid. I have to say hello. To Jennifer: *"Hi, are you new here?"*

JENNIFER: To herself: Oh no, don't talk to me. I don't know what to say. To Kristin: *"No, I was here last year."* To herself: Sure, nobody ever notices me.

KRISTEN: To herself: Great, now I look like a jerk for not recognizing her. Now what do I do? To Jennifer: *"Oh, I guess we've never met. I'm Kristen."*

JENNIFER: To herself: When is the bell going to ring? To Kristin: *"I'm Jennifer. I've seen you before."*

KRISTEN: To Jennifer: *"Oh, weren't you in my study hall? With Mr. Holt?"* To herself: I hope she doesn't remember when I got sick in there. Why did I bring up study hall?

JENNIFER: To herself: She was so popular, I can't talk to her. She thinks I'm a nerd 'cause I sat by myself all year. To Kristen: *"Yes, I was in there. I have to go now."* To herself: I have to get out of here. I can't take this anymore.

KRISTIN: To herself: Oh boy, she thinks I'm weird, she does remember, I'm so embarrassed. I bet my face is all red. To Jennifer: *"Okay, see you."* To herself: I'm glad that's over.

(Adapted from "Therapist's Manual: Cognitive-Behavioral Group Treatment of Adolescent Social Phobias," by A. M. Albano, P. A. Marten, and C. S. Holt., 1991, p. 18, unpublished manual. Department of Psychology, University of Louisville, KY. Reprinted by permission.)

sources of anxiety at this age include consolidation of identity, sexuality, social acceptance, and conflict about independence; the symptoms of anxiety they most frequently report include fears of public speaking, blushing, excessive worry about past behavior, and self-consciousness (Bell-Dolan et al., 1990). The prevalence of social phobia appears to increase with age, although more information is needed to determine the natural course of the disorder and its long-term outcome (Neal & Edelmann, 2003).

Selective Mutism

Keisha
Mum's the Word

Keisha, age 6, doesn't speak at kindergarten to teachers or peers and did not do so during her 2 years in preschool. Two years ago she had difficulties being left at preschool and it took about 2 months before she could be left without crying. Although she doesn't talk to other children, she interacts with them and participates in school activities. Keisha speaks openly to all family members at home but does not speak to them in public if others might hear her. She says that she does not know why she doesn't talk, but has told her mother that she feels scared. Her mother says Keisha is shy and is a worrier. (Adapted from Leonard & Dow, 1995)

Children with **selective mutism** fail to talk in specific social situations, even though they may speak loudly and frequently at home or in other settings. This disorder is uncommon and is estimated to occur in about 0.5% of all children (Bergman, Piacentini, & McKracken, 2002). Although not included as an anxiety disorder in DSM-IV-TR, selective mutism has many factors in common with the anxiety disorders (Leonard & Dow, 1995). For example, 90% of young children with selective mutism meet diagnostic criteria for a social phobia in ways other than their reluctance to speak (Black & Uhde, 1995). Based on these similarities it has been hypothesized that selective mutism may be an extreme type of social phobia rather than a unique disorder (Anstendig, 1999; Dummit et al., 1997). However, there are also some differences between the two disorders, for example, oppositional features and nonverbal social engagement occur in selective mutism (Yeganeh, Beidel, Turner, Pina, & Silverman, 2003). Children with selective mutism may fail to talk in some settings because they are socially anxious, but there may be other reasons as well. Thus, it would be premature to conclude that selective mutism and social phobia are the same disorder.

SECTION SUMMARY

- Children with social phobia fear being the focus of attention or scrutiny, or of doing something in public that will be intensely humiliating.

- Social phobias occur in 1% to 3% of children, affecting slightly more girls than boys.

- They generally develop after puberty, at a time when most teens experience heightened self-consciousness and worries about what others think of them.

- Children with selective mutism fail to talk in specific social situations, even though they may speak loudly and frequently at home or in other settings.

Obsessive-Compulsive Disorder

Insanity: doing the same thing over and over again and expecting different results.

—Albert Einstein

Paul
Stuck in a Doorway

At almost any hour, Paul, age 16, could be found in a doorway, slightly swaying back and forth, with his eyes fixed at the upper corner of the doorframe. "What are you doing?" a ward attendant would ask. "I'm stuck," Paul whispered back, without moving. "I have to do it over again to get it right; I have to do it a certain, special way." "Have to do what?" the attendant would ask. "Get through the door right," Paul would answer. (Adapted from Rapoport, 1989)

Paul has an **obsessive-compulsive disorder (OCD)**, which is an unusual disorder of ritual and doubt. Children and adolescents with OCD experience recurrent, time-consuming (take more than 1 hour a day), and disturbing obsessions and compulsions (Piacentini & Bergman, 2000). **Obsessions** are persistent and intrusive thoughts, ideas, impulses, or images. Most children describe their obsessions as very similar to worries. However, obsessions are much more than heightened worries about everyday problems, such as homework or popularity. They are excessive and irrational, and are focused on improbable or unrealistic events, or on greatly exaggerated real-life events. Children with OCD may complain about being unable to stop "hearing" recurring rhymes or songs, or fears of having a serious disease such as cancer, or of being attacked by an intruder. The most common obsessions in children and adolescents focus on contamination, fears of harm to self or others, concerns with symmetry, and sexual, somatic, and religious preoccupations (B. Geller et al., 1998). Since these and other obsessions create considerable anxiety and distress, children with OCD go to great lengths to try to neutralize them with another action, known as a compulsion (Henin & Kendall, 1997).

Compulsions are repetitive, purposeful, and intentional behaviors (e.g., handwashing) or mental acts (e.g., repeating words silently) that are performed in response to an obsession. For example, as a result of an obsession with germs, a child with OCD may feel compelled to clean, check for dirt, or engage in some other ritual as a way of decreasing anxiety. For example, one 7-year-old boy felt compelled to wash his homework! Multiple compulsions are the norm, with the most common being excessive washing and bathing (occurring in about 85% of cases), repeating, checking, touching, counting, hoarding,

and ordering or arranging (B. Geller et al., 1998). The belief that drives OCD is similar to the superstitious "Step on a crack, break your mother's back" and similar rituals and superstitions. Paul, the boy with OCD who got stuck in doorways, reported that "cracks in the sidewalk were also big problems." "Not the little way they are for some kids," he said, "but in a very big way" (Rapoport, 1989, p. 75). The DSM criteria for OCD are shown in Table 7.7.

Most children with OCD have multiple obsessions and compulsions, and certain compulsions are commonly associated with specific obsessions. For example, washing and cleaning rituals are likely to be associated with contamination obsessions, such as a concern or disgust with body wastes or secretions (e.g., urine, feces, saliva), a concern with dirt or germs, or an excessive concern about chemical or environmental contamination. Compulsions

Table 7.7
Main Features of Diagnostic Criteria for Obsessive-Compulsive Disorder

A. Either obsessions or compulsions:

Obsessions as defined by (1), (2), (3), and (4):

(1) Recurrent and persistent thoughts, impulses, or images that are experienced, at some time during the disturbance, as intrusive and inappropriate and that cause marked anxiety or distress

(2) The thoughts, impulses, or images are not simply excessive worries about real-life problems

(3) The person attempts to ignore or suppress such thoughts, impulses, or images, or to neutralize them with some other thought or action

(4) The person recognizes that the obsessional thoughts, impulses, or images are a product of his or her own mind (not imposed from without as in thought insertion)

Compulsions as defined by (1) and (2):

(1) Repetitive behaviors (e.g., hand washing, ordering, checking) or mental acts (e.g., praying, counting, repeating words silently) that the person feels driven to perform in response to an obsession, or according to rules that must be applied rigidly

(2) The behaviors or mental acts are aimed at preventing or reducing distress or preventing some dreaded event or situation; however, these behaviors or mental acts either are not connected in a realistic way with what they are designed to neutralize or prevent or are clearly excessive

B. At some point during the course of the disorder, the person has recognized that the obsessions or compulsions are excessive or unreasonable.
Note: This does not apply to children.

Source: Reprinted with permission from *Diagnostic and Statistical Manual of Mental Disorders, DSM-IV-TR, Text Revision, Fourth Edition.* Copyright 2000 by the American Psychiatric Association.

involving counting over and over to a certain number are frequently related to a concern about harm—that something terrible might happen like the death of a parent or a fire. Obsessions with symmetry, exactness, or order are often associated with compulsions for arranging and ordering, such as repeatedly packing and unpacking a suitcase or rearranging drawers (Piacentini, 1997).

How can children with OCD be so reasonable about some things yet so disturbed with respect to their obsessions and compulsions? Most children over age 8 persist in their obsessions or compulsions even though they recognize them as excessive and unreasonable (children ordinarily use the word *dumb* or *stupid*). However, OCD is extremely resistant to reason, even when the child recognizes the "silliness" of the routines. For example, one of 10-year-old Emilio's obsessive thoughts is that a long, flexible, pipe-like structure protrudes from his chest. He knows this is not so, but he must behave as if the pipe is there and move in such a way that no person or object comes too close in front of him (Despert, 1955).

Children with OCD often involve family members in their rituals; for example, demanding that their clothes be washed 2 or 3 times a day, not allowing others to eat certain foods for fear of illness or contamination, or having a parent get up at 5 a.m. to assist them in dressing rituals that may take hours to complete (Piacentini, 1997; Waters & Barrett, 2000). Some children with OCD insist that certain phrases be repeated or that questions be answered in a certain way. Consider this exchange between Heather, age 11, and her mother.

> HEATHER: You said before that we were having dessert. Now you say we're having ice cream. Which one is it?
> MOTHER: Ice cream is dessert.
> HEATHER: But which one is right?
> MOTHER: Both.
> HEATHER: But are we having ice cream or dessert?
> MOTHER: We're having ice cream.
> HEATHER: So why did you say we were having dessert?

Heather became so argumentative, insistent, and persistent that her mother thought she had a severe behavior problem. However, with further assessment, it became clear that Heather's oppositional behavior was an expression of OCD. When interviewed about her problem, Heather said: "I can't help it. When I'm with my mother, I have to make her say things 'just right' or I feel terrible."

Compulsions are intended to neutralize or reduce the anxiety and tension of the obsessions, or to prevent some dreaded event or situation from happening. Although rituals may provide temporary relief from anxiety, in the long run they fail to achieve their intended purpose. As a result, children with OCD increasingly become trapped in a time-consuming and never-ending cycle of obsessions

Haunted by their habits: washing, checking, and symmetry.

and compulsions (Carter & Pollock, 2000). Many hours each day are dominated by disabling, alarming, and sometimes ridiculous thoughts, and by repeated compulsive behaviors. The child's preoccupation with obsessions and rituals makes it extremely difficult, if not impossible, to focus on anything else. As we saw with Paul, even a simple activity like walking into a room may become an insurmountable problem.

As a result of such excessive preoccupations, normal activities of children with OCD are reduced, and health, social, and family relations and school functioning can be severely disrupted (Carter et al., 1995). Cleaning or washing rituals may lead to health problems, such as skin irritation of the hands and forearms as a result of prolonged washing, or gum lesions as a result of prolonged toothbrushing. Dressing or washing rituals may result in chronic lateness. Counting and checking rituals and intrusive thoughts may prevent concentration at school and interfere with schoolwork. These rituals may require the child to check and recheck every answer on a test so often that he or she is unable to finish it. Homework may become a daily struggle, as the child spends hours repeatedly checking and correcting the work. Bedtime rituals may preclude inviting friends to sleep over and cause repeated refusals to accept similar invitations from friends. Contamination fears may interfere with school attendance and social activities, such as going to the movies or participating in sports (Piacentini, 1997).

Because of the odd and senseless nature of OCD symptoms, many children try to mask or hide their rituals, especially in social situations or at school (Rapoport et al., 2000). In less severe cases, teachers, friends, and family members may be unaware of the child's OCD for months or even years. However, as the rituals become more elaborate and time-consuming, they become increasingly difficult to conceal. With considerable effort, children with OCD may muster the energy to supress their symptoms for brief periods. However, suppression commonly has a rebound effect, with increased symptoms once the child is in a safe place. As the child becomes too overwhelmed by anxiety to cope, or when magazine articles or TV shows about OCD bring the problem into focus, others become more and more aware of its seriousness (Piacentini, 1997).

Prevalence and Comorbidity

The prevalence of OCD in children and adolescents is 2% to 3%, suggesting that it occurs about as often in young people as in adults (Piacentini & Graae, 1997). Clinic-based studies of younger children suggest that OCD is about twice as common in boys than in girls. However, this gender difference has not been observed in community samples of adolescents, which may be a function of age differences, referral bias, or both (Albano et al., 2003). The most common comorbidities are other anxiety disorders, depressive disorders, especially in older children

with OCD, and disruptive behavior disorders (C. G. Last & Strauss, 1989a; Piacentini & Graae, 1997). Substance-use disorders, learning disorders, and eating disorders are also overrepresented in children with OCD, as are vocal and motor tics (Piacentini & Graae, 1997).

Onset, Course, and Outcome

The mean age of onset of OCD is 9–12 years with two peaks, one in early childhood and another in early adolescence (Hanna, 1995). Children with an early onset of OCD (age 6–10) are more likely to have a family history of OCD than children with a later onset, suggesting a greater role of genetic influences in such cases (Swedo, Rapoport, Leonard, Lenane, & Cheslow, 1989). These children may have prominent motor patterns, engaging in compulsions without obsessions and displaying odd behaviors, such as finger licking or compulsively walking in geometric designs.

The developmental course of OCD in young children indicates that they typically have obsessions that are more vague than those of older children, and are less likely to feel that their obsessions are abnormal. Young children with OCD often ask their parents endless questions related to their obsessions and make no effort to hide their discomfort. Most children over age 8 are aware that their obsessions are abnormal, and they are usually uncomfortable talking about them. They may try to hide or minimize them or deny they have them, which frustrates parents who know that something is wrong and want to help.

One-half to two-thirds of children with OCD continue to meet the criteria for the disorder 2–14 years later. Although most children, including those treated with medication show some improvement in symptoms, fewer than 10% show complete remission. Predictors of poor outcome include a poor initial response to treatment, a lifetime history of tic disorder, and parental psychopathology at the time of referral. Thus, OCD remains a serious and chronic disorder for a significant number of children (Albano, Knox, & Barlow, 1995).

SECTION SUMMARY

- Youngsters with obsessive-compulsive disorder (OCD) experience repeated, intrusive, and unwanted thoughts or obsessions that cause anxiety, often accompanied by ritualized behaviors or compulsions to relieve the anxiety.

- Among the most common obsessions in children are contamination and fears of harm to self and others. Among the most common compulsions are washing and bathing, and repeating, checking, and arranging.

- OCD has a mean age of onset of 9–12 years and affects about 2% to 3% of all children. Children with an early onset are more likely to have a family history of the disorder than are those with a later onset.

- OCD is a serious and chronic disorder, with as many as two-thirds of children continuing to have the disorder 2–14 years after being diagnosed.

Panic

Panic Attacks

- "When my heart starts pounding, I feel like I'm going to die."
- "No one really knows how terrified I am when I have these attacks."
- "I can't help being so frightened. My dad says I should snap out of it. I wish I could."

The word *panic* originates from the name "Pan," the goat-like Greek god of nature. Pan terrified travelers who dared to disturb his roadside nap by surprising them with a bloodcurdling scream. So intense was this scream that it sometimes scared the intruders to death. An unexpected and devastating feeling of terror came to be known as panic.

A **panic attack** is a sudden and overwhelming period of intense fear or discomfort that is accompanied by four or more physical and cognitive symptoms characteristic of the fight/flight response (see Table 7.8). Usually, a panic attack is short, with symptoms reaching maximal intensity in 10 minutes or less and then diminishing slowly over the next 30 minutes or the next few hours. Panic attacks are accompanied by an overwhelming sense of imminent danger or impending doom, and by an urge to escape. Although they are brief, they can occur several times a week

or month. It is important to remember that although the symptoms are dramatic, they are not physically harmful or dangerous.

Panic attacks are easily identified in adults, but some controversy exists over how often they occur in children and adolescents (Kearney & Allan, 1995). Although panic attacks are extremely rare in young children, they are common in adolescents (Mattis & Ollendick, 2002; Ollendick, 1998). One explanation is that young children lack the cognitive ability to make the catastrophic misinterpretations (e.g., that a rapid heartbeat signals a heart attack) that usually accompany panic attacks (Nelles & Barlow, 1988). However, research suggests that young children may in fact be capable of such misinterpretations (Mattis & Ollendick, 1997a).

If limited cognitive capacity is not the primary reason that panic attacks are so rare in young children, what is? In a revealing study, the relationship between the occurrence of panic attacks and pubertal stage was assessed in 754 girls in the sixth and seventh grades. Importantly, increasing rates of panic were related to pubertal development, not to increasing age (Hayward et al., 1992). The significance of pubertal development and anxiety disorders in females is more generally supported by findings

---

Table 7.8

Main Features of Diagnostic Criteria for a **Panic Attack**

A discrete period of intense fear or discomfort, in which four or more of the following symptoms developed abruptly and reached a peak within 10 minutes:

- **(1)** Palpitations, pounding heart, or accelerated heart rate
- **(2)** Sweating
- **(3)** Trembling or shaking
- **(4)** Sensations of shortness of breath
- **(5)** Feeling of choking
- **(6)** Chest pain or discomfort
- **(7)** Nausea or abdominal distress
- **(8)** Feeling dizzy, unsteady, lightheaded, or faint
- **(9)** Derealization (feelings of unreality) or depersonalization (being detached from oneself)
- **(10)** Fear of losing control of going crazy
- **(11)** Fear of dying
- **(12)** Paresthesias (numbness or tightening sensations)
- **(13)** Chills or hot flashes

Note: A panic attack is not, in and of itself, a diagnosable disorder.

Source: Reprinted with permission from *Diagnostic and Statistical Manual of Mental Disorders, DSM-IV-TR, Text Revision, Fourth Edition.* Copyright 2000 by the American Psychiatric Association.

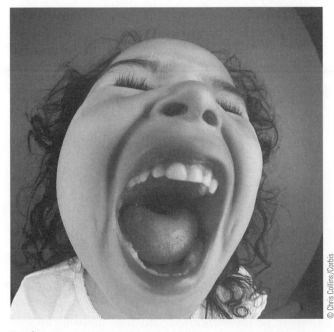

Panic

© Chris Collins/Corbis

that sixth- to eighth-grade females who developed internalizing symptoms were on average 5 months earlier in their pubertal development than females who did not develop symptoms (Hayward, Killen, Wilson, & Hammer, 1997). Given that spontaneous panic attacks are rare before puberty and are related to pubertal stage, and that adolescence is the peak time for the onset of the disorder, the physical changes that take place around puberty seem critical to the occurrence of panic.

Why do the physical symptoms of the fight/flight response occur if an adolescent is not initially frightened? One possibility is that things other than fear can produce these symptoms. A youngster may be distressed for a particular reason, and stress can increase production of adrenalin and other chemicals that may produce physical symptoms of panic. Increased adrenalin may be chemically maintained in the body even after the stress is no longer present. Another possibility is that the youngster may breathe a little too fast (subtle hyperventilation), which also can produce symptoms. Because the overbreathing is very slight, the child gets used to it and doesn't realize that he or she is hyperventilating. A third possibility is that some youngsters are experiencing normal bodily changes but, because they are constantly monitoring their bodies (as adolescents are prone to do), they notice these sensations far more readily (Barlow, 2002).

Panic Disorder

Claudia

An Attack Out of Nowhere

Claudia, age 16, was watching TV after a noneventful day at school. She suddenly felt overwhelmed by an intense feeling of lightheadedness and a smothering sensation, as if she couldn't get any air to breathe. Her heart started to pound rapidly, as if it would explode. The attack came on so fast and was so intense that Claudia panicked and thought she was having a heart attack that would kill her. She began to sweat and tremble, and she felt the room was spinning. These feelings reached a peak within 2 minutes . . . but this was the seventh attack that Claudia had experienced this month. She frantically ran to her mother and pleaded to be taken to the hospital emergency room—again.

Some adolescents who experience repeated severe panic attacks have no other symptoms. Others, like Claudia, have a progression of distressing symptoms and develop a panic disorder (see Box 7.3). Adolescents with **panic disorder (PD)** display recurrent unexpected attacks followed by at least 1 month of persistent concern about having another attack, constant worry about the conse-

A Closer Look

BOX 7.3 Did Darwin Have a Panic Disorder?

Charles Darwin (1809–1882) was a gregarious and daring traveler and outdoorsman in his college days. However, in his late twenties—just a year after returning to England after a 5-year voyage to South America and the Pacific aboard HMS *Beagle*—he started to complain of an "uncomfortable palpitation of the heart." The symptoms arose shortly after he began keeping a secret notebook that, 22 years later, would become his book-length elaboration of the theory of evolution, *On the Origin of Species*. Over the years his affliction was described as a case of bad nerves, a tropical disease, intellectual exhaustion, arsenic poisoning, suppressed gout, and a host of other complaints. However, in his journal Darwin described his malady as a "sensation of fear . . . accompanied by troubled beating of the heart, sweat, trembling of muscles."

Source: Desmond & Moore, 1991.

quences, or a significant change in their behavior related to the attacks. This type of worry is referred to as *anticipatory anxiety*. Those who suffer many panic attacks develop considerable secondary anxiety and may feel anxious most of the time.

Adolescents with PD may avoid locations where they've had a previous panic attack, or situations or activities in which they fear an attack might occur, or situations in which help may not be available. An adolescent with PD like Claudia might think: "It would be bad enough to have an attack at all, but it would be really dangerous if I had one while riding my bike to school. I'd be totally preoccupied with the attack and would have an accident. I'd probably destroy my bike and wind up seriously hurting myself or someone else in the process!" Claudia's avoidance of riding a bike to school could be misinterpreted as a fear of bike riding when it is actually a fear of having a panic attack while riding the bike.

If not recognized and treated, PD and its complications can seriously interfere with relationships at home and at school, and with school performance. Some adolescents with PD may be reluctant to go to school or be separated from their parents. In severe cases, the tendency to avoid everyday life circumstances may increase and generalize, to the point that the older adolescent with PD becomes terrified to leave the house at all. This pattern, characterized by a fear of being alone in and avoiding certain places or situations, is called **agoraphobia**. Agoraphobia, which usually doesn't develop until age 18 or older, is related to a fear of having a panic attack in situations where escape would be difficult or help is unavailable. An older adolescent with agoraphobia who dares to venture into a feared situation does so only with great distress, or when accompanied by a family member or a friend.

Prevalence and Comorbidity

Whereas panic attacks are common among adolescents, affecting about 3% to 4% of teens, PD is less common (Goodwin & Gotlib, 2004; Ollendick, Mattis, & King, 1994). Adolescent females are more likely than adolescent males to experience panic attacks, and a fairly consistent association has been found between panic attacks and stressful life events (N. J. King, Ollendick, & Mattis, 1994; C. G. Last & Strauss, 1989b). About one-half of adolescents with PD have no other disorder, and for the remaining adolescents an additional anxiety disorder and depression are the most common secondary diagnoses (Kearney, Albano, Eisen, Allan, & Barlow, 1997; C. G. Last & Strauss, 1989b). After months or years of unrelenting panic attacks and the restricted lifestyle that results from avoidance behavior, adolescents and young adults with PD may develop severe depression and may be at risk for suicidal behavior. Others may begin to use alcohol or drugs as a way of alleviating their anxiety.

Onset, Course, and Outcome

The average age of onset for a first panic attack in adolescents with PD is 15–19 years, and 95% of adolescents with the disorder are postpubertal (Bernstein, Borchardt, & Perwien, 1996; Kearney & Allan, 1995). PD occurs in otherwise emotionally healthy youngsters about half the time. The most frequent prior disturbance, if one exists, is a depressive disorder (C. G. Last & Strauss, 1989b). Unfortunately, children and adolescents with PD have the lowest rate of remission for any of the anxiety disorders (C. G. Last et al., 1996).

Although panic attacks are extremely rare in prepubertal children, it has been proposed that separation anxiety disorder (SAD) may be a possible early form of panic and that it could develop into PD in later adolescence and adulthood (Mattis & Ollendick, 1997b). However, research does not currently support SAD as a specific precursor for PD, since SAD is a precursor for numerous later conditions, including other anxiety disorders and depression (Aschenbrand et al., 2003).

SECTION SUMMARY

- A panic attack is a sudden and overwhelming period of intense fear or discomfort accompanied by physical and cognitive symptoms.
- Adolescents who experience repeated panic attacks and persistently worry about the possible implications and consequences of having another attack have a panic disorder (PD).
- Many postpubertal adolescents experience panic attacks, but PD is much less common.

Post–traumatic and Acute Stress Disorders

Children with **post–traumatic stress disorder (PTSD)** display persistent anxiety following an overwhelming traumatic event that occurs outside the range of usual human experience (Lonigan, Phillips, & Richey, 2003). When the diagnosis of PTSD was first introduced, the reference points were catastrophic events, such as war, torture, rape, natural disasters (e.g., earthquakes and hurricanes), and disasters of human origin (e.g., fires and automobile accidents). A distinction is made between these types of trauma and other very stressful life events, such as illness or family breakup. The traumatic experiences associated with PTSD are likely to exceed and overwhelm the coping abilities of most humans.

The experiences associated with PTSD involve actual or threatened death or injury, or a threat to one's physical integrity. PTSD is most common among children exposed to major accidents, natural disasters, kidnapping, brutal physical assaults, war and violence, or sexual abuse (see Chapter 14) (L. Davis & Siegel, 2000). Among the specific traumatic events that have been associated with the onset of PTSD in children are Hurricane Andrew, the Oklahoma City bombing, the school shootings in Littleton, Colorado, and the 9/11 terrorist attacks. As a result of exposure to war during the past decade, more than 2 million children world-wide have been killed, approximately 6 million have been injured or permanently disabled, 1 million have been orphaned, and 20 million have been displaced (Barenbaum, Ruchkin, & Schwab-Stone, 2004).

Many others have been injured by land mines or targeted for ethnic cleansing and genocide. Millions of other children have been exposed to bombing, shelling, sniper fire, and terrorist attacks resulting in untold loss of family, friends, and community support (Bellamy, 2002; Machel, 2001; UNICEF, 1996). The tragedy of these events underscores the need to understand how they affect children's mental health, and, more importantly, to find effective ways of helping the child victims of such atrocities (Barenbaum et al., 2004).

The three core features of PTSD are persistent (for more than 1 month):

- Reexperiencing of the traumatic event
- Avoidance of associated stimuli and numbing of general responsiveness
- Symptoms of extreme arousal

Marcie
Not the Only Victim

While accompanying her mother to a neighbor's house, Marcie, age 6, was viciously mauled in the face by a large German shepherd. Her brother Jeff, age 7, and her two younger sisters observed the incident. Although the mother warned the children to keep away from the dog, Marcie and Jeff let it approach and Jeff was able to pet the dog. Marcie then bent toward the dog to pet it, and the dog attacked. The mother immediately applied pressure to the bleeding wound, as the two youngest children clung to their mother's legs. The dog's owner (who had followed the dog down the driveway) panicked and ran to the children's home to get their father, leaving the dog unleashed and barking at the frightened family for about 20 minutes. The father took the family home, cleaned Marcie's wound, and then took her for emergency medical treatment. Marcie received stitches in her face while she was strapped down and in extreme distress.

Following the incident, all the children displayed some fear and reverted to behaviors displayed at a younger age, such as bed-wetting and finger sucking. They also displayed irritability and developed varying degrees of sleep disturbances and nightmares. Moreover, Marcie developed an intense fear of medical procedures or any situation that reminded her of a medical procedure. Thus, intense fear and panic reactions accompanied follow-up visits to the plastic surgeon. Excessive distress was shown in everyday first-aid situations such as caring for a minor scratch or scrape. (Adapted from "Behavioral Assessment and Treatment of PTST in Prepubertal Children: Attention to Developmental Factors and Innovative Strategies in the Case Study of a Family," by A. M. Albano, P. P. Miller, T. Zarate, G. Cote, and D. H. Barlow, 1997, pp. 245–262, *Cognitive and Behavioral Practice, Vol. 2,* Copyright © 1997 by the Association for Advancement of Behavior Therapy. Reprinted by permission.)

Symptoms of PTSD are both conspicuous and complex (Anthony, Lonigan, & Hecht, 1999). They include intense fear, helplessness, and horror, which in children may be expressed as agitated behavior and disorganization. Children with PTSD show many of the same symptoms as combat soldiers exposed to the horrors of war. They may have nightmares, fears, and panic attacks for many years. They may regress developmentally and display age-inappropriate behaviors, such as a fear of strangers. Children with PTSD avoid situations that could remind them of the traumatic event or they may reenact the event in play. They may feel pessimistic, vulnerable, or numb, and have problems in school.

Some key symptoms are expressed differently in children than in adults. For example, instead of flashbacks and waking recall of the traumatic event, young children are likely to reexperience trauma in nightmares. Initially, the nightmares reflect the traumatic event, but over time they may become nonspecific. Similarly, daytime recall may be expressed in play or through reenactment of the event or related themes. Trauma reactions of preschool children may include repetitive drawing and play focused on trauma-related themes, regressive behavior, antisocial or aggressive behavior, and destructive behavior (Perrin, Smith, & Yule, 2000).

Acute stress disorder is characterized by the development during or within 1 month after exposure to an extreme traumatic stressor of at least three of the following dissociative symptoms: an absence of emotional responsiveness, derealization, a reduced awareness of surroundings, depersonalization, or dissociative amnesia. The traumatic event is persistently reexperienced, and the child displays marked avoidance of stimuli that arouse memories of it. These disturbances last for at least 2 days, but do not persist longer than a month (APA, 2000). Acute stress disorder is short-lived and emphasizes acute dissociative reactions to the trauma, whereas PTSD has long-lasting effects (Harvey & Bryant, 2002).

Prevalence and Comorbidity

In a large national sample of over 4,000 adolescents ages 12–17 in the United States, the six-month prevalence of PTSD was 3.7% for boys and 6.3% for girls. In addition, nearly 75% of these youngsters displayed a comorbid diagnosis of depression and/or substance abuse (Kilpatrick et al., 2003). Thus, PTSD is common in children exposed to traumatic events (S. Perrin, Smith, & Yule, 2000), and there is some evidence that rates are increasing (Amaya-Jackson & March, 1995). The prevalence of PTSD symptoms is greater in children who are exposed to life-threatening events than children who are not. For example, nearly 40% of children exposed to the Buffalo Creek dam collapse in 1972 showed probable PTSD symptoms 2 years after the disaster (K. E. Fletcher, 2003). PTSD in children is also strongly correlated with degree of

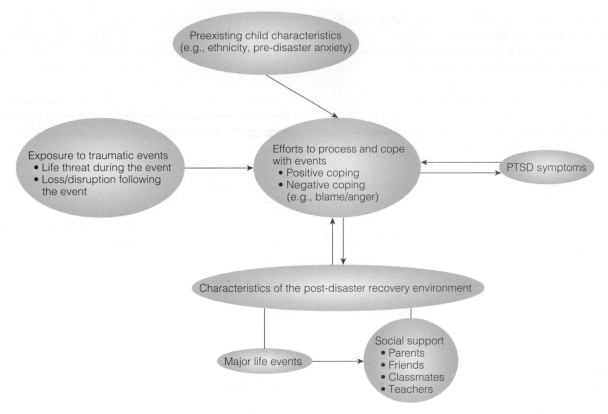

Figure 7.1. Predicting children's reactions to Hurricane Andrew

Source: From "Symptoms of Posttraumatic Stress in Children After Hurricane Andrew: A Prospective Study," by A. M. La Greca, W. K. Silverman, E. M. Vernberg, and M. J. Prinstein 1996, *Journal of Consulting and Clinical Psychology, 64,* 712–723. Copyright © 1996 American Psychological Association. Reprinted by permission of the author.

exposure. In children exposed to a schoolyard sniper attack, proximity to the attack was directly related to the risk of developing PTSD symptoms (Pynoos et al., 1987). Traumatized children frequently exhibit symptoms of disorders other than PTSD (e.g., depression), and children with other disorders may have PTSD as a comorbid diagnosis (Famularo, Fenton, Kinscherff, & Augustyn, 1996). The PTSD that occurs in children traumatized by fires, hurricanes, or chronic maltreatment may worsen or lead to disruptive behavior disorders (Amaya-Jackson & March, 1995).

Onset, Course, and Outcome

PTSD can strike at any time during childhood. Its course depends on the age of the child when the trauma occurred and the nature of the trauma. Since the traumatic experience is filtered cognitively and emotionally before it can be appraised as an extreme threat, how trauma is experienced depends on the child's developmental level (Meiser-Stedman, 2002). Furthermore, some children appear to have different trauma thresholds—some seem more protected, others seem more vulnerable to extremely stressful situations (Pynoos, Steinberg, & Piacentini, 1999). De-

spite these differences, exposure to horrific events is traumatic to nearly all children.

Many children thought they might die during Hurricane Andrew, and as many as 30% reported symptoms of severe PTSD. About 12% of the children continued to report severe to very severe levels of PTSD symptoms nearly a year after the disaster, especially symptoms related to re-experiencing the trauma. Even among the 90% of the children who were on the road to recovery, more than 75% reported at least one PTSD symptom 10 months after the hurricane (La Greca, Silverman, Vernberg, & Prinstein, 1996).

Several factors are important in predicting children's course of recovery from PTSD following exposure to a natural disaster (La Greca, Silverman, & Wasserstein, 1998). These factors are highlighted in Figure 7.1. Efforts to help children cope with their feelings and reactions following a disaster often focus on these same factors, see Box 7.4 (La Greca, Silverman, Vernberg, & Roberts, 2002; S. Perrin et al., 2000).

Longitudinal findings suggest that PTSD can become a chronic psychiatric disorder for some children, persisting for decades and in some cases for a lifetime (K. E. Fletcher, 2003; Nader, Pynoos, Fairbanks, & Frederick,

BOX 7.4 Helping Children Following a Disaster

A catastrophe such as an earthquake, hurricane, tornado, fire, or flood is frightening to children and adults alike. It is important to acknowledge the frightening parts of the disaster when talking with a child about it. Falsely minimizing the danger will not end a child's concerns.

The way children see and understand their parents' response is very important. Children are aware of their parents' worries most of the time, but they are particularly sensitive during a crisis. Parents should admit their concerns to their children, and also stress their abilities to cope with the situation.

A child's reaction also depends on how much destruction he or she sees during and after the disaster. If a friend or family member has been killed or seriously injured, or if the child's school or home has been severely damaged, there is a greater chance that the child will experience difficulties.

A child's age affects how the child will respond to the disaster. For example, 6-year-olds may show their concerns about a catastrophe by refusing to attend school, whereas adolescents may minimize their concerns but argue more with parents and show a decline in school performance.

Source: Adapted from *Facts for Families #36: Helping Children After a Disaster,* 1995, American Academy of Child and Adolescent Psychiatry. Adapted by permsision.

1990; Terr, 1983). Children with chronic PTSD may display a developmental course marked by remissions and relapses. In a delayed variant, children exposed to a traumatic event may not exhibit symptoms until months or years later when a situation that resembles the original trauma triggers the onset of PTSD. For example, sexual violence during adulthood may trigger PTSD in a survivor of childhood sexual abuse.

SECTION SUMMARY

- Youngsters with post–traumatic stress disorder (PTSD) display persistent frightening thoughts following overwhelming traumatic events, such as threatened death or injury, natural disasters, or sexual abuse.
- Children with PTSD re-experience the traumatic event, avoid associated stimuli, and display symptoms of extreme arousal.
- An acute distress disorder is short-lived and emphasizes acute dissociative reactions, whereas PTSD has long-lasting effects.

- Several factors appear to be important in children's course of recovery from PTSD including the nature of the traumatic event, preexisting child characteristics, and social support.

Associated Characteristics

Children with anxiety disorders display a number of associated characteristics including cognitive disturbances, physical symptoms, social and emotional deficits, and anxiety and depression.

Cognitive Disturbances

For most children, the development of cognitive maturity is associated with a reduction in fears. However, children with anxiety disorders continue to evaluate nonthreatening events as threatening, which suggests a disturbance in how they perceive and process information (Alfano, Beidel, & Turner, 2002; Vasey & MacLeod, 2001).

Intelligence and Academic Achievement Children with anxiety disorders typically have normal intelligence, and there is little evidence of a strong relationship between anxiety and IQ. However, excessive anxiety may be related to deficits in specific areas of cognitive functioning, such as memory, attention, and speech or language. High levels of anxiety can interfere with academic performance. One study found that anxiety in the first grade predicted anxiety in the fifth grade, and significantly influenced fifth-grade achievement (Ialongo, Edelsohn, Werthamer-Larsson, Crockett, & Kellam, 1995). The specific mechanisms involved could include anything from frequent absences to direct interference on cognitive tasks, such as writing a test or solving a math problem. Youngsters with anxiety disorders, particularly generalized social anxiety, may also fail to reach their academic potential because they drop out of school prematurely (Van Ameringen, Mancini, & Farvolden, 2003).

Attentional Biases Children with anxiety disorders selectively attend to information that may be potentially threatening (e.g., an angry looking face)—a tendency referred to as anxious vigilance or hypervigilance (Hadwin et al., 2003; Vasey, El-Hag, & Daleiden, 1996). Anxious vigilance permits the child to avoid potentially threatening events by early detection, with minimal anxiety and effort. Although this may benefit the child in the short term, it has the unfortunate long-term effect of maintaining and heightening anxiety by interfering with the information-processing and coping responses needed to learn that many potentially threatening events are not so dangerous after all (Vasey et al., 1996).

Cognitive Errors and Biases   When faced with a clear threat, both nonanxious and anxious children use rules to confirm information about danger, and minimize information about safety. However, highly anxious children often do this in the face of less obvious threats, suggesting that their perceptions of threats activate danger-confirming thoughts (Muris, Rapee, Meesters, Schouten, & Geers, 2003). You may recall from our discussion of children with conduct problems (Chapter 6) that they too put a negative spin on ambiguous events. The main difference is that anxious children select avoidant solutions in response to perceived threat, whereas children with conduct problems select aggressive solutions (Bell-Dolan, 1995; Chorpita, Albano, & Barlow, 1996).

Although cognitive errors and distortions are associated with anxiety in children, the precise nature of these errors across anxiety disorders and their possible role in causing anxiety has not yet been established (Alfano et al., 2002). In general, children with anxiety disorders see themselves as having less control over anxiety-related events than do other children (Weems, Silverman, Rapee, & Pina, 2003). However, different types and degrees of cognitive errors may occur in children with different anxiety disorders, for example, higher ratings of responsibility in children with OCD (Barrett & Healy, 2003).

Physical Symptoms

As we have seen, many children with anxiety disorders have somatic problems, such as stomachaches or headaches. These complaints are more common in youngsters with PD and SAD than in youngsters with a specific phobia. Somatic complaints are also more frequent in adolescents than in younger children, and in children who display school refusal. Youngsters with anxiety disorders may display sleep disturbances, such as difficulty initiating sleep and poor sleep quality (Garland, 2001). Some may experience *nocturnal panic*, an abrupt waking in a state of extreme anxiety that is similar to a daytime panic attack. Nocturnal panic attacks usually occur in adolescents who suffer from PD. They prevent a return to sleep and are vividly recalled the next day (Craske & Rowe, 1997).

Social and Emotional Deficits

Since anxious children expect danger in social situations, it's not surprising that they experience difficulties in their interactions with other children, including siblings (Fox, Barrett, & Shortt, 2002). In fact, they display low social performance and high social anxiety, and their parents and teachers are likely to view them as anxious and socially maladjusted (Chansky & Kendall, 1997; Krain & Kendall, 2000). Compared to their peers, these children are more likely to see themselves as shy and socially withdrawn, and to report low self-esteem, loneliness, and difficulties in starting and maintaining friendships.

Some difficulties with peers and siblings may be related to specific deficits in understanding emotion, particularly in hiding and changing emotions (Southam-Gerow & Kendall, 2000) and in differentiating between thoughts and feelings (Alfano et al., 2002). Findings regarding how children with anxiety disorders are viewed by other children are mixed (P. C. Kendall, Panichelli-Mindel, Sugarman, & Callahan, 1997). It appears that childhood anxiety disorders are most likely associated with diminished peer popularity when they coexist with depression (C. C. Strauss, Lahey, Frick, Frame, & Hynd, 1988).

Anxiety and Depression

We have already discussed co-occurring disorders in relation to each anxiety disorder, and it is important to keep in mind that a child's risk for accompanying disorders will vary with the type of anxiety disorder. Social phobia, GAD, and SAD are more commonly associated with depression than is specific phobia. Depression is also diagnosed more often in children with multiple anxiety disorders and in children who show severe impairments in their everyday functioning (Bernstein, 1991). The pattern of covariation among symptoms of depression and anxiety disorder symptoms may also reflect different developmental pathways. For example, one study found two pathways from anxiety to depression, one a *genetically* mediated pathway beginning with early GAD and phobic symptoms, and the other a *shared environment* pathway reflecting persistent SAD and later occurring GAD (Silberg, Rutter, & Eaves, 2001).

The strong and undeniable relationship between anxiety and depression in children and adolescents merits further discussion (P. C. Kendall & Brady, 1995; Mesman & Koot, 2000a, 2000b). Does anxiety lead to depression, are anxiety and depression the same disorder with different clinical features, are they on a continuum of severity, or are they distinct disorders with different causes but some overlapping features? (L. D. Seligman & Ollendick, 1998; Zahn-Waxler, Klimes-Dougan, & Slattery, 2000).

Children with anxiety and depression are older at age of presentation than children with only anxiety, and in most cases symptoms of anxiety both precede and predict symptoms of depression (Avenevoli, Stolar, Li, Dierker, & Merikangas, 2001; Brady & Kendall, 1992; Roza et al., 2003). Symptoms of anxiety and depression may form a single indistinguishable dimension in younger children, but are increasingly distinct in older children and children with at least one diagnosable disorder (D. A. Cole, Truglio, & Peeke, 1997; Gurley, Cohen, Pine, & Brook, 1996).

The concept of negative affectivity is useful in understanding the nature of the link between anxiety and depression (N. J. King, Ollendick, & Gullone, 1991a; V. V. Wolfe & Finch, 1987). **Negative affectivity** is a persistent negative mood, as reflected in nervousness, sadness, anger, and guilt. In contrast, **positive affectivity** includes states such as joy, enthusiasm, and energy. Negative affectivity is related to both anxiety and depression, whereas positive affectivity is negatively correlated with depression, but is independent of anxiety symptoms and diagnoses (Laurent & Ettelson, 2001; Lonigan, Phillips, & Hooe, 2003). In general, children with anxiety do not differ from children with depression in their negative affect, which suggests that a general underlying dimension of negative affectivity is common to both anxiety and depression (Chorpita, 2002). Rather, the difference between children who are anxious and children who are depressed may be the greater positive affectivity in those who are anxious.

Consistent with the idea of anxiety and depression as distinct dimensions with different developmental pathways are findings that some of the predictors and environmental influences associated with anxiety are different from those of depression. In terms of predictors, social and externalizing problems predict later anxiety disorders, whereas mood disorders are better predicted by internalizing symptoms (Roza et al., 2003). In terms of environmental influences, threatening life events such as physical jeopardy or the risk of losing a parent are related to symptoms of anxiety but not depression. In contrast, life events involving loss and stress, such as the death of a family member or family stress, are associated with depression but not anxiety (Eley & Stevenson, 2000).

Keep in mind that the associations between anxiety and other characteristics may be different in children seen in service versus research clinics. For example, although the two groups may be similar with respect to internalizing symptoms, children treated in service clinics display more co-morbid conduct problems and are more likely to come from low-income single-parent families (Southam-Gerow, Weisz, & Kendall, 2003).

SECTION SUMMARY

- Children with anxiety disorders may display deficits in specific areas of cognitive functioning, such as memory, attention, and speech and language.

- They selectively attend to information that may be potentially threatening, a tendency referred to as anxious vigilance.

- These children often have somatic problems, such as stomachaches or headaches, and may experience sleep disturbances.

- Children with anxiety disorders report being socially withdrawn and lonely, and may be viewed by others as socially maladjusted.

- There is a strong and undeniable relationship between anxiety and depression in children and adolescents. The

difference between children who are anxious and those who are depressed may be the greater positive affectivity in those who are anxious.

Gender, Ethnicity, and Culture

Studies have found a preponderance of anxiety disorders in girls during childhood and adolescence (Lewinsohn, Gotlib, Lewinsohn, Seeley, & Allen, 1998; Mackinaw-Koons & Vasey, 2000). By age 6, twice as many girls as boys have experienced symptoms of anxiety, and this discrepancy persists through childhood, adolescence, and young adulthood (Roza et al., 2003; see Figure 7.2). The fact that girls are more likely than boys to report anxiety may contribute to this variation, although how much is not known. For adolescents with anxiety, the variations between genders cannot be accounted for solely by variations in psychosocial factors such as stress, self-perceived social competence, or emotional reliance. This suggests that female vulnerability to anxiety may be related more to genetic influences than to varying social roles and experiences (Lewinsohn, Gotlib, et al., 1998).

One study of gender role orientation in children with anxiety disorders found that self-reported masculinity was negatively related to overall levels of fearfulness, as well as specific fears of failure and criticism, medical fears, and fears of the unknown (Ginsburg & Silverman, 2000). In contrast, no relation was found between self-reported

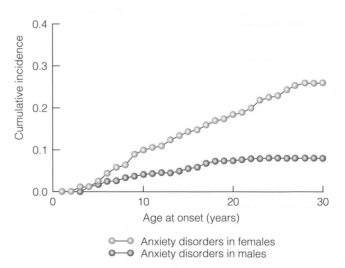

Figure 7.2. **Cumulative incidence of anxiety disorders in females and males**
Source: Roza, S. J., Hofstra, M. B., van der Ende, J., Verhulst, F. C. (2003). Stable prediction of mood and anxiety disorders based on behavioral and emotional problems in childhood: A 14-year follow-up during childhood, adolescence, and young adulthood. *American Journal of Psychiatry, 160,* 2116–2121.

femininity and fearfulness. This suggests that gender role orientation, especially masculinity, may play a role in the development and persistence of fearfulness in children.

Research into the relationship between ethnocultural factors and childhood anxiety disorders is limited and inconclusive. Studies comparing the number and nature of fears in both African American and white youngsters have found the two groups to be quite similar (Ginsburg & Silverman, 1996; Treadwell, Flannery-Schroeder, & Kendall, 1994). However, African American children report more symptoms of anxiety than do white children (D. A. Cole, Martin, Peeke, Henderson, & Harwell, 1998). White children endorse more symptoms of social phobia and fewer symptoms of separation anxiety than African American children (Compton, Nelson, & March, 2000). The underrepresentation of minorities and lower SES children for certain anxiety disorders such as OCD could reflect a bias in which minority lower-income children are less likely to be referred for treatment (Neal & Turner, 1991).

Among the children who are referred for anxiety disorders, whites are more likely to present with school refusal and higher severity ratings, while African Americans are more likely to have a history of PTSD and a slightly greater number of fears (C. G. Last & Perrin, 1993). Although anxiety may be similar in the two groups, patterns of referral, help-seeking behaviors, diagnoses, and treatment processes are likely to differ. For example, African Americans who need help with their child's OCD symptoms may be more likely to turn to members of their informal social network, such as clergy or medical personnel, than to mental health professionals (Hatch, Friedman, & Paradis, 1996). Their family members are also less likely to be drawn into the child's OCD symptoms. Although ethnicity is not related to outcomes in the treatment of anxiety disorders, it may be related to premature termination of treatment (P. C. Kendall & Flannery-Schroeder, 1998).

Research comparing phobic and anxiety disorders in Hispanic and white children finds marked similarities in age at intake, gender, primary diagnoses, proportion of school refusal, and proportion with more than one diagnosis. Hispanic children are more likely to have a primary diagnosis of SAD. Hispanic parents also rate their children as more fearful than do white parents (Ginsburg & Silverman, 1996). Few studies have examined anxiety disorders in Native American children. Prevalence estimates from one study of Native American youth in Appalachia (mostly Cherokee) indicate rates of anxiety disorders similar to those for white youth, with the most common disorder for both groups being SAD. Rates of SAD were slightly higher for Native American youth, especially girls (Costello, Farmer, Angold, Burns, & Erkanli, 1997).

The experience of anxiety is pervasive across cultures. Although cross-cultural research into anxiety disorders in children is limited, specific fears in children have been studied and documented in virtually every culture. Developmental fears (e.g., a fear of loud noises or of separation from the primary caregiver) occur in children of all cultures at about the same age. The details may vary from culture to culture, but the number of fears in children tends to be highly similar across cultures, as does the presence of gender differences in pattern and content.

Nevertheless, the expression, developmental course, and interpretation of symptoms of anxiety are affected by culture (Barlow, 2002; Ingman, Ollendick, & Akande, 1999). For example, Native Hawaiian adolescents display rates of OCD that are twice as high as other ethnic groups (Guerrero et al., 2003). When attempting to explain such differences, it is important to keep in mind that genetic and/or environmental risk factors may play a role.

Cultural differences in traditions, beliefs, and practices about children can affect the occurrence of anxiety and related symptoms and how they are perceived by others (Wang & Ollendick, 2001). Increased levels of fear in children are found in cultures that favor inhibition, compliance, and obedience (Ollendick, Yang, King, Dong, & Akande, 1996). Chinese cultural values, such as human malleability and self-cultivation may heighten levels of general distress and specific fears (e.g., social evaluative) (Dong, Yang, & Ollendick, 1994). Children in Thailand have been found to display more symptoms of anxiety, such as shyness and somatic complaints, than children in the United States (Weisz, Weiss, Suwanlert, Chaiyasit, 2003). Perhaps the most accurate way to analyze cultural differences in anxiety is using Weisz and colleagues' (2003, p. 384) **Behavior + Lens principle**, which states that child psychopathology reflects a mix of actual child behavior and the lens through which it is viewed by others in a child's culture.

SECTION SUMMARY

- About twice as many girls as boys experience symptoms of anxiety, and this difference is present in children as young as 6 years of age.
- Children's ethnicity and culture may affect the expression and developmental course of fear and anxiety.

Theories and Causes

Over the years, numerous theories and causes have been proposed to explain the origins of fear and anxiety in children, including brain disease, mental strain, parenting practices, conditioning, and instinct (Treffers & Silverman, 2001). The recent study of fear and anxiety in children dates back to Freud's (1909/1953) classic account of the case of Little Hans, J. B. Watson and Rayner's (1920) conditioning of a fear in Little Albert, and Bowlby's (1973) monumental works on early attachment and loss. Although each early theory has been debated since it was introduced, all have had a lasting impact on how we think about anxiety.

Early Theories

Classical psychoanalytic theory viewed anxieties and phobias as defenses against unconscious conflicts rooted in the child's early upbringing. Certain drives, memories, and feelings are so painful that they must be repressed and displaced onto an external object, or symbolically associated with the real source of anxiety. Thus, anxiety and phobias will protect the child against unconscious wishes and drives. Freud's most famous case of a phobia was Little Hans, a 5-year-old who feared horses. According to Freud, Little Hans unconsciously felt that he was in competition with his father for his mother's love and feared his father's revenge (the Oedipus complex). Hans's fear was repressed and displaced onto horses, a symbol of his castrating father. Having something specific to fear was less stressful for Hans than suffering from anxiety without apparent cause.

Behavioral and learning theories held that fears and anxieties were learned through classical conditioning. In the case of Little Albert, J. B. Watson and Rayner (1920) created what looked very much like a rat phobia, and claimed that fears were learned by association. Operant conditioning has been cited in explaining why fears persist once they are established. The principle is that behavior will continue if it is reinforced or rewarded. Once something has become frightening, there is the automatic reward of instant relief whenever the child avoids the feared object or situation. Thus, through negative reinforcement, avoidance of a feared stimulus becomes a learned response, which serves to maintain the child's fear even while not exposed to it. The combination of classical and operant conditioning in the learning and maintenance of fears is called the **two-factor theory** (Mowrer, 1947).

Bowlby's theory of attachment (1973) presents a very different explanation for children's fears. According to attachment theory, fearfulness in children is biologically rooted in the emotional attachment needed for survival. Infants must be close to their caregivers if their physical and emotional needs are to be met. Attachment behaviors, such as crying, fear of strangers, and distress, represent active efforts by the infant to maintain or restore proximity to the caregiver. Separation gradually becomes more tolerable as the child gets older. However, children who are separated from their mothers too early, who are treated harshly, or who fail to have their needs met consistently show atypical reactions to separation and reunion. Early insecure attachments become internalized and determine how children see the world and other people. Children who view the environment as undependable, unavailable,

hostile, or threatening may later develop anxiety and avoidance behavior.

No single theory is sufficient to explain the various anxiety disorders in children, the differences among children in the expression of these disorders, or the variations in outcomes over time. It is important to recognize that different anxiety disorders may require different causal models. In contrast to early theories, current models of anxiety emphasize the importance of interacting biological and environmental influences (Zahn-Waxler et al., 2000). Clearly articulated causal models for anxiety disorders in children are just beginning to emerge (Albano et al., 2003).

Temperament

Once I visited with a group of preschool children from the campus day care center when I noticed a little Caucasian boy slowly sneaking up behind a little Chinese girl who was walking in front of him. The boy came to within 2 feet of the girl, his presence still undetected, stopped, and then screamed at the top of his lungs, "Boo!" Even though I saw it coming, the intensity of the boy's scream startled me a bit. However, much to my surprise, the intended victim showed hardly any reaction. Instead, this pint-sized version of Lara Croft paused for a moment, slowly turned, looked at the boy (who appeared dumbfounded by this unexpected display of fearlessness), and with a relaxed smile on her face, calmly said, "I'm used to that sort of thing." She then turned and continued on her way, with the little boy trailing behind like a puppy dog (I think he was in love).

The lesson of this story is that children (like adults) differ markedly in their reactions to novel or unexpected events, perhaps because of their wiring, gender, cultural background, prior experience (in this example, perhaps with a pesky little brother?), or a combination of factors. How would you react if someone snuck up behind you and yelled "Boo!!"?

Readiness to react to unfamiliar or discrepant events is one distinguishing feature of all mammals. Orienting, attending, vigilance, wariness, and motor readiness in response to the unfamiliar are important mechanisms for survival. From an evolutionary perspective, abnormal fears and anxieties reflect variation among infants in their initial behavioral reactions to novelty (Kagan, 1997).

Early differences in temperament may predispose some children to develop anxiety disorders.

This variation is partly the result of inherited differences in the neurochemistry of brain structures thought to play an important role in detecting discrepant events. These brain structures include the amygdala and its projections to the motor system, the cingulate and frontal cortex, the hypothalamus, and the sympathetic nervous system (Schwartz, Wright, Shin, Kagan, & Rauch, 2003). Children with a high threshold to novelty, such as the little Chinese girl in the story, are presumed to be at low risk for developing anxiety disorders. Other children are born with a tendency to become overexcited and to withdraw in response to novel stimulation as infants, a tendency to be fearful and anxious as toddlers, and a tendency to be socially wary or withdrawn in unfamiliar situations as young children. This type of temperament is called **behavioral inhibition (BI)**, an enduring trait for some and a possible risk factor for the development of later anxiety disorders (Kagan & Snidman, 1999; Rubin, Burgess, Kennedy, & Stewart, 2003; Schwartz, Snidman, & Kagan, 1999).

However, the road from BI during infancy and childhood to a later anxiety disorder is neither direct nor straightforward. Although BI may contribute to later anxiety disorders, it is not an inevitable outcome (Prior, Smart, Sanson, & Oberklaid, 2000). Such an outcome probably depends on whether the inhibited child grows up in an environment that fosters this tendency (Kagan,

Snidman, & Arcus, 1992). For example, a parent's use of firm limits that teach children how to cope with stress may reduce their risk for anxiety. In contrast, it is possible that well-meaning but overprotective parents who shield their sensitive child from stressful events may inadvertently cause timidity to persist by preventing the child from confronting fears. By not confronting them, they cannot eliminate them. Such tendencies in the parents of inhibited children may be common (Hirshfeld et al., 1992; Rosenbaum et al., 1991b). Thus, inhibited children may be at high risk not only because of their inborn temperament, but also because of their elevated risk of exposure to anxious, overprotective parenting (S. M. Turner, Beidel, & Wolff, 1996).

Genetic and Family Risk

"I was always considered shy . . . Now I see my daughter is just like I was. Did I do something to cause this?" (Beidel & Turner, 1998, p. 67)

Family and twin studies suggest a biological vulnerability to anxiety disorders, indicating that children's general tendencies to be inhibited, tense, or fearful are inherited (DiLalla, Kagan, & Reznick, 1994). However, little research exists now to support a direct link between specific genetic markers and specific types of anxiety disorders. Contributions from multiple genes seem related to anxiety only when certain psychological and social factors are also present.

Studies of twins have generally found overall concordance rates for anxiety disorders that are significantly higher for monozygotic (MZ) twins than for dizygotic (DZ) twins (Eley, 1999). However, MZ twins pairs do not typically have the same types of anxiety disorders. This finding is consistent with the view that a disposition to become anxious is inherited, with the form of the disorder determined by environmental influences. Importantly, the amount of genetic influence has been found to vary with the type of anxiety, being highest for obsessive-compulsive behaviors and shyness/inhibition (Eley et al., 2003; Silberg, Rutter, Neale, & Eaves, 2001). In contrast, shared environmental influences seem to play a relatively stronger role for specific fears and separation anxiety, suggesting that these may be learned from parents (Muris & Merckelbach, 2001).

In general, findings from twin and adoption studies of anxiety in children and adolescents indicate that (Eley, 1999):

- There is a moderate genetic influence on anxiety in childhood that accounts for about one-third of the variance in most cases, but varies with the disorder.

- The genetic contribution for anxiety may increase with age.
- Heritability for anxiety may be greater for girls than boys.
- Shared environmental influences, or experiences that make children in the same family resemble one another, such as maternal psychopathology, ineffective parenting, or poverty, have a significant influence on anxiety disorders in children and adolescents.

Two lines of evidence suggest that anxiety disorders run in families. First, parents of children with anxiety disorders have increased rates of current and past anxiety disorders. Second, children of parents with anxiety disorders have an increased risk for anxiety disorders (Merikangas, Avenevoli, Dierker, & Grillon, 1999). In general, family studies consistently show a relationship between an anxiety disorder in the child and anxiety disorders in first-degree relatives. Children of parents with anxiety disorders are about 5 times more likely to have anxiety disorders than are children of parents without anxiety disorders (Beidel & Turner, 1997). However, they are not necessarily the same disorders (Mancini, van Ameringen, Szatmari, Fugere, & Boyle, 1996). Nearly 70% of children of parents with agoraphobia meet diagnostic criteria for disorders such as anxiety and depression, and report more fear and anxiety and less control over various risks than do children of comparison parents. However, the fears of parents with agoraphobia and the fears of their children are no more closely aligned than those of nonanxious parents and their children, once again supporting the view that for most anxiety disorders it may be a general predisposition for anxiety that is perpetuated in families (Capps, Sigman, Sena, & Henker, 1996).

Specific gene studies have suggested that variants in the CRH (corticotropin-releasing hormone) gene may be associated with a proneness to anxiety (Smoller et al., 2003). CRH is a key factor in mediating the response to stress through its effects on the hypothalamic-pituitary-adrenal axis (HPA-axis) and limbic brain systems, which implicates these systems in anxious and avoidant behavior. High levels stress may increase CRH in the central nucleus of the amygdala, which may lead to heightened levels of fearfulness.

Neurobiological Factors

The parts of the brain most often connected with anxiety involve neural circuits related to potential threat and fear conditioning—the HPA-axis, the limbic system (particularly the amygdala) that acts as a mediator between the brain stem and the cortex, the prefrontal cortex, and other cortical and subcortical structures (Coplan et al., 2002; Pine, 2003). Potential danger signals are monitored and sensed by the more primitive brain stem, which then relays the signals to the higher cortical centers through the limbic system. This brain system is referred to as the behavioral inhibition system (BIS) and is believed to be overactive in children with anxiety disorders.

Particularly noteworthy are findings that the regulation of these brain circuits can be shaped by early life stress, thus providing a possible biological basis for an increased vulnerability to later stress and the development of anxiety disorders (Heim & Nemeroff, 2001). Early life stress may also produce lasting hyper-reactivity of corticotrophin-releasing factor (CRF) systems, which are closely related to the HPA-axis, as well as alterations in other neurotransmitter systems that create a heightened response to stress (Pine, 2003). CRF has emerged as a neurotransmitter that plays a very key role in anxiety (Barlow, 2002).

Brain scans of children with GAD and PTSD suggest abnormalities (larger volume) in brain regions associated with social information processing and fear conditioning (amygdala and superior temporal gyrus) (De Bellis, Keshavan, Frustaci et al., 2002; DeBellis, Keshavan, Shifflett et al., 2002). These studies also report more pronounced right > left hemisphere asymmetries in children with GAD and PTSD, which have also been reported in children who are behaviorally inhibited or anxious/depressed (Kagan & Snidman, 1999). An over-excitable amygdala has also been implicated in children who are behaviorally inhibited (Schwartz et al., 2003).

The neurotransmitter system that has been implicated most often in anxiety disorders is the γ-aminobutyric acidergic (GABA-ergic) system. Neuropeptides are generally viewed as anticipatory stress modulators whose abnormal regulation may play a role in anxiety disorders (Sallee & Greenawald, 1995). A group of neurons known as the locus ceruleus ("deep blue place") is a major brain source for norepinephrine, an inhibitory neurotransmitter. Overactivation of this region is presumed to lead to a fear response, and underactivity to inattention, impulsivity, and risk-taking. Abnormalities of these systems may be related to anxiety states in children (Sallee & Greenawald, 1995).

Variants in the serotonin transporter gene (5-HTT) have been implicated in anxiety-related personality traits in adults. Although they account for only a small amount of inherited variance, these variants are of interest because transporter-facilitated uptake of serotonin has been implicated in anxiety, and is the site of action for widely used anti-anxiety and antidepressant medications (Lesch et al., 1996).

New findings using brain scans have increased our understanding of the neurobiological mechanisms in anxiety disorders. However, research with children is quite limited and difficult to conduct. Nevertheless, the brain regions we have described have been consistently implicated in fear and anxiety. While acknowledging that pathways are likely to be complex, the plasticity of these neural systems during early development makes research into possible mechanisms a priority for both understanding and preventing later anxiety disorders in children.

Family Influences

Parenting practices such as rejection, overcontrol, overprotection, and modeling of anxious behaviors have all been suggested as contributors to childhood anxiety disorders (Rapee, 2002; Wood, McLeod, Sigman, Hwang, & Chu, 2003). Parents of anxious children are often described as overinvolved, intrusive, or limiting of their child's independence. Observations of interactions between 9–12-year-old children with anxiety disorders and their parents found that parents of children with anxiety disorders were rated as granting less autonomy to their children than other parents; the children rated their mothers and fathers as being less accepting (Siqueland, Kendall, & Steinberg, 1996). Other studies have found that mothers of children previously identified as BI or anxious are more likely to be critical and to be less positive when interacting with their children (Whaley, Pinto, & Sigman, 1999). Emotional overinvolvement by parents is also associated with an increased occurrence of SAD in their children (Hirshfeld, Biederman, Brody, & Faraone, 1997; Hirshfeld, Biederman, & Rosenbaum, 1997). These findings generally support the association between excessive parental control and anxiety disorders in children, although the causal mechanisms are not yet known (Chorpita & Barlow, 1998; Rapee, 1997; Wood et al., 2003).

Not only are parents of children with anxiety disorders more controlling than other parents, they also have different expectations. For example, when they thought the child was being asked to give a videotaped speech, mothers of children with anxiety disorders expected their children to become upset and had low expectations for their children's coping (Kortlander, Kendall, & Panichelli-Mindel, 1997). It is likely that parental attitudes shape, and are shaped by, interactions with the child, during which parent and child revise their expectations and behavior as a result of feedback from each other (Barrett, Rapee, Dadds, & Ryan, 1996; Dadds, Barrett, & Rapee, 1996).

Parental anxiety disorder alone may not lead to an elevated risk of anxiety disorders in children of high or middle SES parents, but may increase risk in children of low SES parents (Beidel & Turner, 1997). These findings are consistent with the idea that some children have a genetic vulnerability to anxiety, which may be actualized in the context of specific life circumstances, such as the stressful conditions that are often present in low SES families. Children with an initial disposition to develop high levels of fear may be especially vulnerable to the type of power-assertive parenting often used by low SES parents. These children may be particularly sensitive to punishment and, when exposed to physical discipline, may become hypervigilant to hostile cues, and develop a tendency to react defensively or aggressively (Colder, Lochman, & Wells, 1997).

Insecure attachments may be a risk factor for the development of later anxiety disorders (Dadds, 2002; Manassis & Bradley, 1994), and are associated with anxiety disorder symptoms in early adolescence (Muris & Meesters, 2002). Mothers with anxiety disorders have been found to have insecure attachments themselves, and 80% of their children are also insecurely attached (Manassis, Bradley, Goldberg, Hood, & Swinson, 1994). Infants who are ambivalently attached have more anxiety diagnoses during childhood and adolescence (Bernstein et al., 1996). Although it is a risk factor, insecure attachment may be a nonspecific factor because many infants with insecure attachments develop disorders other than anxiety (e.g., disruptive behavior disorder), and many do not develop disorders.

In concluding this section on theories and causes, there is much debate regarding the distinctness of the DSM anxiety disorders for children, with some emphasizing the similarities among these disorders and others emphasizing the differences (Pine, 1997). An emphasis on similarities is consistent with the strong associations among the different disorders, the presence of shared risk factors such as female gender, and evidence of a broad genetic predisposition for anxiety. An emphasis on differences is consistent with different developmental progressions and outcomes that we have discussed, as well as differences in the biological correlates of anxiety disorders in children and adults (Pine, Cohen, Cohen, & Brook, 2000). Children with anxiety disorders will most likely display features that are shared across the various disorders, as well as other features that are unique to their particular disorder (Eley et al., 2003).

In the absence of an integrative model to account for anxiety disorders in children, we present the possible developmental pathway shown in Figure 7.3. Children with an inborn predisposition to be anxious or fearful who sense that the world is not a safe place may develop a psychological vulnerability to anxiety. Once anxiety occurs, it feeds on itself. The anxiety and avoidance continue long after the stressors that provoked them are gone. Keep in mind that many children with anxiety disorders do not continue to experience problems as adults. Therefore, it will be important to identify risk and protective factors that would explain these differences in outcomes (Pine & Grun, 1999). In addition, this model is an oversimplification, since different developmental pathways are likely for children with different anxiety disorders, or even for those with the same disorder (Ollendick & Hirshfeld-Becker, 2002).

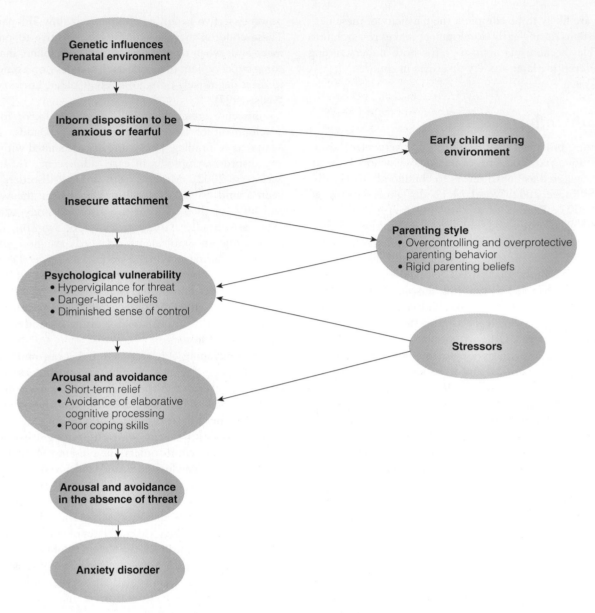

Figure 7.3. A possible developmental pathway for anxiety disorders

SECTION SUMMARY

- No single theory can explain the many different forms of anxiety disorder in children.

- Early theories viewed anxiety as a defense against unconscious conflicts, a learned response, or an adaptive mechanism needed for survival.

- Some children are born with a tendency to become overexcited and to withdraw in response to novel stimulation (behavioral inhibition), an enduring trait for some, and a possible risk factor for later anxiety disorders.

- Family and twin studies suggest a moderate biological vulnerability to anxiety disorders.

- Anxiety is associated with specific neurobiological processes. The potential underlying vulnerability of children at risk for anxiety is most likely localized to brain circuits involving the brain stem, the limbic system, and the frontal cortex.

- Parenting styles characterized by overcontrol and rigid beliefs are often associated with anxiety disorders in children.

- Children with anxiety disorders will likely display features that are shared across the various disorders, as well as other features that are unique to their particular disorder.

Treatment

Candy

Afraid to Swallow

Candy, age 11, was hospitalized for dehydration. Her voice trembled and her eyes widened with fear as she described being rushed to the emergency room in an ambulance after she fainted. She was embarrassed that something as simple as eating was so hard for her, but it terrified her to even think about trying. Candy detested being thin, and desperately wanted to be "just like other kids." After talking with Candy, it was clear that she dreaded eating because she was afraid of vomiting in public. Her fear began when she couldn't eat in front of other kids in the school cafeteria, but advanced quickly to her not being able to eat at all. Candy doesn't have an eating disorder—she has a severe social phobia.

Since most fears and anxieties are not associated with serious disturbances, deciding whether a child's anxiety is serious enough to warrant treatment is seldom easy. Although anxiety disorders are extremely disabling for the child and family, they are rarely life threatening. Children with anxiety disorders can be extremely quiet, shy, compliant, eager to please, or secretive, and their distress may go unnoticed. Sometimes a severe disruption to a normal routine may be needed before a parent seeks help. If a child is so afraid of spiders or dogs that she is terror-stricken when going outside, regardless of whether a spider or dog is nearby, then treatment may be needed. Treatment may also be required when parents repeatedly make important decisions that interfere with family life to accommodate a child's fears, such as not going camping, not traveling by airplane, or not driving on holidays. Unlike children who provoke or offend others, children with anxiety disorders typically don't cause trouble, and as a result they receive far less professional attention than children with conduct problems. This situation is unfortunate, because many of these children can be helped with treatment (P. C. Kendall, Chu, Pimental, & Choudhury, 2000; Labellarte, Ginsburg, Walkup, & Riddle, 1999; Prins & Ollendick, 2003).

In 1924, Mary Cover Jones worked with 3-year-old Peter who was afraid of a rabbit. She eliminated Peter's fear by gradually exposing him to the rabbit when he was relaxed, by having him watch other children play with a rabbit, and by rewarding him for approaching the rabbit. These treatment techniques are still used today. Teaching children to use behavioral and cognitive coping skills to reduce anxious avoidance also increases the child's options and opportunities (P. C. Kendall, 1992). In this regard, in addition to reducing or preventing symptoms of anxiety, early intervention may prevent future problems, such as loss of friends, failure to reach social and academic potential, low self-esteem, and depression (Rapee, 2002; Spence & Dadds, 1996). Universal programs of primary prevention have also had some success in decreasing symptoms of anxiety (Hudson, Flannery-Schroeder, & Kendall, 2004; Lowry-Webster, Barrett, & Lock, 2003).

Overview

"Timidity will always diminish if the occasions that produce it be skillfully repeated, until they cease to cause surprise, for the timid apprehend the unexpected."

(Yoritomo-Tashi, 1916)

Decades of research from almost every perspective imaginable corroborate the popular adage that the best way to defeat your fears is to face them. Although specific procedures may vary, exposing children to the situations, objects, and occasions that produce anxiety is the main line of attack in any treatment for anxiety disorders (Barrios & O'Dell, 1998; M. Moore & Carr, 2000). As described in Box 7.5, when former three-time world heavyweight boxing champion Evander Holyfield was only 17 years old, he faced his fears—and was never afraid again.

Treatments for anxiety are directed at modifying four primary problems (Barlow, 2002):

- Distorted information processing
- Physiological reactions to perceived threat
- Sense of a lack of control
- Excessive escape and avoidance behaviors

Treatments approach these central problems from different directions (Ollendick & King, 1998). It is important that treatments be matched to the child's symptoms (Eisen & Silverman, 1993). In the following sections, we present an overview of the most commonly used treatments for anxiety disorders including behavior therapy, cognitive-behavioral therapy (CBT), medications, and family interventions. Typically, combined forms of treatment are used.

Behavior Therapy

The main technique of behavior therapy for phobias and anxiety disorders is **exposure,** causing children to face with what frightens them, while providing ways of coping other than escape and avoidance. About 75% of children with anxiety disorders are helped by this treatment (W. K. Silverman & Kurtines, 1996b).

Usually the process is gradual, and referred to as **graded exposure.** The child and therapist make a list of

BOX 7.5 **Evander Holyfield:
The Best Way to Defeat
Fear Is to Face It**

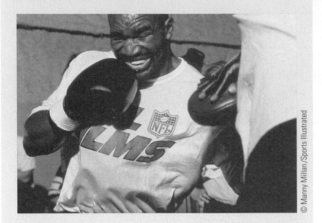

Evander Holyfield, a former three-time world heavyweight boxing champion, has the reputation of having no fear of failure or injury. In fact, Holyfield is amazed by his courage, since he used to be paralyzed by fear. From age 8, when he began boxing, until he was 17, he knew nothing but the constant anxiety of being bullied. "I was scared at everything I did, but especially boxing," he says. "I don't know how I ever got started, but I was scared. I don't know why I stayed. But I won a lot of fights, never got hurt, and as much torment as I was living in, I just assumed I would quit before I got to, say, 18. From watching the older kids box, I knew there came a time when you could get hurt, your nose would be bloody, your eye cut. I'd quit before that happened to me."

However, at 17, he suddenly found himself looking at a left hook from nowhere. Holyfield, then a slim 147 pounds of quivering nerves, was knocked unconscious, more or less, but he rose from the deck and charged his opponent. It was quite a little amateur fight.

The fight came back to him in a dream that night, after his head had cleared. He had been knocked down, yes, but he had gotten up and fought, after a fashion. Amazingly, he remembered nothing from the experience except numbness; it hadn't hurt at all. "I was never afraid again" he says.

Source: Reprinted courtesy of *Sports Illustrated,* June 30, 1997, pp. 24–25. Copyright © 1997, Time, Inc. "Lovestruck" by Richard Hoffer. All rights reserved.

feared situations, from least to most anxiety-producing, and the child is asked to rate the distress caused by each situation on a scale from 1 to 10; this is called a Subjective Units of Distress Scale (SUDS) or fear thermometer. The child is then exposed to each situation, beginning

BOX 7.6 **Sample Fear Hierarchy**

WAYMAN: OCD

SITUATION	SUDS RATING
Not checking class schedule	10
Leaving bedroom closet door open	8
Not arranging books in bookbag	7
Not arranging items in bathroom	6
Not rewriting homework	5
Not flipping light on and off three times	3

Source: Adapted from "An Update on the Treatment of OCD in Children and Adolescents," by J. Piacentini, 1997, *Masters in Psychiatry,* pp. 9–12. Copyright © 1997 by Cliggot Communications. Adapted by permission.

with the least distressing and moving up the hierarchy as the level of anxiety permits. A fear hierarchy, for Wayman, aged 10, who has OCD, is presented in Box 7.6.

For Wayman, leaving his bedroom closet door open was an anxiety-provoking situation with a SUDS rating of 8. Exposure was achieved by asking him to imagine being in this bedtime situation.

> THERAPIST: It is nighttime. Your parents have tucked you in and have gone to bed themselves. You reach over to shut off the light on the nightstand, and you notice that your bedroom closet door is open just a bit, just enough for something to crawl out and into your room. It's dark in that corner and you think you see something. You shut off the light and lie down. You hear a strange, scratching noise coming from the closet. It sounds like something is moving. What's your SUDS rating?
>
> WAYMAN: (Points to fear thermometer.) It's a seven.
>
> THERAPIST: Stay with it. Tell me about what happens next.
>
> WAYMAN: The closet door creaks open a bit more, and now I know that something is there. It can come get me. It's a monster.
>
> THERAPIST: You begin to sweat. You want so badly to go and shut that door, but you stay in bed. You close your eyes, but the sound doesn't stop. It seems to be getting closer. You look over and see a horrible face, with red eyes staring at you. You want to scream, but you know you can't. What's your SUDS rating now?
>
> WAYMAN: Eight. This is the worst part.
>
> THERAPIST: Okay, good, stay with the image. Stay with it. What's your SUDS rating now?
>
> WAYMAN: Five.

With repeated exposure to the fear, Wayman's SUDS ratings continued to decrease, and he was able to leave his bedroom closet door open without feeling anxious.

(Adapted from Albano et al., 1995)

A second behavior therapy technique for treating children's fears and anxiety is **systematic desensitization,** which consists of three steps: teaching the child to relax, constructing an anxiety hierarchy, and presenting the anxiety-provoking stimuli sequentially while the child remains relaxed. With repeated presentation, the child feels relaxed in the presence of stimuli that previously provoked anxiety.

In a third technique known as **flooding,** exposure is carried out in prolonged and repeated doses. Throughout the process, the child remains in the anxiety-provoking situation and provides anxiety ratings until the levels diminish. Flooding is typically used in combination with **response prevention,** which prevents the child from engaging in escape or avoidance behaviors. More than other approaches, flooding may create distress, especially during the early stages of treatment. This procedure must be used carefully, especially with young children who may not understand the rationale.

In exposure-based therapies, the feared object can be confronted many ways, including real-life, role playing, and imagining, or by observing others in contact with the feared object or situation (modeling). There is also evidence that exposure through virtual reality is effective (B. O. Rothbaum, Hodges, & Smith, 2000).

The most effective procedures for treating specific phobias involve participant modeling and reinforced practice (Ollendick & King, 1998). Using these procedures, the therapist models the desired behavior (e.g., approaching the feared object), encourages and guides the child in practicing this behavior, and reinforces the child's efforts. Although all exposure procedures are effective, real-life or in vivo exposure works best, although it is not always easy to implement. Once the child faces her fear in a real-life situation with no adverse consequences, she is more confident of doing it again.

Other useful behavior therapies are directed at reducing the physical symptoms of anxiety. These include muscle relaxation and special breathing exercises. Children who are anxious often take rapid shallow breaths (hyperventilation) that can produce increased heartbeat, dizziness, and other symptoms. Relaxation procedures are often used with gradual exposure.

Cognitive-Behavioral Therapy (CBT)

The most effective procedure for treating most anxiety disorders is cognitive-behavioral therapy (CBT) (Prins & Ollendick, 2003). CBT teaches children to understand how thinking contributes to anxiety, and how to modify their maladaptive thoughts to decrease their symptoms (P. C. Kendall et al., 2000). For example, as part of a comprehensive CBT for panic disorder, a teen who becomes lightheaded during a panic attack and fears she is going to die may be helped by a clinical strategy in which the therapist asks her to spin in a circle until she becomes dizzy. When she becomes alarmed and thinks, "I'm gonna die," she learns to replace this thought with one that is more appropriate; for example, "It's just a little dizziness—I can handle it" (E. C. Hoffman & Mattis, 2000). Making the youngster aware of thought patterns and ways to change them complement exposure and other behavior therapy procedures, such as positive reinforcement and relaxation. CBT and exposure-based treatments are almost always used in combination. An example of a combined approach for treating adolescents with social phobia is presented in Box 7.7 (Albano, 2003).

The CBT treatment program *Coping Cat,* developed by Philip Kendall and his colleagues, is one of the most carefully evaluated treatments for youngsters 7–13 years old with GAD, SAD, and social phobia (P. C. Kendall, Aschenbrand, & Hudson, 2003). A teen version is available,

THE FAR SIDE® **BY GARY LARSON**

Professor Gallagher and his controversial technique of simultaneously confronting the fear of heights, snakes, and the dark.

BOX 7.7 Cognitive-Behavioral Therapy for Adolescent Social Phobia

Ann Marie Albano and her colleagues have developed a comprehensive group CBT treatment program for adolescents with a social phobia (Albano & Barlow, 1996; Albano, 2000). Treatment is carried out in small groups of 4–6 teens and involves sixteen 90-minute sessions. The treatment includes a number of important elements (Albano, Detweiler, & Logsdon-Conradsen, 1999).

Psychoeducational

In this phase, teens are informed about the nature of anxiety. A model emphasizing the cognitive, physiological, and behavioral symptoms increases their awareness and understanding of what provokes and maintains their symptoms. They are taught self-monitoring to help them identify anxiety triggers and reactions. To help the teens identify their symptoms, they are placed in anxiety-provoking situations, such as entering a classroom late, and asked to describe their physical, cognitive, and behavioral reactions:

THERAPIST: What would you be feeling? (physical)
CHILD: Butterflies, dizziness, shortness of breath.
THERAPIST: What would you be thinking? (cognitive)
CHILD: Everyone will be looking at me. What if the teacher yells at me? My face will be all red; they'll see it.
THERAPIST: What would you do? (behavioral)
CHILD: Skip the class. Not look up at anyone. Go to the nurse's office instead.

(Adapted from Albano et al., 1991)

Skill Building

In this phase, teens learn cognitive restructuring, social skills, and problem-solving skills. Adolescents are taught to identify cognitive distortions, or errors in thinking that perpetuate anxiety. Systematic rational responses are developed to replace these cognitions. Modeling, role-playing, and systematic exposure exercises are used.

Specific social skills for interpersonal interactions, maintenance of relationships, and assertiveness are identified and taught. Adolescents first identify behaviors that negatively influence social interactions, such as not smiling, making nervous gestures, not showing interest, speaking too softly, or criticizing or ignoring others. They then practice better forms of social interaction (Marten, Albano, & Holt, 1991).

Problem Solving

In this phase, a model for identifying problems and developing realistic goals is presented and rehearsed. The teen is taught how to cope by using a proactive approach rather than avoidance. Two therapists roleplay in a situation that produces social anxiety. They verbalize their automatic thoughts and rational coping responses to model stages of cognitive restructuring. One therapist verbalizes the automatic thoughts, and the other therapist acts as the "rational responder," as illustrated in the following example:

Scene: You have been called on to give a brief talk in front of your class.
T1: "Oh no, I can't do this!"
T2: "Okay, calm down, stay cool. Don't think so negatively."
T1: "Everyone will be looking at me. I'll mess up."
T2: "They have to do this too. We're all a little nervous."
T1: "What will I say? I can't think!"
T2: "Okay, I can say things clearly, I know this stuff."
T1: "My heart is beating so fast, I'm gonna be sick."
T2: "I feel nervous, but it will pass. I'll be fine."
T1: "Boy, I'm glad that's over, I'll never do this again."
T2: "Alright! I did it! That was okay. I made it!"

(Adapted from Albano et al., 1991)

Therapists then discuss the role play with the group, drawing on the members' experiences in similar situations.

Exposure

In this phase, teens develop a fear and avoidance hierarchy of social situations, which serves as the focus of in-session exposures. Group members and therapists simulate the situations. Exposures target the behavioral avoidance and cognitive component of anxiety, showing that anxiety will dissipate with habituation.

Generalization and Maintenance

To enhance generalization and maintenance of treatment effects, the prosocial and coping behaviors that the teen learns in the group are modeled and practiced during snack-time sessions. In addition, to increase generalization to the home setting, the program also includes a component for active parent participation (Marten et al., 1991).

When asked how she had changed following treatment for her social phobia, here's what one girl said:

> "Well, my friends told me that when they used to ask my opinion about something, I would always say, 'I don't care' or 'I don't know.' Now when they ask me, I give them my opinion. They said they like me much better now because I say what I think." (Beidel & Turner, 1998, p. 223).

as is an Australian adaptation (*Coping Koala*). This approach emphasizes learning processes and the influence of contingencies and models, as well as the pivotal role of information processing. Treatment is directed at decreasing negative thinking, increasing active problem solving, and providing the child with a functional coping outlook. The intervention creates behavioral experiences with emotional involvement while simultaneously addressing thought processes (P. C. Kendall et al., 2003).

Skills training and exposure are used to combat the problematic thinking that contributes to anxious distress and the behavioral avoidance that serves to maintain it. A variety of effective techniques include modeling, role play, exposure, and relaxation training. Therapists use social reinforcement to encourage and reward the children, who are also taught to reward themselves for successful coping. Children first learn to use the following four steps of a FEAR plan (Kendall et al., 2003, p. 87):

F = Feeling frightened? (recognizing physical symptoms of anxiety)

E = Expecting bad things to happen? (recognizing anxious cognitions)

A = Attitudes and actions that will help (coping self-talk and behavior to use when anxious)

R = Results and rewards (evaluating performance and administering self-reward for effort)

After children learn the FEAR plan, the second part of the program is devoted to exposure and practice. Children attend 16 to 20 sessions over a period of 8 weeks. To enhance the skills learned in therapy, they must practice using them in anxiety-producing situations at home and school. Controlled evaluations of this approach have found it to be extremely effective in the short term. Most children show reductions in anxiety with 71% of children freed of their primary diagnosis at the end of treatment, and 54% not meeting criteria for any anxiety disorder. These gains have been maintained for periods of 1 to 3 years following treatment (Kendall et al., 2003). Children who are younger, have fewer internalizing symptoms, and whose mothers do not display depressive symptoms generally show more favorable outcomes (Southam-Gerow, Kendall, & Weersing, 2001).

Although CBT is effective in treating childhood anxiety disorders, studies have not tested whether its effectiveness is by changes in the hypothesized key components—child's cognitions and coping skills (Prins & Ollendick, 2003). Thus, CBT works, but we don't yet know why.

Medications

A variety of medications have been used to treat the symptoms of anxiety in children and adolescents, the most common ones being selective serotonin reuptake inhibitors (SSRIs), tricyclic antidepressants, and benzodiazepines (Varley & Smith, 2003). Medications are typically combined with CBT, or when CBT proves unsuccessful. Some children who are severely anxious may require medication before they are able participate in CBT. To date, there have been relatively few controlled studies of the effectiveness of medications for the treatment of anxiety disorders in children; however, clinical trials and a growing number of controlled studies provide some knowledge about the use of these compounds (Kearney & Silverman, 1998; Varley & Smith, 2003).

The strongest evidence for the effectiveness of medication is for OCD, where the SSRIs are the treatment of choice (Liebowitz et al., 2002; March et al., 1998). Combining SSRIs with exposure and response prevention may be most effective, since children treated with either method alone continue to experience some OCD symptoms (R. A. King, Leonard, & March, 1998). Combined approaches may also increase compliance and minimize relapse when medication is terminated (Piacentini & Graae, 1997).

Findings regarding the effectiveness of medications for treating anxiety disorders other than OCD have been less consistent (P. C. Kendall et al., 1997). However, recent studies suggest the potential use of medications in managing the symptoms of anxiety for youngsters with social phobia, SAD, and GAD (The Research Unit on Pediatric Psychopharmacology Anxiety Study Group, 2001), particularly when they are used as part of a more comprehensive treatment plan (Varley & Smith, 2003).

Family Interventions

Anxiety disorders often occur in a context of parental anxiety and problematic family relationships, which may influence the effectiveness of any of the treatment approaches. In some cases, child-focused treatment may have spillover effects into the family. For example, as children come to view themselves as more competent and less avoidant, parents' perceptions about what their child can and can't do change as well. As a result, parents may begin to respond differently to their child, and their own feelings and functioning are improved (P. C. Kendall & Flannery-Schroeder, 1998).

Addressing children's anxiety disorders in a family context may result in more dramatic and lasting effects than only focusing on the child (Barrett & Shortt, 2003; Howard & Kendall, 1996a, 1996b). In one study it was found that nearly 70% of the children with anxiety disorders who completed individual or family treatment did not meet criteria for any anxiety disorder at posttreatment. The addition of a family component that focuses on interactions, managing emotion, communication, and problem solving significantly enhances short-term outcome and long-term maintenance (Barrett, Dadds, & Rapee, 1996).

Given the important role of the family in childhood OCD, treatments for OCD have increasingly emphasized family involvement (Waters & Barrett, 2000). The primary treatment for children with OCD helps them learn to confront their worse fears gradually (graded exposure) while being prevented from engaging in their rituals (response prevention) (Albano, March, & Piacentini, 1999; March & Mulle, 1998; Shafron, 1998). Family treatment for OCD provides education about the disorder and helps families cope with their feelings, such as helplessness in not being able to relieve the child's pain, frustration that the child cannot "just stop," jealousy from siblings, and disappointment that the child is not "normal" (Piacentini, Jacobs, & Maidment, 1997). Both individual and family-based treatments have proven to be effective in treating children with OCD (Barrett, Healy-Farrell, & March, 2004; Rapoport & Inoff-Germain, 2000).

SECTION SUMMARY

- Exposing youngsters to the situations, objects, and occasions that produce their anxiety is the main line of attack in treating fears and anxieties.
- The most effective procedures for treating specific phobias involve participant modeling and reinforced practice.
- Cognitive-behavioral treatments (CBT) teaches children to understand how their thinking contributes to anxiety, how to change maladaptive thoughts to decrease their symptoms, and how to cope with their fears and anxieties other than by escape and avoidance.
- Medications such as SSRIs are effective in treating children with OCD. However, findings for the effectiveness of medications used to treat other anxiety disorders have been inconsistent.
- Family interventions for anxiety disorders may result in more dramatic and lasting effects than focusing only on the child.

Key Terms

 InfoTrac College Edition

To research recent articles on the subject, go to:
www.infotrac-college/thomsonlearning.com

Enter search terms: ANXIETY IN CHILDREN, SEPARATION ANXIETY, SCHOOL PHOBIA, TEST ANXIETY, SELECTIVE MUTISM, OBSESSIVE COMPULSIVE DISORDER, PANIC ATTACKS, POST–TRAUMATIC STRESS DISORDER.

Mood Disorders

*Some are unhappy through illness, some are
ill through unhappiness.*

—Sir Walter Langdon Brown

Donna

Desperate Despair

Donna, age 12, says, "Sometimes I feel like jumping off the roof or finding some other way to hurt myself." Over the past 3 months Donna has become more and more withdrawn, and her feelings of sadness, worthlessness, and self-hatred scare her. Her teacher describes Donna as "a loner who seems very troubled and unhappy." She's always been a good student, but she is now having difficulty concentrating, is failing tests, and feels totally unmotivated. At home, Donna is having trouble sleeping, has no appetite, and frequently complains of headaches. Most days she stays in her room and does nothing. When her mother asks her to do something, Donna becomes extremely upset. She says she is "moody and irritable most of the time."

Mick

Up and Down

Mick, age 16, is moody all of the time. Sometimes he is sad, sullen, and apathetic. At other times he is full of life and energy, or intensely angry. When full of energy, he can go with little or no sleep for days without feeling tired. He moves constantly, talks incessantly, and cannot be interrupted. These extreme changes in mood make Mick feel out of control, and sometimes he thinks about hurting himself. He is frightened by his thoughts and drinks or uses drugs when they are available to reduce the pain.

Perhaps you know a child or teen who seems constantly unhappy, shows little enthusiasm for anything, is moody, or, at worst, thinks life just isn't worth living. This child may have a **mood disorder** (also called an *affective disorder*), in which a disturbance in mood is the central feature. Mood is broadly defined as a feeling or emotion, for example, sadness, happiness, anger, elation, or crankiness. Children with mood disorders suffer from extreme, persistent, or poorly regulated emotional states, such as excessive unhappiness or swings in mood from deep sadness to high elation. Mood disorders are one of the most common, chronic, and disabling illnesses in young people, affecting about 6% of all children at any given time (Costello et al., 2002; NIMH, 2003).

Mood disorders come in several brands. At one end of the spectrum are children who experience severe depression. Like Donna, these children suffer from **dysphoria,** a state of prolonged bouts of sadness. They feel little joy in anything they do and lose interest in nearly all activities, a state known as **anhedonia.** In the words of one depressed teen:

"Depression makes you lose interest in all the stuff you used to think was fun. You might quit playing guitar or drop out of yearbook, and claim that you just don't have the energy or desire to pursue extracurricular activities—or curricular activities, for that matter." (From "I Did Not Want to Live," by Sabrina Solin, 1995. *Seventeen,* April 1, 1995, pp. 154–156, 176. Copyright © 1995 by Primedia Corp. Reprinted by permission.)

Many youngsters with depression express these combined feelings of sadness and loss of interest. However, some never report feeling sad. Rather, they express their depression through their irritable mood. Others may describe them as cranky, grouchy, moody, short-fused, or easily upset. Being around these children is difficult because any little thing can set them off. Irritability is one of the most common symptoms of depression, occurring in about 80% of clinic-referred youngsters with depression (Goodyer & Cooper, 1993).

At the opposite end of the spectrum is a smaller number of youngsters, those like Mick, who also experience episodes of **mania,** an abnormally elevated or expansive mood, and feelings of **euphoria,** which is an exaggerated sense of well-being. They suffer from an ongoing combination of extreme highs and extreme lows, a condition known as **bipolar disorder (BP)** or *manic-depressive illness.* Their highs may alternate with lows, or they may feel both extremes at about the same time.

DSM-IV-TR divides mood disorders into two general categories, depressive disorders and bipolar disorder (BP) (APA, 2000). We will discuss each of these primary mood disorders in the sections that follow.

SECTION SUMMARY

- Children with mood disorders suffer from extreme, persistent, or poorly regulated emotional states, for example, excessive unhappiness or swings in mood from deep sadness to high elation.

- Mood disorders are common and among the most persistent and disabling illnesses in young people, affecting about 6% of all children.

- There are two major types of mood disorders: depressive disorders and bipolar disorder (BP).

Depressive Disorders

"And how are you?" said Winnie-the-Pooh.

Eeyore shook his head from side to side.

"Not very how," he said. "I don't seem to have felt at all how for a long time."

—*A. A. Milne, Winnie-the-Pooh (1926)*

Depression refers to a pervasive unhappy mood, the kind of gloomy feeling displayed by Eeyore, the sad and indecisive old gray donkey in *Winnie-the-Pooh*. The symptoms of depression are so universal that depression is sometimes called "the common cold of psychopathology." Everyone feels sad, blue, out of sorts, or "down in the dumps" at times. (Even reading or writing about depression can be a real downer—can anyone think of a way to put a positive spin on feelings of dejection, hopelessness, worry, loneliness, or self-blame?) Sometimes our sadness is a normal reaction to an unfortunate event in our lives like losing a friend or a job. At other times we may feel depressed without really knowing why. These feelings soon pass, however, and we resume our normal activities. Clinical depression, in contrast, is more severe than the occasional blues or mood swings that everyone gets from time to time.

Childhood is usually thought of as a happy and carefree time, a period unfettered by the worries, burdens, and responsibilities of adulthood. We tend to think of young people as positive and upbeat, not depressed. In fact, a common reaction to hearing that a child is depressed is "What does she have to be depressed about?" Even when children experience disappointment, disapproval, or other negative events in their lives that are inevitable, their sadness, frustration, and anger are expected to be short-lived. When children become sad, irritable, or upset, parents often attribute the negative moods to temporary factors, such as a lack of sleep or not feeling well, and expect the moods to pass. Thus, for a long time it was thought that children didn't get depressed, and when they did, it would be short-lived. We now know this is not true (Shaffer & Waslick, 2002). Over 800,000 teens in the United States suffer from depression each year, and more than 500,000 make a suicide attempt that requires medical attention (NIMH, 2003).

Unlike most children who bounce back quickly when they are sad, children who are depressed can't seem to shake their sadness, and it begins to interfere with their daily routines, social relationships, school performance, and overall functioning. Depressed youngsters often have accompanying problems, such as anxiety or conduct disorders. Although clinical depression may resemble the normal emotional dips of childhood, for some youngsters it is pervasive, disabling, long-lasting, and life-threatening (Kovacs & Devlin, 1998). Unfortunately, depression often goes unrecognized and untreated because parents and, in some cases teachers, may not recognize the child's underlying subjective negative mood (Mesman & Koot, 2000a, 2000b; Wu et al., 1999).

Main Features

Depression affects children and adolescents in many areas of functioning (Oster & Montgomery, 1995, pp. 47–48):

- *Mood.* Children with depression experience feelings of sadness that are more exaggerated and more persistent than normal sad feelings. Feelings of irritability, guilt, and shame may also accompany depression.

- *Behavior.* They may display increased restlessness and agitation, reduced activity, slowed speech, or excessive crying. Along with decreased activity comes less frequent social contact. At times, youngsters who are depressed may express their sadness through verbal sarcasm, screaming, or destructive behavior. Adolescents with depression may abuse alcohol or other drugs as a way to feel better.

- *Changes in attitude.* They experience feelings of worthlessness and low self-esteem. They see themselves as inadequate and believe that others view them this way. Their attitudes toward school may change, and school performance may suffer. They begin to dread the future and are convinced they are doomed to failure, often asking, "Why should I even bother?" or "What's the use in trying?" When these attitudes and feelings intensify, the risk for suicidal behavior may increase.

- *Thinking.* They are preoccupied with their inner thoughts and tensions. This self-focus may cause them to be extremely self-critical and self-conscious. Thought patterns are slowed, reasoning is distorted, and pessimistic views about the future are expressed. They may have difficulty concentrating, remembering, and making decisions, then may blame themselves for every bad outcome.

- *Physical changes.* They experience disruptions in eating and sleeping. Appetite loss and early morning or frequent wakening are common, as are reports of feeling tired all the time. Physical complaints such as headaches and stomachaches, nausea, persistent aches and pains, and loss of usual energy also occur.

We may think of children with depression as tearful and quietly sobbing alone in their rooms, but the reality is that many show their depression in other ways. Children with depression may be irritable or cranky, and become upset by little disappointments, like losing an article of clothing. They can be extremely argumentative, making it difficult for others to be around them. Some children express their disturbed mood with temper tantrums or angry outbursts, behaviors that may elicit anger in others and scapegoating of the child. Acting out may be a way to avoid the painful feelings of depression. Because the youngster may not seem sad, parents and teachers may not realize that angry behavior could be a sign of depression (W. M. Reynolds & Johnston, 1994b). In the words of one mother:

"My son attempted to gain some control over his life by becoming the bad guy at school and at home. . . . He lashed out at everyone who came near, and we were too angry to think about the possibility that he was depressed." (From "Childhood Depression," by K. Levine, pp. 42–45. *Parents,* October 1995. Copyright © 1995 by Gruner & Jahr USA Publishing. Reprinted by permission of the author.)

Depression in children goes well beyond normal mood swings.

History

Not long ago, people doubted the existence of depression in children. This mistaken belief was rooted in traditional psychoanalytic theories, which viewed depression as a result of hostility or anger turned inward, usually caused by actual or perceived loss. Because children lacked sufficient superego development to permit aggression to be directed against the self, it was believed that they were incapable of experiencing depression (Rochlin, 1959). In another mistaken view, symptoms of depression were considered normal and passing expressions of certain stages of development, a belief that also has proved false. Depression in young people is a recurrent problem, as it is for adults (Lewinsohn, Rohde, & Seeley, 1998).

As depression in children was acknowledged, a popular view emerged that children express depression much differently than adults, in ways that are often indirect and hidden. This idea came to be known as *masked depression.* It was thought that any known clinical symptom in children, including hyperactivity, learning problems, aggression, bed-wetting, separation anxiety, sleep problems, and running away, could be a sign of an underlying but masked depression (Cytryn & McKnew, 1974). Because this concept is too encompassing to be useful, the once popular notion of masked depression has been rejected. Depression in children isn't masked, but may simply be

overlooked because it frequently co-occurs with more visible disorders, such as conduct problems (Hammen & Compas, 1994).

Depression in Young People

Almost all youngsters experience some symptoms of depression, and as many as 5% of children and 10% to 20% of adolescents experience significant depression (W. M. Reynolds & Johnston, 1994b). These children display lasting depressed mood while facing real or perceived distress, and display disturbances in their thinking, physical functioning, and social behavior (R. C. Harrington, Fudge, Rutter, Pickles, & Hill, 1990). Suicide among teens, which is frequently associated with depression, has also skyrocketed in recent years (Beautrais, 2003).

Even when children recover from their depression, they are likely to experience recurrent bouts and continued impairments (Lewinsohn, Roberts et al., 1994). As many as 90% of these youngsters show significant impairment in daily functions (Simonoff et al., 1997). The long-lasting emotional suffering, problems in everyday living, and heightened risk of these youngsters to suicide, substance abuse, and BP make depression in young people a very serious concern (Fombonne, Wostear, Cooper, Harrington, & Rutter, 2001a, 2001b).

The occurrence of depression in young people is increasing, while the age of onset is decreasing (Fombonne, 1999). Although the precise reasons for the increase in depression are not known, one factor that has been implicated is rapid social change. Overcrowded cities, family breakup, increased drug use, and shifts in occupational and employment patterns may increase their levels of stress. These changes may also make children more vulnerable to stress due to a loss of protective factors such as family support (Kovacs, 1997).

Depression and Development

Children express and experience depression differently at different ages (Weiss & Garber, 2003). An infant may show sadness by being passive and unresponsive; a preschooler may appear withdrawn and inhibited; a school-age child may be argumentative and combative; a teenager may express feelings of guilt and hopelessness (Herzog & Rathbun, 1982). These examples are not various types of depressions, they likely represent different stages in the developmental course of the same process.

No one pattern fits all children within a particular age group or developmental period, and not until children are older is depression recognizable as a clinical disorder using DSM criteria. However, recent studies have suggested that age-related modifications in diagnostic criteria may be used to identify a significant depressive syndrome in children as young as 3–5 years (Luby et al., 2002). Although depression in children under the age of 7 is diffuse and less easily identified, it is important to recognize depressive symptoms in young children, since their less visible symptoms may develop into depressive disorders during late childhood or early adolescence (Cantwell, 1990).

We know the least about depression in infants. In the 1940s, René Spitz described a condition he called **anaclitic depression,** in which infants raised in a clean but emotionally cold institutional environment displayed reactions that resembled a depressive disorder (Spitz & Wolf, 1946). They displayed weeping, withdrawal, apathy, weight loss, sleep disturbance, overall decline in development, and in some cases, death. Although Spitz attributed this depression to an absence of mothering and the lack of opportunity to form an attachment, other factors, such as physical illness and deprivation, may also have played a role.

It also became clear that similar symptoms could occur even in noninstitutionalized infants raised in severely disturbed families in which their mother was depressed, psychologically unavailable, or physically abusive. These infants may experience sleep disturbances, loss of appetite, increased clinging, apprehension, crying, and sadness (S. H. Goodman & Gotlib, 2002; see Chapter 14).

Preschool children who are depressed may appear extremely somber and tearful. They generally lack the exuberance, bounce, and enthusiasm in their play that characterize most preschoolers. They may display excessive clinging and whiny behavior around their mothers, as well as fears of separation or abandonment. In addition to getting upset when things don't go their way, many are irritable for no apparent reason. Negative and self-destructive verbalizations may occur, and physical complaints such as stomachaches are common (Luby, Heffelfinger, Mrakotsky, Brown, Hessler, Wallis, & Spitznagel, 2003).

School-age children with depression display many of the symptoms of preschoolers in addition to increasing irritability, disruptive behavior, temper tantrums, and combativeness. A parent may say, "Nothing ever pleases my child—she hates herself and everything around her." School-age children may look sad, but are often unwilling to talk about their sad feelings. Physical complaints may include weight loss, headaches, and sleep disturbances. Academic difficulties and peer problems are also common, and may include frequent fighting and complaints of not having friends or being picked on. Suicide threats may also begin to occur at this age.

Preteens with depression display many of the symptoms of younger children in addition to increasing self-blame and expressions of low self-esteem, persistent sadness, and social inhibition. A child may say "I'm stupid," or "Nobody likes me." Feelings of isolation from family are also common. The preteen may also experience an inability to sleep or may sleep excessively. Disturbances in eating are also common. Teens show increased irritability, loss of feelings of pleasure or interest, and worsening

Depression in insitutionalized infants: A physical appearance that in an adult might be described as depression.

school performance. Angry discussions with parents regarding normal parent–teen issues, such as choice of friends or curfew, are also more common. Other symptoms at this age include a negative body image and self-consciousness, physical symptoms such as excessive fatigue and energy loss, feelings of loneliness, guilt, and worthlessness, and suicidal thoughts and attempts.

Many of these symptoms and behaviors may also occur in children who are developing normally or occur in children with other disorders or conditions. Therefore, the presence of sad mood, loss of interest, or irritability is essential for diagnosing depression. In addition, regardless of the child's age, the symptoms must reflect a change in behavior, persist over time, and cause significant impairment in functioning.

Anatomy of Depression

The term *depression* has been used in various ways. It is important to distinguish between depression as a symptom, depression as a syndrome, and depression as a disorder (Cantwell, 1990).

As a *symptom,* depression refers to feeling sad or miserable. Depressive symptoms often occur without the existence of a serious problem, and are relatively common at all ages, occurring in 40% or more of children and adolescents (Rutter, Tizard, & Whitmore, 1970). For most children, symptoms of depression are temporary, related to events in the environment, and not part of any disorder.

As a *syndrome,* depression is more than a sad mood. A syndrome refers to a group of symptoms that occur together more often than by chance. Sadness may also occur with a reduced interest in activities, cognitive and motivational changes, and somatic and psychomotor changes. The occurrence of depression as a syndrome is far less

less common than isolated depressive symptoms, and often includes mixed symptoms of anxiety and depression, which tend to cluster on a single dimension of negative affect (Ollendick, Seligman, Goza, Byrd, Singh, 2003; L. D. Seligman & Ollendick, 1998). The syndrome can also occur along with other disorders, such as conduct disorder or ADHD. At times, a depressive syndrome may occur following certain life events, for example, as a normal grief reaction following the loss of a loved one. However, bereavement is regarded as a clinical syndrome only if the symptoms persist or reoccur beyond a reasonable adjustment period.

As a *disorder*, depression involves a syndrome that has a minimum duration of 2 weeks and is associated with significant impairments in functioning. The disorder of depression may be associated with common causes, associated features, and a characteristic course, outcome, and response to treatment. As we discuss next, depression as a disorder is defined using the DSM criteria for major depressive disorder and for dysthymic disorder.

SECTION SUMMARY

- Depression in young people involves numerous and persistent symptoms, including impairments in mood, behavior, attitudes, thinking, and physical functioning.

- For a long time it was mistakenly believed that depression didn't exist in children in a form comparable to depression in adults.

- It is now known that depression in young people is prevalent, disabling, increasing in frequency, and often underreferred and undertreated.

- The way in which children express and experience depression changes with age.

- It is important to distinguish between depression as a symptom, syndrome, and disorder.

Major Depressive Disorder (MDD)

Joey

Feeling Worthless and Hopeless

Ten-year-old Joey's mother and teacher are concerned about his irritability and temper tantrums at home and school. With little provocation, he bursts into tears, yells, and throws objects. In class he seems to have difficulty concentrating and seems easily distracted. Increasingly shunned by his peers, he plays by himself at recess, and at home spends most of his time in his room watching TV. His mother notes that he has been sleeping poorly and has gained 10 pounds over the past couple of months from constant snacking. The school psychologist has ruled out learning disabilities or ADHD; instead, she says Joey is a deeply unhappy child who expresses feelings of worthlessness and hopelessness, and even a wish that he would die. These feelings began about 6 months ago, when Joey's father, divorced from his mother for several years, remarried and moved to another town and now spends far less time with Joey. (Adapted from Hammen & Rudolph, 2003)

Alison

"I Couldn't Take It Any More"

Alison, age 17, gets high grades, is a talented musician, and is attractive. However, for the past 3 years she has been fighting to stay alive. "There are times when I was in school and I would start to cry—I had no idea why. My friends would say, 'What have you got to be depressed about, Alison? You're smart, talented, and can have any boy you want.' When my closest friend moved away 3 years ago, I was really lonely," says Alison. "I'd write notes about suicide and talk about killing myself. I couldn't eat and was tired most of the time. Even the smallest decision was overwhelming. Some days I'd never get out of bed I was so depressed. I couldn't stand school and hated everyone." Alison's feelings of hopelessness lasted for days, then weeks, then months. Finally, "I couldn't take it anymore," says Alison. "I wanted to die—so I tried to kill myself."

Although Joey and Alison differ in age and symptoms, both display the key features of **major depressive disorder (MDD):** sadness, loss of interest or pleasure in nearly all activities, irritability, plus a number of additional specific symptoms that are present for at least 2 weeks. These symptoms must also represent a change from previous functioning. DSM criteria for a major depressive episode are presented in Table 8.1.

A diagnosis of MDD depends on the presence of a major depressive episode plus the exclusion of other conditions, such as the prior occurrence of a manic episode. (In this case, a diagnosis of BP would be made.) It also requires ruling out organic factors that may have caused or prolonged the depression, a depression that is part of normal bereavement, and underlying thought disorders.

The cases of Joey and Alison highlight three important points about the diagnosis of MDD in children and adolescents (Hammen & Rudolph, 2003):

- The same DSM criteria can be used to diagnose school-age children and adolescents as to diagnose adults.

Five (or more) of the following symptoms are present during the same 2-week period and represent a change from previous functioning; at least one symptom is either (1) depressed mood or (2) loss of interest or pleasure.

Note: Do not include symptoms that are clearly due to a general medical condition, or mood-incongruent delusions or hallucinations.

(1) Depressed mood most of the day, nearly every day, as indicated by subjective account (e.g., feels sad or empty) or observations by others (e.g., appears tearful).

Note: In children and adolescents, can be irritable mood.

(2) Markedly diminished interest or pleasure in all, or almost all, activities most of the day, nearly every day (as indicated by subjective account or observations by others).

(3) Significant weight loss when not dieting or weight gain (e.g., a change of more than 5% of body weight in a month), or decrease or increase in appetite nearly every day.

Note: In children, consider failure to make expected weight gains.

(4) Insomnia or hypersomnia nearly every day.

(5) Psychomotor agitation or retardation nearly every day (observable by others, not merely subjective feelings of restlessness or being slowed down).

(6) Fatigue or loss of energy nearly every day.

(7) Feelings of worthlessness or excessive or inappropriate guilt (which may be delusional) nearly every day (not merely self-reproach or guilt about being sick).

(8) Diminished ability to think or concentrate, or indecisiveness, nearly every day (either by subjective account or as observed by others).

(9) Recurrent thoughts of death (not just fear of dying), recurrent suicidal ideation without a specific plan, or a suicide attempt or a specific plan for committing suicide.

- Because children's disruptive behaviors attract more attention, or are more easily observed compared with internal, subjective suffering, depression in children can be easily overlooked.
- Some features of depression are likely more common in children and adolescents than in adults—notably, irritable mood.

There are some differences in expression of symptoms between children and adults with MDD. Depressed appearance, separation anxiety, phobias, somatic complaints, and behavioral problems occur more frequently in younger than older individuals. In contrast, symptoms of anhedonia, psychomotor retardation, suicide attempts, and impairment of functioning will increase with age (G. A. Carlson & Kashani, 1988; Hammen & Rudolph, 2003).

Children and adolescents with MDD frequently display similar symptoms and have comparable rates of comorbidity and recurrence as adults (Birmaher et al., 2004). However, relative to adults, clinic-referred youngsters with MDD have almost exclusively first-episode depressions, will recover somewhat faster from their episode of MDD, and are at greater risk for developing a BP. Children who develop MDD suffer from their disorder for many years longer than adults, making early-onset MDD a particularly severe form of affective illness (Kovacs, 1996).

Prevalence

Between 2% and 8% of all children ages 4–18 experience MDD (Poznanski & Mokros, 1994). Depression is rare among preschool (less than 1%) and school-age children (about 2%) (NIMH, 2003), but increases two- to three-fold by adolescence (Rudolph, Hammen, & Daley, in press). Since depression comes and goes, prevalence estimates vary with the length of the time during which symptoms are assessed. For example, in 14 to 18-year-old adolescents, the prevalence of depression is about 3% when taken at a single point in time and about 8% when taken over a 1-year period. However, the lifetime prevalence in adolescents—whether a youngster has ever been depressed—is as high as 20% (Lewinsohn, Clarke, Seeley, & Rohde, 1994). This rate is similar to the prevalence for adults and suggests that depression in adults may originate during adolescence (Glowinski, Madden, Bucholz, Lynskey, & Heath, 2003).

Despite these high rates, they may underestimate the problem. First, the estimates using a formal diagnosis of MDD might be lower than the self-reported symptoms of depression. Second, many youngsters who just barely fail to meet diagnostic criteria for MDD still show significant impairments in their social competence, cognitive attributions, coping skills, family relations, and experience of stress. They are also at greater risk than other youths for developing future depression and other disorders, such as substance abuse (Gotlib, Lewinsohn, & Seeley, 1995; Herman-Stahl & Petersen, 1996).

The modest increase in depression from preschool to elementary school is likely not biologically based, but rather is a reflection of the school-age child's growing self-awareness and cognitive capacity, verbal ability to report symptoms, and increased performance and social pressures. In contrast, the sharp increase in depression in adolescence appears to be the result of biological maturation at puberty interacting with important developmental changes that occur during this tumultuous time period. This hypothesis is supported by the emergence of large sex differences in depression after puberty (discussed on p. 227), the emergence of BP, and the relative stability in rates of MDD through adolescence (Birmaher et al., 1996b).

Comorbidity

Raymond	Raymond, age 16, lives alone with

Raymond

Depressed and Enraged

Raymond, age 16, lives alone with his single mother. For the past few months he has been persistently sad and unhappy, overcome with feelings of worthlessness. He is socially withdrawn, and spends most of his time alone at home or avoiding contact with peers on those days when he manages to attend school. He is constantly tired but still finds it difficult to sleep, lying awake at night for hours and then struggling to drag himself from bed in the morning. Both he and his mother are concerned about his weight, which has increased substantially due to his inability to control his appetite for chips, candy, and soda. Even if he makes it to school, he finds he is unable to concentrate on his work.

Raymond's listlessness and withdrawal are countered, however, by his repeated outbursts of anger and aggression. He frequently lashes out in rage at his mother, recently punching his fist through a wall and a door at home. He also has been in several fights with other students at school as a result of being teased by his peers. He rarely complies with rules and limits at home or at school, leading to frequent conflicts with his mother and with school authorities. The event that precipitated Raymond's current referral was his arrest for shoplifting at a local store. (Adapted from Compas & Hammen, 1994)

Like Raymond, who has MDD and a co-occurring conduct disorder, as many as 70% of youngsters with MDD have one or more other disorders (Simonoff et al., 1997). The most frequent co-occurring disorders in *clinic-referred* youngsters with MDD are anxiety disorders, particularly GAD, specific phobias, and SAD (Compas & Oppedisano, 2000; L. D. Seligman & Ollendick, 1998). Depression and anxiety become more visible as separate but co-occurring disorders as the severity of the child's problem increases and as the child gets older (Gurley, Cohen, Pine, & Brook, 1996). Dysthymia, conduct problems, ADHD, and substance use disorder are also common in clinic-referred youngsters with MDD (Birmaher et al., 1996b; Simonoff et al., 1997).

As many as 20% of adolescents with MDD in community samples also have a co-occurring disorder, which are most commonly anxiety disorders, disruptive behavior disorders, and substance use disorder (Beyers & Loeber, 2003; Lewinsohn, Rohde, Seeley, & Hops, 1991; Rao, Daley, & Hammen, 2000). Further, about 60% of adolescents with MDD have a comorbid personality disorder, which is most commonly borderline personality disorder—characterized by instability of interpersonal relationships, self-image, affects, and marked impulsivity (Birmaher et al., 1996b).

MDD in young people is more likely to occur after rather than before the onset of all other psychiatric disorders except panic disorder and alcohol or substance abuse, which usually begin during the middle to late teens. Most co-occurring disorders are present before MDD and are likely to persist after the child is no longer depressed (Birmaher et al., 1996b). The presence of a co-occurring disorder is significant because it can increase the risk for recurrent depression, the duration and severity of the depressive episode, and suicide attempts. The presence of another disorder also decreases the youngster's response to treatment and is related to less effective outcomes (Birmaher et al., 1996b).

Onset, Course, and Outcome

Onset of depression in adolescence may be gradual or sudden. Either way, a youngster typically has a history of milder episodes of depression (Gotlib & Hammen, 1992). Subthreshold refers to other episodes that do not meet formal diagnostic criteria. Most adults with depression report having their first depressive episode between the ages of 15 and 19 (Burke, Burke, Regier, & Rae, 1990). However, prospective studies of children and adolescents usually find earlier ages of onset, most commonly between the ages of 13 and 15 (Lewinsohn, Hops, et al., 1993). Children with an onset of depression before or after puberty display similar symptoms, duration, severity of first episode, rates of recovery and recurrence, comorbid disorders, and parental psychiatric history (Birmaher et al., 2004).

The average episode of MDD in children and adolescents lasts about 8 months, with longer episodes if a parent has a history of depression (Kaminski & Garber, 2002). For children identified through a community sample, the first depressive episode lasted 26 weeks on average, with a median duration of 8 weeks (Lewinsohn, Clarke, Seeley, & Rohde, 1994). MDD that is severe enough to result in referral for treatment usually lasts about a year. About 90% of children recover from their episode of MDD within 1–2 years following onset, but the rest may experience a prolonged episode and remain depressed (Birmaher et al., 2004; Kovacs, Obrosky, Gatsonis, & Richards, 1997).

Although almost all youngsters eventually recover from their initial depressive episode, their disorder does not go away (Birmaher, Arbelaez, & Brent, 2002). MDD is a recurrent condition with a chance of recurrence of about 25% within 1 year, 40% within 2 years, and 70% within 5 years. A significant number of youngsters develop a chronic, relapsing disorder that persists into young adulthood (Fombonne et al., 2001a; Rao, Hammen, & Daley, 1999). For youngsters hospitalized for depression, nearly one-half will be rehospitalized within 2 years following remission. In addition, about 30% of adolescents with MDD will develop a BP within 5 years after the onset of their depression, known as a "bipolar switch" (DelBello et al., 2003; McCauley et al., 1993).

For most adolescents, their depressive episode will likely continue for several months, and youngsters with early-onset depression will experience many episodes (Strober, Lampert, Schmidt, & Morrell, 1993). Although rates of recovery are high, so too are rates of relapse (Goodyer, Germany, Gowrusankur, & Altham, 1991). Thus, depression is a condition that endures over the course of development, creating a long-term social, emotional, and economic burden for the child and the family (Kovacs, 1997).

Why do depressive episodes reoccur, and why does the length of time between episodes get progressively shorter? One possible explanation is that the first episode may sensitize the youngster to future episodes (Hammen, Henry, & Daley, 2000). According to this idea, the first episode may be linked to a specific stressor (Lewinsohn, Allen, Seeley, & Gotlib, 1999), and is accompanied by lasting changes in biological processes and changes in the child's sensitivity to future stressors (Post et al., 1996). In addition, the initial externally produced changes in the brain can be conditioned so that following the first depressive episode, even minor events that resemble loss or stress experiences may result in depression. This phenomenon is known as *kindling* (Kovacs, 1997; Post & Weiss, 1998).

Even after recovery from their depressive episode, many youths continue to show milder symptoms of depression and experience adjustment and health problems and chronic stress (Birmaher et al., 1996b; Rohde, Lewinsohn, & Seeley, 1994). This is a significant concern because these problems are risk factors for future depressive episodes (Daley, Hammen, & Rao, 2000).

In addition to their recurring bouts of depression, the immediate and long-term prospects for children with MDD include many other negative outcomes. For example, adolescents who are depressed have a greater than normal risk for delinquency, arrest and conviction, school dropout, and unemployment (Lewinsohn, Roberts, et al., 1994). A history of depression during the school years also increases the risk for later substance use disorder, suicidal behavior, poor work record, and marital problems (Gotlib, Lewinsohn, & Seeley, 1998).

The overall outcome for young people with MDD is not optimistic. They continue to be at high risk for later episodes of mood and other disorders and for impaired social and academic functioning. One mother of a depressed teen paints a bleak picture of the long-term outcome for a child who suffers from MDD and, unfortunately, one that is not too far off the mark:

"Depression in kids, when it hits them in their teens, leaves a hole in their lives. When they're young and just starting out in life, they're supposed to become independent. But that doesn't happen with depressed kids. They're out of synch and get left behind. And they never really catch up. That leaves a permanent scar." (Adapted from Owen, 1993, p. C1)

As adults, children and adolescents with MDD continue to experience many negative long-term outcomes that include a high rate of suicide and suicide attempts, recurrence of MDD, high rates of psychiatric and medical hospitalizations, alcohol abuse/dependence, psychosocial impairments, employment problems, and lower educational achievement (Fombonne et al., 2001b; Weissman, Wolk, et al., 1999a, 1999b).

Gender and Ethnicity

In what has been called depression's double standard, females are twice as likely as males to suffer from depression, are more susceptible to milder mood disorders, and are more likely to experience recurrent episodes (Lewinsohn, Pettit, Joiner, & Seeley, 2003; Zahn-Waxler, Race, & Duggal, in press). However, this sex difference is not present among children ages 6 to 11, where depression is equally common in boys and girls (Speier, Sherak, Hirsch,

Teenage girls are particularly vulnerable to depression.

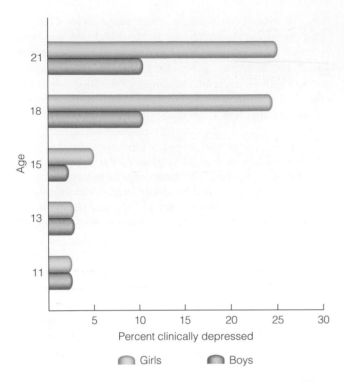

Figure 8.1. The overall rate of depression and the proportion of females with depression increases dramatically during adolescence.

(Adapted from "Development of Depression from Preadolescence to Young Adulthood: Emerging Gender Differences in a 10-Year-Longitudinal Study," by B. L. Hankin, L. Y. Abramson, T. E. Moffitt, P. A. Silva, R. McGee, and K. E. Andell, 1998, *Journal of Abnormal Psychology, 107,* 128–140. Copyright © 1998 by the American Psychological Association. Reprinted by permission of the author.)

& Cantwell, 1995). It is important to note, however, that sex differences in specific symptoms that forecast later depression (e.g., fearfulness, feelings of inadequacy, negative self-evaluation, and negative affect) may in fact be present by 10 years of age, with girls reporting significantly more of these symptoms than boys (Rudolph et al., in press).

Sex differences in diagnosable depression begin between ages 13 and 15, when the rate rises for girls (Wade, Cairney, & Pevalin, 2002). As shown in Figure 8.1, rates of depression as well as gender differences in rates increase dramatically between ages 15 and 18 (Hankin et al., 1998). The ratio of girls to boys is about 2:1 to 3:1 after puberty, a pattern that continues throughout adolescence and adulthood.

Although depression occurs more frequently in girls than boys, it is noteworthy that symptom presentation is quite similar for both sexes. (Slightly more girls than boys report symptoms related to weight and appetite disturbances and worthlessness/guilt) (Kovacs, 2001; Lewinsohn et al., 2003). However, the correlates of depression may differ for the sexes. For example, depression has been found to be more highly related to school-related stress in boys than in girls (Sund, Larsson, & Wichstrom, 2003).

The increase in depression during adolescence, and the emergence of sex differences in depression at this time, have led to a special interest in this developmental period (Petersen et al., 1993; Rudolph et al., in press). Many physical, psychological, and social changes during adolescence may heighten the risk for depression in girls. Hormonal changes in estrogen and testosterone may affect brain function, increasing sexual maturity may affect social roles, interpersonal changes and expectations may result in heightened exposure to stressful life events, and non-normative changes such as early maturation may lead to isolation from one's peer group.

These changes may diminish self-worth, lead to dysphoric mood, and evoke self-focused attention. It is also thought that females may be at higher risk than males because they have a greater orientation toward cooperation and sociality. They also use ruminative coping styles to deal with stress, especially stress involving interpersonal loss and disruptions. These characteristics may put girls at a disadvantage during adolescence, when they face somewhat greater biological and stressful role-related challenges than boys (Rudolph & Hammen, 1999; Zahn-Waxler et al., in press). Interpersonal stress and a lack of social support appear to be particularly salient aspects of depression for adolescent girls (Rudolph, 2002; Schraedley, Gotlib, & Hayward, 1999).

Research suggests that increased levels of testosterone and estrogen at puberty, particularly when they occur in combination with social stress, increase the risk for depression in girls who are vulnerable (Angold, Worthman, & Costello, 2003). Hormones and sleep cycles, which can alter mood, differ dramatically between males and females. One study of blood flow in regions of the brain during periods of sadness in men and in women found that although men and women considered themselves to be equally sad, their brain activity differed. When asked to feel sad, both sexes activated regions of the prefrontal cortex, but women showed a much wider activation of the limbic system. These findings with adults suggest that sex differences in depression may be partly rooted in biological differences in the brain processes that regulate emotions (George, Ketter, Parekh, Herscovitch, & Post, 1996).

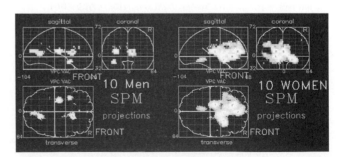

PET scans reveal that during sadness, the limbic system in women's brains (right) becomes metabolically more active than that area in men's brains (left).

The incidence of depression has been found to vary across regions worldwide (Culbertson, 1997; Leutwyler, 1997); however, few studies have examined ethnic or cultural differences in children and adolescents. One study compared the prevalence of major depression across nine ethnic groups in a large community sample of children in grades 6 to 8 (R. E. Roberts, Roberts, & Chen, 1997). Of these groups, African American and Mexican American youths both had significantly higher rates of depression, possibly related to SES effects. However, only Mexican American youths with depression showed an elevated risk for impaired functioning. In another study, pubertal status was found to be a better predictor of depressive symptoms than chronological age in Caucasian girls, but not in African American or Hispanic girls (Hayward, Gotlib, Schraedley, & Litt, 1999).

A large community study of high school students found that non-White (African American, Hispanic, and Asian) adolescents reported more symptoms of depression than White adolescents (Rushton, Forcier, & Schectman, 2002). However, these differences likely reflect differences in SES, since depression and lower SES are related. Future studies will be needed to sort out differences in depression related to culture versus those due to adverse conditions that are known to be associated with race and ethnic status.

SECTION SUMMARY

- The key features of major depressive disorder (MDD) are sadness, loss of interest or pleasure in nearly all activities, irritability, plus many specific symptoms that are present for a duration of at least 2 weeks.

- The overall prevalence of MDD for children ages 4–18 is between 2% and 8%, with rates that are low during childhood but increasing dramatically during adolescence.

- The most frequent accompanying disorders in youngsters with MDD are anxiety disorders, dysthymia, conduct problems, ADHD, and substance use disorder.

- Almost all youngsters recover from their initial depressive episode, but about 70% have another episode within 5 years and many develop BP.

- Depression in preadolescent children is equally common in boys and girls, but the ratio of girls to boys is about 2:1 to 3:1 after puberty.

- The relation between depression and race and ethnicity during childhood is an understudied area.

In the next section we discuss dysthymic disorder (DD), a milder but more chronic form of depression about which we know relatively little compared to MDD. Many children with DD eventually develop MDD, therefore, DD and MDD are related.

Dysthymic Disorder (DD)

Deborah

Lost Childhood

A few months ago, my mother unearthed some pictures of me as a baby, which I had never seen before. One showed me at about 9 months old, crawling on the grass of Golden Gate Park. I was looking directly at the camera, my tongue sticking out of the corner of my mouth, and I was laughing happily. My face was lit from within, and looked more than a little mischievous. I was absolutely transfixed by that photo for days. I would continually take it out of my wallet and stare at it, torn between laughter and tears. For a while I couldn't figure out what it was about the picture that drew me. Finally it hit me; this was the only picture of myself as a child that I had seen which showed me laughing. All the photos I had ever seen depicted a child staring solemnly or smiling diffidently, but never laughing. I looked at the Golden Gate Park picture and wished that I had remained that happy, and that depression had not taken away my childhood. When I first was diagnosed with depression at age 24, I discussed my childhood with my doctor. Although it is hard to diagnose a child from 20 years in the past, it seemed clear to both of us that I had suffered from dysthymia (mild, long-term depression) probably from the time I was a small child. (From Internet Web site, "A Childhood without Laughter," by D. M. Deren. Copyright © 1996, 1997 by Deborah M. Deren, Revised June 8, 1997. Reproduced by permission.)

Like Deborah, youngsters who suffer from **dysthymic disorder (DD) or dysthymia** display depressed mood for most of the day, on most days, for at least 1 year. They are unhappy or irritable most of the time. Although their symptoms are chronic, they are less severe than those for children with MDD. DSM criteria for DD are shown in Table 8.2.

Children with DD are characterized by poor emotion regulation, which includes constant feelings of sadness, feelings of being unloved and forlorn, self-deprecation, low self-esteem, anxiety, irritability, anger, and temper tantrums (Masi et al., 2003; Renouf & Kovacs, 1995). Some may experience **double depression,** where a major depressive episode is superimposed on the child's previous DD, causing the child to present with both disorders (Lewinsohn et al., 1991).

The chronic nature of DD raises the issue of whether it is considered to be a mood disorder or a general personality style (Daley et al., 1999). For example, we all know people we would describe as "sad sacks"—nothing ever seems to make them happy. DD seems to follow a chronic course that is typical of mood disorders, and the

A. Depressed mood for most of the day, for more days than not, as indicated by either subjective account or by observation by others, for at least 2 years.
Note: In children and adolescents, mood can be irritable and duration must be at least 1 year.

B. Presence, while depressed, of two (or more) of the following:

(1) Poor appetite or overeating

(2) Insomnia or hypersomnia

(3) Low energy or fatigue

(4) Low self-esteem

(5) Poor concentration or difficulty making decisions

(6) Feelings of hopelessness

C. During the 2-year period (1 year for children or adolescents) of the disturbance, the person has never been without the symptoms in Criteria A and B for more than 2 months at a time.

Source: Reprinted with permission from *Diagnostic and Statistical Manual of Mental Disorders, DSM-IV-TR, Text Revision, Fourth Edition.* Copyright 2000 by the American Psychiatric Association.

similarities between DD and MDD in young people suggest that DD is a mood disorder, not a personality style (Renouf & Kovacs, 1995). One study found that children and adolescents with either MDD or DD alone did not differ in their clinical features, demographics, or associated characteristics, leading to unanswered questions about the validity of this distinction. However, children with both disorders were more severely impaired than children with just one of the disorders (Goodman, Schwab-Stone, Lahey, Shaffer, & Jensen, 2000).

Prevalence and Comorbidity

Rates of DD are lower than those of MDD, with approximately 1% of children and 5% of adolescents displaying the disorder (Birmaher et al., 1996b; Lewinsohn, Hops, et al., 1993). About 5% have an episode of DD by the end of adolescence (lifetime prevalence) (Renouf & Kovacs, 1995).

The most prevalent co-occurring diagnosis with DD is MDD (Renouf & Kovacs, 1995). During the course of their DD, as many as 70% of children may have an episode of major depression (Renouf & Kovacs, 1995). About one-half of the children with DD also have one or more co-occurring nonaffective disorders that preceded DD, including anxiety disorders, CD, and ADHD (Kovacs et al., 1994).

Onset, Course, and Outcome

DD develops about 3 years earlier than MDD, most commonly around 11–12 years of age (Kovacs et al., 1997). Since DD frequently precedes MDD, it could be a precursor to its development (Lewinsohn, Hops, et al., 1993). Childhood-onset DD has a prolonged duration, with an average episode length of 2–5 years (Lewinsohn et al., 1991). Children with DD who have co-occurring conduct problems require more time to recover (Kovacs et al., 1997).

Almost all youngsters eventually recover from DD. On the other hand, they also have an extremely high risk of developing other disorders, especially MDD, anxiety disorders (SAD and GAD are the most common) (Masi et al., 2003), and conduct disorder. They are also at increased risk for the subsequent development of BP and substance use disorder (Kovacs et al., 1994).

Adolescents with a history of DD report receiving less social support from friends. This finding appears to be unique to children with DD when compared to children with MDD (D. N. Klein, Lewinsohn, & Seeley, 1997). Those who recover from their DD have the same family relationships, cognitive styles, and school functioning as other children. The only area that continues to be affected is psychosocial functioning (D. N. Klein et al., 1997). However, it is not known whether deficits in psychosocial functioning precede or follow DD. They may be a predisposing factor for the development of DD, or a lasting scar of the illness (Renouf & Kovacs, 1995).

The early onset and extended duration of DD make it a serious problem. Youngsters who develop DD at age 9, then recover 4 years later will have spent more than 30% of their entire lives and over 50% of their school-age years being depressed. Since depression is associated with many other academic, cognitive, family, and social problems, these long-lasting episodes of dysthymia can have extremely harmful effects on development (Renouf & Kovacs, 1995). Since early-onset DD is almost always followed by MDD and sometimes by a BP, early diagnosis of DD may help to identify youngsters at risk for later mood disorders and has important implications for prevention.

SECTION SUMMARY

- Children with dysthymic disorder (DD) display depressive symptoms on most days for at least 1 year.

- About 5% of children and adolescents have an episode of dysthymia by the end of adolescence.

- The most common accompanying disorders with DD are superimposed MDD, anxiety disorders, conduct disorder, and ADHD.

- The most common age of onset for DD is between 11 and 12 years, with an average episode length of between 2 and 5 years.

- Almost all youngsters eventually recover from their dysthymia, but many will develop MDD.
- Children who recover from their DD don't differ from other children on any measures except psychosocial functioning.

Now that we have a good understanding of MDD and DD, we next consider the associated characteristics and possible causes for these disorders.

Associated Characteristics of Depressive Disorders

Youngsters with depression also experience deficits in intellectual performance and academic achievement, and disturbances in self-perceptions, self-esteem, social problem-solving and behavior, and life stressors (Garber & Kaminskey, 2000; Kovacs & Goldston, 1991). However, since depression often occurs with anxiety and other disorders we don't know whether these associated problems are specific to depression, or related to the presence of psychopathology in general (Lewinsohn, Gotlib, & Seeley, 1997). In addition, it is often difficult to know whether cognitive and psychosocial deficits are an outcome or a cause of depression (D. A. Cole, Martin, Powers, & Truglio, 1996).

Intellectual and Academic Functioning

Certain depressive symptoms—difficulty concentrating, loss of interest, and slowness of thought and movement—are most likely to have a harmful effect on a youngster's intellectual and academic functioning. The overall intellectual potential of depressed youngsters is comparable to the potential of those who are not depressed. The association between severity of depression and children's overall intelligence is weak, suggesting that the effects of depression on cognitive functions may be selective. For example, depression may be associated with impairments on nonverbal tasks that require attention, coordination, and speed, but not necessarily on those that require verbal skills or intelligence (Kovacs & Goldston, 1991).

Youngsters with MDD perform more poorly than others in school. They score lower on standard achievement tests, are rated by their teachers as achieving less academically, and have lower levels of grade attainment (D. A. Cole, 1990; D. A. Cole et al., 1996). Poor concentration and thinking ability, psychomotor retardation or agitation, fatigue, insomnia, and somatic complaints may lead to repeating a grade, being late or skipping school, failure to complete homework, and dissatisfaction with or refusal of school (Kearney, 1993; Lewinsohn, Roberts, et al., 1994). Jenn, a 15-year-old girl with MDD, and her mother had this to say about school:

"School is a big waste of time," says Jenn. "I don't want to be there. I don't have the energy or motivation for school. I just say I'm sick so I can stay at home in bed and sleep all day." Jenn's mother says, "We used to fight about school so much that eventually I'd let her stay home—just to avoid having another fight."

It is unclear whether MDD has an enduring effect on school performance. Some studies find that school difficulties do not occur following the child's recovery from depression, while others report that academic problems continue even after recovery (Kovacs & Goldston, 1991). In general, the association between depression and school difficulties is not as strong as the association between depression and social dysfunction (Lewinsohn et al., 1997).

Cognitive Disturbances

"Good morning, Pooh Bear," said Eeyore gloomily. "If it is a good morning," he said. "Which I doubt."

—A. A. Milne, Winnie-the-Pooh (1926)

Ellie
Life's Hardly Worth It

". . . like everything's worthless, like it's just not worth it to even be . . . It's—it seems like it's a silly thing to even go through life and exist. And from one day to the next you're always wondering if you're going to make it to the next day if it's—if you can stand it, if it's worth trying to get to tomorrow . . . It's just—just, I feel like—I feel mostly like I'm worthless, like there's something wrong with me. It's really not a pleasant feeling to know that you're a total failure, a complete nothing, and I get the feeling that I never do nothing right or worthwhile or anything." (Adapted from McKnew, Cytryn, & Yahraes, 1983)

Many youngsters with depression experience deficits and distortions in their thinking (Kaslow, Adamson, & Collins, 2000). Some cognitive disturbances, such as Ellie's painful feelings of worthlessness, are part of the diagnosis of depression. Negative beliefs ("I never do nothing right") and attributions of failure ("I'm a total failure") are not part of the diagnosis but typically accompany the disorder. Negative thoughts that are self-critical and automatic, such as "I'm a real loser," "I'm ugly," or "I'm gonna fail," are common. Unfortunately, these thoughts can't simply be swept aside by suggesting to a depressed youngster that she or he "look at the bright side."

"We all have different pain thresholds"

Peanuts, *Reprinted by permission of United Feature Syndicate, Inc.*

Depressed youngsters often devalue their own performance by not acknowledging their accomplishments. They dismiss praise when it is given and frequently make inaccurate interpretations of their experiences (Fichman, Koestner, & Zuroff, 1996). To focus narrowly on negative events for long periods is referred to as a *depressive ruminative style* (Nolen-Hoeksema, Girgus, & Seligman, 1992). These youngsters view themselves as ineffective in most areas of their lives, and make self-directed disparaging comments when faced with further failure or rejection (e.g., "It must be my fault"). They misread situations, feel slighted by otherwise harmless remarks, and are easily frustrated—small setbacks are seen as major catastrophes. Negative thinking and faulty conclusions are generalized across situations, so the depressed youngster sees no hope of gaining any pleasure or satisfaction.

It is not unusual for youngsters with depression to think that no one can help them out of their misery. Many report hopelessness, or negative expectations about the future (Abela, 2001) that are related to diminished self-esteem, and to suicide ideation and attempts (Kazdin, French, Unis, Esveldt-Dawson, & Sherick, 1983; Marciano & Kazdin, 1994). Since feelings of hopelessness dominate their lives, they experience a vicious downward cycle in which self-defeating negative thoughts become pervasive and impair performance at school and home. As performance deteriorates, they perceive more failure, receive, and even seek, further negative feedback (Joiner, Katz, & Lew, 1997). These outcomes maintain their low self-opinion and view of an inability to change, which lead to further impairments in functioning.

Their pessimistic outlook also places them at greater risk for depressive symptoms, especially in response to stressful life events (Robinson, Garber, & Hilsman, 1995; Rudolph et al., in press). Since their pessimism may continue after remission of depressive symptoms, they remain at risk for future depressive episodes (Gotlib, Lewinsohn, Seeley, Rohde, & Redner, 1993).

We will return to the role of cognitive disturbances in depression in a later section on cognitive theories.

Negative Self-Esteem

Eeyore, the old grey Donkey, stood by the side of the stream and looked at himself in the water.

"Pathetic," he said. "That's what it is. Pathetic."

—A. A. Milne, Winnie-the-Pooh (1926)

Farah
Never Good Enough

15-year-old Farah's mother says that Farah is a "model daughter" who is near the top of her class, active in school activities, and extremely popular. Her mother is concerned about "how hard Farah is on herself, thinking that she has to be perfect." If Farah doesn't get the highest grade on a test, she won't allow herself to see her friends for a week, and spends most of the time in her room studying. Farah acknowledges that she sets very high standards for herself and if she fails to meet these standards becomes extremely self-critical and self-punitive. She has even slapped herself in the face after what she saw as academic "failure" (getting an A— rather than an A). Farah's accomplishments bring her little satisfaction, and any perceived failure leads to immediate self-condemnation. Farah's overall self-worth is low and her sense of self, which is based on competency in academic achievement, is highly vulnerable.

Almost all youngsters with depression experience negative self-esteem (Mitchell et al., 1988; Renouf & Harter, 1990). In fact, low self-esteem is the symptom that seems most specifically related to depression in adolescents (Lewinsohn et al., 1997). Self-esteem in youngsters with depression is also highly reactive to daily life events, and such daily fluctuations in self-esteem appear to be related to depression following exposure to major life stresses (R. E. Roberts & Gotlib, 1997). Thus, both low self-esteem and unstable self-esteem seem to play an important role in depression.

Since physical appearance and approval from peers are especially important as sources of self-esteem for most adolescents, perceived incompetence in these areas may heighten the risk for depression. The fact that self-esteem problems in adolescent girls are often related to a negative body image may partly contribute to their higher risk for depression (Hankin & Abramson, 2001; Petersen, Sarigiani, & Kennedy, 1991).

An interesting developmental model of self-esteem and depression hypothesizes that children seek and receive feedback from others about their competence or incompetence in several domains: academics, social relations, sports, conduct, and physical appearance. Self-views are constructed from this feedback, and the outcome may be a varied and positive self-view leading to optimism, energy, and enthusiasm. Or it may be a narrow and negative self-view leading to pessimism, a sense of helplessness, and possibly, depression (Jordan & Cole, 1996; Seroczynski, Cole, & Maxwell, 1997). Youngsters whose self-views are negative and narrowly focused in one domain—for example, in academics—may show instability in their self-esteem because they lack alternative compensatory areas of functioning—for example, sports or social relations). This may make them vulnerable to developing depression when faced with stress in their primary domain (Jordan & Cole, 1996).

Social and Peer Problems

Youngsters who are depressed have few friends or close relationships, feel lonely and isolated, and feel that others do not like them (which, unfortunately, often becomes a reality) (Rudolph et al., in press). Those who report poor friendships at the time of referral have a reduced likelihood of recovery from depression (Goodyer, Herbert, Tamplin, Secher, & Pearson, 1997). Even when youngsters recover from their depression, they continue to experience some social impairment (Kovacs & Goldston, 1991).

Other than dysphoric mood, social withdrawal is the symptom that most distinguishes youngsters with depression from those with other disorders (Goodyer & Cooper, 1993; Kovacs, 1987). They often spend significant amounts of time alone, show little interest in seeing friends, and engage in few activities. Their social withdrawal may reflect an inability to maintain social interactions, which is possibly related to negative, irritable, and aggressive behavior toward others, and deficits in initiating conversations or making friends (Altmann & Gotlib, 1988). These factors can seriously interfere with social development. Thus, youngsters with depression may fail to experience the social exchanges that lead to effective

social skills and healthy social relationships (Kovacs, 1997; Kovacs & Goldston, 1991).

Youngsters who are depressed use ineffective styles of coping in social situations. For example, they use less active and problem-focused coping, and more passive, avoidant, ruminative, or emotion-focused coping (Hammen & Rudolph, 2003). Depressed teens may also make poor choices in dealing with social problems, such as turning to alcohol or drugs in response to a break-up with a boy- or girlfriend. In the words of Page, age 17:

I was so unhappy that I didn't care about myself—even about being safe. I was out drinking a lot, doing a lot of pot. Sometimes I would just black out and not know what was happening. One night I think a bunch of guys had sex with me when I passed out, I don't know. I never remembered anything, it was all hearsay the next day. I made some really bad boyfriend choices. I would date guys who reinforced my view of myself as ugly, stupid, and uncool. I dropped my preppy boyfriend and started dating a 20-year-old guy who was living in his own apartment and playing in a band. He had tattoos on his arms and stomach. I would date guys just so I could get a ride, even though I didn't like them. I would pick boyfriends who were depressed or ones that my parents really didn't like." (From "I Did Not Want to Live," by Sabrina Solin, 1995. *Seventeen,* April 1, 1995, pp. 154–156, 176. Copyright © 1995 by Primedia Corp. Reprinted by permission.)

Interestingly, the basic understanding required for appropriate social relations appears to be relatively intact in youngsters with depression. They are generally capable of providing cognitive solutions to interpersonal problems and doing as well as others on tasks of social cognition (Kovacs & Goldston, 1991). However, as with Page, their deficits in social behavior are in sharp contrast to their social understanding.

Family Problems

Youngsters with depression experience poor relationships and conflict with their parents and siblings (Chiariello & Orvaschel, 1995). They report feeling socially isolated from their families and prefer to be alone rather than with them (Larson, Raffaelli, Richards, Ham, & Jewell, 1990). In family situations, the child's social isolation may not be a social skill deficit, but rather a reflection of the child's desire to avoid conflict. Family relationship difficulties have been found to persist, even when children are no longer depressed (Giaconia et al., 1994).

During interactions they may be quite negative toward their parents, and their parents in turn may respond in a negative, dismissing, or harsh manner (Coyne, Downey, & Boergers, 1992). When repeated over time, these interactions may adversely affect the family relationships. Children with depression who are irritable, unresponsive, and unaffectionate provide little positive reinforcement for their parents, and frustrate their parent's desire for satisfaction in the parenting role (Kovacs, 1997). Importantly, family conflict and perceptions of negative parenting have been shown to mediate the influence of maternal depression on child depression, and directly affect their children's social competence and stressors (Rudolph et al., in press).

Suicide

Carla
"It Became Too Much"

Carla, age 12, was admitted to the intensive care unit unconscious and unstable after ingesting eight of her mother's 50-mg Elavil™ tablets, an unknown quantity of antidepressants, and approximately 20 tablets of Tylenol 3™. This suicide attempt, her first, came after arguing with her father over chores and restrictions imposed because her grades were so bad. Carla said she went to the medicine cabinet and ingested everything she could find because "it became too much" and she "did not want to live." For the previous month, she had displayed a noticeable change of mood, behaving with more instability and depression, feeling worthless and hopeless. In this period she had lost her appetite and had dropped two dress sizes. She increasingly had isolated herself, staying alone in her room. Her school performance, for which her father had restricted her, had declined from B's the previous term to D's. (From *Adolescent Suicide: Assessment and Intervention*, by A. L. Berman and D. A. Jobes, 1991, p.144. Copyright © 1991 by the American Psychological Association. Reprinted by permission of the author.)

Carla's case illustrates the profound feelings of hopelessness, helplessness, and despair that often lead a youngster with depression to attempt suicide. Most youngsters with depression report suicidal thinking, and between 16% and 30% who think about killing themselves actually attempt it (Kovacs, Goldston, & Gatsonis, 1993). Drug overdose and wrist cutting are the most common methods for adolescents who attempt suicide. For children who complete suicide the most common methods are firearms (57%), hanging or suffocation (28.4%), and poisoning or overdose (7.6%) (CDC, 2002).

The link between depression, suicidal behavior, and completed suicide is undeniable, strong, and sobering (Beautrais, 2003; Pfeffer, 2002). Although suicidal ideation (e.g., thinking about killing oneself) is common across many different types of disorders, actual suicide attempts seem to be specific to depression (see Box 8.1). In one 7 to

---

A Closer Look

BOX 8.1 Depressive Disorder Is Associated with Suicide Thoughts and Suicide Attempts. Teri: What's the Use?

> What's the use?
> I look ~~erou~~ around here and all I see,
> Is a school and a world that could do without me.
> I've gotten here but only by fate.
> My death, I'm sure, will not come late.
> I try each day to see the use of being here.
> There is none.
> I try to find a meaning,
> But the wars have been fought, my battle is yet to come.
> When I close my eyes the pain goes.
> When I open them again the pain. snows.
> I try to not cry aloud,
> Wouldn't matter anyway I'm lost in this crowd.
> You can pretend I don't live,
> But I'll keep living 'till my life gives.

Teri's note
Source: Berman & Jobes, 1991.

Teri, age 15, had been depressed since her father died when she was 11. According to her mother, over the past 14 months her behavior had gone from moody to sullen. She had disobeyed restrictions imposed as punishments, and had run away from home on several occasions. She labeled herself as "stupid," spoke and wrote often of death and suicide (see accompanying note). On three occasions she had cut her wrists, albeit only superficially. Her school performance had declined and she spoke now of hating school. Her peer associations were almost exclusively with other alienated teens, described by her as "punks and other anarchists."

Source: From *Adolescent Suicide: Assessment and Intervention*, by A. L. Berman and D. A. Jobes, 1991, p. 95. Copyright ©1991 by the American Psychological Association. Reprinted by permission of the author and the publisher.

9-year follow-up of children with psychiatric disorders, 84% of all suicide attempts were found to occur for depressive disorders (Shaffer, Gould, et al., 1996).

About 30% of youngsters who are clinically depressed attempt suicide by 17 years of age (N. D. Ryan et al., 1987). Unfortunately, about one-half of them eventually make further attempts (Kovacs et al., 1993). The suicide attempts of youngsters with depression almost never occur during times when they are symptom-free—90% or more have depressive features at the time of their suicidal episode. Finally, among youngsters who kill themselves, the odds of having major depression are 27 times higher than among controls (Brent et al., 1993; Shaffer, Gould, et al., 1996).

In general, young females with depression show more suicidal ideation and attempt suicide about 9 times more often than young males. However, since girls typically don't use guns, they are usually less successful in completing suicide than boys (Goldston, Daniel, & Arnold, in press). Ages 13 and 14 are peak periods for a first suicide attempt by youngsters with depression. In adolescents with depression, suicide attempts double during the teen years, but show an abrupt decline after age 17 or 18. It is possible that as young people mature, they are better able to tolerate their negative mood states, and acquire more resources for coping, thus making it less likely that they will attempt suicide during periods of sadness (Borowsky, Ireland, & Resnick, 2001; Kovacs et al., 1993).

SECTION SUMMARY

- Youngsters with depression have normal intelligence, although certain symptoms such as difficulty concentrating, loss of interest, and slowness of thought may negatively affect intellectual functioning.

- They perform more poorly than others in school, score lower on standard achievement tests, and have lower levels of grade attainment.

- They often experience deficits and distortions in their thinking, including negative beliefs, attributions of failure, and self-critical automatic negative thoughts.

- Almost all youngsters with depression experience low or unstable self-esteem.

- Youngsters with depression have few friends and close relationships, feel lonely and isolated, and feel that others do not like them.

- They experience poor relations and conflict with their parents and siblings, who in turn may respond in a negative, dismissing, or harsh manner.

- Most youngsters with depression report suicidal thinking, and between 16% and 30% who think about killing themselves actually attempt it.

Theories of Depression

Many theories have been proposed to explain the onset and course of depression. Until recently, however, most were developed to explain depression in adults, then directly applied to children with minimal regard for developmental differences (Garber & Horowitz, 2002). In the sections that follow we consider several of these theories. Keep in mind, however, that depression is likely a final, common pathway for interacting influences that predispose a child to develop the disorder (Hammen & Rudolph, 2003). No one theory can explain all the forms of depressive disorders and differences in symptoms and severity within the same disorder. An overview of the primary theories of depression is presented in Table 8.3.

Table 8.3
Overview of Theories of Depression

Psychodynamic	Introjection of the lost object; anger turned inward; excessive severity of the superego; loss of self-esteem
Attachment	Insecure early attachments; distorted internal working models of self and others
Behavioral	Loss of reinforcement or quality of reinforcement; deficits in skills needed to obtain reinforcement
Cognitive	Depressive mindset; distorted or maladaptive cognitive structures, processes, and products; negative view of self, world, and future; poor problem-solving ability
Self-Control	Problems in organizing behavior toward long-term goals; deficits in self-monitoring, self-evaluation, and self-reinforcement
Interpersonal	Impaired interpersonal functioning related to grief over loss; role dispute and conflict, role transition, interpersonal deficit, single parenting; social withdrawal; interaction between mood and interpersonal events
Socioenvironmental	Stressful life circumstances and daily hassles as vulnerability factors; social support, coping, and appraisal as protective factors
Neurobiological	Neurochemical and receptor abnormalities; neurophysiological abnormalities; neuroendocrine abnormalities

---

Source: Adapted from "A Developmental Cognitive Model of Unipolar Major Depression," by D. J. A. Dozois, unpublished manuscript. Adapted by permission of the author.

Psychodynamic

Early psychodynamic theories viewed depression as the conversion of aggressive instinct into depressive affect. Depression is presumed to result from the loss of a love object that is loved ambivalently. This loss can be actual, in the case of the death of a parent, or symbolic, as a result of emotional deprivation, rejection, or inadequate parenting. The individual's subsequent rage toward the love object is then turned against the self. Since children and adolescents were believed to have inadequate development of the superego or conscience, the hostility directed against internalized love objects that have disappointed or abandoned them does not produce guilt, so they do not become depressed (Bemporad, 1994; Poznanski, 1979). The fact that depression occurs in many youngsters who do not experience loss or rejection, and doesn't occur in many children who do, casts doubt on the psychodynamic model. Furthermore, contrary to this theory, many children do experience clinical depression.

Attachment

Attachment theory focuses on parental separation and disruption of an attachment bond as predisposing factors for depression. John Bowlby hypothesized that a child confronted with unresponsive and emotionally unavailable care-giving goes through a typical sequence involving protest, despair, and detachment (Bowlby, 1961). A parent's consistent failure to meet the child's needs is associated with the development of an insecure attachment, a view of self as unworthy and unloved, and a view of others as threatening or undependable. These factors may place the child at risk for later depression, particularly in the context of stressful interpersonal relationships (Rudolph, Hammen, & Burge, 1997). Attachment relationships also serve to regulate biological and behavioral systems related to emotion, for example, when a secure attachment can be used to reduce distress. Thus, insecure attachments may lead to difficulties in regulating emotion, which also may become a risk factor for later depression. In support of this theory, children with insecure attachments are more likely than children with secure attachments to display symptoms of depression (e.g., Toth & Cicchetti, 1996), and children with MDD are more likely to experience disturbances in attachment than children without MDD (D. Stein et al., 2000).

Behavioral

Behavioral views emphasize the importance of learning, environmental consequences, and skills and deficits during the onset and maintenance of depression. Depression is related to a *lack of response-contingent positive reinforcement* (Lewinsohn, 1974). This lack of positive reinforcement may occur for three reasons. First, a youngster may be unable to experience available reinforcement, often due to interfering anxiety. Second, changes in the environment, such as the loss of a significant person in the child's life, may result in a lack of availability of rewards. Finally, a youngster may lack the skills needed to have rewarding and satisfying social relationships.

Children may also receive sympathy for their sadness, which produces the desired attention and concern. However, this sympathy is usually short-lived because even people who care about the youngster begin to avoid him or her. This reduction in attention may then lead to withdrawal, functional impairment, and heightened feelings of depression. Few studies have tested specific behavioral hypotheses with children, and this model seems incomplete in the light of what is known about other factors that may lead to a vulnerability to depression. Nevertheless, the behavioral model highlights the importance of learning processes in the emergence, expression, and outcome of depression in young people.

Cognitive

Cognitive theories focus on the relation between negative thinking and mood (Hammen, 1992). The underlying assumption is that how young people view themselves and their world will influence their mood and behavior. A variety of negative cognitions, attributions, misperceptions, and deficiencies in cognitive problem-solving skills are related to depression in young people (Kaslow et al., 2000). Cognitive theories emphasize **depressogenic cognitions**, which are the negative perceptual and attributional styles and beliefs associated with depressive symptoms.

Depression-prone individuals tend to make **internal, stable, and global attributions** to explain the causes of negative events. In other words, when something bad happens, they think they are responsible (internal attribution), the reason they are to blame won't change over time (stable attribution), and the reason that something bad happened applies to most things they do and in most situations (global attribution) (Abramson, Seligman, & Teasdale, 1978). In contrast they attribute positive events to something outside themselves (external), which is not likely to happen again (unstable), and is seen as unique to this event (specific). A *negative attributional style* results in the individual's taking personal blame for negative events in his or her life and leads to helplessness and avoidance of these events in the future. Helplessness may in turn lead to hopelessness about the future, which promotes further depression (Abramson, Metalsky, & Alloy, 1989).

The cognitive model developed by Aaron Beck (1967) proposes that depressed individuals make negative interpretations about life events because they use biased and negative beliefs as interpretive filters for understanding these events. Depressed individuals show cognitive problems in three areas.

First, they display *information-processing biases,* or errors in their thinking in specific situations, called *negative automatic thoughts.* These often include thoughts of physical and social threat, personal failure, and hostility (Schniering & Rapee, 2004). They may selectively attend to negative information, assume blame for negative events, maximize and exaggerate negative events, and minimize positive events. They also assign negative labels to events, and then react emotionally to the label rather than the event. For example:

> EVENT: Child didn't receive an invitation to Henry's party.
> LABEL: "I didn't receive an invitation because Henry doesn't like me. Nobody likes me."
> EMOTIONAL REACTION: Unhappiness and depression.

Second, depression is believed to be associated with a negative outlook in the following three areas, referred to as the **negative cognitive triad** (see Figure 8.2).

- Negative views about *oneself* (e.g., "I'm no good," "I'm boring")
- Negative views about the *world* (e.g., "They're no good," "It's too hard")
- Negative views about the *future* (e.g., "It's always going to be this bad," "I'll never graduate")

These negative views maintain feelings of helplessness, undermine the youngster's mood and energy level, and are related to the child's severity of depression (Stark, Schmidt, & Joiner, 1996).

Third, depressed youngsters have **negative cognitive schemata,** which are stable structures in memory that guide information processing, including self-critical beliefs and attitudes. These schemata are rigid and resistant to change even in the face of contradictory evidence, and may heighten the youngster's sensitivity to depression, especially when activated by stress.

Applying cognitive theories to depression in young people raises questions about the cognitive capacities of children at various stages of development, and the development and stability of cognitive structures that may be involved in their depressive thinking (Gotlib & Sommerfeld, 1999). A well-developed sense of self and a time perspective for the future are needed to experience depression; these cognitive processes are still developing in children. In addition, many of the cognitive errors and distortions discussed so far, such as illogical thinking or faulty attributions, are normal ways of thinking in young children!

Cognitive errors and distortions also must be considered in relation to the child's developing sense of personal

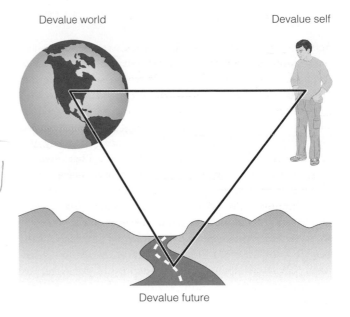

Devalue world Devalue self

Devalue future

Figure 8.2. The Negative Cognitive Triad: Depression is related to a devaluation of self, the world, and the future.
Source: Based on D. Murdoch, 1997.

competence (Seroczynski et al., 1997). For example, during the transition from preoperational to concrete operational thinking during middle childhood, children begin to develop the capacity to reflect on their own thinking (metacognition). Prior to this age, children can make social comparisons, but not as a basis for making self-evaluations. With the emergence of concrete operational thinking, however, children begin to compare themselves to others in a self-evaluative way. Also around this time depression begins to be characterized by negative self-esteem as well as mood disturbance (Rehm & Carter, 1990). Thus, a vulnerability for depressive thinking may begin with emerging views of personal competence during middle childhood and, once developed, may remain relatively stable throughout adolescence (Garber, Weiss, & Shanley, 1993; McGrath & Repetti, 2002).

Although higher rates of negative thinking are found in youngsters with depression, there are still many unanswered questions about the relation between cognition and depression (Kaslow et al., 2000). More information is needed about how negative cognitions develop. Are they the result of parental rejection and negative parenting practices? Is there a relation between maternal and child cognitions, as suggested by the relationship between mothers' and children's negative thinking (Stark, Schmidt, & Joiner, 1996)? How does a cognitive vulnerability for depression interact with stress to result in depression (Hammen & Rudolph, 2003)? Longitudinal studies are needed to answer these and other questions concerning the role of cognition in the development of depression in young people.

Other Theories

Self-control theories view youngsters with depression as having difficulty organizing their behavior in relation to long-term goals, and display deficits in self-monitoring, self-evaluation, and self-reinforcement. As a result, they selectively attend to negative events and to the immediate consequences of their behavior. These youngsters set excessively high standards for performance, make negative causal attributions, administer insufficient self-rewards, and use excessive self-punishment. Research suggests that children with depression display some of these deficits, although findings are limited (Rehm & Sharp, 1996).

Interpersonal models view disruptions in interpersonal relationships, especially with family and peers, as the basis for the onset and maintenance of depression (Hammen, 1999). The behaviors of a depressed youngster are unpleasant to others, leading family members and others to become annoyed and frustrated. As the youngster becomes more aware of how others are reacting, he or she feels even more needy, then unthinkingly and annoyingly seeks excessive reassurance, which in turn leads to further interpersonal rejection (Joiner, 1999). Interpersonal models also propose that the child's depression may serve a function in the family, for example, to reduce conflict between parents.

Socioenvironmental models examine the relationship between stressful life events and depression. Some life events related to the onset of depression are social disadvantage, unemployment, single-parent status, large family, and poor social support (Compas, Grant, & Ey, 1994). Stressful life events may be linked to depression in several ways (Biederman & Spencer, 1999b). First, depression can be a direct reaction to the occurrence of stressful life events, such as the loss of a parent. Second, the impact of stress may be moderated by individual risk factors, such as genetic risk. This is referred to as the **diathesis-stress model of depression** because the occurrence of depression depends on the interaction between the youngster's personal vulnerability (diathesis) and life stress. Third, negative environmental events may be internalized as negative cognitions, which then predispose the child to develop depression. Finally, depression may result in impairments in functioning that generate stressful life circumstances that in turn lead to depressive reactions (Hammen & Rudolph, 2003; Rudolph et al., 2000).

Neurobiological models of depression in young people focus on genetic vulnerabilities and neurobiological processes. Several neurobiological abnormalities have been identified, although findings are far less consistent for children than for adults (NIMH, 2003). We consider possible biologic factors in the next section on causes.

SECTION SUMMARY

- Psychodynamic theories presume that depression results from the actual or symbolic loss of a love object, and view depression as the conversion of aggressive instinct into depressive affect.

- Behavioral views emphasize the importance of learning, environmental consequences (particularly a lack of response-contingent reinforcement), and skills and deficits during the onset and maintenance of depression.

- Cognitive theories of depression focus on the relation between negative thinking and mood, with the underlying assumption that how young people view themselves and their world will influence their mood and behavior.

- Other theories of depression have emphasized the role of deficits in self-control, interpersonal disturbances, stressful life events, and genetic and neurobiological processes.

Causes of Depression

In light of the many vulnerability, risk, and protective factors that have been implicated, an integrative framework is necessary to account for depression in young people, and for its nonoccurrence in the presence of risk (Hammen & Rudolph, 2003). The framework presented in Figure 8.3 highlights possible causes of depression in young people and the interplay among genetic, neurobiological, family, cognitive, emotional, interpersonal, and environmental factors. Given these many interacting influences, multiple pathways are likely (Eaves, Silberg, & Erkanli, 2003).

Within this framework, genetic risk influences neurobiological processes, and is reflected in an early temperament characterized by oversensitivity to negative stimuli, high negative emotionality, and a disposition to feeling anxious (Clark, Watson, & Mineka, 1994). These early dispositions increase exposure to and are shaped by experiences within the family, and continue to exert influence throughout development. Core beliefs about self and others develop as a result of experiences within the family. Parenting that is insensitive, disengaged, or rejecting may lead to a view of self as incompetent, other people as threatening or unresponsive, and relationships as negative and unpredictable. Negative family experiences may also create an inconsistent emotional and social environment, which makes it difficult for the child to effectively regulate emotions and interpersonal behavior and to cope with stress (Compas, Connor-Smith, Saltzman, Thomsen, & Wadsworth, 2001).

Cognitive, emotional, and interpersonal problems may lead directly to depression. Or, they may elicit conflict, rejection by others, and social isolation, which will eventually lead to depression. In other instances, negative beliefs, poor social relationships, and difficulty in regulating emotions may create a vulnerability to develop depression when confronted with life stress. In any of these scenarios the child's depression may then interfere with future development by further disrupting interpersonal relationships, damaging existing competencies, producing

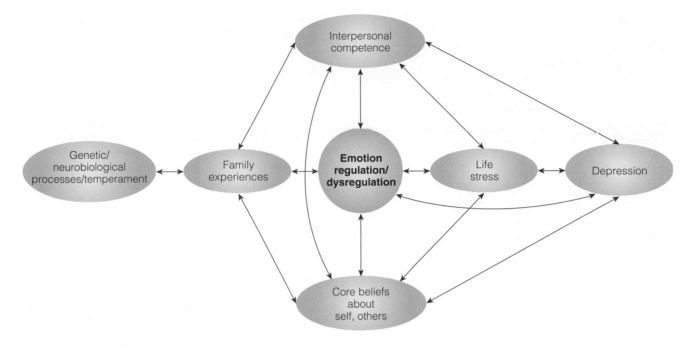

Figure 8.3. A developmental framework for depression in young people.

further difficulties in regulating emotions, creating additional stress, and confirming the child's already negative views about self and others (Hammen & Rudolph, 2003).

In the sections that follow we examine several of these possible causal influences for depression.

Genetic and Family Risk

Findings from twin studies suggest a moderate genetic influence on depression in community samples of children and adolescents, with heritability estimates ranging from 35% to 75% across studies (Eley, 1999; Glowinski et al., 2003). Twin studies or adoption studies of youngsters diagnosed with MDD have not been conducted, thus the extent to which clinical depression in young people is a genetically influenced disorder is not known (Rice, Harold, & Thapar, 2002). Nevertheless, there is consistent evidence that MDD in young people is familial. Children with a parent who suffered from depression as a child are 14 times more likely than controls to become depressed themselves before the age of 13 (Weissman, Warner, Wickramaratne, & Prusoff, 1988). The presence of MDD also increases the chances of other internalizing and externalizing disorders in both the child and family members, suggesting that there is also a family liability for comorbid problems (Burcusa, Iacono, & McGue, 2003).

Children of parents with depression have about 2–3 times the risk of having depression compared with children of parents having no psychiatric disorders (Beardslee, Versage, & Gladstone, 1998; Weissman, Warner, Wickramaratne, Moreau, & Olfson, 1997). The child's risk for depression is even higher when both parents have a mood disorder. Children of depressed parents also have an earlier age of onset for their depression (by about 3 years), and are more likely to show an onset before puberty than children of nondepressed parents (Weissman et al., 1997). This is a significant factor, because a family history of MDD is most likely associated with recurrence of MDD, and a continuation of MDD into adulthood for children with an onset of MDD before puberty (Klein, Lewinsohn, Rohde, Seeley, & Durbin, 2002; Wickramaratne, Greenwald, & Weissman, 2000).

The lifetime prevalence of MDD in mothers of children with MDD is also high, about 50% to 75% (Kovacs, 1997). A family history of depression is also greater in first-degree relatives of children with MDD than in children without MDD (Wickramaratne et al., 2000).

Although depression in young people is a family disorder, the extent to which transmission in families is genetic, psychosocial, or both is not yet known. Causal influences may also differ with development, with support for a greater role for shared environmental influences for depression during childhood, in contrast to a greater genetic influence during adolescence (Scourfield et al., 2003). In general, family and twin studies suggest that a vulnerability to negative affect may be inherited, and that certain environmental stressors may be required for these vulnerabilities to result in depression (Eley & Stevenson, 2000; Rice, Harold, & Thapar, 2003). In support of genetic vulnerability, a recent study found that individuals with abnormalities in the serotonin transporter (5-HTT) gene displayed more depressive symptoms, diagnosable depression, and suicidality in relation to stressful life events than those who did not (Caspi et al., 2003).

Neurobiological Influences

Although we can't point to one part of the brain that causes a young person to be depressed, abnormalities in the structure and function of several brain regions have been implicated. Brain scan studies (mostly with adults) have identified multiple abnormalities in limbic and prefrontal cortical brain structures (Davidson, Pizzagalli, & Nitschke, 2002). In general, brain activity has been found to be less active in regions of the brain associated with attention and sensory processes, but more active than normal in regions involved in recognizing and regulating emotions, mediating stress responses, and learning and recalling emotion-arousing memories. For example, the amygdala may overstimulate brain structures involved in forming certain types of memories, perhaps accounting for the tendency of depressed youngsters to ruminate on past negative life events. Overactivity of the amygdala may also affect the recognition and consolidation of social stimuli (e.g, faces, tone of voice) so that ordinary interpersonal events are seen or recalled as aversive or emotionally arousing (NIMH, 2003).

The hippocampus, one of the brain's memory centers, has also been implicated in depression. Parts of the hippocampus are involved in recognizing the contexts for reward or danger, and brain scan studies of depressed adults have found a reduced hippocampal size. This reduction may result from hyperactivity of the corticotrophin releasing hormone (CRH), or other disturbances in mechanisms of the HPA-axis. Because of abnormalities in the hippocampus, individuals with depression may experience a constant state of anxiety and have difficulty recognizing situations that are safe (Davidson et al., 2002).

Other studies into the neurobiological correlates of depression in young people have focused on the HPA-axis, sleep architecture, growth hormone, and the brain neurotransmitters dopamine, serotonin, and norepinephrine, which are widely spread throughout brain circuits thought to underlie mood disorders (Armitage et al., 2000; Birmaher & Ryan, 1999). However, studies of these neurobiological correlates in children are few in number, and the findings are far less consistent than for adults (Birmaher et al., 1996b; Kaufman, Martin, King, & Charney, 2001). For example, although elevated HPA-axis reactivity is one of the most consistent findings for depressed adults, findings for children and adolescents are much less clear. One study, for example, found that depressed preschoolers showed altered patterns of HPA-axis activity relative to psychiatric and normal controls, but not the types of elevations in activity that were predicted (Luby, Heffelfinger, Mrakotsky, Brown, Hessler, & Spitznagel, 2003).

Although HPA-axis and other neurobiological findings in children and adolescents are inconsistent as compared with adults, there is strong interest in the impact of early exposure to stress on later negative moods. Since brain structure and function are under construction in children, failure to find consistent HPA abnormalities such as those for adults does not preclude the importance of these systems. As we discussed in Chapter 7, mounting evidence suggests that early adversity (e.g., prenatal stress, harsh or neglectful parenting) may produce HPA-axis abnormalities (e.g., alterations in corticotrophin releasing hormone (CRH) circuits), which sensitize the child to later stress, thus increasing the risk for developing depression (Goodman, 2002; Heim & Nemeroff, 2001; Huizink, Mulder, & Buitelaar, 2004). Infants of depressed mothers show higher levels of salivary cortisol (the stress hormone) and less frontal lobe electrical activity than infants of mothers without depression (G. Dawson, Frey, Panagiotides, Osterling, & Hessl, 1997). Like higher levels of cortisol, atypical frontal lobe activity may also be a vulnerability factor for negative emotional states (G. Dawson et al., 1999). These and other findings suggest that interactions between mothers and their infants may produce biochemical and neurological changes that form and perpetuate a lasting basis for depressive disorder (Cytryn & McKnew, 1996; Post et al., 1996).

In summary, findings from studies of neurobiological correlates suggest that youngsters with depression may have a heightened sensitivity to stress. Repeated neuroendocrine activation related to stress may increase youngsters' susceptibility to chronic depressive symptoms, which in turn may lead to further extreme biological activation and psychosocial stress (Birmaher et al., 1996b). Preliminary neurobiological findings are suggestive, but additional brain scan studies will be needed to clarify the specific neural circuits underlying depression in young people (Kaufman et al., 2001).

Family Influences

"I was always able to explain away my daughter's symptoms," says the mother of a 12-year-old. "When she was 10 and fought with me about everything, I just wrote it off as preadolescent hissy fits. When she dropped out of gymnastics—which had been her raison d'etre—and started losing weight, I told myself she was just searching for a new identity. But when her best friend came to me and told me that my daughter was talking about suicide, I was forced to face the truth. I keep blaming myself. What did I do to cause this depression? What could I have done to prevent it?"

(From "Childhood Depression," by K. Levine, pp. 42–45. *Parents*, October 1995. Copyright © 1995 by Gruner & Jahr USA Publishing. Reprinted by permission of the author.)

Several parent and family characteristics are associated with depression in young people. One way of examining these characteristics looks at families of children with depression; the second way considers families of parents who are depressed.

When Children Are Depressed Families of children with depression display more critical and punitive behavior toward their depressed child than toward other children in the family. Compared to families of youngsters without depression, these families display more anger and conflict, greater use of control, poorer communication, more overinvolvement, and less warmth and support (Chiariello & Orvaschel, 1995; Lewinsohn, Roberts, et al., 1994; Stein et al., 2000). They often experience high levels of stress, disorganization, marital discord, and a lack of social support (Messer & Gross, 1995; Slavin & Rainer, 1990). Youngsters with depression describe their families as less cohesive and more disengaged than do youngsters without depression (Kashani, Allan, Dahlmeier, Rezvani, & Reid, 1995).

Research points strongly to the link between childhood depression and family dysfunction. One longitudinal study found that less support and more conflict in the family were associated with more depressive symptoms in adolescents both concurrently and prospectively over a 1-year period. In contrast, more depressive symptoms did not predict a worsening of family relationships over the same time period. Thus, family problems precede and may be directly related to the development of depressive symptoms (Sheeber, Hops, Alpert, Davis, & Andrews, 1997).

When Parents Are Depressed

Mrs. D.	Mrs. D. is depressed and has been helpless and needy for most of her 5-year-old daughter Maria's life. She moves ever so slowly to prepare breakfast for Maria and herself. Wringing her hands, she
Not Up to Mothering	

pays little attention to events around her. Maria has been tugging at her mother for some time, apparently wanting food. Mrs. D. mumbles something, sobs continuously, and wipes tears from her cheek as she moves between the cupboard and kitchen table. Maria persists in trying to gain her mother's attention, and finally Mrs. D. hugs her and strokes her hair. At first Maria pulls back; then she snuggles against her mother's legs. Finally Mrs. D. fills a bowl with cereal, and she and Maria sit down to eat in total silence, during which Mrs. D. looks sadly at her daughter. Deep bouts of depression periodically incapacitate Mrs. D., and any problem that Maria has sends her to bed. Mostly, Maria is left on her own to handle problems. (Adapted from Radke-Yarrow & Zahn-Waxler, 1990)

Depression interferes with the parent's ability to meet the needs of the child (Radke-Yarrow, 1998). Mothers who suffer from depression often create a child-rearing environment teeming with negative mood, irritability, helplessness, and unpredictable displays of affection. They also display less energy in stimulating play, less consistent discipline, less involvement, poor communication, lack of affection, and more criticism and resentment of their children than well mothers (Kovacs, 1997; Reissland, Shepherd, & Herrera, 2003). High levels of marital conflict, family discord, and stress may also be present in the home when a parent is depressed (Beardslee & Wheelock, 1994; Kaslow et al., 1994).

Depressed mothers also differ from one another in their styles of interaction; some are more withdrawn and others are more intrusive. These differences are important because they may be associated with different child outcomes. For example, as early as infancy, children of depressed mothers display atypical patterns of jealousy, with their avoidance and "tuning out" associated with an intrusive maternal style, and a heightened sociability toward strangers associated with a withdrawn maternal style (Hart, Jones, Field, 2003). Thus, the offspring of mothers with depression attempt to cope with the unpredictability of their environment in different ways, which are often maladaptive and show reactions ranging from aggressive behavior to withdrawal, failure to thrive, school refusal, depression, even suicidal behavior (Brennan et al., 2000; Nelson, Hammen, Brennan, & Ullman, 2003; Klimes-Dougan et al., 1999). Like Maria, they must take care of themselves and learn how to handle their own problems. It is not surprising that infants and toddlers of mothers with depression show emotional delays, separation difficulties, and insecure attachments (Field, 2000). Children of mothers with depression tend to be self-critical and have difficulties regulating their own emotions. As a result, the children are ill equipped to cope effectively with stressful events, which may subsequently place them at risk for depression and other impairments (S. H. Goodman & Gotlib, 2002).

Follow-up studies of these children confirm the risks associated with growing up in a family with a depressed parent (Gotlib & Goodman, 1999). One study found adolescents of depressed mothers to be twice as likely to develop a diagnosable depression by age 15, with the adolescent's risk for depression increasing with the chronicity of the mother's depression (Hammen & Brennan, 2003). Over a 10-year period, children of depressed parents not only had increased rates of MDD, particularly before puberty, but also higher rates of phobias, panic disorder, and alcohol dependence (Weissman et al., 1997). Relative to controls, offspring of depressed parents received more outpatient treatment over 10 years, and had poorer overall functioning in work, family, and marital relationships. The findings from this study are sobering in documenting the serious long-term negative outcomes and impairments in the children whose parents suffer from depression.

On a more positive note, low levels of parental psychological control and maternal overinvolvement, and high levels of maternal warmth have been found to predict better outcomes in children of depressed mothers (Brennan, Brocque, & Hammen, 2003). Such findings suggest that interventions that focus on parent-child relationship qualities could serve to reduce negative outcomes in children of depressed mothers.

Several issues regarding the relationship between child depression, maternal depression, and family factors need to be considered. First, the kinds of family difficulties we have described are related to many other child disorders, and may not be specific to depression (Downey & Coyne, 1990; Goodyer et al., 1997). Second, it is difficult to know whether family problems are the result of a co-occurring condition such as child conduct problems, or maternal anxiety disorder rather than depression. Third, most studies are correlational, making it impossible to determine the direction of influence. An adverse family environment can lead to depression, but depression may also evoke negative and critical reactions from family members and produce distress in others. Finally, another factor, such as genetic risk, may account for both depression and family disturbances. Some support exists for all these mechanisms of family influence in child depression.

Stressful Life Events

Carline
How Depression Acts

I don't feel depressed all the time. It comes and goes. Usually it takes something to set it off. It could be something big, like when we moved, but anything, no matter how small, can really get to me, and then I start feeling bad and can't do anything. So today things are OK and I don't feel so bad. But tomorrow, or the next day, something might happen, no matter how minor, and I just might not want to get out of bed, or do anything.

Depression is associated with severe stressful life events (Rudolph et al., 2000). These events may include a move to a new neighborhood, a change of schools, a serious accident or family illness, an extreme lack of family resources, a violent family environment, or parental conflict or divorce (Gilman, Kawachi, Fitzmaurice, & Buka, 2003; Goodyer et al., 1997). They may occur alone or in combination with other risk factors, such as a lack of social support or inadequate parental care. At times, nonsevere stressful events, or daily hassles, such as a poor grade on a test, an argument with a parent, criticism from a teacher, a fight with a boyfriend, or a broken date, may also result in depression. Relative to nondepressed young-

sters, those who become depressed experience significantly more severe and nonsevere stressful events in the year preceding their depression—especially events related to romantic relationships, education, relationships with friends or parents, work, and health (Birmaher et al., 1996b). Chronic interpersonal difficulties are especially associated with adolescent depression in the children of depressed mothers (Hammen, Shih, Altman, & Brennan, 2003).

Triggers for depression often involve interpersonal stress or actual or perceived personal losses, such as the death of a loved one, abandonment, rejection, or a threat to one's self-esteem (Eley & Stevenson, 2000; Goodyer, 1999). For example, a recent relationship break-up seems to be an especially significant predictor for first versus later episodes of MDD during adolescence (Monroe, Rohde, Seeley, & Lewinsohn, 1999). Sadness and depression following loss are common. In children ages 5–12 who had recently suffered the most horrible loss, the loss of a parent, all experienced sadness and grief, and about 40% developed major depression (Weller, Weller, Fristad, & Bowes, 1991). Thirty percent of adolescents who had lost a friend or peer through suicide developed a depressive disorder within 6 months following the loss (Brent et al., 1992). Yet depressive disorder is not an inevitable outcome to personal losses—more than 60% of children who experience the loss of a parent or friend do not develop major depression.

Emotion Regulation

Emotion regulation refers to the processes by which emotional arousal is redirected, controlled, or modified to facilitate adaptive functioning (Cicchetti et al., 1991) and refers to the balance maintained among positive, negative, and neutral mood states (Kopp, 1992). Youngsters demonstrate wide differences in regulating their emotions and managing their negative mood states (Keenan, 2000). For example, if a favorite playmate cannot be found, one child may cry and cannot be comforted, another may cry for a short time then find someone else to play with, and another child may look to an adult for comfort. Children's strategies for self-regulation play a crucial role in overcoming, maintaining, or preventing negative emotional states (Garber, Braafladt, & Zeman, 1991). As we have discussed, young children who experience prolonged periods of emotional distress and sadness may have problems regulating negative emotional states, and may be prone to the development of depression (Zahn-Waxler, Klimes-Dougan, & Slattery, 2000).

A variety of skills are necessary to manage one's own emotions. These include recognizing changes in emotion, accurately interpreting the conditions that led to mood change, setting goals to change one's mood, and implementing effective coping responses (Kazdin & Marciano, 1998). Youngsters with depression may show deficits in one or more of these regulatory skills and, as a result, may have difficulty overcoming their negative moods (Sheeber, Allen, Davis, & Sorensen, 2000). They may use avoidance or negative behavior to regulate their distress, rather than more problem-focused and adaptive coping strategies (Garber et al., 1991). Since emotion regulation encompasses neurobiological regulatory processes, acquired behavioral and cognitive strategies, and external resources for coping, depression may result from difficulties in any one or more of these areas (R. A. Thompson, 1994b).

SECTION SUMMARY

- Depression is likely a final common pathway for interacting influences that predispose a child to develop the disorder.

- Family and twin studies suggest that what may be inherited is a vulnerability to depression and anxiety, and that certain environmental stressors may be required to express these disorders.

- Youngsters with depression may experience heightened reactions to stress that increase their vulnerability to depression. Studies of neurobiological correlates have focused on limbic and prefrontal neural circuits, hypothalamic-pituitary-adrenal axis (HPA-axis), sleep architecture, growth hormone, and the neurotransmitters dopamine, serotonin, and norepinephrine.

- Families of children with depression display anger and conflict, greater use of control, less effective communication, more overinvolvement, and less warmth and support than families of children who are not depressed.

- Children of depressed parents experience increased rates of MDD before puberty, and higher rates of phobias, panic disorder, and alcohol dependence as adolescents and adults.

- Depression is associated with severe stressful life events, such as a move to a new neighborhood, the death of a loved one, or a serious accident or family illness.

- Young children who experience prolonged periods of emotional distress and sadness may have problems in regulating their negative emotional states, and may be prone to the development of depression.

Treatment of Depression

Leeta

Feeling Better

Leeta, age 16, sat slumped in her chair. Disheveled and distracted, she answered questions in a vague and unfocused manner. She was admitted to the hospital after she slit her wrists with a knife; she had become despondent, irritable, and out of control at home. Leeta's thoughts and reasoning were distorted. She expressed a pervasive sense of hopelessness and was certain that she would remain in hospitals for the rest of her life.

Fortunately, this was not the case. She became involved in cognitive-behavior therapy that focused on accurate reasoning, a more positive self-image, and ways to lessen family turmoil, and was also treated with antidepressant medication. One year later, Leeta entered our office for a follow-up interview with energy and excitement. "I never thought that I would feel like hanging out with friends and doing things again. It's not that I don't get sad once in a while, but it doesn't take over my whole life." (Adapted from Oster & Montgomery, 1995)

Although the prevalence of depression in young people is about 2% to 8%, each year only about 1% of children in the United States receive outpatient treatment for depression (Olfson, Gameroff, Marcus, & Waslick, 2003). Despite the availability of effective treatments, only 20% to 30% of young people with depression receive help (Lewinsohn et al., 1991). In one study of adolescents who killed themselves, most of whom had a depressive disorder, only 7% had been in treatment prior to their suicide (Brent et al., 1988).

The high comorbidity, associated deficits, and recurrence of depression in children and adolescents require a combination of treatments, with an emphasis on maintaining positive outcomes and preventing relapse (Hammen, Rudolph, Weisz, Rao, & Burge, 1999; Michael & Crowley, 2002). Cognitive-behavioral therapy (CBT), the treatment used with Leeta, has shown the most short- and long-term success, with about 70% of youngsters with depression responding to it (Kaslow & Thompson, 1998; Reinecke, Ryan, & DuBois, 1998). CBT is also more effective than either family therapy or nondirective supportive therapy in treating the symptoms of depression (Brent et al., 1997). In addition, when CBT is used as a maintenance therapy following the remission of depression, it has also been found to reduce the likelihood of relapse (Kroll, Harrington, Jayson, Fraser, & Gowers, 1996). Although it is effective, we don't yet know whether improvements in depression following treatment are the result of changes in the cognitive distortions that CBT is designed to correct (Kolko, Brent, Baugher, Bridge, & Birmaher, 2000).

Tricyclic antidepressant medications (TCAs) have not proven to be nearly as effective for depressed young people as for adults (B. Geller, Reising, Leonard, Riddle, & Walsh, 1999). Newer antidepressants, especially the SSRIs, have proven useful in controlled studies (Elliott & Smiga, 2003), although there are recently voiced concerns about possible serious side effects for some of the SSRIs. Treatments that emphasize increasing parental involve-

Table 8.4
Treatments for Youngsters with Depression

Behavior Therapy	Aims to increase behaviors that elicit positive reinforcement, and reduce punishment from the environment. May involve teaching social and other coping skills, and using anxiety management and relaxation training.
Cognitive Therapy	Focuses on helping the youngster with depression become more aware of pessimistic and negative thoughts, depressogenic beliefs and biases, and casual attributions of self-blame for failure. Once these self-defeating thought patterns are recognized, the child is taught to change from a negative, pessimistic view to a more positive, optimistic one.
Cognitive Behavior Therapy (CBT)	The most common form of psychosocial intervention. Combines elements of behavioral and cognitive therapies in an integrated approach. Attribution retraining may also be used to challenge the youngster's pessimistic beliefs (Jaycox, Reivich, Gillham, & Seligman, 1994).
Interpersonal Therapy	Explores family interactions that maintain depression. Family sessions are supplemented with individual sessions in which youngsters with depression are encouraged to understand their own negative cognitive style and the effects of their depression on others, and to increase pleasant activities with family members and peers (Mufson & Dorta, 2003).
Supportive Therapy	Provides therapeutic support to create a safe environment that allows depressed youngsters to feel connected to and supported by others. Attempts to increase adolescents' self-esteem and to decrease depressive symptoms (Fine, Forth, Gilbert, & Haley, 1991).
Medications	Treats mood disturbances and other symptoms of depression using antidepressants, especially selective serotonin reuptake inhibitors (SSRIs) and to a lesser extent tricyclic antidepressants (TCAs).

ment, improving interpersonal relationships, and increasing social and academic functioning are also useful (Birmaher, Ryan, Williamson, Brent, & Kaufman, 1996a; Diamond, Reis, Diamond, Siqueland, & Isaacs, 2002; Mufson & Dorta, 2003).

An early onset of depression places youngsters at greater risk for experiencing multiple episodes of major depression throughout their lives. Therefore, it is critical that treatment begin as soon as possible; very early and aggressive intervention is warranted to reduce the length of a depressive episode, prevent any future episodes, minimize associated impairments in functioning, and reduce the risk of suicide. An overview of the main treatments for youngsters with depression is presented in Table 8.4.

Psychosocial Interventions

Most psychosocial treatments for depression in young people use an integrated CBT approach derived from two traditions—cognitive therapy and behavior therapy (Weisz, Valeri, McCarty, & Moore, 1999). These two approaches were originally developed for depressed adults, but have since been adapted and applied with children and adolescents (Lewinsohn & Clarke, 1999).

Cognitive therapy teaches youngsters with depression to identify, challenge, and modify negative thought processes such as misattributions, negative self-monitoring, short-term focus, excessively high performance standards, and a failure to self-reinforce. They are taught to identify and eliminate negative thoughts, such as "It's my fault," or "What's the point?" and taught to replace them with positive thoughts, such as "She really likes me," or "I'm an interesting person." A child who has been rejected by a friend might be encouraged to think, "She was in a bad mood," rather than "She hates me." When youngsters are presented with specific situations and examples of irrational negative thinking, they are taught to substitute alternative logical explanations that are more positive. For example:

SITUATION: Two girls, Diana and Colleen, both ask friends to get together with them after school. Both girls' friends say they can't because they have too much homework to do.

IRRATIONAL THINKING: Diana feels rejected and thinks, "Because my friend won't get together with me, she doesn't like me, and she'll never want to do anything with me again."

RATIONAL THINKING: In contrast, Colleen thinks, "Well, my friend is busy today, but we can get together some other time. She's still my best friend."

Behavior therapy maintains that depression results from and is sustained by a lack of reinforcement due to a restricted range of potential reinforcers, few available reinforcers, or inadequate skills for obtaining rewards (Lewinsohn, 1974). The treatment focuses on increasing pleasurable activities and events, and provides the youngster with the skills needed to obtain more reinforcement. Interventions such as social skills training teach children assertiveness, communication, ways to accept and give feedback, social problem solving, and conflict resolution skills in order to increase positive social interactions (e.g., Fine et al., 1991).

In practice, cognitive therapy and behavior therapy are integrated into a unified treatment approach in which more adaptive cognitions are hypothesized to lead to more adaptive behavior, and vice versa (Stark, Sander, Yancy, Bronick, & Hoke, 2000). Examples of these integrated CBT treatment approaches for children and adolescents follow.

Primary and Secondary Control Enhancement Training (PASCET).

John Weisz and his colleagues (Weisz, Southam-Gerow, Gordis, & Connor-Smith, 2003) have developed a 15-session, individualized CBT-based program for youngsters ages 8–15 with depression. In treatment sessions and in take-home assignments, youngsters learn and practice two types of coping skills:

- *Primary control skills* (ACT skills) for changing objective events in their lives (e.g., the activities they engage in, learning to relax) to conform with one's wishes
- *Secondary control skills* (THINK skills) for altering the subjective impact of stressful life events (e.g., altering their negative thoughts and feelings)

The focus of the PASCET program is to help the child change conditions that are changeable, and to change the subjective impact of those that are not. Parents are also involved in the program and encouraged to support their children in using these coping skills. PASCET is an excellent example of a program that has evolved since its initial use in the schools to reduce depressive symptoms. It is now being implemented and evaluated in community mental health clinics with youngsters who have been referred for depression.

Taking Action.

Kevin Stark, Philip Kendall, and their colleagues have developed a comprehensive CBT approach for children with depression and their families (Stark & Kendall, 1996). Like the PASCET program, *Taking Action* uses a holistic approach that involves both child and family. The ACTION acronym is used to nourish the idea that youngsters can have an impact on their moods, and it is presented to them as follows (Stark & Kendall, 1996, p. 14):

A = Always find something to do to feel better.
C = Catch the positive.
T = Think about it as a problem to be solved.
I = Inspect the situation.
O = Open yourself to the positive.
N = Never get stuck in the negative muck.

Multiple treatment procedures are used to reduce the child's mood disturbances, behavioral deficits, and cognitive symptoms:

- *Dysphoria, anger, anhedonia, and excessive anxiety* are treated by educating the child about the relation between mood, thinking, and behavior, and by using anger management procedures, scheduling pleasant activities, and relaxation training.
- *Interpersonal deficits* are treated using social skills training.
- *Cognitive distortions and negative and self-critical thinking* are addressed by using cognitive-restructuring procedures and training in effective problem-solving and self-control procedures.

Interventions are carried out in both individual and group formats and make use of a workbook that includes a variety of exercises such as this one:

SITUATION: You accidentally drop your books . . . a group of classmates are talking and laughing at the other side of the room.
NEGATIVE THINKING: Now look at what I've done. They must think I'm a complete idiot.
COPING RESPONSE: No, they're probably laughing at something else. Besides, I know them. They're not like that. It's not like I'm the first person ever to drop her books. It's really no big deal.

Interventions with family members are used to facilitate the child's use of effective coping strategies outside of treatment, and to change events that may contribute to and prolong the child's problems. Since negative parent–child interactions may result in negative thinking, changing maladaptive patterns within the family is an important feature of the Taking Action program. Several methods are used to change parental and family cognitions and behavior, including teaching parents effective forms of discipline, ways to manage anger, and ways to change negative thinking. Interventions with the entire family teach negotiation and conflict resolution skills, recreational planning, and effective problem solving and family communication (Stark, Swearer, Kurowski, Sommer, & Bowen, 1996). The Taking Action program is a promising intervention built on a sound theoretical and research base, but requires further evaluation as a comprehensive treatment package for depression.

Adolescent Coping with Depression Program (CWDA).

One of the most well-established and comprehensive CBT programs for the treatment of depression in adolescents is the Adolescent Coping with Depression Program (CWDA) (Clarke, Lewinsohn, & Hops, 2001; Clarke, DeBar, & Lewinsohn, 2003). CWDA is a nonstigmatizing psychoeducational approach that emphasizes skills training to promote adolescents' control over their moods, and enhancement of their ability to cope with problematic situations. Treatment is provided in 16 2-hour sessions over an 8-week period for groups of up to 10 adolescents ages 13 to 18. Adolescents use a workbook that includes brief readings, short quizzes, structured learning tasks, and forms for homework assignments for each session. The core treatment sessions with adolescents involve group activities and role playing. In addition, complementary therapy with the youngsters' parents is carried out to accelerate and support the learning of new skills, and to assist in applying the skills learned in the group to everyday life situations. Periodic "booster sessions" help to maintain the skills taught during treatment (Clarke et al., 2003).

Initially, adolescents learn that depression can result from many causes, including inherited tendencies, stress, and excessive negative thinking. Relaxation training is then used to quickly provide a successful experience and some immediate relief. Subsequent sessions include the following components (Clarke et al., 2003):

- Self-change skills are taught, such as self-monitoring of mood and behavior, and ways to establish realistic goals.

- Pleasurable activities and opportunities for reinforcement are increased.

- Positive thinking is increased by identifying, challenging, and changing negative cognitions.

- Training in social, communication, and problem-solving skills is integrated throughout the program.

- Specific skills are taught, such as conversational skills, ways to plan social activities, and ways to make friends.

- Goal setting is used to identify short and long-term life goals, and potential barriers.

- Final sessions emphasize integrating the skills learned and making plans for the future.

The CWDA progam has demonstrated beneficial treatment and prevention effects in many controlled studies by its developers. However, as with the other treatments we have discussed, there is a need for further evaluation by independent investigators and for extending its use to a wider variety of depressed youngsters (Clarke et al., 2003).

Medications

"I kept hearing about Prozac in the news," says one father, "and when we finally brought my 9-year-old to a psychiatrist, I thought he could just give her this pill and change our lives. After a year, I can say that things are a bit better. But it took lots of trials with lots of different pills."

(From "Childhood Depression," by K. Levine, pp. 42–45. *Parents,* October 1995. Copyright © 1995 by Gruner & Jahr USA Publishing. Reprinted by permission of the author.)

Antidepressant medications are commonly used to treat children and adolescents with depression, and nearly 60% of those treated in outpatient settings are filling prescriptions for these drugs (Olfson, Gameroff, et al., 2003). For many youngsters, antidepressant medications can shorten a depressive episode and return them to the important developmental tasks of childhood and adolescence (Ambrosini, Bianchi, Rabinovich, & Elia, 1993). As we have noted, although TCAs are very effective with adults, the controlled studies with children are far less conclusive (Emslie & Mayes, 2001). In fact, TCAs have consistently failed to demonstrate any advantage over placebo in treating depression in young people, and may have some potentially serious cardiovascular side effects (B. Geller et al., 1999).

SSRIs have clearly become the first-line of drug treatment for youngsters with depression, with one national survey reporting that over 90% of prescriptions written for these youngsters were for SSRIs (Olfson, Gameroff, et al., 2003). A growing number of controlled investigations have demonstrated that SSRIs can be effective in reducing symptoms of depression in children and adolescents (Emslie & Mayes, 2001; Elliott & Smiga, 2003). The only SSRI that is currently FDA approved for the treatment of depression in children is fluoxetine (Prozac™). Prozac now comes in peppermint flavor, and nearly three-quarters of a million prescriptions for SSRIs for children ages 6–18 were written in 1996—an 80% increase in only 2 years (*APA Monitor,* December 1997). The use of Prozac and other SSRIs has increased dramatically in the past few years (Elliott & Smiga, 2003).

Other SSRIs such as sertraline (Zoloft™) and paroxetine (Paxil™) have also shown some benefits, with new medications coming along all the time (Emslie & Mayes, 2001). However, both professional and public concerns indicate that these benefits do include some risks (Kluger, 2003). One concern relates to possible serious side-effects such as suicidal thoughts and self harm. In fact, in 2003 the FDA advised against the use of Paxil in children and adolescents, and both British and Canadian drug regulators have made similar recommendations regarding Paxil and other SSRIs. Another important concern relates to the lack of information we have regarding the long-term effects of these medications on the developing brain. In addition, although research findings are promising, further evidence for the effectiveness of SSRIs relative to placebo is needed, and many youngsters show only partial or no improvement in response to medication treatment. Finally, in light of the demonstrated effectiveness of the psychosocial treatments for depression in children that we have discussed, the use of medications seems to exceed recommended practice guidelines, which raises concerns about overuse.

Nothwithstanding these concerns, untreated depression has profound long-term consequences, including a

off the mark by Mark Parisi

THAT'S THE WAY, UH, HUH UH, HUH...
I LIKE IT!
UH, HUH UH, HUH...

www.offthemark.com

ATLANTIC FEATURE © 1996 MARK PARISI

EEYORE WHEN HE
REMEMBERS HIS PROZAC

Cartoon copyrighted by Mark Parisi. Use without permission is prohibited.

high risk for suicide. There is some evidence that regional increases in the use of antidepressant medications are associated with decreases in rates of adolescent suicide (Olfson, Shaffer, Marcus, & Greenberg, 2003). Thus, there are possible risks that go along with not using medications, especially when numerous research and clinical studies indicate that many young people benefit from drug treatment (Elliott & Smiga, 2003).

In the absence of better data regarding drug effects and side effects with children, there are currently no easy answers to this dilemma. Some say it is unethical to treat children using medications in light of the potential dangers. Others say that the risks associated with drug treatment are no greater than risks for other treatments and that it is unethical to withhold treatment in light of the known benefits. Given the many social, political, and economic implications surrounding the use of medications to treat depression in young people, we are likely to hear a lot more about this issue for some time to come (e.g., Riddle, 2004).

Prevention

In view of the recurring nature of depression, successful efforts during childhood and adolescence to prevent the onset of depression may reduce a lifelong risk of illness and reduce the use of health care resources (Gillham, Shatte, & Freres, 2000; Schraedley et al., 1999). Group CBT with relaxation and group problem-solving therapy may prevent the recurrence of depression in adolescents with depressive symptoms for up to 2 years after treatment (Lewinsohn, Clarke, & Rohde, 1994). Prevention studies with grade school and high school students with subclinical symptoms of depression have also found CBT/ problem solving approaches effective in reducing depressive symptoms and lowering risk for developing depression up to 2 years after treatment (Gillham & Reivich, 1999; Shochet et al., 2001). Nevertheless not all programs have reported lasting benefits (e.g., Spence, Sheffield, & Donovan, 2003).

Other large-scale prevention efforts (*Teen Screen*) have been directed at the early detection of high school students at risk for depression and suicide, to ensure these students receive help (Shaffer et al., 2004). The importance of school-based screening is highlighted by the finding that although 90% of parents report that they are confident in their ability to tell if their child is thinking about suicide, only about one-third of teens with mental health problems are known to their parents.

Psychotherapy with toddlers and their depressed mothers has been successful in preventing the declines in cognitive development observed in toddlers of depressed mothers who did not receive psychotherapy (Cicchetti, Rogosch, & Toth, 2000). Finally, other interventions aimed at families with parents with depression have reported increased family communication, better adaptation, and greater understanding of the parent's illness by their children following intervention (Beardslee, Gladstone, Wright, & Cooper, 2003).

A high priority must be assigned to the development and continued refinement of identification and prevention efforts for youngsters at risk for depressive disorders (Coyle et al., 2003; NIMH, 2003). The use of computer-based interactive programs in the schools with further access to Internet resources for help has been suggested as a promising future direction (Andrews, Szabo, & Burns, 2002).

SECTION SUMMARY

- Cognitive-behavioral therapy has had the most success in treating depression in young people.

- Antidepressants are very effective with adults, but controlled studies with children are inconclusive. SSRIs have been recommended as the first line of drug treatment for depression because they have fewer side effects, equal effectiveness, and greater convenience of use than antidepressants, but concerns have recently been raised about their use.

- A high priority needs to be given to programs aimed at preventing depression in young people.

Bipolar Disorder (BP)

In a sense, depression is a view of the world through a dark glass, and mania is that seen through a kaleidoscope—often brilliant but fractured.

(Jamison, 1997, p. 48)

Ben

Extreme Mood Swings

Ben, age 14, was living in a residential treatment center. He had a history of moodiness, hyped-up activity, sleeplessness, and a sexual preoccupation with girls in his class—he had even approached his teacher with offers of sexual intimacy. Ben's thoughts raced, his speech was rapid and fragmented, and he had wide mood swings. At the high extreme Ben rarely slept and yelled, sang, and disturbed everyone—charging about the residence day and night with a seemingly endless supply of energy. He felt "absolutely terrific" at these times and thought he could fly. The low extreme found Ben curled up in a ball beneath a stack of blankets, a withdrawn and hopeless young man who expressed feelings of worthlessness and thoughts of suicide.

In the past, bipolar disorder (BP) was generally considered an adult illness, receiving very little attention in children and adolescents (G. A. Carlson, 2002; Geller & DelBello, 2003). However, there has been a recent upsurge of professional and public interest in pediatric BP, as reflected in the increasing rates of diagnosis, treatment, and media coverage (Kluger & Song, 2002; Weckerly, 2002; Youngstrom, Findling, & Calabrese, in press). BP in young people is difficult to identify because it has a low base rate of occurrence, extreme variability of clinical presentation within and across episodes, and overlap in symptoms with more common childhood disorders such as ADHD (Leibenluft, Charney, Towbin, Bhangoo, & Pine, 2003).

Although rare in young children, BP increases significantly after puberty. It is at once remarkable and almost inconceivable how a young person like Ben, with this disorder, can be so manic, elated, and wild at one moment, so depressed and immobile the next, and at other times seem so normal (B. Geller & Luby, 1997). Ben displays the essential features of BP: a striking period of abnormally and persistently elevated, expansive, or irritable mood, alternating with or accompanied by one or more major depressive episodes. The two mood states associated with BP are elation and euphoria. However, these feelings can quickly change to anger and hostility if the youngster's behavior is impeded. Since many youngsters with BP have simultaneous feelings of depression, they are easily reduced to tears.

Youngsters with BP show severe and cyclical mood changes and outbursts. Mania typically occurs in episodes, with an onset and offset. Thus, in its fully developed state it is clearly different from a youngster's usual condition (G. A. Carlson, 2002). During a manic episode, youngsters with BP may display intense symptoms, such as irritability and rage. Or they may show silly, giddy, overexcited, overtalkative behavior coupled with expansive, grandiose beliefs (e.g., a teen who feels he or she has a special connection to God). It is normal for children to pretend to have special powers or abilities, but a youngster with BP, during a manic episode, will actually believe he is Spiderman or Jackie Chan and that he is all-powerful. He might believe he can walk on water, control traffic, or jump off buildings without hurting himself—and kill himself in the process.

Restlessness, agitation, and sleeplessness are also typical of youngsters with BP. Sexual disinhibition (like Ben's propositioning his teacher) may also occur when the youngster becomes uncharacteristically preoccupied with sexual themes, sexually touching others, or "talking dirty." Youngsters with BP may experience unrealistic elevations in self-esteem (believing they are "the chosen one") and vast surges of energy; they may go with little or no sleep for days without feeling tired. They may be able to concentrate for hours on one activity that interests them, such as drawing or becoming engrossed in a mentally demanding fantasy game. At the same time, however, they may be highly distractible, constantly jumping from one thing to another (B. Geller & Luby, 1997).

The elated mood of youngsters with mania may (erroneously) give them the appearance of being happy and cheerful. Like Ben, they may say, "I feel absolutely terrific." It is difficult to recognize that a laughing, happy youngster also has a history of misery and distress. For this reason, evaluating a youngster's current mood in relation to his or her developmental history is essential, particularly when there is an inconsistency between the child's elated mood and his or her history of trouble at home or school (Youngstrom et al., in press).

Although not without problems, the diagnosis of BP in young people can be made using the same DSM criteria used for adults (G. A. Carlson, Pine, Nottelmann, & Leibenluft, 2004). Current research suggests that BP with an onset prior to age 18 is essentially the same disorder that occurs in adults, although possible differences in long-term outcomes and associated characteristics are not known. There are several subtypes of BP, based on whether the youngster displays a *manic, mixed,* or *hypomanic* episode. The DSM criteria for each episode are presented in Table 8.5, and the criteria for the different types of BP are presented in Table 8.6. A diagnosis of BP requires evidence for a manic or mixed episode in the case of **bipolar I disorder,** a hypomanic episode (episode of manic symptoms where the disturbance is not severe enough to cause marked impairments in life functioning

Table 8.5

Main Features of DSM-IV Criteria for
Manic, Mixed, and Hypomanic Episodes

DSM-IV-TR Criteria for a Manic Episode

A **manic episode** is the hallmark characteristic of bipolar disorder and is defined as follows:

A distinct period of abnormally and persistently elevated, expansive, and/or irritable mood, lasting at least 1 week (or any duration if hospitalization is necessary).

During the period of mood disturbance, three (or more) of the following symptoms have persisted (four if the mood is only irritable) and are present to a significant degree:

(1) Inflated self-esteem or grandiosity

(2) Decreased need for sleep (e.g., feels rested after only 3 hours of sleep)

(3) More talkative than usual, or pressure to keep talking

(4) Flight of ideas or subjective experience that thoughts are racing

(5) Distractibility (i.e., attention too easily drawn to unimportant or irrelevant external stimuli)

(6) Increase in goal-directed activity (socially, at work or school, or sexually) or psychomotor agitation

(7) Excessive involvement in pleasurable activities that have a high potential for painful consequences (e.g., engaging in unrestrained buying sprees, sexual indiscretions, or foolish business investments)

DSM-IV-TR Criteria for a Mixed Episode

A mixed episode is diagnosed when criteria are met for a manic episode and a major depressive episode over at least a 1-week period.

DSM-IV-TR Criteria for a Hypomanic Episode

A hypomanic episode has similar features to a manic episode but differs in the severity, duration, and degree of impairment criteria. The symptoms must be present for at least 4 days and must produce an unequivocal change in functioning that is uncharacteristic of the person when not symptomatic. However, by definition, there is no marked deterioration in functioning, need for hospitalization, or psychotic symptoms; otherwise a diagnosis of manic episode applies.

Source: Adapted with permission from *Diagnostic and Statistical Manual of Mental Disorders, DSM-IV-TR, Text Revision, Fourth Edition.* Copyright 2000 by the American Psychiatric Association.

---

or to require hospitalization) in the case of **bipolar II disorder,** or subthreshold manic symptoms in the case of **cyclothymic disorder.**

Youngsters with mania often present with atypical symptoms (Biederman et al., 2000). Changes in mood, psychomotor agitation, and mental excitation are often volatile and erratic rather than persistent. Irritability, belligerence, and mixed manic-depressive features occur more frequently than euphoria. Unlike adults, developmental limitations and the social environment place constraints on children's reckless behaviors, which typically involve school failure, fighting, dangerous play, and inappropriate sexual conduct. Thus, classic manic symptoms of grandiosity, psychomotor agitation, and reckless behavior must be differentiated from manic symptoms of common childhood disorders, such as ADHD, and from normal childhood behaviors, such as bragging, imaginary play, overactivity, and youthful blunders (American Academy of Child and Adolescent Psychiatry [AACAP], 1997).

How are some of the more notable symptoms of mania expressed in youngsters with BP? When in a manic state, youngsters show great conviction about the correctness or importance of their ideas. Adolescents with BP may show grand delusions—illogical and strong beliefs

Table 8.6

Subtypes of Bipolar Disorder

· **Bipolar I Disorder**

To have a bipolar I disorder, the individual has a clinical course characterized by one or more manic or mixed episodes, and one or more major depressive episodes.

· **Bipolar II Disorder**

Individuals with bipolar II disorder have a clinical course of one or more major depressive episodes accompanied by at least one hypomanic episode. The presence of a manic or mixed episode precludes the diagnosis of a bipolar II disorder.

· **Cyclothymic Disorder**

For children and adolescents, cyclothymia is diagnosed when there have been periods of 1 year or more (2 years in adults) where there are numerous hypomanic and depressive symptoms that do not meet full criteria for either a manic episode, mixed episode, or major depressive disorder. The symptoms must be present for most of the defined 1-year period, with no more than 2 consecutive symptom-free months, and must cause significant distress or impairment in functioning.

Source: Based on DSM-IV-TR 2000 by APA.

that lead to poor judgment and impulsive behavior (Jamison, 1997). For example, they may badger their teachers about how to teach. This badgering may become so intense that teachers contact the parents, pleading with them to ask their children to cease. Youngsters with BP may intentionally fail subjects, acting on their illogical belief that children can choose what to pass or fail, because they believe they are not being taught correctly. They may steal expensive items, and be unresponsive to efforts by police or parents to explain that their actions are wrong and illegal. Although these youngsters know that stealing is illegal for others, they believe they are above the law. They may believe that they will achieve great fame, for example, as a surgeon, even though they are failing all of their classes at school. Similarly, a youngster with BP who is short, clumsy, and lacks any athletic ability may practice basketball with great fervor, and strongly believe that he will become the next Michael Jordan (G. A. Carlson, 1994; B. Geller & Luby, 1997).

In contrast to youngsters with depression who can't fall asleep and may lie in bed for hours fretting and brooding, those with mania show high levels of activity at bedtime, spend very little time in bed, and require very little sleep. A child with mania might spend several hours at bedtime rearranging clothes in a dresser or closet, or an adolescent may wait until his or her parents are asleep then sneak out of the house to a party.

For children with mania, their words, thoughts, and actions occur in fast motion. Increased verbal production with puns, word plays, and incessant speech are common. At all ages, children with mania show *pressured speech*—they talk too much and too fast, change topics too quickly, and cannot be interrupted. They also have *racing thoughts* that they may describe in concrete terms—for example, by saying they can't do their schoolwork because their thoughts keep interrupting. In the words of one teen, "I wish I had a switch on my forehead so I could turn off my racing thoughts" (B. Geller & Luby, 1997). Like an adult with BP, a child with the disorder also shows a *flight of ideas*, which is an illogical jump from one idea to another. For example, in reply to the question, "Do you live in Los Angeles?" the child may reply, "Some people like to swim in the ocean. Do you have a dog?"

For manic children of all ages, even slight changes in their surroundings can lead to significant distractibility. Heightened psychomotor agitation and goal-directed actions resemble normal activities carried out in excess, with a seemingly endless supply of energy. During a brief period of time, a manic youngster might draw several pictures, read a book, work on the computer, prepare a snack, make multiple phone calls, write a letter, and vacuum the house.

Accepting dares is common for youngsters with BP. In older adolescents, this may appear as reckless driving that results in multiple tickets for speeding or driving under the influence. In preadolescents, it may be expressed as grandiose delusions of being able to jump out the window because they believe they can fly. They also may push the limits on usual childhood climbing on things, based on the strong belief that they are above the possibility of danger (B. Geller & Luby, 1997). In extreme cases, they may experience violent agitation with delusional thinking as well as visual and auditory hallucinations.

Prevalence

The lifetime prevalence of BP in young people is estimated to be about 0.4% to 1.2% (Costello et al., 2002; Lewinsohn, Seeley, Buckley, & Klein, 2002). However, because of the complicated presentation of symptoms and the difficulties in making an accurate diagnosis, it is possible that BP in young people is more common and occurs at a younger age than previously thought (Youngstrom et al., in press). The duration of manic symptoms in young people often does not meet the 1-week duration requirement of DSM to be a manic episode. Therefore, the most common diagnoses are the milder bipolar II disorder and cyclothymic disorder, rather than bipolar I disorder (Lewinsohn et al., 1995). Children are also likely to present with rapid cycling episodes (at least 4 mood episodes of a mood disturbance over a 1-year period), with about 80% of children showing this course (B. Geller et al., 1995).

Despite anecdotal accounts of the onset of mania in children as young as 5 or 6 years old, the incidence of BP prior to puberty is extremely rare, but it increases during adolescence (Lewinsohn, Klein, & Seeley, 2000). In fact, the prevalence of BP during adolescence is at least as high as it is for adults and, similar to depression, may be on the rise, with an earlier age of onset (B. Geller & Luby, 1997).

In sharp contrast to the effects of depression, BP affects males and females equally. However, in studies of youngsters with early-onset BP, boys seem to be affected more often than girls, especially when the age of onset is younger than 13 years. Rates of BP have not been found to differ by ethnicity or culture, but few studies have investigated this issue in children and adolescents (AACAP, 1997).

Comorbidity

Some youngsters with BP have normal histories prior to the onset of their illness. However, preexisting behavior problems, such as ADHD and disruptive behavior disorders, are present in a significant number of cases. Premorbid anxiety and emotional problems are also common, as is a prior major depressive episode (Akiskal, 1995). High rates of co-occurring disorders are extremely common in children with BP, with the most typical being ADHD, disruptive behavior disorders, and learning disorders (Biederman, 1998; Wilens et al., 1999). Co-occurring substance use disorders are also common, as are suicidal thoughts and ideation, and anxiety disorders (B. Geller et al., 2002; B. Geller & Luby, 1997; Kim & Miklowitz, 2002; Weckerly, 2002).

Youngsters with BP frequently display co-occurring symptoms of ADHD, such as poor judgment, distractibility, inattention, irritability, hyperactivity, anger, poor impulse control, demanding behaviors, and the tendency to jump from one topic or activity to another. For youngsters first seen because of symptoms of BP, about 60% to 90% of prepubertal children and 30% of adolescents also have ADHD (B. Geller & Luby, 1997).

Oppositional and conduct disorders occur in about 20% of children and adolescents with BP. Symptoms of grandiosity, mania, and poor judgment in BP may be confused with symptoms of conduct problems. For example, one 11-year-old boy with BP, who believed he would be a famous rock star, stole several hundred dollars' worth of CDs and was totally unaffected when questioned by the police. Conduct disorder overlaps with BP on symptoms such as running away, driving under the influence, substance abuse, sexual promiscuity, and stealing. Similarly, the flight of ideas and or pressured speech associated with mania may be mistaken for a language disorder (G. A. Carlson, 2002; B. Geller & Luby, 1997).

Onset, Course, and Outcome

About 20% of all patients with BP experience their first episode during adolescence, with a peak age of onset between 15 and 19 years old (AACAP, 1997). Onset prior to age 10 is extremely rare. Youngsters with BP may first present with either depressive or manic episodes. Most youngsters report that their first mood episode was major depression. This is consistent with the reported high rates of switching from depression to mania (B. Geller & Luby, 1997). In children with MDD who later develop BP, 80% are age 12 or younger at the time of onset of their depression (V. Geller, Fox, & Clark, 1994).

Risk factors for eventual mania include a major depressive episode characterized by rapid onset, psychomotor retardation, and psychotic features, and a family history of mood disorders, especially BP (AACAP, 1997). When a young person presents with a first episode of obvious mania, it's very likely that further manic episodes will follow. Bipolar episodes are generally shorter than major depressive episodes, lasting from 4 to 6 months if left untreated. About 75% of adolescents recover within 6 months (G. A. Carlson, 1994).

Adolescents with mania often have complex presentations that include psychotic symptoms, such as hallucinations, paranoia, and thought disorder. They also have unstable moods with mixed manic and depressive features, and severe deterioration in behavior. These diverse forms of presentation may result in an underdiagnosis of BP in teens, which is often misdiagnosed as schizophrenia.

Because of the difficulty in recognizing symptoms of BP in young people, it is common for the symptoms to be noticed well before a youngster is treated or hospitalized, but not labeled as BP (Youngstrom et al., in press). A look back at the histories of adults with BP symptoms often shows that mood swings began around puberty; however, there is frequently a 5 to 10-year lag between the onset of symptoms, and display of the disorder serious enough to be recognized and treated (G. A. Carlson, 1994).

An early onset and course of BP is chronic and resistant to treatment, with a poor long-term prognosis similar to that in adults (AACAP, 1997). In a 5-year prospective follow-up study of adolescents with BP, nearly 50% of all patients had a relapsing course or never achieved complete remission (Strober et al., 1995). Compared with adults, adolescents with BP may have a more prolonged early course and a poorer response to treatment. However, long-term prognosis appears to be similar to that for adults, with about 50% of all patients showing significant functional impairment relative to premorbid functioning. The long-term impact of BP on development is likely to be great, but has received little systematic study to date (G. Carlson, 2002; B. Geller & Delbello, 2003).

Causes

Jessi

Runs in the Family

"Jessi's father had been an alcoholic and a manic depressive," says her mother, "probably since he was an adolescent. He died of dehydration that occurred during a manic episode. His illness had been a mystery to us.

Growing up, Jessi knew her father was ill, and when she was older, she began to worry about what his sickness might mean for her. I worried too," says Jessi's mother. "By the time Jessi was in her early twenties, something was clearly wrong. At first, I noticed only that she had become less reliable—forgetting things, arriving late, and occasionally missing appointments with me. Frequently, she complained of fatigue, a cold, flu, or a stomachache. Increasingly, her responses were brief, perfunctory. Though we didn't know it then, Jessi was experiencing a huge mood shift that was taking months to complete itself. Jessi had MDD, without the manic swings of the bipolar disorder her father had suffered from." (Adapted from C. Dowling, 1992)

Few studies have examined the causes of BP in young people, although research with adults indicates that BP is one of the most heritable forms of mental disorder (McInnis et al., 2003). Findings from familial and gene studies with adults indicate that BP is the result of a genetic vulnerability combined with environmental factors, such as life stress or disturbances in the family. When an identical twin has BP, there is only a 65% chance that the other twin will have it too, suggesting that in addition to genes, other factors are important. Although BP can affect anyone, it has definitely been shown to be a familial disorder. If one or both parents have BP, the chances are about 5 times greater that their children will also develop BP, or like Jessi, often another mood disorder (Hodgins, Faucher, Zarac, & Ellenbogen, 2002).

Besides mood disorder, children at risk for BP by virtue of having parents with the disorder also display a wide range of psychopathology, particularly conduct problems and ADHD. Relatives of youngsters with BP also have a higher incidence of BP. Family incidence is highest in cases of early-onset BP, with lifetime prevalence rates of about 15% in first-degree relatives (AACAP, 1997). This rate is 15 times greater than the prevalence of the disorder in the general population. Increasing evidence suggests that BP arises from multiple genes (McInnis et al., 2003). There is likely a complex mode of inheritance rather than a single dominant gene. Individuals with a genetic predisposition do not necessarily develop BP, since environmental factors play an important role in determining how genes are expressed (B. Geller & Luby, 1997).

Brain scans have found that BP in adolescents is related to reduced volumes of certain brain structures, particularly the amygdala (Blumberg et al., 2003). As you may recall, we discussed the importance of the amygdala for recognizing and regulating emotions in relation to depression.

Treatment

Treatment of BP in children and adolescents is an understudied area (Hellander, 2002). BP generally requires a multimodal treatment plan that includes education of the patient and the family about the illness, medications such as lithium, and psychotherapeutic interventions to address the youngster's symptoms and related psychosocial impairments (Fristad & Goldberg Arnold, 2004). The general goals of treatment are to decrease BP symptoms and to prevent relapse, while also reducing long-term illness and enhancing the youngster's normal health and development (AACAP, 1997).

Numerous youngsters with BP have been given multiple medications, however, there are currently no drugs that are FDA approved for the treatment of BP in children (Hellander, 2002). Medications are typically used to address manic or mixed symptoms and depressive symptoms, or to prevent relapse. Although clinical trials of medication have had some success, at this time, controlled studies of medication treatment for children and adolescents with BP are limited to non-existent (G. A. Carlson et al., 2003). The current recommended treatments are based on findings with adults, and as we saw with tricyclic antidepressants, such an extrapolation may not be warranted (B. Geller et al., 1998; B. Geller & Luby, 1997). There is currently little information concerning recommended treatments in the psychosocial realm.

In general, lithium is the first agent of choice in the treatment of BP, although many other medications have been used, including SSRIs (Biederman, Mick, Spencer, Wilens, & Faraone, 2000; Frazier, et al., 1999; Hellander, 2002). Lithium is a common salt that is widely present in the natural environment—for example, in drinking water—usually in amounts too small to have any effects. However, the side effects of therapeutic doses of lithium can be serious, especially when used in combination with other medications, and may include toxicity (poisoning), renal and thyroid problems, and substantial weight gain (Gracious et al., 2004). It can be given to young people when used with the same safety precautions and similar careful monitoring used for adults. However, lithium cannot be given to children in chaotic families or to children who are unable to keep the multiple appointments needed for monitoring potentially dangerous side effects (G. A. Carlson, 1994; B. Geller & Luby, 1997).

Medications may decrease symptoms of BP but do not help with the associated functional impairments, which include preexisting or co-occurring substance use disorders, learning and behavior problems, and family- and peer-related issues. Psychosocial interventions focus on providing information to the child and family about the disorder, symptoms and course, possible impact on family functioning, and heritability of the disorder. Nonadherence to medication has been shown to be a major contributor to relapse. Thus, the family must be educated about the negative effects of nonadherence to medications and to recognize possible symptoms of relapse (Fristad & Goldberg Arnold, 2004; B. Geller & Luby, 1997). Unfortunately, there is little research available on psychosocial interventions for youngsters with BP, and no psychotherapy available that is specific to the treatment of mania.

SECTION SUMMARY

- Youngsters with bipolar disorder (BP) show periods of abnormally and persistently elevated, expansive, and/or irritable mood.

- They may display symptoms such as an inflated self-esteem, decreased need for sleep, pressured speech, flight of ideas, distractibility, and reckless behavior.

- BP is far less common than MDD in young people, with prevalence estimates of 1% or lower.

- BP has a peak age of onset in late adolescence and affects males and females about equally. The most common accompanying disorders are anxiety disorders, ADHD, conduct disorders, and substance abuse.

- Very few studies have examined the causes of BP in children and adolescents. Family and gene studies with adults indicate that BP is the result of a genetic vulnerability in combination with environmental factors, such as life stress or disturbances in the family.

- BP in young people requires a multimodal treatment plan with education of the patient and the family about the illness, medication, and psychotherapeutic interventions to address the youngster's symptoms and related psychosocial impairments.

Key Terms

 InfoTrac College Edition

To research recent articles on the subject, go to:
www.infotrac-college/thomsonlearning.com

Enter search terms: DEPRESSION IN CHILDREN, DEPRESSION IN ADOLESCENTS, BIPOLAR DISORDER, SUICIDE, ANTIDEPRESSANTS AND CHILDREN, COGNITIVE-BEHAVIORAL THERAPY.

Mental Retardation

You judge a person by how they look or how they talk or what the tests show, but you can never really tell what is inside the person.

—Ed, 27 years old, who was labeled mentally retarded and placed in a state institution at age 15.
(Bogdan & Taylor, 1982)

The scientific history of idiocy has yet to be produced; its data are scarce, and the study has not many charms.

—*P. M. Duncan & W. Millard, 1866*

So lamented the authors of one of the first professional books on the topic of mental retardation, or "idiocy," as it was called almost 150 years ago. Until the mid-19th century, children and adults who today would be diagnosed as having mental retardation were often lumped together with persons suffering from mental disorders or medical conditions. They were typically ignored or feared, even by the medical profession, because their differences in appearance and ability were so little understood.

Although age-old fears, resentment, and scorn continue to overshadow many important discoveries about subnormal intelligence, the field of mental retardation has experienced monumental gains during the 20th century in determining causes and providing services. Advances in understanding the development of children with mental retardation, along with research in genetics, psychopathology, and other areas, have changed the face of this field dramatically. An appreciation of the rapid improvements in knowledge and treatment of mental retardation, as well as an understanding of the prejudice and ignorance that had to be overcome, can be gained by looking at how the disorder has been viewed over the years.

Intelligence and Mental Retardation

Early references to persons with intellectual impairments have been traced to the Romans, who sometimes kept "fools" for the amusement of the household and its guests

Ignorance resulted in the segregation of children with mental retardation, who were subjected to treatment that today would be considered inhumane.

(Kanner, 1964). When kept by the wealthy, these individuals were generally treated well. Throughout recorded history, however, the vast majority of persons with intellectual and other disabilities received scorn, not assistance, from fellow townspeople. Martin Luther, the German theologian who initiated the Protestant Reformation in 1517, explained how the odd appearance and behavior of a child (most likely with mental retardation, but this disorder was not known at the time) was attributed to possession by the devil:

"He was twelve years old, had the use of his eyes and all his senses, so that one might think that he was a normal child. But he did nothing but gorge himself as much as four peasants or threshers. He ate, defecated, and drooled and, if anyone tackled him, he screamed. If things didn't go well, he wept. . . . For it is in the Devil's power that he corrupts people who have reason and souls when he possesses them. The Devil sits in such changelings where their soul should have been!"

(From *A History of the Care and Study of the Mentally Retarded,* by L. Kanner, 1964, p. 7. Courtesy of Charles C. Thomas, Publishers, Springfield, Illinois.)

The prevailing misunderstanding and mistreatment of children with mental retardation began to change toward the end of the 18th century, fueled by the discovery of feral children such as Victor, the "wild boy of Aveyron" (discussed in Chapter 1), and by the expansion of humanitarian efforts to assist other oppressed or neglected groups, such as slaves, prisoners, the mentally ill, and per-

sons with physical disabilities. By the mid-19th century, the concept of mental retardation had spread from France and Switzerland to much of Europe and North America. During the same period, Dr. Samuel G. Howe convinced his contemporaries that training and educating the feeble-minded was a public responsibility and opened the first humanitarian institution in North America for persons with mental retardation—the Massachusetts School for Idiotic and Feeble-Minded Youth.

By the late-19th century, treatment of persons with intellectual disabilities and special educational needs had become the responsibility of state-run schools and institutions. However, the initial optimism for curing mental retardation was fading. As admissions rapidly increased, it became clear that many individuals had no prospect of returning to their families or communities. Within approximately two decades, institutional inmates were considered lifelong residents, and an emphasis on teaching them basic occupational skills such as cleaning or cooking (to be used in service to the institution, in many cases) replaced their basic academic education (Kuhlmann, 1940).

It is the parents of children with mental retardation who can be credited with advancing a perspective and response to the need for long-term care that was completely different from that of the prevailing public and professional opinions. By the 1940s, parents began to meet in groups and to create local diagnostic and guidance centers to increase the availability of humane care. These groups organized in 1950 to form the National Association for Retarded Children, which quickly established a scientific board made up of representatives from every specialty possible to assist in the study, prevention, and care of persons with mental retardation (Kanner, 1964). These efforts gained momentum when President John F. Kennedy, who had a sister with mental retardation, formed the President's Panel on Mental Retardation in 1962 and called for a national program to combat mental retardation.

In the mid-1960s, a young New York reporter named Geraldo Rivera and U.S. Senator Robert Kennedy exposed the deplorable conditions in many institutions for persons with mental retardation. The ensuing controversy inspired Professor Burton Blatt to ask his friend, freelance photographer Fred Kaplan, to accompany him on a tour of the back wards of similar institutions. With a hidden camera strapped to Kaplan's waist, they were able to take pictures of the cruelty they observed. Their photographs brought the plight of many residents in these institutions to the attention of the public. Administrators stated that the use of solitary confinement and restraints was attributed to staff shortages: "What can one do with those patients who do not conform? We must lock them up, or restrain them, or sedate them, or put fear into them" (Blatt & Kaplan, 1966). As a result of these exposés, public awareness and outrage at the treatment of persons with mental retardation reached an all-time high.

The Eugenics Scare

"Three generations of imbeciles are enough."

—Justice Oliver Wendell Holmes Jr., commenting
on the Supreme Court's (1927) decision
to uphold eugenics sterilization laws

Evolutionary degeneracy theory, a pervasive 19th-century phenomenon, attributed the intellectual and social problems of children with mental retardation to regression to an earlier period in human evolution (Bowler, 1989). In fact, mental deficiency experts in the 19th century believed they had found the "missing link" between humans and lower species (Gelb, 1995). J. Langdon H. Down, best known for the clinical description of the genetic syndrome that bears his name, interpreted the "strange anomalies" among his medical sample of persons with mental retardation as an evolutionary throwback to the Mongol race (Down, 1866). Down believed that parents in one racial group might give birth to a child with mental retardation who was a "retrogression" to another group. While grounded in speculation and misinformed conclusions, evolutionary degeneracy theory and its notion of inferiority received growing support as an explanation for insanity, mental deficiency, and social deviance by the late-19th century. Box 9.1 depicts how this popular theory was conveniently used to explain undesirable human characteristics.

By 1910, the eugenics movement was gaining momentum. **Eugenics** was first defined by Sir Francis Galton (Charles Darwin's cousin) in 1883 as "the science which deals with all influences that improve the inborn qualities of a race" (cited in Kanner, 1964, p. 128). Public and professional emphasis shifted away from the needs of persons with mental retardation toward a consideration of the needs of society; society was to be protected from the presumable harm done by the presence of these persons in the community. Leo Kanner, a pioneer in the study of autism and mental retardation, aptly describes the prevailing sentiment:

> "A feeling that society was in serious danger created an atmosphere of growing alarm. The mental defectives were viewed as a menace to civilization, incorrigible at home, burdens to the school, sexually promiscuous, breeders of feebleminded offspring, victims and spreaders of poverty, degeneracy, crime, and disease."
>
> (From *A History of the Care and Study of the Mentally Retarded*, by L. Kanner, 1964, p. 7. Courtesy of Charles C. Thomas, Publishers, Springfield, Illinois.)

Consequently, persons with mental retardation were often blamed for the social ills of the time, which is a powerful example of how labeling a problem can quickly become an explanation for it. Box 9.2, in fact, shows a 1912 *New York Times* article reflecting this public sentiment.

BOX 9.1 The Infamous Kallikaks

Psychologist Henry Goddard, who began one of the largest training schools for the mentally retarded in the early 20th century, was also a proponent of the popular degeneracy theory and eugenics movement. In his book *The Kallikak Family: A Study in the Heredity of Feeble-Mindedness* (1912), Goddard traced two lines of descendants from a Revolutionary War soldier, Martin Kallikak who fathered a child by a feebleminded barmaid during the war, which began the first line, and then fathered other children by a "respectable girl" he married after the war. The name Kallikak was invented by Goddard from a combination of two Greek words: *kalos,* meaning "attractive, pleasing," and *kakos,* meaning "bad, evil."

Goddard reported that many descendants of the first union were feebleminded, delinquent, poor, and alcoholic, whereas those of the second union were of good reputation. He claimed this outcome was evidence for the inheritance of intelligence, although he overlooked the two families' obvious environmental differences (Achenbach, 1982). A closer look at the disclaimer from the preface to the book is telling: "It is true that we have made rather dogmatic statements and have drawn conclusions that do not seem scientifically warranted by the data."

The appearance, ability, and behavior of persons with mental retardation were considered evidence of their lack of moral fiber, a belief that led to the diagnostic term *moral imbecile,* or *moron,* used to describe and explain their differences. This concept became a straightforward explanation for acts of deviance, and justified wide-ranging attempts to identify and control such individuals. Morons, considered the least intellectually impaired (roughly comparable to mild mental retardation today) were seen as a threat to society because, unlike the insane, they could easily pass for normal (Gelb, 1995). The intellectually impaired and other "undesirables" were once again seen as a public menace, to be feared and ostracized.

Meanwhile, early developmental psychologists proposed that children between the ages of 8 and 12 pass through an "ancestral stage," during which moral reasoning emerges. As G. Stanley Hall, a prominent psychologist who was instrumental in the development of educational psychology, described it, children of this age were "mature savages" who required strong social forces to ensure that they advanced beyond this stage and became fit for civilized life (Gelb, 1995). Persons with different abilities or less social status—especially members of minority groups, women, children, and the physically and mentally challenged—were considered less capable of judgment or reasoning, which of course provided further justification for restricting their rights and opportunities for advancement.

Defining and Measuring Children's Intelligence and Adaptiveness

Around 1900, the pioneering work of two French educators, Alfred Binet and Theophile Simon, led to some of the first major advancements in the field of children's intellectual functioning. Binet and Simon were asked to develop a way to identify schoolchildren who might need special help in school. They approached this monumental task by developing the first intelligence tests to measure judgment and reasoning, which they believed were basic processes of higher thought. These early test questions asked children to manipulate unfamiliar objects, such as blocks or figures, and to solve puzzles and match familiar parts of objects. The test later became the Stanford-Binet scale, which remains one of the most widely used intelligence tests.

From these beginnings in intellectual testing, **general intellectual functioning** is now defined by an intelligence quotient (IQ or equivalent) that is based on assessment with one or more of the standardized, individually administered intelligence tests, such as the Wechsler Intelligence Scales for Children (WISC-IV), the Stanford-Binet (SB5), and the Kaufman Assessment Battery for Children (KABC-II). These tests assess various verbal and visual-spatial skills in the child, such as knowledge of the world, reasoning, similarities and differences, and mathematical concepts, which together are presumed to constitute the general construct known as intelligence.

By convention, intelligence test scores (with a mean of 100 and standard deviation of 15) are derived from a standardized table based on a person's age and test score (Neisser et al., 1996). Because intelligence is defined along a normal distribution, approximately 95% of the population has scores within 2 standard deviations of the mean (that is, between 70 and 130). Subaverage intellectual functioning is defined, accordingly, as an IQ of about 70 or below (approximately 2 standard deviations below the mean).

As we will discuss later in this chapter, the definition of mental retardation includes not only subaverage intellectual functioning, but also a subaverage level of adaptive functioning. **Adaptive functioning** refers to how effectively individuals cope with ordinary life demands, and how capable they are of living independently and abiding by community standards (Hodapp & Dykens, 2003). Two of the many tests available to assess adaptive abilities in children are the Vineland Adaptive Behavior Scales and the AAMD Adaptive Behavior scales, which each address about ten content areas of adaptive abilities. Note that some children and adolescents may learn to adapt quite well to their environment despite their lowered intelligence as measured by an IQ test, and therefore would not be considered to have mental retardation. Table 9.1 gives examples of several content areas that comprise adaptive behavior.

The Controversial IQ

If a person's intelligence is relatively stable over time, it would be tempting to conclude that it is largely innate and fixed. On the other hand, if intellectual and cognitive development are significantly shaped by environment, per-

Table 9.1	
Examples of Content Areas within Adaptive Behavior Assessment	

CONTENT AREA	EXAMPLES
Basic developmental skills	Sensory development, motor development
Communication	Expressive language, receptive language, writing and spelling skills
Emotional and personal adjustment	Coping, entering a new school or job, interpersonal conflict
Social and inter-personal skills	Basic interaction skills, group participation, play activities and skills
Self-help skills	Dressing, eating, toileting, personal hygiene and grooming
Consumer skills	Money handling, banking, budgeting, purchasing
Domestic skills	Kitchen skills, household cleaning, household management, maintenance and repair, laundering and clothing care

Source: From *Contemporary Assessment for Mentally Retarded Adolescents and Adults* by A. S. Halpern, J. P. Lehmann, and L. K. Irvin, and T. J. Heiry, 1982, p. 10. Copyright © 1982 by University of Oregon. Reprinted by permission.

haps cognitive growth can be stimulated at an early age and the level of mental retardation decreased.

Because intelligence is measured in relation to age-mates, IQ is generally stable from childhood through adulthood (Canivez & Watkins, 1999). One exception to this general rule is IQ that is measured during early infancy, when considerable fluctuation can still occur. For typically developing children, IQ measured prior to the first birthday has virtually no correlation with the IQ score achieved at age 12; however, by the time children are 4 years old the correlation with IQ 12 years later is high ($r = .77$) (Neisser et al., 1996).

The picture is dramatically different, however, for infants and children with developmental delays or mental retardation. At the lower IQ levels (say, below 50), even the youngest infants show IQ stability over time, with correlations between infant and childhood test scores ranging from .50 to .97 (Sattler, 2002). Researchers have discovered a similar pattern of IQ stability from middle childhood to young adulthood among children with mild to moderate intellectual delays (B. H. King, State, Shaw, Davanzo, & Dykens, 1997; Mortensen, Andresen, Kruuse, Sanders, & Reinisch, 2003).

Even though the IQ of cognitively delayed infants and young children is unlikely to change, proper environmental circumstances will help children reach their fullest po-

tential. Since the early 1960s, researchers in child development and retardation have been investigating ways to provide early stimulation programs that will help children with developmental delays and environmental disadvantages build on their existing strengths. Despite its strong genetic component, mental ability is always modified by experience. Not surprisingly, infancy through early childhood offer the most significant opportunity for influencing intellectual ability, due to the young child's rapid brain development and response to environmental stimulation (Campbell, Ramey, Pungello, Sparling, & Miller-Johnson, 2002).

The importance of genetic makeup notwithstanding, IQ can and does change for some individuals by 10–20 points between childhood and adolescence (Simonoff, Bolton, & Rutter, 1996). Differences in outcome vary widely in relation to opportunities for each child to learn and develop. Children who live in healthy environments, where caregivers provide appropriate levels of stimulation and help them manage ambient levels of stress, are most likely to reach their full potential. Moreover, tests can sample only a limited spectrum of intellectual ability, and are incapable of accounting for each individual's unique learning history (Flynn, 1999).

Are We Really Getting Smarter? Scores have risen sharply since the beginning of IQ testing, ranging from 5 to 25 points in a single generation (Kanaya, Scullin, & Ceci, 2003). When James Flynn brought this phenomenon of rising IQ scores to the attention of scientists in 1987, it became known as the "Flynn effect." The gain has averaged about 3 IQ points per decade, adding up to more than a full standard deviation since the 1940s. Once a test is re-normed (about every 15 to 20 years) the mean is re-set to 100, resulting in a brief reversal of this gain in IQ scores.

In attempting to explain the Flynn effect, scientists have considered the rising standards of living, better schooling, better nutrition, medical advances, more stimulating environments, even the influence of computer games and complex toys. IQ tests themselves have once again come under scrutiny, as have children's exposure to problems similar to those on the tests—like the mazes and puzzles they see on their cereal boxes and fast-food bags. Yet the consistent IQ gains are too large to be the result simply of increased familiarity with testing methods.

Although the exact cause of the effect remains unknown, experts on children's intelligence suspect the gains reflect a meaningful aspect of intellectual growth and development. A relatively permissive and child-focused parenting style has emerged during recent decades, which may have given children greater facility with language and stronger overall cognitive capacity. Moreover, there are unprecedented cultural differences between successive generations, as daily life and occupational experiences are far more complex today. There is a possible downside to the Flynn effect, however. Test scores drop an average of 5.6 points among persons with borderline and mild mental retardation after a test is re-normed, which can have a significant impact on a child's eligibility for proper educational placement and other related services (Kanaya et al., 2003).

Are IQ Tests Biased or Unfair? Concern has been expressed over the relatively low mean of the distribution of intelligence test scores of African Americans. Although studies using different tests and samples yield a range of results, the mean of African Americans is typically about 1 standard deviation (about 15 IQ points) below that of whites (Jencks & Phillips, 1998). In a controversial article titled "How Much Can We Boost IQ and Scholastic Achievement?" Arthur Jensen (1969) argued that the heritability of IQ was high among both white and black populations (approximately 80%), and therefore the mean IQ difference between them was probably primarily genetically determined. This conclusion led to critical analysis of the environmental enrichment programs that were just beginning to gain foothold in various communities. Many academics viewed Jensen's findings and conclusions (which, in retrospect, were premature and based on incomplete studies) as poor science at best and racism at worst.

In spite of the controversy, economic and social inequality—not test bias or racial differences—is the simplest explanation for existing group differences in test performance between blacks and whites (Brooks-Gunn, Klebanov, Smith, Duncan, & Lee, 2003). Any person, regardless of race or intelligence level, can benefit from appropriate environmental interventions, which have proven meaningful effects on IQ (Landesman Ramey & Ramey, 1999). However, a much higher proportion of African Americans and other ethnic minorities are poor, and poverty is linked to poor nutrition, inadequate prenatal care, fewer intellectual resources, and similar realities that can have negative effects on children's developing intelligence (Turkheimer, Haley, Waldron, D'Onofrio, & Gottesman, 2003).

Nevertheless, the differential in IQ scores appears to be diminishing. Since 1980, the mean score of African Americans has consistently been over 90, and the differential has been less than 10. Some of the gains can be attributed to the many programs implemented during the past two decades that were geared to the education of minority children (Neisser et al., 1996).

SECTION SUMMARY

- The early history of mental retardation was plagued by ignorance and blame.
- By the mid-20th century, progress toward understanding mental retardation moved more rapidly, as parents, researchers, politicians, and the public sought better answers regarding its causes and ways to assist both children and adults with mental retardation.

- Mental retardation refers to limitations in both intelligence and adaptive behavior. However, many persons with this disorder are capable of learning and of living fulfilling lives.

- Despite its drawbacks, the IQ has become a principle standard for diagnosing mental retardation combined with other skills and abilities of the child.

Features of Mental Retardation

Mental retardation encompasses perhaps the widest variation in cognitive and behavioral abilities of any childhood disorder. Some children function quite well in school and the community, whereas others, those with significant physical and cognitive impairments, require daily supervision and assistance. The situations of Matthew, age 6, and Vanessa, age 8, illustrate some of the unique challenges children with mental retardation face every day.

Matthew
Gaining at His Own Pace

Matthew was almost 6 years old when he was referred for a psychological assessment. His brief school record described him as "developmentally delayed," and the school was concerned that his speech and social skills were very limited. He also had temper tantrums at home, and his new first-grade teacher had expressed concerns about his aggressive behavior with children in his class.

I first met with Matt in his home. "Show me some of your favorite toys or games," I suggested, unsure of how comfortable he was with a stranger at his home. He was a thin boy, with curly hair and a cautious, reserved expression. He looked me over for what must have been several minutes while I spoke with his mother and father. Although he said "OK," I wasn't sure he meant it—he stayed put and seemed uninterested in my request. Matt had turned 6 a few months ago, but I noticed that his clothes, games, and vocabulary were closer to those of my 3-year-old daughter. "I don't want to talk about school stuff!" he exclaimed, quite loudly, when I asked about his favorite subjects. "I only like recess and lunchtime—the stuff they won't let you do till the bell rings!" There was a certain degree of truth, and humor, to his statement, although I don't think he intended it as such. . . .

Matt became a bit more interested when I brought out some testing materials. He completed with ease a puzzle designed for toddlers, and was able to make the sounds of animals in the puzzle. But his emotional expression remained subdued, with little spontaneous laughter or joy. He seemed watchful and cautious. "Tell me about this story," I said to Matt, holding up a card showing some animals arguing over a ball. "What do you think is going on in this picture, and what are the characters, like the elephant and the zebra, thinking and feeling?" Matt started right in: "He's mad 'cuz the zebra grabbed the ball and ran away with it into the woods. That's all I see." My attempts to elicit more detail were met with only an inquisitive look.

After a few minutes of this, we took a break and brought out his toys. "Do you like *Harry Potter?*" he asked. We found some common ground among the characters in the book, and under these "ideal" conditions, Matt's communication became more at ease and spontaneous. He expressed a wide range of emotion throughout the interview, and settled in to his own comfortable level of relating. Gradually, his language production increased as we continued with the more relaxed play sessions.

In private, Matt's mother told me about his behavior problems around other children, such as hitting, biting, throwing objects, and demanding attention. I saw a brief episode of it myself, when his 3-year-old sister came into the room: "Get out! This man is here to play with me!" Overall, Matt behaved much like a younger child—for example, by shouting or pushing when he couldn't get his way immediately. When we met for the second time, in my office, Matt's WISC-IV full-scale IQ was assessed at 64, and his adaptive abilities score was 68, based on his mother's report on the Vineland Adaptive Behavior Scales. Despite his mild mental retardation, however, Matt has been gaining over the past year in school, and he is showing a healthy gain in his developmental milestones as well.

Vanessa

Gaining at Home

Vanessa is an 8-year-old girl with moderate mental retardation (IQ = 52) and limited communication skills. She was diagnosed prior to her fourth birthday, after medical and psychological examinations were undertaken to determine why she was not making many speech sounds or learning basic self-help skills. Vanessa's mother told us about how her daughter's special needs were poorly met while she was a resident in a special school for the mentally retarded, and how this led to their decision to raise Vanessa at home with the help of their community:

"When our family moved here in 1990, we were told that we would receive $55 per month to care for

her at home, or she could live at the Children's Training Center. Vanessa had been diagnosed with moderate mental retardation prior to her fourth birthday, and we knew that we could not care for her daily needs at home with the limited assistance being offered. So we made the difficult decision to place her at the training center. But, even though Vanessa came home every weekend, we felt there was something missing from her life; something beyond staff care and attention was needed to foster her growth.

"About 2 years later, things changed dramatically. Vanessa was injured by another resident, and we decided that she should return home once and for all. We made every effort to find services she needed for her training and education in our own community. She now attends an integrated classroom at the same school as her older brother, and her teachers have noticed strong gains in her behavior and language. She participates in recreational programs, and has become an accomplished swimmer and basketball player."

Matthew was diagnosed as having mild mental retardation. Although delayed in his speech and language development, he was developing effective verbal skills and was capable of attending a regular classroom. Establishing friendships with children at school was sometimes problematic because he was often slow at understanding the rules of games and was teased by some children because of his slowness.

Vanessa was diagnosed as having moderate mental retardation. She could feed and dress herself with minimum assistance, and she communicated in short sentences, although her speech was not always discernible to people outside her family. Vanessa required more daily assistance to complete her routines, but she too was able to attend a local school during part of the day. As these cases show, the special needs of both children were sometimes overshadowed by economic and educational limitations, which required creativity and coordinated assistance on the part of parents, teachers, and other professionals.

Clinical Description

When the psychiatrist interviewed me he had my records in front of him—so he already knew I was mentally retarded. It's the same with everyone. If you are considered mentally retarded there is no way you can win. There is no way they give you a favorable report.

—Ed, describing part of his intake interview at the state institution. (Bogdan & Taylor, 1982)

Children with mental retardation show a considerable range of abilities and interpersonal qualities. With proper assistance, children with mild intellectual impairments, like Matthew, can carry out their daily routine much like other children. They can attend a regular classroom, adjust to the demands of physical and intellectual challenges, and develop meaningful and lasting relationships with peers and adults. Many show normal physical development and can learn physical coordination to ride a bike. Others, like Vanessa, who have more severe impairments, will require greater daily supervision and care throughout their childhood and sometimes into early adulthood, at which time they may have developed the necessary skills to live more independently.

Both Matthew and Vanessa, however, experience limitations that involve most areas of daily living. Their most obvious difficulties are learning to communicate effectively, due to their limited speech and language skills. Although Matthew eventually learned effective verbal communication, for several years Vanessa had to rely on sign language and nonverbal expressions or gestures to express her needs. Both children had problems developing friendships with other children because of their limited ability to comprehend what other children were expressing, especially during games and social activities that require stamina and formal rules. Many cognitive abilities such as language and problem solving are affected, therefore most children have difficulty with some aspect of learning. The degree of difficulty depends on the extent of cognitive impairment, which is the primary reason current definitions of mental retardation emphasize this aspect.

Table 9.2 summarizes the DSM-IV-TR diagnostic criteria for mental retardation. These criteria consist of three core features that describe this disorder in both children and adults. First, such individuals must have "significantly subaverage intellectual functioning," determined by formal intelligence testing or clinical judgment (in the case of an infant or an untestable subject). An individual must have an IQ score of approximately 70 or below to meet this first criterion, which falls 2 standard deviations below the average IQ score of 100 and thereby includes roughly 2% to 3% of the population.

The second criterion for diagnosing mental retardation requires "concurrent deficits or impairments in adaptive functioning," which refers to the ability to perform daily activities. In effect, an IQ score of 70 or below is not sufficient to receive a diagnosis of mental retardation. A person must also show significant limitations in at least two areas of adaptive behavior, such as communication, self-care, social/interpersonal skills, or functional academic or work skills. This aspect of the definition is important because it specifically excludes persons who may function well in their own surroundings, yet for various reasons may not perform well on standard IQ tests. Importantly, whether a child or adolescent exhibits these various adaptive skills is related not only to ability, but

also to experience and opportunity. Using public transportation, walking to a neighborhood store, and making simple purchases can all be affected by the individual's place of residence (urban versus rural, for example), or their concerns about neighborhood safety. Clinicians and educators must make educated guesses regarding a person's potential for performing a certain task if the person has not had experience with a particular skill on the test.

The final criterion for mental retardation stipulates that the child's below-average intellectual and adaptive abilities must be evident prior to age 18. The purpose of establishing this upper limit for the age of onset is twofold. First, it acknowledges that mental retardation is a developmental disorder that is evident during childhood and adolescence. Problems in learning and comprehension are most likely to occur during this time of rapid brain development. Second, this age criterion rules out persons who may show mental deficiencies caused by adult-onset degenerative diseases, such as Alzheimer's disease, or by head trauma.

The definition of mental retardation continues to be somewhat inaccurate and arbitrary, largely because it is based on a statistical concept—a cutoff IQ score—rather than on the nature or qualities of the person (B. H. King et al., 1997). Those with more severe cognitive impairments are more likely to be correctly diagnosed; however, the majority of persons diagnosed with mental retardation fall into the mild range. The ramifications of diagnosing someone with mental retardation can be serious. As Ed described so well, a careful balance must be struck between identifying the special needs of persons with intellectual disabilities, and labeling them as having mental retardation on the basis of somewhat arbitrary criteria (MacDonald & MacIntyre, 1999).

Additionally, the definition and identification of mental retardation depend somewhat on our social institutions. When children enter the school system, it is a significant point at which children's abilities are compared and deficiencies are most likely to be detected. If children are placed in a poorly matched learning environment, their developmental progress can be disrupted. Following their school years, persons with mild mental retardation often blend back into the larger population, and their "diagnosis" no longer has as much meaning to either their education or training (Hodapp & Dykens, 2003).

Degrees of Impairment

Children with mental retardation vary widely in their degree of disability. Some show cognitive impairments from early infancy, such as limited vocalizations or poor self-regulation, whereas other impairments may go relatively unnoticed through the elementary school years. Because of the wide variation in cognitive functioning and impairment, classification systems for mental retardation have always attempted to delineate various degrees of cognitive impairment. The DSM-IV-TR has continued the tradition by designating retardation as mild, moderate, severe, or profound; these designations are based primarily on IQ scores. The American Association on Mental Retardation (AAMR, 2002), in contrast, has restructured its description of varying degrees of mental retardation, choosing to base its categories on the level of support or assistance the person needs, rather than on IQ.

According to the DSM-IV-TR definition (APA, 2000), persons with **mild mental retardation** (IQ level of 55–70) constitute the largest group, estimated to be as many as 85% of persons with the disorder. Children with mild mental retardation often show small delays in development during the preschool years, but typically are not identified until academic or behavior problems emerge during the early elementary years. This category also has an overrepresentation of minority group members.

As a group, children with mild mental retardation typically develop social and communication skills during the preschool years (ages 0–5 years), perhaps with modest delays in expressive language. They usually have minimal or no sensorimotor impairment, and engage with peers readily. Like Matthew, however, some may find school and peer relationships to be challenging. By their late teens, these children can acquire academic skills up to approximately the sixth-grade level. During their adult years, they usually achieve social and vocational skills adequate for minimum self-support, but may need supervision, guidance, and assistance, especially when under unusual social or economic stress. With appropriate supports, individuals with mild mental retardation usually live successfully in the community, either independently or in supervised settings.

Persons with **moderate mental retardation** (IQ level of 40–54) constitute about 10% of those with mental retardation. Individuals at this level of impairment are more intellectually and adaptively impaired than someone with mild mental retardation, and are usually identified during the preschool years when they show delays in reaching early developmental milestones. By the time they enter school, they may communicate through a combination of single words and gestures, and show self-care and motor skills similar to an average 2- to 3-year-old. Many persons with Down syndrome function at the moderate level of retardation. Some of these individuals may require only a few supportive services to function on a daily basis, but others may continue to require some help throughout life.

Like Vanessa, most individuals with this level of mental retardation acquire limited communication skills during their early years, and by age 12 may be using practical communication skills. They benefit from vocational training and, with moderate supervision, can attend to their personal care. They can also benefit from training in social and occupational skills, but are unlikely to progress beyond the second-grade level in academic subjects. Adolescents with moderate mental retardation often have difficulty recognizing social conventions, such as appropriate dress or humor, which interferes with peer relationships. By adulthood, persons with moderate mental retardation typically adapt well to living in the community, and can perform unskilled or semiskilled work under supervision in sheltered workshops (specialized manufacturing facilities that train and supervise persons with mental retardation) or in the general workforce.

Those with **severe mental retardation** (IQ level of 25–39) constitute approximately 3% to 4% of persons with mental retardation. Most of these individuals suffer one or more organic causes of retardation, such as genetic defects, and are identified at a very young age because they have substantial delays in development and visible physical features or anomalies. Milestones such as standing, walking, and toilet training may be markedly delayed, and basic self-care skills are usually acquired by about age 9. In addition to intellectual impairment, they may have problems with physical mobility or other health-related problems, such as respiratory, heart, or physical complications.

Most persons functioning at this severe level of mental retardation require some special assistance throughout their lives. During early childhood they acquire little or no communicative speech; by age 12, they may use some two- to three-word phrases. Between 13 and 15 years of age, their academic and adaptive abilities are similar to those of an average 4- to 6-year-old. They profit to a limited extent from instruction in preacademic subjects, such as familiarity with the alphabet and simple counting, and can master skills such as sight reading "survival" words, like hot, danger, and stop. During their adult years, they may be able to perform simple tasks in closely supervised settings. Most adapt well to life in the community, in group homes or with their families, unless they have an associated disability that requires specialized nursing or other care (B. H. King et al., 1997).

Persons with **profound mental retardation** (IQ level below 20 or 25) constitute approximately 1% to 2% of those with mental retardation. Such individuals are typically identified as infants because of marked delays in development and biological anomalies such as asymmetrical facial features. During early childhood they show considerable impairments in sensorimotor functioning; by the age of 4 years, for example, their responsiveness is similar to that of a typical 1-year-old. They are able to learn only the rudiments of communication skills, and they require intensive training to learn basic eating, grooming, toileting, and dressing behaviors.

Persons with profound mental retardation require lifelong care and assistance. Almost all of these individuals show organic causes for their retardation, and many have severe co-occurring medical conditions, such as congenital heart defect or epilepsy, that sometimes lead to death during childhood or early adulthood. Most of these individuals live in supervised group homes or small, specialized facilities. Optimal development may occur in a highly structured environment with constant aid and supervision and an individualized relationship with a caregiver. Motor development as well as self-care and communication skills may improve if appropriate training is provided. For example, persons with profound mental retardation can usually perform simple tasks, such as washing their hands and changing their clothes, provided they have close supervision.

Level of Needed Supports

The DSM-IV-TR categories have been criticized as potentially stigmatizing and limiting because they emphasize the degree of impairment. This criticism provided the major impetus for the AAMR focus on levels of needed support and assistance (Luckasson et al., 2002). Rather than use the traditional IQ-based levels of impairment, the AAMR categorizes persons with mental retardation according to their need for supportive services: intermittent, limited, extensive, and pervasive. Table 9.3 defines these AAMR categories. Although similarities do exist between these levels of support and the DSM-IV levels of impairment, the major difference concerns the AAMR emphasis on the interaction between the person and the environment in determining his or her level of functioning. Defined in this manner, mental retardation is determined not so much by the ability of the person alone (as in the DSM-IV-TR definition), but by the level of support the person needs to function adaptively in the community (Hodapp & Dykens, 2003).

The AAMR approach underscores the areas of assis-

Table 9.3
American Association on Mental Retardation: Definition of Needed Supports

Intermittent:

Support on an "as needed" basis, such as following loss of job or during a medical crisis

Limited:

Support that is more consistent over time, such as time-limited employment training or during transition from school to work

Extensive:

Support characterized by regular (daily) involvement in at least some environments, such as work or home, and not time-limited

Pervasive:

Support that is constant and of high intensity, provided across several settings and possibly life-sustaining

Source: From *Mental Retardation: Definition, Classification, and Systems of Support,* 9th ed., by R. Luckasson, D. L. Coulter, E. A. Polloway, S. Reiss, R. L. Schalock, M. E. Snell, D. Spitalnik, and J. A. Stark, 1992, p. 26. Copyright © 2002 by the American Association on Mental Retardation. Reprinted by permission.

tance the child needs, which can be translated into specific training goals. Instead of a diagnosis of moderate mental retardation, Vanessa might receive the following AAMR diagnosis: "Vanessa is a child with mental retardation who needs limited supports in home living, academic skills, and development of self-help skills." Matthew's diagnosis might state: "Matt is a child with mental retardation who requires support on an as-needed basis, especially during stressful or demanding times—for example, during the transition to school, when making new friends, and when faced with new academic challenges." Like the DSM-IV-TR's degrees of impairment, the AAMR's levels of needed support have value in describing persons with mental retardation, yet face similar challenges in surmounting the unfortunate pressures of stigmatization.

Prevalence

Based on available evidence and estimates, the total number of children and adults with mental retardation most likely falls between 1% and 3% of the entire population (Szymanski & King, 1999). Recall that the number of persons diagnosed with mental retardation depends on the point at which the line is drawn for cutoff scores for IQ and adaptive behavior. Even with a stable IQ criterion of 70 and below, however, the number of persons with mental retardation is open to debate. Each person applies his or her own cognitive abilities in unique ways that may be more or less adaptive in her or his own environment.

Slightly more males than females are currently considered to fall within the range of mental retardation (B. H. King et al., 1997; C. C. Murphy, Yeargin-Allsopp, Decoufle, & Drews, 1995). Similar to racial differences in the diagnosis of mental retardation, however, this gender difference may be an artifact of identification and referral patterns. Boys are referred more often than girls for psychometric testing (usually in relation to behavioral disturbances), and are somewhat more likely than girls to fail on adaptive functioning tests (Vardill & Calvert, 2000). If a true male excess of mental retardation does exist, researchers suspect this may be due to the occurrence of X-linked genetic disorders, such as fragile-X syndrome (discussed later in the chapter), which affect males more prominently than females (E. Anderson, 1994).

It is a well-established finding that mental retardation is more prevalent among children of lower socioeconomic status (SES) and children from minority groups. This link is found primarily among children in the mild mental retardation range; children with more severe levels are identified almost equally in different racial and economic groups. Whether or not signs of organic etiology are present, diagnoses of mild mental retardation increase sharply from near zero among children from higher SES to about 2.5% in the lowest SES category (APA, 2000). These figures indicate that SES factors play a suspected role both in the cause of mental retardation and in the identification and labeling of persons with mental retardation (B. H. King et al., 1997; Stromme & Magnus, 2000).

The overrepresentation of minority and low SES children in the group with mild mental retardation is a complicated and unresolved issue. As we noted, average IQ levels for the African American population are lower than IQ levels found in the white population, resulting in more African American children among samples of mild mental retardation. What specific environmental circumstances might create such an imbalance in IQ findings? To answer this question, Brooks-Gunn et al. (2003), tested the theory that the differences can be partially explained based on social and economic disadvantage. They accounted for initial African American versus white child IQ differences of over 17 points by the independent effects of economic deprivation, home environment, and maternal characteristics. As shown in Figure 9.1, initial IQ differences were almost 18 points between a sample of African American and white children at 5 years of age, controlling for gender and birth weight. However, these differences were reduced by about 71% after adjusting for differences in poverty and home environment.

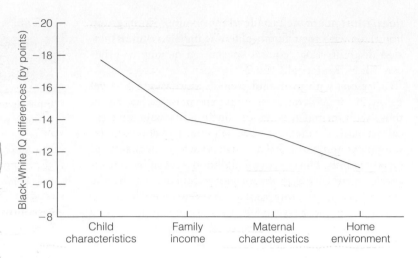

Figure 9.1 Factors accounting for differences in IQ scores between white and African American children.
Source: (Data from Brooks-Gunn, J., Klebanov, P. K., Smith, J., Duncan, G. J., & Lee, K. (2003). The Black-White test score gap in young children: Contributions of test and family characteristics. *Applied Developmental Science,* 7(4), pp. 239–252.)

SECTION SUMMARY

- The DSM-IV-TR criteria for mental retardation consist of subaverage intellectual functioning (defined as an IQ of 70 or below), deficits or impairments in adaptive functioning, and onset before age 18.

- Children with mental retardation vary widely in their degree of disability or level of functioning.

- The DSM-IV-TR describes a person's level of functioning in terms of degrees of impairment—mild, moderate, severe, or profound—based on ranges in IQ scores.

- The American Association on Mental Retardation (AAMR) describes a person's level of functioning in terms of needed levels of support or assistance rather than on IQ. The AAMR levels are intermittent, limited, extensive, and pervasive.

- Mental retardation occurs in an estimated 1% to 3% of the population, more often among males than females.

- Mental retardation occurs more often among children from lower socioeconomic and minority groups. Economic disadvantage and discrimination practices often account for the latter findings.

Developmental Course and Adult Outcomes

To appreciate the manner in and extent to which children with mental retardation achieve various developmental milestones, consider how typically developing children express themselves. An infant exploring his or her world relies on primitive sensorimotor functions—touching, tasting, and manipulating objects—to learn about the environment. At this stage of development everything is new, and the brain is establishing literally millions of new connections each day.

Then, between 18 and 24 months, the toddler begins to acquire language and to draw on memories of past experience to aid in understanding the present. For an intellectually normal child, it is during this stage that the child's environmental conditions and opportunities are known to play a crucial role in fostering enthusiasm for learning, and in establishing the roots of intellectual sophistication. Although the majority of children with mental retardation progress through each developmental milestone in roughly the same manner as their nonretarded counterparts, important differences in their developmental accomplishments are evident.

Much of the knowledge about other issues involved in the developmental course and adult outcomes for children with mental retardation is derived from studies of children with Down syndrome. Chromosome abnormalities are the single most common cause of severe mental retardation. **Down syndrome** is the most common disorder resulting from these abnormalities. These children, along with their parents, have frequently participated in studies comparing their development with that of their normally developing peers.

Dan, a 15-year-old with Down syndrome, describes how his early development was similar to, but much slower than, that of his younger brother.

Dan
With His Brother's Help

When I was almost 3 and my sister was 5, we had a baby brother. I helped feed him and take care of him until he was almost 3. I was 5 by then, and could do most of the things he could do, but about that time he caught up to me. I could still do some things he couldn't, but not many. He could do some things I had trouble with. We became good friends. Every time he learned a new skill, I would either learn it with him, or he would teach me later. I was really little for my age, so we were pretty close in size. We shared a bunk bed, toys, and clothes. We learned to do a lot of things together. When he learned to ride a bike, and I wasn't ready to learn yet, mom and dad got me a Powerwheel motorized bike so I could ride, too. When he learned to read, he taught me how, too. When he played baseball and football, he took me with him.

In those days, I still went to school in another district, so most of my friends were his friends. Now that we go to the same school it is sometimes hard for him to remember that I have my own friends, too. I have to tell him I am the big brother. He sometimes gets teased at school because he is my brother, but he is learning to explain instead of fight. Mostly, the kids are all nice to us.

Dan, with moderate mental retardation, is describing how his younger brother Brian, with normal intelligence, caught up with him by the time Brian was 2 years old, and progressed through developmental milestones at a faster pace. Does Dan's development follow the same organized sequence as Brian's? Will his development show specific deficits in certain intellectual abilities such as language, or will he eventually catch up? This case illustrates the developmental versus difference controversy (B. Weiss, Weisz, & Bromfield, 1986), an issue that has intrigued those in the field of child development and mental retardation for some time. Simply stated, the **developmental versus difference controversy** is this: Do all children—regardless of intellectual impairments—progress through the same developmental milestones in a similar sequence, but at different rates? Or does the development of children with mental retardation proceed in a different, less sequential, and less organized fashion?

The developmental position, which applies primarily to individuals not suffering from organic impairment, consists of two primary hypotheses. First, the *similar sequence hypothesis* argues that all children, with or without mental retardation, pass through stages of cognitive development in an identical (invariant) order; they differ only in their rate and upper limit of development (Hodapp & Zigler, 1995). Second, the *similar structure hypothesis* suggests that children with mental retardation demonstrate the same behaviors and underlying processes as typically developing children at the same level of cognitive functioning (such as Dan and his younger brother were at ages 5 and 2). That is, if children with mental retardation are matched to nonretarded children by their mental age, then the children with mental retardation will show equivalent performance on cognitive tasks, such as problem solving, spelling, and moral reasoning. The developmental position rejects the notion of a specific deficit or difference among children with mental retardation, and instead emphasizes how these children traverse the stages more slowly and attain a lower developmental ceiling than typically developing children (Hodapp & Zigler, 1995).

In contrast, the **difference viewpoint** argues that cognitive development of children with mental retardation differs from that of children without mental retardation in more than a developmental rate and upper limit. According to this position, even when his mental age is matched to his younger brother's, Dan will show qualitatively different reasoning and problem-solving strategies, and he may never be able to accomplish some tasks beyond a certain level.

Although this issue has not been entirely resolved, ample evidence supports the developmental hypothesis for children with familial, as opposed to organic, types of retardation (both are discussed in the section on causes). Specifically, children with familial mental retardation generally follow developmental stages in an invariant order, the same as nonretarded children, with the possible exception of some children with co-occurring brain abnormalities or autism (Hodapp & Zigler, 1995). The similar structure hypothesis has also been supported for children with familial mental retardation, with some exceptions. Children with familial mental retardation show slight deficits in memory and information processing when compared with mental age-matched, nonretarded children (Weiss et al., 1986). These deficits may be due to the children's difficulty in staying motivated to perform repetitive, boring tasks (Weisz, 1999).

The picture for children with organically based mental retardation (such as Dan, who has Down syndrome) is more straightforward. They often have one or more specific deficit areas that cause them to perform worse than mental age-matched, nonretarded children. Thus, Dan is likely to show some differences in his performance in certain areas of development, including his expressive language. Nevertheless, he will likely pass through the same developmental sequences as his younger brother, but at a slower pace.

Motivation

Many children who fall within the mild range of mental retardation are bright enough to learn and to attend regular schools and classrooms. However, they are more susceptible to a sense of helplessness and frustration, which places additional burdens on their social and cognitive development. As a consequence, they begin to expect failure, even for tasks they can master; in the absence of proper instruction, their motivation to tackle new demands decreases (Hodapp & Zigler, 1995).

Ed, describing his memory of comments made by his teacher in elementary school, expresses this phenomenon well:

"Her negative picture of me stood out like a sore thumb. That's the problem with people like me—the schools and teachers find out we have problems, they notice them, and then we are abandoned. That one teacher was very annoyed that I was in her class. She had to put up with me." (Bogdan & Taylor, 1982)

Consequently, compared with typically developing children of their same mental age, children with mental retardation expect little success, set lower goals for themselves, and settle for minimal success when they are able to do better (Weisz, 1999). This learned helplessness may be unwittingly condoned by adults. When they are told a child is "retarded," adults are less likely to urge that child to persist following failure than urge a normal child at the same level of cognitive development. On the other hand, young children with mild mental retardation improve in their ability to remain on task and develop goal-directed behavior when provided with stimulating environments and caregiver support (Blair, Greenberg, & Crnic, 2001).

"Acknowledge our children's differences but respect their uniqueness."—Parent of a child with Down syndrome

Changes in Progress

Mental retardation is not necessarily a lifelong disorder. Although it is a relatively stable condition from childhood into adulthood, any individual's IQ score can fluctuate in relation to level of impairment and type of retardation. Children who have mild mental retardation, like Matthew, with appropriate training and opportunities may develop good adaptive skills in other domains, and may no longer have the level of impairment required for a diagnosis of mental retardation (APA, 2000).

The major cause of a child's mental retardation certainly affects the degree to which his or her IQ and adaptive abilities may change. Children with Down syndrome, who are not representative of the course of mental retardation in general, may plateau during the middle childhood years, and then decrease in IQ over time. For example, from 1 to 6 years of age, children with Down syndrome often show significant age-related gains in adaptive functioning, but as they grow older, their pace of development levels off or even declines. Similarly, as they grow older, a deceleration is often seen in their rate of social development (Roizen & Patterson, 2003). This observation has been termed the *slowing and stability hypothesis* (Hodapp & Dykens, 2003), and affirms that children with Down syndrome may alternate between periods of gain and functioning and periods of little or no advance. Although these children continue to develop in intelligence, they do so at progressively slower rates throughout the childhood years.

Language and Social Behavior

Research on language development and social functioning among children and adolescents with Down syndrome suggests that their development follows a largely predictable and organized course (Cicchetti, Toth, & Bush, 1988). Because their cognitive development, play, self-knowledge, and knowledge of others are interrelated in organized and meaningful ways, the underlying symbolic abilities in children with Down syndrome are believed to be largely intact (Cicchetti et al., 1988).

However, important differences in language development exist between children with Down syndrome and their typically developing age-mates. Perhaps the most striking difference is the considerable delay in expressive language development for children with Down syndrome, which is necessary to establish independent living skills. Their expressive language is often much weaker than receptive language, especially as they attain communication abilities beyond the 24-month level (Miller, 1999).

In addition to the development of symbolic and language skills, a major milestone during infancy and early childhood development concerns the ability to form a secure attachment relationship with one's primary caregivers. Although slower than normal, many children with Down syndrome form secure attachment relationships with their caregivers by 12–24 months of developmental age (Cicchetti et al., 1988). Still, a significant number may have problems in developing a secure attachment because they express less emotion than other children. In one study, children with Down syndrome were not picked up and held by either the mother or the stranger in the strange situation to the same extent as nondelayed children. Even when these children made approaches with appropriate signals for contact, mothers and strangers rarely completed the contact, presumably because the children did not show the distress signals of crying, reaching, or holding on that typically tell the parent "I want to be picked up!" (B. E. Vaughn, Contreras, & Seifer, 1994). This finding has important implications for parents of young children with Down syndrome: Even though they may show few signals of distress or desire for contact, these infants and toddlers need to be held and nurtured just as others do.

Following the attachment period, the next important developmental milestones relate to the emergence of a sense of self, which establishes the early foundations of personality. Like other children, toddlers with Down syndrome begin to delight at recognizing themselves in mirrors and photos, although this milestone is often delayed. The experience of self-recognition in most infants is immediately met with smiles and laughter, a finding that is repeated among toddlers with Down syndrome as well (Mans, Cicchetti, & Sroufe, 1978). This positive affect accompanying their visual self-recognition suggests that these children feel good about themselves (Cicchetti et al., 1988). However, as toddlers and preschoolers, children with Down syndrome show delayed and aberrant functioning in their *internal state language*, the language that reflects the emergent sense of self and others (through the use of words such as mad and happy). Because internal state language is critical to regulating social interaction and providing a foundation for early self-other understanding, these children may be at increased risk for subsequent problems in the development of the self-system (Beeghly & Cicchetti, 1997).

Children with mental retardation, especially those with moderate to mild impairments, learn symbolic play—games, puppets, and sports—in much the same manner as other children. Nevertheless, they often fail to gain their peers' acceptance in regular education settings, because they may have deficits in social skills and social-cognitive ability (Bebko et al., 1998). Concerns about the social development of children with mental retardation are increasing as a result of the movement to include children with different levels of ability in regular classrooms and schools, rather than only placing them in institutions or specialized facilities. Typically developing children seem to prefer playing with other typically developing children, and as a result, children with mental retardation are more socially isolated from other children their age (Guralnick, 1999; Kemp & Carter, 2002). Despite their limited social skills, these integrated classrooms allow children with intellectual disabilities to interact with typically developing peers, and positively affect their social status (Kemp & Carter, 2002).

Emotional and Behavioral Problems

Pattie

Disturbed or Disturbing?

Pattie was labeled mentally retarded and lived in over 20 homes and institutions before being committed to a state school at age 10. At the age of 20, she discussed some of her experiences and feelings: "I guess I was very disturbed. I call it disturbed, but it was when I was very upset. A lot of people at (the institution) . . . told me I was disturbed—that I was disturbed and that I was retarded—so I figure that all through my life I was disturbed. Looking at the things I done, I must have been disturbed. . . . Upset and disturbed are the same in my mind. Crazy to me is something else. It is somebody that is really gone. I mean really out. Just deliberately kill somebody just to do it. That is what I call crazy. I guess what I was was emotionally disturbed—yeah. Emotionally disturbed is a time when too many things are bothering me. They just build up till I get too nervous or upset. My mind just goes through all these changes and different things. So many things inside that were bothering me." (Bogdan & Taylor, 1982)

Pattie's description of her feelings while living in various institutions illuminates how "disturbing" her behavior could be. But are her feelings a function of her environment and personal limitations? Many children and adolescents with mental retardation have to face many obstacles related to their intellectual, physical, and social impairments, and often they have little control over their own lives.

In the early 1970s, a major study was conducted (Rutter, Tizard, Yule, Graham, & Whitmore, 1976) to gain some understanding of the extent of psychiatric disorders among children and adults with and without mental retardation. Ratings by parents and teachers each revealed that about one-third of the children with mild mental retardation and one-half of the children with more severe forms of mental retardation showed major signs of emotional disturbance, suggesting these problems are common. Since then, research has estimated the rate of emotional and behavioral disturbances is about four times greater than in the general population (Emerson, 2003; Hodapp & Dykens, 2003).

The general sense is that the nature and course of psychiatric disorders in children and adolescents with and without mental retardation is very similar, except for those diagnosed with more severe and profound levels (Hodopp, Kazemi, Rosner, & Dykens, in press). The most common psychiatric diagnoses given to children with mental retardation involve impulse control disorders, anxiety disorders, and mood disorders (Bouras, 1999). Although these problems are sometimes severe and often require intervention, they are considered part of the spectrum of problems that coexist with mental retardation, not indicators of other psychiatric illnesses (Hodapp & Dykens, 2003).

Adjustments are usually needed in how DSM-IV-TR diagnostic criteria for other mental disorders are applied, however. The frequency of temper tantrums, hyperactivity, and mood disorders among these children requires consideration of what is normal or typical for other children with similar levels of retardation. For example, recall that the diagnosis of ADHD (Chapter 5) requires behavioral disturbance that is inappropriate for an individual's developmental level. Among individuals with profound mental retardation, their attention spans, distractibility, and on-task behaviors vary considerably. An individual with profound mental retardation must be compared to other children with profound mental retardation for the purpose of diagnosing any other psychiatric disturbance (Benson & Aman, 1999).

Internalizing Problems Adolescence is a developmental period of increased risk for mood disorders and other internalizing symptoms, which is also true for those with mental retardation. Dykens, Shah, Sagun, Beck, and King (2002), for example, noted that average Internalizing scores for adolescents with mental retardation on the Child Behavior Checklist were almost twice that of younger children. Like their normally developing peers, adolescents with Down syndrome and other forms of mental retarda-

tion may show a decline in their previously sociable and cheerful behaviors, and in some cases suffer from significant symptoms of depression and social withdrawal.

ADHD-related Symptoms Teachers and parents of children with mental retardation commonly report ADHD-related symptoms that require adjustments in instruction and child management strategies (Dykens, 2000; Pearson, Norton, & Farwell, 1997). When a teacher is present to prompt the appropriate behavior and participate in the activity, children with mental retardation with and without ADHD will generally remain on task. However, when instructed to work on their own without teacher assistance, differences between those with and without ADHD emerge during these independent tasks (Handen, McAuliffe, Janosky, Feldman, & Breaux, 1994). When children with mental retardation and ADHD are placed on stimulant medication, they are able to remain on task for longer periods and their accuracy on cognitive tasks improves, although their responses are more varied than responses of normal-IQ children (Aman, Buican, & Arnold, 2003).

Other Symptoms Children and adults with mental retardation may show additional symptoms that can be particularly troublesome. Pica (discussed in Chapter 13), which can result in the ingestion of caustic and dangerous substances, is seen in its more serious forms among children and adults with mental retardation. **Self-injurious behavior (SIB)** is a serious and sometimes life-threatening problem that affects about 8% of persons across all ages and levels of retardation (Rojahn & Esbensen, 2002). Some common forms of SIB include head banging, eye gouging, severe scratching, rumination, some types of pica, and inserting objects under the skin. The long-term prognoses for pica and SIBs are not favorable. An 18-year study indicates that emotional withdrawal, stereotypies (frequent repetition of the same posture, movement, or form of speech, e.g., head banging, hand or body movements), and avoidance of eye contact were still evident 18 years later among persons with severe mental retardation (A. H. Reid & Ballanger, 1995).

Thus, children with mental retardation may show emotional and behavioral problems that require special recognition and learning strategies. In general, these problems do not constitute major psychiatric disorders, but they do reflect the greater challenges these children may have in learning to express their needs and adapting to their surroundings. A 7-year-old girl with mild mental retardation, for instance, may be at a developmental level comparable to a typically developing 4-year-old. In the classroom, therefore, she may have difficulty sitting in her seat and remaining on task. She may not always control her emotions or her behavior as well as other 7-year-olds in the class, leading to occasional outbursts of laughter or anger. It is important to keep these problems within a developmental perspective. We would not expect a 4-year-

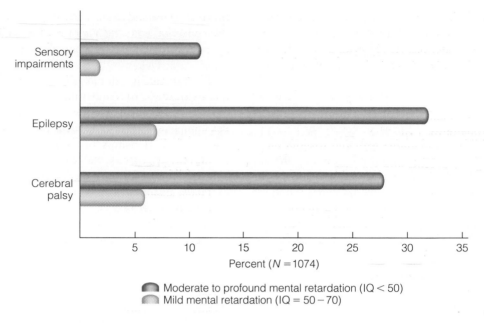

Figure 9.2 Physical disabilities among children with mental retardation.
(Data from C. C. Murphy et al., 1995)

old to behave as well in the classroom as an older child, and expectations and teaching methods have to be adjusted accordingly. As expressed so well by Ed and Pattie, labeling a child with a diagnostic term that implies pathology or inability is often ill-conceived and counterproductive. Such terms must be used sparingly—only in instances, such as self-injurious behaviors, where special attention is warranted.

Other Disabilities

Children with mental retardation may also suffer other physical and developmental disabilities that can affect their health and development in pervasive ways. Such disabilities are usually related to the degree of intellectual impairment. Figure 9.2 shows how often some of the more common developmental disabilities are noted among children with moderate to profound mental retardation (IQ < 50) and those with mild mental retardation (IQ = 50–70), based on a large sample of schoolchildren (C. C. Murphy et al., 1995). Overall, 12% of the children with mild mental retardation and 45% of those with moderate to profound mental retardation had at least one other disability, such as a sensory impairment, cerebral palsy, or epilepsy.

Despite major co-occurring physical and intellectual disabilities, children and adults with Down syndrome now have greater life expectancy (median life expectancy was 49 years in 1997) (Yang, Rasmussen, & Friedman, 2002). About two-thirds of adults with Down syndrome survive beyond 30 years of age, largely as a result of better medical treatments for respiratory infections and congenital

heart disorders. However, most individuals with Down syndrome who live beyond the age of 40 demonstrate cognitive decline (much like Alzheimer's disease) due to gene damage on chromosome 21 (Lendon, Ashall, & Goate, 1997). Moreover, increased life expectancy is more dramatic for whites than for minorities across various countries, due to fewer financial and social supports and less access to quality health care (Yang et al., 2002).

SECTION SUMMARY

- Children with mental retardation follow developmental stages in the same order as typically developing children. However, their goals and motivation are reduced over time because of feelings of frustration, which often lead to expectations of failure.

- Adaptive skills and level of impairment may improve over time, especially for children with mild mental retardation, if appropriate training and opportunities are provided.

- Developmental disabilities are common, such as speech and language problems and behavioral disturbances. Emotional and behavioral problems are considered part of the spectrum of problems coexisting with mental retardation, rather than indicators of mental disorder.

- Children with mental retardation have a greater chance of having other physical and developmental disabilities such as sensory impairments, cerebral palsy, and epilepsy that can affect their health and development in pervasive ways.

Causes

It is astounding to consider that there are over 1,000 genetic disorders associated with mental retardation (King, Hodapp, & Dykens, in press), in addition to other organic causes. Yet, despite the number of known causes, scientists cannot account for mental retardation in the majority of cases, especially the milder forms. A genetic or environmental cause is known for almost two-thirds of individuals with moderate to profound mental retardation, whereas only about one-quarter of those causes are known for mild mental retardation (Raynham, Gibbons, Flint, & Higgs, 1996). Some causes happen before birth (prenatal), as is the case with all genetic disorders and accidents in the womb. Other causes are birth-related (perinatal) insults, such as prematurity or a lack of oxygen (anoxia) at birth. Still other causes are an inflammation of the brain lining (meningitis), head trauma, and other factors that occur after birth (postnatal).

To make sense of these different causes, researchers have proposed a two-group approach to mental retardation—the organic group and the cultural-familial group. The definitions, characteristics, and causes of mental retardation as viewed from the two-group approach are summed up in Table 9.4. The **organic group** (sometimes referred to as pathological) has a clear biological cause and is usually associated with severe and profound mental retardation, whereas the **cultural-familial group** has no clear organic cause and is usually associated with mild mental retardation (Zigler, 1967; Zigler & Hodapp, 1986).

Considerable knowledge exists about organic mental retardation due to the strong biological factors involved.

In stark contrast, the cultural-familial group remains somewhat of a mystery, although it comprises one-half to two-thirds of all persons with mental retardation (Hodapp & Dykens, 2003). The prime suspects are environmental and situational factors such as poverty, inadequate child care, poor nutrition, and parental psychopathology, which affect the psychological (not biological) development of the child. However, more specific cause-and-effect relationships have not been determined.

Certainly, genetic factors still play some role in cultural-familial forms of mental retardation, as suggested by family histories. The chance of a child having mental retardation increases geometrically if both parents have normal IQ but one parent has a sibling with mental retardation (13%), if one parent has mental retardation (20%), and if both parents have mental retardation (42%) (Reed & Reed, 1965). Accordingly, both genetic and environmental factors are implicated in milder forms of mental retardation, but in a manner as yet to be determined (State, King, & Dykens, 1997).

The two-group distinction also contends that mild mental retardation should be conceptualized along a continuum that varies from lesser to greater degrees of intellectual ability, similar to a bell curve. In contrast, the more severe forms of mental retardation are categorical—present or absent—due to unusual events that have powerful influences on development. Figure 9.3 shows that an unexpected excess of low-range IQ scores opposes the assumption of a normal distribution. Significant organic causes, in all probability, account for these additional low-range scores.

The relative importance of the environment also stands out in the two-group distinction. The socio-

---

Table 9.4
The Two-Group Approach to Mental Retardation

	ORGANIC	CULTURAL-FAMILIAL
Definition	Individual shows a clear organic cause of mental retardation.	Individual shows no obvious cause of retardation. Other family member may have mental retardation.
Characteristics	More prevalent in moderate, severe, and profound mental retardation. Equal or near-equal rates across all ethnic and SES levels. More often associated with other physical disabilities.	More prevalent in mild mental retardation. Higher rates within minority groups and low SES groups. Few associated physical and medical disabilities.
Causes[1]	Prenatal (genetic disorders, accidents in utero). Perinatal (prematurity, anoxia). Postnatal (head trauma, meningitis).	Polygenic (i.e., parents of low IQ). Environmentally deprived. Undetected organic conditions.

[1] Causes are suspected for cultural-familial mental retardation.

Source: From "Mental Retardation," by R. M. Hodapp and E. M. Dykens, 1996, p. 378. In E. J. Mash and R. A. Barkley (Eds.) *Child Psychopathology.* Copyright © 1996 The Guilford Press. Reprinted by permission.

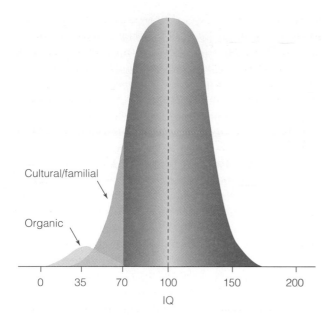

Figure 9.3 The approximate distribution of Stanford-Binet IQs. In practice, more children get low IQs than is predicted by this distribution. The excess of very low IQs has important implications for the two-group explanations of mental retardation—cultural-familial and organic.

Source: Adapted from *Understanding Mental Retardation,* by E. Ziegler and R. J. Hodapp, p. 73. Copyright © 1986 by Cambridge University Press. Adapted by permission.

Inheritance and the Role of the Environment

The study of human intelligence has received the lion's share of attention in terms of the underlying processes involved in genetic makeup, and the environmental factors that influence genetic expression. Still, the long-standing debate concerning the relative contributions of genes and environment is far from being fully resolved (McGue, 1997). Conceivably, genetic influences on development are potentially modifiable by environmental input, although the practicality of the modifications is another matter. Similarly, environmental influences on development involve the genes or structures to which the genes have contributed (Neisser et al., 1996). Simply stated, children do not inherit an IQ—they inherit a **genotype,** which is a collection of genes that pertain to intelligence. The expression of the genotype in the environment—the gene–environment interaction—is referred to as the **phenotype.** The **heritability** of a trait describes the proportion of the variation of a trait attributable to genetic influences in the population (Neisser et al., 1996). Heritability of any given trait, therefore, can range from none (0%) to 100% genetically determined.

Is it possible to estimate the heritability of intelligence and, by implication, the heritability of mental retardation? This intriguing question can now be answered with some degree of confidence, but little fanfare. The overwhelming evidence points to a heritability of intelligence of approximately 50%; that is, both genetic and nongenetic factors play a powerful role in the makeup and expression of intelligence (McGue, Bouchard, Iacono, & Lykken, 1993; Plomin & Neiderhiser, 1991).

There are so many specific genetic causes of mental retardation that some skepticism about the importance of environmental effects still remains. The difficulty of identifying, pinpointing, and measuring specific, nongenetic variables certainly adds to this dilemma (Hodapp & Des-Jardin, 2002). Considerable evidence has demonstrated, however, that major environmental variations do affect cognitive performance in children from disadvantaged backgrounds (Ramey, Campbell, & Ramey, 1999). For example, children born to socially disadvantaged parents and then adopted into more privileged homes have significantly higher IQ scores than siblings reared by their disadvantaged, biological parents (Capron & Duyme, 1989).

economic background of the organic group is about the same as for the general population, which fits with the notion that severe forms of mental retardation can affect anyone, regardless of SES. The familial group is overrepresented by those of lower SES and social disadvantage, and is significantly related to a family history of mental retardation. This fits with the assertion that an impoverished social environment can influence intellectual growth and ability in subtle, yet crucial, ways.

In most cases, the two-group approach has been supported empirically, with some adjustments (Simonoff et al., 1996). First, the percentage of individuals with a clear organic cause has increased over the last few decades, due to the greater knowledge of genetic and organic causes (Dykens et al., 2000). As well, the original assumption that mild mental retardation is not due to organic causes had to be tempered by findings that epilepsy, cerebral palsy, and other organic disorders are found more often among persons with mild mental retardation than among those without (Sabaratnam, Laver, Butler, & Pembrey, 1994). After factoring in the overlap between the two groups, however, this approach to the etiology of mental retardation has persevered.

The Buckets *reprinted by permission of United Feature Syndicate, Inc.*

The prenatal environment may influence IQ to a greater extent than previously appreciated. A review of studies of twins and non-twin siblings revealed that the shared prenatal environment (i.e., all children shared the same mother) accounted for 20% of IQ similarity in twins but only 5% among non-twin siblings (Devlin, Daniels, & Rodin, 1997). These findings imply that prenatal influences such as nutrition, hormone levels, and toxic substances may be misidentified as genetic when in fact they are environmental (McGue, 1997). The practical benefits of this research are important to consider: If early environmental (prenatal) influences have a significant impact on intellectual functioning, then expanding public health initiatives aimed at improving maternal nutrition and reducing prenatal exposure to toxins may not only improve maternal prenatal care, but may unexpectedly improve children's intellectual and cognitive functioning as well.

Genetic and Constitutional Factors

Despite the rapid expansion of knowledge regarding the genetic mechanisms underlying conditions associated with mental retardation, the actual biological mechanisms that cause impaired intellect are poorly understood (Hodapp & Dykens, 2003). Identification of abnormal genes, or genes involving an increased risk for particular disorders, is invaluable for genetic screening and counseling, but the identification does not specify a more effective treatment mode for mental retardation.

Because so many conditions cause mental retardation, the focus in this section will be on several different disorders or classes of disorder including: Down syndrome, fragile-X syndrome, Prader-Willi and Angelman syndromes, and single-gene conditions. Each disorder illustrates different aspects of genetic mechanisms. The various ways in which genes may interact with environmental influences are also highlighted.

Chromosome Abnormalities   The most common disorder that results from chromosome abnormalities is Down syndrome. These abnormalities can also occur in the number of sex chromosomes, resulting in mental retardation syndromes such as Klinefelter's (XXY, a disorder in which males have an extra X chromosome) and Turner's (XO, a disorder in which women are missing a second X chromosome). These latter disorders are somewhat common—about 1 in 400 live births—but they are generally less devastating than genetic irregularities in their effects on intellectual functioning (Simonoff et al., 1996).

The number of children with Down syndrome has gradually decreased from 1 in 700 births to 1 in 1000 births over the last two decades, due to increased prenatal screening and terminated pregnancies diagnosed with Down syndrome (Roizen & Patterson, 2003). The syndrome produces several distinguishing physical features including: a small skull; a large tongue protruding from a small mouth; almond-shaped eyes with sloping eyebrows; a flat nasal bridge; a short, crooked fifth finger; and broad, square hands with a simian (monkeylike) crease across the palm. These physical features are sometimes inconspicuous, and can appear to varying degrees.

In most Down syndrome cases, the extra chromosome results from **nondisjunction**, which is the failure of the 21st pair of the mother's chromosomes to separate during meiosis. When the mother's two chromosomes join with the single 21st chromosome from the father, the result is three number 21 chromosomes instead of the normal two (known as trisomy 21). Because nondisjunction is strongly related to maternal age, the incidence of Down syndrome increases from about 1 per 1000 live births for mothers less than 35 years old to about 20 per 1000 when the mother is 45 years of age or older (Morris, Wald, Mutton & Alberman, 2003).

Although the chromosomal basis of Down syndrome is well understood, the specific cause of mental retardation in these children is not known. Based on recent gene mapping of chromosome 21, it is believed that some genes may have localized effects on brain development (Roizen & Patterson, 2003). Testing this theory from a functional perspective, Pennington, Moon, Edgin, Stedron, and Nadel (2003) recently pinpointed differences in hippocampal function among young children with and without Down syndrome based on neuropsychological testing. Because the hippocampus plays an important role in long-term memory, these findings help to explain some of the underlying processes that affect the ability of children with Down syndrome to acquire normal language skills (a fundamental aspect of IQ).

Fragile-X syndrome is the most common cause of inherited mental retardation. Down syndrome occurs more frequently but is rarely inherited. This disorder affects about 1 in 4000 males (Turner, Web, Wake, & Robinson, 1996) and 1 in 8000 females (Crawford et al., 1999). Physical features are more subtle than in Down syndrome, and may include a large forehead, a prominent jaw, and low, protruding ears. Mental retardation is generally in the mild to moderate range, although some children are profoundly handicapped and others have normal intelligence (Simonoff et al., 1996). Fragile-X syndrome has a more detrimental effect on males, causing mental retardation in most cases (Bailey, Hatton & Skinner, 1998) compared to about half of females (Mazzocco, 2000).

Although the gene for fragile-X syndrome, known as the FMR-1 gene, is located on the X chromosome, this syndrome does not follow a traditional X-linked inheritance pattern. About one-third to one-half of the females who carry and transmit the disorder are themselves affected with a variant of the syndrome, and show a slight degree of cognitive or emotional impairment. Further, about 20% of males with the FMR-1 gene transmit the disorder but are not affected themselves (E. Anderson, 1994).

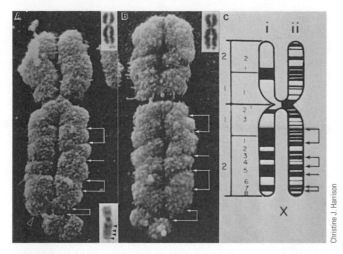

Micrograph showing the "pinched chromosome" found in fragile-X syndrome.

The behavioral characteristics of fragile-X syndrome are often subtle but distinctive. The majority of affected males have unusual social and communication patterns marked by shyness and poor eye contact, as well as significant delays in cognitive and communication development (Bailey, Hatton, & Skinner, 1998). Social anxiety and avoidance are also common in girls with this disorder, even if unaccompanied by mental retardation (Lesniak-Karpiak, Mazzocco & Ross, 2003). Notably, most males and about one-third of females with fragile-X syndrome show some autism-like behaviors, such as flapping hands, biting themselves, repetitive actions, and walking on toes, and about 33% of children with Fragile X receive a formal diagnosis of autism (Rogers, Wehner, & Hagerman, 2001).

Prader-Willi syndrome is a complex genetic disorder that includes short stature, mental retardation or learning disabilities, incomplete sexual development, low muscle tone, and an involuntary urge to eat constantly (Akefeldt & Gillberg, 1999). The syndrome is rare and estimated to affect only about 5 to 10 per 100,000 births (Dykens & Shah, 2003). Between ages 2 and 6, children with this syndrome develop extreme overeating, foraging, and hoarding. They need fewer calories than normal to maintain an appropriate weight because they are small, and they invariably become obese (Butler et al., 2002).

Angelman syndrome is associated with mental retardation that is usually moderate to severe. The behavior of children with this disorder is characterized by ataxia (awkward gait), jerky movements, hand flapping, seizures, and the absence of speech. Distinctive facial features include a large jaw and an open-mouthed expression.

Both Prader-Willi and Angelman syndromes are associated with an abnormality of chromosome 15, but they are not considered inherited conditions. Rather, these syndromes are believed to be spontaneous genetic birth defects that occur at or near the time of conception. For reasons that are still not well understood, genes in the affected region on the mother's chromosome 15 are not expressed (functional). This lack of a gene or genes that are very close to each other appears to be the cause of the related syndromes. The origin—whether maternal or paternal—of the absent genetic material is the likely cause of the marked phenotypic differences.

Much is being discovered about the genetic influences on intelligence and adaptive abilities. Because these influences are by no means uniform or exact, a challenge remains in accounting for the mechanisms that cause these effects on intelligence and the variations in phenotypic expression. Even with Down syndrome, for example, the range in IQ extends into mild mental retardation, and some individuals have an IQ within the normal range. Molecular genetic and biological techniques are beginning to make it possible to understand why such variation occurs, although knowledge to date is extremely limited (State et al., 1997).

Single-Gene Conditions Other syndromes affecting intelligence and cognitive functioning can result from genetically based metabolic defects, known as inborn errors of metabolism. Such defects cause excesses or shortages of certain chemicals that are necessary during particular stages of development. Inborn errors of metabolism account for 3% to 7% of cases of severe mental retardation (Moser et al., 1990).

One of the best understood examples of a single-gene condition is *phenylketonuria* (PKU), a rare disorder occurring in approximately 1 in 10,000 individuals (DiLella & Woo, 1987). Unlike chromosomal abnormalities that cause Down syndrome, the cause of PKU is a recessive gene transmitted by typical Mendelian mechanisms. Children receive the gene from both parents—neither of whom need have PKU—which results in a lack of liver enzymes

Children and adolescents with fragile-X syndrome.

necessary for converting the amino acid phenylalanine into tyrosine, another essential amino acid. Tyrosine is normally converted into other chemicals needed for physical development. Because the individual is unable to metabolize phenylalanine, which is found in many foods, it accumulates in the body and is converted to phenylpyruvic acid, another abnormal metabolite. This metabolite, in turn, causes brain damage, mental retardation, musty body odor, hyperactivity, seizures, and dry, bleached skin and hair.

PKU is a good example of a genetic disorder that can be treated successfully by environmental changes. All infants are now screened at birth for the presence of this defect, and immediately placed on a restricted diet if necessary. However, now that affected individuals have received early treatment, young women with PKU have begun to reproduce, resulting in high rates of birth defects and subsequent mental retardation in their offspring. Severe dietary restriction, begun prior to conception, is currently the best precaution for these problems (Walter et al., 2002).

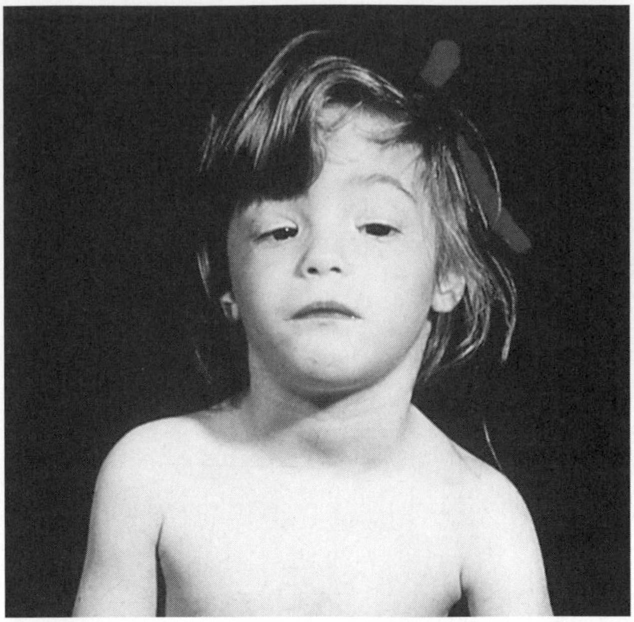
K. L. Jones/LLR Research

Characteristics of children with fetal alcohol syndrome include skin folds at the corner of the eye, low nasal bridge, short nose, groove between nose and upper lip, small head circumference, small eye opening, small midface, and thin upper lip.

Neurobiological Influences

Fetal and infant development also can be affected by adverse biological conditions such as malnutrition, exposure to toxic substances, and various prenatal and perinatal stressors. These conditions directly or indirectly cause lowered intelligence and mental retardation in some, but by no means all, circumstances. The affects often depend on the degree of insult to the fetus and the time of fetal development (the first trimester being the period of greatest susceptibility). Pregnancy and delivery are times of greatest susceptibility to trauma, infections, or other complications that account for about 10% of mental retardation overall (APA, 2000). Other general medical conditions acquired during infancy or childhood, such as infections, traumas, and accidental poisonings, account for about 5% or so of suspected or known causes of mental retardation (APA, 2000).

Prenatal exposure to alcohol is preventable, yet is considered one of the most widely recognized causes of mental retardation, especially if the mother drinks heavily during pregnancy. *Fetal Alcohol Spectrum Disorder* (FASD) is an umbrella term that covers the range of outcomes associated with all levels of prenatal alcohol exposure (Sokol, Delaney-Black, & Nordstrom, 2003). Even small amounts of prenatal alcohol may have negative effects on growth and intellectual abilities. For example, significant deficits in physical development were found among adolescents with prenatal alcohol exposure when mothers had less than one drink per day (Day et al., 2002).

The most extreme form of FASD is **fetal alcohol syndrome,** considered to be a leading known cause of mental retardation because of its clear link to intellectual impairment. Fetal alcohol syndrome is estimated to occur in about 5 to 20 cases per 10,000 births (Morbidity and mortality weekly report [MMWR], 2002). Alarmingly, the incidence of this disorder is about 4 times higher among African Americans and 16 times higher for Native Americans when compared with majority populations (MMWR, 2002). Despite over two decades of public health warnings about abstaining from alcohol immediately before and during pregnancy, fetal alcohol spectrum disorders have not declined, most likely because women at greatest risk are not heeding such warnings (Sokol et al., 2002).

Fetal alcohol syndrome is characterized by central nervous system (CNS) dysfunction, abnormalities in facial features, and growth retardation below the 10th percentile. The mechanism that causes the abnormalities is not clear but is believed to involve the *teratogenic* (damage to fetal development) effects of alcohol on the development of the central nervous system, and the related damage from metabolic and nutritional problems associated with alcoholism (Steinhausen, Willms, & Spohr, 1994). On average, for children and youths with this disorder their IQ is in the mild range of mental retardation (Streissguth, Barr, Bookstein, Sampson, & Olson, 1999). In addition to intellectual deficits, they often have long-term difficulties that resemble ADHD, including attention deficits, poor impulse control, and serious behavior problems, which often persist into adulthood (Sokol et al., 2003).

Several teratogens other than alcohol are known to increase the risk of mental retardation because of their effect on central nervous system development. Viral infections, such as rubella (German measles), contracted by the mother during the first 3 months of pregnancy can cause severe defects in the fetus. However, immunization has virtually eliminated this cause of retardation in most developed countries. Syphilis, scarlet fever, tuberculosis of the nervous system, degenerative diseases of the nerves, and sometimes measles and mumps can lead to mental retardation. It can also be caused by X rays, certain drugs taken by the mother during pregnancy, mechanical pressure on the child's head during birth, lack of oxygen due to delays in breathing at birth, poisons such as lead and carbon monoxide, and tumors and cysts in the head (Hodapp & Dykens, 2003). In essence, any biochemical or infectious substance that cannot be destroyed or regulated by the mother's immune system or regulatory system can pose a risk to fetal development and, in turn, intellectual ability.

Social and Psychological Dimensions

The final group of factors that cause mental retardation, or occur in association with it, is perhaps the least understood and most diverse. Broadly defined, these factors include many environmental influences, such as deprived physical and emotional care and stimulation of the infant, and other mental disorders that are often accompanied by mental retardation, such as autistic disorder. Together these events account for about 15% to 20% of mental retardation (APA, 2000). Although quite broad in scope, these influences are largely indirect and unproven because they are often embedded in different layers and degrees of individual and family circumstances. In this section we focus on the role of the caregivers and the family in supporting the development of a child with mental retardation, as well as the stress and challenges that may interfere with this role. Parental deviance, such as abuse or neglect, and how it can affect intellectual and behavioral development are discussed in greater detail in Chapter 14.

Parents not only provide their children with their genes, but also provide the child-rearing environment and atmosphere that serve to direct and shape the child's psychological development right from the beginning. Consider the comments by the father of a young child with Down syndrome, who had to learn how to ask for proper assistance and to connect with other families of Down syndrome children:

"I will never forget when the nurse told us how much these children can achieve. Her advice to contact a local association for children with Down syndrome was an important beginning. Other parents at the association helped me understand that Down syndrome was a chromosomal aberration and not a disease, and [gave advice on] how to look for help. My son was hardly a month old when he began physiotherapy to help him learn and interact with others. Jake is 3 years old now and he is full of life. He walks, repeats several words, and understands directions." (Adapted from Martin, 1995)

How do families who have a child with mental retardation contribute to the child's healthy development or, alternatively, to his or her decline? The field of mental retardation in recent years has shown a major change in how this question is addressed. Rather than focusing only on the family's negative influence, researchers are interested in learning more about the successful ways some families cope with the additional stress and demands of raising a child with mental retardation. As is the case when dealing with other stressors, individual members and the family unit can be affected negatively as well as positively, such as when the couple is brought closer together by caring for a difficult child (Fidler, Hodapp, & Dykens, 2000).

One way parents adapt successfully to a child with special needs is to use social supports and community resources, although individual preferences regarding type of support may vary, and supports that help mothers may not help fathers. Mothers are often concerned about how raising a child with mental retardation may affect their personal relationships with their husbands, and about the restrictions the child's care may place on their role in the family, whereas fathers worry about not feeling close to the child or being reinforced by the child (Krauss, 1993). Thus, mothers and fathers differ in how they understand and relate to the child with mental retardation, the aspects of raising the child they see as stressful, and the factors that best alleviate stress (Weinger, 1999).

An understanding of the social and independent functioning of young people with Down syndrome has helped us understand the factors that affect their adjustment to community living. Not surprisingly, early cognitive development is a strong predictor of developmental progress and self-sufficiency among such children, as shown in areas such as language (Sloper & Turner, 1996). However, family factors are also important, particularly mothers' strategies for coping with their children's problems and the families' level of social support.

SECTION SUMMARY

- The two-group approach emphasizes the important etiological differences between organic and cultural-familial causes of mental retardation.
- Causes of organic forms include genetic and constitutional factors, such as chromosome abnormalities, single gene conditions, and neurobiological influences.
- Suspected causes of cultural-familial forms include economic deprivation and genetic inheritance of intelligence.

- Social and psychological causes of mental retardation include diverse environmental influences, and focusing particularly on the quality of physical and emotional care and stimulation of the infant and small child.

Prevention, Education, and Treatment

We plead for those who cannot plead for themselves.

—Motto of Highgate, the first public institution for persons with mental retardation, established in London, England, October 1847

As we turn our discussion toward treatment methods for children with mental retardation, consider for a moment how you would apply your knowledge of psychological and educational treatments to best assist a child like Vanessa or Matthew. Would you start with Matthew's behavior problems and try to get them under control first, and then teach him other skills? Would Vanessa likely benefit from individualized treatment that emphasizes gradual speech training and self-help skills?

As is true for several other disorders we have discussed, such as ADHD and some types of conduct disorders, the primary presenting problems—in this case, intellectual retardation and limited adaptive abilities—are chronic conditions that pose limitations across many important areas of development. Consequently, programs often must be designed to fit the educational and developmental levels of each individual child even more so than, say, treatment programs for children with behavior or anxiety problems. It is useful to begin this task with an overview of major environmental and individual characteristics that may increase the risk of adjustment problems or serve to protect the child from such problems. Figure 9.4 shows these major factors.

As shown in the figure, the child's overall adjustment is a function of parental participation, family resources, and social supports (on the environmental side), combined with his or her level of intellectual functioning, basic temperament, and other specific deficits (on the individual side). Treatment can be designed to build on the child's existing resources and strengths in an effort to bolster particular skill areas or learning abilities. In other words, it is not necessary to focus attention primarily on what the child lacks, but rather on how best to match teaching and therapeutic methods to the child's own levels and abilities to accomplish realistic, practical goals. Thus, treatment and education for children with mental retardation involves a multi-component, integrated strategy that considers children's needs within the context of their individual development, their family or institutional setting, and their community.

The severity of mental retardation can be prevented or reduced in some instances by taking proper precautions. Therefore, we begin this section by discussing cur-rent health care practices involving parental education and prenatal screening. These procedures, implemented in many communities, are designed to inform parents of proper prenatal care and risks and to detect abnormal fetal development. We then turn to psychosocial treatments for children with mental retardation and their families, which have become a common part of many treatment and education plans. In short, treatment focuses on teaching the child necessary skills and abilities, such as language, personal care and hygiene, and social skills, as well as teaching skills and providing supports to parents and other caregivers.

Psychopharmacological interventions for children and adults with mental retardation are presently very limited (Matson et al., 2000). The effective use of medications with this population has been hindered by both professional and public perceptions that psychotropic drugs are used to control behavior, a view based on unfortunate and inappropriate use in the past and on the drugs' major side effects (M. H. Lewis, Aman, Gadow, Schroeder, & Thompson, 1996). Although many newer classes of compounds that reduce unpleasant side effects have become available over the past decade, these compounds have not been systematically studied in treating people with mental retardation. Nevertheless, drug treatment is beneficial in some cases. As with other childhood disorders, drug treatment can be targeted at desirable changes in specific behaviors or dimensions, such as compulsions, aggression, or self-injury, rather than at treating the underlying disorder itself (M. H. Lewis et al., 1996). Children with both mental retardation and ADHD often benefit from either fenfluramine (pondimin) or methylphenidate (Ritalin) (Aman et al., 2003), although fenfluramine must be monitored carefully because of the possibility of side effects such as drowsiness, dizziness, and anorexia (Aman, Kern, Osborne, & Tumuluru, 1997).

Prenatal Education and Screening

One of the best opportunities to promote healthy child outcomes occurs during prenatal development (Hodapp & Dykens, 2003). Although not all forms of mental retardation can be prevented prenatally, many debilitating forms related to fetal alcohol syndrome, lead poisoning, or rubella, can be easily prevented if proper precautions are taken. A much larger number of children are affected by prenatal education and health care if one includes not only the prevention of specific risks, but also the promotion of proper child care, especially during the child's first two years.

Not too long ago, a pregnant woman would have seen her doctor for several visits prior to childbirth, and may have gained additional knowledge through reading and from family members. At that time the focus was largely on the medical needs of the pregnancy, with little opportunity to consider what it means to raise a child and

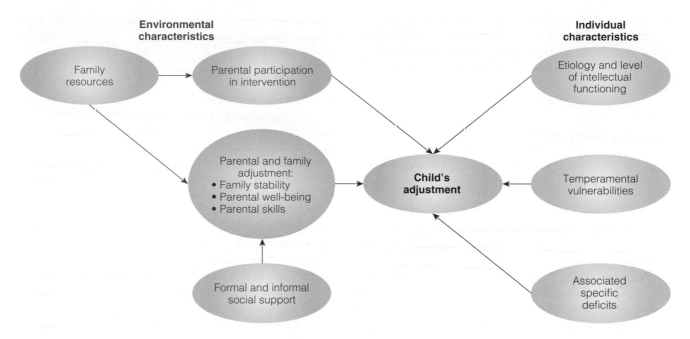

Figure 9.4. Risk and protective factors affecting the psychological adjustment of intellectually disabled children. (based on Lacharité et al., 1995).

to prepare for the added stress and complexity that child care involves.

Today, almost all communities have prenatal programs for parents, and fathers have taken on a much larger role as well. Parents are provided with information about the different periods of fetal development and are cautioned about the use of alcohol, tobacco, nonprescribed drugs, and caffeine during pregnancy. These programs, often run by public health nurses, community colleges, churches, and other community organizations, have filled much of the gap in services between basic medical care and basic child care that parents need, prior to the birth of a baby. The stresses of childbirth and postnatal adjustment are described, with opportunities for parents to consider the additional supports they may need and the changes they may need to make to ensure the child's health and safety. Many programs also include discussion of children with special needs, so that parents are not left feeling confused and alone (Ramey et al., 2000).

In providing these important prenatal services, there is an increasing multicultural focus which sensitively and appropriately considers the cultural background of the recipients (Coates & Vietze, 1996). We now recognize that family members make choices based on cultural influences. To be of most help, prenatal and postnatal services must be culturally diverse and culturally sensitive. Meeting this goal involves working with informal support and assistance networks, such as churches, community and spiritual leaders, and community organizations, in ways that extend self-determination. Prenatal programs are increasingly breaking away from a set curriculum and are being modified to establish a better fit with each cultural group or community, for example, by providing information on ways to access health care and family services for persons with limited transportation, limited income, and so forth.

Prenatal screening constitutes a particular form of genetic screening that is used to determine whether a fetus has a genetic abnormality, such as Down syndrome, that would lead to a seriously handicapping condition. Ultrasound scanning can detect many conditions associated with physical defects, and testing of amniotic fluid during fetal development assists the prenatal diagnosis of chromosomal abnormalities and genetic diseases identifiable at the DNA level (Cooley & Graham, 1991). The next decade will probably see substantial advances in genetic screening, which will allow for much greater precision in genetic counseling. For example, there is hope new molecular genetic techniques will replace invasive techniques such as amniocentesis, and will allow for quicker diagnosis of a broad range of genetic disorders (Abbott & Benn, 2002). Ethical and practical guidelines must first be developed, however, because there is a fundamental difference between using genetic information to prevent an illness or disease and altering genetic material to promote desired (or get rid of undesired) personal characteristics (Sutton, 1995).

Psychosocial Treatments

The first psychosocial treatment we consider involves intensive, broad-ranging, early-intervention services for families with young children that are designed to reduce risk factors and promote healthy child development. Although expensive to deliver, these services are proving to be of considerable benefit to children and families over the long term, and accomplish a great deal more than only reducing intellectual deficits. We then take a close look at the existing educational and therapeutic methods that have successfully benefited children with various levels of mental retardation. We discuss the application of behavioral, cognitive-behavioral, and family-oriented interventions, with an emphasis on the task of integrating known treatments that best match the different needs of these children.

As a prelude to the discussion of psychosocial treatments, we acknowledge the importance of community-based activities that offer people with disabilities a choice of ways to develop their interpersonal and practical skills and self-confidence. For example, a study involving over 100 athletes who participated in the 1993 Special Olympics World Games in Austria found that athletes scored higher on measures of social competence and had more positive self-perceptions than a matched, nonathlete comparison group (Dykens & Cohen, 1996).

Early Intervention   For over 25 years, the involvement of caregivers and other adults in intensive, child-focused activities from an early point in time has been one of the most promising methods for enhancing the intellectual and social skills of young children with developmental disabilities, including children with mental retardation, learning disabilities, and lack of environmental stimulation (Blair & Wahlsten, 2002). Many of these children would be described as disadvantaged or high-risk, synonymous terms referring to family circumstances such as low income, insufficient health care, poor housing, child characteristics such as low IQ, poor adaptive abilities, physical or health disabilities, or a combination of both (Ramey, Mulvihill, & Ramey, 1996). Early educational intervention consists of systematic efforts to provide high-risk children with supplemental educational experiences before they enter school, and the intervention frequently includes other family and child services.

One of the more successful examples of an early educational intervention is the Carolina Abecedarian project (F. A. Campbell & Ramey, 1995). The intervention is offered to children of poor families, who are provided with enriched environments from early infancy through preschool years. Results show that by age 2, test scores of children in the enrichment group are already higher than test scores of children in control groups, and they remain some 5 points higher at age 15, 10 years after the end of the program. At age 15, members of the treated group are less likely to score in the mentally retarded or low-normal range of intellectual functioning. The enrichment group also outperformed the control groups in academic achievement through 10 years in school for both reading

BOX 9.3 Practical Recommendations for Enhancing Children's Lives Through Early Intervention

- *Encouragement of exploration.* Children are encouraged by adults to explore and gather information about their environments.
- *Mentoring in basic skills.* A trusted, familiar adult teaches children basic cognitive skills such as labeling, sorting, sequencing, and comparing.
- *Celebration of developmental advances.* Family and others who know the child celebrate and reinforce each of the child's accomplishments.
- *Guided rehearsal and extension of new skills.* Responsible others assist the child in rehearsing and extending newly acquired skills.
- *Protection from harmful displays of disapproval, teasing, or punishment.* Constructive criticism and negative consequences for unacceptable behaviors are used.
- *A rich and responsive language environment.* Adults provide a predictable and understandable environment for communication. Spoken and written language are used to convey information, provide social awards, and encourage the learning of new material and skills.

Source: C. T. Ramey and S. L. Ramey (1992)

and mathematics, and there were fewer instances of grade retention or special education classes (Ramey et al., 1999; Ramey et al., 2000).

Based on these and related findings, the optimal timing for intervention appears to be during the preschool years (Ramey et al., 1996). Early education programs such as the Abecedarian project are highly relevant to the issue of environmental effects in mental retardation, because they involve children from socially disadvantaged backgrounds, who have a much higher risk of retardation. Although the programs clearly are effective, the lasting benefits depend on the stability and continuation of environmental changes that foster healthy child development. Box 9.3 offers a set of practical recommendations for enhancing children's lives through early intervention.

Dan's mother added some additional ideas, based on her own experiences:

"Be creative. He learns by repetition, so the more closely you follow the "house" system and coordinate all the topics of all the classes, the easier he and the other students can learn. He can learn spelling words of items he touches in science lab. He can learn history related to his library book of the week. Combine the lesson plans to touch all phases of the subject."

Behavioral Treatments   As noted earlier, for many years the mode for dealing with problems faced by persons with mental retardation was to isolate them from society by placing them in institutions or separate schools, a practice that curtailed their ability to interact with typically developing peers. Behavioral interventions first emerged in the context of these restricted settings, and were initially seen primarily as a means to control or redirect negative behaviors, such as aggression or self-injurious behavior.

Through the efforts of concerned behavior therapists, important principles were established concerning the implementation of behavioral methods with children and other persons who are unable to provide fully informed consent. The Association for Behavior Analysis (ABA) Task Force stipulated that each individual has the right to the least restrictive effective treatment, as well as a right to treatment that results in safe and meaningful behavior change (Van Houten et al., 1988). These efforts, coupled with continued input from parents and educators, led to a greater emphasis on positive methods for teaching basic academic and social skills in both schools and communities to help children and adolescents with mental retardation adapt in the most normal fashion (Gardner, Graeber-Whalen, & Ford, 2001).

Vanessa's treatment plan typifies how several important behavioral methods are successfully applied. Language training is often considered a fundamental starting point for teaching more advanced skills to children with mental retardation, and behavioral methods are well suited for this purpose (Matson & Coe, 1991). The plan developed for Vanessa offers a useful example of how these methods are applied. Vanessa participated in one-to-one therapy sessions, during which she was reinforced (by edibles and praise) for emitting sounds that imitated the therapist's sounds. The speech therapist used a _shaping_ procedure that began by forming a list of responses (such as "ge," "ga," "oh") that were progressively more similar to the target response (in this case, the word _go_). After Vanessa mastered the first sound, she was reinforced only for attempts at the next sound on the list, and so on, until the desired sound or word was gradually shaped.

To encourage her speech sounds and simple words to become functional speech and language, the therapist taught Vanessa to imitate the names of pictures shown to her. If she said the name of the picture, such as "dog", within a few seconds, she received social rewards and, if necessary, tangible rewards such as candy. As Vanessa became more adept at naming the pictures, the therapist began to use some of the trained words in response to questions he would pose, such as "What is this?" Gradually, Vanessa's mother and father were brought into the sessions with the therapist to begin asking her similar questions and promoting her use of functional speech. As her speech grew, new words and short sentences were introduced—ones that would be of most use to Vanessa on a daily basis at home, at the cafeteria, and when asking to use the bathroom.

Vanessa's behavior during mealtimes also presented considerable problems for her parents. She had difficulty getting food onto her fork or spoon, so her parents were taught to use simple methods of _modeling_ and _graduated guidance_ to assist. After demonstrating how to hold a spoon, they would show her how to pick up her food and bring it to her mouth. They carefully demonstrated each step involved, from dipping the spoon to placing it in the mouth, each time praising her for her attempts. As required, they would guide her hand to show her how each step was done.

Unfortunately, without much warning, Vanessa would sometimes throw or spit her food, so her parents were also taught how to respond to such outbursts. Their first attempt to stop this problem was to remove her food for half a minute or so. If this tactic did not settle the behavior, or if she became more aggressive, they used time-out from reinforcement. They provided a short reprimand ("Don't throw food!") and told her why she was in time-out. Without ceremony, they turned her chair into the corner for about a minute. At the first sign of settling her behavior, they turned Vanessa around in her chair to face them and returned to a positive, guided method of helping her to learn to feed herself.

In addition to their training in basic skills to promote language and readiness to learn, many older children and adolescents with mental retardation benefit from training

Social and sports events are an important way of fostering independence, social competence, and self-esteem in persons with mental retardation.

in specific social skills to promote their integration into regular classrooms and other activities. As mentioned previously, individuals with mental retardation have various degrees of difficulty in communication, self-control, anger management, correct recognition and labeling of affect in others, social problem-solving, and a host of other interpersonal limitations (Matson & Hammer, 1996).

Tailored to each student's individual needs, social skills training uses positive reinforcement strategies to teach and reward important interpersonal skills such as smiling, sharing, asking for help, attending, taking turns, following directions, and solving problems (McEvoy, Shores, Wehlby, Johnson, & Fox, 1990). Nondisabled peers can also be taught effective ways to increase opportunities for social interaction of children with mental retardation, a method known as social network intervention. This method is successful in increasing the quantity and quality of interactions between children with disabilities and their nondisabled peers, and it promotes the development of friendships (Haring & Breen, 1992).

Cognitive-Behavioral Therapy   The same theories that led to the development of cognitive therapy techniques for children with other types of learning and behavior problems generally apply to children with mental retardation as well. These methods are most effective for children with some receptive and expressive language skills, like the skills Vanessa acquired after careful and prolonged training through the use of visual and physical prompts. Once children are able to follow adult verbal directives and to verbally describe their own actions, they are in a position to benefit from verbal self-regulation training programs (Whitman, Scherzinger, & Sommer, 1991). Self-instructional training is most beneficial for children who have developed some language proficiency, but still have difficulty understanding and following directions. **Self-instructional training** teaches children to use verbal cues to process information, which are initially taught by the therapist or teacher, to keep themselves on task ("I'm not gonna look. I'm gonna keep working.") and to remind themselves of how to approach a new task ("What do I have to do here? First, I have to . . .").

Education of children with mental retardation has been plagued by the fact that specific cognitive skills can be taught, yet children often lack the higher-order (metacognitive) capabilities to apply these skills in new situations. Children with mental retardation use fewer, simpler, and more passive cognitive strategies in memory and learning task situations than do nonretarded children (Gardner et al., 2001). Therefore, instructional methods developed to assist the average or above-average learner are often ineffective. Coupled with this concern is the continued reliance on verbal instruction to teach behavioral and cognitive skills to normal and exceptional children.

Language problems may require verbal instructional techniques to be replaced by methods that capitalize on a particular child's strongest learning channels. These methods often rely less on verbal, symbolic representation and more on perceptual, visually oriented techniques such as modeling and picture cuing.

Specific learning techniques can also be used to improve memory and learning. **Metacognitive training** (also known as executive functioning training) has expanded the value of specific self-management skills by coordinating these skills across learning situations. For example, in addition to being taught various basic math skills, students learn to identify the type of math problem they confront, and then to choose the appropriate strategy for solving the problem. The goal of this training is, first, to teach the child to be *strategical*—to use cognitive strategies—and then to be *metastrategical*—to make discriminations regarding how to apply different strategies in different situations. This method has been successful in teaching children with intellectual impairments a range of adaptive skills, such as math and language (Benson & Valenti-Hein, 2001; Levy, Tennebaum, & Ornoy, 2003).

Family-Oriented Strategies   The presence in the family of a child with mental retardation is a challenge but not an insurmountable problem. Families are central to the development of any child, but for families of a child with mental retardation, child care involves an expanded commitment of time, energy, and skills (B. L. Baker, 1996). The needs of the child often dictate that family members participate in various community services and educational systems with which they may be quite unfamiliar. In the end, the majority of parents of children with mental retardation come to see their child as a positive contributor to their family and quality of life, although the family experiences a higher-than-average level of stress and parental depressive symptoms (Fidler et al., 2000; Weinger, 1999). This view of the child as a positive contributor is reassuring, given the finding that individual services provided for the child are usually more effective when family members are active participants (Gardner et al., 2001).

What exactly do the parents of a child with mental retardation need to be most effective? Family members need support and guidance, access to necessary services, opportunities for a short caregiving break, such as a weekend, and the availability of goal-oriented counseling to cope with the practical difficulties of demanding caregiving tasks, sleep disruption, marital discord, and restricted leisure and social opportunities. Short-term, problem-focused behavior therapy for the parents is one of the most successful approaches. Each family's treatment goals are developed individually; then parents are provided with solutions matched to their needs. For example, parents may be taught assertiveness skills or behavior management techniques (discussed in the next section). In some instances, the solutions involve obtaining new resources from teachers or day-care staff or from neighbors and extended family.

Parent training has been widely used to assist parents of children with mental retardation. As opposed to the focus of many other applications of parent training, when the child has mental retardation the primary focus on behavior change is skill acquisition rather than behavior problem reduction (B. L. Baker, 1996). The parents' roles as primary teachers often continue well past the normal childhood years, so parent training often entails a relevant focus on development to prepare the family to tackle each new challenge.

The Portage Project is an exemplary program that has been in existence for over 30 years and implemented in several countries (Copa, Lucinski, Olsen, & Wollenburg, 1999). Children with mental retardation are taught at home by their parents, from infancy through age 6. A therapist visits the family each week in the home to observe, give feedback, evaluate progress, and model ways to teach new behaviors. The program is set up in a series of sequenced behaviors in the five skill areas of cognition, language, self-help, motor skills, and socialization. Each skill is broken down into very small and discrete steps, therefore the program is relatively easy to learn and implement, and both the parents and the child increase their competence.

There are three critical, but not exclusive, periods during the family life cycle in which parent training and family counseling are most beneficial. The first occurs during the child's infancy and toddlerhood, when parents are coming to terms with the child's disability and may need assistance in learning ways to provide adequate stimulation of early language formation and similar developmental skills. A second critical time is during the preschool and school years, when parents often want to know more about the best way to teach their child basic academic and social skills. Intensive programs, which demand a considerable amount of the parents' time, are usually best suited during the preschool years when the family is most focused on child developmental issues (C. E. Cunningham, Bremner, & Secord-Gilbert, 1993). Finally, parental concerns reemerge during the child's emergence into young adulthood. At this age, the child is no longer eligible for funded schooling, and new issues of housing, employment, relationships, and financial planning associated with independent living become concerns (B. L. Baker, 1996).

Some children and adolescents with mental retardation benefit from **residential care,** or out-of-home placement, which also carries with it unique responsibilities of family members. Residential care services are seldom a full replacement for the love and attention of the family, yet they may be necessary and beneficial under some circumstances, such as aggressive behavior of the child or the need for specialized language or social skills training that cannot be provided adequately in the home or regular school setting. Residential care may range from part-time care, when the child returns home each evening or weekend, to full-time care, when home visits are less frequent. Some residential programs may serve only a few children at a time, much like a group home; others may be large, multidisciplinary tertiary care facilities serving persons of all ages with various disabilities.

Whether the child or adolescent with mental retardation lives at home or in a community residential setting, he or she is likely to attend a regular school, at least for a part of each day. The **inclusion movement** calls for integration of individuals with disabilities in regular classroom settings, regardless of the severity of the disability. The school curriculum must be adaptable to meet the individual needs and abilities of children with mental retardation. For example, because children with Down syndrome often have strong visual short-term memories, a visually based approach to teach them how to read has been determined more effective than traditional phonetic approaches (Hodapp and Desjardin, 2002). Furthermore, this movement has raised anew the issue of how persons with disabilities are perceived and treated by professionals and peers.

Regardless of the structure of the residential program, research has determined that family involvement plays a critical role in children's adaptation to and benefit from such settings. Facilities that offer ways to promote family involvement, such as weekend visits and participation in classroom activities, strengthen the important attachment between children with mental retardation and their families (B. L. Baker & Blacher, 1993). Because one goal of residential care is often to enable the child to live at home or in a family-like community setting, efforts to maintain family involvement are invaluable (Young, 2003). Mental health professionals seeking to maximize the chances of social acceptance of such individuals must contend with the myriad issues that emerge in integrated settings (Kavale & Forness, 2000).

SECTION SUMMARY

- Intervention efforts are most successful when offered at the earliest point in time, especially through the preschool years.
- Interventions for children with mental retardation are matched to the child's individual needs and abilities, and are integrated with the family, school, and community.
- Successful interventions often include behaviorally based training and educational components that teach specific skills and reduce undesired behavior.

Key Terms

 InfoTrac College Edition

To research recent articles on the subject, go to:
www.infotrac-college/thomsonlearning.com

Enter search terms: MENTAL RETARDATION, INTELLIGENCE LEVELS, INTELLIGENCE TESTING, DOWN SYNDROME, FETAL ALCOHOL SYNDROME, PRENATAL SCREENING.

Autism and Childhood-Onset Schizophrenia

It wasn't just that she didn't understand language. She didn't seem to be aware of her surroundings. She wasn't figuring out how her world worked, learning about keys that fit into doors, lamps that turned off because you pressed a switch, milk that lived in the refrigerator . . . If she was focusing on anything, it was on minute particles of dust or hair that she now picked up from the rug, to study with intense concentration. Worse, she didn't seem to be picking up anyone's feelings.

—(Maurice, 1993a, pp. 32–33)

Autism

The compelling description that begins this chapter, from a mother talking about her 2-year-old daughter, offers a first glimpse into the mystery of autism, perhaps the most captivating and telling of all childhood disorders. **Autistic disorder** or **autism** is a severe developmental disorder characterized by abnormalities in social functioning, language and communication, and unusual behaviors and interests. It touches every aspect of the child's interaction with his or her world, involves many parts of the brain, and undermines the traits that make us human—our social responsiveness, ability to communicate, and feelings for other people.

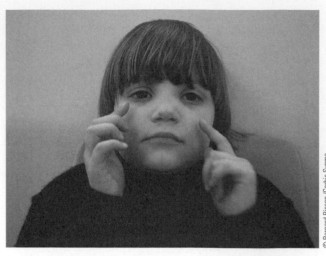

Children with autism behave in unusual and frequently puzzling ways.

Description and History

Imagine yourself the parent of an infant or toddler who won't cuddle, look into your eyes, or respond to your affection or touching. Unlike other children, your child doesn't seem to form a loving relationship with you as you interact with him. In fact, he seems incapable of forming a normal relationship or communicating with anyone. As he grows older, he rarely speaks. When he does speak, he talks in unusual ways, for example, by parroting what you say to him or blurting out seemingly meaningless phrases, such as "dinosaurs don't cry." Your child doesn't use facial expressions or gestures to communicate his needs or to tell you how he feels—no smiles, no nods, no head shakes, no holding up toys for you to look at. Nor does he seem to understand the smiling faces that you and others make as you try to engage him socially. Your child shows little interest in sharing pride or pleasure with you or anyone else. Over the first few years of life he becomes more and more isolated, caught up in his own little world of rituals and interests, which when interrupted, cause him to become extremely upset. Something is seriously wrong.

Autism is one of several **pervasive developmental disorders (PDDs)**, also called **autistic spectrum disorders (ASDs)**, all characterized by significant impairments in social and communication skills, and stereotyped patterns of interests and behaviors (Volkmar, Lord, Bailey, Schultz, & Klin, 2004). As we shall see, children with PDDs vary significantly in the form, pervasiveness, and severity of their symptoms and abilities. We devote most of this chapter to autistic disorder because it is the most common and most studied PDD. Other PDDs that now receive increasing attention are described following our discussion of autism. Although it is not a PDD, we conclude the chapter with a discussion of *childhood-onset schizophrenia*. For most of the 20th century, autism and schizophrenia that occurred during childhood were mistakenly thought of as a single condition, but it is now clear that they are distinct disorders, with different family histories, outcomes, and associated features (J. Asarnow & R. Asarnow, 2003).

Ancient myths suggest that children with autism have been around for centuries. For example, stories of elfin children, left in the place of real human babies who were stolen away by the "little people," describe these "changelings" as strange and remote, much like a child with autism (Wing & Potter, 2002). The factual history of autism begins in 1943, when psychiatrist Leo Kanner described 11 children who, in the first few years of life, withdrew into shells, disregarded people for objects, avoided eye contact, lacked social awareness, had limited or no language, and displayed stereotyped motor activities. They also exhibited **preservation of sameness**, which is an anxious and obsessive insistence on the maintenance of sameness in daily routines and activities, which no one but the child may disrupt. Their parents described them as "like in a shell," "acting as if people weren't there," and "oblivious to everything around him" (Kanner, 1943, p. 242).

Kanner (1943, 1944) called this disorder *early infantile autism* (autism literally means "within oneself"). He viewed the core feature of autism as the children's "inability to relate themselves in the ordinary way to people and situations from the beginning of life" (1943, p. 242). There is, said Kanner, "an extreme autistic aloneness that, whenever possible, disregards, ignores, shuts out anything that comes to the child from outside" (p. 242). The early onset of this disorder led Kanner to conclude that autism resulted from an inborn inability to form loving relationships with other people.

Kanner described the parents of the children he observed as highly intelligent and obsessive people who were cold, mechanical, and detached in their relationships—called the "refrigerator parent." Although he clearly saw autism as an inborn deficit, he also planted the seeds for the psychoanalytic view that "the precipitating factor in infantile autism is the parent's wish that his child should not exist" (Bettelheim, 1967, p. 125). However, this early view that autism resulted from a child's defensive withdrawal from an intellectual, cold-hearted, and hostile parent has found no support (Rutter, 1999). Children with autism have not withdrawn from reality because of a mental disorder—rather, they have failed to enter reality because of widespread and serious disturbances in their development (Rutter, 1991a). Or, as Clara Clark, mother of a child with autism, put it, "You can't say autistic children are withdrawn, because they were never there to begin with" (Adler, 1994, p. 248). Autism is now recognized as a biologically based lifelong developmental disability that is present in the first few years of life (Rutter, 2000a).

Jay

Not Normal and Knowing It

My 8-year-old son, Jay, is autistic. Autism is blatantly wrong. It is maladaptive. I know it; Jay knows it. He wants out. "Are you normal yet?" he says, as his hands flap in wing beats below his chin. He toe-steps in place. "'Am I,'" I correct. "Am I normal yet?" His high-pitched voice is raspy. Blue eyes probe me with intensity. "Not when you scream, kick, and bite people," I say. "You want to be normal!" he screeches. Flopping to the floor, he flails his legs in the air. "Normal, normal. This program has also been made possible with financial support of viewers like you. This program has also been made possible by . . . Stop! No more." I hold my ears and rock slightly, modeling his technique.

When he awakens, Jay charges out of bed to the stereo where he slips on headphones and listens intently to *Phantom of the Opera*. If the selection on the CD player is anything other than *Phantom*, he shrieks while kicking tables, flipping chairs, and striking out at anyone within reach. Then abruptly he begins to weep, a timeless wailing, unchildlike in its profound grief. Later he adds and subtracts numbers in his workbooks or obsessively lists the previous day's events. With his uneven motor control, he inscribes letters and numbers hieroglyphic-like on endless pages. Throughout the day he searches for apostrophes. He locates them on signs, cereal boxes, books. "Is that an apostrophe?" His body trembles; his eyes wet with joy. But his real friends are the newscasters. He tracks their appearance and mourns their absence. For special occasions his conversations with them include Spanish. "Jane Pauley will be sitting in for Tom Brokaw tomorrow. Tom, are you sick? See you Lunes. See you manana, Jane Pauley." His vision of order is sacred. I never dare trespass on it. (Adapted from Swackhamer, 1993)

Children with autism behave in unusual and frequently puzzling ways. They may squeal with excitement at the sight or sound of a wheel spinning on a toy car, yet ignore or have a full-blown tantrum if someone attempts to play

with them. At times they may look through you as if you are a pane of glass, but other times stare directly into your face or tug on your arm to lead you to something they want. When you speak to a child with autism, she may act as if she is deaf, but then quickly turn in the direction of the faint crinkling sound of a candy wrapper in another room.

Many children with autism display extreme fear or avoidance of noisy or moving objects, such as running water, swings, elevators, battery-operated toys, or even the wind. One child was so afraid of a vacuum cleaner that he would not go anywhere near the closet where it was kept. When someone used it in the house, he ran to the garage and covered his ears with his hands. Yet the same child was oblivious to the sounds of traffic roaring by him on a dangerous freeway. Although children with autism fear many things, they are also attracted to and preoccupied with other objects and activities—for example, a rotating fan, a flickering light, or in Jay's case, TV newscasters. These children often develop unusual attachments or reactions to odd objects, such as a rubber band, a piece of sandpaper or string, or, like Jay, apostrophes.

Children with autism may scream, kick, and lash out at others if a chair is moved from its usual location in their room or, like Jay, if something other than a favorite musical selection is playing on the CD player. They may spend hour after hour playing in a corner of their room, engaged in stereotyped or repetitive motor activities, such as rocking, lining up objects, or repeatedly flapping their hands and fingers as they flip through pages of a magazine. Rather than seeing the big picture, children with autism are much more likely to fixate on a minuscule object or event in their world, such as a tiny spot on their shirt. Whereas most of us see the hugeness of trees in the forest, a child with autism is more likely to fixate on one pine needle.

SECTION SUMMARY

- Autism is one of the pervasive developmental disorders (PDDs), also called autistic spectrum disorders (ASDs), which are characterized by severe and widespread impairments in social interaction and communication skills, and by stereotyped patterns of behaviors, interests, and activities.
- Autism and schizophrenia in childhood were previously lumped together as a single condition; now, however, they are recognized as separate disorders.
- Autism has increasingly come to be recognized as a biologically based lifelong developmental disability that is present in the first few years of life.
- Children with autism behave in unusual and frequently puzzling ways.
- They may spend hours engaging in stereotyped or repetitive motor activities, or focus on minuscule details of their world rather than their entire environment.

DSM-IV-TR: Defining Features

The DSM-IV-TR criteria for autistic disorder are presented in Table 10.1. In addition to the core symptoms of the disorder, the child must also show delays or abnormal functioning in social interaction, language used for social communication, or symbolic or imaginative play with onset prior to age 3 years.

Table 10.1

Main Features of DSM-IV-TR Diagnostic Criteria for Autistic Disorder

A total of six (or more) items from (1), (2), and (3), with at least two from (1), and one each from (2) and (3).

(1) Qualitative impairment in social interaction, as manifested by at least two of the following:
  - **(a)** Marked impairment in the use of multiple nonverbal behaviors such as eye-to-eye gaze, facial expressions, body postures, and gestures to regulate social interaction
  - **(b)** Failure to develop peer relationships appropriate to developmental level
  - **(c)** A lack of spontaneous seeking to share enjoyment, interests, or achievements with other people (e.g., by a lack of showing, bringing, or pointing out objects of interest)
  - **(d)** Lack of social or emotional reciprocity

(2) Qualitative impairments in communication as manifested by at least one of the following:
  - **(a)** Delay in, or total lack of, the development of spoken language (not accompanied by an attempt to compensate through alternative modes of communication such as gesture or mime)
  - **(b)** In individuals with adequate speech, marked impairment in the ability to initiate or sustain a conversation with others
  - **(c)** Stereotyped and repetitive use of language or idiosyncratic language
  - **(d)** Lack of varied, spontaneous make-believe play or social imitative play appropriate to developmental level

(3) Restricted repetitive and stereotyped patterns of behavior, interests, and activities, as manifested by at least one of the following:
  - **(a)** Encompassing preoccupation with one or more stereotyped and restricted patterns of interest that is abnormal either in intensity or focus
  - **(b)** Apparently inflexible adherence to specific, nonfunctional routines or rituals
  - **(c)** Stereotyped and repetitive motor mannerisms (e.g., hand or finger flapping or twisting, or complex whole-body movements)
  - **(d)** Persistent preoccupation with parts or objects

Source: Reprinted with permission from *Diagnostic and Statistical Manual of Mental Disorders, DSM-IV-TR, Text Revision, Fourth Edition.* Copyright 2000 by the American Psychiatric Association.

Dustin Hoffman with Tom Cruise in *Rain Man:* Although some individuals with autism display the special talents that are portrayed in the movies, most do not.

Autism Across the Spectrum

When we hear the term *autism* we may think of Raymond in the movie *Rain Man*, the young man with an encyclopedic memory and amazing math skills portrayed by Dustin Hoffman in his Academy Award-winning performance. Although a few individuals with autism may possess special talents like Raymond's, most do not. As we have noted, autism is a spectrum disorder, which means that its symptoms, abilities, and characteristics are expressed in many different combinations and in any degree of severity (Lord, Cook, Leventhal, & Amaral, 2000). At one end of the spectrum we may find a mute child, crouched in a corner of his room, spinning a paper clip over and over again for hours; at the other end of the spectrum is a university researcher who is also able to hold corporate jobs—as long as they don't require interacting with customers.

Not only do children with autism vary widely in their cognitive, language, and social abilities, they also display many features not specific to autism—most commonly, mental retardation and epilepsy. Thus, children with a diagnosis of autism can be vastly different from one another. To illustrate this point, let's compare and contrast two children, Lucy and John, both diagnosed with autism:

Lucy
Autism with Mental Retardation

Lucy's parents watched her development right from the start, because there had been so many difficulties during pregnancy and delivery. Labor began 3 weeks early, and lasted 23 hours, so that forceps were needed to assist the delivery. She had to have oxygen to revive her, spent 4 days in the special-care unit, and received treatment for jaundice.

Indeed, it seemed that everything in Lucy's development was troubling. For example, she was always too distressed to feed or she fed so ravenously and quickly that she vomited. Nights were no better—she took hours to settle, and always woke early. By her first birthday she had only just started to sit up, and was still not crawling. Their family physician said that she was indeed delayed in her development. At 14 months she began to crawl (6 months is typical), and at 19 months she pulled herself up on the furniture (most children do this around 12 months); she made little progress in other areas.

At 2 years Lucy still did not use any words, and was unresponsive to her parents' attempts to engage her in simple games like peek-a-boo. At 30 months she started to walk (most children walk by 14 months). However, her main sounds were a strange clicking noise made with the back of her tongue, and a variety of screams. She still seemed oblivious to people around her (including her parents) unless they had something she wanted. A pediatrician thought the delay in her development might be due to the difficulties with her delivery and suggested that Lucy be checked every 12 months.

She loved to play with a particular blue and red rattle that she would shake or spin for hours. Once she had the rattle she did not look at anyone, and if someone tried to take it from her she screamed and banged her head on the floor. Understandably, this devastated her parents. Lucy took great interest in odors, sniffing food, toys, clothes, and (to her parents' embarrassment) people. She also liked to feel things, and often tried to stroke stockings on women's legs, even of complete strangers. If they tried to stop her, she had a tantrum.

When Lucy was 4 years old, the pediatrician suspected she suffered from autism, and referred her to a psychologist for a detailed assessment. The diagnosis was confirmed, and her parents were told that Lucy was generally delayed in her development. They were heartbroken, but they felt that finally Lucy would get the help she desperately needed. (Reprinted from *Autism: The Facts,* by S. Baron-Cohen and P. Bolton, 1993, pp. 5–8, by permission of Oxford University Press.)

John

Autism with Average Intelligence

John was born after a normal pregnancy and delivery. As an infant, he was easy to feed and slept well. He seemed happy and content to lie in his crib for hours. He sat unsupported at 6 months (which is in the normal range), and soon after, he crawled. His parents saw him as independent and willful. However, his grandmother thought John lacked interest in people.

John walked on his first birthday (in sharp contrast to Lucy, who did not walk until 30 months); yet during his second year he did not progress as well as expected. Although he made sounds, he did not use words. Indeed, his ability to communicate was so limited that even when he was 3 years old his mother still found herself trying to guess what he wanted (as if he were a much younger child). Occasionally he would grab hold of her wrist and drag her over to the sink, yet he never said anything like "drink."

At this time his parents also became concerned about John's extreme independence. Even when he fell down and hurt himself, he would not come to his parents for help. He never became upset when his mother had to go out and leave him with a neighbor or relative. In fact, he seemed to be more interested in his toy bricks than in people. He spent hours lining the bricks up in exactly the same way and in precisely the same sequence of colors.

After his third birthday his parents became increasingly concerned, despite reassurances from their doctor. John used no words and showed no interest in other children. He did not wave bye-bye or show any real joy when they tried to play peek-a-boo. John always wriggled away from his mother's cuddles, and only seemed to like rough-and-tumble play with his father. His mother worried that she had done something wrong, and felt depressed, rejected, and guilty.

When John was 3.5 years old, he was referred to a child psychiatrist who told his parents that John had autism, but added that his abilities in spatial tasks (such as jigsaw puzzles) suggested normal intelligence in these areas. Although it was still too early to tell how John would progress, there were indications he would do better than most children with autism. John received speech therapy, and a psychologist helped his parents plan ways of encouraging communication and reducing temper tantrums.

At age 4, John suddenly began to speak in complete sentences. However, his speech was quite unusual. For example, he often repeated back word for word whatever his parents had said. If they asked him "Do you want a drink?" he would say "you want a drink" in reply. At other times, John made rather surprising remarks. For instance, he would say "You really tickle me" in a tone of voice exactly similar to that of a family friend who had first used the expression some days before. However, his use of this phrase, and most of his speech, was usually inappropriate to the setting, and lacked any clear meaning. (Reprinted from *Autism: The Facts,* by S. Baron-Cohen and P. Bolton, 1993, pp. 1–5. Reprinted by permission of Oxford University Press.)

Lucy and John both display the DSM-IV-TR defining features of autism. They failed to develop normal two-way social relationships and communication in the first few years of life, and displayed repetitive interests and preoccupations. When Lucy was young, her parents described her as "living in a glass bubble." Extreme social unresponsiveness is typical of many children with autism. John is more socially outgoing and talkative when he approaches others, however, his efforts at social contact are repetitive and unnatural. These abnormalities in communication are less obvious than his social deficits, and consist of speaking in one-sided and stereotyped phrases. In contrast, Lucy is seriously lacking in her ability to communicate and is silent most of the time (Baron-Cohen & Bolton, 1993).

In addition to their abnormalities in social and language development, John and Lucy both display ritualistic behavior. Lucy checks the location of little pieces of thread that she has tied on all the chairs in her house, and John insists on taking exactly the same route to school each day. John and Lucy also have repetitive interests: John likes nothing better than counting lampposts, while Lucy, if allowed to do so, watches the same video over and over again. Both children can spend hours absorbed in nothing but these narrow interests, and the obsessions may lead to other problems. For example, John or Lucy may scream intensely if even a minor change occurs in one of their daily routines (Baron-Cohen & Bolton, 1993).

Despite the similarities shown by John and Lucy, their stories also show how children with autism can be quite different from one another. Three critical factors contribute to these differences:

- *Level of intellectual ability*: from profound retardation to above-average intelligence. John is of average intelligence, whereas Lucy has severe mental retardation. Because of her mental handicap, Lucy was slow to develop in all areas. As a result of Lucy's limited overall level of functioning, she shows a much narrower range of interests and activities than John shows.
- *Severity of their language problems*: John speaks quite a lot, whereas Lucy is mute. Children with autism can fall anywhere between these two extremes.
- *Behavior changes with age*: Some children make little progress, whereas others develop speech or become more outgoing. When significant gains are made, they are usually made by children like John, who have average or above-average intelligence and acquire speech at a young age.

SECTION SUMMARY

- In DSM-IV-TR, autism is a severe disorder, with an onset before age 3 years, that is characterized by abnormalities in social functioning, language and communication, and by unusual interests and behaviors.

- Autism is a spectrum disorder, which means that its symptoms and characteristics are expressed in many different combinations and in any degree of severity.

Core Deficits of Autism

Despite more than 60 years of research, considerable debate continues today about the core deficits of autism. Because autism is a relatively rare disorder that can affect children in vastly different ways, it is difficult to study. Autism most likely consists of several deficits, not one primary deficit, which affect the child's social-emotional, language, and cognitive development (Romanczyk, Weiner, Lockshin, & Ekdahl, 1999). As we discuss each core deficit of autism, keep in mind that these aspects of development are interconnected—they do not develop in isolation (Klinger, Dawson, & Renner, 2003).

Social Impairments

Children with autism experience profound difficulties in relating to other people, even when they have average or above-average intelligence (Klin, Jones, Schultz, Volkmar, & Cohen, 2002). From a young age, they show deficits in many skills that are crucial for early social development: imitating others, orienting to social stimuli, sharing a focus of attention with others, understanding emotions of others, and engaging in make-believe play (Ozonoff & South, 2001). As they grow older, they initiate few social behaviors and seem unresponsive to other people's feelings.

Social expressiveness and sensitivity to social cues are limited, and little sharing of experiences or emotions with other people takes place. Children with autism display deficits in recognizing faces (Joseph & Tanaka, 2003), and experience great difficulties integrating the social, communicative, and emotional behaviors that are required when greeting a familiar person. Their lack of understanding of people as social partners may lead to their treating people as objects, or to directing their actions at the body parts of people, as when the child attacks a restraining hand rather than the person (Phillips, Gomez, Baron-Cohen, Laa, & Riviere, 1995).

Children with autism display impairments in **joint social attention,** which is the ability to coordinate one's focus of attention on another person and an object of mutual interest (G. Dawson, Meltzoff, Osterling, Rinaldi, & Brown, 1998). Joint social attention, which normally develops by 12–15 months of age, involves making a social connection with another person by directing that person's attention to objects or people by pointing, showing, and looking, and by communicating shared interest. Although children with autism may bring an object to a person, or point to an object when they want something done for them, they show little desire to share interest and attention with another person for the sheer pleasure of interaction. Deficits in joint attention in infants with autism at 20 months, have been found to predict greater problems in language, communication, and social behavior at age 42 months (Charmin, 2003).

Children with autism process social information in unusual ways. At a young age, they may have greater difficulty imitating other people's actions or orienting to social versus nonsocial stimuli (G. Dawson, 1996) than do typically developing children or children with other developmental disorders (Rogers, Hepburn, Stackhouse, & Wehner, 2003). In processing information about the human face, they may overemphasize one part of the face, such as the mouth, rather than attending to its overall shape (Joseph & Tanaka, 2003). They may not show the typical preference of most children for speech over nonspeech sounds (Klin, 1991).

Although it was once thought that these children failed to form a social bond with their parents, or that they could not tell the difference between their parents and other adults, research has proved this wrong (Dissanayake & Sigman, 2000). Most children with autism are more re-sponsive to their caregivers than to unfamiliar adults, directing more social behavior and seeking to be closer to them than to strangers after a brief separation (Sigman & Mundy, 1989). In addition, once the children's disoriented and disorganized repetitive motor behaviors are taken into account, children with autism display slightly lower but comparable rates of secure attachment to their mothers as normal controls (Capps, Sigman, & Mundy, 1994). They show a preference for their mother over a stranger, use their mother as a secure base for exploration, and are comforted by their mother when distressed.

It is not a global deficit in their ability to form attachments that children with autism suffer from. Rather, the deficit seems to be in their ability to understand and respond to social information (Rogers, Ozonoff, & Maslin-Cole, 1993). As shown in Box 10.1, a child with autism will likely notice when his mother leaves the room and will look for her, both signs of attachment. However, unlike a normal child, he may have little understanding of the event or how to respond in order to change the situation, making it seem as if he has no attachment.

In addition to their social difficulties, children with autism have difficulty processing emotional information

---

BOX 10.1 **Children in a Social Situation**

This young boy with autism notices that his mother has left the room. He wanders around the room looking for her, but there's essentially no change in his expression. He doesn't seem to know what to do to change the event.

A child his age without autism is likely to react like this:

© 1991 Alvin Perlmutter (all)

This child's facial expression changes in ten seconds from "Oh no, they're not really leaving me" to "You gotta be kidding" to "Oh my god, they're gone." He's crying, but as soon as his mother returns, he's comforted and he's fine.

Source: Behavior Disorders of Childhood, produced by Alvin H. Perlmutter, Inc. in association with Toby Levine Communications. Reproduced with permission.

Autism and Childhood-Onset Schizophrenia **289**

contained in body language, gestures, facial expressions, or the voice. Preschool-age children with autism do not look for or attend to the emotional cues provided by other people, for example, whether the other person is happy, sad, interested, or annoyed. In contrast to other children of the same mental age, they may sort pictures of people according to the type of hat these people are wearing rather than by their emotional expressions (Weeks & Hobson, 1987).

In addition to difficulties in understanding emotional information, their own bodily expressions of emotion are very different from those of normal children, often characterized by limited spontaneous use of expressive gestures, and bizarre, rigid, or mechanical facial expressions (Loveland et al., 1994; Macdonald et al., 1989). Thus, children with autism both process and express emotional information in unusual ways. It is not yet known whether they also experience emotions differently than do other children.

Communication Impairments

For 2 years the mother of a young man with autism would correct her son by saying, "Don't do that. It doesn't look normal." The son would stop the inappropriate behavior. Then she would add, "You want to look normal, don't you?" The son would say, "Yes." Then one day it occurred to the mother to ask her son, "Do you know what normal means?" "Yes," he said, and the mother was impressed. She pushed for his definition. He said, "It's the second button from the left on the washing machine."

(From "Our Old Ways Just Aren't Working," by
A. M. Donnellan, 1988, *Dialect*, February 1988.
Reprinted by permission of the Saskatchewan
Association for Community Living.)

Children with autism display serious abnormalities in communication and language that appear early in childhood and persist. Before children learn to talk, they have at their disposal a rich array of facial expressions, vocalizations, and gestures to communicate their needs, interests, and feelings. One of the first signs of their language impairment is the inconsistent use of these early preverbal communications. For example, a typical child with autism may point to a stuffed animal she wants that is out of reach. By doing this, she is demonstrating the ability to use **protoimperative gestures**—gestures or vocalizations that are used to express needs. However, this child will fail to use **protodeclarative gestures**—gestures or vocalizations that direct the visual attention of other people to objects of shared interest.

The primary purpose of protodeclarative gestures is to engage other people in interaction; for example, a toddler excitedly points to a dog to direct her mother's attention to this fascinating creature that she sees. The use of protodeclarative gestures requires shared social attention and an implicit understanding of what other people are thinking—abilities that are lacking in children with autism. They are also missing other declarative gestures, for example, the *showing gesture,* which young children without autism use to show someone else something of interest, like a newly discovered object (or a handful of shaving cream; see Box 10.2).

As many as one-half of all children with autism do not develop useful language, including some children who begin to speak and then regress in their speech development, usually between 12 and 30 months of age. Children with autism with no speech or only limited speech do not use gestures to communicate. Instead, they rely on primitive forms of communication, such as pulling their mother's hand in a desired direction or bringing her an orange to be peeled or a box to be opened. Children with autism may use *instrumental gestures* to get someone else to do something for them immediately, but they fail to use *expressive gestures* to convey feelings (U. Frith, 2003). These two types of gestures are illustrated in Figure 10.1.

Children with autism who develop language usually do so before age 5. Although almost all children with autism show delays in their language development, it is their

Instrumental Gestures

Expressive Gestures

Figure 10.1. Instrumental and expressive gestures. Children with autism may use gestures to get others to do things for them but not to convey feelings.
(Based on U. Frith, 1989)

BOX 10.2 **Early Communication**

When a dab of shaving cream is put in the hand of this child with autism, he pays attention to the shaving cream, and that's all he pays attention to. He is oblivious to the fact that his father is a foot away and his mother is close by. He shows no signs of wanting to share his experience with others.

This normally developing child is delighted with the shaving cream, and immediately incorporates everyone into his experience by showing his mother what he has in his hand. He has something to communicate and wants to let everyone in on it.

Source: Behavior Disorders of Childhood, produced by Alvin H. Perlmutter, Inc.

© 1991 Alvin Perlmutter (all)

use of qualitatively deviant forms of communication that is most striking (Boucher, 2003). The rhythm and intonation of their speech is often unusual (McCann & Peppe, 2003), but most noticeable is their lack of social chatter—failure to use language for social communication. Parents and teachers of children with autism describe their communications as nonsensical, silly, incoherent, and irrelevant, having little meaningful connection with the situation in which they occur. This is illustrated in the following interview with Jerry, a 5-year-old boy with autism who has a great deal of expressive language (Bemporad, 1979, pp. 183–184):

> INTERVIEWER: "Would you draw a man or a woman?"
> JERRY: "A man was business to a lady."
> INTERVIEWER: "What does that mean?"
> JERRY: "No, a man is present to a lady, yes, yes, yes. A radio. Lady gives the pedal. Great big handkerchief and napkin, all tucked in. So see, there it is. We'll paint the picture and put it in a frame."

Other common qualitative language impairments in children with autism include pronoun reversals and echolalia. **Pronoun reversals** occur when the child repeats personal pronouns exactly as heard, without changing them to suit the situation. For example, a child named Tim when asked, "What's your name?" answered, "Your name is Tim," rather than "My name is Tim." **Echolalia** can be either immediate or delayed and is the child's parrot-like repetition of words or word combinations that she or he has heard. A child who is asked the question "Do you want a cookie?" responds by repeating "Do you want a cookie?" Although echolalia was once thought

Autism and Childhood-Onset Schizophrenia **291**

Figure 10.2. Children with autism have difficulty with the pragmatic use of language.
(Based on U. Frith, 1989)

to be pathological, it may actually be a critical first step in language acquisition for many children with autism. Echolalia and other unconventional verbal behavior, such as *perseverative speech*—incessant talking about one topic and incessant questioning—may serve a variety of communicative and developmental functions for children with autism. These behaviors may reflect the child's desire to communicate, although in a very primitive way (Prizant, 1996; Prizant & Wetherby, 1989).

The primary difficulty for children with autism who develop language is not so much with the computational (sounds, words, and grammar) or the semantic (meaning) use of language. Rather, these children display profound impairments in **pragmatics,** which is the appropriate use of language in social and communicative contexts. An example of pragmatics, or, in this case the lack of it, is shown in Figure 10.2. The point of the question "Can you get the phone?" is to request that an action be taken, not to request information about one's ability to pick up a receiver. To understand this, a child must know more than what words mean—a child must "read" the context in which words are used. Lacking in pragmatic competence, children with autism often have difficulty understanding nonliteral statements or adjusting their language to fit the situation (G. Dawson, 1996; Tager-Flusberg, 1993).

Children with autism also use language in a literal fashion. Often the meaning of a word becomes inflexible and cannot be used apart from its original acquired meaning. For example, a child with autism who learns to use the word *yes* when put on his father's shoulders, may take the word *yes* to mean only the desire to be put on his father's shoulders. The child does not detach the meaning of the word *yes* from the specific context and has difficulty using it as a general affirmation. As we saw earlier, the

word *normal* may be used only in reference to a button on the washing machine!

High-functioning children with autism who have mastered word order and have large vocabularies may continue to display impairments in pragmatics. In addition, they continue to show both verbal and nonverbal deficits that reflect a basic failure to recognize the thoughts, feelings, and intentions of other people. At a nonverbal level, their monotone voice and lack of gestures suggest difficulty in communicating emotions. At a verbal level, they display problems with narrative discourse, including impoverished stories and difficulty providing sufficient information to others. As they get older, children with autism make little use of language for social convention, for example, to greet others or to be polite. It has been suggested that the common element underlying all the communication deficits in autism is a general failure to understand that language can be used to inform and influence other people (Tager-Flusberg, 1996, 2000).

Repetitive Behaviors and Interests

Children with autism often display narrow patterns of interests that include a fascination with arithmetic, repetitive behaviors or stereotyped body movements (M. Turner, 1999). They seem driven to engage in and maintain these behaviors. Some may perform stereotyped movements, such as rocking or flapping their hands and arms, with such intensity that they begin to perspire; others may react explosively to a minor change in their routine. They may show stereotyped and repetitive behaviors at times when they are not explicitly directed to engage in another activity, suggesting a possible deficit in their ability to initiate activities on their own. Other stereotyped behaviors

Pamela engaging in self-stimulation as a 7-year-old child and 20 years later as an adult.

occur in unpredictable, or demanding situations, and may provide the child with a sense of control over the environment and a way to cope with changes that are not understood (Klinger et al., 2003).

Self-stimulatory behaviors are stereotyped as well as repetitive body movements or movements of objects, for example, hand flapping or pencil spinning. Although self-stimulatory behaviors also occur in children with other forms of developmental disability, they are especially common and persistent in children with autism. A particular behavior, such as moving the fingers in front of the eyes, may persist from childhood through adulthood. In the accompanying photos of Pamela, taken 20 years apart, her self-stimulatory behavior looks amazingly similar.

Self-stimulation may involve one or more of the senses, for example, staring at lights, rocking, or smelling objects. The same stereotyped behavior, such as spinning a spoon on a table, may involve more than one sense—seeing the movement of the spoon and hearing the sound that it makes.

The exact reasons that children with autism engage in self-stimulatory and other repetitive behaviors are not known, although many theories have been advanced (M. Turner, 1999). One theory is that these children crave stimulation, and self-stimulation serves to excite their nervous system. Another theory is their environment may be too stimulating, and they engage in repetitive self-stimulation as a way of blocking out and controlling unwanted stimulation. Other theories maintain that self-stimulation is maintained by the reinforcement it provides. In the case of an individual child, any one of these explanations may apply.

SECTION SUMMARY

- Children with autism experience profound difficulties in relating to other people, including deficits in orienting to social stimuli, imitating others, sharing a focus of attention with others, and noticing and understanding other people's feelings.

- They display serious abnormalities in communication and language, including deficits in the use of preverbal vocalizations and gestures, language oddities such as pronoun reversal and echolalia, and difficulties with the appropriate use of language in social contexts.

- They display stereotyped and repetitive patterns of behaviors, interests, and activities that include obsessive routines and rituals, abnormal preoccupations, insistence on sameness, or stereotyped body movements.

Associated Characteristics of Autism

In addition to their core deficits, children with autism display a number of associated characteristics. These include intellectual deficits and strengths, sensory and perceptual impairments, cognitive deficits, physical chacteristics, and family stress.

Intellectual Deficits and Strengths

Children with autism vary widely in intelligence, from profound mental retardation to superior ability. Those with superior abilities often capture media attention, yet in reality, about 70% of children with autism have mental retardation. Of those children, approximately 40% have severe to profound intellectual impairments with IQs less than 50, and 30% have mild to moderate intellectual impairments with IQs between 50 and 70. The remaining 30% have average intelligence or above (Fombonne, 2003).

Most children with mental retardation without autism show a general delay across all areas of intellectual functioning. In contrast, the performance of children with

(Age 5)

Figure 10.3. Drawing of horse by Nadia at age 5.
(From *Nadia, A Case of Extaordinary Drawing Ability in an Autistic Child,* by L. Selfe. Copyright © 1977 by Academic Press, Ltd. Reprinted by permission).

In addition, about 5% of children with autism develop an isolated and often remarkable talent that far exceeds normally developing children of the same age. These children, referred to as *autistic savants,* display supernormal abilities in calculation, memory, jigsaw puzzles, music, or drawing. One boy with autism had an IQ of 60 but could recite the daily lottery numbers for the past 5 years. Another boy learned to play the piano by reproducing any tune he heard on the radio, from Brahms to Bacharach. Psychologists who studied this boy estimated that he had more than 2000 tunes in his head (Gzowski, 1993, p. 91). Nadia, a girl with autism, was obsessed with horses; she drew hundreds of pictures of them with incredible vividness and accuracy when she was only 3 years old. One of Nadia's drawings at age 5 is reproduced in Figure 10.3. After seeing a picture of a horse in a story, Nadia could generate endless images of what this horse would look like in any pose (Baron-Cohen & Bolton, 1993).

It is not clear whether the special talents of a few children with autism reflect intact abilities or indicate a cognitive deficit. One idea is that autistic savants tend to segment information into parts rather than looking at the whole, which leads to exceptional performance in certain domains (Pring, Hermelin, & Heavey, 1995). Another explanation is that children with autism think in images rather than abstract ideas, which allows them to remember material like a camera or a recorder (Hurlbert, Happe, & Frith, 1994). Unfortunately, despite the fascination and appeal of the skills of autistic savants or the more common splinter skills, in most cases the skills are not used constructively to enhance everyday living.

Sensory and Perceptual Impairments

Many sights, sounds, smells, or textures that most children find normal, can be confusing or even painful to children with autism. A child with autism may perceive and react to a specific person's voice as a loud shriek, to a gentle stroke on the arm as a sharp pain, or to a ringing telephone as the sound of a power drill next to the ear. These sensory abnormalities and deficits are common in children with autism. They include oversensitivities or undersensitivities to certain stimuli, overselective and impaired shifting of attention to sensory input, and impairments in mixing across sensory modalities, for example, an inability to simultaneously see the movement and hear the sound of a person's clapping.

Children with autism may display sensory-perceptual deficits such as sensory dominance and stimulus overselectivity. *Sensory dominance* is the tendency to focus on certain types of sensory input over others, for example, a preference for sights over sounds. *Stimulus overselectivity* is the tendency to focus on one feature of an object or event in the environment while ignoring other equally important features. A selective focus on one narrow part of

autism tends to be uneven across different IQ subtests. One common pattern is a relatively low score on verbal subtests such as Comprehension, and relatively high scores on nonverbal subtests involving short-term memory for strings of numbers (Digit Span), or arranging blocks to form a specific pattern (Block Design) (Happe, 1994b).

Low intellectual ability in children with autism, particularly low verbal IQ, is generally associated with more severe symptoms and poorer long-term outcomes (Bolton et al., 1994). Only those children with average intelligence or above have the potential to achieve relatively independent living status as adults. IQ scores of children with autism are typically stable over time and are good predictors of their level of educational attainment.

Despite their intellectual deficits, a small but significant number of children with autism develop *splinter skills,* or *islets of ability.* Their special talents may be in spelling, reading, arithmetic, music, or drawing. As many as 25% of children with autism display a special cognitive skill that is above average for the general population, and well above their own general level of intellect (Goode, Rutter, & Howlin, 1994).

the environment while ignoring other important features gives children with autism the appearance of having tunnel vision or tunnel hearing, and makes it very difficult for them to learn about their world (Klinger et al., 2003).

Cognitive Deficits

Two types of cognitive limitations proposed to underlie autism are: (1) specific cognitive deficits in processing social-emotional information, and (2) more general cognitive deficits in information processing, planning, and attention.

Deficits in Processing Social-Emotional Information
The social and communication deficits of children with autism have generated much interest in how they process social-emotional information, such as emotional expressions, voice and facial cues, and internal mental states. Their unusual social behavior suggests a significant impairment in their social sensitivities (Sigman, 1995). Social interaction is not entirely absent or impaired, but rather that they have great difficulty in situations that require social understanding.

At around 12 months, most normally developing infants can tell when they and another person are attending to the same thing. They begin to recognize that people's actions are driven by desires and directed at goals. This ability contributes to the emergence of pretend, or "as if," play. Young children with autism, however, don't understand pretense, nor do they engage in pretend play (Rutherford & Rogers, 2003). For example, a normally developing child may give a doll a drink of water from an empty cup while making the appropriate slurping sounds, whereas a child with autism may simply spin the cup repetitively (U. Frith, 1993).

The deficits in spontaneous pretend play in young children with autism led to the hypothesis that these children would also display impairments in their understanding of beliefs and desires or other mental states in themselves or others that cannot be seen directly. The development of such an awareness of the mental states in themselves and others is referred to as **mentalization** or **theory of mind (ToM)** (Baron-Cohen, 1995; Morton & Frith, 1995; Baron-Cohen, 2000b; Baron-Cohen, Tager-Flusberg, & Cohen, 2000). By age 4, most children can comprehend what others might know, think, and believe, something that even older individuals with autism have great difficulty doing (Baron-Cohen, 1995). The ToM hypothesis of autism begins with the premise that the ability to read the intentions, beliefs, feelings, and desires of others from their external behavior has adaptive significance in human evolution. ToM proposes that all humans are, by nature, mind readers. We spend our waking lives reading subtle cues that enable us to fill in the blanks about other people's beliefs and intentions. We do this automatically and with little conscious effort.

Suppose, for example, that a student walked into your class about 10 minutes after it began, looked around the room, and then left. How would you explain the student's behavior? As a mind reader, you may have thought: "Maybe she was *trying* to find a book she lost, and she *thought* she left it in this classroom," or "Maybe she *wanted* to find a friend who was taking this class, but *realized* that her friend was not in class that day." No doubt you can come up with many explanations for this student's behavior, and most will be based on her mental states (the words in italics). You may not be 100% certain of the reason, but chances are you can easily generate many possibilities.

It has been proposed that the primary problems of individuals with autism stem from a deficit in their ToM mechanism. In other words, children with autism suffer in varying degrees from "mindblindness"; that is, "they fail to develop the capacity to mindread in the normal way" (Baron-Cohen, 1995, p. 5). Interestingly, when asked what brains do, most 5-year-olds say that brains are for thinking, dreaming, keeping secrets, and so on. But when children with autism are asked this question, they may say that the brain is what makes people move—expressing nothing about mental activity (Baron-Cohen, 1995). A child with ToM deficits may be able to learn, remember, and know things about the social world but has little understanding of their meaning.

The original test used to determine children's ability to detect mental states of others was called the Sally-Anne Test. A similar test is described in Box 10.3. This test, which is extremely simple, illustrates what it means to have an everyday ToM.

A small but significant number of children with autism (estimates range widely, from 15% to 60%) demonstrate some knowledge of ToM—they pass the Sally-Anne Test or tests like it (Happe, 1995a). In contrast to the children with autism who do not pass false-belief tests, those children with autism who pass the tests display insightful and interactive behavior and have better verbal and communication abilities (U. Frith & Happe, 1994). They also display far more verbal ability than other children of the same chronological age, suggesting that they may work out ToM tasks in a conscious and logical way (Happe, 1995a, 1995b). All children who succeed at ToM tasks, including children with autism, usually understand metaphors, irony, and a range of speaker emotions, such as the intention to lie or tell a joke. However, youngsters with autism who understand a false belief give laborious explanations for their insights, suggesting the use of conscious and deliberate strategies to discern mental states. In contrast, understanding a false belief may be so natural, automatic, and unconscious for most children that they may have difficulty explaining how they come up with their answer (Happe, 1995a). Even youngsters with autism who pass ToM tests tend to show impairments on

BOX 10.3 The Sally-Anne Test: What It Means to Have a Theory of Mind

Two dolls, Sally and Anne, are used as props. Sally has a basket; Anne has a box. Sally puts a marble in her basket and covers it, then leaves the room. Anne takes the marble from the basket and hides it in her own box. Next, Sally comes back from her walk and wants to play with her marble. The critical question is: Where will Sally look for her marble?

Most 4-year-olds can answer this question reliably. Sally will look for her marble in her basket where she put it. Even children with mental retardation realize that Sally will think that the marble is where she had left it. They also indicate that Sally did not know what Anne did because she was out of the room when Anne moved the marble.

This understanding demonstrates that young children have attributed a mental state to another person. They grasp that someone can have a false belief about a situation. The **false belief** [boldface added] is a mental state, not a physical state, and can very helpfully explain and predict behavior—for instance, that Sally will look for her marble in her basket. Understanding false belief naturally implies an understanding of true belief, of knowledge and ignorance, and of intentions and feelings. This is a theory of mind (ToM).

Most children with autism, even of a mental age far in excess of 4 years, find the simple Sally-Anne test a great puzzle and tend to get it wrong. They say that Sally will look for the marble in Anne's box (where it really is)—even though they remember correctly that Sally had put the marble into her basket, and was not present when Anne transferred it to her box. Despite remembering the simple sequence of events, they cannot make sense of them by inferring that Sally has a false belief—so they do not take into account at all what Sally thinks; they miss the important change (her previously correct belief is now wrong). Thus, they cannot predict Sally's behavior. Their lack of understanding of false belief reflects a lack of understanding of others' mental states. Hence the claim that individuals with autism do not have a theory of mind (ToM).

Source: Adapted from U. Frith, 1997.

complex tests that use more real-life situations (Happe, 1994a).

Brain scan studies suggest that the ability to mentalize is associated with one specific region of the brain that is connected to a widespread network of brain regions involved in social cognition (Gallagher & Frith, 2003). Re-

garding the difficulties displayed by children with autism, these findings may have implications for understanding the neural basis of autism, which we will return to in a later section. Although specific socio-emotional cognitive deficits, as in ToM, are very common in children with autism, the fact that they do not occur in all of these children suggests that mechanisms other than ToM may be needed to explain the cognitive deficits in autism.

General Deficits   It has been suggested that children with autism display a general deficit in higher-order planning and regulatory behaviors (Russell, 1997). These processes, called *executive functions,* (See Chapter 5) permit us to maintain effective problem solving by inhibiting inappropriate behaviors, engaging in thoughtful actions, sustaining task performance and self-monitoring, using feedback, and flexibly shifting from one task to another. This presence of a general deficit in executive functioning is suggested by their difficulties in cognitive functions such as planning and organizing, changing to a new cognitive set, disengaging from salient stimuli, processing information in novel and unpredictable environments, and generalizing previously learned information to new situations (Hill, 2004). As we saw with ADHD, there are many types of executive functions so it will be important to identify which deficits in executive function are specific to individuals with autism (Ozonoff, 1997; Zelazo & Mueller, 2002).

Another general cognitive deficit hypothesized to underlie autism is a weak drive for **central coherence,** which refers to the strong tendency of humans to interpret stimuli in a relatively global way that takes the broader context into account (U. Frith, 1993). By doing this, we can extract meaning from complex sets of information and remember the main points rather than the precise details. It has been proposed that individuals with autism have a weak tendency for central coherence and tend to process information in bits and pieces rather than looking at the big picture (U. Frith & Happe, 1994). Understanding other peoples' words, gestures, or feelings can be extremely difficult for someone lacking in central coherence, as reflected in this statement by Donna Williams, an adult with autism who has written extensively about what it is like to have this disorder:

> It is hard to care or be interested in what a person feels when you perceive a body and then a hand and an eye and a nose and other bits all moving but not perceived in any connected way, with no perception of the context. (Nemeth, 1994, p. 49)

Consistent with a general deficit in central coherence, individuals with autism perform surprisingly well on tasks in which a focus on parts of a stimulus, rather than the overall pattern, serves to facilitate performance. One such task, the Embedded Figures Test (Jolliffe & Baron-Cohen,

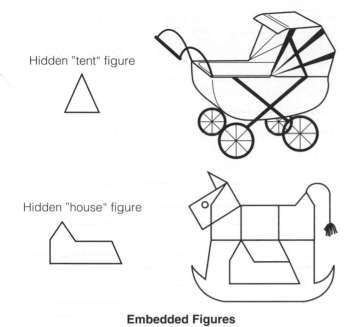

Hidden "tent" figure

Hidden "house" figure

Embedded Figures

Figure 10.4. Embedded Figures Test: Children with autism perform relatively well on tasks that require attention to details of a figure rather than the overall pattern.

(From *A Manual for the Embedded Figures Test* by H. A. Witkin, P. K. Oltman, E. Raskin, and S. A. Karp, pp. 21–26. Consulting Psychologists Press, Inc. Copyright © 1971 by Stephen Karp. Reprinted by permission of S. A. Karp.)

1997) is shown in Figure 10.4. The advantage for individuals with autism on this task may be caused by their spontaneous mental segmentation of the figures into unconnected and meaningless units. This segmentation happens to facilitate the identification of the figure embedded in the whole pattern, resulting in higher scores on this task.

Are These Cognitive Deficits Specific to Autism? Of the cognitive deficits that we have described, a ToM deficit seems to be the one most specific to children with autism compared with children with mental retardation or specific language deficits. However, ToM has not been studied extensively in children with other conditions, such as ADHD and conduct disorder, and, as we know, these children also have difficulties in accurately interpreting other people's intentions. Deficits in processing socio-emotional information appear to be less specific to autism than ToM deficits, occurring in many other conditions, including schizophrenia and mental retardation. There is even less diagnostic specificity for deficient executive functioning, which occurs in many other clinical groups of children, including those with ADHD and conduct disorder (Griffith, Pennington, Wehner, & Rogers, 1999). However, since executive functioning encompasses many different processes, further work is needed to determine whether the

kinds of deficits in executive functioning in children with autism differ from deficits in executive functioning in children with other problems (Hill, 2004).

Are These Cognitive Deficits Found in All Individuals with Autism? As we have noted, some individuals with autism pass ToM tests. However, it is not yet clear whether normal-IQ individuals with autism have actually developed a ToM. The fact that many of these individuals still display severe social impairments in everyday life suggests that they have not developed a ToM, but may have learned to use an alternative strategy to solve ToM tasks.

It seems unlikely that a single cognitive abnormality can explain all the deficits present in children with autism (U. Frith, 2000). The presence of multiple cognitive deficits, some specific and some general, may help us explain why autism exists in so many forms and levels of severity. Finally, although we have discussed the general and specific deficits in cognitive functioning in autism individually, they are related to one another. For example, there is likely a link between the development of certain executive functions and the emergence of children's theory of mind (ToM) (Carlson & Moses, 2001).

Physical Characteristics

A small percentage of children with autism, no more than about 10%, have a coexisting medical condition that may play a causal role in their autism (Challman, Barbaresi, Katusic, & Weaver, 2003; Fombonne, 2003). About 25% or more of individuals with autism also develop epilepsy. Compared with individuals with mental retardation who typically display epilepsy at a young age, those with autism are more likely to have an onset of epilepsy in late adolescence or early adulthood. When epilepsy occurs in young children with autism, it is usually associated with profound mental retardation. However, apart from this latter association, the risk of epilepsy in children with autism is not strongly associated with IQ (A. Bailey, Phillips, & Rutter, 1996).

Children with autism are usually described as having a normal or attractive physical appearance, and do not display the visible physical deviations that often accompany severe mental retardation that is not associated with autism. They may have subtle but distinctive minor physical anomalies, such as facial asymmetries, which suggest the influence of genetic or other prenatal factors in autism (Bryson, 1996).

About 20% of individuals with autism have a larger-than-normal head size that places them in the upper 3% of the general population (Fombonne, Roge, Claverie, Courty, & Fremolle, 1999). This characteristic is more common in higher-functioning individuals and distinguishes them from individuals with mental retardation, language disorder, and ADHD (Gillberg & de Souza, 2002; Woodhouse et al., 1996). Interestingly, one recent study found that infants with autism tend to have a much smaller than average head size at birth, but then show an excessive increase in growth during their first 12 months, leading to the larger than normal head size observed at a later age (Courchesne, Carper, & Akshoomoff, 2003). The cause of this rapid growth is not known, and these findings require further study, but one implication is that the overproduction of brain connections too quickly makes it difficult for developing children with autism to adapt to and make sense out of their experiences.

rapid growth, little pruning

Family Stress

Emilie	
Hard on the Family	Emilie, age 4, can spend the whole day flipping the pages of a catalogue, just staring into space. Or she'll twirl her skipping rope in the air, over and over again, never noticing the bins of brightly colored blocks and puzzles her mother has collected for

her. She is driven to climb—onto the stove, the fridge, the highest dresser. Twice she has brought the television set down on top of herself. All the doors in the house have hooks on them. If she's not strapped into the stroller, she'll dart out into traffic—if the front door is left open, she'll bolt out. Emilie is a whirlwind in need of constant attention. She gets up in the middle of the night several times a week, wide awake, humming loudly, tossing toys, tugging on her sleeping brother in the upper bunk. (From Susan Semenak, *The Gazette*, November 21, 1996 p. A15. Reprinted by permission.)

Life for the parents of a child with autism can be a daily grind, a completely draining, sleepless, relentless effort to prevent their child from self-harm, guess their child's needs, and search for ways to prevent their child from withdrawing. Initially, parents may experience delays before their concerns are seriously considered by professionals, and may be frustrated by additional delays before receiving help. Developing working relationships with professionals and coordinating services across various agencies also places enormous time and energy demands on parents and other family members (Webster, Feiler, Webster, & Lovell, 2004).

> In the midst of these tantrums that come 5, 10, 20 times a day, strangers stare at her and shake their heads. "What a spoiled brat," they mutter so she can hear. *(From Susan Semenak,* The Gazette, *November 21, 1996 p. A 1. Reprinted by permission.)*

Parents of children with autism may experience social ostracism from friends who find it difficult to be around demanding children, or from strangers who may be unaware of the context for the child's disruptive behavior or the parent's efforts to control these behaviors.

Accompanying Disorders and Symptoms

The two disorders that most often accompany autism are mental retardation and epilepsy (Fombonne, 2003). Additional behavioral and psychiatric symptoms may include hyperactivity, learning disabilities, anxieties and fears, and mood problems (Kim, Szatmari, Bryson, Streiner, & Wilson, 2000; Ghaziuddin, Ghaziuddin, & Greden, 2002). Some children with autism also engage in extreme and sometimes potentially life-threatening *self-injurious behavior* (SIB)—any self-inflicted behavior that can cause tissue damage to the child's own body (see Chapter 9). The most common forms of SIB are head banging, hand or arm biting, and excessive scratching and rubbing. Head banging, if not prevented, can be severe enough to produce bleeding or even brain injury. SIB may occur for a variety of reasons—self-stimulation, to gain attention, or to eliminate unwanted demands—or, it may occur for no apparent reason (J. E. Dawson, Matson, & Cherry, 1998). In some instances, SIB may be related to the presence of a subclinical seizure or a middle ear infection (Carr, 1977).

Differential Diagnosis

The social deficits of children with autism and low IQs may be difficult to distinguish from those of children with severe or profound mental retardation without autism. However, even children with profound mental retardation display simple social behaviors, such as smiling and eye contact, which are appropriate to their mental age. Children with mental retardation also do not display the deficits in joint attention or theory of mind (ToM) observed in children with autism (Charman et al., 1997). Both groups display self-stimulation and SIBs, which appear to be primarily a function of mental age than of diagnosis.

Distinguishing between autism and developmental language disorders (Chapter 11) can be difficult, especially in young children. Both groups show similar delays in babbling, language acquisition, length of utterance, and grammatical complexity. However, children with autism use more atypical forms of language, such as echolalia and pronoun reversals, display less spontaneous social conversation, and show greater impairment in nonverbal communication (Cantwell, Baker, Rutter, & Mawhood, 1989).

SECTION SUMMARY

- About 70% of children with autism also have mental retardation; about 40% have IQs less than 50, and 30%

have IQs between 50 and 70. The remaining 30% have average intelligence or above.

- Sensory-perceptual abnormalities and deficits are common in children with autism and include oversensitivities or undersensitivities to certain stimuli, and a tendency to focus on one feature of a stimulus while ignoring others.

- Children with autism display a deficit in theory of mind (ToM)—the ability to understand other people's and one's own mental states, including beliefs, intentions, feelings, and desires.

- Children with autism display a general deficit in higher-order planning and regulatory behaviors (e.g., executive functions).

Prevalence and Course of Autism

For decades, autism was thought to be a rare disorder affecting about 4 children per 10,000 (Tanguay, 2000). However, recent findings throughout the world indicate a much higher prevalence—about 16 children per 10,000, or, as high as 30–60 children per 10,000 for all forms of PDD (Fombonne, 2003; Lingam et al., 2003; Yeargin-Allsopp et al., 2003). Many causes for this dramatic increase have been proposed—vaccines, mercury, diet, antibiotics, allergies, environmental pollutants, and electromagnetic radiation—but none have been scientifically substantiated to date (Wing & Potter, 2002). It seems likely that most, if not all, of the rise in prevalence is caused by a broadening of the criteria used to diagnose autism over the years and to the greater recognition of milder forms of autism (Bryson & Smith, 1998; Wing & Potter, 2002). However, whether there is also a real increase in prevalence due to an unidentified cause remains an open question.

Autism is found in all social classes and has been identified worldwide. It is about 3 to 4 times more common in boys than in girls, a ratio that has remained fairly constant over the years, even with increasing prevalence estimates (Fombonne, 2003). The sex difference is most apparent among children with IQs in the average or above range, perhaps being as high as 10:1 in higher-functioning individuals. However, among children with autism and profound mental retardation, the numbers of boys and girls are similar. Thus, although girls are less often affected by autism than are boys, when they are affected, they tend to have more severe intellectual impairments (Koenig & Tsatsanis, in press).

In considering the high ratio of males to females with autism, Simon Baron-Cohen (2002) has proposed the *extreme male brain (EMB) theory of autism*. Those with autism are presumed to fall at the extreme high end of a continuum of cognitive abilities associated with systemizing (constructing systems that helps us understand the inanimate world), and at the extreme low end of abilities associated with empathizing (identifying emotions and thoughts that helps us understand our social world). Both abilities are present in all males and females, but males are presumed to show relatively more systemizing and females show more empathizing. Frequent interests and behaviors that occur among individuals with autism (e.g., attention to detail, collecting, interest in mathematics, mechanical knowledge, scientific and technical information) are presumed to reflect an extreme on the systemizing dimension of the male brain, and a relative absence of empathizing (e.g., mindreading, empathy, eye contact, communication) (Baron-Cohen, Richler, Bisarya, Gurunathan, & Wheelright, 2003). The EMB theory is intriguing but somewhat controversial. Further research into the neurocognitive aspects of these dimensions in individuals with autistic spectrum disorders will be needed before we can infer that they are "from Mars and not Venus."

Age of Onset

Anne-Marie
First Birthday

We were celebrating Anne-Marie's first birthday and had just paraded in, bearing the cake with much fanfare. Daniel, her big brother, almost two and a half years old, and greatly excited, joined us in singing. Anne-Marie, in her highchair, gazed solemnly at the cake, her baby body still, her mouth unsmiling. . . . I couldn't help once again making a silent comparison to her brother, who at his first birthday party had squealed with delight. . . . Who knows, really, what the first sign was, at what point Anne-Marie began to slip away from us? Was it around that first celebration, or after or before? (Maurice, 1993b)

The age at which symptoms of autism first appear is uncertain (Koenig, Rubin, Klin, & Volkmar, 2000). Most parents of children with autism become seriously concerned during the months preceding their child's second birthday. At this time, their child's lack of progress in language, imaginative play, and social relations stands in sharp contrast to rapid developments in these areas by other children of the same age. Although deficits of autism become increasingly noticeable around age 2, elements are probably present and noticed much earlier, as reflected in Anne-Marie's solemn reaction to her first birthday party.

In a revealing study, home videotapes of the first birthday parties of infants later diagnosed with autism, mental retardation, or as typically developing were coded (Osterling, Dawson, & Munson, 2002). Infants with autism looked at others and oriented to their names less frequently than infants with mental retardation. Compared with typically developing infants, those with autism and those with mental retardation used gestures and looked at objects held by others less frequently, and engaged in repetitive motor actions more frequently. Thus, autism can be differentiated from both mental retardation and typical development by 12 months of age.

At present, the period from 12 to 18 months seems to be the earliest point in development that autism can be reliably detected (Bryson, Rogers, & Fombonne, 2003). However, with increasing research into key early social indicators and with systematic screening, it is possible that autism will one day be detected much earlier in development (Baron-Cohen, Cox, et al., 1996; Dawson et al., 2002; Filipek et al., 1999).

Course and Outcome

The symptoms of children with autism change over time. Most symptoms show a gradual improvement with age, even though children continue to experience many problems. During adolescence, some symptoms, such as hyperactivity, self-injury, and compulsivity, may worsen. During later adolescence and adulthood, abnormalities such as stereotyped motor movements, anxiety, and socially inappropriate behaviors are common, even in high-functioning individuals who also often experience loneliness, social problems, and work difficulties. Complex obsessive-compulsive rituals may develop, and talking may be characterized by idiosyncratic and perseverative speech, monotonous tone, and self-talk (Newsom & Hovanitz, in press).

Findings from early studies of children with autism who received limited help indicated that an overwhelming majority (70% or more) showed poor outcomes with limited progress and continuing handicaps that did not permit them to lead an independent existence (Lotter, 1978). Recent follow-up studies report slightly better, but quite similar, outcomes (Howlin, Goode, Hutton, & Rutter, 2004). A small percentage of adults with autism achieved high levels of independence. At age 29, most remained quite dependent on their family and other support services, with no permanent job, and few friends. They continued to display problems in communication, stereotyped behaviors and interests, and poor reading and spelling abilities. In general, children who were more verbal and had IQ scores above 70 generally showed better outcomes, but outcomes were variable, even for high-functioning children.

For most individuals, especially those with severe or profound mental retardation, autism is a chronic and life-long condition. Without intensive early intervention, most

children with autism show some gradual improvement in symptoms with age, but will continue to display the cognitive, language, and social impairments that make them different from others throughout their lives (Piven, Harper, Palmer, & Arndt, 1996).

SECTION SUMMARY

- Autism is a rare disorder that affects 16 children per 10,000 or more. It is 3 to 4 times more common in boys than girls. Autism is found across all social classes and has been identified in every country in which it has been studied.

- Autism is most often identified around age 2 years or older, although elements are probably present at a much earlier age. Most children with autism show gradual improvement of their symptoms with age, although they continue to display social impairments that make them different from other people throughout their lives.

- The two strongest predictors of adult outcomes in children with autism are IQ and language development.

Causes of Autism

No single abnormality can likely account for all the impairments associated with autism, or for the many forms of the disorder, ranging from mild to severe (Eigisti & Shapiro, 2003). Although the precise causes of autism are still not known, our understanding of possible mechanisms has increased dramatically (Gillberg, 1999; Nicolson & Szatmari, 2003). These advances are evident when we consider that, not long ago, autism was being attributed to cold and unloving parents.

It is now generally accepted that autism is a biologically based neurodevelopmental disorder with multiple causes (Dawson et al., 2002; Trottier, Srivastava, & Walker, 1999). This does not rule out environmental risk factors, especially physical events that occur during prenatal development (e.g., anti-seizure medication taken during pregnancy). To understand autism we must consider problems in early development, genetic influences, and neuropsychological and neurobiological findings.

Problems in Early Development

Children with autism experience more health problems during pregnancy, at birth, or immediately following birth than other children (Rodier & Hyman, 1998). Premature birth, bleeding during pregnancy, toxemia (blood poisoning), viral infection or exposure, and a lack of vigor after birth have been identified in a small percentage of children with autism (Wilkerson, Volpe, Dean, & Titus, 2002). Although these problems during pregnancy and birth are not the primary cause of autism, they do suggest that fetal or neonatal development has been somewhat compromised (Bolton et al., 1997; Piven et al., 1993).

A controversial proposal is that some cases of autism in children, who speak only a few words and have other social-communicative behaviors that disappear in the second year of life, may be linked to vaccinations. The most attention has been given to combination vaccines for measles, mumps, and rubella (MMR) (Kawahima et al., 2000; A. J. Wakefield et al., 2000). However, current evidence does not support an association between MMR vaccines and autism (Wilson, Mills, Ross, McGowan, & Jadad, 2003).

Genetic Influences

The study of specific chromosomal anomalies and gene disorders, and findings from family and twin studies, indicate a substantial role for genetic factors in the etiology of autism (Folstein & Rosen-Sheidley, 2001; Rutter, 2000a).

Chromosomal and Gene Disorders   The discovery of the fragile-X anomaly (see Chapter 9) in about 2% to 3% of children with autism led to increased attention to this and other chromosomal defects that might be related to autism (Turk & Graham, 1997). In general, individuals with autism have an elevated risk of about 5% for chromosomal anomalies (Barton & Volkmar, 1998; Dykens & Volkmar, 1997). However, these anomalies alone do not indicate the specific gene sites underlying the disorder, because autism has been associated with anomalies involving several chromosomes (Gillberg, 1998).

Autism is also associated with *tuberous sclerosis,* a rare single-gene disorder. The manifestations of this disorder can vary widely from mild to severe, and may include neural deficits, seizures, and learning disabilities. Most cases are derived from new mutations with no family history of the disorder (Bailey et al., 1996). About 25% or more of children with tuberous sclerosis also have autism. This makes the association between autism and tuberous sclerosis greater than that for any other genetically based condition. Although the underlying mechanisms are not known, autism could arise if the tuberous sclerosis gene mutations occur during critical stages of neural development in brain regions critical to the development of autism (Smalley, 1998).

Family and Twin Studies   Family studies indicate that about 3% to 7% of siblings and extended family members of individuals with autism also have the disorder (Le Couteur et al., 1996). Thus, the likelihood that autism will occur twice in the same family is 50 to 100 times greater than would be expected by chance alone (Bolton et al., 1994). Twin studies have reported concordance rates for autism in identical twins ranging from 60% to 90%, in contrast to near zero rates for fraternal twins (Bailey et al., 1996). Taken together, family and twin studies suggest that the heritability of an underlying liability to autism is above 90% (Rutter, 2000a).

Family members of children with autism also display higher than normal rates of social and language deficits, and unusual personality features that are very similar to those found in autism, but less severe (Lainhart et al., 2002; Spiker, Lotspeich, Dimiceli, Myers, & Risch, 2002). Referred to as the *broader autism phenotype,* these deficits include social oddities such as aloofness, lack of tact, and rigidity; pragmatic language problems such as over- or undercommunicativeness; and poor verbal comprehension. Family members with the broader phenotype do not, however, display the atypical language (e.g., echolalia), extreme stereotyped repetitive behavior, or mental retardation and epilepsy associated with a formal diagnosis of autism (Rutter, 2000a). These findings are consistent with a general family risk for autism that is genetically mediated (Piven, 1999).

Molecular Genetics   Exciting new research using molecular genetics has pointed to particular areas on many different chromosomes, especially chromosomes 2, 7, 13, and 15, as possible locations for *susceptibility genes* for autism (Barnby & Manaco, 2003; Yonan et al., 2003). However, actual susceptibility genes have not yet been identified (International Molecular Genetic Study of Autism Consortium, 1998). Susceptibility genes are causally implicated in the liability to autism but do not cause it directly on their own. The identification of specific genes in autism may greatly enhance our understanding of this disorder and its specific components (Stodgell, Ingram, & Hyman, 2000). However, initial steps in identifying a gene for autism address only a small part of the genetic risk for autism. Similar searches will be needed to identify other genes, and multiple interacting genes are a far more probable cause than a single gene (Rutter, 2000a).

Brain Abnormalities

Although there is no known biological marker for autism, impressive advances have been made in documenting the biological basis of the disorder (Volkmar et al., 2004). Elevated rates of epilepsy and the occurrence of EEG abnormalities in about one-half of all individuals with autism provide general evidence of abnormal brain functioning. In addition, several brain abnormalities have been identified that are generally consistent with an early disturbance in neural development occurring prior to 30 weeks before birth (Gillberg, 1999; Minshew, Johnson, & Luna, 2000).

Neuropsychological impairments in autism occur in many domains, including verbal intelligence, orienting and selective attention, memory, pragmatic language, and executive functions (Dawson, 1996). The widespread nature of these deficits suggests multiple regions of the brain are involved at both the cortical and subcortical levels (Dawson et al., 2002; Happe & Frith, 1996). The types of neuropsychological deficits also vary as a function of the severity of the child's disorder. For example, low-functioning children with autism may show impairments in basic memory functions, such as visual recognition memory, which are mediated by the brain's medial temporal lobe (Barth, Fein, & Waterhouse, 1995). In contrast, high-functioning children may have more subtle deficits in working memory or in encoding complex verbal material, suggesting the involvement of higher cortical functions (Dawson, 1996).

Biological Findings   Brain imaging studies have looked for structural and functional abnormalities in brain development, or consistently localized brain lesions associated with the symptoms of autism (Brambilla et al., 2003; Rumsey & Ernst, 2000). Abnormalities in the frontal lobe cortex are consistently found in individuals with autism (Carper & Courchesne, 2000; Mundy, 2003). Studies have also consistently identified structural abnormalities in the cerebellum and in the medial temporal lobe and related limbic system structures (Saitoh & Courchesne, 1998).

The *cerebellum*, a relatively large part of the brain located near the brain stem, is most frequently associated with motor movement. However, it is also partially involved in language, learning, emotion, thought, and attention (Courchesne, Townsend, & Chase, 1995). Specific areas of the cerebellum are found to be significantly smaller than normal in a majority of individuals with autism (Courchesne et al., 1995). It has been proposed that cerebellar abnormalities may underlie the problem that children with autism have in rapidly shifting their attention from one stimulus to another.

A second localized brain abnormality is in the medial temporal lobe and connected limbic system structures such as the amygdala and hippocampus (Baron-Cohen et al., 2000; Howard et al., 2000). These areas of the brain are associated with functions that are often disturbed in children with autism, for example, emotion regulation, learning, and memory. The amygdala plays an especially important role in recognizing the emotional significance of stimuli, in orienting toward social stimuli, the perception of eye gaze direction, and, with the hippocampus, in long-term memory. Findings from brain scan studies suggest both structural and functional abnormalities in the amygdala of those with autism, although not in all cases (Salmond, de Haan, Friston, Gadian, & Vargha-Khadem, 2003).

Studies of brain metabolism in individuals with autism suggest decreased blood flow in the frontal and temporal lobes. Studies have also found a decrease in the functional connections between cortical and subcortical regions, and a delay in the maturation of the frontal cortex, as indicated by reduced cerebral blood flow in the frontal brain regions of preschool-age children with autism (see Figure 10.5). These findings suggest a possible delay in the maturation of the frontal lobes that is consistent with clinical findings related to deficits in executive functions in autism (Zilbovicius et al., 1995).

Numerous hypotheses concerning neurotransmitter abnormalities in autism have been proposed (E. H. Cook, 1990; Narayan, Srinath, Anderson, & Meundi, 1993). The most consistent finding is that about one-third of individuals with autism show elevated levels of whole blood serotonin (E. H. Cook & Leventhal, 1996). However, the significance of this finding in relation to associated behaviors or treatment has yet to be demonstrated.

Autism as a Disorder of Brain Development

Collectively, biological findings support the presence of a pervasive abnormality in brain development in autism that produces generalized impairments in complex information-processing abilities (Gillberg, 1999). Several events in neuronal brain organization have been implicated, including dendritic and axonal development, the establishment of synaptic contacts, and programmed cell death and selective elimination of neuronal processes (Minshew, 1996). Given the difficulties in processing social information, it has been suggested that autism may involve dysfunction of a brain system that is specialized for social cognition, possibly the medial temporal lobe and orbital frontal lobe (Baron-Cohen et al., 1999). With regard to possible neural substrates for the early symptoms of autism, the amygdala in particular seems to be connected with early deficits in orienting to social stimuli, motor imitation, joint attention, and empathy (Dawson et al., 2002).

SECTION SUMMARY

- Autism is a biologically based neurodevelopmental disorder that may result from multiple causes.

- Autism is a genetic condition, although the specific genes have yet to be identified.

- Nonautistic relatives of individuals with autism display higher than normal rates of social, language, and cognitive deficits that are similar in quality to those found in autism, but are less severe and are not associated with intellectual deficits or epilepsy.

- Neuropsychological impairments occur in many areas of functioning, including intelligence, attention, memory, language, and executive functions.

Child with autism

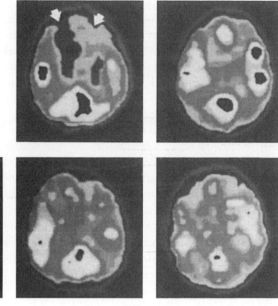

Comparison children

1 year   3 years   6 years

Figure 10.5. Regional blood flow images illustrate the transient frontal hypoperfusion (reduced cerebral blood flow) observed in children with autism. *Top row:* A child with autism at 3 and 6 years of age. SPECT examination at 3 years showed a clear bilateral frontal hypoperfusion (white arrows), while the exam at 6 years revealed normal frontal perfusion. *Bottom row:* Three normal comparison children. SPECT images show frontal hypoperfusion at 1 year (white arrows) but normal perfusion by age 3. These differences suggest a possible delay in frontal brain maturation in children with autism, a finding that is consistent with findings related to deficits in executive functions. (Zilbovicius et. al., 1995)

- Structural abnormalities in the cerebellum and the medial temporal lobe and related limbic system structures have been found, particularly in the amygdala.

Treatment of Autism

I have not counted the trials of medication, the diets, the neurosurgery, the behavioral programs. If they total five hundred, there are five hundred fewer to try. . . . I'm a believer. . . . I believe my son can get well.

(Swackhamer, 1993, p. 312)

Autistic people suffer from a biological defect. Although they cannot be cured, much can be done to improve their lives.

(U. Frith, 1997, p. 92)

These two sentiments, the first by the mother of a child with autism, the second by an autism expert, underscore the promise, pain, and uncertainty that surround efforts to help children with autism and their families. The limited success of current treatments in completely eliminating the symptoms of autism makes many parents vulnerable

to new claims of dramatic improvements. This is especially true for widely publicized treatments such as dietary modifications (e.g., gluten-free and casein-free diets), secretin (a hormone that controls digestion), auditory training, sensory integration, and facilitated communication. These treatments have not lived up to their claims under close scientific scrutiny (Gresham, Beebe-Frankenberger, & MacMillan, 1999; Jacobson, Mulick, & Schwartz, 1995; Volkmar, 1999).

Although behavioral, educational, and medical treatments may improve learning and behavior, and may permit a few children to achieve near-normal functioning, there is no known cure for autism. Most treatments are directed at maximizing the child's potential and helping the child and family cope more effectively with the disorder (Volkmar, Cook, Pomeroy, Realmuto, & Tanguay, 1999). Promising new programs of early intervention, community-based education, and community living options are all reasons for optimism about improving outcomes for children with autism (Newsom & Hovanitz, in press). Most children treated using these newer methods show significant developmental gains, particularly in measured IQ (gains from 7 to 28 points). Nevertheless, controlled studies are needed before long-term outcomes can be fully assessed (T. Smith, 1999).

Different Children, Different Treatments

Given the extensive variability in severity of symptoms, degree of language impairments, and level of intellectual functioning found in children with autism, it is not surprising that variations in these factors relate to expected gains in treatment.

The stories of Pamela and Ricky illustrate this point (see Box 10.4). Both received intensive treatment when they were 7–8 years old. As a child, Ricky had higher intellectual ability and more language than Pamela, and his adult outcome and living arrangements are consistent with his higher overall level of functioning. Pamela, in contrast, had lower intellectual ability and less language as a child than Ricky, and as an adult she requires a more closely supervised living arrangement. These two cases illustrate how treatment strategies, goals, and expectations vary considerably for different children with autism.

Goals for Low-Functioning Children Children with autism and profound or severe mental retardation will likely require supervised living and work arrangements throughout their lives. The prognosis is especially poor for those who fail to develop speech by age 5 years, display profound social impairments, show clear signs of neurological problems, and have confirmed chromosomal abnormalities or significant delays in motor development.

Treatments for lower-functioning children generally emphasize the elimination of harmful behavior and efforts to teach the child self-help skills, compliance with simple requests and rules, basic social and emotional behaviors, communication of needs, and appropriate play. As these children get older, an increasing emphasis is placed on teaching domestic and work-related skills to prepare them for supervised living or work settings. Work with the parents of low-functioning children must walk a fine line between avoiding expectations for dramatic improvement and not creating excessive pessimism. The emphasis is on rewarding progress, no matter how gradual, and on enjoyment of the child for his or her uniqueness (Newsom & Hovanitz, in press).

Goals for High-Functioning Children The long-term outlook for children with autism who function within the moderately retarded to normal range of intelligence depends on when their treatment begins and how intensive it is. High-functioning children who receive concentrated doses of early intervention and who show rapid learning early in treatment are most likely to achieve near-normal outcomes.

In addition to the goals for low-functioning children, goals for high-functioning children include teaching language fluency, age-appropriate social interactions with normal peers, and the behaviors and skills expected in typical classrooms. Extensive parental involvement and support, and help from in-home therapy aides, are common. For high-functioning older children who have not received early intervention, goals include successful functioning in their special education classrooms and elaboration of their language, social, community, and work skills. In general, outcomes for high-functioning children can be extremely variable depending on the child, family, quality of early treatment and education, and later opportunities (Newsom & Hovanitz, in press).

Overview

Emilie

A Full-Time Job

When Emilie was 2 she was diagnosed with autism, Emilie's mother recalled, her eyes brimming with tears. "We've been relying on ourselves ever since." Emilie's mother and father have read about children with autism who became accomplished scientists and musicians—but progress for Emilie, now age 4, has been slow.

Two months ago they hired a specialist to teach them a new one-on-one approach for getting through to Emilie with a reward system. Pictures of food are taped to hallway walls. On the fridge is a cut-out of a glass of milk. After years of shrieking and kicking for what she wants Emilie is learning to express her needs. When she points to what she wants, she gets a reward—a potato chip or an activity she likes. Every afternoon mother and daughter spend 2 hours on the floor, face to face, their legs interlocked. "Listen to maman, Emilie. Look at me. Look at me. Say 'yes.' Say 'yes.' Do you like chips, Emilie? You can have one if you just say the word, 'yes.'"

Emilie's mother coaxes patiently, firmly, holding out a bowl of chips. But Emilie runs to the radiator and climbs it, teetering there. When her mother pulls her down Emilie shrieks, kicks, and falls to the floor crying. In a minute the episode is over, and the lesson begins again. This time Emilie looks at her mother, says "yes," and holds out her hand for a chip. "Bravo, sweetheart. You did it. I knew you could," her mother beams. Emilie's mother has used the reward system to build Emilie's vocabulary to 22 words. That, to her parents, has been a monumental breakthrough.

"We have to motivate her," says her mother, whose only respite is an evening out once or twice a month with her husband. "If we let her be, she'd just climb or hide under the cover all day long. That's my nightmare, that she'll end up in a psychiatric hospital, withdrawn from the world. I can see that we are slowly beginning to get through to her," Emilie's mother says with a deep sigh. "She didn't pay any attention to us at all before. She never showed any affection or made eye contact. But now she looks at me and says maman. Sometimes she hugs me. It doesn't happen every day. But it grabs my heart when it does." (Adapted from Susan Semenak, *The Gazette*, November 21, 1996, p. A1, A15. Reprinted by permission.)

BOX 10.4 Pamela and Ricky: Living with a Lifelong Disorder

In 1964, psychologist Ivar Lovaas started a long-term research and treatment program at UCLA. Pamela and Ricky were among the first children with autism to receive intensive behavioral interventions.

At ages 7 and 8, Pamela and Ricky had made significant improvements, but still had language and social skill deficits. Unfortunately, after 14 months, they were discharged to a state hospital, to allow treatments to be offered to other children. The staff at the state hospital did not have the resources to follow through with the behavioral treatment. Sadly, both Pamela and Ricky lost most of their gains. In recent years, however, the state hospital has developed behavioral treatment programs, and Pamela and Ricky have both benefited.

Pamela at age 7.

Pamela at age 27.

Pamela has remained in the state hospital. She is able to carry out some basic household tasks, although she has lost much of her appropriate speech.

Ricky lives in a small teaching home in the community. He has lost most of his language skills and spontaneity.

Ricky at age 8.

Ricky at age 28.

Unlike Pamela, Ricky has developed some recreational skills, such as rug hooking. With assistance, he participates in the community.

Source: Behavior Treatment of Autism, produced by E. L. Anderson. All photos © 1988 Edward L. Anderson by permission of Sinclair Institute.

Emilie's case captures the demands, frustrations, aspirations, and hopes of a family trying to do the best possible for their child with autism. An overview of the most effective treatments for helping children with autism, like Emilie, and their families is shown in Table 10.2. The treatments include general strategies for engaging children in treatment, specific techniques to decrease disruptive behaviors, and programs for teaching appropriate social behavior and communication skills. Family interventions enable parents to participate fully in their child's treatment and to cope with the substantial demands associated with raising a child with autism. These treatments are often used in the context of comprehensive programs of early intervention (Carr et al., 2002). In addition, educational interventions are commonly used, and for some children, medications (e.g., risperidone) may help to decrease interfering behavioral symptoms (Bryson et al., 2003).

Treatments focus on the specific social, communication, cognitive, and behavioral deficits of autism that we have discussed throughout this chapter. Because these children have great difficulty making changes and general-

Table 10.2

Overview of Treatments for Autism

Initial Stages of Treatment
  Building rapport with the child
  Teaching learning readiness skills
  Reducing or eliminating disruptive behavior

Teaching Appropriate Social Behavior
  Teaching imitation and observational learning
  Expressing affection
  Social play and social skills groups
  Peer-mediated interventions
    Peer-initiated procedures
    Child-initiated procedures
  Sibling-mediated procedures

Teaching Appropriate Communication Skills
  Operant speech training
    Verbal imitation
    Receptive labeling
    Expressive labeling
    Incidental teaching
  Sign language training

Family Intervention
  Behavioral parent training
  Parent counseling

Early Intervention
  Preschool programs
  Home-based programs

Educational Interventions

Psychopharmacological/Somatic Interventions

(Newsom 1998)

izing previously learned skills to new environments, these areas must be directly addressed in treatment. It is also critical that treatment be tailored to meet the needs of the individual child and the family, thus making it possible for each child to meet his or her full potential.

Initial Stages Initially, treatment focuses on building rapport and teaching the child learning-readiness skills. Various procedures help the child feel comfortable being physically close to the therapist and to identify rewards to strengthen the child's social behavior, affection, and play. Imitating the child's use of toys may increase eye contact, touching, and vocalizations directed toward the therapist. Prompting the child to engage in play with a preferred toy may decrease social avoidance.

Children with autism must learn to sit in a chair, come when called, and attend to their teacher if they are to progress. These readiness skills are taught in one step-by-step approach to presenting a stimulus and requiring a specific response, which is a procedure called **discrete trial training.** Other procedures attempt to strengthen behavior by capitalizing on naturally occurring opportunities, referred to as **incidental training.** Successful interventions use a combination of these approaches.

Reducing Disruptive Behavior Young children with autism display many disruptive and interfering behaviors, such as tantrums or throwing objects, as well as self-stimulation, aggression, and self-injury. These behaviors are common reactions to demands on the child that are made early in treatment, and must be eliminated if the child is to learn more adaptive forms of social interaction and communication. Many procedures are effective in eliminating disruptive behavior, including rewarding competing behaviors, ignoring, and mild punishment.

Teaching Appropriate Social Behavior Teaching appropriate social behavior is a high treatment priority (Rogers, 2000). The salience of social cues may be increased by pairing people with actions, activities, and events that the child finds pleasant or useful. Children are also taught ways to express affection through smiling, hugging, tickling, or kissing—behaviors that enable them to return affection they receive from others. Other efforts to enhance social interaction have included teaching social toy play, social pretend play, and specific social skills such as initiating and maintaining interactions, taking turns and sharing, and including others in activities.

One strategy for teaching appropriate social behavior to children with autism involves teaching normal or mildly handicapped peers to interact with them. Peers are taught to initiate age-appropriate social behaviors such as playing with toys, commenting about activities, or acknowledging their partner's responses. Teachers may signal and reward the peers' social initiations with the child with autism. Other strategies use prompts and rewards for teaching the child with autism to initiate interactions, and in some cases to involve siblings as trainers (Strain, Kohler, & Goldstein, 1996).

Teaching Appropriate Communication Skills Several strategies are used to help children with autism communi-

The mother of Emilie, a 4-year-old girl with autism, spends hours each day on the floor in face-to-face communication with her daughter.

cate more appropriately. **Operant speech training** is a step-by-step approach that first increases the child's vocalizations, then teaches imitation of sounds and words, the meanings of words, labeling objects, making verbal requests, and expressing desires. The emphasis is on teaching the child to use language more spontaneously and more functionally in everyday life situations to influence others and to communicate better (Koegel & Koegel, 1996; Newsom & Hovanitz, in press).

Another approach to teaching language to children with autism is *sign language training,* since many find it easier to learn through nonverbal methods. However, since verbal communication is the norm, speech training is recommended first for most children. If the child does not progress using only verbal methods, then simultaneous communication training (verbal and signing) is used. Mute children who are poor verbal imitators are initially more likely to learn language using simultaneous communication training or sign-only training than with verbal training.

Early Intervention

As the methods to identify autism at a very young age are developed, possibilities for early intervention increase dramatically (Erba, 2000). The promise of early intervention derives from the plasticity of neural systems early in development (Mundy & Neal, 2000), and the yet-to-be tested hypothesis that providing very young children with autism with intensive and highly structured experiences may alter their developing brains in ways that permit outcomes that are not otherwise possible (Dawson, Ashman, & Carver, 2000).

The average age of children with autism entering early intervention programs has been 3–4 years or younger. Children have an average IQ in the mid-50s, although many are not testable at the time of their intake for treatment. Early intervention provides direct one-to-one work with the child for 15–40 hours per week and active involvement of the family. In effect, these programs become a way of life for the family—24 hours a day, 7 days a week. Programs are carried out at home and in the preschool, and efforts are made to include the child in interactions with normal peers, especially later in treatment.

Comprehensive reviews of outcomes for children completing early intervention programs find that many of them are able to function in regular educational placements, although the type of setting and amount of support services needed varied considerably. Most children also show developmental gains, as reflected in improvements in their IQ scores, scores on developmental tests, and classroom observations (G. Dawson & Osterling, 1997; Smith, 1999).

The UCLA Young Autism Project   The UCLA Young Autism Project began about 40 years ago under the direction of Ivar Lovaas. It is the most detailed and labor intensive of the early intervention programs that begins the earliest, and is the only program with outcomes evaluated against a control group of similar-age children receiving less intensive intervention (McEachin, Smith, & Lovaas, 1993; T. Smith & Lovaas, 1998). Outcomes for three children with different levels of functioning who were treated in the project are described in Box 10.5.

The program includes many of the key elements of early intervention and is based on principles of *applied behavioral analysis* (ABA), including the use of rewards and punishment, and shaping by successive approximation (Lovaas, 2003). Parents are taught to act as the primary therapists for their children, with direction and help from students who work with them in the home. The average age of children entering the program is 32 months.

In a landmark research investigation, children with autism were assigned to one of three groups. Although this assignment was not carried out randomly, the groups were found to be comparable with respect to age, language, intellectual functioning, and other measures prior to intervention. The experimental group of 19 children received 40 hours per week of intensive intervention. Control group 1 consisted of 19 children who attended special education classes and received 10 hours per week of one-to-one instruction. Control group 2 consisted of 21 children from a larger study who also attended special education classes but received no one-to-one instruction.

For children in the experimental condition, the first year of the program emphasized reducing disruptive behaviors and teaching appropriate behaviors such as compliance, imitation, and appropriate toy play. The second year emphasized expressive and abstract language and interactive play. Children were also taught how to function in a preschool group and, if possible, were enrolled in regular education preschool. The third year of the program emphasized the appropriate expression of emotions, preacademic tasks, assertiveness, and observational learning.

The first outcome data were obtained when the children were 7 years old. Remarkably, 47% of the children in the experimental group were found to be educationally and intellectually normal. They successfully completed a regular 1st-grade class without support, were recommended for promotion by their teachers to a regular 2nd-grade class, and had scored at or above average on standardized IQ tests. On average, IQ scores of these children increased by 37 points from 70 to 107; overall, the experimental group children showed an increase in mean IQ from 53 to 83. Children in the two control conditions did not fare nearly as well, resulting in only 1 of 40 children placed in a regular 1st-grade class; overall, these children showed only minimal increases in IQ scores. The experimental group children were assessed again when their average age was 13 years, with similar results. The nine children who were placed in regular classrooms were virtually indistinguishable from same-age normal peers.

Nearly all children with autism benefit from early

BOX 10.5 Chris, Val, and Neils: The UCLA Young Autism Project

Chris: Autism with Moderate Mental Retardation

Pretreatment	Current Functioning	Language Skills	Future Plans

Chris stopped talking at 18 months. At pretreatment he would not respond to his name. He had no toy play, no peer play, spun tops and knobs, and sifted sand. He had frequent temper tantrums. If angry, Chris would bite his mother or brother.

During a 10-year period, Chris received over 15,000 hours of one-to-one instruction. Chris's IQ remained unchanged, but his adaptive and self-help skills improved, so that now he is actively involved in family life.

Mother: *Language skills are very difficult for Chris, so we pair up the signed word and the spoken word. Over the last 10 years Chris has learned about 200 words. We chose these words because we felt they were important for him to use in his everyday living.*

Mother: *We've been working very hard over the last 10 years, some of which has been a struggle. We hope that by the age of 20 Chris will be employed as a bus boy or a chef's helper, or perhaps a gardening job. He could live in our home, or he could live in a community group home; it's still open.*

Val: Autism with Mild Mental Retardation

Pretreatment	Current Functioning	Language Skills	Future Plans

Val was echolalic, very aggressive, had no toy play or peer play, and rejected affection. He excessively flapped his hands while gazing at them, smelled objects, and paced in patterns across the floor.

After treatment, Val's IQ rose 23 points, from 34 to 57, and he improved sufficiently to be placed in classes with language or mildly delayed children.

Mother: *His language is pretty good now but I know that he needs to improve more. . . . Because when he talks . . . he has a hard time to get the words together.*

Val converses with his therapist.
V: What did you do—the weekend?
T: I went to Disneyland.
V: And what did you ride?
T: What did I ride? Let's see. I went on Pirates of the Caribbean, and the Matterhorn.
V: I didn't ride on Matterhorn.
T: You didn't? Why?
V: Cause I'm scared.

Mother: *I don't know about school, if he'll be able to finish school, but I have the feeling he'll probably be able to work. For the kind of work my husband does, he doesn't need to know a lot of things. The only thing he needs to know how to do—math, is he has to know how to charge. But you know, to set up tile, I think, it's not too hard. And I think he'll be able to do that.*

Neils: Autism Without Mental Retardation

Pretreatment	Current Functioning	Language Skills	Future Plans

Neils had no toy play or peer play, acted as if he were blind and deaf, and rejected adult attention. He stared at rotating fans, paced, spun himself, and lined objects. His mother was particularly concerned that he did not speak or interact with any other children.

Mother: *He was nonverbal, or didn't talk. He just sort of lived in his own little world. He'd sit out in the sand box and sift sand.*

Following intensive treatment, Neils' IQ rose from the retarded to the superior range.

Mother: *He is going to gifted and talented classes here in school and they consider him gifted in the areas of mathematics and science. Neils is one of these three boys. Nine years after treatment at age 14 he is indistinguishable from other boys his age.*

Neils' language skills appear to be normal:

Interviewer: *Are there any things that bother you, that you worry about?*

Neils: *I guess, uh, not making very good grades and not being able to get into a place I want to go after I graduate from high school. . . . I think I'm a more outgoing person, because of the therapy. And if I didn't have the therapy I'd be clammed up, hiding in a corner all my life.*

Neils: *When I graduate from high school the reason I want to go to the air force academy is my dad served in the air force for over 20 years, and I think I have a pretty good chance of getting in.*

Source: Behavior Treatment of Autistic Children, produced by E. L. Anderson. All photos © 1988 Edward L. Anderson by permission of Sinclair Institute.

intervention, but it remains unclear how much the rate of progress depends on the child's IQ and language ability, and what the long-term outcomes will be (Rogers, 1998; T. Smith, Eikeseth, Klevstrand, & Lovaas, 1997). Several anecdotal accounts and research reports claim that some children with autism can achieve normal functioning if given intensive intervention before age 3 (Maurice, 1993b; McEachin et al., 1993). However, the question of whether they can achieve full recovery is a matter of some debate (Gresham & MacMillan, 1997a, 1997b; T. Smith & Lovaas, 1997).

SECTION SUMMARY

- Treatments for autism are directed at maximizing the child's potential and helping the child and family cope more effectively with the disorder.

- The most effective treatments use highly structured skills-oriented strategies that are tailored to the individual child and provide education and supportive counseling for the family.

- Nearly all children with autism benefit from early intervention, however, controlled studies are needed to evaluate long-term outcomes.

Other Pervasive Developmental Disorders (PDD)

Other PDDs have been studied much less than autism. Although all PDDs have some clinical features in common which constitutes the autistic spectrum, how they are related is not yet known. In addition to autism, DSM-IV-TR specifies four other PDDs.

Asperger's Disorder (AD)

Asperger's disorder (AD) is characterized by major difficulties in social interaction and unusual patterns of interest and behavior in children with relatively intact cognitive and communication skills (Klin, Volkmar, & Sparrow, 2000; Gillberg, 2002). They display the same social impairments and the restricted, stereotyped interests as children with autism but not the same general delays in language, cognitive development, development of age-appropriate self-help skills, adaptive behavior (other than social interaction), or curiosity about the environment.

A current conservative estimate of the prevalence of AD is about 2.5 per 10,000 (Fombonne, 2003). However, rates are likely to be much higher, as we learn more about this disorder. Individuals with AD are higher functioning that those with autism, but in many ways, they are very similar. One study found few clinical differences between individuals with AD and those with autism. Individuals

with autism showed greater language delay, but as many as 43% of individuals with AD also had a delayed onset of language. Children with AD have a higher verbal mental age, less language delay, and greater interest in social contact (Eisenmajer et al., 1996).

Generally, individuals with AD tend to be egocentric, socially inept, and preoccupied with abstract, narrow interests that cause them to appear eccentric. Their preoccupations may include topics such as the weather, facts about TV stations, or maps, which are learned in rote fashion and reflect poor understanding. Other common clinical features of AD include clumsy and ill-coordinated movements and an odd posture. These youngsters lack empathy, engage in inappropriate, one-sided social interaction, show little ability to form friendships, and are socially isolated. They display poor nonverbal communication, pedantic and flat speech, and may ramble on about topics that have little interest to anyone but themselves. Older children and adults with AD display marked difficulties with conversational skills and other pragmatic abilities, even when other aspects of language are intact (Volkmar et al., 1996). Also common in adults with AD are anxiety disorders, particularly social phobias and obsessive-compulsive symptoms (Soderstrom, Rastam, & Gillberg, 2002).

Our knowledge of AD is limited but increasing (Gillberg, 2002). Boys are more likely affected than girls, although the precise ratio of boys to girls is unknown. We also know little about possible genetic links that increase the likelihood of finding similar conditions in other family members, which may be stronger for AD than for autism (Volkmar, Klin, & Pauls, 1998). The higher intellectual functioning in children with AD suggests a better long-term outcome than is typically seen in autism. Preliminary findings for Asperger's disorder suggest that brain abnormalities in the cerebellum and limbic system are similar to those for autism, but less severe (M. L. Bauman, 1996). This selective involvement may underlie the prominent social and pragmatic language difficulties of individuals with AD, despite their strong cognitive skills.

There is ongoing debate about whether AD is a variant of autism or simply describes higher-functioning individuals with autism (Volkmar & Klin, 2000). To some extent the resolution of this debate will depend on how the AD diagnosis is used, since no official definition for AD existed until it was introduced in DSM-IV in 1994 (Volkmar & Klin, 1998). Another issue of high interest is whether AD should be viewed as a "disorder" or as an extreme on a continuum of social behavior (Baron-Cohen, 2000a).

Rett's Disorder

Rett's disorder is a severe and disabling neurological developmental disorder that predominantly affects females. The disorder was discovered by Andreas Rett (1966) in his clinic in Vienna, Austria, when he observed two girls in his waiting room making identical stereotyped hand-washing movements. Only female cases have been reported to date, although variants of the disorder have been reported in a few males (Leonard et al., 2001). After examining these children, Rett noted a remarkably similar pattern of early development and symptoms. Girls with Rett's disorder have a normal head circumference at birth. However, following a period of apparently normal prenatal and early development for the first 6 to 12 months of life, they begin to display a specific pattern of deficits that includes:

- Deceleration of head growth between ages 5 months and 48 months
- Loss of previously acquired purposeful hand skills between ages 5 months and 30 months with the subsequent development of stereotyped hand movements (e.g., hand-wringing or hand-washing)
- Loss of social engagement early in the course (although social interaction often develops later)
- Appearance of poorly coordinated gait or trunk movements
- Severely impaired expressive and receptive language development with severe psychomotor retardation
  (Reprinted with permission from *Diagnostic and Statistical Manual of Mental Disorders, DSM-IV-TR, Text Revision, Fourth Edition.* Copyright 2000 by the American Psychiatric Association.)

Rett's disorder occurs in about 1–4 per 10,000 females (Fombonne, Simmons, Ford, Meltzer, & Goodman, 2003). It is a severe neurological developmental disorder, caused by specific X-linked gene mutations found in more than 80% of those affected (Huppke, Held, Laccone, & Hanefeld, 2003). These mutations are usually lethal to the male fetus, therefore Rett's occurs almost exclusively in females (Bienvenu et al., 2000). Although the most dramatic effects of these mutations occur between 8 and 18 months, recent findings suggest that more subtle effects may occur earlier in development than previously thought and are present at birth (Huppke et al., 2003). Although the presentation of Rett's disorder can vary, ranging from extremely severe with almost no development to mild mental handicap, most of those affected experience a variety of serious problems, including severe or profound mental retardation, epileptic seizures, motor handicaps, and difficulties with communication (Hagberg, 1995; Huppke et al., 2003). *Apraxia,* the inability to execute desired movements, is common in girls with Rett's; 25% of the girls may never walk, and about 50% of those who do walk will lose the ability. Most girls with Rett's disorder are severely impaired and are likely to need assistance with all activities of daily living, including feeding, dressing, and toileting.

Girls with Rett's disorder have brains that are 12% to 34% smaller than other children's brains, with reduced size and increased density of neuronal cells found extensively throughout the forebrain (D. D. Armstrong, 1992; M. L. Bauman, Kemper, & Arin, 1995). Decreased length and complexity of dendritic branching have been found in all areas of the cortex, suggesting deficiencies in dendritic and synaptic development (D. D. Armstrong, 1992). The brain abnormalities in Rett's disorder appear to be diffuse, which suggests a reduction in brain maturation prior to birth (M. L. Bauman, 1996).

Childhood Disintegrative Disorder (CDD)

Childhood disintegrative disorder (CDD) describes children who evidence a significant loss of previously acquired skills prior to age 10. This regression follows a period of apparently normal development in verbal and nonverbal communication, social relationships, play, and adaptive behavior for the first 2 years of life. Children with CDD show losses in at least two of the following areas: expressive or receptive language, social skills or adaptive behavior, bowel or bladder control, play, or motor skills (Mouridsen, 2003). In addition, abnormalities in two of the three following areas of functioning are also present:

- Qualitative impairment in social interaction (e.g., impairment in nonverbal behaviors, failure to develop peer relationships, lack of social or emotional reciprocity)
- Qualitative impairments in communication (e.g., delay or lack of spoken language, inability to initiate or sustain a conversation, stereotyped and repetitive use of language, lack of varied make-believe play)
- Restricted, repetitive, and stereotyped patterns of behavior, interests, and activities, including motor stereotypes and mannerisms
  (Reprinted with permission from *Diagnostic and Statistical Manual of Mental Disorders, DSM-IV-TR, Text Revision, Fourth Edition.* Copyright 2000 by the American Psychiatric Association.)

CDD is a very rare condition, with a prevalence rate of about .2 per 10,000 children (Fombonne et al., 2003). For this diagnosis to be made, the disturbances cannot be better attributed by another specific PDD or by schizophrenia. The symptoms, degree of impairment, and outcomes for children with CDD appear similar to those for most children with autism, with the exception of age of onset and a period of normal development, typically for the first 2–4 years of life (Hendry, 2000; Malhotra & Gupta, 1999). However, the inclusion of CDD (and Rett's disorder) with the other PDDs has been questioned, because the former are neurodegenerative diseases with seemingly different causes and courses than autism and AD (Malhotra & Gupta, 2002).

Pervasive Developmental Disorder-Not Otherwise Specified (PDD-NOS)

Pervasive developmental disorder-not otherwise specified (PDD-NOS) describes children who display the social, communication, and behavioral impairments associated with PDD but do not meet criteria for other PDDs, schizophrenia, or other disorders (Volkmar, Shaffer, & First, 2000). PDD-NOS might better be called *atypical autism*, since the category is often used to diagnose children who fail to meet criteria for autistic disorder because of their late age of onset, atypical symptoms, subthreshold symptoms, or a combination of these. Concern has been expressed that this category as currently defined in DSM may be too broad (Volkmar et al., 2000).

SECTION SUMMARY

- Asperger's disorder is characterized by major difficulties in social interaction and by unusual patterns of interest and behavior in children with relatively intact cognitive and communication skills.

- Rett's disorder is a severe neurological developmental disorder in girls, the result of a specific gene mutation.

- Children with childhood disintegrative disorder (CDD) show a significant loss of previously acquired language, social skills, and adaptive behavior prior to age 10 that follows a period of apparently normal development.

- Children with pervasive developmental disorder—not otherwise specified (PDD-NOS) display the social, communication, and behavioral impairments associated with PDD but do not meet criteria for other PDDs, schizophrenia, or other disorders.

Childhood-Onset Schizophrenia

I have a special power in my nose and I can control what's on TV and what people say or do.

(From "Schizophrenia: Hidden Torment," by M. Nichols, Macleans, January 30, 1995, p. 73 Copyright © 1995 by Maclean's. Reprinted by permission.)

This statement by a young girl with schizophrenia highlights the seriousness of this disorder. **Schizophrenia** is a disorder of the brain that is expressed in abnormal mental functions and disturbed behavior (Remschmidt, 2001). It is characterized by severe psychotic symptoms, including: bizarre delusions (false beliefs), hallucinations (false perceptions), thought disturbances, grossly disorganized behavior or catatonic behavior (motor dysfunctions ranging from wild agitation to immobility), extremely inappropriate or flat affect, and significant deterioration or impairment in functioning.

The term *childhood schizophrenia* was previously applied to a highly diverse mix of children with little in common other than their experience of a profound and chronic disturbance during early childhood (Rutter, 1972). The label was often given to children who displayed borderline or no psychotic symptoms and who by today's standards would likely be diagnosed with autism or another PDD. Several factors distinguish children with schizophrenia from children with autism. These factors include: a later age of onset of their problem, less intellectual impairment, less severe social and language deficits, hallucinations and delusions as the child gets older, and periods of remission and relapse (J. R. Asarnow & Asarnow, 2003).

Earlier approaches to diagnosis attempted to construct a category for childhood schizophrenia distinct from the category of schizophrenia in adults. However, current thinking is that the criteria used to diagnose schizophrenia in adults can also be used to diagnose this disorder in children (Asarnow, Tompson, & McGrath, 2004). Rather than being a distinct form of schizophrenia, early-onset or *childhood-onset schizophrenia (COS)* appears to be a more severe form of adult-onset schizophrenia.

In the initial stages of schizophrenia, the afflicted youngster may have difficulty concentrating, sleeping, or doing schoolwork, and may start to avoid friends. As the illness progresses, she or he may begin to speak incoherently and see or hear things that no one else does. Periods of improvement may be followed by terrifying relapses, characterized by disordered thinking in which the youngster leaps illogically from one idea to another. The youngster may experience hallucinations, paranoia, and delusions. During their psychotic phases, youngsters with schizophrenia may be convinced that they have godlike powers or that people are spying on them. When in the grip of a psychosis, they may behave unpredictably and may become violent and suicidal.

Several of the clinical features of COS are illustrated in the case of Mary, a girl who first began to display symptoms of the disorder when she was about 10 years old.

Mary

Depressed, Disorderly, Doomed

Mary had always been a very shy child. At times, she would become mute, had severe difficulty making friends, was frequently oppositional, and occasionally wet the bed. By age 10, Mary had problems in school in addition to her continuing social isolation. She became depressed, felt that the devil was trying to make her do bad things, believed that her teacher was trying to hurt her, and became preoccupied with germs. Her behavior became increasingly disorganized; she talked of killing herself, appeared disheveled, and ran in front of a moving car in an apparent suicide attempt.

This episode precipitated an inpatient psychiatric evaluation, where Mary continued to show bizarre behavior. She lapsed into periods of intense anxiety and had one episode of uncontrolled screaming. At times she would stare blankly into space and was frequently mute. Although Mary's functioning improved during hospitalization and she returned to her family, throughout her childhood and adolescence she was tormented by fears, hallucinations, the belief that others were out to get her, and occasional bouts of depression often accompanied by suicide attempts. She continued to be socially isolated and withdrawn and to perform poorly at school. At age 17, after several brief inpatient hospitalizations, Mary was admitted to a state hospital where she remained until the age of 19. During this period her affect was increasingly flat, and her psychotic symptoms persisted. One week after discharge from the hospital, Mary went into her room, locked the door, and overdosed on her medications. She was found dead the next morning. (Adapted from J. R. Asarnow & Asarnow, 2003)

Mary's tragic story illustrates several key features of COS.

- Although most cases have their onset during late adolescence or early adulthood, schizophrenia does occur during childhood (Nicolson & Rapoport, 1999).
- COS has a gradual rather than sudden onset in childhood, with the child displaying a wide range of impairments that precede his or her psychotic symptoms (Nicolson et al., 2000).
- When the disorder is present in childhood, the symptoms likely will persist into adolescence and adulthood.
- COS has a profound negative impact on the child's developing social and academic competence.

Mary's futile 10-year struggle with schizophrenia underscores the tremendous pain and personal suffering experienced by youngsters with this illness.

DSM-IV-TR: Defining Features

DSM-IV-TR criteria for schizophrenia are presented in Table 10.3. For an accurate diagnosis, continuous signs of disturbance must persist for at least 6 months. In addition, after the onset of the disturbance, the youngster must show a significant decrement in one or more areas of functioning or a failure to achieve expected levels of interpersonal, academic, or occupational achievement. The disorder cannot be attributable to mood disorder or schizoaffective disorder, and is not due to substance use or a general medical condition. If there is a history of autism or another PDD, the additional diagnosis of schizophrenia is made only if prominent delusions or hallucinations are also present for at least a month.

The use of the same diagnostic criteria for children and adults facilitates comparisons between cases of childhood- and adult-onset schizophrenia and the identification of continuities in the disorder during the course of development. However, schizophrenia may be expressed differently at different ages. For example, hallucinations, delusions, and formal thought disturbances are extremely rare and difficult to diagnose before the age of 7; when they do occur, they may be less complex and reflect childhood themes (Caplan, 1994). A failure to adjust diagnostic criteria for developmental changes, such as social withdrawal or peer problems, may overlook children who show early signs of schizophrenia, but may not develop the full-blown adult type until a later age (McClellan, Breiger, McCurry, Hlastala, 2003).

Other developmental considerations may also come into play in making a diagnosis. For example, it is sometimes difficult to distinguish between pathological symptoms, such as delusions, and the rich imaginative fantasies typical of many young children. One difference between children and adults with schizophrenia is that young children may not experience their psychotic symptoms as distressing or disorganizing. Thus, when psychotic symptoms appear early in development, children may have difficulty distinguishing them from normal experience (A. T. Russell, 1994).

Table 10.3

Main Features of DSM-IV-TR Criteria for Schizophrenia

Characteristic symptoms: At least two or more of the following symptoms are present for a significant portion of time during a 1-month period.

(1) Delusions

(2) Hallucinations

(3) Disorganized speech (e.g., frequent derailment or incoherence)

(4) Grossly disorganized or catatonic behavior

(5) Negative symptoms (e.g., affective flattening, alogia, or avolition)

If delusions are bizarre or if hallucinations consist of a running commentary about the person or two or more conversing voices, then only one of these symptoms is required to make the diagnosis.

Source: Reprinted with permission from *Diagnostic and Statistical Manual of Mental Disorders, DSM-IV-TR, Text Revision, Fourth Edition.* Copyright 2000 by the American Psychiatric Association.

BOX 10.6 Psychotic Symptoms in Children with Schizophrenia

Hallucinations

An 8-year-old boy stated: "I once heard a noise coming from the south and the east; one told me to jump off the roof and one told me to smash my mom."

A 9-year-old boy reported voices calling him bad names, and threatening that if he doesn't do what he is told something bad will happen to him.

A 12-year-old boy saw a ghost (man) with red, burned, scarred, and cut face on multiple occasions and in different locations. He had been seeing this since age 5.

An 8-year-old boy felt the devil touching him and moving his body "so he can make me come and live with him."

An 8-year-old girl reported feeling an angel, babies and devil inside her arm, and that she could feel them fighting.

Delusions

A 9-year-old boy was convinced he was a dog (his parents were German Shepherds) and was growing fur, and on one occasion, refused to leave a veterinarian's office unless he received a shot.

An 11-year-old boy described "waste" produced when the good and bad voices fought with each other; the "waste" came out of his feet when he swam in chlorinated pools.

An 8-year-old girl believed that people outside of her house were staring and pointing at her trying to send her a message to come outside. She also believed that people on the TV were talking to her because they used the word "you."

An 11-year-old boy had the firm belief that he was "different" and able to kill people. He felt that when "God zooms through me [him]" he became very strong and developed big muscles.

A 10-year-old girl believed that the "evil one" was trying to poison her orange juice.

Thought Disorder

"I used to have a Mexican dream. I was watching TV in the family room. I disappeared outside of this world and then I was in a closet. Sounds like a vacuum dream. It's a Mexican dream. When I was close to that dream earth, I was turning upside down. I don't like to turn upside down. Sometimes I have Mexican dreams and vacuum dreams. It's real hard to scream in dreams."

Source: Adapted from "The Clinical Presentation of Childhood-Onset Schizophrenia," by A. T. Russell, 1994, *Schizophrenia Bulletin, 20,* 631–646. Adapted by permission of the author.

Psychotic Symptoms Youngsters with COS may display psychotic symptoms such as delusions and hallucinations. **Delusions** are disturbances in thinking involving disordered thought content and strong beliefs that are misrepresentations of reality. **Hallucinations** are disturbances in perception in which things are seen, heard, or otherwise sensed even though they are not real or present. The most common presenting symptom for children with schizophrenia is auditory hallucinations, which occur in about 80% of cases with an onset prior to age 11. About 40% to 60% of children with schizophrenia also experience visual hallucinations, delusions, and thought disorder (Caplan, 1994; Caplan, Guthrie, Tang, Komo, & Asarnow, 2000; Russell, Bott, & Sammons, 1989). Examples of psychotic symptoms reported by children with schizophrenia are presented in Box 10.6.

SECTION SUMMARY

- Schizophrenia is a disorder of the brain that is expressed in abnormal mental functions and disturbed behavior.
- Unlike children with autism, children with schizophrenia have a later age of onset, show less intellectual impairment, display less severe social and language deficits, develop hallucinations and delusions as they get older, and experience periods of remission and relapse.

- Childhood-onset schizophrenia (COS) is a more severe form of adult-onset schizophrenia, rather than a different disorder.
- Youngsters with COS may display psychotic symptoms such as delusions and hallucinations.

Related Symptoms and Comorbidities

Children with schizophrenia often display other symptoms and disorders, such as depression, ADHD, conduct problems, and suicidal tendencies. About 70% of the children meet criteria for another diagnosis, most commonly oppositional/conduct disorder or mood disorder (A. T. Russell, Bott, & Sammons, 1989). Given the links historically made between autism and schizophrenia, it is of interest that children with COS do not show an elevated risk of autism or other PDDs.

For a majority of children with COS, the onset of their disorder is gradual rather than sudden, with nearly 90% showing a clear history of behavioral and psychiatric disturbances before the onset of psychosis (A. T. Russell, 1994). For example, Mary was oppositional and had difficulty making friends well before she began to display her psychotic symptoms. Given this kind of developmental history, it can be difficult to determine whether early conduct, mood, and other symptoms are signs of COS or co-occurring conditions (J. R. Asarnow & Asarnow, 2003).

Prevalence

Schizophrenia is extremely rare in children under 12 years of age, it increases in frequency in adolescence, and has a modal age of onset between 20 and 25 years (Remschmidt, Schulz, Martin, Warnke, & Trott, 1994):

- Prevalence estimates of COS range from .14 to 1.0 child in 10,000 (J. R. Asarnow & Asarnow, 2003).
- These estimates suggest that schizophrenia occurs at least 100 times more often in adults than in children (Bromet & Fennig, 1999).
- COS has an earlier age of onset (2–4 years) in boys (Hafner, Hambrecht, Loffler, Munk-Jorgenson, & Reichler-Rossier, 1998), and is about twice as common in boys as in girls. However, this sex difference disappears in adolescence (Frazier et al., 1997).

The reasons that more males have COS are not known; a greater general biological vulnerability of males for neurological disorders and different causes have both been suggested as possibilities. For adults, the rates of schizophrenia are higher in lower socioeconomic groups. However, there is little information regarding the relationship between social class and COS. In a related vein, the incidence rates and pattern of symptoms in adults with schizophrenia are similar across cultures, countries, and racial groups (Bromet & Fennig, 1999), but little information regarding cross-cultural patterns is available for COS (J. R. Asarnow & Asarnow, 1994).

SECTION SUMMARY

- Schizophrenia is extremely rare in children under 12 years of age, occurring much less often than in adolescents and adults.
- COS has an earlier age of onset in boys, and is about twice as common in boys as in girls.

Causes and Treatment

Causes

Current views regarding the causes of schizophrenia are based on a **vulnerability-stress model** that emphasizes the interplay among vulnerability, stress, and protective factors, within the context of developmental maturation of brain circuitry. Vulnerability factors are predisposing conditions, such as genetic risk, central nervous system impairment, inadequate learning opportunities, or deviant patterns of family interaction. Stressors are events that heighten the likelihood of a schizophrenic episode and may be both prenatal stressors as well as major life-change events, such as the death of a parent, or chronic stressors, such as ongoing child abuse. Protective factors are conditions that reduce the risk of a schizophrenic episode in individuals at risk, and may include intelligence, social competence, or supportive family relationships.

A vulnerability-stress model recognizes the complex and diverse pathways that may lead to schizophrenia. For example, a child who has a genetic risk for schizophrenia may experience central nervous system impairments that lead to deficits in attention and information processing. These deficits in a child of low intelligence who is exposed to a deviant family environment may increase the risk of a schizophrenic episode, whereas the same impairments in a child of high intelligence with a supportive family environment may not. Thus, the onset of schizophrenia will depend on the interactions among enduring psychobiological vulnerabilities, environmental and biological stressors, and the protective effects of child and family competencies and resources for coping. Although a genetic predisposition exists for schizophrenia, schizophrenic episodes are likely to occur only in vulnerable individuals exposed to stress and who possess few resources for coping (J. R. Asarnow & Asarnow, 2003; Sullivan, Kendler, & Neale, 2003).

Biological Factors Preliminary evidence suggests a strong genetic contribution to schizophrenia in childhood, more prevalent than for adults (R. F. Asarnow et al., 2001; Tsuang, 2000). For example, the rate of schizophrenia among relatives of children with COS is about double the rate for family members of adults with schizophrenia. One early twin study found concordance rates of 88% and 23%, respectively, for identical versus fraternal twins with schizophrenia with an onset prior to 15 years of age (Kallman & Roth, 1956). These findings generally suggest that COS is a more severe form of adult-onset schizophrenia (Rosenthal, 1970). Although many potential vulnerability genes have been reported for adults with schizophrenia (Pulver, 2000), less is known about vulnerability genes in children (Gordon, Krasnewich, White, Lenane, & Rapoport, 1994).

The presence of central nervous system dysfunction among individuals with schizophrenia, and the dramatic improvements associated with medication suggest that schizophrenia is a disorder of the brain (D. A. Lewis & Lieberman, 2000). Brain scan studies of youngsters with COS suggest a shrinkage in brain gray matter that spreads across the brain during adolescence, beginning in the rear brain structures involved in attention and perception, and spreading to the frontal parts of the brain involved in executive functions such as planning and organization (Thompson et al., 2001). However, no single brain lesion has been identified in all cases, and the lesions that have been found in some cases are not specific to schizophrenia.

A key issue in understanding schizophrenia is why

a genetically based, neurobiological disorder is not expressed clinically until 15–20 years after birth, at which time it progressively disables its victims. In understanding this issue, investigators have proposed a *neurodevelopmental model* of schizophrenia in which a genetic vulnerability and early neurodevelopmental insults result in impaired connections between many brain regions that include the prefrontal cortex and parts of the limbic system (Raedler, Knable, & Weinberger, 2000; Selemon & Goldman-Rakic, 1999). This defective neural circuitry is then vulnerable to dysfunction until it is revealed by developmental processes and events during puberty (e.g., synaptic and hormonal changes) and by exposure to stress (D. A. Lewis & Lieberman, 2000). This model of early-occurring neural pathology in schizophrenia is consistent with the findings that infants and children often display developmental impairments well before the onset of their psychotic symptoms, including deficits in motor, language, cognitive, and social functioning (Marenco & Weinberger, 2000).

Few autopsy, brain scan, or neurochemical studies of children with schizophrenia have been conducted. However, consistent with the findings for older adolescents and adults, the limited evidence that is available suggests the presence of diverse anatomical and neurological anomalies (Sowell, Toga, & Asarnow, 2000). For example, an autopsy study of a man who died at age 22 and had his first onset of schizophrenia at age 10 found abnormalities in several brain regions, including the brain stem, thalamus, and frontal cortex (Casanova, Carosella, & Kleinman, 1990). Findings from brain scan studies of children with schizophrenia are highly suggestive of disruptions in early brain development (Alaghband-Rad, Hamburger, Giedd, Frazier, & Rapoport, 1997; Rapoport et al., 1999).

Neuropsychological findings indicate that children with schizophrenia show many of the same deficits in attention and information processing found in adults with schizophrenia. Their performance on information-processing tasks is disrupted, more than that of other children, by increasing the amount of information to be processed. Moreover, recordings of brain activity during task performance suggest limitations in resources available for cognitive processing (Strandburg, Marsh, Brown, Asarnow, & Guthrie, 1994). In general, neuropsychological findings suggest a deficit in central nervous system structures involved in recruiting and allocating resources for processing information (R. F. Asarnow et al., 1994).

Environmental Factors   COS is a familial disorder, but the less than 100% concordance rates for identical twins suggest that nongenetic influences contribute to the likelihood for a child to develop schizophrenia. Nongenetic factors, including exposure to infectious, toxic, or traumatic insults, and stress during the prenatal or postnatal development, may play a role in schizophrenia, perhaps through subtle effects on neurodevelopment (Marcelis et al., 1998). In considering other nongenetic influences,

the elevated likelihood of psychiatric illness in parents of children with schizophrenia will likely have a negative effect on parental role functioning.

The influence of psychosocial stress in the etiology of schizophrenia is most apparent in studies of high-risk samples in which the onset of schizophrenia is associated with significant stress on the family. Because of its rarity, very few cases of COS have been identified in high-risk samples. There was one report of two high-risk children who developed schizophrenia at age 10 (Fish, 1987). Clearly, conclusions cannot be drawn from only two children. However, it is of interest they were the only children in the sample who had been physically abused, both were raised by mothers with schizophrenia, and both showed delays and disorganization in their gross motor and/or visual motor development and delays in physical growth (Fish, 1987).

A study of the home environments of siblings and fraternal twins of children with schizophrenia found an association between family disturbances and schizophrenia-spectrum outcomes (Kallman & Roth, 1956). More than 80% of the homes of twins and siblings diagnosed as schizoid or schizophrenic included a disturbed or inadequate parent, economic distress, or a broken home, in contrast to 65% of the homes of twins and siblings with healthy outcomes. The generally high level of problems in these families may reflect the fact that all included at least one child with schizophrenia.

A series of interesting studies were conducted to describe the family environments of children with schizophrenia and those with *schizotypal personality disorder (SPD)* (J. R. Asarnow, Tompson, & Goldstein, 1994). Youngsters with SPD show social and interpersonal deficits marked by acute discomfort with close relationships and by cognitive and perceptual distortions and eccentricities. Although the diagnosis of SPD is controversial in childhood, schizotypal symptoms such as social isolation and thought disturbance may be precursors of schizophrenia (J. R. Asarnow, 1988). For example, raters were able to distinguish between children who later developed schizophrenia as adults and their healthy siblings by observing home movies that were made before the age of 8 years (Grimes & Walker, 1994; E. Walker & Lewine, 1990).

Parents of children with schizophrenia or SPD score higher than parents of children with depression on **communication deviance,** which is a measure of interpersonal signs of attentional and thought disturbance. Children from families with high communication deviance showed the most severe impairment and the poorest attentional functioning. These findings suggest that communication deviance may be associated with a severe form of schizophrenia, or that family interaction may worsen the severity of dysfunction (J. R. Asarnow, Goldstein, & Ben-Meir, 1988). Parents of children with schizophrenia are more likely to use harsh criticism of their children than are parents of depressed children or normal controls.

In general, family findings highlight the stress, distress, and personal tragedy often experienced by families of children with schizophrenia (J. R. Asarnow & Asarnow, 2003). In the words of June Beeby, the mother of 17-year-old Matthew, who was diagnosed with schizophrenia and believed that God wanted his mother and his sister to die:

> "It's quite horrendous. First of all, you've got somebody that you love, a child that you've raised. And then suddenly, the child becomes a crazy person" (M. Nichols, 1995, p. 70). On a dark and cold winter day, June Beeby arrived home to find her son dead in a pool of blood. "He had taken two ordinary dinner knives . . . and plunged them into his eyes until they pierced his brain" (p. 70). In a diary entry that he had made 2 years before he took his life, Matthew had described an encounter with God: "He used his power and he controlled my brain for nine months. . . . God wanted me to feel that I would die, in order for individuals to live forever in heaven" (p. 74).

Treatment

As a parent you feel you have a tremendous responsibility to keep a son or daughter safe. . . . But when your child is schizophrenic you can't do that, because the person doesn't want help.

(From "Schizophrenia: Hidden Torment," by M. Nichols, *Macleans*, January 30, 1995, p. 73 Copyright © 1995 by Maclean's. Reprinted by permission.)

COS is a chronic disorder with a poor long-term outcome for most sufferers, although some youngsters may display more positive outcomes (Eggers, Bunk, & Ropcke, 2002). In either case, outcomes for most afflicted individuals are vastly improved over what they once were. Current treatments emphasize the use of antipsychotic medications combined with psychotherapeutic, and social and educational support programs (J. R. Asarnow et al., 2004; McClellan et al., 2001). Although we know far less about the use of antipsychotic medications with children than with adults, they are widely used to treat children with schizophrenia (J. R. Asarnow et al., 2004). Medications effectively help control psychotic symptoms in children with schizophrenia. However, the need for psychosocial treatments, such as family intervention, social skills training, and educational support is also widely recognized in clinical practice (Asarnow et al., 2004). Many advances have occurred in the psychosocial treatment of adults with schizophrenia; however, few controlled studies have been conducted with children.

SECTION SUMMARY

- Current views regarding the causes of schizophrenia are based on a vulnerability-stress model that emphasizes the interplay among vulnerability, stress, and protective factors.
- Schizophrenia is a disorder that involves multiple genes and is associated with environmental and developmental vulnerability factors.
- Although medications may help control psychotic symptoms in children with schizophrenia, psychosocial treatments, such as social skills training, family intervention, and special school placement, are also needed.

Key Terms

 InfoTrac College Edition

To research recent articles on the subject, go to:
www.infotrac-college/thomsonlearning.com

Enter search terms: AUTISM, AUTISTIC CHILDREN, AUTISTIC SPECTRUM DISORDERS, ASPERGER'S DISORDER, PERVASIVE DEVELOPMENTAL DISORDER, SCHIZOPHRENIA IN CHILDREN.

Communication and Learning Disorders

If you can read this, thank a teacher.

—Anonymous

Everyone has important needs and ideas: Imagine not being able to get them across. Sights and sounds surround you, but you cannot focus your attention long enough to make sense of them. When you are shown how to read or add, you find that the letters and numbers look and sound too much alike. Although these difficulties vary from person to person, they are common daily experiences of many children and adolescents with communication and learning disorders. Everyday tasks can be confusing and frustrating, and sometimes result in a cycle of academic failure and lowered self-esteem.

Children with communication or learning disorders can learn, and they are as intelligent as anyone else. The disorders usually affect only certain limited aspects of learning; rarely are they severe enough to impair the pursuit of a normal life, but they can be very stressful. Consider the experiences of James and Francine:

James, age 9, was a growing concern for his teacher: "James is obviously a very bright boy, and he wants to do well. I've noticed that he likes art, and is always wanting to draw. But he gets really upset when I ask him to do some work in class. He looks like he dreads coming to school. And he complains that some words he tries to read don't make sense to him. I'm worried that his increasing frustration is going to cause other problems in school or with friends. Sometimes he gets mad at something and he has trouble calming down. If he is trying to create something that doesn't turn out the way he envisioned it, he explodes and slams his fist against the wall."

What James's mother heard was all too familiar. She knew that her son would get involved in something only if he could do it his own way. Her mind wandered briefly to when he was a toddler and sometimes got so anxious and worried about something that he had trouble sleeping or felt sick. She shared with his teacher her frustration at trying to find out what the problem was: "Getting him to read at home is like pulling teeth. He won't read at all on his own because he knows he can't read many of the words."

Francine, age 7, was entering a new school for the second time in 2 years. The first school was too challenging, and the other kids teased her because she "doesn't know what 2 plus 2 is." She is content to play for hours by herself and is not interested in the things that other kids her age are doing. "Most of the time," her mother explained, "Francine seems sad and in a bit of a fog." Although school performance was a major concern, her mother was also quite worried about Francine's lack of friends and the way other children treated her.

Her mother and father proudly shared their daughter's early childhood history and developmental milestones with me during our first interview. "Francine walked before she was a year old, and was a very talkative baby and toddler, who picked up new words quite quickly. She was a healthy and normal baby—we can't figure out why she seems so uninterested in school and other kids." They went on to explain: "When she entered preschool and kindergarten, she seemed uninterested in making friends. The other kids basically ignored her, even though she didn't do anything to bother them. My husband and I didn't think much of it at first. In fact, we bragged about how she took an early interest in reading and would spend a lot of her time alone with a book or magazine, even when she was 4 or 5, although she didn't usually understand what she read. But we grew more concerned around age 5 because she paid little attention to popular movies, toys, and things other kids her age played with. When she was a preschooler, we also noticed that she had trouble with numbers and understanding concepts like "more," "less," or "bigger." She knows what these words mean now, but she is still confused when we ask her to count something.

Yesterday I gave her her allowance and just for the heck of it, I used pennies, nickels, and dimes to see if she could add them up. No matter how hard we tried, she became confused, switching from one coin to the other, and she thought she had a bigger allowance if I stacked the pennies up! And if you ask her to arrange something, like setting the table for dinner, you never know what you'll end up with!"

James and Francine have different learning problems. James' are with language and reading. His ability to distinguish the different sounds (phonemes) of language is underdeveloped, which is the primary reason for his poor word recognition and writing ability. Francine's problems are mostly with nonverbal learning, such as math. She can read quite well, although she has difficulty understanding some of the subtleties of facial expressions and gestures. She also confuses terms and instructions that describe spatial or numerical relationships.

The field of learning and communication disorders, broadly referred to as "learning disabilities," has changed dramatically during the last 10 years. For many years, learning problems were often attributed to poor motivation or poor instruction. Fortunately, breakthroughs in neuroimaging techniques led to increased recognition of differences in the neurological makeup and development of children with problems in language and related cognitive tasks. With recent advances in detection and intervention aimed at early language development, signs of communication problems are detected at an early age and children are provided with alternative teaching methods that build on their developmental strengths.

In this chapter, we emphasize the relationship between language development and the subsequent appearance of a learning problem once the child enters school. We put these problems in a developmental context by showing how communication disorders (diagnosed primarily in early childhood), and learning disorders (identified most often during early school years) have interconnected features and underlying causes. As a case in point, preschoolers with communication disorders are more likely to de-

Slowly but surely, most children learn the letters of the alphabet and how to use them to read and write words. For children with certain learning disabilities, however, the shapes and sounds of different letters continue to be confusing.

velop a learning disability by middle childhood or early adolescence (Beitchman et al., 2001; Tallal, 2003).

Definitions and History

Learning disability is the general term for learning problems that occur in the absence of other obvious conditions, such as mental retardation or brain damage. The term has been replaced in the DSM-IV-TR by two more specific terms, *learning disorders* and *communication disorders*, but the common use of the term requires that it be clarified and defined.

A learning disability affects how individuals with normal or above-average intelligence take in, retain, or express information. Incoming or outgoing information can be scrambled as it passes between the senses and the brain. Unlike most physical disabilities, a learning disability is a hidden handicap, and is often undetected in young children (Lyon, Fletcher, & Barnes, 2003). Thus, children with learning disabilities often must cope with their limitations in reading, writing, or math, and with the frustration of convincing others that their problems are as legitimate as visible disabilities.

Learning difficulties often show up in schoolwork and can impede a child's ability to learn to read or write or do math, but also can affect many other parts of life, including work, daily routines, family life, and friendships. Some learning problems are specific and affect a narrow range of ability, whereas others may affect many different tasks and social situations. Each type of learning disability, whether it is related to reading, writing, math, or

Few realize that Albert Einstein had early speech and language difficulties, given his monumental contributions to society.

language, is characterized by distinct definitions and diagnoses.

Knowledge of communication and learning disorders is growing rapidly as a result of increased scientific interest and research support. We now recognize that a learning disability, though challenging, does not have to be a handicap. Many well-known people with learning problems, for example, used their talents in exceptional ways (International Dyslexia Association, 2004):

Thomas Edison, inventor

Albert Einstein, physicist

Winston Churchill, British Prime Minister

Woodrow Wilson, U.S. president

Tom Cruise, actor

Whoopi Goldberg, actor and comedian

For all intents and purposes, the terms *learning disorders* and *learning disabilities* are used interchangeably. Simply stated, the main characteristic shared by all children with learning disabilities is not performing up to their expected level in school. Otherwise, symptoms vary tremendously (Toppelberg & Shapiro, 2000). The recognition of learning disorders has brought needed attention to many children and adults who are unable to acquire academic skills at a normal rate.

Children with learning disabilities constitute the majority of children in North America who receive special education services (C. R. Johnson & Slomka, 2000). Yet, experts still struggle to adequately define learning disabilities because of their many forms and overlapping symptoms, which you will note in the following definitions:

Learning disabilities is a general term that refers to significant problems in mastering one or more of the following skills: listening, speaking, reading, writing, reasoning, and mathematics. Learning disabilities do not include problems primarily attributed to visual, hearing, or motor handicaps, mental retardation, emotional disturbance, or environmental disadvantage. Emotional and social disturbances and other adaptive deficiencies may occur with learning problems, but they do not by themselves constitute a learning disability (adapted from the Individuals with Disabilities Education Act [IDEA], 1997).

In Chapter 9 we described intelligence as involving basic cognitive abilities that include problem solving, verbal skills, and mental reasoning. The term *multiple intelligence*, described in Box 11.1, implies there are diverse forms of intelligence, and suggests that each type is as important as the others, but for different reasons. Broadening the concept of intelligence to include more than logical, mathematical, or language abilities helps focus attention on individual strengths. For example, we are all stronger in some areas of learning and performance than others (we enjoy writing and reading, but don't ask us to fix your car). Similarly, children with learning disorders, who have normal intelligence, show a pattern of relative strengths and weaknesses that can make some learning tasks much more difficult. This pattern is noteworthy mostly because it is so extreme and unexpected for a child who otherwise shows normal cognitive and physical development.

Communication disorders is a diagnostic term that refers to the difficulty in

- producing speech sounds (phonological disorder)
- speech fluency (stuttering),
- using spoken language to communicate (expressive language disorder),
- understanding what other people say (mixed expressive-receptive language disorder)

These disorders are developmentally connected to the later onset of learning disorders.

Learning disorders is a diagnostic term that refers to specific problems in

- reading (disorder of reading, **dyslexia**)
- math (disorder of mathematics)
- writing ability (disorder of written expression)

These disorders are determined by achievement test results that are substantially below what is expected for the child's age, schooling, and intellectual ability.

A Closer Look

BOX 11.1 Aspects of Multiple Intelligence

- *Linguistic:* A sensitivity to the meaning, function, and grammatical rules of words, as in writing an essay.
- *Musical:* A sensitivity and creativity in hearing and manipulating tones, rhythms, musical patterns, pitch, and timbre, as in composing a symphony.
- *Logical/mathematic:* The ability to solve problems and see abstract relationships, as in calculus or engineering.
- *Spatial:* A sensitivity to the perception, manipulation, and creation of different forms and contexts, as in painting.
- *Bodily/kinesthetic:* The ability to use the body and the relevant part of the brain to coordinate movements in special and highly coordinated ways, as in dance and athletics.
- *Intrapersonal:* The ability to recognize, define, and pursue inner feelings and thoughts, as in poetry and self-knowledge.
- *Interpersonal:* The ability to sense the moods, feelings, and actions of other people, as in teaching, parenting, and politics.

Source: Based on Gardner, 1993.

An unexpected pattern of strengths and weaknesses in learning was first noted and studied by physicians during the late 19th century who were treating patients with medical injuries (Hammill, 1993). Franz Joseph Gall, a pioneer of language disorders, was struck by what he observed among some of his brain-injured patients: They had lost the capacity to express their feelings and ideas clearly through speech, yet they did not seem to suffer any intellectual impairments. One of his patients could not speak, but had no problem writing his thoughts on paper. Because he knew that this patient had normal speech before the head injury, Gall reasoned that the problem must have resulted from brain damage that had disrupted the neurological processes related to speech. For the first time, scientists began to pinpoint areas in the brain that control the ability to express and receive language processes.

These early observations, based on known medical injuries, raised the possibility that people with learning disabilities differ from people with mental retardation in terms of relative strengths and deficits. They have normal intellectual processes in most areas but are relatively weaker in others, known as an **unexpected discrepancy** between measured ability and actual performance. This premise remains at the foundation of today's definition of learning disorders. However, debate now focuses on whether the discrepancy is necessary for distinguishing learning disabilities (Siegel, 2003), a point we will return to later in the chapter.

The links between mental retardation, organic brain damage, and learning problems fascinated scientists, who had a firmer understanding of brain–behavior relationships by the 1940s. During that time, the question still remained as to why some children who did not fit the definition of mental retardation based on IQ had significant problems in learning. Could mental retardation be restricted to certain intellectual abilities but not others? Were academic problems the same as those assessed by measures of general intelligence?

A. A. Straus and H. Werner (1943) shed light on this issue by pointing out that children learn in individual ways, challenging the concept that learning is a relatively uniform, predictable process in nonretarded children. Three important concepts from this period continue to influence the field to this day (Lyon et al., 2003):

1. Children approach learning in different ways, so each child's individual learning style and uniqueness should be recognized and used to full advantage.

2. Educational methods should be tailored to an individual child's pattern of strengths and weaknesses; one method should not be imposed on everyone.

3. Children with learning problems might be helped by teaching methods that strengthen existing abilities rather than emphasize weak areas.

By the early 1960s, the modern learning disabilities movement had begun. Parents and educators were dissatisfied with the fact that children often had to be diagnosed with mental retardation to receive special education services. A category was needed to describe learning problems that could not be explained on the basis of mental retardation, lack of learning opportunities, psychopathology, or sensory deficits (Lyon et al., 2003).

Thus, the emerging concept of learning disabilities made intuitive sense to many who were familiar with the varied needs of children, and was welcomed as states and provinces began to support special education programs and services. The domination of physicians and psychologists in the field gave way to greater input from educators, parents, and clinicians. Teacher training expanded to include new ways to teach youngsters who could not respond to typical classroom methods. Professionals trained in speech and language pathology became an important part of school-based services.

As the focus of the learning disabilities movement shifted from the clinic to the classroom, parents and educators assumed a major role in programming and placement. They were encouraged by the fact that the term *learning disabled* did not stigmatize children, but rather brought them needed services (Hammill, 1993). The fact that these children had normal intelligence gave parents and teachers hope that difficulties in reading, writing, and math could be overcome if only the right set of instruc-

tional conditions and settings could be identified (Lyon et al., 2003). Thus, with the collaborative leadership of parents, educators, and specially trained professionals, the field of learning disabilities grew from its beginning in the 1960s to the major aspect of educational services it is today.

SECTION SUMMARY

- *Learning disabilities* is a general term for communication and learning problems that occur in the absence of other obvious conditions, such as mental retardation or brain damage.

- Children and adults with learning disabilities show specific deficits in using spoken or written language, often referred to as relative strengths and weaknesses.

- Parents and educators assumed a major role in bringing recognition and services to children with learning disabilities.

Language Development

From birth, infants selectively attend to parental speech sounds and soon learn to communicate with basic gestures and sounds of their own. Usually, by their first birthday they can recognize several words and use a few of their own to express their needs and emotions. Over the next 2 years their language development proceeds at an exponential pace, and their ability to formulate complex ideas and express new concepts is a constant source of amazement and amusement for parents. Adults play an important role in encouraging language development by providing clear examples of language and enjoying the child's expressions.

Language consists of **phonemes**, which are the basic sounds (such as sharp *ba*'s and *da*'s and drawn-out *ee*'s and *ss*'s) that make up language. When a child hears a phoneme over and over, receptors in the ear stimulate the

From an early age, children love to express themselves.

formation of dedicated connections to the brain's auditory cortex. A perceptual map forms that represents similarities among sounds and helps the infant learn to discriminate different phonemes. These maps form quickly; 6-month-old children of English-speaking parents already have auditory maps different from infants in Swedish homes, as measured by neuron activity in response to different sounds (Kuhl, 1995). By their first birthday, the maps are complete, and infants have lost the ability to discriminate sounds that are not important in their own language.

Rapid development of a perceptual map is why learning a second language after, rather than with, the first language is difficult—brain connections are already wired for English, and the remaining neurons are less able to form basic new connections for, say, Swedish. Once the basic circuitry is established, infants can turn sounds into words, and the more words they hear, the faster they learn language. The sounds of words serve to strengthen and expand neural connections that can then process more words. Similar cortical maps are formed for other highly refined skills, such as musical ability. A young child who learns to play a musical instrument may strengthen the neural circuits that underly not only music, but verbal memory as well (Ho, Cheung, & Chan, 2003).

Phonological Awareness

Not all children progress normally through the milestones of language development. Some are noticeably delayed, continuing to use gestures or sounds rather than speech. Others progress normally in some areas, such as following spoken directions and attending to commands, but have trouble finding the words to express themselves clearly.

Although the development of language is one of the best predictors of school performance and overall intelligence (Sattler, 2002), delays or differences in development are not a definitive sign of intellectual retardation or cognitive disorder. Rather, such deviations from normal may be just that—deviations—and may be accompanied by superior abilities in other areas of cognitive functioning. Albert Einstein, who is considered an intellectual genius, began speaking late and infrequently, causing his parents to worry that he was "subnormal." According to family members, when his father asked his son's headmaster what profession his son should adopt, the answer was simply, "It doesn't matter, he'll never make a success of anything" (R. W. Clark, 1971, p. 10).

Since language development is an indicator of general mental development, children who fail to develop language or who show severe delay in acquiring language are considered at risk of having a language-based learning disability. Albert Einstein notwithstanding, early language problems are considered highly predictive of subsequent

communication and learning disorders (Benasich & Tallal, 2002; Dale, Price, Bishop, & Plomin, 2003).

Phonology is the ability to learn and store phonemes as well as the rules for combining the sounds into meaningful units or words. Deficits in phonology are a chief reason that most children and adults with communication and learning disorders have problems in language-based activities such as learning to read and spell (Snowling, Gallagher, & Frith, 2003).

A young child is required to recognize that speech is segmented into phonemes (English language contains about 42, such as *ba, ga, at,* and *tr*). The difficulty of this task for many children is the fact that speech does not consist of separate phonemes produced one after another. Instead, sounds are *co-articulated* (overlapped with one another) to permit rapid communication, rather than pronounced sound by sound (Liberman & Shankweiler, 1991). About 80% of children can segment words and syllables into their proper phonemes by the time they are 7 years old. The other 20% cannot, and it is these children who struggle hardest to read (Vellutino, Fletcher, Snowling, & Scanlon, 2004).

Generally, early language problems surface as learning problems when children enter school, because now children are taught to connect spoken and written language. Those who do not easily learn to read and write often have difficulty learning the alphabetic system—the relationship of sounds to letters. They also cannot manipulate sounds within syllables in words, which is called a lack of phonological awareness and is a precursor to reading problems (Frost, 1998).

Phonological awareness is a broad construct that includes recognition of the relationship that exists between sounds and letters, detection of rhyme and alliteration, and awareness that sounds can be manipulated within syllables in words. Primary-grade teachers detect phonological awareness as they ask children to rhyme words and manipulate sounds. For example, the teacher can say "hat" and ask the child to say the word without the *h* sound, or say "trip" and have the child say the word without the *p*. To assess the child's ability to blend sounds, teachers can say, for example, the three sounds *t, i,* and *n* and see if the child can pull the sounds together to say "tin."

In addition to serving as a prerequisite for basic reading skills, phonological awareness and processing also appear highly related to expressive language development (Pennington & Lefly, 2001). Readers with core deficits in phonological processing problems have difficulty segmenting and categorizing phonemes, retrieving the names of common objects and letters, storing phonological codes in short-term memory, and producing some speech sounds. Reading and comprehension depend on the rapid and automatic ability to decode single words. Children who are slow and inaccurate at decoding have the most difficulties in reading comprehension (Lyon et al., 2003).

- Language development is based on innate ability and environmental opportunities to learn, store, and express important sounds in the language, which also proceeds very rapidly during infancy.

- Deficits in phonological awareness—the ability to distinguish the sounds of language—have been identified as a major cause of both disorders in communication and learning.

COMMUNICATION DISORDERS

Children with communication disorders (formerly known as developmental speech and language disorders) have difficulty producing speech sounds, using spoken language to communicate, or understanding what other people say. In DSM-IV-TR, communication disorders include the diagnostic subcategories of *expressive language disorder, phonological disorder, mixed receptive-expressive disorder,* and *stuttering.* These subcategories are distinguished by the exact nature of the child's impairment.

Recall that during development phonological problems appear before problems in language reception or expression, yet they have strong similarities. The following discussion focuses on expressive language disorder in an effort to highlight early childhood problems that represent the fundamental features of communication disorders. (Stuttering has a unique clinical feature and developmental course, so it is discussed separately.)

Consider Jackie's communication problems at age 3 years:

Jackie
Screaming, Not Talking

Jackie's mother explained with no hesitation why she asked for help: "My 3-year-old daughter is a growing concern. Since she was a baby, she has been plagued by ear infections and sleep problems. Some nights she screams for hours on end, usually because of the ear infections. She has violent temper outbursts and refuses to do simple things that I ask her to do, like get dressed or put on her coat."

The child, waiting in the playroom, could be heard screaming over her mother's voice. Jackie was asking my assistant for something, but she could not make out what Jackie was saying. It was pretty obvious how frustrated both the child and her mother must feel on occasion. Her mother explained how she and Jackie's father had divorced when Jackie was less than 2 years old, and

that after weekend exchanges it sometimes took a few days for Jackie's routine to return to some degree of normalcy.

I opened the letter she had brought from Jackie's preschool teacher, someone who I knew had a great deal of experience with children of this age. "Jackie is a bright and energetic child," the letter began, "but she is having a great deal of difficulty expressing herself with words. When she gets frustrated, she starts to give up or becomes angry—she won't eat her meals or she fights with staff at nap time, even if she is hungry or tired. If a new teacher at day care is introduced, it takes Jackie a long time to get used to the new person. Jackie seems to understand what she is being asked, but can't find the words to express herself, which understandably leads to an emotional reaction on her part."

Expressive Language Disorder

Jackie's problems met criteria for an **expressive language disorder,** which is a communication disorder characterized by deficits in expression despite normal comprehension of speech. As a result of these deficits, Jackie showed her frustration loudly and inappropriately.

Children's language development follows specific steps, although each child may proceed through the steps at a different rate. Normal variations can make it difficult to predict that a given child's early communication problems will become major problems in learning later on. A common example is the child who points to different objects and makes grunting or squealing noises that the parent quickly recognizes as "more milk" or "no peas." Prior to age 3 or so, many children communicate this way unless parents actively encourage using words and discourage nonverbal communications. Nevertheless, despite plenty of verbal examples and proper language stimulation, some children fail to develop in some areas of speech and language, and later have problems in school. This developmental connection makes the study of communication disorders highly pertinent to the understanding and treatment of subsequent learning problems.

Children with an expressive language disorder, like Jackie, do not suffer from mental retardation or one of the pervasive developmental disorders that affect speech and language (see Chapters 9 and 10). A defining characteristic of expressive language disorder is the discrepancy between what children understand (receptive language) and what they are able to say (expressive language). For example, when asked by her parents to go upstairs, find her socks, and put them on, Jackie was quite capable of

Table 11.1
Main Features of DSM-IV-TR Diagnostic Criteria for Expressive Language Disorder

A. The scores obtained from standardized individually administered measures of expressive language development are substantially below those obtained from standardized measures of both nonverbal intellectual capacity and receptive language development.

B. The difficulties with expressive language interfere with academic or occupational achievement or with social communication.

Source: Reprinted with permission from *Diagnostic and Statistical Manual of Mental Disorders, DSM-IV-TR, Fourth Edition.* Copyright © 2000 by the American Psychiatric Association.

complying. When asked by her mother to describe what she has just done, however, she might respond simply, "find socks." Table 11.1 shows the major features of the DSM-IV-TR diagnostic criteria for expressive language disorder.

The linguistic abilities of children with expressive language disorders vary significantly, based on the severity of the disorder and the age of the child. Most often these children begin speaking late and progress slowly in their speech development. Their vocabulary is often limited and is marked by short sentences and simple grammatical structure, as in Jackie's response. To fit the diagnostic criteria, these problems must be so severe that they interfere with pre-academic or academic achievement or the ability to communicate in everyday social situations.

Two closely related types of communication disorders deserve clarification. A **mixed receptive-expressive language disorder** may be present if speaking problems are coupled with the difficulty in understanding some aspects of speech. Although their hearing is normal, children with this disorder cannot make sense of certain sounds, words, or sentences. They may have difficulty understanding particular types of words or statements, such as complex if-then sentences. In severe cases, the child's ability to understand basic vocabulary or simple sentences may be impaired, and there may be deficits in auditory processing of sounds and symbols, storage, recall, and sequencing (APA, 2000). Understandably, these problems make the child seem inattentive or noncompliant, and the disorder can be easily misdiagnosed.

Imagine how it would feel to be in Greece visiting an English-speaking host and her Greek husband. Unless your host is present, trying to engage in friendly conversation can be frustrating and uncomfortable. Even if both you and the husband can understand a few words each other is saying, you probably cannot actually converse. If you have ever faced a similar communication barrier, you probably have a greater appreciation of the frustration

and discomfort that accompany an expressive language disorder.

When the developmental language problem involves articulation or sound production rather than word knowledge, a **phonological disorder** may be an appropriate diagnosis. Children with this disorder have trouble controlling their rate of speech, or lag behind playmates in learning to articulate certain sounds. The most frequently misarticulated sounds such as *l, r, s, z, th,* and *ch* are acquired later in the developmental sequence (APA, 2000). Depending on the severity of the disorder, the speech quality of these children may be unusual, even unintelligible. For example, at age 6, James still said "wabbit" instead of "rabbit" and "we-wind" for "rewind." Preschoolers, of course, often mispronounce words or confuse the sounds that they hear, which is a normal part of learning to speak. When these problems persist beyond the normal developmental range or interfere with academic and social activities, they deserve separate attention.

Prevalence and Course

Children usually reveal problems in speech articulation and expression as they attempt to tackle new sounds and express their own concepts. Even though prevalence estimates account for normal variation in language development and are based on individuals who meet specific diagnostic criteria, the degree of severity can vary considerably. For example, in early childhood, milder forms of phonological disorder are relatively common, affecting close to 10% of preschoolers. However, many of these children outgrow their earlier difficulties, so by the time they are 6 or 7 years old only 2% to 3% meet the criteria for phonological disorder. Similarly, expressive language disorder (affecting 2% to 3%) and mixed expressive-receptive disorder (affecting less than 3%) are both common among younger school-age children (APA, 2000; Tallal & Benasich, 2002).

Communication disorders are identified only slightly more often in boys (8%) than girls (6%) (Shriberg, Tomblin, & McSweeny, 1999). However, because boys show more behavior problems accompanying their language difficulties, they are referred and diagnosed with communication learning disorders more often than girls (Vellutino et al., 2004). Fortunately, by mid- to late adolescence, most children with a developmental communication disorder have acquired normal language (APA, 2000). About 50% fully outgrow their problems, whereas the other 50% may show considerable improvement but still have some degree of impairment until late adolescence. In contrast, the course and prognosis for children with an acquired type of communication disorder (caused by some event unrelated to development, such as brain lesions, head trauma, or stroke) depend highly on the severity and location of the injury, the child's age and extent of language development at the time of the event (APA, 2000).

Even though language problems usually disappear or diminish with time, children with communication disorders often have higher than normal rates of negative behaviors that began at an early age (Beitchman et al., 2001; Toppleberg & Shapiro, 2000). Associated behavior problems, such as ADHD, can add to communication problems, which further alters the course of development in terms of how they relate to peers or keep up with educational demands. To give children with special needs the opportunity to interact with typically developing children, school systems have begun to include these children with different needs into regular, rather than segregated, classrooms. **Inclusion education strategies** are based on the premise that the abilities of children with special needs will improve from associating with normally developing peers and be spared the effects of labeling and special placements.

Causes

Notable findings that support the role of genetics, brain function, and environmental risk factors associated with higher incidence of learning disorders are discussed in the following sections (Shriberg et al., 1999; Campbell et al., 2003).

Genetics   Language processes appear to be heritable to a significant degree, although the specific genetic underpinnings are difficult to pinpoint. About 50% (Stromswald, 1998) to 75% (Spitz, Tallal, Flax, & Benasich, 1997) of all children with specific language disorders show a positive family history with some type of learning disability. Twin studies (Bishop et al., 1999; Bishop, 2003) and adoption studies (Felsenfeld & Plomin, 1997) also suggest a genetic connection.

Scientists are zeroing in on specific deficits in brain functioning that lead to communication disorders and may be heritable. Studies comparing language-impaired children with and without an affected parent suggest that *temporal processing deficits* occur significantly more often in children with a positive family history for a language-based learning disability (Flax et al., 2003; Keen & Lovegrove, 2000). That is, affected children have more difficulty deciphering certain speech sounds because of subtle but important differences in the way neurons fire in response to various sounds. In a twin study, Bishop, Bishop, et al., (1999) found that the variation in temporal processing was due to enviromental factors and not genetics because twin-twin correlations were similar for MZ and DZ twins. However, what does appear to be genetic is a deficit in phonological short-term memory.

The Brain   Language functions develop rapidly and are housed primarily in the left temporal lobe of the brain (see Figure 11.1). A circular feedback loop helps strengthen the developmental process of language reception and expression. The better children comprehend spoken language, the better they will be able to at express themselves. Feedback from their own vocalizations, in turn, helps shape their subsequent expression. Lack of comprehension and absence of feedback reduces verbal output, and thus interferes with the development of articulation skills (Vellutino et al., 2004).

Anatomical and neuroimaging studies show that deficits in phonological awareness and segmentation are related to problems in the functional connections between brain areas, not to a specific dysfunction of any single area of the brain (Lyon et al., 2003). Recent brain imaging studies indicate that poor performance on tasks demanding phonological awareness is associated with less brain activity in the left temporal region, suggesting that phonological problems may stem from neurological deficits or deviations in posterior left-hemisphere systems that control the ability to process phonemes (S. Shaywitz, 2003; Tallal, 2003). We return to these findings on brain function later on in our discussion of reading disorders.

Ear Infections   Another biological cause of expressive language impairment may be recurrent otitis media (middle ear infection) in the first year of life, because hearing loss accompanies frequent or long bouts of infections. Otitis media that occurs during a critical period may cause early language problems that improve relatively quickly, whereas in the absence of such a history, the causes are likely to be more neurological and long lasting (Shriberg et al., 2000). Children with chronic otitis media still face some delays in their social development, however, as they attempt to catch up to their peers in learning appropriate forms of verbal communication (Shriberg, Friel-Patti, Flipsen, & Brown, 2000).

In summary, although biological findings point to abnormal brain functioning, how this abnormality originates is still unclear. The best guess is that communication disorders result from an interaction of genetic influences, slowness or abnormalities of brain maturation, and, possibly, minor brain lesions that escape clinical detection (S. Shaywitz & Shaywitz, 1999).

Home Environment   How much does the home environment contribute to communication disorders? Do some parents fail to provide adequate examples to stimulate their children's language? Because of the important role parents play in children's development, psychologists have studied this issue carefully.

We noticed when we first visited Jackie that her stepfather was a very quiet man who often communicated nonverbally—a gesture, a frown, a short phrase. Her mother used very simple speech when talking to Jackie but not when talking to Jackie's 6-year-old sister. These observations match those of Whitehurst and his colleagues

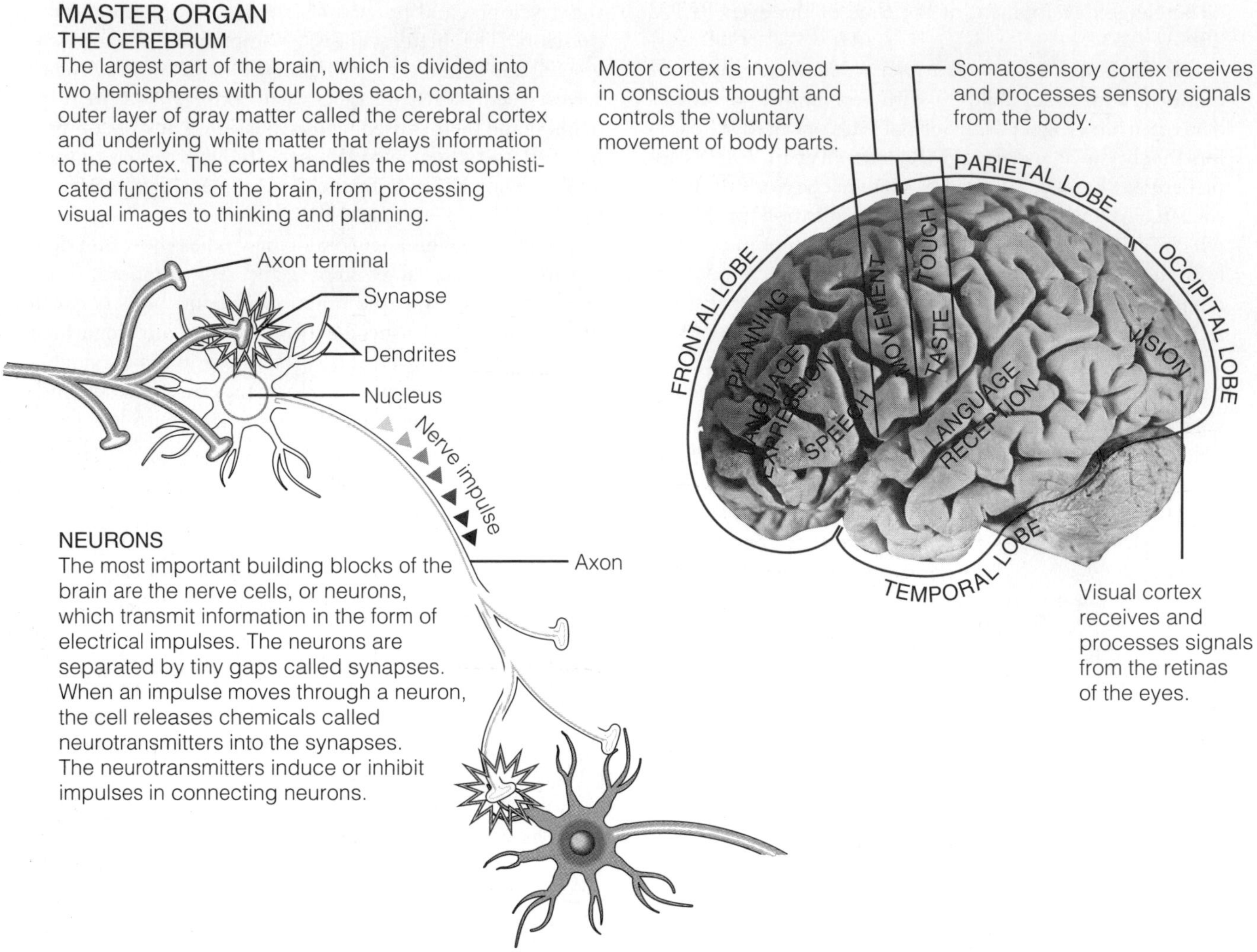

MASTER ORGAN
THE CEREBRUM

The largest part of the brain, which is divided into two hemispheres with four lobes each, contains an outer layer of gray matter called the cerebral cortex and underlying white matter that relays information to the cortex. The cortex handles the most sophisticated functions of the brain, from processing visual images to thinking and planning.

Axon terminal

Synapse

Dendrites

Nucleus

Nerve impulse

NEURONS

The most important building blocks of the brain are the nerve cells, or neurons, which transmit information in the form of electrical impulses. The neurons are separated by tiny gaps called synapses. When an impulse moves through a neuron, the cell releases chemicals called neurotransmitters into the synapses. The neurotransmitters induce or inhibit impulses in connecting neurons.

Axon

Motor cortex is involved in conscious thought and controls the voluntary movement of body parts.

Somatosensory cortex receives and processes sensory signals from the body.

PARIETAL LOBE

FRONTAL LOBE

OCCIPITAL LOBE

PLANNING

LANGUAGE EXPRESSION

SPEECH

MOVEMENT

TASTE

TOUCH

VISION

LANGUAGE RECEPTION

TEMPORAL LOBE

Visual cortex receives and processes signals from the retinas of the eyes.

Figure 11.1. Areas of the brain involved in language functions.

(Illustration of brain and text copyright © 1996 Time, Inc. Reprinted by permission of *Time,* Inc. (Canadian edition 7/5/95, U. S. edition 1/31/96). Copyright © *Time* 1996.)

(1988), who compared verbal interactions of families with and without a child who had an expressive language disorder. They found that parents changed the way they spoke to their children, depending on their children's abilities. When the child spoke in simple, two- or three-word sentences, the parents adjusted their speech accordingly. Note that, except in extreme cases of child neglect or abuse, it is unlikely that communication disorders are caused by parents. Parental speech and language stimulation may affect the pace and range of language development, but not the specific impairments that characterize the disorders (Flax et al., 2003; Tallal & Benasich, 2002).

Treatment

Fortunately, expressive language disorder and similar communication disorders usually self-correct by the age of 6 and may not require intervention. Even so, parents may

seek help in understanding their child's speech delays and to ensure that they are doing everything possible to stimulate language development. Specialized preschools, for example, have had good results using a combination of computer- and teacher-assisted instruction to teach early academic skills to young children, which helps to pace the child's practice of new skills (Eikeseth & Nesset, 2003; Hatcher, Hulme, & Snowling, 2004).

A home-based parent training package has also shown success in teaching various ways to improve the child's expressive speech (Whitehurst, Fischel, Arnold, & Lonigan, 1992). For Jackie, for example, we designed ways that her parents and day-care teachers could build on her existing strengths. Her day-care teacher had an excellent idea: Because Jackie loved to draw and to talk about her artwork, why not use her interest in drawing to increase her enthusiasm for speaking? When I visited her class, she ran up to show me her drawing, exclaiming, "I draw picture of mom, dad, kitty, and lake." We agreed that her behavior problems could be managed by simple forms of ignoring and distracting and the occasional time-out. Jackie became attached to computer graphics and images, and soon was able to identify letters and small words and to move shapes around the screen. All the while, her expressive language improved, and by age 5 she could pronounce all the letters of the alphabet and was eager to start kindergarten.

more aware that Sayad's peers tease and imitate him. She explained why she came for an assessment: "We were on the way to the store when Sayad kept saying 'where' over and over. After I stopped the car and unfastened his seatbelt, he finished his question—'is daddy?' After that, I gave up on my 'leave it alone' notion and began trying ways to slow Sayad down a bit."

Stuttering

Stuttering is the repeated and prolonged pronunciation of certain syllables that interferes with communication. It is quite normal for children, who are still learning to speak, to go through a period of nonfluency, or unclear speech, as part of their development. It takes practice and patience for a child to develop the coordination for the tongue, lips, and brain to work in unison to produce unfamiliar or difficult combinations of sounds. For most children, this period of speech development passes without notice, and for most parents it is full of wonder and amusement as their children wrestle with new words. Some children, however, progress slowly through this stage, repeating *(wa-wa-wa)* or prolonging *(n-ah-ah-ah-o)* sounds; they struggle to continue or develop ways to avoid or compensate for certain sounds or words. Four-year-old Sayad has speech problems that typify the pattern of stuttering:

Sayad
Family Legacy

Sayad's parents had received a lot of informal advice from friends and relatives about their son's speech problems, but most of what they said was worrisome. "He'll struggle with this for most of his life," his grandmother had warned. "If something isn't done right away, he'll become a stutterer, and be so self-conscious that he won't be able to keep up in school or with his friends."

Sayad started repeating and prolonging some of his words when he was about 2, but by now his problem had grown more noticeable. As he spoke, he pursed his lips, closed his eyes, and shortened his breathing, seeming to tense up his face. Yet his interactions with me were friendly and at ease. "M-m-m-m-y words get stuck in m-m-m-m-y m-m-mouth," he explained, "and I-I-I-I talk t-t-t-too fast. Wh-wh-wh-why can't I talk right?" I soon discovered why his grandmother was so concerned: The child's great-grandfather and great-uncle both stuttered, and Sayad's father had been a stutterer until he was a teenager.

Sayad's mother had been trying to ignore the problem and not draw attention to it, but she was growing

Prevalence and Course

Stuttering has a gradual onset between the ages of 2 and 7 years, usually peaking at age 5 (APA, 2000). A large population-based study estimated the incidence of stuttering to be about 3% in children, with males affected about 3 times more often than females (Craig, Hancock, Tran, Craig, & Peters, 2002). However, few children actually receive this diagnosis because most children recover from stuttering. This developmental course is important for treatment considerations, because almost 80% of children who stutter before age 5 will no longer stutter once they attend school for a year or so (Packman & Onslow, 2002).

Causes and Treatment

Many myths and falsehoods surround stuttering. The widely held view that stuttering is caused by an unresolved emotional problem or by anxiety, is countered by the lack of supportive evidence (Packman & Onslow, 2002). Because the problem runs in families, researchers have focused on family characteristics as the major causes. However, it is not likely this behavior is acquired primarily as a function of the child's linguistic environment. Sayad's grandmother and mother would be relieved to know that the communicative behavior of mothers does not significantly contribute to the development of stuttering (Smits-Bandstra & Yovetich, 2003).

Genetic factors play a strong role in the etiology of stuttering. According to one major study, heritability accounts for 71% of the variance in the causes of stuttering, and the remaining 29% are the result of the environment (Andrews, Morris-Yates, Howie, & Martin, 1991). Genetic factors most likely influence speech by causing an abnormal development in the location of the most prominent speech centers in the brain, which are usually in the left hemisphere. This biological source for stuttering explains many of its clinical features, including the loss of spontaneity and occasional problems in self-esteem (Packman & Onslow, 2002).

Since most children outgrow stuttering, one of the most frustrating problems for parents and therapists is to decide whether therapy would be intervention or interference. Therapy is usually recommended if sound and syllable repetitions are frequent, if the parent or child is concerned about the problem, or if the child shows facial or vocal tension, like Sayad. A common psychological treatment for children who stutter is to teach parents how to speak to their children slowly, use short and simple sentences, and consequently remove the pressure the child may feel about speaking (Smits-Bandstra & Yovetich, 2003). Contingency management procedures have also been beneficial in teaching language-fluency training to younger children, by using positive consequences for fluency and negative consequences for stuttering (Butcher, McFadden, Quinn, & Ryan, 2003).

SECTION SUMMARY

- Speech and language problems that emerge during early childhood include difficulty producing speech sounds, speech fluency, using spoken language to communicate, or understanding what other people say.

- Even though most children with communication disorders acquire normal language by mid- to late adolescence, early communication disorders are developmentally connected to the later onset of learning disorders.

- Expressive language disorder is a communication disorder defined as a discrepancy between receptive language and expressive language.

- Causes of communication disorders include genetic influences and slow or abnormal brain maturation. Early ear infections may play a causal role in some cases.

- Treatment of children with communication disorders is often unnecessary, since many of these problems are self-correcting soon after children begin attending school.

- Stuttering, or speech dysfluency, occurs mostly in younger children, peaking around age 5. Recovery usually occurs once the child enters school.

LEARNING DISORDERS

People do not understand what it costs in time and suffering to learn how to read. I have been working at it for eighty years, and I still can't say that I've succeeded.

—Goethe (1749–1832)

Whether we are studying Roman history or calculus, applying ourselves to the task of learning requires exertion and concentration. Like physical activities, some learning activities are more difficult than others, especially for younger children who have not developed a foundation of good study habits and successful learning experiences. Parents and teachers may notice that a child is struggling unusually hard to master a particular skill, such as reading, and wonder why. The problem may be formally assessed by an IQ test and various standardized tests that assess abilities in specific academic areas.

When achievement in reading, math, or writing is substantially below expectations for the child's age, schooling, and intellectual ability, he or she may be diagnosed with a learning disorder. In practice, *substantially below* is defined as a discrepancy of more than 2 standard deviations between the IQ findings and the actual achievement test findings. In other words, a child with a learning disorder is bright enough to learn the subject material, but does not appear able to do so. However, as we note in the following example there is some debate as to the validity of using a discrepancy formula to define learning disorders (Siegel, 2003).

Let's return to James, the 9-year-old with reading problems:

James
Strong Points Shine

The look on the 9-year-old's face said it all—he did not want to be here. "I'm tired of talking to people" was his terse greeting. I wondered for a moment whether he would talk to me at all, but as soon as he saw my computer, he brightened a bit. To allow time for him to feel more comfortable, I invited James to play a quick game or two. His skill at the action games told me a lot about his basic energy and problem-solving ability—he was a whiz at figuring out the rules of each game and getting a high score. We spoke casually during the warm-up, but it was clear to me that he preferred to concentrate on the game.

A half hour passed, with little more than a few sentences exchanged. A quick trip to the snack bar gave us the common ground we needed to open up and talk a bit. "Why does my teacher want me to come here?" he reasonably asked. As he listened and replied to my explanation, his language problems stood out. His sentences were short, simple, and rapid. Here is an example:

"James, tell me something about your favorite story or a recent movie you've seen."

"I like the movie. Lots of dogs."

"What movie is that, James?"

"Dog movie."

During testing, James often tried to start before I had finished telling him what to do. He was eager to do what I asked, but he stopped abruptly as soon as he had trouble. James could focus on only one sound at a time, so if he missed early cues or initial instructions, he would become disoriented, frustrated, and uncooperative. James wanted to do well, but I could see he was struggling. He completed the WISC-IV in less than an hour, hurrying almost as if to escape his own mistakes. His measured general intelligence was within the normal range, but his performance abilities (performance IQ = 109) were much stronger than his verbal abilities (verbal IQ = 78). It was obvious as well that the test underestimated his true ability, as a result of his eagerness to finish and his difficulty with understanding some of the instructions.

To my surprise, James was ready to continue on to the next test after only a short computer game break. He explained why this was so. "I put things together, like puzzles. I make cars and planes at my house." As long as I gave him small breaks on the computer, he was willing to tackle the material on the tests. Some of his spelling errors stood out immediately, such as *skr* for *square*, and *srke* for *circle*. When asked to write the sentence *he shouted a warning*, he wrote *he shtd a woin*. He read *see the black dog* as "see the black pond," and *she wants a ride to the store* as "she was rid of the store." He seemed to use a "best guess" strategy in tackling reading, based on the sounds that he knew: When asked to write the word *bigger*, he wrote just *her*. But I noticed that James's enthusiasm picked up a bit as he began telling stories from pictures he was shown, and he marveled at his own ability to rotate shapes on the computer to complete a picture. He left my office more animated and talkative than when he arrived, which showed how nice it must have felt for him to experience success.

Compare James's reading problems with those of Tim, a 7-year-old who has a great deal of trouble with math and drawing:

Tim
Warming with Interest

When I first saw Tim, he seemed aloof and disinterested. His eyes stayed focused on the floor, and his body remained expressionless, as if to say, "Leave me alone, and let me outta here." As I searched for something to say, I asked Tim to tell me a little about his family: "Do you have any brothers or sisters? Does your family like to do anything special together?" His tired response, "I have two brothers, my father works all day, mom plays piano. We want a boat," sent me a clear message as to his mood and interest in this activity. My usual ploy of turning on the computer games fell flat—"I hate computers" was Tim's preemptive response. I wondered, "Is he depressed, angry, hurt, frustrated? Just what is going on here?"

Having looked at his school record, I knew he was struggling, especially in math and physical sciences, but his speech and affect expressed more than only academic problems. His school records flashed the news that Tim had a learning disorder, as evidenced by his WISC-IV performance score of 79 that fell in the borderline- to low-average range, and his verbal score of 108 that fell in the average range. The test administrator had politely described Tim's test-taking approach as "reluctant." Notes by teachers indicated that he commonly had problems on tasks involving drawing, particularly if they required memory, and his math and social skills were far below those of others in his class.

I pulled out my *Where's Waldo?* book and we began looking at it together. In addition to being fun, looking for Waldo and his friends (small figures amidst millions of figures and colors) required Tim to be patient. At first he balked, but I noticed that he improved if he used his own verbally mediated strategy to solve the problem. Tim talked to himself as he thought aloud: "Look around the edges first, then start to look closer and closer to the middle of the page. Look for Waldo's red and white shirt—look closely at each section!" The more interested he was, the more he would talk. Once he warmed up, his smile appeared, along with his admission that "this sure beats math lesson."

Tim's problems are in the areas of spatial orientation and mathematical reasoning, and further achievement testing confirmed that they fit the diagnostic criteria for a learning disorder in mathematics. However, his academic problems were almost masked by his frustration and low self-esteem. Emotional problems are often seen in children who are bright enough to recognize that their performance is below that of others.

James' pattern of strengths and weaknesses shows that although he has reading problems, other strengths compensate for this disability. He has strong talents for figuring out how things work and for drawing ideas on paper. Tim has several strengths, too, especially in linguistic skills such as word recognition, sentence structure, and reading. In contrast to James, Tim has problems primarily in the visual, spatial, and organizational spheres, which show up as difficulties with tactile (touch) perception, psychomotor activity (e.g., throwing and catching), and nonverbal problem solving (e.g., figuring out math problems and assembling things). The limitations of both children can affect every aspect of their formal education as well as their interpersonal abilities, and therefore require comprehensive and ongoing treatment plans.

To better understand the nature of learning disorders, picture yourself asking for directions at a gas station in an unfamiliar town. The attendant says: "Go out the driveway and turn right. Go till you reach the second light, turn left, and look for the sign to Amityville. It's about 3 miles down the road. You'll pass a cemetery and a red schoolhouse, and go under a railroad trestle before you get to Highway 18. When you see the sign, turn right." We all have some difficulty processing such information and recalling it accurately; we drive away repeating to ourselves,

For children with learning disorders, following simple instructions can be confusing and frustrating.

Table 11.2

Main Features of DSM-IV-TR Diagnostic Criteria for Learning Disorders: **Reading Disorder, Mathematics Disorder, and Disorder of Written Expression** *

A. Reading achievement/mathematical ability/writing skill, as measured by individually administered standardized tests, is substantially below that expected given the person's chronological age, measured intelligence, and age-appropriate education.

B. The disturbance in criterion A significantly interferes with academic achievement or activities of daily living that require reading skills/mathematical ability/composition of written texts.

* *Because the basic criteria are identical, the three separate learning disorders are combined here, with the exception of the specific ability that is affected.*

Source: Adapted with permission from *Diagnostic and Statistical Manual of Mental Disorders, DSM-IV-TR, Fourth Edition.* Copyright © 2000 by the American Psychiatric Association.

"Stop light, go left, cemetery, highway, turn at schoolhouse?" Our driving companions, who heard the same instructions, may recall a different route.

This situation demonstrates that even simple verbal instructions can easily be jumbled. Children and adults with learning disorders experience similar confusion in the everyday situations of processing new information or understanding what they are reading. These learning problems can be difficult to recognize because, for most of us, the material in question is straightforward and simple. The child may be blamed for not listening, not paying attention, or for being "slow," which further disguises the true nature of the learning problems.

Disabilities in reading, mathematics, and written expression are characterized by an individual's performance below that expected for someone the same age. Main features of DSM-IV-TR criteria are shown in Table 11.2. To be classified as a disability, the performance problems must significantly interfere with academic achievement or daily living. (Some children and adults have found ways to compensate for their learning problems and therefore do not display a disability, despite their test findings of poor achievement.) Finally, the disability cannot be related to a sensory problem, such as impaired hearing or sight, unless it goes well beyond what children typically experience.

Because many aspects of speaking, listening, reading, writing, and arithmetic overlap and build on the same functions of the brain, it is not surprising that a child or adult can have more than one form of learning disorder. Recall that phonological awareness facilitates the ability to speak and, later on, to read and write. A single gap in the brain's functioning can disrupt many types of cognitive activity. These disruptions, in turn, can interfere with the development of important fundamental skills and compound the learning difficulties in a short time. Moreover, as we saw with both James and Tim, numerous secondary problems can emerge, such as temper outbursts and withdrawal from social situations, as a result of frustration and lack of success.

Reading Disorder

He has only half learned the art of reading who has not added to it the more refined art of skipping and skimming.

—*Arthur James Balfour*

Children are naturally attracted to reading, and its importance in our society is unequaled by any other academic accomplishment. We are surrounded by written signs and messages and, by about age 5 or so, most children want to know what they mean. (Capitalizing on this natural curiosity, advertisers have become expert in pairing recognizable symbols with the names of their product or establishment so that children can "read" more quickly.) By the first grade, natural interest and developmental readiness are channeled into formally learning how to read. For many children this process is difficult and tedious; for a sizeable minority, however, it can be confusing and upsetting. The role of parents in this process is critical, because children need positive feedback and to feel satisfied with their performance, regardless of their speed and accuracy.

When you consider everything involved in learning the basics of reading, such as associating shapes of letters (graphemes) with sounds (phonemes), it is not surprising that some children have difficulty and can quickly fall behind. Read the following sentence: "I believe that abnormal child psychology is one of the most fascinating and valuable courses I have taken." As you read the sentence, did you notice that you had to simultaneously

- Focus attention on the printed marks and control your eye movements across the page?
- Recognize the sounds associated with letters?
- Understand words and grammar?
- Build ideas and images?
- Compare new ideas with what you already know?
- Store ideas in memory?

Most of us have forgotten all the effort that goes into reading, especially in the beginning. Not surprisingly, children's initial attempts are laborious and monotonous as they wrestle with the sounds and complexities of combined letters. Such mental processing requires a complex intact network of nerve cells that connect our vision, language, and memory centers (Grigorenko, 2001; Tallal, 2003). A small problem in any area can cause reading difficulties. The most common underlying feature of reading disorder, however, is an inability to distinguish or to separate the sounds in spoken words. Phonological skills are fundamental to learning to read, and therefore this deficit is critical.

To assess a child's need for additional practice in mastering phonemes and words, there are two systems that operate when one reads words, which are essential in the development of reading. The first system operates on individual units (phonemes) and is relatively slow; the second system operates on whole words more quickly. In normal readers, whole words are learned through the development of phonologically based word analysis. However, persistently poor readers seem to rely on rote memory for recognizing words (S. E. Shaywitz, B. A. Shaywitz, et al., 2003).

Many clinical signs of reading disorders are first evident only to a trained eye. Some testing methods developed by teachers and school psychologists show how children with reading disorders function in the classroom. They often have trouble learning basic sight words, especially what is phonetically irregular and must be memorized, such as *the, who, what, where, was, laugh, said,* and so forth. These children have developed their own unique and peculiar reading patterns, which signal the need for different teaching methods. Typical errors include *reversals (b/d; p/q), transpositions* (sequential errors such as *was/saw, scared/sacred), inversions (m/w; u/n),* and *omissions* (reading *place* for *palace* or *section* for *selection*). However, these errors are common in many younger children who are just learning to read and write, and do not necessarily imply a reading disorder.

To assess a child's need for additional practice in certain areas, teachers may log the types of errors the child makes while reading out loud. In addition to decoding words, reading comprehension is assessed by having the student retell a story or suggest the next episode. Average readers rely heavily on auditory and visual modalities for gathering new information, but children with reading disorders may prefer a mode of touch or manipulation, to assist them in learning. These various patterns of strengths and weaknesses, if adequately assessed, can then be used to the child's advantage in planning additional teaching methods such as computer-based learning (Lyons et al., 2003; Pennington & Lefly, 2001).

The core deficits in reading disorders are in **decoding**—breaking a word into parts rapidly enough to read the whole word—coupled with difficulty reading single, small words (Vellutino et al., 2004). When a child cannot detect the phonological structure of language and automatically recognize simple words, reading development will very likely be impaired (Pennington, 1999). The slow and labored decoding of single words requires substantial effort and detracts from the child's ability to retain the meaning of a sentence, much less a paragraph or page. The child with a reading disorder lacks the critical language skills required for basic reading, reading comprehension, spelling, and written expression.

Mathematics Disorder

During their preschool years, children are not as naturally drawn to mathematical concepts as they are to reading. This changes rapidly as they discover that they need to count and add to know how much money it takes to buy something or how many days remain until vacation. As in reading, the need to know propels children to learn new and difficult concepts, and little by little their new skills help them understand the world better.

For some children, like Francine and Tim, this curiosity about numbers is compromised by their inability to grasp the abstract concepts inherent in many forms of numerical and cognitive problem solving. Francine's difficulty with numbers and concepts began to show up well before she attended school, which is typically the case. When she encountered math concepts in second grade that required some abstract reasoning, she fell further and further behind.

Many skills are involved in arithmetic: recognizing numbers and symbols, memorizing facts (the multiplication table), aligning numbers, and understanding abstract concepts such as place value and fractions. Any or all may be difficult for children with a mathematics disorder (Lyon et al., 2003). The DSM-IV-TR criteria for mathematics disorder, like the criteria for learning disorders, are based on assumptions of normal or above-average intelligence that is assessed by IQ, normal sensory function, adequate educational opportunity, and the absence of developmental disorders and emotional disturbance. Children

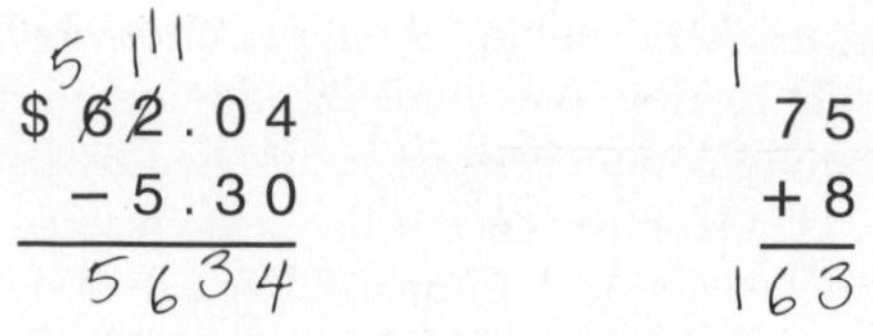

$$\begin{array}{r} {}^{5}\;{}^{|11} \\ \$6\cancel{2}.04 \\ -\;5.30 \\ \hline 5634 \end{array} \qquad \begin{array}{r} {}^{|} \\ 75 \\ +\;8 \\ \hline 163 \end{array}$$

Figure 11.2. Errors in math computation by a 10-year-old girl with a mathematics disorder. (From "Learning Disabilities," by H. G. Taylor, 1988, p. 422. In E. J. Mash and L. G. Terdal (Eds.) *Behavioral Assessment of Childhood Disorders,* 2nd ed. Copyright © 1988 The Guilford Press. Reprinted by permission.)

and adults with this disorder may have difficulty not only in math, but also in comprehending abstract concepts or in visual-spatial ability. Historically, these characteristics were termed *developmental dyscalculia*, which is defined as the failure to develop arithmetic competence, but the term is seldom used today. Examples of calculation errors typical of children with a mathematics disorder are shown in Figure 11.2, an example that points out errors that suggest spatial difficulties and directional confusion.

Children with mathematics disorders typically have core deficits in arithmetic calculation and/or mathematics reasoning abilities, which include naming amounts or numbers; enumerating, comparing, and manipulating objects; reading and writing mathematical symbols; understanding concepts and performing calculations mentally; and performing computational operations (Lyon et al., 2003). These deficits imply that the neuropsychological processes underlying mathematical reasoning and calculation are underdeveloped or impaired.

Writing Disorder

Carlos

Slowly Taking Shape

Carlos, age 7, was about to finish second grade when his teacher and parents met to discuss his handwriting problems. The year had gone generally well, but his parents were bracing for bad news. Smiling and pulling out some workbooks, Carlos's teacher lined up examples of how he had gradually become able to print some letters over the course of the year. But what his parents saw was self-explanatory: His shapes were very poor and looked more like those of his 3-year-old sister. Sensing both parents' apprehension, his teacher clarified: "Carlos is having a few problems in his fine motor coordination, in activities such as artwork, putting puzzles together, and similar tasks. He goes too fast when trying to do these tasks, and he forgets to be careful or to follow the pattern. He makes a half-hearted attempt on his writing assignments and

then starts talking to his classmates. I'd like him to be seen by a psychologist for testing, and hopefully next fall his new teacher can strengthen his writing and fine motor skills with some additional exercises."

During the initial interview, Carlos took an immediate interest in our computer games, exclaiming how easy it was to use the mouse to draw figures. When asked to use a pencil and paper, however, Carlos balked. We asked him to copy by hand some of the figures he drew on the computer, after first printing them for him on paper. In doing so, he switched to his preferred hand in the middle of the task. He also showed several letter reversals (*b/d; p/q*), and pushed down very hard on the pencil in an attempt to trace or draw the figures. Throughout these tasks he talked freely and asked a lot of questions, making us wonder at times who was assessing whom.

Carlos showed evidence on neuropsychological testing of finger agnosia (he could not tell which finger I touched when his hand was behind his back), especially with his left hand. He also had considerable difficulty copying a triangle, a circle, and a square based on examples shown to him (see Figure 11.3). On the WISC-IV he obtained a performance score of 91 in the low-average range, and a verbal IQ score of 117 in the high-average range. On performance subtests he had particular problems with block design and puzzles, such as object assembly. He had more difficulty with verbal IQ subtests that involved concentration and attention, such as math and digit-span tasks. Throughout the testing, we found Carlos to be impulsive and sometimes quite defiant: If he didn't want to do something, he simply would not do it. These observations were consistent with his parents' frustration at his immature behavior and defiance at home.

Carlos has a learning disorder related to written expression. He has strong language and reasoning abilities, as well as normal problem-solving skills for his age, yet he is considerably weaker in his visual-motor abilities, as shown by his writing, figure copying, and figure rotation. Like reading and math, writing derives from several interconnected brain areas that produce vocabulary, grammar, hand movement, and memory.

Children with writing disorders often have problems with tasks that require eye/hand coordination, despite their normal gross motor development. Teachers notice that, compared with children who have normal writing skills, children with writing disorders produce shorter, less interesting, and poorly organized essays, and are less likely to review spelling, punctuation, and grammar to increase clarity (Hooper et al., 1994). However, spelling errors or poor handwriting that do not significantly in-

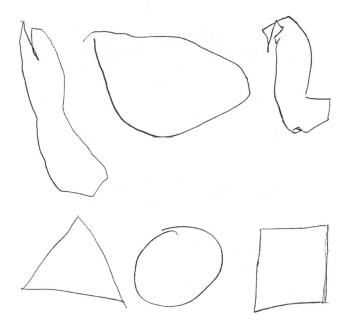

Figure 11.3. *Top:* Drawings produced by Carlos when asked to copy a triangle, a circle, and a square. *Bottom:* Examples of a triangle, circle and square from a normally developing 7-year-old boy.

terfere in daily activities or academic pursuits, do not qualify a child for this diagnosis. In addition, problems in written expression signal the possibility of other learning disorders, because of shared metacognitive processes: planning, self-monitoring, self-evaluation, and self-modification (Tallal & Benasich, 2002). Writing disorders are less understood than other learning disorders, and are often found in combination with learning disorders in reading or mathematics, which also have underlying core deficits in language and neuropsychological development.

Prevalence and Course

Current estimates of the prevalence of all types of learning disorders range from 2% to 10% of the entire population, depending on how the problems are defined and measured (APA, 2000). However, several researchers suggest that due to underreporting, these estimates should be much higher. The prevalence of dyslexia (reading disorder) is estimated to range from 5% to 17% of school-aged children (Lyon et al., 2003; Shaywitz, 1998).

Reading difficulties may be part of a continuum of reading abilities rather than a discrete, all-or-none phenomenon, which would mean that children with reading disorders are essentially those who fall at the lower end of the continuum (Pennington & Lefly, 2001; Snowling et al., 2003). This consideration is useful and important because, clearly, there are strong readers and weak readers, and no definitive cutoff point easily distinguishes the two (Lyon et al., 2003). If prevalence estimates are based

on a continuum of reading problems rather than a diagnostic category, reading disabilities are estimated to affect 1 in 5, or at least 10 million children in the United States (S. E. Shaywitz et al., 1992).

Current estimates of the prevalence of disorders related to mathematics and written expression are highly discrepant due to a lack of epidemiologic studies. Clinical studies put the prevalence of mathematics disorder at about 20% of all children with learning disorders, which means that about 1% of school-age children receive this diagnosis (APA, 2000). If prevalence is estimated on the basis of test scores, however, about 5% to 6% of school-age children would be included (Shalev, Auerbach, Manor, & Gross-Tsur, 2000). Like reading disorder, mathematics disorder usually becomes apparent during second or third grade, once formal mathematics instruction begins. Therefore, prevalence estimates based solely on diagnoses may be unduly conservative.

Finally, disorder of written expression is considered to be rare when not associated with other learning disorders (APA, 2000). However, given the high rate of developmental language disorders in the general population (8% to 15%) and the significantly high rate of disorders in reading skills previously noted, written language disorders probably affect at least 10% of the school-age population (Lyon et al., 2003). Because of their high comorbidity, disorders in math and written expression may best be construed as related features of a generalized problem in learning, rather than selective impairments.

Cultural, Class, and Gender Variations   Social and cultural factors are less relevant to learning disorders than other types of cognitive and behavioral problems; in fact, the diagnostic criteria state that they cannot be attributed to these factors. Nevertheless, some cultural and racial issues may affect how children with learning disorders are identified and treated.

Language development is highly influenced by its context (Tallal & Benasich, 2002), so it is necessary to consider how cultural and ethnic differences in the home may influence a child's language development. F. B. Wood et al., (1991) did an interesting study to illustrate the point that deficits in phonological awareness occur more frequently among populations that use nonstandard English. They followed a random sample of 485 children—Caucasian (55%) and African American (45%)—from first grade through third grade, and found that although African American youngsters read at the same grade level as Caucasian children at the beginning of the first grade, they show marked declines in reading by the third grade and severe declines by the fifth grade.

As emphasized throughout this text, many childhood disorders reflect an interaction between the child's inherent abilities and resources and the opportunities that exist in the child's local environment. In the case of learning to read, some teaching approaches do not explicitly emphasize specific sound–symbol relationships that are inherent in African American children's dialect (F. B. Wood et al., 1991). Greater attention to differences in dialect can lead to better learning opportunities.

Whereas attention to cultural and ethnic issues pertaining to learning disorders is a recent addition to research, sex differences have a long and contentious history. Males are more often diagnosed with learning disorders than females, accounting for 60% to 80% of all children diagnosed (APA, 2000). As with communication disorders, reasons for referral can distort the fact that boys and girls actually have very similar rates of reading problems. It comes as no surprise that schools refer about 4 times as many boys as girls, largely because boys are more likely to show behavior problems. Girls with learning problems are often quiet and withdrawn rather than loud and attention-seeking, and may be overlooked unless educators and parents are well informed. When male–female ratios are derived from epidemiological estimates rather than referrals, boys and girls are represented equally among children with learning disorders in reading, as long as attention-related disorders are taken into account (Cutting & Denckla, 2003; Young, in press).

Development Children with learning disorders often do not know how or why they are different, but they do know how it feels to be unable to keep up with others in the classroom. Hearing themselves described as "slow," "different," or "behind" they may identify more with their disabilities rather than with their strengths. These daily experiences may cause some children to act out by either withdrawing or becoming angry and noncompliant. Like James, they may stop trying to learn. Like Francine, they may become isolated and limit their participation in activities that their peers enjoy.

What can be expected of Francine, James, Tim, and Carlos during their school years? Proper planning and goal setting are the cornerstone of helping strategies at home and at school. Learning disorders are not easily outgrown, but there is reason for optimism. First and foremost, about three-fourths of the children diagnosed with reading disorder in elementary school still have major reading problems in high school and young adulthood (Beitchman et al., 1996; Young et al., 2002). Therefore, developmental expectations and educational planning must be ongoing (Lipka & Siegel, in press).

Do problems continue as a direct and unchangeable result of the disability, or of a failure to identify the learning problem in time to affect its course? The required discrepancy between IQ and performance may hamper early identification, because the assessment often is not done until the child has attempted and failed at reading, usually by the third grade. By that time, the child's achievement may be slow enough to demonstrate the discrepancy, but the child has failed in reading for 2 to 3 years and may have developed other learning problems as a result (Lyon

et al., 2003). Furthermore, the discrepancy requirement for the diagnosis of a learning disorder may not be necessary or meaningful. Researchers are now finding very few differences between discrepant and nondiscrepant readers in many factors such as information processing, genetic variables, neurophysiological response, and so forth (Siegel, 2003; Vellutino et al., 2004). The limitations of this approach should be kept in mind when it is necessary to meet local regulations for determining a child's eligibility for special services.

Children and adolescents with learning disorders are more likely than their peers to show internalizing problems such as anxiety (Beitchman et al., 2001) and mood disorders (Maughan, Rowe, Loeber, & Stouthamer-Loeber, 2003), as well as externalizing behaviors such as overactivity and noncompliance (Cutting & Denkla, 2003). The range and type of problems are generally similar for both younger and older age groups. Accordingly, issues pertaining to both younger and older children and adolescents with learning disorders are considered jointly unless particular developmental differences warrant attention. Many of these issues are common to all types of learning disorders unless otherwise noted.

Psychological and Social Adjustment Students with reading disorders feel less supported by their parents, teachers, and peers than do normal readers, and are more likely to express poor academic or scholastic self-concepts (Boetsch et al., 1996; Kellner, Houghton, & Douglas, 2003). As a case in point, the school dropout rate for adolescents with learning disorders is nearly 40%, or approximately 1.5 times the average (APA, 2000).

The connection between learning disorders and behavioral or emotional disorders has generated considerable interest but only cautious conclusions. Common sense suggests that children with learning disorders are faced with considerable challenges that are likely to take a toll on self-esteem and, in time, their social relationships. However, children's self-concepts in sports and appearance are usually less affected (Lyons et al., 2003).

Parents and teachers describe children with learning disorders as being more difficult to manage than typical children beginning at an early age. Although overall reports of behavior problems increase considerably for all children between early and middle childhood (Achenbach, Howell, Quay, & Conners, 1991), behavior problems among children with learning disorders are about 3 times higher than the norm by 8 years of age (Benasich, Curtiss, & Tallal, 1993) (see Figure 11.4). Most of these problems are not specific to learning disorders, but cover a broad range of problems that overlap 10% to 25% with features of conduct disorder (CD), oppositional defiant disorder (ODD), attention-deficit/hyperactivity disorder (ADHD), and major depressive disorder across all ages (APA, 2000).

These co-occurring problems are often interpreted as

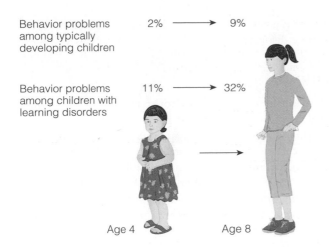

Figure 11.4. Percentage of clinically significant behavior problems among children with and without learning disorders, at 4 years and 8 years of age.
(Data from Benasich et al., 1993)

Behavior problems among typically developing children 2% → 9%

Behavior problems among children with learning disorders 11% → 32%

Age 4   Age 8

individual reactions and coping styles in response to failure, frustration, and, in some instances, punishment and negative attention. In terms of development, however, it is hard to say which comes first: Behavior problems may precede learning problems, may follow them, or occur at the same time (Hinshaw, 1992; Cutting et al., 2003). One explanation for the higher rate of behavior problems in children with learning disorders as they enter school is their impeded intellectual development, which creates additional academic and social pressure (Tallal & Benasich, 2002).

Based on a review of over 150 studies (Kavale & Forness, 1996), about 3 of every 4 students with learning disorders have significant deficits in social skills. As a group, they are more isolated and less popular among peers than other children, and they tend to make negative impressions on others (Vallance, Cummings, & Humphries, 1998). Like Francine, who was described by her mother as "humorless and in a bit of a fog," most children with learning disorders have difficulty grasping the nuances of social interaction and may not know how to greet others, make friends, or join in playground games. Subtle cues of social interaction may be missed or ignored. They may not always interpret correctly or respond appropriately to the frequent nonverbal—but very expressive—communication of other children, such as rolling the eyes to show dislike or disinterest. When children with learning disorders misunderstand the situation and act inappropriately, other children turn away.

A child with a learning disorder can also be an emotional burden for family members. Parents may experience a wide range of emotions, including denial, guilt, blame, frustration, anger, and despair. Brothers and sisters often feel annoyed, embarrassed, or jealous of the attention their sibling receives. Because behavioral problems are usually so disruptive, a child's distress and emotional needs may easily be overlooked; in fact, parents are often more aware of their children's acting-out than of their underlying feelings of sadness and self-doubt (Lardieri, Blacher, & Swanson, 2000).

Adult Outcomes Unfortunately, the social and emotional difficulties connected to communication and learning disorders may continue into adulthood, largely because of inadequate recognition and services (Young et al., 2002). Adults may find ways to disguise their problems, such as watching television news rather than reading newspapers. On the other hand, many excel in nonacademic subjects such as art, music, dance, or athletics. Still others may become outstanding architects and engineers, or they may have extraordinary interpersonal skills (Lyon et al., 2003). Each child and adolescent has many strengths that can be developed to compensate for their known deficits. Thus, despite their earlier risk for academic failure and psychosocial problems, many adults with learning disorders lead successful and productive lives (Werner, 1993).

Men with reading disorders do not differ from their peers regarding feelings of global self-worth; symptoms of depression; feelings of competency and satisfaction with jobs, marriages, and other relationships; or frequency of antisocial behavior (Boetsch et al., 1996). However, men still perceive lower levels of social support from parents and relatives—the only people still in their lives who knew of their problems as children—which confirms the indelible impressions left by early experiences.

One adult describes his own way of compensating for learning problems:

I faked my way through school because I was very bright. I resent most that no one picked up my weaknesses. Essentially I judge myself on my failures. . . . [I] have always had low self-esteem. . . . A blow to my self-esteem when I was in school was that I could not write a poem or a story. . . . I could not write with a pen or pencil. The computer has changed my life. I do everything on my computer. It acts as my memory. I use it to structure my life and for all of my writing since my handwriting and written expression has always been so poor. (Polloway, Schewel, & Patton, 1992, p. 521)

Whereas the long-term outlook for men with learning disorders is generally positive, the troublesome issue of sexism arises when considering how adult women with learning disorders fare over time. As a group, women with learning disorders have more adjustment problems than men as they leave school and face the demands of adult life. Problems and breakdowns in relationships are common, which indicate continued vulnerability (Bruck, 1998), and could very well reflect the lack of opportunity available to these women to achieve in areas that capital-

BOX 11.2 Factors That Increase Resiliency and Adaptation

Several personal characteristics and circumstances aid those with learning disorders in their successful adaptation from childhood, through adolescence, to young adulthood. As part of a longitudinal study of all children born in 1955 on the island of Kauai, Hawaii, E. E. Werner followed 22 children with learning disabilities and 22 matched controls. She found that most children with learning disabilities adapted successfully to adult life. Those who showed the greatest resiliency and flexibility over time had (1) a basic temperament that elicited positive responses from others; (2) a well-developed sense of efficacy, preparedness, and self-esteem that guided their lives; (3) competent caregivers and supportive adults; and (4) opportunities for a second chance if they made mistakes or got into trouble with the law. Although some of the characteristics are present from birth (e.g., temperament), many of the other supportive factors can be increased through the efforts of family members, schools, and communities.

Source: Based on Werner, 1993.

ize on their strengths. Reading problems often cause poorly qualified graduates to take relatively undemanding and unrewarding jobs. Women who lack competitive skills and strong career options due to school failure tend to get involved at an early age in intimate relationships that are generally unsupportive (Fairchild, 2002). Young men, in contrast, have more wide-ranging options once they leave school, which facilitates more positive social functioning in adulthood. Thus, if they are able to select their own environments in adulthood (and women have more obstacles in this regard than men), both men and women with learning disorders can build on their existing strengths, skills, and talents (Maughan & Hagell, 1996).

It is safe to say that even though learning disorders may remain, people who are given proper educational experiences have a remarkable ability to learn throughout their life spans. Box 11.2 describes some of these important opportunities that increase resilience. Adults can learn to read, although it is difficult because brain development slows down after puberty. Current gains in knowledge of the causes and early signs of learning disorders are likely to have a positive impact on early recognition and proper instruction. Nonintrusive electrophysiological measurements of brain reactivity may permit an early diagnosis based on underlying deficits in phonological processing rather than on performance alone (Benasich & Tallal, 2002). Thus, early identification and intervention

may be the key to preventing the long-term consequences of these disorders.

Causes

Most learning disorders do not stem from problems in a single area of the brain, but from difficulties in bringing information from various brain regions together in "convergence zones," where information is integrated and understood (Damasio & Damasio, 2000). Minute disturbances may underlie phonological processing deficits. Emerging evidence points to the conclusion that, in many cases, these subtle disturbances begin very early during development, perhaps prenatally (Benasich & Tallal, 2002; Tallal, 2003).

Recent findings suggest two distinguishable types of reading disorder – those children who are persistently poor readers and those who are accuracy improved (compensated readers) (S. E. Shaywitz, B. A. Shaywitz, et al., 2003). Persistenly poor readers and accuracy-improved readers have comparable reading skills and SES when they begin school, but by the time they are young adults, the accuracy-improved readers show better cognitive ability. The presence of compensatory factors, such as stronger cognitive ability, allowed the accuracy-improved individuals to minimize the consequences of their phonological defect. The accuracy improved group may represent a more genetic type of reading disorder, whereas the persistent group may represent a more enviromentally influenced type.

Genetic and Constitutional Factors Children who lack some of the skills needed for reading, such as hearing the separate sounds of words, are more likely to have a parent with a related problem. Around the turn of the 20th century this problem was studied largely by physicians, who considered reading disorders to be an inherited condition called *congenital word blindness* (W. P. Morgan, 1896). Today, estimates based on behavioral genetic studies indicate that heritability accounts for over 60% of the variance in reading disorders (Bishop, 2003; Viding et al., 2004), although the exact mode of transmission remains undetermined.

Most attention paid to heritability is aimed at genetic transmission of critical brain processes underlying phonetic processing (Vellutino et al., 2004). Because a parent's learning disorder may take a slightly different form in the child—the father may have a writing disorder and his child an expressive language disorder—it seems unlikely that specific types of learning disorders are inherited directly. More likely, what is inherited is a subtle brain dysfunction that, in turn, can lead to a learning disorder (Tallal, 2003). For example, an area has been identified on chromosome 6 that predisposes children to reading disorder (Grigorenko, 2001). Genetic transmission provides a plausible explanation for the high rate of 35% to 45% among family members for learning disorders in reading as well as math (Shalev et al., 2001), which are considerably higher than the estimated base rate of 5% to 10% in the population (Pennington & Lefly, 2001; Snowling et al., 2003).

Neurobiological Factors   Our understanding of learning disorders, particularly reading-based and language-based problems, took an important new direction in the mid-1980s with the discovery that the brains of people with these problems were characterized by cellular abnormalities in the left hemisphere that contains important language centers (Galaburda, Sherman, Rosen, & Geschwind, 1985). The fact that these cellular abnormalities could occur only during the fifth to seventh month of fetal development strengthened the view that learning disorders evolve from subtle brain deficits present at birth (Lyon et al., 2003). Initial autopsy findings were confirmed by sophisticated brain imaging technology that reveals the brain directly at work and makes it possible to detect subtle malfunctions that could never be seen before.

The suspected deficits, which likely are genetically based, involve specific discrimination tasks, such as detecting visual and auditory stimuli, as well as more pervasive visual-organizational deficits associated with reasoning and mathematical ability (Tallal & Benasich, 2002). A probable location of these deficits is a structure called the *planum temporale,* a language-related area in both sides of the brain. In a normal brain, the left side of the planum temporale is usually larger than the right side; however, in the brain of an individual with a reading disorder, both sides are equal size (Tallal, 2003). An immature form of EEG activation has also been found in children with learning problems. Specifically, these children have been found to have a greater expression of slow frequencies in EEGs of the frontal areas of their cortex, suggesting a retardation in the growth of the brain structures that are responsible for attention and organization of information (Kiroi, Ermakov, Belova, & Samoilina, 2002).

S. E. Shaywitz, B. A. Shaywitz et al., (2002) found lower activation in numerous sites, primarily the left hemisphere of the brains of dyslexic children compared to nonimpaired children, including the inferior frontal, parieto-temporal, and occipito-temporal gyri. These three areas of the brain are respectively responsible for understanding phonemes, analyzing words, and automatically detecting words (Shaywitz, 2003).

We have stressed that most children with reading and writing disorders have difficulty distinguishing phonemes that occur rapidly in speech. But why is this so? Consider what is involved, as shown in Figure 11.5. The sound must be processed by various brain areas as it is carried by nerve impulses from the ear to the thalamus to the nerve cells within the auditory cortex, where it is matched to existing patterns, or phonic bins, that have been previously formed and stored.

Compare this process to listening to music. When you first hear a new song, do you recognize aspects that resemble other recordings by that group or another group? Can you distinguish the music of one group from another? As we listen, we tend to cluster sounds into various categories, acquiring our taste for music as we store more collections and melodies into memory. Each time we hear new music, we match it to what we already know and appreciate. Young people are particularly adept at assimilating new sounds, thereby broadening their tastes. In contrast, people who have already formed specific musical tastes tend to stick to what they know, rejecting unrecognizable sounds. This gap in music appreciation is analogous to the gap researchers describe in the phonic abilities of children with learning disorders—they lack certain auditory sites that allow certain sounds to be recognized, so their appreciation of certain words is compromised.

Each neuron in the language processing areas of the brain has immense specificity. Some neurons fire when you silently name an object but not when you read the object's name out loud, and vice versa. Certain neurons are activated when bilingual people speak one language, but not when they speak the other (Ojemann, 1991). Someone can have an expressive language problem despite full comprehension, because the same neurons that are active when a person hears a word are not active when that person speaks it.

In the visual system, different aspects of what you see, such as form, color, and motion, are routed to different regions of the visual cortex. When something moves in your visual field, the region of the cortex that responds to visual motion—labeled V5—is activated. Eden et al., (1996) discovered that adults with reading disorders show no activation in this V5 area when asked to view randomly moving dots. They proposed that a V5 defect in perception of visual motion may be a marker of a general deficit in timing, which affects many different brain functions (C. Frith & Frith, 1996). To detect differences between consonant sounds—such as *b* or *t*—we must be able to distinguish between very rapid changes in sound frequency. A subtle neurological deficit in sensitivity could prohibit this distinction, which would then show up clinically as problems in reading and phonological processing (Agnew, Dorn, & Eden, 2004).

Thus, two major findings implicate specific biological underpinnings of reading disorders: (1) the language difficulties for people with reading disorders are specifically associated with the neurological processing of phonology; and (2) behavioral and physiological abnormalities are found in the processing of visual information. It is not surprising, therefore, that phonological and visual processing problems often coexist among people with reading disorders (Eden et al., 1996).

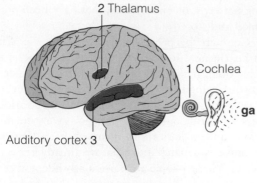

2 Thalamus

1 Cochlea

ga

Auditory cortex 3

Making sense of spoken words
1. A sound, like the phonic syllable **ga**, hits the ear and is sent as nerve impulses to the brain.

2. In the brain, the thalamus processes incoming signals and sends them to the auditory cortex.

3. The nerve cells within the auditory cortex match incoming signals with patterns the cortex has previously stored.

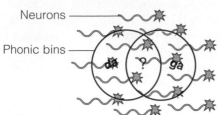

Neurons

Phonic bins

da ? ga

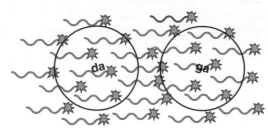

da ga

Why do language-impaired children confuse sounds?
By repeated exposure to spoken language, the neurons in the brain form patterns, or phonic bins, associated with particular sounds. When children have difficulty distinguishing between rapid acoustic cues, like the consonants in **ga** and **da**, those bins may overlap. Some scientists believe this overlap may be the key to language-based learning disabilities.

Can you retrain the brain?
Researchers at Rutgers and the University of California at San Francisco found that when children are taught to distinguish sounds that have been slowed down and exaggerated, their brains form new phonic bins. The scientists hypothesize that these new bins may be larger and no longer overlap. Eventually, the children learn to distinguish **ga** and **da** in ordinary speech.

Figure 11.5. How the brain processes speech.

("How the Brain Processes Speech" Copyright © 1996 *Time,* Inc. Reprinted by permission.)

Studies of the causes of learning disorders mostly involve children with reading disorders, but the findings apply to disorders in written expression and mathematics as well. Many—but not all—disabled writers show deficits in reading (Lyon et al., 2003), and some mathematical concepts require reading and writing as well as mathematics skills. In contrast to these language-based disorders, however, are various nonverbal learning disabilities (Rourke et al., 2002). **Nonverbal learning disabilities (NLD) are** deficits related to right-hemisphere brain functioning, and are characteristic of children who perform considerably worse at math than reading. These deficits involve social skills, spatial orientation, problem solving, and the recognition of nonverbal cues such as body language. In addition to math deficiencies, nonverbal learning disorders may be accompanied by neuropsychological problems such as poor coordination, poor judgment, and difficulties adapting to novel and complex situations (Cornoldi, Rigoni, Tressoldi, & Vio, 1999; Lyon et al., 2003).

Recall that Francine had well-developed word recognition and spelling abilities, but significantly worse mechanical arithmetic skills. Mathematics disorder, and perhaps that of written expression as well, are known to be associated with brain deficits that differ from deficits described for language-based learning disorders. These deficits are largely found in areas not related to verbal ability, which has led to use of the term nonverbal learning disorders.

The search for suspected causes for this nonverbal pattern of learning disabilities focuses on neurological diseases of childhood and developmental disabilities that impair brain functioning. Fetal alcohol syndrome, insulin-dependent diabetes, autism, irradiation (for treatment of various forms of cancer), and several other fetal and early childhood diseases and trauma have been linked to nonverbal learning disorders (Collins & Rourke, 2003; Rourke & Del Dotto, 1994). The common element among these various diseases and traumas—the final common pathway leading to the nonverbal learning disorder syndrome—is that they impair development and functioning of the brain.

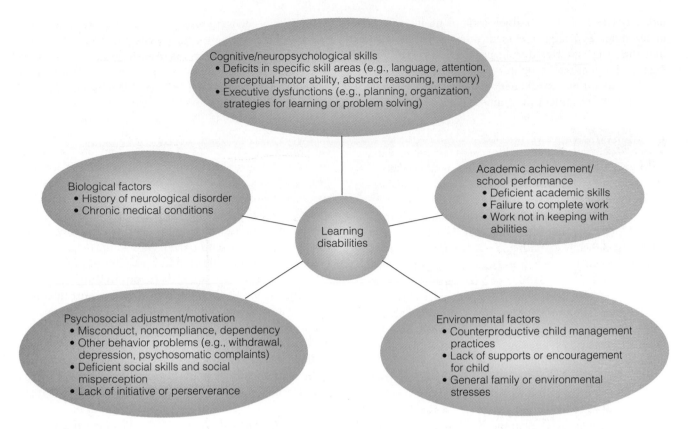

Figure 11.6. A biobehavioral systems model of major areas influencing the development and expresion opf learning disorders.

(From "Learning Disabilities," by H. G. Taylor, 1989. In E. J. Mash and L. G. Terdal, 1989, *Treatment of Childhood Disorders,* pp. 347–380. Copyright © 1989 by Guilford Publications. Reprinted by permission.)

Social and Psychological Factors Emotional disturbances and other signs of poor adaptive ability often accompany learning disorders, perhaps because the underlying causes are the same. The overlap between dyslexia and ADHD, for example, ranges from 30% to 70% depending on how ADHD is defined (Fletcher et al., 1999). Although this degree of overlap suggests that behavioral and learning problems have certain common aspects, they are still distinct and separate disorders (Lyon et al., 2003). Reading disorder is commonly associated with deficits in phonological awareness, whereas ADHD has more variable effects on cognitive functioning, especially in areas of rote verbal learning and memory (Hinshaw, 1992a). ADHD, moreover, is relatively unrelated to phonological awareness tasks (F. B. Wood et al., 1991). However, some children with learning disorders show symptoms similar to ADHD, including inattention, restlessness, and hyperactivity (Cutting et al., 2003; Vellutino et al., 2004).

As a summary and integration of this section, Figure 11.6 presents a biobehavioral systems model depicting possible ways in which major biological, cognitive, academic, environmental, and psychosocial factors interact to cause learning disorders (H. G. Taylor, 1989).

Prevention and Treatment

Although learning disorders have strong biological underpinnings, intervention methods rely primarily on educational and psychosocial methods. Psychosocial treatments for James, Francine, Carlos, and Tim must be comprehensive and ongoing, with each new task broken down into manageable steps, including examples, practice, and ample feedback. Combined with proper teaching strategies, children and their families may benefit from counseling aimed at helping the children develop greater self-control and a more positive attitude toward their own abilities. Support groups for parents can also fill an important gap between the school and the home by providing information, practical suggestions, and mutual understanding.

Someday, breakthroughs in brain research may lead to new medical interventions, but at present no biological treatments exist for speech, language, and academic disabilities. Where significant problems coexist in concentration and attention, some children respond favorably to stimulant medications that may temporarily improve attention, concentration, and the ability to control their impulsivity (see Chapter 5), albeit little or no improvement in learning. Typically, the medication schedule ensures that the drug is active during peak school hours, when reading and math are taught.

Consider the coordinated planning and effort that went into the treatment programs for Francine:

Francine
Slowly but Surely Improving

To reduce Francine's difficulties with math and, especially, with peer relationships, we considered several factors. First, we decided that teaching should be primarily verbal, with an understanding that she would have the most difficulty in math and science. Her teachers favored allowing Francine to use a calculator and a computer to assist her in learning new concepts. An emphasis on physical education was also planned, to help her with her visual-motor coordination. Her math teacher agreed that using graph paper might help her visualize numerical relationships, which led to noticeable improvements in her schoolwork.

Francine's problems in making friends were a major concern to everyone, and we believed that they were directly linked to her learning disability. A cognitive-behavioral intervention plan was developed in conjunction with her educational program. Because of Francine's strong verbal skills, we taught her to problem solve through role playing, and encouraged her mother to invite one child at a time for her to play with so that she could practice her skills. Francine had drifted into being a loner and seemed disinterested in looking after herself, so we also discussed ways to develop better self-care at home by giving her an allowance for completing household chores. We spent considerable time explaining the nature of her problems to her parents, and this guidance led to relief and understanding.

We saw the family once again 1 year later; although some of Francine's problems still existed, her social abilities had improved. She still had difficulties in developing friendships and tended to prefer being alone, but the problem had clearly lessened from the previous year.

Francine was able to get help because her problems were detected; recall, however, that by the time she was referred, she had already begun to fail at formal schooling. The first step in solving any problem is to realize that it exists. The nature of learning disorders makes this difficult for many children and parents. Although numerous signs of language-based learning disorders are present from early childhood, sophisticated means of assessing problems are not yet available until children are old enough to be formally tested.

Issues of identification are important because a brief window of opportunity may exist for successful treatment. If a problem is detected in early childhood—say, by kindergarten—then language-based deficits can often be remediated successfully. If the problem is not detected until age 8 or so, response to treatment is much lower (Hatcher et al., 2004). This is why prevention of reading difficulties is a hot topic: Training children in phonological awareness activities at an early age may prevent subsequent reading problems among children at risk (Foorman, Francis, Beeler, Winikates, & Fletcher, 1997). These activities consist of games that involve listening, rhyming, identifying sentences and words, and analyzing syllables and phonemes. For example, the child might analyze *sand* as *s-and* and then synthesize it into *sand,* or colored alphabet blocks might be used to break the word into separate phonetic sounds *(s-a-n-d)* (Lyon & Cutting, 1998).

Knowledge of communication and learning disorders has played leapfrog with the philosophy and practice of classroom instruction during the last decade. Discoveries in neurosciences, as noted above, challenged some prevailing educational practices, and today considerable disagreement remains as to the best way of assisting children with learning disorders.

The Regular Education Initiative Placing children with special educational needs in regular classrooms is now the norm in North America. The groundwork for this *inclusion movement,* which began during the 1950s, was based on studies showing that segregated classes for students with disabilities were ineffective and possibly harmful (Baldwin, 1958). Resource rooms and specially trained teachers replaced the special classes that had been in vogue, a change that had the further advantage of removing the need to label and categorize children. The Education for All Handicapped Children Act of 1975 in the United States (replaced by the 1997 Individuals with Disabilities Education Act, [IDEA]), and the Education Act of 1982 in Canada mandated that children with special needs must be afforded access to all educational services, regardless of their handicaps.

By the late 1980s, the inclusion movement expanded to become the **regular education initiative (REI)**, whereby students with learning disabilities are placed in general classrooms, and general and special education teachers share the responsibility for student instruction. Most prominently, the programs—rather than the children—are labeled (Hammill, 1993). In principle, the REI is attractive and promising, because it allows children with special needs to receive services without being diagnosed or labeled as mentally retarded, learning disabled, and so forth. However, implementation and teacher training, as well as the question of whether the REI succeeds in meeting the special needs of students, continue to be unresolved (Kavale & Forness, 2000; Miller, 2002).

Instructional Methods Although controversy remains over the practical aspects of including all children in regular classrooms, most educators today favor direct instruction for children with learning disorders. **Direct instruction** is a straightforward approach to teaching based on the premise that to improve a skill, the instructional activities must approximate those of the skill being taught (Hammill, Mather, Allen, & Roberts, 2002). Direct instruction in word structure is necessary because of the child's phonological deficits (Pennington & Lefly, 2001; Tallal & Benasich, 2002). Direct instruction in reading emphasizes the specific learning of word structure and the decontextualization of reading until the skill is learned. This method is based on the premise that a child's ability to decode and recognize words accurately and rapidly must be acquired before reading comprehension can occur (Hammill et al., 2002; Hatcher et al., 2004).

To prevent dyslexia, it is important to provide early interventions that teach both phonologic and verbal abilities. Children must be able to learn the sounds of words to decode them, but they must also understand the meaning of the word to understand the message of the text (Shaywitz et al., 2003). The techniques that have been demonstrated to work are practicing manipulating phonemes, building vocabulary, increasing comprehension, and improving fluency, which helps strengthen the brain's ability to link letters to sounds (Shaywitz, 2003; Tallal, 2003).

In brief, the components of effective reading instruction are the same whether the focus is prevention or intervention—phonemic awareness and phonemic decoding skills, fluency in word recognition, construction of meaning, vocabulary, spelling, and writing (Foorman & Torgesen, 2001). Evidence-based evaluations show dramatic reductions in the incidence of reading failure when direct and explicit instruction in these components are provided by the classroom teacher (Agnew et al.,, 2004; Foorman & Torgesen, 2001; Tallal & Benasich, 2002). Empirical support for teaching phonics from an early age is also emerging from recent brain imaging studies, as described in Figure 11.7 (Eden & Moats, 2002; Temple et al., 2003).

We now turn to some practical examples of how reading, writing, and math can be taught by applying well-established principles of learning. Behavioral and cognitive-behavioral strategies have been highly beneficial in remediating the problems of children with communication and learning disorders (Lyon et al., 2003). In addition, new methods based on the use of technology offer some children additional ways to acquire basic and advanced academic skills.

Behavioral Strategies Many problems that children with communication and learning disorders have stem from the fact that the material is simply presented too fast for them (Tallal & Benasich, 2002). Thus, a strategy to provide children with a set of verbal rules that can be writ-

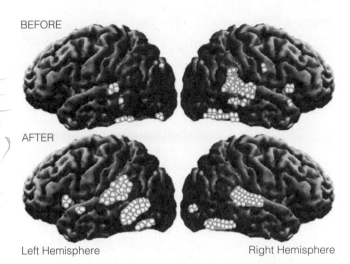

BEFORE

AFTER

Left Hemisphere   Right Hemisphere

Figure 11.7. Brain activation maps from a child with severe dyslexia before and after an 8-week intense intervention in which word reading skills moved into the average range. The upper panel shows the typical brain activation map from magnetic source imaging studies of dyslexia, with predominant activity in temporal and parietal areas of the right hemisphere, but little activation in homologous areas of the left hemisphere. In the lower panel there is a significant increase in the activaton of these left tempoparietal areas associated with the significant improvement in word reading accuracy that parallels the patterns observed in proficient readers. (From "Specific Reading Disability" by Fran R. Vellutino, et al. in *Journal of Child Psychology & Psychiatry,* 45:1, p. 2–40. © 2004 Blackwell Publishing. Reprinted with permission.)

ten out and reapplied may be more beneficial than one that relies on memory, or on grasping the concept all at once. Tried and true behavioral principles of learning are well suited to this task of teaching systematically.

In addition to academic concepts, some of the associated problems with peers can be addressed in the same fashion, as we saw with Francine. A simple, gradual approach is more beneficial than an approach that tries to solve the problem all at once. Children also need help learning to generalize new information to different situations. An individualized, skills-based approach does not have to be boring or routine; in fact, speech and language therapists are skilled at providing a stimulating but structured environment for hearing and practicing language patterns. During an engaging activity with a younger child, the therapist may talk about toys, then encourage the child to use the same sounds or words. The child may watch the therapist make the sound, feel the vibration in the therapist's throat, then practice making the sounds before a mirror.

Behavioral methods are often used in conjunction with a complete program of direct instruction, which typ-

BOX 11.3 Steps in Direct Behavioral Instruction

1. Review the child's existing abilities.
2. Develop a short statement of goals at the beginning of each lesson.
3. Present new concepts and material in small steps, each followed by student practice.
4. Provide clear and detailed instructions and explanations.
5. Provide considerable practice for all students.
6. Check student understanding of concepts continually, in response to teacher questions.
7. Provide explicit guidance for each student during initial practice.
8. Provide systematic feedback and corrections.
9. Provide explicit instruction and practice for exercises completed by students at their desks.

Source: From "Treatment of Learning Disabilities," by G. R. Lyons and L. Cutting, 1998. In E. J. Mash and L. C. Terdal (Eds.), *Treatment of Childhood Disorders.* Copyright © 1998 Guilford Publications. Reprinted by permission.

ically proceeds in a cumulative, highly structured manner (Wright & Jacobs, 2003), as shown in Box 11.3. Because this method places a strong emphasis on the behavior of the teacher in terms of explicit correction, reinforcement, and practice opportunities, it is sometimes referred to as "faultless instruction": Each concept should be so clearly presented that only one interpretation is possible. Each lesson is structured according to field-tested scripts. Teachers work with one small group of students at a time, and shoot questions at them at a rate as high as 10–12 per minute.

This highly structured, repetitive method is clearly effective. Students who receive direct behavioral instruction typically outperform students who receive standard classroom instruction by almost 1 standard deviation on various learning measures (Lyons et al., 2003).

Cognitive-Behavioral Interventions Cognitive-behavioral interventions are also highly suited for children with learning disorders. Like behavioral methods, these procedures actively involve students in learning, particularly in monitoring their own thought processes. Considerable emphasis is placed on self-control by using strategies such as self-monitoring, self-assessment, self-recording, self-management of reinforcement, and so on (Eikeseth & Nesset, 2003). Essentially, children are taught to ask themselves several questions as they progress, to make themselves more aware of the material (Magliano & Millis, 2003). Try it yourself: "Why am I reading this? What's the main idea the authors are trying to get across? Where can

I find the answer to this question? How does this follow from what I learned a minute ago?"

Carlos's treatment program shows how some of these procedures were applied to his particular writing problems:

Carlos

PLANS

In third grade, Carlos's treatment plan was to integrate a cognitive-behavioral approach into regular teaching methods. Rather than using one-to-one instruction, we discussed with his teacher ways of blending some behavioral methods into the classroom. For example, his strengths are in the areas of thinking and speaking, so we discussed using computers and tape recorders to help him learn the materials. He seemed to like these methods, and they helped him bypass some aspects of his writing disability. We discussed practice strategies for visual-motor integration, such as drawing and tracing, and gradually made the task more complex. Because cursive writing is often easier for children than printing, we suggested that Carlos bypass learning to print. A continuous pattern of output is easier for Carlos to plan and produce than a discrete form of output, such as printing.

To help Carlos write a paper, we adopted a basic planning strategy from Graham, MacArthur, Schwatz, and Voth (1992), which helped him structure the tasks into related subproblems: The acronym PLANS helps him to remember to:

Pick goals (related to length, structure, and purpose of the paper)
List ways to meet goals
And
make **N**otes
Sequence notes

This mnemonic was used in a three-step writing strategy to assist Carlos to (1) do PLANS, (2) write and say more, and (3) evaluate whether he is successful in achieving his goals.

Computer-Assisted Learning Studies conducted in over 60 schools and clinics have shown that a similar level of efficacy in phonetic ability can be achieved by teachers as well as clinicians (Merzenich, Saunders, Jenkins, Miller, Peterson, & Tallal, 1999), which has led to a growing number of computer and internet training programs. One problem in reading instruction is maintaining a balance between the basic, but dull, word decoding and the complex, but engaging, text comprehension. Not all the issues have been resolved, but computer-assisted methods for spelling, reading, and math provide more academic en-

New research raises cautious hope that computer games and exercises can help children with learning disabilities develop key mental skills.

gagement and achievement than traditional pencil-and-paper methods.

Computers have been used as simple instructional tools to deliver questions and answers since the 1970's. Since discovering phonological awareness and timing problems in the brain, researchers are now testing whether computers can remedy some basic auditory problems. Some children with communication and learning disorders are unable to process information that flashes by too quickly, such as the consonant sounds *ba* and *da*, and this deficit interferes with vital speech processes.

In a test to determine whether computers could help these children by delivering the sounds more slowly, children ages 5 to 10 played simple computer games in which they won points for distinguishing various sounds (Tallal et al., 1996). Computers stretched consonant sounds to half the normal speed. As the children improved, the games got harder, with sounds becoming shorter in duration and spaced closer together. The results were striking: Children who were 1 to 3 years behind in language ability improved by a full 2 years after only 4 weeks, and these gains remained 6 weeks later. The training did not simply supply the children with tricks for performing exercises, but actually improved their language understanding. Further studies support the value of using acoustically modified speech and computer-assisted instruction for improving children's early academic and speech abilities (Hitchcock & Noonan, 2000; Temple et al., 2003).

In summary, treatment methods for communication and learning disorders are varied and beneficial. Box 11.4 reviews some of the basic elements of a successful beginning reading program, elements that apply to other disabilities as well. For children with reading disorders to learn how to read, they must receive a balanced intervention program composed of direct and explicit instruction in phonemic awareness, a systematic way to generalize this learning to the learning of sound–symbol relation-

BOX 11.4 Critical Elements for a Successful Beginning Reading Program

1. *Provide direct instruction in language analysis.* Identify at-risk children early in their school careers—preferably in kindergarten—and teach phonological awareness skills directly.

2. *Provide direct teaching of the alphabetic code.* Code instruction should be structured and systematic, in a sequence that goes from simple to more complex. Teach the regularities of the English language before introducing the irregularities. Nothing should be left to guesswork—be as explicit as possible. Teach a child who is overly reliant on letter-by-letter decoding to process larger and larger chunks of words.

3. *Teach reading and spelling in coordination.* Children should learn to spell correctly the words they are reading.

4. *Provide intensive reading instruction.* Children may need 3 or more years of direct instruction in basic reading skills to ensure competency. As they progress, they should practice more and more reading that is contextualized. Reading materials should have controlled vocabularies that contain mostly words the children can decode. As children develop a core sight vocabulary, introduce only those irregular words that can be read with high accuracy. Guessing is counterproductive.

5. *Teach for automaticity.* Once basic decoding is mastered, children must be exposed to words often enough that they become automatically accessible. This usually requires a great deal of practice, which should be as pleasant and rewarding as possible.

Source: From "Effects of Instruction on the Decoding Skills of Children with Phonological-Processing Problems," by R. H. Felton, 1993, *Journal of Learning Disabilities, 26,* 583–589. Copyright © 1993 PRO-ED. Reprinted by permission.

ships (phonics), and many opportunities to practice these coding skills by reading meaningful, interesting, and controlled texts. The sooner this intervention occurs in schools, the better (Lyon & Cutting, 1998).

SECTION SUMMARY

- Learning disorders consist of specific problems in reading, mathematics, or writing ability, with reading disorders as the most common. Mathematics and writing disorders overlap considerably with reading disorders.

- Although learning disorders overlap with behavioral disorders, they are distinct problems. Opportunities to develop and use particular strengths lead to more success-ful adult outcomes.

- Learning disorders in reading may be caused by phono-logical problems that arise from physiological abnor-malities in the processing of visual information in the brain. These deficits are believed to be largely inherited.

- Treatments for children with communication and learn-ing disorders involve educational strategies that capital-ize on existing strengths, and behavioral strategies in-volving direct instruction.

- Cognitive-behavioral techniques and computer-assisted instruction are also used successfully.

Key Terms

communication disorder, p. 320
decoding, p. 331
direct instruction, p. 341
dyslexia, p. 320
expressive language disorder, p. 323
inclusion, p. 325
learning disability, p. 320
learning disorder, p. 320
mixed receptive-expressive language disorder, p. 324
nonverbal learning disability (NLD), p. 338
phonemes, p. 321
phonological awareness, p. 322

phonological disorder, p. 324
regular education initiative (REI), p. 340
unexpected discrepancy, p. 320

 InfoTrac College Edition

To research recent articles on the subject, go to:
www.infotrac-college/thomsonlearning.com

Enter search terms: LEARNING DISABILITIES, LEARNING DISABLED, READING DISABILITY, LANGUAGE ACQUISITION, LANGUAGE DIS-ORDERS IN CHILDREN.

Health-Related and Substance Use Disorders

How I hate this world. I would like to tear it apart with my own two hands if I could. I would like to dismantle the universe star by star, like a treeful of rotten fruit.

—Author Peter De Vries, after his daughter died of leukemia

Jeremiah

Breath Is Life

Jeremiah Jager, four, loves blue. He drinks blue soda pop, picks the blue marshmallows out of his Magic Stars cereal, and grabs the blue crayon. But when he got croupy and turned his favorite color this past winter—lips, cheeks, nose—his mother panicked. It was Jeremiah's eighth visit to the ER. And the scariest. "When he turned blue, I said 'I want some answers,'" says Cathy, who figured that, like relatives on both sides of his family, Jeremiah was developing asthma. She called the 800 number for Lung Line at the National Jewish Medical and Research Center in Denver. "This is going to cost twice as much as our car," says Cathy. "But why give birth to them if you're not going to do all you can for them?" Within a week, the Jagers left Alliance, Nebraska, for the long drive to Denver. They had to find out what was wrong with their child. ("An epidemic of Sneezing and Wheezing, " by C. G. Dowling and A. Hollister, *Life Magazine,* May 1997, p. 79. Copyright © 1997 Time Inc. Reprinted by permission.)

Freddie

Too Worried to Sleep

Freddie, age 12, had considerable difficulty falling asleep. Each night it would take him an hour or two to fall asleep, which made it very difficult for him to get up for school at 6:00 the next morning. His typical nighttime routine was to watch television downstairs until 9:00 p.m. and then get ready for bed. Once in bed, he read for a while before turning out the lights. He explains: I start to get sleepy when I'm reading, but as soon as I turn off the lights I'm wide awake. I can't stop from thinking about things, especially stuff that bothers me at school, like homework and making friends. My dad told me I would get sick because I don't sleep enough, and now I'm afraid I'll catch "mono" like a friend of mine has at school. No matter what I do, I can't seem to just fall asleep like I used to. (Adapted from Bootzin & Chambers, 1990)

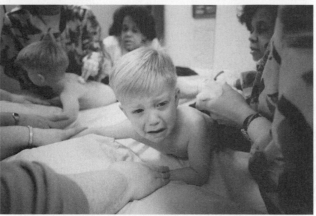

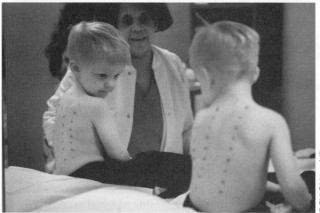

Jeremiah and Fire Bear (top) wait for a test. The boy's back is dotted with solutions of common allergens to see if he gets raised bumps, but he does not.

What do Jeremiah and Freddie have in common? To varying degrees, these children must face situations that affect their health and well-being; as a result, they and their family members are continually distressed and worried. Jeremiah's parents want answers for his breathing problems, which seem to occur without warning. Because doctors are unable to explain his episodes, Jeremiah's parents secretly wonder whether his breathing problems may be due to psychological causes. Similarly, Freddie's sleep problems are intermingled with worries, brought on by his father's comments about him failing to get enough sleep. What role, if any, do psychological factors play in Jeremiah's and Freddie's development and adaptation to their health-related problems?

Children, parents, and other family members are all deeply affected by children's health-related problems, which is why they have considerable psychological importance. The problems discussed in this chapter are not typically viewed as mental health disorders, but rather as health-related problems and medical stressors. Some stressors are mild, like Freddie's problems falling asleep and sleeping through the night, but problems, like Jeremiah's asthma, can be life-threatening and highly disruptive, and involve complicated and intrusive medical interventions.

Pediatric health-related disorders is a distinct area of specialization, but covers a wide range from relatively minor concerns such as enuresis (bed-wetting) and encopresis (soiling), to chronic illnesses such as cancer and diabetes (Roberts, 2003). Health-related disorders are often viewed differently from child psychopathology in general because children's adjustment problems are more directly connected to the impact of the physical illness. Moreover, the field of pediatric psychology stresses the interaction between physical and mental health, since the various disorders and developmental problems all share medical, psychological, and psychosocial components (Peterson, Reach, & Grube, 2003). The involvement of psychologists and other mental health professionals in children's health-related problems has led to many highly successful ways to assist children and family members in coping with and adapting to their circumstances.

History

Although psychological approaches to aiding children with health-related problems have gained considerable momentum over the past two decades, a long history preceded these developments. Ever since Greek philosophers first suggested that pain and disease were caused by an imbalance in the body's basic elements of fire, air, water, and earth, various cultures have been fascinated and perplexed by the interrelationship between the mind and the body. During the medieval period, these early philosophies were overshadowed by the belief that mental and physical illnesses were caused by demonic possession, requiring a quick and gruesome dispatch of the afflicted person.

Scientific interest in the relationship between emotional and physical well-being remained largely dormant until the late 19th century, when Charcot and Freud brought forth their theories on the nature of hysteria and conversion disorders. Psychodynamic theory and the emerging discoveries of modern medicine often clashed during the early years of the 20th century, however, as debates emerged over the relative importance of the mind–body dichotomy (Siegel, Smith, & Wood, 1991).

Partially as a result of these developments, an early distinction emerged between disorders caused by physical factors and those caused by emotional or psychological factors (Peterson et al., 2003). Physical disorders that stem from, or are affected by, psychological and social factors were referred to as *psychosomatic* and later, *psychophysiological,* which meant that psychological factors affected somatic (physical) function. These terms are no longer used, however, because they wrongly implied that a person's physical symptoms were caused solely by mental problems, especially without medical evidence.

Until 50 years ago, attention was rightfully placed on the acute, infectious diseases such as smallpox, tuberculosis, diphtheria, and typhus, which claimed the lives of 1 in 4 children before their ninth birthday (Pollock, 1987). This statistic—simple, unemotional, impartial—belies the emotional toll this high infant and child mortality rate must have had on our ancestors. In fact, some historians argue that prior to the mid-19th century, children's highly unpredictable lifespans contributed to a diminished emotional investment in children among parents and society (Garrison & McQuiston, 1989). It is difficult to conceive of these circumstances today in Western society, even though high child mortality rates still exist in other countries around the world.

The health-related problems addressed in this chapter—sleep disorders, elimination disorders, chronic illness, and substance use disorders—are good examples of how poorly understood physical symptoms can be misattributed primarily to psychological causes. Moreover, diverse childhood experiences underscore how reliance on fashionable cures and untested folk wisdom, rather than on scientific findings, can be viewed by subsequent generations as unwise and sometimes harmful.

Consider children's sleep and elimination disorders. For centuries, these relatively common afflictions were unfairly attributed to children's inherent stubbornness and laziness. Societal attitudes varied from severe to lenient and were similar to the responses elicited by mental retardation. By the turn of the 20th century, according to professional and public opinion, enuresis, like childhood masturbation, was a potential sign of emotional and behavioral disturbance. Early psychodynamic theory was gaining in popularity and proposed that toileting difficulties reflected unconscious conflicts that, if unresolved, could turn into troublesome personality styles. The sources of the underlying conflict were numerous: lack of parental love, the guilt value of feces, separation anxiety, pregnancy wishes, response to family problems, and traumatic separation from mother between the oral and anal stages of psychosexual development (Fielding & Doleys, 1988).

By the 1920s, the *Infant Care Bulletin,* the official publication of the U.S. Children's Bureau, reflected the harsh stance of society toward children's developmental problems. It advised parents to force their children to have bowel movements on a strict, regular schedule, and to complete toilet training by 8 months of age at the latest! If the baby did not go along with this plan, elimination was induced by inserting a stick of soap into the rectum (Achenbach, 1982).

Fortunately, by the 1940s this advice mellowed toward more natural, developmentally sensitive approaches that allowed children's maturity to dictate when parents could shift from diapers to toileting, which occurred between 12 and 30 months of age. Toilet training issues once again emerged during the rebellious 1960s, when renowned pediatrician Benjamin Spock was blamed for many social problems in North America because his advice on toileting and early childhood discipline from the 1940s on was considered too lenient. Spock had made it clear, though, that "the child supplies the power but the parents have to do the steering" (1955).

The Society of Pediatric Psychology was established in 1968 to connect psychology and pediatrics, which established the *Journal of Pediatric Psychology* in 1976. These two landmark events broadened the research and theory on physical outcomes of child health disorders to encompass the psychosocial effects of illness and the interplay between the two (Roberts, 2003).

How children adapt to the many situational, developmental, and chronic stressors affecting their health and well-being is a primary interest of pediatric health psychology. We begin by discussing sleep disorders, pausing to consider how important sleep is to our psychological and physical development and its regulation from birth. From there we discuss elimination disorders and chronic illness in children and adolescents, areas in which monumental gains have been made in recent years in helping children overcome or adapt to these challenges. How health-related problems interact with children's and adolescents' psychological well-being, and how they and their families adapt in response, are central themes throughout this chapter.

SECTION SUMMARY

- For centuries, poorly understood physical symptoms have been misattributed to psychological causes.
- Today, pediatric health psychologists study how children's health-related problems interact with their psychological well-being, and how they and their families adapt in response.

Sleep Disorders

A professor is one who talks in someone else's sleep.

—Anonymous

We all have problems sleeping at one time or another. Usually, the problems are not serious and do not interfere with the next day's activities, but sometimes sleep problems can seriously affect our physical and psychological health and well-being. As any parent, sibling, or roommate can attest, these problems can have a major impact on them as well. In fact, problems such as resistance at bedtime, difficulty settling at bedtime, night waking, difficulty waking up, and fatigue are among the most common complaints or concerns expressed by parents of young children (Blader, Koplewicz, Abikoff, & Foley, 1997).

Arguably, sleep is the *primary* activity of the brain during the early years of development. Consider this: By 2 years of age the average child has spent almost 10,000 hours (nearly 14 months) asleep, and approximately 7500 hours (about 10 months) in waking activities (Anders, Goodlin-Jones, & Sadeh, 2000). During those 2 years, the brain has reached 90% of adult size, and the child has attained remarkable complexity in cognitive skills, language, concept of self, socioemotional development, and physical skills (Dahl, 1996). Yet, during most of the time these maturational advances were occurring, the child was asleep.

Gradually, by age 5 or so, a more even balance emerges between sleep and wakefulness. Still, by the time they begin school, children have spent more time asleep than in social interactions, exploration of the environment, eating, or any other single waking activity. Why has evolution favored sleep over these important activities? Wouldn't it be to our advantage to have more waking time to learn language, acquire knowledge, and develop similar adaptive skills? Apparently, sleep serves a fundamental role in brain development and regulation (Dahl,

1996). This role explains why sleep disturbances can affect overall physical and mental health and well-being, and why sleep disorders are important to abnormal child psychology.

Perhaps you have noticed how sleep problems co-occur with many different disorders, including ADHD (Corkum, Moldofsky, Hogg-Johnson, Humphries, & Tannock, 1999; Gruber et al., 2000), depression and anxiety (Johnson, Chilcoat, Breslau, 2000), autism (Richdale, 1999), and conduct problems (Lavigne et al., 1999). This connection raises an important consideration: Do sleep problems cause or result from other disorders? The answer to this question requires an understanding of how sleep problems interact with a person's psychological well-being. Because our own experience has been that sleep problems commonly arise from particular stressors—an upcoming exam or a relationship problem—we tend to think that sleep difficulties are secondary symptoms of a more primary problem. However, the relationship between sleep problems and psychological adjustment is bidirectional.

Sleep problems may themselves cause emotional and behavioral problems among children and adolescents, and they can be caused directly by a psychological disorder. In some circumstances, sleep problems might result from some underlying factor that is common to both sleep problems and other disorders. Remember that in Chapter 7 on anxiety, we saw how problems in the brain's arousal and regulatory systems can cause increased anxiety. Stress-related events, especially those that affect the child's safety, such as war, disaster, and child abuse, increase arousal and interfere with normal sleep patterns (Sadeh et al., 2000). Simply stated, sleep disorders can cause other psychological problems, or can result from other disorders or conditions. Sleep disorders have considerable importance to abnormal child psychology because they mimic or worsen many of the symptoms of major disorders (Chervin, Dillon, Archbold, & Ruzicka, 2003; Paavonen et al., 2002).

The Regulatory Functions of Sleep

We tend to think that sleep is a time when not much is happening—the "lights are on but nobody's home." This lack of activity and nearly complete loss of awareness during sleep gives us the impression that sleep regulation has little to do with psychological processes such as attention, arousal, emotions, and behavior. So why does the brain—particularly, the developing brain—require long periods of relative inactivity?

Opposing the popular image of sleep as simply rest is the growing awareness that sleep, arousal, affect, and attention are all closely intertwined in a dynamic regulatory system (Dahl, 1996). When the central nervous system (CNS) must increase arousal in response to possible danger, the system must recover soon thereafter and restore the balance between sleep and arousal. It is fascinating how the system changes with development: During infancy the balance is skewed in favor of more sleep, because safety and other needs are provided for by the child's caregivers. As children mature, they start looking after their own needs, becoming more alert and attentive to danger. Gradually, the cycle between sleep and arousal becomes skewed more in favor of arousal, which by then is adaptive and necessary, and the dynamic patterns of sleep help restore the balance.

Most students suffer sleep loss or disruption as a result of all-night study sessions or late-night partying, so you are probably familiar with sleep's important role in regulating states of emotional arousal and restoration. The giddiness, silliness, and impulsive behaviors children and adults show if sleep-deprived signify impairment in the prefrontal cortex functions. As noted in earlier chapters, the prefrontal cortex is an important *executive control* center in the brain—it's in charge of processing emotional signals and making critical decisions for response—so impairment results in signs of decreased concentration and diminished ability to inhibit, or control, basic drives, impulses, and emotions.

The prefrontal cortex is uniquely situated in the brain where it can integrate thoughts (higher cortical functions) with emotions (basic CNS functions). If a person is sleep-deprived or otherwise impaired, the first functions affected are the more complex, demanding tasks that require integrating cognitive, emotional, and social input rapidly and accurately (Dahl, 1996). Ask any parent or teacher and they can tell you: Children with disrupted or inadequate sleep show less executive control the next day; they are more cranky, impulsive, distractible, and emotionally labile, meaning they switch abruptly from, say, laughing to crying. These symptoms are easily confused with those of ADHD, although sleep problems usually self-correct within a day or two (Gruber et al., 2000).

The physiology of sleep also has a fascinating connection to developmental problems that occur during childhood, and it further underscores the crucial role of sleep in restoring balance. Specific stages of sleep are believed to produce an active *uncoupling,* or disconnection, of neurobehavioral systems (Dahl, 1996). In effect, separate aspects of the central nervous system take a break from their constant duty. Think about how your nervous system must continuously maintain an active, close connection while you are awake, which is achieved through electrical signals. As we noted in our discussion of learning disorders (Chapter 11), these signals require that we maintain precise timing and frequency.

Sleep researcher R. E. Dahl (1996) describes the uncoupling process by comparing sleep's role to that of tuning instruments in a large orchestra: Tuning cannot be accomplished while the instrument is continuously playing, or "coupling," with the other instruments in the orches-

Sleep problems occur across a number of behavioral and emotional problems in children and adolescents.

tra. Likewise, retuning or recalibration of the components of the CNS may require temporary uncoupling, or disconnection from other systems. Further, the uncoupling may be particularly critical for children. As children mature, regions of the brain rapidly differentiate and establish specific functions and patterns of interconnection within the CNS (P. Levitt, 1995), which requires considerable recalibration or retuning. In Dahl's music analogy, a new instrument must be retuned more often than one that has been broken in.

Maturational Changes   Our sleep patterns and needs change dramatically during the first few years of life, then gradually settle into a stable pattern as we reach adulthood (Mindell, Owens, & Carskadon, 1999). Newborns sleep about 16 to 17 hours each day, and 1-year-olds sleep about 13 hours a day, including daytime naps that range from 1 to over 2 hours (Anders & Eiben, 1997). These maturational changes partially explain why infants and children have sleep problems different from those of older children, adolescents, and adults. Infants and toddlers have more night-waking problems, preschoolers have more falling-asleep problems, and younger school-age children have more going-to-bed problems. In contrast, sleep problems among adolescents and adults typically involve difficulty going to or staying asleep (insomnia), or not having enough time to sleep (Carskadon, 2002; R.E. Roberts, Roberts, & Chen, 2002; Sadeh et al., 2000).

Paradoxically, adolescents have an increased physiological need for sleep, but many get significantly less sleep during early childhood. This results in many teens' being chronically sleep-deprived with daytime symptoms of fatigue, irritability, emotional lability, difficulty concentrating, and falling asleep in class (Wolfson & Carskadon, 1998). The bottom line? Let sleeping teens lie—they need to catch up on their sleep!

© ZITS Partnership. Reprinted with special permission of King Features Syndicate.

Features of Sleep Disorders

Primary sleep disorders are presumed to be a result of abnormalities in the body's ability to regulate sleep-wake mechanisms and the timing of sleep, as opposed to sleep problems related to a medical disorder, a mental disorder, or the use of medications. The DSM-IV-TR divides primary sleep disorders into two major categories: dyssomnias and parasomnias (APA, 2000). **Dyssomnias** are disorders of initiating or maintaining sleep, characterized by difficulty getting enough sleep, not sleeping when you want to, not feeling refreshed from sleeping, and so forth. **Parasomnias,** in contrast, are sleep disorders in which behavioral or physiological events intrude on ongoing sleep. Whereas dyssomnias involve disruptions in the sleep process, parasomnias involve physiological or cognitive arousal at inappropriate times during the sleep-wake cycle, which can result in sleepwalking or in nightmares that jolt someone from sleep. Persons suffering from parasomnia sleep disorders often complain of unusual behaviors while asleep, rather than sleepiness or insomnia.

Dyssomnias   Dyssomnias, many of which are common during certain times of development, are disturbances in the amount, timing, or quality of sleep. Freddie, for example, suffered from a common form of childhood insomnia in which he had difficulty getting to sleep. Fortunately, many sleep problems resolve themselves as the child matures, especially if parents are given basic information and guidance, such as to refrain from yelling at the child to go to sleep, and to adhere to a bedtime routine (Blader et al., 1997).

Table 12.1 provides a descriptive overview of childhood dyssomnias. For the most part, dyssomnias are common childhood afflictions, with the exception of narcolepsy, which is rare and primarily affects adolescents and adults. Breathing-related sleep disorders are somewhat less common and can affect children of various ages as a result of allergies, asthma, or swollen tonsils and adenoids. Although relatively common, dyssomnias can sometimes

have a significant impact on children's behavior and emotional state, much like they impact adult behavior.

Parasomnias   Parasomnias are somewhat common afflictions during early to mid-childhood and, we might add, are a bit easier to understand because of their more familiar terms and our experiences. They include **nightmares** (repeated awakenings, with frightening dreams that you usually remember), **sleep terrors** (abrupt awakening, accompanied by autonomic arousal but no recall), and **sleepwalking** (getting out of bed and walking around, but with no recall the next day). Nightmares are referred to as *REM parasomnias* because they occur during REM (dream) sleep, usually during the second half of the sleep period. Sleep terrors and sleepwalking, in contrast, are referred to as *arousal parasomnias* because they occur during deep sleep in the first third of the sleep cycle when the person is so soundly asleep that he or she is difficult to arouse, and has no recall of the episode the next morning (Dahl, 1999). Fortunately, as with the dyssomnias, children typically grow out of parasomnias or recover from sleep disruption or sleep loss and do not develop a chronic condition that interferes with daily activities. Characteristics of parasomnia sleep disorders are shown in Table 12.2.

DSM-IV-TR criteria for sleep disorders typically are not met in full by younger children because of the transitory nature of their sleep problems (Anders & Eiben, 1997). Refer to Tables 12.1 and 12.2, in lieu of the specific criteria for children, to aid in understanding the major features and differences of the various sleep disorders. Also, note two considerations concerning diagnostic criteria: In addition to the symptoms pertaining to each sleep disorder, as listed in Tables 12.1 and 12.2, DSM diagnostic criteria for all sleep-related disorders emphasize (1) the presence of clinically significant distress or impairment in social, occupational, or other important areas of functioning; and (2) the requirement that the sleep disturbance cannot be better accounted for by another mental disorder, the direct physiological effects of a substance, or a general medical condition (other than a breathing-related

Table 12.1
Dyssomnias

SLEEP DISORDER	DESCRIPTION	PREVALENCE AND AGE	TREATMENT
Protodyssomnia	Difficulty initiating or maintaining sleep, or sleep that is not restorative; in infants, repetitive night waking and inability to fall asleep.	25% to 50% of 1- to 3-year-olds.	Behavioral treatment, family guidance.
Hypersomnia	Complaint of excessive sleepiness that is displayed as either prolonged sleep episodes or daytime sleep episodes.	Common among young children.	Behavioral treatment, family guidance.
Narcolepsy	Irresistible attacks of refreshing sleep occurring daily, accompanied by brief episodes of loss of muscle tone (cataplexy).	<1% of children and adolescents.	Structure, support, psychostimulants, antidepressants.
Breathing-related sleep disorder	Sleep disruption leading to excessive sleepiness or insomnia that is caused by sleep-related breathing difficulties.	1% to 2% of children; preschool, elementary ages.	Removal of tonsils and adenoids.
Circadian rhythm sleep disorder	Persistent or recurrent sleep disruption leading to excessive sleepiness or insomnia due to a mismatch between the sleep-wake schedule required by a person's environment and his or her internal sleep cycle (circadian rhythm); late sleep onset (after midnight), difficulty awakening in morning, sleeping in on weekends, resistance to change.	Unknown; possibly 7% of adolescents.	Behavioral treatment, chronotherapy.

Table 12.2
Parasomnias

SLEEP DISORDER	DESCRIPTION	PREVALENCE AND AGE	TREATMENT
REM PARASOMNIA			
Nightmare disorder	Repeated awakenings with detailed recall of extended and extremely frightening dreams, usually involving threats to survival, security, or self-esteem; generally occurs during the second half of the sleep period.	Common between ages 3 and 8.	Provide comfort, reduce stress.
AROUSAL PARASOMNIAS			
Sleep terror disorder	Recurrent episodes of abrupt awakening from sleep, usually occurring during the first third of the major sleep episode and beginning with a panicky scream; autonomic discharge, racing heart, sweating, vocalized distress, glassy-eyed staring, difficult to arouse, inconsolable, disoriented; no memory of episodes in morning.	3% of children; ages 18 months to 6 years.	Reduce stress and fatigue; add late afternoon nap.
Sleepwalking disorder	Repeated episodes of arising from bed during sleep and walking for periods of 5 seconds to 30 minutes, usually during the first third of the major sleep episode; poorly coordinated, difficult to arouse, disoriented; no memory in morning.	15% of children have one attack; 1% to 6% have one to four attacks per week; age 4–12 years, rare in adolescence.	Take safety precautions, reduce stress and fatigue, add late afternoon nap.

disorder) (APA, 2000). These considerations apply to all the disorders discussed in this chapter.

Treatment

Sleeping difficulties in infants and toddlers often subside on their own, but any parent who has been awakened night after night by a screaming child can attest that "waiting for them to grow out of it" seems like forever. If going to sleep or staying asleep becomes difficult, the goal of behavioral interventions is to teach parents to attend to the child's need for comfort and reassurance, but to gradually withdraw more quickly from the child's room after saying goodnight. (This is an example of *extinction*, since parental attention is being removed.)

Parents can also be taught to establish good sleep hygiene appropriate to their child's developmental stage and the family's cultural values. Once established, positive reinforcement methods, such as praise or star charts, can be used to reward the child for efforts to follow the bedtime routine (Bootzin & Rider, 1997). Sleep hygiene may involve identifying suspected causes of disrupted sleep and involving other family members in maintaining a chosen routine. For example, individualized bedtime rituals, such as reading, singing, or playing a quiet game, establish a positive transition to bedtime, and regular bedtimes and waking times establish a consistent routine (Owens, Palermo, & Rosen, 2002).

Treatment of circadian rhythm sleep disorders requires a highly motivated adolescent and a supportive family because there are no shortcuts or medications that can easily restore a disrupted sleep-wake cycle. The goal of behavioral intervention is twofold: to eliminate the sleep deprivation and to restore a more normal sleep and wake routine. The adolescent is asked to keep a sleep-wake and daily activity log, with regular bedtimes and rise times. If begun early in the disorder, such supportive behavioral methods are often effective.

In contrast to treatment for some dyssomnias, prolonged treatment of child and adolescent parasomnias is usually not necessary, particularly if the episodes of sleep intrusion occur infrequently (Owens et al., 2003). Treatment of nightmares consists of providing comfort at the time of occurrence and making every attempt to reduce daytime stressors. If nightmares or sleep terrors are intense and persistent, daytime stresses at school, family conflicts, or emotional disturbance may be implicated (Sadeh et al., 2000). If sleepwalking is suspected, parents are usually first asked to record episodes at home using a camcorder. If sleepwalking is confirmed, parents must take precautions to reduce the chance of injury to a child who may fall or bump into objects. Because of the possibility of fire or other emergencies, children should never be locked in their rooms. Excessive fatigue or unusual stresses during the daytime often precipitate sleepwalking. Therefore, brief afternoon naps can be beneficial.

Elimination Disorders

"Step 1: Before you begin, remove all stubbornness from the child." These instructions were provided by a popular toilet training manual years ago, apparently without a hint of irony. For generations, parents have half-jokingly referred to the bathroom, and toilet training in particular, as the "combat zone," where parental right meets child's might. Teaching toddlers how to use the toilet is one of the more significant challenges of parenting, but whether it truly deserved the disproportionate amount of attention it received in the early abnormal child psychology literature is unlikely.

Thanks to a better understanding of the biological and psychological underpinnings of elimination disorders, attention has been directed away from the child's personality or emotional trauma. However, for a significant minority of children, the problems associated with toileting continue well past the age when most children have achieved freedom and independence. Elimination problems can turn into distressing and chronic difficulties, and can affect participating in educational and social activities, camps, sleepovers, and so forth. In extreme cases, toileting accidents can precipitate physical child abuse (R. C. Herrenkohl, Herrenkohl, & Egolf, 1983).

Two elimination problems that occur during childhood and adolescence are **enuresis,** the involuntary discharge of urine during the day or night, and **encopresis,** the passage of feces into inappropriate places, such as clothing or the floor. Child psychologists have studied and treated these elimination problems among children because they can have strong implications on the development of self-competence and self-esteem. Even though most children eventually outgrow problems of enuresis or encopresis by age 10 or so, they may have suffered years of embarrassment and peer rejection that remain troublesome. Fortunately, in most instances the problems can be alleviated through education and retraining efforts involving both parents and children. These disorders are one of the few areas of abnormal child psychology in which early referral and treatment can virtually eliminate long-term consequences.

Enuresis

As many as 7 million children in the United States and Canada go through the same routine each night: turn off the lights, go to sleep, wet the bed. Most of the time the child cannot control the discharge, but on occasion it may be intentional. Although the problem is relatively common, it is stressful for parents and children.

Concerns about correcting children's bed-wetting have perplexed professionals and parents for generations. Here is how Thomas Phaer, "the father of English pediatrics," explained the early cure to physicians in his Boke of Children (1544):

Of Pyssying in the Bedde Many times for debility of vertus retentive of the reines or blader, as wel olde men as children are oftentimes annoyed, whan their urine issueth out either in theyre slepe or waking against theyr wylles, having no power to reteine it whan it cometh, therfore yf they will be holpen, fyrst they must avoid al fat meates, til ye vertue be restored againe, and to use this pouder in their meates and drynkes. (Cited in Glicklich, 1951, p. 862)

The "pouder" was derived from the trachea of a cock or the "stones of a hedge-hogge." This remedy seems tame in view of more "enlightened" mechanical and surgical approaches to enuresis that emerged by the 18th century— yokes made of iron (mercifully covered with velvet) that prevented urination and steel spikes placed on the child's back to prevent lying on the back, the position believed to stimulate bladder function during sleep. If you didn't want your child to be outfitted for one of these devices, other forms of treatment were available. Medicinals like strychnine, belladonna, sacral plasters, and chloral hydrate were used presumably to stimulate the bladder (regardless of poisonous side effects), or the orifice of the urethra was cauterized (partially closed) with silver nitrate to make it more tender and responsive to passage of urine (Glicklich, 1951). Throughout history, the treatment of childhood bed-wetting reflects society's generally poor un-

derstanding and sensitivity to children's needs and problems at the time.

Most children have bed-wetting accidents until age 5 or so, therefore DSM-IV-TR has narrowed the criteria to reflect the developmental nature of this disorder. The criteria stipulate that the problem be frequent (at least twice a week for 3 consecutive months), or accompanied by significant distress or impairment in social, academic, or other important areas of functioning. A chronological age of 5 years, or the equivalent developmental level, was arbitrarily chosen as a developmental benchmark for the point at which most children achieve urinary continence. Finally, the voiding of urine into bed or clothes must not be due exclusively to a general medical condition, or the result of a diuretic, which is a drug that reduces water retention.

DSM-IV-TR distinguishes between three subtypes of enuresis (APA, 2000). *Nocturnal only* is the most common subtype, in which wetting occurs only during sleep at night, typically during the first third of the night. Sometimes the child is dreaming of urinating, which indicates that the voiding took place during REM sleep. *Diurnal only* is defined as the passage of urine during waking hours, most often during the early afternoon on school days (APA, 2000). Diurnal enuresis is more common in females than males and is uncommon after age 9. Because of these features, suspected causes of diurnal enuresis often indicate a child's reluctance to use the toilet because of social anxiety or a preoccupation with a school event. Finally, *nocturnal* and *diurnal* can exist in combination.

Prevalence and Course

Between 13%–33% of 5-year-old children wet their beds (Butler, 1998), boys more often than girls, which makes enuresis a common problem among younger school-age children. The prevalence of enuresis declines rapidly with maturity: By age 10, only 3% of males and 2% of females are affected, and this evens out to 1% of males and less than 1% of females by late adolescence (Houts, 2003). Diurnal enuresis is much less common, and is estimated to affect 3% of 6-year-olds (Peterson et al., 2003). However, prevalence of both forms of enuresis is higher among less educated, lower socioeconomic groups as well as institutionalized children, perhaps due to less structure in their daily routines and added environmental stressors (APA, 2000).

Approximately 85% of children with enuresis have *primary enuresis,* because they have never attained at least 6 months of continuous nighttime control. By definition, primary enuresis starts at age 5. In contrast, *secondary enuresis,* is less common and refers to children who have previously established urinary continence but then relapse, usually between the ages of 5 and 6 years (APA, 2000). Children with secondary enuresis often take a longer time establishing initial nighttime continence, or face a higher

Waking up to a wet bed is upsetting, and can affect a young child's self-confidence if poorly managed.

dose of stressful life events (Houts, 2003). Most children do eventually stop bed-wetting, but for those who do not remit on their own, treatment is particularly beneficial in preventing a lengthy and disruptive problem.

You can imagine how younger children are treated when peers discover that they have wet themselves in class or while sleeping over. Teasing, name calling, and social stigmatization are common peer reactions to this unfortunate problem. Although enuresis is a physical condition, it is often accompanied by some degree of psychological distress. The impact of this distress often depends on three features related to the nature of the enuresis: (1) limitations imposed on social activities, such as sleeping away from home; (2) effects on self-esteem, including the degree of social ostracism imposed by peers; and (3) parental reactions, such as anger, punishment, and rejection (Houts, 2003). Parents are often poorly informed about the nature of enuresis and may respond by punishing or humiliating the child who suffers from it. Fortunately, these consequences are not inevitable or long-lasting. Many children with enuresis are able to establish their self-esteem and peer relationships despite their occasional embarrassment or anxiety. For others, treatment for bed-wetting usually has a positive impact on their self-concept and peer relations (Fritz, Rockney, et al., 2004).

Causes and Treatment

For most children with enuresis, one specific etiology cannot be identified (Fritz et al., 2004). Children with nocturnal enuresis need to urinate at night, but they don't wake up when they need to urinate. By age 5 or so, most children have made the transition from urinating around the clock, as they did in infancy, to urinating only during waking hours.

Children who continue to need to urinate at night may have a deficiency during sleep of an important hormone known as *antidiuretic hormone (ADH)*. ADH helps concentrate urine during sleep hours, meaning that the urine contains less water and has therefore decreased volume. For normal children, this decreased volume usually means that their bladders do not overfill while they are asleep, unless they drank excessive fluids before bed. For children with enuresis, they do not show the usual increase in ADH during sleep (Norgaard, Pederson, & Djurhuus, 1985). They continue to produce more urine during the hours of sleep than their bladders can hold, and if they fail to wake up, bed-wetting results.

The reason children with enuresis fail to wake up when they need to urinate can also be explained by developmental and biological factors. Older children and adolescents are able to sense a full bladder at night, which activates a nerve impulse from the bladder to the brain. This signal may initiate dreams about water or going to the toilet, which usually wakes them up. This signaling mechanism matures during early childhood, so infants understandably have very little ability to detect the need to urinate. Some children with primary enuresis, however, lack normal development of this signal processing in the brain (Ornitz et al., 1999).

Primary enuresis, the most common type, is decidedly not due to stress or child obstinence. To the contrary, this trait appears to be inherited. If both parents were enuretic, 77% of their children are too; if only one parent was enuretic, then 44% of their offspring are also. If neither parent had this problem, only about 15% of their children develop enuresis. Concordance rates of enuresis for monozygotic (68%) and dyzygotic (36%) twins also verify this connection (Bakwin, 1973).

Treatments for children with nocturnal enuresis have perhaps the most comprehensive evaluation track record of any psychological intervention for childhood problems (Houts, 2003). Dozens of promising behavioral methods have been investigated by hundreds of studies over several decades; they are joined by many other studies of pharmacological agents. Fortunately, these efforts have led to some strong conclusions as to what works best. (This example provides a good lesson in how long it often takes to verify successful treatment methods for psychological disorders.)

The standard behavioral intervention, based on classical conditioning principles, is using an alarm that sounds at the first detection of urine. Bed-wetting alarms have been around since O. H. Mowrer and W. M. Mowrer (1938) first invented the "bell and pad" (a battery-operated device that produced a loud sound as soon as a drop of urine closed the electrical circuit), and they are among the safest and most effective treatments. Modern alarms have a simple moisture sensor that snaps into a child's pajamas, with a small speaker attached to the shoulder to awaken the child. A single drop of urine completes the electronic circuit, setting off a piercing alarm that causes the child to tense and reflexively stop urinating. The one drawback to this method is the alarm's unpopularity with other household members. For the alarm to be effective, an adult must wake the child up, which usually isn't easy, walk him to the bathroom, get him to finish urinating in the toilet, and then reset the alarm. If this ritual is carefully followed, the alarm will begin to wake the child directly within 4–6 weeks, and by 12 weeks he will likely master nighttime bladder control and no longer need the alarm. The modern urine alarm, when used in conjunction with other behavioral activities (e.g., monitoring and intermittent reinforcement), has been as recommended by the *American Academy of Child and Adolescent Psychiatry* as a minimal standard in the treatment of enuresis (i.e., should apply in at least 95% of enuresis cases) (Fritz et al., 2004).

Another behavioral method, based on operant conditioning principles, involves variations of *dry-bed training*. Children, like adults, wake up more easily when the day holds promise and excitement. Reward systems, such as star charts or other tokens, capitalize on this anticipation. Dry-bed training was originally developed as a brief but intensive intervention in response to parents' frustration over the more intrusive and drawn-out urine alarm (Azrin & Foxx, 1974). During a single office visit, parents are instructed in bladder retention control training by having their child drink more and more fluids during the day, and then delay urination for longer periods (in an effort to strengthen bladder control), hourly wakings for trips to the toilet, a cleanup routine for accidents (overcorrection, or having the child clean more than just the sheets), and positive reinforcement contingent on dry nights. This routine is practiced nightly for 1 or 2 weeks.

Dry-bed training methods combined with an alarm (referred to today as *full-spectrum home training*) are still commonly used, resulting in a success rate of about 3 in 4 children (Mellon & McGrath, 2000), and a relapse rate of 10% after 1 year (Houts, 2003). In less severe or prolonged cases of primary enuresis, a simple incentive such as earning stars or similar tokens for dry nights is often enough to make children responsive to nighttime bladder fullness. Other children, however, may require the alarm treatment to get the message firmly implanted, coupled with close professional monitoring to help parents adhere to the training methods.

In the mid-1980s, desmopressin, a synthetic ADH, became available as a treatment for enuresis, and is a simple nasal spray administered before bedtime. Within a few days, about 70% of children using desmopressin can avoid bed-wetting, with another 10% or so showing significant improvement in the number of dry nights (Rap-paport, 1993). Although desmopressin works very well while children are on the medicine, the difficulty comes in keeping them dry when they stop the medication: the relapse rate can be as high as 80% (Fritz et al., 2004). Unlike alarm systems, which have most children cured of bed-wetting within 12 weeks, treatment with medication often requires some additional behavioral treatment before children are able to stop taking the medicine (Thompson & Rey, 1994).

Psychological treatments for enuresis, especially the urine alarm, have been more effective overall than pharmacological treatments (Houts, 2003). In particular, urine alarm treatment was found to be superior to any other type of intervention. At the end of treatment, which generally lasts 12 weeks, children treated with a urine alarm or with desmopressin are equally likely to have ceased bed-wetting; however, at their 3-month follow-up, children treated with a urine alarm are almost twice as likely to have ceased bed-wetting as children who received other treatments, including desmopressin. On average, almost one-half of all children treated with alarms remain dry at follow-up, compared with about one-third treated with other behavior therapies and one-quarter treated with tricyclic medications (Houts, 2003). Treatment of enuresis is one of the few treatments in which psychological interventions are clearly superior to drug therapies, and should be used instead of waiting for the child to grow out of the problem because of the distress it causes the child and family (Peterson et al., 2003).

Encopresis

Encopresis refers to the passage of feces into inappropriate places, such as clothing or the floor. Like enuresis, this act is usually involuntary, but may occasionally be done intentionally. The diagnostic criteria stipulate that this event must occur at least once per month for at least 3 months, and that the child must be 4 years old or older (if the child is developmentally delayed, a mental age of at least 4 years is used). Fecal incontinence must not be due to an organic or general medical condition.

Two subtypes of encopresis are described in DSM-IV-TR: with or without constipation, and overflow incontinence. Essentially, encopresis results from constipation that produces fecal impaction. Liquid stool above the impaction gradually develops sufficient pressure to leak around the impaction, thereby producing overflow incontinence in most cases (Cox, Sutphen, Ling, Quillian, & Borowitz, 1996).

Prevalence and Course

An estimated 1.5% to 3% of children have encopresis (Sprague-McRae, Lamb, & Homer, 1993). Again, this disorder is 5 to 6 times more common in boys than in girls

(Schroeder & Gordon, 1991), and it decreases rapidly with age. Like enuresis, encopresis can be categorized as primary or secondary. Children with primary encopresis have reached age 4 without establishing fecal continence, whereas children with secondary encopresis have established a period of continence before the current episode of encopresis began.

As many as 1 in 5 children with encopresis show significant psychological problems, but these problems more likely result from, rather than initially cause, the encopresis (Peterson et al., 2003). Understandably, they may feel ashamed and try to avoid situations, like camp or school, that might lead to embarrassment. As with enuresis, the degree of children's impairment and associated psychological distress is partially a function of social ostracism by peers, as well as anger, punishment, and rejection on the part of caregivers.

Causes and Treatment

Overly aggressive or early toilet training, family disturbance and stress, and child psychopathology have all been thought to cause encopresis at one time or another (Peterson et al., 2003). However, like enuresis, encopresis is a physical disorder that can lead to, but seldom results from only psychological factors. The sooner it is diagnosed and treated, the less likely the child will suffer any lasting emotional scars or disruptions in social relationships. Exceptions, of course, are children with oppositional defiant and conduct disorders (discussed in Chapter 6), in which encopresis and enuresis may occur as secondary symptoms of broader behavior patterns.

Understanding the etiology of encopresis leads to a discussion of toilet training, where children first learn to control bowel movements. Children must learn how to recognize signals from the muscles and nerves that tell them when it is time for a bowel movement. Sometimes they try to avoid or suppress these signals, especially if something more enjoyable is going on. Some children attempt to suppress their feces to avoid having an accident; this allows feces to build up in the colon over a period of time, causing *megacolon*. If uncleared, the feces that stay in the bowel become large, hard, and dry, which causes further bowel movements to be painful. Over time, the stretched muscles and nerves give fewer and fewer signals to the child about the need to have a bowel movement. This decrease in signals results in stool accidents, and the colon and rectum often do not empty as they should.

About one-half of all children who develop this pattern of avoidance also have abnormal *defecation dynamics;* that is, they contract rather than relax the external sphincter when they attempt to defecate (Borowitz, Cox, & Sutphen, 1999; Peterson et al., 2003). Combined with avoidance tactics, an increased risk of chronic constipation and encopresis develops. In case you're wondering how such dynamics develop, consider how some children

(and adults) avoid using a bathroom if they are in a strange place, or if they have been told that public toilets should be avoided because they are germ-infested. Anxiety about defecating in a particular place, or because their toileting experiences were stressful and harsh, can cause chronic constipation. Without reversing this pattern of retention, the child becomes less able to perform the many skills required for successful toileting, including recognizing body cues, undressing, going into the bathroom, sitting on the toilet chair, and relaxing the appropriate muscles (Peterson et al., 2003).

Optimal treatment of encopresis involves both medical and behavioral interventions to help the child learn to empty the colon to allow it to return to normal size and function (Stark et al., 1997). To get the process moving, fiber, enemas, laxatives, or lubricants may be given to disimpact the rectum. Then, to establish a better routine and healthy pattern of elimination, behavioral methods are used in combination with laxatives or similar agents. Laxatives alone do not address the underlying behavioral mechanisms. Children who have large and impacted stools will find defecation frightening and painful, which further encourages them to ignore early rectal distention cues (the urge to defecate) and avoid going to the toilet (Cox, Borowitz, Kovatchev, & Ling, 1998).

Behavioral methods involve teaching a toilet-training procedure that encourages detection of and response to rectal distention cues, parental efforts to praise the child's clean pants and toilet use, and regularly scheduled toilet times after meals. During these times, children practice tensing and relaxing their external anal sphincter for several minutes; the practice time is often followed by fun time of reading or playing games to desensitize children to sitting on the toilet. They are then taught to strain and attempt to have a bowel movement. With a combination of laxatives and behavioral treatment, most children improve significantly within the first 2 weeks of treatment, and over 75% maintain these improvements (Cox et al., 1996; 1999). Whether the intervention is medical or behavioral in nature, positive reinforcement adds incremental benefits (McGrath, Mellon, & Murphy, 2000).

SECTION SUMMARY

- Enuresis is the involuntary discharge of urine during the day or night.
- Encopresis is the passage of feces into inappropriate places, such as clothing or the floor.
- Primary enuresis has a strong genetic component, whereas encopresis results from children's efforts to avoid defecation, resulting in chronic constipation.
- Combined pharmacological and psychological treatments of elimination problems are often very successful.

Chronic Illness

Who has not feared that the very worst could somehow single out a family member? Who does not worry as a toddler wanders toward the curb, or as a preschooler climbs a playground ladder, or as a teenager suddenly begins having severe headaches and dizziness? Chronic illnesses and medical conditions affect over 11 million children and adolescents in North America, so it is likely that we will frequently hear about these sad events.

A **chronic illness** is one that persists longer than 3 months in a given year, or requires a period of continuous hospitalization of more than 1 month. Chronic medical

Chronic illness and medical conditions affect over 11 million children and adolescents in North America.

conditions—the wide range of complications relating to physical growth, function, and development, such as a visual or hearing impairment—are part of this picture as well. About 10% to 20% of youths under the age of 18 years will experience one or more chronic health conditions, with approximately 2% to 4% of these children suffering from a disease so severe that it regularly interferes with their daily activities, such as forming friendships, attending school, and simply pursuing a normal quality of life (Brown & Macias, 2001).

Children and adolescents whose health and functional ability is compromised by a chronic medical condition face numerous challenges to their development and adjustment. Each day, children with insulin-dependent diabetes must monitor their blood glucose level and diet, and administer insulin through injections. Children with asthma cautiously navigate new situations, on the alert for an attack that can literally leave them breathless, and children with cancer must cope with the stares or comments from peers, who have little understanding or compassion for why another child looks different or seems frail. Like other developmental disorders, these conditions impact not only the child but peers and family members as well. This impact, in turn, affects the child's ability to adapt to the condition.

The DSM-IV-TR addresses the mental health issues pertaining to health-related disorders in children and adults indiscriminantly, relying mainly on two quite distinct categories: somatoform disorders and psychological factors affecting physical condition. We briefly discuss these DSM categories to provide an understanding of their meaning and limited applicability to pediatric populations.

Somatoform disorders are a group of related problems involving physical symptoms that resemble or suggest a medical condition, but lack organic or physiological evidence (APA, 2000). Somatization (i.e., expression of feelings through physical symptoms), hypochondriasis (i.e., preoccupation with real or fancied ailments), and pain disorders (e.g., recurring stomach pains) are examples of somatoform disorders. The diagnostic criteria involve a clustering of complaints with pain, and gastrointestinal, sexual, and pseudoneurological symptoms that exist at any time during the course of the disturbance. These symptoms are not intentionally produced or feigned, and they are real enough to cause significant distress or impairment to the individual. For some somatoform disorders, a strong presumption of a psychological component to the symptom is required for the diagnosis.

Somatoform disorders have been studied largely with adult populations, especially because they imply a chronic, established pattern that is often not detected until young adulthood (Peterson et al., 2003). Thus, their diagnostic applicability in reference to children and adolescents is questionable and seldom used (Fritz, Fritsch, & Hagino, 1997). Nonetheless, we raise this topic primarily because the multiple somatic complaints from children, especially recurrent abdominal pain, may be developmental precursors to adult somatoform disorders (Garber, Van Slyke, & Walker, 1998; Neeleman, Systema, & Wadsworth, 2002).

The second category, **psychological factors affecting physical condition,** refers to disorders in which psychological factors are presumed to cause or exacerbate a physical condition. DSM criteria primarily address situations in which a person's medical condition is adversely affected by psychological factors, such as a person with diabetes who is depressed and refuses to monitor and regulate her glucose level. However, this diagnostic category does not apply to most children with chronic health conditions, because it is the medical condition and its limitations that affect their psychological adjustment, not the other way around. Psychological symptoms develop in response to the stress of having or being diagnosed with a general medical condition. Rather than depression affecting the course of diabetes, as in the previous example, it is more likely that diabetes causes adjustment difficulties, which sometimes (but by no means always) include clinical disorders, such as depression. Thus, some children and adolescents with chronic illness accompanied by significant adjustment or behavioral problems may receive a diagnosis of adjustment disorder, which better accounts for the nature of the stressor (APA, 2000).

Progress in the development of effective medical treatments and cures for children with chronic illness has been spectacular over the past three decades, greatly prolonging the lives of many who previously would have died during infancy or childhood. Remarkably, the survival rate for certain types of cancer, such as acute lymphoblastic leukemia, has increased from about 1 in 5 children in the 1950s to 4 in 5 children today (Peterson et al., 2003). At the same time, however, these advances and improved survival rates have led to greater child and adult morbidity. **Morbidity** refers to the various forms of physical and functional consequences and limitations that result from an illness. Increased morbidity implies that more children and adolescents are adapting to the challenges of a chronic illness. For these children, illness has become a chronic life situation and stressor, and can have repercussions well into adulthood. For example, survivors of childhood cancer have a greater risk of developing a physical or mental illness as adults compared to their siblings; approximately 50% will develop a major illness in adulthood, most often chronic anxiety or infertility problems (Hudson et al., 2003).

As children's survival has improved and life-threatening illnesses are better controlled, attention has moved away from the acute, infectious diseases to a broader emphasis on promoting children's health and development, and assisting in the care of children with chronic illness or handicapping conditions (Black, Danseco, & Krishnakumar, 1998). Pediatric health psychologists are particularly active in helping children with chronic health disorders successfully adapt and attain an optimal quality of life.

To increase our awareness of the ways children with chronic disease learn to cope and adapt to physical and social challenges, we take a look at how children normally think of and express health concerns. This awareness provides a developmentally sensitive context for distinguishing between adaptive and maladaptive coping reactions among children with chronic illness.

Normal Variations in Children's Health

We now recognize that children can communicate about their pain and discomfort about as well as adults, but this was not always true. It was thought that infants did not experience pain at all, and that children were far less sensitive to pain than adults. Because children seemed less able to communicate about their pain, it was wrongly concluded that they had higher pain thresholds than adults. However, children do have a good concept of what pain is, and how to express it (McAlpine & McGrath, 1999). Their concepts of pain and its causes, their descriptions of pain, and their specific pain experiences seem remarkably well formed by an early age, both for boys and girls.

Consider these comments:

It [stomachache] was like bees in your stomach—stinging your stomach, yellow jackets going ping, pong, bop inside—like something just chopped down your stomach. [6-year-old boy]. It [earache] felt like something is inside your ear like a sticker from a rose bush poking deep inside your ear, like way harder than just pricking. [9-year-old boy] (D. M. Ross & Ross, 1984, p. 184)

Further, it is unlikely that children simply pick up pain descriptions from their parents or others. Consider the childlike imagery used by a 7-year-old boy in describing a headache:

Like there's this big monster in there, see, and he's growing like crazy and there's no room and he's pulling the two sides of my head apart he's getting so big. (D. M. Ross & Ross, 1984, p. 189).

Picture this common scene: Since age 6, Jackie has informed her parents from time to time that she was "too sick" to go to school. She would then carefully provide them with a list of her symptoms: "My tummy hurts, I feel hot, my throat hurts, I can't feel my toes." Careful questioning would usually result in a further list of symptoms— in fact, most were suggested by one of her parents "Does your leg hurt too?" [yes]; "How does your head feel?" [achey]; "What does your skin feel like?" [stingy]. The astute reader might note that these symptoms emerged at about the time Jackie was entering the first grade. Would you consider this situation to be typical of how children learn about physical symptoms and their connection to life's responsibilities?

Are somatic complaints in children (such as those expressed by Jackie) normal and commonplace? To no one's surprise, about a third of typical school-aged children report using pain for secondary gains, such as increased parental and peer attention, and avoidance of school and athletic activities. Undeniably, one of the most common ways children express their fears, dislikes, and avoidance is to complain of aches and pains, often of uncertain or dubious origin.

Girls and boys show interesting differences in this respect. When they are asked, girls report more symptoms of pain and anxiety than do boys. Under stressful circumstances, girls are more likely to cry, cling, and seek emotional support, and boys are more likely to be uncooperative, avoidant, and stoic. Similarly, excessive somatic complaints are associated with emotional disorders in girls and disruptive behavior disorders in boys (Egger, Costello, Erkanli, & Angold, 1999), as well as shyness (Chung & Evans, 2000). Does this imply that girls are somehow more sensitive to pain or less able to manage their fear and anxiety than boys? Not likely. These gender differences probably stem from socialization expectations, not physiological differences. We are all familiar with the ways boys are encouraged to adopt stoic attitudes about pain, whereas girls are reinforced for passive, affective expression (McGrath, 1993). Both boys and girls are reactive to distress, but they express it according to how they have been taught and what they wish to receive. Therefore, these complaints are developmentally within the normal range and do not merit a psychiatric label.

Some children may be more likely than others to experience recurrent pain and physical symptoms because of their family influences (Peterson, Harbeck, Farmer, & Zink, 1991). For example, children with functional abdominal pain and similar forms of recurrent unexplained pain are more likely to identify someone in their family who often expresses pain than are children whose pain is due to known organic causes (Osborne, Hatcher, & Richtsmeier, 1989). In addition, children of mothers with a somatic disorder are 4 times more likely to express physical symptoms when emotionally upset (Craig, Cox, & Klein, 2002). These unexplained, recurrent pain symptoms among children, therefore, seem to originate primarily from family *pain models* (Peterson et al., 2003). Children also learn healthy adaptational patterns at home and elsewhere. Children with well-developed social and academic competence, for instance, are less likely to respond to negative life events, like divorce or hospitalizations, with amplified stress and pain reactions (Walker, Garber, & Greene, 1994).

Let's turn our attention now to those children who have chronic health problems or conditions. Each chronic illness has unique challenges. Children with diabetes face daily medical routines, but they have a relatively pre-

dictable prognosis; children with cancer experience unpleasant side effects of treatment and must also cope with the uncertain prognosis of their illness.

The one important thing that all chronic illnesses and medical conditions have in common is that they constitute a major stressor that challenges and absorbs both the child's and the family's available coping resources. Viewing chronic illness in this way—as a form of major stress requiring adaptation—has allowed researchers to identify factors that promote successful adaptation to chronic illness. This view has also advanced new ways to assist children in coping with these challenges, as we will see.

The number of children with any chronic health-related disorder or condition is quite high, varying from 10 to 20% of the child population of North America (Drotar, 2000). Of these children, about two-thirds have mild conditions; the remainder has conditions that result in moderate to severe activity restrictions and bothersome treatment regimens (Peterson et al., 2003). Asthma is the most common chronic illness in childhood, followed by neurological and developmental disabilities and behavioral disorders. Fortunately, severe forms of chronic illnesses—those that pose major physical and intellectual limitations that interfere with children's daily lives—are relatively rare, but their combined rates are sizeable. About 2 out of every 100 children in the general population are significantly affected by a chronic illness or medical condition (Thompson & Gustafson, 1996).

Table 12.3 shows the prevalence of selected chronic childhood diseases and medical conditions. Survival rates for many of these illnesses have improved, therefore, prevalence rates reflect a large proportion of children who

---

Table 12.3

Estimated Population Prevalence of Selected Chronic Diseases and Conditions in Children, Ages 0–20, in the United States

	PREVALENCE ESTIMATES PER 1000	PERCENTAGE SURVIVING TO AGE 20
Moderate to severe asthma	10.0	98
Congenital heart disease	7.0	65
Cystic fibrosis	.20	60
Diabetes mellitus	1.8	95
Hemophilia	.15	90
Leukemia	.11	40
Muscular dystrophy	.06	25
Sickle-cell anemia	.28	90

Source: Adapted from Gortmaker & Sappenfield, 1984; Gortmaker, 1985.

have survived these childhood illnesses until age 20 or longer. Many of these illnesses are approaching their maximum (100%) survival rates (Gortmaker, 1985). The impact of living with HIV and AIDS, currently the sixth leading cause of death among 15–24 year-olds in the United States, will likely be a major health issue in the years to come (Brown, Lourie, & Pao, 2000).

Chronic childhood illnesses do not discriminate in terms of social class and ethnicity—they affect all children equally. The only exceptions are the specific conditions genetically determined by racial or ethnic descent. For example, cystic fibrosis affects primarily Caucasians, and sickle-cell disease affects primarily persons of African descent (Thompson & Gustafson, 1996). However, a troubling connection exists between socioeconomic status (SES) and survival rates, among children and adults with cancer, in particular (Mackillop, Zhang-Salomons, Groome, Paszat, & Holowaty, 1997). Despite the attempts to achieve more equitable health care delivery, residents of poorer communities still may receive inferior quality of care, even in publicly funded, single-tier health care systems like that in Canada. In addition, the poor may have other ailments that make cancer survival more difficult, or parents may be less inclined to seek medical attention if they have other major life stressors, or they are not aware of critical symptoms (Mackillop et al., 1997). People with adequate means generally enjoy a greater degree of empowerment—self-guidance and choices—over their lives, which translates into greater opportunities for proper medical care for their children. Later in this chapter we consider some ways to empower families and achieve a greater balance in their roles and resources.

We now take a closer look at two specific illnesses, diabetes mellitus and childhood cancer, that are representative of the course and patterns of adaptation faced by children with chronic illness.

Diabetes Mellitus

Amanda

Daily Struggle with Diabetes

Amanda, age 14, was diagnosed with insulin-dependent diabetes mellitus about a year ago. Like most teenagers, she leads an active life, and eating the proper foods is difficult enough without the added burden of daily glucose monitoring and insulin injections. She shared with us some of the ways this disease has affected her life, and how she copes with its demands and limitations:

Becoming diabetic has completely changed my life. My best friend is the insulin I take and the machine. I use the machine to test my blood sugar four times a day by poking my finger and putting blood on a test strip.

From the reading I am able to adjust my insulin and what I must eat. I am forced to eat a healthy balanced meal regularly about six times every day. I try not to have a negative attitude because I now realize just how lucky I am. I do not know what I would do if I did not have my machine or all of the sugar-free foods that are now available. Not only did diabetes change my physical life, but it altered my mental life as well. It helped me look at my life and realize what was important to me. My close friend, Germaine, helped me get through the first year at school, when some of the other kids wondered why I had to use needles and couldn't eat the same things they do. My parents have been great, and even my younger brother lays off me when he knows I'm having a particularly bad day. In a way, I'm more aware of how important health is to us than most kids at school, and I don't take things for granted the way I used to.

Amanda suffers from **insulin-dependent diabetes mellitus (IDDM)**, a lifelong metabolic disorder in which the body is unable to metabolize carbohydrates as a result of inadequate pancreatic release of insulin. This lack of insulin has a domino effect on the body's ability to regulate appetite, metabolize carbohydrates into necessary energy, and maintain a balance of blood chemistry. The lack of insulin prohibits glucose from entering the cells, which forces glucose to accumulate in the bloodstream and cause *hyperglycemia*. Glucose also tells the regulatory cells of the hypothalamus when a person is hungry or full, so without this information, the person tends to eat constantly but does not gain weight (Thompson & Gustafson, 1996). A treatment regimen consisting of insulin injections, diet, and exercise is necessary to approximate a normal metabolic state. Although current treatment regimens have greatly improved the health status of people with IDDM, the condition is still associated with significant morbidity and mortality.

IDDM affects boys and girls equally (Johnson, 1998). Initial symptoms often include fatigue, thirst, hunger, frequent urination, and weight loss despite excessive eating. IDDM is a progressive disease, with the more chronic complications that occur during young adulthood or beyond, including circulatory problems that can lead to blindness, kidney failure, and accelerated cardiovascular disease (Arslanian, Becker, & Drash, 1995). Life expectancy for persons with this disorder is one-third less than life expectancy of the general population (Silverstein, 1994). Given the seriousness of the illness and the long-standing, intrusive treatment requirements, it is understandable that children with diabetes and their families have an increased risk for conflict and adjustment problems (Martin, Miller-Johnson, Kitzmann, & Emery, 1998).

Children with IDDM face daily treatment tasks to maintain their metabolic control, such as blood glucose monitoring, dietary restraints, insulin injections, and learning how to balance energy demands and insulin needs (Peterson et al., 2003). **Metabolic control** is the degree to which the patient's glucose levels are maintained within the normal range. Children and adolescents must carefully monitor their insulin levels—too little insulin can result in a diabetic coma, too much insulin can result in an insulin reaction called *hypoglycemia*. Hypoglycemic episodes are extremely unpleasant and can include irritability, headaches, and shakiness. Adding to the complexity is the fact that illness and stress can upset the relationship between glucose and required insulin levels (Arslanian et al., 1995).

Children and teens must carefully follow the instructions given to them by their physician; that is, they must practice careful *regimen adherence*. Good regimen adherence and metabolic control are linked to the individuals' correct knowledge about their disease and its treatment, their belief that adherence is important, and adequate problem-solving skills (Drotar, 2000). As we saw with Amanda, adolescence is a particularly difficult period because of the impact that the illness can have on self-esteem and social and educational experiences—adolescence is difficult enough without the added burden of these daily treatment tasks. Therefore, psychologists have become active in developing ways to promote regimen adherence and metabolic control by helping family members adapt favorably to the demands of the condition (Stewart et al., 2000). Behavioral strategies have been quite successful in this regard, especially methods that reinforce symptom reduction or medication use, and self-control methods that teach patients to regulate dosage and monitor their symptoms, blood glucose, and medications (Drotar, 1999; Wysocki et al., 2000).

Childhood Cancer

Chen

A Determined Boy Fighting Leukemia

Chen, age 9, explains his feelings about childhood leukemia and its impact on his family and peer relations:

I've had cancer now for three years. They're still trying to fight it with the right medicine but nothing has worked yet. My friends come visit me—they're pretty OK with everything. But sometimes if you try and tell other kids about it they don't understand because they don't have it. To them we're normal. They don't have any kind of problems that hold them back from doing things. They don't have to worry about being in the hospital, checkups and

things, to see how you're doing. You can tell your friends why you have to stop and rest awhile, but they don't really understand—they don't really want to—they want to keep on going. I've got lots of family who care about me and I worry for them. I guess I'm used to all the doctors and medicines I take. Not that I like them but I know it's the only thing that might help. But I liked having the ability to do anything with my friends (or even my parents). I want to be able to get up and go. I'd tell someone else going through this to stay strong and keep the faith. And speak up when you need something!

Chen's mother explains the ordeal he and his family have undergone since his diagnosis:

Chen received a bone marrow transplant from his brother over a year ago and, thankfully, his leukemia went into remission. But when we went back one year later for a checkup we were told Chen had suffered a relapse—the cancer had overtaken the bone marrow, and his prognosis is poor. Now our family focuses on enjoying our time together and doing things with Chen. We are fortunate—my employer has gone out of their way to help me stay at home with Chen. Their support over the past year has been incredible. In fact, our whole community has shown tremendous support to our family. But his turn for the worst has made it difficult for us to do the things we have done over the past few weeks. We are angry, hopeful, depressed, joyous, saddened all the time. It is the worst roller coaster that we have ever ridden. Yet, Chen's medical condition has made us more determined to do more than we had ever hoped for, and the kindness shown toward our family has been overwhelming.

It is difficult for most of us to imagine what Chen and his family have experienced. Their words acknowledge the importance of their strength and determination and their human kindness when faced with a serious childhood illness, which in this case was terminal. Cancer can strike children very suddenly, more so than with adults. Children are also often at a more advanced stage of cancer when they are first diagnosed: Whereas only 20% of adults with cancer show evidence that the disease has spread at the time of diagnosis, this figure is fourfold in children (National Childhood Cancer Foundation, 1997).

The most common form of childhood cancer is *acute lymphoblastic leukemia* (ALL), which accounts for close to one-half of all forms of childhood cancer (Thompson & Gustafson, 1996). ALL is actually a group of heterogeneous diseases in which there is a malignancy of the bone marrow that produces blood cells. The bone marrow produces malignant cells called *lymphoblasts* that progressively replace normal bone marrow with fewer red blood cells and more white blood cells, causing anemia, infection, and easy bruising or excessive bleeding (Friedman, Latham, & Dahlquist, 1998). Childhood cancer used to be fatal, but advances in medical treatment have resulted in dramatic improvements in survival rates. Still, long-term complications such as recurrent malignancy, growth retardation, neuropsychological deficits, cataracts, and infertility pose a risk to survival.

Like those with diabetes, children with cancer undergo complicated medical treatment regimens, especially during the first 2–3 years. In addition, they face school absences, significant treatment side effects, and an uncertain prognosis. Chemotherapy and radiation therapy can cause hair loss and weight changes, as well as nausea, vomiting, increased fatigue, endocrine and growth retardation, and a depressed immune system (Friedman et al., 1998). Children with cancer must also cope with painful medical procedures, such as venipuncture, bone marrow aspirations, and lumbar punctures. Treatment requires children to be away from friends and some family members, which hinders their psychosocial development. Therefore, the psychosocial aspects of pediatric cancer have focused on management of distress related to the multiple diagnostic and treatment procedures these children face.

Although approximately 80% of pediatric cancer patients survive, 50% will have a serious physical or mental illness as adults. The most commonly occurring illnesses include infertility, chronic anxiety, and recurrent cancers (Hudson, Mertens, Yasui, Hobbie, Chen, Gurney, et al., 2003). Many patients require long-term care into adulthood after never learning the life-skills necessary for self-care.

Development and Course

Children with chronic illnesses are more likely to suffer emotional and behavioral adjustment problems stemming from the burden of their disease and its treatment. The Ontario Child Health Study (Cadman, Boyle, Szatmari, & Offord, 1987) was a major undertaking designed, in part, to determine the connection between medical conditions and psychological adaptation among a representative sample of 4- to 16-year-olds. Parents and teachers completed a mental health survey that contained information on children's illnesses and psychological adjustment. Children were then classified into one of three levels of physical health: chronic illness with physical disability, chronic illness without disability, and physically healthy. Psychiatric disorders, if any, were also determined from parent and teacher data.

Figure 12.1 shows the percentages of children with at least one psychiatric disorder across these three levels of physical health. Overall, children with chronic illness, regardless of degree of disability, had a risk for psychiatric

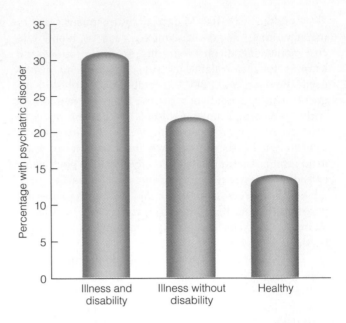

Figure 12.1 Percentages of children with a psychiatric disorder among three groups: with chronic illness and disability, with illness and no disability, and physically healthy.
(Data from Cadman et al., 1987)

disorder that was 2.4 times that of healthy children. However, children with chronic illness accompanied by disability were at greatest risk for other disorders. These disorders appeared primarily as internalizing problems, such as anxiety and depression, but externalizing problems, such as ADHD, were evident as well. Understandably, children whose normal functional abilities are limited face the greatest challenges in everyday activities, which in turn increases behavioral, social, and school adjustment difficulties. These findings were mirrored by the U.S. National Health Survey, where chronic physical conditions posed a significant risk factor for behavior problems, above and beyond socioeconomic status effects (Gortmaker, Walker, Weitzman, & Sobol, 1990).

Thus, children with chronic physical illnesses, especially those with physical disabilities, have an increased risk of secondary psychological adjustment difficulties (Hoekstra-Webers, Jasper, Kamps, & Klip, 1999), which refer to problems suspected to be due to the primary medical condition, rather than the reverse. These problems are most often expressed as internalizing symptoms, such as anxiety and depression, or a combination of both internalizing and externalizing problems (Boekaerts & Roeder, 1999; Lavigne & Faier-Routman, 1992).

To keep these symptoms in perspective, one must recognize that adjustment of children with chronic illness is typically better than that of other children referred to mental health clinics for non-health-related problems

(Eiser, Hill, & Vance, 2000; Wallander & Varni, 1998). For the most part, these children are exhibiting stress-related symptoms; the incidence of DSM-IV-TR-type disorders among children with chronic illness is actually low. For example, the prevalence of depression among children with various chronic health conditions averages only 9% across studies, an encouraging indication of successful adaptation among the vast majority of these children (Bennett, 1994). Moreover, children with diabetes (Holmes, Yu, & Frentz, 1999; Kovacs et al., 1990) and children with cancer (Eiser et al., 2000) on average report symptoms of anxiety, depression, and low self-esteem within the normal range for their age and gender.

Although chronically ill populations of children have increased risk of initial adjustment difficulties, it is difficult to say what causes particular symptoms, or why some children adapt more successfully than others. When one considers how these children must cope with unpredictable events and challenges almost every day, it is understandable that they would show an increase in stress-related symptoms. It is especially encouraging to know that most can adapt successfully to the course and consequences of their illness. Symptoms of anxiety, depression, and anger can be thought of as normal responses to stressful experiences associated with the long-term illness and treatment regimens, rather than psychiatric disorders (Eiser et al., 2000). This is similar to the adjustment problems faced by children with mental retardation and children who have been abused or neglected. Most children with chronic illness show considerable resilience in the face of stressful experiences associated with their condition, and we should exercise caution in applying psychiatric labels or descriptors that fail to capture the context and nature of their circumstances.

Effect on Family Members The field of pediatric health psychology has clearly adopted a focus on the important role of family functioning in the adjustment of children with chronic illness. The child's circumstances may result in family cohesion and support, as we saw in Amanda's and Chen's families, or result in family disruption and crisis. As parents try to understand and cope with the news of their child's diagnosis, they must at the same time start to accept that their child might always be different from other children. How they react and accept these realities determines, to a large extent, how their child and other siblings will react and adapt. Parents who fail to resolve this crisis are more likely to have problems with attachment and child-rearing (Goldberg, Gotowiec, & Simmons, 1995; Sheeran, Marvin, & Pianta, 1997), which further complicates the stressful nature of the child's illness.

Learning that a child has a life-threatening disease causes trauma and stress to all family members and, in fact, qualifies as a traumatic event that can precipitate post-traumatic stress disorder (PTSD) (APA, 2000). A mother of an infant born with a chronic disability describes her initial reaction:

I felt like I was bouncing around on a raft in the middle of a terrible storm. I didn't know where I was, where I was going, or what wave was going to break over my head next. Most of the time, I just hung on. Hanging on, I discovered, is the key to survival. (Medvescek, 1997, p. 67)

Many parents of children with chronic illness report that their fears resurface and memories return whenever their child has only a common illness, like a cold or flu. About 10% of mothers and fathers suffer symptoms of PTSD, a rate that is comparable to other types of traumatic stress exposure (Kazak et al., 1997). Fortunately, the children themselves do not typically suffer PTSD-related symptoms connected to learning of their disorder, probably because they were very young at the time of diagnosis. However, children's memory of stressful procedures plays a role in their experience of distress (Chen, Zeltzer, Craske, & Katz, 2000), and some survivors of childhood cancer recall disturbing memories of the medical procedures as much as 12 years later (Stuber, Christakis, Houskamp, & Kasak, 1996).

Families exert a significant impact on the behavior of children with chronic health problems, as they do with healthy children. No one type of chronic illness poses a significantly greater risk of adjustment than any other. Thus, factors associated with children's situations—like family stress and resources—may be more critical to their adaptation than the challenges posed by the illness alone (Lavigne & Faier-Routman, 1992). Also, the degree to which parents can assist their children in developing more autonomy and control over their treatment regimens in a non-conflictual manner, predicts the likelihood that the teen will adhere to the treatment regimen. The normal conflict observed in parent–teenager relationships is heightened in families where the teen is trying to incorporate a treatment regimen into a changing lifestyle. For example, drinking alcohol is a significant risk for teens with diabetes; therefore conversations and parent expectations regarding experimentation with substance use are often heightened because alcohol use is more deleterious (Murata et al., 2000).

It is not the amount of concordance between parent and teen perceptions of who is making decisions about treatment that predicts adherence to treatments; it is the degree of conflict in the parent–teen relationship (Miller & Drotar, 2003), Thus, parents who can help their teen maintain adherence in a non-confrontational manner (regardless of whether they agree with their child about who is in fact making treatment decisions), will increase their teens' health and adaptation. In general, the following stress factors that parents face are quite similar across all types of pediatric chronic illness: financial and physical burdens, changes in parenting roles, sibling resentment, child adjustment problems, social isolation, frequent hospitalizations, and grief (Wallander & Robinson, 1999). It comes as no surprise, therefore, that couples with chronically ill children report more marital conflict, poor communication, role incongruity, and a lack of intimacy and positive affect (Gordon-Walker, Johnson, Manion, & Cloutier, 1996; Holmes, Yu, & Frentz, 1999).

The point is worth repeating: Despite these psychological and tangible repercussions, many children with chronic illness adapt favorably to these challenges, as do their families. Perceived social support and parental adaptation are key components aiding their adaptation (Skinner, John, & Hampson, 2000), since primary caregivers play an important role in their children's stress and coping abilities. Specifically, mothers who perceive lower levels of illness-related stress, use more adaptive and active ways to cope with stress and problems, and perceive their families as more supportive than conflictual are more likely to show normal adjustment levels themselves (Thompson & Gustafson, 1996). Regardless of the circumstances, we often see this connection: When maternal abilities remain intact, child and family functioning is less impaired. This illustrates the reciprocal relationship between children's adjustment and parental stress and distress—healthy parental adjustment is related to healthy child adjustment, and vice versa. (Most research has considered only the role of mothers on child adjustment, but the specific influence of fathers on children's coping and adaptation to chronic illness may also be prominent.) Thus, parental adjustment is one of the important correlates of children's adjustment with chronic illness.

Siblings of children with a chronic illness also experience heightened social and mental health problems. They tend to have more internalizing symptoms, such as depression and anxiety, lower cognitive scores, and fewer peer activities (Sharpe & Rossiter, 2002). These outcomes are worse for chronic illnesses that require daily treatment regimens, which suggests the increased caregiving demands faced by parents and subsequent decreased amounts of parental attention for siblings contribute to their maladjustment. Interestingly, the effect of having a sibling with a chronic illness itself is positive (Sharpe & Rossiter, 2002), suggesting that the sibling relationship is a paradox, and requires further investigation to fully understand its effects on both siblings' adjustment.

Social Adjustment and School Performance   Children's adjustment to chronic illness is reflected not only in terms of psychological distress, but also through developmental accomplishments in social adjustment, peer relationships, and school performance. Because chronic illness results in lifestyle interruptions that interfere with opportunities for social interaction (La Greca & Thompson, 1998), children with more severe, disruptive illnesses tend to suffer primarily in social adjustment (Meijer, Sinnema, Bijstra, Mellenbergh, & Wolters, 2000a). This maladjustment is often expressed by displaying more submissive behavior with their peers, and engaging in less social activities overall (Meijer et al., 2000a; Meijer, Sinnema, Bijstra, Mellenbergh, & Wolters, 2000b). However, peer support does facilitate disease adaptation for youngsters, and can help with treatment regimens, particularly when peer-crowd affiliations (e.g., "brains," "jocks") are linked with health-promoting behaviors (La Greca, Bearman, & Moore, 2002).

Consider child cancer patients' peer relationships. Chen explained how the other children did not understand why he could not join in or behave the same as they did—to them he looked normal, so he must be okay. Negative or ill-informed reactions from peers and others are, unfortunately, a fact of life for some children with chronic illness. In a longitudinal study of children with cancer, adolescents were perceived by their teachers as less sociable, less prone toward leadership, and more socially isolated and withdrawn than their peers (Noll, LeRoy, Bukowski, Rogosch, & Kulkarni, 1991). Similar problems in social adjustment are evident among those children with illnesses that affect primarily the central nervous system—cerebral palsy, spina bifida, and brain tumors—because of the impact of these disorders on cognitive abilities such as social judgment (Mulhern et al., 1999).

School adjustment and performance is another domain in which children and adolescents with chronic illness are at increased risk for adjustment difficulties. Risk may stem from two sources: primary effects of the illness or its treatment, and secondary consequences of the illness, such as fatigue, absenteeism, or psychological stress (Witt, Riley, & Coiro, 2003). Primary effects of the illness on school performance are especially evident among children with brain-related illnesses. They must undergo aggressive treatment regimens that put a heavy toll on the central nervous system, especially younger children (Brown, Sawyer, Antoniou, Toogood, & Rice, 1999). The most common neurocognitive effects appear in nonverbal abilities and attention or concentration functions (Mulhern et al., 1999). Short-term memory, speed of processing, visuomotor coordination, and sequencing ability are also frequently affected. Thus, about one-half of the children with brain-related illnesses are placed in special education settings or do not attend school. In contrast, children with physical, non-brain-related illnesses tend to have normal educational placements; however, they continue to have problems in reading, which may be one indirect effect of chronic illness and school absence (Witt et al., 2003).

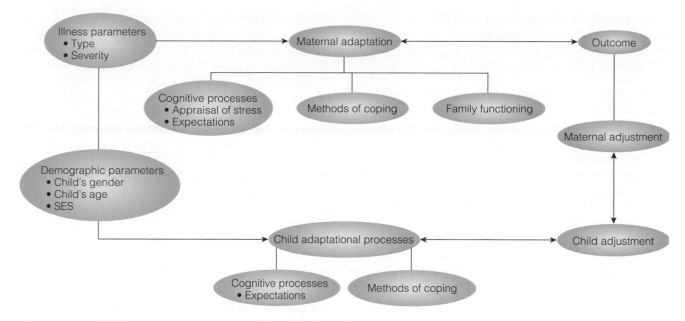

Figure 12.2 The transactional stress and coping model for chronic childhood illness.

Source: Adapted from "Change Over a 12-Month Period in the Psychological Adjustment of Children and Adolescents with Cystic Fibrosis," by R. J. Thompson, Jr., K. E. Gustafson, L. K. George and A. Spock, 1994, *Journal of Pediatric Psychology,* 19 pp. 189–203. Copyright © 1994 by the American Psychological Association. Reprinted by permission of the author.

How Children Adapt: A Biopsychosocial Model

We described the adjustment difficulties of children with chronic illness in general terms, but we know that each child's illness and family situation is different. Some children, like Amanda and Chen, have supportive families with adequate resources, but others may not. Countless events can influence children's adaptation to chronic illness; no single factor explains why some children adjust more readily than others.

How do we make sense of the numerous factors influencing children's adjustment? When a single-factor theory is not a sufficient explanation, researchers often develop multifactorial theories that link the most important variables in conceptual and meaningful ways. Figure 12.2 depicts the *transactional stress and coping model* developed by Thompson and colleagues (Thompson, Gil, Burbach, Keith, & Kinney, 1993; Thompson, Gustafson, George, & Spock, 1994), which shows how children's adaptation to chronic illness is influenced not only by the nature of the illness itself, but also by personal and family resources. This model helps make sense of the complicated processes that shape children's outcomes.

The transactional stress and coping model emphasizes the stressful nature of chronic illness, which compels the child and family members to adapt. How they accomplish the adaptation is a key factor in children's outcomes.

Illness parameters encompass the type of illness and the severity of the illness, including visible disfigurement and functional impairment (MacLean, Perrin, Gortmaker, & Pierre, 1992; Mulhern, Carpentieri, Shema, Stone, & Fairclough, 1993). *Demographic parameters* include gender, age, and SES of the child, which also can affect the impact of the illness. The model then proposes that important child and family processes mediate the illness–outcome relationship, beyond the illness and demographic factors. Important psychological mediators involve parental adjustment, child adjustment, and their interrelationship, as described next.

Illness Parameters One would expect that children's psychosocial adjustment varies as a function of their medical condition. Some illnesses have an uncertain course and others have dire effects on everyday activities, adding stress along the way. Different chronic illnesses have many features in common, though, so it often makes sense to study children's adjustment in relation to illness-related dimensions, or parameters, rather than specific illnesses. The common dimensions that vary among different illnesses include things such as the extent to which the illness:

- Is visible to others, or involves physical deformity
- Is severe and life-threatening
- Has a worsening or fatal prognosis versus a stable or improving prognosis

- Requires intrusive or painful procedures
- Affects the child's functional status, such as physical or cognitive impairments that affect performance of everyday tasks (Thompson & Gustafson, 1996)

Children with chronic illness face different challenges along each of these dimensions, so naturally their adjustment may be affected accordingly. Across all medical conditions, the illness parameters that play the most significant role in children's adjustment are *severity, prognosis,* and *functional status* (Lavigne & Faier-Routman, 1993). Functional status seems to be especially important in terms of cognitive impairments, such as conditions that involve the brain and central nervous system.

Personal Characteristics Chronic medical conditions require both children and family members to accept and cope with considerable stress and uncertainty. What child characteristics and resources might favor successful adaptation? A child's sex is one consideration: Boys with chronic illness show more adjustment problems overall than girls. However, this sex difference depends on the dimension of adjustment and who is reporting the information. Boys are described by parents and teachers as having more behavior problems than girls (E. C. Perrin, Ayoub, & Willett, 1993). However, girls are more likely than boys to self-report anxiety, depression, and negative perceptions of physical appearance (La Greca, Swales, Klemp, Madigan, & Skyler, 1995), and more likely to describe themselves as less socially competent (Holden, Chmielewski, Nelson, & Kager, 1997). This gender difference reflects two common findings: Girls are more willing to acknowledge and report symptoms than boys (Achenbach, McConaughy, & Howell, 1987), and girls react to stress with internalizing symptoms, whereas boys react with more externalizing symptoms (Egger et al., 1999).

Although children's overall adjustment seldom differs as a function of current age or age at the onset of the illness (Peterson et al., 2003), economic and health disparities that exist among ethnic minority children and their families play a contributing role (Willis, 2002). These disparities not only affect the course and treatment of chronic illnesses, but also have a pronounced affect on quality of life and risk of disease and disability. Being poor is a risk factor for many stressful life events, but being poor and having a health problem greatly increases distress and adjustment problems (Willis, 2002). Similarly, treatment studies on chronic illness in children and adolescents have generally failed to address important cultural issues that affect treatment outcome, especially compliance with the treatment regime (Clay, Mordhorst, & Lend, 2002).

Not surprisingly, children with greater intellectual ability and acquired strengths in their self-concept and coping skills also show more positive psychological adjustment, regardless of medical condition (Compas Harding & Thomsen, 1999). Specifically, children's accurate appraisal of perceived stress—how they interpret and react to daily events and hassles associated with illness management—leads to a better sense of well-being and fewer symptoms of distress and maladjustment (Frank, Blount, & Brown, 1997). Chen states this well:

> I now realize that life is full of a series of tests. You never know what is around the corner, but you have to take it as it comes. A positive attitude, and remembering that I have friends and family for support, helps me get through some of the rough days.

Family Adaptation and Functioning If chronic illness is considered a stressor affecting all family members to some extent, then child adjustment depends in part on the degree of stress and symptoms experienced by other family members, especially the primary caregiver. Undeniably, the family environment assumes greater importance in the lives of children with a chronic illness, in part because a closer parent–child interaction often is necessary to manage the disease.

The transactional model shown in Figure 12.2 considers parental adaptation to be a key mediator of the relationship between child illness and adjustment for both child and parent. How does a parent "adapt" in a way that favors healthy outcomes? According to the model, parental adaptation is a function of three major processes: (1) how they manage daily stress and view their self-efficacy, as seen with Chen's mother; (2) whether they use active, solution-focused coping; and (3) family functioning and perceived support. Successful parental adaptation, in turn, leads to better parental adjustment and healthier family communication and conflict resolution skills (Wysocki et al., 2000). Ultimately, of course, parents' positive adjustment greatly increases the likelihood of more positive child outcomes. Parent perceptions of illness are one aspect of parental adaptation that plays a key role in promoting their child's health. Perceptions of child vulnerability are related to increased social anxiety in their children and more school absences (Anthony, Gil, & Schnanberg, 2003).

Family functioning is often defined in terms of the availability of two types of primary family resources: *utilitarian* and *psychological*. Utilitarian family resources relate to the practical demands of caring for a child with a disability, such as financial resources and parental education, which influence their ability to understand the illness and seek beneficial assistance for their child. Psychological resources are less tangible but often considered far more important—how family members support one another, relate to each other and to persons outside the family, and resolve conflicts. Together these two types of family resources account for considerable variance in behavioral and social adjustment of chronically ill children (Wallander & Robinson, 1999).

Intervention

The psychological impact of chronic illness occurs through the disruption of normal processes of child development and family functioning. Fortunately, this impact can be lessened and adaptation can be strengthened by the use of psychosocial interventions that reduce stress, enhance social problem-solving skills, and promote effective child-rearing methods. These various methods often entail stress management and skill-building components to assist children and family members in their continuous process of adaptation.

The basic goal of intervention is to enhance the quality of life for the children and their families. Ways to achieve this goal have taken a dramatic shift over the past two decades, given the strong interest of pediatric and health psychologists. Prior to the mid-1970s, intervention efforts were primarily based on a child-centered, medically based model. The health professional was the expert, the child was the patient, and parents were passive observers. However, the passage of the Education for All Handicapped Children Act in 1975 and the more recent Individuals with Disabilities Education Act in the U.S. (IDEA; Public Law 101–476) created new expectations for parents to participate in the decision-making process and their child's educational planning. This started a philosophical shift from child-centered to family-centered intervention, which was furthered by the 1986 Handicapped Infant and Toddler Program (Bazyk, 1989). For the first time families were properly recognized as the constant in children's lives, and their role as consumers of services and decision makers was deemed worthy of support and assistance.

Empowering Families   These developments and others eventually led to the current trend toward health promotion and empowerment for families and children, which refer to encouraging changes, opportunities, and competence to achieve one's health potential (Peterson et al., 2003). This perspective recognizes the importance of attaining a balance between the abilities of the individual or family, and the challenges and risks of the environment. The role of health care provider thus began to shift from expert to consultant—someone who seeks to establish a collaborative relationship that supports parents in meeting their goals. In effect, families are now recognized as important resources, and seen as part of the solution; they are kept in the forefront of children's intervention needs, not in the background.

This underlying philosophy of family empowerment reduces stress and dependency, and enables families to obtain the necessary information to make informed decisions and take competent actions (Varni, LaGreca, & Spirito, 2000). Chen's family members, for example, took an active role in enhancing his quality of life and were not frightened away or uninformed about his needs and their opportunities. His mother explains:

Physiotherapy has helped Chen be less dependent on mom and dad. The goal is for him to think ahead and be prepared to do things on his own. An example is at bedtime getting his clothes out and onto the bed for the following morning. Then in the morning he can get himself dressed and transferred into his chair by himself.

Support groups and educational programs of various types offered considerable benefits to children and other family members. Helping families connect with one another and share their common experiences and concerns generates both personal power and important resources for change (Plante, Lobato, & Engel, 2001). Participation is the active agent in empowerment, and a cooperative health professional–family model encourages individuals to support one another while providing a venue for modeling positive attitudes and values. Similarly, educational programs that provide information and skills training to family members are often beneficial. The most beneficial promote knowledge and self-management of the illness, reintegration of children into the school setting, and support and coordination of care among parents of children with chronic illness (Plante et al., 2001). Gaining more knowledge about their child's disease promotes greater parental understanding of the child and the overall effect of the disease on the family.

In short, treatment-related activities for children with chronic illness are often based on the needs of the entire family. However, these efforts must fit the degree to which parents want to be, and realistically can be, involved in their child's overall care. Intervention methods that favor these adaptive processes adhere to medical regimens and psychologically based approaches, to help children cope with pain that is associated with invasive medical procedures and illness, as described in the next section.

Helping Children Cope   Throughout our discussion of children with chronic illness we have seen how they must cope with numerous stressful circumstances, ranging from painful medical procedures to peer rejection and functional limitations. For this reason, considerable effort has been placed on ways to enhance their successful coping through support groups (see Box 12.1) and recreational activities (see Box 12.2). Much of this work focuses on coping with painful medical procedures, yet these methods also apply to settings and circumstances, at school or during home routines. Parent involvement and maternal adaptation are, once again, key components in children's

BOX 12.1 **Virtual Support Groups**

In her private room at New York City's Mount Sinai Medical Center, 12-year-old Lauren peers intently into the colorful screen of a computer monitor. Lauren was diagnosed with a malignant tumor in her right wrist; 9 months of chemotherapy followed, and the radius bone in her right forearm was replaced with a metal rod. But today her mischievous brown eyes and smile light up the room as she plays. Finally tiring of the game, she clicks her way out and uses the computer to place a video call to one of her friends. "I've had bothersome moments," Lauren says after completing the call. "Like when I was in intensive care, and I wasn't allowed to do anything or see anyone. But this system lets me talk to kids from other hospitals who have the same thing as I do. I realized I'm not alone, and that made me feel better."

The system that cheers Lauren and children like her is an interactive network called STARBRIGHT World (SBW). For some of the children, SBW helps speed their recovery; for those less fortunate, it helps provide a measure of pleasure, comfort, diversion, and solace in their last months and weeks. SBW is a safe and secure online community where kids and teens living with serious ill-

Child with chronic illness speaking to others via Web technology.

nesses can connect with each other. Kids on SBW can chat, read and post to bulletin boards, email, search for friends with similar illnesses, participate in fun events and contests, surf pre-screened Web sites and play games.

Source: www.starbright.org.

---

coping; to effectively assist their children, parents must maximize their sense of control over the outcome and progress of their children's health (Kibby, Tyc, & Mulhern, 1998).

Enhancing adaptation and quality of life of children with chronic illness similarly requires that children comply as much as possible with medical regimens, both in and outside the doctor's office. Since children often don't comply with even simpler tasks, like following directions, eating what they should, or getting ready for school, how can we expect them to comply with the unpleasant demands of medical procedures? The significance of these procedures has caused the emphasis in pediatric health psychology to shift to helping children and their parents cope with necessary protocols, rather than developing ways to make them comply.

Evidence suggests that most children and adults do best if a stressful medical procedure is explained first, and they are given an opportunity to see what is going to happen. Accordingly, interventions for reducing stress and managing pain during pediatric procedures have applied behavioral and cognitive approaches that emphasize *coping and stress management* (McQuaid & Nassau, 1999). Children who actively seek information about impending painful events show improved adjustment and less distress (Blount, Smith, & Frank, 1999). In addition, maternal

and family functioning, effective child-rearing strategies to reinforce desired behaviors, and a positive doctor–patient relationship all contribute to children's improved adherence to the requirements of monitoring and treating their illness (Drotar, 2000; Wallander & Robinson, 1999).

In general, there are two main psychological approaches to helping children cope with stressful medical procedures and chronic and recurrent pain: providing information and training in coping skills (Thompson & Gustafson, 1996). *Information strategies* offer verbal explanations and demonstrations as well as modeling the procedure, which reduce distress because the medical procedure is more predictable (Dahlquist, 1999). Inexperienced patients often prefer modeling and receiving information about the unfamiliar medical procedure to alleviate their anxiety, whereas experienced children prefer specific training to cope with the bothersome procedures (Dahlquist, 1989).

Coping strategies involve teaching the various coping skills of deep breathing, attention distraction, muscle relaxation, relaxing imagery, emotive imagery, and behavioral rehearsal. For example, children may be asked to imagine themselves as superheroes undergoing a test of their powers, similar to the strategy used by the boy in the dentist chair (Dahlquist, 1999). Children are encouraged

BOX 12.2 **A Summer Retreat**

Promoting social adjustment among children with a chronic illness can be difficult, but enrolling them in summer camps for children with similar illnesses is one way of encouraging social interaction with peers. Camp Oochigeas, the first residential camp for pediatric cancer patients in Canada, is an example of a place children with similar medical issues can come together and share their experiences. Campers come for a free 2-week stay and participate in a number of camping activities with rest hours and medical regimens built in to their schedule. A team of oncologists and 180 volunteers received over 200 children in 2003, referred from the local children's hospital. Many of the volunteers were once campers themselves, and serve as role models and success stories for the campers.

Going away to summer camp provides these children with a chance to interact with their peers and be accepted, and to realize they are not the only ones coping with a chronic illness. It boosts their confidence and self-esteem and provides them with a social network that is often missing due to being out of school, or feeling different from everyone else. "At a camp like Oochigeas, no one really pays attention to the fact that you have cancer because everyone does." It also gives their families a much needed break from the responsibility of caring for a child with a chronic illness; and encourages the child to develop some independence and self-care skills. Often, the developmental task of gaining self-care skills and autonomy from parents delayed for these children, due to the nature of their illness. Camp is a way for both the child and parents to have a positive separation experience (in contrast to hospital visits), and to recognize the need for appropriate levels of independence.

Courtesy Camp Oochigeas

Child with chronic illness attending summer camp.

Source: http://www.ooch.org/about_overview.html

to identify specific stressors associated with their illness (e.g., giving themselves an injection), and to learn ways to handle those stressors and prevent distress or failure. Amanda, for instance, coped with her injections by thinking of positive things in her life. Parents can serve as coaches during the stress and coping procedures and help their children rehearse coping skills both at home and in the clinic (Powers, Blount, Bachanas, Cotter, & Swan, 1993; Varni et al., 2000). Using these coping skills leads to the reduction of pain and physical symptoms, but it also has a wide range of benefits that include fewer health care contacts and school absences and less interference with family functioning (Gil, Anthony, & Carson, 2001).

To help their children cope with invasive medical procedures, parents should be encouraged to use distraction, contingent praise, and active directives ("take a deep breath now"), but they should avoid explanations, vague commands, or criticism (Dahlquist et al., 2001). Because of its demonstrated benefit, cognitive-behavioral therapy for children with chronic medical conditions that require painful medical procedures has become routine (Slifer, Tucker, & Dahlquist, 2002).

SECTION SUMMARY

- Children with chronic illness are at increased risk for psychosocial problems, which generally reflect their attempts to cope with stress.

- Children respond to the stress of chronic conditions very differently, and adjustment problems are more likely among children with increased disability. Adjustment problems may appear in the form of behavioral and emotional distress symptoms, such as low self-esteem, lack of social competence, poor school performance, and, sometimes, psychiatric disorders.

- Many children and their families adapt favorably to the challenges associated with chronic illness. Perceived social support and maternal adaptation are key components aiding their adaptation.

- Recent shifts to greater family empowerment and parental involvement have resulted in innovative ways to help children cope with the challenges of chronic illness. Psychosocial interventions assist children's adaptation to chronic illness by enhancing their social problem-solving skills and coping skills and by reinforcing effective child-rearing methods.

Adolescent Substance Use Disorders

Researchers have discovered that chocolate produces some of the same reactions in the brain as marijuana. The researchers also discovered other similarities between the two but can't remember what they are.

—Matt Lauer

Let's begin this section with a short quiz. Many of us believe we have a good understanding of the nature and extent of substance use in our peer culture, so please look at Box 12.3 before reading this section to see if you agree with the facts! As you probably will discover, many myths and facts remain about substance use that merit greater education and awareness, especially among the most vulnerable youth. Although most adolescents experiment with substances ranging from cigarettes to street drugs without experiencing adverse effects, the risks of substance include increased mortality and morbidity related to impaired driving, unsafe sexual practices, aggression, and similar concerns (Williams, Holmbeck, & Greenley, 2002). Frequent and prolonged consumption not only increases their risk of developing a substance use disorder, but interferes with the development of important psychosocial skills (Chassin, Ritter, Trim, & King, 2003).

An increasing area of concern, particularly in adolescents, is the use and abuse of substances (e.g., nicotine, alcohol, marijuana, and other drugs). The abuse of such substances has physical implications for the developing child or adolescent, and may produce symptoms that mimic other psychopathological behaviors. Substance abuse is also related to a wide variety of psychological disorders.

Substance use disorders (SUDs) during adolescence include substance dependence and substance abuse, which result from the self-administration of any substance that alters mood, perception, or brain functioning (Brown, Aarons, & Abrantes, 2001). Whereas almost all abused substances can lead to psychological dependence, some also extend to physical dependence. Psychological dependence refers to the subjective feeling of needing the substance to adequately function. Physical dependence occurs when the body adapts to the substance's constant presence, and tolerance refers to requiring more of the substance to experience an effect once obtained at a lower dose. Another aspect of physical dependence is the experience of withdrawal, an adverse physiological symptom that occurs when consumption of an abused substance is abruptly ended and thus removed from the body.

Diagnostic criteria for the two types of SUDs (abuse and dependence) are shown in Tables 12.4 and 12.5, based on the DSM-IV-TR (APA, 2000). To receive a diagnosis of **substance dependence**, an adolescent (or adult) must show a maladaptive pattern of substance use for at least 12 months, accompanied by three or more significant clinical signs of distress—tolerance (the need for increased amounts to achieve intoxication), withdrawal (cognitive and physiological changes upon discontinuation of the drug), and other indices of compulsive use. Substance dependence is also characterized as with or without physiological dependence (i.e., with or without evidence of tolerance or withdrawal). Criteria for **substance abuse**, in contrast, involve one or more harmful

More serious

Table 12.4
DSM-IV Criteria for Substance Dependence

A. A maladaptive pattern of substance use, leading to clinically significant impairment or distress, as manifested by three (or more) of the following, occurring at any time in the same 12-month period:

(1) tolerance, as defined by either of the following:

    a. a need for markedly increased amounts of the substance to achieve intoxication or desired effect

    b. markedly diminished effect with continued use of the same amount of the substance

(2) withdrawal, as manifested by either of the following:

    a. the characteristic withdrawal syndrome for the substance

    b. the same (or a closely related) substance is taken to relieve or avoid withdrawal symptoms

(3) the substance is often taken in larger amounts or over a longer period than was intended

(4) there is a persistent desire or unsuccessful efforts to cut down or control substance use

(5) a great deal of time is spent in activities necessary to obtain the substance (e.g., visiting multiple doctors or driving long distances), use the substance (e.g., chain-smoking), or recover from its effects

(6) important social, occupational, or recreational activities are given up or reduced because of substance use

(7) the substance is continued despite knowledge of having a persistent or recurrent physical or psychological problem that is likely to have been caused or exacerbated by the substance (e.g, current cocaine use despite recognition of cocaine-induced depression, or continued drinking despite recognition that an ulcer was made worse by alcohol consumption)

Source: Reprinted with permission of *Diagnostic and Statistical Manual of Mental Disorders, DSM-IV-TR, Text Revision, Fourth Edition.* Copyright 2000 by the American Psychiatric Association.

Table 12.5
DSM-IV Criteria for Substance Abuse

A. A maladaptive pattern of substance use leading to clinically significant impairment or distress, as manifested by one (or more) of the following, occurring within a 12-month period:

(1) recurrent substance use resulting in a failure to fulfill major role obligations at work, school, or home (e.g., repeated absences or poor work performance related to substance use; substance-related absences, suspensions, or expulsions from school; neglect of children or household)

(2) recurrent substance use in situations in which it is physically hazardous (e.g., driving an automobile or operating a machine when impaired by substance use)

(3) recurrent substance-related legal problems (e.g., arrests for substance-related disorderly conduct)

(4) continued substance use despite having persistent or recurrent social or interpersonal problems caused or exacerbated by the effects of the substance (e.g., arguments with spouse about consequences of intoxication, physical fights)

B. The symptoms have never met the criteria for Substance Dependence for this class of substance.

Source: Reprinted with permission of *Diagnostic and Statistical Manual of Mental Disorders, DSM-IV-TR, Text Revision, Fourth Edition.* Copyright 2000 by the American Psychiatric Association.

features associated with substance abuse and/or withdrawal, such as disorientation or mood swings.

SUDs among youths also differ from that of adults in terms of their pattern of use, which is likely a function of the restrictions on availability. For example, adolescents tend to drink less often, but drink larger amounts at any one time than adults drink (i.e., binge drinking), which is associated with acute health and social risks (Chassin et al., 2003). Adolescents' substance use is also strongly influenced by peers, their desire for autonomy and experimentation with adult "privileges," and the level of parental supervision they received (Williams et al., 2002). These influences affect the expression and features of the SUDs in ways that differ from adults.

Prevalence and Course

It should come as little surprise that alcohol remains the most prevalent substance used, and abused, by adolescents. As shown in Figure 12.3, about 4 in 5 high school seniors, 2 in 3 tenth graders, and one-half of those in eighth grade report having used alcohol (Monitoring the Future, 2002). About one-third of these teens report a history of binge drinking, defined as episodic heavy drinking of 5 or more drinks in a row. Cigarettes are the second most commonly used substance among adolescents, with

and repeated negative consequences of substance use over the last 12 months. Because substance dependence is the more serious of the two, a diagnosis of substance abuse would not be given if an individual met criteria for substance dependence.

As with other disorders described in this textbook, these criteria do not adequately consider important developmental differences between adults and adolescents (Brown et al., 2001). Whereas substance-abusing adolescents experience withdrawal symptoms, their physiological dependence and symptoms are less common than the same among adults (Brown & Abrantes, in press). Adolescents are more likely to show cognitive and affective

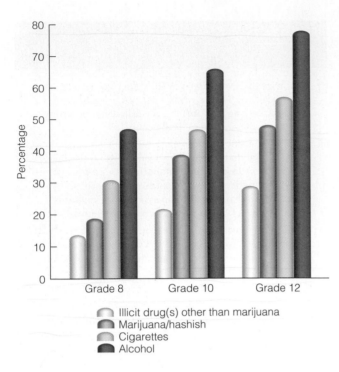

Figure 12.3 Rates of lifetime substance use among high school students.
(Data from Monitoring the Future, 2002)

about 60% of high school seniors reporting lifetime use of nicotine, and one-third smoking cigarettes in the last month.

Illicit substance use is also common among these age groups, with over one-half of high school seniors reporting the lifetime use of a drug other than alcohol or cigarettes (typically, marijuana). One substance use problem

Rates of substance use among adolescent girls have increased over the last decade to a level similar to that of boys.

of great concern among youths during the last decade is the increase in illicit drugs other than marijuana. The number of adolescents who have used MDMA (i.e., Ecstasy), opiates, cocaine, and crack has been increasing, yet, adolescents using hallucinogens and inhalants has decreased somewhat (Monitoring the Future, 2002).

Given the relatively high levels of substance use among adolescents, it is not surprising that a significant portion meet criteria for a substance abuse or dependence diagnosis. The 2001 National Household Survey on Drug Abuse, which involves a community-based sample of youths, found that close to 8% of adolescents aged 12 to 17 met criteria for substance abuse or dependence (Substance Abuse and Mental Health Services Administration [SAMHSA], 2002). Not surprisingly, much higher rates of these disorders (about one in three) are reported among youths with histories of other mental health problems, or with involvement in the child welfare or juvenile justice systems (Aarons, Brown, Hough, Garland, & Wood, 2001).

Age of Onset   A certain amount of substance use during adolescence is normative behavior, therefore researchers have looked at several factors that may differentiate trajectories of use that are relatively benign from those that have lasting significance. One of the most widely supported risk factors for the onset of substance use problems and subsequent disorders is age of first use (Brown & Abrantes, in press). The National Longitudinal Survey of Youth (NLSY), for example, found that the odds of developing alcohol dependence decreased by 9% for each year that the onset of drinking was delayed (Grant, Stinson, & Harford, 2001). In general, researchers find that alcohol use before age 14 is a strong predictor of subsequent alcohol abuse or dependence (Grant & Dawson, 1997), especially when early drinking is followed by rapid escalation in the quantity of alcohol consumption (Chassin, Pitts, & Prost, 2002).

Sex and Ethnicity   Although past surveys have found that girls typically use fewer types of drugs and use them less often than boys, sex differences in the lifetime prevalence rates of substance use are converging, due mostly to increased substance use among girls (Wallace et al., 2003). Similarly, rates of diagnoses for SUDs no longer differ significantly between boys and girls (about 8%) (SAMHSA, 2002). Notable ethnic differences in prevalence rates of substance use and abuse have been found, however. Based on a large U.S. sample of adolescents, substance use (as indicated by alcohol, marijuana, and smoking) are highest among Native American boys and girls, a bit lower among White, Hispanic/Latina and African Americans, and lowest among Asian American adolescents (Wallace et al., 2003).

Course   Typically, rates of substance use peak around late adolescence and then begin to decline during young

© Benelux Press / Taxi / Getty Images

adulthood, in conjunction with adult roles of work, marriage, and parenthood (Brown & Abrantes, in press). For some youths, however, a pronounced pattern of early-onset risk-taking may signal a more troublesome course that can threaten their well-being in both the short and long term. As we noted in Chapter 6 on conduct disorders, concern is particularly warranted when high-risk behaviors begin well before adolescence, are ongoing rather than occasional, and occur among a group of peers who engage in the same activities (Lerner & Galambos, 1998). Indeed, most adolescent risk and problem behaviors co-occur, so an indication of one problem is often a signal that others may be happening or on their way (Hamburg, 1997).

Although experimentation with substances is commonplace among teenagers, it is not harmless; substance use lowers inhibitions, reduces judgment, and increases the risk of physical harm (Kilpatrick, Acierno, Saunders, Resnick, & Best, 2000). A survey of Canadian high school students found that alcohol use influenced the practice of, or involvement in, many other high-risk behaviors (Feldman, Harvey, Holowaty, & Shortt, 1999), most notably unsafe sexual activity, smoking, and drinking and driving. Moreover, girls who report dating aggression are 5 times more likely to use alcohol than girls in non-violent relationships, whereas boys are 2.5 times more likely (Pepler, Craig, Connolly, & Henderson, 2002). Teens who use alcohol and drugs are more likely to have sexual intercourse at an earlier age, have more sexual partners, and have greater risk of sexually transmitted diseases (Connolly, Furman, & Konarski, 2000). Substance use is also a risk factor for unhealthy weight control (such as taking diet pills or laxatives), suicidality, and mood and anxiety disorders (Rohde, Lewinsohn, & Seeley, 1996).

Associated Characteristics Turning more specifically to adolescents diagnosed with substance use disorders, many related symptoms and behaviors have been noted. These youths tend to use more than one drug simultaneously, with marijuana and alcohol the most common combination, followed by alcohol and hallucinogens (Chassin et al., 2003). They also have problems related to poor academic achievement, higher rates of academic failure, higher rates of delinquency, and more parental conflict (Chassin et al., 2003). Emerging research also suggests that heavy drinking may be physically more dangerous at 15 years of age than a few years later at age 20, because it may disrupt or disturb ongoing neurodevelopmental processes of myelination and synaptic pruning. When compared to teens with lower substance use levels, teens with long histories of heavy drinking performed poorly on tests of memory and attention, in addition to other signs of abnormal neurological development (Tapert, Granholm, Leedy, & Brown, 2002). Given these characteristics associated with SUDs, it comes as no surprise that there is high co-morbidity with many disorders covered in

Associating with deviant and substance-using peers increases access to, and adoption of, beliefs supporting drug use.

this textbook, especially ADHD and conduct problems (Brown & Abrantes, in press).

Causes

Personality Characteristics Similar to conduct disorders, several pathways and various risk factors have been associated with problematic substance use in adolescents, including personality characteristics, family history, family functioning, and peer involvement. Personality characteristics that may predispose a teen to substance use stem from basic temperament characteristics, such as increased sensation seeking (Wills & Dishion, 2004). Sensation seeking has been described as a preference for novel, complex and ambiguous stimuli, and has been linked to a range of high-risk behaviors. Although originally identified as a personality characteristic, recent debate has arisen about whether sensation seeking is better understood as a more complex phenomenon that has hereditary components, but is also influenced by socialization (Donahew et al., 1999). The implication of the more expanded conceptualization of sensation seeking is that it is a behavior that can be changed or shaped.

Regardless of whether sensation seeking is a personality trait or learned behavior, it has a clear link to adolescent substance use. A recent longitudinal study looking at two samples of adolescents between grades 8 and 10 found sensation seeking had strong predictive value for

Health-Related and Substance Use Disorders   **373**

both current and future marijuana and alcohol use (Crawford, Pentz, Chou, Li, & Dwyer, 2003). The relationship between sensation seeking and substance use was strongest for predicting marijuana, followed by alcohol, and to a lesser extent, cigarette use. Furthermore, there were both sex and ethnicity differences in levels of sensation seeking—males tended to score higher than females, and Caucasian adolescents tended to score higher than adolescents with other ethnic backgrounds. One of the most important findings from this study indicated sensation seeking was not stable over time, suggesting that there may be a window of opportunity to intervene and prevent sensation seeking.

There are also many attitudes that predict substance use; some relate directly to substance use and others are more general attitudes. Positive attitudes about substance use (i.e., high perceived benefit and acceptability, low perceived risk) and having friends who hold similar views, are attitudes and beliefs found to be associated with substance use (SAMSHA, 2002). Perceiving oneself to be physically older than same-age peers and striving for adult social roles are also risky attitudes. Finally, the way adolescents feel about school—in particular, how connected they feel to their school community predicts a lower risk for use of substances (Williams, Holmbeck, & Greenley, 2002). This concept of school connectedness is a nonspecific risk factor; that is, adolescents who feel engaged with and supported by their school tend to exhibit lower levels of risk behavior in a variety of domains (e.g., substance use, violence, sexual behavior, suicidality). In contrast, youths who are more alienated and not involved in school tend to report higher levels of these behaviors.

Family Functioning The lack of parental involvement and parent–child affection, inconsistent parenting and poor monitoring, and negative parent–child and interparent interactions are all factors that increase the risk of substance use (Brown & Abrantes, in press). An investigation of drinking initiation among sixth graders found that low parental expectations for abstaining from alcohol predicted earlier onset of drinking, and interacted with adolescents' own expectations. That is, if teens held positive expectancies about alcohol use and believed their parents did not hold strong expectations for them not to drink, they were much more likely to initiate alcohol use during grade 6. If they held these same beliefs but thought that their parents had clear expectations for them not to use alcohol, they were not as likely to initiate (Simons-Morton, 2004). This finding was present for males, females, Caucasian, and African American youths and demonstrates that even at a time when youths are turning toward their peers for cues about acceptable behavior, parent attitudes still play an important role.

Low parental monitoring, or the extent to which parents do not know "where their adolescents are and who they are with" has consistently emerged as a predictor of adolescent substance use (DiClemente et al., 2001; Jacob & Johnson, 1999). Interestingly, it seems to be the teens' perception of parental monitoring that is important. Presumably there is a correlation between adolescent perceptions of parental monitoring and actual parental practices. For example, research with six cross-sectional data sets (including 1200 low income African American youths) found a significant protective effect of perceived parental monitoring in predicting lower levels of substance use in each of the six cohorts (Rai et al., 2003).

Some researchers have found sex differences in the relationship between parental monitoring and substance use. For example, a study of 700 ninth and tenth graders found higher levels of parental monitoring were associated with less alcohol use in males, but had no affect on females' behavior (Borawski et al., 2003). In this same study, trust between adolescent females (but not males) and their parents was a strong deterrent for risk behaviors. Other family characteristics that have been linked to adolescent substance use include a parental history of substance abuse, poor parent–teen communication, and family conflict (Fergusson & Horwood, 1999).

Peers Given the importance that peers generally play in adolescents' lives, it is not surprising that peer influences play a large role in determining substance use. The role of peers seems to operate in more than one way. For example, associating with deviant and substance using peers causes youths to likely adopt beliefs supporting drug use (we tend to have similar beliefs to our friends). At the same time, affiliation with these peers also increases access to substances. In addition, the idea of a false consensus (i.e., the belief that everyone is doing it) exerts pressure on youths to engage in substance use. The extent to which individual teens think that their peer group is using substances is related to the individual's decision to use or not use substances (Musher-Eizenman, Holub, & Arnett, 2003).

Treatment and Prevention

Treatment outcomes for adolescents with SUDs have been somewhat disappointing. Approximately one-half of adolescents receiving treatment for substance use disorders (SUDs) relapse within the first 3 months following treatment, and only 20% to 30% remain abstinent at 1 year (Cornelius et al., 2003). Despite limitations, among the more promising treatments for adolescent substance abuse are those that involve the larger systems affecting the adolescent's behavior. Derived from interventions for conduct disorders, family-based approaches seek to modify negative interactions between family members, improve communication between members, and develop effective problem-solving skills to address areas of conflict (Brown & Abrantes, in press; Robbins et al., 2003; Williams & Chang, 2000). Multisystemic Therapy (MST), for example, involves intensive intervention that targets family, peer, school, and community systems, and has been especially effective in the treatment of SUDs among delinquent adolescents (Henggeler, Clingempeel, Brondino, & Pickrel, 2002; Randall & Cunningham, 2003). In general, the type of treatment indicated depends on levels of use and the individual's home environment. Adolescents with low to moderate levels of abuse and a more stable home environment are reasonable candidates for outpatient treatment, whereas those with more severe levels of abuse, an unstable living situation, or comorbid psychopathology may require an inpatient or residential setting (Brown & Abrantes, in press).

Because adolescence is a time of rapid, major transitions and changes in physical, emotional and social domains, prevention efforts related to substance use are being increasingly introduced at the elementary and secondary school levels. Facilitating successful transitions, for example, in the areas of romantic and peer relationships, sexual behavior, and healthy lifestyle choices, has the added major benefit of reducing multiple problematic outcomes in later life. Critical health-damaging behaviors that are preventable include substance use and abuse, unsafe sexual practices, and abusive behavior, which have a common context of peer and dating relationships (Wolfe, Jaffe, & Crooks, in press). These efforts are being recognized as having important payoffs in terms of reductions in future health problems and enhancement of personal goals (Irwin, Burg, & Cart, 2002).

Effective approaches to adolescent substance abuse prevention have addressed multiple risk factors from influences of the individual, peer, family, school, and community. Life Skills Training, a detailed and well-evaluated program, emphasizes building drug resistance skills, personal and social competence, and altering cognitive expectancies around substance use (Botvin & Griffin, 2002; Griffin, Botvin, Nichols, & Doyle, 2003). Because adolescents must receive consistent messages and reinforcement regarding pressures to use alcohol and drugs as well as develop effective refusal skills, societal messages about responsible use are emphasized to influence students' behavior (Perry et al., 2000). Prevention programs also target the social environment through the community and school norms and their efficacy to enact change, and they often include some level of parent involvement and education to improve parent-child communication about substance use (Greenberg, Domitrovich, & Bumbarger, 2000).

Key Terms

chronic illness, p. 357

dyssomnias, p. 350

encopresis, p. 352

enuresis, p. 352

insulin-dependent diabetes mellitus (IDDM), p. 360

metabolic control, p. 361

morbidity, p. 358

nightmares, p. 350

parasomnias, p. 350

psychological factors affecting physical condition, p. 358

sleep terrors, p. 350

sleepwalking, p. 350

somatoform disorders, p. 357

substance abuse, p. 370

substance dependence, p. 370

substance use disorders (SUDs), p. 370

InfoTrac College Edition

To research recent articles on the subject, go to:
www.infotrac-college/thomsonlearning.com

Enter search terms: TOILET TRAINING, SLEEP DISORDERS IN CHILDREN, HEALTH BEHAVIOR IN CHILDREN, CHILDREN (DISEASES SUBDIVISION), CHILDREN (HEALTH ASPECTS SUBDIVISION), PAIN IN CHILDREN, CANCER IN CHILDREN, DIABETES IN CHILDREN.

13 Eating Disorders and Related Conditions

"I feel like I'm disappearing, getting smaller every day but I look in the mirror—I'm bigger in every way"

—Lyrics from *Tunic (Song for Karen),* Sonic Youth. Written in memory of singer Karen Carpenter, who died of anorexia.

Although serious eating problems have only recently been considered mental disorders, bizarre and unusual eating habits have been documented for many centuries. The ancient Egyptians believed that illness could be avoided through monthly purges. The ancient Romans built the aptly described "vomitorium," where men purged their stomachs after overindulging in a heavy banquet—before returning to eat more. For centuries, voluntary as well as forced starvation has had both saintly and evil guises, whether as religious fasting or as a way to put an end to individuals who seemed possessed and bewitched. Today, as always, eating and starvation are connected to mental health problems and unusual cultural practices.

This chapter addresses several eating disorders and their related conditions. We begin with a discussion of disorders that occur during infancy or early childhood, followed by the developmental significance of childhood obesity, with rates that have reached epidemic proportions in recent decades (Lissau et al., 2004). Obesity is not a psychiatric disorder, nor is it associated with greater psychopathology (Brownell & Wadden, 1992). However, children with obesity are at risk of establishing unhealthy dieting patterns, often caused by social discrimination, that sometimes lead to chronic health problems and eating disorders.

The last section of the chapter addresses the two major eating disorders of adolescence and young adulthood: anorexia nervosa and bulimia nervosa. Anorexia nervosa emerges primarily among adolescent girls and may continue into young adulthood. It is often marked by an obsession with food and a drive for thinness that causes the person to lose sight of what is healthy. Bulimia nervosa is characterized by binge eating, followed by an effort to compensate, usually through self-induced vomiting but sometimes by fasting, by misusing laxatives, diuretics, or other medications, or by exercising excessively. Individuals with bulimia are also obsessed with food and with losing weight, but they do not experience the excessive weight loss associated with anorexia. Most persons with bulimia are within 10% of their normal weight, whereas individuals with anorexia refuse to maintain even a minimally normal weight.

Eating disorders have traditionally been only a medical concern. Studies of their etiology and treatment have focused on physiological mechanisms and the serious biological consequences associated with these disorders. Over the last quarter century, as mental health professionals began to study psychosocial factors—genetic makeup, cognitive and social development, and everyday experiences between infant and caregivers—they discovered that many of the same factors underlying other major childhood disorders significantly influence early feeding and eating disorders.

Unlike most disorders of childhood and adolescence described in this text, however, the causes of major eating disorders seem to be disproportionately related to sociocultural influences, rather than psychological and biological influences. What makes these disorders particularly unusual is that they are so closely linked to Western culture, where food is plentiful and a person's appearance, especially among young women, is so highly valued. The various types of eating disorders have increasingly become a problem for adolescents in Western society: It is the third most common illness in adolescent females (Fisher et al., 1995; Leichner, 2002).

How Eating Patterns Develop

Anyone who has ever watched a 2-year-old eat spaghetti knows that learning to feed oneself is not a simple process. In fact, feeding and eating problems are a normal part of development for most children as they learn through gradual approximations.

Normal Development

Troublesome eating habits and limited food preferences are among the most distinguishing characteristics of early childhood. Almost one-third of young children (under age 10) are described as picky eaters by their mothers. Picky eating is more common among girls than boys (Rydell, Dahl, & Sundelin, 1995; Marchi & Cohen, 1990), but its relationship to the emergence of eating disorders during adolescence or adulthood is unclear (Jacobi, Hayward, de Zwaan, Kraemer, & Agras, 2004). Beginning around age 9, girls are more anxious than boys about losing weight (O'Dea & Abraham, 1999).

These typical developmental patterns are, in part, a function of societal norms and expectations, especially for girls, as portrayed through images of thinness and attractiveness in magazines, television, and movies (Harrison, 2000). In addition, normal concerns about weight and appearance can be either reduced or increased by the comments of parents, friends, and romantic partners (Vincent & McCabe, 2000). The effects of the early parent–child relationship on fundamental biological processes such as eating and growth patterns are of paramount importance. Entering school is the next significant developmental landmark because of increasing social pressure to conform to narrow perceptions of desirable body type. Significantly, the desire to achieve an ideal image can turn into an obsession during adolescence (Sands, 2000).

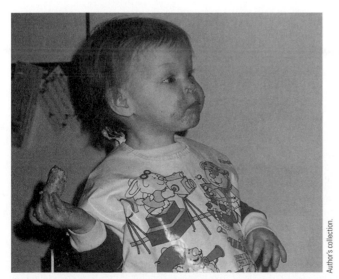

Eating disorders should not be confused with disorderly eating, a normal part of early development.

Author's collection.

Developmental Risk Factors

A developmental perspective of eating problems and eating disorders raises the intriguing possibility of a continuum of "eating pathology," that ranges from dieting to clinical syndromes, across all developmental periods (Attie & Brooks-Gunn, 1995). Figure 13.1 illustrates how problem-eating from a young age may contribute to being overweight or obese during childhood. For example, peers in elementary school often tease or reject overweight children, which, in turn, may cause a drive for thinness with the intention of improving their negative body image and acceptance (Lunner et al., 2000). **Drive for thinness** is a key motivational variable that underlies dieting and body image, among young females in particular, whereby the individual believes that losing more weight is the answer to overcoming their troubles and to achieving success (Sands, 2000). Such behavior, however, often creates the negative side effects of weight preoccupation, concern with appearance, and restrained eating, which increase the risk of an eating disorder (Polivy & Herman, 1999).

Early Eating Habits, Attitudes, and Behaviors Disturbed **eating attitudes** describe a person's belief that cultural standards for attractiveness, body image, and social acceptance are closely tied to one's ability to control diet and weight gain. Even among 7- to 10-year-olds, concerns about weight, dieting, and physique are common, suggesting that Western sociocultural values and preoccupation with body weight and dieting—factors that lead to eating disorders among vulnerable adolescents—may be internalized and expressed at a very early age (Griffiths et al., 2000; Thompson, Rafiroiu, & Sargent, 2003).

Researchers following samples of children and adolescents over several years have documented the continuity between eating problems during childhood (such as struggles at mealtime or disinterest in food) and the subsequent onset of a disorder. Examining patterns of eating problems over 8 years among normal adolescent girls, Graber, Brooks-Gunn, Paikoff, and Warren (1994) discovered that about 25% of them showed signs of a serious eating problem at each assessment. These teens had earlier pubertal maturation, higher percentages of body fat, concurrent psychological problems (especially depression), and poorer body image than teens without eating problems. Weight concerns (such as fear of weight gain, worry over weight and body shape, diet history, and perceived fatness), and body image, in particular, appear to be significantly related to the onset of eating problems and eating disorders during adolescence (Byely, Archibald, Graber, & Brooks-Gunn, 2000; Killen et al., 1996; Kotler, Cohen, Davies, Pine, & Walsh, 2001; Striegel-Moore et al., 2000). This constellation of physical and psychological factors, linked to early eating problems and distorted beliefs, signifies a considerable risk pattern for the development of persistent and possibly severe eating problems (Jacobi et al., 2004). The desire to appear thin may be responsible for the near-epidemic rates of referral of young people with eating disorders, especially bulimia, since the mid-1970s throughout Western society.

Transition into Adolescence Passage from childhood to early adolescence is full of unexpected challenges, not the least of which is undergoing the significant changes in body shape that require considerable adjustments in self-image. Along with pubertal development, dieting and weight concerns intensify during early adolescence, especially for girls, who experience a "fat spurt" associated with puberty that adds an average of 11 kilograms of body fat (Brooks-Gunn & Warren, 1985). The timing of matu-

Eating Problems

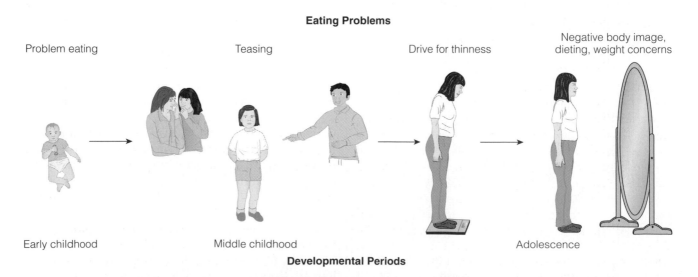

Problem eating   Teasing   Drive for thinness   Negative body image, dieting, weight concerns

Early childhood   Middle childhood   Adolescence

Developmental Periods

Figure 13.1 A developmental continuum of eating habits and disorders.

ration also affects dieting behavior, because girls who mature early are likely to be heavier than their late-maturing peers (Tyrka et al., 2000).

As we saw with younger children, girls report feeling worse about themselves than do boys, most likely because girls place greater emphasis on their self-image, including their body image. Although they readily acknowledge their interpersonal and social abilities, many postpubescent girls say they frequently feel fat and unattractive. In contrast, boys see themselves in a more positive light with respect to achievement, academic aspirations, self-assertion, and body image (O'Dea & Abraham, 1999). Contradictory societal messages implying that women must be successful in traditionally feminine and traditionally masculine roles place added pressure on young women to aspire to some elusive superwoman caricature (M. L. Levine & Smolak, 1992). Female adolescents who describe themselves in superwoman terms are more likely to associate thinness with autonomy, success, and recognition for their independent achievements; however, they are also significantly more at risk for eating disorders (Steiner-Adair, 1990; Striegel-Moore & Steiner-Adair, 1998).

The all-too-familiar interaction of pubertal weight gain, beginning of social dating, and threats to achievement status often promote body dissatisfaction, distress, and perceived loss of control in young adolescents, especially because they occur cumulatively over a relatively short period (M. L. Levine & Smolak, 1992). As you might expect, these changes also encourage smoking and other substance use among teenage girls, who feel that it protects them from the impulse to binge eat and the consequences of weight gain (Crisp, Sedgwick, Halek, Joughin, & Humphrey, 1999). (The importance of one's perceived body image is discussed later in the sections on anorexia and bulimia.)

Dieting and Weight Concerns Restrictive dieting has become a North American pastime, especially among youths, choosing to diet at very young ages. A large-scale survey of students in grades 5 through 8 found that approximately 60% had tried to lose weight in the past 7 days (Thompson et al., 2003), which is consistent with the notion these concerns often begin as early as elementary school and increase steadily throughout adolescence (Huon & Walton, 2000). A significant number of these students report feeling depressed after overeating and choose strict dieting as a form of weight control (Stice, Hayward, Cameron, Killen, & Taylor, 2000).

Chronic dieting seems strongly related to both gender and developmental factors. By mid-adolescence, about two-thirds of girls report being on a diet during the previous year, which is a twofold increase over elementary school. Among those who diet, about 10% of girls are chronic dieters—that is, someone who continuously remains on a diet or diets sporadically more than 10 times

during the year (French, Story, Downes, Resnick, & Blum, 1995). In contrast, only 2% of boys are chronic dieters.

Why does dieting sometimes lead to overeating? Decreasing caloric intake reduces a person's metabolic rate, which allows fat to remain in the cells, so weight loss is in fact impeded. This failure to lose weight sets the stage for a vicious cycle of increased commitment to dieting and vulnerability to binge eating. Psychological consequences also contribute to this cycle by creating what some researchers call the "false hope syndrome"—an initial commitment to change one's appearance leads to short-term improvements in mood and self-image, but this hope declines as feelings of failure and loss of control increase (Polivy & Herman, 1999). Loss of control may lead to binge eating, and purging is seen as a way to counteract the perceived effects of binge eating on weight gain. **Purging** is the voluntary use of vomiting, laxatives, or other methods to rid the body of food. It is invariably followed by disgust and self-recrimination, which prompts renewed vows of abstinence and sets the stage for the whole cycle of dieting, overeating, dietary failure, and affective distress to begin again (Heatherton & Polivy, 1992; McFarlane, Polivy, & McCabe, 1999).

Although dieting is clearly a risk factor in relation to the onset of eating disorders (Jacobi et al., 2004) it should be viewed in perspective: Many young persons diet in order to influence body weight and shape, yet only a small minority develop eating disorders (Garner, 1993a). Dieting can be harmful or beneficial, depending on the individual and the conditions. It is important to distinguish between dieting in individuals (especially children) who are not overweight, and dieting in individuals whose excess weight increases medical or psychological risk (Brownell & Rodin, 1994). There is a critical difference between watching your weight as part of a health-conscious lifestyle and chronic, unrealistic dieting that upsets your body's natural rhythm and balance.

A developmental approach to researching and treating eating disorders in youths is essential, yet few researchers have adopted a developmental perspective in their studies (Pratt, Phillips, Greydanus, & Patel, 2003). While many of the symptoms exhibited are similar to adult symptoms, the effects of those symptoms may have lasting and significant effects on adolescents' growth and development (Fisher et al., 1995). Adolescents with an eating disorder may be deprived of key social, emotional, and biological developmental processes that normally develop during this period (Bulik, 2002).

Biological Regulators

How do we know when to eat and how much to eat? For most of us, eating, like sleeping, is a natural process, controlled by biorythyms that have adapted successfully over time to the stress and strain of our individual lives. However, normal patterns of eating and growth, as well as the disorders based on disturbances in these patterns, are influenced by physical and psychological processes that continuously interact. In essence, your particular growth and weight pattern is based on the relation between your genes and your constitution, which governs your ability from early infancy to self-regulate your sleep and elimination patterns, appetite, and past and current nutritional patterns.

Metabolic rate, or balance of energy expenditure, is established based on individual genetic and physiological makeup as well as eating and exercise habits. Individual metabolism, in turn, serves to self-monitor and self-regulate behavior, which is why we may have trouble maintaining changes in weight or exercise. If you burn more energy than you take in, a state of chronic negative energy balance, or hypocaloric malnutrition, can occur. Malnutrition, even for brief periods of time, is followed by physical attempts to adapt, which can produce significant biological, behavioral, and psychological effects, including loss of circadian rhythm, increase in the release of growth hormones, dermatological changes with the loss of fatty tissue or hair pigmentation, and emotional and behavioral changes such as lethargy, depression, and apathy (Woolston, 1991). These changes can have long-term consequences if they occur during crucial developmental stages, or during the acquisition of fundamental cognitive abilities. Feeding and eating disorders thus merit careful study, because these problems can be overlooked when they are accompanied by more pronounced emotional and behavioral problems.

Body Weight Anyone who has tried dieting knows how hard it is to lose weight and keep it off. Weight loss is rapid for the first few weeks, but most of the lost weight returns with time. In fact, 90% to 95% of those who lose weight regain it within several years (Garner & Wooley, 1991). Why is body weight so resistant to change? For years the blame was primarily placed on the dieter's weak resolve or lack of willpower, but today researchers place more credence in the view that each person is biologically and genetically programmed to weigh within a certain, natural weight range. A person's natural weight is regulated around his or her own **set point,** which is a comfortable range of body weight that the body tries to "defend" and maintain (Garner, 1997).

In effect, people who gain or lose weight will experience metabolic changes that strive to bring the body back to its natural weight. If fat levels decrease below our body's normal range, the brain (specifically, the hypothalamus) compensates by slowing metabolism. We begin to feel lethargic, we increase our sleep, and our body temperature decreases slightly to conserve energy (which is why many persons with anorexia complain of being cold). In this state of relative deprivation, uncontrollable urges to binge are common because our bodies are telling us that they need more food than they are getting to function properly.

Similarly, the body fights against weight gain by increasing metabolism and raising body temperature in an effort to burn off extra calories. (Admittedly, this valiant effort is seldom enough to conquer the force of holidays and other feasts.) Because of its responsivity to change, researchers often compare the body's set point to the setting on a thermostat that regulates room temperature. When room temperature falls below a certain range, the thermostat automatically sends a signal to the heating system to increase the heat level until it again reaches the established temperature setting. Human bodies respond similarly to deviations in body weight by turning their metabolic "furnace" up or down (Garner, 1997).

Growth Under normal conditions, the biological mechanisms of growth are like the well-orchestrated ecosystem of a forest or a lake—a system of feedback loops, messenger signals, and major organs that work together to maintain a healthy balance. For humans, the biology of growth fundamentally involves the manner in which circulating hormones interact with available nutritional resources to produce changes throughout the skeletal system. The most significant hormonal determinants of growth rate during childhood are the *growth hormone* (GH) and *thyroid hormone,* with additional gonadal steroids kicking in during adolescence to produce a further growth spurt and skeletal maturation. From 50% to 75% of growth hormone production occurs after the onset of deep sleep in children and young adults (Woolston, 1991), which may explain why eating and sleep disorders coexist in some younger children (Lyons-Ruth, Zeanah, & Benoit, 1996).

Thus, individual growth depends on GH circulating throughout the body. The release of GH from the pituitary gland is determined by the hypothalamus and the higher brain structures that affect it (the limbic cortex and amygdala). These higher brain structures are involved in emotional sensation and response, which may account for the connection between eating and emotional disorders (discussed in the following section). Just as a thermostat determines the need to increase or decrease temperature, the hypothalamus senses the need to release more or less GH throughout the body. To accomplish this task, the hypothalamus releases two controlling hormones that exert opposite effects. The *growth hormone inhibiting factor* (i.e., somatostatin) essentially inhibits the GH response to internal signals of hunger, so we stop eating. In contrast, the *growth hormone releasing factor* has the specific function of telling our body when, how, and where to grow by releasing growth hormone from the pituitary.

Familiarity with these biological processes makes it easier to understand how the biological substrates of growth and metabolism can be thrown off balance by many factors that cause behavioral and physiological changes in children or young adults. Although we do not know if the majority of eating disorders are caused by biological abnormalities, or if the disorder itself creates a biological disruption, these underlying biological mechanisms influencing weight regulation are important to the understanding of eating disorders discussed in the remainder of this chapter.

SECTION SUMMARY

- Eating problems are common among children.
- Normal concerns about weight and appearance can be unduly influenced by parents and peers, sometimes resulting in eating disturbances.
- Early eating habits, attitudes, and behaviors that place undue concern on body image and a drive for thinness increase the risk of eating disorders.
- Increased dieting and weight concerns often accompany the transition into adolescence, especially for girls, which can lead to the emergence of unhealthy eating patterns.
- Attempts to reduce weight by dieting can lead to a vicious cycle of weigh loss and weight gain. Chronic dieting is associated with the onset of adolescent eating disorders.
- Normal patterns of eating and growth, as well as the later emergence of eating disorders, are influenced by biological processes such as one's metabolic rate and set point.

Feeding and Eating Disorders

Feeding and eating disorders that occur during infancy or early childhood constitute a general diagnostic category that includes several different developmental and behavioral problems associated with eating and growth that are evident from a very young age.

Feeding Disorder of Infancy or Early Childhood

Feeding disorder of infancy or early childhood is characterized by a sudden or marked deceleration of weight gain in an infant or a young child (under age 6) and a slowing or disruption of emotional and social development. This disorder can lead to physical and mental retardation and even death.

Prevalence and Development

Feeding disorders and failure to gain weight are relatively common, affecting up to one-third of young children (Lyons-Ruth et al., 1996). If not identified early, feeding disorders are particularly troublesome because they can have lasting effects on growth and development. Feeding disorders are equally common among males and females.

There is no typical developmental outcome among children with feeding disorders, probably because many of the factors that initially led to the problem in the first place also affect the course of the illness. However, the onset of feeding disorder commonly occurs during the first 2 years of life, which can lead to malnutrition with serious developmental consequences. If there is no medical reason for the failure to gain weight, such early onset is often associated with poor caregiving that includes abuse and neglect (APA, 2000). Thus, feeding disorder can lead to, or be the result of, a failure to thrive. As expected, the factors that lead to more serious problems over time include the degree and chronicity of malnutrition, the degree and chronicity of developmental delay, the severity and duration of the problems in the infant–caregiver relationship (Drotar, 1991).

Causes and Treatment

The etiology of feeding disorder has been studied from both biological and psychosocial perspectives, and the best conclusion at present is that many interacting risk factors influence how a child adapts to a certain level of caloric intake, and influence whether the child shows normal or abnormal behavioral development. Because feeding disorder has long been associated with family disadvantage, poverty, unemployment, social isolation, and parental mental illness, considerable attention has been focused on those concerns.

Maternal eating disorders have been identified as a specific risk factor for an infant's eating or feeding disorder. A failure of children to thrive by their first birthday has been associated with mothers who have a history of anorexia nervosa (Brinch, Isager, & Tolstrup, 1988) and disturbed maternal eating habits and attitudes (A. Stein, Murray, Copper, & Fairburn, 1995). Because the mother–child relationship during the early stages of attachment is critical, eating disorders shown by infants and young children may be symptomatic of a fundamental problem in this relationship (Lyons-Ruth et al., 1996). Thus, treatment regimens involve a detailed assessment of feeding behavior and parent–child interactions like smiling, talking, and soothing, while allowing the parents to play a role in the infant's recovery (D. A. Wolfe & St. Pierre, 1989).

Pica

Pica is the ingestion of inedible substances, such as hair, insects, or chips of paint, and primarily affects very young children and those with mental retardation. Infants and toddlers typically put things into their mouths, since taste

Infants and toddlers with pica may develop the disorder as a result of poor stimulation and supervision. They are at considerable risk of lead poisoning or intestinal obstruction.

and smell are their preferred ways of exploring the physical world. This disorder is one of the more common and usually less serious eating disorders found among very young children, yet an infant or young child who eats inedible, nonnutritive substances for a period of 1 month or longer may have a more serious problem (Linscheid & Murphy, 1999).

Although children with pica are also interested in eating normal foods, they persist in consuming inedible items as well. In most reported cases, the disorder begins during infancy and lasts for several months, at which time it remits on its own or in conjunction with added infant stimulation and improved environmental conditions. For individuals with mental retardation, however, pica may continue into adolescence before it begins to diminish gradually.

Prevalence and Development

Pica is more prevalent among institutionalized children and adults, especially persons with more severe impairments and mental retardation (Matson & Bamburg, 1999). Among children and adults with intellectual disabilities, the prevalence of pica ranges from 0.3% to 14.4% in the community, and 9% to 25% in institutions (Ali, 2001). The degree of severity is often related to the degree of environmental deprivation and mental retardation in individuals suffering from the more extreme forms of pica.

Causes and Treatment

Historically, pica was sometimes encouraged by fashions and social pressures that were similar to those affecting body image and appearance today. During the 18th and 19th centuries, for example, young girls sometimes ate lime, coal, vinegar, and chalk, because these substances were believed to produce a fashionably pale complexion (Parry-Jones & Parry-Jones, 1994).

Specific causes of pica have not been isolated. Pica may appear during the first and second years of life, even among otherwise normally developing infants and toddlers. The only distinguishing characteristic of these children is that they typically have poor stimulation in their home environment and may be poorly supervised. Because of the risk of lead poisoning or of obstruction in their intestine, pica can become a very serious and substantial problem for this group of infants or toddlers (Linscheid & Murphy, 1999; Woolston, 1991).

Researchers have also suspected and in some cases discovered vitamin or mineral deficiencies among persons with pica, although no specific biological abnormalities have shown a causal link to the disorder (Vyas & Chandra, 1984). Individual case studies have effective treatment of pica with vitamin supplements (e.g., Pace & Toyer, 2000). There is no evidence, except in cases of mental retardation, that genetic factors play a role in the etiology of the disorder. As mentioned earlier, however, pica in childhood constitutes a risk factor for the development of bulimia in adolescence.

Because of the limited number of treatment studies, no conclusions can be drawn about the relative success of any treatment for pica. Most clinical interventions for children with pica emphasize operant conditioning procedures, in which caregivers are shown how to reinforce the child for desirable behaviors such as exploring the room or playing with objects. Positive forms of attention, including smiling, laughing, and tickling, provide additional stimulation and are especially beneficial, because the disorder is often related to inadequate interaction with caregivers (L. Burke & Smith, 1999). Caregivers are also taught to keep the child's environment tidy and to remove or safely store dangerous substances.

Failure to Thrive

Failure to thrive (FTT) is a growth disorder associated with early feeding disturbances, which can have severe consequences for a child's physical and psychological development. Like feeding disorder, this associated disorder is embedded in social and economic disadvantage, and is often connected to inadequate or abusive caregiving that originates during early infancy. FTT is considered the final common pathway for multiple biological, psychological, and social factors that influence growth and viability of the infant or toddler (Attie & Brooks-Gunn, 1995).

Prevalence

FTT is characterized by weight below the 5th percentile for age and/or a deceleration of at least 2 standard deviations in the rate of weight gain from birth to the present, using standard growth charts for comparison (Budd et al., 1992; Lyons-Ruth et al., 1996). The eating and feeding disorders of early childhood previously described can lead to, coexist with, or be the result of failure to thrive.

Causes

A prominent controversy concerns the significance of emotional deprivation (lack of love) and malnutrition (lack of food). Investigators have argued that the infant with failure to thrive has been deprived of maternal stimulation and love, which results in emotional misery, developmental delays, and eventually, physiological changes. In one study, mothers of infants diagnosed with FTT were found to be more insecurely attached than mothers of normal infants. Mothers of failure-to-thrive infants were also more passive and confused, and either became intensely angry when discussing past and current attachment relationships or dismissed the attachments as unimportant and noninfluential (Benoit, Zeanah, & Barton, 1989). Children who have suffered from FTT as a result of early abuse exhibit poorer outcomes 20 years later than children whose FTT resulted from neglect, lack of parenting, or feeding difficulties (Iwaniec, Sheddon, & Allen, 2003).

These findings support the notion that eating and growth disorders during early infancy are highly related to the poor quality of the caregiver–child attachment, which is likely to reflect the insensitive treatment the caregiver received as a child. Poverty, family disorganization, and limited social support contribute to the likelihood of malnutrition and growth failure, as do infants who are difficult to feed and nurture because of temperament and acute physical illnesses (Budd et al., 1992; Drotar, 1991). Hospitalization to achieve weight gain, without consideration of ways to improve the parent–child relationship, is often insufficient to protect the child from further harm.

What is particularly striking about FTT is that a child's developmental outcome is highly related to the child's home environment. Significant changes in quality of care and in the emotional environment results in better adjustment 20 years later, even for children who failed to thrive because of abuse (Iwaniec et al., 2003). Moreover, early FTT may affect physical growth in childhood, but there is no evidence that it affects future cognitive functioning (Boddy, Skuse, & Andrews, 2000; Drewett, Corbett, & Wright, 1999; Mackner Black, & Starr, 2003). For these reasons, much of the etiology of FTT has focused on parental psychopathology that results in maltreatment of the child. In short, these associated feeding disorders may be a biological outcome of child abuse and neglect.

SECTION SUMMARY

- Pica is the eating of inedible substances. It affects mostly infants, toddlers, and some children with mental retardation.
- Feeding disorder of infancy or early childhood is characterized by a sudden or rapid deceleration of weight gain and a disruption in major developmental milestones. The disorder can have serious consequences.
- Feeding disorder of early childhood can lead to or result from failure to thrive (FTT), characterized by weight below the fifth percentile for age.

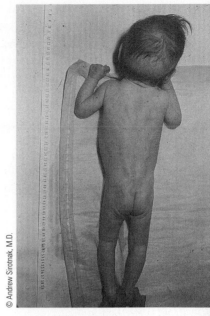

© Andrew Sirotnak, M.D.

This 4-month-old infant stopped gaining weight and developed failure to thrive.

Obesity

Childhood obesity is considered to be a chronic medical condition similar to hypertension or diabetes, and is characterized by excessive body fat. Persons with obesity regulate their weight appropriately, but their set point is elevated. Obesity is usually defined in terms of a *body mass index* (BMI), essentially a height-to-weight ratio, which is above the 95th percentile, based on norms for the child's age and sex.

As we have seen, more and more children and adolescents are caught up in a dieting cycle, and the reasons for wanting to lose weight are compelling. Obesity is severely stigmatized in North American society and carries many social and health hazards. Herein lies a fundamental conflict: The mass media powerfully promote the thin ideal in a land where fast food is widely available and accessible. Although obesity is clearly not a mental disorder, it can significantly affect a child's psychological and physical development. Obese children and adolescents are five times more likely than healthy children to experience an impaired quality of life, similar to children with cancer (Schwimmer, Burwinkle, & Varni, 2003).

Ellen, an 18-year-old who first became aware of her obesity when she was 9, describes her thoughts and feelings with respect to her weight:

It does matter to me what people say and think about my size. I guess the whole self-esteem thing began when I was little and other kids made fun of me for being fat—which basically I feel has continued until about a year ago. OK, fine, that is other people's rudeness and lack of sensitivity about someone's problem. Because of these a_holes I have always had to try harder at everything to prove I wasn't just a fat blob—there was a person living, breathing, caring inside that has to be dealt with. . . .

. . . I fell into the trap from about age 5 of letting others' images of a fat me be my own self-image. I have now let myself get to the point of only accepting others' concept of my new getting-thin person and don't allow myself to think thin. There are times when I get what I need—either trying a smaller-sized outfit, having a total stranger compliment me or a friend tell me I'm looking nice that day—I get high on those compliments and I can be fueled on them for a day or so and then I'm back to square one—who is this person in the picture?

I am scared. All my life I have wanted to be thin. . . . I know the day I weigh 170 . . . the number isn't going to make my mind snap into line and make me happy with my accomplishment.

The whole self-esteem thing seems as difficult if not more so than the actual weight loss. To lose weight you eat the right foods and exercise—the weight falls off—but to change how you feel about yourself is a whole different ball of wax. How do you change approximately 18 years of thinking about yourself one way when you are really no longer that person? How do I convince myself—do I write 500 times a day I am thin, worthwhile, nice, organized, good worker, pleasant personality, pretty, smart, logical mind, good advice giver? I know all these things about myself, but they are shadows of the tower of this whole f_ing weight thing. I need a bulldozer to knock over that tower. Where does the bulldozer come from—from inside? But where is it buried, where are the good feelings, the easiness with myself, the self-confidence that I do look nice and desirable? (From "Obesity," by J. P. Foreyt and J. H. Cousins, 1987, pp. 502–503. In M. Hersen and V. B. Van Hasselt (Eds.) *Behavior Therapy with Children and Adolescents.* Copyright © 1987 by John Wiley & Sons, Inc. Reprinted by permission of John Wiley & Sons, Inc.)

Ellen's self-disclosure captures the social and emotional dilemma that overweight children and adolescents so often face, which she characterizes as "the self-esteem thing." Many obese children and adults suffer the consequences of Western cultural attitudes that equate attractiveness and competence with thinness. As early as first grade, children are less likely to befriend overweight peers (Goldfield & Chrisler, 1995), and these attitudes intensify during adolescence (Striegel-Moore et al., 2000). Although her weight losses were slow, with the help of group and individual therapy, Ellen defeated the critical messages that had plagued her since childhood, allowing her to maintain her realistic goal of 170 pounds.

Prevalence and Development

For the past decade, alarm bells have been sounding over the fact that the number of children who are overweight or obese is increasing. For example, the proportion of children in North America who are overweight jumped from 5% in the 1960s to nearly 15% in the 1990s (Ogden, Flegal, Carroll, & Johnson, 2002). The obesity rate among boys age 7–13 nearly tripled between the early 1980s and the mid-1990s, while the prevalence of obesity among girls of the same age more than doubled (M. S. Tremblay & Willms, 2000). Even 10% of toddlers are considered to be very overweight or obese (Ogden et al., 2002).

Figure 13.2 discusses how children's meal portions make a huge difference in their caloric intake, which may account for the jump in the percentages of boys and girls who are overweight, especially over the last decade (see "Unsafe at any age"). This figure also shows how the BMI index is calculated and plotted (see "Is your child overweight?"). Note how the BMI rate is expected to increase with age, especially during adolescence. The exponential increase in fast-food restaurants and convenient junk foods can also contribute to the rise in obesity rates. On any given day, 30% of American children eat fast food (Bowman et al., 2004), and 50% of the caloric intake of youths in the United States comes from added sugar and fat (Muñoz, Krebs-Smith, Ballard-Barbash, & Cleveland, 1997).

Although obesity during infancy and obesity during later childhood are not strongly related, *childhood-onset* obesity is more likely to persist into adolescence and adulthood (Troiano, Kuczmarski, Johnson, Flegal, & Campbell, 1995). Even during their youth, individuals with obesity risk many health concerns, such as cardiovascular problems and elevated cholesterol and triglycerides (Hayman, Meininger, Coates, & Gallagher, 1995). Obesity during childhood may have long-term effects in that many lifestyle and behavioral choices associated with obesity develop during the school-age years (Carter, 2002). In fact, obesity is a major factor in one out of every 10 adult deaths in North America (Katzmarzyk & Ardern, 2004).

One troubling finding is that preadolescent obesity is a risk factor in the later emergence of eating disorders, especially for females, primarily due to the manner in which peers ignore or tease children who are obese. Obesity is strongly correlated with teasing by age-mates at an early

It's hard for children to stay lean when portions keep growing. A look at what Americans are eating, and how it's changing the shape of our bodies:

■ A traditional McDonald's burger with a 16-ounce Coke and a small order of fries carries 627 calories and 19 grams of fat.

■ Upgrade to a Big Xtra! with cheese, and 'super size' the drink and fries. Now your lunch packs 1,805 calories and 84 grams of fat.

Unsafe at any age: The percentage of American kids who are overweight has more than doubled since the 1960s.

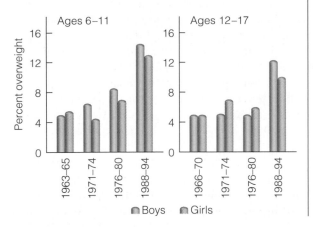

Is your child overweight? To find out, calculate the child's BMI, and plot it by age on one of the two graphs below:

$$\boxed{} \div \boxed{} \div \boxed{} \times 703 = \boxed{}$$

Child's weight in pounds — Height in inches — Height in inches again — Child's BMI

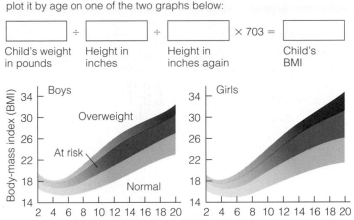

Figure 13.2 Bigger meals, bigger kids

Source: Newsweek, July 3, 2000, p. 43. Data from Centers for Disease Control and Prevention, and McDonald's.

age; teasing, in turn, predicts overall dissatisfaction with appearance and body image, and sets in motion a chain of restrictive and high-risk eating practices (Eisenberg, Neumark-Sztainer, & Story, 2003). Overweight children and adolescents may require assistance at an early age in developing a healthy, acceptable body image and eating patterns to resist the harmful and cruel pressures of early adolescence (Tanofsky-Kraff et al., 2004).

Similarly, in a 10-year follow-up of children who had received prior treatment for obesity, L. H. Epstein, Klein, and Wisniewski (1994) found the occurrence of bulimia to be 6% among the girls, which is 2–6 times the rate in the general population. Overweight students in middle- and high-schools use fewer healthy weight-control strategies (e.g., physical activity, healthier eating), and more unhealthy strategies (e.g., vomiting, diet pills, laxatives) than non-overweight students (Boutelle, Neumark-Sztainer, Story, & Resnick, 2002). Thus, a childhood pattern of being overweight may make it more difficult during adolescence and adulthood to achieve or maintain the culturally valued degree of thinness. The individual may then engage in the more extreme weight-control measures that may lead to an eating disorder.

Culture and SES While the percentage of overweight or obese children in the United States increased 3% to 5% in the 1990s alone, an alarming trend is the 10% increase

for African Americans and Mexican Americans over the same brief period (Ogden et al., 2002). Rates of obesity and eating disorders seem to increase upon exposure to Western culture (Becker, Burwell, Herzog, Hamburg, & Gilman, 2002; Walcott, Pratt, & Patel, 2003). A recent survey of 15 industrialized countries found that the United States had the highest percentage of overweight children, whether compared to age (13 vs. 15 years) or gender (Lissau et al,. 2004). Figure 13.3 shows how the United States compares with the next highest countries and the country with the lowest percentage of obese youths (Lithuania). It could be that the massive Western influence and globalization of the fast-food industries may continue to fuel the rapid rise in obesity rates. Other countries, however, have obesity rates that are catching up. For example, up to 10% of Chinese children are now overweight, and that number is expected to double within the next decade (*Time,* Aug. 25, 2003).

Minorities make up a significant proportion of low SES populations in North America. Fast food and junk food tends to be relatively inexpensive, thus rates of consumption of these foods are higher in low SES groups (Crister, 2003). An additional problem for low SES groups is that many of their neighborhoods are unsafe, and parents may keep their children at home out of safety concerns, which severely limits the child's opportunities for physical activities (Crister, 2003).

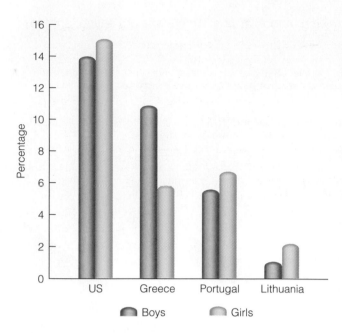

Figure 13.3 Childhood obesity among boys and girls in the United States, Greece, and Portugal (countries with the highest rates) compared to Lithuania (lowest rate).

Causes

Body weight, like height and hair color, is to a large extent a function of pedigree. By age 17, a child of two obese parents has 3 times the chance of being obese as a child of lean parents; moreover, if one sibling is obese, there is a 40% chance that a second sibling will also be obese (Garn & Clark, 1976). Although heritability may account for a substantial proportion of the variance in obesity, other individual and family-related factors, such as dietary and lifestyle preferences, also play a role (Klump, McGue, & Iacono, 2000).

Researchers have identified an obesity gene among mice that carries instructions to produce a protein called *leptin* (J. Friedman & Burley, 1995). Leptin deficiencies have been found among children with severe obesity (Montague et al., 1997). Persons with obesity are somehow resistant to leptin's effect, a situation similar to adult diabetes, in which a person usually produces insulin but it fails to work properly, causing sugar levels to go out of control. Leptin levels decrease with dieting, so leptin is less likely to provide feedback to the hypothalamus. Paradoxically, this connection between dieting and lower leptin levels may explain why dieting increases hunger and slows metabolism, and results in gaining back the lost weight (Laessle, Wurmser, & Pirke, 2000).

Despite strong biological forces, proper diet and exercise still play a critical role in determining a child's level of obesity. We not only inherit our biochemical makeup from our parents, we also look to them as routine instructors and role models as we develop our attitudes toward food and eating (Baker, Whisman, & Brownell, 2000). Parents determine what food is available, and they model an approach to exercise and diet. Inexperienced or highly pressured parents, however, may respond to any sign of distress in the infant or toddler by attempts to feed, by neglect, or by both reactions. Moreover, parents of obese children sometimes have greater difficulty setting limits, which has obvious implications for the child's tendency to overeat (J. B. Sherman, Liao, Alexander, Kim, & Kim, 1995). Like many other childhood disorders, obesity and poor eating habits are related to the degree of family disorganization, ranging from poor communication and a lack of perceived family support, to sexual and physical abuse (Neumark-Sztainer, Story, Hannan, Beuhring, & Resnick, 2000).

Treatment

Because of the combination of health and social consequences, the effort for prevention or intervention of childhood obesity consider not only the individual's health but also the family's resources. Except when there are serious medical complications, pediatricians often recommend proper nutrition to arrest weight gain until the child's height and weight are proportional. Note, however, that this nutrition program does not involve putting the child on a diet, since energy-restricted or unbalanced diets can place a child in jeopardy of medical or learning problems.

Family functioning not only influences eating patterns and obesity, it can also be instrumental in its prevention and treatment. To no one's surprise, any decrease in physical activity relative to food intake, such as eating while viewing television, can result in increased weight. Thus, efforts to curb childhood obesity often focus on addressing parents' knowledge of nutrition and increasing children's physical activity (Gable & Lutz, 2000).

Treatment should instill active, less sedentary routines. Obese and overweight children need parental encouragement, so many effective weight-loss programs teach parents and children ways to be more active (L. Epstein, Paluch, Gordy, Saelens, & Ernst, 2000). Children who are taught to be active and reinforced for being less sedentary (such as playing outdoors rather than watching television) increase their liking for high-intensity activity, which in turn reduces weight (L. H. Epstein et al., 1995). Similarly, pitfalls of weight-control plans must be anticipated and removed to allow the child's environment and daily routines to be altered. For example, parents may be advised not to bring high-calorie snack foods into the house and to monitor what they eat in front of their children, as obese children are highly sensitive to food cues in their environments (Braet & Crombez, 2003).

Other behavioral interventions focus on the goal of making the child's eating behaviors and physical activity patterns more adaptive and self-managed. Self-control procedures encourage children to set their own goals for diet, weight, and exercise, and teach them the necessary skills to achieve these goals with minimal outside directives from parents or therapists. For example, children may be taught to monitor the quantity and nature of their food, when they eat it, and who shared the meal; similar self-monitoring is encouraged for exercise goals (Foreyt & Cousins, 1989). Even if some children are unable to reach or maintain their intended goal of weight loss, self-control training encourages a greater sense of perceived control among children with obesity (Israel, 1999).

Lately, schools have begun to take a bigger role in helping young children develop a healthy body image and promote healthy eating habits (Kater, Rohwer, & Levine, 2000). The increase in the involvement of educators was sparked by the alarming number of overweight children over the past decade, as well as their concern that children may be inundated by cultural forces that place undue value on dieting and appearance. Given the greater awareness of the importance of early eating habits and the influence of cultural expectations, school-based programs now address children's and teens' desire for knowledge and support in developing a healthy body image and eating attitudes (Neumark-Sztainer, Martin, & Story, 2000; O'Dea & Abraham, 2000). As shown in Box 13.1, schools have been active in developing educational strategies that involve the whole school environment, from classroom education to cafeteria and vending machine selections, to training staff to recognize signs of disordered eating, and promote healthy eating attitudes (Littleton & Ollendick, 2003).

SECTION SUMMARY

- Childhood obesity is defined by a body mass index above the 95th percentile for children of the same age and sex.

- Obesity is not a mental disorder, but it can affect a child's psychological and physical development in significant ways.

- Obesity poses a risk for unhealthy dieting patterns, chronic health problems, and later-onset eating disorders.

- Obesity rates have increased dramatically in the past few decades, with a steeper increase in U.S. minority populations.

- The causes of obesity and related conditions (such as disturbed eating attitudes) include genetic predisposition and family influences such as poor communication, lack of support, and in extreme cases, sexual and physical abuse.

- Treatment and prevention efforts are often aimed at helping parents take an active role in children's proper nutrition and activity level. Schools contribute to this

A Closer Look

BOX 13.1 Junk Food Corporations in Schools

As education resources have decreased in recent years, schools boards have increasingly felt the need to seek funding elsewhere. Corporate sponsors have been quick to jump on board and sign contracts with school districts, allowing their products to be sold exclusively within the schools. In 2002, there were 240 U.S. school districts that had exclusive contracts with soft drink companies, and 60% of U.S. middle and high schools had soft-drink vending machines (Fried & Nestle, 2002). Junk food is readily available in most school cafeterias and vending machines, and is often cheaper than healthy foods.

The plethora of junk food and rising obesity rates have led to criticisms of corporate contracts, and some districts are starting to take action. In 2001, California passed a bill placing nutrition regulations on all foods sold in public schools (California State Education Code, §27), and Refreshments Canada, which represents 30 soft drink companies, announced in 2004 that it would voluntarily remove all soda drinks from Canadian elementary schools (Ministry of Education, Jan.6, 2004).

Source: Newsweek, July 3, 2000, p. 43.

effort by educating children in nutrition, exercise, and awareness of healthy eating attitudes and body image.

Eating Disorders of Adolescence

Eating disorders (EDs), as well as eating-related problems such as dieting and bingeing, are most likely to appear during two important periods of adolescent development: the early passage into adolescence and the movement from later adolescence to young adulthood (Attie & Brooks-Gunn, 1995). Early- and middle-childhood risk factors, such as eating problems, dieting patterns, and negative body image, clash with the ongoing challenges that confront adolescents. This clash leads some teens, particularly girls, to exert excessive control over their eating in a misguided effort to manage stress and physical changes. In some instances this controlled pattern of eating, coupled with other ill-conceived efforts to overcompensate for eating and weight changes (such as excessive exercise), leads to major eating disorders such as anorexia nervosa and bulimia nervosa.

Anorexia nervosa gained medical attention in 1873, when two doctors first described the disorder. Sir William Gull, an English physician, named the malady and described it for the first time as a specific disease. About the same time, in Paris, psychiatrist Charles Lasegue described anorexia from a social and psychological standpoint. Both investigators observed that the disease was most prevalent in the wealthiest social classes, which prompted Lasegue to propose a connection between a lack of parental affection (believed to be relatively common among wealthy families) and a preoccupation with food. Conflict between parents and children could drive some teenage girls to refuse food as an expression of their feelings of rejection. Accordingly, by the turn of the century, the prescribed treatment for anorexia was a "parentectomy," the removal of the child from the family home, which was combined with forcefeeding by any means necessary (R. Epstein, 1990).

References to the disorder we now refer to as bulimia date back to 6th-century descriptions of more than 40 individuals who displayed symptoms described as "insatiable voracity, morbid or canine appetite, with or without vomiting" (Parry-Jones & Parry-Jones, 1994, p. 288). Interestingly, almost all of these historical cases described males, perhaps because overeating was socially accepted as a sign of wealth or success, a reversal of the pattern today.

Ideal body sizes change with the times and with cultural preferences. Rubenesque figures were considered highly attractive and desirable until the late 19th century, when body image preferences were usurped by major cultural changes. During the Victorian period, refusing food was in keeping with prevailing social pressures. A hearty appetite was considered a wanton expression of sexuality and lack of self-restraint; women were expected to be passively uninterested in both sex and food. Thus, it became morally, spiritually, and socially desirable for women to refuse food, in response to shifting cultural norms for women's appearance and behavior (Brumberg, 1988).

According to physicians around the turn of the 20th century, anorexia nervosa was a symptom of inappropriate romantic choices, blocked educational or social opportunities, and conflicts with parents. Slimness symbolized asexuality and gentility, which implied a respectable amount of social distance from the working classes (Attie & Brooks-Gunn, 1995). Originating in the 1930s, today's attitudes and beliefs about women's ideal body size and appearance have been shaped by advertisers, film stars, clothing designers, and similar forces resulting in a prevailing cultural preference for slimness.

The meaning of food and eating for female identity, the role of family and social class in determining body image and food choices, and the use of weight regulation as a substitute for self-regulation and control in adolescence remain salient causes of eating disorders to this day. Within the last quarter century, additional aspects of eating disorders, such as the chronic refusal of food, emphasis on overactivity, and bulimic symptoms of bingeing and purging, have gained recognition as significant and potentially dangerous complications (Tyrka et al., 2000).

Anorexia Nervosa

Martha at age 16, on the road to a full recovery from anorexia nervosa

© M. Duisterhof

Martha

Obsessed with Food and Weight

At 14, Martha was five-foot-two and 69 pounds. And she thought that was normal. "I feel like I don't need to gain weight, like I'm at a reasonable weight now," reads her journal entry. Martha was in the hospital's Eating Disorders Program because her dieting, which had begun six months earlier as a health kick, had evolved into anorexia: an obsession with food and weight that was consuming her life and threatening to kill her.

"It started when I was 13," Martha explains. "Before I left for camp I had a physical, and the doctor said I should start eating more because I hadn't started menstruating. At camp, Martha started eating "kind of the way a dieter would. In the morning I would eat a bowl of peaches. And at first I'd eat the hot entrees, but then I started just having salads. My friends would say, 'Gosh, you're a healthy eater.' Martha staved off her period, but she embarked on a food fixation that would stay with her for years. Along with the new eating regimen came a strict exercise program. "It was gradual, but I really got into it: get home, no snack, do homework. In the afternoon, jump rope for ten minutes. Eat dinner. Every night I would do situps, leg lifts and jumping jacks. Fifty of each—no more, no less."

Her mother tried everything to get her daughter to eat. The dinner table became a nightly battleground as everyone focused on Martha's stubborn refusal to eat. "I wanted to eat, to be like other people, but I couldn't," she explains. "I thought a lot about the things that I wasn't going to allow myself to eat each day. I felt like eating was something I had total control of, and I didn't want to let go of that control."

No one was able to convince Martha that she was in danger. Finally, her doctor insisted that she be hospitalized and carefully monitored for treatment of her illness. It took a lengthy hospitalization and a good deal of individual and family outpatient therapy for Martha to face and solve her problems.

Today, at age 16, she weighs 100 pounds and [is] gaining. Martha plans to attend medical school and go into pediatrics—undaunted by the fact that she'll be in school for many, many years to come. "I'm not afraid to work really hard," she says. "I'm good at that." (Solin, 1995)

Martha is suffering from the restricting type of **anorexia nervosa (AN)**, an eating disorder characterized by

- the refusal to maintain a minimally normal body weight.
- an intense fear of gaining weight.
- a significant disturbance in the individual's perception and experiences of his or her own size.

As Martha's story shows, anorexia nervosa is a severe eating disorder with serious health and mental health consequences if left untreated. One of the most notable features of the psychopathology of the disease is that persons who have it deny they are too thin or that they have a weight problem. As a result, friends or family members often must insist on taking them to see a physician. Diagnostic criteria for anorexia nervosa are shown in Table 13.1.

Although the word *anorexia* literally means "loss of appetite," that definition is misleading because the person with this disorder rarely suffers appetite loss. Weight loss is accomplished deliberately through a very restricted diet, purging, or exercise. Although many persons occasionally use these methods to lose weight, the individual with anorexia intensely fears obesity and pursues thinness relentlessly.

Young persons who suffer from anorexia show a major distortion in how they experience their weight and shape. They may become obsessed with measuring themselves to see whether the "fat" has been eliminated. Thus, how they see themselves and how they relate to others

is often a function of their perceived shape and weight. To such an individual, weight loss is a triumph of self-discipline. Martha expressed this perfectly: "When I lose weight, I look better and I feel better." But with anorexia there is never enough weight loss: The person always wants to lose more weight to be on the safe side, and if not enough weight is lost one day, the person may panic and work extra hard to lose weight the next day.

The DSM-IV-TR specifies two subtypes of AN based on the methods used to limit caloric intake. This distinction has to do with possible differences in etiology and treatment avenues. In the **restricting type,** individuals seek to lose weight primarily through diet, fasting, or excessive exercise; in the **binge-eating/purging type,** the individual regularly engages in episodes of binge eating or purging, or both. Compared with persons with bulimia, those with the binge-eating/purging type of anorexia eat relatively small amounts of food and commonly purge more consistently and thoroughly. Approximately one-half of the individuals meeting criteria for AN engage in binge-eating and purging behavior (APA, 2000).

The significantly different characteristics exhibited by the two subtypes have clinical implications. Individuals who regularly binge and purge tend to have stronger personal and family histories of obesity, and higher rates of

BOX 13.2 Anorexia Danger Signals

- Losing a great deal of weight in a relatively short period
- Continuing to diet, although bone-thin
- Reaching a diet goal and then immediately setting another for further weight loss
- Being dissatisfied with appearance, even after reaching a weight-loss goal
- Preferring to diet in isolation rather than with a group
- Experiencing the loss of monthly menstrual periods
- Engaging in strange eating rituals and/or eating extremely small amounts of food
- Becoming a secret eater
- Being obsessive about exercising
- Experiencing long-lasting depressions
- Engaging in bingeing and purging

Source: American Anorexia/Bulimia Association (1996)

---

so-called impulsive disorders that include stealing, drug misuse, self-harm, and mood problems. In contrast, the restricting subtypes are highly controlled, rigid, and often obsessive individuals (Garner, 1993b).

Finally, the initial clinical presentation of persons with anorexia is usually quite distinctive, as serious medical complications due to malnutrition are imminent. By the time most individuals are brought to a professional, their average weight is 25% to 30% below normal for their age and height (Hsu, 1990). Accordingly, many physical symptoms of starvation are usually evident. Cessation of menstrual cycle (amenorrhea) is invariably present in postmenarcheal young women, as are dry and sometimes yellowish skin; fine downy hair on the trunk, face, and extremities; a sensitivity to cold; and cardiovascular and gastrointestinal problems. Box 13.2 lists anorexia danger signals that suggest the need for further assessment and intervention.

Bulimia Nervosa

Phillipa
A Well-Kept Secret

Phillipa developed bulimia nervosa at 18. Like Martha, her strange eating behavior began when she started to diet. But Phillipa began gaining weight because she was eating a lot at night. With the extra weight came self-loathing. "I felt like my body was in the way of me being successful at school, and getting dates. I looked in the mirror several times a day, thinking 'I don't even want to

be in this body.' There wasn't a minute in my life that I didn't think about some aspect of how I looked."

Although Phillipa dieted and exercised to lose weight, unlike Martha she regularly ate huge amounts of food and maintained her normal weight by forcing herself to vomit. Phillipa often felt like an emotional powder keg—angry, frightened, and depressed. Unable to understand her own behavior, Phillipa thought no one else would either. She felt isolated and lonely. Typically, when things were not going well, she would be overcome with an uncontrollable desire for sweets. She would eat pounds of candy and cake at a time, and often not stop until she was exhausted or in severe pain. Then, overwhelmed with guilt and disgust, she would make herself vomit.

Her eating habits so embarrassed her that she kept them secret until, depressed by her mounting problems, she attempted suicide. Fortunately, she didn't succeed. While recuperating in the hospital, Phillipa was referred to an eating disorders clinic where she became involved in group therapy. There she received medications to treat the illness, and the understanding and help she so desperately needed from others who had the same problem. With a smile, Phillipa explains: "It taught me that my self-worth is not absolutely correlated with my appearance or what others may think of me." (National Institute of Mental Health [NIMH], 1994b)

Of the two major forms of eating disorders afflicting adolescents and young adults, **bulimia nervosa (BN)** is far more common than anorexia. The DSM-IV-TR diagnostic criteria listed in Table 13.2 note that the primary hallmark of bulimia nervosa is binge eating. Because most of us overeat certain foods at certain times, you may ask "What exactly is a binge?" As noted in the criteria, a **binge** is an episode of overeating that must involve an objectively large amount of food (more than most people would eat under the circumstances), and lack of control.

No specific quantity of food constitutes a binge—it is the context of the behavior that must also be considered. Overeating at celebrations or holiday feasts, for example, is not considered bingeing. Although most binge eaters report overeating junk food rather than fresh fruits and vegetables, the amounts of food they consider a binge vary widely. On average, eaters consumed roughly 1500 calories during a binge, about 5 times more than they normally ate at one time (Rosen, Leitenberg, Fisher, & Khazam, 1986).

Persons with bulimia attempt to conceal binge eating out of shame. Although binges are not planned, a ritual may form wherein the person, sensing no one around, makes a split-second decision (on the way home from a late-night party, for example) to stop, purchase, and con-

Table 13.2

Main Features of DSM-IV-TR Diagnostic Criteria for Bulimia Nervosa

A. Recurrent episodes of binge eating. An episode of binge eating is characterized by both of the following:

(1) Eating, in a discrete period of time (e.g., within any 2-hour period), an amount of food that is definitely larger than most people would eat during a similar period of time and under similar circumstances

(2) A sense of lack of control over eating during the episode (e.g., a feeling that one cannot stop eating or control what or how much one is eating)

B. Recurrent inappropriate compensatory behavior in order to prevent weight gain, such as self-induced vomiting; the misuse of laxatives, diuretics or enemas, or other medications; fasting; or excessive exercise.

C. The binge eating and inappropriate compensatory behaviors both occur, on average, at least twice a week for 3 months.

D. Self-evaluation is unduly influenced by body shape and weight.

E. The disturbance does not occur exclusively during episodes of anorexia nervosa.

Specify type:

Purging Type: During the current episode of bulimia nervosa, the person has regularly engaged in self-induced vomiting or the misuse of laxatives, diuretics, or enemas.

Nonpurging Type: During the current episode of bulimia nervosa, the person has used other inappropriate compensatory behaviors, such as fasting or excessive exercise, but has not regularly engaged in self-induced vomiting or the misuse of laxatives, diuretics, or enemas.

Source: Reprinted with permission from *Diagnostic and Statistical Manual of Mental Disorders, DSM-IV-TR, Fourth Edition, Text Revision,* Copyright 2000 by the American Psychiatric Association.

sume massive quantities of food. Typically, binge eating follows changes in mood or interpersonal stress, but it may also be related to intense hunger from dieting or to feelings about personal appearance or body shape. Although these feelings may dissipate for awhile, the depressed mood and self-criticism usually return (R. A. Gordon, 2000).

The second important part of the diagnostic criteria involves the individual's attempts to compensate somehow for a binge. **Compensatory behaviors** are intended to prevent weight gain following a binge episode, and include self-induced vomiting, fasting, exercising, and the misuse of diuretics, laxatives, enemas, or diet pills. The

criteria subdivides bulimia into *purging type,* in which there is regular self-induced vomiting or regular overuse of laxatives or diuretics to reduce fluids and solids, and *nonpurging type,* in which the individual uses other forms of compensation, such as fasting or excessive exercise.

Approximately two-thirds of persons with bulimia engage in purging. By far the most common compensatory technique after an episode of binge eating is induced vomiting—stimulating the gag reflex with the fingers or another instrument—a method reported by 80% to 90% of individuals with bulimia who seek treatment. Vomiting produces immediate relief from physical discomfort and reduces fear of gaining weight.

A different pattern of compensatory behavior is reported among community samples of individuals who fit criteria for BN (i.e., individuals who have not sought help but are identified through random interviews by phone or in person). Figure 13.4 shows the various compensatory behaviors of males and females who met all criteria for bulimia nervosa, based on their responses to part of the Ontario Health Survey, in which over 8000 individuals were interviewed in person about their health habits. Among these nonreferred subjects, vigorous exercise and strict diet are the preferred means of compensating for bingeing. In contrast to clinical samples, only 1 in 5 reported vomiting as a compensatory behavior (Garfinkel et al., 1995).

Research with community (nonclinical) samples has not identified any significant differences between persons with bulimia who purge and those who do not (Stice & Fairburn, 2003). Subtypes of BN that have been found in both community and clinical samples are dietary and

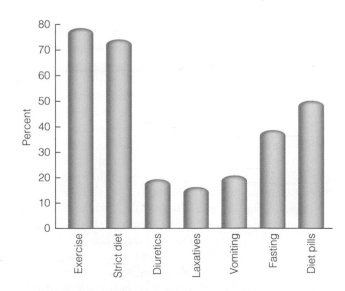

Figure 13.4 Compensatory behaviors of full-syndrome bulimia nervosa among community samples.
(Data from Garfinkel et al., 1995)

dietary-depressive subtypes (Grilo, Masheb, & Berman, 2001; Stice & Agras, 1999; Stice & Fairburn, 2003). Dietary symptoms (e.g., restraint, purging) are central features of BN, but only a subset of people with BN exhibit both dietary restraint and depressive affect. Young women who have the dietary-depressive subtype exhibit more eating pathology, social impairment, psychiatric comorbidity, and persistence of bulimic symptoms over 5 years than women with only the dietary subtype (Stice & Fairburn, 2003).

Like those with anorexia, adolescents and adults with bulimia are often described as rigid and absolutistic (displaying an all-or-nothing attitude) in their thinking (Joiner, Katz, & Heatherton, 2000; Lilenfeld et al., 2000). They see themselves as either completely in control or completely out of control, and view everyday events in extremes of either black or white. Martha revealed such thinking by her comment, "I felt like eating was something I had total control of, and I didn't want to let go of that control." Phillipa also expressed absolutistic thinking, attributing her woes to one thing and one thing only: "I felt like my body was in the way of me being successful at school, and getting dates." These beliefs relate to the DSM-IV-TR criteria, which stress the importance of body shape and weight to self-evaluation. Young women with bulimia, as well as those with anorexia, have greater dissatisfaction with their body proportions and distort their true body size, behaviors that are more strongly connected to cognitive factors, such as biases in attention, memory, and selective interpretation or judgment, than with any actual problem with perceptual ability (Cash & Deagle, 1997).

The medical consequences of chronic BN can be significant, although they are not as severe as the consequences that result from anorexia. Common physical complaints include fatigue, headaches, puffy cheeks (due to enlarged salivary glands). The permanent or significant loss of dental enamel, especially from the inside surface of the front teeth, is due to the contact of the acidic stomach contents with the teeth. Among females, menstrual irregularity or amenorrhea may occur, although it is not clear whether these disturbances are related to weight fluctuations, other nutritional deficiencies, or stress. Electrolyte imbalances due to purging behavior are sometimes severe enough to cause significant medical problems. Box 13.3 lists bulimia danger signals that point to the need for further assessment and intervention.

Binge eating disorder (BED) (APA, 2000) has become increasingly widespread during this age of abundant fast food and obesity. Although similar to the binge eating found in bulimia, BED is without the compensatory behaviors. It involves periods of eating more than other people would with a feeling of a loss of control. Researchers differ on whether binge episodes are objective overeating (e.g., over 1000 calories) or an individual, subjective feeling of losing control (e.g., eating two cookies on a

strict diet). Youths define overeating in a variety of ways, including the amount and types of food eaten, emotional consequences after the binge (e.g., feeling guilty), and the individual's reasons for overeating (Neumark-Sztainer & Story, 1998).

The prevalence of BED among youth is approximately 3.1% for girls, and 0.9% for boys (Ackard, Neumark-Sztainer, Story, & Perry, 2003). The mounting concern over BED is justified not only by the higher rates of obesity and weight loss attempts (Ackard et al., 2003), but also for the negative mental health correlates. Youths with BED score lower on body satisfaction and self-esteem, higher on depressive mood, and are more likely to report that weight and shape are very important to their overall feelings about themselves (Ackard et al., 2003). Perhaps the most shocking finding in this study was that over 25% of both boys and girls meeting criteria for BED reported that they had attempted suicide.

Binge eating also highlights difficulties within obese populations. In a study of obese children and adolescents seeking treatment for obesity, those who binged more often had lower self-esteem, although they did not differ in weight (DeCaluwe, Braet, & Fairburn, 2003). It could be that the subjective loss of control during binges is more damaging to mental health than the overeating itself.

Prevalence and Development of Anorexia and Bulimia

Distinguishing between the two major eating disorders of adolescents and young adults can be difficult, because anorexia and bulimia share many features. Members of both groups have distorted body images and nervous feelings after eating. Whereas persons with anorexia are 15% or more below normal weight, persons with bulimia are within 10% of normal weight. Also, persons with anorexia engage in binge eating only occasionally and typically avoid forbidden food, whereas those with bulimia binge frequently on forbidden food, then purge to control their weight.

Eating disorders can overlap with other mental disorders, such as depression and schizophrenia, making some features obscured and the disorder misdiagnosed (Foreyt & Mikhail, 1997). However, in terms of cognitive beliefs and self-image, only patients with anorexia show an intense drive for thinness and a disturbance in their perception of body image.

Among female adolescents and young adults, studies have estimated the prevalence of anorexia nervosa at 0.3% (van Hoeken, Seidell, & Hoek, 2003) and bulimia nervosa at around 1% (Gowers & Bryant-Waugh, 2004). Both disorders are more rare among males, with an estimated female to male ratio of 11:1 for AN and about 30:1 for BN (van Hoeken et al., 2003). However, the prevalence of all forms of eating disorders, specifically among children and adolescents, may be much higher. A community study of 14- and 15-year-old Norwegians revealed prevalence rates of any ED of 8% in girls and 2.5% in boys, and lifetime (i.e., ever experienced) prevalence rates of 17.9% and 6.5%, respectively (Kjelsås, Bjørnstrøm, & Götestan, 2004).

The diagnosis of eating disorders is difficult among youths who are still maturing physically, cognitively, and emotionally. For example, the vast majority of the disorders found in the previous study were diagnosed as **Eating Disorders—Not Otherwise Specified (EDNOS)** (APA, 2000), a category of eating disorders that includes problems that do not quite fulfill criteria for AN or BN. The EDNOS category is less stringent than DSM-IV-TR criteria for AN or BN, and therefore is sometimes more appropriate for adolescents (Lock & le Grange, in press). Because about one-half of adolescents with eating problems don't meet the diagnostic criteria for BN or AN (Turner & Bryant-Waugh, in press), professional organizations, such as the Society for Adolescent Medicine, have advised clinicians to set lower thresholds for diagnosing adolescents with eating disorders (i.e., not requiring they meet all the DSM criteria) (Golden et al., 2003; Reijonen, Pratt, Patel, & Greydanus, 2003).

There is increased recognition that eating disorders are more common among young men than originally believed. Males are also subjected to powerful media images, although not to the same extent as females. The increasingly muscular male body ideal may be contributing to body dissatisfaction, disordered eating, and harmful weight-control or body-building behaviors (Labre, 2002). Young men with eating disorders show the same clinical features as young women. However, men show less of a preoccupation with food or a drive for thinness, and place more emphasis on athletic appearance or attractiveness as the rationale for their disturbed eating behavior (Geist, Heinmaa, Katzman, & Stephens, 1999). Because eating disorders are considered a problem affecting primarily women, young men may be underdiagnosed (Nelson, Hughes, Katz, & Searight, 1999).

Ethnic and Cross-Cultural Considerations Although eating disorders have long been associated with Caucasian females, it is difficult to make simple generalizations regarding ethnicity (Jacobi et al., 2004). In their review of eating disturbances among American minorities, Crago, Shisslak, and Estes (1996) found that Hispanics had equal, Blacks and Asians lower, and Native American women higher rates compared to Caucasians. Some types of eating problems also differ among ethnic groups. For example, African Americans have lower rates of body dissatisfaction and weight concerns than Caucasians, but similar rates of bingeing (Streigel-Moore et al., 2000).

Cross-culturally, there is some support for the belief that exposure to Western ideals of weight and appearance (known as *acculturation*) leads to increased rates of eating disorders and disturbances in other cultures (Lake, Staiger, & Glowinski, 2000). Minority adolescents from upper-middle-class families are particularly at risk because of their motivation to be accepted into the dominant White culture, or as a result of being caught between two different sets of cultural values (Yates, 1989).

Like African American women, Latina women were thought to possess a kind of cultural immunity to eating disorders, but current trends disprove that.

Developmental Course Anorexia nervosa usually strikes during adolescence, between the ages of 14 and 18, although it does occasionally affect older women, men, and prepubertal children. It often begins insidiously with dieting that gradually leads to life-threatening starvation (Lock & le Grange, in press). Sometimes the onset of this dieting and starvation pattern is linked to stressful events, such as being teased about weight, onset of menses, school transitions, and so forth.

Although the symptoms of anorexia are quite specific and well defined, its developmental course and outcome are highly variable. Findings averaged across 119 studies of persons with anorexia show that the rate of mortality is

cathy®
by Cathy Guisewite

Significant (5%); of the survivors fewer than one-half show full recovery, one-third show fair improvement, and one-fifth continue on a chronic course (Steinhausen, 2002).

Most common is a fluctuating pattern that involves a restoration of normal weight followed by relapse (Eckert, Halmi, Marchi, Grove, & Crosby, 1995). As the individual loses weight and becomes dangerously malnourished, she is hospitalized and begins to show signs of improvement. A significant number of patients—between 6% (Sullivan, 1995) and 10% (APA, 2000; Herzog, Kronmueller, Hartmann, Bergman, & Kroeger, 2000)—die from medical complications or suicide. Features correlated with fatal outcome are longer duration of illness, bingeing and purging, comorbid substance abuse, and comorbid affective disorders (Herzog et al., 2000). Although the disorder itself is rare, it has the highest mortality rate of any psychiatric disorder and is a leading cause of death for females 15–24 years old in the general population (Sullivan, 1995).

Full-blown symptoms of BN usually emerge in late adolescence and young adulthood, although episodes of bingeing and purging and a preoccupation with weight begin much earlier (Lock & le Grange, in press). A noteworthy aspect of bulimia is that binge eating often develops during or after a period of restrictive dieting (Hsu, 1990). Because of the guilt and discomfort caused by binge eating, purging follows as compensation (Wilson, Becker, & Heffernan, 2003). Bulimia can either follow a chronic course or occur intermittently, with periods of remission alternating with binge eating and purging (Fairburn, Cooper, Doll, Norman, & O'Connor, 2000). However, it is not easy to reverse the developmental course. Because the habits and cultural influences that led to the disorder are so powerful, a chronic pattern of disturbed

eating may be established, such as secretive bingeing at social gatherings, which in turn leads to further problems.

Follow-up studies of patients with bulimia indicate that they have a greater chance of recovery than patients with anorexia—between 50% and 75% show full recovery over several years (Collings & King, 1994; Herzog et al., 1999). The best predictors of a more favorable outcome were younger age at onset and higher social class. A family history of alcohol abuse suggests that once the teen left the negative family circumstances, improvement was made (Collings & King, 1994). Importantly, bulimia responds favorably to treatment that disrupts its cyclical course.

Similar to the study of long-term outcomes of persons with bulimia, studies of eating behaviors and attitudes among college student populations suggest that maturing into adulthood and getting away from powerful social pressures that emphasize thinness help many women escape from chronic dieting and abnormal eating. A 10-year follow-up study of body weight, dieting, and symptoms of eating disorders among male and female college students found both encouraging and discouraging results (Heatherton, Mahamedi, Striepe, Field, & Keel, 1997). On a positive note, women reduced their eating disorder behaviors and increased their body satisfaction ratings. However, body dissatisfaction and desires to lose weight still remained relatively high, and one-fifth of the women who met clinical criteria for an eating disorder in college also met criteria 10 years later. Men, on the other hand, were prone to weight gain after college, and many reported increased dieting or disordered eating in the 10 years following college. Although disordered eating tends to decline during the transition to early adulthood, body dissatisfaction remains an issue for many young adults (Heatherton et al., 1997).

Causes

Why would people starve themselves to near emaciation or eat to the point of illness? The dramatic effects on physical and psychological well-being that can result from eating disorders have inspired many theories. No single factor has been isolated as the major cause of any type of eating disorder, and searching for causes is complicated by the "chicken and egg" problem of causation: Do neurobiological processes disrupt eating patterns, or do eating problems lead to changes in neurobiology?

Explaining the gradual degenerative process of forming an eating disorder requires acknowledging the contribution of all three major etiological domains—biological, sociocultural (including family and peers), and psychological—which can operate singly or in combination to disturb self-regulation in any given individual. We are all familiar with the cultural emphasis on thinness, self-control, and exercise, which creates idealized images that define attractiveness. We'll see that these sociocultural aspects play a very powerful role in initiating disturbed eating patterns.

Biological Dimension   There is reasonable agreement that neurobiological factors play only a minor role in precipitating anorexia and bulimia. However, these factors may contribute to the maintenance of the disorder because of their effects on appetite, mood, perception, and energy regulation (Lock & le Grange, in press).

It makes sense to suspect that biological mechanisms (a gene? a neurochemical process?) acting together or alone are responsible for corrupting normal regulatory functions. A slight twist places the problem on the individual who disrupts his or her normal regulatory processes in an ill-conceived attempt to achieve weight or diet goals. This disruption may cause biological changes throughout the central nervous and neuroendocrine systems that, in turn, create more disruption. Thus, it also makes sense that success at controlling important bodily functions like hunger or appetite may lead to unnatural eating habits resulting in an abusive eating pattern.

Genetic and Constitutional Factors.   Eating disorders tend to run in families. Research conducted over the past decade has found that relatives of patients with anorexia or bulimia, especially female relatives, are 4–5 times more likely than persons in the general population to develop an eating disorder (Kaye et al., 2000; Strober, Freeman, Lampert, Diamond, & Kaye, 2000). Studies on twins, in which genetic factors are better controlled, indicate that the heritability of anorexia is estimated to fall between 58% (Wade, Bulik, Neale, & Kendler, 2000) and 88% (Jacobi et al., 2004), suggesting that shared genetic and environmental risk factors both play an etiological role. Heritability of binge eating and vomiting have been estimated at 46% and 70%, respectively (Sullivan, Bulik, & Kendler, 1998).

If bulimia and anorexia are connected to genetic factors, what exactly is inherited? Some people may have a biological vulnerability that interacts with social and psychological factors to increase their chances of their developing an eating disorder (Bulik, Sullivan, Wade, & Kendler, 2000). For example, inherited personality traits, such as emotional instability and poor self-control, would predispose an individual to be emotionally reactive to stress, which, in turn, could lead to impulsive eating in an attempt to relieve the feelings associated with stress.

Neurobiological Factors.   Because serotonin regulates hunger and appetite, this neurotransmitter has been focused on as a possible cause of both anorexia and bulimia (Monteleone, Brambilla, Bortolotti, & Maj, 2000). Essentially, the presence of serotonin leads to a feeling of fullness and a desire to decrease food intake, so a decrease in serotonin leads to continuous hunger and greater consumption of food at one time—the perfect condition for bingeing.

One of the strongest findings in support of the serotonin explanation for bulimia comes from studies investigating the relationship of diet to the availability in the brain of the serotonin precursor *tryptophan*. Meals that are rich in protein or low in carbohydrates decrease tryptophan; carbohydrate-rich meals increase it. Put another way, bingeing on sweet and starchy foods creates conditions in the brain that produce more serotonin, which, eventually, leads to a sense of fullness. Binge eating (which usually involves high-carbohydrate food), especially for women, may increase the availability of tryptophan, thereby temporarily increasing brain serotonin and forestalling the compensatory response (Cowen, Anderson, & Fairburn, 1992). It is still not known, however, whether problems related to the availability of serotonin in the brain are due to dieting or are a premorbid characteristic (Jacobi et al., 2004).

Because of their similarities to other types of addictions, researchers have questioned whether anorexia and bulimia are a form of "food addiction." Such an addiction may be biochemically caused (say, by a serotonin imbalance), or could even be sociocultural—women suffer from eating disorders more often than men, while men suffer more often from substance use disorders and gambling (M. Reid & Burr, 2000). Although eating disorders do not have the same dependency features as other addictions, they tend to be associated with substance abuse and dependence in clinical and community samples (Wilson, 1999). This connection is not causal, however, and it is more likely that their co-occurrence is related to personality or other characteristics.

In addition to connections between depression and eating disorders, scientists have found biochemical similarities between people with eating disorders and people with obsessive-compulsive disorder (OCD). Just as serotonin levels are known to be abnormal in people with de-

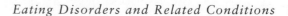

pression and people with eating disorders, they are also abnormal in patients with OCD (Rastram, 1992). Moreover, many persons with bulimia show obsessive-compulsive behavior as severe as that shown among patients diagnosed with OCD, and patients with OCD often have abnormal eating behaviors.

In summary, some neurobiological abnormalities are found among persons with eating disorders, although these problems are probably the result, rather than the primary cause, of semistarvation or the binge/purge cycle. Understanding how normal eating patterns may initially become disturbed requires a close look at the cultural and psychological components of eating disorders.

Social Dimension The features of contemporary Western culture could be considered prerequisites for eating disorders (Pinel, Assanand, & Lehman, 2000). Personal freedom, an emphasis on instant gratification, the availability of food any time of night or day, lack of supervision, and the cultural ideal of diet and exercise for weight loss add up to powerful influences (Attie & Brooks-Gunn, 1995). These factors contribute to a drive for thinness and an emphasis on body image and appearance as key to success. There is some evidence that bulimia, but not anorexia, is related primarily to Western culture. Examination of history and of other cultures reveals instances of anorexic behaviors fo physical appearance or control issues; however, this is not the case for bulimia (Keel & Klump, 2003).

Sociocultural Factors. Adolescents' concerns about undereating and overeating are legendary, which causes us to question: What aspects of Western culture drive someone, most likely a young woman, to overcome the body's natural rhythm and force it into a punishing and dangerous routine of semistarvation or frequent purging?

It is well known that for most young white females in middle- and upper-class society, self-worth, happiness, and success are determined primarily by physical appearance, and most eating disorders represent an attempt to feel good with respect to personal appearance and self-control. In reality, body size itself has little or no long-term correlation with personal happiness and success; one's self-concept and self-efficacy are more important. However, as Brownell (1991) explains, a collision may be occurring between our culture and our physiological boundaries, because the average North American woman between the ages of 17 and 24 is heavier by 5 to 6 pounds than 20 years ago, and she is not satisfied with her body image.

It appears that as fashion models and media images of women have gotten smaller, adolescent girls have become unhappier. Today, only 15% of teenage girls feel happy "the way I am" (USA Weekend, 1998), compared to 29% just 10 years earlier (Brown & Gilligan, 1992). The pursuit of the thin ideal is so pervasive that girls today consider weight loss and being skinny to be more important than sexual issues, alcohol and drug abuse, mental health, disease, and environmental issues (Vagisil Women's Health Center, 2000). Perhaps this accounts for the abundance of "pro-eating disorders" websites that are gaining in popularity (see Box 13.4).

Few would argue that eating disorders are more common in women because of sex-role identification. Images of women in the 21st century and assumptions about what it is to be feminine are based largely on the idea that girls must be pretty (i.e., not fat) to draw attention and praise from others, whereas boys are admired for their athletic or academic accomplishments. Body build and self-esteem are correlated for girls, but not for boys, by the time they reach the fourth grade (Striegel-Moore, Silberstein, & Rodin, 1986). This finding endorses the view that the relationships on which young women's identity and self-worth depend are overly influenced by physical attractiveness and body image.

Sex-role identification is closely tied to cultural norms and expectations, so it is not surprising that women in different cultures do not share the same perception of ideal body weight. Cogan, Bhalla, Sefa-Dedeh, and Rothblum (1996) looked at cross-cultural trends in attitudes on obesity and thinness and how they affect dieting patterns in young women from the United States and Ghana. Ghanaian women, compared with American women, rated larger body sizes as ideal for both sexes. American women scored higher on measures of eating restraint and eating-disordered behavior, and perceived the experience of being overweight as interfering with social acceptance. A disturbing trend indicates that a greater drive for thinness is emerging among young African American girls in the United States in relation to increased peer criticism about weight and appearance (Streigel-Moore et al., 2000).

The forces of culture, combined with gender-based expectations, are powerful determinants of one's perception of ideal body size and associated eating and dieting patterns. Fortunately, these sociocultural patterns may be gradually shifting toward more healthy norms of eating behaviors and lifestyle choices. Eating disorder symptoms, dieting, and body dissatisfaction declined significantly on college campuses between 1982 and 1992 (Heatherton, Nichols, Mahamedi, & Keel, 1995). The increase in public health advertisements, talk shows and television shows devoted to discussions of eating disorders and to healthy lifestyles, may be responsible for raising awareness and prevention of these various disorders and dieting patterns (Heatherton et al., 1995). Perhaps as a further result of these awareness efforts, sociocultural messages about the importance of proper nutrition and body satisfaction are changing as well.

Family Influences. Researchers and clinicians have placed considerable importance on the role of the family, and parental psychopathology in particular, in considering causes of eating disorders. They have argued that alliances, conflicts, or interactional patterns within a family

BOX 13.4 **Pro-eating Disorders Websites**

The Internet can be a good source of information, but it can also help people who are isolated by a disorder to seek out similar others for mutual support, and not necessarily in healthy ways. With the advent of widespread Internet use has come a proliferation of pro-anorexia and pro-bulimia websites, or "pro-ana" and "pro-mia" as referred to on these sites. People on these sites reinforce each other's views, share tips on purging and fooling others, and defend their "lifestyle choice." Disturbingly, pro-ana websites are much more numerous than pro-recovery or professional services websites (Chesley, Alberts, Klein, & Kreipe, 2003). Web servers, recognizing the potential harm, quickly shut down these sites on their servers, but many are still out there.

Excerpts from pro-ana websites and on-line journals:

"You'll be FAT if you eat today. Just put it off one more day.

Guys will want to get to know you, not laugh at you and walk away.

Starve off the parts you don't need. They're ugly and drag you down.

Nothing tastes as good as thin feels."

"What's the nutritional information for the chocolate laxatives? If anyone knows, please let me know. I can't believe I'm obsessing over the calorie and carb[ohydrate] content of a laxative."

"I crave to stop eating all together [sic]. But my boyfriend would give me those sad looks again when my shirt's off and my ribs are protruding and each vertabrae is perfectly noticeable. I miss the bones, I miss them I miss them."

"I was doing good fasting wise today til [sic] my friend was waving sour gummy worms in my face (they are a weakness . . .). I had a few, fat free, but still I should have been stronger . . . So I'm all pissed at myself now . . . I'll prob. [sic] take a laxi [sic] to make me feel

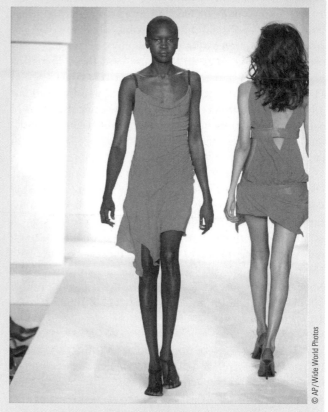

© AP / Wide World Photos

"That's the designer's dream size . . . On their sketches, the body is like a hanger. The smaller the sample, the better it drapes—the natural shape of the body distorts their clothing . . . It's almost like the body is not present." (Cosmopolitan, 2001).

better . . . sometimes I am SO happy to have ana/mia, my loving sisters . . . but then the other ½ it's like I feel so f—cked up and I wish to be normal . . . we have such a love-hate relationship . . . love thy bones ladies!"

---

may play a causal role in the development of eating disorders among some individuals (Minuchin, Rosman, & Baker, 1978). Accordingly, a teen's eating disorder may be functional in that it directs attention away from basic conflicts in the family to the teen's more obvious (symptomatic) problem.

Because of the importance of the family in shaping a young adolescent's values, it is understandable that family processes may contribute to an overemphasis on weight and dietary control. For example, a mother who is critical of her daughter's weight or who diets frequently herself and encourages her daughter to diet, may unintentionally become a co-conspirator in the development of an eating

disorder (Fairburn, 1994). Similarly, parents who drink heavily or abuse drugs (Garfinkel et al., 1995) or who are often absent, uninterested, demanding, or critical (Fairburn, 1994) may lay the groundwork for the emergence of bulimia and other disorders in their children. Young people recovering from an eating disorder may also face scrutiny and criticism by other family members, which can lead to poorer recovery (Herzog, Kronmueller, Hartmann, Bergmann, & Kroeger, 2000).

Early clinical suspicions that child sexual abuse could be a risk factor for eating disorders have been supported by ongoing investigations of this important issue (Jacobi et al., 2004). Based on a general population sample, women with bulimia were about 3 times more likely to have been sexually abused as children (35%) than were women without the disorder (12.5%) (Garfinkel et al., 1995). Similar findings have been reported among population samples of school-aged youths, whereby youths at risk for disordered eating reported more negative perceptions of their families and parents, and more sexual or physical abuse experiences (Neumark-Sztainer, Story, Hannan, Beuhring, & Resnick, 2000). In addition, sexually abused children report many of the early risk signs of eating disorders, such as higher levels of weight dissatisfaction and purging and dieting behavior (Wonderlich et al., 2000).

This connection between abuse and eating disorders should be tempered by the awareness that childhood sexual abuse is a general risk factor for psychopathology, rather than a specific risk factor for eating disorders. Such events are not uncommon in the backgrounds of individuals with eating disorders, as well as those with other psychiatric disorders (Fairburn, 1994). Presumably, childhood sexual abuse is associated with many undesirable adolescent and adult outcomes, of which eating disorders are prominent. (These issues are discussed further in Chapter 14.)

The importance of family factors has led to valuable treatment approaches, as we will see later in this chapter. Nonetheless, family factors must be considered in conjunction with individual and sociocultural factors to explain why the particular features of eating disorders emerge in some families with such dynamics but not in others.

Psychological Dimension Understanding the role of psychological processes in the expression of eating disorders requires keeping in mind the powerful social and cultural forces noted previously. External pressures to look thin and be in control of one's weight and appearance interact with certain psychological characteristics to increase the risk of an eating disorder, especially during important developmental transitions. This is a complex, interactive process embedded in multiple layers of biological, familial, personality, and environmental factors. Understandably, this complexity makes causal connections difficult to pinpoint.

Consideration of the psychological dimensions related to eating disorders grew out of the pioneering efforts of Hilda Bruch (1962, 1973), who was the first to propose that self-starvation among persons with anorexia was related to their struggle for autonomy, competence, control, and self-respect. She linked this struggle most closely to parental failure to recognize and confirm their child's emerging independent needs. This set in motion further confusion that can lead to the principal symptoms of anorexia—disturbance in body image, the inability to recognize and respond to internal sensations, to emotions; and the all-pervasive feelings of ineffectiveness and loss of

self-control. Her early work set the stage for the cognitive-behavioral interventions used today. She proposed gradual but deliberate relabeling of misconceptions and errors in thinking resulting from faulty developmental experiences, and encouraged patients to learn healthy ways of expressing their thoughts and feelings in a genuine and more direct fashion (J. A. Silverman, 1997).

Arthur Crisp, another pioneer in the understanding and treatment of eating disorders, considers anorexia to be a type of phobic avoidance disorder in which the phobic objects are normal adult body weight and shape. He describes this fear metaphorically as a flight from growth (Crisp, 1997). As a result of family and cultural influences, a young female may begin to perceive herself as being fat as she reaches puberty and starts to change into a more adult size and weight. In response, she tries to pursue and maintain her prepubertal weight as a way to avoid the unwelcome aspects of her own growth. This pursuit becomes a vicious cycle, of course, because trying to maintain one's prepubertal body weight meets powerful biological resistance, so she continues her pursuit of weight loss as "insurance" against these unrelenting forces of nature. In effect, a person with anorexia fears loss of control over her attempts to avoid growth, which often translates into a fear of weight gain above 95–100 pounds. Like Hilda Bruch's insights, this explanation has led to important treatment efforts.

Adolescents with anorexia are clinically described as being obsessive and rigid, showing emotional restraint, preferring the familiar, having a high need for approval, and showing poor adaptability to change (Casper, Hedeker, & McClough, 1992). The psychological dimensions underlying these clinical features constitute a triad of personality features: avoidance of harm, low novelty seeking, and reward dependence (Strober, 1991). These features render persons vulnerable to developmental events, like puberty, that disrupt their carefully maintained sense of self.

In a 10-year follow-up of anorexia patients, their obsessions, compulsions, and social interaction persisted, even among those who had their weight restored, leading the researchers to conclude that these problems may be constitutional rather than a result of the disorder (Nilsson, Gillberg, Gillberg, & Rastam, 1999). Moreover, more than 4 out of 5 persons with adolescent-onset anorexia experienced at least one episode of major depression or dysthmia within 10 years after onset (Ivarsson, Rastam, Wentz, Gillberg, & Gillberg, 2000). Researchers believe the common association between anorexia and depression may be due to genetic or neurobiologic factors that increase the risk of both disorders (Wade et al., 2000).

Adolescents with bulimia exhibit somewhat different personality characteristics involving mood swings, poor impulse control, and obsessive-compulsive behaviors (Aragona & Vella, 1998). In the study by Garfinkel et al., (1995), persons with bulimia had a threefold increase in the lifetime occurrence of major depression and at least a doubling of the rate for anxiety disorders. Specific phobias, agoraphobia, panic disorder, generalized anxiety disorder, and alcohol dependence were all more elevated among bulimic individuals than nonbulimic community members. Moreover, abuse of alcohol or stimulants to control appetite is also present in about one-third of the clinical samples of adolescents with bulimia (APA, 2000). Depression, in particular, may co-occur with bulimic symptoms in adolescent girls because they are reciprocally related—each one increases the risk for onset of the other disorder (Stice, Burton, & Shaw, 2004). Finally, sex differences also emerge in relation to psychological factors. Females with chronic bulimic symptoms report more drive for thinness than do males with similar chronic symptoms, but these same males report more perfectionism and interpersonal distrust (Joiner, Katz, & Heatherton, 2001).

Eating disorders are almost always accompanied by other disorders. Community samples, in which adolescents are randomly selected and interviewed for psychiatric disorders, reveal that almost 90% of persons fitting the criteria for an eating disorder also have other Axis I disorders, usually depression, anxiety, or OCD (Lewinsohn, Striegel-Moore, & Seeley, 2000; Zaider, Johnson, & Cockell, 2000). Although genetic links certainly play a role, researchers have also focused on personality characteristics, such as perfectionism, rigidity, or neuroticism, which may be a common link between these disorders (Goldner, Srikameswaran, Schroeder, Livesley, & Birmingham, 1999; Podar, Hannus, & Allik, 1999). For example, persons who are high on the need for perfectionism and who also experience high levels of daily stress are more likely to exhibit symptoms of depression (Hewitt & Flett, 1993). Similarly, individuals who score high on perfectionism and also perceive themselves as being overweight have a greater risk of bulimic symptoms (Joiner, Heatherton, Rudd, & Schmidt, 1997). Simply stated, a discrepancy between one's actual self (in this case, perceived weight) and ideal self (a strive toward perfectionism) increases the likelihood of eating problems, especially among women.

Let's look at a practical example of how the preceding information can be put into dynamic perspective. The adolescent with bulimia or anorexia feels her efforts to restrict her diet and lose weight are ways of gaining control over her life and of becoming a better person, beliefs that were formed during childhood and become operational when she faces the challenges of early adolescence. What develops into the rigidity of anorexia or the battle for control of bulimia may begin as a moderate diet. A teenager may unwittingly begin a dangerous eating pattern because of her dissatisfaction with body weight and shape, and her efforts initially are rewarded by weight loss and a sense of greater control and self-worth, such as former gymnast Erica Stokes describes in Box 13.5.

The transition from dieting to eating disorder may be prompted by the extra attention from peers for what appears to be dramatic willpower and weight loss. Therefore, powerful psychological needs may be at the root of the eating disorder, because the disorder itself is a way to cope with strong feelings that the person otherwise does not know how to express or resolve (Maloney & Kranz, 1991). This dynamic process accounting for the many determinants of eating disorders is depicted visually in Figure 13.5.

Because of high-profile cases of gymnasts and other performers with eating disorders, the demands of competitive sports and performing arts have been blamed for these problems. Both types of activities emphasize appearance, so involvement in them has been cited as a risk factor for developing an eating disorder because of the pressure to be thin (Owens & Slade, 1987). Although elevated rates of subclinical symptoms of eating disorders have been found among female dancers and other athletes involved in weight-related sports, athletes are not any more likely to have full syndromes of AN or BN (Jacobi et al., 2004).

Among high-school samples of adolescents, sports participation is a weak predictor of symptoms of eating disorders (French, Perry, Leon, & Fulkerson, 1994; Fulker-

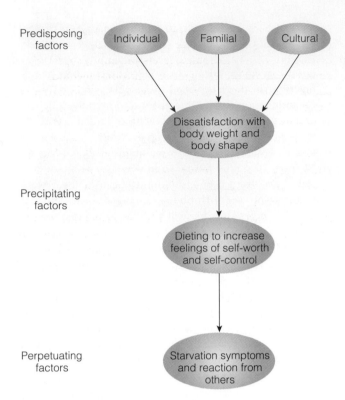

Figure 13.5 A dynamic perspective on the determinants of eating disorders.

Source: From "Pathogenesis of Anorexia Nervosa," by D. M. Garner, 1993, Lancet, 341, 1631–1635. Copyright © 1993 by Lancet. Reprinted by permission.

son, Keel, Leon, & Dorr, 1999). The psychological, social, and environmental variables we have discussed, such as self-esteem and the pressure to dress and behave in a certain manner, explain a larger proportion of the variance for being at risk than explained by dietary and physical activity variables. Like any other students, athletes who show even mild signs of an eating disorder should be given immediate attention (Garner, Rosen, & Barry, 1998).

Treatment

Psychological interventions for eating disorders often include some form of individual and/or family-based psychotherapy, sometimes accompanied by medical interventions. However, the evidence base for the effectiveness of any form of intervention is surprisingly weak, especially for anorexia nervosa (Gowers & Bryant-Waugh, 2004; p. 63). The discouraging news, based on a systematic review of treatment studies, is very limited evidence exists to support specific interventions for AN at any age, especially for adolescents (Treasure & Schmidt, 2003). The benefits of psychological treatments for BN, on the other hand, are more encouraging. More than 30 controlled studies have supported the efficacy of cognitive-behavioral approaches that focus on modifying abnormal eating be-

haviors and related cognitions (Fairburn & Harrison, 2003).

Most adolescents with AN, BN, and related eating disorders can be managed on an outpatient basis. Hospitalization is usually only required for a small percentage of adolescents with anorexia who have serious complications due to comorbid diagnoses, or are at high physical and/or psychiatric risk. Inpatient treatment is usually brief, as long as psychological counseling and outpatient psychotherapy are made available (Gowers & Bryant-Waugh, 2004). However, because psychological treatments are under pressure to show effectiveness in increasingly briefer periods of time, there is growing concern that high-risk patients are released too soon, before they reach their normal body weight (Becker, Grinspoon, Klibanski, & Herzog, 1999), primarily to reduce costs (Pratt et al., 2003).

Pharmacological Pharmacological treatments are gaining recognition for assistance in the management of eating disorders, although they are not considered to be the initial treatment of choice (Gowers & Bryant-Waugh, 2004). Because of the strong association between anorexia and bulimia and the affective disorders, serotonin-reuptake inhibitors (SSRIs) such as fluoxetine (Prozac) have been used to treat eating disorders and some forms of obesity (Dunner et al., 1999). The weight-loss benefits of this drug were discovered serendipitously during clinical trials of the drug's ability to regulate mood. It was believed that people with obesity load up on carbohydrates to elevate mood, and that a sense of well-being could be achieved artificially by regulating serotonin levels.

To date, however, no drug has proved useful or effective for treating symptoms of anorexia among adolescents, and none has consistently improved long-term weight maintenance, changed a distorted self-image, or prevented relapse (Lock & le Grange, in press). In contrast, there is a consensus that antidepressants have a useful role in the treatment of bulimia, but probably not as the initial treatment of choice (Compas et al., 1998). Persons with bulimia may respond favorably to antidepressants and serotonin-reuptake inhibitors, as long as they are continued for 6 months or so, and are accompanied by psychosocial treatments with proven effectiveness, as described in the next section (Agras et al., 1994; Leitenberg et al., 1994). Although drug therapy has its use, especially in cases that are not responding to psychological therapy, cognitive-behavior therapy (CBT) remains a more effective choice than medication alone (Ferguson & Pigott, 2000; Gowers & Bryant-Waugh, 2004).

Psychosocial The presence of both emotional and physiological problems in eating disorders requires a comprehensive treatment plan, which ideally consists of a treatment team with an internist, a nutritionist, a psychotherapist, and a psychopharmacologist. Once an eating disorder has been diagnosed and any other illness has been medically ruled out, the clinician determines whether the individual can be treated as an outpatient. Family engagement then may become necessary, to assist family members in managing their fears and worries, as well as to enlist their cooperation. For younger patients, family involvement is often necessary and practical, since parents are responsible for their child's well-being and can offer important directives and guidance that increase successful treatment. In some cases, resolution of family problems, such as parental psychopathology, family isolation, and a poor parent–child relationship, are crucial to recovery from an eating disorder. Recovered patients consider the resolution of family and interpersonal problems as pivotal to their recovery (Lock & le Grange, in press).

The etiology and course of anorexia result in a disorder that is less responsive to treatment than bulimia; nevertheless, inroads are certainly being made. The initial phase of treatment must involve the restoration of weight and the monitoring of any medical complications that might arise. However, restoring a patient's weight may be the easier part of the process. Many patients regain weight initially (especially if placed in hospital), but the pattern of weight loss and distorted beliefs returns, unless careful attention is paid to family and individual factors that initially led to the overemphasis on control of eating.

The lack of empirical support for any treatment for AN is partially due to the difficulty of randomly assigning individuals with this life-threatening condition to a control group. Nonetheless, the "best practices" for treating this disorder have evolved based on existing clinical wisdom and modified research designs. One alternative is to assign patients to two different "known" treatment conditions to compare their relative effectiveness (without a no-treatment or placebo control group). Robin, Siegel, and Moye (1995), for example, compared behavioral family systems therapy (BFST) with ego-oriented individual therapy (EOIT) over a 16-month treatment regimen that involved 22 adolescents with anorexia. BFST emphasized parental control over eating, cognitive restructuring, and problem-solving communication training, whereas EOIT emphasized building ego strength, adolescent autonomy, and insight. Both treatments led to improvements in body mass and restoration of menstruation, and produced significant reductions in negative communication and parent–adolescent conflict. These changes were maintained 1 year later, which is a critical period for recovery, and were replicated in more recent work (Robin et al., 1999).

As mentioned, family therapy is the initial treatment of choice for persons with anorexia who are younger and living at home. The facade of togetherness expressed by family members of girls with anorexia is often seen by clinicians as an attempt to disguise covert or overt aggression and avoid conflict. Family-based interventions, therefore, are often required to restore healthy communication patterns (Lock, 2002). By involving the whole family, therapists can attend to the family's attitudes toward body shape and body image that, to an adolescent, can be perceived as subtle but critical judgments. Once weight is restored to within acceptable levels and family support becomes more available, cognitive-behavioral methods similar to the methods described previously can focus more specifically on the patient's rigid beliefs, self-esteem, and self-control processes.

Family therapy does not necessarily mean that all family members are seen at the same time (i.e., conjoint family therapy); in some cases seeing family members separately is the best approach. For instance, instead of challenging family members' negative interaction patterns, such as conflict avoidance and alliances (similar to the early work of Minuchin et al., 1978), therapists encourage parents to mobilize the family's resources to take control of their adolescent's eating patterns, raise parents' morale, and engage all members in further therapy. Focusing on the nature of the illness and its treatment helps to avoid further criticizing of the child and placing blame on family members (Dare & Eisler, 1997). Working with parents separately from their teenage daughters (which of course makes it impossible to challenge interaction patterns and alliances) has been effective as conjoint methods, and has been even more beneficial for families with high levels of criticism and hostility (Le Grange, Lock, & Dymek, 2003; Eisler et al., 1998; 2000).

As noted, the most effective current therapies for bulimia involve cognitive-behavioral treatment delivered individually, or by involving the family unit (Fairburn & Harrison, 2003; Pike, Walsh, Vitousek, Wilson, & Bauer, in press). Cognitive-behavioral therapists change eating behaviors by rewarding or modeling appropriate behaviors, and help patients change distorted or rigid thinking patterns that may contribute to their obsession. CBT has become the standard treatment for bulimia nervosa, and forms the theoretical base for much of the treatment for anorexia (Garner & Needleman, 1997). This evidence-based method is the treatment that patients choose whose age does not mandate family therapy, and whose symptoms are moderate to severe.

The clinical application of CBT has been expanded to address specific cues that trigger the urge to binge or to vomit; it also addresses the underlying interpersonal issues that bother some patients. The goals of CBT are to modify abnormal cognitions on the importance of body shape and weight, and to replace efforts at dietary restraint and purging with more normal eating and activity patterns (W. G. Johnson et al., 1996). CBT for treatment of bulimia includes several components (Gowers & Bryant-Waugh, 2004). Patients are taught at first to self-monitor their food intake and bingeing and purging episodes, as well as any thoughts and feelings that trigger these episodes. This is combined with regular weighing; specific recommendations on how to achieve desired goals, such as the introduction of avoided foods and meal planning, designed to normalize eating behavior and curb restrictive dieting; cognitive restructuring aimed at habitual reasoning errors and underlying assumptions relevant to the development and maintenance of the eating disorder; and regular review and revision of these procedures to prevent relapse.

Some evidence indicates that other psychotherapeutic approaches besides standard CBT are also effective for treating BN. One favored approach is to offer interpersonal therapy that addresses situational and personal issues contributing to the development and maintenance of the disorder (McIntosh, Bulik, McKenzie, Luty, & Jordan, 2000). Studies that involve random assignment of BN patients to CBT or interpersonal therapy conditions suggest that both approaches are equally beneficial, especially those that are long-term (Agras, Walsh, Fairburn, Wilson, & Kramer, 2000; Fairburn, Marcus, & Wilson, 1993; Fairburn et al., 1995).

Treatment of bulimia has progressed rapidly over the course of two decades, and CBT has emerged as a strong treatment of choice for this disorder (Compas et al., 1998). Nevertheless, on average, just over one-half of persons with bulimia who are treated with CBT remain in complete remission at follow-up (Lock & le Grange, in press).

SECTION SUMMARY

- Anorexia nervosa is characterized by a refusal to maintain body weight, an intense fear of gaining weight or becoming fat, a distorted body image, and amenorrhea.

- Bulimia nervosa involves recurrent episodes of binge eating, followed by an effort to compensate by self-induced vomiting or other means of purging. Individuals with bulimia are also unduly influenced by body shape and weight, and are obsessed with food.

- Anorexia is less common than bulimia, and has an earlier onset (ages 14–18). Bulimia affects 1% to 3% of mostly older adolescents. These disorders are much more common in girls than boys, although the rates of EDs in males appears to be increasing.

- If untreated, both disorders can become chronic and pose serious threats to health; bulimia has a higher rate of recovery than anorexia.

- Biological factors likely do not precipitate eating disorders, but their effects on appetite, mood, perception, and energy regulation contribute to the maintenance of the disorder.

- Features of Western culture and family life play a significant causal role in eating disorders. Emphasis on dieting and physical appearance can lead to a drive for thinness.

- Eating disorders have one of the highest rates of comorbidity. The most common co-existing disorders are depression (including dysthymia) and anxiety (including OCD).

- Adolescents with anorexia are clinically described as being obsessive and rigid, preferring the familiar, having a high need for approval, and showing poor adaptability to change.

- Adolescents with bulimia are more likely to show mood swings, poor impulse control, and obsessive-compulsive behaviors.

- Psychosocial and pharmacological treatments for anorexia are limited, with no form of intervention particularly beneficial. Clinical approaches often emphasize the importance of changes in family communication patterns.

- Cognitive-behavioral treatments that focus on the attitudes, beliefs, and behaviors supporting dieting, binge eating, or purging are supported as the most effective psychosocial treatments for bulimia. Pharmacological intervention is sometimes used as a corollary treatment for comorbid disorders, such as depression.

Key Terms

anorexia nervosa (AN), p. 389
binge, p. 390
binge eating disorder (BED), p. 392
binge-eating/purging type, p. 389
bulimia nervosa (BN), p. 390
childhood obesity, p. 383
compensatory behavior, p. 391
drive for thinness, p. 378
eating attitudes, p. 378
eating disorders—not otherwise specified (ENOS), p. 393
failure to thrive (FTT), p. 382
feeding disorder of infancy or early childhood, p. 381

metabolic rate, p. 380
pica, p. 381
purging, p. 379
restricting type, p. 389
set point, p. 380

 InfoTrac College Edition

To research recent articles on the subject, go to:
www.infotrac-college/thomsonlearning.com

Enter search terms: EATING DISORDERS, FAILURE TO THRIVE, OBESITY IN CHILDREN, BODY IMAGE

Child Maltreatment and Non-Accidental Trauma

Peace in society depends upon peace in the family.

—Augustine

Mary Ellen's Legacy

She is a bright little girl, with features indicating unusual mental capacity, but with a care-worn, stunted, and prematurely old look. Her apparent condition of health, as well as her scanty wardrobe, indicated that no change of custody or condition could be much for the worse.

. . . On her examination [in court] the child made a statement as follows: ". . . I don't know how old I am. . . . I have never had but one pair of shoes, but I cannot recollect when that was. I have had no shoes or stockings on this winter. . . . I am never allowed to play with any children, or to have any company whatever. Mamma has been in the habit of whipping and beating me almost every day. She used to whip me with a twisted whip—a raw hide. The whip always left a black and blue mark on my body. I have now the black and blue marks on my head which were made by mamma, and also a cut on the left side of my forehead which was made by a pair of scissors. She struck me with the scissors and cut me; I have no recollection of ever having been kissed by any one. . . . I have never been taken on my mamma's lap and caressed or petted. . . . I do not know for what I was whipped—momma never said anything to me when she whipped me." *(New York Times, April 10, 1874)*

This heartbreaking and tragic report of the abuse Mary Ellen experienced led to the formation of the New York Society for the Prevention of Cruelty to Children in the winter of 1874, when citizens discovered that animals were protected from mistreatment, but children were not. Sadly, it took another 100 years before legislation was passed that clearly defined and mandated the reporting of child abuse and neglect, finally launching new efforts to identify and assist abused and neglected children in North America. Despite these efforts, child abuse and neglect remain one of the most common causes of nonaccidental child deaths, as Nadine's sorrowful story reveals:

Nadine	Prison was only the last stop on Carla Lockwood's miserable family journey, one that over the years brought the troubled mother and her children into contact with far more institutions than just the city's child welfare agency. Before her daughter, Nadine, 4, was found starved to
What Went Wrong?	

death last week, there were public schools, hospitals and welfare offices, among other social-service agencies, that touched the family. . . . In the end, the mix of bad fortune and good intentions, blessings, mistakes and a mother's apparent act of malice, did not prevent Nadine from dying. (From "For Dead Child's Family, Long History of Troubles," by Joe Sexton. *The New York Times,* September 5, 1996, p. B6. Copyright © 1996 by *The New York Times.* Reprinted by permission.)

Since records of official reports began in the United States 25 years ago, child abuse and neglect has been recognized as a significant problem, and the lives of some children like Nadine end tragically and without purpose. Unfortunately, Nadine is not alone in her tragic end—in fact, it is estimated that each day three children in the United States die at the hands of their parents or caregivers, more often as a result of neglect than any other type of maltreatment (U.S. Department of Health and Human Services [USDHHS] 2003).

In North America, before they reach adulthood, it is estimated that 1 in 5 girls and 1 in 9 boys will experience some form of sexual abuse (Finkelhor, 1994). Each year about 1 of every 10 children receive harsh physical punishment by a parent or other caregiver that puts them at risk of injury or harm (Straus & Stewart, 1999). Countless other children suffer the effects of emotional abuse and neglect, which, like the effects of physical and sexual abuse, can cause known harm to their psychological development.

Violence against children and other family members has been viewed as a private matter for many generations, and its significant negative effects continue to be poorly acknowledged. Until very recently, violence against members of one's family was considered in the eyes of the law to be less consequential, less damaging, and less worthy of

society's serious attention than violence between strangers. Today we know better: Family violence occurs in numerous forms, from mild acts of frightening or yelling at children, to severe acts of assaulting them with fists and weapons. Moreover, violence and abuse wax and wane in a cyclical manner that creates tension, uncertainty, and fear in children, forcing them to cope with harsh realities and fearful demands (Wekerle & Wolfe, 2003).

We devote an entire chapter to maltreatment because severe disturbances in the parent–child relationship, the family, or the community are common causes of abnormal child development. This chapter departs from the traditional taxonomic approach to abnormal child psychology, and considers how disturbed child-rearing environments or unsafe communities play an important role in abnormal development during childhood and adolescence.

Child maltreatment is a generic term that refers to four primary acts: physical abuse, neglect, sexual abuse, and emotional abuse. Maltreatment can take many forms, including acts experienced by the majority of children, such as corporal punishment, sibling violence, and peer assault, as well as acts experienced by a significant minority, such as physical abuse (Finkelhor & Dziuba-Leatherman, 1994). It cuts across all lines of gender, national origin, language, religion, age, ethnicity, disability, and sexual orientation. **Non-accidental trauma** refers to the wide-ranging effects of maltreatment on the child's ongoing physical and emotional development. Children, because of their social and psychological immaturity, are highly dependent on adults. This dependency makes them more vulnerable to different forms of **victimization**, which is defined as the abuse or mistreatment of someone whose ability to protect him- or herself is limited (Finkelhor & Dziuba-Leatherman, 1994).

Child abuse and neglect have considerable psychological importance because they occur within ongoing relationships that are expected to be protective, supportive, and nurturing. Children from abusive and neglectful families grow up in environments that fail to provide consistent and appropriate opportunities that guide their development; instead, these children are placed in jeopardy of physical and emotional harm (Wolfe & Jaffe, 2001). Yet, their ties to their families—even to the abuser—are very important, so child victims may feel torn between a sense of belonging and a sense of fear and apprehension.

A child victim of sexual abuse expressed it this way: "I was afraid. When it happened, [my father] behaved as if it never happened—he made me doubt myself. I was afraid that I would embarrass my father [the abuser] and be a shame to his family" (Sas, Hurley, Hatch, Malla, & Dick, 1993, p. 68).

Because children are dependent on the people who harm or neglect them, they face other paradoxical dilem-

mas as well (Report of the American Psychological Association, 1996):

- *The victim wants to stop the violence but also longs to belong to a family.* Loyalty and strong emotional ties to the abuser are powerful opponents to the victim's desire to be safe and protected.

- *Affection and attention may coexist with violence and abuse.* A recurring cycle may begin, whereby mounting tension characterized by fear and anticipation ultimately gives way to more abusive behavior. A period of reconciliation may follow, with increased affection and attention. Children are always hopeful that the abuse will not recur.

- *The intensity of the violence tends to increase over time, although in some cases physical violence may decrease or even stop altogether.* Abusive behavior may vary throughout the relationship, taking verbal, sexual, emotional, or physical forms, but the adult's abuse of power and control remains the central issue.

Many societies are struggling to balance parental rights (e.g., the right to discipline their children) and the rights of children to be safe and free of harm. Consequently, a significant shift is under way in how child maltreatment is defined and in how its effects are studied. In the past, abuse was defined primarily by visible physical injuries. However, today we recognize that physical injuries are only one of many consequences. Maltreatment can also damage an individual's developing relationships with others and his or her fundamental sense of safety and self-esteem.

We begin our discussion of child abuse and neglect by considering the role of the family in children's healthy socialization, and the need for more clear and well-established boundaries between appropriate and inappropriate actions toward children.

History and Family Context

Society's view of child-rearing and intolerance of abuse and neglect has evolved over a relatively short period. Child maltreatment and non-accidental forms of trauma have always existed, and most likely were even more commonplace in previous generations (Radbill, 1987), but these acts were seldom identified as a problem or concern. For generations, children were viewed as the exclusive property and responsibility of their fathers, who had full discretion as to how punishment could be administered. This right was unchallenged by any countermovement to seek more humane treatment for children up until the recognition of the abuse Mary Ellen experienced, just over 100 years ago.

Ironically, the same legal system that was designed to support and assist the family has tolerated and in some respects condoned the abuse of family members, including children, women, and the elderly (Jaffe, Lemon, Sandler, & Wolfe, 1996). Two major cultural traditions have influenced this position, until recently: absolute authority over the family by the husband, and the right to family privacy. The Roman Law of Chastisement (753 B.C.), for example, required that if a husband intended to beat his wife he should use a stick no bigger around than his right thumb. This "rule of thumb" was later incorporated into Church doctrine, along with the adage "spare the rod and spoil the child" (Jaffe et al., 1996). Sadly, this view of children as personal property to be managed however the parent wishes, is still adhered to throughout many developed and developing societies (Wolfe & Nayak, 2003).

Fortunately, over the last century and a half, particularly the last 30 years, the legal system's response has shifted to one of condemnation of such behavior throughout much of the Western world (albeit with considerable resistance). The Convention on the Rights of the Child (U. N. General Assembly, 1989) spurred counter-efforts to value the rights and needs of children, and to recognize their exploitation and abuse in many developed countries. Today, 32 countries have established an official government policy regarding child abuse and neglect, and about one-third of the world's population is included in the various countries that conduct an annual count of child abuse and neglect cases (Kempe Children's Center, 2002). These efforts provide the critical first steps to identifying the scope of the problem, and justify the implementation of important societal, community, and cultural changes to combat child abuse.

Healthy Families

It is difficult to talk about child abuse and neglect without talking about the importance of families. Family relations are the earliest and most enduring social relationships that also significantly affect a child's competence, resilience, and sense of well-being. For most of us, family influences are positive and beneficial, offering a primary source of support and nurturance that sets the stage for lifetime patterns of secure relationships and well-being. For others, however, family events and experiences are profoundly negative and harmful, providing the context for some of the most severe violence in society (Straus, Gelles, & Steinmetz, 2003).

As parents, we recognize that children require considerable direction and control and sometimes behave in ways that challenge our decisions and interfere with our plans. If you've not experienced this yourself, ask a parent you know if you can take their young child grocery shopping! Individuals who are ill-prepared for the vital and challenging role of being parents may rely heavily on child-rearing methods from their own childhood, without questioning or modifying those methods. Although this approach to parenting is natural and often appropriate, in some cases it can perpetuate undesirable child-rearing methods, such as physical coercion, verbal threats, and neglect of the child's needs (Gershoff, 2002; Wolfe, 1999).

Understanding the dire effects of abuse and neglect on the mental health of children and adults must begin with a discussion of what children should expect from a healthy family environment. For healthy development, children need a caregiving environment that balances their need for control and direction, or "demandingness," with their need for stimulation and sensitivity, or "responsiveness" (Maccoby & Martin, 1983). Determinants of healthy parent–child relationships and family roles derived from these two primary developmental needs include:

- Adequate knowledge of child development and expectations, including knowledge of children's normal sexual development and experimentation
- Adequate skill in coping with stress related to caring for small children, and ways to enhance child development through proper stimulation and attention
- Opportunities to develop normal parent–child attachment and early patterns of communication

- Adequate parental knowledge of home management, including basic financial planning, proper shelter, and meal planning
- Opportunities and willingness to share the duties of child care between both parents, when applicable
- Provision of necessary social and health services

These healthy patterns depend not only on parental competence and developmental sensitivity, but also on family circumstances and the availability of community resources, such as education and child-rearing information, as well as social networks and supports. The family situation itself, including the parents' marital relationship and the child's characteristics, such as temperament, health, and developmental limitations, provides the basic context for child-rearing.

Although we would expect a considerable range in ability and resources among North American families, certain features of a child's environment should be fundamental and expectable (Scarr, 1992). For infants an **expectable environment** requires protective and nurturing adults, as well as opportunities for socialization within a culture. For older children, an expectable environment includes a supportive family, contact with peers, and ample opportunities to explore and master their environment (Cicchetti & Lynch, 1995). Moreover, responsible parenting involves a gradual shifting of control from the parent to the child and the community. Seldom is this process a smooth one, but healthy families learn to move gradually from nearly complete parental control, through shared control, to the child's growing self-control and eventual independence as an adult.

Family Stress and Disharmony

> *You know the only people who are always sure about the proper way to raise children? Those who've never had any.*
>
> —Bill Cosby

Children have an amazing ability to adapt to changing demands, an ability that is essential for healthy development. Nevertheless, they need a basic expectable environment to adapt successfully, or their development may be compromised. All children must cope with various degrees of stress, and these experiences can be strengthening if they do not exceed the child's coping ability (Garmezy, 1983). However, a child's method of adapting to their immediate environmental demands (such as avoiding an abusive caregiver) may later compromise his or her ability to form relationships with others. A child's successful methods of adapting to outbursts of anger and aggression between family members is constantly challenged. Signs of stress appear, such as increased illness, symptoms of fear and anxiety, and problems with peers or school. Even infants as young as 3 months have been found to react with changes in their heart rate to adults' arguing (Cummings, 1997).

Stressful events in the family affect each child in different and unique ways. However, certain situations trigger more intense stress reactions and consequences than others. (Consider, for example, the difference between the stress of moving to a new school and the stress of being bullied by an older child.) Child maltreatment is among the worst and most intrusive forms of stress. It impinges directly on the child's daily life, may be ongoing and unpredictable, and is often the result of actions or inactions of people the child is supposed to trust and depend on. Keep in mind, however, that even traumatic events like abuse, neglect, and family violence do not affect each child in a predictable, characteristic fashion. Rather, their impact depends on the child's makeup and available supports (Masten & Powell, 2003).

A prime factor in how children respond to various forms of stress is the degree of support and assistance they receive from their parents to help them cope and adapt. Parents provide a model that teaches the child how to exert some control even in the midst of confusion and upheaval. Understandably, a warm relationship with an adult who provides a predictable routine and consistent, moderate discipline, and who buffers the child from unnecessary sources of stress, is a valuable asset. Maltreated children may have the hardest time adapting appropriately to any form of stress when they are deprived of positive adult relationships, effective models of problem solving, and a sense of personal control or predictability (Luthar, 2003).

Continuum of Care

Most of us agree that children who lack the basic necessities of life—food, affection, medical care, education, and intellectual and social stimulation—are placed in jeopardy, but different cultural values, community standards, and personal experiences make one person's abuse another person's discipline or education (Korbin, 2002).

Figure 14.1 depicts a hypothetical range of child care from healthy to abusive and neglectful, which provides some guidelines and boundaries for acceptable behavior between parents and children (Wolfe, 1991). At the child-centered end of this continuum we see appropriate and healthy forms of child-rearing actions that promote child development. Competent parents encourage their child's development in a variety of ways, and match their demands and expectations to the child's needs and abilities. Of course, parents are human, and many on occasions will scold, criticize, or even show insensitivity to the child's state of need; in fact, discipline often requires such firm control, with accompanying verbal statements and affect.

Child-Centered	Borderline	Inappropriate/Abusive/Neglectful
· Provides a variety of sensory stimulation and positive emotional expressions · Engages in highly competent, child-centered interactions · Communicates to child about normal sexuality and healthy relationships · Makes rules for safety and health · Occasionally scolds, criticizes, interrupts child activity · Uses emotional delivery and tone that are sometimes harsh	· Shows rigid emotional expression and inflexibility in responding to child · Uses verbal and nonverbal pressure to achieve unrealistic expectations · Frequently uses verbal and non-verbal coercive methods and minimizes child's competence · Is insensitive to child's needs · Makes unfair comparisons · Takes advantage of or ignores child's dependency status · Impinges on the child's personal need for privacy	· Denigrates, insults child · Expresses conditional love and ambivalent feelings toward child · Emotionally or physically rejects child's attention · Uses cruel and harsh control methods · Shows no sensitivity to child's needs · Intentionally seeks out ways to frighten, threaten, or provoke child · Responds unpredictably with emotional discharge · Takes advantage of child's dependency status through coercion, threats, or bribes · Is sexually or physically coercive and intrusive

Figure 14.1 Continuum of parental emotional sensitivity and expression
Source: (From *Preventing Physical and Emotional Abuse of Children* by D. A. Wolfe, p. 13. Copyright © 1991 Guilford Press. Reprinted with permission.)

Borderline actions, however, represent greater degrees of irresponsible and harmful child care. Parents who show any discernable degree of these actions toward their child often need instruction and assistance in effective child care methods. Finally, parents who violate their child's basic needs and dependency status in a physical, sexual, or emotional manner are engaging in inappropriate and abusive behavior. Similarly, their failure to respond to a child's needs is the cornerstone of neglect.

SECTION SUMMARY

- Child maltreatment refers to four primary acts: physical abuse, neglect, sexual abuse, and emotional abuse.
- Child abuse has always existed, but until fairly recently it was seldom identified as a problem or concern.
- Child maltreatment represents one of the greatest failures of the child's expectable environment. It is among the worst and most intrusive forms of stress, and often leads to poor adaptive outcomes.
- Maltreating families fail to provide many of the expected emotional and physical necessities for children, and offer few supports and opportunities for children to explore and master their environment.
- Child care can be described along a hypothetical continuum ranging from healthy to abusive and neglectful.
- Boundaries between appropriate and inappropriate behavior toward children are not always clear or well established, but an awareness of what is right and what is wrong can go a long way in preventing maltreatment.

Types of Maltreatment

Have you ever baby-sat a young child or been in charge of a group of children at a camp or school? If you saw bruises on a child, what would you do? You should be aware that all states and provinces in North America have civil laws, or statutes, that obligate persons who come in contact with children as part of their job or volunteer work (bus drivers, day care workers, teachers, baby-sitters, and so forth) to report known or suspected cases of abuse to the police or child welfare authorities. These statutes also provide criteria for removing children from their homes if they are suspected of being maltreated. Criminal statutes further specify the forms of maltreatment that are criminally punishable.

The incidents of maltreatment that affect children's health and well-being involves abuse and neglect by adults, not abnormal child behavior or psychological disorders. Thus, specific definitions of types of child maltreatment do not appear in DSM-IV-TR. Instead, DSM-IV-TR considers severe maltreatment (of an adult or a child) under the Axis I category "Other conditions that may be a focus of clinical attention." If a child who was abused is also suffering from a clinical disorder, such as depression (Axis I), the maltreatment would be noted on Axis IV (psychosocial and environmental problems), because maltreatment may affect the diagnosis, treatment, and prognosis of the child's depression.

The definition of each type of maltreatment has been established by three National Incidence Studies (NIS) conducted by the U.S. Department of Health and Human Services since 1980. NIS estimates of maltreatment are derived from official reports as well as a nationally representative sample of professionals who come in contact with children in a variety of settings.

Physical Abuse

> **Milton**
>
> **Abused and Abusive**
>
> Four-year-old Milton's rambunctious nature and his mother's hair-trigger temper were an explosive mix. He was constantly in trouble at home and was often spanked, yelled at, and locked in his room. One evening his baby-sitter took him to the emergency department because she thought he had a bad cold. During the examination the doctor discovered that Milton had a fracture to his left forearm that was a couple of weeks old. There was a goose egg on Milton's forehead and multiple bruises on his face at various stages of healing, as well as bruises on his back.
>
> Several people had noticed Milton's aggressive behavior—pushing other children or hitting them with something at preschool—but no one had realized that he was being abused. His preschool teacher told investigators, "I'm never sure from one minute to the next how Milton will react to the other children. He could be playing and suddenly become angry at something and start to destroy things or hit someone. I've also seen him become frightened—at what I don't know—and withdraw into a corner. I've tried several times to discuss these things with his mother, but she says he's just trying to get his way all the time."

Milton has been physically abused. His behavior is indicative of growing up in an environment with punitive disciplinary methods that are the norm and are detrimental to child-centered stimulation and appropriate limit setting. **Physical abuse** is multiple acts of aggression that include punching, beating, kicking, biting, burning, shaking, or otherwise physically harming a child. In most cases the injuries from physical abuse are not intentional, but they occur as a result of overdiscipline or severe physical punishment. The severity and nature of the injuries vary considerably, as shown by these sobering examples of physical abuse from the NIS (Sedlak & Broadhurst, 1996):

- A 1-year-old child who died of a cerebral hemorrhage after being shaken by her father

- A teen whose mother punched her and pulled out her hair
- A child who sustained second- and third-degree "stocking" burns to the feet after being held in hot water

As a result of their harsh and insensitive treatment, physically abused children like Milton are often described as more disruptive and aggressive than their age-mates, with disturbances that reach across a broad spectrum of emotional and cognitive functioning (Cicchetti, Toth, & Maughan, 2000). Physical injuries may range from minor (bruises, lacerations), to moderate (scars, abrasions), to severe (burns, sprains, or broken bones). These physical signs represent only the visible injuries; we will see later in this chapter that the psychological development of physically abused children is often impaired in less visible, but very serious, ways as well. We ask you to keep Milton's case in mind, since we refer to him several times throughout the chapter.

Neglect

> **Jane and Matt**
>
> **Used to Neglect**
>
> Although Janet had worked for child protective services for over 10 years, she still cringed when she described the conditions of the home from which she had just removed two young siblings. "Neighbors and relatives have complained about the parents' never being around much, and how they often hear children crying," Janet explained during our interview. "I've been to the home before, and usually it stays clean for a few days after my visit. But this time the children were left with a teenaged baby-sitter, who went off to play in an arcade. They walked out of the home, and had to be returned by the police. What I saw this time was worse than before. Little Matt, who's almost 3 years old, was running around in soiled diapers, crawling across broken dishes and spilled food, putting things in his mouth. His sister Jane, who turns 6 next month, was dressed in dirty clothes and looked like she hadn't eaten in a week. The odor from the house forced me to step outside for air. The children seemed used to it—they just moved things out of their way and didn't seem to care."
>
> I met with both children once they were settled into a foster home, and offered ways for the foster parents to manage Jane's strong-willed behavior and Matt's delay in speech and toileting. The foster mother noted how both children seemed to need "constant attention and control," and how neither had knowledge of typical routines like sitting down together for dinner, cleaning up, bed times, basic hygiene, and the need to wear clean clothing.

These two children suffered the effects of physical and emotional neglect, characterized by a failure to provide for their basic physical, educational, or emotional needs. **Physical neglect** includes refusal or delay in seeking health care, expulsion from the home or refusal to allow a runaway to return home, abandonment, and inadequate supervision. **Educational neglect** involves actions such as allowing chronic truancy, failing to enroll a child in school who is of mandatory school age, and failing to attend to a child's special educational need. **Emotional neglect,** one of the most difficult categories to define, includes actions such as marked inattention to the child's needs for affection, refusal or failure to provide needed psychological care, spousal abuse in the child's presence, and permission of drug or alcohol use by the child.

The determination of child neglect requires consideration of cultural values and standards of care, as well as recognition that the failure to provide the necessities of life may be related to poverty. The following examples are actual cases of the three forms of neglect (Sedlak & Broadhurst, 1996):

Physical Neglect

- A 2-year-old who was found wandering in the street late at night, naked and alone
- An infant who had to be hospitalized for near-drowning after being left alone in a bathtub
- Children who were living in a home contaminated with animal feces and rotting food

Educational Neglect

- An 11-year-old and a 13-year-old who were chronically truant
- A 12-year-old whose parents permitted him to decide whether to go to school, how long to stay there, and in which activities to participate
- A special education student whose mother refused to believe he needed help in school

Emotional Neglect

- Siblings who were subjected to repeated incidents of family violence between their mother and father
- A 12-year-old whose parents permitted him to drink and use drugs
- A child whose mother helped him shoot out the windows of a neighbor's house

Neglected children may suffer physical health problems, limited growth, and increased complications in other health conditions, such as diabetes, allergies, and failure-to-thrive (Lyons-Ruth, Zeanah, & Benoit, 2003). They may also show behavior patterns that vacillate between undisciplined activity and extreme passivity (Hildyard & Wolfe, 2002), due to their ways of adapting to an unresponsive caregiver. As toddlers, they show little persistence and enthusiasm; as preschoolers, neglected children show poor impulse control and are highly dependent

© Arthur Tress/Photo Researchers, Inc.

Child neglect, the most common form of maltreatment, is tied to poverty, substance abuse, and parental indifference.

on teachers for support and nurturance (M. R. Erickson and Egeland, 2002).

Note that emotional neglect also includes children who witness parental violence. Passive recipients of violence and abuse are affected in much the same way as other victims of maltreatment (Fantuzzo & Mohr, 1999). Younger abused children are fearful and often show regressive and somatic signs of distress, such as sleep problems, bed-wetting, headaches, stomachaches, diarrhea, ulcers, and enuresis. Older boys tend to be more aggressive with peers and dating partners; girls tend to be more passive, withdrawn, and low in self-esteem (Grych, Jouriles, Swank, McDonald, & Norwood, 2000; Wolfe, Crooks, Lee, McIntyre-Smith, & Jaffe, 2003).

Sexual Abuse

Rosita

No Haven at Home

Rosita was not quite 4 years old when her family doctor suspected that something was going on that troubled her. He expressed his concerns to child welfare, and Rosita reenacted several sexual acts for them, using dolls depicting her father and herself. "Daddy said I can play a game, and it's OK 'cause grownups do it," she hesitantly explained. Rosita made the dolls kiss, then the male doll rubbed the female doll's vagina. "But he hurt me, and it made me scared. I didn't want to get in trouble." To make matters worse, her mother became furious with Rosita and the agency when she heard the accusations, and was unwilling to ensure her daughter's protection and safety at home. "Rosita just wants a lot of attention—she's said this stuff before and I don't believe her one minute," was her mother's only comment.

Rosita was sexually abused by her father and disbelieved by her mother; as a result, she faces many ongoing psychological complications. Because Rosita was seen several times throughout the course of her childhood and adolescent development, her case is discussed further in a later section of this chapter on the course of development of children and adolescents who have been sexually abused.

Sexual abuse includes fondling a child's genitals, intercourse with the child, incest, rape, sodomy, exhibitionism, and commercial exploitation through prostitution or the production of pornographic materials. The actual number of sexual abuse cases may be underreported because of the secrecy or "conspiracy of silence" that so often characterizes these cases, making determination of abuse difficult (Haugaard, 2000). The following are cases of sexual abuse reported in the NIS (Sedlak & Broadhurst, 1996):

- A 10-year-old girl who was raped by her father
- Two sisters and a brother who were sexually molested by their mother's live-in boyfriend
- A 4-year-old who was fondled by his father during weekend visitations

The behavior and development of sexually abused children may be significantly affected, especially in relation to the duration or frequency of abuse, the use of force, penetration, and a close relationship to the perpetrator (Berliner & Elliott, 2002). The physical health of these children may be compromised by urinary tract problems, gynecological problems, sexually transmitted diseases (including AIDS), and pregnancy (National Research Council, 1993).

About one-third of sexually abused children report or exhibit no visible symptoms, and about two-thirds of those who do show symptoms recover significantly during the first 12–18 months following the abuse (Kendall-Tackett, Williams, & Finkelhor, 1993). Nonetheless, the possibility of delayed emergence of symptoms is becoming more widely recognized (L. M. Williams, 2003). Children's reactions to and recovery from sexual abuse vary, depending on the nature of the sexual assault and the response of their important others, especially the mother. Many acute symptoms of sexual abuse resemble children's common reactions to stress, such as fears, increased anger, anxiety, fatigue, depression, passivity, difficulties focusing and sustaining attention, and withdrawal from usual activities.

In reaction to an abusive incident, it is common for younger children to regress temporarily, such as becoming enuretic or easily upset, or having problems sleeping. In later childhood and early adolescence, these signs of distress may take the form of acting-out behaviors, such as delinquency, drug use, promiscuity, or self-destructive behavior (Wekerle & Wolfe, 2003). Some sexually abused children may exhibit sexualized behaviors with other children or toys that may include excessive masturbation, age-inappropriate knowledge of sexual activity, and/or pro-

nounced seductive or promiscuous behavior. Any of these symptoms of distress may be associated with a decline or sudden change in school performance, behavior, and peer relations.

Unlike physical abuse and neglect, sexual abuse has no connection to child-rearing, discipline, or inattention to developmental needs. Rather, it constitutes a breach of trust, deception, intrusion, and exploitation of a child's innocence and status. Whereas all types of maltreatment share a common ground in relation to the abuse of power by an adult over a child, sexual abuse stands out from physical abuse and neglect in terms of these specific dynamics.

Emotional Abuse

Evan

If This Is Love . . .

Evan described himself as "an eleven-year-old boy who can be good when he tries really hard, but most of the time he makes bad choices." One of these bad choices was to put paint in the teacher's coffee cup, leading to his suspension from school. Evan also started stealing and drinking beer. The school says he was threatening other kids, wanting their money. To document their plight, his parents volunteered to have a television documentary made about their "trouble with Evan," using motion-sensitive cameras in two rooms in their home. What emerged from the tapes, however, were repeated episodes of emotional abuse toward Evan by his stepfather and mother. Below are some illustrative conversations:

Evan's stepfather: "I would like to lock you up in a cage and let everybody look at you like you are an animal. I am fed up with this sh_. I can't put up with it no more and neither can your mother. And if you think I am talking to the wall, I am talking to you, beef head. If you'd of been me, you'd of been dead because my father would have killed you. Your insubordination is going to get you a hook on the side of your f_ing head. If you don't like it the door is right there."

Evan's parents were convinced that he was stealing money from them, and his mother's confrontation follows: "We already know that you are lying so you f_ing tell me the truth NOW! Everything. Go take a look in the mirror. Go take a look in the mirror and then come back here. You look guilty as sin. [Turns to husband] I am going to hit him. Now that is not how you normally look, is it? That is not a normal look for a child, is it? You have got great big letters written all over your face that spell guilty." Evan's mother then discovered she had miscounted the money. (Transcribed quote from "The Trouble with Evan," for the television program *The Fifth Estate,* executive producer, David Studer for the Canadian Broadcasting Corporation, originally aired on March 25, 1994.)

Evan experienced very harsh, emotionally abusive threats and put-downs from his parents, which can be as harmful to a child's development as physical abuse or neglect. **Emotional abuse** includes repeated acts or omissions by the parents or caregivers that have caused, or could cause, serious behavioral, cognitive, emotional, or mental disorders. For example, the parents or caregivers may use extreme or bizarre forms of punishment, such as confinement of a child in a dark closet. Emotional abuse also includes verbal threats and put-downs like those Evan experienced, as well as habitual scapegoating, belittling, and name-calling. Emotional abuse exists, to some degree, in all forms of maltreatment, so the specific psychological consequences of this form of maltreatment are poorly understood (Glaser, 2002).

The following cases reported in the NIS tend to be more severe forms of emotional abuse because of the definitional requirement that the acts have caused, or could cause, serious harm (Sedlak & Broadhurst, 1996):

- A young child strapped in a high chair all day while her parents went to work
- A 4-year-old who was locked in a closet as a means of discipline
- Children traumatized when their father took them to a store to buy a gun with which he threatened to kill them and their mother

Exploitation

Children also suffer trauma from commercial or other sexual exploitation, such as child labor and child prostitution. Globally, as many as 10 million children may be victims of child prostitution, the sex industry, sex tourism, and pornography, although accurate statistics are not available (WHO, 1999). Sadly, many exploited children began as victims of abuse and rape in their homes, and are forced into commercial sexual activity at a young age (9–13 years old) (UNICEF, 2000). Rates of child prostitution tend to be higher in Asia and Latin America, but an alarming growth has been recorded in Africa, North America, and Europe. Eastern Europe has recently emerged as the newest market in the worldwide sexual exploitation of children (Wolfe & Nayak, 2003). Poverty is the greatest factor in the child prostitution explosion, as migration of families from the rural areas into cities creates unemployment, the breakdown of family structures, homelessness and, inevitably, an increase in child prostitution.

SECTION SUMMARY

- Physical abuse includes acts of aggression such as punching, beating, kicking, biting, burning, shaking, or otherwise physically harming a child.
- Child neglect is a failure to provide for a child's basic physical, educational, or emotional needs.

- Sexual abuse ranges from sexual touching to exhibitionism, sexual intercourse, and commercial exploitation (pornography, prostitution).
- Emotional abuse includes acts or omissions that could cause serious behavioral, cognitive, emotional, or mental disorders.
- Exploitation of children includes child labor and child prostitution, which are recognized as a significant form of trauma to children and adolescents worldwide.

Prevalence and Context

When the *battered child syndrome* (the early term for physical abuse) was first described in the early 1960s (Kempe, Silverman, Steele, Droegenmueller, & Silver, 1962), it was believed that this phenomenon applied to fewer than 300 children in the United States. Today, state child protective services agencies investigate close to 3 million suspected cases of child abuse and neglect each year, of which about a one-third are confirmed (USDHHS, 2003).

Incidence of Abuse and Neglect in North America

About 1 million children in the United States were confirmed to be victims of child maltreatment in 2001, which is a rate of 12.4 per 1000 children in the population (USDHHS, 2003). By comparison, Canada's substantiated incidence of maltreatment is 9.7 per 1000 children (Trocmé & Wolfe, 2001). The difference in incidence between these otherwise similar countries is due to a higher number of neglect cases in the United States, which may be a function of higher poverty rates and less access to medical services.

Figure 14.2 shows the proportion of each subtype of abuse and neglect. This pattern has remained fairly constant over the past decade, although there has been a slight decline in the overall rate of child maltreatment during the latter part of the 1990s (especially in child sexual abuse), for reasons that are presently unknown (L. Jones & Finkelhor, 2003). Child neglect (including medical neglect) continues to be a worrisome problem, accounting for close to 60% of all documented cases of maltreatment in the United States. Almost 20% of the children suffered physical abuse, and nearly 10% were sexually abused. In addition, about 1 in 4 of these children suffered more than one form of maltreatment.

Incidence of child maltreatment can also be estimated from large-scale community or nationwide surveys that represent of societal views and which avoid some factors that may inhibit children or adults from reporting maltreatment to officials. Consequently, asking representative

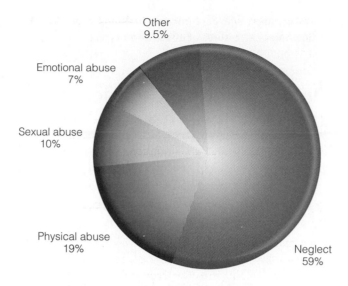

Figure 14.2 Percentages of types of maltreatment
U.S. Department of Health and Human Services (USDHHS, 2001).
Note: "Other" forms of maltreatment include abandonment, threats of harm to the child, and congenital drug addiction. The percentages total more than 100% because children may have been victims of more than one type of maltreatment.

samples of parents about their various child-rearing methods anonymously results in much higher estimates of the number of children at risk of maltreatment each year than the estimates provided by official reports. Based on telephone interviews with over 3500 families in the United States in 1985 and 1995, about 10% of parents admitted using some method in the past year to control their child that amounted to a severe violent act, such as hitting with an object, pushing, or scalding their child (Straus & Gelles, 1986; Straus & Stewart, 1999).

Lifetime prevalence estimates of maltreatment are derived by asking adults if they experienced particular forms of maltreatment as children. These studies have been conducted almost exclusively on sexual abuse, perhaps because discrete sexual acts are more readily defined than other forms of abuse and neglect. A notable exception is the Ontario Health Supplement, a general population survey of nearly 10,000 residents of Ontario, Canada, in which people 15 years and older were asked about physical and sexual abuse during childhood (H. L. MacMillan et al., 1997). A history of physical abuse during childhood was reported more often by males (31.2%) than females (21.1%), whereas sexual abuse during childhood was more commonly reported by females (12.8%) than males (4.3%). Keep in mind that these figures are estimates only. Retrospective reports of childhood experiences are inexact, and it is rarely possible to corroborate episodes of maltreatment to get precise accounts (Hardt & Rutter, 2004). Nevertheless, these incidence and prevalence data indicate a substantial problem that, until quite recently, was disregarded.

Characteristics of Victimized Children

Are some children more likely than others to be abused or neglected than others because of their age, race, or gender? Incidence studies have consistently found that children's sex and age are related to risk of maltreatment, but ethnic identity is not related once other factors such as poverty and homelessness are taken into account (USDHHS, 2003; Trocmé & Wolfe, 2001).

Child maltreatment occurs at all ages, but there is correspondence between certain types of maltreatment and children's age. Younger children, who have the greatest need for care and supervision, are the most common victims of physical neglect. Along with young adolescents, toddlers and preschoolers are the most common victims of physical and emotional abuse, which corresponds to the emergence of greater independence and parental conflict during these developmental periods. Sexual abuse incidence, in contrast, is relatively constant beginning at age 3, which attests to children's vulnerability from early preschool years throughout childhood.

Sex differences in maltreatment rates are generally few, with the important exception of sexual abuse, where girls account for about 80% of the reported victims (USDHHS, 2003). Moreover, the dynamics of sexual abuse differ considerably for boys and girls. Although boys as well as girls are more likely to be abused by someone they know and trust than by a stranger, boys are more likely to be abused by male nonfamily members—camp staff, teachers, scout leaders—whereas girls are more likely to be sexually abused by male family members (Berliner & Elliott, 2002; Wolfe & Trocmé, 2001). This finding suggests different patterns of vulnerability for boys and girls and has implications for safety and prevention.

Characteristics of Family and Perpetrator

Family characteristics remind us of the cultural and social forces that shape child-rearing methods. Most significant is the well-established finding that maltreatment is more common among the poor and disadvantaged (although it also occurs among higher income families). This connection is not likely due to a reporting bias because it has remained constant for the past 30 years, despite increased awareness and reporting (USDHHS, 2003). What it does imply, however, is that the economically based context of maltreatment—restricted child care opportunities, crowded and unsafe housing, lack of health care, to name a few conditions—is a powerful backdrop to the high incidence rates.

Family structure is also connected to the probability of child maltreatment. Children living with a single parent are at significantly greater risk of both physical abuse and neglect. Those living with single fathers are almost twice as likely to be physically abused than those living with single mothers (Sedlak & Broadhurst, 1996; Trocmé & Wolfe, 2001). Maltreatment—especially physical and educational neglect—is more common in larger families, where additional children in the household mean additional tasks, responsibilities, and demands.

Who commits these acts? It shouldn't surprise you that 85% of the victims are maltreated by one or both parents, across all forms of maltreatment. However, there are important exceptions, as well as key sex differences in the nature of abuse or neglect. Nearly 50% of sexually abused children are abused by persons other than parents or parent figures, compared with only a fraction in other categories. Child neglect is committed predominantly—about 90% of the time—by mothers, which fits with the fact that mothers and mother substitutes tend to be primary caregivers. In contrast, sexual abuse is committed more often—also about 90% of the time—by males, about 50% of whom are the child's father or father figure. While males are the dominant perpetrators in sexual abuse, the most common perpetrator pattern overall is a female parent acting alone, who is typically younger than 30 years of age (USDHHS, 2003).

Cross-Cultural Comparisons

How do children fare in other Western countries and in other countries around the world? Although it is difficult to draw comparisons between countries because of the differences in defining and reporting the cases of child maltreatment, what little is known about the prevalence of maltreatment in other countries suggests that physical and sexual abuse are at epidemic proportions in many societies worldwide.

The World Health Organization (WHO) estimates that 40 million children by the age of 14 are victims of child abuse and neglect annually around the world (WHO, 1999), confirming suspicions that child abuse is found in all societies and is almost always a highly guarded secret. Studies in which children or young adults were interviewed about their childhood experiences further confirm that rates of child sexual abuse in other Western societies are comparable to those rates in North America, which cluster around 20% for females, and between 3% and 11% for males (Finkelhor, 1994).

SECTION SUMMARY

- Child abuse and neglect are at epidemic proportions in the United States, Canada, and many other countries worldwide.
- Physical neglect is most common among younger children.
- Physical and emotional abuse are most common among toddlers, preschoolers, and young adolescents.
- Sexual abuse affects children, mostly girls, beginning at age 3.

- Poverty and single parenthood are the most prominent demographic features of abuse and neglect.

Developmental Course and Psychopathology

The child trapped in an abusive environment is faced with formidable tasks of adaptation. She must find a way to preserve a sense of trust in people who are untrustworthy, safety in a situation that is unsafe, control in a situation that is terrifyingly unpredictable, power in a situation of helplessness.

(Herman, 1992, p. 98)

This statement by prominent clinician and researcher Judith Herman captures the essence of the world of maltreated children and youth. Abuse and neglect are more than physical pain and transitory fear; to a child or adolescent, these events often represent threats to their emerging sense of self, their world, and their feelings of safety and well-being. We return to Rosita's case to illustrate this dramatic impact:

Rosita
Feeling Trapped

At age 6, Rosita was brought to the hospital following two suicidal/self-harm gestures. While camping, she wrapped a rope that hung from a tree around her neck and her foster mother grabbed it and untangled it. She did not appear to be hurt, but she sat and cried for a long time while her foster mother cuddled her.

"Rosita is preoccupied with themes of death and self-harm, in her drawings, stories at school, and even with her classmates," her teacher explained. "She has problems making friends, because she acts silly when she tries to join their games. More than once she's asked other children to touch her vagina, and she has tried to put her finger in one girl's vagina. Needless to say, this has alarmed other parents and teachers. But she's such a needy child—she'll go from a temper tantrum to becoming clingy in a matter of seconds."

Rosita's life became more settled, and by age 9 her school performance had improved noticeably. However, at age 15 her psychological condition rapidly grew worse. She made suicide attempts and began cutting her arm with glass and other sharp objects. When I saw her following her release from the hospital she was very distraught, and felt unloved and abandoned. Her feelings of depression and anxiety were evident: "I'll jump or get really scared, for no reason. I just want to go somewhere and hide, and get away from people," she explained. "I can't trust anybody except for my friend Mary—but even she thinks I'm weird when I get like this. It's like I'm trapped or caught, and can't get away." My interview went on to reveal Rosita's sleeping problems and her constant crying and sadness.

Rosita had never forgotten the abuse she experienced as a child, and sometimes had intrusive reminders of what happened. "I feel tied in a knot, and I feel like I'm going crazy or something. That's when I might start cutting on my arm or something, just to feel like I'm not dreaming, that I'm real." Sometimes she even blamed herself for losing her family years ago, explaining that "no matter how bad it was I wish no one had ever found out, because it wasn't worth all the pain I'm going through."

Rosita lacks a sense of self-esteem and a sense of the future. She is very vulnerable to recurring victimization because she lacks self-awareness and has limited self-protection skills. She feels a terrible loss and ambivalence over her family, sometimes blaming herself for the abuse or wishing it had never been discovered. Although she is a verbal and insightful young woman, she is often overcome with worries, anxiety, fear, and emotional distress related to her current circumstances.

Resilience and Adaptation

What happens to the development of children who were abused or neglected during their important formative years? Recall from Chapter 1 how normal development follows a predictable, organized course, beginning with the child's mastery of physiological regulation (eating, sleeping), and continuing throughout the development of higher skills, such as problem solving and peer relationships. However, under abnormal and unusual circumstances, especially abuse and neglect, predictability and organization are disrupted and thrown off course, which results in developmental failure and limited adaptation.

Maltreated children not only must face acute and unpredictable parental outbursts or betrayal, but also must adapt to environmental circumstances that pose developmental challenges. These influences include the more dramatic events, such as marital violence and separation of family members, as well as the mundane but important everyday activities that may be disturbing or upsetting, such as unfriendly interactions, few learning opportunities, and a chaotic lifestyle. Children who are sexually abused undergo pronounced interruptions in their developing view of themselves and the world, which result in significant emotional and behavioral changes indicative of their attempts to cope with such events. Because the source of stress and fear is centralized in their family, children who are maltreated are challenged regularly to find

ways to adapt that pose the least risk, and offer maximum protection and opportunity for growth (Trickett, Kurtz, & Pizzigati, 2004).

Child maltreatment, like other forms of adversity and trauma during childhood, does not affect each child in a predictable or consistent fashion. To the contrary, the impact of maltreatment depends not only on the severity and chronicity of the specific events but also on how the events interact with the child's individual and family characteristics. Without proper support and assistance, young children who may have initially achieved normal developmental milestones can show a dramatic downturn in their developmental progress as a result of chronic or acute maltreatment and similar types of stress (E. A. Carlson et al., 1999). Consequently, their core developmental processes are impaired, which results in emotional and behavioral problems ranging from speech and language delays to criminal behavior. However, one prospective study found that about 1 in 5 maltreated children were considered resilient adults, defined as no period of homelessness, consistent employment, and no juvenile or adult arrests (McGloin & Widom, 2001).

Children may be protected in part from the effects of maltreatment by a positive relationship with at least one important and consistent person in their lives who provides support and protection (Trickett et al., 2004). This person is typically their mother (Leifer, Kilbane, & Kalick, 2004; Toth, Cicchetti, & Kim, 2002), but the person could also be the identified maltreating parent, a notion that at first may be hard to comprehend. However, maltreated children do not think of their parents as abusive; rather, they adapt to their own experiences as best as possible. Loyalty to one's parents is a powerful emotional tie, so from the child's point of view, a parent who at times yells, hits, and castigates, may at other times be a source of connection, knowledge, or love (Wekerle & Wolfe, 2003). Personality characteristics such as positive self-esteem and sense of self are also related to fewer negative

Young Jason never goes unarmed. Grabbing his plastic gun and rubber knife, he tells his mother, "If daddy comes, I'll be able to stop him."

outcomes among maltreated children (Cicchetti & Rogosch, 1997).

Simply stated, if children are raised in environments where love and positive attention are expressed rarely or inconsistently, the children have no other standard of comparison. Their natural inclination is to distort their view of their parents as being more like others'—positive, well meaning, and all important. It may be more adaptive for children to focus on what their parents provide, rather than what they don't provide because this focus will allow themselves to seem normal and accepted. This view has important implications for intervention efforts, because some interventions, such as removing children from their families, can become another source of stress and disruption with undesired side effects (Wilson & Melton, 2002).

Developmental Consequences

Understanding the major consequences of the maltreatment of children requires consideration of the basic developmental processes that are impaired or delayed among this population. We begin by focusing on early attachment and affect regulation—the building blocks of the development of important self-regulatory and interpersonal competencies.

Early Attachment and Emotion Regulation Episodes of child abuse and neglect, whether chronic or sporadic, can disrupt the important process of attachment, and interfere with children's ability to seek comfort and to regulate their own physiological and emotional processes. As a result, maltreated children are more likely than other children to show an absence of an organized attachment strategy (Lyons-Ruth, Yellin, Melnick, & Atwood, 2003).

Parent–child attachment and the home climate play a critical role in emotion regulation, another early developmental milestone. **Emotion regulation** refers to the ability to modulate or control the intensity and expression of feelings and impulses, especially intense ones, in an adaptive manner (Cicchetti, Ganiban, & Barnett, 1990; Maughan & Cicchetti, 2002). Without consistent stimulation, comfort, and routine to aid in the formation of secure attachment, maltreated infants and toddlers have considerable difficulty establishing a reciprocal, consistent pattern of interaction with their caregivers. Instead, they show a pattern described as *insecure-disorganized attachment,* characterized by a mixture of approach and avoidance, helplessness, apprehension, and a general disorientation (Barnett, Ganiban, & Cicchetti, 1999). The lack of a secure, consistent basis for relationships places maltreated children at greater risk of falling behind in their cognitive and social development, and can result in problems regulating their emotions and behavior with others (Sroufe, Carlson, Levy, & Egeland, 1999). Emotions serve as important internal monitoring and guidance systems

designed to appraise events as beneficial or dangerous, and provide motivation for action.

Because emotions provide important signals about our internal and external worlds, children must learn to interpret and respond to them appropriately. Most children learn this naturally through the emotional expressions and explanations given by their caregivers. Maltreated children, on the other hand, live in a world of emotional turmoil and extremes, making it difficult for them to understand, label, and regulate their internal states (Shipman, Zeman, Penza, & Champion, 2000). Expressions of affect, such as crying or signals of distress, may trigger disapproval, avoidance, or abuse, so maltreated youngsters tend to inhibit their emotional expression and regulation, and remain more fearful and on alert (Klorman, Cicchetti, Thatcher, & Ison, 2003; Pollak, Cicchetti, Hornung, & Reed, 2000). Similarly, they show increased attention to anger- and threat-related signals like facial expressions, and less attention to other emotional expressions (Pollak & Tolley-Schell, 2003). When a new situation that involves a stranger or peer triggers emotional reactions, they do not have the benefit of a caring smile or words from a familiar adult to assure them that things are okay.

Difficulties modulating emotions can be expressed as depressive reactions as well as intense angry outbursts (Wekerle & Wolfe, 2003). Accordingly, as maltreated children grow older and face new situations involving peers and other adults, poor emotional regulation becomes more and more problematic, resulting in unusual and self-harmful behaviors, such as Rosita's attempts to cut herself (Rodriguez-Srednicki, 2001). Over time, this inability to regulate emotions is associated with internalizing disorders, such as depression and fearfulness, as well as externalizing disorders, such as hostility, aggression, and various forms of acting-out (Cicchetti & Rogosch, 2001).

Brain Development Neuroscientists have connected the behavioral signs of poor emotion regulation among maltreated children to alterations in the developing brain. Studies with maltreated children and adults with a history of childhood abuse show long-term alterations in the hypothalamic-pituitary-adrenal (HPA) axis and norepinephrine systems, which have a pronounced affect on one's responsiveness to stress (Bremner & Vermetten, 2001; Nemeroff, 2004). Brain areas implicated in the stress response include the hippocampus (involved in learning and memory), the prefrontal cortex, and the amygdala, which can lead to long-term mental health problems (Bremner 2003).

In effect, acute and chronic forms of stress associated with maltreatment may cause changes in brain development and structure. As we noted in Chapter 2, the neuroendocrine system is designed to handle sudden stressful events by releasing cortisol to produce a fight-or-flight response. However, after prolonged and unpredictable stressful episodes associated with all forms of child abuse and neglect, cortisol levels become depleted and the feedback systems that control hormone levels in the brain may not function correctly. Stress floods the brain with cortisol; the brain, in turn, resets the threshold at which cortisol is produced, so that ultimately it circulates at a dramatically low level. As a result, the neuroendocrine system becomes highly sensitive to stress (De Bellis, Keshavan, Spencer, & Hall, 2000). These neurobiological changes that occur in response to untoward early-life stress may partially account for the psychiatric problems that emerge throughout the lives of maltreated children as described in the following section.

Emerging View of Self and Others   As normal development progresses, regulation of affect and behavior becomes less dependent on the caregiver and more and more autonomous (parents often use the vernacular expression, "terrible twos"). Toddlers' developing self-regulation is now applied to new situations, which further strengthens their emerging view of themselves and others. Importantly, children form complex mental representations of people, relationships, and the world during this developmental period. Their emerging view of themselves and their surroundings is fostered by healthy parental guidance and control that invoke concern for the welfare of others. Because these opportunities are seldom available to maltreated children, emotional and behavioral problems are more likely to appear as a result of their maladaptive view of themselves and others.

Representational models of oneself and others are significant because they contain experience, knowledge, and expectations that carry forward to new situations (Cicchetti & Lynch, 1995). For example, consider how a child's internalized belief that "my mother is usually there for me when I need her" or that "I am loved and worthy of love" shapes his basic beliefs about himself and others, and how these ideas reflect a sense of well-being and connection. Maltreated children, in contrast, often lack these core positive beliefs about themselves and their world (Cicchetti, Rogosch, Maughan, Toth, & Bruce, 2003; Weinfield, Sroufe, & Egeland, 2000). Instead, they may develop negative representational models of themselves and others based on a sense of inner "badness," self-blame, shame, or rage, all of which further impair their ability to regulate their affective responses (Feiring, Taska, & Lewis, 2002).

One male survivor of child sexual abuse explains this feeling of inferiority: "I could not see anybody loving me. I could not see anybody liking me or wanting to be with me, I could not see myself as significant to the point where I would actually be in a relationship with someone else." (Lisak, 1994, p. 542).

Feelings of powerlessness and betrayal are often described by children and adults who have been victims of maltreatment—feelings that become salient components of their self-identity (Finkelhor & Browne, 1988; Wolfe, Jaffe, Jette, & Poisson, 2003). In a situation of powerlessness, the child's will, desire, and sense of self-efficacy are thwarted and rebuked, which is often linked to fears, worries, and depression. In the words of one survivor, "It's as if the world was evil, it's coming to get you, and you could do almost nothing to defend from it" (Lisak, 1994, p. 533). **Betrayal** involves the degree to which the child feels the perpetrator gained their confidence through manipulation and coercion, as well as the position of trust or authority held by the perpetrator. As a consequence, the child's emotional needs may be compromised by intense and contradictory feelings of the need for closeness and the fear of it.

One's sense of personal power or self-efficacy can be undermined by physical and verbal abuse as well as by physical and emotional neglect; this maltreatment devalues the child as a person. Feelings of betrayal can also challenge an individual's sense of self, because the person the individual depended on violated that trust and confidence. Such feelings may not be identified until years later, once the individual reaches an age whereby he or she can recognize this betrayal dynamic as the source of feelings of self-blame, guilt, and powerlessness (L. M. Williams, 2003).

The following are typical of children's and adolescents' descriptions of having their sense of safety and self-esteem undermined by the sexual abuser (Sas et al., 1993, p. 68):

"I was scared that if someone else found out, that my father would believe that we had told and that he would kill our mother."

"I was embarrassed, worried, especially as I was a boy, I was being molested by a man. I thought people might think I was gay or my parents might not believe me."

Emotional reactions elicited by harsh punishment or sexual exploitation require the child to search for an answer to a fundamental question concerning responsibility and blame: "Why did this happen to me?" The previous quotes about self-esteem illustrate how some sexually abused children feel responsible for failing to recognize the abuse, participating in the abuse, causing their families' reactions to disclosure, failing to avoid or control the abuse, and failing to protect themselves. Rather than acknowledge or believe that one's own parents or a trusted adult could be the person at fault, some maltreated children may ascribe nonmalevolent intentions to the offender, which can then be used to explain and justify to others their family problems and disruption. Shifting the blame to themselves or to situational factors that are less important than one's own parents provides a more acceptable explanation (McGee, Wolfe, & Olson, 2001). One male survivor describes this attribution of blame: "I had to make sense out of what was going on. And the sense I made out of this was that I'm not really a good person. There's something different about me and something wrong" (Lisak, 1994, p. 541).

Girls and boys tend to differ in the ways they process and express their turmoil. Maltreated girls tend to show more internalizing signs of distress, such as shame and self-blame (Quas, Goodman, & Jones, 2003; Wolfe, Sas, & Wekerle, 1994); boys, on the other hand, tend to show heightened levels of physical and verbal aggression (S. J. Kaplan, Pelcovitz, & Labruna, 1999).

Emotional and Behavioral Problems   It comes as no surprise that the relationships maltreated children have with their peers and teachers typically mirror the models of relationships they know best. Instead of a healthy sense of autonomy and self-respect, their models of relationships have elements of being a victim and a victimizer—those who rule and those who submit—and during interactions with peers, maltreated children may alternate between being the aggressor and being the victim (Dodge, Pettit, & Bates, 1994a). Their strategies for adaptation, such as hypervigilance and fear, evolve to become highly responsive to threatening or dangerous situations. These strategies conflict, however, with the new challenges of school and peer groups. As a result, some maltreated children, especially those with histories of physical abuse and neglect, may be more distracted by aggressive stimuli, and misread the intentions of their peers and teachers as being more hostile than they actually are (Dodge et al., 1994a).

The development of empathy and social sensitivity for others during the preschool years are prerequisites for the development of positive, reciprocal peer relationships. Physically abused and neglected children, however, show less skill at recognizing or responding to distress in others, since this has not been their experience (Smetana et al., 1999). Observational studies of the behavior of maltreated children and their nonmaltreated peers reveal that physically abused children engaged in more stealing behavior, and neglected children engaged in more cheating behavior and less rule-compatible behavior (Koenig, Cicchetti, & Rogosch, 2004).

This is how one 2-year-old boy who had been physically abused by his parents responded to a crying child:

He then turned away from her to look at the ground and while looking at the ground began vocalizing "Cut it out! Cut it out!" with increasing agitation, each time speaking more loudly and more quickly. He patted the child on the back, but when this disturbed her he retreated from her, hissing and baring his teeth. He again

---

began patting her on the back, but this time his patting turned into beating. He continued beating the little girl despite her screams. (Main & Goldwyn, 1984, p. 207)

Thomas, an abused 1-year-old, exhibits disturbing signs of fearful distress when he hears a child crying in the distance:

Suddenly, Thomas becomes a statue. His smile fades and his face takes on a look of distress also. He sits very still, his hand frozen in the air. His back is straight, and he becomes more and more tense as the crying continues. . . . The (distant) crying diminishes. Suddenly Thomas is back to normal, calm, mumbling, and playing in the sand. (Main & George, 1985, p. 410)

These quotes illustrate a lack of social sensitivity as well as a disorganized, victim–victimizer reaction to peer distress. The nonabused children in these studies typically showed concern or attempted to provide comfort to the distressed child, but not one maltreated child exhibited a concerned response at witnessing the distress of another toddler. Maltreated children not only failed to show concern, but actively responded to distress in others with fear, physical attack, or anger. Can you see the continuity between their own experiences and their behavior with peers?

The general nature of maltreated children's peer relationships can be organized into two prominent themes (Cicchetti & Lynch, 1995). First, maltreated children, particularly physically abused children and those who witness violence between parents, are more physically and verbally aggressive toward their peers (S. J. Kaplan et al., 1999; Wolfe et al., 2003). They are more likely to respond with anger and aggression equally to friendly overtures from peers and to signs of distress in other children (Shields & Cicchetti, 1998). As a result they are less popular and have atypical social networks marked by aggression and negative attention-seeking, which appear to grow worse over time (Haskett & Kistner, 1991). Given their propensity to mistakenly attribute hostile intent to others and their lack of empathy and social skill, it is not surprising that abused and neglected children are rejected by their peers (Bolger & Patterson, 2001; Shields, Ryan, & Cicchetti, 2001).

The second theme is that maltreated children, especially neglected children, withdraw from and avoid peer interactions. Neglected preschool and school-age children tend to remain isolated and passive during opportunities for free play with other children, and seldom display overtures of affection or initiate play with their mothers or peers (Hildyard & Wolfe, 2002).

Children with histories of neglect stand out as having the most severe and wide-ranging problems in school and interpersonal adjustment. They perform worse than other

Table 14.1
Range of Child Characteristics Associated with Physical Abuse, Neglect, and Sexual Abuse

DIMENSION OF DEVELOPMENT	PHYSICAL ABUSE	NEGLECT	SEXUAL ABUSE
Physical	Minor: Bruises, lacerations, abrasions Major: Burns, brain damage, broken bones	Failure-to-thrive symptoms: Slowed growth, immature physical development	Physical symptoms: Headaches, stomachaches, appetite changes, vomiting; gynecological complaints
Cognitive	Mild delay in areas of cognitive and intellectual functioning; academic problems; difficulties in moral reasoning	Mild delay in areas of cognitive and intellectual functioning; academic problems; difficulties in moral reasoning	No evidence of cognitive impairment; self-blame; guilt
Behavioral	Aggression; peer problems; "compulsive compliance"	Passivity; "hyperactivity"	Fears, anxiety, PTSD-related symptoms; sleep problems
Socioemotional	Social incompetence; hostile intent attributions; difficulties in social sensitivity	Social incompetence; withdrawal, dependence; difficulties in social sensitivity	Symptoms of depression and low self-esteem; "sexualized" behavior; behaviors that accommodate to the abuse (e.g., passive compliance; no or delayed disclosure)

Source: From "Child Maltreatment" by C. Wekerle and D. A. Wolfe, in E. J. Mash and R. A. Barkley (Eds.), *Child Psychopathology, 2nd Edition*, p. 644. Copyright © 2003 Guilford Press. Reprinted with permission.

maltreated children on standardized tests of reading, language, and math (Eckenrode, Laird, & Doris, 1993). They are described by teachers unaware of their backgrounds as lacking maturity and academic readiness. These descriptions indicate problems completing schoolwork, lack of initiative, overreliance on teachers for help, and behavior that is both aggressive toward and withdrawn from their peers (Egeland, Yates, Appleyard, & van Dulmen, 2002). This pattern of poor adjustment often persists, leading to higher rates of personality disorders in early adulthood (J. J. Johnson, Smailes, Cohen, Brown, & Bernstein, 2000).

Sexually abused children also have problems with peers and school adjustment, although this varies considerably. Unaware of their maltreatment status, teachers describe them as more anxious, inattentive, and unpopular, and having less autonomy and self-guidance in completing schoolwork (Erickson et al., 1989). Children with histories of sexual abuse are more likely than nonabused children to suffer in their academic performance and their ability to focus on tasks, be frequently absent from school, and receive teacher ratings of shyness-anxiousness (Trickett, McBride-Chang, & Putnam, 1994; Wekerle & Wolfe, 2003). As a useful summary of this information, Table 14.1 shows the major dimensions of development that are affected by physical abuse, neglect, and sexual abuse.

Psychopathology and Adult Outcomes

The body mends soon enough. The broken spirit, however, takes the longest to heal.

—Adult survivor of sexual abuse

The developmental disruptions and impairments that accompany child abuse and neglect set in motion a series of events that increase the likelihood of failure and future maladaptations. As stated earlier, not all maltreated children who face these developmental challenges will develop psychopathology—let alone the same form of psychopathology—but they are at a much greater risk for significant emotional and adjustment problems (Cicchetti et al., 2000; Kilpatrick et al., 2003).

Adolescents and adults with histories of physical abuse and exposure to violence between parents are at increased risk to develop interpersonal problems accompanied by their own acts of aggression and violence (Egeland et al., 2002; Ulman & Straus, 2003). This relationship between being abused as a child and becoming abusive toward others as an adult is known as the **cycle-of-violence hypothesis**, which infers that victims of violence become perpetrators of violence (Widom, 1989b). In contrast, persons with histories of sexual abuse are more likely to develop chronic impairments in self-esteem, self-concept, and emotional and behavioral self-regulation, including severe outcomes such as PTSD, depression, and dissociative states (Banyard, Williams, & Siegel, 2002; Koenig, Doll, O'Leary, & Pequegnat, 2004).

As adulthood approaches, developmental impairments that stem from child maltreatment can lead to more pervasive and chronic psychiatric disorders, including anxiety and panic disorders, depression, eating disorders, sexual problems, and personality disturbances (J. Brown, Cohen, Johnson, & Smailes, 1999; Kendler et al., 2000). In the following section, we examine four prominent developmental outcomes of maltreatment—mood and affect disturbances, post-traumatic stress-related problems, sexual adjustment, and criminal and antisocial behavior—and note the similarities and differences in the outcomes according to particular forms of abuse whenever appropriate.

Mood and Affect Disturbances The following comment is from an adult survivor of sexual abuse:

> I trusted him so I think that it was confusing that he was doing this to me. I think that when I got older I was afraid more often than I was confused. I was really afraid. I really didn't want him to come near me. I'd try to avoid the situation and try to pretend that I was asleep so that he wouldn't come in to the room or anything like that, but it never worked. I felt helpless, which gradually turned into hopelessness and despair. (Transcribed from *The Nature of Things with David Suzuki*, executive producer, Michael Alder for the Canadian Broadcasting Corporation, originally aired on 10/6/94.)

Some say that child maltreatment affects children to their very soul, since it disrupts and impairs so many sig-

nificant childhood memories and experiences. Perhaps this is why symptoms of depression, emotional distress, and suicidal ideation are common among children with histories of physical, emotional, and sexual abuse (Wekerle & Wolfe, 2003). On a more positive note, the causes of these symptoms can sometimes be avoided if children are provided with available support from nonoffending family members, and are given opportunities to develop healthy coping strategies and social supports (Leifer et al.,2004). If symptoms of depression and mood disturbance go unrecognized, however, they are likely to increase during late adolescence and adulthood, and can lead to life-threatening suicide attempts and self-mutilating behavior (S. J. Kaplan, Pelcovitz, Salzinger, Mandel, & Weiner, 1997), especially among those sexually or physically abused since childhood (Brown et al., 1999; Kolko, 2002).

Similarly, teens with histories of maltreatment have a much greater risk of substance abuse (Kilpatrick et al., 2003), which, in turn, increases the risk of other adjustment problems. Perhaps as a result of their chronic emotional pain, some teens and adults attempt to cope with unpleasant memories and current stressors by abusing alcohol and drugs, in a futile effort to reduce or avoid their distress. Substance abuse may also temporarily bolster self-esteem and reduce feelings of isolation (Bensley, Eenwyk, & Simmons, 2000; Kendler et al., 2000).

Celia
Walled Away

"What I would end up doing was separating from the physical feeling and couldn't comprehend the physical pain and emotional sensation. The only word I can use now—I didn't have the word when I was five—the word I use now is rape, and the only way I could deal with that was I would separate into the wallpaper and the wallpaper was all different ballerinas and different poses and what I could see from them was that they didn't move. They were always smiling or they always had this look on their face and they couldn't be touched. They just stood still. So I would become this ballerina and I couldn't be touched and whatever he did to me I couldn't feel it because I was in the wall." Transcribed from *The Nature of Things with David Suzuki*, executive producer, Michael Adler Canadian Broadcasting Corporation, originally aired on 10/6/1994.

© Roy Morsch/Corbis

Many women, as well as men, with histories of child sexual abuse face lifelong struggles in establishing close and trusting relationships.

Post-traumatic Stress-Related Problems A significant number of men and women who have been subjected to severe physical or sexual abuse during childhood suffer long-term stress-related disorders, which we described in Chapter 7. Like Rosita, these adults may be haunted by intrusive thoughts or feelings of being trapped or, like Celia, they may dissociate or become emotionally numb, as they had done originally to escape from the pain and fear.

As we noted in Chapter 13, child sexual abuse can also lead to eating disorders, such as anorexia nervosa and bulimia nervosa (Wunderlich et al., 2001).

Between 20% and 50% of children and adolescents with histories of maltreatment involving sexual abuse or combined sexual and physical abuse meet criteria for post-traumatic stress disorder (PTSD) (McCloskey & Walker, 2000; Scott, Wolfe, & Wekerle, 2003). The prevalence among adults is equally disturbing: About one-third of the childhood victims of sexual abuse, physical abuse, or neglect meet criteria for lifetime PTSD (Kilpatrick et al., 2003; Widom, 1999). The course of this disorder may begin during childhood with abuse-specific fears, such as fear of being alone and fear of men, as well as idiosyncratic fears related to specific events of abuse, such as fear of sleeping (Terr, 1991). PTSD-related symptoms are also more likely to occur if the abuse was chronic and the perpetrator relied on a method of coercion or trickery to force compliance (Rodriguez, Ryan, Vande-Kemp, & Foy, 1997; Williams, 2003).

In reaction to emotional and physical pain from abusive experiences, children may voluntarily or involuntarily induce an altered state of consciousness known as **dissociation,** which can be adaptive when neither resistance nor escape are possible (Herman, 1992). The process allows the victim to feel detached from the body or self, as if what is happening is not happening to him or her. Almost all people dissociate in minor ways, such as daydreaming, but abuse victims may rely on this form of psychological escape to the extent that profound disruptions to self and memory can occur (Macfie, Cicchetti, & Toth, 2001). Over time, this fragmentation of experience and affect can progress into borderline disorder or multiple personality disorder (Briere, 2002; Ogawa, Sroufe, Weinfield, Carlson, & Egeland, 1997).

Sexual Adjustment   Sexual abuse can also lead to **traumatic sexualization,** in which a child's sexual knowledge and behavior are shaped in developmentally inappropriate ways. About 35% of preschoolers who have been sexually abused show age-inappropriate sexual behavior, such as French-kissing, open masturbation, and genital exposure (Friedrich & Trane, 2002). These signs of traumatic sexualization are more likely to occur following a situation during which a sexual response was evoked from the child, or he or she was enticed or forced to participate (Finkelhor & Browne, 1988).

For some children, the offenders' means of enticement—gifts, privileges, affection, and special attention—teaches them that their own sexual behavior is a means to an end. Thus, the abused child may attempt to sexualize interpersonal relationships by indiscriminantly hugging and kissing strange adults and children, something that is relatively uncommon among nonsexually abused children (Cosentino et al., 1995). For others, however, sexual behavior is associated with strong emotions, such as fear,

disgust, shame, and confusion. These feelings may translate into distorted views about the body and sexuality, in some cases leading to weight problems, eating disorders, poor physical health care, and physically self-destructive behaviors (Friedrich & Trane, 2002; Noll, Trickett, & Putnam, 2003).

Although sexualized behaviors are more common among younger abused children, they sometimes reemerge during adolescence or young adulthood in the guise of promiscuity, prostitution, sexual aggression, and victimization of others (Noll, Horowitz, Bonanno, Trickett, & Putnam, 2003). In fact, a history of any type of maltreatment among males is a significant risk factor for inappropriate sexual behaviors, alienation, and social incompetence during adolescence (Salter et al., 2003; D. A. Wolfe, Scott, Wekerle, & Pittman, 2001). Women with childhood histories of sexual abuse, in particular, are more likely to report difficulties during adulthood related to sexual adjustment that range from low sexual arousal to intrusive flashbacks, disturbing sensations, and feelings of guilt, anxiety, and low self-esteem concerning their sexuality (Banyard et al., 2002; Merrill, Guimond, Thomsen, & Milner, 2003).

Because their normal development of self-awareness and self-protection was severely compromised, adult survivors of child sexual abuse may become less capable of identifying risk situations or persons, or knowing how to respond to unwanted sexual or physical attention. Consequently, they are more likely to fall victim to further trauma and violence during adulthood, such as rape or domestic violence (Noll et al., 2003; Tyler, Hoyt, & Whitbeck, 2000).

Criminal and Antisocial Behavior   Does violence beget violence, as predicted by the cycle-of-violence hypothesis mentioned earlier? Although many persons convicted of heinous crimes and child abuse report significant histories of child abuse and neglect, most abused children do not go on to commit crimes. How do we reconcile this obvious, but complicated, connection between victim and victimizer roles?

Consider the developmental importance of adolescence. This developmental stage may represent a critical transition between being a victim of child maltreatment and the future likelihood of becoming abusive or being abused as an adult (Scott et al., 2003). Social dating, a favorite—and significant—adolescent pastime, can be a testing ground whereby one's knowledge and expectations about relationships are played out. Youths who have learned to adapt to violence and intimidation as a way of life, and who lack suitable alternative role models or experiences, are more likely to enter the social dating arena with inappropriate expectations about relationships.

Indeed, youths (girls as well as boys) who grew up in violent homes report more violence—especially verbal abuse and threats—toward their dating partners and to-

Child Maltreatment and Non-Accidental Trauma   **421**

BOX 14.1 What Are the Long-Term Criminal Consequences of Child Maltreatment?

This important question has plagued the field and the general public, from therapists and educators to policy makers and criminal justice officials. Cathy Widom (1996) addressed this question by examining the criminal records of over 900 individuals subjected as children to physical or sexual abuse or neglect prior to age 12, along with a matched cohort of nonmaltreated children. Both groups were followed into adolescence and early adulthood to determine whether they engaged in criminal or delinquent behavior as adolescents or adults.

The results are telling: Of the people who experienced any type of child maltreatment (physical abuse, sexual abuse, or neglect), 27% were arrested as juveniles, compared with 17% of their nonabused counterparts. The same pattern continued into adulthood: 42% of the abused/neglected group, compared with 33% of the controls, had arrest records as adults. Consistent with the cycle-of-violence hypothesis, those with histories of physical abuse (21%), neglect (20%), or both (16%) were particularly likely to be arrested for a violent crime (Maxfield & Widom, 1996).

One disturbing result is that women with histories of physical abuse and neglect were significantly more likely than nonmaltreated women to be arrested for a violent act (7% versus 4%, respectively), whereas this relationship was barely significant for men (26% versus 22%, respectively). Notably, persons with histories of sexual abuse were no different from the other maltreated children in their rates of criminal offenses.

But what about sex crimes? Are persons who were sexually abused during childhood more likely to commit sexual offenses, as suggested by the backgrounds of the known sexual offenders? If all types of abuse and neglect are combined, the odds of being arrested for a sex crime were 2 times greater for maltreatment victims than for

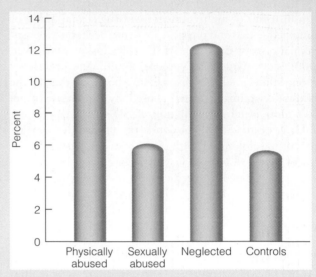

Sex crimes and maltreatment backgrounds
(Data from Widom, 1996)

nonvictims. However, if maltreatment backgrounds were broken down by type, only those with physical abuse and neglect backgrounds were associated with increased arrest for sex crimes; those with sexual abuse backgrounds were not (this finding remained when only male subjects were compared). Children who were sexually abused were about as likely as the controls to be arrested later for any sex crime, and less likely than victims of physical abuse and neglect (see the accompanying figure).

Thus, although any type of maltreatment puts victims at higher risk for criminal behavior, persons who were sexually abused in childhood are less likely than victims of physical abuse or neglect to commit a sex crime, and no more likely than demographically similar individuals.

---

ward themselves (Wolfe et al., 2001; Wolfe, Wekerle, Scott, Straatman, & Grasley, in press). Dating violence that occurs during adolescence, combined with a past history of violence in their own family, are strong prerelationship predictors of intimate violence during early adulthood and marriage (O'Leary, Malone, & Tyree, 1994; White & Widom, 2003). Thus, adolescence may be the middle stage, or initiation period, in the formation of a violent dynamic in intimate partnerships.

As we said, many children with maltreatment histories do not become violent offenders. Yet there is a significant connection between these events and subsequent arrests as a juvenile or an adult, even among girls (Siegel

& Williams, 2003; Widom, 1989a), or engaging in sexual and physical violence as a young adult, especially for males (Egeland et al., 2002). A history of maltreatment is associated with an earlier mean age at first offense and a higher frequency of offenses, as well as a higher proportion of chronic offenders (Widom, 1989b). Box 14.1 describes a study that links childhood violence and adult violence.

Although most child victims of maltreatment do not grow up to be perpetrators of violence, a disturbingly high number—approximately 30%—carry the pattern into adolescence and adulthood (J. L. Kaufman & Zigler, 1989). Growing up with power-based, authoritarian methods can be toxic to relationship and social patterns even if they don't result in physical injuries or identified maltreatment. Even the amount of routine violence— frequently being hit with objects or physically punished— that one experiences as a child is significantly associated with violent delinquent behavior later in life (Straus, 2001).

SECTION SUMMARY

- Child maltreatment disrupts the normal course of development; therefore, maltreated children show a wide range of different problems.

- Children may be protected in part from the effects of maltreatment by a positive relationship with at least one important and consistent person in their lives who provides support and protection.

- Early child maltreatment can disrupt caregiver–infant attachment, thus interfering with the child's ability to seek comfort and to regulate his or her emotions and behavior.

- Emotion regulation refers to the ability to modulate or control the intensity and expression of feelings and impulses.

- By early childhood, maltreated children show deficits in sensitivity to others, including problems with empathy, interpersonal trust, and mood.

- Impairments in cognitive and moral development often lead to problems in social judgment, communication, and school performance, as well as problems in self-control and aggression with peers.

- Child maltreatment can result in significant negative repercussions that persist into adulthood, including mood disturbances, PTSD, difficulties in sexual adjustment, and criminal and antisocial behavior.

Causes

My father was frightened of his mother. I was frightened of my father and I am damn well going to see to it that my children are frightened of me.

—*George V, King of England (1865–1936)*

Why do some family relationships give rise to pain and conflict instead of support and harmony? There is no simple answer to this question, so we must rely on a combination of theory, clinical observations, and empirical findings. For physical abuse and neglect, an important fact is that they are **relational disorders**. These forms of maltreatment occur most often during periods of stressful role transitions for parents, such as the postnatal attachment period, the early childhood and early adolescence "oppositional" periods of testing limits, and the times of

family instability and disruption (Milner, 2003). The caregivers' failure to provide nurturant, sensitive, available, and supportive care, especially during critical periods, is a fundamental feature of maltreatment.

Notwithstanding the critical role of the adult offender, abuse and neglect are rarely caused by a single risk factor. In addition, even though the risk signs and indicators are present, it is still very difficult to predict who will become abusive and who will not. Remember that child maltreatment is an event, not a uniform disorder; therefore it is necessary to consider multiple causes that interact unpredictably. Like a tornado that arises from just the right conditions of heavy wind, atmospheric pressure, and open terrain, child maltreatment may emerge in any given family if the "right" conditions exist. These causal conditions stem largely from the interaction of child, familial, and cultural influences, but it is not possible to predict with precision where and when they will detonate (Cicchetti et al., 2000).

Stress is one of those forces of nature and humankind that can convert static, stable conditions into dynamic, chaotic patterns. For example, physical abuse and neglect occur most often in the context of social and economic family deprivation, which can transform any predisposed, high-risk parents into abusive or neglectful ones. The greater degree of stress in the social environment that the abusive parent experiences will increase the probability that violence will surface as an attempt to gain control or cope with irritating, stressful events. In the case of neglect, stress may be so severe that parents withdraw from their child care responsibilities.

Sexual abuse is also influenced by cultural and familial practices, as well as the dynamic forces of stress. However, unlike physical abuse and neglect, sexual abuse is primarily a premeditated act, during which the adult offender plays a purposeful and intentional role. The abuser plans ways to circumvent the child's natural resistance and self-protection, and controls the situation to avoid detection. In the following sections we address these important causal issues in relation to psychological, social, and cultural dimensions.

Maltreatment is seldom caused by severe forms of adult psychopathology (Wolfe, 1999). Fewer than 10% of maltreating parents have a primary psychiatric illness, such as paranoid schizophrenia or Factitious disorder by proxy (formerly Munchausen by proxy; see Box 14.2), which might cause them to harm a child. However, these parents are likely to have a history of learning and intellectual deficits and personality disorders that impede their day-to-day abilities to cope successfully with child-related and other stressors (Kolko, 2002).

Similarly, child sexual abuse perpetrators often show various personality disorders related to immaturity and interpersonal adjustment, but these disorders do not fit a homogeneous pattern (Fagan, Wise, Schmidt, & Berlin,

2002). We begin to unravel this complicated story by looking at the important psychological dimensions that contribute to these adult behaviors toward children.

BOX 14.2 Factitious Disorder by Proxy—The Deadly Game

After 22 months of unsuccessful diagnostic procedures in a hospital setting in England to determine the cause of a baby's breathing problem, staff concealed a video camera in the baby's hospital room, and a policewoman and a nurse jointly monitored the scene. The following events occurred:

Sixteen hours after the onset of video monitoring, the child was asleep in his cubicle with only his mother in attendance. She moved the chair away from the cot and lowered the cot sides. She then placed a soft garment (a T-shirt) on the bedding close to the child's face. Five minutes later she placed the garment over his nose and mouth and forced his head onto the mattress. He awoke immediately and struggled violently. After ten seconds the officer alerted the nurses who went into the cubicle. . . . In this first episode the police officer had intervened prematurely [by legal standards] because of her own distress at what she had seen. She decided to continue surveillance. Twenty minutes later, when the child was asleep on his side and the mother was again alone in the cubicle, she placed him in a supine position with his face upright and tucked his arms under the bedding. Ten minutes later she again applied the garment to his nose and mouth and forced his head onto the mattress. The child struggled violently. Forty-two seconds later the nursing staff were alerted by the police and went into the cubicle. . . . The mother claimed that he had woken screaming and that she was comforting him. (Schreier & Libow, 1993, p. 40)

Munchausen is the name of an 18th-century military mercenary who became famous for his wartime tales, suspected to be fabrications. As an adult disorder, Munchausen syndrome (now called Factitious disorders) refers to an intentional fabrication of illness. As a form of child abuse, it refers to physical and psychological harm either through direct attack by the parent (which can be life-threatening) or as a function of being subjected to painful and numerous medical assessment procedures. Although the disorder is more likely to involve the mother, the father may be a passive colluder and an uninvolved or absent parent. Little is known of this form of abuse, other than over 95% of known cases are perpetrated by women (Schreier, 2002).

Source: Schreier, & Libow, 1993.

Physical Abuse and Neglect

Brenda
Unhappy Childhood, Unhappy Motherhood

Milton's mother, Brenda, described her childhood as one of harsh discipline and physical abuse. "My father was an alcoholic, and when he was drunk he'd start picking on one of us—me, my older brother, or my mom," Brenda explained. "After being pushed around and beaten for so long, I took off and left home as soon as I was able to, when I was 15. I lived with friends until I was old enough to get welfare; then I hooked up with Milton's father. He was good to me at first, but it wasn't long until he started hitting me, just like my dad had done." In recounting her background, Brenda would sometimes grow quiet and sad, but this soon was overpowered by her efforts to force herself back to her complaints about her son. Her affect changed rapidly to one of hostility and annoyance, which spilled over into her actions with Milton.

To many parents like Brenda, child-rearing is a difficult and aversive event that can escalate unpredictably into a sudden abusive incident, or more gradually turn into avoidance and neglect. Lacking experience and guidance in child-rearing and facing overwhelming stress, these parents cannot think of ways to best handle the situation. Instead, they succumb to the irritation of the moment—the child—and respond emotionally, without thinking.

Brenda's history and situation is very typical: How would she know how to raise her child, given her own childhood experiences? Many abusive and neglectful parents had little past or present exposure to positive parental models and supports. Their own childhoods were often full of difficult, sometimes very traumatic, episodes of family violence, alcoholism, and harsh family circumstances related to frequent moves, unemployment, and poverty (Wolfe, 1999). As adults, they find daily living stressful and irritating, and prefer to avoid potential sources of support because it takes additional energy to maintain social relationships. Chronic physical ailments and a pervasive mood of discontentment are common complaints, which are understandable in light of the circumstances and limited coping resources.

Offender Characteristics Maltreatment doesn't happen accidentally, but it is rarely a planned or intentional act. One parent described it this way:

"I felt I was spinning out of control. Everywhere I went, things just built up and tension mounted. When I tried to quiet my kids down, I would start shouting. When I tried to run away, everything followed me like a trail of debris. I just wanted the craziness to stop."

Like a chain reaction, a tragic combination of events can cause some predisposed individuals to maltreat a child in their care. Most of these events have one factor in common: They pose added stress for an individual who has already reached his or her limit.

Because abuse and neglect usually occur in relation to child-rearing demands, it is not surprising that both neglectful and abusive parents interact less often with their children than other parents during everyday activities involving their children. In general, neglectful parents actively avoid interacting with their children, even when the child appropriately seeks attention, most likely because social interaction is unfamiliar and even unpleasant. Physically abusive parents, in contrast, tend to deliver a lot of threats or angry commands when interacting with their children that exceed the demands of the situation, rather than offer their children positive forms of guidance and praise (Azar & Wolfe, in press).

Let's return to Brenda's situation and consider how her learning history, combined with her situational events, became a recipe for disaster. When her son misbehaved, she responded with a harsh combination of emotional and physical threats—the methods most familiar to her. At first, the physical punishment would stop Milton's misbehavior, but over time it led to a standoff, forcing her to increase the severity of her punishment and the child to escalate his aversiveness.

Her cognitive perceptions and distortion of events also played a significant role in this coercive process. The effect of **information-processing disturbances,** causes maltreating parents to misperceive or mislabel typical child behavior in ways that lead to inappropriate responses and increased aggression (Azar, 2002; Milner, 2003). They are unfamiliar with their role as parents and what is developmentally appropriate behavior for a child at a given age. Brenda believed that her son was able to understand—at age 4—what she was thinking and feeling, and to put her needs ahead of his own.

Over time, Brenda thought Milton was misbehaving intentionally, presumably because, in her mind, he should have known better. ("I can never get him to listen—he's a troublemaker, and he knows how to push my buttons.") Some parents apply the same faulty reasoning to their own behavior as well, which results in lowered self-efficacy. ("I'm not a good mother; other mothers can get their children to do these things.") These unrealistic expectations and negative intent attributions can lead to greater punishment for child misbehavior, and less reliance on explanation and positive teaching methods (Azar & Wolfe, in press). Children are seen as deserving of harsh punishment, and its use is rationalized as a way to maintain control. By now you can see where this process might end up.

Neglectful parents have received far less research attention than physically abusive ones, perhaps because omissions of proper caretaking behaviors are more difficult to describe and detect than commissions. Personality characteristics and lifestyle choices of abusive and neglectful parents overlap considerably, as a group. However, neglectful parents have more striking personality disorders and inadequate knowledge of children's needs, and they suffer more chronic patterns of social isolation than both abusive and nonmaltreating parents (Wolfe, 1999). Furthermore, neglectful caregivers typically disengage when they are under stress, whereas abusive parents become emotionally and behaviorally reactive (Azar, 2002). Neglectful parents try to cope with the stress of child-rearing and related family matters through escape and avoidance, which can lead to severe consequences for the child and to higher risk of substance abuse and similar coping failures for the parents (Crittenden & Claussen, 2002).

Like a tropical storm with an unpredictable course, a conflict between the parent and child can suddenly increase in intensity and turn into a damaging hurricane, or it can simply blow over. Negative arousal and emotions are highly "conditionable," so that salient events can later trigger the same feelings. This conditioning may occur gradually and build into uncontrollable outbursts, or occur suddenly during highly stressful, provocative episodes of conflict (Averill, 2001).

To illustrate, picture yourself trying to get your child ready for school each day, and going through the same frustrating chain of events: You're late for work and under pressure to get to a meeting when your preschooler starts to fuss about wearing his boots or combing her hair. For all but a hearty few, this combination of stress and all-too-familiar child demands spells anger and frustration. While most of us manage to control our emotions to deal with the situation in the best possible way, parents who have deficits in child-rearing and information-processing skills may see the child as intentionally causing them to be late. Anger and arousal are powerful emotions, so rational problem solving can quickly give way to emotional and reflexive reactions.

Anger and rage are highly dependent on situational cues, which usually stem from prior emotionally arousing events. In Brenda's case, certain "looks" that her son gave led her to believe that he wasn't going to comply. We discovered this interaction by videotaping the two of them playing together and then having Brenda ask Milton to straighten up the room. We played the tape back and asked Brenda to tell us whenever she felt that Milton was doing something that bothered her. She stopped the tape at several different points, telling us that "he's giving me that look," or "I know what he's thinking—why should I have to do what she says?" At this point, Brenda's tone of voice would become more tense and frustrated, and her instructions to Milton more forceful and abrupt.

Although Brenda could acknowledge she was getting

very angry, she was not able at first to interrupt this process and calm herself down. This demonstrates how parental arousal can be triggered by events, including past memories and current emotional tension, that may be highly specific to a particular parent–child relationship. This may lead, of course, to an overgeneralized—more angry, more aggressive—parental response, because the parent is responding impulsively to cues that have been previously associated with frustration and anger.

Child and Family Influences Do certain child characteristics or behaviors increase the likelihood of abusive or neglectful care? Children have an uncanny ability to figure out what their parents are going to do before they actually do it, and they become amazingly accomplished at weighing the odds for desired outcomes. However, even though children might do things that are annoying, adults are fully responsible for abuse and neglect. No child—no matter how difficult to manage or how challenging to teach—ever deserves to be mistreated. Children's behavior or developmental limitations may increase the potential for abuse, but only if accompanied by the other critical factors noted previously.

With the important exception of girls being sexually abused more often than boys, no child characteristic, such as conduct problems, has been associated with the risk of maltreatment, once environmental and adult factors are controlled (USDHHS, 2003). Unintentionally, however, the child may still play a role in the continuation or escalation of abusive or neglectful relationships. For example, children with disabilities such as mental retardation or physical impairments were 3 times more likely to be abused than were their nondisabled peers, based on a large population-based sample (Sullivan & Knutson, 2000).

The kind of coercive family interactions that we discussed in Chapter 6 with regard to aggressive children frequently occur in abusive families (Wolfe, 1999). Physi-

cally abused or neglected children, for example, may learn from an early age that misbehaving often elicits a predictable parent reaction—even though it's negative—which gives the child some sense of control. If crying and clinging are the only ways to get a parent's attention, these behaviors may escalate in intensity over time, especially if the parent fails to provide appropriate child stimulation and control.

This type of coercive interaction explains why abusive incidents occur most often during difficult, but not uncommon, episodes of child behavior such as disobedience, fighting and arguing, accidents, and dangerous behavior, which may produce anger and tension in some adults. In contrast, circumstances surrounding incidents of neglect relate more to chronic adult inadequacy, which spills over into daily family functioning (B. C. Herrenkohl, Herrenkohl, & Egolf, 1983). Neglected children's early feeding problems or irritability may place an increased strain on the parents' limited child care abilities, again setting in motion an escalation in the child's dependency needs and demands, accompanied by further parental withdrawal (Drotar, 1999).

Family circumstances, most notably conflict and marital violence, also have a causal connection to child maltreatment. In about one-half of the families in which adult partners are violent toward one another, one or both parents have also been violent toward a child at some point during the previous year (Edleson, 1999). Domestic conflicts and violence against women most often arise during disagreements over child-rearing, discipline, and each partner's responsibilities in child care (Edleson, Mbilinyi, Beeman, & Hagemeister, 2003). Children may be caught in the cross fire between angry adults, or in some cases, instigate a marital conflict by misbehaving or demanding attention. In either case, an escalating cycle of family turmoil and violence begins, whereby children's behavioral and emotional reactions to the violence create additional stress on the marital relationship, further aggravating an already volatile situation.

The physical and psychological consequences of violence, moreover, cause abused women to be less capable of responding to their children's needs, which again increases pressure on the family system. Tragically, not only do marital violence and family turmoil frighten and disturb children in a direct manner, but the resulting fallout from these events—ranging from changes in financial status and living quarters to loss of family unity and safety—prolongs the stress and thus the harmful impact on children's development (Margolin, Gordis, Medina, & Oliver, 2003).

An Integrated Model In a dynamic process, parental and situational factors interact over time to either increase or decrease the risk of physical abuse or neglect. Figure 14.3 depicts this dynamic process in relation to three hypothetical transitional stages. These stages suggest that

"I hate you! Never come back to my house," screamed an 8-year-old at his father as police arrested the man for attacking his wife.

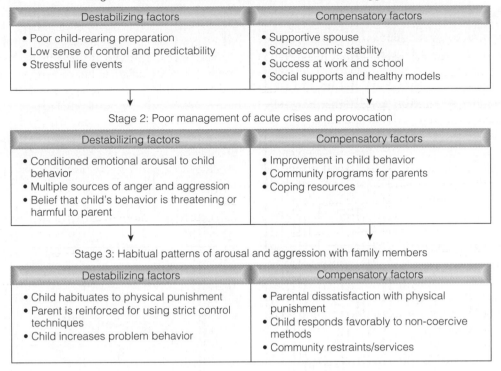

Stage 1: Reduced tolerance for stress and disinhibition of aggression

Destabilizing factors	Compensatory factors
• Poor child-rearing preparation • Low sense of control and predictability • Stressful life events	• Supportive spouse • Socioeconomic stability • Success at work and school • Social supports and healthy models

Stage 2: Poor management of acute crises and provocation

Destabilizing factors	Compensatory factors
• Conditioned emotional arousal to child behavior • Multiple sources of anger and aggression • Belief that child's behavior is threatening or harmful to parent	• Improvement in child behavior • Community programs for parents • Coping resources

Stage 3: Habitual patterns of arousal and aggression with family members

Destabilizing factors	Compensatory factors
• Child habituates to physical punishment • Parent is reinforced for using strict control techniques • Child increases problem behavior	• Parental dissatisfaction with physical punishment • Child responds favorably to non-coercive methods • Community restraints/services

Figure 14.3 An integrated model of physical child abuse.
(Wolfe, 1999)

maladaptive interaction patterns, like adaptive ones, develop not simply because of the predilections of the parent or child. To the contrary, these patterns are the result of complex interactions between child characteristics, parental personality and style, the history of the parent–child relationship, and the supportive or nonsupportive nature of the broader social context within which the family is embedded (Wolfe, 1999). This process, moreover, includes both destabilizing and compensatory factors that can influence the likelihood of abuse or neglect in a negative or positive fashion, respectively.

Sexual Abuse

Those seeking explanations for child sexual abuse have looked for evidence of deviant sexual histories of the adult offender, as well as environmental and cultural risk factors that play a role in the sexual exploitation of children. Yet, similar to physical abusers of children, sexual abusers are a very mixed group who defy all personality labels or psychiatric descriptors. Some are described as timid and unassertive, whereas others show a pattern of poor impulse control and domineering interpersonal style. Their common ground is a preference for sexual exploitation of children and adolescents who, because of their age and innocence, cannot consent to the activities or easily disclose the abuse to someone.

Offender Characteristics Sexual abusers of children come from many walks of life, and they are seldom discernable based on personality traits, occupation, or age (other than the conclusion that the vast majority of offenders are male). As a group, these offenders are more likely to have significant social and relationship deficits, including social isolation, difficulty forming emotionally close, trusting relationships, and low self-esteem (Berliner & Elliott, 2002; Marshall, Marshall, Sachdev, & Kruger, 2003b). Comorbid psychiatric disorders and substance abuse also emerge as proximate risk factors for sexual abuse of children (Fagan et al., 2002).

Sexual offenders of children usually meet DSM-IV-TR criteria for **pedophilia,** defined as sexual activity or sexually arousing fantasies involving a prepubescent child (generally age 13 years or younger), by someone who is at least 16 years old and at least 5 years older than the child. Some persons with pedophilia are sexually attracted only to children (exclusive type), whereas others are also attracted to adults (nonexclusive type).

Persons who commit pedophilia may limit their activities to incest that involves their own children, stepchildren, or other relatives, or they may victimize children outside their families (APA, 2000; Fagan et al., 2002). Significantly, over 50% of individuals who are pedophiles report an awareness of their pedophilic interests before they turn 17 years old (63% of those who target male chil-

Child Maltreatment and Non-Accidental Trauma **427**

BOX 14.3 Abuse in the Catholic Church

John Geoghan, below, stands out as one of the worst serial molesters in the recent history of the Catholic Church in America. For three decades, Geoghan preyed on young boys in a half-dozen parishes in the Boston area while church leaders looked the other way. Despite his disturbing pattern of abusive behavior, Geoghan was transferred from parish to parish for many years before the church finally defrocked him in 1998.

Source: http://www.boston.com/globe/spotlight/abuse/geoghan/

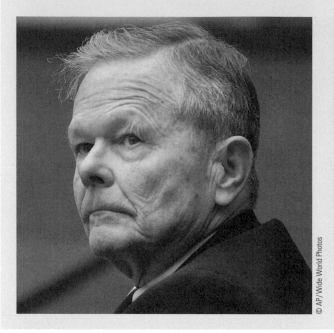

© AP/Wide World Photos

© AP/Wide World Photos

Bernie McDaid and Gary Bergeron, right, say they were molested by Rev. Joseph Birmingham in the 1960s.

---

dren and 50% of those who target female children), which they begin to act out on average by their late teens or early twenties (Abel, Osborn, & Twigg, 1993).

Those who victimize children develop complicated techniques to gain access and compliance from the child, which emphasizes the sexually opportunistic and predatory nature of this behavior. Pedophiles may win the trust of the child's mother or marry a woman with an attractive child. They may use methods to lower a child's resistance, such as initiating a friendship, playing games or giving presents, having hobbies or interests that appeal to the child, and using peer pressure (Wekerle & Wolfe, 2003).

Sexual offenders seldom resort to violence or force to gain the child's compliance; rather, they are attentive to the child's needs to gain the child's affection, interest, and loyalty, and to reduce the chances that the child will report the sexual activity. Typically, sexual behavior takes place only after a period of "grooming" with a gradual indoctrination into sexual activity, which underscores how sex offenders of children are "sophisticated, calculating, and patient" (Singer, Hussey, & Strom, 1992, p. 884). As one offender asserted, "You can spot the child who is unsure of himself and target him with compliments and positive attention" (Elliott et al., 1995, p. 584).

A perpetrator's efforts to establish a relationship with the child or youth, such as spending time alone or singling the child out as favored or special, may also reduce the child's internal inhibition by distorting the roles of the relationship and blurring interpersonal boundaries. His special status as a teacher, religious figure, or scout leader may cover his intentions with a sense of entitlement or privilege with a child, distorting his role into one that is a central part of the child's life (Wolfe et al., 2003). Sadly, children made more than 11,000 allegations of sexual abuse by over 4000 priests between 1950 and 2002, which represents about 4% of the 110,000 priests who served during the 52 years covered by the study (U.S. Conference of Catholic Bishops, 2004) (see Box 14.3).

Like the backgrounds of physical abusers, the backgrounds of sexual abusers of children reveal a link between being abused during childhood and perpetrating abuse against others, although this link is by no means well understood or inevitable. One possibility is that negative childhood experiences—sexual abuse, as well as other forms of maltreatment—set in motion a cautious, distrustful approach to intimate relationships (Fagan et al., 2002; Marshall et al., 2003a).

An adolescent male with a history of unhealthy or exploitative relationships, for example, may justify using co-ercive and abusive actions toward others who are smaller or weaker, because his other attempts at closeness have failed (S. M. Hudson & Ward, 1997). His sexual interests and arousal become fused with his need for emotional closeness, which can lead to sexual preoccupation, pro-miscuity, and the possibility of increasing sexual deviancy as his attempts to gain intimacy escalate through sexual contact (Marshall et al., 2003b).

Family and Situational Influences   Like sexual offend-ers, incestuous families do not fit a uniform profile. The most common elements of incestuous families such as greater social isolation, restricted personal autonomy, and deference to strict morality and religiosity tend to protect the "family secret" and to maintain control and domina-tion by the abuser (Howes, Cicchetti, Toth, & Rogosch, 2000). Not surprisingly, marital couples report significant levels of relationship distress and dissatisfaction, includ-ing sexual discontentment (Berliner & Elliott, 2002). As in other maltreating families, these characteristics reflect a climate of domination and abuse of power in which children are powerless at controlling unpleasant events. However, because these studies are frequently based on families after the discovery of incest, there is no way of knowing which came first—the abuse or the poor family functioning.

Certain situational factors increase children's vulner-ability to sexual abuse, a fact that offenders exploit to their advantage. Offenders see children as more vulner-able if they have family problems, spend a lot of time alone, and seem unsure of themselves; they also admit to preferring victims who are attractive, trusting, and young (Elliott, Browne, & Kilcoyne, 1995). To gain access to the child, the offenders look for circumstances that create lax supervision or opportunities for them to become involved, such as parental unavailability, illness, stress, spousal abuse, or lack of emotional closeness to the child. Low in-come and social isolation also increase a child's risk of sexual abuse, if parents lack the resources or opportuni-ties for suitable child care and safety precautions (Wekerle & Wolfe, 2003).

Social and Cultural Dimensions

What role does our culture play in the abuse and neglect of children? Intuitively, a primary focus on individual fac-tors as causes of child abuse and neglect is very limiting, since we live in a society that not only condones violence but also glorifies it directly and indirectly.

Consider how the entertainment industry, including many aspects of the media and professional sports, earns billions of dollars in profits from exploiting our interests in violence in all of its forms. Equally disturbing is the por-trayal of sex roles by society's envoys in the media and the entertainment industry: Females are stereotypically pre-sented as relatively powerless and passive, and men as vested with power; women are encouraged to defer to the benevolence of powerful men, and men are encouraged to challenge the autonomy of powerful and assertive women (Hedley, 1994). These cultural phenomena are ingrained through years of repeated imagery, and are presumed to be the basis for the motivation of some men to maintain control and power in a relationship (Williams, 2003).

At the family level, we have noted that child mal-treatment usually occurs in the context of homes and neighborhoods with multiple problems where poverty, so-cial isolation, and wide acceptance of corporal punish-ment significantly influence child development. These fac-tors stem from racism and inequality, which are arguably the major sociocultural factors contributing to abuse and neglect, not only of children, but of many adults and members of minority groups. The extent to which a soci-ety deems any particular group as being less worthy of recognition and economic or political support represents the level of vulnerability for that group to violence and a host of other indignities.

Poverty and Social Isolation   Although child maltreat-ment is certainly not limited by the boundaries of socio-economic status, the problem must be considered in the context of poverty and environmental stress. Poverty is associated with severe restrictions within the child's ex-pectable environment, such as lack of adequate day care, safety, and housing, which often impair or impede the de-velopment of healthy parent–child relationships. In addi-tion, adults who exist below poverty level suffer more in-dividual and family problems, such as substance abuse and emotional disorders. This is reflected by the fact that, on average, 40% of substantiated child maltreatment cases involve substance abuse (Wekerle & Wall, 2002).

Although the relationship between poverty and child maltreatment is a fact, this explanation is not sufficient. To fully explain this connection requires consideration of the psychological dimensions noted previously. Social and cultural disadvantage amounts to an extra burden of stress and confusion, and a limited number of alterna-tives. The coping abilities of family members are impaired by their circumstances and further constrained by their resources.

Perhaps as a result of cultural and social factors, mal-treating families often lack significant social connections to others within their extended families, neighborhoods, and communities, as well as to social assistance agencies (Korbin, 2003; R. A. Thompson & Flood, 2002). Unfor-tunately, maintaining family privacy and isolation may re-sult in restricted access to healthier child-rearing models and social supports. Neglectful families are especially prone to isolation and insularity, which may be directly related to the parents' significant interpersonal problems (Gaudin, Polansky, Kilpatrick, & Shilton, 1996).

Child-Rearing Practices and Family Privacy Child-rearing practices have been changing dramatically over the past 50 years or so. Today's parents are expected to appreciate their child's developmental strengths and limitations, and to move away from total reliance on disciplinary control methods toward methods that encourage the child's emerging independence and self-control. However, hypocrisy emerges when attempting to differentiate child abuse from child discipline, because cultural norms in many countries have long accepted corporal punishment as a primary, even necessary, component of discipline. As a result, four out of five 3-year-old children in the United States are physically punished by their parents during any given year, and about one in ten receive discipline so severe that they are at considerable risk of physical and emotional harm (Straus & Stewart, 1999).

Whether it is acceptable to spank children has become very controversial among lay and professional audiences in recent years (Benjet & Kazdin, 2003; Gershoff, 2002). Does corporal punishment, however, influence the likelihood of child abuse? The tentative answer is yes, but only indirectly. Most parents who use physical discipline are not abusing their children in either the physical or psychological sense. However, a change in circumstances—increased stress, more difficult child behavior—can up the ante quite suddenly.

Acceptance of corporal punishment leaves it up to local standards and parental judgment to define what is reasonable punishment, because no universal standard exists. Cultural values, historical precedent, and community standards, therefore, may set the stage for one person's abuse as being another person's discipline. Thus, child maltreatment occurs to a certain extent because of limited cultural opportunities to learn about appropriate child-rearing and to receive necessary education and supports, as well as long-held social customs that endorse the use of physical force to resolve child conflicts. Given increasing evidence that corporal punishment of children is harmful (Gershoff, 2002), a growing number of countries are choosing to abolish the practice (see Box 14.4).

Cultural norms and practices influence the prevalence of sexual abuse as well. The erotic portrayal of children, not only in pornography, but also in mainstream advertising raises many concerns about personal boundaries and appropriate messages. There is also grave concern stemming from the quantity of child pornography circulating on the Internet, where sexual abusers of children share information, exchange pornography, and make contact with potential child victims. Children exposed to pornography may be desensitized and socialized into believing that the activity is normal (Mitchell, Finkelhor, & Wolak, 2003). Children used in the production of pornography show psychological symptoms such as emotional withdrawal, anti-

social behavior, mood swings, depression, fear and anxiety, and disorders such as PTSD (Bowkett, 2003).

A Closer Look

BOX 14.4 Mounting Evidence Against Corporal Punishment of Children

A recent meta-analysis examined the long-range effects (positive as well as negative) of parental corporal punishment on key aspects of development and behavior. Negative or undesirable outcomes were found in terms of:

- decreased moral internalization
- increased child aggression
- increased child delinquent and antisocial behavior
- decreased quality of relationship between parent and child
- decreased child mental health
- increased risk of being a victim of physical abuse
- increased adult aggression
- increased adult criminal and antisocial behavior
- decreased adult mental health
- increased risk of abusing own child or spouse.

Corporal punishment was associated with only one desirable behavior: increased immediate compliance on the part of the child (which is often why parents say they rely on this method). Although causal relationships cannot be firmly established by these results, the findings are fairly evident that the use of corporal punishment is a risk factor for a number of undesired outcomes in child- and adulthood.

Source: Gershoff, 2002

Given the accumulating evidence, several countries have abolished the use of corporal punishment of children by parents or other caregivers (date of abolition is in parentheses):

Austria (1989)	Finland (1983)	Latvia (1998)
Croatia (1999)	Germany (2000)	Norway (1987)
Cyprus (1994)	Israel (2000)	Sweden (1979)
Denmark (1997)	Iceland (2003)	

SECTION SUMMARY

- Abusive and neglectful parents have often had little past or present exposure to positive parental models and supports.

- Parental lack of knowledge of child-rearing and ways of coping with anger and arousal play prominent roles in physical abuse and neglect.

- Mental disorders are seldom responsible for child abuse and neglect; however, stress-filled environments contribute to poor coping and social isolation.

- A sexual offender's preference for sexual exploitation of children and adolescents is a primary cause of sexual abuse.
- Sexual offenders of children usually meet DSM-IV-TR criteria for pedophilia, defined as sexual activity or sexually arousing fantasies involving a child.
- Child maltreatment also stems from poverty and inequality, social isolation, and unhealthy cultural norms concerning child-rearing practices and family privacy.

Prevention and Treatment

It should come as no surprise that child maltreatment exacts an enormous toll on society, in terms of both human suffering as well as economic loss. The costs of medical, legal, educational, and child welfare services related to maltreatment are estimated to be a staggering $94 billion a year in the United States (Prevent Child Abuse America, 2001; see Table 14.2). Accordingly, there is a sense of urgency in addressing this issue at all levels of prevention and intervention.

Consider these obstacles to intervention and prevention services for maltreating families: (1) Those most in need are least likely to seek help on their own; (2) they are brought to the attention of professionals as a result of someone else's concern, usually after they have violated expected norms or laws; and (3) parents do not want to admit to problems because they fear losing their children

Table 14.2.
Total Annual Cost of Child Abuse and Neglect in the United States

DIRECT COSTS	
	Estimated Annual Cost
Hospitalization	$6,205,395,000
Chronic Health Problems	2,987,957,400
Mental Health Care System	425,110,400
Child Welfare System	14,400,000,000
Law Enforcement	24,709,800
Judicial System	341,174,702
Total Direct Costs	*$24,384,347,302*

INDIRECT COSTS	
Special Education	$223,607,830
Mental Health and Health Care	4,627,636,025
Juvenile Delinquency	8,805,291,372
Lost Productivity to Society	656,000,000
Adult Criminality	55,380,000,000
Total Indirect Costs	*$69,692,535,227*
TOTAL ESTIMATED COST	**$94,076,882,529**

Source: Prevent Child Abuse America, 2001.

or being charged with a crime (fears that are, of course, realistic).

Many children and adults who seek treatment related to child abuse and neglect are under some form of legal constraint. Similar to other psychological interventions, child abuse treatments are based on the principle of beneficial assistance—but who wants assistance for something they won't admit to being a problem? As a result, treatments for child abuse and neglect have languished because of this basic dilemma: Access to treatment and prevention depends on admitting to or recognizing one's own culpability (Azar & Wolfe, in press).

Despite these obstacles, children and youths who have grown up with violence can make major shifts through treatment in how they relate to others, especially if treatment is begun early (Saunders, Berliner, & Hanson, 2003). Seeing their strengths and abilities, rather than their deficits, is a plausible approach to preventing physical abuse, neglect, and related social problems. Fifteen years after receiving pre- and postnatal home-visitation services to establish resource linkages and learn about their child's developmental needs, first-time parents—who were initially at risk of maltreatment based on either low socioeconomic status, young age (under 19 years), or unmarried status—gained over controls on important dimensions such as better family planning concerning number and spacing of children, less need for welfare, less child maltreatment, and fewer arrests of their children during adolescence (Olds et al., 1997).

Clearly, efforts to enhance positive experiences at an early stage in the development of the parent–child relationship hold considerable promise for prevention of child maltreatment and the reduction of its consequences. Similarly, programs that instruct children and their parents on how to avoid and report sexual abuse will improve children's responses to victimization, especially those programs that encourage children to actively participate in prevention activities (M. K. Davis & Gidycz, 2000; MacIntyre & Carr, 2000). Formal treatment efforts also increase the chances of overcoming the harmful effects of abuse and neglect. We discuss these treatments for physical abuse and neglect in the same section because of their close connection to child-rearing disturbances. Treatment of child sexual abuse is presented separately because of its unique nature and course.

Physical Abuse and Neglect

Treatment of child abuse and neglect can be delivered in many ways: to individual parents, to children, to parents and children together, or to the entire family. Despite how it is delivered, treatment of physical abuse usually attempts to change how parents teach, discipline, and attend to their children, most often by training parents in basic child-rearing skills accompanied by cognitive-behavioral methods that target specific anger patterns or distorted beliefs.

Similarly, treatment for child neglect focuses on parenting skills and expectations, coupled with training in social competence, which may include home safety, family hygiene, finances, medical needs, drug and alcohol counseling, marital counseling, and similar efforts to manage family resources and attend to the needs of the children (Azar & Wolfe, in press). Although most interventions emphasize the needs of the parents, desired changes in parenting can have a pronounced effect on their children's development as well.

Because maltreating parents place too much emphasis on control and discipline, or ways to avoid contact and responsibilities, they seldom know how to enjoy their child's company. Treatment, therefore, often begins with efforts designed to increase positive parent–child interactions and pleasant experiences. Parents are shown, through modeling, role playing, and feedback, how to engage in daily activities with their child that serve to strengthen the child's areas of deficiency, and to promote adaptive functioning (Wolfe, 1991). Activities are selected to maximize the child's attention and provide ample opportunity for pleasant interchanges. Milton's treatment plan illustrates this important initial step:

Milton's Treatment— Session 1

It didn't take long to see what Brenda faced at home. Partway through our first session, Milton (age 4) wanted his mother's attention and became quite angry when she was asked to leave the room for a few minutes. During this outburst he pushed an easy chair over and tried to hit Brenda with a rolled-up poster. She happily left for the observation room, leaving him and me together for the first time. I found a game and some puppets that he liked and began the process of establishing a relationship. As soon as Milton started to lose interest, I switched to a new activity. I modeled for Brenda some ways to simply observe Milton's behavior and express my interest:

"Milton likes to explore everything! Look! I have a talking doll! Can you make him say something? Excellent—he spoke to you!" (Milton starts to go for the toy chest). "Look, Milton! I have a puppet. Would you like to hold him? Good, you're coming back to play with me. After we play with the puppet, mommy will come in and play too! When we're all done, we'll go get a drink. Can you stack these blocks? Oops, you knocked them down; that looked like fun. Let's try again; only this time, you put one on here for me." I closely guided Milton to new activities to reduce his distractibility, all the time talking aloud so that his mother could hear in the adjoining room where she was observing the interaction.

Once parents learn a more flexible, adaptive teaching style that suits their child's development, efforts are begun to strengthen the child's compliance and self-control. Parents observe while the therapist models positive ways to encourage the child's attention and appropriate behavior, followed by practice and feedback. Therapists model for the parent how to express positive affect—with smiles, hugs, physical affection, praise—and how to show dismay or concern when necessary with appropriate facial expression, firmer voice tone, and similar cues that express disapproval.

Parent training seldom goes smoothly, especially with multiproblem families. What do you do when a child just "acts himself" and doesn't follow your directions, while his parent watches? These situations are often valuable for helping a parent apply the new skills under the naturalistic, this-is-what-it's-really-like conditions. Serendipitously, the value of modeling how to handle such a challenge was discovered a few sessions later:

Milton's Treatment— Session 4

Milton was tired of following my directions. Unaware that his mother was watching, he seized the opportunity to have some fun. He picked up toys and tossed them, and turned the light switch off and on. I thought I could simply get Milton to settle down by taking him down from his chair (which he was using to reach the light switch) and bringing him back to the couch. I was wrong. He started throwing a tantrum and screaming violently. With no other choice (child psychologists know when they're licked), I decided to talk above the noise so that his mother could hear how I was feeling and what I thought I might do: "I'm not sure just what to do yet. Milton seems to be uninterested in listening at the moment. Rather than getting angry, I think I'll wait a minute or two and try again. I've seen my 3-year-old do this, and I know you can't always expect kids to listen."

Brenda, familiar with this behavior at home, thought the situation was priceless—"Now you know what I have to deal with!" In lighthearted defense, I explained how there may not be an easy solution for these situations, which is why it is so important to maintain your composure and not expect or demand cooperation from Milton immediately. Tongue-in-cheek, I reminded her of Murphy's law of child behavior—"Anything that can go wrong, will"—and its corollary, "Just because it worked last time doesn't mean it will work every time!"

From this and similar misadventures, we discovered how familiar problems that emerge during treatment delivery will add authenticity for parents (and conveniently happen whether or not we plan them!). These situations, as well as less stressful ones, are also used to teach parents how to manage themselves calmly, yet firmly. Therapists model how parents can express frustration and annoyance without becoming abusive and harsh, and parents are then encouraged to discuss and rehearse how they can handle the situation. Gradually, they learn to replace physical punishment or apathy with more positive approaches. This process takes time, and parental frustration and impatience are to be anticipated.

On the whole, evaluations of interventions for physical abuse and neglect indicate that for several valid reasons, cognitive-behavioral approaches are the most widely supported methods for assisting maltreating parents (Saunders et al., 2003). Most significantly, these methods are effective (relative to standard protective-service interventions that involve brief counseling and monitoring) in modifying parental behaviors most relevant to child maltreatment, such as appropriate child-rearing and self-control skills. Techniques such as relaxation and self-management skills training, cognitive restructuring (viewing child behavior more appropriately), problem-solving training, and stress and anger management training are often combined with structured training in basic child-rearing skills. These methods, either alone or in combination, have been successful at teaching coping and problem-solving skills to abusive and neglectful parents (Kolko, 2002; Wolfe & Wekerle, 1993).

In addition to learning new ways to stimulate child development and structure child activities, neglectful parents often require very basic education and assistance in managing everyday demands, such as financial planning and home cleanliness. Programs like Project SafeCare provide multicomponent interventions that address the various needs of neglectful and multiproblem families, such as marital counseling, financial planning, lessons on cleanliness, and similar concerns (Gershater-Molko, Lutzker, & Wesch, 2003). Treatment services for abused or neglected children are less common than parent-oriented interventions, largely because parental behavior is often the primary concern. We have seen, however, that maltreated children often lag in important developmental competencies, which is a strong rationale for focusing additional attention on these areas.

The programmatic efforts of John Fantuzzo and his colleagues provide an excellent example of a developmentally focused intervention for maltreated children. Day care activities are coupled with resilient peer treatment (RPT), a peer-mediated classroom intervention that involves pairing withdrawn children (some with maltreatment histories) with resilient peers who are exceptionally strong at positive play activities (Coolahan, Fantuzzo, Mendez, & McDermott, 2000). Play activities are specifically targeted in this program, because play is a primary means for younger children to develop peer relationship skills. Competent "players" are encouraged to interact with less competent children in special play areas where adults participate in a minimal role. As a result, withdrawn children have the uncommon experience of being the center of another child's attention and experiencing a resilient child's repertoire of tactics for creating play and getting along with others (Coolahan et al., 2000).

The results of this series of studies have been impressive: Relative to controls, withdrawn children with histories of abuse or neglect show improvement in social behavior, cognitive development, and self-concept, and reduction in aggressive and coercive behaviors. A further strength of this intervention is that it can be conducted in community settings, such as Head Start classrooms, that offer comprehensive services for disadvantaged children and their families (Fantuzzo, Weiss, & Coolahan, 1998).

Sexual Abuse

What allowed this to happen was that so many people were silent about it.

—Adult sexually abused as a child

Sexually abused children have experienced a world of secrecy, silence, and isolation. After they break that silence by disclosing the abuse, or the abuse is discovered by accident, the path toward healing can be difficult. They must access not only unpleasant memories, but also buried feelings of guilt, confusion, fear, and low self-worth.

Despite advances in understanding the prevalence and impact of sexual abuse of children, children's treatment programs are only beginning. Like physical abuse and neglect, sexual abuse carries a special treatment challenge: Sexually abusive experiences affect each child unpredictably, which leads to diverse short- and long-range outcomes. As a result, treatments must match the needs of a wide age range of children who may show all kinds of symptoms or no symptoms at all (Berliner & Elliott, 2002).

Moreover, sexual abuse, like many other problems of childhood, occurs in the context of other individual, family, and community problems that affect its impact and treatment. Elements of family functioning, especially maternal support and help-seeking in response to the crisis, are known to affect children's level of distress and aid in their recovery, so treatment often must address these situational issues as well.

Treatment programs for children who have been sexually abused usually provide several crucial elements to restore the child's sense of trust, safety, and guiltlessness (Berliner & Elliott, 2002; Saywitz, Mannarino, Berliner, & Cohen, 2003). One major element of treatment involves education and support to help these children understand why this happened to them, and how they can learn to feel safe once again. Information and education about the nature of sexual abuse helps clarify false beliefs that might lead to self-blame, and children's feelings of stigma and isolation are often addressed through reassurance or group therapy that involves other child victims. Animated films and videos offer ways for child victims to acknowledge and validate their feelings and help them talk about their feelings, which allows them to move toward the future with a sense of hope and empowerment. Children are also taught ways to prevent sexual abuse and restore their sense of personal power and safety. Through the use of animated films and behavioral rehearsal children learn how to distinguish appropriate from inappropriate touches (M. K. Davis & Gidycz, 2000).

Cognitive-behavioral methods are particularly valuable in achieving these goals (Saywitz et al., 2003). Preferably, education and support are provided not only to the child victim, but to (nonoffending) parents as well. The secretive betrayal that underlies the nature of sexual abuse causes some parents to feel ambivalent about whether to believe their child or how they feel about the alleged perpetrator, whom they may have trusted. Parents may need advice on ways to understand and manage their child's behavior that may involve regressive or sexual behaviors due to the abuse. Parents often experience their own fears and worries as a result of the disclosure, and discussion with other parents and therapists can provide valuable support.

In conjunction with education and support, sexually abused children must express their feelings about the abuse and its aftermath—anger, ambivalence, fear—within a safe and supportive context. Younger children, for example, often cannot report their psychological reactions to the trauma unless they are asked specifically about the aspects of the trauma (Wolfe et al., 1994). Sexual abuse elicits attempts by children to cope with powerful and confusing feelings, and it is understandable that some will use every method possible to avoid these feelings. However, attempts to escape or avoid internal states of fear and anxiety can paradoxically make them worse.

For these reasons, controlled-exposure techniques, similar to those discussed in Chapter 7, have been adapted for child sexual abuse victims. The child is asked to gradually recall her memories of events, often to the point of feeling distressed, to allow the powerful emotions to be extinguished with repeated exposure. In addition, she learns to cope with negative thoughts and feelings about the abuse by using positive statements and imagery. Gradual exposure, modeling, education, coping, and prevention skills training with the child may be important in the treatment of PTSD-related symptoms (Deblinger, Stauffer, & Steer, 2001; Saywitz et al., 2003).

There is strong agreement that successful interventions for sexually abused children should result in several important outcomes (Berliner & Elliott, 2002). Treatment

services should help children understand that what happened to them was abuse, that it was wrong, and that it may have caused them some temporary problems. Emotional and behavioral problems that may have arisen from the abuse should subside, and children should have the personal resources to handle future problems. Importantly, they should have supportive relationships in place, especially with parents and other caregivers who have received adequate knowledge and assistance to understand the possible impact the abuse may have on their children's behavior and adjustment. Finally, successful treatment outcome results in children's regaining their normal rate of development.

Twenty years ago, psychology textbooks never discussed these issues. We had little knowledge of the devastating developmental, mental health, and societal consequences of abuse and neglect, and very few treatments were available. Since that time, considerable progress has been made in understanding and helping children who have been abused and neglected and their families. Most importantly, broader efforts at prevention and family support may help reduce or eliminate the likelihood of such unnecessary and harmful mistreatment of children and youths.

SECTION SUMMARY

- Treatment services for maltreating families have been limited, in part, due to the difficulty of parents' acknowledging their own weaknesses and seeking help without coercion.

- Prevention of maltreatment holds considerable promise, especially if begun early in the formation of the parent–child relationship.

- Interventions for physical abuse and neglect emphasize parent- and family-focused training in child-rearing and stress management. This method also benefits the child as a result of improved parental care.

- Treatment of physical abuse involves training parents in more positive child-rearing skills, accompanied by cognitive-behavioral methods to target specific anger patterns or distorted beliefs.

- Treatment for child neglect focuses on parenting skills and expectations, coupled with training in social competence and household management.

- Interventions for children who have been sexually abused emphasize the children's needs for safety, understanding, and expression of emotional consequences.

- Cognitive-behavioral methods have shown value in working with sexually abused children, especially when accompanied by education and support to supportive caregivers as well.

Key Terms

 InfoTrac College Edition

To research recent articles on the subject, go to:
www.infotrac-college/thomsonlearning.com

Enter search terms: CHILD ABUSE, FAMILY VIOLENCE, POST-TRAUMATIC STRESS DISORDER IN CHILDREN, PEDOPHILIA

Epilogue

Photo: Annie, age 3

Annie

I feel peaceful and safe

I feel peaceful and
Safe in my house. I
feel peaceful and
Safe in my colleg.
I feel peaceful and
Safe with my moma
and my DaDa. I feel
peaceful and Safe with
my sister and my
brother. I feel peaceful and
Safe in my bed. I
feel peaceful and Safe
with my teddy bear.

I feel peaceful and
Safe with my friends.
I feel peaceful and
Safe when the
Sun is up. I
feel peaceful and
Safe when it is
Quiet. I feel peaceful
and Safe when I
am working. I feel
peaceful and Safe
when I am whering
Soft Slipers. I feel
peaceful and Safe when I am
With My family.

Annie Legate-Wolfe, age 7

Glossary

acute stress disorder A form of anxiety disorder characterized by the development of anxiety, dissociation, and other symptoms within 1 month following exposure to an extremely traumatic stressor.

adaptational failure Failure to master or progress in accomplishing developmental milestones.

adaptive functioning The ability to cope effectively with ordinary life demands, to live independently, and to abide by community standards. Adaptive functioning is a necessary component for defining levels of mental retardation.

ADHD: combined type (ADHD-C) A subtype of attention-deficit/hyperactivity disorder characterized by a combination of inattentive symptoms and hyperactive-impulsive symptoms.

ADHD: predominantly hyperactive-impulsive type (ADHD-HI) A subtype of attention-deficit/hyperactivity disorder characterized by predominantly hyperactive-impulsive symptoms.

ADHD: predominantly inattentive type (ADHD-PI) A subtype of attention-deficit/hyperactivity disorder characterized by predominantly inattentive symptoms.

adolescent-limited (AL) path A developmental pathway to antisocial behavior whereby the child's antisocial behavior begins around puberty, continues into adolescence, and later desists in young adulthood.

adolescent-onset conduct disorder A specific type of conduct disorder for which the characteristics are not exhibited prior to 10 years of age.

agoraphobia A form of anxiety characterized by a fear of being alone in, and avoiding, certain places or situations from which escape may be difficult or embarrassing, or in which help may be unavailable in the event of a panic attack.

amplifier hypothesis The premise that stress may serve to amplify the maladaptive predispositions of parents, thereby disrupting family management practices and compromising the parents' ability to be supportive of their children.

anaclitic depression A condition described by Renee Spitz in the 1940s in which infants raised in a clean but emotionally cold institutional environment displayed reactions that resembled a depressive disorder, including weeping, withdrawal, apathy, weight loss, sleep disturbance, an overall decline in development, and in some cases even death.

analogue research Research that evaluates a specific variable of interest under conditions that only resemble or approximate the situation to which one wishes to generalize.

Angelman syndrome A genetic disorder associated with an abnormality of chromosome 15. Children with Angelman syndrome typically suffer from moderate to severe mental retardation, ataxia (awkward gait), jerky movements, hand flapping, seizures, the absence of speech, and distinctive facial features such as a large jaw and open-mouthed expression.

anhedonia A negative mood state characterized by a lack of enjoyment in anything one does and a loss of interest in nearly all activities.

anorexia nervosa A severe eating disorder characterized by the refusal to maintain a minimally normal body weight, an intense fear of gaining weight, and a significant disturbance in the individual's perception and experiences of his or her own size.

antisocial behavior See *conduct problems.*

antisocial personality disorder (APD) An adult disorder characterized by a pervasive pattern of disregard for, and violation of, the rights of others, as well as engagement in multiple illegal behaviors.

anxiety A mood state characterized by strong negative affect, bodily symptoms of tension, and apprehensive anticipation of future danger or misfortune.

anxiety disorder A disorder in which the child experiences excessive and debilitating anxiety.

apprehensive expectation Excessive and exaggerated worry and tension in the absence of conditions that would normally provoke such a reaction.

Asperger's disorder (AD) A pervasive developmental disorder characterized by major difficulties in social interaction and unusual patterns of interest and behavior in children with relatively intact cognitive and communication skills.

assent Evidence of some form of agreement on the part of a child to participate in a research study without the child's having the full understanding of the research that would be needed to give informed consent.

attachment The process of establishing and maintaining an emotional bond with parents or other significant care givers. This process is ongoing, typically beginning between 6 and 12 months of age, and provides infants with a secure, consistent base from which to explore and learn about their worlds.

attentional capacity The amount of information in short-term memory to which one can attend.

attention-deficit/hyperactivity disorder (ADHD) A disorder in which the individual consistently and repeatedly shows age-inappropriate behaviors in the two general categories of inattention and hyperactivity-impulsivity.

autism A pervasive developmental disorder characterized by abnormalities in social functioning, language and communication, and unusual interests and behaviors. More specifically, autism affects every aspect of the child's interaction with his or her world, involves many parts of the brain, and undermines the very traits that make us human—our social responsiveness, ability to communicate, and feelings for other people.

autistic disorder DSM-IV diagnostic category used to describe children with autism.

Behavior + Lens principle A principle which states that child psychopathology reflects a mix of actual child behavior and the lens through which it is viewed by others in a child's culture.

behavior analysis or functional analysis of behavior An effort to identify as many factors as possible that could be contributing to a child's problem behavior, thoughts, and feelings, and to develop hypotheses about which ones are the most important and/or most easily changed.

behavioral activation system (BAS) A subsystem of the brain that activates behavior in response to cues of reward or nonpunishment.

behavioral assessment The evaluation of the child's thoughts, feelings, and behaviors in specific settings, based on which hypotheses are formulated about the nature of the problem and what can be done about it.

behavioral genetics A branch of genetics that investigates possible connections between a genetic predisposition and observed behavior.

behavioral inhibition The ability to delay one's initial reactions to events or to stop behavior once it has begun.

behavioral inhibition system (BIS) A subsystem of the brain that produces anxiety and inhibits ongoing behavior in the presence of novel events, innate fear stimuli, and signals of nonreward or punishment.

betrayal The degree to which a child feels a perpetrator gained his or her confidence through manipulation and coercion, as well as the position of trust or authority held by the perpetrator. As a consequence, the child's emotional needs may be compromised by intense and contradictory feelings of the need for closeness and the fear of it.

binge Overeating that involves both excessive amounts of food and a lack of control.

binge eating disorder (BED) A disorder that involves periods of excessive eating with a feeling of a loss of control. It is similar to binge eating but without the compensatory behaviors and has become increasingly widespread during this age of abundant fast food and obesity.

binge-eating/purging A type of anorexia whereby the individual regularly engages in episodes of binge eating or purging, or both.

bipolar disorder (BP) A type of mood disorder characterized by an ongoing combination of extreme highs and extreme lows. An episode of mania is an abnormally elevated or expansive mood, and feelings of euphoria are an exaggerated sense of well-being. The highs may alternate with lows, or both extremes may be felt at about the same time.

bipolar I disorder A form of bipolar disorder characterized by one or more manic or mixed episodes, usually accompanied by major depressive episodes.

bipolar II disorder A form of bipolar disorder characterized by one or more major depressive episodes, accompanied by at least one hypomanic episode.

brain circuits Paths made up of clustering neurons that connect one part of the brain to another.

bulimia nervosa (BN) An eating disorder that involves recurrent episodes of binge eating, followed by an effort to compensate by self-induced vomiting or other means of purging. Individuals with bulimia are also unduly influenced by body shape and weight, and are obsessed with food.

bullying When one or more children expose another child, repeatedly and over time, to negative actions, such as physical contact, words, making faces or dirty gestures, and intentional exclusion from a group.

callous and unemotional interpersonal style A mode of social interaction that is characterized by such traits as the absence of feelings of guilt, not showing empathy, and not showing emotions.

case study An intensive and usually anecdotal observation and analysis of an individual subject.

categorical classification The diagnostic systems that are primarily based on informed professional consensus, which is an approach that has dominated and continues to dominate the field of child (and adult) psychopathology.

central coherence The strong tendency of humans to interpret stimuli in a relatively global way that takes the broader context into account.

child maltreatment The abuse and neglect of children by parents or by others responsible for their welfare. Child maltreatment is a generic term used to refer to the four primary acts of physical abuse, neglect, sexual abuse, and emotional abuse of persons less than 18 years of age.

childhood disintegrative disorder A pervasive developmental disorder characterized by a significant loss of previously acquired skills, as well as the presence of abnormalities in two of the following three areas of functioning: social interaction, communication, and patterns of behavior, interests, and activities.

childhood obesity A chronic medical condition characterized by an excessive

accumulation of body fat relative to gender- and age-based norms.

childhood-onset conduct disorder A specific type of conduct disorder whereby the child displays at least one characteristic of the disorder prior to 10 years of age.

chronic illness An illness that is long lasting and often irreversible.

classification A system for representing the major categories or dimensions of child psychopathology, and the boundaries and relations among them. One definition of diagnosis is the assignment of cases to categories of the classification system.

clinical assessment A process of differentiating, defining, and measuring the behaviors, cognitions, and emotions that are of concern, as well as the environmental circumstances that may be contributing to these problems.

clinical description A summary of unique behaviors, thoughts, and feelings that together make up the features of a given psychological disorder.

code-emphasis approach Approaches to reading instruction that emphasize the specific learning of word structure and the decontextualization of reading until the skill is learned. Code-emphasis methods are based on the premise that the ability to decode and recognize words accurately and rapidly must be acquired before reading comprehension can occur.

coercion theory A developmental theory proposing that coercive parent–child interactions serve as the training ground for the development of antisocial behavior. Specifically, it is proposed that through a four-step escape-conditioning sequence, the child learns how to use increasingly intense forms of noxious behavior to escape and avoid unwanted parental demands.

cohort A group of individuals who are followed over time and who experience the same cultural or historical events during the same time period.

communication deviance A measure of interpersonal attentional and thought disturbance observed in families of children with schizophrenia or schizotypal personality disorder. Children from families with high communication deviance show the most severe impairment and the poorest attentional functioning.

communication disorders A diagnostic term that refers to difficulty producing speech sounds (phonological disorder) or with speech fluency (stuttering); with using spoken language to communicate (expressive language disorder); or with understanding what other people say (mixed expressive-receptive language disorder).

comorbidity The overlapping of two or more disorders at a rate that is greater than would be expected by chance alone.

compensatory behavior Behavior shown by persons suffering from bulimia nervosa to prevent weight gain following a binge episode. Compensatory behaviors include self-induced vomiting, fasting, exercising, and the misuse of diuretics, laxatives, enemas, or diet pills. (Also see *purging*.)

competence The ability to adapt to one's environment. Children's competence involves their performance relative to their same-age peers as well as to their individual course of development.

compulsions Repetitive, purposeful, and intentional behaviors or mental acts that are performed in response to an obsession.

conduct disorder (CD) A form of disruptive behavior disorder in which the child exhibits an early, persistent, and extreme pattern of aggressive and antisocial acts that involve the infliction of pain on others or interference with others' rights through physical and verbal aggression, stealing, vandalism, truancy, or running away.

conduct problems (antisocial behavior) Age-inappropriate actions and attitudes that violate family expectations, societal norms, and the personal or property rights of others.

continuity of development A theoretical position for explaining development which proposes that normal and abnormal developmental changes are gradual and quantitative. Continuity theorists argue that development is an additive process that is ongoing rather than occurring in distinct stages.

correlation coefficient A number that describes the degree of association between two variables of interest.

cortisol A stress hormone produced by the adrenal glands.

cross-sectional research A method of research whereby different individuals at different ages/stages of development are studied at the same point in time.

cultural-familial group Mental retardation in which there is no evidence of organic brain damage (usually associated with mild MR).

cycle-of-violence hypothesis The repetition of patterns of violent behavior across generations. For example, persons who are abused as children are more likely to be abusive toward others as adults.

cyclothymic disorder A form of bipolar disorder characterized by at least 1 year (2 years in adults) of numerous periods of hypomanic symptoms that do not meet criteria for a manic episode, and numerous periods of depressive symptoms that do not meet criteria for a major depressive episode.

decoding A skill necessary for reading that involves breaking words down into parts.

delinquent The legal term used to describe antisocial behavior.

delusions Disturbances in thinking involving disordered thought content and strong beliefs that are misrepresentations of reality.

depressogenic cognitions The negative perceptual and attributional styles and beliefs associated with depressive symptoms.

destructive-nondestructive dimension An independent dimension of antisocial behavior consisting of a continuum ranging from acts such as cruelty to animals or destruction of property at one end, to nondestructive behaviors such as arguing or irritability at the other.

developmental coordination disorder (DCD) A disorder characterized by marked motor incoordination (e.g., clumsiness and delays in achieving motor milestones).

developmental history or family history Information obtained from the parents about potentially significant historical milestones and events that might have a bearing on the child's current difficulties.

developmental pathway A concept to describe the sequence and timing of particular behaviors, and to highlight the known and suspected relationships of behaviors over time.

developmental psychopathology An approach to describing and studying disorders of childhood and adolescence in a manner that emphasizes the importance of developmental processes and tasks. This approach uses abnormal development to inform normal development and vice versa.

developmental tasks Psychosocial tasks of childhood that reflect broad domains of competence and tell us how children typically progress within each of these domains as they grow.

developmental tests Tests used to assess infants and young children that are generally carried out for the purposes of screening, diagnosis, and evaluation of early development.

developmental-versus-difference controversy A debate regarding the developmental progression of children with mental impairments. The developmental position argues that all children, regardless of intellectual impairments, progress through the same developmental stages in the same sequence, but at different rates. The difference position argues that the development of children with mental impairments proceeds in a different, less sequential, and less organized fashion than that of children without impairments.

diagnosis The identification of a disorder from an examination of the symptoms.

diathesis-stress model of depression A theory of depression proposing that the impact of stress is moderated by individual risk factors and that the occurrence of depression depends on the interaction between the subject's personal vulnerability and life stress.

difference viewpoint The view that cognitive development of children with mental retardation differs from that of normally developing children in more ways than merely differences in developmental rate and upper limit.

dimensional classification An empirically based approach to the diagnosis and classification of child psychopathology which assumes that there are a number of independent dimensions or traits of behavior and that all children possess these to varying degrees.

direct instruction An approach to teaching children with learning disorders based on the premise that to improve a skill the instructional activities have to approximate those of the skill being taught.

discontinuity of development A theoretical position for explaining development proposing that normal and abnormal developmental changes are abrupt and qualitative. Discontinuity theorists, such as Piaget and Erickson, argue that children pass through developmental stages that are qualitatively different from each other.

discrete trial training A method of teaching readiness skills or other desired behaviors that involves a step-by-step approach to presenting a stimulus and requiring a specific response.

disruptive behavior disorders A DSM-IV-TR category for persistent patterns of antisocial behavior that includes oppositional defiant disorder, and conduct disorder.

dissociation An altered state of consciousness in which the individual feels detached from the body or self. This process may be voluntary or involuntary, and can be adaptive when resistance or escape from a life-threatening situation is not possible.

distractibility A term used to describe deficits in selective attention.

double depression An instance in which a major depressive episode is superimposed on the subject's previous dysthymic disorder.

Down syndrome A chromosomal abnormality in which there are three 21st chromosomes rather than the normal two. Children with Down syndrome typically function at the moderate level of mental retardation, have an increased likelihood of medical problems, and have unusual physical features. This syndrome is also called trisomy 21.

drive for thinness A motivational variable underlying dieting and body image, among young females in particular, whereby the individual believes that losing more weight is the answer to overcoming their troubles and achieving success.

dyslexia Disorder of reading not due to low intelligence. (Also see *reading disorder*.)

dysphoria A negative mood state characterized by prolonged bouts of sadness.

dyssomnias A category of sleep disorders involving difficulties initiating or maintaining sleep. Such disorders are often characterized by problems getting enough sleep, not sleeping when one wants to, and not feeling refreshed after sleeping.

dysthymic disorder (DD) A form of depressive disorder characterized by at least 1 year (2 years in adults) of depressed mood for more days than not, accompanied by additional depressive symptoms that do not meet criteria for a major depressive episode. In comparison to major depressive disorder, dysthymia is milder, but more long-term.

eating attitudes A person's belief that cultural standards for attractiveness, body image, and social acceptance are closely tied to the ability to control one's diet and weight gain.

eating disorders—not otherwise specified (EDNOS) A category of eating disorders that includes problems that do not quite fulfill criteria for anorexia nervosa or bulimia nervosa. The EDNOS category is less stringent than DSM-IV-TR criteria for anorexia nervosa or bulimia nervosa, and therefore is sometimes more appropriate for adolescents.

echolalia A child's immediate or delayed parrot-like repetition of words or word combinations.

eclectic The approaches that are identified by clinicians who work with children and families as different approaches for different problems and circumstances.

educational neglect Failure to provide for a child's basic educational needs, including allowing chronic truancy, failing to enroll a child of mandatory school age in school, and failing to attend to a special educational need.

electroencephalogram (EEG) An electrophysiological measure of brain functioning whereby electrodes are taped to the surface of the subject's scalp to record the electrical activity of the brain. EEG recordings are sensitive to changes in state and emotionality, thereby making them particularly useful for studying social and emotional processes.

emotion reactivity A dimension of emotional processes associated with individual differences in the threshold and intensity of emotional experience.

emotion regulation The processes by which emotional arousal is redirected, controlled, or modified to facilitate adaptive functioning.

emotional abuse Abusive behavior that involves acts or omissions by parents or care-givers that cause, or could cause, serious behavioral, cognitive, emotional, or mental disorders.

emotional neglect Failure to provide for a child's basic emotional needs, including marked inattention to the child's needs for affection, refusal of or failure to provide needed psychological care, spousal abuse in the child's presence, and permission of drug or alcohol use by the child.

encopresis The passage of feces into inappropriate places, such as clothing, whether involuntary or intentional.

enuresis Involuntary discharge of urine occuring in persons over 5 years of age or the developmental equivalent.

epidemiological research The study of the incidence, prevalence, and co-occurrence of childhood disorders and competencies in clinic-referred and community samples.

epinephrine A hormone produced by the adrenal glands that is released into the bloodstream in response to stress in order to energize and prepare the body for a possible threat. This hormone is also known as adrenaline.

equifinality The concept that similar outcomes may stem from different early experiences.

etiology The study of the causes of disorders. With respect to childhood disorders, etiology considers how biological, psychological, and environmental processes interact.

euphoria An exaggerated sense of well-being.

executive functions Higher-order mental processes that enable a child to maintain a problem-solving set in order to attain a future goal. Examples of executive functions include working memory, mental computation, flexibility of thinking, internalization of speech, response inhibition, motor coordination, self-regulation of arousal level, and mature moral reasoning, among others.

expectable environment External conditions or surroundings that are considered to be fundamental and necessary for healthy development. The expectable environment for infants includes protective and nurturant adults and opportunities for socialization; for older children it includes a supportive family, contact with peers, and ample opportunities to explore and master the environment.

exposure A behavior therapy technique for treating anxiety disorders that exposes the subject to the source of his or her fear while providing appropriate and effective ways of coping with the fear (other than through escape and avoidance).

expressive language disorder A form of communication disorder characterized by deficits in expression despite normal comprehension of speech.

external validity The degree to which findings can be generalized or extended to people, settings, times, measures, and characteristics other than the ones in the original study.

externalizing behavior A continuous dimension of behavior that includes a mix of impulsive, overactive, aggressive, and delinquent acts.

externalizing problems Problem behaviors that begin during childhood and encompass more acting-out behaviors such as aggression and delinquent behavior.

failure to thrive Characterized by weight below the fifth percentile for age, and/or deceleration in the rate of weight gain from birth to the present of at least 2 standard deviations, using standard growth charts for comparison.

false belief An incorrect assumption about a situation. Once a child recognizes that another person may have a false belief, he or she is better able to explain and predict the other's behavior. Understanding false beliefs is central to the development of theory of mind.

family systems Theory that the behavior of an individual can be most accurately understood in the context of the dynamics of his or her family.

fear An alarm reaction to current danger or life-threatening emergencies marked by strong escape-oriented tendencies and a surge in the sympathetic nervous system.

feeding disorder of infancy or early childhood A disorder characterized by a sudden or marked deceleration of weight gain in an infant or a young child (under age 6) and a slowing or disruption of emotional and social development.

fetal alcohol syndrome A disorder stemming from extensive prenatal exposure to alcohol. Children with this disorder typically suffer from problems in intellectual functioning, central nervous system dysfunction, cranial feature defects, behavior problems, growth retardation, and physical abnormalities of the face.

fight/flight response The immediate reaction to perceived danger or threat whereby efforts are directed toward protecting against potential harm, either by confronting the source of danger (fight), or by escaping from the situation (flight).

flooding A procedure for treating anxiety that involves prolonged and repeated exposure to the anxiety-provoking situation until the subject's level of anxiety has diminished.

fragile-X syndrome A chromosomal abnormality in which one area on the X chromosome is pinched. Children with fragile-X syndrome typically suffer from moderate mental retardation.

frontal lobes Four areas of each cerebral hemisphere; responsible for the functions underlying much of our thinking and reasoning abilities, including memory.

frontostriatal circuitry A structure of the brain consisting of the prefrontal cortex and the basal ganglia; it is associated with attention, executive functions, delayed response, and response organization. Abnormalities with this structure have been linked to ADHD.

general intellectual functioning One's general level of intellectual ability, defined by an intelligence quotient (IQ or equivalent) derived from an assessment with one or more of the standardized, individually administered intelligence tests.

generalized anxiety disorder (GAD) A form of anxiety disorder in which the subject experiences chronic or exaggerated worry and tension, almost always anticipating disaster, even in the absence of an obvious reason to do so. The worrying is often accompanied by physical symptoms such as trembling, muscle tension, headache, and nausea.

generalized social phobia A severe form of social phobia in which the subject fears most social situations, is afraid to meet or talk with new people, avoids contact with anyone outside his or her family, and finds it extremely difficult to attend school, participate in recreational activities, or socialize at all.

genotype An individual's specific genetic makeup.

goodness of fit The extent to which two things are suited. For instance, with respect to child psychopathology, one might use the term to refer to the extent to which the child's early temperament and the parent's style of interaction are suited to each other.

graded exposure Gradual exposure of a subject to a feared situation.

hallucinations Disturbances in perception in which things are seen, heard, or otherwise sensed even though they are not real or present.

health promotion An approach to the prevention of disease that involves education, public policy, and similar actions to promote health.

heritability The proportion of the variance of a trait that is attributable to genetic influences.

hostile attributional bias The tendency of aggressive children to attribute negative intent to others, especially when the intentions of another child are unclear (e.g., when a child accidentally bumps into them, they are likely to think the other child did it on purpose).

hyperactive Displaying an unusually high level of energy and an inability to remain still or quiet.

hypothalamic-pituitary-adrenal (HPA) axis A regulatory system of the brain made up of the hypothalamus control center and the pituitary and adrenal glands; it influences a person's response to stress and his or her ability to regulate emotions.

idiographic An approach to case formulation or assessment that emphasizes the detailed representation of the individual child or family as a unique entity. This approach is in contrast to the nomothetic approach, which instead emphasizes the general laws that apply to all individuals.

impulsive Prone to acting with little or no consideration of possible consequences. This term is frequently used to describe children who suffer from attention-deficit/hyperactivity disorder.

inattentive Lacking the ability to focus or sustain one's attention. Children who are inattentive find it difficult to sustain mental effort during work or play and behave carelessly, as if they are not listening.

incidence rate The rate at which new cases of a disorder appear over a specified period of time.

incidental training A method of teaching readiness skills or other desired behaviors that works to strengthen the behavior by capitalizing on naturally occurring opportunities.

inclusion The education strategies that are based on the premise that the abilities of children with special needs will improve from associating with normally developing peers and be spared the effects of labeling and special placements.

inclusion movement The integration of individuals with disabilities in regular classroom settings, regardless of the severity of the disability. The school curriculum must be adaptable to meet the individual needs and abilities of these children.

information-processing disturbances Cognitive misperceptions and distortions in the way events are perceived and interpreted.

informed consent An individual's expressed willingness to participate in a research study, based on an understanding of the nature of the research, the potential risks and benefits involved, the expected outcomes, and possible alternatives.

insulin-dependent diabetes mellitus A lifelong metabolic disorder in which the body is unable to metabolize carbohydrates due to inadequate pancreatic release of insulin.

interdependent Applies to the assumption that abnormal child behavior is determined by both the child and his or her environment, and that these two factors are interconnected (also see *transaction*).

internal validity The extent to which an intended manipulation of a variable, rather than extraneous influences, accounts for observed results, changes, or group differences.

internal, stable, and global attributions Assignment of responsibility for an event whereby the child believes that he or she is responsible (internal attribution), that the event is likely to occur again, that when it does he or she will again be responsible (stable attribution), and that the reason he or she is responsible applies to most other situations (global attribution). Depending on the nature of the event in question, internal, stable, and global attributions can be either good or bad. Internal, stable, and global attributions regarding negative events are characteristic of depressed individuals.

internalizing problems Problem behaviors that begin during childhood and include anxiety, depression, somatic complaints, and withdrawn behavior.

intervention A broad concept that encompasses many different theories and methods with a range of problem-solving strategies directed at helping the child and family adapt more effectively to their current and future circumstances.

joint social attention The ability to coordinate one's focus of attention on another person and an object of mutual interest.

learning disabilities A general term that refers to significant problems in mastering one or more of the following skills: listening, speaking, reading, writing, reasoning, mathematics.

learning disorders A diagnostic term that refers to specific problems in reading (disorder of reading), math (disorder of mathematics), or writing ability (disorder of written expression), as deter-

mined by achievement test results that are substantially below what would be expected for the child's age, schooling, and intellectual ability.

life-course-persistent (LCP) path A developmental pathway to antisocial behavior in which the child engages in antisocial behavior at an early age and continues to do so into adulthood.

longitudinal research A method of research whereby the same individuals are studied at different ages/stages of development.

macroparadigm A broad philosophical framework that combines several approaches to the study of a phenomenon.

maintenance Efforts to increase adherence to treatment over time in order to prevent a relapse or recurrence of a problem.

major depressive disorder (MDD) A form of depressive disorder characterized by one or more major depressive episodes that last for at least 2 weeks and are accompanied by additional symptoms such as sleep disturbances or thoughts of suicide.

mania An abnormally elevated or expansive mood.

mediator variables The process, mechanism, or means through which a variable produces a specific outcome.

mental status exam An assessment of a subject's general mental functioning, typically carried out during an interview in which questions are asked and systematic observations of the subject are made in the areas of appearance and behavior, thought processes, mood and affect, intellectual functioning, and sensorium.

mentalization Awareness of other people's and one's own mental states. Also referred to as *theory of mind*.

metabolic control The degree to which an individual's glucose level is maintained within the normal range (in reference to diabetes mellitus).

metabolic rate The body's balance of energy expenditure. Metabolic rate is determined by genetic and physiological makeup, along with eating and exercise habits.

metacognitive training Instruction in techniques that help to improve memory and learning, including how to coordinate learned skills across learning situations.

methylphenidate The stimulant medication most commonly used in treating children with attention-deficit/

hyperactivity disorder. It is sold under the name Ritalin.

mild mental retardation An IQ level of 50–55 to approximately 70.

mixed receptive-expressive language disorder A form of communication disorder characterized by deficits in expressive language coupled with a difficulty in understanding some aspects of speech (i.e., deficits in receptive language).

moderate mental retardation An IQ level of 35–40 to 50–55.

moderator variables A factor that influences the direction or strength of a relationship between variables.

molecular genetics The methods of genetics that directly assess the association between variations in DNA sequences and variations in particular trait(s). More than an association, variations in genetic sequences are thought to cause the variations in the trait(s). These methods offer more direct support for genetic influences on child psychopathology.

mood disorder A disorder in which the subject suffers from extreme, persistent, or poorly regulated emotional states.

morbidity The various forms of physical and functional consequences and limitations that result from an illness.

multiaxial system A classification system consisting of several different domains (axes) of information about the subject that may assist a clinician in planning the treatment of a disorder. The DSM-IV is an example of a multiaxial classification system.

multifinality The concept that various outcomes may stem from similar beginnings.

multimethod assessment approach A clinical assessment that emphasizes the importance of obtaining information from different informants, in a variety of settings, using a variety of procedures that include interviews, observations, questionnaires, and tests.

multiple-baseline design A single-case experimental design in which the effect of a treatment is shown by demonstrating that behaviors in more than one baseline change as a result of the institution of a treatment.

multisystemic treatment (MST) An approach to treatment that attempts to address the multiple determinants of problematic behavior by involving family members, school personnel, peers, juvenile justice staff, and others in the child's life, and by drawing on multiple techniques such as parent-management training, cognitive problem-solving skills training, and marital therapy, as well as specialized interventions such as special education placements, referral to substance abuse treatment programs, or referral to legal services.

natural experiment An experiment in which comparisons are made between preexisting conditions or treatments (i.e., random assignment is not used).

naturalistic observation The unstructured observation of a child in his or her natural environment.

negative affectivity A persistent negative mood evidenced by nervousness, sadness, anger, and guilt.

negative cognitive schemata Stable structures in memory that guide information processing, including self-critical beliefs and attitudes, in a way that is consistent with the negative self-image of the subject. These cognitive schemata are rigid and resistant to change even in the face of contradictory evidence.

negative cognitive triad Negative views about oneself, the world, and the future that are characteristic of youngsters with depression. These views maintain feelings of helplessness, undermine the child's mood and energy level, and are related to the severity of depression.

neural plasticity The malleable nature of the brain, evidenced throughout the course of development (use-dependent). Although infants are born with basic brain processes, experience leads to anatomical differentiation. That is, certain synapses of the brain are strengthened and stabilized, while others regress and disappear.

neuroimaging A method of examining the structure and/or function of the brain. Neuroimaging procedures include magnetic resonance imaging (MRI), coaxial tomographic scan (CT), positron emission tomography (PET), and functional magnetic resonance imaging (fMRI).

neuropsychological assessment A form of assessment that attempts to link brain functioning with objective measures of behavior known to depend on an intact central nervous system.

neurotic paradox The pattern of self-perpetuating behavior in which children who are overly anxious in various situations, even while being aware that the anxiety may be unnecessary or excessive, find themselves unable to abandon their self-defeating behaviors.

nightmares A form of parasomnia that occurs during REM sleep and is charac-

terized by repeated awakenings with detailed recall of extended and extremely frightening dreams, usually involving threats to survival, security, or self-esteem.

nomothetic An approach to case formulation or assessment that emphasizes general principles that apply to all people. This approach contrasts with the idiographic approach, which instead emphasizes a detailed representation of the individual or family as a unique entity.

non-accidental trauma The wide-ranging effects of maltreatment on the child's ongoing physical and emotional development.

nondisjunction The failure of the 21st pair of the mother's chromosomes to separate during meiosis. In most Down syndrome cases, the extra chromosome results from this failure of the chromosomes to separate.

nonshared environment A subtype of environmental influences that refers to the environmental factors that produce behavioral differences among siblings in the same family. Nonshared environmental influence can be estimated and is calculated by subtracting the MZ twin correlation from 1.0.

nonverbal learning disabilities Learning disabilities characterized by deficits relating to right hemisphere brain functioning, such as problems in social skills, spatial orientation, problem solving, and the recognition of nonverbal cues such as body language.

nosologies Efforts to classify psychiatric disorders into descriptive categories.

obsessions Persistent, intrusive, and irrational thoughts, ideas, impulses, or images that focus on improbable or unrealistic events or real-life events that are greatly exaggerated.

obsessive-compulsive disorder (OCD) A form of anxiety disorder in which the subject experiences repeated, intrusive, and unwanted thoughts that cause anxiety and often engages in ritualized behavior to relieve this anxiety.

operant speech training A strategy used to help children use language more appropriately; it involves a step-by-step approach that successively increases the child's vocalizations, teaches the child to imitate sounds and words, teaches the meanings of words, and teaches the child to use language expressively to label objects, make verbal requests, and express desires. This training is often employed for children with autism.

oppositional defiant disorder (ODD) The least severe form of disruptive behavior disorder, in which children show an age-inappropriate and persistent pattern of irritable, hostile, oppositional, and defiant behavior.

optimal stimulation theory A theory of attention-deficit/hyperactivity disorder that contends that hyperactivity arises from a low level of arousal and is simply an under-aroused child's effort to maintain an optimal level of arousal through self-stimulation.

organic group Mental retardation stemming from clear organic (physical) causes such as brain damage or improper CNS development.

organization of development The assumption that early patterns of adaptation evolve over time and transform into higher-order functions in a structured manner. For instance, infant eye contact and speech sounds evolve and transform into speech and language.

overt-covert dimension An independent dimension consisting of a continuum of antisocial behavior ranging from overt forms such as physical aggression at one end, to covert forms (i.e., hidden or sneaky acts) at the other. The overt forms of antisocial behavior correspond roughly to those on the aggressive subdimension of the externalizing dimension, whereas the covert behaviors correspond roughly to those on the delinquent subdimension of the externalizing dimension.

panic A group of unexpected physical symptoms of the fight/flight response that occur in the absence of any obvious threat or danger.

panic attack A sudden and overwhelming period of intense fear or discomfort accompanied by four or more physical and cognitive symptoms characteristic of the fight/flight response.

panic disorder (PD) A form of anxiety disorder characterized by panic attacks and sudden feelings of terror that strike repeatedly and without warning. Physical symptoms include chest pain, heart palpitations, shortness of breath, dizziness, and abdominal stress. There is also persistent concern about having another attack and the possible implications and consequences it would bring.

parasomnias A category of sleep disorders in which behavioral or physiological events intrude on ongoing sleep. Persons suffering from parasomnias often complain of unusual behaviors during sleep such as sleepwalking and nightmares.

parent management training (PMT) A program aimed at teaching parents to cope effectively with their children's difficult behavior and their own reactions to it.

pedophilia Sexual activity or sexually arousing fantasies involving a prepubescent child, by someone who is at least 16 years old and at least 5 years older than the child.

pervasive developmental disorder not otherwise specified (PDD-NOS) A disorder in which the child displays social, communication, and behavioral impairments associated with PDD, but does not meet the criteria for PDD, schizophrenia, or other disorders.

pervasive developmental disorders (PDDs) A category of disorders characterized by severe and extensive impairments in social interaction and communication skills, along with stereotyped patterns of behaviors, interests, and activities.

phenotype An individual's observable characteristics or behavior (the expression of one's genotype in the environment).

phobia Fear that occurs at an inappropriate age, persists, is irrational or exaggerated, leads to avoidance of the object or event, and causes impairment in normal routines.

phonemes The basic sounds that make up language.

phonological awareness A broad construct that includes recognition of the relationship that exists between sounds and letters, detection of rhyme and alliteration, and awareness that sounds can be manipulated within syllables in words.

phonological disorder A form of communication disorder characterized by difficulties in articulation or sound production, but not necessarily in word expression.

physical abuse The infliction or endangerment of physical injury as a result of punching, beating, kicking, biting, burning, shaking, or otherwise intentionally harming a child.

physical neglect Failure to provide for a child's basic physical needs, including refusal of or delay in seeking health care, inadequate provision of food, abandonment, expulsion from the home or refusal to allow a runaway to return home, inadequate supervision, and inadequate provision of clean clothes.

pica A form of eating disorder in which the infant or toddler persists in eating inedible, nonnutritive substances. This disorder is one of the more common and usually less serious eating disorders found among very young children.

positive affectivity A persistent positive mood as reflected in states such as joy, enthusiasm, and energy.

positive illusory bias A person's report of higher self-esteem than is warranted by his or her behavior. This exaggeration of one's competence may, for example, cause a child with ADHD to perceive their relationships with their parents no differently than do control children, even though their parents see things in a more negative light.

post-traumatic stress disorder (PTSD) A form of anxiety disorder whereby the child displays persistent anxiety following exposure to or witnessing of an overwhelming traumatic event that is outside the range of usual human experience.

Prader-Willi syndrome A complex genetic disorder associated with an abnormality of chromosome 15. Children with Prader-Willi syndrome typically suffer from short stature, mental retardation or learning disabilities, incomplete sexual development, certain behavior problems, low muscle tone, and an involuntary urge to eat constantly.

pragmatics The aspect of language that focuses on its appropriate use in social and communicative contexts.

preservation of sameness A characteristic of children with autistic disorder who show an anxious and obsessive insistence on the maintenance of sameness that no one but the child may disrupt. Changes in daily routine, arrangement of objects, or the wording of requests, or the sight of anything broken or incomplete, will produce tantrums or despair.

prevalence rates The number of cases of a disorder, whether new or previously existing, that are observed during a specified period of time.

prevention Activities directed at decreasing the chances that undesired future outcomes will occur.

problem-solving skills training (PSST) Instruction aimed at targeting the cognitive deficiencies and distortions displayed by children and adolescents who experience conduct problems in interpersonal situations, particularly those children who are aggressive.

profound mental retardation An IQ level below 20 or 25.

prognosis The prediction of the course or outcome of a disorder.

pronoun reversal The repetition of personal pronouns exactly as heard, without changing them according to the person being referred to. For example, if asked "Are you hungry?", one might reply "You are hungry," rather than "I am hungry."

protective factor A variable that precedes a negative outcome of interest and decreases the chances that the outcome will occur.

protodeclarative gestures Gestures or vocalizations that direct the visual attention of other people to objects of shared interest, such as pointing to a dog; done with the prime purpose of engaging another person in interaction.

protoimperative gestures Gestures or vocalizations used to express needs, such as pointing to an object that one desires but cannot reach.

psychological disorder A pattern of behavioral, cognitive, or physical symptoms that includes one or more of the following prominent features: (a) some degree of distress in the subject; (b) behavior indicating some degree of disability; and (c) an increased risk of suffering, death, pain, disability, or an important loss of freedom.

psychological factors affecting physical condition Psychological disorders or conditions that are presumed to cause or exacerbate a physical condition.

psychopathy A pattern of deceitful, callous, manipulative, and remorseless behavior.

purging Behavior aimed at ridding the body of consumed food, including self-induced vomiting and the misuse of laxatives, diuretics, or enemas. Also see compensatory behaviors.

qualitative research Research for which the purpose is to describe, interpret, and understand the phenomenon of interest in the context in which it is experienced.

random assignment The assignment of research participants to treatment conditions whereby each participant has an equal chance of being assigned to each condition. Random assignment increases the likelihood that characteristics other than the independent variable will be equally distributed across treatment groups.

real-time prospective design A research design in which the research sample is identified and then followed longitudinally over time, with data collected at specified time intervals.

reciprocal influence The theory that the child's behavior is both influenced by and itself influences the behavior of other family members.

regular education initiative A program implemented by some school systems that involves the placement of children with disabilities in the same classrooms as normal students, with general and special education teachers sharing responsibility for student instruction. Also see *mainstream education*.

reinforcement trap The process by which parents who are involved in coercive interactions with their child find themselves trapped by the consequences of their own behavior.

relational disorders Disorders that occur in the context of relationships, such as child abuse and neglect. Relational disorders signify the connection between children's behavior patterns and the availability of a suitable childrearing environment.

reliability The extent to which the result of an experiment is consistent or repeatable.

residential care A living arrangement in which a child whose family or school cannot adequately provide for him or her is cared for in a specialized out-of-home setting.

resilience The ability to avoid negative outcomes despite being at risk for psychopathology.

response prevention A procedure used in the treatment of anxiety that prevents the child from engaging in escape or avoidance behaviors. This procedure is usually used in conjunction with flooding.

response-cost procedure A technique for managing a subject's behavior that involves the loss of reinforcers such as privileges, activities, points, or tokens in response to inappropriate behavior.

restricting Behavior exhibited by people suffering from anorexia whereby dieting, fasting, or excessive exercise is used to lose or avoid gaining weight.

retrospective design A research design in which the research sample is asked to provide information relating to an earlier time period.

Rett's disorder A pervasive developmental disorder characterized by a deceleration of head growth in the early years, a loss of previously acquired purposeful hand skills with subsequent development of stereotyped hand movements, a loss of social engagement, poorly coordinated gait or trunk move-

ments, severe impairments in expressive and receptive language development, and severe psychomotor retardation.

risk factor A variable that precedes a negative outcome of interest and increases the chances that the outcome will occur.

schizophrenia A form of psychotic disorder that involves characteristic disturbances in thinking (delusions), perception (hallucinations), speech, emotions, and behavior.

school refusal behavior A form of anxious behavior in which the child refuses to attend classes or has difficulty remaining in school for an entire day.

screening Identification of subjects at risk for a specific negative outcome.

selective attention The ability to concentrate exclusively on relevant stimuli and to avoid distraction by irrelevant stimuli in the environment.

selective mutism The inability or refusal to talk in social situations, despite the fact that the subject may talk at home or in other settings.

self-injurious behavior Severe and sometimes life-threatening acts that cause damage to the subject's own body, such as head banging, eye gouging, severe scratching, rumination, some types of pica, and inserting objects under the skin.

self-instructional training Teaching children to use verbal cues to process information, which are initially taught by the therapist or teacher, to keep themselves on task.

self-stimulatory behaviors Repetitive body movements or movements of objects, such as hand flapping or spinning a pencil.

semistructured interviews Interviews that include specific questions designed to elicit information in a relatively consistent manner regardless of who is doing the interview. The interview format usually ensures that the most important aspects of a particular disorder are covered.

sensitive periods Windows of time during which environmental influences on development (both good and bad) are heightened, thus providing enhanced opportunities to learn.

separation anxiety disorder (SAD) A form of anxiety disorder in which the subject displays age-inappropriate, excessive, and disabling anxiety about being apart from his or her parents or away from home.

set point A comfortable range of body weight that the body tries to "defend" and maintain.

severe mental retardation An IQ level of 20–25 to 35–40.

sexual abuse Abusive acts that are sexual in nature, including fondling a child's genitals, intercourse, incest, rape, sodomy, exhibitionism, and commercial exploitation through prostitution or the production of pornographic materials.

shared environment A subtype of environmental influences that refers to the environmental factors that produce similarities in developmental outcomes among siblings in the same family. If siblings are more similar than expected from only their shared genetics, this implies an effect of the environment both siblings share, such as being exposed to marital conflict or poverty, or being parented in a similar manner.

single-case experimental design A type of research design most frequently used to evaluate the impact of a clinical treatment on a subject's problem. Single-case experimental designs involve repeated assessment of behavior over time, the replication of treatment effects on the same subject over time, and the subject serving as his or her own control by experiencing all treatment conditions.

sleep terrors A form of parasomnia that occurs during deep sleep and is characterized by abrupt awakening, accompanied by autonomic arousal but no recall.

sleepwalking A form of parasomnia occurring during deep sleep in which the individual gets out of bed and walks around, but has no recall the next day.

social anxiety See *social phobia*.

social cognition A construct to describe how people think about themselves in relation to others, and how they interpret ambiguous events and solve problems.

social learning A theoretical approach to the study of behavior that is interested in both overt behaviors and the role of possible cognitive mediators that may influence such behaviors directly or indirectly.

social phobia A marked and persistent fear of social or performance situations in which the subject is exposed to possible scrutiny and embarrassment.

social selection hypothesis The premise that people tend to select environments in which there are other people similar to themselves.

somatoform disorders   A group of related problems involving physical symptoms that resemble or suggest a medical condition, but lack organic or physiological evidence: somatization (i.e., expression of feelings through physical symptoms), hypochondriasis (i.e., preoccupation with real or fancied ailments), and pain disorders (e.g., recurring stomach pains).

specific phobia   A marked and persistent fear of clearly discernible, circumscribed objects or situations.

spectrum disorder   Disorder in which the symptoms and characteristics are expressed in many different combinations and in any degree of severity.

standardization   The process by which a set of standards or norms is specified for a measurement procedure so that it can be used consistently across different assessments.

stigma   A cluster of negative attitudes and beliefs that motivates fear, rejection, avoidance, and discrimination against people with mental illnesses.

stimulant medications   Drugs that alter the activity in the frontostriatal region of the brain by impacting three or more neurotransmitters important to the functioning of this region—dopamine, norepinephrine, and epinephrine, and possibly serotonin.

structured observation   Observation of a subject, usually occurring in a clinic or laboratory, in which the subject is given specific tasks or instructions to carry out, and researchers look for specific information.

substance abuse   In contrast to substance dependence, this diagnosis involves one or more harmful and repeated negative consequences of substance use over the last 12 months. Because substance dependence is the more serious diagnosis, a diagnosis of substance abuse is not given if an individual meets criteria for substance dependence.

substance dependence   A diagnosis of an adolescent (or adult) who must show a maladaptive pattern of substance use for at least 12 months, accompanied by three or more significant clinical signs of distress—tolerance (the need for increased amounts to achieve intoxication), withdrawal (cognitive and physiological changes upon discontinuation of the drug), and other indices of compulsive use. Substance dependence is also characterized as with or without physiological dependence (i.e., with or without evidence of tolerance or withdrawal).

substance use disorders (SUDs)   Disorders that occur during adolescence and include substance dependence and substance abuse, which result from the self-administration of any substance that alters mood, perception, or brain functioning.

subtype   A group of people with a specific disorder who have something in common, such as symptoms, etiology, problem severity, or likely outcome, that makes them distinct from people with other subtypes of the same disorder.

sustained attention   The ability to maintain a persistent focus of attention over time or when fatigued.

systematic desensitization   A three-step behavior therapy technique for treating anxiety whereby (1) the child is taught to relax, (2) an anxiety hierarchy is constructed, and (3) the anxiety-provoking stimuli are presented sequentially while the child remains relaxed.

target behaviors   Behaviors that are the primary problems of concern.

temperament   The child's innate reactivity and self-regulation with respect to the domains of emotions, activity level, and attention; the child's organized style of behavior that appears early in development, such as fussiness or fearfulness, which shapes the child's approach to his or her environment and vice versa.

test   A task or set of tasks given under standard conditions with the purpose of assessing some aspect of the subject's knowledge, skill, personality, or condition.

test anxiety   The experience of intense somatic, cognitive, and behavioral symptoms of anxiety during test-taking situations that usually interferes with test performance.

theory of mind (ToM)   The cognition and understanding of mental states that cannot be observed directly, such as beliefs and desires, both in one's self and in others.

tic disorders   Disorders characterized by sudden, repetitive, nonrhythmic motor movements or phonic productions, such as eye blinking, facial grimacing, throat clearing, and grunting or other sounds.

transaction   The process by which the subject and environment interact in a dynamic fashion to contribute to the expression of a disorder (also see *interdependent*).

traumatic sexualization   One possible outcome of child sexual abuse, whereby the child's sexual knowledge and behavior are shaped in developmentally inappropriate ways.

treatment   Corrective actions that will permit successful adaptation by eliminating or reducing the impact of an undesired outcome that has already occurred.

treatment effectiveness   The degree to which a treatment can be shown to work in actual clinical practice, as opposed to controlled laboratory conditions.

treatment efficacy   The degree to which a treatment can produce changes under well-controlled conditions that depart from those typically used in clinical practice.

treatment planning   The process of using assessment information to generate a treatment plan and evaluate its effectiveness.

true experiment   An experiment in which the researcher has maximum control over the independent variable or conditions of interest, and in which the researcher can use random assignment of subjects to groups, can include needed control conditions, and can control possible sources of bias.

two-factor theory   Theory used to explain the learning and maintenance of fears through a combination of classical and operant conditioning.

unexpected discrepancy   A basic premise of current definitions of learning disorders that denotes a disparity or discrepancy between an individual's measured ability and actual performance.

validity   The extent to which a measure actually assesses the dimension or construct that the researcher sets out to measure.

victimization   Abuse or mistreatment of someone whose ability to protect himself or herself is limited (e.g., the mistreatment of a child by his or her parents).

vulnerability-stress model   An approach to understanding the development of a disorder that emphasizes the interplay among vulnerability factors (e.g., genetic risk, deviant family interactions), stressors (e.g., ongoing child abuse, death of a parent), and protective factors (e.g., intelligence, supportive family relationships). The advantage of this model is that it recognizes the many diverse and complex pathways that may lead to a disorder.

References

Aaron, P. G., Joshi, R. M., Palmer, H., Smith, N., & Kirby, E. (2002). Separating genuine cases of reading disability from reading deficits caused by predominantly inattentive ADHD behaviour. *Journal of Learning Disabilities, 35,* 425.

Aarons, G. A., Brown, S.A., Hough, R. L., Garland, A. F., & Wood, P.A. (2001). Prevalence of adolescent substance use disorders across five sectors of care. *Journal of the American Academy of Child and Adolescent Psychiatry, 40,* 419–426.

Abbott, M. A., & Benn, P. (2002). Prenatal genetic diagnosis of Down's syndrome. *Expert Review of Molecular Diagnostics, 2,* 605–615.

Abel, C. G., Osborn, C. A., & Twigg, D. A. (1993). Sexual assault through the life span: Adult offenders with juvenile histories. In H. E. Barbaree, W. L. Marshall, & S. M. Husdon (Eds.), *The juvenile sex offender* (pp. 104–117). New York: Guilford Press.

Abela, J. R. Z. (2001). The hopelessness theory of depression: A test of the diathesis-stress and causal mediation components in third and seventh grade children. *Journal of Abnormal Child Psychology, 29,* 241–254.

Abikoff, H. B., Jensen, P. S., Arnold, L. E., Hoza, B., Hechtman, L., Pollack, S., et al., (2002). Observed classroom behavior of children with ADHD: Relationship to gender and comorbidity. *Journal of Abnormal Child Psychology, 30,* 349–359.

Abikoff, H., Courtney, M., Pelham, W., & Koplewicz, H. (1993). Teachers' ratings of disruptive behaviors: The influence of halo effects. *Journal of Abnormal Child Psychology, 21,* 519–533.

Abramson, L. Y., Metalsky, G. I., & Alloy, L. B. (1989). Hopelessness depression: A theory-based subtype of depression. *Psychological Review, 96,* 358–372.

Abramson, L. Y., Seligman M. E., & Teasdale, J. D. (1978). Learned helplessness in humans: Critique and reformulation. *Journal of Abnormal Psychology, 37,* 49–74.

Achenbach, T. M. (2000). Assessment of psychopathology. In A. Sameroff, M. Lewis, & S. Miller (Eds.), *Handbook of developmental psychopathology* (2nd ed., pp. 41–56). New York: Plenum.

Achenbach, T. M. (1982). *Developmental psychopathology* (2nd ed.). New York: Wiley.

Achenbach, T. M. (1985). *Assessment and taxonomy of child and adolescent psychopathology.* Beverly Hills, CA: Sage.

Achenbach, T. M. (1990). Conceptualization of developmental psychopathology. In M. Lewis & S. M. Miller (Eds.), *Handbook of developmental psychopathology* (pp. 3–14). New York: Plenum.

Achenbach, T. M. (1991a). *Manual for the Child Behavior Checklist/4–18 and 1991 profile.* Burlington: University of Vermont, Department of Psychiatry.

Achenbach, T. M. (1991b). *Manual for the Youth Self-Report and 1991 profile.* Burlington: University of Vermont, Department of Psychiatry.

Achenbach, T. M. (1993). *Empirically based taxonomy: How to use syndromes and profile types derived from the CBCL/4–18, TRF, and YSR.* Burlington: University of Vermont, Department of Psychiatry.

Achenbach, T. M. (1995). Developmental issues in assessment, taxonomy, and diagnosis of child and adolescent psychopathology. In D. Cicchetti & D. J. Cohen (Eds.), *Developmental psychopathology: Vol. 1. Theory and methods* (pp. 57–80). New York: Wiley.

Achenbach, T. M. (1997). What is normal? What is abnormal? Developmental perspectives on behavioral and emotional problems. In S. S. Luthar, J. A. Burack, D. Cicchetti, & J. R. Weisz (Eds.), *Developmental psychopathology: Perspectives on adjustment, risk, and disorder* (pp. 93–114). New York: Cambridge University Press.

Achenbach, T. M. (1998). Diagnosis, assessment, taxonomy, and case formulations. In T. H. Ollendick & M. Hersen (Eds.), *Handbook of child psychopathology* (3rd ed., pp. 63–87). New York: Plenum Press.

Achenbach, T. M. (1999). The Child Behavior Checklist and related instruments. In M. E. Maruish (Ed.), *The use of psychological testing for treatment planning and outcomes assessment* (2nd ed., pp. 429–466). Mahwah, NJ: Erlbaum.

Achenbach, T. M., & Edelbrock, C. (1981). Behavioral problems and competencies reported by parents of normal and disturbed children aged four through sixteen. *Monographs of the Society for Research in Child Development, 46* (Serial No. 188, Whole No. 1).

Achenbach, T. M., Howell, C. T., Quay, H. C., & Conners, C. K. (1991). National survey of problems and competencies among four- to sixteen-year-olds: Parents' reports for normative and clinical samples. *Monographs of the Society for Research in Child Development, 56* (Serial No. 225, Whole No. 3).

Achenbach, T. M., McConaughy, S. H., & Howell, C. T. (1987). Child/adolescent behavioral and emotional problems: Implications of cross-informant correlations for situational specificity. *Psychological Bulletin, 101,* 213–232.

Ackard, D. M., Neumark-Sztainer, D., Story, M., & Perry, C. (2003). Overeating among adolescents: Prevalence and associations with weight-related characteristics and psychological health. *Pediatrics, 111,* 67–74.

Adelman, A. (1995). Traumatic memory and the intergenerational transmission of Holocaust narratives. *Psychoanalytic Study of the Child, 50,* 343–367.

Adler, T. (1994). Comprehending those who can't relate. *Science News, 145,* 248–249.

Agnew, J. A., Dorn, C., & Eden, G. F. (2004). Effect of intensive training on auditory processing and reading skills. *Brain & Language, 88,* 21–25.

Agras, W. S., Rossiter, E. M., Arnow, B., Telch, C. F., Raeburn, S. D., Bruce, B., Koran, L. M. (1994). One-year follow-up of psychosocial and pharmacologic treatments for bulimia nervosa. *Journal of Clinical Psychiatry, 55* (5), 179–183.

Agras, W. S., Walsh, B. T., Fairburn, C. G., Wilson, C. T., & Kramer H.C. (2000) A multicenter comparison of cognitive-behavioral therapy and interpersonal psychotherapy for bulimia nervosa. *Archives of General Psychiatry, 57,* 459–466.

Ainsworth, M.D.S., Blehar, M. C., Waters, E., & Wall, S. (1978). *Patterns of attachment: A psychological study of the strange situation.* Hillsdale, NJ: Erlbaum.

Akefeldt, A., & Gillberg, C. (1999). Behavior and personality characteristics of children and young adults with Prader-Willi syndrome: A controlled study. *Journal of the American Academy of Child and Adolescent Psychiatry, 38,* 761–769.

Akiskal, H. S. (1995). Developmental pathways to bipolarity: Dysthymic, cyclothymic and bipolar II disorders in the "borderline realm." *Psychiatric Clinics of North America, 4,* 25–46.

Alaghband-Rad, J., Hamburger, S. D., Giedd, J. N., Frazier, J., & Rapoport, J. L. (1997). Childhood-onset schizophrenia: Biological markers in relation to clinical characteristics. *American Journal of Psychiatry, 154,* 64–68.

Albano, A. M. (1995). Treatment of social anxiety in adolescents. *Cognitive and Behavioral Practice, 2,* 271–298.

Albano, A. M. (2003). Treatment of social anxiety disorder. In M. A. Reinecke & F. M. Dattilio (Eds.), *Cognitive therapy with children and adolescents: A casebook for clinical practice* (2nd ed., pp. 128–161). New York: Guilford.

Albano, A. M., Chorpita, B. F., & Barlow, D. H. (2003). Childhood anxiety disorders. In E. J. Mash & R. A. Barkley (Eds.), *Child psychopathology* (2nd ed., pp. 279–329). New York: Guilford.

Albano, A. M., Detweiler, M. F., & Logsdon-Conradsen, S. (1999). Cognitive-behavioral interventions with socially phobic children. In S. W. Russ & T. H. Ollendick (Eds.), *Handbook of psychotherapies with children and families* (pp. 255–280). New York: Plenum Press.

Albano, A. M., Knox, L. S., & Barlow, D. H. (1995). Obsessive-compulsive disorder. In A. R. Eisen, C. A. Kearney, & C. A. Schaefer (Eds.), *Clinical handbook of anxiety disorders in children and adolescents* (pp. 282–316). Northvale, NJ: Jason Aronson.

Albano, A. M., March, J. S., & Piacentini, J. (1999). Obsessive-compulsive disorder. In R. T. Ammerman & M. Hersen (Eds), *Handbook of prescriptive treatments for children and adolescents* (2nd ed., pp. 193–213). Needham Heights, MA: Allyn & Bacon.

Albano, A. M., Miller, P. P., Zarate, R., Cote, G., & Barlow, D. H. (1997). Behavioral assessment and treatment of PTSD in prepubertal children: Attention to developmental factors and innovative strategies in the case study of a family. *Cognitive and Behavioral Practice, 4,* 245–262.

Alfano, C. A., Beidel, D. C., & Turner, S. M. (2002). Cognition in childhood anxiety: Conceptual, methodological, and developmental issues. *Clinical Psychology Review, 22,* 1209–1238.

Ali, Z. (2001). Pica in people with intellectual disability: A literature review of aetiology, epidemiology and complications. *Journal of Intellectual & Developmental Disability, 26,* 205–215.

Althoff, R. R., Rettew, D. C., & Hudziak, J. J. (2003). Attention-deficit/hyperactivity disorder, oppositional defiant disorder, and conduct disorder. *Psychiatric Annals, 33, 4 ,* 245–252.

Altmann, E. O., & Gotlib, I. H. (1988). The social behavior of depressed children: An observational study. *Journal of Abnormal Child Psychology, 16,* 29–44.

Aman, M. G., Buican, B., & Arnold, L. E. (2003). Methylphenidate treatment in children with borderline IQ and mental retardation: Analysis of three aggregated studies. *Journal of Child and Adolescent Psychopharmacology, 13,* 29–40.

Aman, M., Kern, R. A., Osborne, P., & Tumuluru, R. (1997). Fenfluramine and methylphenidate in children with mental retardation and borderline IQ: Clinical effects. *American Journal on Mental Retardation, 101,* 521–534.

Amaya-Jackson, L., & March, J. S. (1995). Posttraumatic stress disorder. In J. S. March (Ed.), *Anxiety disorders in children and adolescents* (pp. 276–300). New York: Guilford Press.

Ambrosini, P. J., Bianchi, M. D., Rabinovich, H., & Elia, J. (1993). Antidepressant treatments in children and adolescents: I. Affective disorders. *Journal of the American Academy of Child and Adolescent Psychiatry, 32,* 1–6.

American Academy of Child and Adolescent Psychiatry. (1997). AACAP official action: Practice parameters for the assessment and treatment of children and adolescents with bipolar disorder. *Journal of the American Academy of Child and Adolescent Psychiatry, 36,* 138–157.

American Academy of Pediatrics. (2000). Clinical practice guideline: Diagnosis and evaluation of the child with attention-deficit/hyperactivity disorder. *Pediatrics, 105,* 1158–1170.

American Association on Mental Retardation (AAMR). (2002). *Mental retardation: Definition, classification, and systems of support* (10th ed.). Washington, DC: Author.

American Psychiatric Association. (1952). *Diagnostic and statistical manual of mental disorders.* Washington, DC: Author.

American Psychiatric Association. (1968). *Diagnostic and statistical manual of mental disorders* (2nd ed.). Washington, DC: Author.

American Psychiatric Association. (1980). *Diagnostic and statistical manual of mental disorders* (3rd ed.). Washington, DC: Author.

American Psychiatric Association. (1994). *Diagnostic and statistical manual of mental disorders* (4th ed.). Washington, DC: Author.

American Psychiatric Association [APA] (2000). *Diagnostic and statistical manual of mental disorders DSM-IV-TR (Text Revision).* Washington, DC: Author.

American Psychological Association. (1996). *Violence and the family.* (Report of the American Psychological Association Presidential Task Force on Violence and the Family). Washington, DC: Author.

American Psychological Association (2002). *Ethical principles of psychologists and code of conduct.* Washington, DC: Author. Available online at: http://www.apa.org/ethics/

American Psychological Association (APA). (2002). *Developing adolescents: A reference for professionals.* Washington, DC: Author.

American Psychological Association (2003). Senate introduces bill to provide incentives to increase the ranks of child mental health providers. Public Policy Office. Available: *http://www .apa.org/ppo/issues/es12230603.html*

Anastopoulos, A. D., & Farley, S. E. (2003). A cognitive-behavioral training program for parents of children with attention-deficit/hyperactivity disorder. In A. E. Kazdin & J. R. Weisz (Eds.), *Evidence-based psychotherapies for children and adolescents* (pp. 187–203). New York: Guilford Press.

Anastopoulos, A. D., Spisto, M. A., & Maher, M. C. (1994). The WISC-III Freedom from Distractibility factor: Its utility in identifying children with attention deficit hyperactivity disorder. *Psychological Assessment, 6,* 368–371.

Anders, T. F., & Eiben, L. A. (1997). Pediatric sleep disorders: A review of the past 10 years. *Journal of the American Academy of Child and Adolescent Psychiatry, 36,* 9–20.

Anders, T., Goodlin-Jones, B., & Sadeh, A. (2000). Sleep disorders. In C. H. Zeanah, Jr. et al. (Eds.), *Handbook of infant mental health* (2nd ed., pp. 326–338). New York: Guilford Press.

Anderson, C. A., & Bushman, B. J. (2002). The effects of media violence on society. *Science, 295,* 2377–2379.

Anderson, E. (1994, May). The code of the streets. *Atlantic Monthly, 273(5),* 81–94.

Anderson, K. E., Lytton, H., & Romney, D. M. (1986). Mothers' interactions with normal and conduct-disordered boys: Who affects whom? *Developmental Psychology, 22,* 604–609.

Andrade, A. R., Lambert, E. W., & Bickman, L. (2000). Dose effect in child psychotherapy: Outcomes associated with negligible treatment. *Journal of the American Academy of Child and Adolescent Psychiatry, 39,* 161–168.

Andrews, G., Morris-Yates, A., Howie, P., & Martin, N. G. (1991). Genetic factors in stuttering confirmed. *Archives of General Psychiatry, 48,* 1034–1035.

Andrews, G., Szabo, M., & Burns, J. (2002). Preventing major depression in young people. *British Journal of Psychiatry, 181,* 460–462.

Angold, A., & Costello, E. J. (1996). Toward establishing an empirical basis for the diagnosis of oppositional defiant disorder. *Journal of the American Academy of Child and Adolescent Psychiatry, 35,* 1205–1212.

Angold, A., & Costello, E. J. (2001). The epidemiology of disorders of conduct: Nosological issues and comorbidity. In J. Hill & B. Maughan (Eds.), *Conduct disorders in childhood and adolescence* (pp. 126–168). Cambridge: Cambridge University Press.

Angold, A., Costello, J., Burns, B. J., Erkanli, A., & Farmer, E.M.Z. (2000). Effectiveness of nonresidential specialty mental health services for children and adolescents in the "real world." *Journal of the American Academy of Child and Adolescent Psychiatry, 39,* 154–160.

Angold, A., Erkalni, A., Egger, H., & Costello, E. J. (2000). Stimulant treatment for children: A community perspective. *Journal of the American Academy of Child and Adolescent Psychiatry, 39*, 975–984.

Angold, A., Erkanli, A., Farmer, E.M.Z., Fairbank, J. A., Burns, B. J., Keeler, G., & Costello, E. J. (2002). Psychiatric disorder, impairment, and service use in rural African-American and White youth. *Archives of General Psychiatry, 59*, 893–904.

Angold, A., Worthman, C., & Costello, E. J. (2003). In C. Hayward (Ed.), *Gender differences at puberty* (pp. 137–164). New York: Cambridge University Press.

Annin, P. (1996, January 22). Superpredators arrive. *Newsweek, 127*, p. 57.

Anstendig, K. D. (1999). Is selective mutism an anxiety disorder? Rethinking its DSM-IV classification. *Journal of Anxiety Disorders, 13*, 417–434.

Anthony, J. L., Lonigan, C. J., & Hecht, S. A. (1999). Dimensionality of posttraumatic stress disorder symptoms in children exposed to disaster: Results from confirmatory factor analyses. *Journal of Abnormal Psychology, 108*, 326–336.

Anthony, K. K, Gil, K. M., & Schanberg, L. E. (2003). Brief report: Parent perceptions of child vulnerability in children with chronic illness. *Journal of Pediatric Psychology, 28*, 185–190.

Antrop, I., Roeyers, H., Van Oost, P., & Buysse, A. (2000). Stimulation seeking and hyperactivity in children with ADHD. *Journal of Child Psychology and Psychiatry, 41*, 225–231.

Applegate, B., Lahey, B. B., Hart, E. L., Biederman, J., Hynd, G. W., Barkley, R. A., et al., (1997). Validity of the age-of-onset criterion for ADHD: A report from the DSM-IV field trials. *Journal of the American Academy of Child and Adolescent Psychiatry, 36*, 1211–1221.

Aragona, M., & Vella, G. (1998). Psychopathological considerations on the relationship between bulimia and obsessive-compulsive disorder. *Psychopathology, 31*, 197–205.

Aries, P. (1962). *Centuries of childhood.* New York: Vintage Books.

Armbruster, P., & Kazdin, A. E. (1994). Attrition in child psychotherapy. *Advances in Clinical Child Psychology, 16*, 81–108.

Armitage, R., Emslie, G. J., Hoffmann, R. F., Weinberg, W. A., Kowatch, R. A., Rintelmann, J., & Rush, A. J. (2000). Ultradian rhythms and temporal coherence in sleep EEG in depressed children and adolescents. *Biological Psychiatry, 47*, 338–350.

Armstrong, D. D. (1992). The neuropathology of Rett Syndrome. *Brain and Development, 14 (Suppl.)*, 89–98.

Armstrong, T. (1995). *The myth of the A.D.D. child: 50 ways to improve your child's behavior and attention span without drugs, labels or coercion.* New York: Dutton.

Arnold, L. E. (1999). Treatment alternatives for attention-deficit/hyperactivity disorder (ADHD). *Journal of Attention Disorders, 3*, 30–48.

Arnold, L. E., Abikoff, H. B., Cantwell, D. P., Conners, C. K., Elliott, G., Greenhill, L. L., et al., (1997). National Institute of Mental Health Collaborative Multimodal Treatment Study of Children with ADHD (the MTA): Design challenges and choices. *Archives of General Psychiatry, 54*, 865–870.

Arslanian, S., Becker, D., & Drash, A. (1995). Diabetes mellitus in the child and adolescent. In M. S. Kappy, R. M. Blizzard, & C. J. Migeon (Eds.), *The diagnosis and treatment of endocrine disorders in childhood and adolescence* (4th ed., pp. 961–1026). Springfield, IL: Charles C. Thomas.

Asarnow, J. R. (1988). Children at risk for schizophrenia. *Schizophrenia Bulletin, 14*, 613–631.

Asarnow, J. R., & Asarnow, R. F. (2003). Childhood-onset schizophrenia. In E. J. Mash & R. A. Barkley (Eds.), *Child psychopathology* (2nd ed., pp. 455–485). New York: Guilford.

Asarnow, J. R., Goldstein, M. J., & Ben-Meir, S. (1988). Parental communication deviance in childhood-onset schizophrenia spectrum and depressive disorders. *Journal of Child Psychology and Psychiatry, 29*, 825–838.

Asarnow, J. R., Scott, C. V., & Mintz, J. A. (2002). Combined cognitive-behavioral family education intervention for depression in children: A treatment development study. *Cognitive Therapy and Research, 26*, 221–229.

Asarnow, J. R., Tompson, M., & Goldstein, M. J. (1994). Childhood-onset schizophrenia: A follow-up study. *Schizophrenia Bulletin, 20*, 599–618.

Asarnow, J. R., Tompson, M. C., & McGrath, E. P. (2004). Childhood-onset schizophrenia: Clinical and treatment issues. *Journal of Child Psychology and Psychiatry, 45*, 180–194.

Asarnow, R. F., Asamen, J., Granholm, E., Sherman, T., Watkins, J. M., & Williams, M. E. (1994). Cognitive/neuropsychological studies of children with a schizophrenic disorder. *Schizophrenia Bulletin, 20*, 647–670.

Asarnow, R. F., & Asarnow, J. R. (1994). Childhood-onset schizophrenia. *Schizophrenia Bulletin, 20*, 591–598.

Asarnow, R. F., Nuechterlein, K. H., Fogelson, D., Subotnik, K. L., Payne, D. A., Russell, A. T., Asamen, J., Kuppinger, H., & Kendler, K. S. (2001). Schizophrenia and schizophrenia-spectrum personality disorders in the first-degree relatives of children with schizophrenia: The UCLA family study. *Archives of General Psychiatry, 58*, 581–588.

Aschenbrand, S. G., Kendall, P. C., Webb, A., Safford, S. M, & Flannery-Schroeder, E. (2003). Is childhood separation anxiety disorder a predictor of adult panic disorder and agoraphobia? A seven-year longitudinal study. *Journal of the American Academy of Child and Adolescent Psychiatry, 42*, 1478–1485.

Attie, I., & Brooks-Gunn, J. (1995). The development of eating regulation across the life span. In D. Cicchetti & D. J. Cohen (Eds.), *Developmental psychopathology: Vol. 2. Risk, disorder, and adaptation* (pp. 332–368). New York: Wiley.

Avenevoli, S., Stolar, M., Li, J., Dierker, L., & Merikangas, K. R. (2001). Comorbidity of depression in children and adolescents: Models and evidence from a prospective high-risk family study. *Biological Psychiatry, 49*, 1071–1081.

Averill, J. R. (2001). Studies on anger and aggression: Implications for theories of emotion. In: W. Parrott (Ed.), *Emotions in social psychology: Essential readings* (pp. 337–352). Philadelphia, PA: Psychology Press.

Axline, V. M. (1947). *Play therapy: The inner dynamics of childhood.* Boston: Houghton Mifflin.

Azar, S. T. (2002). Parenting and child maltreatment. In M. H. Bornstein (Ed.), *Handbook of parenting: Vol. 4: Social conditions and applied parenting* (2nd ed., pp. 361–388); Mahwah, NJ: Lawrence Erlbaum Associates.

Azar, S. T., & Wolfe, D. (in press). Child physical abuse and neglect. In E. J. Mash & R. A. Barkley (Eds.), *Treatment of childhood disorders* (3rd ed.). New York: Guilford Press.

Azrin, N. H., & Foxx, R. M. (1974). *Toilet training in less than a day.* New York: Simon & Schuster.

Bailey, A., Phillips, W., & Rutter, M. (1996). Autism: Towards an integration of clinical, genetic, neuropsychological, and neurobiological perspectives. *Journal of Child Psychology and Psychiatry, 37*, 89–126.

Bailey, D. B., Jr., Hatton, D. D., & Skinner, M. (1998). Early developmental trajectories of males with fragile X syndrome. *American Journal of Mental Retardation: AJMR, 103*, 29–39.

Baker, B. L. (1996). Parent training. In J. W. Jacobson & J. A. Mulick (Eds.), *Manual of diagnosis and professional practice in mental retardation* (pp. 289–299). Washington, DC: American Psychological Association.

Baker, B. L., & Blacher, J. B. (1993). Out-of-home placement for children with mental retardation. *American Journal on Mental Retardation, 98*, 368–377.

Baker, C. W., Whisman, M. A., & Brownell, K. D. (2000). Studying intergenerational transmission of eating attitudes and behaviors: Methodological and conceptual questions. *Health Psychology, 19*, 376–381.

Bakwin, H. (1973). The genetics of enuresis. In I. Kolvin, R. C. MacKeith, & R. Meadow (Eds.), *Bladder control and enuresis* (pp. 73–77). Philadelphia: Lippincott.

Baldwin, W. K. (1958). The social position of mentally handicapped children in the regular class in the public schools. *Exceptional Children, 25*, 106–108.

Banaschewski, T., Brandeis, D., Heinrich, H., Albrecht, B., Brunner, E., & Rothenberger, A. (2003). Association of ADHD and conduct disorder: Brain electrical evidence for the existence of a distinct subtype. *Journal of Child Psychology and Psychiatry, 44,* 356–376.

Bandura, A. (1977). *Social learning theory.* Englewood Cliffs, NJ: Prentice Hall.

Bandura, A. (1986). *Social foundations of thought and action: A social cognitive theory.* Englewood Cliffs, NJ: Prentice Hall.

Banyard, V. L., Williams, L. M., & Siegel, J. A. (2002). Retraumatization among adult women sexually abused in childhood: Exploratory analyses in a prospective study. *Journal of Child Sexual Abuse, 11,* 19–48.

Barber, M. A., Milich, R., & Welsh, R. (1996). Effects of reinforcement schedule and task difficulty on the performance of attention deficit hyperactivity disordered and control boys. *Journal of Clinical Child Psychology, 25,* 66–76.

Barenbaum, J., Ruchkin, V., & Schwab-Stone, M. (2004). The psychosocial aspects of children exposed to war: Practice and policy initiatives. *Journal of Child Psychology and Psychiatry, 45,* 41–62.

Barkley, R. A. (1988). The effects of methylphenidate on the interactions of preschool ADHD children with their mothers. *Journal of the American Academy of Child and Adolescent Psychiatry, 26,* 336–341.

Barkley, R. A. (1995). *Taking charge of ADHD: The complete, authoritative guide for parents.* New York: Guilford Press.

Barkley, R. A. (1997a). *ADHD and the nature of self-control.* New York: Guilford Press.

Barkley, R. A. (1997b). Attention-deficit/hyperactivity disorder. In E. J. Mash & L. G. Terdal (Eds.), *Behavioral assessment of childhood disorders* (3rd ed., pp. 71–129). New York: Guilford Press.

Barkley, R. A. (1997d). Behavioral inhibition, sustained attention, and executive functions: Constructing a unifying theory of ADHD. *Psychological Bulletin, 121,* 65–94.

Barkley, R. A. (1997e). *Defiant children: A clinician's manual for assessment and parent training* (2nd ed.). New York: Guilford Press.

Barkley, R. A. (1998a). Attention-deficit/hyperactivity disorder. In E. J. Mash & R. A. Barkley (Eds.), *Treatment of childhood disorders* (2nd ed., pp. 55–110). New York: Guilford Press.

Barkley, R. A. (1998b). *Attention-deficit hyperactivity disorder: A handbook for diagnosis and treatment* (2nd ed.). New York: Guilford Press.

Barkley, R. A. (2001). The inattentive type of ADHD as a distinct disorder: What remains to be done. *Clinical Psychology: Science and Practice, 8,* 489–493.

Barkley, R. A. (2003). Attention-deficit/hyperactivity disorder. In E. J. Mash & R. A. Barkley (Eds.), *Child psychopathology* (pp. 75–143). New York: Guilford.

Barkley, R. A., & Biederman, J. (1997). Toward a broader definition of the age-of-onset criterion for attention-deficit-hyperactivity disorder. *Journal of the American Academy of Child and Adolescent Psychiatry, 36,* 1204–1210.

Barkley, R. A., Cook, E. H., Dulcan, M., Campbell, S., Prior, M., Atkins, et al., (2002). International consensus statement on ADHD. *Clinical Child and Family Psychology Review, 5,* 89–111.

Barkley, R. A., DuPaul, G. J., & McMurray, M. B. (1990). A comprehensive evaluation of attention deficit disorder with and without hyperactivity. *Journal of Consulting and Clinical Psychology, 58,* 775–789.

Barkley, R. A., Fischer, M., & Fletcher, K. (1997). *Young adult outcome of hyperactive children diagnosed by research criteria.* NIMH Grant, University of Massachusetts Medical Center.

Barkley, R. A., Fischer, M., Edelbrock, C. S., & Smallish, L. (1990). The adolescent outcome of hyperactive children diagnosed by research criteria, I: An 8-year prospective follow-up study. *Journal of the American Academy of Child and Adolescent Psychiatry, 29,* 546–557.

Barkley, R. A., Fischer, M., Edelbrock, C. S., & Smallish, L. (1991). The adolescent outcome of hyperactive children diagnosed by research criteria, III: Mother-child interactions, family conflicts, and maternal psychopathology. *Journal of Child Psychology and Psychiatry, 32,* 233–256.

Barkley, R. A., Fischer, M., Smallish, L., & Fletcher, K. (2002). The persistence of attention-deficit/hyperactivity disorder into young adulthood as a function of reporting source and definition of disorder. *Journal of Abnormal Psychology, 111,* 279–289.

Barkley, R. A., Grodzinsky, G., & DuPaul, G. J. (1992). Frontal lobe functions in attention deficit disorder with and without hyperactivity: A review and research report. *Journal of Abnormal Child Psychology, 20,* 163–188.

Barkley, R. A. (in press). Attention-Deficit/Hyperactivity Disorder in adolescents. In D. A. Wolfe & E. J. Mash (Eds.), *Behavioral and emotional problems in adolescents.* New York: Guilford Press.

Barkley, R. A., Murphy, K. R., DuPaul, G. R., & Bush, T. (2002). Driving in young adults with attention deficit hyperactivity disorder: Knowledge, performance, adverse outcomes and the role of executive functions. *Journal of the International Neuropsychological Society, 8,* 655–672.

Barkley, R. A., Shelton, T. L., Crosswait, C., Moorehouse, M., Fletcher, K., Barrett, S., Jenkins, L., & Metevia, L. (2002). Preschool children with high levels of disruptive behavior: Three-year outcomes as a function of adaptive disability. *Development and Psychopathology, 14,* 45–68.

Barlow, D. H., & Hersen, M. (1984). *Single case experimental designs: Strategies for studying behavior change* (2nd ed.). Elmsford, NY: Pergamon Press.

Barlow, D. H. (2002). *Anxiety and its disorders: The nature and treatment of anxiety and panic* (2nd ed.). New York: Guilford Press.

Barnby, G., & Manaco, A. P. (2003). Strategies for autism candidate gene analysis. *Novartis Foundation Symposium, 251,* 48–63.

Barnett, D., Ganiban, J., & Cicchetti, D. (1999). Maltreatment, negative expressivity, and the development of Type D attachments from 12 to 24 months of age. *Monographs of the Society for Research in Child Development, 64,* 97–118.

Baron-Cohen, S. (1995). *Mindblindness: An essay on autism and theory of mind.* Cambridge, MA: MIT Press.

Baron-Cohen, S. (2000a). Is Asperger syndrome/high functioning autism necessarily a disability? *Development and Psychopathology, 12,* 489–500.

Baron-Cohen, S. (2000b). Theory of mind and autism: A review. *International Review of Research in Mental Retardation, 23,* 170–184.

Baron-Cohen, S. (2002). The extreme male brain theory of autism. *Trends in Cognitive Sciences, 6,* 248–254.

Baron-Cohen, S., & Bolton, P. (1993). *Autism: The facts.* Oxford, England: Oxford University Press.

Baron-Cohen, S., Cox, A., Baird, G., Swettenham, J., Nightingale, N., Morgan, K., Drew, A., & Charman T. (1996). Psychological markers in the detection of autism in infancy in a large population. *British Journal of Psychiatry, 168,* 158–163.

Baron-Cohen, S., Richler, J., Bisarya, D., Gurunathan, N., & Wheelright, S. (2003). The systemizing quotient: An investigation of adults with Asperger syndrome or high-functioning autism, and normal sex differences. *Philosophical Transactions of the Royal Society: Biological Sciences, 358,* 361–374.

Baron-Cohen, S., Ring, H. A., Bullmore, E. T., Wheelwright, S., Ashwin, C., & Williams, S. C. (2000). The amygdala theory of autism. *Neuroscience Biobehavioral Review, 24,* 355–364.

Baron-Cohen, S., Ring, H. A., Wheelright, S., Bullmore, E. T., Brammer, M. J., Simmons, A., & Williams, S. C. (1999). Social intelligence in the normal and autistic brain: An fMRI study. *European Journal of Neuroscience, 11,* 1891–1898.

Baron-Cohen, S., Tager-Flusberg, H., & Cohen, D. (2000). *Understanding other minds: Perspectives from developmental cognitive neuroscience.* Oxford: Oxford University Press.

Barrett, J. (1998). Psychological and social function before and after phalloplasty. *International Journal of Transgenderism, 2 (1).*

Barrett, P., Healy-Farrell, L., & March, J. S. (2004). Cognitive-behavioral family treatment of childhood obsessive-compulsive disorder. A controlled trial. *Journal of the American Academy of Child and Adolescent Psychiatry, 43,* 46–62.

Barrett, P., & Shortt, A. L. (2003). Parental involvement in the treatment of anxious children. In A. E. Kazdin & J. R. Weisz (Eds.), *Evidence-based psychotherapies for children and adolescents* (pp. 101–119). New York: Guilford Press.

Barrett, P. M., Dadds, M. R., & Rapee, R. M. (1996). Family treatment of childhood anxiety: A controlled trial. *Journal of Consulting and Clinical Psychology, 64,* 333–342.

Barrett, P. M., & Healy, L. J. (2003). An examination of the cognitive processes involved in childhood obsessive-compulsive disorder. *Behaviour Research and Therapy, 41,* 285–299.

Barrett, P. M., Rapee, R. M., Dadds, M. M., & Ryan, S. M. (1996). Family enhancement of cognitive style in anxious and aggressive children. *Journal of Abnormal Child Psychology, 24,* 187–203.

Barrios, B. A., & Hartmann, D. P. (1997). Fears and anxieties. In E. J. Mash & L. G. Terdal (Eds.), *Assessment of childhood disorders* (3rd ed., pp. 230–327). New York: Guilford Press.

Barrios, B. A., & O'Dell, S. L. (1998). Fears and anxieties. In E. J. Mash & R. A. Barkley (Eds.), *Treatment of childhood disorders* (pp. 249–337). New York: Guilford Press.

Barter, C., & Renold, E. (2000). 'I wanna tell you a story': Exploring the application of vignettes in qualitative research with children and young people. *International Journal of Social Research Methodology: Theory & Practice, 3,* 307–323.

Barth, C., Fein, D., & Waterhouse, L. (1995). Delayed match-to-sample performance in autistic children. *Developmental Neuropsychology, 11,* 53–69.

Barton, M., & Volkmar, F. (1998). How commonly are known medical conditions associated with autism? *Journal of Autism and Developmental Disorders, 28,* 273–278.

Bates, J. E., Bayles, K., Bennett, D. S., Ridge, B., & Brown, N. M. (1991). Origins of externalizing behavior problems at eight years of age. In D. J. Pepler & K. H. Rubin (Eds.), *The development and treatment of childhood aggression* (pp. 93–120). Hillsdale, NJ: Erlbaum.

Bauman, M. L. (1996). Neuroanatomic observations of the brain in pervasive developmental disorders. *Journal of Autism and Developmental Disorders, 26,* 199–203.

Bauman, M. L., Kemper, T. L., & Arin, D. M. (1995). Pervasive neuroanatomic abnormalities of the brain in three cases of Rett's syndrome. *Neurology, 45,* 1581–1586.

Baumeister, R. F., Bushman, B. J., & Campbell, W. K. (2000). Self-esteem, narcissism, and aggression: Does violence result from low self-esteem or from threatened egotism? *Current Directions in Psychological Science, 9,* 26–29.

Baumeister, R. F., Smart, L., & Boden, J. M. (1996). Relation of threatened egotism to violence and aggression: The dark side of high self-esteem. *Psychological Review, 103,* 5–33.

Baving, L., Laucht, M., & Schmidt, M.H. (2003). Frontal EEG correlates of externalizing spectrum behaviors. *European Child & Adolescent Psychiatry, 12,* 36–42.

Bazyk, S. (1989). Changes in attitudes and beliefs regarding parent participation in home programs: An update. *American Journal of Occupational Therapy, 43,* 723–728.

Beardslee, W. R., Gladstone, T.R.G., Wright, E. J., & Cooper, A. B. (2003). A family-based approach to the prevention of depressive symptoms in children at risk: Evidence of parental and child change. *Pediatrics, 112,* e119–e131.

Beardslee, W. R., Versage, E. M., & Gladstone, T. R. (1998). Children of affectively ill parents: A review of the past 10 years. *Journal of the American Academy of Child and Adolescent Psychiatry, 37,* 1134–1141.

Beardslee, W. R., & Wheelock, I. (1994). Children of parents with affective disorders: Empirical findings and clinical implications. In W. M. Reynolds & H. F. Johnston (Eds.), *Handbook of depression in children and adolescents* (pp. 463–479). New York: Plenum.

Beauchaine, T. P., Katkin, E. S., Strassberg, Z., & Snarr, J. (2001). Disinhibitory psychopathology in male adolescents: Discriminating conduct disorder from attention-deficit/hyperactivity disorder through concurrent assessment of multiple autonomic states. *Journal of Abnormal Psychology, 110,* 610–624.

Beauchaine, T.P. (2003). Taxometrics and developmental psychopathology. *Development & Psychopathology,* Special Issue: Conceptual, methodological, and statistical issues in developmental psychopathology: A special issue in honor of Paul E. Meehl, *15, 3,* 501–527.

Beautrais, A. L. (2003). Suicide and serious suicide attempts in youth: A multiple group comparison study. *American Journal of Psychiatry, 160,* 1093–1099.

Bebko, J. M., Wainwright, J. A., Brian, J. A., Coolbear, J., Landry, R., & Vallance, D. D. (1998). Social competence and peer relations in children with mental retardation: Models of the development of peer relations. *Journal on Developmental Disabilities. 6,* 1–31.

Beck, A. T. (1967). *Depression: Clinical, experimental, and theoretical aspects.* Philadelphia: University of Pennsylvania Press.

Beck, S. J. (2000). Behavioral assessment. In M. Hersen & R. T. Ammerman (Eds.). *Advanced abnormal child psychology* (2nd ed., pp. 177–195). Mahwah, NJ: Erlbaum.

Becker, A. E., Burwell, R. A., Herzog, D. B., Hamburg, P., & Gilman, S. E. (2002). Eating behaviours and attitudes following prolonged exposure to television among ethnic Fijian adolescent girls. *British Journal of Psychiatry, 180,* 509–514.

Becker, A. E., Grinspoon, S. K., Klibanski, A., & Herzog, D.B. (1999). Current concepts: Eating disorders. *New England Journal of Medicine, 340,* 1092–1098.

Beeghly, M., & Cicchetti, D. (1997). Talking about self and other: Emergence of an internal state lexicon in young children with Down syndrome. *Development and Psychopathology, 9,* 729–748.

Beidel, D. C., Silverman, W. K., & Hammond-Laurence, K. (1996). Overanxious disorder: Subsyndromal state or specific disorder? A comparison of clinic and community samples. *Journal of Clinical Child Psychology, 25,* 25–32.

Beidel, D. C., & Turner, S. M. (1988). Comorbidity of test anxiety and other anxiety disorders in children. *Journal of Abnormal Child Psychology, 16,* 275–287.

Beidel, D. C., & Turner, S. M. (1997). At risk for anxiety: I. Psychopathology in the offspring of anxious parents. *Journal of the American Academy of Child and Adolescent Psychiatry, 36,* 918–924.

Beidel, D. C., & Turner, S. M. (1998). *Shy children, phobic adults: Nature and treatment of social phobia.* Washington, DC: American Psychological Association.

Beidel, D. C., Turner, S. M., Morris, T. L. (1999). Psychopathology of childhood social phobia. *Journal of the American Academy of Child and Adolescent Psychiatry, 38,* 643–650.

Beidel, D. C., Turner, S. M., & Taylor-Ferreira, J. C. (1999). Teaching study skills and test-taking strategies to elementary school students: The Testbusters program. *Behavior Modification, 23,* 630–646.

Beitchman, J. H., Wilson, B., Brownlie, E. B., Walters, H., Inglis, A., & Lancee, W. (1996). Long-term consistency in speech/language profiles: II. Behavioral, emotional, and social outcomes. *Journal of the American Academy of Child and Adolescent Psychiatry, 35,* 815–825.

Beitchman, J. H., Wilson, B., Johnson, C. J., Atkinson, L., Young, A., Adlaf, E., et al. (2001). Fourteen-year follow-up of speech/language-impaired and control children: Psychiatric outcome. *Journal of the American Academy of Child & Adolescent Psychiatry, 40,* 75–82.

Bell, D., Foster, S. L., & Mash, E. J. (Eds.). (in press). *Handbook of behavioral and emotional problems in girls.* New York: Kluwer Academic..

Bellack, A. S., & Hersen, M. (Eds.). (1998). *Behavioral assessment: A practical handbook* (4th ed.). Needham Heights, MA: Allyn & Bacon.

Bellamy, C. (2002). *The state of the world's children 2002: Leadership.* New York: United Nations Children's Fund.

Bell-Dolan, D. J. (1995). Social cue interpretation of anxious children. *Journal of Clinical Child Psychology, 24,* 1–10.

Bell-Dolan, D. J., Last, C. G., & Strauss, C. C. (1990). Symptoms of anxiety disorders in normal children. *Journal of the American Academy of Child and Adolescent Psychiatry, 29,* 759–765.

Bemporad, J. R. (1979). Adult recollections of a formerly autistic child. *Journal of Autism and Developmental Disorders, 9,* 179–197.

Bemporad, J. R. (1994). Dynamic and interpersonal theories of depression. In W. M. Reynolds & H. F. Johnston (Eds.), *Handbook of depression in children and adolescents* (pp. 81–95). New York: Plenum.

Benasich, A. A., Curtiss, S., & Tallal, P. (1993). Language, learning, and behavioral disturbances in childhood: A longitudinal perspective. *Journal of the American Academy of Child and Adolescent Psychiatry, 32,* 585–594.

Benasich, A. A., & Tallal, P. (2002). Infant discrimination of rapid auditory cues predicts later language impairment. *Behavioural Brain Research, 136,* 31–49.

Benjamin, J., Li, L., Patterson, C., Greenberg, B. D., Murphy, D. L., & Hamer, D. H. (1996). Population and familial association between the D4 dopamine receptor gene and measures of novelty seeking. *Nature Genetics, 12,* 81–84.

Benjamin, L. T., Jr. & Shields, S. A. (1990). Leta Stetter Hollingworth (1886–1939). In O' Connell A. N. & Russo, N. F. (Eds.),*Women in psychology: A bio-biographic sourcebook* (pp.173–183). Westport, CT: Greenwood Press.

Benjet, C., & Kazdin, A. E. (2003). Spanking children: The controversies, findings, and new directions. *Clinical Psychology Review, 23,* 197–224.

Bennett, D. S. (1994). Depression among children with chronic medical problems: A meta-analysis. *Journal of Pediatric Psychology, 19,* 149–170.

Benoit, D., Zeanah, C. H., & Barton, L. M. (1989). Maternal attachment disturbances in failure to thrive. *Infant Mental Health Journal, 10,* 185–202.

Bensley, L. S., Eenwyk, J. V., & Simmons, K. W. (2000). Self-reported childhood sexual and physical abuse and adult HIV-risk behaviors and heavy drinking. *American Journal of Preventive Medicine, 18,* 151–158.

Benson, B. A., & Aman, M.G. (1999). Disruptive behavior disorders in children with mental retardation. In H. C. Quay & A. E. Hogan (Eds.), *Handbook of disruptive behavior disorders* (pp. 559–578). New York: Kluwer Academic/Plenum.

Benson, B., & Valenti-Hein, D. (2001). Cognitive and social learning treatments. In A. Dosen & K. Day (Eds.), *Treatment of mental illness and behavior disorders in children and adults with mental retardation* (pp. 101–118). Washington, DC: American Psychiatric Press.

Berg, B. L. (1998). *Qualitative research methods for the social sciences* (3rd ed.). Needham Heights, MA: Allyn & Bacon.

Bergman, R. L., Piacentini, J., & McKracken, J. T. (2002). Prevalence and description of selective mutism in a school-based sample. *Journal of the American Academy of Child and Adolescent Psychiatry, 41,* 938–946.

Berliner, L., & Elliot, D. (2002). Sexual abuse of children. In J. E. B. Myers, L. Berliner, J. Briere, C. T. Hendrix, C. Jenny, & T. A. Reid (Eds.), *The APSAC handbook on child maltreatment* (2nd ed., pp. 55–78). Thousand Oaks, CA: Sage

Berman, A. L., & Jobes, D. A. (1991). *Adolescent suicide: Assessment and intervention.* Washington, DC: American Psychological Association.

Bernstein, G. A. (1991). Comorbidity and severity of anxiety and depressive disorders in a clinic sample. *Journal of the American Academy of Child and Adolescent Psychiatry, 30,* 43–50.

Bernstein, G. A., Borchardt, C. M., & Perwien, A. R. (1996). Anxiety disorders in children and adolescents: A review of the past 10 years. *Journal of the American Academy of Child and Adolescent Psychiatry, 35,* 1110–1119.

Bernstein, G. A., Borchardt, C. M., Perwien, A. R., Crosby, R. D., Kushner, M. D., Thuras, P. D., & Last, C. G. (2000). Imipramine plus cognitive behavioral therapy in the treatment of school refusal. *Journal of the American Academy of Child and Adolescent Psychiatry, 39,* 276–283.

Bettelheim, B. (1967). *The empty fortress: Infantile autism and the birth of the self.* New York: Free Press.

Beyers, J. M., & Loeber, R. (2003). Untangling developmental relations between depressed mood and delinquency in male adolescents. *Journal of Abnormal Child Psychology, 31,* 247–266.

Bickett, L. R., Milich, R., & Brown, R. T. (1996). Attributional styles of aggressive boys and their mothers. *Journal of Abnormal Child Psychology, 24,* 457–472.

Biederman, J. (1998). Resolved: Mania is mistaken or ADHD in prepubertal children. *Journal of the American Academy of Child and Adolescent Psychiatry, 35,* 997–1008.

Biederman, J., Faraone, S. V., & Lapey, K. (1992). Comorbidity of diagnosis in attention-deficit hyperactivity disorders. In G. Weiss (Ed.), *Child and adolescent psychiatric clinics of North America: Attention-deficit hyperactivity disorder* (pp. 335–360). Philadelphia: Saunders.

Biederman, J., Faraone, S. V., Mick, E., Spencer, T., Wilens, T., Kiely, K., et al., (1995). High risk for attention deficit hyperactivity disorder among children of parents with childhood onset of the disorder: A pilot study. *American Journal of Psychiatry, 152,* 431–435.

Biederman, J., Faraone, S. V., Milberger, S., Jetton, J. G., Chen, L., Mick, E., et al. (1996). Is childhood oppositional defiant disorder a precursor to adolescent conduct disorder? Findings from a four-year follow-up study of children with ADHD. *Journal of the American Academy of Child and Adolescent Psychiatry, 35,* 1193–1204.

Biederman, J., Faraone, S. V., Monuteaux, M. C., Plunkett, E. A., Gifford, J., & Spencer, T. (2003). Growth deficits and attention-deficit/hyperactivity disorder revisited: Impact of gender, development, and treatment. *Pediatrics, 111,* 1010–1016.

Biederman, J., Mick, E., & Faraone, S. V. (1998). Depression in attention deficit hyperactivity disorder (ADHD) children: "True" depression or demoralization? *Journal of Affective Disorders, 47,* 113–122.

Biederman, J., Mick, E., Faraone, S. V., Braaten, E., Doyle, A., Spencer, T., et al., (2002). Influence of gender on attention deficit hyperactivity disorder in children referred to a psychiatry clinic. *American Journal of Psychiatry, 159,* 36–42.

Biederman, J., Mick, E., Spencer, T. J., Wilens, T. E., & Faraone, S. V. (2000). Therapeutic dilemmas in the pharmacotherapy of bipolar depression in the young. *Journal of Child and Adolescent Psychopharmacology, 10,* 185–192.

Biederman, J., Rosenbaum, J. F., Bolduc-Murphy, E. A., Faraone, S. V., Chaloff, J., Hirshfeld, D. R., & Kagan, J. (1993a). A three-year follow-up of children with and without behavioral inhibition. *Journal of the American Academy of Child and Adolescent Psychiatry, 32,* 814–821.

Biederman, J., & Spencer, T. (1999a). Attention-deficit/hyperactivity disorder (ADHD) as a noradrenergic disorder. *Biological Psychiatry, 46,* 1234–1242.

Biederman, J., & Spencer, T. (1999b). Depressive disorders in childhood and adolescence: A clinical perspective. *Journal of Child and Adolescent Psychopharmacology, 9,* 233–237.

Bienvenu, T., Carrie, A., de Roux, N., Vinet, M. C., Jonveaux, P., Couvert, P., et al. (2000). MECP2 mutations account for most cases of typical forms of Rett syndrome. *Human Molecular Genetics, 9,* 1377–1384.

Biglan, A., Metzler, C. W., Wirt, R., Ary, D., Noel, J., Ochs, L., French, C., & Hood,

D. (1990). Social and behavioral factors associated with high-risk sexual behavior among adolescents. *Journal of Behavioral Medicine, 15,* 245–261.

Biklen, D. (1990). Communication unbound: Autism and praxis. *Harvard Educational Review, 60,* 291–314.

Biklen, D., & Cardinal, D. N. (Eds.). (1997). *Contested words, contested science: Unraveling the facilitated communication controversy.* New York: Teacher's College Press.

Bingham, C. Raymond, Loukas, A., Fitzgerald, H. E., Zucker, R. A. (2003). Parental ratings of son's behavior problems in high-risk families: Convergent validity, internal structure, and interparent agreement *Journal of Personality Assessment, 80,* 3, 237–251.

Bird, H. R., Canino, G. J., Davies, M., Zhang, H., Ramirez, R., & Lahey, B. B. (2001). Prevalence and correlates of antisocial behaviors among three ethnic groups. *Journal of Abnormal Child Psychology, 29,* 465–478.

Birmaher, B. (2003). Treatment of psychosis in children and adolescents. *Psychiatric Annals, 33 (4),* 257–264.

Birmaher, B., Arbelaez, C., & Brent, D. A. (2002). Course and outcome of child and adolescent major depressive disorder. *Child and Adolescent Psychiatric Clinics of North America, 11,* 639–648.

Birmaher, B., & Ryan, N. D. (1999). Neurobiological factors. In C. A. Essau & F. Petermann (Eds.), *Depressive disorders in children and adolescents: Epidemiology, risk factors, and treatment* (pp. 287–318). Northvale, NJ: Jason Aronson.

Birmaher, B., Ryan, N. D., Williamson, D. E., Brent, D. A., & Kaufman, J. (1996a). Childhood and adolescent depression: A review of the past 10 years: Part II. *Journal of the American Academy of Child and Adolescent Psychiatry, 35,* 1575–1583.

Birmaher, B., Ryan, N. D., Williamson, D. E., Brent, D. A., Kaufman, J., Dahl, R. E., Perel, J., & Nelson, B. (1996b). Childhood and adolescent depression: A review of the past 10 years: Part I. *Journal of the American Academy of Child and Adolescent Psychiatry, 35,* 1427–1439.

Birmaher, B., Williamson, D. E., Dahl, R. E., Axelson, D. A., Kaufman, J., Dorn, L. D., & Ryan, D. (2004). Clinical presentation and course of depression in youth: Does onset in childhood differ from onset in adolescence. *Journal of the American Academy of Child and Adolescent Psychiatry, 43,* 63–70.

Bishop (2003). Genetic and environmental risks for specific language impairment in children. *International Congress Series 1254,* 225–245.

Bishop, D.V.M., Bishop, S. J., Bright, P., James, C., Delaney, T., & Tallal, P. (1999). Different origin of auditory and phonological processing problems in children with language impairment: Evidence from a twin study. *Journal*

of Speech, Language, & Hearing Research, 42, 155–168.

Bjorklund, D. F. (1995). *Children's thinking: Developmental function and individual differences* (2nd ed.). Pacific Grove, CA: Brooks/Cole.

Bjorkqvist, K., & Niemela, P. (Eds.). (1992). *Of mice and women: Aspects of female aggression.* San Diego, CA: Academic Press.

Black, B., & Uhde, T. W. (1995). Psychiatric characteristics of children with selective mutism: A pilot study. *Journal of the American Academy of Child and Adolescent Psychiatry, 29,* 36–44.

Black, M. M., Danseco, E. R., & Krishnakumar, A. (1998). Understanding pediatric health concerns in a social-ecological context: A review of intervention research. *Children's Services: Social Policy, Research, and Practice, 1,* 111–126.

Blader, J. C., Koplewicz, H. S., Abikoff, H., & Foley, C. (1997). Sleep problems of elementary school children. *Archives of Pediatric Adolescent Medicine, 151,* 473–480.

Blair, C., Greenberg, M., & Crnic, K. (2001). Age-related increases in motivation among children with mental retardation and MA- and CA-matched controls. *American Journal on Mental Retardation, 106,* 511–524.

Blair, C., & Wahlsten, D. (2002). Why early intervention works: A reply to Baumeister and Bacharach. *Intelligence, 30,* 129–140.

Blanck, P. D., Bellack, A. S., Rosnow, R. L., Rotheram-Borus, M. J., & Schooler, N. R. (1992). Scientific rewards and conflicts of ethical choices in human subjects research. *American Psychologist, 47,* 959–965.

Blatt, B., & Kaplan, F. (1966). *Christmas in purgatory: A photographic essay on mental retardation.* Boston: Allyn & Bacon.

Block, J., Block, J. H., & Gjerde, P. F. (1986). The personality of children prior to divorce: A prospective study. *Child Development, 57,* 827–840.

Blount, R. L., Smith, A. J., & Frank, N. C. (1999). Preparation to undergo medical procedures. In A. J. Goreczny & M. Hersen (Eds.), *Handbook of pediatric and adolescent health psychology* (pp. 305–326). Boston: Allyn & Bacon.

Blumberg, H. P., Kaufman, J., Martin, A., Whiteman, R., Zhang, J. H., Gore, J. C., Charney, D. S., Krystal, J. H., & Peterson, B. S. (2003). Amygdala and hippocampal volumes in adolescents and adults with bipolar disorder. *Archives of General Psychiatry, 60,* 1201–1208.

Boddy, J., Skuse, D., & Andrews, B. (2000). The developmental sequelae of nonorganic failure to thrive. *Journal of Child Psychology & Psychiatry & Allied Disciplines, 41,* 1003–1014.

Boekaerts, M. & Roeder, I. (1999). Stress, coping, and adjustment in children with a chronic disease: A review of the literature. *Disability and Rehabilitation, 21,* 311–337.

Boetsch, E. A., Green, P. A., & Pennington, B. F. (1996). Psychosocial correlates of dyslexia across the life span. *Development and Psychopathology, 8,* 539–562.

Bogdan, R., & Taylor, S. J. (1982). *Inside out: The social meaning of mental retardation.* Toronto: University of Toronto Press.

Bolger, K. E., & Patterson, C. J. (2001). Developmental pathways from child maltreatment to peer rejection. *Child Development, 72,* 549–568.

Bolton, P., MacDonald, H., Pickles, A., Rios, P., Goode, S., Crowson, M., Bailey, A., & Rutter, M. (1994). A case-control family history study of autism. *Journal of Child Psychology and Psychiatry, 35,* 877–900.

Bolton, P., Murphy, M., Macdonald, H., Whitlock, B., Pickles, A., & Rutter, M. (1997). Obstetric complication in autism: Consequences or causes of this condition? *Journal of the American Academy of Child and Adolescent Psychiatry, 36,* 272–281.

Boney-McCoy, S., & Finkelhor, D. (1995). Psychosocial sequelae of violent victimization in a national youth sample. *Journal of Consulting and Clinical Psychology, 63,* 726–736.

Bongers, I. L., Koot, H. M., van der Ende, J., & Verhulst, F. C. (2003). The normative development of child and adolescent problem behaviour. *Journal of Abnormal Psychology, 112,* 179–192.

Bootzin, R. R., & Chambers, M. J. (1990). Childhood sleep disorders. In A. M. Gross & R. S. Drabman (Eds.), *Handbook of clinical behavioral pediatrics* (pp. 205–227). New York: Plenum.

Bootzin, R. R. & Rider, S.P.C. (1997). Behavioral techniques and biofeedback for insomnia. In M. R. Pressman & W. C. Orr (Eds.), *Understanding sleep: The evaluation and treatment of sleep disorders. Application and practice in health psychology* (pp. 315–338). Washington, DC: American Psychological Association.

Borawski, E. A., Ievers-Landis, C. E., Lovegreen, L. D., & Trapl, E. S. (2003). Parental monitoring, negotiated unsupervised time, and parental trust: The role of perceived parenting practices in adolescent health risk behaviors *Journal of Adolescent Health, 33,* 60–70.

Borkovec, T. D., Ray, W. J., & Stoeber, J. (1998). Worry: A cognitive phenomenon intimately linked to affective, physiological, and interpersonal behavioral processes. *Cognitive Therapy and Research, 22,* 561–576.

Borkovec, T. M., & Inz, J. (1990). The nature of worry in generalized anxiety disorder: A predominance of thought activity. *Behaviour Research and Therapy, 28,* 153–158.

Borkovec, T. M. (1994). The nature, functions, and origins of worry. In G.C.L. Davey & F. Tallis (Eds.), *Worrying: Perspectives on theory, assessment and treatment* (pp. 5–33). Chichester, England: Wiley.

Borowitz, S. M., Cox, D. J., & Sutphen, J. L. (1999). Differences in toileting habits between children with chronic encopresis, asymptomatic siblings, and asymptomatic nonsiblings. *Journal of Developmental and Behavioral Pediatrics, 20,* 145–149.

Borowsky, I. W., Ireland, M., & Resnick, M. D. (2001). Adolescent suicide attempts: Risks and protectors. *Pediatrics, 107,* 485–493.

Borstelmann, L. J. (1983). Children before psychology: Ideas about children from antiquity to the late 1800s. In W. Kessen (Vol. Ed.), *Handbook of child psychology* (4th ed.): Vol. I. History, theory, and methods (pp. 1–40). New York: Wiley.

Botvin, G.J., & Griffin, K.W. (2002). Life skills training as a primary prevention approach for adolescent drug abuse and other problem behaviors. *International Journal of Emergency Mental Health, 4,* 41–48.

Boucher, J. (2003). Language development in autism. *International Congress Series, 1254,* 247–253.

Bouras, N. (Ed.). (1999). *Psychiatric and behavioural disorders in developmental disabilities and mental retardation.* New York: Cambridge University Press.

Boutelle, K., Neumark-Sztainer, D., Story, M., & Resnick, M. (2002). Weight control behaviors among obese, overweight, and nonoverweight adolescents. *Journal of Pediatric Psychology, 27,* 531–540.

Bowkett, S. (2003). Child abuse on the internet: Ending the silence. *Clinical Child Psychology & Psychiatry, 8,* 556–557.

Bowlby, J. (1961). Childhood mourning and its implications for psychiatry. *American Journal of Psychiatry, 118,* 481–498.

Bowlby, J. (1973). *Attachment and loss: Vol. 2. Separation: Anxiety and anger.* New York: Basic Books.

Bowlby, J. A. (1988). *A secure base: Parent–child attachment and healthy human development.* New York: Basic Books.

Bowler, P. J. (1989). Holding your head up high: Degeneration and orthogenesis in theories of human evolution. In J. R. Moore (Ed.), *History, humanity, and evolution: Essays for John C. Greene* (pp. 329–353). Cambridge, England: Cambridge University Press.

Bowman, S. A., Gortmaker, S.L., Ebbeling, C. B., Pereira, M. A., & Ludwig, D. S. (2004). Effects of fast-food consumption on energy intake and diet quality among children in a national household survey. *Pediatrics, 113,* 112–118.

Boyle, M. H., & Jadad, A. R. (1999). Lessons from large trials: The MTA study as a model for evaluating the treatment of childhood psychiatric disorder. *Canadian Journal of Psychiatry, 44,* 991–998.

Bradley, R. H., Corwyn, R. F., McAdoo, H. P., & Garcia Coll, C. (2001). The home environments of children in the United States. Part 1: Variations by age, ethnicity, and poverty status. *Child Development, 72,* 1844–1867.

Brady, E., & Kendall, P. C. (1992). Comorbidity of anxiety and depression in children and adolescents. *Psychological Bulletin, 3,* 244–255.

Braet, C., & Crombez, G. (2003). Cognitive interference due to food cues in childhood obesity. *Journal of Clinical Child and Adolescent Psychology, 32,* 32–39.

Brambilla, P., Hardan, A., Ucelli di Nemi, S., Perez, J., Soares, J. C., & Barale, F. (2003). Brain anatomy and development in autism: Review of structural MRI studies. *Brain Resarch Bulletin, 61,* 557–569.

Bramble, D. (2003). The use of psychotropic medications in children: A British view. *Journal of Child Psychology and Psychiatry, 44,* 169–179.

Brame, B., Nagin, D. S., & Tremblay, R. E. (2001). Developmental trajectories of physical aggression from school entry to late adolescence. *Journal of Child Psychology and Psychiatry, 42,* 503–512.

Breggin, P. (1998). *Talking back to Ritalin.* Monroe, ME: Common Courage Press.

Brehaut, J. C., Miller, A, Raina, P., & McGrail, K. M. (2003). Childhood behavior disorders and injuries among children and youth. *Pediatrics, 111,* 262–269.

Bremner, J. D. (2003). Long-term effects of childhood abuse on brain and neurobiology. *Child & Adolescent Psychiatric Clinics of North America, 12,* 271–292.

Bremner, J. D. & Vermetten, E. (2001). Stress and development: Behavioral and biological consequences. *Development & Psychopathology Special Issue: Stress and development: Biological and psychological consequences, 13,* 473–489.

Brener, N. D., Simon, T. R., Krug, E. G., & Lowry, R. (1999). Recent trends in violence-related behaviors among high school students in the United States. *Journal of the American Medical Association, 282,* 440–446.

Brennan, P. A., Brocque, R. L., & Hammen, C. (2003). Maternal depression, parent-child relationships, and resilient outcomes in adolescence. *Journal of the American Academy of Child and Adolescent Psychiatry, 42,* 1469–1477.

Brennan, P. A., Hall, J., Bor, W., Najman, J. M., & Williams, G. (2003). Integrating biological and social processes in relation to early-onset persistent aggression in boys and girls. *Developmental Psychology, 39,* 309–323.

Brennan, P. A., Hammen, C., Andersen, M. J., Bor, W., Najman, J. M., & Williams, G. M. (2000). Chronicity, severity, and timing of maternal depressive symptoms: Relationships with child outcomes at age 5. *Developmental Psychology, 36,* 759–766.

Brent, D. A., Holder, D., Kolko, D., Birmaher, B., Baugher, M., Roth, C., Iyengar, S., & Johnson, B. A. (1997). A clinical psychotherapy trial for adolescent depression comparing cognitive, family, and supportive therapy. *Archives of General Psychiatry, 54,* 877–885.

Brent, D. A., Perper, J. A., Goldstein, C. E., Kolko, D. J., Allan, M. J., Allman, C. J., & Zelenak, J. P. (1988). Risk factors for adolescent suicide: A comparison of adolescent suicide victims with suicidal inpatients. *Archives of General Psychiatry, 45,* 581–588.

Brent, D. A., Perper, J. A., Moritz, G., Allman, C., Friend, A., Roth, C., Schweers, J., Balach, L., & Baugher, M. (1993). Psychiatric risk factors for adolescent suicide: A case control study. *Journal of the American Academy of Child and Adolescent Psychiatry, 32,* 521–529.

Brent, D. A., Perper, J. A., Moritz, G., Allman, C., Friend, A., Schweers, J., et al. (1992). Psychiatric effects of exposure to suicide among the friends and acquaintances of adolescent suicide victims. *Journal of the American Academy of Child and Adolescent Psychiatry, 31,* 629–640.

Brestan, E. V., & Eyberg, S. M. (1998). Effective psychosocial treatments of conduct-disordered children and adolescents: 29 years, 82 studies, and 5,272 kids. *Journal of Clinical Child Psychology, 27,* 180–189.

Bretherton, I. (1995). Attachment theory and developmental psychopathology. In D. Cicchetti & S. Toth (Eds.), *Emotion and representation in developmental psychopathology* (Rochester Symposium on Developmental Psychopathology). Rochester, NY: University of Rochester Press.

Breton, J., Bergeron, L., Valla, J. P., Berthiaume, C., Gaudet, N., Lambert, J., et al. (1999). Quebec children mental health survey: prevalence of DSM-III-R mental health disorders. *Journal of Child Psychology and Psychiatry, 40,* 375–384.

Briere, J. (2002). Treating adult survivors of severe childhood abuse and neglect: Further development of an integrative model. In J.E.B. Myers, L. Berliner, J. Briere, C. Hendrix, C. Jenny, & T.A. Reid (Eds.), *The APSAC handbook on child maltreatment* (2nd ed., pp. 175–203). Thousand Oaks, CA: Sage Publications.

Briggs-Gowan, M. J., Horwitz, S. M., Schwab-Stone, M. E., Leventhal, J. M., & Leaf, P. J. (2000). Mental health in pediatric settings: Distribution of disorders and factors related to service use. *Journal of the American Academy of Child and Adolescent Psychiatry, 39,* 841–849.

Brinch, M., Isager, T., & Tolstrup, K. (1988). Anexoria nervosa and motherhood: Reproduction pattern and mothering behavior of 50 women. *Acta Psychiatrica Scandinavica, 77,* 611–617.

Brinkmeyer, M. Y., & Eyberg, S. M. (2003). Parent-child interaction therapy for oppositional children. In A. E. Kazdin & J. R. Weisz (Eds.), *Evidence-based psychotherapies for children and adolescents* (pp. 204–223). New York: Guilford Press.

Broidy, L. M., Nagin, D. S., Tremblay, R. E., Bates, J. E., Brame, B., Dodge, K. A., et al. (2003). Developmental trajectories of childhood disruptive behaviors and adolescent delinquency: A six-site, cross-national study. *Developmental Psychology, 39*, 222–245.

Bromet, E. J., & Fennig, S. (1999). Epidemiology and natural history of schizophrenia. *Biological Psychiatry, 46*, 871–881.

Bromfield, R., Weisz, J. R., & Messer, I. (1986). Children's judgments and attributions in response to the mental retarded label. *Journal of Abnormal Psychology, 95*, 81–87.

Bronfenbrenner, U. (1977). Toward an experimental ecology of human development. *American Psychologist, 52*, 513–531.

Brook, J. S., Whiteman, M., Finch, S. J., & Cohen, P. (1996). Young adult drug use and delinquency: Childhood antecedents and adolescent mediators. *Journal of the American Academy of Child and Adolescent Psychiatry, 35*, 1584–1592.

Brooks-Gunn, J., & Duncan, G. J. (1997). The effects of poverty on children. *The Future of Children, 7(2)*, 55–71.

Brooks-Gunn, J., Klebanov, P. K., Smith, J., Duncan, G. J., & Lee, K. (2003). The Black-White test score gap in young children: Contributions of test and family characteristics. *Applied Developmental Science, 7*, 239–252.

Brooks-Gunn, J., & Warren, M. P. (1985). Effects of delayed menarche in different contexts: Dance and nondance students. *Journal of Youth and Adolescence, 14*, 285–300.

Brown, J., Cohen, P., Johnson, J. G., & Smailes, E. M. (1999). Childhood abuse and neglect: Specificity and effects on adolescent and young adult depression and suicidality. *Journal of the American Academy of Child and Adolescent Psychiatry, 38*, 1490–1496.

Brown, L. K., Lourie, K. J., & Pao, M. (2000). Children and adolescents living with HIV and AIDS: A review. *Journal of Child Psychology and Psychiatry, 41*, 81–96.

Brown, L. M., & Gilligan, C. (1992). *Meeting at the crossroads: Women's psychology and girls' development.* Cambridge, MA: Harvard University Press.

Brown, R.T., & Macias, M. (2001). Chronically ill children and adolescents. In J. N. Hughes, A. M. La Greca, & J. C. Conoley (Eds.), *Handbook of psychological services for children and adolescents* (pp.353–372). London: Oxford University Press.

Brown, R. T., Sawyer, M. G., Antoniou, G., Toogood, I., & Rice, M. (1999). Longitudinal follow-up of the intellectual and academic functioning of children receiving central nervous system-

prophylactic chemotherapy for leukemia: A four-year final report. *Journal of Developmental and Behavioral Pediatrics, 20*, 373–377.

Brown, S. A., Aarons, G. A., & Abrantes, A. M. (2001). Adolescent alcohol and drug abuse. In C. E. Walker & M. C. Roberts (Eds.), *Handbook of clinical child psychology, 3rd edition* (pp. 757–775).

Brown, S. A., & Abrantes, A. M. (in press). Substance use disorders. In D. A. Wolfe & E. J. Mash (Eds.), *Behavioral and Emotional Disorders in Adolescence.* New York: Guilford Press.

Brown, T. (Ed.). (2000). *Attention deficit disorders and comorbidities in children, adolescents, and adults.* Washington, DC: American Psychiatric Press.

Brownell, K. D. (1991). Dieting and the search for the perfect body: Where physiology and culture collide. *Behavior Therapy, 22*, 1–12.

Brownell, K. D., & Rodin, J. (1994). The dieting maelstrom: Is it possible and advisable to lose weight? *American Psychologist, 49*, 781–791.

Brownell, K. D., & Wadden, T. A. (1992). Etiology and treatment of obesity: Understanding a serious, prevalent, and refractory disorder. *Journal of Consulting and Clinical Psychology, 60*, 505–517.

Bruch, H. (1962). Perceptual and conceptual disturbances in anorexia nervosa. *Psychosomatic Medicine, 24*, 187–194.

Bruch, H. (1973). *Eating disorders: Obesity, anorexia nervosa and the person within.* New York: Basic Books.

Bruck, M. (1998). Outcomes of adults with childhood histories of dyslexia. In C. Hulme, R. Joshi, & R. Malatesha (Eds) *Reading and spelling: Development and disorders* (pp. 179–200). Mahwah, NJ: Erlbaum.

Bruer, J. T. (2001). A critical and sensitive period primer. In: D. B. Bailey, Jr., J. T. Bruer, F. J. Symons, & J. W. Lichtman (Eds.), *Critical thinking about critical periods (3–26).* Baltimore, MD: Paul H. Brookes Publishing Co.

Brumberg, J. J. (1988). *Fasting girls: The emergence of anorexia nervosa as a modern disease.* Cambridge, MA: Harvard University Press.

Bryson, S. E. (1996). Epidemiology of autism. *Journal of Autism and Developmental Disorders, 26*, 165–167.

Bryson, S. E., Rogers, S. J., & Fombonne, E. (2003). Autism spectrum disorders: Early detection, intervention, education, and psychopharmacological management. *Canadian Journal of Psychiatry, 48*, 506–515.

Bryson, S. E., & Smith, I. M. (1998). Epidemiology of autism: Prevalence, associated characteristics, and implications for research and service delivery. *Mental Retardation and Developmental Disabilities Research Reviews, 4*, 97–103.

Budd, K. S., McGraw, T. E., Farbisz, R., Murphy, T. M., Hawkins, D., Heilman, N., Werle, M., & Hochstadt, N. J. (1992). Psychosocial concomi-

tants of children's feeding disorders. *Journal of Pediatric Psychology, 17*, 81–94.

Buka, S. L., Stichick, T. L., Birdthistle, I., & Earls, F. J. (2001). Youth exposure to violence: Prevalence, risks and consequences. *American Journal of Orthopsychiatry, 71*, 298–310.

Bulik, C. M. (2002). Eating disorders in adolescents and young adults. *Child & Adolescent Psychiatric Clinics of North America, 11*, 201–218.

Bulik, C. M., Sullivan, P. F., Wade, T. D., & Kendler, K. S. (2000). Twin studies of eating disorders: A review. *International Journal of Eating Disorders, 27*, 2–20.

Bullock, B. M., & Dishion, T. J. (2002). Sibling collusion and problem behavior in early adolescence: Toward a process model for family mutuality. *Journal of Abnormal Child Psychology, 30*, 143–153.

Burcusa, S. L., Iacono, W. G., & McGue, M. (2003). Adolescent twins discordant for major depressive disorder: Shared familial liability to externalizing and other internalizing disorders. *Journal of Child Psychology and Psychiatry, 44*, 997–1005.

Burd, L., Klug, M. G., Coumbe, M. J., & Kerbeshian, J. (2003). Children and adolescents with attention deficit-hyperactivity disorder: 1. Prevalence and cost of care. *Journal of Child Neurology, 18*, 555–561.

Burgess, K. B., Marshall, P. J., Rubin, K. H., Fox, N. A. (2003). Infant attachment and temperament as predictors of subsequent externalizing problems and cardiac physiology. *Journal of Child Psychology and Psychiatry, 44*, 819–831.

Burke, J. D., Loeber, R., & Lahey, B. B. (2001). Which aspects of ADHD are associated with tobacco use in early adolescence? *Journal of Child Psychology and Psychiatry, 42*, 493–502.

Burke, K. C., Burke, J. D., Regier, D. A., & Rae, D. S. (1990). Age at onset of selected mental disorders in five community populations. *Archives of General Psychiatry, 47*, 511–518.

Burke, L., & Smith, S. L. (1999). Treatment of pica: Considering least intrusive options when working with individuals who have a developmental handicap and live in a community setting. *Developmental Disabilities Bulletin, 27*, 30–46.

Burns, G. L., Boe, B., Walsh, J. A., Sommers-Flannagan, R., & Teegarden, L. A. (2001). A confirmatory factor analysis on the DSM-IV ADHD and ODD symptoms: What is the best model for the organization of tehse symptoms? *Journal of Abnormal Child Psychology, 29*, 339–349.

Burns, G. L., & Walsh, J. A. (2002). The influence of ADHD-hyperactivity/impulsivity symptoms on the development of oppositional defiant disorder symptoms in a two-year longitudinal study. *Journal of Abnormal Child Psychology, 30*, 245–256.

Burns, G. L., Walsh, J. A., Patterson, D. R., Holte, C. S., Somers-Flanagan, R., & Parker, C. M. (1997). Internal validity of the disruptive behavior disorder symptoms: Implications from parent ratings for a dimensional approach to symptom validity. *Journal of Abnormal Child Psychology, 25,* 307–319.

Burt, S. A., Krueger, R. F., McGue, M., & Iacono, W. G. (2001). Sources of co-variation among attention-deficit hyper-activity disorder, oppositional defiant disorder, and conduct disorder: The importance of shared environment. *Journal of Abnormal Psychology, 110,* 516–525.

Burton, L. M., & Jarrett, R.L. (2000). In the mix, yet on the margins: The place of families in urban neighborhood and child development research. *Journal of Marriage & the Family, 62,* 1114–1135.

Bussing, R., Zima, B. T., Gary, F. A., Mason, D. M., Leon, C. E., Sinha, K., & Garvan, C. W. (2003). Social networks, caregiver strain, and utilization of mental health services among elementary school students at high risk for ADHD. *Journal of the American Academy of Child and Adolescent Psychiatry, 42,* 842–850.

Butcher, C., McFadden, D., Quinn, B., & Ryan, B. P. (2003). The effects of language training on stuttering in young children, without and with contingency management. *Journal of Developmental & Physical Disabilities, 15,* 255–280.

Butcher, J. N., Williams, C. L., Graham, J. R., Archer, R. P., Tellegen, A., Ben-Porath, Y. S., & Kaemmer, B. (1992). *MMPI-A, Minnesota Multiphasic Personality Inventory—Adolescent: Manual for administration, scoring, and interpretation.* Minneapolis: University of Minnesota Press.

Butler, J. V., Whittington, J. E., Holland, A. J., Boer, H., Clarke, D., & Webb, T. (2002). Prevalence of, and risk factors for, physical ill-health in people with Prader-Willi syndrome: A population-based study. *Developmental Medicine and Child Neurology, 44,* 248–255.

Butler, R. J. (1998). Annotation: Night wetting in children: Psychological aspects. *Journal of Child Psychology and Psychiatry & Allied Disciplines, 39,* 453–463.

Byely, L., Archibald, A. B., Graber, J., & Brooks-Gunn, J. (2000). A prospective study of familial and social influences on girls' body image and dieting. *International Journal of Eating Disorders, 28,* 155–164.

Cabrera, N. J., Tamis-LeMonda, C. S., Bradley, R. H., Hofferth, S., & Lamb, M. E. (2000). Fatherhood in the twenty-first century. *Child Development, 71,* 127–136.

Cadman, D., Boyle, M., Szatmari, P., & Offord, D. R. (1987). Chronic illness, disability, and mental and social well-being: Findings of the Ontario Child Health Study. *Pediatrics, 79,* 805–813.

Calder, J. (1980). *RLS: A life study.* London: Hamish Hamilton.

Camic, P. M., Rhodes, J. E., & Yardley, L. (2003). Naming the stars: Integrating qualitative methods into psychological research. In P. M. Camic, J. E. Rhodes, & L. Yardley (Eds.), *Qualitative research in psychology: Expanding perspectives in methodology and design,* (pp.3–15). Washington, DC: American Psychological Association.

Campbell, F. A., & Ramey, C. T. (1995). Effects of early intervention on intellectual and academic achievement: A follow-up study of children from low-income families. *Child Development, 65,* 684–698.

Campbell, F. A., Ramey, C. T., Pungello, E., Sparling, J., & Miller-Johnson, S. (2002). Early childhood education: Young adult outcomes from the Abecedarian Project. *Applied Developmental Science, 6,* 42–57.

Campbell, S. B. (2000a). Attention-deficit/hyperactivity disorder: A developmental view. In A. J. Sameroff & M. Lewis (Eds.), *Handbook of developmental psychopathology* (2nd ed., pp. 383–401). New York: Kluwer Academic/Plenum.

Campbell, S. B. (2000b). Special issue: Child and family characteristics as predictors and outcomes in the multimodal treatment study of ADHD (MTA Study). *Journal of Abnormal Child Psychology, 28,* 481–599.

Campbell, S. B. (2002). *Behavior problems in preschool children: Clinical and developmental issues* (2nd ed.). New York: Guilford Press.

Campbell, S. B., March, C. L., Pierce, E. W., Ewing, L. J., & Szumowski, E. K. (1991). Hard-to-manage preschool boys: Family context and the stability of externalizing behavior. *Journal of Abnormal Child Psychology, 19,* 301–318.

Campbell, S. B., Shaw, D. S., & Gilliom, M. (2000). Early externalizing behavior problems: Toddlers and preschoolers at risk for later maladjustment. *Development and Psychopathology, 12,* 467–488.

Campbell, T. F., Dollaghan, C. A., Rockette, H. E., Paradise, J. L., Feldman, H. M., Shriberg, L. D., et al. (2003). Risk factors for speech delay of unknown origin in 3-year-old children. *Child Development, 74,* 346–357.

Campbell, V. A., Baker, D. B., & Bratton, S. (2000). Why do children drop-out from play therapy? *Clinical Child Psychology and Psychiatry, 5,* 133–138.

Canino, I. A., & Spurlock, J. (1994). *Culturally diverse children and adolescents: Assessment, diagnosis, and treatment.* New York, New York: Guilford Press, xii, 196.

Canivez, G. L., & Watkins, M. W. (1999) Long-term stability of the Wechsler Intelligence Scale for Children-Third Edition among demographic subgroups: Gender, race/ethnicity, and age. *Journal of Psycho-educational Assessment, 17,* 300–313.

Cantwell, D. P. (1990). Depression across the early life span. In M. Lewis & S. M. Miller (Eds.), *Handbook of developmental psychopathology* (pp. 293–309). New York: Plenum.

Cantwell, D. P., & Baker, L. (1992). Association between attention deficit-hyperactivity disorder and learning disorders. In S. E. Shaywitz & B. A. Shaywitz (Eds.), *Attention deficit disorder comes of age: Toward the twenty-first century* (pp. 145–164). Austin, TX: Pro-ed.

Cantwell, D. P., Baker, L., Rutter, M., & Mawhood, L. (1989). Infantile autism and developmental receptive dysphasia: A comparative follow-up into middle childhood. *Journal of Autism and Developmental Disorders, 19,* 19–31.

Capaldi, D. M., Conger, R. D., Hops, H., & Thornberry, T. P. (2003). Introduction to special section on three-generation studies. *Journal of Abnormal Child Psychology, 31,* 123–125.

Capaldi, D. M., Crosby, L., & Stoolmiller, M. (1996). Predicting the timing of first sexual intercourse for at-risk adolescent males. *Child Development, 67,* 344–359.

Capaldi, D. M., & Patterson, G. R. (1994). Interrelated influences of contextual factors on antisocial behavior in childhood and adolescence. In D. Fowles, P. Sutker, & S. Goodman (Eds.), *Psychopathy and antisocial personality: A developmental perspective* (pp. 165–198). New York: Springer.

Caplan, R. (1994). Communication deficits in childhood schizophrenia spectrum disorders. *Schizophrenia Bulletin, 20,* 671–684.

Caplan, R., Guthrie, D., Tang, B., Komo, S., Asarnow, R. F. (2000). Thought disorder in childhood schizophrenia: Replication and update of concept. *Journal of the American Academy of Child and Adolescent Psychiatry, 39,* 771–778.

Capps, L., Sigman, M., & Mundy, P. (1994). Attachment security in children with autism. *Development and Psychopathology, 6,* 249–261.

Capps, L., Sigman, M., Sena, R., & Henker, B. (1996). Fear, anxiety and perceived control in children of agoraphobic parents. *Journal of Child Psychology and Psychiatry, 37,* 445–452.

Capron, C., & Duyme, M. (1989). Assessment of the effects of socioeconomic status on IQ in a full cross-fostering study. *Nature, 340,* 552–554.

Carlson, C. L., & Mann, M. (2002). Sluggish cognitive tempo predicts a different pattern of impairment in the attention deficit hyperactivity disorder, predominantly inattentive type. *Journal of Clinical Child and Adolescent Psychology, 31,* 123–129.

Carlson, C. L., & Tamm, L. (2000). Responsiveness of children with attention deficit-hyperactivity disorder to reward and response cost: Differential impact on performance and motivation. *Journal of Consulting and Clinical Psychology, 68,* 73–83.

Carlson, C. L., Tamm, L., & Hogan, A. E. (1999). The child with oppositional defiant disorder and conduct disorder in the family. In H. C. Quay & A. E. Hogan (Eds.), *Handbook of disruptive behavior disorders* (pp. 337–352). New York: Kluwer Academic/Plenum.

Carlson, E. A., & Sroufe, L. A. (1995). Contribution of attachment theory to developmental psychopathology. In D. Cicchetti & D. J. Cohen (Eds.), *Developmental psychopathology: Vol. 1. Theory and methods* (pp. 581–617). New York: Wiley.

Carlson, E. A., Sroufe, L. A., Collins, W. A., Jimerson, S., Weinfield, N., Henninghausen, K., et al. (1999). Early environmental support and elementary school adjustment as predictors of school adjustment in middle adolescence. *Journal of Adolescent Research, 14,* 72–94.

Carlson, G. A. (1994). Adolescent bipolar disorder: Phenomenology and treatment implications. In W. M. Reynolds & H. F. Johnston (Eds.), *Handbook of depression in children and adolescents* (pp. 41–60). New York: Plenum.

Carlson, G. A. (2002). Bipolar disorder in children and adolescents: A critical review. In D. Shaffer & B. Waslick (Eds.), *The many faces of depression in children and adolescents* (pp. 105–128). Washington, DC: American Psychiatric Publishing.

Carlson, G. A., Jensen, P. S., Findling, R. L., Meyer, R. E., Calabrese, J., DelBello, M. P., et al. (2003). Methodological issues and controversies in clinical trials with child and adolescent patients with bipolar disorder: Report of a consensus conference. *Journal of Child and Adolescent Psychopharmacology, 13,* 13–27.

Carlson, G. A., & Kashani, J. (1988). Phenomenology of major depression from childhood through adulthood: Analysis of three studies. *American Journal of Psychiatry, 145,* 1222–1225.

Carlson, G. A., Pine, D. S., Nottelmann, E., & Leibenluft, E. (2004). Defining subtypes of childhood bipolar illness: Response and commentary. *Journal of the American Academy of Child and Adolescent Psychiatry, 43,* 3–4.

Carlson, S. M., & Moses, L. J. (2001). Individual differences in inhibitory control and children's theory of mind. *Child Development, 72,* 1032–1053.

Carper, R. A., & Courchesne, E. (2000). Inverse correlation between frontal lobe and cerebellum sizes in children with autism. *Brain, 123,* 836–844.

Carr, E. G. (1977). The motivation of self-injurious behavior: A review of some hypotheses. *Psychological Bulletin, 84,* 800–811.

Carr, E. G., Dunlap, G., Horner, R. H., Koegel, R. L., Turnbull, A. P., Sailor, W., et al. (2002). Positive behavior support: Evolution of an applied science. *Journal of Positive Behavior Interventions, 4,* 4–16.

Carskadon, M. A. (2002). Factors influencing sleep patterns of adolescents. In M. A. Carskadon (Ed.), *Adolescent sleep patterns: Biological, social, and psychological influences,* (pp.4–26). New York: Cambridge University Press.

Carter, A. S., Pauls, D. L., & Leckman, J. F. (1995). The development of obsessionality: Continuities and discontinuities. In D. Cicchetti & D. Cohen (Eds.), *Handbook of developmental psychopathology* (Vol. 2, pp. 609–632). New York: Wiley.

Carter, A. S., & Pollock, R. A. (2000). Obsessions and compulsions: The developmental and familial context. In A. J. Sameroff & M. Lewis (Eds.), *Handbook of developmental psychopathology* (2nd ed., pp. 549–566). New York: Kluwer Academic/Plenum.

Carter, R.C. (2002). The impact of public schools on childhood obesity. *Journal of the American Medical Association, 288,* 21–80.

Casanova, M. F., Carosella, N., & Kleinman, J. E. (1990). Neuropathological findings in a suspected case of childhood schizophrenia. *Journal of Neuropsychiatry and Clinical Neurosciences, 2,* 313–319.

Casey, B. J., Castellanos, F. X., Giedd, J. N., Marsh, W. L., Hamburger, S. D., Schubert, A. B. et al., (1997). Implication of right frontostriatal circuitry in response inhibition and attention-deficit/hyperactivity disorder. *Journal of the American Academy of Child and Adolescent Psychiatry, 36,* 374–383.

Cash, T. F., & Deagle, E. A. (1997). The nature and extent of body-image disturbances in anorexia nervosa and bulimia nervosa: A meta-analysis. *International Journal of Eating Disorders, 22,* 107–125.

Casper, R., Hedeker, D., & McClough, J. F. (1992). Personality dimensions in eating disorders and their relevance for subtyping. *Journal of the American Academy of Child and Adolescent Psychiatry, 31,* 830–840.

Caspi, A., Elder, G. H., Jr., & Bem, D. J. (1987). Moving against the world: Life-course patterns of explosive children. *Developmental Psychology, 23,* 308–313.

Caspi, A., Harrington, H., Milne, B., Amell, J. W., Theodore, R. F., & Moffitt, T. E. (2003). Children's behavioral styles at age 3 are linked to their adult personality traits at age 26. *Journal of Personality, 71,* 495–513.

Caspi, A., Henry, B., McGee, R. O., Moffitt, T., & Silva, P. A. (1995). Temperamental origins of child and adolescent behavior problems: From age three to age fifteen. *Child Development, 66,* 55–68.

Caspi, A., Lynam, D., Moffitt, T. E., & Silva, P. A. (1993). Unraveling girls' delinquency: Biological, dispositional, and contextual contributions to adolescent misbehavior. *Developmental Psychology, 29,* 19–30.

Caspi, A., McClay, J., Terrie E. Moffitt, T. E., Mill, J., Martin, J., Craig, I. W., Taylor, A., & Poulton, R. (2002). Role of genotype in the cycle of violence in maltreated children. *Science, 297,* 851–854.

Caspi, A., & Moffitt, T. E. (1995). The continuity of maladaptive behavior: From description to understanding in the study of antisocial behavior. In D. Cicchetti & D. J. Cohen (Eds.), *Developmental psychopathology: Vol. 2. Risk, disorder, and adaptation* (pp. 472–511). New York: Wiley.

Caspi, A., Sugden, K., Moffitt, T. E., Taylot, A., Craig, I. W., Harrington, H., et al. (2003). Influence of life stress on depression: Moderation by a polymorphism in the 5-HTT gene. *Science, 301,* 386–389.

Caspi, A., Taylor, A., Moffitt, T. E., & Plomin, R. (2000). Neighborhood deprivation affects children's mental health: Environmental risks identified in a genetic design. *Psychological Science, 11,* 338–342.

Cass, L. K., & Thomas, C. B. (1979). *Child psychopathology and later adjustment.* New York: Wiley.

Cassidy, J., & Shaver, P. R. (Eds.). (2002). *Handbook of attachment: Theory, research, and clinical applications.* New York: Guilford Press.

Castellanos, F. X., Lee, P. P., Sharp, W., Jeffries, N. O., Greenstein, D. K., Clasen, L. S., et al., (2002). Developmental trajectories of brain volume abnormalities in children and adolescents with attention-deficit/hyperactivity disorder. *JAMA: Journal of the American Medical Association, 288,* 1740–1748.

Castellanos, F. X., Sharp, W. S., Gottesman, R. F., Greenstein, D. K., Giedd, J. N., & Rapoport, J. L. (2003). Anatomic brain abnormalities in monozygotic twins discordant for attention deficit hyperactivity disorder. *American Journal of Psychiatry, 160,* 1693–1696.

CDC (Centers for Disease Control and Prevention). (2002). Centers for Disease Control and Prevention web-based injury statistics query and reporting system (WASQARS) [online]. Available online: http://www.cdc.gov/ncipc/wisqars.

Challman, T. D., Barbaresi, W. J., Katusic, S. K., & Weaver, A. (2003). The yield of the medical evaluation of children with pervasive developmental disorders. *Journal of Autism and Developmental Disorders, 33,* 187–192.

Chan, E., Zhan, C., & Homer, C. J. (2002). Health care use and costs for children with attention-deficit/hyperactivity disorder: National estimates from the medical expenditure panel study. *Archives of Pediatrics and Adolescent Medicine, 156,* 504–512.

Chandler, L.A., & Johnson, V. J. (1991). Using projective techniques with children: A guide to clinical assessment. Springfield, IL: Charles C. Thomas.

Chansky, T. E., & Kendall, P. C. (1997). Social expectancies and self-perceptions in anxiety-disordered children. *Journal of Anxiety Disorders, 11*, 347–363.

Charman, T., Swettenham, J., Baron-Cohen, S., Cox, A., Baird, G., & Drew, A. (1997). Infants with autism: An investigation of empathy, pretend play, joint attention, and imitation. *Developmental Psychology, 33*, 781–789.

Charmin, T. (2003). Why is joint attention a pivotal skill in autism? *Philosophical Transactions of the Royal Society: Biological Sciences, 358*, 315–324.

Chassin, L., Pitts, S., & Prost, J. (2002). Heavy drinking trajectories from adolescence to young adulthood in a high risk sample: Predictors and substance abuse outcomes. *Journal of Consulting and Clinical Psychology, 70*, 67–78.

Chassin, L., Ritter, J., Trim, R. S., & King, K. M. (2003). Adolescent substance use disorders. In E. J. Mash & R. A. Barkley (Eds.), *Child psychopathology* (2nd ed., pp. 199–230). New York: Guilford Press.

Chen, E., Zeltzer, L. K., Craske, M. G., & Katz, E. R. (1999). Alteration of memory in the reduction of children's distress during repeated aversive medical procedures. *Journal of Consulting and Clinical Psychology, 67*, 481–490.

Chen, X., Rubin, K. H., Li, B., & Li, D. (1999). Adolescent outcomes of social functioning in Chinese children. *International Journal of Behavioral Development, 23*, pp. 199–223.

Chen, X., Rubin, K. H., & Li, Z. Y. (1995). Social functioning and adjustment in Chinese children: A longitudinal study. *Developmental Psychology, 31*, 531–539.

Chervin, R. D., Dillon, J. E., Archbold, K. H., & Ruzicka, D. L. (2003). Conduct problems and symptoms of sleep disorders in children. *Journal of the American Academy of Child & Adolescent Psychiatry, 42*, 201–208.

Chesley, E. B., Alberts, J. D., Klein, J. D., & Kreipe, R. E. (2003). Pro or con? Anorexia nervosa and the Internet. *Journal of Adolescent Health, 32*, 123–124.

Chess, S. (1960). Diagnosis and treatment of the hyperactive child. *New York State Journal of Medicine, 60*, 2379–2385.

Chess, S., & Thomas, A. (1984). *Origins and evolution of behavior disorders.* New York: Brunner/Mazel.

Chethik, M. (2000). *Techniques of child therapy: Psychodynamic strategies* (2nd ed.). New York: Guilford.

Chhabildas, N., Pennington, B. F., & Willcutt, E. G. (2001). A comparison of the neuropsychological profiles of the DSM-IV subtypes of ADHD. *Journal of Abnormal Child Psychology, 29*, 529–540.

Chiariello, M. A., & Orvaschel, H. (1995). Patterns of parent-child communication: Relationship to depression. *Clinical Psychology Review, 15*, 395–407.

Child Medication Safety Act (2003). *Child medication safety act of 2003.* 108th U.S. Congress, 1st Session, H. R. 1170 [Report No. 108–121]. Union Calendar No. 62.

Children's Defense Fund. (2002). *The state of children in America's union: A 2002 action guide to leave no child behind®.* Washington, DC: Author. Available: *http://www.childrensdefense.org/pdf/minigreenbook.pdf*

Chorpita, B. F. (2002). The tripartite model and dimensions of anxiety and depression: An examination of structure in a large school sample. *Journal of Abnormal Child Psychology, 30*, 177–190.

Chorpita, B. F., Albano, A. M., & Barlow, D. H. (1996). Cognitive processing in children: Relation to anxiety and family in influences. *Journal of Clinical Child Psychology, 25*, 170–176.

Chorpita, B. F., & Barlow, D. H. (1998). The development of anxiety: The role of control in the early environment. *Psychological Bulletin, 124*, 3–21.

Chorpita, B. F., Tracey, S. A., Brown, T. A., Collica, T. J., & Barlow, D. H. (1997). Assessment of worry in children and adolescents: An adaptation of the Penn State Worry Questionnaire. *Behaviour Research and Therapy, 35*, 569–581.

Christian, R. E., Frick, P. J., Hill, N. L., Tyler, L., & Frazer, D. R. (1997). Psychopathy and conduct problems in children: II. Implications for subtyping children with conduct problems. *Journal of the American Academy of Child and Adolescent Psychiatry, 36*, 233–241.

Chung, J. Y., & Evans, M. A. (2000). Shyness and symptoms of illness in young children. *Canadian Journal of Behavioural Science, 32*, 49–57.

Cicchetti, D., & Cannon, T. D. (1999). Neurodevelopmental processes in the ontogenesis and epigenesis of psychopathology. *Development and Psychopathology, 11*, 375–393.

Cicchetti, D., Ganiban, J., & Barnett, D. (1990). Contributions from the study of high-risk populations to understanding the development of emotion regulation. In J. Garber & K. A. Dodge (Eds.), *The development of emotion regulation and dysregulation* (pp. 15–48). Cambridge, England: Cambridge University Press.

Cicchetti, D., Ganiban, J., & Barnett, D. (1991). Contributions from the study of high-risk populations to understanding the development of emotion regulation. In J. Garber & K. A. Dodge (Eds.), *The development of emotion regulation and dysregulation* (pp. 15–48). Cambridge, England: Cambridge University Press.

Cicchetti, D., & Hinshaw, S. P. (2003). Conceptual, methodological, and statistical issues in developmental psycho-pathology: A special issue in honor of Paul E. Meehl, *Development and Psychopathology, 15* (Whole No. 3).

Cicchetti, D., & Lynch, M. (1995). Failures in the expectable environment and their impact on individual development: The case of child maltreatment. In D. Cicchetti & D. J. Cohen (Eds.), *Developmental psychopathology: Vol. 2. Risk, disorder, and adaptation* (pp. 32–71). New York: Wiley.

Cicchetti, D., Rappaport, J., Sandler, I., & Weissberg, R.P. (Eds.). (2000). *The promotion of wellness in children and adolescents.* Washington, DC: Child Welfare League of America, Inc.

Cicchetti, D., & Richters, J. E. (1993). Developmental considerations in the investigation of conduct disorder. *Development and Psychopathology, 5*, 331–344.

Cicchetti, D., & Rogosch, F. A. (1996). Equifinality and multifinality in developmental psychopathology. *Development and Psychopathology, 8*, 597–600.

Cicchetti, D., & Rogosch, F. A. (1997). The role of self-organization in the promotion of resilience in maltreated children. *Development and Psychopathology, 9*, 797–815.

Cicchetti, D., & Rogosch, F. A. (2001). The impact of child maltreatment and psychopathology on neuroendocrine functioning. *Development and Psychopathology, 13*, 783–804.

Cicchetti, D., & Rogosch, F. A. (2002). A developmental psychopathology perspective on adolescence. *Journal of Consulting & Clinical Psychology, 70*, 6–20.

Cicchetti, D., Rogosch, F. A., & Toth, S. L. (2000). The efficacy of toddler-parent psychotherapy for fostering cognitive development in offspring of depressed mothers. *Journal of Abnormal Child Psychology, 28*, 135–148.

Cicchetti, D., Rogosch, F. A., Maughan, A., Toth, S. L., & Bruce, J. (2003). False belief understanding in maltreated children. *Development & Psychopathology Special Issue: Experiments of nature: Contributions to developmental theory, 15*, 1067–1091.

Cicchetti, D., & Sroufe, L. A. (2000). Editorial: The past as prologue to the future: The times, they've been a-changin'. *Development and Psychopathology, 12*, 255–264.

Cicchetti, D., Toth, S., & Bush, M. (1988). Developmental psychopathology and incompetence in childhood: Suggestions for intervention. In B. B. Lahey & A. E. Kazdin (Eds.), *Advances in clinical child psychology* (Vol. 11, pp. 1–77). New York: Plenum.

Cicchetti, D., Toth, S. L., & Maughan, A. (2000). An ecological-transactional model of child maltreatment. In A. J. Sameroff, M. Lewis, & S. Miller (Eds.), *Handbook of developmental psychopathology* (2nd ed., pp. 689–722). New York: Plenum.

Clark, L. A., Watson, D., & Mineka, S. (1994). Temperament, personality, and the mood and anxiety disorders. *Journal of Abnormal Psychology, 103,* 103–116.

Clark, R. W. (1971). *Einstein: The life and times.* New York: World.

Clarke, G. N., DeBar, L. L., & Lewinsohn, P. M. (2003). Cognitive-behavioral group treatment for adolescent depression. In A. E. Kazdin & J. R. Weisz (Eds.), *Evidence-based psychotherapies for children and adolescents* (pp. 120–134). New York: Guilford Press.

Clarke, G. N., Lewinsohn, P. M., & Hops, H. (2001). *Instructor's manual for Adolescent Coping with Depression course.* Retrieved February 10, 2004 from Kaiser Permanente Center for Health Research website: *http://www.kpchr.org/public/acwd/acwd.html*

Clay, D. L., Mordhorst, M. J., & Lend, L. (2002). Empirically supported treatments in pediatric psychology: Where is the diversity? *Journal of Pediatric Psychology, 27,* 325–337.

Clementz, B. A., & Iacono, W. G. (1993). Nosology and diagnosis. In A. S. Bellack & M. Hersen (Eds.), *Psychopathology in adulthood* (pp. 3–20). Needham Heights, MA: Allyn & Bacon.

Cleveland, H. H., Weibe, R. P., van den Oord, E. J. C. G., & Rowe, D. C. (2000). Behavior problems among children from different family structures: The influence of genetic self-selection. *Child Development, 71,* 733–751.

Coates, D. L., & Vietze, P. M. (1996). Cultural considerations in assessment, diagnosis, and intervention. In J. W. Jacobson & J. A. Mulick (Eds.), *Manual of diagnosis and professional practice in mental retardation* (pp. 243–263). Washington, DC: American Psychological Association.

Cogan, J. C., Bhalla, S. K., Sefa-Dedeh, A., & Rothblum, E. D. (1996). A comparison study of United States and African students on perceptions of obesity and thinness. *Journal of Cross Cultural Psychology, 27,* 98–113.

Cohen, M. (1998). The monetary value of saving a high-risk youth. *Journal of Quantitative Criminology, 14,* 5–33.

Cohen, M. A., Miller, T. R., & Rossman, S. B. (1994). The costs and consequences of violent behavior in the United States. In A. J. Reiss, Jr., & J. A. Roth (Eds.), *Understanding and preventing violence, Vol. 4: Consequences and control* (pp. 67–166). Washington, DC: National Academy Press.

Cohen, N. J., Vallance, D. D., Barwick, M., Im, N., Menna, R., Horodezky, N. B., & Isaacson, L. (2000). The interface between ADHD and language impairment: An examination of language, achievement, and cognitive processing. *Journal of Child Psychology and Psychiatry, 41,* 353–362.

Cohen, P., Cohen, J., & Brook, J. S. (1993). An epidemiological study of disorders in late childhood and adolescence: II. Persistence of disorders. *Journal of Child Psychology and Psychiatry, 34,* 869–877.

Cohen, P., & Kasen, S. (1999). The context of assessment: Culture, race, and socioeconomic status as influences on the assessment of children. In D. Shaffer & C. P. Lucas (Eds.), *Diagnostic assessment in child and adolescent psychopathology* (pp. 299–318). New York: Guilford Press.

Coie, J. D. (1997, August). *Testing developmental theory of antisocial behavior with outcomes from the Fast Track prevention project.* Paper presented at the annual meeting of the American Psychological Association, Chicago.

Colapinto, J. (1993, November). The trouble with Nick. *Redbook,* pp. 121–123, 145, 151–153.

Colder, C. R., Lochman, J. E., & Wells, K. C. (1997). The moderating effects of children's fear and activity level on relations between parenting practices and childhood symptomatology. *Journal of Abnormal Child Psychology, 25,* 251–263.

Cole, D. A. (1990). The relation of social and academic competence to depressive symptoms in childhood. *Journal of Abnormal Psychology, 99,* 422–429.

Cole, D. A., Martin, J. M., Peeke, L., Henderson, A., & Harwell, J. (1998). Validation of depression and anxiety measures in White and Black youths: Multitrait-multimethod analyses. *Psychological Assessment, 10,* 261–276.

Cole, D. A., Martin, J. M., Powers, B., & Truglio, R. (1996). Modeling causal relations between academic and social competence and depression: A multitrait-multimethod longitudinal study of children. *Journal of Abnormal Psychology, 105,* 258–270.

Cole, D. A., Truglio, R., & Peeke, L. (1997). Relation between symptoms of anxiety and depression in children: A multitrait-multimethod-multigroup assessment. *Journal of Consulting and Clinical Psychology, 65,* 110–119.

Collings, S., & King, M. (1994). Ten-year follow-up of 50 patients with bulimia nervosa. *British Journal of Psychiatry, 164,* 80–87.

Collins, D. W. & Rourke, B. P. (2003). Learning-disabled brains: A review of the literature. *Journal of Clinical & Experimental Neuropsychology, 25,* 1011–1034.

Compas, B. E., Connor-Smith, J. K., Saltzman, H., Thomsen, A. H., & Wadsworth, M. E. (2001). Coping with stress during childhood and adolescence: Problems, progress, and potential in theory and research. *Psychological Bulletin, 127,* 87–127.

Compas, B. E., Grant, K. E., & Ey, S. (1994). Psychosocial stress and child and adolescent depression: Can we be more specific? In W. M. Reynolds & H. F. Johnston (Eds.), *Handbook of depression in children and adolescents* (pp. 509–523). New York: Plenum.

Compas, B. E., Haaga, D. A. F., Keefe, F. J., Leitenberg, H., & Williams, D. A. (1998). Sampling of empirically supported psychological treatments from health psychology: Smoking, chronic pain, cancer, and bulimia nervosa. *Journal of Consulting and Clinical Psychology, 66,* 89–112.

Compas, B. E., & Hammen, C. L. (1994). Child and adolescent depression: Covariation and comorbidity in development. In R. J. Haggerty, L. R. Sherrod, N. Garmezy, & M. Rutter (Eds.), *Stress, risk, and resilience in children and adolescents: Processes, mechanisms, and interventions* (pp. 225–267). New York: Cambridge University Press.

Compas, B. E., & Harding Thomsen, A. (1999). Coping and responses to stress among children with recurrent abdominal pain. *Journal of Developmental and Behavioral Pediatrics, 20,* 323–324.

Compas, B. E., & Oppedisano, G. (2000). Mixed anxiety/depression in childhood and adolescence. In A. J. Sameroff & M. Lewis (Eds.), *Handbook of developmental psychopathology* (2nd ed., pp. 531–548). New York: Kluwer Academic/Plenum.

Compton, S. N., Nelson, A. H., & March, J. S. (2000). Social phobia and separation anxiety symptoms in community and clinical samples of children and adolescents. *Journal of the American Academy of Child and Adolescent Psychiatry, 39,* 1040–1046.

Conduct Problems Prevention Research Group. (1992). A developmental and clinical model for the prevention of conduct disorder: The FAST Track program. *Development and Psychopathology, 4,* 509–527.

Conduct Problems Prevention Research Group. (1999a). Initial impact of the Fast Track prevention trial for conduct problems: I. The high-risk sample. *Journal of Consulting and Clinical Psychology, 67,* 631–647.

Conduct Problems Prevention Research Group. (1999b). Initial impact of the Fast Track prevention trial for conduct problems: II. Classroom effects. *Journal of Consulting and Clinical Psychology, 67,* 648–657.

Conduct Problems Prevention Research Group. (2000). Merging universal and indicated prevention programs: The Fast Track model. *Addictive Behaviors, 25,* 913–927.

Conduct Problems Prevention Research Group (2002a). The implementation of the Fast Track program: An example of a large-scale prevention science efficacy trial. *Journal of Abnormal Child Psychology, 30,* 1–17.

Conduct Problems Prevention Research Group (2002b). Evaluation of the first 3 years of the Fast Track prevention trial with children at high risk for adolescent conduct problems. *Journal of*

Abnormal Child Psychology, 30, 19–35.

Conger, R. D., Ge, X., Elder, G. H., Lorenz, F. O., & Simons, R. L. (1994). Economic stress, coercive family process, and developmental problems of adolescents. *Child Development, 65,* 541–561.

Conners, C. K. (1980). *Food additives and hyperactive children.* New York: Plenum.

Connolly J., Furman, W., & Konarski, R. (2000). The role of peers in the emergence of heterosexual romantic relationships in adolescence. *Child Development, 71,* 1395–408.

Connor, D. F., Edwards, G., Fletcher, K. E., Baird, J., Barkley, R. A., & Steingard, R. J. (2003). Correlates of comorbid psychopathology in children with ADHD. *Journal of the American Academy of Child and Adolescent Psychiatry, 42,* 193–200.

Cook, E. H., & Leventhal, B. L. (1996). The serotonin system in autism. *Current Opinion in Pediatrics, 8,* 348–354.

Cook, E. H. (1990). Autism: Review of neurochemical investigation. *Synapse, 6,* 292–308.

Cook, E. H., Stein, M. A., Krasowski, M. D., Cox, N. J., Olkon, D. M., Kiefer, J. E., & Leventhal, B. L. (1995). Association of attention-deficit disorder and the dopamine transporter gene. *American Journal of Human Genetics, 56,* 993–998.

Coolahan, K., Fantuzzo, J., Mendez, J., & McDermott, P. (2000). Preschool peer interactions and readiness to learn: Relationships between classroom peer play and learning behaviors and conduct. *Journal of Educational Psychology, 92,* 458–465.

Cooley, W. C., & Graham, J. M., Jr. (1991). Common syndromes and management issues for primary care physicians: Down syndrome—An update and review for the primary pediatrician. *Clinical Pediatrics, 30,* 233–253.

Coolidge, F. L., Thede, L. L., & Young, S. E. (2000). Heritability and the comorbidity of attention deficit hyperactivity disorder with behavioral disorders and executive function deficits: A preliminary investigation. *Developmental Neuropsychology, 17,* 273–287.

Copa, A., Lucinski, L., Olsen, E., & Wollenburg, K. (1999). Promoting professional and organizational development: A reflective practice model. *Zero to Three, 20,* 3–9.

Coplan, J. D., Moreau, D., Chaput, F., Martinez, J. M., Hoven, C. W., Mandell, D. J., et al. (2002). Salivary cortisol concentrations before and after carbon-dioxide inhalations in children. *Biological Psychiatry, 51,* 326–333.

Corkum, P., Moldofsky, H., Hogg-Johnson, S., Humphries, T., & Tannock, R. (1999). Sleep problems in children with attention-deficit/hyperactivity disorder: Impact of subtype, comorbidity, and stimulant medication. *Journal of the*

American Academy of Child and Adolescent Psychiatry, 38, 1285–1293.

Corkum, P., Tannock, R., & Moldofsky, H. (1988). Sleep disturbances in children with attention-deficit/hyperactivity disorder. *Journal of the American Academy of Child and Adolescent Psychiatry, 37,* 637–646.

Cornelius, J. R., Maisto, S. A., Pollock, N. K., Martin, C. S., Salloum, I. M., Lynch, K. G., & Clark, D. B. (2003). Rapid relapse generally follows treatment for substance use disorders among adolescents. *Addictive Behaviors, 28,* 381–386.

Corrigan, P. W. (2000). Mental health stigma as social attribution: Implications for research methods and attitude change. *Clinical Psychology: Science and Practice, 7,* 48–67.

Cosentino, C. E., Meyer-Bahlburg, H. F., Alpert, J., Weinberg, S. L., & Gaines, R. (1995). Sexual behavior problems and psychopathology symptoms in sexually abused girls. *Journal of the American Academy of Child and Adolescent Psychiatry, 34,* 1033–1042.

Costello, E. J. (1989). Developments in child psychiatric epidemiology. *Journal of the American Academy of Child and Adolescent Psychiatry, 28,* 836–841.

Costello, E. J. (1990). Child psychiatric epidemiology: Implications for clinical research and practice. In B. B. Lahey & A. E. Kazdin (Eds.), *Advances in clinical child psychology* (Vol. 13, pp. 53–90). New York: Plenum.

Costello, E. J., & Angold, A. (1995). Developmental epidemiology. In D. Cicchetti & D. J. Cohen (Eds.), *Developmental psychopathology: Vol. 1. Theory and methods* (pp. 23–56). New York: Wiley.

Costello, E. J., & Angold, A. C. (2000). Developmental epidemiology: A framework for developmental psychopathology. In A. Sameroff, M. Lewis, & S. Miller (Eds.), *Handbook of developmental psychopathology* (2nd ed., pp. 57–73). New York: Plenum.

Costello, E. J., Farmer, E.M.Z., Angold, A., Burns, B. J., & Erkanli, A. (1997). Psychiatric disorders among American Indian and white youth in Appalachia: The Great Smoky Mountains Study. *American Journal of Public Health, 87,* 827–832.

Costello, E J., Messer, S. C., Bird, H. R., Cohen, P., & Reinherz, H .Z. (1998). The prevalence of serious emotional disturbance: A re-analysis of community studies. *Journal of Child & Family Studies, 7,* 411–432.

Costello, E. J., Pine, D. S., Hammen, C., March, J. S., Plotsky, P. M., Weissman, M. M., Biederman, J., Goldsmith, H. H., Kaufman, J., Lewinsohn, P. M., Hellander, M., Hoagwood, K., Koretz, D. S., Nelson, C. A., & Leckman, J. F. (2002). Development and natural history of mood disorders. *Biological Psychiatry, 52,* 529–542.

Courchesne, E., Carper, R., & Akshoomoff, N. (2003). Evidence of brain overgrowth in the first year of life in autism. *Journal of the American Medical Association, 290,* 337–344,

Courchesne, E., Townsend, J. P., & Chase, C. (1995). Neurodevelopmental principles guide research on developmental psycho-pathologies. In D. Cicchetti & D. Cohen (Eds.), *Developmental psychopathology: Vol. 1. Theories and methods* (pp. 195–226). New York: Wiley.

Cowan, P. A., & Cowan, C. P. (2003). Normative family transitions, normal family processes, and healthy child development. In: Walsh, F. (Ed.), *Normal family processes: Growing diversity and complexity (3/e),* pp. 424–459. New York: Guilford Press.

Cowen, P. J., Anderson, I. M., & Fairburn, C. G. (1992). Neurochemical effects of dieting: Relevance to eating and affective disorders. In G. H. Anderson & S. H. Kennedy (Eds.), *The biology of feast and famine: Relevance to eating disorders* (pp. 269–284). New York: Academic Press.

Cox, D. J., Borowitz, S., Kovatchev, B., & Ling, W. (1998). Contribution of behavior therapy and biofeedback to laxative therapy in the treatment of pediatric encopresis. *Annals of Behavioral Medicine, 20,* 70–76.

Cox, D. J., Sutphen, J., Ling, W., Quillian, W., & Borowitz, S. (1996). Additive benefits of laxative, toilet training, and biofeedback therapies in the treatment of pediatric encopresis. *Journal of Pediatric Psychology, 21,* 659–670.

Cox, D. L., Stabb, S. D., & Bruckner, K. H. (1999) *Women's anger: Clinical and developmental perspectives.* Philadelphia: Brunner/Mazel, Inc.

Coyle, J. T., Pine, D. S., Charney, D. S., Lewis, L., Nemeroff, C. B., Carlson, G. A., Joshi, P. T., Reiss, D., Todd, R. D., Hellander, M., & The Depression and Bipolar Support Alliance Consensus Development Panel (2003). Depression and bipolar support alliance consensus statement on the unmet needs in diagnosis and treatment of mood disorders in children and adolescents. *Journal of the American Academy of Child and Adolescent Psychiatry, 42,* 1494–1503.

Coyne, J. C., Downey, G., & Boergers, J. (1992). Depression in families: A systems perspective. In D. Cicchetti & S. L. Toth (Eds.), *Rochester symposium on developmental psychopathology: Vol. 4. Developmental perspectives on depression* (pp. 211–249). New York: University of Rochester Press.

Crago, M., Shisslak, C. M., & Estes, L. S. (1996). Eating disturbances among American minority groups: A review. *International Journal of Eating Disorders, 19,* 239–248.

Craig, A., Hancock, K., Tran, Y., Craig, M., & Peters, K. (2002). Epidemiology of stuttering in the community across the entire life span. *Journal of Speech, Language, & Hearing Research, 45,* 1097–1105.

Craig, T. K., Cox, A. D., & Klein, K. (2002). Intergenerational transmission of somatization behaviour: A study of chronic somatizers and their children. *Psychological Medicine, 32,* 805–816.

Craske, M. G., & Rowe, M. K. (1997). Nocturnal panic. *Clinical Psychology: Science and Practice, 4,* 153–174.

Crawford, A. M., Pentz, M. A., Chou, C., Li, C., & Dwyer, J. H. (2003). Parallel developmental trajectories of sensation seeking and regular substance use in adolescents. *Psychology of Addictive Behaviors, 17,* 179–192.

Crawford, D. C., Meadows, K. L., Newman, J. L., Taft, L. F., Pettay, D. L., Gold, L. B., Hersey, S. J., Hinkle, E. F., Stanfield, M. L., Holmgreen, P., Yeargin-Allsopp, M., Boyle, C., & Sherman, S. L (1999). Prevalence and phenotype consequence of FRAXA and FRAXE alleles in a large, ethnically diverse, special education-needs population. *American Journal of Human Genetics, 64,* 495–507.

Crick, N. R. (1995). Relational aggression: The role of intent attributions, feelings of distress, and provocation type. *Development and Psychopathology, 7,* 313–322.

Crick, N. R. (1997). Engagement in gender normative versus nonnormative forms of aggression: Links to social-psychological adjustment. *Developmental Psychology, 33,* 610–617.

Crick, N. R., Bigbee, M. A., & Howes, C. (1996). Gender differences in children's normative beliefs about aggression: How do I hurt thee? Let me count the ways. *Child Development, 67,* 1003–1014.

Crick, N. R., & Dodge, K. A. (1994). A review and reformulation of social-information-processing mechanisms in children's social adjustment. *Psychological Bulletin, 115,* 74–101.

Crick, N. R., & Dodge, K. A. (1996). Social information-processing mechanisms on reactive and proactive aggression. *Child Development, 67,* 993–1002.

Crick, N. R., & Nelson, D. A. (2002). Relational and physical victimization within friendships: Nobody told me there'd be friends like these. *Journal of Abnormal Child Psychology, 30,* 599–607.

Crick, N. R., Nelson, D. A., Morales, J. R., Cullerton-Sen, C., Casas, J. F., & Hickman, S. E. (2001). Relational victimization in childhood and adolescence: I hurt you through the grapevine. In J. Juvonen, & S. Graham, Graham (Eds.), *Peer harassment in school: The plight of the vulnerable and victimized* (pp. 196–214). New York: Guilford Press.

Crick, N. R., & Rose, A. J. (2000). Toward a gender-balanced approach to the study of social-emotional development: A look at relational aggression. In P. H.

Miller & E. Kofsky Scholnick (Eds.), *Toward a feminist developmental psychology* (pp. 153–168). Florence, KY: Taylor & Francis/Routledge.

Crick, N. R., & Zahn-Waxler, C. (2003). The development of psychopathology in females and males: Current progress and future challenges. *Development & Psychopathology* Special Issue: Conceptual, methodological, and statistical issues in developmental psychopathology: A special issue in honor of Paul E. Meehl, *15,* 719–742.

Crijnen, A.A.M., Achenbach, T. M., & Verhulst, F. C. (1997). Comparisons of problems reported by parents of children in 12 cultures: Total problems, externalizing, and internalizing. *Journal of the American Academy of Child and Adolescent Psychiatry, 36,* 1269–1277.

Crisp, A., Sedgwick, P., Halek, C., Joughin, N., & Humphrey, H (1999). Why may teenage girls persist in smoking? *Journal of Adolescence, 22,* 657–672.

Crisp, A. H. (1997). Anorexia nervosa as flight from growth: Assessment and treatment based on the model. In D. M. Garner and P. E. Garfinkel (Eds.), *Handbook of treatment for eating disorders* (2nd ed., pp. 248–277). New York: Guilford Press.

Crister, G. (2003). *Fat land: How Americans became the fattest people in the world.* Boston: Houghton Mifflin.

Crittenden, P. M., & Claussen, A. H. (2002). Developmental psychopathology perspectives on substance abuse and relationship violence. In C. Wekerle & A. M. Wall (Eds), *The violence and addiction equation: Theoretical and clinical issues in substance abuse and relationship violence* (pp. 44–63). New York: Brunner-Routledge.

Crone, E. A., Jennings, J. R., & van der Molen, M. (2003). Sensitivity to interference and response contingencies in attention-deficit/hyperactivity disorder. *Journal of Child Psychology and Psychiatry, 44,* 214–226.

Crystal, D. S., Ostrander, R., Chen, R. S., & August, G. J. (2001). Multimethod assessment of psychopathology among DSM-IV subtypes of children with attention-deficit/hyperactivity disorder: self-, parent, and teacher reports. *Journal of Abnormal Child Psychology, 29,* 189–205.

Cuellar, I. (2000). Acculturation as a moderator of personality and psychological assessment. In: R. H. Dana, Ed., *Handbook of cross-cultural and multicultural personality assessment* (pp. 113–129). Mahwah, NJ: Lawrence Erlbaum Associates.

Cuffe, S. P., McCullough, E. L., & Pumariega, A. J. (1994). Comorbidity of attention deficit hyperactivity disorder and post-traumatic stress disorder. *Journal of Child and Family Studies, 3,* 327–336.

Culbertson, F. M. (1997). Depression and gender: An international review. *American Psychologist, 52,* 25–31.

Cummings, E. M. (1997). Marital conflict, abuse, and adversity in the family and child adjustment: A developmental psychopathology perspective. In D. A. Wolfe, R. J. McMahon, & R. Dev Peters (Eds.), *Child abuse: New directions in prevention and treatment across the lifespan* (pp. 1–24). Thousand Oaks, CA: Sage.

Cummings, E. M., & Davies, P. T. (2002). Effects of marital conflict on children: Recent advances and emerging themes in process-oriented research. *Journal of Child Psychology & Psychiatry & Allied Disciplines, 43,* 31–63.

Cummings, E. M., & Davies, P. T., Campbell, S. B. (2000). *Developmental psychopathology and family process: theory, research, and clinical implications.* New York: Guilford Press.

Cunningham, C. E. (1999). In the wake of the MTA: Charting a new course for the study and treatment of children with attention-deficit hyperactivity disorder. *Canadian Journal of Psychiatry, 44,* 999–1006.

Cunningham, C. E., Boyle, M., Offord, D., Racine, Y., Hundert, J., Secord, M., & McDonald, J. (2000). Tri-ministry study: Correlates of school-based parenting course utilization. *Journal of Consulting and Clinical Psychology, 68,* 928–933.

Cunningham, C. E., Bremner, R., & Secord-Gilbert, M. (1993). Increasing the availability, accessibility, and cost efficacy of services for families of ADHD children: A school-based, systems-oriented parenting course. *Canadian Journal of School Psychology, 9,* 1–15.

Cunningham, P. B., Henggeler, S. W., Brondino, M., & Pickrel, S. G. (1999). Testing underlying assumptions of the family empowerment perspective. *Journal of Child and Family Studies, 8,* 437–449.

Curtis, W. J., & Cicchetti, D. (2003). Moving research on resilience into the 21st century: Theoretical and methodological considerations in examining the biological contributors to resilience. *Development and Psychopathology, 15,* 773–810

Cutting, L. E., & Denckla, M.B. (2003). Attention: Relationships between attention-deficit hyperactivity disorder and learning disabilities. In L. H. Swanson & K. R. Harris (Eds.), *Handbook of learning disabilities* (pp. 125–139). New York: Guilford Press.

Cytryn, L., & McKnew, D. H. (1974). Factors influencing the changing clinical expression of the depressive process in children. *American Journal of Psychiatry, 131,* 879–881.

Cytryn, L., & McKnew, D. H. (1996). *Growing up sad: Childhood depression and its treatment.* New York: Norton.

Dadds, M. R. (2002). Learning and intimacy in the families of anxious children. In R. J. McMahon & R. DeV. Peters (Eds.), *The effects of parental dysfunction on children* (pp. 87–94). New York: Kluwer Academic/Plenum Publishers.

Dadds, M. R., Barrett, P. M., Rapee, R. M. (1996). Family process and child anxiety and aggression: An observational analysis. *Journal of Abnormal Child Psychology, 24*, 715–734.

Dahl, R. E. (1996). The regulation of sleep and arousal: Development and psychopathology. *Development and Psychopathology, 8*, 3–27.

Dahl, R. E. (1999). Parasomnias. In R. T. Ammerman, M. Hersen, & C. G. Last (Eds.), *Handbook of prescriptive treatments for children and adolescents* (2nd ed. pp.244–260). Needham Heights, MA: Allyn & Bacon.

Dahlquist, L. M. (1989). Cognitive-behavioral treatment of pediatric cancer patients' distress during painful and invasive medical procedures. In M. C. Roberts & C. E. Walker (Eds.), *Casebook of child and pediatric psychology* (pp. 360–379). New York: Guilford Press.

Dahlquist, L. M. (1999). *Pediatric pain management.* New York: Plenum.

Dahlquist, L. M., Pendley, J. S., Power, T. G., Landthrip, D. S., Jones, C. L. & Steuber, C. P. (2001). Adult command structure and children's distress during the anticipatory phase of invasive cancer procedures. *Children's Health Care, 30*, 151–167.

Dale, P. S., Price, T. S., Bishop, D. V. M., & Plomin, R. (2003). Outcomes of early language delay: I. Predicting persistent and transient language difficulties at 3 and 4 years. *Journal of Speech, Language, & Hearing Research, 46*, 544–560.

Daley, S. E., Hammen, C., Burge, D., Davila, J., Paley, B., Lindberg, N., & Herzberg, D. S. (1999). Depression and Axis II symptomatology in an adolescent community sample: Concurrent and longitudinal associations. *Journal of Personality Disorders, 13*, 47–59.

Daley, S. E., Hammen, C., & Rao, U. (2000). Predictors of first onset and recurrence of major depression in young women during the 5 years following high school graduation. *Journal of Abnormal Psychology, 109*, 525–533.

Dalsgaard, S., Mortensen, P. B., Frydenberg, M., & Thomsen, P. H. (2002). Conduct problems, gender and adult psychiatric outcome of children with attention-deficit hyperactivity disorder. *British Journal of Psychiatry, 181*, 416–421.

Daly, J. M., Biederman, J., Bostic, J. Q., Maraganore, A. M., Lelon, E., Jellinek, M., & Lapey, A. (1996). The relationship between childhood asthma and attention deficit hyperactivity disorder: A review of the literature. *Journal of Attention Disorders, 1*, 31–40.

Damasio, A., & Damasio, H. A. (2000). Language and the brain. In K. Emmorey & H. Lane (Eds.), *The signs of language revisited: An anthology to honor Ursula Bellugi and Edward Klima* (pp. 477–491). Mahwah, NJ: Lawrence Erlbaum Associates.

Danforth, J. S., Barkley, R. A., & Stokes, T. F. (1991). Observations of parent-child interactions with hyperactive children: Research and clinical implications. *Clinical Psychology Review, 11*, 703–727.

Dare, C., & Eisler, I. (1997). Family therapy for anorexia nervosa. In D. M. Garner & P. E. Garfinkel (Eds.), *Handbook of treatment for eating disorders* (2nd ed., pp. 307–324). New York: Guilford Press.

David, C. F., & Kistner, J. A. (2000). Do positive self-perceptions have a "dark side"? Examination of the link between perceptual bias and aggression. *Journal of Abnormal Child Psychology, 28*, 327–337.

Davidson, R. J., Pizzagalli, D., & Nitschke, J. (2002). The representation and regulation of emotion in depression: Perspectives from affective neuroscience. In I. H. Gotlib & C. L. Hammen (Eds.), *Handbook of depression* (pp. 219–244). New York: Guilford.

Davis, L., & Siegel, L. J. (2000). Posttraumatic stress disorder in children and adolescents: A review and analysis. *Clinical Child and Family Psychology Review, 3*, 135–154.

Davis, M. K. & Gidycz, C. A. (2000). Child sexual abuse prevention programs: A meta-analysis. *Journal of Clinical Child Psychology, 29*, 257–265.

Dawson, G. (1996). Neuropsychology of autism: A report on the state-of-the-science. *Journal of Autism and Developmental Disorders, 2*, 179–181.

Dawson, G., Ashman, S. B., & Carver, L. J. (2000). The role of early experience in shaping behavioral and brain development and its implications for social policy. *Development and Psychopathology, 12*, 695–712.

Dawson, G., Frey, K., Panagiotides, H., Osterling, J., & Hessl, D. (1997). Infants of depressed mothers exhibit atypical frontal brain activity: A replication and extension of previous findings. *Journal of Child Psychology and Psychiatry, 38*, 179–186.

Dawson, G., Frey, K., Self, J., Panagiotides, H., Hessl, D., Yamada, E., & Rinaldi, J. (1999). Frontal brain electrical activity in infants of depressed and non-depressed mothers: Relations to variations in infant behavior. *Development and Psychopathology, 11*, 589–605.

Dawson, G., Meltzoff, A. N., Osterling, J., Rinaldi, J., Brown, E. (1998). Children with autism fail to orient to naturally occurring social stimuli. *Journal of Autism and Developmental Disorders, 28*, 479–485.

Dawson, G., & Osterling, J. (1997). Early intervention in autism: Effectiveness and common elements of current approaches. In M. J. Guralnick (Ed.), *The effectiveness of early intervention: Second generation research* (pp. 307–326). Baltimore: Brookes.

Dawson, G., Webb, S., Schellenberg, G. D., Dager, S., Friedman, S., Aylward, E., & Richards, T. (2002). Defining the broader phenotype of autism: Genetic, brain, and behavioral perspectives. *Development and Psychopathology, 14*, 581–611.

Dawson, J. E., Matson, J. L., & Cherry, K. E. (1998). An analysis of maladaptive behaviors in persons with autism, PDD-NOS, and mental retardation. *Research in Developmental Disabilities, 19*, 439–448.

Day, N. L., Leech, S. L., Richardson, G. A., Cornelius, M. D., Robles, N., & Larkby, C. (2002). Prenatal alcohol exposure predicts continued deficits in offspring size at 14 years of age. *Alcoholism: Clinical and Experimental Research, 26*, 1584–1591.

Day, N. L., Richardon, G. A., Goldschmidt, L., & Cornelius, M. D. (2000). Effects of prenatal tobacco exposure on preschoolers' behavior. *Journal of Developmental & Behavioral Pediatrics, 21*, 180–188.

De Bellis, M. D., Keshavan, M. S., Frustaci, K., Shifflett, H., Iyengar, S., Beers, S. R., & Hall, J. (2002). Superior temporal gyrus volumes in maltreated children and adolescents with PTSD. *Biological Psychiatry, 51*, 544–552.

De Bellis, M. D., Keshavan, M. S., Shifflett, H., Iyengar, S., Dahl, R. E., Axelson, D. A., et al. (2002). Superior temporal gyrus volumes in pediatric generalized anxiety disorder. *Biological Psychiatry, 51*, 553–562.

De Bellis, M., Burke, L., Trickett, P., & Putnam, F. (1996). Antinuclear antibodies and thyroid function in sexually abused girls. *Journal of Traumatic Stress, 9*, 369–378.

De Bellis, M. D., Keshavan, M. S., Spencer, S., & Hall, J. (2000). N-acetylaspartate concentration in the anterior cingulate of maltreated children and adolescents with PTSD. *American Journal of Psychiatry, 157*, 1175–1177.

Dean, R. R., Kelsey, J. E., Heller, M. R., & Ciaranello, R. D. (1993). Structural foundations of illness and treatment: Receptors. In D. L. Dunner (Ed.), *Current psychiatric therapy*. Philadelphia: Saunders.

Deater-Deckard, K., & Dodge, K. A. (1997). Externalizing behavior problems and discipline revisited: Nonlinear effects and variation by culture, context, and gender. *Psychological Inquiry, 8*, 161–175.

Deblinger, E., Stauffer, L. B., & Steer, R. A. (2001). Comparative efficacies of supportive and cognitive behavioral group therapies for young children who have been sexually abused and their nonoffending mothers. *Child Maltreatment: Journal of the American Professional Society on the Abuse of Children, 6*, 332–343.

DeCaluwe, V., Braet, C., & Fairburn, C. G. (2003). Binge eating in obese children and adolescents. *International*

Journal of Eating Disorders, 33, 78–84.

DeGrandpre, R. J. (2000). A science of meaning: Can behaviorism bring meaning to psychological science? *American Psychologist, 55,* 721–739.

DeKlyen, M., Speltz, M. L., Greenberg, M. T. (1998). Fathering and early onset conduct problems: Positive and negative parenting, father-son attachment, and the marital context. *Clinical Child and Family Psychology Review, 1,* 3–21.

DelBello, M. P., Carlson, G. A., Tohen, M., Bromet, E. J., Schwiers, M., & Strakowski, S. M. (2003). Rates and predictors of developing a manic or hypomanic episode 1 to 2 years following a first hospitalization for major depression with psychotic features. *Journal of Child and Adolescent Psychopharmacology, 13,* 173–185.

Demaray, M. K., & Elliot, S. N. (2001). Perceived social support by children with characteristics of attention-deficit/hyperactivity disorder. *School Psychology Quarterly, 16,* 68–90.

Denham, S. A., Workman, E., Cole, P. M., Weissbrod, C., Kendziora, K.T., & Zahn-Waxler, C. (2000). Prediction of externalizing behavior problems from early to middle childhood: The role of parental socialization and emotion expression. *Development & Psychopathology, 12,* 23–45.

Denzin, N. K., & Lincoln, Y. S. (Eds.). (1994). *Handbook of qualitative research.* Thousand Oaks, CA: Sage.

Deren, D. M. (1997, June). *A childhood without laughter.* (From http://members.aol.com/depress/children.htm# Introduction). Copyright © 1996, 1997 Deborah M. Deren. Revised June 8, 1997. Retrieved October 22, 1997.

Derryberry, D., & Reed, M. A. (1994). Temperament and the self-organization of personality. *Development and Psychopathology, 6,* 653–676.

Despert, J. L. (1955). Differential diagnosis between obsessive-compulsive neurosis and schizophrenia in children. In P. Hoch & J. Zubins (Eds.), *Psychopathology of childhood* (pp. 241–253). New York: Grune & Stratton.

Deutsch, C. K., & Kinsbourne, M. (1990). Genetics and biochemistry in attention deficit disorder. In M. Lewis & S. M. Miller (Eds.), *Handbook of developmental psychopathology* (pp. 93–107). New York: Plenum.

Devlin, B., Daniels, M., & Rodin, K. (1997). The heritability of IQ. *Nature, 388,* 468–471.

Diamond, G. S., Reis, B. F., Diamond, G. M., Siqueland, L., & Isaacs, L. (2002). Attachment-based family therapy for depressed adolescents: A treatment development study. *Journal of the American Academy of Child and Adolescent Psychiatry, 41,* 1190–1196.

DiClemente, C. C., Marinilli, A. S., Singh, M., & Bellino, L. E. (2001). The role of feedback in the process of health behavior change. *American Journal of Health Behavior, 25,* 217–227.

DiLalla, L. F., Kagan, J., & Reznick, J. S. (1994). Genetic etiology of behavioral inhibition among 2-year-old children. *Infant Behavior and Development, 17,* 405–412.

DiLella, A., & Woo, S. L. C. (1987). Molecular basis of phenylketonuria and its clinical applications. *Biology and Medicine, 4,* 183–192.

Dillon, K. M. (1993). Facilitated communication, autism, and Ouija. *Skeptical Inquirer, 17,* 281–287.

Dion, R., Gotowiec, A., & Beiser, M. (1998). Depression and conduct disorder in native and non-native children. *Journal of the American Academy of Child & Adolescent Psychiatry, 37,* 736–742.

Dionne, G., Tremblay, R., Boivin, M., LaPlante, D., & Perusse, D. (2003). Physical aggression and expressive vocabulary in 19-month-old twins. *Developmental Psychology, 39,* 261–273.

Dishion, T. J., & Andrews, D. W. (1995). Preventing escalation in problem behaviors with high-risk young adolescents: Immediate and 1-year outcomes. *Journal of Consulting and Clinical Psychology, 63,* 538–548.

Dishion, T. J., Andrews, D. W., & Crosby, L. (1995). Antisocial boys and their friends in early adolescence: Relationship characteristics, quality, and interactional process. *Child Development, 66,* 139–151.

Dishion, T. J., & Bullock, B. M. (2002). Parenting and adolescent problem behavior: An ecological analysis of the nurturance hypothesis. In J. G. Borkowski, S. L. Ramey, & M. Bristol-Power (Eds.), *Parenting and the child's world: Influences on academic, intellectual, and social-emotional development* (pp. 231–249). Mahwah, NJ: Erlbaum.

Dishion, T. J., Bullock, B. M., & Granic, I. (2002). Pragmatism in modeling peer influence: Dynamics, outcomes and change processes. *Development and Psychopathology, 14,* 969–981.

Dishion, T. J., French, D. C., & Patterson, G. R. (1995). The development and ecology of antisocial behavior. In D. Cicchetti & D. J. Cohen (Eds.), *Developmental psychopathology: Vol. 2. Risk, disorder, and adaptation* (pp. 421–471). New York: Wiley.

Dishion, T. J., & Granic, I. (2004). Naturalistic observation of relationship processes. In S. N. Haynes & E. M. Heiby (Eds.), *Comprehensive handbook of psychological assessment, Volume 3: Behavioral assessment* (pp. 143–161). New York: Wiley.

Dishion, T. J., & Kavanagh, K. (2003). *Intervening in adolescent problem behavior: A family-centered approach.* New York: Guilford Press.

Dishion, T. J., McCord, J., & Poulin, F. (1999). When interventions harm: Peer groups and problem behavior. *American Psychologist, 54,* 755–764.

Dishion, T. J., & Patterson, G. R. (1992). Age effects in parent training outcome. *Behavior Therapy, 23,* 719–729.

Dissanayake, C., & Sigman, M. (2000). Attachment and emotional responsiveness in children with autism. *International Review of Research in Mental Retardation, 23,* 239–266.

Dodge, K. A. (1989). Problems in social relationships. In E. J. Mash & R. A. Barkley (Eds.), *Treatment of childhood disorders* (pp. 222–244). New York: Guilford Press.

Dodge, K. A., Lansford, J. E., Burks, V. S., Bates, J. E., Pettit, G. S., Fontaine, R., & Price, J. M. (2003). Peer rejection and social information-processing factors in the development of aggressive behavior problems in children. *Child Development, 74,* 374–393.

Dodge, K. A., & Pettit, G. S. (2003). A biopsychosocial model of the development of chronic conduct problems in adolescence. *Developmental Psychology Special Issue: Violent children, 39,* 349–371.

Dodge, K. A., Pettit, G. S., & Bates, J. E. (1994a). Effects of physical maltreatment on the development of peer relations. *Development and Psychopathology, 6,* 43–55.

Dodge, K. A., Pettit, G. S., & Bates, J. E. (1994b). Socialization mediators of the relation between socioeconomic status and child conduct problems. *Child Development, 65,* 649–665.

Dodge, K. A., Pettit, G. S., Bates, J. E., & Valente, E. (1995). Social information-processing patterns partially mediate the effect of early physical abuse on later conduct problems. *Journal of Abnormal Psychology, 104,* 632–643.

Donahew, L., Hoyle, R. H., Clayton, R., Skinner, W. F., Colon, S. E., & Rice, R. E. (1999). Sensation seeking and drug use by adolescents and their friends: Models for marijuana and alcohol. *Journal of Studies on Alcohol, 60,* 622–631.

Dong, Q., Yang, B., & Ollendick, T. H. (1994). Fears in Chinese children and adolescents and their relations to anxiety and depression. *Journal of Child Psychology and Psychiatry, 35,* 351–363.

Donnellan, A. M. (1988, February). *Our old ways just aren't working.* Dialect. [Newsletter of the Saskatchewan Association for the Mentally Retarded]. Available from Saskatchewan Association for Community Living, 3031 Louise Street, Saskatoon, SK S7J 3L1.

Donohue, B., Hersen, M., & Ammerman, R. T. (2000). Historical overview. In M. Hersen & R. Ammerman (Eds.), *Abnormal child psychology* (2nd ed., pp. 3–14). Mahwah, NJ: Erlbaum.

Douglas, V. I. (1972). Stop, look, and listen: The problem of sustained attention and impulse control in hyperactive and normal children. *Canadian Journal of Behavioural Science, 4,* 259–282.

Douglas, V. I. (1988). Cognitive deficits in children with attention deficit disorder with hyperactivity. In L. M. Bloomingdale & J. A. Sergeant (Eds.), *Attention deficit disorder: Criteria, cognition, intervention* (pp. 65–82). London: Pergamon Press.

Douglas, V. I. (1999). Cognitive control processes in attention deficit/hyperactivity disorder. In H. C. Quay & A. E. Hogan (Eds.), *Handbook of disruptive behavior disorders* (pp. 105–138). New York: Kluwer Academic/Plenum.

Douglas, V. I., & Parry, P. A. (1994). Effects of reward and nonreward on frustration and attention in attention deficit disorder. *Journal of Abnormal Child Psychology, 22,* 281–302.

Dowling, C. (1992, January 20). Rescuing your child from depression. *New York,* pp. 45–51.

Dowling, C. G., & Hollister, A. (1997, May). An epidemic of sneezing and wheezing. *Life,* pp. 76–92.

Down, J. L. H. (1866). Observations on an ethnic classification of idiots. *Clinical Lectures and Reports (London Hospital), 3,* 259–262.

Downey, G., & Coyne, J. C. (1990). Children of depressed parents: An integrative review. *Psychological Bulletin, 108,* 50–76.

Doyle, A. E., Faraone, S. V., DuPre, E. P., & Biederman, J. (2001). Separating attention deficit hyperactivity disorder and learning disabilities in girls: A familial risk analysis. *American Journal of Psychiatry, 158,* 1666–1672.

Dozois, D. J. A. (1997). *A developmental cognitive model of unipolar major depression.* Unpublished manuscript, University of Calgary, Calgary, Alberta.

Draguns, J. G., & Tanaka-Matsumi, J. (2003). Assessment of psychopathology across and within cultures: Issues and findings. *Behaviour Research & Therapy Special Issue: Cross cultural assessment and abnormal psychology, 41,* 755–776.

Drewett, R. F., Corbett, S. S., & Wright, C. M. (1999). Cognitive and educational attainments at school age of children who failed to thrive in infancy: A population-based study. *Journal of Child Psychology & Psychiatry & Allied Disciplines, 40,* 551–561.

Drotar, D. (1991). The family context of nonorganic failure to thrive. *American Journal of Orthopsychiatry, 61,* 23–34.

Drotar, D. (1999a). Child neglect in the family context: Challenges and opportunities for management in pediatric settings. *Children's Health Care, 28,* 109–121.

Drotar, D. (1999b). Psychological interventions for children with chronic physical illness and their families: Toward integration of research and practice. In S. W. Russ, & T. H. Ollendick (Eds.), *Handbook of psychotherapies with children and families. Issues in clinical child psychology* (pp. 447–461). New York: Plenum.

Drotar, D. (Ed.) (2000). *Promoting adherence to medical treatment in chronic childhood illness: Concepts, methods, and interventions.* Mahwah, NJ: Erlbaum.

Ducharme, J. M., Atkinson, L., Poulton, L. (2000). Success-based, noncoercive treatment of oppositional behavior in children from violent homes. *Journal of the American Academy of Child and Adolescent Psychiatry, 39,* 995–1004.

Duel, B. P., Steinberg-Epstein, R., Hill, M., & Lerner, M. (2003). A survey of voiding dysfunction in children with attention deficit-hyperactivity disorder. *Journal of Urology, 170,* 1521–1524.

Dummit, E. S., Klein, R. G., Tancer, N. K., Asche, B., Martin, J., & Fairbanks, J. A. (1997). Systematic assessment of 50 children with selective mutism. *Journal of the American Academy of Child and Adolescent Psychiatry, 36,* 653–660.

Duncan, G. J., & Brooks-Gunn, J. (2000). Family poverty, welfare reform, and child development. *Child Development, 71,* 188–196.

Duncan, P. M., & Millard, W. (1866). *A manual for the classification, training, and education of the feeble-minded, imbecile, and idiot.* London: Longmans, Green.

Dunlap, K. (1932). *Habits: Their making and unmaking.* New York: Liveright.

Dunner, D. L., Greden, J. F., Greist, J. H., Rosenbaum, J. F., Schatzberg, A. F., & Zajecka, J. M. (1999). Special uses of SSRIs. *Journal of Clinical Psychiatry Monograph Series, 17,* 42–52.

DuPaul, G. J. (2003). Assessment of ADHD symptoms: Comment on Gomez et al. (2003). *Psychological Assessment, 15,* 115–117.

DuPaul, G. J., & Eckert, T. L. (1997). The effects of school-based interventions for attention deficit hyperactivity disorder: A meta-analysis. *School Psychology Digest, 26,* 5–27.

DuPaul, G. J., Guevremont, D. C., & Barkley, R. A. (1992). Behavioral treatment of attention-deficit hyperactivity disorder in the classroom: The use of the attention training system. *Behavior Modification, 16,* 204–225.

DuPaul, G. J., McGoey, K. E., Eckert, T. L., & VanBrakle, J. (2001). Preschool children with attention-deficit/hyperactivity disorder: impairments in behavioral, social, and school functioning. *Journal of the American Academy of Child and Adolescent Psychiatry, 40,* 508–515.

DuPaul, G. J., & Stoner, G. (2003). *ADHD in the schools (2nd ed.).* New York: Guilford.

Dykens, E. M. (2000). Psychopathology in children with intellectual disabilities. *Journal of Child Psychology and Psychiatry, 41,* 407–417.

Dykens, E. M., & Cohen, D. J. (1996). Effects of Special Olympics International on social competence in persons with mental retardation. *Journal of the American Academy of Child and Adolescent Psychiatry, 35,* 223–229.

Dykens, E. M., Hodapp, R. M. & Finucane, B. M. (2000). *Genetics and mental retardation syndromes: A new look at behavior and interventions.* Baltimore, MD: Paul H. Brookes Publishing Co.

Dykens, E. M., & Shah, B. (2003). Psychiatric disorders in Prader-Willi Syndrome: Epidemiology and management. *CNS Drugs, 17,* 167–178.

Dykens, E. M., Shah, B., Sagun, J., Beck, T., & King, B. Y. (2002). Maladaptive behavior in children and adolescents with Down syndrome. *Journal of Intellectual Disability Research, 46,* 484–492.

Dykens, E. M., & Volkmar, F. (1997). Medical conditions associated with autism. In D. J. Cohen & F. R. Volkmar (Eds.), *Handbook of autism and pervasive developmental disorders* (pp. 388–410). New York: Wiley.

Eaves, L., Silberg, J., & Erkanli, A. (2003). Resolving multiple epigenetic pathways to adolescent depression. *Journal of Child Psychology and Psychiatry, 44,* 1006–1014.

Ebstein, R. P., Novick, O., Umansky, R., Priel, B., Osher, Y., Blaine, D., et al., (1996). Dopamine D4 receptor (D4DR) exon III polymorphism associated with the human personality trait of Novelty Seeking. *Nature Genetics, 12,* 78–80.

Eckenrode, J., Laird, M., & Doris, J. (1993). School performance and disciplinary problems among abused and neglected children. *Developmental Psychology, 29,* 53–62.

Eckert, E. D., Halmi, K. A., Marchi, P., Grove, W., & Crosby, R. (1995). Ten-year follow-up of anorexia nervosa: Clinical course and outcome. *Psychological Medicine, 25,* 143–156.

Edelbrock, C., Crnic, K., & Bohnert, A. (1999). Interviewing as communication: An alternative way of administering the Diagnostic Interview Schedule for Children. *Journal of Abnormal Child Psychology, 27,* 447–453.

Edelbrock, C. S., Rende, R., Plomin, R., & Thompson, L. A. (1995). A twin study of competence and problem behavior in childhood and early adolescence. *Journal of Child Psychology and Psychiatry, 36,* 775–786.

Eden, G. F., & Moats, L. (2002). The role of neuroscience in the remediation of students with dyslexia. *Nature Neuroscience Special Issue: Beyond the bench: The practical promise of neuroscience, 5,* 1080–1084.

Eden, G. F., VanMeter, J. W., Rumsey, J. M., Maisog, J. M., Woods, R. P., & Zeffiro, T. A. (1996, July 4). Abnormal processing of visual motion in dyslexia revealed by functional brain imaging. *Nature, 382,* 66–69.

Edleson, J. L. (1999). The overlap between child maltreatment and woman battering. *Violence Against Women, 5,* 134–154.

Edleson, J. L., Mbilinyi, L. F., Beeman, S. K., & Hagemeister, A. K. (2003). How children are involved in adult domestic violence: Results from a four-city telephone survey. *Journal of Interpersonal Violence, 18,* 18–32.

Edwards, F., Barkley, R., Laneri, M., Fletcher, K., & Metevia, L. (2001). Parent-adolescent conflict in teenagers with ADHD and ODD. *Journal of Abnormal Child Psychology, 29,* 557–572.

Egeland, B., Yates, T., Appleyard, K., & van Dulmen, M. (2002). The long-term consequences of maltreatment in the early years: A developmental pathway model to antisocial behavior. *Children's Services: Social Policy, Research, & Practice, 5,* 249–260.

Egger, H. L., Costello, E. J., Erkanli, A., & Angold, A. (1999). Somatic complaints and psychopathology in children and adolescents: Stomach aches, musculoskeletal pains, and headaches. *Journal of the American Academy of Child and Adolescent Psychiatry, 38,* 852–860.

Eggers, C., Bunk, D., & Ropcke, B. (2002). Childhood and adolescent onset schizophrenia: Results from two long-term follow-up studies. *Neurology, Psychiatry and Brain Research, 9,* 183–190.

Eigisti, I. M., & Shapiro, T. (2003). A systems neuroscience approach to autism: Biological, cognitive and clinical perspectives. *Mental Retardation and Developmental Disabilities Research Reviews, 9,* 205–215.

Eikeseth, S. & Nesset, R. (2003). Behavioral treatment of children with phonological disorder: The efficacy of vocal imitation and sufficient-response-exemplar training. *Journal of Applied Behavior Analysis, 36,* 325–337.

Eisen, A. R., & Engler, L. B. (1995). Chronic anxiety. In A. R. Eisen, C. A. Kearney, & C. A. Schaefer (Eds.), *Clinical handbook of anxiety disorders in children and adolescents* (pp. 223–250). Northvale, NJ: Jason Aronson.

Eisen, A. R., Kearney, C. A., & Schaefer, C. E. (1995). *Clinical handbook of anxiety disorders in children and adolescents.* Northvale, NJ: Jason Aronson.

Eisen, A. R., & Silverman, W. K. (1993). Should I relax or change my thoughts? A preliminary examination of cognitive therapy, relaxation training, and their combination with overanxious children. *Journal of Cognitive Psychotherapy: An International Quarterly, 7,* 256–279.

Eisenberg, M., Neumark-Sztainer, D., & Story, M. (2003). Associations of weight-based teasing and emotional well-being among adolescents. *Archives of Pediatric and Adolescent Medicine, 157,* 733–738.

Eisenberg N., Pidada S., & Liew J. (2001). The relations of regulation and negative emotionality to Indonesian children's social functioning. *Child Development, 72,* 1747–1763.

Eisenmajer, R., Prior, M., Leekam, S., Wing, L., Gould, J., Welham, M., & Ong, B. (1996). Comparison of clinical symptoms in autism and Asperger's disorder. *Journal of the American Academy of Child and Adolescent Psychiatry, 35,* 1523–1531.

Eiser, C., Hill, J. J., & Vance, Y. H. (2000). Examining the psychological consequences of surviving childhood cancer: Systematic review as a research method in pediatric psychology. *Journal of Pediatric Psychology, 25,* 449–460.

Elder, G. H., Jr., Caspi, A., & Van Nguyen, T. (1986). Resourceful and vulnerable children: Family influence in hard times. In R. K. Silbereisen, K. Eyferth, & G. Rudinger (Eds.), *Development as action in context: Problem behavior and normal youth development* (pp. 167–186). New York: Springer-Verlag.

Elder, G. H., Jr., Robertson, E. B., & Ardelt, M. (1994). Families under economic pressure. In R. D. Conger, G. H. Elder, Jr., F. O. Lorenz, R. L., Simons, & L. B. Whitbeck (Eds.), *Families in troubled times: Adapting to change in rural America* (pp. 79–103). New York: Aldine de Gruyter.

Eley, T. C. (1999). Behavioral genetics as a tool for developmental psychology: Anxiety and depression in children and adolescents. *Clinical Child and Family Psychology Review, 2,* 21–36.

Eley, T. C., Bolton, D., O'Conner, T. G., Perrin, S., Smith, P., & Plomin, R. (2003). A twin study of anxiety-related behaviours in pre-school children. *Journal of Child Psychology and Psychiatry, 44,* 945–960.

Eley, T. C., Lichenstein, P., & Stevenson, J. (1999). Sex differences in the etiology of aggressive and nonaggressive antisocial behavior: Results from two twin studies. *Child Development, 70,* 155–168.

Eley, T. C., Lichenstein, P., & Moffitt, T. E. (2003). A longitudinal behavioral genetic analysis of the etiology of aggressive and nonaggressive antisocial behavior. *Development and Psychopathology, 15,* 383–402.

Eley, T. C., & Stevenson, J. (2000). Specific life events and chronic experiences differentially associated with depression and anxiety in young twins. *Journal of Abnormal Child Psychology, 28,* 383–394.

Ellinwood, C. G., & Raskin, N. J. (1993). Client-centered/humanistic psychotherapy. In T. R. Kratochwill & R. J. Morris (Eds.), *Handbook of psychotherapy with children and adolescents.* Needham Heights, MA: Allyn & Bacon.

Elliott, D. S., Huizinga, D., & Ageton, S. S. (1985). *Explaining delinquency and drug use.* Beverly Hills, CA: Sage.

Elliott, D. S., Huizinga, D., & Menard, S. (1989). *Multiple problem youth: Delinquency, substance use, and mental health problems.* New York: Springer-Verlag.

Elliott, M., Browne, K., & Kilcoyne, J. (1995). Child sexual abuse prevention: What offenders tell us. *Child Abuse and Neglect, 19,* 579–594.

Ember, C. R., & Ember, M. (1994). War, socialization, and interpersonal violence: A cross-cultural study. *Journal of Conflict Resolution, 38,* 620–646.

Emde, R. N., & Spicer, P. (2000). Experience in the midst of variation: New horizons for development and psychopathology. *Development and Psychopathology, 12,* 313–331.

Eme, R. F., & Kavanaugh, L. (1995). Sex differences in conduct disorder. *Journal of Clinical Child Psychology, 24,* 406–426.

Emerson, E. (2003). Prevalence of psychiatric disorders in children and adolescents with and without intellectual disability. *Journal of Intellectual Disability Research, 47,* 51–58.

Emery, R. E. (1999). Postdivorce family life for children: An overview of research and some implications for policy. In R. A. Thompson & P. R. Amato (Eds.), *The postdivorce family: Children, parenting, and society* (pp. 3–27). Thousand Oaks, CA: Sage.

Emery, R. E., & Laumann-Billings, L. (1998). An overview of the nature, causes, and consequences of abusive family relationships: Toward differentiating maltreatment and violence. *American Psychologist, 53,* 121–135.

Emery, R. E., Waldron, M., Kitzmann, K. M., & Aaron, J. (1999). Delinquent behavior, future divorce or nonmarital childbearing, and externalizing behavior among offspring: A 14-year prospective study. *Journal of Family Psychology, 13,* 568–579.

Emslie, G. J., & Mayes, T. L. (2001), Mood disorders in children and adolescents: Psychopharmacological treatment. *Biological Psychiatry, 49,* 1082–1090.

Epstein, L. H., Klein, K. R., & Wisniewski, L. (1994). Child and parent factors that influence psychological problems in obese children. *International Journal of Eating Disorders, 15,* 151–158.

Epstein, L. H., Valoski, A. M., Vara, L. S., McCurley, J., Wisniewski, L., Kalarchian, M. A., Klein, K. R., & Shrager, L. R. (1995). Effects of decreasing sedentary behavior and increasing activity on weight change in obese children. *Health Psychology, 14,* 109–115.

Epstein, L., Paluch, R., Gordy, C., Saelens, B., & Ernst, M. (2000). Problem solving in the treatment of childhood obesity. *Journal of Consulting and Clinical Psychology, 68,* 717–721.

Epstein, R. (1990). *Eating habits and disorders.* New York: Chelsea House.

Erba, H. W. (2000). Early intervention programs for children with autism: Conceptual frameworks for implementation. *American Journal of Orthopsychiatry, 70,* 82–94.

Ergene, T. (2003). Effective interventions on test anxiety reduction: A meta-analysis. *School Psychology International, 24,* 313–328.

Erhardt, D., & Hinshaw, S. P. (1994). Initial sociometric impressions of attention-deficit hyperactivity disorder and comparison boys: Predictions from social behaviors and from nonbehavioral variables. *Journal of Consulting and Clinical Psychology, 62,* 833–842.

Erickson, M. R., & Egeland, B. (2002). Child neglect. In J.E.B. Myers, L. Berliner, J. Briere, C. T. Hendrix, C. Jenny, & T.A. Reid (Eds.), *The APSAC handbook on child maltreatment* (pp. 3–20). Thousand Oaks, CA: Sage.

Erickson, M. F., Egeland, B., & Pianta, R. (1989). The effects of maltreatment on the development of young children. In D. Cicchetti & V. Carlson (Eds.), *Child maltreatment: Theory and research on the causes and consequences of child abuse and neglect* (pp. 647–684). New York: Cambridge University Press.

Eslinger, P. J. (1996). Conceptualizing, describing, and measuring components of executive function: A summary. In G. R. Lyon & N. A. Krasnegor (Eds.), *Attention, memory, and executive function* (pp. 367–395). Baltimore: Brookes.

Essau, C. A., Conradt, J., & Petermann, F. (2000a). Frequency, comorbidity, and psychosocial impairment of specific phobia in adolescents. *Journal of Clinical Child Psychology, 29*, 221–231.

Essau, C. A., Conradt, J., & Petermann, F. (2000b). Frequency, comorbidity, and psychosocial impairment of anxiety disorders in German adolescents. *Journal of Anxiety Disorders, 14*, 263–279.

Essau, C. A., Conradt, J., Petermann, F. (1999). Frequency and comorbidity of social phobia and social fears in adolescents. *Behaviour Research and Therapy, 37*, 831–843.

Evans, D. W., Gray, F. L., & Leckman, J. F. (1999). The rituals, fears and phobias of young children: Insights from development, psychopathology and neurobiology. *Child Psychiatry and Human Development, 29*, 261–276.

Evans, D. W., Leckman, J. F., Carter, A., Reznick, J. S., Henshaw, D., King, R. A., & Pauls, D. (1997). Ritual, habit, and perfectionism: The prevalence and development of compulsive-like behavior in normal young children. *Child Development, 68*, 58–68.

Evans, I. M. (1999). Child-focused behavioral assessment and modification. *Journal of Clinical Child Psychology, 28*, 493–501.

Fagan, P. J., Wise, T. N., Schmidt, C. W., Jr., & Berlin, F. S. (2002). Pedophilia. *JAMA: Journal of the American Medical Association, 288*, 2458–2465.

Fairburn, C., Cooper, Z., Doll, H., Norman, P., & O'Connor, M. (2000). The natural course of bulimia nervosa and binge eating disorder in young women. *Archives of General Psychiatry, 57*, 659–665.

Fairburn, C. G. (1994, May). *The aetiology of bulimia nervosa.* Paper presented at the Sixth International Conference on Eating Disorders, New York.

Fairburn, C. G., & Harrison, P. J. (2003). Eating disorders. *The Lancet, 361*, 407–416.

Fairburn, C. G., Marcus, M. D., & Wilson, G. T. (1993). Cognitive-behavioral therapy for binge eating and bulimia nervosa: A comprehensive treatment manual. In C. G. Fairburn & G. T. Wilson (Eds.), *Binge eating: Nature, assessment, and treatment* (pp. 361–404). New York: Guilford Press.

Fairburn, C. G., Norman, P. A., Welch, S. L., O'Connor, M. E., Doll, H. A., & Peveler, R. C. (1995). A prospective study of outcome in bulimia nervosa and the long-term effects of three psychological treatments. *Archives of General Psychiatry, 52*, 304–312.

Fairchild, S. R. (2002). Women with disabilities: The long road to equality. *Journal of Human Behavior in the Social Environment, 6*, 13–28.

Falicov, C. J. (2003). Culture, society and gender in depression. *Journal of Family Therapy, 25 (4)*, 371–387.

Famularo, R., Fenton, T., Kinscherff, R., & Augustyn, M. (1996). Psychiatric comorbidity in childhood posttraumatic stress disorder. *Child Abuse and Neglect, 20*, 953–961.

Fantuzzo, J. W. & Mohr, W. K. (1999). Prevalence and effects of child exposure to domestic violence. *Future of Children, 9*, 21–32.

Fantuzzo, J. W., Weiss, A. D., & Coolahan, K. C. (1998). Community-based partnership-directed research: Actualizing community strengths to treat child victims of physical abuse and neglect. In J. R. Lutzker (Ed.), *Handbook of child abuse research and treatment* (pp. 213–237). New York: Plenum.

Faraone, S. V., & Biederman, J. (1997). Do attention deficit hyperactivity disorder and major depression share familial risk factors? *Journal of Nervous and Mental Disease, 185*, 533–541.

Faraone, S. V., & Beiderman, J. (1998). Neurobiology of attention deficit hyperactivity disorder. *Biological Psychiatry, 44*, 951–958.

Faraone, S. V., Biederman, J., Chen, W. J., Krifcher, B., Keenan, K., Moore, C., Sprich, S., & Tsuang, M. T. (1992). Segregation analysis of attention deficit hyperactivity disorder. *Psychiatric Genetics, 2*, 257–275.

Faraone, S. V., Biederman, J., Keenan, K., & Tsuang, M. T. (1991a). A family-genetic study of girls with DSM-III attention deficit disorder. *American Journal of Psychiatry, 148*, 112–117.

Faraone, S. V., Biederman, J., Mick, E., Williamson, S., Wilens, T., Spencer, T., Weber, W., Jetton, J., Kraus, I., Pert, J., & Zallen, B. (2000). Family study of girls with attention deficit hyperactivity disorder. *American Journal of Psychiatry, 157*, 1077–1083.

Faraone, S. V., Biederman, J., & Monuteaux, M. C. (2000). Attention-deficit disorder and conduct disorder in girls: Evidence for a familial subtype. *Biological Psychiatry, 48*, 21–29.

Faraone, S. V., Biederman, J., & Monuteaux, M. C. (2001). Attention deficit hyperactivity disorder with bipolar disorder in girls: Further evidence for a familial subtype? *Journal of Affective Disorders, 64*, 19–26.

Faraone, S. V., Glatt, S. J., & Tsuang, M. T. (2003). The genetics of pediatric-onset bipolar disorder. *Biological Psychiatry, 53*, 970–977.

Farmer, J. E., & Muhlenbruck, L. (2000). Pediatric neuropsychology. In R. G. Frank & T. R. Elliott (Eds.), *Handbook of rehabilitation psychology* (pp. 377–397). Washington, DC: American Psychological Association.

Farrington, D. P. (1986). Age and crime. In M. Tonry & N. Morris (Eds.), *Crime and justice: An annual review of research* (Vol. 7, pp. 189–250). Chicago: University of Chicago Press.

Farrington, D. P. (1991). Childhood aggression and adult violence: Early precursors and later life outcomes. In D. J. Pepler & K. H. Rubin (Eds.), *The development and treatment of childhood aggression* (pp. 5–29). Hillsdale, NJ: Erlbaum.

Fauber, R. L., & Kendall, P. C. (1992). Children and families: Integrating the focus of interventions. *Journal of Psychotherapy Integration, 2*, 107–123.

Fauber, R. L., & Long, N. (1991). Children in context: The role of the family in child psychotherapy. *Journal of Consulting and Clinical Psychology, 59*, 813–820.

Feiring, C., Taska, L., & Lewis, M. (2002). Adjustment following sexual abuse discovery: The role of shame and attributional style. *Developmental Psychology, 38*, 79–92.

Feldman, L., Harvey, B., Holowaty, P., & Shortt, L. (1999) Alcohol use beliefs and behaviors among high school students. *Journal of Adolescent Health, 24*, 48–58.

Felsenfeld, S., & Plomin, R. (1997). Epidemiological and offspring analyses of developmental speech disorders using data from the Colorado Adoption Project. *Journal of Speech, Language, and Hearing Research: JSLHR, 40*, 778–791.

Felton, R. H. (1993). Effects of instruction on the decoding skills of children with phonological-processing problems. *Journal of Learning Disabilities, 26*, 583–589.

Ferguson, C. P., & Pigott, T. A. (2000). Anorexia and bulimia nervosa: Neurobiology and pharmacotherapy. *Behavior Therapy, 31*, 237–263.

Fergusson, D. M., & Horwood, L. J. (1999). Prospective childhood predictors of deviant peer affiliations in adolescence. *Journal of Child Psychology and Psychiatry and Allied Disciplines, 40*, 581–592.

Fergusson, D. M., & Horwood, L. J. (2002). Male and female offending trajectories. *Development and Psychopathology, 14*, 159–177.

Fergusson, D. M., Horwood, L. J., & Lloyd, M. (1991). Confirmatory factor analysis of attention deficit and conduct disorder. *Journal of Child Psychology and Psychiatry, 32*, 257–274.

Fergusson, D. M., Horwood, L. J., & Lynskey, M. T. (1993). Early dentine lead levels and subsequent cognitive and behavioural development. *Journal of Child Psychology and Psychiatry, 34,* 215–227.

Fernandez-Ballesteros, R. (2004). Self-report questionnaires. In S. N. Haynes & E. M. Heiby (Eds.), *Comprehensive handbook of psychological assessment, Volume 3: Behavioral assessment* (pp. 194–221). New York: Wiley.

Fichman, L., Koestner, R., & Zuroff, D. C. (1996). Dependency, self-criticism, and perceptions of inferiority at summer camp: I'm even worse than you think. *Journal of Youth and Adolescence, 25,* 113–126.

Fidler, D. J., Hodapp, R. M., & Dykens, E. M. (2000). Stress in families of young children with Down syndrome, Williams syndrome, and Smith-Magenis syndrome. *Early Education and Development. 11,* 395–406.

Field, T. M. (2000). Infants of depressed mothers. In S. L. Johnson & A. M. Hayes (Eds.), *Stress, coping, and depression* (pp. 3–22). Mahwah, NJ: Erlbaum.

Fielding, D. M., & Doleys, D. M. (1988). Elimination problems: Enuresis and encopresis. In E. J. Mash & L. G. Terdal (Eds.), *Behavioral assessment of childhood disorders* (2nd ed., pp. 586–623). New York: Guilford Press.

Fiese, B. H., & Bickham, N. L. (1998). Qualitative inquiry: An overview for pediatric psychology. *Journal of Pediatric Psychology, 23,* 79–86.

Fiese, B. H., Wilder, J., & Bickham, N.L. (2000). Family context in developmental psychopathology. In A. J. Sameroff, (Ed.), & M. Lewis (Ed.), *Handbook of developmental psychopathology (2nd ed.),* 115–134. Dordrecht, Netherlands: Kluwer Academic Publishers, xxxi, 813.

Filipek, P. A., Accardo, P. J., Baranek, G. T., Cook, E. H., Jr., Dawson, G., Gordon, B., et al. (1999). The screening and diagnosis of autistic spectrum disorders. *Journal of Autism and Developmental Disorders, 29,* 439–484.

Filipek, P. A., Semrud-Clikeman, M., Steingard, R. J., Renshaw, P. F., Kennedy, D. N., & Biederman, J. (1997). Volumetric MRI analysis comparing subjects having attention-deficit hyperactivity disorder with controls. *Neurology, 48,* 589–601.

Fine, S., Forth, A., Gilbert, M., & Haley, G. (1991). Group therapy for adolescent depressive disorder: A comparison of social skills training and therapeutic support. *Journal of the American Academy of Child and Adolescent Psychiatry, 30,* 79–85.

Finkelhor, D. (1994). The international epidemiology of child sexual abuse. *Child Abuse and Neglect,* 18, 409–417.

Finkelhor, D., & Browne, A. (1988). Assessing the long-term impact of child sexual abuse: A review and conceptualization. In L. Walker (Eds.), *Handbook on sexual abuse of children* (pp. 55–71). New York: Springer.

Finkelhor, D., & Dziuba-Leatherman, J. (1994). Victimization of children. *American Psychologist, 49,* 173–183.

Fischer, M., Barkley, R. A., Edelbrock, C. S., & Smallish, L. (1990). The adolescent outcome of hyperactive children diagnosed by research criteria, II: Academic, attentional, and neuropsychological status. *Journal of Consulting and Clinical Psychology, 58,* 580–588.

Fischer, M., Barkley, R. A., Smallish, L., & Fletcher, K. (2002). Young adult follow-up of hyperactive children: Self-reported psychiatric disorders, comorbidity, and the role of childhood conduct problems and teen CD. *Journal of Abnormal Child Psychology, 30,* 463–476.

Fish, B. (1987). Infant predictors of the longitudinal course of schizophrenic development. *Schizophrenia Bulletin, 13,* 395–410.

Fisher, C. B. (1991). Ethical considerations for research on psychosocial intervention for high-risk infants and children. *Register Reporter, 17(2),* 9–12.

Fisher, M., Golden, N.H., Katzman, D. K., Kreipe, R. E., Rees, J., Schebendach, J., et al. (1995). Eating disorders in adolescents: A background paper. *Journal of Adolescent Health, 16,* 420–437.

Flax, J. F., Realpe-Bonilla, T., Hirsch, L. S., Brzustowicz, L. M., Bartlett, C. W., & Tallal, P. (2003). Specific language impairment in families: Evidence for co-occurrence with reading impairments. *Journal of Speech, Language, & Hearing Research, 46,* 530–543.

Fletcher, J. M., Shaywitz, S. E., & Shaywitz, B. A. (1999). Comorbidity of learning and attention disorders: Separate but equal. *Pediatric Clinics of North America, 46,* 885–897.

Fletcher, J. M., & Taylor, H. G. (1997). Children with brain injury. In E. J. Mash & L. G. Terdal (Eds.), *Assessment of childhood disorders* (3rd ed., pp. 453–480). New York: Guilford Press.

Fletcher, K. E. (2003). Childhood post-traumatic stress disorder. In E. J. Mash & R. A. Barkley (Eds.), *Child psychopathology* (2nd ed., pp. 330–371). New York: Guilford Press.

Flory, K., & Lynam, D. R. (2003). The relation between attention deficit hyperactivity disorder and substance abuse: What role does conduct disorder play? *Clinical Child and Family Psychology Review, 6,* 1–6.

Flynn, J. R. (1999). Searching for justice: The discovery of IQ gains over time. *American Psychologist. 54,* 5–20.

Folstein, S. E., & Rosen-Scheidley, B. (2001). Genetics of autism: Complex aetiology for a heterogeneous disorder. *Nature Reviews, 2,* 943–954,

Fombonne, E. (1999). Time trends in affective disorders. In P. Cohen & C. Slomkowski (Eds.), *Historical and geographical influences on psychopathology* (pp. 115–139). Mahwah, NJ: Lawrence Erlbaum Associates Publishers.

Fombonne, E. (2003). Epidemiological surveys of autism and other pervasive developmental disorders: An update. *Journal of Autism and Developmental Disorders, 33,* 265–284.

Fombonne, E., Roge, B., Claverie, J., Courty, S., & Fremolle, J. (1999). Microcephaly and macrocephaly in autism. *Journal of Autism and Developmental Disorders, 29,* 113–119.

Fombonne, E., Simmons, H., Ford, T., Meltzer, H., & Goodman, R. (2003). Prevalence of pervasive developmental disorders in the British nationwide survey of child mental health. *International Review of Psychiatry, 15,* 158–165.

Fombonne, E., Wostear G., Cooper V., Harrington R., & Rutter, M. (2001a). The Maudsley long-term follow-up of child and adolescent depression: 1. Psychiatric outcomes in adulthood. *British Journal of Psychiatry, 179,* 210–217.

Fombonne, E., Wostear G., Cooper V., Harrington R., & Rutter, M. (2001b). The Maudsley long-term follow-up of child and adolescent depression: 2. Suicidality, criminality and social dysfunction in adulthood. *British Journal of Psychiatry, 179,* 218–223.

Fonagy, P., & Target, M. (2000). The place of psychodynamic theory in developmental psychopathology. *Development and Psychopathology, 12,* 407–425.

Foorman, B. R., Francis, D. J., Beeler, T., Winikates, D., & Fletcher, J. M. (1997). Early interventions for children with reading problems: Study designs and preliminary findings. *Learning Disabilities: A Multidisciplinary Journal, 8,* 63–72.

Foorman, B. R., & Torgesen, J. (2001). Critical elements of classroom and small-group instruction promote reading success in all children. *Learning Disabilities Research & Practice Special Issue: Emergent and early literacy: Current status and research directions, 16,* 203–212.

Forehand, R. L., & Kotchick, B. A. (1996). Cultural diversity: A wake-up call for parent training. *Behavior Therapy, 27,* 171–186.

Foreyt, J. P., & Cousins, J. H. (1987). Obesity. In M. Hersen & V. B. Van Hasselt (Eds.), *Behavior therapy with children and adolescents: A clinical approach* (pp. 485–511). New York: Wiley.

Foreyt, J. P., & Cousins, J. H. (1989). Obesity. In E. J. Mash & R. A. Barkley (Eds.), *Treatment of childhood disorders* (pp. 405–422). New York: Guilford Press.

Foreyt, J. P., & Mikhail, C. (1997). Anorexia nervosa and bulimia nervosa. In E. J. Mash & L. G. Terdal (Eds.), *Assessment of childhood disorders* (3rd ed., pp. 683–716). New York: Guilford Press.

Foster, S. L., & Robin, A. L. (1988). Family conflict and communication in adolescence. In E. J. Mash & L. G. Terdal (Eds.), *Behavioral assessment of childhood disorders* (2nd ed., pp. 717–775). New York: Guilford Press.

Foster, S. L., & Robin, A. L. (1998). Parent-adolescent conflict and relationship discord. In E. J. Mash & R. A. Barkley (Eds.), *Treatment of childhood disorders* (2nd ed., pp. 601–646). New York: Guilford Press.

Fowles, D. C. (2001). Biological variables in psychopathology: A psychobiological perspective. In P. Sutker & H. E. Adams (Eds.), *Comprehensive handbook of psychopathology* (3rd ed., pp. 85–104). New York: Kluwer Academic/Plenum Press.

Fox, N. A., Calkins, S. D., & Bell, M. A. (1994). Neural plasticity and development in the first two years of life: Evidence from cognitive and socioemotional domains of research. *Development and Psychopathology, 6,* 677–696.

Fox, T. L., Barrett, P. M., & Shortt, A. L. (2002). Sibling relationships of anxious children: A preliminary investigation. *Journal of Clinical Child and Adolescent Psychology, 31,* 375–383.

Francis, G., Last, C. G., & Strauss, C. C. (1987). Expression of separation anxiety disorder: The roles of age and gender. *Child Psychiatry and Human Development, 18,* 82–89.

Francis, S. E., & Chorpita, B. F. (2004). Behavioral assessment of children in outpatient settings. In S. N. Haynes & E. M. Heiby (Eds.), *Comprehensive handbook of psychological assessment, Volume 3: Behavioral assessment* (pp. 291–319). New York: Wiley.

Frank, N. C., Blount, R. L., & Brown, R. T. (1997). Attributions, coping, and adjustment in children with cancer. *Journal of Pediatric Psychology, 22,* 563–576.

Frank, Y., Lazar, J. W., & Seiden, J. A. (1992). Cognitive event-related potentials in learning-disabled children with or without attention-deficit hyperactivity disorder. *Annals of Neurology, 32,* 478 (abstract).

Frazier, J. A., Alaghband-Rad, J., Jacobsen, L., Lenane, M. C., Hamburger, S., Albus, K., et al. (1997). Pubertal development and onset of psychosis in childhood onset schizophrenia. *Psychiatry Research, 70,* 1–7.

Frazier, J. A., Meyer, M. C., Biederman, J., Wozniak, J., Wilens, T. E., Spencer, T. J., Kim, G. S., & Shapiro, S. (1999). Risperidone treatment for juvenile bipolar disorder: A retrospective chart review. *Journal of the American Academy of Child and Adolescent Psychiatry, 38,* 960–965.

French, D. C., & Dishion, T. (2003). Predictors of early initiation of sexual intercourse among high-risk adolescents. *Journal of Early Adolescence, 23,* 295–315.

French, S. A., Perry, C. L., Leon, G. R., & Fulkerson, J. A. (1994). Food preferences, eating patterns, and physical activity among adolescents: Correlates of eating disorders. *Journal of Adolescent Health, 15,* 286–294.

French, S. A., Story, M., Downes, B., Resnick, M. D., & Blum, R. W. (1995). Frequent dieting among adolescents: Psychosocial and health behavior correlates. *American Journal of Public Health, 85,* 695–710.

French, V. (1977). History of the child's influence: Ancient Mediterranean civilizations. In R. Q. Bell & L. V. Harper (Eds.), *Child effects on adults* (pp. 3–29). Hillsdale, NJ: Erlbaum.

Freud, S. (1909/1953). Analysis of a phobia in a five-year-old boy. In J. Strachey (Ed.), *The standard edition of the complete psychological works of Sigmund Freud* (Vol. 10, pp. 3–149). London: Hogarth Press.

Frick, P. J., Cornell, A. H., Bodin, S. D., Dane, H. E., Barry, C. T., & Loney, B. R. (2003). Callous–unemotional traits and developmental pathways to severe conduct problems. *Developmental Psychology, 39,* 246–260.

Frick, P. J., & Ellis, M. (1999). Callous-unemotional traits and subtypes of conduct disorder. *Clinical Child and Family Psychology Review, 2,* 149–168.

Frick, P. J., & Jackson, Y. K. (1993). Family functioning and childhood antisocial behavior: Yet another reinterpretation. *Journal of Clinical Child Psychology, 22,* 410–419.

Frick, P. J., Kamphaus, R. W., Lahey, B. B., Christ, M.A.G., Hart, E. L., & Tannenbaum, T. E. (1991). Academic underachievement and the disruptive behavior disorders. *Journal of Consulting and Clinical Psychology, 59,* 289–294.

Frick, P. J., Lahey, B. B., Loeber, R., Stouthamer-Loeber, M., Christ, M.A.G., & Hanson, K. (1992). Familial risk factors to oppositional defiant disorder and conduct disorder: Parental psychopathology and maternal parenting. *Journal of Consulting and Clinical Psychology, 60,* 49–55.

Frick, P. J., Lahey, B. B., Loeber, R., Tannenbaum, L, Van Horn, Y, Christ, M.A.G., Hart, E. L., & Hanson, K. (1993). Oppositional defiant disorder and conduct disorder: A meta-analytic review of factor analyses and cross-validation in a clinic sample. *Clinical Psychology Review, 13,* 319–340.

Frick, P. J., Lilienfeld, S. O., Ellis, M., Loney, B., & Silverthorn, P. (1999). The association between anxiety and psychopathy dimensions in children. *Journal of Abnormal Child Psychology, 27,* 383–392.

Frick, P. J. (2000). A comprehensive and individualized treatment approach for children and adolescents with conduct disorders. *Cognitive and Behavioral Practice, 7,* 30–37.

Fried, E. J., & Nestle, M. (2002). The growing political movement against soft drinks in schools. *Journal of the American Medical Association, 288,* 21–81.

Friedman, A. G. Latham, S. A., Dahlquist, L. M. (1998). Childhood cancer. In T. H. Ollendick & M. Hersen (Eds.), *Handbook of child psychopathology*

(3rd ed., pp. 435–461). New York: Plenum Press.

Friedman, H. S., Tucker, J. S., Schwartz, J. E., Tomlinson-Keasey, C., Martin, L. R., Wingard, D. L., & Criqui, M. H. (1995). Psychosocial and behavioral predictors of longevity: The aging and death of the "termites." *American Psychologist, 50,* 69–78.

Friedman, J., & Burley, S. K. (1995). *Leptin helps body regulate fat, links to diet* [On-line]. Available: http://www.rockefeller.edu/pubinfo/leptinlevel.nr.html. Rockefeller University and Howard Hughes Medical Institute Press Release.

Friedrich, W. N., & Trane, S. T. (2002). Sexual behavior in children across multiple settings. *Child Abuse & Neglect, 26,* 243–245.

Friman, P. C., Larzelere, R., & Finney, J. W. (1994). Exploring the relationship between thumbsucking and psychopathology. *Journal of Pediatric Psychology, 19,* 431–441.

Fristad, M. A., & Goldberg Arnold, J. S. (2004). *Raising a moody child: How to cope with depression and bipolar disorder.* New York: Guilford Press.

Frith, C., & Frith, U. (1996). A biological marker for dyslexia. *Nature, 382,* 19–20.

Frith, U. (1989). *Autism: Explaining the enigma.* Oxford, England: Basil Blackwell.

Frith, U. (1993, June). Autism. *Scientific American,* pp. 108–114.

Frith, U. (1997). Autism. *Scientific American [Special Issue],* pp. 92–98.

Frith, U. (2000). Cognitive explanations of autism. In K. Lee (Ed.), *Childhood cognitive development: The essential readings. Essential readings in development psychology;* (pp. 324–337). Malden, MA: Blackwell.

Frith, U. (2003). *Autism: Explaining the enigma (2nd ed.).* Oxford, England: Blackwell.

Frith, U., & Happe, F. (1994). Autism: Beyond "theory of mind." *Cognition, 50,* 115–132.

Fritz, G. K., Fritsch, S., & Hagino, O. (1997). Somatoform disorders in children and adolescents: A review of the past 10 years. *Journal of the American Academy of Child and Adolescent Psychiatry, 36,* 1329–1338.

Fritz, G., Rockney, R., & the Work Group on Quality Issues (2004). Summary of the practice parameter for the assessment and treatment of children and adolescents with enuresis. *Journal of the American Acadamy of Child and Adolescent Psychiatry, 43,* 123–125.

Fromm, S. (2001). *Total estimated cost of child abuse and neglect in the United States: Statistical evidence.* Available: http://www.preventchildabuse.org/learn_more/research_docs/cost_analysis.pdf.

Frost, R. (1998). Toward a strong phonological theory of visual word recognition: True issues and false trails. *Psychological Bulletin, 123,* 71–99.

Fulkerson, J. A., Keel, P. K., Leon, G. R., & Dorr, T. (1999). Eating-disordered behaviors and personality characteristics of high school athletes and nonathletes. *International Journal of Eating Disorders, 26,* 73–79.

Fuster, J. M. (1989). *The prefrontal cortex.* New York: Raven.

Gabel, S., & Shindledecker, R. (1993). Characteristics of children whose parents have been incarcerated. *Hospital and Community Psychiatry, 44,* 656–660.

Gable, S., & Lutz, S. (2000). Household, parent, and child contributions to childhood obesity. *Family Relations: Interdisciplinary Journal of Applied Family Studies, 49,* 293–300.

Gadow, K. D., & Nolan, E. E. (2002). Differences between preschool children with ODD, ADHD and ODD+ADHD symptoms. *Journal of Child Psychology and Psychiatry, 43,* 191–201.

Gadow, K. D., & Sprafkin, J. (1993). Television "violence" and children with emotional and behavioral disorders. *Journal of Emotional and Behavioral Disorders, 1,* 54–63.

Gadow, K. D., Sprafkin, J., & Nolan, E. E. (2001). DSM-IV symptoms in community and clinic preschool children. *Journal of the American Academy of Child and Adolescent Psychiatry, 40,* 1383–1392.

Galaburda, A. M., Sherman, G. F., Rosen, G. D., & Geschwind, A. F. (1985). Developmental dyslexia: Four consecutive patients with cortical anomalies. *Annals of Neurology, 18,* 222–223.

Galatzer-Levy, R. M., Bachrach, H., Skolnikoff, A., & Waldron, S. (2000). *Does psychoanalysis work?* New Haven, CT: Yale University Press.

Gallagher, H. L., & Frith, C. C. (2003). Functional imaging of 'theory of mind.' *Trends in Cognitive Sciences, 7,* 77–83.

Garber, J., & Flynn, C. (1998). Origins of the depressive cognitive style. In D. K. Routh & R. J. DeRubeis (Eds.), *The science of clinical psychology: Accomplishments and future directions* (pp. 53–93). Washington, DC: American Psychological Association.

Garber, J., Braafladt, N., & Zeman, J. (1991). The regulation of sad affect: An information-processing perspective. In J. Garber & K. Dodge (Eds.), *The development of emotion regulation and dysregulation* (pp. 208–240). New York: Cambridge University Press.

Garber, J., & Horowitz, J. L. (2002). Depression in children. In I. H. Gotlib & C. Hammen (Eds.), *Handbook of depression* (pp. 510–540). New York: Guilford Press.

Garber, J., & Kaminsky, K. M. (2000). Laboratory and performance based measures of depression in children and adolescents. *Journal of Clinical Child Psychology, 29,* 509–525.

Garber, J., Van Slyke, D. A., & Walker, L. S. (1998). Concordance between mothers' and children's reports of somatic and emotional symptoms in patients with recurrent abdominal pain or emotional disorders. *Journal of Abnormal Child Psychology, 26,* 381–391.

Garber, J., Weiss, B., & Shanley, N. (1993). Cognitions, depressive symptoms, and development in adolescents. *Journal of Abnormal Psychology, 102,* 47–57.

Garcia Coll, C., Akerman, A., & Cicchetti, D. (2000). Cultural influences on developmental processes and outcomes: Implications for the study of development and psychopathology. *Development and Psychopathology, 12,* 333–356.

Gardner, H. (1993). *Multiple intelligences: The theory in practice.* New York: Basic Books.

Gardner, W. I., Graeber-Whalen, J. L., & Ford, D. R. (2001). Behavioral therapies: Individualizing interventions through treatment formulations. In A. Dosen & K. Day, (Eds), *Treating mental illness and behavior disorders in children and adults with mental retardation* (pp. 69–100). Washington, DC: American Psychiatric Publishing.

Garfinkel, P. E., Lin, E., Goergin, P., Spegg, C., Goldbloom, D. S., Kennedy, S., Kaplan, A. S., & Woodside, D. B. (1995). Bulimia nervosa in a Canadian community sample: Prevalence and comparison of subgroups. *American Journal of Psychiatry, 152,* 1052–1058.

Garland, E. J. (2001). Sleep disturbances in anxious children. In G. Stores & L. Wiggs (Eds.), *Sleep disturbance in children and adolescents with disorders of development: Its significance and management* (pp. 155–160). New York: Cambridge University Press.

Garmezy, N. (1983). Stressors of childhood. In N. Garmezy & M. Rutter (Eds.), *Stress, coping, and development in children* (pp. 43–84). New York: McGraw-Hill.

Garmezy, N. (1991). Resiliency and vulnerability to adverse developmental outcomes associated with poverty. *American Behavioral Scientist, 34,* 416–430.

Garn, S. M., & Clark, D. C. (1976). Trends in fatness and the origins of obesity: Ad hoc committee to review the ten-state nutrition survey. *Pediatrics, 57,* 443–456.

Garner, D. M. (1993a). Binge eating in anorexia nervosa. In C. G. Fairburn & G. T. Wilson (Eds.), *Binge eating: Nature, assessment and treatment* (pp. 50–76). New York: Guilford Press.

Garner, D. M. (1993b). Pathogenesis of anorexia nervosa. *Lancet, 341,* 1631–1635.

Garner, D. M. (1997). Psychoeducational principles in treatment. In D. M. Garner and P. E. Garfinkel (Eds.), *Handbook of treatment for eating disorders* (2nd ed., pp. 145–177). New York: Guilford Press.

Garner, D. M., & Needleman, L. D. (1997). Sequencing and integration of treatments. In D. M. Garner and P. E. Garfinkel (Eds.), *Handbook of treatment for eating disorders* (2nd ed., pp. 50–63). New York: Guilford Press.

Garner, D. M., Rosen, L. W., & Barry, D. (1998). Eating disorders among athletes: Research and recommendations. *Child and Adolescent Psychiatric Clinics of North America, 7,* 839–857.

Garner, D. M., & Wooley, S. C. (1991). Confronting the failure of behavioral and dietary treatments for obesity. *Clinical Psychology Review, 11,* 729–780.

Garrison, W. T., & McQuiston, S. (1989). *Chronic illness during childhood and adolescence: Psychological aspects.* Newbury Park, CA: Sage.

Gaub, M., & Carlson, C. L. (1997b). Gender differences in ADHD: A meta-analysis and critical review. *Journal of the American Academy of Child and Adolescent Psychiatry, 36,* 1036–1045.

Gaudin, J. M., Polansky, N.A., Kilpatrick, A. C., & Shilton, P. (1996). Family functioning in neglectful families. *Child Abuse & Neglect, 20,* 363–377.

Geist, R., Heinmaa, M., Katzman, D., & Stephens, D. (1999). A comparison of male and female adolescents referred to an eating disorder program. *Canadian Journal of Psychiatry, 44,* 374–378.

Gelb, S. A. (1995, February). The beast in man: Degenerationism and mental retardation, 1900–1920. *Mental Retardation, 33,* 1–9.

Geller, B., Cooper, T. B., Zimerman, B., Frazier, J., Williams, M., Heath, J., & Warner, K. (1998). Lithium for prepubertal depressed children with family history predictors of future bipolarity: A double-blind, placebo-controlled study. *Journal of Affective Disorders, 51,* 165–175.

Geller, B., Craney, J. L., Bolhofner, K., Nickelsburg, M. J., Williams, M., & Zimmerman, B. (2002). Two-year prospective follow-up of children with a prepubertal and early adolescent bipolar disorder phenotype. *American Journal of Psychiatry, 159,* 927–933.

Geller, B., & DelBello, M. P. (Eds.). (2003). *Bipolar disorder in childhood and early adolescence.* New York: Guilford.

Geller, B., & Luby, J. (1997). Child and adolescent bipolar disorder: A review of the past 10 years. *Journal of the American Academy of Child and Adolescent Psychiatry, 36,* 1168–1176.

Geller, B., Reising, D., Leonard, H. L., Riddle, M. A., & Walsh, B. T. (1999). Critical review of tricyclic antidepressant use in children and adolescents. *Journal of the American Academy of Child and Adolescent Psychiatry, 38,* 513–528.

Geller, B., Sun, K., Zimerman, B., Luby, J., Frazier, J., & Williams, M. (1995). Complex and rapid cycling in bipolar children and adolescents. *Journal of Affective Disorders, 34,* 259–268.

Geller, V., Fox, L. W., & Clark, K. A. (1994). Rate and predictors of prepubertal bipolarity during follow-up of 6- to 12-year-old children. *Journal of American Academy of Child and Adolescent Psychiatry, 33,* 461–468.

George, M. S., Ketter, T. A., Parekh, P. I., Herscovitch, P., & Post, R. M. (1996). Gender differences in regional cerebral blood flow during transient self-induced sadness or happiness. *Biological Psychiatry, 40,* 859–871.

Gerdes, A. C., Hoza, B., & Pelham, W. E. (2003). Attention-deficit/hyperactivity disordered boy's relationships with their mothers and fathers: Child, mother, and father perceptions. *Development and Psychopathology, 15,* 363–382.

Gershater-Molko, R. M., Lutzker, J. R., & Wesch, D. (2003). Project SafeCare: Improving health, safety, and parenting skills in families reported for, and at-risk for child maltreatment. *Journal of Family Violence, 18,* 377–386.

Gershoff, E. T. (2002). Corporal punishment by parents and associated child behaviors and experiences: A meta-analytic and theoretical review. *Psychological Bulletin, 128,* 539–579.

Gershon, J. (2002). A meta-analytic review of gender differences in ADHD. *Journal of Attention Disorders, 5,* 143–154.

Ghazziuddin, M., Ghazziuddin, N., & Greden, J. (2002). Depression in persons with autism: Implications for research and clinical care. *Journal of Autism and Developmental Disorders, 32,* 299–306.

Giaconia, R. M., Reinherz, H. Z., Silverman, A. B., Pakiz, B., Frost, A. K., & Cohen, E. (1994). Ages of onset of psychiatric disorders in a community population of older adolescents. *Journal of the American Academy of Child and Adolescent Psychiatry, 33,* 706–717.

Gil, K. M., Anthony, K. K., & Carson, J. (2001). Daily coping practice predicts treatment effects in children with sickle cell disease. *Journal of Pediatric Psychology, 26,* 163–173.

Gill, M., Daly, G., Heron, S., Hawi, Z., & Fitzgerald, M. (1997). Confirmation of a dissociation between attention deficit hyperactivity disorder and a dopamine transporter polymorphism. *Biological Psychiatry, 2,* 311–313.

Gillberg, C. (1998). Chromosomal disorders and autism. *Journal of Autism and Developmental Disorders, 28,* 415–425.

Gillberg, C. (1999). Neurodevelopmental processes and psychological functioning in autism. *Development and Psychopathology, 11,* 567–587.

Gillberg, C. (2002). *A guide to Asperger syndrome.* New York: Cambridge University Press.

Gillberg, C. (2003a). ADHD and DAMP: A general health perspective. *Child and Adolescent Mental Health, 8,* 106–113.

Gillberg, C. (2003b). Emerging evidence that AD/HD and DCD interact multiplicatively. *Child and Adolescent Mental Health, 8,* 117.

Gillberg, C., & de Souza, L. (2002). Head circumference in autism, Asperger syndrome, and ADHD: A comparative study. *Developmental Medicine and Child Neurology, 44,* 296–300.

Gillham, J. E., & Reivich, K. J. (1999). Prevention of depressive symptoms in school children: A research update. *Psychological Science, 10,* 461–462.

Gillham, J. E., Shatte, A. J., & Freres, D. R. (2000). Preventing depression: A review of cognitive behavioral and family interventions. *Applied and Preventive Psychology, 9,* 63–88.

Gilman, S. E., Kawachi, I., Fitzmaurice, G. M., & Buka, S. (2003). Family disruption in childhood and risk of adult depression. *American Journal of Psychiatry, 160,* 939–946.

Gilvarry, E. (2000). Substance abuse in young people. *Journal of Child Psychology and Psychiatry, 41,* 55–80.

Ginsburg, G. S., La Greca, A. M., & Silverman, W. K. (1998). Social anxiety in children with anxiety disorders: Relation with social and emotional functioning. *Journal of Abnormal Child Psychology, 26,* 175–185.

Ginsburg, G. S., & Silverman, W. (1996). Phobic and anxiety disorders in Hispanic and Caucasian youth. *Journal of Anxiety Disorders, 10,* 517–528.

Ginsburg, G. S., & Silverman, W. K. (2000). Gender role orientation and fearfulness in children with anxiety disorders. *Journal of Anxiety Disorders, 14,* 57–67.

Glaser, D. (2002). Emotional abuse and neglect (psychological maltreatment): A conceptual framework. *Child Abuse & Neglect, 26,* 697–714.

Glicklich, L. B. (1951). An historical account of enuresis. *Pediatrics, 8,* 859–876.

Glover, S. H., & Pumariega, A. J. (1998). The importance of children's mental health epidemiological research with culturally diverse populations. In Hernandez, M. (Ed), & Isaacs, M. R. (Ed), *Promoting cultural competence in children's mental health services,* 271–303, Baltimore, MD, US: Paul H. Brookes Publishing Co.

Glowinski, A. L., Madden, P.A.F., Bucholz, K. K., Lynskey, M. T., & Heath, A. C. (2003). Genetic epidemiology of self-reported lifetime DSM-IV major depressive disorder in a population-based twin sample of female adolescents. *Journal of Child Psychology and Psychiatry, 44,* 988–996.

Glutting, J. J., Youngstrom, E. A., Ward, T., Ward, S., & Hale, R. (1997). Incremental efficacy of WISC-III factor scores in predicting achievement: What do they tell us? *Psychological Assessment, 9,* 295–301.

Goldberg, L. R. (1992). The development of markers for the big-five factor structure. *Psychological Assessment, 4,* 26–42.

Goldberg, S., Gotowiec, A., & Simmons, R. J. (1995). Infant-mother attachment and behavior problems in healthy and medically compromised preschoolers. *Development and Psychopathology, 7,* 267–282.

Golden, N. H., Katzman, D. K., Kreipe, R. E., Stevens, S. L., Sawyer, S. M., Rees, J., et al. (2003). Eating disorders in adolescents: Position paper of the Society for Adolescent Medicine. *Journal of Adolescent Health, 33,* 496–503.

Goldentyer, T. (1994). *Gangs.* Austin, TX: Steck-Vaughn.

Goldfield, A., & Chrisler, J. C. (1995). Body stereotyping and stigmatization of obese persons by first graders. *Perceptual and Motor Skills, 81,* 909–910.

Goldner, E. M., Srikameswaran, S., Schroeder, M. L., Livesley, W. J., & Birmingham, C. L. (1999). Dimensional assessment of personality pathology in patients with eating disorders. *Psychiatry Research, 85,* 151–159.

Goldston, D. B., Daniel, S. S., & Arnold, E. M. (in press). Suicidal and non-suicidal self-harm behaviors. In D. A. Wolfe & E. J. Mash (Eds.), *Behavioral and emotional disorders in adolescents: Nature, assessment, and treatment.* New York: Guilford Press.

Gomez, R., Burns, G. L., Walsh, J. A., & Alves de Moura, M. (2003). A multitrait-multisource confirmatory factor analytic approach to the construct validity of ADHD rating scales. *Psychological Assessment, 15,* 3–16.

Goode, S., Rutter, M., & Howlin, P. (1994). *A twenty-year follow-up of children with autism.* Paper presented at the 13th biennial meeting of the ISSBD, Amsterdam, the Netherlands.

Goodman, S. (2002). Depression and early adverse experiences. In I. H. Gotlib & C. Hammen (Eds.), *Handbook of depression* (pp. 245–267). New York: Guilford.

Goodman, S. H., & Gotlib, I. H. (Eds.). (2002). *Children of depressed parents: Mechanisms of risk and implications for treatment.* Washington, DC: American Psychological Association.

Goodman, S. H., Schwab-Stone, M., Lahey, B., Shaffer, D., & Jensen, P. (2000). Major depression and dysthymia in children and adolescents: Discriminant validity and differential consequences in a community sample. *Journal of the American Academy of Child and Adolescent Psychiatry, 39,* 761–770.

Goodwin, R. D., & Gotlib, I. H. (2004). Panic attacks and psychopathology among youth. *Acta Psychiatrica Scandinavica, 109,* 216–221.

Goodyer, I. M. (1999). The influence of recent life events on the onset and outcome of major depression in young people. In C. Essau & F. Petermann (Eds.), *Depressive disorders in children and adolescents: Epidemiology, risk factors, and treatment* (pp. 237–260). Northvale, NJ: Jason Aronson.

Goodyer, I. M., & Cooper, P. (1993). A community study of depression in adolescent girls: II. The clinical features of identified disorder. *British Journal of Psychiatry, 163,* 374–380.

Goodyer, I. M., Germany, E., Gowrusankur, J., & Altham, P. (1991). Social influences on the course of anxious and depressive disorders in school-age children. *British Journal of Psychiatry, 158,* 676–684.

Goodyer, I. M., Herbert, J., Tamplin, A., Secher, S. M., & Pearson, J. (1997). Short-term outcome of major depression: II. Life events, family dysfunction, and friendship difficulties as predictors of persistent disorder. *Journal of the American Academy of Child and Adolescent Psychiatry, 36,* 474–480.

Gordon, C. T., Krasnewich, D., White, B., Lenane, M., & Rapoport, J. L. (1994). Translocation involving chromosomes 1 and 7 in a boy with childhood-onset schizophrenia. *Journal of Autism and Developmental Disorders, 24,* 537–545.

Gordon, R. A. (2000). *Eating disorders: Anatomy of a social epidemic* (2nd ed.). Malden, MA: Blackwell.

Gordon-Walker, J., Johnson, S., Manion, I., & Cloutier, P. (1996). Emotionally focused marital intervention for couples with chronically ill children. *Journal of Consulting and Clinical Psychology, 64,* 1029–1036.

Gorman, B. J. (1999). Facilitated communication: Rejected in science, accepted in court—A case study and analysis of the use of FC evidence under Frye and Daubert. *Behavioral Sciences and the Law, 17,* 517–541.

Gortmaker, S. L. (1985). Demography of chronic childhood diseases. In N. Hobbs & J. M. Perrin (Eds.), *Issues in the care of children with chronic illness: A sourcebook of problems, services, and policies* (pp. 135–154). San Francisco: Jossey-Bass.

Gortmaker, S. L., Walker, D. K., Weitzman, M., & Sobol, A. M. (1990). Chronic conditions, socioeconomic risks and behavioral problems in children and adolescents. *Pediatrics, 85,* 267–276.

Gotlib, I. H., Goodman, S. H. (1999). Children of parents with depression. In W. K. Silverman & T. H. Ollendick (Eds.), *Developmental issues in the clinical treatment of children* (pp. 415–432). Needham Heights, MA: Allyn & Bacon.

Gotlib, I. H., & Hammen, C. L. (Eds.) (1992). *Psychological aspects of depression: Toward a cognitive-interpersonal integration.* London: Wiley.

Gotlib, I. H., Lewinsohn, P. M., & Seeley. J. R. (1995). Symptoms versus a diagnosis of depression: Differences in psychosocial functioning. *Journal of Consulting and Clinical Psychology, 63,* 90–100.

Gotlib, I. H., Lewinsohn, P. M., & Seeley, J. R. (1998). Consequences of depression during adolescence: Marital status and marital functioning in early adulthood. *Journal of Abnormal Psychology, 107,* 686–690.

Gotlib, I. H., Lewinsohn, P. M., Seeley, J. R., Rohde, P., & Redner, J. E. (1993).

Negative cognitions and attributional style in depressed adolescents: An examination of stability and specificity. *Journal of Abnormal Psychology, 102,* 607–615.

Gotlib, I. H., & Sommerfeld, B. K. (1999). Cognitive functioning in depressed children and adolescents: A developmental perspective. In C. Essau & F. Petermann (Eds.), *Depressive disorders in children and adolescents: Epidemiology, risk factors, and treatment* (pp. 195–236). Northvale, NJ: Jason Aronson.

Gottfredson, D. C., Gottfredson, G. D., & Hybel, L. G. (1993). Managing adolescent behavior: A multi-year, multi-school study. *American Educational Research Journal, 30,* 179–215.

Gottlieb, G., & Halpern, C. T. (2002). A relational view of causality in normal and abnormal development. *Development and Psychopathology, 14,* 421–435.

Gowers, S., & Bryant-Waugh, R. (2004). Management of child and adolescent eating disorders: the current evidence base and future directions. *Journal of Child Psychology and Psychiatry 45:1,* pp 63–83.

Graber, J. A., Brooks-Gunn, J., Paikoff, R. L., & Warren, M. P. (1994). Prediction of eating problems: An 8-year study of adolescent girls. *Developmental Psychology, 30,* 823–834.

Gracious, B. L., Findling, R. L., Seman, C., Youngstrom, E. A., Demeter, C. A., & Calabrese, J. R. (2004). Elevated thyrotropin in bipolar youths prescribed both lithium and divalproex sodium. *Journal of the American Academy of Child and Adolescent Psychiatry, 43,* 215–220.

Graham, S., MacArthur, C., Schwartz, S., & Voth, T. (1992). Improving LD student's compositions using a strategy involving product and process goal-setting. *Exceptional Children, 58,* 322–334.

Granger, D. A., Shirtcliff, E. A., Zahn-Waxler, C., Usher, B., Klimes-Dougan, B., & Hastings, P. (2003). Salivary testosterone diurnal variation and psychopathology in adolescent males and females: Individual differences and developmental effects. *Development and Psychopathology, 15,* 431–449

Granic, I., & Dishion, T. J. (2003). Deviant talk in adolescent friendships: A step toward measuring a pathogenic attractor process. *Social Development, 12,* 314–334.

Grant, B. F., & Dawson, D. A. (1997). Age of onset of alcohol use and its association with DSM-IV alcohol abuse and dependence: Results from the National Longitudinal Epidemiologic Survey. *Journal of Substance Abuse, 9,* 103–110.

Grant, B. F., Stinson, F. S., & Harford, T. C. (2001). Age of onset of alcohol use and DSM-IV alcohol abuse and dependence: A 12-year follow-up. *Journal of Substance Abuse, 13,* 493–504.

Grattan, L. M., & Eslinger, P. J. (1991). Frontal lobe damage in children and

adults: A comparative review. *Developmental Neuropsychology, 7,* 283–326.

Greenberg, M. T., DeKlyen, M., Speltz, M. L., & Endriga, M. C. (1997). The role of attachment processes in externalizing psychopathology in young children. In L. Atkinson & K. J. Zucker (Eds.), *Attachment and psychopathology* (pp. 196–222). New York: Guilford Press.

Greenberg, M. T., Domitrovich, C., & Bumbarger, B. (2000). *Preventing mental disorders in school-aged children: A review of the effectiveness of prevention programs.* Washington, DC: Substance Abuse Mental Health Services Administration, U.S. Department of Health and Human Services.

Greenberg, M. T., Lengua, L. J., Coie, J. D., & Pinderhughes, E. (1999). Predicting developmental outcomes at school entry using a multiple risk model: Four American communities. *Developmental Psychology, 35,* 403–417.

Greene, R. W., Biederman, J., Faraone, S. V., Ouellette, C. A., Courtney, P., & Griffin, S. M. (1996). Toward a new psychometric definition of social disability in children with attention-deficit hyperactivity disorder. *Journal of the American Academy of Child and Adolescent Psychiatry, 35,* 571–578.

Greene, R. W., & Doyle, A. E. (1999). Toward a transactional conceptulization of oppositional defiant disorder: Implications for assessment and treatment. *Clinical Child and Family Psychology Review, 2,* 129–148.

Greey, M. (1995, November). Special families, special needs: The rigours and rewards of raising children with disabilities. *Today's Parent,* 96–106.

Gresham, F. M., Beebe-Frankenberger, M. E., & MacMillan, D. L. (1999). A selective review of treatments for children with autism: Description and methodological considerations. *School Psychology Review, 28,* 559–575.

Gresham, F. M., & Macmillan, D. L. (1997a). Autistic recovery? An analysis and critique of the empirical evidence. *Behavioral Disorders, 22,* 185–201.

Gresham, F. M., & Macmillan, D. L. (1997b). Denial and defensiveness in the place of fact and reason: Rejoinder to Smith and Lovaas. *Behavioral Disorders, 22,* 219–230.

Gresham, F. M., MacMillan, D. L., Bocian, K. M., Ward, S. L., & Forness, S. R. (1998). Comorbidity of hyperactivity-impulsivity-inattention and conduct problems: Risk factors in social, affective, and academic domains. *Journal of Abnormal Child Psychology, 26,* 393–406.

Griffin, K. W., Botvin, G. J., Nichols, T. R., & Doyle, M. M. (2003). Effectiveness of a universal drug prevention approach for youth at high risk for substance abuse initiation. *Preventive Medicine, 36,* 1–7.

Griffith, E. M., Pennington, B. F., Wehner, E. A., & Rogers, S. J. (1999). Executive functions in young children with autism. *Child Development, 70,* 817–832.

Griffiths, R., Mallia-Blanco, R., Boesenberg, E., Ellis, C., Fischer, K., Taylor, M., & Wyndham, J. (2000). Restrained eating and sociocultural attitudes to appearance and general dissatisfaction. *European Eating Disorders Review, 8,* 394–402.

Grigorenko, E. L. (2001) Developmental dyslexia: An update on genes, brains, and environments. *Journal of Child Psychology and Psychiatry, and Allied Disciplines, 42,* 91–125.

Grilo, C. M., Masheb, R. M., & Berman, R. M. (2001). Subtyping women with bulimia nervosa along dietary and negative affect dimensions: A replication in a treatment-seeking sample. *Eating & Weight Disorders, 6,* 53–58.

Grimes, K., & Walker, E. F. (1994). Childhood emotional expressions, educational attainment, and age at onset of illness in schizophrenia. *Journal of Abnormal Psychology, 103,* 784–790.

Grisso, T., Baldwin, E., Blanck, P. D., Rotheram-Borus, M. J., Schooler, N. R., & Thompson, T. (1991). Standards in research: APA's mechanism for monitoring the challenges. *American Psychologist, 46,* 758–766.

Gross, M. D. (1995). Origin of stimulant use for treatment of Attention Deficit Disorder. *American Journal of Psychiatry, 152,* 298–299.

Grossman, A. W., Churchill, J. D., McKinney, B. C., Kodish, I. M., Otte, S. L., & Greenough, W. T. (2003). Experience effects on brain development: Possible contributions to psychopathology. *Journal of Child Psychology and Psychiatry, 44,* 33–63.

Gruber, R., Sadeh, A., & Raviv, A. (2000). Instability of sleep patterns in children with attention-deficit/hyperactivity disorder. *Journal of the American Academy of Child and Adolescent Psychiatry, 39,* 495–501.

Grych, J. H., Jouriles, E. N., Swank, P. R., McDonald, R., & Norwood, W. D. (2000). Patterns of adjustment among children of battered women. *Journal of Consulting and Clinical Psychology, 68,* 84–94.

Guerrero, A.P.S., Hishinuma, E. S., Andrade, N. N., Bell, C. K., Kurahara, D. K., Lee, T. G., Turner, H., Andrus, J., Yuen, N.Y.C., & Stokes, A. J. (2003). Demographic and clinical characteristics of adolescents in Hawaii with obsessive-compulsive disorder. *Archives of Pediatric Adolescent Medicine, 157,* 665–670.

Gullone, E. (1999). The assessment of normal fear in children and adolescents. *Clinical Child and Family Psychology Review, 2,* 91–106.

Guralnick, M. J. (1999). Family and child influences on the peer-related social competence of young children with developmental delays. *Mental Retardation and Developmental Disabilities Research Reviews, 5,* 21–29.

Gurley, D., Cohen, P., Pine, D. S., & Brook, J. (1996). Discriminating depression and anxiety in youth: A role for diagnostic criteria. *Journal of Affective Disorders, 39,* 191–200.

Gurman, A. S., & Kniskern, D. P. (Eds.). (1991). *Handbook of family therapy* (Vol. 2). New York: Brunner/Mazel.

Guskin, S. L., Bartel, N. R., & MacMillan, D. L. (1975). Perspective of the labeled child. In N. Hobbs (Ed.), *Issues in the classification of children* (Vol. 2, pp. 185–212). San Francisco: Jossey-Bass.

Gzowski, P. (1993, April). Gzowski's Canada: Extraordinary guests. *Canadian Living,* p. 91.

Hadwin, J. A., Donnelly, N., French, C. C., Richards, A., Watts, A., & Daley, D. (2003). The influence of children's self-report trait anxiety and depression on visual search for emotional faces. *Journal of Child Psychology and Psychiatry, 44,* 432–444.

Hafner, H., Hambrecht, M., Loffler, W., Munk-Jorgenson, P., & Reichler-Rossier, A. (1998). Causes and consequences of the gender difference in age of onset of schizophrenia. *Schizophrenia Bulletin, 24,* 99–113.

Hagberg, B. (1995). Clinical delineation of Rett Syndrome variants. *Neuropediatrics, 26,* 62.

Hallowell, E. M., & Ratey, J. J. (1994). *Answers to distraction.* New York: Pantheon Books.

Halperin, J. M., & McKay, K. E. (1998). Psychological testing for child and adolescent psychiatrists: A review of the past 10 years. *Journal of the American Academy of Child and Adolescent Psychiatry, 37,* 575–584.

Halpern, A. S., Lehmann, J. P., Irvin, L. K., & Heiry, T. J. (1982). *Contemporary assessment for mentally retarded adolescents and adults.* Baltimore: University Park Press.

Hamalainen, M., & Pulkkinen, L. (1996). Problem behavior as a precursor of male criminality. *Development and Psychopathology, 8,* 443–455.

Hamburg, D. A. (1997). Toward a strategy for healthy adolescent development. *American Journal of Psychiatry, 154,* 7–12.

Hammen, C. (1992). Cognitive, life stress, and interpersonal approaches to a developmental psychopathology model of depression. *Development and Psychopathology, 4,* 191–208.

Hammen, C. (1999). The emergence of an interpersonal approach to depression. In T. Joiner & J. Coyne (Eds.), *The interactional nature of depression: Advances in interpersonal approaches* (pp. 22–36). Washington, DC: American Psychological Association.

Hammen, C., & Brennan, P. A. (2003). Severity, chronicity, and timing of maternal depression and risk fo adolescent offspring diagnoses in a community sample. *Archives of General Psychiatry, 60,* 253–258.

Hammen, C., & Compas, B. E. (1994). Unmasking unmasked depression in children and adolescents: The problem of comorbidity. *Clinical Psychology Review, 14,* 585–603.

Hammen, C., Henry, R., & Daley, S. E. (2000). Depression and sensitization to stressors among young women as a function of childhood adversity. *Journal of Consulting and Clinical Psychology, 68,* 782–787.

Hammen, C., & Rudolph, K. D. (2003). Childhood mood disorders. In E. J. Mash & R. A. Barkley (Eds.), *Child psychopathology* (2nd ed., pp. 233–278). New York: Guilford Press.

Hammen, C., Rudolph, K., Weisz, J., Rao, U., & Burge, D. (1999). The context of depression in clinic-referred youth: Neglected areas in treatment. *Journal of the American Academy of Child and Adolescent Psychiatry, 38,* 64–71.

Hammen, C., Shih, J., Altman, T., & Brennan, P. A. (2003). Interpersonal impairment and the prediction of depressive symptoms in adolescent children of depressed and nondepressed mothers. *Journal of the American Academy of Child and Adolescent Psychiatry, 42,* 571–577.

Hammill, D. D. (1993). A brief look at the learning disabilities movement in the United States. *Journal of Learning Disabilities, 26,* 295–310.

Hammill, D. D., Mather, N., Allen, E. A., & Roberts, R. (2002). Using semantics, grammar, phonology, and rapid naming tasks to predict word identification. *Journal of Learning Disabilities, 35,* 121–136.

Handen, B. L., McAuliffe, S., Janosky, J., Feldman, H., & Breaux, A. M. (1994). Classroom behavior and children with mental retardation: Comparison of children with and without ADHD. *Journal of Abnormal Child Psychology, 22,* 267–280.

Hankin, B. L., & Abramson, L. Y. (2001). Development of gender differences in depression: An elaborated cognitive vulnerability-transactional stress theory. *Psychological Bulletin, 127,* 773–796.

Hankin, B. L., Abramson, L. Y., Moffitt, T. E., Silva, P. A., McGee, R., & Andell, K. E. (1998). Development of depression from preadolescence to young adulthood: Emerging gender differences in a 10-year longitudinal study. *Journal of Abnormal Psychology, 107,* 128–140.

Hanley, G. P., Iwata, B. A., & McCord, B. E. (2003). Functional analysis of problem behavior: A review. *Journal of Applied Behavior Analysis, 36,* 147–185.

Hanna, G. (1995). Demographic and clinical features of obsessive-compulsive disorder in children and adolescents. *Journal of the American Academy of Child and Adolescent Psychiatry, 34,* 19–27.

Happe, F.G.E. (1994a). Current psychological theories of autism: The "theory of mind" account and rival theories. *Jour-*

nal of Child Psychology and Psychiatry, 35, 215–230.

Happe, F.G.E. (1994b). Wechsler IQ profile and theory of mind in autism: A research note. Journal of Child Psychology and Psychiatry, 35, 1461–1471.

Happe, F.G.E. (1995a). The role of age and verbal ability in the theory of mind task performance of subjects with autism. Child Development, 66, 843–855.

Happe, F.G.E. (1995b, March). Wechsler IQ profile and theory of mind in autism. Paper presented at the biennial meeting of the Society for Research in Child Development, Indianapolis, IN.

Happe, F.G.E., & Frith, U. (1996). The neuropsychology of autism. Brain, 119, 1377–1400.

Hardt, J. & Rutter, M. (2004). Validity of adult retrospective reports of adverse childhood experiences: review of the evidence. Journal of Child Psychology & Psychiatry & Allied Disciplines, 45, 260–273.

Hare, R. D. (1993). Without conscience: The disturbing world of the psychopaths among us. New York: Pocketbooks.

Haring, T. G., & Breen, C. G. (1992). A peer-mediated social network intervention to enhance the social integration of persons with moderate and severe disabilities. Journal of Applied Behavior Analysis, 25, 319–333.

Harrington, R. C., Fudge, H., Rutter, M., Pickles, A., & Hill, J. (1990). Adult outcomes of childhood and adolescent depression: Psychiatric status. Archives of General Psychiatry, 47, 465–473.

Harrison, K. (2000). Television viewing, fat stereotyping, body shape standards, and eating disorder symptomatology in grade school children. Communication Research, 27, 617–640.

Hart, E. L., Lahey, B. B., Loeber, R., Applegate, B., Frick, P. J. (1996). Developmental change in attention-deficit hyperactivity disorder in boys: A four-year longitudinal study. Journal of Abnormal Child Psychology, 23, 729–749.

Hart, S., Jones, N. A., & Field, T. (2003). Atypical expressions of jealousy in infants of instrusive- and withdrawn-depressed mothers. Child Psychiatry and Human Development, 33, 193–207.

Hartmann, T. (1993). Attention deficit disorder: A different perception. Lancaster, PA: Underwood-Miller.

Hartung, C. M., & Widiger, T. A. (1998). Gender differences in the diagnosis of mental disorders. Conclusions and controversies of DSM-IV. Psychological Bulletin, 123, 260–278.

Hartung, C. M., Willcutt, E. G., Lahey, B. B., Pelham, W. E., Loney, J., Stein, M. A., & Keenan, K. (2002). Sex differences in young children who meet criteria for attention deficit hyperactivity disorder. Journal of Clinical Child and Adolescent Psychology, 31, 453–464.

Hartup, W. W. (1996). The company they keep: Friendships and their developmental significance. Child Development, 67, 1–13.

Harvey, A. G., & Bryant, R. A. (2002). Acute stress disorder: A synthesis and critique. Psychological Bulletin, 128, 886–902.

Haskett, M. E., & Kistner, J. A. (1991). Social interactions and peer perceptions of young physically abused children. Child Development, 62, 979–990.

Hastings, P. D., Zahn-Waxler, C., Robinson, J., Usher, B., & Bridges, D. (2000). The development of concern for others in children with behavior problems. Developmental Psychology, 36, 531–546.

Hatch, M. L., Friedman, S., & Paradis, C. M. (1996). Behavioral treatment of obsessive-compulsive disorder in African Americans. Cognitive and Behavioral Practice, 3, 303–315.

Hatcher, P.J., Hulme, C., & Snowling, M.J. (2004). Explicit phoneme training combined with phonic reading instruction helps young children at risk of reading failure. Journal of Child Psychology and Psychiatry, 45, 338–358.

Haugaard, J. J. (2000). The challenge of defining child sexual abuse. American Psychologist, 55, 1036–1039.

Hayman, L. L., Meininger, J. C., Coates, P. M., & Gallagher, P. R. (1995). Nongenetic influences of obesity on risk factors for cardiovascular disease during two phases of development. Nursing Research, 44, 277–283.

Hayward, C., Gotlib, I. H., Schraedley, P. K., & Litt, I. F. (1999). Ethnic differences in the association between pubertal status and symptoms of depression in adolescent girls. Journal of Adolescent Health, 25, 143–149.

Hayward, C., Killen, J. D., Hammer, L. D., Litt, I. F., Wilson, D. M., Simmonds, B., & Taylor, C. B. (1992). Pubertal stage and panic attack history in sixth- and seventh-grade girls. American Journal of Psychiatry, 149, 1239–1243.

Hayward, C., Killen, J. D., Wilson, D. M., & Hammer, L. D. (1997). Psychiatric risk associated with early puberty in adolescent girls. Journal of the American Academy of Child and Adolescent Psychiatry, 36, 255–262.

Heatherton, T. F., Mahamedi, F., Striepe, M., Field, A. E., & Keel, P. (1997). A 10-year longitudinal study of body weight, dieting, and eating disorder symptoms. Journal of Abnormal Psychology, 106, 117–125.

Heatherton, T. F., Nichols, P., Mahamedi, F., & Keel, P. K. (1995). Body weight, dieting, and eating disorder symptoms among college students 1982 to 1992. American Journal of Psychiatry, 152, 1623–1629.

Heatherton, T. F., & Polivy, J. (1992). Chronic dieting and eating disorders: A spiral model. In J. H. Crowther, D. L. Tennenbaum, S. E. Hobfall, & M. A. P. Stephens (Eds.), The etiology of bulimia nervosa: The individual and familial

context (pp. 133–155). Washington, DC: Hemisphere.

Hechtman, L. (2000). Assessment and diagnosis of attention-deficit/hyperactivity disorder. Child and Adolescent Psychiatric Clinics of North America, 9, 481–498.

Hedley, M. (1994). The presentation of gendered conflict in popular movies: Affective stereotypes, cultural sentiments, and men's motivation. Sex Roles, 31, 721–740.

Heim, C., & Nemeroff, C. B. (2001). The role of childhood trauma in the neurobiology of mood and anxiety disorders: Preclinical and clinical studies. Biological Psychiatry, 49, 1023–1039.

Hellander, M. (2002). Lithium testing in children: A public health necessity. Washington: DC: Testimony to the Food and Drug Administration. Available at: [http://www.fda.gov/ohrms/dockets/ac/02/slides/3870s1.htm]

Hendren, R. L., De Backer, I., & Pandina, G. J. (2000). Review of neuroimaging studies of child and adolescent psychiatric disorders from the past 10 years. Journal of the American Academy of Child and Adolescent Psychiatry, 39, 815–828.

Hendry, C. N. (2000). Childhood Disintegrative Disorder: Should it be considered a distinct diagnosis? Clinical Psychology Review, 20, 77–90.

Henggeler, S. W. (1991, April). Treating conduct problems in children and adolescents: An overview of the multisystemic approach with guidelines for intervention design and implementation. Division of Children, Adolescents and Their Families, South Carolina Department of Mental Health, Charleston, SC.

Henggeler, S. W. (1996). Treatment of violent juvenile offenders—We have the knowledge: Comment on Gorman-Smith et al. (1996). Journal of Family Psychology, 10, 137–141.

Henggeler, S. W., Clingempeel, W. G., Brondino, M. J., & Pickrel, S. G. (2002). Four-year follow-up of multisystemic therapy with substance-abusing and substance-dependent juvenile offenders. Journal of the American Academy of Child & Adolescent Psychiatry. 41, 868–874.

Henggeler, S. W., & Lee, T. (2003). Multisystemic treatment of serious clinical problems. In A. E. Kazdin & J. R. Weisz (Eds.), Evidence-based psychotherapies for children and adolescents (pp. 301–322). New York: Guilford.

Henggeler, S. W., Melton, G. B., & Smith, L. A. (1992). Family preservation using multisystemic therapy: An effective alternative to incarcerating serious juvenile offenders. Journal of Consulting and Clinical Psychology, 60, 953–961.

Henggeler, S. W., & Santos, A. B. (Eds.). (1997). Innovative approaches for difficult-to-treat populations. Washington, DC: American Psychiatric Press.

Henggeler, S. W., Schoenwald, S. K., Borduin, C. M., Rowland, M. D., & Cunningham, P. B. (1998). Multisystemic *treatment of antisocial behavior in children and adolescents.* New York: Guilford Press.

Henggeler, S. W., Schoenwald, S. K., & Pickrel, S. G. (1995). Multisystemic therapy: Bridging the gap between university- and community-based treatment. *Journal of Consulting and Clinical Psychology, 63,* 709–717.

Henin, A., & Kendall, P. C. (1997). Obsessive-compulsive disorder in childhood and adolescence. *Advances in Clinical Child Psychology, 19,* 75–131.

Henker, B., & Whalen, C. K. (1980). The many messages of medication: Hyperactive children's perceptions and attributions. In S. Salzinger, J. Antrobus, & J. Glick (Eds.), *The ecosystem of the "sick" child: Implications for classification and intervention for disturbed and mentally retarded children* (pp. 141–166). New York: Academic Press.

Henker, B., & Whalen, C. K. (1999). The child with attention-deficit/hyperactivity disorder in school and peer settings. In H. C. Quay & A. E. Hogan (Eds.), *Handbook of disruptive behavior disorders* (pp. 157–178). New York: Kluwer Academic/Plenum.

Henrich, C. C., Brown, J. L., & Aber, J. L. (1999). Evaluating the effectiveness of school-based violence prevention: Developmental approaches. *Social Policy Report: Society for Research in Child Development, 13(3),* 1–17.

Henry, B., Caspi, A., Moffitt, T. E., & Silva, P. A. (1996). Temperamental and familial predictors of violent and nonviolent criminal convictions: Age 3 to age 18. *Developmental Psychology, 32,* 614–623.

Herman, J. L. (1992). *Trauma and recovery: The aftermath of violence—from domestic abuse to political terror.* New York: Basic Books.

Herman-Stahl, M., & Petersen, A. C. (1996). The protective role of coping and social resources for depressive symptoms among young adolescents. *Journal of Youth and Adolescence, 25,* 733–753.

Herrenkohl, R. C., Herrenkohl, E. C., & Egolf, B. P. (1983). Circumstances surrounding the occurrence of child maltreatment. *Journal of Consulting and Clinical Psychology, 51,* 424–431.

Herzog, D. B., Dorer, D. J., Keel, P. K., Selwyn, S. E., Ekeblad, E. R., Flores, A. T., Greenwood, D. N., Burwell, R. A., & Keller, M. B. (1999). Recovery and relapse in anorexia and bulimia nervosa: A 7.5-year follow-up study. *Journal of the American Academy of Child and Adolescent Psychiatry, 38,* 829–837.

Herzog, D. B., & Rathbun, J. M. (1982). Childhood depression: Developmental considerations. *American Journal of Diseases of Children, 136,* 115–120.

Herzog, W., Kronmueller, K. T., Hartmann, M., Bergmann, G., & Kroeger, F. (2000). Family perception of interpersonal behavior as a predictor in eating disorders: A prospective six-year followup study. *Family Process, 39,* 359–374.

Hetherington, E. M., Bridges, M., & Insabella, G. M. (1998). What matters? What does not? Five perspectives on the association between marital transitions and children's adjustment. *American Psychologist, 53,* 167–184.

Hetherington, E. M., Reiss, D., & Plomin, R. (Eds.). (1994). *Separate social worlds of siblings: The impact of nonshared environment on development.* Hillsdale, NJ: Erlbaum.

Hewitt, P. L., & Flett, G. L. (1993). Dimensions of perfectionism, daily stress, and depression: A test of the specific vulnerability hypothesis. *Journal of Abnormal Psychology, 102,* 58–65.

Hildyard, K., & Wolfe, D. A. (2002). Child neglect: Developmental issues and outcomes. *Child Abuse & Neglect, 26,* 679–695.

Hill, D. E., Yeo, R. A., Campbell, R. A., Hart, B., Vigil, J., & Brooks, W. (2003). Magnetic resonance imaging correlates of attention-deficit/hyperactivity disorder in children. *Neuropsychology, 17,* 496–506.

Hill, E. L. (2004). Executive dysfunction in autism. *Trends in Cognitive Sciences, 8,* 26–32.

Hill, J. (2002). Biological, psychological and social processes in the conduct disorders. *Journal of Child Psychology and Psychiatry, 43,* 133–164.

Hinshaw, S. P., & Lee, S. S. (2003). Conduct and oppositional defiant disorders. In E. J. Mash & R. A. Barkley (Eds.), *Child psychopathology* (2nd. ed., pp. 144–198). New York: Guilford.

Hinshaw, S. P. (1987). On the distinction between attentional deficits/hyperactivity and conduct problems/aggression in child psychopathology. *Psychological Bulletin, 101,* 443–463.

Hinshaw, S. P. (1992a). Externalizing behavior problems and academic underachievement in childhood and adolescence: Causal relationships and underlying mechanisms. *Psychological Bulletin, 111,* 127–155.

Hinshaw, S. P. (1992b). Interventions for social competence and social skill. In G. Weiss (Ed.), *Child and Adolescent Psychiatric Clinics of North America* (Vol. 1, 2, October, 539–552). Philadelphia: Saunders.

Hinshaw, S. P. (1994a). *Attention deficits and hyperactivity in children.* Thousand Oaks, CA: Sage.

Hinshaw, S. P. (2000). Attention-deficit/hyperactivity disorder: The search for viable treatments. In P. C. Kendall (Ed.), *Child and adolescent therapy: Cognitive-behavioral procedures* (2nd ed., pp. 88–128). New York: Guilford Press.

Hinshaw, S. P. (2001). Is the inattentive type of ADHD a separate disorder? *Clinical Psychology: Science and Practice, 8,* 498–501.

Hinshaw, S. P., & Blachman, D. R. (in press). Attention-deficit/hyperactivity disorder in girls. In D. Bell, S. L. Foster, & E. J. Mash (Eds.), *Handbook of behavioral and emotional disorders in girls.* New York: Kluwer Academic.

Hinshaw, S. P., Cicchetti, D. (2000). Stigma and mental disorder: Conceptions of illness, public attitudes, personal disclosure, and social policy. *Development and Psychopathology, 12,* 555–598.

Hinshaw, S. P., Lahey, B. B., & Hart, E. L. (1993). Issues of taxonomy and comorbidity in the development of conduct disorder. *Development and Psychopathology, 5,* 31–49.

Hinshaw, S. P., Owens, E. B., Wells, K. C., Kraemer, H. C., Abikoff, H. B., Arnold, L. E., et al., (2000). Family processes and treatment outcome in the MTA: Negative/ineffective parenting practices in relation to multimodal treatment. *Journal of Abnormal Child Psychology, 28,* 555–568.

Hirschi, T., & Gottfredson, M. (1983). Age and the explanation of crime. *American Journal of Sociology, 89,* 552–583.

Hirshfeld, D. R., Biederman, J., Brody, L., & Faraone, S. V. (1997). Associations between expressed emotion and child behavioral inhibition and psychopathology: A pilot study. *Journal of the American Academy of Child and Adolescent Psychiatry, 36,* 205–213.

Hirshfeld, D. R., Biederman, J., & Rosenbaum, J. F. (1997). Expressed emotion toward children with behavioral inhibition: Associations with maternal anxiety disorder. *Journal of the American Academy of Child and Adolescent Psychiatry, 36,* 910–919.

Hirshfeld, D. R., Rosenbaum, J. F., Biederman, J., Bolduc, E. A., Faraone, S. V., Snidman, N., et al. (1992). Stable behavioral inhibition and its association with anxiety disorder. *Journal of the American Academy of Child and Adolescent Psychiatry, 31,* 103–111.

Hitchcock, C. H., & Noonan, M. J. (2000). Computer-assisted instruction of early academic skills. *Topics in Early Childhood Special Education, 20,* 145–158.

Ho, H. Y., Cheung, M. C., & Chan, A. S. (2003). Music training improves verbal but not visual memory: Cross-sectional and longitudinal explorations in children. *Neuropsychology, 17,* 439–450.

Hoagwood, K. (2003). Ethical issues in child and adolescent psychosocial treatment research. In A. E. Kazdin & J. R. Weisz (Eds.), *Evidence-based psychotherapies for children and adolescents* (pp. 60–75). New York: The Guilford Press.

Hodapp, R. M., & DesJardin, J. L. (2002). Genetic etiologies of mental retardation: Issues for interventions and interventionists. *Journal of Developmental & Physical Disabilities, 14,* 323–338.

Hodapp, R. M., & Dykens, E. M. (2003). Mental retardation (intellectual disabilities). In E. J. Mash & R. A. Barkley (Eds.), *Child psychopathology* (2nd edition; pp. 486–519). New York: Guilford Press.

Hodapp, R. M., Kazemi, E., Rosner, B. A., & Dykens, E. M. (in press). In D. A. Wolfe & E. J. Mash (Eds.). *Behavioral and emotional disorders in adolescents: Nature, assessment, and treatment.* New York: Guilford Press.

Hodapp, R. M., & Zigler, E. (1995). Past, present, and future issues in the developmental approach to mental retardation and developmental disabilities. In D. Cicchetti & D. J. Cohen (Eds.), *Developmental psychopathology: Vol 2. Risk, disorder, and adaption* (pp. 299–331). New York: Wiley.

Hodgins, S., Faucher, B., Zarac, A., & Ellenbogen, M. (2002). Children of parents with bipolar disorder: A population at high risk for major affective disorders. *Child and Adolescent Psychiatric Clinics of North America, 11,* 533–553.

Hodgins, S., Kratzer, L., & McNeil, T. F. (2001). Obstetrical complications, parenting, and risk of criminal behavior. *Archives of General Psychiatry, 58,* 746–752.

Hoekstra-Weebers, J.E.H.M., Jasper, J.P.C., Kamps, W. A., & Klip, E. C. (1999). Risk factors for psychological maladjustment of parents of children with cancer. *Journal of the American Academy of Child and Adolescent Psychiatry, 38,* 1526–1535.

Hoffman, E. C., & Mattis, S. G. (2000). A developmental adaptation of panic control treatment for panic disorder in adolescence. *Cognitive and Behavioral Practice, 7,* 253–261.

Hoffmann, H. (1845). *Struwwelpeter.* London and Glasgow: Blackie.

Hofmann, S., Albano, A. M., Heimberg, R. G., Tracey, S., Chorpita, B. F., & Barlow, D. H. (1999). Subtypes of social phobia in adolescents. *Depression and Anxiety, 9,* 15–18

Hogan, A. E. (1999). Cognitive functioning in children with oppositional defiant disorder. In H. C. Quay & A. E. Hogan (Eds.), *Handbook of disruptive behavior disorders* (pp. 317–335). New York: Kluwer Academic/Plenum.

Holden, E. W., Chmielewski, D., Nelson, C. C., & Kager, V. A. (1997). Controlling for general and disease-specific effects in child and family adjustment to chronic childhood illness. *Journal of Pediatric Psychology, 22,* 15–27.

Holmes, C. S., Yu, Z., & Frentz, J. (1999). Chronic and discrete stress as predictors of children's adjustment. *Journal of Consulting and Clinical Psychology, 67,* 411–419.

Holmes, F. B. (1936). An experimental investigation of a method of overcoming children's fears. *Child Development, 7,* 6–30.

Hoon, A. H., & Melhem, E. R. (2000). Neuroimaging: Applications in disorders of early brain development. *Journal of Developmental and Behavioral Pediatrics, 21,* 291–302.

Hooper, S. R., Montgomery, J., Swartz, C., Reed, M., Sandler, A., Levine, M., et al. (1994). Measurement of written language. In G. R. Lyon (Ed.), *Frames of reference for the assessment of learning disabilities: New views on measurement issues* (pp. 375–418). Baltimore: Brookes.

Hoover, D. W., & Milich, R. (1994). Effects of sugar ingestion expectancies on mother-child interactions. *Journal of Abnormal Child Psychology, 22,* 501–514.

Hops, H., Lewinsohn, P. M., Andrews, J. A., & Roberts, R. E. (1990). Psychosocial correlates of depressive symptomatology among high school students. *Journal of Clinical Child Psychology, 19,* 211–220.

Houts, A.C. (2003). Behavioral treatment for enuresis. In A.E. Kazdin & J.R. Weisz (Eds.), *Evidence-based psychotherapies for children and adolescents* (pp. 389–406). New York: Guilford Press.

Howard, B., & Kendall, P. C. (1996a). *Cognitive-behavioral family therapy for anxious children: Therapist manual.* Ardmore, PA: Workbook.

Howard, B. L., & Kendall, P. C. (1996b). Cognitive-behavioral family therapy for anxiety-disordered children: A multiple-baseline evaluation. *Cognitive Therapy and Research, 20,* 423–443.

Howard, M. A., Cowell, P. E., Boucher, J., Broks, P., Mayes, A., Farrant, A., & Roberts, N. (2000). Convergent neuroanatomical and behavioural evidence of an amygdala hypothesis. *Neuroreport, 11,* 2931–2935.

Howes, P. W., Cicchetti, D., Toth, S. L., & Rogosch, F. A. (2000). Affective, organizational, and relational characteristics of maltreating families: A systems perspective. *Journal of Family Psychology, 14,* 95–110.

Howlin, P., Goode, S., Hutton, J., & Rutter, M. (2004). Adult outcome for children with autism. *Journal of Child Psychology and Psychiatry, 45,* 212–229.

Hoza, B., Pelham, W. E., Dobbs, J., Owens, J. S., & Pillow, D. (2002). Do boys with attention-deficit/hyperactivity disorder have positive illusory self-concepts? *Journal of Abnormal Psychology, 111,* 268–278.

Hoza, B., Waschbusch, D. A., Pelham, W. E., Molina, B.S.G., & Milich, R. (2000). Attention-deficit/hyperactivity disordered and control boys' responses to social success and failure. *Child Development, 71,* 432–446.

Hsu, L. K. G. (1990). *Eating disorders.* New York: Guilford Press.

Hudson, J. L., Flannery-Schroeder, E., & Kendall, P. C. (2004). Primary prevention of anxiety disorders. In D. J. A. Dozois & K. S. Dobson (Eds.), *The prevention of anxiety and depression: Theory, research, and practice* (pp. 101–130). Washington, DC: American Psychological Association.

Hudson, M. M., Mertens, A. C., Yasui, Y., Hobbie, W., Chen, H., Gurney, J. G., et al. (2003). Health status of adult long-term survivors of childhood cancer: A report from the childhood cancer survivor study. *JAMA, 290,* 1583–1592.

Hudson, S. M., & Ward, T. (1997). Intimacy, loneliness, and attachment style in sexual offenders. *Journal of Interpersonal Violence, 12,* 323–329.

Huesmann, L. R., Eron, L. D., Lefkowitz, M. M., & Walder, L. O. (1984). Stability of aggression over time and generations. *Developmental Psychology, 20,* 1120–1134.

Huesmann, L. R., Moise-Titus, J., Podolski, C., & Eron, L. D. (2003). Longitudinal relations between children's exposure to TV violence and their aggressive and violent behavior in young adulthood: 1977–1992. *Developmental Psychology, 39,* 201–221.

Huizink, A. C., Mulder, E. J. H, & Buitelaar, J. K (2004). Prenatal stress and risk for psychopathology: Specific effects or induction of general susceptibility. *Psychological Bulletin, 130,* 115–142.

Huon, G., & Walton, C. (2000). Initiation of dieting among adolescent females. *International Journal of Eating Disorders, 28,* 226–230.

Huppke, P., Held, M., Laccone, F., & Hanefeld, F. (2003). The spectrum of phenotypes in females with Rett Syndrome. *Brain & Development, 25,* 346–351.

Hurlbert, R. T., Happe, F., & Frith, U. (1994). Sampling the form of inner experience in three adults with Asperger syndrome. *Psychological Medicine, 24,* 385–395.

Ialongo, N., Edelsohn, G., Werthamer-Larsson, L., Crockett, L., & Kellam, S. (1995). The significance of self-reported anxious symptoms in first grade children: Prediction to anxious symptoms and adaptive functioning in fifth grade. *Journal of Child Psychology and Psychiatry, 36,* 427–437.

Illick, J. E. (1974). Childrearing in seventeenth century England and America. In L. deMause (Ed.), The history of childhood. New York: Psychohistory Press. In T. A. Van Dijk. (Ed.), *Discourse as structure and process: Discourse studies: A multidisciplinary introduction, Vol. 1* (pp. 63–111). Thousand Oaks, CA: Sage.

Inderbitzen-Nolan, H. M., & Walters, K. S. (2000). Social anxiety scale for adolescents: Normative data and further evidence of construct validity. *Journal of Clinical Child Psychology, 29,* 360–371.

Ingman, K. A., Ollendick, T. H., & Akande, A. (1999). Cross-cultural aspects of fears in African children and adolescents. *Behaviour Research and Therapy, 37,* 337–345.

Innocenti, G. M. (1982). Development of interhemispheric cortical connections. *Neurosciences Research Program Bulletin, 20(4),* 532–540.

International Dyslexia Association (2004). *Frequently asked questions about dyslexia.* Available: http://www.interdys.org/servlet/compose?section_id=5&page_id=95. Accessed February 19, 2004.

International Molecular Genetic Study of Autism Consortium (1998). A full genome screen for autism with evidence for linkage to a region on chromosome 7q. *Human Molecular Genetics, 7,* 571–578.

Irwin, C. E., & Duncan, P. (Eds.) (2002). Health futures of youth II: Pathways to adolescent health. *Journal of Adolescent Health, 31* (Supplement).

Irwin, C. E. Jr., Burg, S. J., & Cart, C. U. (2002). America's adolescents: Where have we been, where are we going? *Journal of Adolescent Health, 31,* 91–121.

Israel, A. C. (1999). Commentary: Empirically supported treatments for pediatric obesity: Goals, outcome criteria, and the societal context. *Journal of Pediatric Psychology, 24,* 249–250.

Ivarsson, T., Rastam, M., Wentz, E., Gillberg, I. C., & Gillberg, C. (2000). Depressive disorders in teenage-onset anorexia nervosa: A controlled longitudinal, partly community-based study. *Comprehensive Psychiatry, 41,* 398–403.

Iwaniec, D., Sheddon, H., & Allen, S. (2003). The outcomes of a longitudinal study of non-organic failure-to-thrive. *Child Abuse Review, 12,* 216–226.

Jackson, J. (2000). What ought psychology to do? *American Psychologist, 55,* 328–330.

Jacob, T., & Johnson, S. L. (1999). Family influences on alcohol and substance abuse. In P. J. Ott & R. E. Tarter (Eds.), *Sourcebook on substance abuse: Etiology, epidemiology, assessment, and treatment* (pp. 166–174). Needham Heights, MA: Allyn & Bacon.

Jacobi, C., Hayward, C., de Zwaan, M., Kraemer, H. C., & Agras, S. (2004). Coming to terms with risk factors for eating disorders: Application of risk terminology and suggestions for a general taxonomy. *Psychological Bulletin, 130,* 19–65.

Jacobson, J. W., Mulick, J. A., & Schwartz, A. A. (1995). A history of facilitated communication: Science, pseudoscience, and antiscience. *American Psychologist, 50,* 750–765.

Jacobson, K. C., Prescott, C. A., & Kendler, K. S. (2002). Sex differences in the environmental influences on the development of antisocial behavior. *Development and Psychopathology, 14,* 395–416.

Jacobvitz, D., & Sroufe, L. A. (1987). The early caregiver-child relationship and attention-deficit disorder with hyperac-

tivity in kindergarten: A prospective study. *Child Development, 58,* 1496–1504.

Jacobvitz, D., & Sroufe, L. A., Stewart, M., & Leffert, N. (1990). Treatment of attention and hyperactivity problems in children with sympathomimetic drugs: A comprehensive review. *Journal of the American Academy of Child and Adolescent Psychiatry, 29,* 677–688.

Jaffe, P., Lemon, N., Sandler, J., & Wolfe, D. (1996). *Working together to end domestic violence.* Tampa, FL: Mancorp.

Jaffe, W. B., D'Zurilla, T. J. (2003). Adolescent problem solving, parent problem solving, and externalizing behavior in adolescents. *Behavior Therapy, 34,* 295–311.

Jaffee, S. R., Moffitt, T. E., Caspi, A., & Taylor, A. (2003). Life with (or without) father: The benefits of living with two biological parents depend on the father's antisocial behavior. *Child Development, 74,* 109–126.

Jamison, K. R. (1997, January). Manic-depressive illness and creativity. *Scientific American (Special Issue), 7(1),* 44–49.

Jaycox, L. H., Reivich, K. J., Gillham, J., & Seligman, M.E.P. (1994). Prevention of depressive symptoms in school children. *Behaviour Research and Therapy, 32,* 801–816.

Jencks, C., & Phillips, M. (1998). *The Black–White test score gap.* Washington, DC: Brookings Institution Press.

Jensen, A. R. (1969). How much can we boost IQ and scholastic achievement? *Harvard Educational Review, 39,* 1–23.

Jensen, P. S. (1999). Fact versus fancy concerning the multimodal treatment study for attention-deficit hyperactivity disorder. *Canadian Journal of Psychiatry, 44,* 975–980.

Jensen, P. S. (2000). Commentary. *Journal of the American Academy of Child and Adolescent Psychiatry, 39,* 984–987.

Jensen, P. S. (Ed.). (2001). Special Section: ADHD comorbidity and treatment outcomes in the MTA. *Journal of the American Academy of Child and Adolescent Psychiatry, 40,* 134–179.

Jensen, P. S., Hoagwood, K., & Petti, T. (1996). Outcomes of mental health care for children and adolescents: II. Literature review and application of a comprehensive model. *Journal of the American Academy of Child and Adolescent Psychiatry, 35,* 1064–1077.

Jensen, P. S., Kettle, L., Roper, R. S., Sloan, M. T., Dulcan, M. K., Hoven, C., et al. (1999). Are stimulants overprescribed? Treatment of ADHD in four U.S. communities. *Journal of the American Academy of Child and Adolescent Psychiatry, 38,* 797–804.

Jensen, P. S., Martin, B. A., & Cantwell, D. P. (1997). Comorbidity in ADHD: Implications for research, practice, and DSM-IV. *Journal of the American Academy of Child and Adolescent Psychiatry, 36,* 1065–1079.

Johnson, C. R., & Slomka, G. (2000). Learning, motor, and communication disorders. In M. Hersen, R. T. Ammerman et al. (Eds.), *Advanced abnormal child psychology* (2nd ed., pp. 371–385). Mahwah, NJ: Erlbaum.

Johnson, E. O., Chilcoat, H. D., & Breslau, N. (2000). Trouble sleeping and anxiety/depression in childhood. *Psychiatry Research, 94,* 93–102.

Johnson, J. G., Bromley, E., Bornstein, R. F., & Sneed, J. R. (in press). Adolescent personality disorders. In D. A. Wolfe & E. J. Mash (Eds.), *Behavioral and emotional disorders in adolescents: Nature, assessment, and treatment.* New York: Guilford Press.

Johnson, J. G., Cohen, P., Smailes, E. M., Kasen, S., & Brook, J. S. (2002). Television viewing and aggressive behaviour during adolescence and adulthood. *Science, 295,* 2468–2471.

Johnson, J. G., Smailes, E. M., Cohen, P., Brown, J., & Bernstein, D. P. (2000). Associations between four types of childhood neglect and personality disorder symptoms during adolescence and early adulthood: Findings of a community-based longitudinal study. *Journal of Personality Disorders, 14,* 171–187.

Johnson, S. B. (1998). Juvenile diabetes. In T. H. Ollendick & M. Hersen (Eds.), *Handbook of child psychopathology* (3rd ed., pp. 417–434). New York: Plenum Press.

Johnson, W. G., Tsoh, J. Y., & Vanrado, P. J. (1996). Eating disorders: Efficacy of pharmacological and psychological interventions. *Clinical Psychology Review, 16,* 457–478.

Johnston, C. (1996). Addressing parent cognitions in interventions with families of disruptive children. In K. S. Dobson & K. D. Craig (Eds.), *Advances in cognitive-behavioral therapy* (pp. 193–209). Thousand Oaks, CA: Sage.

Johnston, C., & Freeman, W. (1998). Parent training interventions for sibling conflict. In J. Briesmeister & C. E. Schaefer (Eds.), *Handbook of parent training: Parents as co-therapists for children's behavior problems* (2nd ed., pp. 153–176). New York: Wiley.

Johnston, C., & Leung, D. W. (2001). Effects of medication, behavioral, and combined treatments on parents' and children's attributions for the behavior of children with attention-deficit hyperactivity disorder. *Journal of Consulting and Clinical Psychology, 69,* 67–76.

Johnston, C., & Mash, E. J. (2001). Families of children with attention-deficit hyperactivity disorder: A review and recommendations for future research. *Clinical Child and Family Psychology Review, 4,* 183–207.

Johnston, L. D., O'Malley, P. M., & Bachman, J. (2002). *Monitoring the Future national results on adolescent drug use: Overview of key findings, 2001* (NIH Publication No. 02–5105). Bethesda, MD: National Institute on Drug Abuse.

Johnstone, S. J., Barry, R. J., & Dimoska, A. (2003). Event-related slow-wave activity in two subtypes of attention-deficit/hyperactivity disorder. *Clinical Neurophysiology, 114,* 504–514.

Joiner, T. E., Jr. (1999). A test of interpersonal theory of depression in youth psychiatric inpatients. *Journal of Abnormal Child Psychology, 27,* 77–85.

Joiner, T. E., Heatherton, T. F., Rudd, M. D., & Schmidt, N. B. (1997). Perfectionism, perceived weight status, and bulimic symptoms: Two studies testing a diathesis-stress model. *Journal of Abnormal Psychology, 106,* 145–153.

Joiner, T., Katz, J., & Heatherton, T. (2001). Personality features differentiate late adolescent females and males with chronic bulimic symptoms. *International Journal of Eating Disorders, 27,* 191–197.

Joiner, T. E., Katz, J., & Lew, A. S. (1997). Self-verification and depression among youth psychiatric inpatients. *Journal of Abnormal Psychology, 106,* 608–618.

Jolliffe, T., & Baron-Cohen, S. (1997). Are people with autism and Asperger syndrome faster than normal on the Embedded Figures Test? *Journal of Child Psychology and Psychiatry, 38,* 527–534.

Jones, L. M. & Finkelhor, D. (2003). Putting together evidence on declining trends in sexual abuse: A complex puzzle. *Child Abuse & Neglect, 27,* 133–135.

Jones, M. C. (1924b). The elimination of children's fears. *Journal of Experimental Psychology, 1,* 383–390.

Jordan, A. E., & Cole, D. A. (1996). Relation of depressive symptoms to the structure of self-knowledge in childhood. *Journal of Abnormal Psychology, 105,* 530–540.

Joseph, R. M., & Tanaka, J. (2003). Holistic and part-based face recognition in children with autism. *Journal of Child Psychology and Psychiatry, 44,* 529–542.

Kadesjo, B., & Gillberg, C. (2001). The comorbidity of ADHD in the general population of Swedish school-age children. *Journal of Child Psychology and Psychiatry, 42,* 487–492.

Kagan, J. (1997). Temperament and the reactions to unfamiliarity. *Child Development, 68,* 139–143.

Kagan, J. (2003). Biology, context, and developmental inquiry. *Annual Review of Psychology, 54,* 1–23.

Kagan, J., & Snidman, N. (1999). Early child predictors of adult anxiety disorders. *Biological Psychiatry, 46,* 1536–1541.

Kagan, J., Snidman, N., & Arcus, D. M. (1992). Initial reactions to unfamiliarity. *Current Directions in Psychological Science, 1,* 171–174.

Kagan, J., Snidman, N., Zentner, M., & Peterson, E. (1999). Infant temperament and anxious symptoms in school age children. *Development and Psychopathology, 11,* 209–224.

Kahn, C. A., Kelly, P. C., & Walker, W. O. (1995). Lead screening in children with attention deficit hyperactivity disorder and developmental delay. *Clinical Pediatrics, 34,* 498–501.

Kallman, F. J., & Roth, B. (1956). Genetic aspects of preadolescent schizophrenia. *American Journal of Psychiatry, 112,* 599–606.

Kaminski, K. M., & Garber, J. (2002). Depressive spectrum disorders in adolescents: Episode duration and predictors of time to recovery. *Journal of the American Academy of Child and Adolescent Psychiatry, 41,* 410–418.

Kamphaus, R. W., & Frick, P. J. (1996). *Clinical assessment of child and adolescent personality and behavior.* Needham Heights, MA: Allyn & Bacon.

Kanaya, T., Scullin, M. H., & Ceci, S. J. (2003). The Flynn effect and U.S. policies: The impact of rising IQ scores on American society via mental retardation diagnoses. *American Psychologist, 58,* 778–790.

Kanner, L. (1943). Autistic disturbances of affective contact. *Nervous Child, 2,* 217–250.

Kanner, L. (1944). Early infantile autism. *Journal of Pediatrics, 25,* 211–217.

Kanner, L. (1962). Emotionally disturbed children: A historical review. *Child Development, 33,* 97–102.

Kanner, L. (1964). *A history of the care and study of the mentally retarded.* Springfield, IL: Charles C. Thomas.

Kaplan, R. M. (2000). Two pathways to prevention. *American Psychologist, 55,* 382–396.

Kaplan, S. J., Pelcovitz, D., & Labruna, V. (1999). Child and adolescent abuse and neglect research: A review of the past 10 years. Part I: Physical and emotional abuse and neglect. *Journal of the American Academy of Child and Adolescent Psychiatry, 38,* 1214–1222.

Kaplan, S. J., Pelcovitz, D., Salzinger, S., Mandel, F., & Weiner, M. (1997). Adolescent physical abuse and suicide attempts. *Journal of the American Academy of Child and Adolescent Psychiatry, 36,* 799–808.

Kasen, S., Cohen, P., Brook, J. S., & Hartmark, C. (1996). A multiple-risk interaction model: Effects of temperament and divorce on psychiatric disorders in children. *Journal of Abnormal Child Psychology, 24,* 121–150.

Kashani, J. H., Allan, W. D., Dahlmeier, J. M., Rezvani, M., & Reid, J. C. (1995). An examination of family functioning utilizing the circumplex model in psychiatrically hospitalized children with depression. *Journal of Affective Disorders, 35,* 65–73.

Kaslow, N. J., Adamson, L. B., & Collins, M. H. (2000). A developmental psychopathology perspective on the cognitive components of child and adolescent depression. In A. J. Sameroff, M. Lewis, & S. M. Miller (Eds.), *Handbook of developmental psychopathology* (2nd ed., pp. 491–510). New York: Kluwer/Plenum.

Kaslow, N. J., Brown, R. T., & Mee, L. L. (1994). Cognitive and behavioral correlates of childhood depression: A developmental perspective. In W. M. Reynolds & H. F. Johnston (Eds.), *Handbook of depression in children and adolescents* (pp. 97–122). New York: Plenum.

Kaslow, N. J., & Thompson, M. P. (1998). Applying the criteria for empirically supported treatments to studies of psychosocial interactions for child and adolescent depression. *Journal of Clinical Child Psychology, 27,* 146–155.

Kataoka, S. H., Zhang, L., & Wells, K. B. (2002). Unmet need for mental health care among U.S. children: Variation by ethnicity and insurance status. *American Journal of Psychiatry, 159,* 1548–1555.

Kater, K., Rohwer, J., & Levine, M. (2000). An elementary school project for developing healthy body image and reducing risk factors for unhealthy and disordered eating. *Eating Disorders: The Journal of Treatment and Prevention, 8,* 3–16.

Katzmarzyk, P.T., & Ardern, C.I. (2004). Overweight and obesity mortality trends in Canada, 1985–2000. *Canadian Journal of Public Health, 95,* 16–20.

Kaufman, A. S., & Kaufman, N. L. (2004). KABC-II: Kaufman Assessment Battery for Children, 2nd Ed. Circle Pines, MN: AGS Publishing.

Kaufman, J. L., & Zigler, E. (1989). The intergenerational transmission of child abuse. In D. Cicchetti & V. Carlson (Eds.), *Child maltreatment: Theory and research on the causes and consequences of child abuse and neglect* (pp. 129–150). New York: Cambridge University Press.

Kaufman, J., Martin, A., King, R. A., & Charney, D. (2001). Are child-, adolescent-, and adult-onset depression one and the same disorder? *Biological Psychiatry, 49,* 980–1001.

Kavale, K. A., & Forness, S. R. (1983). Hyperactivity and diet treatment: A meta-analysis of the Feingold hypothesis. *Journal of Learning Disabilities, 16,* 324–330.

Kavale, K. A., & Forness, S. R. (1996). Social skill deficits and learning disabilities: A meta-analysis. *Journal of Learning Disabilities, 29(3),* 226–237.

Kavale, K. A., & Forness, S. R. (2000). History, rhetoric, and reality: Analysis of the inclusion debate. *Remedial and Special Education, 21,* 279–296.

Kawahima, H., Mori, T., Kashiwagi, Y., Takekuma, K., Hoshika, A., & Wakefield, A. (2000). Detection and sequencing of measles virus from peripheral mononuclear cells from patients with inflammatory bowel disease and autism. *Digestive Diseases and Sciences, 45,* 723–729.

Kaye, W. H., Lilenfeld, L. R., Berrettini, W. H., Strober, M., Devlin, B., Klump, K. L., Goldman, D., Bulik, C. M., Halmi, K. A., Fichter, M. M., Kaplan,

A., Woodside, D. B., Treasure, J., Plotnicov, K. H., Pollice, C., Rao, R., & McConaha, C. W. (2000). A search for susceptibility loci for anorexia nervosa: Methods and sample description. *Biological Psychiatry, 47,* 794–803.

Kazak, A. E., Barakat, L. P., Meeske, K., Christakis, D., Meadows, D., Casey, R., et al. (1997). Posttraumatic stress, family functioning, and social support in survivors of childhood leukemia and their mothers and fathers. *Journal of Consulting and Clinical Psychology, 65,* 120–129.

Kazdin, A. E. (1982). *Single-case research designs: Methods for clinical and applied settings.* New York: Oxford University Press.

Kazdin, A. E. (1992). Overt and covert antisocial behavior: Child and family characteristics among psychiatric inpatient children. *Journal of Child and Family Studies, 1,* 3–20.

Kazdin, A. E. (1995). *Conduct disorders in childhood and adolescence (2nd ed.).* Thousand Oaks, CA: Sage.

Kazdin, A. E. (1996a). Combined and multimodal treatments in child and adolescent psychotherapy: Issues, challenges, and research directions. *Clinical Psychology: Science and Practice, 3,* 69–100.

Kazdin, A. E. (1996c). Problem solving and parent management training in treating aggressive and antisocial behavior. In E. D. Hibbs & P. S. Jensen (Eds.), *Psychosocial treatments for child and adolescent disorders: Empirically based strategies for clinical practice* (pp. 377–408). Washington, DC: American Psychological Association.

Kazdin, A. E. (1997a). A model for developing effective treatments: Progression and interplay of theory, research, and practice. *Journal of Clinical Child Psychology, 26,* 114–129.

Kazdin, A. E. (1997b). Parent management training: Evidence, outcomes, and issues. *Journal of the American Academy of Child and Adolescent Psychiatry, 36,* 1349–1365.

Kazdin, A. E. (1998). *Research design in clinical psychology (3rd ed.).* Needham Heights, MA: Allyn & Bacon.

Kazdin, A. E. (2000). *Psychotherapy for children and adolescents: Directions for research and practice.* New York: Oxford University Press.

Kazdin, A. E. (2003a). Problem-solving skills training and parent management training for conduct disorder. In A. E. Kazdin & J. R. Weisz (Eds.), *Evidence-based psychotherapies for children and adolescents* (pp. 241–262). New York: Guilford Press.

Kazdin, A. E. (2003b). Psychotherapy for children and adolescents. *Annual Review of Psychology, 54,* 253–276.

Kazdin, A. E., French, N. H., Unis, A. S., Esveldt-Dawson, K., & Sherick, R. B. (1983). Hopelessness, depression, and suicidal intent among psychiatrically disturbed inpatient children. *Journal of Consulting and Clinical Psychology, 51,* 504–510.

Kazdin, A. E., & Johnson, B. (1994a). Advances in psychotherapy for children and adolescents: Interrelations of adjustment, development, and intervention. *Journal of School Psychology, 32,* 217–246.

Kazdin, A. E., & Kagan, J. (1994b). Models of dysfunction in developmental psychopathology. *Clinical Psychology: Science and Practice, 1,* 35–52.

Kazdin, A. E., & Marciano, P. L. (1998). Child and adolescent depression. In E. J. Mash & R. A. Barkley (Eds.), *Treatment of childhood disorders* (2nd ed., pp. 211–248). New York: Guilford Press.

Kazdin, A. E., Siegel, T. C., & Bass, D. (1990). Drawing upon clinical practice to inform research on child and adolescent psychotherapy. *Professional Psychology: Research and Practice, 21,* 189–190.

Kazdin, A. E., & Wassell, G. (1999). Barriers to treatment participation and therapeutic change among children referred for conduct disorder. *Journal of Clinical Child Psychology, 28,* 160–172.

Kazdin, A. E., & Wassell, G. (2000). Therapeutic changes in children, parents, and families resulting from treatment of children with conduct problems. *Journal of the American Academy of Child and Adolescent Psychiatry, 39,* 414–420.

Kazdin, A. E., & Weisz, J. R. (Eds.) (2003). *Evidence-based psychotherapies for children and adolescents.* New York: Guilford Press, xix, 475.

Kazdin, A. E., & Whitley, M. K. (2003). Treatment of parental stress to enhance therapeutic change among children referred for aggressive and antisocial behavior. *Journal of Consulting and Clinical Psychology, 71,* 504–515.

Kearney, C. A. (1993). Depression and school refusal behavior: A review with comments on classification and treatment. *Journal of School Psychology, 31,* 267–279.

Kearney, C. A. (1995). School refusal behavior. In A. R. Eisen, C. A. Kearney, & C. A. Schaefer, (Eds.), *Clinical handbook of anxiety disorders in children and adolescents* (pp. 19–52). Northvale, NJ: Jason Aronson.

Kearney, C. A. (2001). *School refusal behavior in youth: A functional approach to assessment and treatment.* Washington, DC: American Psychological Association.

Kearney, C. A., & Albano, A. M. (2004). The functional profiles of school refusal behavior: Diagnostic aspects. *Behavior Modification, 28,* 147–161.

Kearney, C. A., Albano, A. M., Eisen, A. R., Allan, W. D., & Barlow, D. A. (1997). The phenomenology of panic disorder in youngsters: An empirical study of a clinical sample. *Journal of Anxiety Disorders, 11,* 49–62.

Kearney, C. A., & Allan, W. D. (1995). Panic disorder with or without agora-

phobia. In A. R. Eisen, C. A. Kearney, & C. A. Schaefer (Eds.), *Clinical handbook of anxiety disorders in children and adolescents* (pp. 251–281). Northvale, NJ: Jason Aronson.

Kearney, C. A., & Silverman, W. K. (1996). The evolution and reconciliation of taxonomic strategies for school refusal behavior. *Clinical Psychology: Science and Practice, 3,* 339–354.

Kearney, C. A., & Silverman, W. K. (1998). A critical review of pharmacotherapy for youth with anxiety disorders: Things are not as they seem. *Journal of Anxiety Disorders, 12,* 83–102.

Keel, P. K., & Klump, K. L. (2003). Are eating disorders culture-bound syndromes? Implications for conceptualizing their etiology. *Psychological Bulletin, 129,* 747–769.

Keen, A. G., & Lovegrove, W. J. (2000). Transient deficit hypothesis and dyslexia: Examination of whole-parts relationship, retinal sensitivity, and spatial and temporal frequencies. *Vision Research, 40,* 705–715.

Keenan, K. (2000). Emotion dysregulation as a risk factor for child psychopathology. *Clinical Psychology: Science and Practice, 7,* 418–434.

Keenan, K., Loeber, R., & Green, S. (1999). Conduct disorder in girls: A review of the literature. *Clinical Child and Family Psychology Review, 2,* 3–19.

Keenan, K., & Shaw, D. (1997). Developmental and social influences on young girls' early problem behavior. *Psychological Bulletin, 121,* 95–113.

Keenan, K., & Wakschlag, L. S. (2000). More than the terrible twos: The nature and severity of behavior problems in clinic-referred preschool children. *Journal of Abnormal Child Psychology, 28,* 33–46.

Keller, M., Lavori, P., Wunder, J., Beardslee, W., Schwartz, C., & Roth, J. (1992). Chronic course of anxiety disorders in children and adolescents. *Journal of the American Academy of Child and Adolescent Psychiatry, 31,* 595–599.

Kellner, R., Houghton, S., & Douglas, G. (2003). Peer-related personal experiences of children with attention-deficit/hyperactivity disorder with and without comorbid learning disabilities. *International Journal of Disability, Development & Education, 50,* 119–136.

Keltner, D., Moffitt, T. E., & Stouthamer-Loeber, M. (1995). Facial expressions of emotion and psychopathology in adolescent boys. *Journal of Abnormal Psychology, 104,* 644–652.

Kemp, C. & Carter, M. (2002). The social skills and social status of mainstreamed students with intellectual disabilities. *Educational Psychology, 22,* 391–411.

Kempe, C. H., Silverman, F. N., Steele, B. F., Droegemueller, W., & Silver, H. K. (1962). The battered child syndrome. *Journal of the American Medical Association, 181,* 17–24.

Kempe Children's Center (2002). *World Perspectives on Child Abuse: The Fifth*

International Resource Book. Carol Stream, IL: International Society for the Prevention of Child Abuse.

Kendall, J. (1999). Sibling accounts of attention deficit hyperactivity disorder (ADHD). *Family Process, 38,* 117–136.

Kendall, P. C. (1992). Childhood coping: Avoiding a lifetime of anxiety. *Behaviour Change, 9,* 229–237.

Kendall, P. C. (2000). Guiding theory for therapy with children and adolescents. In P. C. Kendall (Ed.), *Child and adolescent therapy: Cognitive-behavioral procedures* (2nd ed., pp. 3–27). New York: Guilford Press.

Kendall, P. C. (Ed.). (2000). *Child and adolescent therapy: Cognitive-behavioral procedures (2nd ed.).* New York: Guilford Press.

Kendall, P. C., Aschenbrand, S. G., & Hudson, S. G. (2003). Child-focused treatment of anxiety. In A. E. Kazdin & J. R. Weisz (Eds.), *Evidence-based psychotherapies for children and adolescents* (pp. 81–100). New York: Guilford Press.

Kendall, P. C., & Brady, E. (1995). Comorbidity in the anxiety disorders of childhood. In K. Craig & K. Dobson (Eds.), *Anxiety and depression in adults and children.* Newbury Park, CA: Sage.

Kendall, P. C., Chu, B. C., Pimentel, S. S., Choudhury, M. (2000). Treating anxiety disorders in youth. In P. C. Kendall (Ed.), *Child and adolescent therapy: Cognitive-behavioral procedures* (2nd ed., pp. 235–287). New York: Guilford Press.

Kendall, P. C., & Flannery-Schroeder, E. C. (1998). Methodological issues in treatment research for anxiety disorders in youth. *Journal of Abnormal Child Psychology, 26,* 27–38.

Kendall, P. C., Panichelli-Mindel, S. M., Sugarman, A., & Callahan, S. A. (1997). Exposure to child anxiety: Theory, research, and practice. *Clinical Psychology: Science and Practice, 4,* 29–39.

Kendall-Tackett, K. A., Williams, L. M., & Finkelhor, D. (1993). The impact of sexual abuse on children: A review and synthesis of recent empirical studies. *Psychological Bulletin, 113,* 164–180.

Kendler, K. S., Bulik, C. M., Silberg, J., Hettema, J. M., Myers, J., & Prescott, C. A. (2000). Childhood sexual abuse and adult psychiatric and substance use disorders in women: An epidemiological and cotwin control analysis. *Archives of General Psychiatry, 57,* 953–959.

Kennedy, P., Terdal, L., & Fusetti, L. (1993). *The hyperactive child book.* New York: St. Martin's Press.

Kent, L., & Craddock, N. (2003). Is there a relationship between attention deficit hyperactivity disorder and bipolar disorder? *Journal of Affective Disorders, 73,* 211–221.

Kibby, M. Y., Tyc, V. L., & Mulhern, R. K. (1998). Effectiveness of psychological intervention for children and adolescents with chronic medical illness: A

meta-analysis. *Clinical Psychology Review, 18,* 103–117.

Killen, J. D., Taylor, C. B., Hayward, C., Haydel, K. F., Wilson, D. M., Hammer, L., Kraemer, H., Blair-Greiner, A., & Strachowski, D. (1996). Weight concerns influence the development of eating disorders: A 4-year prospective study. *Journal of Consulting and Clinical Psychology, 64,* 936–940.

Kilpatrick, D. G., Acierno, R., Saunders, B., Resnick, H. S., Best, C. L., & Schnurr, P. P. (2000). Risk factors for adolescent substance abuse and dependence: Data from a national sample. *Journal of Consulting and Clinical Psychology, 68,* 19–30.

Kilpatrick, D. G., Ruggiero, K. J., Acierno, R., Saunders, B. E., Resnick, H. S., & Best, C. L. (2003). Violence and risk of PTSD, major depression, substance abuse/dependence, and comorbidity: Results from the National Survey of Adolescents. *Journal of Consulting and Clinical Psychology, 71,* 692–700.

Kim, E. Y., & Miklowitz, D. J. (2002). Childhood mania, attention deficit hyperactivity disorder and conduct disorder: A critical review of diagnostic dilemmas. *Bipolar Disorder, 4,* 215–225.

Kim, J. A., Szatmari, P., Bryson, S. E., Streiner, D. L., & Wilson, F. J. (2000). The prevalence of anxiety and mood problems among children with autism and Asperger syndrome. *Autism, 4,* 117–132.

Kim, W. J., Kim, L. I., & Rue, D. S. (1997). Korean American children. In G. Johnson-Powell, J. Yamamoto (Ed.) et al, *Transcultural child development: psychological assessment and treatment,* 183–207, New York: John Wiley & Sons, Inc, xix, 378.

King, B. H., Hodapp, R. M., & Dykens, E. M. (in press). Mental retardation. In H.I. Kaplan & B.J. Sadock (Eds.), *Comprehensive textbook of psychiatry (8th ed.).* Baltimore: Williams & Wilkins.

King, B. H., State, M. W., Shah, B., Davanzo, P., & Dykens, E. (1997). Mental retardation: A review of the past 10 years: I. *Journal of the American Academy of Child and Adolescent Psychiatry, 36,* 1656–1663.

King, N. J., Mietz, A., Tinney, L., & Ollendick, T. H. (1995). Psychopathology and cognition in adolescents experiencing severe test anxiety. *Journal of Clinical Child Psychology, 24,* 49–54.

King, N. J., Ollendick, T. H., & Gullone, E. (1991a). Negative affectivity in children and adolescents: Relations between anxiety and depression. *Clinical Psychology Review, 11,* 441–459.

King, N. J., Ollendick, T. H., & Gullone, E. (1991b). Test anxiety in children and adolescents. *Australian Psychologist, 26,* 25–32.

King, N. J., Ollendick, T. H., & Mattis, S. G. (1994). Panic in children and adolescents: Normative and clinical studies. *Australian Psychologist, 29,* 89–93.

King, N., Tonge, B. J., Heyne, D., & Ollendick, T. H. (2000). Research on the

cognitive-behavioral treatment of school refusal: A review and recommendations. *Clinical Psychology Review, 20,* 495–507.

King, R. A., Leonard, H., & March, J. (1998). Practice parameters for the assessment and treatment of children and adolescents with obsessive-compulsive disorder. *Journal of the American Academy of Child and Adolescent Psychiatry, 37(10, Suppl.),* 27S–45S.

Kirk, S. A., & Hutchins, H. (1994, June 20). Is bad writing a mental disorder? *New York Times,* pp. A11, A17.

Kiroi, V. N., Ermakov, P. N., Belova, E. I., & Samoilina, T. G. (2002). Spectral characterization of EEG of young school aged children with learning disorders. *Fiziologiia Cheloveka, 28,* 20–30.

Kjelsås, E., Bjørnstrøm, C., & Götestan, K.G. (2004). Prevalence of eating disorders in female and male adolescents (14–15 years). *Eating Behaviors, 5,* 13–25.

Klein, D. N., Lewinsohn, P. M., & Seeley, J. R. (1997). Psychosocial characteristics of adolescents with a past history of dysthymic disorder: Comparison with adolescents with past histories of major depressive and non-affective disorders, and never mentally ill controls. *Journal of Affective Disorders, 42,* 127–135.

Klein, D. N., Lewinsohn, P. M., Rohde, P., Seeley, J. R., & Durbin, C. E. (2002). Clinical features of major depressive disorder in adolescents and their relatives: Impact on familial aggregation, implications for phenotype definition and specificity of transmission. *Journal of Abnormal Psychology, 111,* 98–106.

Klimes-Dougan, B., Free, K., Ronsaville, D., Stilwell, J., Welsh, J., & Radke-Yarrow, M. (1999). Suicidal ideation and attempts: A longitudinal investigation of children of depressed and well mothers. *Journal of the American Academy of Child and Adolescent Psychiatry, 38,* 651–659.

Klin, A. (1991). Young autistic children's listening preferences in regard to speech: A possible characterization of the symptom of social withdrawal. *Journal of Autism and Developmental Disorders, 12,* 29–42.

Klin, A., Jones, S., Schultz, R., Volkmar, F., & Cohen, D. (2002). Defining and quantifying the social phenotype in autism. *American Journal of Psychiatry, 159,* 895–908.

Klin, A., Volkmar, F. R., & Sparrow, S. S. (Eds.). (2000). *Asperger syndrome.* New York: Guilford Press.

Klinger, L. G., Dawson, G., & Renner, P. (2003). Autistic disorder. In E. J. Mash & R. A. Barkley (Eds.), *Child psychopathology* (2nd ed., pp. 409–454). New York: Guilford Press.

Klorman, R., Cicchetti, D., Thatcher, J. E., & Ison, J. R. (2003). Acoustic startle in maltreated children. *Journal of Abnormal Child Psychology, 31,* 359–370.

Kluger, J., & Song, S. (2002). Young and bipolar. *Time*, August 19, 2002, pp. 38–47, 51.

Kluger, J. (2003). Medicating young minds. *Time Canada*, January 14, 2004, pp. 38–46.

Klump, K., McGue, M., & Iacono, W. (2000). Age differences in genetic and environmental influences on eating attitudes and behaviors in preadolescent and adolescent female twins. *Journal of Abnormal Psychology, 109,* 239–251.

Kochanska, G., De Vet, K., Goldman, M., Murray, K., & Putnam, S. P. (1994). Maternal reports of conscience development and temperament in young chidren. *Child Development, 65, 852–868.*

Kochanska, G., Murray, K., & Coy, K. C. (1997). Inhibitory control as a contributor to conscience in childhood: From toddler to early school age. *Child Development, 68, 263–277.*

Koegel, L. K., & Koegel, R. L. (1996). The child with autism as an active communicative partner: Child-initiated strategies for improving communication and reducing behavior problems. In E. D. Hibbs & P. S. Jensen (Eds.), *Psychosocial treatments for child and adolescent disorders: Empirically based strategies for clinical practice* (pp. 553–572). Washington, DC: American Psychological Association.

Koenig, A. L., Cicchetti, D., & Rogosch, F. A. (2004). Moral development: The association between maltreatment and young children's prosocial behaviors and moral transgressions. *Social Development, 13,* 97–106.

Koenig, K., Rubin, E., Klin, A., & Volkmar, F. R. (2000). Autism and the pervasive developmental disorders. In C. H. Zeanah, Jr. (Ed.), *Handbook of infant mental health* (2nd ed., pp. 298–310). New York: Guilford Press.

Koenig, K., & Tsatsanis, K. D. (in press). Pervasive developmental disorders in girls. In D. Bell, S. L. Foster, & E. J. Mash (Eds.), *Handbook of behavioral and emotional problems in girls.* New York: Kluwer.

Koenig, L. J., Doll, L. S., O'Leary, A., & Pequegnat, W. (2004). *From child sexual abuse to adult sexual risk: Trauma, revictimization, and intervention.* Washington, DC: American Psychological Association.

Kokko, K., & Pulkkinen, L. (2000). Aggression in childhood and long-term unemployment in adulthood: A cycle of maladaptation and some protective factors. *Developmental Psychology, 36,* 463–472.

Kolb, B., Gibb, R., & Robinson, T. E. (2003). Brain plasticity and behavior. *Current Directions in Psychological Science, 12,* 1–4.

Kolko, D. J. (1987). Depression. In M. Hersen & V. B. Van Hasselt (Eds.), *Behavior therapy with children and adolescents: A clinical approach* (pp. 137–182). New York: Wiley-Interscience.

Kolko, D. J. (2002). Child physical abuse. In J.E.B. Myers, L. Berliner, J. Briere, C. T. Hendrix, C. Jenny, & T. A. Reid (Eds.), *The APSAC handbook on child maltreatment* (pp. 21–54). Thousand Oaks, CA: Sage

Kolko, D. J., Brent, D. A., Baugher, M., Bridge, J., & Birmaher, B. (2000). Cognitive and family therapies for adolescent depression: Treatment specificity, mediation, and moderation. *Journal of Consulting and Clinical Psychology, 68,* 603–614.

Koplowicz, S., & Barkley, R. A. (1995). *Sense of time in children with attention deficit hyperactivity disorder and normal children.* Unpublished manuscript, University of Massachusetts Medical Center, Worcester, MA.

Kopp, C. B. (1992). Emotional distress and control in young children. In N. Eisenberg & R. A. Fabes (Eds.), *Emotion and its regulation in early development* (pp. 41–56). San Francisco: Jossey-Bass.

Korbin, J. E. (2002). Culture and child maltreatment: Cultural competence and beyond. *Child Abuse & Neglect, 26,* 637–644.

Korbin, J. E. (2003). Neighborhood and community connectedness in child maltreatment research. *Child Abuse & Neglect, 27,* 137–140.

Korkman, M., Kettunen, S., & Autti-Raemoe, I. (2003). Neurocognitive impairment in early adolescence following prenatal alcohol exposure of varying duration. *Child Neuropsychology, 9,* 117–128.

Kortlander, E., Kendall, P. C., & Panichelli-Mindel, S. M. (1997). Maternal expectations and attributions about coping in anxious children. *Journal of Anxiety Disorders, 11,* 297–315.

Kotler, L. A., Cohen, P., Davies, M., Pine, D. S., & Walsh, B. T. (2001). Longitudinal relationships between childhood, adolescent, and adult eating disorders. *Journal of the American Academy of Child & Adolescent Psychiatry, 40*(12), 1434–1440.

Kotimaa, A. J., Moilanen, I., Taanila, A., Ebeling, H., Smalley, S. L., McGough, J. J., et al. (2003). Maternal smoking and hyperactivity in 8-year-old children. *Journal of the American Academy of Child and Adolescent Psychiatry, 42,* 826–833.

Kovacs, M. (1987). Diagnosis of depressive disorders in children: An interim appraisal of the pertinent DSM-III categories. In G. L. Tischler (Ed.), *Diagnosis and classification in psychiatry: A critical appraisal of DSM-III* (pp. 369–383). New York: Cambridge University Press.

Kovacs, M. (1996). Presentation and course of major depressive disorder during childhood and later years of the life span. *Journal of the American Academy of Child and Adolescent Psychiatry, 35,* 705–715.

Kovacs, M. (1997). Depressive disorders in childhood: An impressionistic landscape. *Journal of Child Psychology and Psychiatry, 38,* 287–298.

Kovacs, M. (2001). Gender and the course of major depressive disorder through adolescence in clinically referred youngsters. *Journal of the American Academy of Child and Adolescent Psychiatry, 40,* 1079–1085.

Kovacs, M., Akiskal, H. S., Gatsonis, C., & Parrone, P. L. (1994). Childhood-onset dysthymic disorder: Clinical features and prospective naturalistic outcome. *Archives of General Psychiatry, 51,* 365–374.

Kovacs, M., & Devlin, B. (1998). Internalizing disorders in childhood. *Journal of Child Psychology and Psychiatry, 39,* 47–63.

Kovacs, M., & Goldston, D. (1991). Cognitive and social cognitive development of depressed children and adolescents. *Journal of the American Academy of Child and Adolescent Psychiatry, 30,* 388–392.

Kovacs, M., Goldston, D., & Gatsonis, C. (1993). Suicidal behaviors and childhood-onset depressive disorders: A longitudinal investigation. *Journal of the American Academy of Child and Adolescent Psychiatry, 32,* 8–20.

Kovacs, M., Iyengar, S., Goldston, D., Stewart, J., Obrosky, D. S., & Marsh, J. (1990). Psychological functioning of children with insulin-dependent diabetes mellitus: A longitudinal study. *Journal of Pediatric Psychology, 15,* 619–632.

Kovacs, M., Obrosky, D. S., Gatsonis, C., & Richards, C. (1997). First-episode major depressive and dysthymic disorder in childhood: Clinical and socio-demographic factors in recovery. *Journal of the American Academy of Child and Adolescent Psychiatry, 36,* 777–784.

Krain, A. L., & Kendall, P. C. (2000). The role of parental emotional distress in parent report of child anxiety. *Journal of Clinical Child Psychology, 29,* 328–335.

Krasner, L. (1991). History of behavior modification. In A. S. Bellack, M. Hersen, & A. E. Kazdin (Eds.), *International handbook of behavior modification and therapy* (2nd ed., pp. 3–25). New York: Plenum.

Kratzer, L., & Hodgins, S. (1997). Adult outcomes of child conduct problems: A cohort study. *Journal of Abnormal Child Psychology, 25,* 65–81.

Krauss, M. W. (1993). Child-related and parenting stress: Similarities and differences between mothers and fathers of children with disabilities. *American Journal on Mental Retardation, 97,* 393–404.

Kroll, L., Harrington, R., Jayson, D., Fraser, J., & Gowers, S. (1996). Pilot study of continuation cognitive-behavioral therapy for major depression in adolescent psychiatric patients. *Journal of the American Academy of Child and Adolescent Psychiatry, 35,* 1156–1161.

Krug, E. G, Dahlberg, L. L., Mercy, J. A., Zwi, A. B., & Lozano, R. (Eds.) (2002). *World report on violence and health.*

Geneva: World Health Organization, 2002.

Kuhl, P. (1995, May). *Speech perception, memory, and cognition: Implications for automatic speech recognition systems.* Paper presented at the annual meeting of the American Speech Association, Washington, DC.

Kuhlmann, F. (1940). One hundred years of special care and training. *American Journal of Mental Deficiency, 45,* 8–24.

Kumpfer, K. L., Alvarado, R., Smith, P., & Bellamy, N. (2002). Cultural sensitivity and adaptation in family-based prevention interventions. *Prevention Science, 3,* 241–246.

Kuntsi, J., & Stevenson, J. (2000). Hyperactivity in children: A focus on genetic research and psychological theories. *Clinical Child and Family Psychology Review, 3,* 1–23.

La Greca, A. M., Bearman, K. J. & Moore, H. (2002). Peer relations of youth with pediatric conditions and health risks: Promoting social support and healthy lifestyles. *Journal of Developmental & Behavioral Pediatrics, 23,* 271–280.

La Greca, A. M., & Lopez, N. (1998). Social anxiety among adolescents: Linkages with peer relations and friendships. *Journal of Abnormal Child Psychology, 26,* 83–94.

La Greca, A. M., Silverman, W. K., Vernberg, E. M., & Prinstein, M. J. (1996). Symptoms of posttraumatic stress in children after Hurricane Andrew: A prospective study. *Journal of Consulting and Clinical Psychology, 64,* 712–723.

La Greca, A., Silverman, W., Vernberg, E., & Roberts, M. C. (Eds.). (2002). *Helping children cope with disasters and terrorism.* Washington, DC: APA Books.

La Greca, A. M., Silverman, W. K., & Wasserstein, S. B. (1998). Children's predisaster functioning as a predictor of posttraumatic stress following Hurricane Andrew. *Journal of Consulting and Clinical Psychology, 66,* 883–892.

La Greca, A. M., Swales, T., Klemp, S., Madigan, S., & Skyler, J. (1995). Adolescents with diabetes: Gender differences in psychosocial functioning and glycemic control. *Children's Health Care, 24,* 61–78.

La Greca, A. M., & Thompson, K. M. (1998). Family and friend support for adolescents with diabetes. *Analise Psicologica, 16,* 101–113.

Labellarte, M. J., Ginsburg, G. S., Walkup, J. T., & Riddle, M. A. (1999). The treatment of anxiety disorders in children and adolescents. *Biological Psychiatry, 46,* 1567–1578.

Labre, M.P. (2002). Adolescent boys and the muscular male body ideal. *Journal of Adolescent Health, 30,* 2002. 233–242.

Lachar, D. (1999). Personality Inventory for Children, Second Edition (PIC-2), Personality Inventory for Youth (PIY), and Student Behavior Survey (SBS). In M. E. Maruish (Ed.), *The use of psychological testing for treatment planning and outcomes assessment* (2nd ed., pp. 399–427). Mahwah, NJ: Erlbaum.

Lacharite, C., Boutet, M., & Proulx, R. (1995). Intellectual disability and psychopathology: Developmental perspective. *Canada's Mental Health, 43,* 2–8.

Laessle, R. G., Wurmser, H., & Pirke, K. M. (2000). Restrained eating and leptin levels in overweight preadolescent girls. *Physiology and Behavior, 70,* 45–47.

LaFreniere, P. J. (1999). *Emotional development.* New York: Wadsworth.

Lahey, B. B., Goodman, S. H., Waldman, I. D., Bird, H., Canino, G., Jensen, P., et al. (1999). Relation of age of onset to type and severity of child and adolescent conduct problems. *Journal of Abnormal Child Psychology, 27,* 247–260.

Lahey, B. B., Hart, E. L., Pliszka, S., Applegate, B., & McBurnett, K. (1993). Neurophysiological correlates of conduct disorder: A rationale and review of current research. *Journal of Clinical Child Psychology, 22,* 141–153.

Lahey, B. B., Loeber, R., Burke, J., & Rathouz, P. J. (2002). Adolescent outcomes of childhood conduct disorder among clinic-referred boys: Predictors of improvement. *Journal of Abnormal Child Psychology, 30,* 333–348.

Lahey, B. B., Loeber, R., Hart, E. L., Frick, P. J., Applegate, B., Zhang, Q., et al. (1995). Four-year longitudinal study of conduct disorder in boys: Patterns and predictors of persistence. *Journal of Abnormal Psychology, 104,* 83–93.

Lahey, B. B., Loeber, R., Quay, H. C., Frick, P. J., & Grimm, S. (1992). Oppositional defiant and conduct disorders: Issues to be resolved for DSM-IV. *Journal of the American Academy of Child and Adolescent Psychiatry, 31,* 539–546.

Lahey, B. B., Miller, T. L., Gordon, R. A., & Riley, A. W. (1999). Developmental epidemiology of the disruptive behavior disorders. In H. C. Quay & A. E. Hogan (Eds.), *Handbook of disruptive behavior disorders* (pp. 23–48). New York: Kluwer Academic/Plenum.

Lahey, B. B., Moffitt, T. E., & Caspi, A. (Eds.). (2003). *Causes of conduct disorder and juvenile delinquency.* New York: Guilford.

Lahey, B. B., Pelham, W. E., Schaughency, E. A., Atkins, M. S., Murphy, H. A., Hynd, G. W., et al. (1988). Dimensions and types of attention deficit disorder with hyperactivity in children: A factor and cluster analytic approach. *Journal of the American Academy of Child and Adolescent Psychiatry, 27,* 330–335.

Lahey, B. B., Piacentini, J. C., McBurnett, K., Stone, P., Hartdagen, S., & Hynd, G. (1988). Psychopathology and antisocial behavior in the parents of children with conduct disorder and hyperactivity. *Journal of the American Academy of Child and Adolescent Psychiatry, 27,* 163–170.

Lahey, B. B., Schwab-Stone, M., Goodman, S. H., Waldman, I. D., Canino, G., Rathouz, P. J., Miller, T. L., Dennis, K. D., Bird, H., & Jensen, P. S. (2000). Age and gender differences in in oppositional behavior and conduct problems: A cross-sectional household study of middle childhood and adolescence. *Journal of Abnormal Psychology, 109,* 488–503.

Lahey, B. B., & Waldman, I. D. (2003). A developmental propensity model of the origins of conduct problems during childhood and adolescence. In B. B. Lahey, T. E. Moffitt, & A. Caspi, (Eds.), *Causes of conduct disorder and juvenile delinquency* (pp. 76–117). New York: Guilford Press.

Lahey, B. B., Waldman, I. D., & McBurnett, K. (1999). The development of antisocial behavior: An integrative causal model. *Journal of Child Psychology & Psychiatry & Allied Disciplines, 40,* 669–682.

Lainhart, J. E., Ozonoff, S., Coon, H., Krasny, L., Dinh, E., Nice, J., & McMahon, W. (2002). Autism, regression, and the broader autism phenotype. *American Journal of Medical Genetics, 113,* 231–237.

Laird, R. D., Jordan, K., Dodge, K. A., Pettit, G. S., & Bates, J. E. (2001). Peer rejection in childhood, involvement with antisocial peers in early adolescence, and the development of externalizing problems. *Development and Psychopathology, 13,* 337–354.

Lake, A., Staiger, P., & Glowinski, H. (2000). Effect of Western culture on women's attitudes to eating and perceptions of body shape. *International Journal of Eating Disorders, 27,* 83–89.

Lambert, N. M., Sandoval, J., & Sassone, D. (1978). Prevalence of hyperactivity in elementary school children as a function of social system definers. *American Journal of Orthopsychiatry, 48,* 446–463.

Landau, S., & Milich, R. (1988). Social communication patterns of attention-deficit-disordered boys. *Journal of Abnormal Child Psychology, 16,* 69–81.

Landau, S., Milich, R., & Diener, M. B. (1998). Peer relations of children with attention-deficit hyperactivity disorder. *Reading and Writing Quarterly: Overcoming Learning Difficulties, 14,* 83–105.

Landesman Ramey, S., & Ramey, C. (1999). Early experience and early intervention for children "at risk" for developmental delay and mental retardation. *Mental Retardation and Developmental Disabilities Research Reviews, 5,* 1–10.

Lang, A. R., Pelham, W. E., Johnston, C., & Gelernter, S. (1989). Levels of adult alcohol consumption induced by interactions with child confederates exhibiting normal versus externalizing behaviors. *Journal of Abnormal Psychology, 98,* 294–299.

Lansford, J. E., Dodge, K. A., Pettit, G. S., Bates, J. E., Crozier, J., & Kaplow, J. (2002). Long-term effects of early child physical maltreatment on psychological, behavioral, and academic problems in adolescence: A 12-year prospective study. *Archives of Pediatrics and Adolescent Medicine, 156,* 824–830.

Lardieri, L. A., Blacher, J., & Swanson, H. L. (2000). Sibling relationships and parent stress in families of children with and without learning disabilities. *Learning Disability Quarterly, 23,* 105–116.

Larson, R. W., Raffaelli, M., Richards, M. H., Ham, M., & Jewell, L. (1990). Ecology of depression in late childhood and early adolescence: A profile of daily states and activities. *Journal of Abnormal Psychology, 99,* 92–102.

Last, C. G. (1988). Separation anxiety. In M. Hersen & C. G. Last (Eds.), *Child behavior therapy casebook* (pp. 11–17). New York: Plenum.

Last, C. G. (1991). Somatic complaints in anxiety disordered children. *Journal of Anxiety Disorders, 5,* 125–138.

Last, C. G., & Perrin, S. (1993). Anxiety disorders in African-American and white children. *Journal of Abnormal Child Psychology, 21,* 153–164.

Last, C. G., Perrin, S., Hersen, M., & Kazdin, A. E. (1992). DSM-III-R anxiety disorders in children: Sociodemographic and clinical characteristics. *Journal of the American Academy of Child and Adolescent Psychiatry, 31,* 1070–1076.

Last, C. G., Perrin, S., Hersen, M., & Kazdin, A. E. (1996). A prospective study of childhood anxiety disorders. *Journal of the American Academy of Child and Adolescent Psychiatry, 35,* 1502–1510.

Last, C. G., & Strauss, C. C. (1989a). Obsessive-compulsive disorder in childhood. *Journal of Anxiety Disorders, 3,* 295–302.

Last, C. G., & Strauss, C. C. (1989b). Panic disorder in children and adolescents. *Journal of Anxiety Disorders, 3,* 87–95.

Last, G., Hansen, C., & Franco, N. (1998). Cognitive-behavioral treatment of school phobia. *Journal of the American Academy of Child and Adolescent Psychiatry, 37,* 404–411.

Laufer, M., Denhoff, E., & Solomons, G. (1957). Hyperkinetic impulse disorder in children's behavior problems. *Psychosomatic Medicine, 19,* 38–49.

Laurent, J., & Ettelson, R. (2001). An examination of the tripartite model of anxiety and depression and its application to youth. *Clinical Child and Family Psychology Review, 4,* 209–230.

Lavigne, J. V., Arend, R., Rosenbaum, D., Smith, A., Weissbluth, M., Binns, H. J., & Christoffel, K. K. (1999). Sleep and behavior problems among preschoolers. *Journal of Developmental and Behavioral Pediatrics, 20,* 164–169.

Lavigne, J. V., & Faier-Routman, J. (1992). Psychological adjustment to pediatric physical disorders: A meta-analytic review. *Journal of Pediatrics, 17,* 133–158.

Lavigne, J. V., & Faier-Routman, J. (1993). Correlates of psychological adjustment to pediatric physical disorders: A meta-

analytic review and comparison with existing models. *Journal of Developmental and Behavioral Pediatrics, 14,* 117–123.

Le Couteur, A., Bailey, A., Goode, S., Pickles, A., Robertson, S., Gottesman, I., & Rutter, M. (1996). A broader phenotype of autism: The clinical spectrum in twins. *Journal of Child Psychology and Psychiatry, 37,* 785–801.

Le Grange, D., Lock, J., & Dymek, M. (2003). Family-based therapy for adolescent with bulimia nervosa. *American Journal of Psychotherapy.*

Leibenluft, E., Charney, D. S., Towbin, K. E., Bhangoo, R. K., & Pine, D. S. (2003). Defining clinical phenotypes of juvenile mania. *American Journal of Psychiatry, 160,* 430–437.

Leibson, C. L., Katusic, S., Barbaresi, W. J., Ransom, J., & O'Brien, P. C. (2001). Use and costs of medical care for children and adolescents with and without attention-deficit/hyperactivity disorder. *JAMA: Journal of the American Medical Association, 285,* 60–66.

Leichner P. (2002). Disordered eating attitudes among Canadian teenagers. *CMAJ, 166,* 707–708.

Leifer, M., Kilbane, T., & Kalick, S. (2004). Vulnerability or resilience to intergenerational sexual abuse: The role of maternal factors. *Child Maltreatment: Journal of the American Professional Society on the Abuse of Children, 9,* 78–91.

Leitenberg, H., & Saltzman, H. (2000). A statewide survey of age at first intercourse for adolescent females and age of their male partners: Relation to other risk behaviors and statutory rape implications. *Archives of Sexual Behavior,* 203–215.

Leland, J. (1995, December 11). Violence, reel to real. *Newsweek,* pp. 46–48.

Lemerise, E. A., & Arsenio, W. F. (2000). An integrated model of emotion processes and cognition in social information processing. *Child Development, 71,* 107–118.

Lendon, C. L., Ashall, F., & Goate, A. M. (1997). Exploring the etiology of Alzheimer's disease using molecular genetics. *Journal of the American Medical Association, 277,* 825–831.

Leonard, H. L., & Dow, S. (1995). Selective mutism. In J. S. March (Ed.), *Anxiety disorders in children and adolescents* (pp. 235–250). New York: Guilford Press.

Leonard, H., Silberstein, J., Falk, R., Houwink-Manville, I., Ellaway, C., Raffaele, L. S., et al. (2001). Occurrence of Rett syndrome in boys. *Journal of Child Neurology, 16,* 333–338.

Lerer, R. J., Lerer, M. P., & Artner, J. (1977). The effects of methylphenidate on the handwriting of children with minimal brain dysfunction. *Journal of Pediatrics, 91,* 127–132.

Lerner, R. M., & Galambos, N. L. (1998). Adolescent development: Challenges and opportunities for research, programs, and policies. *Annual Review of Psychology, 49,* 413–446.

Lesch, K. P., Bengel, D., Heils, A., Sabol, S. Z., Greenberg, B. D., Petri, S., et al. (1996). Association of anxiety-related traits with a polymorphism in the serotonin transporter gene regulatory region. *Science, 274,* 1527–1531.

Lesesne, C. A., Visser, S. N., & White, C. P. (2003). Attention-deficit/hyperactivity disorder in school-age children: Association with maternal mental health and use of health care resources. *Pediatrics, 111,* 1232–1237.

Lesniak-Karpiak, K., Mazzocco, M. M., & Ross, J. L. (2003). Behavioral assessment of social anxiety in females with Turner or fragile X syndrome. *Journal of Autism and Developmental Disorders, 33,* 55–67.

Lesser, S. T. (1972). Psychoanalysis with children. In B. B. Wolman (Ed.), *Manual of child psychopathology* (pp. 847–864). New York: McGraw-Hill.

Leutwyler, K. (1997, January). Depression's double standard. *Scientific American,* 53–54.

Leventhal, T., & Brooks-Gunn, J. (2000). The neighborhoods they live in: The effects of neighborhood residence on child and adolescent outcomes. *Psychological Bulletin, 126,* 309–337.

Leventhal, T., & Brooks-Gunn, J. (2003). Children and youth in neighborhood contexts. *Current Directions in Psychological Science, 12,* 27–31.

Levine, K. (1995, October). Childhood depression. *Parents,* 42–45.

Levine, M., & Levine, A. (1992). *Helping children: A social history.* New York: Oxford University Press.

Levine, M. L., & Smolak, L. (1992). Toward a model of the developmental psychopathology of eating disorders: The example of early adolescence. In J. H. Crowther, D. L. Tennenbaum, S. E. Hobfall, & M. A. P. Stephens (Eds.), *The etiology of bulimia nervosa: The individual and familial context* (pp. 59–80). Washington, DC: Hemisphere.

Levitt, E. E., & French, J. (1992). Projective testing of children. In C. E. Walker & M. C. Roberts (Eds.), *Handbook of clinical child psychology* (2nd ed., pp. 149–162). New York: Wiley.

Levitt, P. (1995). Experimental approaches that reveal principles of cerebral cortical development. In M. S. Gazzaniga (Ed.), *The cognitive neurosciences* (pp. 147–163). Cambridge, MA: MIT Press.

Levy, F., & Hay, D. (2001). *Attention, genes, and ADHD.* Philadelphia, PA: Brunner-Routledge.

Levy, Y., Tennebaum, A., & Ornoy, A. (2003). Repair behavior in children with intellectual impairments: Evidence of metalinguistic competence. *Journal of Speech, Language, & Hearing Research, 46,* 368–381.

Lewin, L. M., Hops, H., Davis, B., & Dishion, T. J. (1993). Multimethod comparison of similarity in school adjustment of siblings and unrelated children. *Developmental Psychology, 29,* 963–969.

Lewinsohn, P. M. (1974). A behavioral approach to depression. In R. Friedman & M. Katz (Eds.), *The psychology of depression: Contemporary theory and research* (pp. 157–185). Washington, DC: Winston-Wiley.

Lewinsohn, P. M., Allen, N. B., Seeley, J. R., & Gotlib, I. H. (1999). First onset versus recurrence of depression: Differential processes of psychosocial risk. *Journal of Abnormal Psychology, 108,* 483–489.

Lewinsohn, P. M., & Clarke, G. N. (1999). Psychosocial treatments for adolescent depression. *Clinical Psychology Review, 19,* 329–342.

Lewinsohn, P. M., Clarke, G. N., & Rohde, P. (1994). Psychological approaches to the treatment of depression in adolescents. In W. M. Reynolds & H. F. Johnston (Eds.), *Handbook of depression in children and adolescents* (pp. 309–344). New York: Plenum.

Lewinsohn, P. M., Clarke, G. N., Seeley, J. R., & Rohde, P. (1994). Major depression in community adolescents: Age at onset, episode duration, and time to recurrence. *Journal of the American Academy of Child and Adolescent Psychiatry, 33,* 809–818.

Lewinsohn, P. M., Gotlib, I. H., & Seeley, J. R. (1997). Depression-related psychosocial variables: Are they specific to depression in adolescents? *Journal of Abnormal Psychology, 106,* 365–375.

Lewinsohn, P. M., Gotlib, I. H., Lewinsohn, M., Seeley, J. R., & Allen, N. B. (1998). Gender differences in anxiety disorders and anxiety symptoms in adolescents. *Journal of Abnormal Psychology, 107,* 109–117.

Lewinsohn, P. M., Hops, H., Roberts, R. E., Seeley, J. R., & Andrews, J. A. (1993). Adolescent psychopathology: I. Prevalence and incidence of depression and other DSM-III-R disorders in high school students. *Journal of Abnormal Psychology, 102,* 133–144.

Lewinsohn, P. M., Klein, D., & Seeley, J. R. (1995). Bipolar disorders in a community sample of older adolescents: Prevalence, phenomenology, comorbidity, and course. *Journal of the American Academy of Child and Adolescent Psychiatry, 34,* 454–463.

Lewinsohn, P. M., Klein, D. N., & Seeley, J. (2000). Bipolar disorder during adolescence and young adulthood in a community sample. *Bipolar Disorder, 2,* 281–293.

Lewinsohn, P. M., Pettit, J. W., Joiner, T. E., & Seeley, J. R. (2003). The symptomatic expression of major depressive disorder in adolescents and young adults. *Journal of Abnormal Psychology, 112,* 244–252.

Lewinsohn, P. M., Roberts, R. E., Seeley, J. R., Rohde, P., Gotlib, I. H., & Hops, H. (1994). Adolescent psychopathology: II. Psychosocial risk factors for depression. *Journal of Abnormal Psychology, 103,* 302–315.

Lewinsohn, P. M., Rohde, P., & Seeley, J. R. (1998). Major depressive disorder in older adolescents: Prevalence, risk factors, and clinical implications. *Clinical Psychology Review, 18,* 765–794.

Lewinsohn, P. M., Rohde, P., Seeley, J. R., & Hops, H. (1991). The comorbidity of unipolar depression: Part 1. Major depression with dysthymia. *Journal of Abnormal Psychology, 100,* 205–213.

Lewinsohn, P. M., Seeley, J. R., Buckley, M. E., & Klein, D. N. (2002). Bipolar disorder in adolescence and young adulthood. *Child and Adolescent Psychiatric Clinics of North America, 11,* 461–476.

Lewinsohn, P. M., Striegel-Moore, R., & Seeley, J. (2000). Epidemiology and natural course of eating disorders in young women from adolescence to young adulthood. *Journal of the American Academy of Child and Adolescent Psychiatry, 39,* 1284–1292.

Lewis, D. A., & Lieberman, J. A. (2000). Catching up on schizophrenia: Natural history and neurobiology. *Neuron, 28,* 325–334.

Lewis, D. O., Yeager, C. A., Cobham-Portorreal, C. S., Klein, N., Showalter, B. A., & Anthony, A. (1991). A follow-up of female delinquents: Maternal contributions to the perpetuation of deviance. *Journal of the American Academy of Child and Adolescent Psychiatry, 30,* 197–201.

Lewis, M. (2000). Toward a developmental psychopathology: Models, definitions, and predictions. In A. Sameroff, M. Lewis, & S. Miller (Eds.), *Handbook of developmental psychopathology* (pp. 3–32). New York: Plenum.

Lewis, M. H., Aman, M. G., Gadow, K. D., Schroeder, S. R., & Thompson, T. (1996). Psychopharmacology. In J. W. Jacobson & J. A. Mulick (Eds.), *Manual of diagnosis and professional practice in mental retardation* (pp. 323–340). Washington, DC: American Psychological Association.

Liberman, I. Y., & Shankweiler, D. (1991). Phonology and beginning reading: A tutorial. In L. Rieben & C. A. Perfetti (Eds.), *Learning to read: Basic research and its implications* (pp. 46–73). Hillsdale, NJ: Erlbaum.

Liebowitz, M. R., Turner, S. M., Piacentini, J., Beidel, D. C., Clarvit, S. R., Davies, S. O., et al. (2002). Fluoxetine in children and adolescents with OCD: A placebo-controlled trial. *Journal of the American Academy of Child and Adolescent Psychiatry, 41,* 1431–1438.

Lilenfeld, L. R. R., Stein, D., Bulik, C. M., Strober, M., Plotnicov, K., Pollice, C., Rao, R., Merikangas, K. R., Nagy, L., & Kaye, W. (2000). Personality traits among current eating disordered, recovered and never ill first-degree female relatives of bulimic and control women. *Psychological Medicine, 30,* 1399–1410.

Lingam, R., Simmons, A., Andrews, N., Miller, E., Stowe, J., Taylor, B. (2003). Prevalence of autism and parentally reported triggers in a north east London population. *Archives of Disease in Childhood, 88,* 666–670.

Linnet, K. M., Dalsgaard, S., Obel, C., Wisborg, K., Henriksen, T. B., Rodriguez, A., et al. (2003). Maternal lifestyle factors in pregnancy risk of attention deficit hyperactivity disorder and associated behaviors: Review of the current evidence. *American Journal of Psychiatry, 160,* 1028–1040.

Linscheid, T. R., & Murphy, L. (1999). Feeding disorders of infancy and early childhood. In S. D. Netherton, D. Holmes et al. (Eds.), *Child and adolescent psychological disorders: A comprehensive textbook. Oxford textbooks in clinical psychology* (pp. 139–155). New York: Oxford University.

Lipka, O., & Siegel, L. S. (in press). Adolescents with learning disabilities. In D. A. Wolfe & E. J. Mash, (Eds.). *Behavioral and emotional disorders in adolescents: Nature, assessment, and treatment.* New York: Guilford.

Lipsey, M. W. (1995). What do we learn from 400 research studies on the effectiveness of treatment with juvenile delinquents? In J. McGuire (Ed.), *What works: Reducing reoffending: Guidelines from research and practice* (pp. 63–78). Chichester, England: Wiley.

Lisak, D. (1994). The psychological impact of sexual abuse: Content analysis of interviews with male survivors. *Journal of Traumatic Stress, 7,* 525–548.

Lissau, I., Overpeck, M.D., Ruan, W.J., Due, P., Holstein, B.E., Hediger, M.L., & the Health Behaviour in School-aged Children Obesity Working Group. (2004). Body mass index and overweight in adolescents in 13 European countries, Israel, and the United States. *Archives of Pediatrics and Adolescent Medicine, 158,* 27–33.

Littleton, H. L., & Ollendick, T. (2003). Negative body image and disordered eating behavior in children and adolescents: What places youth at risk and how can these problems be prevented? *Clinical Child and Family Psychology Review, 6,* 51–66.

Lock, J. (2002). Treating adolescents with eating disorders in the family context: Empirical and theoretical considerations. *Child and Adolescent Psychiatric Clinics of North America, 11,* 331–342.

Lock, J., & Le Grange, D. (in press). Eating disorders in adolescence. In D. A. Wolfe & E. J. Mash (Eds.), *Behavioral and emotional disorders in adolescents: Nature, assessment, and treatment.* New York: Guilford Press.

Loeber, R. (1990). Development and risk factors of juvenile antisocial behavior and delinquency. *Clinical Psychology Review, 10,* 1–42.

Loeber, R., Burke, J. D., Lahey, B. B., Winters, A., & Zera, M. (2000). Oppositional defiant and conduct disorder: A review of the past 10 years, Part 1. *Journal of the American Academy of Child and Adolescent Psychiatry, 39*, 1468–1484.

Loeber, R., Drinkwater, M., Yin, Y., Anderson, S. J., Schmidt, L. C., & Crawford, A. (2000). Stability of family interaction from ages 6 to 18. *Journal of Abnormal Child Psychology, 28*, 353–369.

Loeber, R., & Farrington, D. P. (2000). Young children who commit crime: Epidemiology, developmental origins, risk factors, early interventions, and policy implications. *Development and Psychopathology, 12*, 737–762.

Loeber, R., Green, S. M., Lahey, B. B., Christ, M.A.G., & Frick, P. J. (1992). Developmental sequences in the age of onset of disruptive child behaviors. *Journal of Child and Family Studies, 1*, 21–41.

Loeber, R., Green, S. M., Lahey, B. B., Frick, P. J., & McBurnett, K. (2000). Findings on disruptive behavior disorders from the first decade of the Developmental Trends Study. *Clinical Child and Family Psychology Review, 3*, 37–60.

Loeber, R., Green, S. M., Lahey, B. B., & Kalb, L. (2000). Physical fighting in childhood as a risk factor for later mental health problems. *Journal of the American Academy of Child and Adolescent Psychiatry, 39*, 421–428.

Loeber, R., Lahey, B. B., & Thomas, C. (1991). Diagnostic conundrum of oppositional defiant disorder and conduct disorder. *Journal of Abnormal Psychology, 100*, 379–390.

Loeber, R., Stouthamer-Loeber, M., & Green, S. M. (1991). Age at onset of problem behaviour in boys, and later disruptive and delinquent behaviours. *Criminal Behaviour and Mental Health, 1*, 229–246.

Logan, G. D. (1994). On the ability to inhibit thought and action: A users' guide to the stop signal paradigm. In D. Dagenbach & T. H. Carr (Eds.), *Inhibitory processes in attention, memory, and language* (pp. 189–239). San Diego, CA: Academic Press.

Lonigan, C. J., Phillips, B. M., & Hooe, E. S. (2003). Relations of positive and negative affectivity to anxiety and depression in children: Evidence from a latent variable longitudinal study. *Journal of Consulting and Clinical Psychology, 71*, 465–481.

Lonigan, C. J., Phillips, B. M., & Richey, J. A. (2003). Posttraumatic stress disorder in children: Diagnosis, assessment, and associated features. *Child and Adolescent Psychiatric Clinics of North America, 12*, 171–194.

Lord, C., Cook, E. H., Leventhal, B. L., & Amaral, D. G. (2000). Autism spectrum disorders. *Neuron, 28*, 355–363.

Lotter, V. (1978). Follow-up studies. In M. Rutter & E. Schopler (Eds.), *Autism: A reappraisal of concepts and treatment* (pp. 475–495). New York: Plenum.

Lovaas, O. I. (2003). *Teaching individuals with developmental delays.* Austin, TX: Pro-Ed.

Love, J. M., Harrison, L., Sagi-Schwartz, A., Van IJzendoorn, M. H., Ross, C., Ungerer, et al., (2003). Child care quality matters: How conclusions may vary with context. *Child Development, 74(4)*, 1021–1033.

Loveland, K. A., Tunali-Kotoski, B., Pearson, D. A., Brelsford, K. A., Ortegon, J., & Chen, R. (1994). Imitation and expression of facial affect in autism. *Development and Psychopathology, 6*, 433–444.

Lowe, J. (1998). *Oprah Winfrey speaks: Insight from the world's most influential voice.* New York: John Wiley & Sons, Inc.

Lowry-Webster, H. M, Barrett, P. M., & Lock, S. (2003). A universal prevention trial of anxiety symptomology during childhood: Results at 1-year follow-up. *Behaviour Change, 20*, 25–43.

Luby, J. L., Heffelfinger, A. J., Mrakotsky, C., Hessler, M. J., Brown, K. M., & Hildebrand, T. (2002). Preschool major depressive disorder: A preliminary validation for developmentally modified DSM-IV criteria. *Journal of the American Academy of Child and Adolescent Psychiatry, 41*, 928–937.

Luby, J. L., Heffelfinger, A., Mrakotsky, C., Brown, K., Hessler, M., & Spitznagel, E. (2003). Alterations in stress cortisol reactivity in depressed preschoolers relative to psychiatric and no-disorder comparison groups. *Archives of General Psychiatry, 60*, 1248–1255.

Luby, J. L., Heffelfinger, A., Mrakotsky, C., Brown, K., Hessler. M., Wallis, J., & Spitznagel, E. (2003). The clinical picture of depression in preschool children. *Journal of the American Academy of Child and Adolescent Psychiatry, 42*, 340–348.

Luckasson, R., Borthwick-Duffy, S., Buntinx, W.H.E., Coulter, D. L., Craig, E. M., Reeve, A., Schalock, R. L., Snell, M. E., Spitalnick, D. M., Spreat, S., & Tasse, M. J. (2002). *Mental retardation: Definition, classification, and systems of supports (10th Ed.).* Washington DC: American Association on Mental Retardation.

Lunner, K., Werthem, E., Thompson, J. K., Paxton, S., McDonald, F., & Halvaarson, K. (2000). A cross-cultural examination of weight-related teasing, body image, and eating disturbance in Swedish and Australian samples. *International Journal of Eating Disorders, 28*, 430–435.

Luthar, S. S. (1999). *Poverty and children's adjustment.* Thousand Oaks, CA: Sage.

Luthar, S. S., Burack, J. A., & Cicchetti, D. (Eds.). (1997). *Developmental psychopathology: Perspectives on adjustment, risk, and disorder.* New York: Cambridge.

Luthar, S. S., Cicchetti, D., & Becker, B. (2000). The construct of resilience: A critical evaluation and guidelines for future work. *Child Development, 71*, 543–562.

Luthar, S. S., Ed (2003). *Resilience and vulnerability: Adaptation in the context of childhood adversities.* New York: Cambridge University Press.

Lynam, D., Moffitt, T. E., & Stouthamer-Loeber, M. (1993). Explaining the relation between IQ and delinquency: Race, class, test motivation, school failure, or self-control. *Journal of Abnormal Psychology, 102*, 187–196.

Lynam, D. R., & Henry, B. (2001). The role of neuropsychological deficits in conduct disorders. In J. Hill & B. Maughan (Eds.), *Conduct disorders in childhood and adolescence* (pp. 235–263). Cambridge: Cambridge University Press.

Lyon, G. R., & Cutting, L. (1998). Treatment of learning disabilities. In E. J. Mash & R. A. Barkley (Eds.), *Treatment of childhood disorders (2nd ed.).* New York: Guilford Press.

Lyon, G. R., Fletcher, J. M., & Barnes, M. C. (2003). Learning disabilities. In E. J. Mash & R. A. Barkley (Eds.), *Child psychopathology (2nd ed., pp. 520–586).* New York: Guilford.

Lyons-Ruth, K., Yellin, C., Melnick, S., & Atwood, G. (2003). Childhood experiences of trauma and loss have different relations to maternal unresolved and hostile-helpless states of mind on the AAI. *Attachment & Human Development, 5*, 330–352.

Lyons-Ruth, K., Zeanah, C. H., & Benoit, D. (1996). Disorder and risk for disorder during infancy and toddlerhood. In E. J. Mash & R. A. Barkley (Eds.), *Child psychopathology* (pp. 457–491). New York: Guilford Press.

Lyons-Ruth, K., Zeanah, C.H., & Benoit, D. (2003). Disorder and risk for disorder during infancy and toddlerhood. In E.J. Mash & R.A. Barkley (Eds.), *Child psychopathology (2nd ed., pp 589–631).* New York: Guilford Press.

Lytton, H. (1990). Child and parent effects in boys' conduct disorder: A reinterpretation. *Developmental Psychology, 26*, 683–697.

Maccoby, E. E. (1986). Social groupings in childhood: Their relationship to prosocial and antisocial behavior in boys and girls. In D. Olweus, J. Block, & M. Radke-Yarrow (Eds.), *Development of antisocial and prosocial behavior* (pp. 263–284). Orlando, FL: Academic Press.

Maccoby, E. E., & Martin, J. A. (1983). Socialization in the context of the family: Parent-child interaction. In P. H. Mussen (Ed.), *Handbook of child psychology (4th ed.): Vol. IV. Socialization, personality, and social development* (pp. 1–101). New York: Wiley.

Macdonald, H., Rutter, M., Howlin, P., Rios, P., Le Couteur, A., Evered, C., & Folstein, S. (1989). Recognition and expression of emotional cues by autistic and normal adults. *Journal of Child Psychology and Psychiatry, 30*, 865–877.

MacDonald, J. D., & MacIntyre, P. D. (1999). A rose is a rose: Effects of label change, education, and sex on attitudes toward mental disabilities. *Journal on Developmental Disabilities, 6*, 15–31.

Macfie, J., Cicchetti, D., & Toth, S. L. (2001). The development of dissociation in maltreated preschool-aged children. *Development and Psychopathology, 13,* 233–254.

Machel, G. (2001). *The impact of war on children.* London: Hurst & Company.

MacIntyre, D., & Carr, A. (2000). Prevention of child sexual abuse: Implications of programme evaluation research. *Child Abuse Review, 9,* 183–199.

Mackillop, W. J., Zhang-Salomons, J., Groome, P. A., Paszat, L., & Holowaty, E. (1997). Socioeconomic status and cancer survival in Ontario. *Journal of Clinical Oncology, 15,* 1680–1689.

Mackinaw-Koons, B., & Vasey, M. W. (2000). Considering sex differences in anxiety and its disorders across the life span: A construct-validation approach. *Applied and Preventive Psychology, 9,* 191–209.

Maclean, K. (2003). The impact of institutionalization on child development. *Development and Psychopathology, 15,* 853–884.

MacLean, W. E., Jr., Perrin, J. M., Gortmaker, S., & Pierre, C. B. (1992). Psychological adjustment of children with asthma: Effects of illness severity and recent stressful life events. *Journal of Pediatric Psychology, 17,* 159–172.

MacMillan, H. L., Fleming, J. E., Trocme, N., Boyle, M. H., Wong, M., Racine, Y. A., et al. (1997). Prevalence of child physical and sexual abuse in the community: Results from the Ontario Health Supplement. *Journal of the American Medical Association, 278,* 131–135.

Mackner, L. M., Black, M. M., & Starr, R. H., Jr. (2003). Cognitive development of children in poverty with failure to thrive: A prospective study through age 6. *Journal of Child Psychology & Psychiatry & Allied Disciplines, 44,* 743–751.

Maedgen, J. W., & Carlson, C. L. (2000). Social functioning and emotional regulation in the attention deficit hyperactivity disorder subtypes. *Journal of Clinical Child Psychology, 29,* 30–42.

Magliano, J. P., & Millis, K. K. (2003). Assessing reading skill with a think-aloud procedure and latent semantic analysis. *Cognition & Instruction, 21,* 251–283.

Magnusson, D. (1988). Aggressiveness, hyperactivity, and autonomic activity/reactivity in the development of social maladjustment. In D. Magnusson (Ed.), *Paths through life: Individual development from an interactionary perspective: A longitudinal study* (Vol. 1, pp. 153–175). Hillsdale, NJ: Erlbaum.

Maguire, K., & Pastore, A. L. (1998). *Sourcebook of criminal justice statistics 1997.* Washington, DC: U.S. Department of Justice, Bureau of Justice Statistics.

Main, M., & George, C. (1985). Responses of abused and disadvantaged toddlers to distress in agemates: A study in the daycare setting. *Developmental Psychology, 21,* 407–412.

Main, M., & Goldwyn, R. (1984). Predicting rejecting of her infant from mother's representation of her own experience: Implications for the abused-abusing intergenerational cycle. *Child Abuse and Neglect, 8,* 203–217.

Makari, G. J. (1993). Educated insane: A nineteenth-century psychiatric paradigm. *Journal of the History of the Behavioral Sciences, 29,* 8–21.

Malhotra, S., & Gupta, N. (1999). Childhood disintegrative disorder. *Journal of Autism and Developmental Disorders, 29,* 491–498.

Malhotra, S., & Gupta, N. (2002). Childhood disintegrative disorder: Re-examination of the current concept. *European Child and Adolescent Psychiatry, 11,* 108–114.

Maloney, M., & Kranz, R. (1991). *Straight talk about eating disorders.* New York: Facts on File.

Manassis, K., & Bradley, S. (1994). The development of childhood anxiety disorders: Toward an integrated model. *Journal of Applied Developmental Psychology, 15,* 345–366.

Manassis, K., Bradley, S., Goldberg, S., Hood, J., & Swinson, R. P. (1994). Attachment in mothers with anxiety disorders and their children. *Journal of the American and Adolescent Psychiatry, 33,* 1106–1113.

Mancini, C., van Ameringen, M., Szatmari, P., Fugere, C., & Boyle, M. (1996). A high-risk pilot study of the children of adults with social phobia. *Journal of the American Academy of Child and Adolescent Psychiatry, 35,* 1511–1517.

Mannuzza, S., Klein, R. G., & Moulton, J. L. (2002). Young adult outcome of children with "situational" hyperactivity: A prospective, controlled follow-up study. *Journal of Abnormal Child Psychology, 30,* 191–198.

Mans, L., Cicchetti, D., & Sroufe, L. A. (1978). Mirror reactions of Down's syndrome infants and toddlers: Cognitive underpinnings of self-recognition. *Child Development, 49,* 1247–1250.

Marcelis, M., van Os, J., Sham, P., Jones, P., Gilvarry, C., Cannon, M., McKenzie, K., & Murray, R. (1998). Obstetric complications and familial morbid risk of psychiatric disorders. *American Journal of of Medical Genetics, 81,* 29–36.

March, J. S., Biederman, J., Wolkow, R., Safferman, A., Mardekian, J., Cook, E. H., et al. (1998). Sertraline in children and adolescents with obsessive-compulsive disorder: A multicenter randomized controlled trial. *JAMA: Journal of the American Medical Association, 280,* 1752–1756.

March, J. S., & Mulle, K. (1998). *OCD in children and adolescents: A cognitive-behavioral treatment manual.* New York: Guilford Press.

Marciano, P. L., & Kazdin, A. E. (1994). Self-esteem, depression, hopelessness, and suicidal intent among psychiatrically disturbed inpatient adolescents. *Journal of Clinical Child Psychology, 23,* 151–160.

Marenco, S., & Weinberger, D. R. (2000). The neurodevelopmental hypothesis of schizophrenia: Following a trail of evidence from cradle to grave. *Development and Psychopathology, 12,* 501–527.

Margolin, G., Gordis, E. B., Medina, A. M., & Oliver, P. H. (2003). The co-occurence of husband-to-wife aggression, family-of-origin aggression, and child abuse potential in a community sample: Implications for parenting. *Journal of Interpersonal Violence Special Issue: Children and domestic violence, 18,* 413–440.

Marshall, W. L., Fernandez, Y. M., Serran, G. A., Mulloy, R., Thornton, D., Mann, R. E., & Anderson, D. (2003a). Process variables in the treatment of sexual offenders: A review of the relevant literature. *Aggression & Violent Behavior, 8,* 205–234.

Marshall, W. L., Marshall, L. E., Sachdev, S., & Kruger, R. L. (2003b). Distorted attitudes and perceptions, and their relationship with self-esteem and coping in child molesters. *Sexual Abuse: Journal of Research & Treatment, 15,* 171–181.

Marten, P. A., Albano, A. M., & Holt, C. S. (1991, January). *Cognitive-behavioral group treatment of adolescent social phobia with parent participation.* Unpublished manuscript, University of Louisville, Department of Psychology, Louisville, KY.

Martin, J. F. (1995, Fall/Winter). Life with Karl. *Entourage,* p. 10.

Martin, M. T., Miller-Johnson, S., Kitzmann, K. M., & Emery, R. E. (1998). Parent-child relationships and insulin-dependent diabetes mellitus: Observational ratings of clinically relevant dimensions. *Journal of Family Psychology, 12,* 102–111.

Martin, N., Scourfield, J., & McGuffin, P. (2002). Observer effects and heritability of childhood attention-deficit hyperactivity disorder symptoms. *British Journal of Psychiatry, 180,* 260–265.

Maser, J. D. & Patterson, T. (2002). Spectrum and nosology: Implications for DSM-V. *Psychiatric Clinics of North America, 25,* 855–885.

Mash, E. J. (1998). Treatment of child and family disturbance: A behavioral-systems perspective. In E. J. Mash & R. A. Barkley (Eds.), *Treatment of childhood disorders* (2nd ed., pp. 3–54). New York: Guilford Press.

Mash, E. J., & Barkley, R. A. (Eds.). (1998). *Treatment of childhood disorders* (2nd ed.). New York: Guilford Press.

Mash, E. J., & Dozois, D.J.A. (2003). Child psychopathology: A developmental-systems perspective. In E. J. Mash & R. A. Barkley (Eds.), *Child psychopathology* (2nd ed., pp. 3–71). New York: Guilford Press.

Mash, E. J., & Foster, S. L. (2001). Exporting analogue behavioral observation from research to clinical practice: Useful or cost-defective? *Psychological Assessment, 13,* 86–98.

Mash, E. J., & Hunsley, J. (Eds.). (in press). Special section: Evidence-based assessment of child and adolescent disorders. *Journal of Clinical Child and Adolescent Psychology.*

Mash, E. J., & Johnston, C. (1982). A comparison of mother–child interactions of younger and older hyperactive and normal children. *Child Development, 53,* 1371–1381.

Mash, E. J., & Johnston, C. (1983). Parental perceptions of child behavior problems, parenting self-esteem and mothers' reported stress in younger and older hyperactive and normal children. *Journal of Consulting and Clinical Psychology, 51,* 86–99.

Mash, E. J., & Johnston, C. (1990). Determinants of parenting stress: Illustrations from families of hyperactive children and families of physically abused children. *Journal of Clinical Child Psychology, 19,* 313–328.

Mash, E. J., & Terdal, L. G. (1997a). Assessment of child and family disturbance: A behavioral-systems approach. In E. J. Mash & L. G. Terdal (Eds.), *Assessment of childhood disorders* (3rd ed., pp. 3–68). New York: Guilford Press.

Mash, E. J., & Terdal, L. G. (Eds.). (1997b). *Assessment of childhood disorders (3rd ed.).* New York: Guilford Press.

Masi, G., Millepiedi, S., Mucci, M., Pascale, R. P., Perugi, G., & Akiskal, H. S. (2003). Phenomenology and comorbidity of dysthymic disorder in 100 consecutively referred children and adolescents: Beyond DSM-IV. *Canadian Journal of Psychiatry, 48,* 99–105.

Mason, A. (2003). Melanie Klein, 1882–1960. *American Journal of Psychiatry, 160,* 241.

Masten, A. S. (2001). Ordinary magic: Resilience processes in development. *American Psychologist, 56,* 227–238.

Masten, A. S., & Coatsworth, J. D. (1998). The development of competence in favorable and unfavorable environments: Lessons from research on successful children. *American Psychologist, 53,* 205–220.

Masten, A. S., & Curtis, W. J. (2000). Integrating competence and psychopathology: Pathways toward a comprehensive science of adaption in development. *Development and Psychopathology, 12,* 529–550.

Masten, A. S., Hubbard, J. J., Gest, S. D., Tellegen, A., Garmezy, N., & Ramirez, M. (1999). Adaptation in the context of adversity: Pathways to resilience and maladaptation from childhood to late adolescence. *Development and Psychopathology, 11,* 143–169.

Masten, A. S., & Powell, J. L. (2003). A resilience framework for research, policy, and practice. In S. S. Luthar (Ed.), *Resilience and vulnerability: Adaptation in the context of childhood adversities* (pp. 1–25). New York: Cambridge University Press.

Matson, J. L., & Bamburg, J. W. (1999). A descriptive study of pica behavior in persons with mental retardation. *Journal of Developmental and Physical Disabilities, 11,* 353–361.

Matson, J. L., Bamburg, J. W., Mayville, E. A., Pinkston, J., Bielecki, J., Kuhn, D., et al. (2000). Psychopharmacology and mental retardation: A 10 year review (1990–1999). *Research in Developmental Disabilities, 21,* 263–296.

Matson, J. L., & Coe, D. A. (1991). Mentally retarded children. In T. R. Kratochwill & R. J. Morris (Eds.), *The practice of child therapy* (2nd ed., pp. 298–327). Toronto: Pergamon Press.

Matson, J. L., & Hammer, D. (1996). Assessment of social functioning. In J. W. Jacobson & J. A. Mulick (Eds.), *Manual of diagnosis and professional practice in mental retardation* (pp. 157–163). Washington, DC: American Psychological Association.

Mattis, S. G., & Ollendick, T. H. (1997a). Children's cognitive responses to the somatic symptoms of panic. *Journal of Abnormal Child Psychology, 25,* 47–57.

Mattis, S. G., & Ollendick, T. H. (1997b). Panic in children and adolescents: A developmental analysis. *Advances in Clinical Child Psychology, 19,* 27–74.

Mattis, S. G., & Ollendick, T. H. (2002). Nonclinical panic attacks in late adolescence: Prevalence and associated psychopathology, *Journal of Anxiety Disorders, 16,* 321–367.

Maughan, A. & Cicchetti, D. (2002). Impact of child maltreatment and interadult violence on children's emotion regulation abilities and socioemotional adjustment. *Child Development, 73,* 1525–1542.

Maughan, B., Gray, G., & Rutter, M. (1985). Reading retardation and antisocial behavior: A follow-up into employment. *Journal of Child Psychology and Psychiatry, 26,* 741–758.

Maughan, B., & Hagell, A. (1996). Poor readers in adulthood: Psychosocial functioning. *Development and Psychopathology, 8,* 457–476.

Maughan, B., Rowe, R., Loeber, R., & Stouthamer-Loeber, M. (2003). Reading problems and depressed mood. *Journal of Abnormal Child Psychology, 31,* 219–229.

Maughan, B., & Rutter, M. (2001). Antisocial children grown up. In J. Hill & B. Maughan (Eds.). *Conduct disorders in childhood and adolescence* (pp. 507–552). London: Cambridge.

Maurice, C. (1993a, June). Rescuing my daughter. *McCall's,* pp. 75, 76, 78, 84, 156.

Maurice, C. (1993b). *Let me hear your voice: A family's triumph over autism.* New York: Fawcett Columbine.

Maxfield, M. G., & Widom, C. S. (1996). The cycle of violence: Revisited 6 years later. *Archives of Pediatric and Adolescent Medicine, 150,* 390–395.

Mazzocco, M. M. (2000). Advances in research on the fragile X syndrome. *Mental Retardation and Developmental Disabilities Research Reviews, 6,* 96–106.

McAlpine, L. & McGrath, P. J. (1999). Chronic and recurrent pain in children. In A. R. Block, E. F. Kremer, et al. (Eds.), *Handbook of pain syndromes: Biopsychosocial perspectives* (pp. 529–549). Mahwah, NJ: Erlbaum.

McArthur, D. S., & Roberts, G. E. (1982). *Roberts Apperception Test for children.* Los Angeles: Western Psychological Services.

McBurnett, K. (1992). Psychobiological approaches to personality and their application to child psychopathology. In B. B. Lahey & A. E. Kazdin (Eds.), *Advances in clinical child psychology* (Vol. 14, pp. 107–164). New York: Plenum.

McBurnett, K., & Lahey, B. B. (1994). Neuropsychological and neuroendocrine correlates of conduct disorder and antisocial behavior in children and adolescents. In D. C. Fowles, P. Sutker, & S. H. Goodman (Eds.), *Progress in experimental personality and psychopathology research* (pp. 199–231). New York: Springer.

McBurnett, K., Lahey, B. B., Frick, P. J., Risch, C., Loeber, R., Hart, E. L., Christ, M. A. G., & Hanson, K. S. (1991). Anxiety, inhibition, and conduct disorders in children, II: Relation to salivary cortisol. *Journal of the American Academy of Child and Adolescent Psychiatry, 30,* 192–196.

McBurnett, K., Lahey, B. B., Rathouz, P. J., & Loeber, R. (2000). Low salivary cortisol and persistent aggression in boys referred for disruptive behavior. *Archives of General Psychiatry, 57,* 38–43.

McBurnett, K., Pfiffner, L. J., & Frick, P. J. (2001). Symptom properties as a function of ADHD type: An argument for continued study of sluggish cognitive tempo. *Journal of Abnormal Child Psychology, 29,* 207–213.

McCabe, M. A. (1996). Involving children and adolescents in medical decision making: Developmental and clinical considerations. *Journal of Pediatric Psychology, 21,* 505–516.

McCall, R. B., & Groark, C. J. (2000). The future of applied child development research and public policy. *Child Development, 71,* 197–204.

McCann, J., & Peppe, S. (2003). Prosody in autism spectrum disorders: A critical review. *International Journal of Language and Communication Disorders, 38,* 325–350.

McCauley, E., Myers, K., Mitchell, J., Calderon, R., Scholoredt, K., & Treder, R. (1993). Depression in young people: Initial presentation and clinical course. *Journal of the American Academy of Child and Adolescent Psychiatry, 32,* 714–722.

McClellan, J., Breiger, D., McCurry, C., & Hlastala, S. A. (2003). Premorbid functioning in early-onset psychotic disorders. *Journal of the American Academy of Child and Adolescent Psychiatry, 42*, 666–672.

McClellan, J., Werry, J., Bernet, W., Arnold, V., Beitchman, J., Benson, S., et al. (2001). Practice parameters for the assessment and treatment of children and adolescents with schizophrenia. *Journal of the American Academy of Child and Adolescent Psychiatry, 40 (Suppl. 7)*, 4S–23S.

McCloskey, L. A. & Walker, M. (2000). Posttraumatic stress in children exposed to family violence and single-event trauma. *Journal of the American Academy of Child and Adolescent Psychiatry, 39*, 108–115.

McClure, M. (2000). An integrative ecology. In: P. Reder, M. McClure, & A. Jolley, (Eds.), *Family matters: Interfaces between child and adult mental health* (303–317). New York: Routledge.

McCluskey, K. K., & McCluskey, A. (2000). Excerpts from Butterfly Kisses: Amber's journey through hyperactivity. *The Canadian, 6(2),* 11–15.

McCrae, R. R., Costa, P. T. Jr., Terracciano, A., Parker, W. D., Mills, C. J., De Fruyt, F., & Mervielde, I. (2002). Personality trait development from age 12 to age 18: Longitudinal, cross-sectional and cross-cultural analyses. *Journal of Personality and Social Psychology, 83*, 1456–1468.

McDermott, P. A. (1996). A nationwide study of developmental and gender prevalence for psychopathology in childhood and adolescence. *Journal of Abnormal Child Psychology, 24*, 53–66.

McDermott, P. A., & Weiss, R. V. (1995). A normative typology of healthy, subclinical, and clinical behavior styles among American children and adolescents. *Psychological Assessment, 7*, 162–170.

McEachin, J. J., Smith, T., & Lovaas, O. I. (1993). Long-term outcome for children with autism who received early intensive behavioral treatment. *American Journal on Mental Retardation, 97*, 359–372.

McEvoy, M. A., Shores, R. E., Wehlby, J. H., Johnson, S. M., & Fox, J. J. (1990). Special education teachers' implementation of procedures to promote social interaction among children in integrated settings. *Education and Training in Mental Retardation, 25,* 267–276.

McFadyen-Ketchum, S. A., & Dodge, K. A. (1998). Problems in social relationships. In E. J. Mash & R. A. Barkley (Eds.), *Treatment of childhood disorders* (2nd ed., pp. 338–365). New York: Guilford Press.

McFarlane, T., Polivy, J., & McCabe, R. E. (1999). Help, not harm: Psychological foundation for a nondieting approach toward health. *Journal of Social Issues, 55*, 261–276.

McGee, R. A., Wolfe, D. A., & Wilson, S. K. (1997). Multiple maltreatment ex-periences and adolescent behavior problems: Adolescents' perspectives. *Development and Psychopathology, 9*, 131–149.

McGee, R., & Feehan, M. (1991). Are girls with problems of inattention under-recognized? *Journal of Psychopathology and Behavioral Assessment, 13*, 187–198.

McGee, R., Stanton, W. R., & Sears, M. R. (1993). Allergic disorders and attention deficit disorder in children. *Journal of Abnormal Child Psychology, 21*, 79–88.

McGee, R., Wolfe, D. A., & Olson, J. (2001). Multiple maltreatment, attribution of blame, and adjustment among adolescents. *Development and Psychopathology, 13*, 827–846.

McGloin, J. M. & Widom, C. S. (2001). Resilience among abused and neglected children grown up. *Development and Psychopathology, 13*, 1021–1038.

McGrath, E. P., & Repetti, R. L. (2002). A longitudinal study of children's depressive symptoms, self-perceptions, and cognitive distortions about the self. *Journal of Abnormal Psychology, 111*, 77–87.

McGrath, M.L., Mellon, M.W., & Murphy, L. (2000). Empirically supported treatments in pediatric psychology: Constipation and encopresis. *Journal of Pediatric Psychology, 25*, 225–254.

McGrath, P. A. (1993). Psychological aspects of pain perception. In N. L. Schechter, C. B. Berde, & M. Yaster (Eds.), *Pain in infants, children and adolescents* (pp. 39–63). Baltimore: Williams & Wilkins.

McGroder, S. M. (2000). Parenting among low-income, African-American single mothers with preschool-age children: Patterns, predictors, and developmental correlates. *Child Development, 71*, 752–771.

McGue, M. (1997). The democracy of genes. *Nature, 388*, 417–418.

McGue, M., Bouchard, T. J., Jr., Iacono, W. G., & Lykken, D. T. (1993). Behavioral genetics of cognitive ability: A lifespan perspective. In R. Plomin & G. E. McClearn (Eds.), *Nature, nurture and psychology* (pp. 59–76). Washington, DC: American Psychological Association.

McInnes, A., Humphries, T., Hogg-Johnson, S., & Tannock, R. (2003). Listening comprehension and working memory are impaired in attention-deficit hyperactivity disorder irrespective of language impairment. *Journal of Abnormal Child Psychology, 31*, 427–443.

McInnis, M. G., Dick, D. M., Willour, V. L., Avramopoulos, D., MacKinnon, D. F., & Simpson, S. G. (2003). Genome-wide scan and conditional analysis in bipolar disorder: Evidence for genomic interaction in the national institute of mental health genetics initiative bipolar pedigrees. *Biological Psychiatry, 54*, 1265–1273.

McIntosh, V. V., Bulik, C. M., McKenzie, J. M., Luty, S. E., & Jordan, J. (2000). Interpersonal psychotherapy for anorexia nervosa. *International Journal of Eating Disorders, 27*, 125–139.

McKnew, D. H., Jr., Cytryn, L., & Yahraes, H. (1983). *Why isn't Johnny crying? Coping with depression in children.* New York: Norton.

McLoyd, V. C. (1998). Socioeconomic disadvantage and child development. *American Psychologist, 53*, 185–204.

McMahon, R. J., & Estes, A. M. (1997). Conduct problems. In E. J. Mash & L. G. Terdal (Eds.), *Assessment of childhood disorders* (3rd ed., pp. 130–193). New York: Guilford Press.

McMahon, R. J., & Forehand, R. L. (2003). *Helping the noncompliant child: Family-based treatment for oppositional behavior (2nd ed.).* New York: Guilford.

McMahon, R. J., & Wells, K. C. (1998). Conduct problems. In E. J. Mash & R. A. Barkley (Eds.), *Treatment of childhood disorders* (2nd ed., pp. 111–207). New York: Guilford Press.

McManis, M. H., Kagan, J., Snidman, N. C., & Woodward, S. A. (2002). EEG asymmetry, power, and temperament in children. *Developmental Psychobiology, 41*, 169–177.

McNeil, C. B., Capage, L. C., & Bennett, G. M. (2002). Cultural issues in the treatment of young African American children diagnosed with disruptive behavior disorders. *Journal of Pediatric Psychology. Special Issue: Ethnic Minority and Low Income Children and Families. 27*, 339–350.

McQuaid, E. L., & Nassau, J. H. (1999). Empirically supported treatments of disease-related symptoms in pediatric psychology: Asthma, diabetes, and cancer. *Journal of Pediatric Psychology, 24*, 305–328.

Mead, M. A., Hohenshil, T. H., & Singh, K. (1997). How the DSM system is used by clinical counselors: A national study. *Journal of Mental Health Counseling, 19*, 383–401.

Meaux, J. B., & Bell, P. L. (2001). Balancing recruitment and protection: Children as research subjects. *Issues in Comprehensive Pediatric Nursing, 24*, 241–251.

Medvescek, C. R. (1997, April). Special kids. *Parents*, pp. 67–70.

Meehl, P. E. (1999). Clarifications about taxometric methods. *Applied and Preventive Psychology, 8*, 165–174.

Meichenbaum, D. (1977). *Cognitive-behavior modification: An integrative approach.* New York: Plenum.

Meijer, S. A., Sinnema, G., Bijstra, J. O, Mellenbergh, G. J., & Wolters, W. H. (2000a). Peer interaction in adolescents with a chronic illness. *Journal of Child Psychology & Psychiatry & Allied Disciplines, 29*, 799–813.

Meijer, S. A., Sinnema, G., Bijstra, J. O, Mellenbergh, G. J., & Wolters, W. H.

(2000b). Social functioning in children with a chronic illness. *Journal of Child Psychology & Psychiatry & Allied Disciplines, 41,* 309–317.

Meiser-Stedman, R. (2002). Towards a cognitive-behavioral model of PTSD in children and adolescents. *Clinical Child and Family Psychology Review, 5,* 217–232.

Mellon, M. W., & McGrath, M. L. (2000). Empirically supported treatments in pediatric psychology: Nocturnal enuresis. *Journal of Pediatric Psychology, 25,* 193–214.

Melnick, S. M., & Hinshaw, S. P. (1996). What they want and what they get: The social goals of boys with ADHD and comparison boys. *Journal of Abnormal Child Psychology, 24,* 169–185.

Melnick, S. M., & Hinshaw, S. P. (2000). Emotion regulation and parenting in AD/HD and comparison boys: Linkages with social behaviors and peer preference. *Journal of Abnormal Child Psychology, 28,* 73–86.

Melton, G. B. (1996). The child's right to a family environment: Why children's rights and family values are compatible. *American Psychologist, 51,* 1234–1238.

Melton, G. B. (2000). Privacy issues in child mental health services. In J. J. Gates & B. S. Arons (Eds.), *Privacy and confidentiality in mental health care* (pp. 47–70). Baltimore: Brookes.

Melton, G. B., & Ehrenreich, N. S. (1992). Ethical and legal issues in mental health services for children. In C. E. Walker & M. C. Roberts (Eds.), *Handbook of clinical child psychology* (2nd ed., pp. 1035–1055). New York: Wiley.

Merikangas, K. R., Avenevoli, S., Dierker, L., & Grillon, C. (1999). Vulnerability factors among children at risk for anxiety disorders. *Biological Psychiatry, 46,* 1523–1535.

Merrell, K. W. (2003). *Behavioral, Social, and Emotional Assessment of Children and Adolescents.* (2nd ed.). Mahwah, NJ: Lawrence Erlbaum Associates.

Merrill, L. L., Guimond, J. M., Thomsen, C. J., & Milner, J. S. (2003). Child sexual abuse and number of sexual partners in young women: The role of abuse severity, coping style, and sexual functioning. *Journal of Consulting and Clinical Psychology, 71,* 987–996.

Mervielde, I., Fruyt, F. D. (2002). Assessing children's traits with the hierarchial personality inventory for children. In B. de Raad (Ed.) *Big Five assessment* (129–142). Ashland, OH: Hogrefe & Huber Publishers, x, 491.

Merzenich, M. M., Saunders, G., Jenkins, W. M., Miller, S., Peterson, B., & Tallal, P. (1999). Pervasive developmental disorders: Listening training and language abilities. In S. H. Broman & J. M. Fletcher (Eds.), *The changing nervous system: Neurobehavioral consequences of early brain disorders* (pp. 365–385). London: Oxford University Press.

Mesman, J., & Koot, H. M. (2000a). Child-reported depression and anxiety in preadolescence: I. Associations with parent- and teacher-reported problems. *Journal of the American Academy of Child and Adolescent Psychiatry, 39,* 1379–1386.

Mesman, J., & Koot, H. M. (2000b). Child-reported depression and anxiety in preadolescence: II. Preschool predictors. *Journal of the American Academy of Child and Adolescent Psychiatry, 39,* 1379–1386.

Mesquita, B. & Walker, R. (2003). Cultural differences in emotions: A context for interpreting emotional experiences. *Behaviour Research & Therapy Special Issue: Cross cultural assessment and abnormal psychology, 41,* 777–793.

Messer, S. C., & Gross, A. M. (1995). Childhood depression and family interaction: A naturalistic observation study. *Journal of Clinical Child Psychology, 24,* 77–88.

Michael, K. D., & Crowley, S. L. (2002). How effective are treatments for child and adolescent depression? A meta-analytic review. *Clinical Psychology Review, 22,* 247–269.

Mick, E., Biederman, J., Faraone, S. V., Sayer, J., & Kleinman, S. (2002). Case-control study of attention-deficit hyperactivity disorder and maternal smoking, alcohol use, and drug use during pregnancy. *Journal of the American Academy of Child and Adolescent Psychiatry, 41,* 378–385.

Mick, E., Biederman, J., Jetton, J., & Faraone, S. V. (2000). Sleep disturbances associated with attention deficit hyperactivity disorder: The impact of psychiatric comorbidity and pharmacotherapy. *Journal of Child and Adolescent Psychopharmacology, 10,* 223–231.

Mick, E., Biederman, J., Prince, J., Fischer, M. J., & Faraone, S. V. (2002). Impact of low birth weight on attention-deficit hyperactivity disorder. *Journal of Developmental and Behavioral Pediatrics, 23,* 16–22.

Mick, E., Santangelo, S. L., Wypij, D., & Biederman, J. (2000). Impact of maternal depression on ratings of comorbid depression in adolescents with attention-deficit/hyperactivity disorder. *Journal of the American Academy of Child and Adolescent Psychiatry, 39,* 314–319.

Miles, M. B., & Huberman, A. M. (1994). *Qualitative data analysis: An expanded sourcebook (2nd ed.).* Thousand Oaks, CA: Sage.

Milich, R, Balentine, A. C., & Lynam, D. R. (2001). ADHD combined type and ADHD predominantly inattentive type are distinct and unrelated disorders. *Clinical Psychology: Science and Practice, 8,* 463–488.

Milich, R., & Kramer, J. (1984). Reflections on impulsivity: An empirical investigation of impulsivity as a construct. In K. Gadow & I. Bialer (Eds.), *Advances in learning and behavioral dis-*

abilities (Vol. 3, pp. 57–94). Greenwich, CT: JAI Press.

Milich, R., & Landau, S. (1989). The role of social status variables in differentiating subgroups of hyperactive children. In L. M. Bloomingdale & J. M. Swanson (Eds.), *Attention deficit disorder* (Vol. 4, pp. 1–16). Oxford, England: Pergamon Press.

Milich, R., & Lorch, E. P. (1994). Television viewing methodology to understand cognitive processing of ADHD children. In T. H. Ollendick & R. J. Prinz (Eds.), *Advances in clinical child psychology* (Vol. 16, pp. 177–202). New York: Plenum.

Milich, R., Wolraich, M. C., & Lindgren, S. (1986). Sugar and hyperactivity: A critical review of empirical findings. *Clinical Psychology Review, 6,* 493–513.

Mill, J. S., Caspi, A., McClay, J., Sugden, K., Purcell, S., Asherson, P., et al., (2002). The dopamine D4 receptor and the hyperactivity phenotype: A developmental-epidemiological study. *Molecular Psychiatry, 7,* 383–391.

Miller, A. L., & Olson, S. L. (2000). Emotional expressiveness during peer conflicts: A predictor of social maladjustment among high-risk preschoolers. *Journal of Abnormal Child Psychology, 28,* 339–352.

Miller, C. (2002). Learning from each other: Practitioners in school-based support for chidren with language and communication needs. *Support for Learning, 17,* 187–192.

Miller, J. (1999). Profiles of language development in children with Down syndrome. In J. F. Miller, M. Leddy, & L. A. Leavitt (Eds.), *Improving the communication of people with Down syndrome* (pp. 11–39). Baltimore, MD: Paul H. Brookes Publishing Company.

Miller, J. D., Lynam, D., & Leukefeld, C. (2003). Examining antisocial behavior through the lens of the five factor model of personality. *Aggressive Behavior, 29,* 497–514.

Miller, V., & Drotar, D. (2003). Discrepancies between mother and adolescent perceptions of diabetes-related decision-making autonomy and their relationship to diabetes-related conflict and adherence to treatment. *Journal of Pediatric Psychology, 28,* 265–274.

Milner, J. S. (2003). Social information processing in high-risk and physically abusive parents. *Child Abuse & Neglect, 27,* 7–20.

Mindell, J. A., Owens, J. A., & Carskadon, M. A. (1999). Developmental features of sleep. *Child and Adolescent Psychiatric Clinics of North America, 8,* 699–725.

Ministry of Education. (2004, January 6). "*McGuinty congratulates Canadian soft drink industry*". Available online, accessed January 19, 2004: http://www.premier.gov.on.ca/english/news/RefreshmentsCanada010604.asp

Minshew, N. J. (1996). Brain mechanisms in autism: Functional and structural abnormalities. *Journal of Autism and Developmental Disorders, 26,* 205–209.

Minshew, N. J., Johnson, C., & Luna, B. (2000). The cognitive and neural basis of autism: A disorder of complex information processing and dysfunction of neocortical systems. *International Review of Research in Mental Retardation, 23,* 112–140.

Minuchin, S., Rosman, B. L., & Baker, L. (1978). *Psychosomatic families: Anorexia nervosa in context.* Cambridge, MA: Harvard University Press.

Mitchell, J., McCauley, E., Burke, P. M., & Moss, S. J. (1988). Phenomenology of depression in children and adolescents. *Journal of the American Academy of Child and Adolescent Psychiatry, 27,* 12–20.

Mitchell, K. J., Finkelhor, D., & Wolak, J. (2003). The exposure of youth to unwanted sexual material on the Internet: A national survey of risk, impact, and prevention. *Youth & Society, 34,* 330–358.

Moffitt, T. E. (1990). Juvenile delinquency and attention deficit disorder in boys' developmental trajectories from age 3 to age 15. *Child Development, 61,* 893–910.

Moffitt, T. E. (1993a). Adolescence-limited and life-course-persistent antisocial behavior: A developmental taxonomy. *Psychological Review, 100,* 674–701.

Moffitt, T. E. (1993b). The neuropsychology of conduct disorder. *Development and Psychopathology, 5,* 135–151.

Moffitt, T. E., & Caspi, A. (2001). Childhood predictors differentiate life-course persistent and adolescence-limited antisocial pathways among males and females. *Development and Psychopathology, 13,* 355–375.

Moffitt, T. E., Caspi, A., Belsky, J., & Silva, P. A. (1992). Childhood experience and the onset of menarche: A test of a sociobiological model. *Child Development, 63,* 47–58.

Moffitt, T. E., Caspi, A., Dickson, N., Silva, P., & Stanton, W. (1996). Childhood-onset versus adolescent-onset antisocial conduct problems in males: Natural history from ages 3 to 18 years. *Development and Psychopathology, 8,* 399–424.

Moffitt, T. E., Caspi, A., Harrington, H., & Milne, B. J. (2002). Males on the life-course persistent and adolescent-limited antisocial pathways: Follow-up at age 26 years. *Development and Psychopathology, 14,* 179–207.

Moffitt, T. E., Caspi, A., Rutter, M., & Silva, P. A. (2001). *Sex differences in antisocial behaviour: Conduct disorder, delinquency and violence in the Dunedin Longitudinal Study.* Cambridge: Cambridge University Press.

Moffitt, T. E., & Lynam, D. (1994). The neuropsychology of conduct disorder and delinquency: Implications for understanding antisocial behavior. In D. C. Fowles, P. Sutker, & S. H. Goodman (Eds.), *Progress in experimental personality and psychopathology research* (pp. 233–262). New York: Springer.

Moffitt, T. E., Lynam, D., & Silva, P. A. (1994). Neuropsychological tests predict persistent male delinquency. *Criminology, 32,* 101–124.

Molina, B.S.G., & Pelham, W. E. (2003). Childhood predictors of adolescent substance use in a longitudinal study of children with ADHD. *Journal of Abnormal Psychology, 112,* 497–507.

Monastra, V. J., Lubar, J. F., & Linden, M. (2001). The development of quantitative a electroencephalographic scanning process for attention deficit-hyperactivity disorder: Reliability and validity studies. *Neuropsychology, 15,* 136–144.

Monitoring the Future. (2002). *National Results on Adolescent Drug Use: An Overview of Key Findings.* U.S. Department of Health and Human Services. Available: http://www .monitoringthefuture.org/pubs/ monographs/overview2002.pdf. Accessed February 2004.

Monroe, S. M., Rohde, P., Seeley, J. R., & Lewinsohn, P. M. (1999). Life events and depression in adolescence: Relationship loss as a prospective risk factor for first onset of major depressive disorder. *Journal of Abnormal Psychology, 108,* 606–614.

Montague, C. T., Farooqi, I. S., Whitehead, J. P., Soos, M. A., Rau, H., Wareham, N. J., Sewter, C. P., Digby, J. E., Mohammed, S. N., Hurst, J. A., Cheetham, C. H., Earley, A. R., Barnett, A. H., Prins, J. B., & O'Rahilly, S. (1997). Congenital leptin deficiency is associated with severe early-onset obesity in humans. *Nature, 387,* 903–907.

Monteleone, P., Brambilla, F., Bortolotti, F., & Maj, M. (2000). Serotonergic dysfunction across the eating disorders: Relations to eating behaviour, purging behaviour, and nutritional status and general psychopathology. *Psychological Medicine, 30,* 1099–1110.

Moore, M., & Carr, A. (2000). Anxiety disorders. In A. Carr (Ed.), *What works with children and adolescents?: A critical review of psychological interventions with children, adolescents and their families* (pp. 178–202). New York: Routledge.

Morgan, R. K. (1999). *Case studies in child and adolescent psychopathology.* Upper Saddle River, NJ: Prentice-Hall.

Morgan, W. P. (1896). A case of congenital word-blindness. *British Medical Journal, 2,* 1543–1544.

Morris, J. K., Wald, N. J., Mutton, D. E., & Alberman, E. (2003). Comparison of models of maternal age-specific risk for Down syndrome live births. *Prenatal Diagnosis, 23,* 252–258.

Morris, R. J., & Kratochwill, T. R. (Eds.). (1998). *The practice of child therapy (3rd ed.).* Needham Heights, MA: Allyn & Bacon.

Morrisey-Kane, E., & Prinz, R. J. (1999). Engagement in child and adolescent treatment: The role of parental cognitions and attributions. *Clinical Child and Family Psychology Review, 2,* 183–198.

Mortensen, E. L., Andresen, J., Kruuse, E., Sanders, S. A., Reinisch, J. M. (2003). IQ stability: The relation between child and young adult intelligence test scores in low-birthweight samples. *Scandinavian Journal of Psychology, 44,* 395–398.

Morton, J., & Frith, U. (1995). Causal modeling: A structural approach to developmental psychopathology. In D. Cicchetti & D. J. Cohen (Eds.), *Developmental psychopathology: Vol. 1. Theory and methods* (pp. 357–390). New York: Wiley-Interscience.

Moser, H. W., Ramey, C. T., & Leonard, C. O. (1990). Mental retardation. In A. E. H. Emery & D. L. Rimion (Eds.), *Principles and practice of medical genetics* (2nd ed., pp. 495–511). Edinburgh, Scotland: Churchill-Livingstone.

Mouridsen, S. E. (2003). Childhood disintegrative disorder. *Brain & Development, 25,* 225–228.

Mowrer, O. H. (1947). On the dual nature of learning: A reinterpretation of "conditioning" and "problem solving." *Harvard Educational Review, 17,* 102–148.

Mowrer, O. H. (1950). *Learning theory and the personality dynamics.* New York: Arnold Press.

Mowrer, O. H., & Mowrer, W. M. (1938). Enuresis: A method for its study and treatment. *American Journal of Orthopsychiatry, 8,* 436–459.

Mrazek, P. J., & Haggerty, R. J. (Eds.). (1994). *Reducing risks for mental disorders: Frontiers for preventive intervention.* Washington, DC: National Academy Press

MTA Cooperative Group. (1999a). Fourteen-month randomized clinical trial of treatment strategies for attention-deficit hyperactivity disorder. *Archives of General Psychiatry, 56,* 1073–1086.

MTA Cooperative Group. (1999b). Moderators and mediators of treatment response for children with ADHD: The MTA Study. *Archives of General Psychiatry, 56,* 1088–1096.

Mufson, L., & Dorta, K. P. (2003). Interpersonal therapy for depressed adolescents. In A. E. Kazdin & J. R. Weisz (Eds.), *Evidence-based psychotherapies for children and adolescents* (pp. 148–164). New York: Guilford Press.

Mulhern, R. K., Carpentieri, S., Shema, S., Stone, P., & Fairclough, D. (1993). Factors associated with social and behavioral problems among children recently diagnosed with brain tumor. *Journal of Pediatric Psychology, 18,* 339–350.

Mulhern, R. K., Reddick, W., Palmer, S. L., Glass, J. O., Elkin, T., David, K.L.E., et al. (1999). Neurocognitive deficits in medulloblastoma survivors and white matter loss. *Annals of Neurology, 46,* 834–841.

Mundy, P. (2003). The neural basis of social impairments in autism: The role of the dorsal medial-frontal cortex and anterior cingulate system. *Journal of Child Psychology and Psychiatry, 44,* 793–809.

Mundy, P., & Neal, R. (2000). Neuroplasticity, joint attention and autistic developmental psychopathology. *International Review of Research in Mental Retardation, 20,* 139–168.

Muñoz, K. A., Krebs-Smith, S. M., Ballard-Barbash, R., & Cleveland, L. E. (1997). Food intakes of US children and adolescents compared with recommendations. *Pediatrics, 100,* 323–329.

Murata, C., Suzuki, Y., Muramatsu, T., Taniyama, M., Atsumi, Y., Matsuoka, K., et al. (2000). Inactive aldehyde dehydrogenase 2 worsens glycemic control in patients with type 2 diabetes mellitus who drink low to moderate amounts of alcohol. *Alcoholism: Clinical & Experimental Research, 24,* 5S–11S.

Muratori, F., Picchi, L., Bruni, G., Patarnello, M., & Romagnoli, G. (2003). A two-year follow-up of psychodynamic psychotherapy for internalizing disorders in children. *Journal of the American Academy of Child and Adolescent Psychiatry, 42,* 331–339.

Muris, P., & Meesters, C. (2002). Attachment, behavioral inhibition, and anxiety disorders symptoms in normal adolescents. *Journal of Psychopathology and Behavioral Assessment, 24,* 97–106.

Muris, P., & Merckelbach, H. (2000). How serious are common childhood fears? II. The parent's point of view. *Behaviour Research and Therapy, 38,* 813–818.

Muris, P., & Merckelbach, H. (2001) The etiology of childhood specific phobia: A multifactorial model. In M. W. Vasey & M. M. Dadds (Eds.), *The developmental psychopathology of anxiety* (pp. 355–385). New York: Oxford University Press.

Muris, P., Rapee, R., Meesters, C., Schouten, E., & Geers, M. (2003). Threat perception abnormalities in children: The role of anxiety disorders symptoms, chronic anxiety, and state anxiety. *Journal of Anxiety Disorders, 17,* 271–287.

Murphy, C. C., Yeargin-Allsopp, M., Decoufle, P., & Drews, C. D. (1995). The administrative prevalence of mental retardation in 10-year-old children in metropolitan Atlanta, 1985 through 1987. *American Journal of Public Health, 85,* 319–322.

Murphy, D. A., Pelham, W. W., & Lang, A. R. (1992). Aggression in boys with attention deficit hyperactivity disorder: Methylphenidate effects on naturally occurring observed aggression, response to provocation, and social information processing. *Journal of Abnormal Child Psychology, 20,* 451–465.

Murphy, L. B. (1992). Sympathetic behavior in very young children. *Zero to Three, 12(4),* 1–5.

Murray, I. (1993). Looking back: Reminiscences from childhood and adolescence. In G. Weiss & L. T. Hechtman, *Hyperactive children grown up: ADHD in children, adolescents, and adults* (2nd ed., pp. 301–325). New York: Guilford Press.

Murry, V. M., Bynum, M. S., Brody, G. H., Willert, A., & Stephens, D. (2001). African American single mothers and children in context: A review of studies on risk and resilience. *Clinical Child & Family Psychology Review, 4,* 133–155.

Musher-Eizenman, D. R., Holub, S. C., & Arnett, M. (2003). Attitude and peer influences on adolescent substance use: The moderating effect of age, sex, and substance. *Journal of Drug Education, 33,* 1–23.

Nada-Raja, S., Langley, J. D., McGee, R., Williams, S. M., Begg, D. J., & Reeder, A. I. (1997). Inattentive and hyperactive behaviors and driving offences in adolescence. *Journal of the American Academy of Child and Adolescent Psychiatry, 36,* 515–522.

Nadeau, K., Littman, E. B., & Quinn, P. O. (1999). *Understanding girls with AD/HD.* Silver Spring, MD: Advantage Books.

Nader, K., Pynoos, R., Fairbanks, L., & Frederick, C. (1990). Children's PTSD reactions one year after a sniper attack at their school. *American Journal of Psychiatry, 147,* 1526–1530.

Nagin, D. S., & Tremblay, R. E. (1999). Trajectories of boy's physical aggression, opposition, and hyperactivity on the path to physically violent and nonviolent juvenile delinquency. *Child Development, 70,* 1181–1196.

Nagin, D. S., & Tremblay, R. F. (2001). Parental and early childhood predictors of persistent physical aggression in boys from kindergarten to high school. *Archives of General Psychiatry, 58,* 389–394.

Narayan, M., Srinath, S., Anderson, G. M., & Meundi, D. B. (1993). Cerebrospinal fluid levels of homovanillic acid and 5-hydroxy-indoleacetic acid in autism. *Biological Psychiatry, 33,* 630–635.

National Advisory Mental Health Council Workgroup on Child and Adolescent Mental Health Intervention and Deployment (2001). *Blueprint for change: Research on child and adolescent mental health.* Rockville, MD: National Institute of Mental Health.

National Childhood Cancer Foundation. (1997). *Facts about childhood cancer* [On-line]. Available: http://www.nccf.org/nccf/facts.htm#ped.

National Institute of Justice. (1996). *Victim costs and consequences: A new look.* Washington, DC: Author.

National Institute of Mental Health. (1994a). *Attention deficit hyperactivity disorder: Decade of the brain.* (NIMH Publication No. 94-3572). Washington, DC: Author.

National Institute of Mental Health. (1994b). *Eating disorders.* (DHHS Publication No. NIMH 94-3477). Washington, DC: U.S. Government Printing Office.

National Research Council. (1993). *Understanding child abuse and neglect.* Washington, DC: National Academy Press.

Neal, A. M., & Turner, S. M. (1991). Anxiety disorders research with African Americans: Current status. *Psychological Bulletin, 109,* 400–410.

Neal, J., & Edelmann, R. J. (2003). The etiology of social phobia: Toward a developmental profile. *Clinical Psychology Review, 23,* 761–786.

Needleman, H. L., Reiss, J. A., Tobin, M. J., Biesecker, G. E., & Greenhouse, J. B. (1996). Bone lead levels and delinquent behavior. *Journal of the American Medical Association, 275,* 363–369.

Neeleman, J., Systema, S., & Wadsworth, M. (2002). Propensity to psychiatric and somatic ill-health: Evidence from a birth cohort. *Psychological Medicine, 32,* 793–803.

Neisser, U., Boodoo, G., Bouchard T. J., Jr., Boykin, A. W., Brody, N., Ceci, S. J., et al. (1996). Intelligence: Knowns and unknowns. *American Psychologist, 51,* 77–101.

Nelles, W. B., & Barlow, D. H. (1988). Do children panic? *Clinical Psychology Review, 8,* 359–372.

Nelson, C. A. (1999). How important are the first 3 years of life? *Applied Developmental Science, 3,* 235–238.

Nelson, C. A. (2000). The neurobiological bases of early intervention. In J. P. Shonkoff, S. J. Meisels (Eds.), *Handbook of early childhood intervention (2/e.),* (204–227). New York: Cambridge University Press.

Nelson, C. A., & Bloom, F. E. (1997). Child development and neuroscience. *Child Development, 68,* 970–987.

Nelson, D. R., Hammen, C., Brennan, P. A., & Ullman, J. B. (2003). The impact of maternal depression on adolescent adjustment: The role of expressed emotion. *Journal of Consulting and Clinical Psychology, 71,* 935–944.

Nelson, W. L., Hughes, H. M., Katz, B., & Searight, H. R. (1999). Anorexic eating attitudes and behaviors of male and female college students. *Adolescence, 34,* 621–633.

Nemeroff, C. B. (2004). Neurobiological consequences of childhood trauma. *Journal of Clinical Psychiatry Special Issue: Update on posttraumatic stress disorder, 65,* 18–28.

Nemeth, M. (1994, April 4). Altered states. *Maclean's,* pp. 48–49.

Neumark-Sztainer, D., Martin, S., & Story, M. (2000). School-based programs for obesity prevention: What do adolescents recommend? *American Journal of Health Promotion, 14,* 232–235.

Neumark-Sztainer, D., & Story, M. (1998). Dieting and binge eating among adolescents: What do they really mean? *Journal of the American Dietetic Association, 98,* 446–450.

Neumark-Sztainer, D., Story, M., Hannan, P., Beuhring, T., & Resnick, M. (2000).

Disordered eating among adolescents: Associations with sexual/physical abuse and other familial/psychosocial factors. *International Journal of Eating Disorders, 28,* 249–258.

New York Times. (1946, April 14).

Newcorn, J. H., Halperin, J. M., Jensen, P. S., Abikoff, H. B., Arnold, L. E., Cantwell, D. P., et al., (2001). Symptom profiles in children with ADHD: Comorbidity and gender. *Journal of the American Academy of Child and Adolescent Psychiatry, 40,* 137–146.

Newsom, C., & Hovanitz, C. A. (in press). Autistic spectrum disorders. In E. J. Mash & R. A. Barkley (Eds.), *Treatment of childhood disorders (3rd ed.).* New York: Guilford Press.

Nichols, M. (1995, January 30). Schizophrenia: Hidden torment. *Maclean's,* pp. 70–74.

Nicolson, R., Lenane, M., Singaracharlu, S., Malaspina, D., Giedd, J. N., Hamburger, S. D., et al. (2000). Premorbid speech and language impairments in childhood-onset schizophrenia: Association with risk factors. *American Journal of Psychiatry, 157,* 794–800.

Nicolson, R., & Rapoport, J. L. (1999). Childhood-onset schizophrenia: Rare but worth studying. *Biological Psychiatry, 46,* 1418–1428.

Nicolson, R., & Szatmari, P. (2003). Genetic and neurobiological influences in autistic disorder. *Canadian Journal of Psychiatry, 48,* 526–537.

Nigg, J. T. (2000). On inhibition/disinhibition in developmental psychopathology: Views from cognitive and personality psychology and a working inhibition taxonomy. *Psychological Bulletin, 126,* 220–246.

Nigg, J. T. (2001). Is ADHD an inhibitory disorder? *Psychological Bulletin, 125,* 571–596.

Nigg, J. T. (2003). ADHD: Guides for the perplexed reflect the state of the field. *Journal of Clinical Child and Adolescent Psychology, 32,* 302–308.

Nigg, J. T., Blaskey, L. G., Huang-Pollock, C. L., & Rappley, M. D. (2002). Neuropsychological executive functions in DSM-IV ADHD subtypes. *Journal of the American Academy of Child and Adolescent Psychiatry, 41,* 59–66.

Nilsson, E. W., Gillberg, C., Gillberg, I. C., & Rastam, M. (1999). Ten-year follow-up of adolescent-onset anorexia nervosa: Personality disorders. *Journal of the American Academy of Child and Adolescent Psychiatry, 38,* 1389–1395.

NIMH (National Institute of Mental Health). (2003). *Breaking ground, breaking through: The strategic plan for mood disorders research of the National Institute of Mental Health.* Washington, DC: U.S. Department of Health and Human Services.

Noam, G. G., Chandler, M., & LaLonde, C. (1995). Clinical-developmental psychology: Constructivism and social cognition in the study of psychological dysfunctions. In D. Cicchetti & D. J.

Cohen (Eds.), *Developmental psychopathology: Vol. 1. Theory and methods* (pp. 424–464). New York: Wiley.

Nolen-Hoeksema, S., Girgus, J. S., & Seligman, M.E.P. (1992). Predictors and consequences of childhood depressive symptoms: A 5-year longitudinal study. *Journal of Abnormal Psychology, 101,* 405–422.

Noll, J. G., Horowitz, L. A., Bonanno, G. A., Trickett, P. K., & Putnam, F. W. (2003). Revictimization and self-harm in females who experienced childhood sexual abuse: Results from a prospective study. *Journal of Interpersonal Violence, 18,* 1452–1471.

Noll, J. G., Trickett, P. K., & Putnam, F. W. (2003). A prospective investigation of the impact of childhood sexual abuse on the development of sexuality. *Journal of Consulting and Clinical Psychology, 71,* 575–586.

Noll, R. B., LeRoy, S., Bukowski, W. M., Rogosch, F. A., & Kulkarni, R. (1991). Peer relationships and adjustment in children with cancer. *Journal of Pediatric Psychology, 16,* 307–326.

Norgaard, J. P., Pederson, E. B., & Djurhuus, J. C. (1985). Diurnal antidiuretic hormone levels in enuretics. *Journal of Urology, 134,* 1029–1031.

Nottelman, E. D., & Jensen, P. S. (1995). Comorbidity of disorders in children and adolescents: Developmental perspectives. In T. H. Ollendick & R. J. Prinz (Eds.), *Advances in clinical child psychology* (Vol. 17, pp. 109–155). New York: Plenum.

Nowakowski, R. S., & Hayes, N. L. (1999). CNS development: An overview. *Development and Psychopathology, 11,* 395–417.

Nuffield Council on Bioethics. (2002). *Genetics and human behaviour: The ethical context.* London: Author.

O'Connor, T. G. (2002). Annotation: The 'effects' of parenting reconsidered: Findings, challenges, and applications. *Journal of Child Psychology & Psychiatry & Allied Disciplines, 43,* 555–572.

O'Connor, Thomas G., Plomin, Robert (2000). Developmental behavioral genetics. In A. J. Sameroff, M. Lewis, & S. Miller (Eds.). *Handbook of developmental psychopathology* (2nd ed., pp. 217–235). Dordrecht, Netherlands: Kluwer Academic Publishers.

O'Dea, J., & Abraham, S. (1999). Onset of disordered eating attitudes and behaviors in early adolescence: Interplay of pubertal status, gender, weight, and age. *Adolescence, 34,* 671–679.

O'Dea, J., & Abraham, S. (2000). Improving the body image, eating attitudes, and behaviors of young male and female adolescents: A new educational approach that focuses on self-esteem. *International Journal of Eating Disorders, 28,* 43–57.

Odgers, C. L., & Moretti, M. M. (2002). Aggressive and antisocial girls: Research update and challenges. *International Journal of Forensic Mental Health Services, 1,* 103–119.

Office of the Surgeon General (2001). *Youth violence: A report of the Surgeon General.* Rockville, MD: Department of Health and Human Services, U.S. Public Health Service.

Offord, D. R., Alder, R. J., & Boyle, M. H. (1986). Prevalence and sociodemographic correlates of conduct disorder. *American Journal of Social Psychiatry, 4,* 272–278.

Offord, D. R., Kraemer, H. C., Kazdin, A. E., Jensen, P. S., & Harrington, R. (1998). Lowering the burden of suffering from child psychiatric disorder: Trade-offs among clinical, targeted, and universal interventions. *Journal of the American Academy of Child and Adolescent Psychiatry, 37,* 686–694.

Ogawa, J. R., Sroufe, L. A., Weinfield, N. S., Carlson, E. A., & Egeland, B. (1997). Development and the fragmented self: Longitudinal study of dissociative symptomatology in a nonclinical sample. *Development and Psychopathology, 9,* 855–879.

Ogden, C. L., Flegal, K. M., Carroll, M. D., & Johnson, C. L. (2002). Prevalence and trends in overweight among US children and adolescents, 1999–2000. *Journal of the American Medical Association, 288,* 1728–1732.

Ohan, J. L., & Johnston, C. (2002). Are the performance estimates given by boys with ADHD self-protective? *Journal of Clinical Child Psychology, 31,* 230–241.

Ojemann, G. A. (1991). Cortical organization of language. *Neuroscience, 11,* 2281–2287.

Olds, D., Eckenrode, J., Henderson, C. R., Kitzman, H., Powers, J., Cole, R., et al. (1997). Long-term effects of home visitation on maternal life course and child abuse and neglect: Fifteen-year follow-up of a randomized trial. *Journal of the American Medical Association, 278,* 637–643.

Olfson, M., Gameroff, M. J., Marcus, S. C., Jensen, P. S. (2003). National trends in the treatment of attention deficit hyperactivity disorder. *American Journal of Psychiatry, 160,* 1071–1077.

Olfson, M., Gameroff, M. J., Marcus, S. C., & Waslick, B. D. (2003). Outpatient treatment of child and adolescent depression in the United States. *Archives of General Psychiatry, 60,* 1236–1242.

Olfson, M., Marcus, S. C., Weissman, M. M., & Jensen, P. S. (2002). National trends in the use of psychotropic medications by children. *Journal of the American Academy of Child and Adolescent Psychiatry, 41,* 514–521.

Olfson, M., Shaffer, D., Marcus, S. C., & Greenberg, T. (2003). Relationship between antidepressant medication treatment and suicide in adolescents. *Archives of General Psychiatry, 60,* 978–982.

Ollendick, T. H. (1998). Panic disorder in children and adolescents: New developments, new directions. *Journal of Clinical Child Psychology, 27,* 234–245.

Ollendick, T. H., & Hirshfeld-Becker, D. R. (2002). The developmental psychopathology of social anxiety disorder. *Biological Psychiatry, 51,* 44–58.

Ollendick, T. H., & King, N. J. (1994b). Fears and their level of interference in adolescents. *Behaviour Research and Therapy, 32,* 635–638.

Ollendick, T. H., & King, N. J. (1998). Empirically supported treatments for children with phobic and anxiety disorders: Current status. *Journal of Clinical Child Psychology, 27,* 156–167.

Ollendick, T. H., Mattis, S. G., & King, N. J. (1994). Panic in children and adolescents: A review. *Journal of Child Psychology and Psychiatry, 35,* 113–134.

Ollendick, T. H., Seligman, L. D., Goza, A. B., Byrd, D. A., & Singh, K. (2003). Anxiety and depression in children and adolescents: A factor-analytic examination of the tripartite model. *Journal of Child and Family Studies, 12,* 157–170.

Ollendick, T. H., Yang, B., Dong, Q., Xia, Y., & Lin, L. (1995). Perceptions of fear in older children and adolescents: The role of gender and friendship status. *Journal of Abnormal Child Psychology, 23,* 439–452.

Ollendick, T. H., Yang, B., King, N, J., Dong, Q., & Akande, A. (1996). Fears in American, Australian, Chinese, and Nigerian children and adolescents: A cross-cultural study. *Journal of Child Psychology and Psychiatry, 37,* 213–220.

Olson, S. L., Bates, J. E., Sandy, J. M., & Lanthier, R. (2000). Early developmental precursors of externalizing behavior in middle childhood and adolescence. *Journal of Abnormal Child Psychology, 28,* 119–133.

Olweus, D. (1987). Testosterone adrenaline: Aggressive antisocial behavior in normal adolescent males. In S. A. Mednick, T. E. Moffitt, & S. A. Stack (Eds.), *The causes of crime: New biological approaches* (pp. 263–283). New York: Cambridge University Press.

Olweus, D. (1995). Bullying or peer abuse at school: Facts and intervention. *Current Directions in Psychological Science, 4,* 196–200.

Olweus, D. (2003). Social problems in school. In A. Slater & G. Bremner (Eds). *An introduction to developmental psychology* (pp. 434–454). Malden, MA: Blackwell Publishers.

Oosterlaan, J., Logan, G. D., & Sergeant, J. A. (1998). Response inhibition in AD/HD, CD, comorbid AD/HD + CD, anxious, and control children: A meta-analysis of studies with the Stop Task. *Journal of Child Psychology and Psychiatry, 39,* 411–425.

Ornitz, E. M., Russell, A. T., Hanna, G. L., Gabikian, P., Gehricke, J. G., Song, D., & Guthrie, D. (1999). Prepulse inhibition of startle and the neurobiology of primary nocturnal enuresis. *Biological Psychiatry, 45,* 1455–1466.

Osborne, R. B., Hatcher, J. W., & Richtsmeier, A. J. (1989). The role of social modeling in unexplained pediatric pain. *Journal of Pediatric Psychology, 14,* 43–61.

Osofsky, J. D. (1998). On the outside: Interventions with infants and families at risk. *Infant Mental Health Journal, 19,* 101–108.

Oster, G. D., & Montgomery, S. S. (1995). *Helping your depressed teenager: A guide for parents and caregivers.* New York: Wiley.

Osterling, J. A., Dawson, G., & Munson, J. A. (2002). Early recognition of 1-year-old infants with autism spectrum disorder versus mental retardation. *Development and Psychopathology, 14,* 239–251.

Owen, B. (1993, May 18). Kids in the dumps. *Winnipeg Free Press,* p. C1.

Owens, C., Booth, N., & Briscoe, M. (2003). Suicide outside the care of mental health services: A case-controlled psychological autopsy study. *Crisis, 24,* 113–121.

Owens, E. B., Hinshaw, S. P., Kraemer, H. C., Arnold, L. E., Abikoff, H. B., Cantwell, D. P., et al., (2003). Which treatment for whom for ADHD? Moderators of treatment response in the MTA. *Journal of Consulting and Clinical Psychology, 71,* 540–552.

Owens, J. A., Palermo, T. M., & Rosen, C. L. (2002). Overview of current management of sleep disturbances in children: II-Behavioral interventions. *Current Therapeutic Research, 63 (Supplement B),* B38–B52.

Owens, J. S., & Hoza, B. (2003). The role of inattention and hyperactivity/impulsivity in the positive illusory bias. *Journal of Consulting and Clinical Psychology, 71,* 680–691.

Owens, R. G., & Slade, P. D. (1987). Running and anorexia nervosa: An empirical study. *International Journal of Eating Disorders, 6,* 771–775.

Ozonoff, S., & South, M. (2001). Early social development in young children with autism: Theoretical and clinical implications. In G. Bremner & A. Fogel (Eds.), *Blackwell handbook of infant development* (pp. 565–588). Malden, MA: Blackwell Publishers.

Ozonoff, S. (1997). Components of executive function in autism and other disorders. In J. Russell (Ed.), *Autism as an executive disorder* (pp. 179–211). New York: Oxford University Press.

O'Leary, K. D., Malone, J., & Tyree, A. (1994). Physical aggression in early marriage: Prerelationship and relationship effects. *Journal of Consulting and Clinical Psychology, 62,* 594–602.

O'Malley, P. M., Johnston, L. D., & Bachman, J. G. (1999). Epidemiology of substance abuse in adolescence. In P. J. Ott & R. E. Tarter (Eds), *Sourcebook on substance abuse: Etiology, epidemiology, assessment, and treatment* (pp. 14–31). Boston: Allyn & Bacon.

Paavonen, E. J., Almqvist, F., Tamminen, T., Moilanen, I., Piha, J., Raesaenen, E., & Aronen, E. T. (2002). Poor sleep and psychiatric symptoms at school: An epidemiological study. *European Child & Adolescent Psychiatry, 11,* 10–17.

Pace, G. M., & Toyer, E. A. (2000). The effects of a vitamin supplement on the pica of a child with severe mental retardation. *Journal of Applied Behavior Analysis, 33,* 619–622.

Packman, A., & Onslow, M. (2002). Searching for the cause of stuttering. *Lancet, 360,* 655–656.

Pagani, L., Boulerice, B., Vitaro, F., & Tremblay, R. E. (1999). Effects of poverty on academic failure and delinquency in boys: A change and process model approach. *Journal of Child Psychology and Psychiatry, 40,* 1209–1219.

Parry-Jones, W. L., & Parry-Jones, B. (1994). Implications of historical evidence for the classification of eating disorders: A dimension overlooked in DSM-III-R and ICD-10. *British Journal of Psychiatry, 165,* 287–292.

Patterson, G. R. (1982). *Coercive family process.* Eugene, OR: Castalia.

Patterson, G. R. (1996). Some characteristics of a developmental theory for early-onset delinquency. In M. F. Lenzenweger & J. J. Haugaard (Eds.), *Frontiers of developmental psychopathology* (pp. 81–124). New York: Oxford University Press.

Patterson, G. R., DeGarmo, D. S., & Knutson, N. (2000). Hyperactive and antisocial behaviors: Comorbid or two points in the same process. *Development and Psychopathology, 12,* 91–106.

Patterson, G. R., Reid, J. B., & Dishion, T. J. (1992). *Antisocial boys.* Eugene, OR: Castalia.

Patton, M. Q. (1990). *Qualitative evaluation and research methods (2nd ed.).* Beverly Hills, CA: Sage.

Paul, C., Fitzjohn, J., Herbison, P., & Dickson, N. (2000). The determinants of sexual intercourse before age 16. *Journal of Adolescent Health, 27,* 136–147.

Pearson, D. A., Norton, A. M., & Farwell, E. C. (1997). Attention-deficit/hyperactivity disorder in mental retardation: Nature of attention deficits. In J. A. Burack, J. T. Enns et al. (Eds.), *Attention, development, and psychopathology* (pp. 205–221). New York: Guilford Press.

Peleg-Popko, O., & Dar, R. (2003). Ritual behavior in children and mothers' perceptions of family patterns. *Journal of Anxiety Disorders, 17,* 667–681.

Pelham, W. E. (1993). Pharmacotherapy for children with attention-deficit hyperactivity disorder. *School Psychology Review, 22,* 199–227.

Pelham, W. E. (2001). Are ADHD/I and ADHD/C the same or different? Does it matter? *Clinical Psychology: Science and Practice, 8,* 502–506.

Pelham, W. E., Gnagy, E. M., Greiner, A. R., Hoza, B., Hinshaw, S. P., Swanson, J. M., et al., (2000). Behavioral versus behavioral and pharmacological treatment in ADHD children attending a summer treatment program. *Journal of Abnormal Child Psychology, 28,* 507–525.

Pelham, W. E., Greiner, A. R., Gnagy, E. M., Hoza, B., Martin, L., Sams, S. E., & Wilson, T. (1996). Intensive treatment for ADHD: A model summer treatment program. In M. Roberts & A. LaGreca (Eds.), *Model programs in child and family mental health* (pp. 193–213). Mahwah, NJ: Erlbaum.

Pelham, W. E., & Hoza, B. (1996). Intensive treatment: Summer treatment program for children with ADHD. In E. D. Hibbs & P. S. Jensen (Eds.), *Psychosocial treatment research of child and adolescent disorders: Empirically based strategies for clinical practice* (pp. 311–340). Washington, DC: American Psychological Association.

Pelham, W. E., Jr., & Lang, A. R. (1999). Can your children drive you to drink?: Stress and parenting in adults interacting with children with ADHD. *Alcohol Research and Health, 23,* 1999, 292–298.

Pelham, W. E., Jr. (1999). The NIMH Multimodal Treatment Study for attention-deficit hyperactivity disorder: Just say yes to drugs alone. *Canadian Journal of Psychiatry, 44,* 981–990.

Pelham, W. E., Jr., Wheeler, T., & Chronis, A. (1998). Empirically supported psychosocial treatments for attention deficit hyperactivity disorder. *Journal of Clinical Child Psychology, 27,* 190–205.

Pendergrast, M., Taylor, E., Rapoport, J. L., Bartko, J., Donnelly, M., Zametkin, A., Ahearn, M. B., Dunn, G., & Wieselberg, H. M. (1988). The diagnosis of childhood hyperactivity: A U.S.-U.K. cross-national study of DSM-III and ICD-9. *Journal of Child Psychology and Psychiatry, 29,* 289–300.

Pennington, B.F. (1999). Toward an integrated understanding of dyslexia: Genetic, neurological, and cognitive mechanisms. *Development and Psychopathology, 11,* 629–654.

Pennington, B. F. (2002). *The development of psychopathology: Nature and nature.* New York: Guilford Press.

Pennington, B. F., & Lefly, D. L. (2001). Early reading development in children at family risk for dyslexia. *Child Development, 72,* 816–833.

Pennington, B. F., Moon, J., Edgin, J., Stedron, J., & Nadel, L. (2003). The neuropsychology of Down syndrome: Evidence for hippocampal dysfunction. *Child Development, 74,* 75–93.

Pennington, B. F., & Ozonoff, S. (1996). Executive functions and developmental psychopathology. *Journal of Child Psychology and Psychiatry, 37,* 51–87.

Pepler, D. J., Craig, W. M., Connolly, J., & Henderson, K. (2002). Bullying, sexual harassment, dating violence, and substance use among adolescents. In C. Wekerle & A. Wall (Eds), *The violence and addiction equation: Theoretical and clinical issues in substance abuse and relationship violence* (pp. 153–168). New York: Brunner-Routledge.

Perrin, E. C., Ayoub, C. C., & Willett, J. B. (1993). In the eyes of the beholder: Family and maternal influences on perceptions of adjustment of children with a chronic illness. *Journal of Developmental and Behavioral Pediatrics, 14,* 94–105.

Perrin, S., & Last, C. G. (1997). Worrisome thoughts in children clinically referred for anxiety disorder. *Journal of Clinical Child Psychology, 26,* 181–189.

Perrin, S., Smith, P., & Yule, W. (2000). Practitioner review: The assessment and treatment of post-traumatic stress disorder in children and adolescents. *Journal of Child Psychology and Psychiatry, 41,* 277–289.

Perry, C. L., Williams, C. L., Komro, K. A., Veblen-Mortenson, S., Forster, J. L., Bernstein-Lachter, R., et al. (2000). Project Northland high school interventions: Community action to reduce adolescent alcohol use. *Health Education and Behavior, 27(1),* 29–49.

Petersen, A. C., Compas, B., Brooks-Gunn, J., Stemmler, M., Ey, S., & Grant, K. E. (1993). Depression in adolescence. *American Psychologist, 48,* 155–168.

Petersen, A. C., Sarigiani, P. A., & Kennedy, R. E. (1991). Adolescent depression: Why more girls? *Journal of Youth and Adolescence, 20,* 247–271.

Peterson, B. S. (2003). Conceptual, methodological, and statistical challenges in brain imaging studies of developmentally based psychopathologies. *Development and Psychopathology, 15,* 811–832.

Peterson, B. S., Pine, D. S., Cohen, P., & Brook, J. S. (2001). Prospective, longitudinal study of tic, obsessive-compulsive, and attention-deficit/hyperactivity disorders in an epidemiological sample. *Journal of the American Academy of Child and Adolescent Psychiatry, 40,* 685–695.

Peterson, L., Harbeck, D., Farmer, J., & Zink, M. (1991). Developmental contributions to the assessment of children's pain: Conceptual and methodological implications. In J. P. Bush & S. W. Harkins (Eds.), *Children in pain: Clinical and research issues from a developmental perspective* (pp. 33–58). New York: Springer-Verlag.

Peterson, L., Reach, K., & Grube, S. (2003). Health-related disorders. In E. J. Mash & R. A. Barkley (Eds.), *Child psychopathology* (2nd ed., pp. 716–749). New York: Guilford.

Pettit, G. S., & Dodge, K. A. (2003). Violent children: Bridging development, intervention, and public policy. *Developmental Psychology, 39,* 187–188.

Pfeffer, C. R. (2002). Suicide in mood disordered children and adolescents. *Child and Adolescent Psychiatric Clinics of North America, 11,* 639–648.

Pfiffner, L. J., & Barkley, R. A. (1998). Educational placement and classroom management. In R. A. Barkley, *Attention deficit hyperactivity disorder: A handbook for diagnosis and treatment* (pp. 498–539). New York: Guilford Press.

Phillips, W., Gomez, J. C., Baron-Cohen, S., Laa, V., & Riviere, A. (1995). Treating people as objects, agents, or "subjects": How young children with and without autism make requests. *Journal of Child Psychology and Psychiatry, 36,* 1383–1398.

Piacentini, J. (1997). *Cognitive-behavioral treatment of OCD in children and adolescents.* Unpublished manuscript, UCLA, Los Angeles, Childhood OCD and Related Disorders Program.

Piacentini, J., & Bergman, R. L. (2000). Obsessive-compulsive disorder in children. *Psychiatric Clinics of North America, 23,* 519–533.

Piacentini, J., & Graae, F. (1997). Childhood OCD. In E. Hollander & D. Stein (Eds.), *Obsessive-compulsive disorders: Diagnosis, etiology, treatment* (pp. 23–46). New York: Marcel Dekker.

Piacentini, J., Jacobs, C., & Maidment, K. (1997). *Behavioral family treatment for families of children and adolescents with obsessive-compulsive disorder: Preliminary treatment manual outline.* Unpublished manuscript, UCLA, Los Angeles, Childhood OCD and Related Disorders Program.

Pickles, A., & Angold, A. (2003). Natural categories or fundamental dimensions: On carving nature at the joints and the rearticulation of psychopathology. *Development and Psychopathology* Special Issue: Conceptual, methodological, and statistical issues in developmental psychopathology: A special issue in honor of Paul E. Meehl, *15,* 529–551.

Pike, A., & Plomin, R. (1996). Importance of nonshared environmental factors for childhood and adolescent psychopathology. *Journal of the American Academy of Child and Adolescent Psychiatry, 35,* 560–570.

Pike, K. M., Walsh, B. T., Vitousek, K., Wilson, G. T., & Bauer, J. (in press). Cognitive behavioral therapy in the posthospital treatment of anorexia nervosa. *American Journal of Psychiatry.*

Pine, D. S. (1997). Childhood anxiety disorders. *Current Opinions in Pediatrics, 9,* 329–338.

Pine, D. S. (2003). Developmental psychobiology and response to threats: Relevance to trauma in children and adolescents. *Biological Psychiatry, 53,* 796–808.

Pine, D. S., Cohen, E., Cohen, P., & Brook, J. S. (2000). Social phobia and the persistence of conduct problems. *Journal of Child Psychology and Psychiatry, 41,* 657–665.

Pine, D. S., & Grun, J. (1999). Childhood anxiety: Integrating developmental psychopathology and affective neuroscience. *Journal of Child and Adolescent Psychopharmacology, 9,* 1–12.

Pinel, J. P. J., Assanand, S., & Lehman, D. R. (2000). Hunger, eating, and ill health. *American Psychologist, 55,* 1105–1116.

Piven, J. (1999). Genetic liability for autism: The behavioural expression in relatives. *International Review of Psychiatry, 11,* 299–308.

Piven, J., Harper, J., Palmer, P., & Arndt, S. (1996). Course of behavioral change in autism: A retrospective study of high-IQ adolescents and adults. *Journal of the American Academy of Child and Adolescent Psychiatry, 35,* 523–529.

Piven, J., Simon, J., Chase, G. A., Wzorek, M., Landa, R., Gayle, J., & Folstein, S. (1993). The etiology of autism: Pre-, peri- and neonatal factors. *Journal of the American Academy of Child and Adolescent Psychiatry, 32,* 1256–1263.

Plante, W. A., Lobato, D., & Engel, R. (2001). Review of group interventions for pediatric chronic conditions. *Journal of Pediatric Psychology, 26,* 435–453.

Pliszka, S. R. (1992). Comorbidity of attention-deficit hyperactivity disorder and overanxious disorder. *Journal of the American Academy of Child and Adolescent Psychiatry, 31,* 197–203.

Pliszka, S. R. (2000). Patterns of psychiatric comorbidity with attention-deficit/hyperactivity disorder. *Child and Adolescent Psychiatric Clinics of North America, 9,* 525–540.

Pliszka, S. R., Liotti, M., & Woldorff, M. G. (2000). Inhibitory control in children with attention-deficit/hyperactivity disorder: Event-related potentials identify the processing component and timing of an impaired right-frontal response-inhibition mechanism. *Biological Psychiatry, 48,* 238–246.

Pliszka, S. R., McCracken, J. T., & Maas, J. W. (1996). Catecholamines in attention deficit hyperactivity disorder: Current perspectives. *Journal of the American Academy of Child and Adolescent Psychiatry, 35,* 264–272.

Plomin, R., & Neiderhiser, J. M. (1991). Quantitative genetics, molecular genetics, and intelligence. *Intelligence, 15,* 369–387.

Plomin, R., & Rutter, M. (1998). Child development, molecular genetics, and what to do with genes once they are found. *Child Development, 69,* 1223–1242.

Pnoos, R. S., Steinberg, A. M., & Piacentini, J. C. (1999). A developmental psychopathology model of childhood traumatic stress and intersection with anxiety disorders. *Biological Psychiatry, 46,* 1542–1554.

Podar, I., Hannus, A., & Allik, J. (1999). Personality and affectivity characteristics associated with eating disorders: A comparison of eating disordered, weight-preoccupied, and normal samples. *Journal of Personality Assessment, 73,* 133–147.

Polivy, J., & Herman, C. P. (1999). The effects of resolving to diet on restrained and unrestrained eaters: The "false hope syndrome." *International Journal of Eating Disorders, 26,* 434–447.

Pollak, S. D., Cicchetti, D., Hornung, K., & Reed, A. (2000). Recognizing emotion in faces: Developmental effects of child abuse and neglect. *Developmental Psychology, 36,* 679–688.

Pollak, S. D. & Tolley-Schell, S. A. (2003). Selective attention to facial emotion in physically abused children. *Journal of Abnormal Psychology, 112,* 323–338.

Pollock, L. (1987). *A lasting relationship: Parents and children over three centuries.* Hanover: University of New Hampshire Press.

Polloway, E. A., Schewel, R., & Patton, J. R. (1992). Learning disabilities in adulthood: Personal perspectives. *Journal of Learning Disabilities, 25,* 520–522.

Posner, M. I. (2001). The developing human brain. *Developmental Science, 4,* 253–387.

Post, R. M., & Weiss, S. B. (1998). Sensitization and kindling phenomena in mood, anxiety, and obsessive-compulsive disorders: The role of serotonergic mechanisms in illness progression. *Biological Psychiatry, 44,* 193–206.

Post, R. M., Weiss, S. B., Leverich, G. S., George, M. S., Frye, M., & Ketter, T. A. (1996). Developmental psychobiology of cyclic affective illness: Implications for early intervention. *Development and Psychopathology, 8,* 273–305.

Poulin, F., Dishion, T. J., & Haas, E. (1999). The peer influence paradox: Friendship quality and deviancy training within male adolescent friendships. *Merrill-Palmer Quarterly, 45,* 42–61.

Powers, S., Blount, R., Bachanas, P., Cotter, M., & Swan, S. (1993). Helping preschool leukemia patients and parents cope during injections. *Journal of Pediatric Psychology, 18,* 681–695.

Poznanski, E. O. (1979). Childhood depression: A psychodynamic approach to the etiology of depression in children. In A. French & I. Berlin (Eds.), *Depression in children and adolescents* (pp. 46–68). New York: Human Sciences Press.

Poznanski, E. O., & Mokros, H. B. (1994). Phenomenology and epidemiology of mood disorders in children and adolescents. In W. M. Reynolds & H. F. Johnston (Eds.), *Handbook of depression in children and adolescents* (pp. 19–39). New York: Plenum.

Pratt, H. D., Phillips, E. L., Greydanus, D. E., & Patel, D. R. (2003). Eating disorders in the adolescent population: Future directions. *Journal of Adolescent Research, 18,* 297–317.

President's New Freedom Commission on Mental Health (2003). *Achieving the promise: Transforming mental health care in America.* Available http://www.mentalhealthcommission.gov. Accessed February 16, 2004.

Prevent Child Abuse America (2001). *Total estimated cost of child abuse and neglect in the United States: Statistical evidence.* Available: http://www.preventchildabuse.org/learn_more/research_docs/cost_analysis.pdf.

Prince, J. B., Wilens, T. E., Biederman, J., Spencer, T. J., & Wozniak, J. R. (1996). Clonidine for sleep disturbances associated with attention-deficit hyperactivity disorder: A systematic chart review of 62 cases. *Journal of the American Academy of Child and Adolescent Psychiatry, 35,* 599–605.

Pring, L., Hermelin, B., & Heavey, L. (1995). Savants, segments, art and autism. *Journal of Child Psychology and Psychiatry, 36,* 1065–1076.

Prins, P.J.M., & Ollendick, T. H. (2003). Cognitive change and enhanced coping: Missing mediational links in cognitive behavior therapy with anxiety-disordered children. *Clinical Child and Family Psychology Review, 6,* 87–105.

Prinz, R. J., & Miller, G. E. (1996). Parental engagement in interventions for children at risk for conduct disorder. In R. Dev Peters & R. J. McMahon (Eds.), *Preventing childhood disorders, substance abuse, and delinquency* (Vol. 3, pp. 161–183). Thousand Oaks, CA: Sage.

Prior, M., Smart, D., Sanson, A., & Oberklaid, F. (2000). Does shy-inhibited temperament in childhood lead to anxiety problems in adolescence? *Journal of the American Academy of Child and Adolescent Psychiatry, 39,* 461–468.

Pritchard, J. C. (1837). *A treatise on insanity and other disorders affecting the mind.* Philadelphia: Haswell, Barrington, & Haswell.

Prizant, B. (1996). Communication, language, social, and emotional development. *Journal of Autism and Developmental Disorders, 26,* 173–178.

Prizant, B., & Wetherby, A. (1989). Enhancing language and communication in autism: From theory to practice. In G. Dawson (Ed.), *Autism: Nature, diagnosis, and treatment* (pp. 282–309). New York: Guilford Press.

Pulver, A. E. (2000). Search for schizophrenia vulnerability genes. *Biological Psychiatry, 47,* 221–230.

Pynoos, R. S., Frederick, C., Nader, K., Arroyo, W., Steinberg, A., Eth, S., Nunez, F., & Fairbanks, L. (1987). Life threat and posttraumatic stress in school-age children. *Archives of General Psychiatry, 44,* 1057–1063.

Quas, J. A., Goodman, G. S., & Jones, D.P.H. (2003). Predictors of attributions of self-blame and internalizing behavior problems in sexually abused children. *Journal of Child Psychology & Psychiatry & Allied Disciplines, 44,* 723–736.

Quay, H. C. (1993). The psychobiology of undersocialized aggressive conduct disorder: A theoretical perspective. *Development and Psychopathology, 5,* 165–180.

Quay, H. C. (1997). Inhibition and attention deficit hyperactivity disorder. *Journal of Abnormal Child Psychology, 25,* 7–13.

Rabiner, D., Coie, J. D., and the Conduct Problems Prevention Research Group. (2000). Early attention problems and children's reading achievement: A longitudinal investigation. *Journal of the American Academy of Child and Adolescent Psychiatry, 39,* 859–867.

Radbill, S. X. (1968). A history of child abuse and infanticide. In R. E. Helfer & C. H. Kempe (Eds.), *The battered child* (pp. 3–17). Chicago: University of Chicago Press.

Radbill, S. X. (1987). Children in a world of violence: A history of child abuse. In R. E. Helfer & R. S. Kempe (Eds.), *The battered child* (4th rev. & exp. ed., pp. 3–22). Chicago: University of Chicago Press.

Radke-Yarrow, M. (1998). *Children of depressed mothers: From early childhood to maturity.* New York: Cambridge University Press.

Radke-Yarrow, M., & Zahn-Waxler, C. (1990). Research on children of affectively ill parents: Some considerations for theory and research on normal development. *Development and Psychopathology, 2,* 349–366.

Raedler, R. J., Knable, M. B., & Weinberger, D. R. (2000). Schizophrenia as a developmental disorder of the cerebral cortex. *Current Opinion in Neurobiology, 8,* 157–161.

Rai, A. A., Stanton, B., Wu, Y., Li, X., Galbraith, J., Cottrell, L., et al. (2003). Relative influences of perceived parental monitoring and perceived peer involvement on adolescent risk behaviors: An analysis of six cross-sectional data sets. *Journal of Adolescent Health, 33,* 108–118.

Raine, A. (2002a). Biosocial studies of antisocial and violent behavior in children and adults: A review. *Journal of Abnormal Child Psychology, 30,* 311–326.

Raine, A. (2002b). The role of prefrontal deficits, low autonomic arousal and early health factors in the development of antisocial and aggressive behavior in children. *Journal of Child Psychology and Psychiatry, 43,* 417–434.

Ramey, C. T., Campbell, F. A., Burchinal, M., Skinner, M. L., Gardner, D. M., & Ramey, S. L. (2000). Persistent effects of early childhood education on high-risk children and their mothers. *Applied Developmental Science, 4,* 2–14.

Ramey, C. T., Campbell, F. A., & Ramey, S. L. (1999). Early intervention: Successful pathways to improving intellectual development. *Developmental Neuropsychology, 16,* 385–392.

Ramey, C. T., Mulvihill, B. A., & Ramey, S. L. (1996). Prevention: Social and educational factors and early intervention. In J. W. Jacobson & J. A. Mulick (Eds.), *Manual of diagnosis and professional practice in mental retardation* (pp. 215–227). Washington, DC: American Psychological Association.

Ramey, C. T., & Ramey, S. L. (1992). Effective early intervention. *Mental Retardation, 6,* 337–345.

Randall, J., & Cunningham, P. B. (2003). Multisystemic therapy: A treatment for violent substance-abusing and substance-dependent juvenile offenders. *Addictive Behaviors, 28,* 1731–1739.

Rao, U., Daley, S. E., & Hammen, C. (2000). Relationship between depression and substance use disorders in adolescent women during the transition to adulthood. *Journal of the American Academy of Child and Adolescent Psychiatry, 39,* 215–222.

Rao, U., Hammen, C., & Daley, S. E. (1999). Continuity of depression during the transition to adulthood: A 5-year longitudinal study of young women. *Journal of the American Academy of Child and Adolescent Psychiatry, 38,* 908–915.

Rapee, R. M. (1997). Potential role of childrearing practices in the development of anxiety and depression. *Clinical Psychology Review, 17,* 47–67.

Rapee, R. M. (2002). The development and modification of temperamental risk for anxiety disorders: Prevention of a lifetime of anxiety? *Biological Psychiatry, 52,* 947–957.

Rapee, R. M., Craske, M., & Barlow, D. H. (1996). Psychoeducation. In C. G. Lindemann (Ed.), *Handbook of the treatment of the anxiety disorders* (2nd ed., pp. 311–322). Northvale, NJ: Jason Aronson.

Rapoport, J. L. (1989). *The boy who couldn't stop washing: The experience and treatment of obsessive-compulsive disorder.* New York: Signet.

Rapoport, J. L., Giedd, J., N., Blumenthal, J., Hamburger, S., Jeffries, N., Fernandez, T., et al. (1999). Progressive cortical change during adolescence in childhood-onset schizophrenia: A longitudinal magnetic resonance imaging study. *Archives of General Psychiatry, 56,* 649–654.

Rapoport, J. L., & Inhoff-Germain, G. (2000). Treatment of obsessive-compulsive disorder in children and adolescents. *Journal of Child Psychiatry and Psychiatry, 41,* 419–431.

Rapoport, J. L., Inoff-Germain, G., Weissman, M. M., Greenwald, S., Jensen, P. S., Lahey, B. B., et al. (2000). Childhood obsessive-compulsive disorder in the NIMH MECA study: Parent versus child identification of cases. *Journal of Anxiety Disorders, 14,* 535–548.

Rappaport, L. (1993). The treatment of nocturnal enuresis: Where are we now? *Pediatrics, 92,* 465–466.

Rapport, M., & Chung, K. (2000). Attention deficit hyperactivity disorder. In M. Hersen & R. T. Ammerman (Eds.), *Advanced abnormal child psychology* (2nd ed., pp. 413–440). Mahwah, NJ: Erlbaum.

Rapport, M. D., & Kelly, K. L. (1993). Psychostimulant effects on learning and cognitive function. In J. L. Matson (Ed.), *Handbook of hyperactivity in children* (pp. 97–135). Boston: Allyn & Bacon.

Rapport, M. D., Scanlan, S. W., & Denney, C. B. (1999). Attention-deficit/hyperactivity disorder and scholastic achievement: A model of dual developmental pathways. *Journal of Child Psychology and Psychiatry, 40,* 1169–1183.

Rasmussen, P., & Gillberg, C. (2001). Natural outcome of ADHD with developmental coordination disorder at age 22 years: A controlled, longitudinal, community-based study. *Journal of the American Academy of Child and Adolescent Psychiatry, 39,* 1424–1431.

Rastam, M. (1992). Anorexia nervosa in 51 Swedish adolescents: Premorbid problems and comorbidity. *Journal of the American Academy of Child and Adolescent Psychiatry, 31,* 819–828.

Raynham, H., Gibbons, R., Flint, J., & Higgs, D. (1996). The genetic basis for mental retardation. *Quarterly Journal of Medicine, 89,* 169–175.

Reed, E. W., & Reed, S. G. (1965). *Mental retardation: A family study.* Philadelphia: Saunders.

Reese, L. E., Vera, E. M., Simon, T. R., & Ikeda, R. M. (2000). The role of families and care givers as risk and protective factors in preventing youth violence. *Clinical Child and Family Psychology Review, 3,* 61–77.

Rehm, L. P., & Carter, A. S. (1990). Cognitive components of depression. In M. Lewis & S. M. Miller (Eds.), *Handbook of developmental psychopathology* (pp. 341–351). New York: Plenum.

Rehm, L. P., & Sharp, R. N. (1996). Strategies for childhood depression. In M. A. Reineke, F. M. Dattilio, & A. Freeman (Eds.), *Cognitive therapy with children and adolescents: A casebook for clinical practice* (pp. 103–123). New York: Guilford Press.

Reid, A. H., & Ballanger, B. R. (1995). Behaviour symptoms among severely and profoundly mentally retarded patients: A 16–18 year follow-up study. *British Journal of Psychiatry, 167,* 452.

Reid, J. B., Patterson, G. R., Snyder, J. J. (Eds.). (2002). *Antisocial behavior in children and adolescents: A developmental analysis and model for intervention.* Washington, DC: American Psychological Association.

Reid, M. & Burr, J. (2000). Are eating disorders feminine addictions? *Addiction Research, 8,* 203–210.

Reijonen, J. H., Pratt, H. D., Patel, D. R., & Greydanus, D. E. (2003). Eating disorders in the adolescent population: An overview. *Journal of Adolescent Research, 18,* 209–222.

Reinecke, M. A., Ryan, N. E., & DuBois, D. L. (1998). Cognitive-behavioral therapy of depression and depressive symptoms during adolescence: A review and meta-analysis. *Journal of the American Academy of Child and Adolescent Psychiatry, 37,* 34–36.

Reiss D., & Neiderhiser, J. M. (2000). The interplay of genetic influences and social processes in developmental theory: Specific mechanisms are coming into view. *Development and Psychopathology, 12,* 357–374.

Reissland, N., Shepherd, J., & Herrera, E. (2003). The pitch of maternal voice: A comparison of mothers suffering from depressed mood and non-depressed mothers reading books to their infants. *Journal of Child Psychology and Psychiatry, 44,* 255–261.

Reitan, R. M., & Wolfson, D. (2003). The significance of sensory-motor functions as indicators of brain dysfunction in children. *Archives of Clinical Neuropsychology, 18(1),* 1118.

Remschmidt, H. (Ed). (2001). *Schizophrenia in children and adolescents.* New York: Cambridge University Press.

Remschmidt, H. E., Schulz, E., Martin, M., Warnke, A., & Trott, G. (1994). Childhood-onset schizophrenia: History of the concept and recent studies. *Schizophrenia Bulletin, 20,* 727–746.

Renaud, J., Brent, D. A., Birmaher, B., Chiappetta, L., & Bridge, J. (1999). Suicide in adolescents with disruptive behavior disorders. *Journal of the American Academy of Child and Adolescent Psychiatry, 38,* 846–851.

Rende, R., & Plomin, R. (1995). Nature, nurture, and the development of psychopathology. In D. Cicchetti & D. J. Cohen (Eds.), *Developmental psychopathology: Vol. 1. Theory and methods* (pp. 291–314). New York: Wiley.

Renouf, A. G., & Harter, S. (1990). Low self-worth and anger as components of the depressive experience in young adolescents. *Development and Psychopathology, 2,* 293–310.

Renouf, A. G., & Kovacs, M. (1995). Dysthymic disorder during childhood and adolescence. In J. H. Kocsis & D. N. Klein (Eds.), *Diagnosis and treatment of chronic depression* (pp. 20–40). New York: Guilford Press.

Resnick, M. D., Harris, L. J., & Blum, R. W. (1993). The impact of caring and connectedness on adolescent health and well-being. *Journal of Paediatrics and Child Health, 29 (Suppl. 1),* 3–9.

Reynolds, W. M, & Johnston, H. F. (1994b). The nature and study of depression in children and adolescents. In W. M. Reynolds & H. F. Johnston (Eds.), *Handbook of depression in children and adolescents* (pp. 3–17). New York: Plenum.

Rice, F., Harold, G., & Thapar, A. (2002). The genetic aetiology of childhood depression: A review. *Journal of Child Psychology and Psychiatry, 43,* 65–79.

Rice, F., Harold, G., & Thapar, A. (2003). Negative life events as an account of age-related differences in the genetic aetiology of depression in childhood and adolescence. *Journal of Child Psychology and Psychiatry, 44,* 977–987.

Richdale, A. L. (1999). Sleep problems in autism: Prevalence, causes, and intervention. *Developmental Medicine and Child Neurology, 4,* 60–66.

Richters, J. E., Arnold, L. E., Jensen, P. S., Abikoff, H., Conners, C. K., Greenhill, L. L., et al., (1995). NIMH collabora-tive multisite multimodal treatment study of children with ADHD: I. Background and rationale. *Journal of the American Academy of Child and Adolescent Psychiatry, 34,* 987–1000.

Riddle, M. A. (2004). Letters to the editor: Dr. Riddle replies. *Journal of the American Academy of Child and Adolescent Psychiatry, 43,* 128–130.

Rie, H. E. (1971). Historical perspective of concepts of child psychopathology. In H. E. Rie (Ed.), *Perspectives in child psychopathology* (pp. 3–50). Chicago: Aldine-Atherton.

Rie, H. E. (1980). Definitional problems. In H. E. Rie & E. D. Rie (Eds.), *Handbook of minimal brain dysfunctions: A critical review* (pp. 3–17). New York: Wiley-Interscience.

Rilling, M. (2000). John Watson's paradoxical struggle to explain Freud. *American Psychologist, 55,* 301–312.

Ringel, J. S., & Sturm, R. (2001). National estimates of mental health utilization and expenditures for children in 1998. *Journal of Behavioral Health Services and Research, 28,* 319–333.

Robbins, M. S., Szapocznik, J., Santisteban, D. A., Hervis, O. E., Mitrani, V. B., & Schwartz, S.J. (2003). Brief strategic family therapy for Hispanic youth. In A. E. Kazdin & J. R. Weisz (Eds.), *Evidence-based psychotherapies for children and adolescents* (pp. 407–424). New York: Guilford Press.

Roberts, B. W., & DelVecchio, W. F. (2000). The rank-order consistency of personality traits from childhood to old age: A quantitative review of longitudinal studies. *Psychological Bulletin, 126,* 3–25.

Roberts, M. C. (Ed.). (2003). *Handbook of pediatric psychology (3rd ed.).* New York: Guilford.

Roberts, M. W. & Hope, D. A. (2001). Clinic observations of structured parent-child interaction designed to evaluate externalizing disorders. *Psychological Assessment, 13,* 46–58.

Roberts, R. E., & Gotlib, I. H. (1997). Temporal variability in global self-esteem and specific self-evaluation as prospective predictors of emotional distress: Specificity in predictors and outcomes. *Journal of Abnormal Psychology, 106,* 521–529.

Roberts, R. E., Roberts, C. R., & Chen, Y. R. (1997). Ethnocultural differences in prevalence of adolescent depression. *American Journal of Community Psychology, 25,* 95–110.

Robin, A. L., Siegel, P. T., & Moye, A. (1995). Family versus individual therapy for anorexia: Impact on family conflict. Topical section: Treatment and therapeutic processes. *International Journal of Eating Disorders, 17,* 313–322.

Robin, A. L., Siegel, P. T., Moye, A. W., Gilroy, M., Dennis, A. B., & Sikand, A. (1999). A controlled comparison of family versus individual therapy for adolescents with anorexia nervosa. *Journal of the American Academy of Child and Adolescent Psychiatry, 38,* 1482–1489.

Robins, L. N. (1978). Aetiological implications in studies of childhood histories relating to antisocial personality. In R. D. Hare & D. Schalling (Eds.), *Psychopathic behaviour: Approaches to research* (pp. 255–271). Chichester, England: Wiley.

Robins, L. N. (1991). Conduct disorder. *Journal of Child Psychology and Psychiatry, 32,* 193–212.

Robins, L. N., & Rutter, M. (1990). *Straight and devious pathways from childhood to adulthood.* Cambridge, England: Cambridge University Press.

Robinson, N. S., Garber, J., & Hilsman, R. (1995). Cognitions and stress: Direct and moderating effects on depressive versus externalizing symptoms during the junior high school transition. *Journal of Abnormal Psychology, 104,* 453–463.

Robison, L. M., Skaer, T. L., Sclar, D. A., Galin, R. S. (2002). Is attention deficit hyperactivity disorder increasing among girls in the US? Trends in diagnosis and the prescribing of stimulants. *CNS Drugs 16, 2,* 129–137

Rochlin, G. (1959). The loss complex. *Journal of the American Psychoanalytic Association, 7,* 299–316.

Rodier, P. M., Hyman, S. L. (1998). Early environmental factors in autism. *Mental Retardation and Developmental Disabilities Research Reviews, 4,* 121–128.

Rodkin, P. C., Farmer, T. W., Van Acker, R. P., & Van Acker, R. (2000). Heterogeneity of popular boys: Antisocial and prosocial configurations. *Developmental Psychology, 36,* 14–24.

Rodriguez, N., Ryan, S., Vande Kemp, H., & Foy, D. (1997). Posttraumatic stress disorder in adult female survivors of childhood sexual abuse: A comparison study. *Journal of Consulting and Clinical Psychology, 65,* 53–59.

Rodriguez-Srednicki, O. (2001). Childhood sexual abuse, dissociation and adult self-destructive behavior. *Journal of Child Sexual Abuse, 10,* 75–90.

Roeser, R. W., & Eccles, J. S. (2000). Schooling and mental health. In A. J. Sameroff, M. Lewis, & S. M. Miller (Eds.), *Handbook of developmental psychopathology* (2nd ed., pp. 135–156). New York: Kluwer Academic/Plenum Press.

Rogers, S. J. (1998). Empirically supported comprehensive treatments for young children with autism. *Journal of Clinical Child Psychology, 27,* 168–179.

Rogers, S. J. (2000). Diagnosis of autism before the age of 3. *International Review of Research in Mental Retardation, 23,* 1–56.

Rogers, S. J., Hepburn, S. L., Stackhouse, T., & Wehner, E. (2003). Imitation performance in toddlers with autism and those with other developmental disorders. *Journal of Child Psychology and Psychiatry, 44,* 763–781.

Rogers, S. J., Ozonoff, S., & Maslin-Cole, C. (1993). Developmental aspects of attachment behavior in young children with pervasive developmental disorders. *Journal of the American Academy of Child and Adolescent Psychiatry, 32,* 1274–1282.

Rogers, S. J., Wehner, D. E., & Hagerman, R. (2001). The behavioral phenotype in Fragile X: Symptoms of autism in very young children with Fragile X syndrome, idiopathic autism, and other developmental disorders. *Developmental and Behavioral Pediatrics, 22,* 409–417.

Rohde, P., Lewinsohn, P., & Seeley, J. (1994). Are adolescents changed by an episode of major depression? *Journal of the American Academy of Child and Adolescent Psychiatry, 33,* 1289–1298.

Rohde, P., Lewinsohn, P. M., & Seeley, J. R. (1996). Psychiatric comorbidity with problematic alcohol use in high school students. *Journal of American Academy of Childhood and Adolescent Psychiatry, 35,* 101–109.

Roizen, N. J., & Patterson, D. (2003). Down's syndrome. *Lancet, 361,* 1281–1289.

Rojahn, J., & Esbensen, A. J. (2002). Epidemiology of self-injurious behavior in mental retardation: A review. In S. R. Schroede & M. L. Oster-Granite (Eds.), *Self-injurious behavior: Gene-brain-behavior relationships* (pp. 41–77). Washington, DC: American Psychological Association.

Romanczyk, R. G., Weiner, T., Lockshin, S., & Ekdahl, M. (1999). Research in autism: Myths, controversies, and perspectives. In D. B. Zager (Ed.), *Autism: Identification, education, and treatment* (2nd ed., pp. 23–61). Mahwah, NJ: Erlbaum.

Rosen, J. C., Leitenberg, H., Fisher, C., & Khazam, C. (1986). Binge-eating episodes in bulimia nervosa: The amount and type of food consumed. *International Journal of Eating Disorders, 5,* 255–257.

Rosenbaum, J. F., Biederman, J., Hirshfeld, D. R., Bolduc, E. A., Faraone, S. V., Kagan, J., et al. (1991b). Further evidence of an association between behavioral inhibition and anxiety disorders: Results from a family study of children from a non-clinical sample. *Journal of Psychiatric Research, 25,* 49–65.

Rosenblatt, R. (2000, March 13). The killing of Kayla. *Time,* pp. 16–19.

Rosenstein, D. S., & Horowitz, H. A. (1996). Adolescent attachment and psychopathology. *Journal of Consulting and Clinical Psychology, 64,* 244–253.

Rosenthal, D. (1970). *Genetic theory and abnormal behavior.* New York: McGraw-Hill.

Ross, D. M., & Ross, S. A. (1982). *Hyperactivity: Current issues, research, and theory (2nd ed.).* New York: Wiley.

Ross, D. M., & Ross, S. A. (1984). Childhood pain: The school-aged child's viewpoint. *Pain, 20,* 179–191.

Ross, D. P., Shillington, E. R., & Lockhead, C. (1994). *The Canadian fact book on poverty—1994.* Ottawa: Canadian Council on Social Development.

Rothbart, M. K., & Bates, J. E. (1998). Temperament. In W. Damon (Series Ed.) & N. Eisenberg (Vol. Ed.), *Handbook of child psychology: Vol. 3. Social, emotional, and personality development* (pp. 105–176). New York: Wiley.

Rothbart, M. K., & Mauro, J. A. (1990). Questionnaire measures of infant temperament. In W. J. Fagen & J. Colombo (Eds.), *Individual differences in infancy: Reliability, stability, and prediction* (pp. 411–429). Hillsdale, NJ: Erlbaum.

Rothbaum, B. O., Hodges, L., & Smith, S. (2000). Virtual reality exposure therapy abbreviated treatment manuals: Fear of flying application. *Cognitive and Behavioral Practice, 6,* 234–244.

Rourke, B. P., Ahmad, S. A., Collins, D. W., Hayman-Abello, B. A., Hayman-Abello, S. E., & Warriner, E. M. (2002). Child clinical/pediatric neuropsychology: Some recent advances. *Annual Review of Psychology, 53,* 309–339.

Rourke, B. P., & Del Dotto, J. E. (1994). *Learning disabilities: A neuropsychological perspective.* Thousand Oaks, CA: Sage.

Rowland, M. D., Henggeler, S. W., Gordon, A. M., Pickrel, S. G., Cunningham, P. B., & Edwards, J. E. (2000). Adapting multisystemic therapy to serve youth presenting psychiatric emergencies: Two case studies. *Child Psychology and Psychiatry Review, 5,* 30–43.

Roza, S. J., Hofstra, M. B., van der Ende, J., Verhulst, F. C. (2003). Stable prediction of mood and anxiety disorders based on behavioral and emotional problems in childhood: A 14-year follow-up during childhood, adolescence, and young adulthood. *American Journal of Psychiatry, 160,* 2116–2121.

Rubin, K. H., & Stewart, S. L. (1996). Social withdrawal. In E. J. Mash & R. A. Barkley (Eds.), *Child psychopathology* (pp. 277–307). New York: Guilford Press.

Rucklidge, J. J., & Tannock, R. (2001). Psychiatric, psychosocial, and cognitive functioning of female adolescents with ADHD. *Journal of the American Academy of Child and Adolescent Psychiatry, 40,* 530–540.

Rucklidge, J. J., & Tannock, R. (2002). Neuropsychological profiles of adolescents with ADHD: Effects of reading difficulties and gender. *Journal of Child Psychology and Psychiatry, 43,* 988–1003.

Rudolph, K. D. (2002). Gender differences in emotional responses to interpersonal stress during adolescence. *Journal of Adolescent Health, 30,* 3–13.

Rudolph, K. D., & Hammen, C. (1999). Age and gender as determinants of stress exposure, generation, and reactions to youngsters: A transactional perspective. *Child Development, 70,* 660–677.

Rudolph, K. D., Hammen, C., & Burge, D. (1997). A cognitive-interpersonal approach to depressive symptoms in pre-adolescent children. *Journal of Abnormal Child Psychology, 25,* 33–45.

Rudolph, K. D., Hammen, C., Burge, D., Lindberg, N., Herzberg, D. S., & Daley, S. E. (2000). Toward an interpersonal life-stress model of depression: The developmental context of stress generation. *Development and Psychopathology, 12,* 215–234.

Rudolph, K. D., Hammen, C., & Daley, S. E. (in press). Adolescent mood disorders. In D. A. Wolfe & E. J. Mash (Eds.), *Behavioral and emotional disorders in adolescents: Nature, assessment, and treatment.* New York: Guilford.

Rumsey, J. M., & Ernst, E. M. (2000). Functional neuroimaging of autistic disorders. *Mental Retardation and Developmental Disabilities Research Review, 6,* 171–179.

Rushton, J. L., Forcier, M., & Schectman, R. M. (2002). Epidemiology of depressive symptoms in the National Longitudinal Study of Adolescent Health. *Journal of the Academy of Child and Adolescent Psychiatry, 41,* 199–205.

Russell, A. T. (1994). The clinical presentation of childhood-onset schizophrenia. *Schizophrenia Bulletin, 20,* 631–646.

Russell, A. T., Bott, L., & Sammons, C. (1989). The phenomenology of schizophrenia occurring in childhood. *Journal of the American Academy of Child and Adolescent Psychiatry, 28,* 399–407.

Russell, J. (Ed.). (1997). *Autism as an executive disorder.* New York: Oxford University Press.

Rutherford, M. D., & Rogers, S. J. (2003). Cognitive underpinnings of pretend play in autism. *Journal of Autism and Developmental Disorders, 33,* 289–302.

Rutter, M. (1972). Childhood schizophrenia reconsidered. *Journal of Autism and Childhood Schizophrenia, 2,* 315–337.

Rutter, M. (1989b). Pathways from childhood to adult life. *Journal of Child Psychology and Psychiatry, 30,* 23–51.

Rutter, M. (1991a). Autism: Pathways from syndrome definition to pathogenesis. *Comprehensive Mental Health Care, 1,* 5–26.

Rutter, M. (1999). Psychosocial adversity and child psychopathology. *British Journal of Psychiatry, 174,* 480–493.

Rutter, M. (2000a). Genetic studies of autism: From the 1970s into the millennium. *Journal of Abnormal Child Psychology, 28,* 3–14.

Rutter, M. (2000b). Psychosocial influences: Critiques, findings, and research needs. *Development and Psychopathology, 12,* 375–405.

Rutter, M. (2002). Substance use and abuse: Causal pathways considerations. In M. Rutter & E. Taylor (Eds.), *Child and adolescent psychiatry* (4th ed., pp. 455–462). Oxford, England: Blackwell Scientific.

Rutter, M. (2002). The interplay of nature, nurture, and developmental influences: The challenge ahead for mental health. *Archives of General Psychiatry, 59,* 996–1000.

Rutter, M. (2003a). Commentary: Causal processes leading to antisocial behavior. *Developmental Psychology, 39,* 372–378.

Rutter, M. (2003b). Commentary: Nature-nurture interplay in emotional disorders. *Journal of Child Psychology and Psychiatry, 44,* 934–944.

Rutter, M. (2003c). Poverty and child mental health: Natural experiments and social causation. *Journal of the American Medical Association, 290,* 2063–2064.

Rutter, M., Caspi, A., & Moffitt, T. E. (2003). Using sex differences in psychopathology to study causal mechanisms: Unifying issues and research strategies. *Journal of Child Psychology and Psychiatry, 44,* 1092–1115.

Rutter, M., Giller, H., & Hagell, A. (1998). *Antisocial behaviour by young people.* New York: Cambridge University Press.

Rutter, M., & Maughan, B. (2002). School effectiveness findings 1979–2002. *Journal of School Psychology, 40,* 451–475.

Rutter, M., & Silberg, J. (2002). Gene-environment interplay in relation to emotional and behavioral disturbance. *Annual Review of Psychology, 53,* 463–490.

Rutter, M., & Smith, D. J. (Eds.). (1995). *Psychosocial disorders in young people: Time trends and their causes.* Chichester, England: Wiley.

Rutter, M., & Sroufe, L. A. (2000). Developmental psychopathology: Concepts and challenges. *Development and Psychopathology, 12,* 265–296.

Rutter, M., Tizard, J., & Whitmore, K. (1970). *Education, health, and behavior.* London: Longmans, Green.

Rutter, M., Tizard, J., Yule, W., Graham, P., & Whitmore, K. (1976). Research report: Isle of Wight studies, 1964–1974. *Psychological Medicine, 6,* 313–332.

Ryan, N. D., Puig-Antich, J., Ambrosini, P., Rabinovich, H., Robinson, D., Nelson, B., et al. (1987). The clinical picture of major depression in children and adolescents. *Archives of General Psychiatry, 44,* 854–861.

Rydell, A. M., Dahl, M., & Sundelin, C. (1995). Characteristics of school children who are choosy eaters. *Journal of Genetic Psychology, 156,* 217–229.

Sabaratnam, M., Laver, S., Butler, L., & Pembrey, M. (1994). Fragile X syndrome in North-East Essex: Towards systematic screening: Clinical selection. *Journal of Intellectual Disability Research, 38,* 27–35.

Sadeh, A., Raviv, A., & Gruber, R. (2000). Sleep patterns and sleep disruptions in school-age children. *Developmental Psychology, 26,* 291–301.

Safer, D. J. (2000a). Are stimulants overprescribed for youths with ADHD? *Annals of Clinical Psychiatry, 12,* 55–62.

Safer, D. J. (2000b). Commentary. *Journal of the American Academy of Child and Adolescent Psychiatry, 39,* 989–992.

Saitoh, O., & Courchesne, E. (1998). Magnetic resonance imaging study of the brain in autism. *Psychiatry and Clinical Neurosciences, 52 (Suppl.),* S219–S222.

Sallee, R., & Greenawald, J. (1995). Neurobiology. In J. S. March (Ed.), *Anxiety disorders in children and adolescents* (pp. 3–34). New York: Guilford Press.

Salmond, C. H., de Haan, M., Friston, K. J., Gadian, D. G., & Vargha-Khadem, F. (2003). Investigating individual differences in brain abnormalities in autism. Philosophical Transactions of the Royal Society: *Biological Sciences, 358,* 405–413.

Salter, D., McMillan, D., Richards, M., Talbot, T., Hodges, J., Bentovim, A., et al. (2003). Development of sexual abusive behaviour in sexually victimised males: A longitudinal study. *Lancet, 361,* 471–476.

Samaan, R.A. (2000). The influences of race, ethnicity, and poverty on the mental health of children. *Journal of Health Care for the Poor & Underserved, 11,* 100–110.

Sameroff, A. J. (1995). General systems theories and developmental psychopathology. In D. Cicchetti & D. J. Cohen (Eds.), *Developmental psychopathology: Vol. 1. Theory and methods* (pp. 659–695). New York: Wiley.

Sameroff, A. J. (2000). Developmental systems and psychopathology. *Development and Psychopathology, 12,* 297–312.

Sameroff, A.J., & Fiese, B.H. (2000a). Models of development and developmental risk. In C. J. Zeanah, Jr. (Ed.), *Handbook of Infant mental health,* (2nd ed., pp. 3–19). New York: Guilford Press.

Sameroff, A. J., & Fiese, B. H. (2000b). Transactional regulation: The developmental ecology of early intervention. In Shonkoff, J., & Meisels, S. J. (Eds.), *Handbook of early childhood intervention (2/e),* (135–159). New York: Cambridge University Press.

Sameroff, A. J., & MacKenzie, M. J. (2003). Research strategies for capturing transactional models of development: The limits of the possible. *Development and Psychopathology, 15,* 613–640.

Sampson, R. J. (1992). Family management and child development: Insights from social disorganization theory. In J. McCord (Ed.), *Advances in criminological theory: Facts, frameworks, and forecasts* (Vol. 3, pp. 63–91). New Brunswick, NJ: Transaction.

Sampson, R. J., & Groves, W. B. (1989). Community structure and crime: Testing social-disorganization theory. *American Journal of Sociology, 94,* 774–802.

Sampson, R. J., & Laub, J. H. (1994). Urban poverty and the family context of delinquency: A new look at structure and process in a classic study. *Child Development, 65,* 523–540.

Sampson, R. J., Raudenbush, S. W., & Earls, F. (1997). Neighborhoods and violent crime: A multilevel study of collective efficacy. *Science, 277,* 918–924.

Sanders, M. R. (1999). Triple P-Positive Parenting Program: Towards an empirically validated multilevel parenting and family support strategy for the prevention of behavior and emotional problems in children. *Clinical Child and Family Psychology Review, 2,* 71–90.

Sanders, M. R., & Dadds, M. R. (1992). Children's and parents' cognitions about family interaction: An evaluation of video-mediated recall and thought listing procedures in the assessment of conduct-disordered children. *Journal of Clinical Child Psychology, 21,* 371–379.

Sands, R. (2000). Reconceptualization of body image and drive for thinness. *International Journal of Eating Disorders, 28,* 397–407.

Sanson, A., & Prior, M. (1999). Temperament and behavioral precursors to oppositional defiant disorder and conduct disorder. H. C. Quay & A. E. Hogan (Eds.), *Handbook of disruptive behavior disorders* (pp. 397–417). New York: Kluwer Academic/Plenum.

Sapolsky, R. (1997, October). A gene for nothing. *Discover,* pp. 40–46.

Sas, L., Hurley, P., Hatch, A., Malla, S., & Dick, T. (1993). *Three years after the verdict: A longitudinal study of the social and psychological adjustment of child witnesses referred to the child witness project (FVDS No. 4887-06-91-026).* Health and Welfare Canada, Family Violence Prevention Division.

Sattler, J. M. (1998). *Clinical and forensic interviewing of children and families: Guidelines for the mental health, education, pediatric, and child maltreatment fields.* San Diego, CA: Sattler.

Sattler, J. M. (2001). *Assessment of children: Cognitive applications (4th ed.).* La Mesa, CA: Jerome M. Sattler, Publisher, Inc.

Sattler, J. M. (2002). *Assessment of children: Behavioral and clinical applications (4th ed.).* La Mesa, CA: Jerome M. Sattler, Publisher, Inc.

Sattler, J. M., & Mash, E. J. (1998). Introduction to clinical assessment interviewing. In J. M. Sattler, *Clinical and forensic interviewing of children and families: Guidelines for the mental health, education, pediatric, and child maltreatment fields* (pp. 2–44). San Diego, CA: Sattler.

Saunders, B. E., Berliner, L., & Hanson, R. F. (Eds.). (2003). *Child physical and sexual abuse: Guidelines for Treatment (Final Report: January 15, 2003).* Charleston, SC: National Crime Victims Research and Treatment Center. [Document may be downloaded electronically at: http://www.musc.edu/cvc/]

Saywitz, K. J., Mannarino, A. P., Berliner, L., & Cohen, J. A. (2003). Treatment for sexually abused children and adolescents. In M. E. Hertzig & E. A. Farber (Eds.), *Annual progress in child psychiatry and child development:*

2000–2001 (pp. 455–476). New York: Brunner-Routledge.

Scarr, S. (1992). Developmental theories for the 1990's: Development and individual differences. *Child Development, 63*, 1–19.

Schachar, R. (1986). Hyperkinetic syndrome: Historical development of the concept. In E. A. Taylor (Ed.), *The overactive child* (pp. 19–40). London: MacKeith.

Schniering, C. A., & Rapee, R. M. (2004). The structure of negative self-statements in children and adolescent: A confirmatory factor-analytic approach. *Journal of Abnormal Child Psychology, 32*, 95–109.

Schraedley, P. K., Gotlib, I. H., & Hayward, C. (1999). Gender differences in correlates of depressive symptoms in adolescents. *Journal of Adolescent Health, 25*, 98–108.

Schreier, H. (2002). On the importance of motivation in Munchausen by Proxy: The case of Kathy Bush. *Child Abuse & Neglect, 26*, 537–549.

Schreier, H. A., & Libow, J. A. (1993). *Hurting for love: Munchausen by proxy syndrome.* New York: Guilford Press.

Schroeder, C. S., & Gordon, B. N. (1991). *Assessment and treatment of childhood problems: A clinician's guide.* New York: Guilford Press.

Schroeder, C. S., & Gordon, B. N. (2002). *Assessment and treatment of childhood disorders: A clinician's guide (2nd ed.).* New York: Guilford Press.

Schwab-Stone, M., Ruchkin, V., Vermeiren, R., & Leckman, P. (2001). Cultural considerations in the treatment of children and adolescents: Operationalizing the importance of culture in treatment. *Child & Adolescent Psychiatric Clinics of North America, 10(4)*, 729–743.

Schwartz, C. E., Snidman, N., & Kagan, J. (1999). Adolescent social anxiety as an outcome of inhibited temperament in childhood. *Journal of the American Academy of Child and Adolescent Psychiatry, 38*, 1008–1015.

Schwartz, C. E., Wright, C. I., Shin, L. M., Kagan, J., & Rauch, S. L. (2003). Inhibited and uninhibited infants "grown up": Adult amygdalar response to novelty. *Science, 300*, 1952–1953.

Schwimmer, J.B., Burwinkle, T.M., & Varni, J.W. (2003). Health-related quality of life of severely obese children and adolescents. *Journal of the American Medical Association, 289*, 1813–1819.

Schwoeri, L. D., Sholevar, G. P., & Combs, M. P. (2003). Impact of culture and ethnicity on family interventions. In Sholevar, G. Pirooz (Ed.); *Textbook of family and couples therapy: clinical applications* (pp. 725–745). Washington, DC: American Psychiatric Publishing, Inc.

Scott, K. L., Wolfe, D. A., & Wekerle, C. (2003). Maltreatment and trauma: Tracking the connections in adolescence. *Child and Adolescent Psychiatric Clinics of North America, 12*, 211–230.

Scotti, J. R., Morris, T. L., McNeil, C. B., & Hawkins, R. P. (1996). DSM-IV and disorders of childhood and adolescence: Can structural criteria be functional? *Journal of Consulting and Clinical Psychology, 64*, 1177–1191.

Scourfield, J., Rice, F., Thapar, A., Harold, G. T., Martin, N., & McGuffin, P. (2003). Depressive symptoms in children and adolescents: Changing aetiological influences with development. *Journal of Child Psychology and Psychiatry, 44*, 968–976.

Sedlak, A. J., & Broadhurst, D. D. (1996, September). *Third national incidence study of child abuse and neglect: Final report.* Washington, DC: U.S. Department of Health and Human Services.

Seitz, P. (2001). Cultural and business ethics. *Cross Cultural Management, 8 (1)*, 21–27.

Selemon, L. D., & Goldman-Rakic, P. S. (1999). The reduced neuropil hypothesis: A circuit based model of schizophrenia. *Biological Psychiatry, 45*, 17–25.

Selfe, L. (1977). *Nadia: A case of extraordinary drawing ability in an autistic child.* London: Academic Press.

Seligman, L. D., & Ollendick, T. H. (1998). Comorbidity of anxiety and depression in children and adolescents: An integrative review. *Clinical Child and Family Psychology Review, 1*, 125.

Seligman, M. E. P. (1971). Phobias and preparedness. *Behavior Therapy, 2*, 307–320.

Selman, R. L., Beardslee, W., Schultz, L. H., Krupa, M., & Podorefsky, D. (1986). Assessing adolescent interpersonal negotiation strategies: Toward the integration of structural and functional models. *Developmental Psychology, 22*, 450–459.

Selman, R. L., Schultz, L. H., Nakkula, M., Barr, D., Watts, C., & Richmond, J. B. (1992). Friendship and fighting: A developmental approach to the study of risk and prevention of violence. *Development and Psychopathology, 4*, 529–558.

Semenak, S. (1996, November 21). Coping with autism is a full-time job. *Montreal Gazette*, pp. A1, A15.

Semrud-Clikeman, M., Biederman, J., Sprich-Buckminster, S., Lehman, B. K., Faraone, S. V., & Norman, D. (1992). Comorbidity between ADHD and learning disability: A review and report in a clinically referred sample. *Journal of the American Academy of Child and Adolescent Psychiatry, 31*, 439–448.

Semrud-Clikeman, M., Steingard, R. J., Filipek, P., Biederman, J., Bekken, K., & Renshaw, P. F. (2000). Using MRI to examine brain-behavior relationships in males with attention deficit disorder with hyperactivity. *Journal of the American Academy of Child and Adolescent Psychiatry, 39*, 477–484.

Serbin, L. A., Moskowitz, D. S., Schwartzman, A. E., & Ledingham, J. E. (1991). Aggressive, withdrawn, and aggressive/withdrawn children in adolescence. In

D. J. Pepler & K. H. Rubin (Eds.), *The development and treatment of childhood aggression* (pp. 55–70). Hillsdale, NJ: Erlbaum.

Sergeant, J. (2000). The cognitive-energetic model: An empirical approach to attention-deficit hyperactivity disorder. *Neuroscience and Biobehavioral Reviews, 24*, 7–12.

Serketich, W. J., & Dumas, J. E. (1996). The effectiveness of behavioral parent training to modify antisocial behavior in children: A meta-analysis. *Behavior Therapy, 27*, 171–186.

Seroczynski, A. D., Cole, D. A., & Maxwell, S. E. (1997). Cumulative and compensatory effects of competence and incompetence on depressive symptoms in children. *Journal of Abnormal Psychology, 106*, 586–597.

Shadish, W. R., Matt, G. E., Navarro, A. M., & Phillips, G. (2000). The effects of psychological therapies under clinically representative conditions: A meta-analysis. *Psychological Bulletin, 126*, 512–529.

Shaffer, D., Gould, M., Fisher, P., Trautman, P., Moreau, D., Kleinman, M., & Flory, M. (1996). Psychiatric diagnosis in child and adolescent suicide. *Archives of General Psychiatry, 53*, 339–348.

Shaffer, D., Scott, M., Wilcox, H., Maslow, C., Hicks, R., Lucas, C., Garfinkel, R., & Greenwald, S. (2004). The Columbia Suicide Screen: Validity and reliability of a screen for youth suicide and depression. *Journal of the American Academy of Child and Adolescent Psychiatry, 43*, 71–79.

Shaffer, D., & Waslick, B. D. (Eds.). (2002). *The many faces of depression in children and adolescents.* Washington, DC: American Psychiatric Publishing.

Shafron, R. (1998). Childhood obsessive-compulsive disorder. In P. Graham (Ed.), *Cognitive-behavior therapy for children and families* (pp. 45–73). Cambridge: Cambridge University Press.

Shalev, R. S., Auerbach, J., Manor, O., & Gross-Tsur, V. (2000). Developmental dyscalculia: Prevalence and prognosis. *European Child and Adolescent Psychiatry, 9*, 58–64.

Shalev, R. S., Manor, O., Kerem, B., Ayali, M., Badichi, N., Friedlander, Y., & Gross-Tsur, V. (2001). Developmental dyscalculia is a familial learning disability. *Journal of Learning Disabilities, 34*, 5965.

Sharpe, D. G., Rossiter, L. (2002). Siblings of children with a chronic illness: A meta-analysis. *Journal of Pediatric Psychology, 27*, 699–710.

Shaw, D. S., & Bell, R. Q. (1993). Developmental theories of parental contributors to antisocial behavior. *Journal of Abnormal Child Psychology, 21*, 493–518.

Shaw, D. S., & Vondra, J. I. (1994). Chronic family adversity and early child behavior problems: A longitudinal study of low income families. *Journal of*

Child Psychology and Psychiatry, 35, 1109–1122.

Shaw, D. S., Winslow, E. B., & Flanagan, C. (1999). A prospective study of the effects of marital status and family relations on young children's adjustment among African American and Caucasian families. *Child Development, 70,* 742–755.

Shaywitz, B. A., Shaywitz, S. E., Pugh, K. R., Mencl, W. E., Fulbright, R. K., Skudlarski, P., et al. (2002). Disruption of posterior brain systems for reading in children with developmental dyslexia. *Biological psychiatry, 52,* 101–110.

Shaywitz, S., & Shaywitz, B. (1999). Cognitive and neurobiologic influences in reading and in dyslexia. *Developmental Neuropsychology, 16,* 383–384.

Shaywitz, S. E. (1998). Current concepts: Dyslexia. *New England Journal of Medicine, 338,* 307–312.

Shaywitz, S. E. (2003). *Overcoming dyslexia: A new and complete science-based program for reading problems at any level.* New York: Alfred A. Knopf.

Shaywitz, S. E., Escobar, M. D., Shaywitz, B. A., Fletcher, J. M., & Makuch, R. (1992). Evidence that dyslexia may represent the lower tail of a normal distribution of reading ability. *The New England Journal of Medicine, 326(3),* 145–150.

Shaywitz, S. E., Shaywitz, B. A., Fulbright, R. K., Skudlarski, P., Mencl, W. E., Constable, R. T., et al. (2003). Neural systems for compensation and persistence: Young adult outcome of childhood reading disability. *Biological Psychiatry, 54,* 25–33.

Shea, S. E., Gordon, K., Hawkins, A., Kawchuk, J., & Smith, D. (2000). Pathology in the Hundred Acre Wood: A neurodevelopmental perspective on A.A. Milne. *Canadian Medical Association Journal, 163 (12),* 1557–1559.

Sheeber, L., Allen, N., Davis, B., & Sorensen, E. (2000). Regulation of negative affect during mother-child problem-solving interactions: Adolescent depressive status and family processes. *Journal of Abnormal Child Psychology, 28,* 467–479.

Sheeber, L., Hops, H., Alpert, A., Davis, B., & Andrews, J. (1997). Family support and conflict: Prospective relations to adolescent depression. *Journal of Abnormal Child Psychology, 25,* 333–344.

Sheeran, T., Marvin, R. S., & Pianta, R. C. (1997). Mothers' resolution of their child's diagnosis and self-reported measures of parent stress, marital relations, and social support. *Journal of Pediatric Psychology, 22,* 197–212.

Sherman, J. B., Liao, Y. C., Alexander, M., Kim, M., & Kim, B. D. (1995). Family factors related to obesity in Mexican-American and Anglo preschool children. *Family and Community Health, 18,* 28–36.

Shields, A., & Cicchetti, D. (1998). Reactive aggression among maltreated children: The contributions of attention and emotion dysregulation. *Journal of Clinical Child Psychology, 27,* 381–395.

Shields, A., Ryan, R. M., & Cicchetti, D. (2001). Narrative representations of caregivers and emotion dysregulation as predictors of maltreated children's rejection by peers. *Developmental Psychology, 37,* 321–337.

Shiner, R., & Caspi, A. (2003). Personality differences in childhood and adolescence: Measurement, development, and consequences. *Journal of Child Psychology and Psychiatry, 44,* 2–32.

Shipman, K., Zeman, J., Penza, S., & Champion, K. (2000). Emotion management skills in sexually maltreated and nonmaltreated girls: A developmental psychopathology perspective. *Development and Psychopathology, 12,* 47–62.

Shochet, I. M., Dadds, M. R., Holland, D., Whitefield, K., Harnett, P. H., & Osgarby, S. M. (2001). The efficacy of a universal school-based program to prevent adolescent depression. *Journal of Clinical Child Psychology, 30,* 303–315.

Shriberg, L.D., Friel-Patti, S., Flipsen, P.Jr., & Brown, R.L. (2000). Otitis media, fluctuant hearing loss, and speech-language outcomes: A preliminary structural equation model. *Journal of Speech Language and Hearing Research, 43,* 100–120.

Shriberg, L. D., Tomblin, J. B., & McSweeny, J. L. (1999) Prevalence of speech delay in 6-year-old children and comorbidity with language impairment. *Journal of Speech, Language, and Hearing Research, 42,* 1461–1481.

Siegel, J. A., & Williams, L. M. (2003). The relationship between child sexual abuse and female delinquency and crime: A prospective study. *Journal of Research in Crime & Delinquency, 40,* 71–94.

Siegel, L. J. (2003). IQ-Discrepancy Definitions and the Diagnosis of LD: Introduction to the Special Issue. *Journal of Learning Disabilities, 36,* 2–3.

Siegel, L. J., Smith, K. E., & Wood, T. A. (1991). Children medically at risk. In T. R. Kratochwill & R. J. Harris (Eds.), *The practice of child therapy* (2nd ed., pp. 328–363). Toronto: Pergamon Press.

Sigman, M. (1995). Behavioral research in childhood autism. In M. Lenzenweger & J. Haugaard (Eds.), *Frontiers of developmental psychopathology* (pp. 190–206). New York: Springer-Verlag.

Sigman, M., & Mundy, P. (1989). Social attachments in autistic children. *Journal of the American Academy of Child and Adolescent Psychiatry, 28,* 74–81.

Silberg, J. L., Parr, T., Neale, M. C., Rutter, M., Angold, A., & Eaves, L. J. (2003). Maternal smoking during pregnancy and risk to boys' conduct disturbance: An examination of the causal hypothesis. *Biological Psychiatry, 53,* 130–135.

Silberg, J., Rutter, M., & Eaves, L. (2001). Genetic and environmental influences on the temporal association between earlier anxiety and later depression in girls. *Biological Psychiatry, 49,* 1040–1049.

Silberg, J., Rutter, M., D'Onofrio, B., Eaves, L. (2003). Genetic and environmental risk factors in adolescent substance use. *Journal of Child Psychology and Psychiatry, 44,* 664–676.

Silberg, J., Rutter, M., Neale, M., & Eaves, L. (2001). Genetic moderation of environmental risk for depression and anxiety in adolescent girls. *British Journal of Psychiatry, 179,* 116–121.

Silverman, J. A. (1997). Anorexia nervosa: Historical perspective on treatment. In D. M. Garner and P. E. Garfinkel (Eds.), *Handbook of treatment for eating disorders* (2nd ed., pp. 3–10). New York: Guilford Press.

Silverman, W. K., & Ginsburg, C. S. (1995). Specific phobia and generalized anxiety disorder. In J. S. March (Ed.), *Anxiety disorders in children and adolescents* (pp. 151–180). New York: Guilford Press.

Silverman, W. K., & Kurtines, W. M. (1996b). Transfer of control: A psychosocial intervention model for internalizing disorders in youth. In E. D. Hibbs & P. S. Jensen (Eds.), *Psychosocial treatments for child and adolescent disorders: Empirically based strategies for clinical practice* (pp. 63–81). Washington, DC: American Psychological Association.

Silverman, W. K., La Greca, A. M., & Wasserstein, S. (1995). What do children worry about? Worries and their relation to anxiety. *Child Development, 66,* 671–686.

Silverman, W. K., & Nelles, W. B (1989). An examination of the stability of mothers' ratings of child fearfulness. *Journal of Anxiety Disorders, 3,* 1–5.

Silverman, W. K., & Treffers, P.D.A. (Eds.). (2001). *Anxiety disorders in children and adolescents: Research, assessment, and intervention.* New York: Cambridge University Press.

Silverstein, J. (1994). Diabetes: Medical issues. In R. A. Olson, L. L. Mullins, J. B. Gillman, & J. M. Chaney (Eds.), *The sourcebook of pediatric psychology* (pp. 111–117). Boston: Allyn & Bacon.

Silverthorn, P., & Frick, P. (1999). Developmental pathways to antisocial behavior: The delayed-onset pathway in girls. *Development and Psychopathology, 11,* 101–126.

Silverthorn, P., Frick, P. J., Kuper, K., & Ott, J. (1996). Attention deficit hyperactivity disorder and sex: A test of two etiological models to explain the male predominance. *Journal of Clinical Child Psychology, 25,* 52–59.

Simmons, R. (2002). *Odd girl out: The hidden culture of aggression in girls.* New York: Harcourt, Inc.

Simon, T. R., Dent, C. W., & Sussman, S. (1997). Vulnerability to victimization, concurrent problem behaviors, and peer influence as predictors of in-school weapon carrying among high school students. *Violence and Victims, 12,* 277–289.

Simonoff, E. (2001). Gene-environment interplay in oppositional defiant and conduct disorder. *Child and Psychiatric Clinics of North America, 10,* 351–374.

Simonoff, E., Bolton, P., & Rutter, M. (1996). Mental retardation: Genetic findings, clinical implications and research agenda. *Journal of Child Psychology and Psychiatry, 37,* 259–280.

Simonoff, E., Pickles, A., Meyer, J. M., Silberg, J. L., Maes, H. H., Loeber, R., et al. (1997). The Virginia Twin Study of adolescent behavioral development: Influences of age, sex, and impairment on rates of disorder. *Archives of General Psychiatry, 54,* 801–808.

Simons-Morton, B. (2004). Prospective association of peer influence, school engagement, drinking expectancies, and parent expectations with drinking initiation among sixth graders. *Addictive Behaviors, 29,* 299–309.

Simos, P. G., Fletcher, J. M., Bergman, E., Breier, J. I., Foorman, B. R., Castillo, E. M., et al. (2002). Dyslexia-specific brain activation profile becomes normal following successful remedial training. *Neurology, 58,* 1203–1213.

Singer, L. T., Hawkins, S., Huang, J., Davillier, M., & Baley, J. (2001). Developmental outcomes and environmental correlates of very low birthweight, cocaine-exposed infants. *Early Human Development, 64,* 91–103.

Singer, M. I., Hussey, D. L., & Strom, K. J. (1992). Grooming the victim: An analysis of a perpetrator's seduction letter. *Child Abuse and Neglect, 16,* 877–886.

Siqueland, L., Kendall, P. C., & Steinberg, L. (1996). Perceived family environment and observed family interaction styles. *Journal of Clinical Child Psychology, 25,* 225–237.

Sites, P. (1967). *Lee Harvey Oswald and the American dream.* New York: Pageant Press.

Skiba, R. J., Knesting, K., & Bush, L. D. (2002). Culturally competent assessment: More than nonbiased tests. *Journal of Child and Family Studies, 11,* 61–78.

Skinner, T. C., John, M., & Hampson, S. E. (2000). Social support and personal models of diabetes as predictors of self-care and well-being: A longitudinal study of adolescents with diabetes. *Journal of Pediatric Psychology, 25,* 257–267.

Slavin, L. A., & Rainer, K. (1990). Gender differences in emotional support and depressive symptoms among adolescents: A prospective analysis. *American Journal of Community Psychology, 18,* 407–421.

Slifer, K. J., Tucker, C. L., & Dahlquist, L. M. (2002). Helping children and caregivers cope with repeated invasive procedures: How are we doing? *Journal of Clinical Psychology in Medical Settings, 9,* 131–152.

Sloper, P., & Turner, S. (1996). Progress in social-independent functioning of young people with Down's syndrome. *Journal of Intellectual Disability Research, 40,* 39–48.

Smalley, S. L. (1998). Autism and tuberous sclerosis. *Journal of Autism and Developmental Disorders, 28,* 407–414.

Smalley, S. L., McGough, J. J., Del'Homme, M., NewDelman, J., Gordon, E., Kim, T., et al., (2000). Familial clustering of symptoms and disruptive behaviors in multiplex families with attention-deficit/hyperactivity disorder. *Journal of the American Academy of Child and Adolescent Psychiatry, 39,* 1135–1143.

Smetana, J. G., Daddis, C., Toth, S. L., Cicchetti, D., Bruce, J., & Kane, P. (1999). Effects of provocation on maltreated and nonmaltreated preschoolers' understanding of moral transgressions. *Social Development, 8,* 335–348.

Smith, B. H., Waschbusch, D. A., Willoughby, M. T., & Evans, S. (2000). The efficacy, safety, and practicality of treatments for adolescents with attention-deficit/hyperactivity disorder (ADHD). *Clinical Child and Family Psychology Review, 3,* 243–260.

Smith, P. K., Morita, Y., Junger-Tas, J., Olweus, D., Catalano, R. F., Slee, P. (Eds.). (1999). *The nature of school bullying: A cross-national perspective.* London: Routledge.

Smith, T. (1999). Outcome of early intervention for children with autism. *Clinical Psychology: Science and Practice, 6,* 33–49.

Smith, T., Eikeseth, S., Klevstrand, M., & Lovaas, O. I. (1997). Intensive behavioral treatment for preschoolers with severe mental retardation and pervasive developmental disorder. *American Journal on Mental Retardation, 102,* 238–249.

Smith, T., & Lovaas, O. I. (1997). The UCLA Young Autism Project: A reply to Gresham and Macmillan. *Behavioral Disorders, 22,* 202–218.

Smith, T., & Lovaas, O. I. (1998). Intensive early behavioral intervention with autism: The UCLA Young Autism Project. *Infants and Young Children, 10,* 67–78.

Smits-Bandstra, S. M. & Yovetich, W. S. (2003). Treatment effectiveness for school age children who stutter. *Journal of Speech-Language Pathology and Audiology, 27,* 125–133.

Smoller, J. W., Rosenbaum, J. F., Biederman, J., Kennedy, J., Dai, D., Racette, S. R., et al. (2003). Association of a genetic marker at the coritcotropin-releasing hormone locus with behavioral inhibition. *Biological Psychiatry, 54,* 1376–1381.

Snowling, M. J., Gallagher, A., & Frith, U. (2003). Family risk of dyslexia is continuous: Individual differences in the precursors of reading skill. *Child development, 74,* 358–373.

Snyder, H. N., & Sickmund, M. (1999). *Juvenile offenders and victims: 1999 national report.* Pittsburgh, PA: National Center for Juvenile Justice, U.S. Department of Justice.

Snyder, J. (1991). Discipline as a mediator of the impact of maternal stress and mood on child conduct problems. *Development and Psychopathology, 3,* 263–276.

Society for Research in Child Development. (1996). Ethical standards for research with children. In *SRCD: Directory of members* (pp. 337–339). Ann Arbor, MI: Author.

Soderstrom, H., Rastam, M., & Gillberg, C. (2002). Temperament and character in adults with Asperger syndrome. *Autism, 6,* 287–297.

Sokol, R. J., Delaney-Black, V., & Nordstrom, B. (2003). Fetal alcohol spectrum disorder. *JAMA, 290,* 2996–2999.

Solanto, M. V., Abikoff, H., Sonuga-Barke, E., Schachar, R., Logan, G. D., Wigal, T., et al., (2001). The ecological validity of delay aversion and response inhibition as measures of impulsivity in AD/HD: A supplement to the NIMH Multimodal Treatment Study of ADHD. *Journal of Abnormal Child Psychology, 29,* 215–228.

Solin, S. (1995, April 1). I did not want to live. *Seventeen,* pp. 154–156, 176.

Sondheimer, D. L., Schoenwald, S. K., & Rowland, M. D. (1994). Alternatives to the hospitalization of youth with a serious emotional disturbance. *Journal of Clinical Child Psychology, 23,* 7–12.

Sonuga-Barke, E.J.S., Daley, D., & Thompson, M. (2002). Does maternal ADHD reduce the effectiveness of parent training for preschool children's ADHD? *Journal of the American Academy of Child and Adolescent Psychiatry, 41,* 696–702.

Southam-Gerow, M. A., & Kendall, P. C. (2000). A preliminary study of the emotion understanding of youths referred for treatment of anxiety disorders. *Journal of Clinical Child Psychology, 29,* 319–327.

Southam-Gerow, M. A., & Kendall, P. C. (2002). Emotion regulation and understanding: Implications for child psychopathology and therapy. *Clinical Psychology Review, 22,* 189–222.

Southam-Gerow, M. A., Kendall, P. C., & Weersing, R. V. (2001). Examining outcome variability: Correlates of treatment response in a child and adolescent anxiety clinic. *Journal of Clinical Child Psychology, 30,* 422–436.

Southam-Gerow, M. A., Weisz, J. R., & Kendall, P. C. (2003). Youth with anxiety disorders in research and service clinics: Examining client differences and similarities. *Journal of Clinical Child and Adolescent Psychology, 32,* 375–385.

Sowell, E. R., Toga, A. W., & Asarnow, R. (2000). Brain abnormalities observed in childhood-onset schizophrenia: A review of the structural magnetic resonance imaging literature. *Mental Retardation and Developmental Disabilities Research Reviews, 6,* 180–185.

Speier, P. L., Sherak, D. L., Hirsch, S., & Cantwell, D. P. (1995). Depression in children and adolescents. In E. E. Beckham & W. R. Leber (Eds.), *Handbook of depression* (2nd ed., pp. 467–493). New York: Guilford Press.

Speltz, M. L., DeKlyen, M., Calderon, R., Greenberg, M. T., & Fisher, P. A. (1999). Neuropsychological characteristics and test behaviors of boys with early onset conduct problems. *Journal of Abnormal Psychology, 108*, 315–325.

Speltz, M. L., DeKlyen, M., & Greenberg, M. T. (1999). Attachment in boys with early onset conduct problems. *Development and Psychopathology, 11*, 269–285.

Speltz, M. L., McClellan, J., DeKlyen, M., & Jones, K. (1999). Preschool boys with oppositional defiant disorder: Clinical presentation and diagnostic change. *Journal of the American Academy of Child and Adolescent Psychiatry, 38*, 838–845.

Spence, S. H., & Dadds, M. R. (1996). Preventing childhood anxiety disorders. *Behaviour Change, 13*, 241–249.

Spence, S. H., Donovan, C., & Brechman-Toussaint, M. (2000). The treatment of childhood social phobia: The effectiveness of a social skills training-based, cognitive-behavioural intervention, with and without parental involvement. *Journal of Child Psychology & Psychiatry & Allied Disciplines, 41*, 713–726.

Spence, S. H., Sheffield, J. K., & Donovan, C. L. (2003). Preventing adolescent depression: An evaluation of the Problem Solving For Life program. *Journal of Consulting and Clinical Psychology, 71*, 3–13.

Spencer, T. J., Biederman, J., Coffey, B., Geller, D., Wilens, T., & Faraone, S. (1999). The 4-year course of tic disorders in boys with attention-deficit/hyperactivity disorder. *Archives of General Psychiatry, 56*, 842–847.

Spencer, T. J., Biederman, J., Harding, M., O'Donnell, D., Faraone, S. V., & Wilens, T. E. (1996). Growth deficits in ADHD children revisited: Evidence for disorder-associated growth delays? *Journal of the American Academy of Child and Adolescent Psychiatry, 35*, 1460–1469.

Spencer, T. J., Biederman, J., & Wilens, T. (2000). Pharmacotherapy of attention deficit hyperactivity disorder. *Child and Adolescent Psychiatric Clinics of North America, 9*, 77–97.

Spencer, T. J., Wilens, T., Biederman, J., Wozniak, J., & Harding-Crawford, M. (2000). Attention-deficit/hyperactivity disorder with mood disorders. In T. E. Brown (Ed.), *Attention-deficit disorders and comorbidities in children, adolescents, and adults* (pp. 79–124). Washington, DC: American Psychiatric Press.

Spiker, D., Lotspeich, L. J., Dimiceli, S., Myers, R. M., & Rische, N. (2002). Behavioral phenotypic variation in autism multiplex families: Evidence for a con-

tinuous severity gradient. *American Journal of Medical Genetics, 114*, 129–136.

Spitz, R. (1945). Hospitalism: An inquiry into the genesis of psychiatric conditions in early childhood. *Psychoanalytic Study of the Child, 1*, 53–74.

Spitz, R. A., & Wolf, M. (1946). Anaclitic depression: An enquiry into the genesis of psychiatric conditions in early childhood: II. *Psychoanalytic Study of the Child, 2*, 342–363.

Spitz, R. V., Tallal, P., Flax, J., & Benasich, A. A. (1997). Look who's talking: A prospective study of familial transmission of language impairments. *Journal of Speech Language and Hearing Research, 40*, 990–1001.

Spock, B. (1955). *Baby and child care.* London: Bodley Head.

Sprague-McRae, J. M., Lamb, W., & Homer, D. (1993). Encopresis: A study of treatment alternatives and historical and behavioral characteristics. *Nurse Practitioner, 18*, 52–53; 56–63.

Sprich, S., Biederman, J., Crawford, M. H., Mundy, E., & Faraone, S. V. (2000). Adoptive and biological families of children and adolescents with ADHD. *Journal of the American Academy of Child and Adolescent Psychiatry, 39*, 1432–1437.

Sroufe, L. A. (1997). *Emotional development: The organization of emotional life in the early years (Cambridge studies in social and emotional development).* New York: Cambridge University Press.

Sroufe, L. A., Carlson, E. A., Levy, A. K., & Egeland, B. (1999). Implications of attachment theory for developmental psychopathology. *Development and Psychopathology, 11*, 1–13.

Stark, K. D., & Kendall, P. C. (1996). *Treating depressed children: Therapist manual for "Taking ACTION."* Ardmore, PA: Workbook.

Stark, K. D., Sander, J. B., Yancy, M. G., Bronik, M. D., & Hoke, J. A. (2000). Treatment of depression in childhood and adolescence: Cognitive-behavioral procedures for the individual and family. In P. C. Kendall (Ed.), *Child and adolescent therapy: Cognitive-behavioral procedures* (2nd ed., pp. 173–234). New York: Guilford Press.

Stark, K. D., Schmidt, K. L., & Joiner, T. E., Jr. (1996). Cognitive triad: Relationship to depressive symptoms, parents' cognitive triad, and perceived parental messages. *Journal of Abnormal Child Psychology, 24*, 615–631.

Stark, K. D., Swearer, S., Kurowski, C., Sommer, D., & Bowen, B. (1996). Targeting the child and the family: A holistic approach to treating child and adolescent depressive disorders. In E. D. Hibbs & P. S. Jensen (Eds.), *Psychosocial treatments for child and adolescent disorders: Empirically based strategies for clinical practice* (pp. 207–238). Washington, DC: American Psychological Association.

Stark, L. J., Opipari, L. C., Donaldson, D. L., Danovsky, M. B., Rasile, D. A., & DelSanto, A. F. (1997). Evaluation of a standard protocol for retentive encopresis: A replication. *Journal of Pediatric Psychology, 22*, 619–633.

State, M., King, B. H., & Dykens, E. (1997). Mental retardation: A review of the past 10 years: II. *Journal of the American Academy of Child and Adolescent Psychiatry, 36*, 1664–1671.

State, M. W., Lombroso, P. J., Pauls, D. L., & Leckman, J. F. (2000). The genetics of childhood psychiatric disorders: A decade of progress. *Journal of the American Academy of Child and Adolescent Psychiatry, 39*, 946–962.

Statistics Canada. (2003). *Persons in low income before tax.* Cat. No. 75-202-XIE. Available: http://www.statcan.ca/english/Pgdb/famil41a.htm. Accessed February 17, 2004. Ottawa, ON: Author.

Steege, M. W., Wacker, D. P., Cigrand, K. C., Berg, W. K., Novak, C. G., Reimers, et al.,(1990). Use of negative reinforcement in the treatment of self-injurious behavior. *Journal of Applied Behavior Analysis, 23*, 459–467.

Stein, A., Murray, L., Copper, P., & Fairburn, C. G. (1996). Infant growth in the context of maternal eating disorders and maternal depression: A comparative study. *Psychological Medicine, 26*, 569–574.

Stein, D., Williamson, D. E., Birmaher, B., Brent, D. A., Kaufman, J., Dahl, R. E., et al. (2000). Parent-child bonding and family functioning in depressed children and children at high risk and low risk for future depression. *Journal of the American Academy of Child and Adolescent Psychiatry, 39*, 1387–1395.

Stein, M. A., Szumoski, E., Blondis, T. A., & Roizen, N. J. (1995). Adaptive skills dysfunction in ADD and ADHD children. *Journal of Child Psychology and Psychiatry, 36*, 663–670.

Steinberg, L., & Avenevoli, S. (2000). The role of context in the development of psychopathology: A conceptual framework and some speculative propositions. *Child Development, 71*, 66–74.

Steiner-Adair, C. (1990). The body politic: Normal female adolescent development and the development of eating disorders. In C. Gilligan, N. P. Lyons, & T. J. Hammer (Eds.), *Making connections: The relational worlds of adolescent girls at Emma Willard School* (pp. 162–182). Cambridge, MA: Harvard University Press.

Steinhauer, P. D. (1996). *Model for the prevention of delinquency.* Ottawa: National Crime Prevention Council.

Steinhauer, P. D. (1998). Developing resiliency in children from disadvantaged populations. In *Canadian health action: Building on the legacy: Vol. 1. Children and youth* (pp. 47–102). Sainte-Foy, Quebec: Editions Multimondes.

Steinhausen, H. C., Dreschler, R., Foldenyi, M., Imhof, K., & Brandeis, D. (2003). Clinical course of attention-deficit/

hyperactivity disorder toward early adolescence. *Journal of the American Academy of Child and Adolescent Psychiatry, 42,* 1085–1092.

Steinhausen, H. C., Willms, J., & Spohr, H. (1994). Correlates of psychopathology and intelligence in children with Fetal Alcohol Syndrome. *Journal of Child Psychology and Psychiatry, 35,* 323–331.

Sternberg, E. M., & Gold, P. W. (1997). The mind body interaction in disease. *Scientific American,* pp. 8–15.

Stewart, S. M., Lee, P.W.H., Low, L.C.K, Cheng, A., Yeung, W., Huen, K. F., & O'Donnell, D. (2000). Pathways from emotional adjustment to glycemic control in youths with diabetes in Hong Kong. *Journal of Pediatric Psychology, 25,* 393–402.

Stice, E., & Agras, W. S. (1999). Subtyping bulimic women along dietary restraint and negative affect dimensions. *Journal of Consulting and Clinical Psychology, 67,* 460–469.

Stice, E., Burton, E. M., & Shaw, H. (2004). Prospective relations between bulimic pathology, depression, and substance abuse: Unpacking comorbidity in adolescent girls. *Journal of Consulting and Clinical Psychology, 72,* 62–71.

Stice, E., & Fairburn, C. G. (2003). Dietary and dietary-depressive subtypes of bulimia nervosa show differential symptom presentation, social impairment, comorbidity, and course of illness. *Journal of Consulting and Clinical Psychology, 71,* 1090–1094.

Stice, E., Hayward, C., Cameron, R., Killen, J., & Taylor, C. B. (2000). Body-image and eating disturbances predict onset of depression among female adolescents: A longitudinal study. *Journal of Abnormal Psychology, 109,* 438–444.

Still, G. F. (1902). Some abnormal psychical conditions in children. *Lancet, 1,* 1008–1012, 1077–1082, 1163–1168.

Stodgell, C. J., Ingram, J. L., & Hyman, S. L. (2000). The role of candidate genes in unraveling the genetics of autism. *International Review of Research in Mental Retardation, 23,* 57–82.

Strain, P. S., Kohler, F. W., & Goldstein, H. (1996). Learning experiences . . . An alternative program: Peer-mediated interventions for young children with autism. In E. D. Hibbs & P. S. Jensen (Eds.), *Psychosocial treatments for child and adolescent disorders: Empirically based strategies for clinical practice* (pp. 573–587). Washington, DC: American Psychological Association.

Strandburg, R. J., Marsh, J. T., Brown, W. S., Asarnow, R. F., & Guthrie, D. (1994). Information processing deficits across childhood- and adult-onset schizophrenia: ERP correlates. *Schizophrenia Bulletin, 20,* 685–696.

Straus, M. (2001). *Beating the devil out of them: Corporal punishment in American families and its effects on children.* New Brunswick, NJ: Transaction.

Straus, M. A., & Gelles, R. J. (1986). Societal change and change in family violence from 1975 to 1985 as revealed by two national surveys. *Journal of Marriage and the Family, 48,* 465–479.

Straus, M. A., Gelles, R. J., & Steinmetz, S. K. (2003). The marriage license as a hitting license. In M. Silberman (Ed.), *Violence and society: A reader* (pp. 125–135). Upper Saddle River, NJ: Prentice Hall.

Straus, M. A., & Stewart, J. H. (1999). Corporal punishment by American parents: National data on prevalence, chronicity, severity, and duration, in relation to child and family characteristics. *Clinical Child and Family Psychology Review, 2,* 55–70.

Strauss, A. A., & Lehtinen, L. E. (1947). *Psychopathology and education of the brain-injured child.* New York: Grune & Stratton.

Strauss, A. A., & Werner, H. (1943). Comparative psychopathology of the brain-injured child and the traumatic brain-injured adult. *American Journal of Psychiatry, 19,* 835–838.

Strauss, C. C., Lahey, B. B., Frick, P., Frame, C. L., & Hynd, G. W. (1988). Peer social status of children with anxiety disorders. *Journal of Consulting and Clinical Psychology, 56,* 137–141.

Strauss, C. C., & Last, C. G. (1993). Social and simple phobias in children. *Journal of Anxiety Disorders, 7,* 141–152.

Strauss, C. C., Last, C. G., Hersen, M., & Kazdin, A. E. (1988). Association between anxiety and depression in children and adolescents with anxiety disorders. *Journal of Abnormal Child Psychology, 16,* 57–68.

Strauss, C. C., Lease, C. A., Last, C. G., & Francis, G. (1988). Overanxious disorder: An examination of developmental differences. *Journal of Abnormal Child Psychology, 16,* 433–443.

Steinhausen, H. (2002). The outcome of anorexia nervosa in the 20th century. *American Journal of Psychiatry, 159(8),* 1284–1293.

Streissguth, A. P., Barr, H. M., Bookstein, F. L., Sampson, P. D., & Olson, H. C. (1999). The long-term neurocognitive consequences of prenatal alcohol exposure: A 14-year study. *Psychological Science, 10,* 186–190.

Striegel-Moore, R. H., Leslie, D., Petrill, S. A., Garvin, V., & Rosenheck, R. A. (2000). One-year use and cost of inpatient and outpatient services among female and male patients with an eating disorder: Evidence from a national database of health insurance claims. *International Journal of Eating Disorders, 27,* 381–389.

Striegel-Moore, R. H., Silberstein, L. R., & Rodin, J. (1986). Toward an understanding of risk factors for bulimia. *American Psychologist, 41,* 246–263.

Striegel-Moore, R. H., & Steiner-Adair, C. (1998). The prevention of eating disorders. In W. Vandereycken & G. Noordenbos (Eds.), *Studies in eating disorders: An international series* (pp. 1–22). New York: New York University Press.

Strober, M. (1991). Disorders of the self in anorexia nervosa: An organismic-developmental paradigm. In C. Johnson (Ed.), *Psychodynamic treatment of anorexia nervosa and bulimia* (pp. 354–373). New York: Guilford Press.

Strober, M., Freeman, R., Lampert, C., Diamond, J., & Kaye, W. (2000). Controlled family study of anorexia nervosa and bulimia nervosa: Evidence of shared liability and transmission of partial syndromes. *American Journal of Psychiatry, 157,* 393–401.

Strober, M., Lampert, C., Schmidt, S., & Morrell, W. (1993). The course of major depressive disorder in adolescents: Recovery and risk of manic switching in a 24-month prospective, naturalistic follow-up of psychotic and nonpsychotic subtypes. *Journal of the American Academy of Child and Adolescent Psychiatry, 32,* 34–42.

Strober, M., Schmidt-Lackner, S., Freeman, R., Bower, S., Lampert, C., & DeAntonio, M. (1995). Recovery and relapse in adolescents with bipolar affective illness: A five-year naturalistic, prospective follow-up. *Journal of the American Academy of Child and Adolescent Psychiatry, 34,* 724–731.

Stromme, P., & Magnus, P. (2000). Correlations between socioeconomic status, IQ, and aetiology in mental retardation: A population-based study of Norwegian children. *Social Psychiatry and Psychiatric Epidemiology, 35,* 12–18.

Stromswold, K. (1998). Genetics of spoken language disorders. *Human Biology, 70,* 293–320.

Stuber, M., Christakis, D., Houskamp, B., & Kazak, A. (1996). Post trauma symptoms in childhood leukemia survivors and their parents. *Psychosomatics, 37,* 254–261.

Substance Abuse and Mental Health Services Administration (2002). *Results from the 2001 National Household Survey on Drug Abuse: Volume 1.* Summary of National Findings (Office of Applied Studies, NHSDA Series H-17, DHHS Publication No. SMA 02–3758). Rockville, MD.

Sullivan, P. F. (1995). Mortality in anorexia nervosa. *American Journal of Psychiatry, 152,* 1073–1074.

Sullivan, P. F., Bulik, C. M., & Kendler, K. S. (1998). Genetic epidemiology of binging and vomiting. *British Journal of Psychiatry, 173,* 75–79.

Sullivan, P. F., Kendler, K. S., & Neale, M. C. (2003). Schizophrenia as a complex trait: Evidence from a meta-analysis of twin studies. *Archives of General Psychiatry, 60,* 1187–1192.

Sullivan, P. M., & Knutson, J. F. (2000). Maltreatment and disabilities: A population-based epidemiological study. *Child Abuse and Neglect, 24,* 1257–1273.

Sund, A. M., Larsson, B., & Wichstrom, L. (2003). Psychosocial correlates of depressive symptoms among 12-14-year-old Norwegian adolescents. *Journal of Child Psychology and Psychiatry, 44,* 588–597.

Sutker, P. B. (1994). Psychopathy: Traditional and clinical antisocial concepts. In D. C. Fowles, P. Sutker, & S. H. Goodman (Eds.), *Progress in experimental personality and psychopathology research* (pp. 73–120). New York: Springer.

Sutton, A. (1995). The new gene technology and the difference between getting rid of illness and altering people. *European Journal of Genetics and Society, 1,* 12–19.

Suzuki, D. (1994, October 6). *The nature of things with David Suzuki: Easy targets.* Ottawa: Canadian Broadcasting Corporation.

Swackhamer, K. (1993). Believer. *Journal of the American Medical Association, 270,* 312.

Swanson, D. P., Spencer, M. B., Harpalani, V., Dupree, D., Noll, E., Ginzburg, S., & Seaton, G. (2003). Psychosocial development in racially and ethnically diverse youth: Conceptual and methodological challenges in the 21st century. *Development and Psychopathology, 15,* 743–810.

Swanson, J., Castellanos, F. X., Murias, M., LaHoste, G., & Kennedy, J. (1998). Cognitive neuroscience of attention deficity hyperactivity disorder and hyperkinetic disorder. *Current Opinion in Neurobiology, 8,* 263–271.

Swanson, J. M., Arnold, L.E., Vitiello, B., Abikoff, H. B., Wells, K. C., Pelham, W. E., et al., (2002). Response to commentary on the Multimodal Treatment Study of ADHD (MTA): Mining the meaning of the MTA. *Journal of Abnormal Child Psychology, 30,* 327–332.

Swanson, J. M., McBurnett, K., Christian, D. L., & Wigal, T. (1995). Stimulant medications and the treatment of children with ADHD. In T. H. Ollendick & R. J. Prinz (Eds.), *Advances in clinical child psychology* (Vol. 17, pp. 265–322). New York: Plenum.

Swedo, S. E., Rapoport, J. L., Leonard, H., Lenane, M., & Cheslow, D. (1989). Obsessive-compulsive disorder in children and adolescents: Clinical phenomenology of 70 consecutive cases. *Archives of General Psychiatry, 46,* 335–341.

Szapocznik, J., & Williams, R. A. (2000). Brief Strategic Family Therapy: Twenty-five years of interplay among theory, research and practice in adolescent behavior problems and drug abuse. *Clinical Child and Family Psychology Review, 3,* 117–134.

Szatmari, P. (1992). The epidemiology of attention-deficit hyperactivity disorders. In G. Weiss (Ed.), *Child and adolescent psychiatric clinics of North America: Attention deficit hyperactivity disorder* (pp. 361–372). Philadelphia: Saunders.

Szatmari, P., Offord, D. R., & Boyle, M. H. (1989). Correlates, associated impairments, and patterns of service utilization of children with attention deficit disorders: Findings from the Ontario Child Health Study. *Journal of Child Psychology and Psychiatry, 30,* 205–217.

Szymanski, L. & King, B. H. (1999). Practice parameters for the assessment and treatment of children, adolescents, and adults with mental retardation and comorbid mental disorders. *Journal of the American Academy of Child and Adolescent Psychiatry, 38,* (12, Suppl.), 5S–31S.

Tager-Flusberg, H. (1993). What language reveals about the understanding of minds in children with autism. In S. Baron-Cohen, H. Tager-Flusberg, & D. J. Cohen (Eds.), *Understanding other minds: Perspectives from autism* (pp. 138–157). Oxford, England: Oxford University Press.

Tager-Flusberg, H. (1996). Brief report: Current theory and research on language and communication in autism. *Journal of Autism and Developmental Disorders, 26,* 169–172.

Tager-Flusberg, H. (2000). Understanding the language and communicative impairments in autism. *International Review of Research in Mental Retardation, 23,* 185–207.

Tallal, P. (2003). Language learning disabilities: Integrating research approaches. *Current Directions in Psychological Science, 12,* 206–211.

Tallal, P., & Benasich, A.A. (2002). Developmental language learning impairments. *Development and Psychopathology, 14,* 559–579.

Tallal, P., Miller, S. L., Bedi, G., Byma, G., Wang, X., Nagarajan, S. S., et al. (1996). Language comprehension in language-learning impaired children improved with acoustically modified speech. *Science, 271,* 81–84.

Tanguay, P. E. (2000). Pervasive developmental disorders: A 10-year review. *Journal of the American Academy of Child and Adolescent Psychiatry, 39,* 1079–1095.

Tannock, R. (1998). Attention deficit hyperactivity disorder: Advances in cognitive, neurobiological, and genetic research. *Journal of Child Psychology and Psychiatry, 39,* 65–99

Tannock, R. (2000). Language, reading, and motor control problems in ADHD: A potential behavioral phenotype. In L. L. Greenhill (Ed). *Learning disabilities: Implications for psychiatric treatment* (pp. 129–167). Washington, DC: American Psychiatric Publishing.

Tannock, R., & Brown, T. E. (2000). Attention deficit disorders with learning disorders in children and adolescents. In T. E. Brown (Ed.), *Attention deficit disorders and comorbidities in children, adolescents and adults* (pp. 231–295). Washington, DC: American Psychiatric Press.

Tannock, R., Fine, J., Heintz, T., & Schachar, R. J. (1995). A linguistic approach detects stimulant effects in two children with attention-deficit hyperactivity disorder. *Journal of Child and* Adolescent Psychopharmacology, 5, 177–189.

Tannock, R., Purvis, K., & Schachar, R. (1993). Narrative abilities in children with attention deficit hyperactivity disorder and normal peers. *Journal of Abnormal Child Psychology, 21,* 103–117.

Tanofsky-Kraff, M., Yanovski, S. Z., Wilfley, D. E., Marmarosh, C., Morgan, C. M., & Yanovski, J. A. (2004). Eating-disordered behaviors, body fat, and psychopathology in overweight and normal-weight children. *Journal of Consulting and Clinical Psychology, 72, 1,* 53–61.

Tapert, S. F., Granholm, E., Leedy, N. G., & Brown, S. A. (2002). Substance use and withdrawal: Neuropsychological functioning over 8 years in youth. *Journal of the International Neuropsychological Society, 8,* 873–883.

Tapscott, M., Frick, P. J., Wootton, J., & Kruh, I. (1996). The intergenerational link to antisocial behavior: Effects of paternal contact. *Journal of Child and Family Studies, 5,* 229–240.

Tarver-Behring, S., Barkley, R. A., & Karlsson, J. (1985). The mother-child interactions of hyperactive boys and their normal siblings. *American Journal of Orthopsychiatry, 55,* 202–209.

Tate, D. C., Reppucci, N. D., & Mulvey, E. P. (1995). Violent juvenile delinquents: Treatment effectiveness and implications for action. *American Psychologist, 50,* 777–781.

Taylor, E. (1995). Dysfunctions of attention. In D. Cicchetti & D. J. Cohen (Eds.), *Developmental psychopathology: Risk disorder, and adaptation* (Vol. 2, pp. 243–273). New York: Wiley-Interscience.

Taylor, E. (1999). Developmental neuropsychology of attention deficit and impulsiveness. *Development and Psychopathology, 11,* 607–628.

Taylor, H. G. (1988). Learning disabilities. In E. J. Mash & L. G. Terdal (Eds.), *Behavioral assessment of childhood disorders* (2nd ed., pp. 402–450). New York: Guilford Press.

Taylor, H. G. (1989). Learning disabilities. In E. J. Mash & R. A. Barkley (Eds.), *Treatment of childhood disorders* (pp. 347–380). New York: Guilford Press.

Taylor, J., Iacono, W. G., & McGue, M. (2000). Evidence for a genetic etiology of early-onset delinquency. *Journal of Abnormal Psychology, 109,* 634–643.

Teicher, M. H., Andersen, S. L., Polcari, A., Anderson, C. M., & Navalta, C. P. (2002). Developmental neurobiology of childhood stress and trauma. *Psychiatric Clinics of North America, 25,* 397–426.

Teicher, M. H., Ito, Y., Glod, C. A., & Barber, N. I. (1996). Objective measurement of hyperactivity and attentional problems in ADHD. *Journal of the American Academy of Child and Adolescent Psychiatry, 35,* 334–342.

Temple, E., Deutsch, G.K., Poldrack, R.A., Miller, S.L., Tallal, P., Merzenich, M.M., & Gabrieli, J.D.E. (2003). Neural deficits in children with dyslexia ameliorated by behavioral remediation: Evidence from functional MRI. *Proceedings of the National Academy of Sciences, 100*, 2860–2865.

Terr, L. C. (1983). Chowchilla revisited: The effects of psychic trauma four years after a school-bus kidnapping. *American Journal of Psychiatry, 140*, 1543–1550.

Terr, L. C. (1991). Childhood traumas: An outline and overview. *American Journal of Psychiatry, 148*, 10–20.

Thapar, A. J. (2003). Attention deficit hyperactivity disorder: New genetic findings, new directions. In R. Plomin & J. C. DeFries (Eds.), *Behavioral genetics in the postgenomic era* (pp. 445–462). Washington, DC: Psychological Association.

Thatcher, R. W. (1994). Psychopathology of early frontal lobe damage: Dependence on cycles of development. *Development and Psychopathology, 6*, 565–596.

The Research Unit on Pediatric Psychopharmacology Anxiety Study Group (2001). Fluvoxamine for the treatment of anxiety disorders in children and adolescents. *New England Journal of Medicine, 344*, 1279–1285.

Thomas, A., & Chess, S. (1977). *Temperament and development.* New York: Brunner/Mazel.

Thompson, P. M., Giedd, J. N., Woods, R. P., MacDonald, D. E., Alan, C., & Toga, A. W. (2000). Growth patterns in the developing brain detected by using continuum mechanical tensor maps. *Nature, 404*, 190–193.

Thompson, P., Vidal, C., Giedd, J. N., Gochman, P., Blumenthal, J., Nicolson, R., et al. (2001). Mapping adolescent brain change reveals dynamic wave of accelerated gray matter loss in very early-onset schizophrenia. *Proceedings of the National Academy of Sciences, 98*, 11650–11655.

Thompson, R. A. (1994b). Social support and the prevention of child maltreatment. In G. B. Melton and F. D. Barry (Eds.), *Protecting children from abuse and neglect: Foundations for a new national strategy* (pp. 40–130). New York: Guilford Press.

Thompson, R. A. (2001). Sensitive periods in attachment. In Bailey, D. B. Jr., Bruer, J. T., Symons, F. J., & Lichtman, J. W. (Eds.), *Critical thinking about critical periods* (83–106). Baltimore, MD: Paul H. Brookes Publishing Co.

Thompson, R. A., & Flood, M.F.A. (2002). Toward a child-oriented child protection system. In G. B. Melton, R. A. Thompson, & M. A. Small (Eds.), *Toward a child-centered, neighborhood-based child protection system: A report of the consortium on children, families, and the law* (pp. 155–194). Westport, CT: Praeger Publishers/Greenwood Publishing Group.

Thompson, R. J., Jr., Gil, K. M., Burbach, D. J., Keith, B. R., & Kinney, T. R. (1993). Role of child and maternal processes in the psychological adjustment of children with sickle cell disease. *Journal of Consulting and Clinical Psychology, 61*, 468–474.

Thompson, R. J., Jr., & Gustafson, K. E. (1996). *Adaptation to chronic childhood illness.* Washington, DC: American Psychological Association.

Thompson, R. J., Jr., Gustafson, K. E., George, L. K., & Spock, A. (1994). Change over a 12-month period in the psychological adjustment of children and adolescents with cystic fibrosis. *Journal of Pediatric Psychology, 19*, 189–203.

Thompson, S., & Rey, J. M. (1994). Functional enuresis: Is desmopressin the answer? *Journal of the American Academy of Child and Adolescent Psychiatry, 34*, 266–271.

Thompson, S. H., Rafiroiu, A. C., & Sargent, R. G. (2003). Examining gender, racial, and age differences in weight concern among third, fifth, eighth, and eleventh graders. *Eating Behaviors, 3*, 307–323.

Time (2003, August 25). "The fat Earth: Obesity goes global".

Toch, T. (1993, November 8). Violence in schools. *U.S. News & World Report*, pp. 31–36.

Tolan, P. H., Gorman-Smith, D., & Henry, D. B. (2003). The developmental ecology of urban males' youth violence. *Developmental Psychology, 39*, 274–291.

Tolan, P. H., & Guerra, N. (1994, July). *What works in reducing adolescent violence: An empirical review of the field.* Boulder, CO: Center for the Study and Prevention of Violence.

Tolan, P. H., Guerra, N. G., & Kendall, P. C. (1995). A developmental-ecological perspective on antisocial behavior in children and adolescents: Toward a unified risk and intervention framework. *Journal of Consulting and Clinical Psychology, 63*, 579–584.

Toppelberg, C. O., & Shapiro, T. (2000). Language disorders: A 10-year research update review. *Journal of the American Academy of Child and Adolescent Psychiatry, 39*, 143–152

Toth, S. L., & Cicchetti, D. (1996). Patterns of relatedness, depressive symptomatology, and perceived competence in maltreated children. *Journal of Consulting and Clinical Psychology, 64*, 32–41.

Toth, S. L., Cicchetti, D., & Kim, J. (2002). Relations among children's perceptions of maternal behavior, attributional styles, and behavioral symptomatology in maltreated children. *Journal of Abnormal Child Psychology, 30*, 487–501.

Toupin, J., Dery, M., Pauze, R., Mercier, H., & Fortin, L. (2000). Cognitive and familial contributions to conduct disorder in children. *Journal of Child Psychology and Psychiatry, 41*, 333–344.

Treadwell, K. H., Flannery-Schroeder, E. C., & Kendall, P. C. (1994). Ethnicity and gender in a sample of clinic-referred anxious children: Adaptive functioning, diagnostic status, and treatment outcome. *Journal of Anxiety Disorders, 9*, 373–384.

Treasure, J., & Schmidt, U. (2003). Treatment overview. In J. Treasure, U. Schmidt, & E. van Furth (Eds.), *Handbook of eating disorders* (2nd ed., 207–217). Chichester: Wiley.

Treffers, P.D.A., & Silverman, W. K. (2001). Anxiety and its disorders in children and adolescents before the twentieth century. In W. K. Silverman & P.D.A. Treffers (Eds.), *Anxiety disorders in children and adolescents: Research, assessment, and intervention* (pp. 1–22). New York: Cambridge University Press.

Tremblay, M. S., & Willms, J. D. (2000). Secular trends in the body mass index of Canadian children. *Canadian Medical Association Journal, 163*, 1429–1433.

Tremblay, R. E. (2000). The development of aggressive behaviour during childhood: What have we learned in the past century? *International Journal of Behavioral Development, 24*, 129–141.

Tremblay, R. E., Japel, C., Perusse, D., McDuff, P., Boivin, M., Zoccolillo, M., & Montplaisir, J. (1999). The search for the age of 'onset' of physical aggression: Rousseau and Bandura revisited. *Criminal Behaviour and Mental Health, 9*, 8–23.

Tremblay, R., Pihl, R. O., Vitaro, F., & Dobkin, P. L. (1994). Predicting early onset of male antisocial behaviour from preschool behaviour. *Archives of General Psychiatry, 51*, 732–739.

Treuting, J. J., & Hinshaw, S. P. (2001). Depression and self-esteem in boys with attention-deficit/hyperactivity disorder: Associations with comorbid aggression and explanatory attributional mechanisms. *Journal of Abnormal Child Psychology, 29*, 23–39.

Trickett, P. K., Kurtz, D. A., Pizzigati, K. (2004). Resilient outcomes in abused and neglected children: Bases for strengths-based intervention and prevention policies. In K.I. Maton, C. J. Schellenbach, B.J. Leadbeater, & A.L. Solarz (Eds.), *Investing in children, youth, families, and communities: Strengths-based research and policy* (pp. 7395). Washington, DC: American Psychological Association.

Trickett, P. K., McBride-Chang, C., & Putnam, F. W. (1994). The classroom performance and behavior of sexually abused females. *Development and Psychopathology, 6*, 183–194.

Trocmé, N., & Wolfe, D.A. (2001). *Child maltreatment in Canada: Selected results from the Canadian Incidence Study of Reported Child Abuse & Neglect.* Ottawa, ON: Minister of Public Works and Government Services Canada. Available: http://www.hc-sc.gc.ca/pphb-dgspsp/publicat/cissr-ecirc/index.html

Troiano, R. P., Kuczmarski, R. J., Johnson, C. L., Flegal, K. M., & Campbell, S. M. (1995). Overweight prevalence and trends for children and adolescents: The National Health and Nutrition Examination Surveys, 1963 to 1991. *Archives of Pediatrics and Adolescent Medicine, 149,* 1085–1091.

Trottier, G., Srivastava, L., & Walker, C. D. (1999). Etiology of infantile autism: A review of recent advances in genetic and neurobiological research. *Journal of Psychiatry and Neuroscience, 24,* 103–115.

Tsuang, M. (2000). Schizophrenia: Genes and environment. *Biological Psychiatry, 47,* 210–220.

Turk, J., & Graham, P. (1997). Fragile X syndrome, autism and autistic features. *Autism, 1,* 175–197.

Turkheimer, E., Haley, A., Waldron, M., D'Onofrio, B., & Gottesman, I. I. (2003). Socioeconomic status modified heretability of IQ in young children. *Psychological Science, 14,* 623–628.

Turner, B. G., Beidel, D. C., Hughes, S., & Turner, M. W. (1993). Test anxiety in African American school children. *School Psychology Quarterly, 8,* 140–152.

Turner, G., Webb, T., Wake, S., & Robinson, H. (1996). Prevalence of fragile X syndrome. *American Journal of Medical Genetics, 64,* 196–197.

Turner, H., & Bryant-Waugh, R. (in press). Eating disorder not otherwise specified (EDNOS). Profiles of clients presenting at a community eating disorder service. *European Eating Disorders Review.*

Turner, M. (1999). Repetitive behaviour in autism: A review of psychological research. *Journal of Child Psychology and Psychiatry, 40,* 839–849.

Turner, S. M., Beidel, D. C., & Wolff, P. L. (1996). Is behavioral inhibition related to the anxiety disorders? *Clinical Psychology Review, 16,* 157–172.

Tyler, K. A., Hoyt, D. R., & Whitbeck, L. B. (2000). The effects of early sexual abuse on later sexual victimization among female homeless and runaway adolescents. *Journal of Interpersonal Violence, 15,* 235–250.

Tyrka, A. R., Graber, J. A., & Brooks-Gunn, J. (2000). The development of disordered eating: Correlates and predictors of eating problems in the context of adolescence. In A. J. Sameroff, M. Lewis, & S. Miller (Eds), *Handbook of developmental psychopathology* (2nd ed., pp. 607–624). New York: Plenum.

U.S. Department of Health and Human Services (2001). *Youth violence: A report of the Surgeon General.* Rockville, MD: Author.

Ulman, A., & Straus, M. A. (2003). Violence by children against mothers in relation to violence between parents and corporal punishment by parents. *Journal of Comparative Family Studies Special Issue: Violence against women in the family, 34,* 41–60.

U.N. Convention on the Rights of the Child (1989). UN General Assembly Document A/RES/44/25.

Underwood, M. K. (2003). *Social aggression among girls.* New York: Guilford Press.

UN General Assembly. (1989, November). *Adoption of a convention on the rights of the child.* (UN Doc. A/Res/44/25). New York: Author.

UNICEF. (1996). *State of the world's children.* New York: Oxford University Press.

UNICEF (2000, April 12). *Report of the Executive Director: Progress and achievements against the medium-term plan.* New York: Author.

United States Public Health Service Office of the Surgeon General (2001a). *Report of the surgeon general's conference on children's mental health: A national action agenda.* Rockville, MD: Department of Health and Human Services, U.S. Public Health Service.

United States Public Health Service Office of the Surgeon General (2001b). *Mental health: culture, race, and ethnicity: A supplement to mental health: A Report of the Surgeon General.* Rockville, MD: Department of Health and Human Services, U.S. Public Health Service.

U.S. Bureau of the Census (2003). *Small Area Income and Poverty Estimates Program.* Available: www.census.gov/hhes/www/saipe.html (accessed January 10, 2003).

U.S. Conference of Catholic Bishops. http://edition.cnn.com/2004/US/02/16/church.abuse/. Tuesday, February 17, 2004 Posted: 1354 GMT (9:54 PM HKT).

U.S. Department of Health and Human Services (2003). *Emerging practices in the prevention of child abuse and neglect.* Washington DC: Administration for Children and Families, Administration on Children, Youth and Families, Children's Bureau, Office on Child Abuse and Neglect.

U.S. Department of Health and Human Services [USDHHS] (2003). *Child Maltreatment 2001.* Administration on Children, Youth and Families, Washington, DC: U.S. Government Printing Office.

USA Weekend (1998, May 1). "Teens and self-image: Survey results."

Vagisil Women's Health Center (2000, June 27). "Teenage girls today more independent, yet lack self-esteem." *New Updates.*

Vallance, D. D., Cummings, R. L., & Humphries, T. (1998). Mediators of the risk for problem behavior in children with language learning disabilities. *Journal of Learning Disabilities, 31,* 160–171.

Van Ameringen, M., Mancini, C., & Farvolden, P. (2003). The impact of anxiety disorders on educational achievement. *Journal of Anxiety Disorders, 17,* 561–571.

van Hoeken, D, Seidell, J., & Hoek, H. (2003). Epidemiology. In J. Treasure, U. Schmidt, & E. van Furth (Eds.), *Handbook of eating disorders* (2nd ed., 11–34). Chichester: Wiley.

Van Houten, R., Axelrod, S., Bailey, J. S., Favell, J. E., Foxx, R. M., Iwata, B. A., & Lovaas, I. (1988). The right to effective behavioral treatment. *The Behavior Analyst, 11,* 111–114.

van Ijzendoorn, M. H., Schuengel, C., & Bakermans-Kranenburg, M. J. (1999). Disorganized attachment in early childhood: Meta-analysis of precursors, concomitants, and sequelae. *Development and Psychopathology, 11,* 225–249.

Vardill, R. & Calvert, S. (2000). Gender imbalance in referrals to an educational psychology service. *Educational Psychology in Practice, 16,* 213–223.

Varley, C. K., & Smith, C. J. (2003). Anxiety disorders in the child and teen. *Pediatric Clinics of North America, 50,* 1107–1138.

Varni, J. W., La Greca, A. M., & Spirito, A. (2000). Cognitive-behavioral interventions for children with chronic health conditions. In P.C. Kendall (Ed.), *Child and adolescent therapy: Cognitive-behavioral procedures* (2nd ed., pp. 291–333). New York: Guilford Press.

Vasey, M. W. (1993). Development and cognition in childhood anxiety: The example of worry. In T. H. Ollendick & R. Prinz (Eds.), *Advances in clinical child psychology* (Vol. 15, pp. 1–39). New York: Plenum.

Vasey, M. W. (1995). Social anxiety disorders. In A. R. Eisen, C. A. Kearney, & C. A. Schaefer (Eds.), *Clinical handbook of anxiety disorders in children and adolescents* (pp. 131–168). Northvale, NJ: Jason Aronson.

Vasey, M. W., & Dadds, M. R. (Eds.). (2001). *The developmental psychopathology of anxiety.* New York: Oxford University Press.

Vasey, M. W., & Daleiden, E. L. (1994). Worry in children. In G.C.L. Davey & F. Tallis (Eds.), *Worrying: Perspectives on theory, assessment and treatment* (pp. 185–207). Chichester, England: Wiley.

Vasey, M. W., El-Hag, N., & Daleiden, E. L. (1996). Anxiety and the processing of emotionally threatening stimuli: Distinctive patterns of selective attention among high- and low-test anxious children. *Child Development, 67,* 1173–1185.

Vasey, M. W., & MacLeod, C. (2001). Information-processing factors in childhood anxiety: A review and developmental perspective. In M. W. Vasey & M. R. Dadds (Eds.), *The developmental psychopathology of anxiety* (pp. 253–277). New York: Oxford University Press.

Vaughn, B. E., Contreras, J., & Seifer, R. (1994). Short-term longitudinal study of maternal ratings of temperament in samples of children with Down Syndrome and children who are developing normally. *American Journal on Mental Retardation, 98,* 607–618.

Velez, C. N., Johnson, J., & Cohen, P. (1989). A longitudinal analysis of selected risk factors for childhood psychopathology. *Journal of the American Academy of Child and Adolescent Psychiatry, 28,* 861–864.

Vellutino, F. R., Fletcher, J. M., Snowling, M. J., & Scanlon, D. M. (2004). Specific reading disability (dyslexia): What have we learned in the past four decades? *Journal of Child Psychology & Psychiatry & Allied Disciplines, 45,* 2–40.

Verma, S. K. (2000). Some popular misconceptions about inkblot techniques. *Journal of Projective Psychology and Mental Health, 7,* 79–81.

Viding, E., Spinath, F. M., Price, T. S., Bishop, D.V.M., Dale, P. S., & Plomin, R. (2004). Genetic and environmental influence on language development in 4-year-old same-sex and opposite-sex twins. *Journal of Child Psychology and Psychiatry, 45,* 315–325.

Vincent, M., & McCabe, M. (2000). Gender differences among adolescents in family, and peer influences on body dissatisfaction, weight loss, and binge eating behaviors. *Journal of Youth and Adolescence, 29,* 205–221.

Vitaro, F., Brendgen, M., & Tremblay, R. E. (2000). Influence of deviant friends on delinquency: Searching for moderator variables. *Journal of Abnormal Child Psychology, 28,* 313–325.

Volkmar, F. (1999). Lessons from secretin. *New England Journal of Medicine, 341,* 1842–1844.

Volkmar, F., Cook, E. H. Jr., Pomeroy, J., Realmuto, G., & Tanguay, P. (1999). Practice parameters for the assessment and treatment of children, adolescents, and adults with autism and other pervasive developmental disorders. *Journal of the American Academy of Child and Adolescent Psychiatry, 38 (Suppl.),* 32S–54S.

Volkmar, F. R., & Klin, A. (1998). Asperger syndrome and nonverbal learning disabilities. In E. Schopler, G. B. Mesibov, & L. J. Kunce (Eds.), *Asperger syndrome or high-functioning autism?* (pp. 107–121). New York: Plenum.

Volkmar, F. R., & Klin, A. (2000). Asperger's Disorder and higher functioning autism: Same or different? *International Review of Research in Mental Retardation, 23,* 83–111.

Volkmar, F. R., Klin, A., & Pauls, D. (1998). Nosological and genetic aspects of Asperger syndrome. *Journal of Autism and Developmental Disorders, 28,* 457–463.

Volkmar, F. R., Klin, A., Schultz, R., Bronen, R., Marans, W. D., Sparrow, S., & Cohen, D. J. (1996). Grand rounds: Asperger's syndrome. *Journal of the American Academy of Child and Adolescent Psychiatry, 35,* 118–123.

Volkmar, F. R., Lord, C., Bailey, Schultz, R. T., & Klin, A. (2004). Autism and pervasive developmental disorders. *Journal of Child Psychology and Psychiatry, 45,* 135–170.

Volkmar, F. R., Shaffer, D., & First, M. (2000). PDD-NOS in DSM-IV. *Journal of Autism and Developmental Disorders, 30,* 74–75.

Volkow, N. D., Wang, G., Fowler, J. S., Logan, J., Angrist, B., Hitzemann, R., et al., (1997). Effects of methylphenidate on regional brain glucose metabolism in humans: Relationship to dopamine D2 receptors. *American Journal of Psychiatry, 154,* 50–55.

Vyas, D., & Chandra, R. K. (1984). Functional implications of iron deficiency. In A. Stekel (Ed.), *Iron nutrition in infancy and childhood* (pp. 45–59). New York: Raven.

Waddell, C., & Shepherd, C. (2002). *Prevalence of mental disorders in children and youth: A research update prepared for the British Columbia Ministry of Children and Family Development.* Vancouver, BC: The University of British Columbia. Available: http://www.mcf.gov.bc.ca/mental_health/mh_publications/02a_cymh.pdf

Wade, T. D., Bulik, C. M., Neale, M., & Kendler, K. S. (2000). Anorexia nervosa and major depression: Shared genetic and environmental risk factors. *American Journal of Psychiatry, 157,* 469–471.

Wade, T. J., Cairney, J., & Pevalin, D. J. (2002). Emergence of gender differences in depression during adolescence: National panel results from three countries. *Journal of the Academy of Child and Adolescent Psychiatry, 41,* 190–198.

Wagner, B. M., & Reiss, D. (1995). Family systems and developmental psychopathology: Courtship, marriage, or divorce? In D. Cicchetti & D. J. Cohen (Eds.), *Developmental psychopathology: Vol. 1. Theory and methods* (pp. 696–730). New York: Wiley.

Wagner, E. F., Swenson, C. C., & Henggeler, S. W. (2000). Practical and methodological challenges in validating community-based interventions. *Children's Services: Social Policy, Research, and Practice, 3,* 211–231.

Wagner, K. D. (2003). Major depression in children and adolescents. *Psychiatric Annals, 33(4),* 266–270.

Wakefield, A. J., Anthony, A., Murch, S. H., Thomson, M., Montgomery, S. M., Davies, S., et al. (2000). Enterocolitis in children with developmental disorders. *American Journal of Gastroenterology, 95,* 2285–2295.

Walcott, D. D., Pratt, H. D., & Patel, D. R. (2003). Adolescents and eating disorders: Gender, racial, ethnic, sociocultural and socioeconomic issues. *Journal of Adolescent Research, 18,* 223–243.

Waldman, I. D., & Lilienfeld, S. O. (1995). Diagnosis and classification. In M. Hersen & R. T. Ammerman (Eds.), *Advanced abnormal child psychology* (pp. 21–36). Hillsdale, NJ: Erlbaum.

Walker, E. F. (2002). Adolescent neurodevelopment and psychopathology. *Current Directions in Psychological Science, 11,* pp. 24–28.

Walker, E., & Lewine, R. J. (1990). Prediction of adult-onset schizophrenia from childhood home movies of the patients. *American Journal of Psychiatry, 147,* 1052–1056.

Walker, L. S., Garber, J., & Greene, J. W. (1994). Somatic complaints in pediatric patients: A prospective study of the role of negative life events, child social and academic competence, and parental somatic symptoms. *Journal of Consulting and Clinical Psychology, 62,* 1213–1221.

Wallace, J. M., Jr., Bachman, J. G., O'Malley, P. M., Schulenberg, J. E., Cooper, S. M., & Johnston, L D. (2003). Gender and ethnic differences in smoking, drinking, and illicit drug use among American 8th, 10th, and 12th, grade students, 1976–2000. *Addiction, 98,* 225–234.

Wallander, J. L. & Robinson, S. L. (1999). Chronic medical illness. In R. T. Ammerman, M. Hersen et al. (Eds.), *Handbook of prescriptive treatments for children and adolescents* (2nd ed., pp. 364–380). Boston: Allyn & Bacon.

Wallander, J. L. & Varni, J. W. (1998). Effects of pediatric chronic physical disorders on child and family adjustment. *Journal of Child Psychology and Psychiatry and Allied Disciplines, 39,* 29–46.

Wallis, C. (1994, July 18). Life in overdrive. *Time,* pp. 42–50.

Walter, J. H., White, F. J., Hall, S. K., MacDonald, A., Rylance, G., Boneh, A., et al. (2002). How practical are recommendations for dietary control in phenylketonuria? *Lancet, 360,* 55–57.

Wang, Y., & Ollendick, T. H. (2001). A cross-cultural and developmental analysis of self-esteem in Chinese and Western children. *Clinical Child and Family Psychology Review, 4,* 253–271.

Wangbson, M., Bergman, L. R., & Magnusson, D. (1999). Development of adjustment problems in girls: What syndromes emerge? *Child Development, 70,* 678–699.

Waschbusch, D. (2002). A meta-analytic examination of comorbid hyperactive-impulsive-attention problems and conduct problems. *Psychological Bulletin, 128,* 118–150.

Waschbusch, D. A., & Hill, G. P. (2003). Empirically supported, promising, and unsupported treatments for children with attention-deficit/hyperactivity disorder. In S. O. Lilienfeld & S. J. (Eds), *Science and pseudoscience in clinical psychology* (pp. 333–362). New York: Guilford Press.

Waschbusch, D. A., Kipp, H. L., & Pelham, W. E., Jr. (1998). Generalization of behavioral and psychostimulant treatment of attention-deficit/hyperactivity disorder (ADHD): Discussion and examples. *Behaviour Research and Therapy, 36,* 675–694.

Waters, E., Merrick, S., Treboux, D., Crowell, J., & Albersheim, L. (2000). Attachment security in infancy and early adulthood: A twenty-year longitudinal study. *Child Development, 71,* 684–689.

Waters, E., Weinfield, N. S.; & Hamilton, C. E. (2000) The stability of attachment security from infancy to adolescence and early adulthood: General discussion. *Child Development, 71(3),* 703–706.

Waters, T. L., & Barrett, P. M. (2000). The role of the family in childhood obsessive-compulsive disorder. *Clinical Child and Family Psychology Review, 3,* 173–184.

Watkins, C. E., Campbell, V. L., Nieberding, R., & Hallmark, R. (1995). Contemporary practice of psychological assessment by clinical psychologists. *Professional Psychology: Research and Practice, 26,* 54–60.

Watson, J. B. (1925). *Behaviorism.* New York: People's Institute Publishing.

Watson, J. B., & Rayner, R. R. (1920). Conditioned emotional reactions. *Journal of Experimental Psychology, 3,* 1–14.

Watson, R. R. (1996, August). I am the mother of a behaviorist's sons. *Parent's Magazine, 50.* (Original article published August 1930)

Webster, A., Feiler A., Webster V., & Lovell C. (2004). Parental perspectives on early intensive intervention for children diagnosed with autistic spectrum disorder. *Journal of Early Childhood Research, 2,* 25–49.

Webster-Stratton, C. (1996). Early-onset conduct problems: Does gender make a difference? *Journal of Consulting and Clinical Psychology, 64,* 540–551.

Webster-Stratton, C., & Herbert, M. (1994). *Troubled families—problem children: Working with parents: A collaborative process.* New York: Wiley.

Webster-Stratton, C., & Reid, M. J. (2003). The incredible years parents, teachers, and children training series: A multifaceted treatment approach for young children with conduct problems. In A. E. Kazdin & J. R. Weisz (Eds.), *Evidence-based psychotherapies for children and adolescents* (pp. 224–249). New York: Guilford.

Wechsler, D. (1974). *Manual for the Wechsler Intelligence Scale for Children—Revised (WISC-R).* New York: Psychological Corporation.

Weckerly, J. (2002). Pediatric bipolar mood disorder. *Journal of Developmental and Behavioral Pediatrics, 23,* 42–56.

Weeks, S. J., & Hobson, R. P. (1987). The salience of facial expression for autistic children. *Journal of Child Psychology and Psychiatry, 28,* 137–152.

Weems, C. F., Silverman, W. K., & La Greca, A. M. (2000). What do youth referred for anxiety problems worry about? Worry and its relation to anxiety and anxiety disorders in children and adolescents. *Journal of Abnormal Child Psychology, 28,* 63–72.

Weems, C. F., Silverman, W. K., Rapee, R. M., & Pina, A. A. (2003). The role of control in childhood anxiety disorders. *Cognitive Therapy and Research, 27,* 557–568.

Wegner, D. M., Fuller, V. A., & Sparrow, B. (2003). Clever hands: Uncontrolled intelligence in facilitated communication. *Journal of Personality and Social Psychology, 85,* 5–19.

Weinberg, N. Z., Rahdert, E., Colliver, J. D., & Glantz, M. D. (1998). Adolescent substance abuse: A review of the past 10 years. *Journal of the American Academy of Child and Adolescent Psychiatry, 37,* 252–261.

Weinfield, N. S., Sroufe, L. A., & Egeland, B. (2000). Attachment from infancy to early adulthood in a high-risk sample: Continuity, discontinuity, and their correlates. *Child Development, 71,* 695–702.

Weinger, S. (1999). Views of the child with retardation: Relationship to family functioning. *Family Therapy, 26,* 63–79.

Weiss, B., Catron, T., & Harris, V. (2000). A 2-year follow-up of the effectiveness of traditional child psychotherapy. *Journal of Consulting and Clinical Psychology, 68,* 1094–1101.

Weiss, B., Catron, T., Harris, V., & Phung, T. M. (1999). The effectiveness of traditional child psychotherapy. *Journal of Consulting and Clinical Psychology, 67,* 82–94.

Weiss, B., & Garber, J. (2003). Developmental differences in the phenomenology of depression. *Development and Psychopathology, 15,* 403–430.

Weiss, B., Weisz, J. R., & Bromfield, R. (1986). Performance of retarded and nonretarded persons on information-processing tasks: Further tests of the similar structure hypothesis. *Psychological Bulletin, 100,* 157–175.

Weiss, G., & Hechtman, L. T. (1993). *Hyperactive children grown up: ADHD in children, adolescents, and adults (2nd ed.).* New York: Guilford Press.

Weiss, L. (1992). *Attention deficit disorder in adults.* Dallas, TX: Taylor.

Weissman, M. M., McAvay, G., Goldstein, R. B., Nunes, E. V., Verdeli, H., & Wickramaratne, P. J. (1999). Risk/protective factors among addicted mothers' offspring: A replication study. *American Journal of Drug and Alcohol Abuse, 25,* 661–679.

Weissman, M. M., Warner, V., Wickramaratne, P., & Prusoff, B. A. (1988). Early-onset major depression in parents and their children. *Journal of Affective Disorders, 15,* 269–277.

Weissman, M. M., Warner, V., Wickramaratne, P., Moreau, D., & Olfson, M. (1997). Offspring of depressed parents: 10 years later. *Archives of General Psychiatry, 54,* 932–940.

Weissman, M. M., Wolk, S., Goldstein, R. B., Moreau, D., Adams, P., Greenwald, S., Klier, C. M., Ryan, N. D., Dahl, R. E., & Wickramaratne, P. (1999a). Depressed adolescents grown up. *Journal of the American Medical Association, 281,* 1707–1713.

Weissman, M. M., Wolk, S., Wickramaratne, P., Goldstein, R. B., Adams, P., Greenwald, S., Ryan, N. D., Dahl, R. E., & Steinberg, D. (1999b). Chil-

dren with prepubertal-onset major depressive disorder and anxiety grown up. *Archives of General Psychiatry, 56,* 794–801.

Weisz, J. R. (1998). Empirically supported treatments for children and adolescents: Efficacy, problems, and prospects. In K. S. Dobson & K. D. Craig (Eds.), *Empirically supported therapies: Best practice in professional psychology* (pp. 66–92). Newbury Park, CA: Sage.

Weisz, J. R. (1999). Cognitive performance and learned helplessness in mentally retarded persons. In E. Zigler & D. Bennett-Gates (Eds), *Personality development in individuals with mental retardation* (pp. 17–46). New York: Cambridge University Press.

Weisz, J. R., Chayaisit, W., Weiss, B., Eastman, K. L., & Jackson, E. W. (1995). A multimethod study of problem behavior among Thai and American children in school: Teacher reports versus direct observations. *Child Development, 66,* 402–415.

Weisz, J. R., Donenberg, G. R., Han, S. S., & Weiss, B. (1995). Bridging the gap between laboratory and clinic in child and adolescent psychotherapy. *Journal of Consulting and Clinical Psychology, 63,* 688–701.

Weisz, J. R., Southam-Gerow, M. A., Gordis, E. B., & Conner-Smith, J. (2003). Primary and secondary control enhancement training for youth depression: Applying the deployment-focused model of treatment development and testing. In A. E. Kazdin & J. R. Weisz (Eds.), *Evidence-based psychotherapies for children and adolescents* (pp. 165–183). New York: Guilford Press.

Weisz, J. R., Valeri, S. M., McCarty, C. A., & Moore, P. S. (1999). Interventions for depression: Features, effects, and future directions. In C. A. Essau & F. Petermann (Eds.), *Depressive disorders in children and adolescents: Epidemiology, risk factors, and treatment* (pp. 383–435). Northvale, NJ: Jason Aronson.

Weisz, J. R., & Weiss, B. (1993). *Effects of psychotherapy with children and adolescents.* Newbury Park, CA: Sage.

Weisz, J. R., Weiss, B., Suwanlert, S., & Chaiyasit, W. (2003). Syndromal structure of psychopathology in children of Thailand and the United States. *Journal of Consulting and Clinical Psychology, 71,* 375–385.

Wekerle, C., & Wall, A. M. (2002). The overlap between intimate violence and substance abuse. In C. Wekerle & A. M. Wall (Eds.), *The violence and addiction equation: Theoretical and clinical issues in substance abuse and relationship violence* (pp. 1–21). New York: Brunner-Routledge.

Wekerle, C., & Wolfe, D. A. (2003). Child maltreatment. In E. J. Mash & R. A. Barkley (Eds). *Child Psychopathology* (2nd ed., pp. 632–684). New York: Guilford Press.

Weller, R. A., Weller, E. B., Fristad, M. A., & Bowes, J. M. (1991). Depression in recently bereaved prepubertal children. *American Journal of Psychiatry, 148,* 1536–1540.

Welsh, M. C., & Pennington, B. F. (1988). Assessing frontal lobe functioning in children: Views from developmental psychology. *Developmental Neuropsychology, 4,* 199–230.

Wender, P. H. (2000). *ADHD: Attention-deficit hyperactivity disorder in children and adults.* New York: Oxford University Press.

Werner, E. E. (1993). Risk and resilience in individuals with learning disabilities: Lessons learned from the Kauai Longitudinal Study. *Learning Disabilities Research and Practice, 8,* 28–34.

Werner, E. E. (1995). Resilience in development. *Current Directions in Psychological Science, 4,* 81–85.

Werner, E.E., & Smith, R.S. (2001). *Journeys from childhood to midlife: Risk, resilience, and recovery.* Ithaca, NY: Cornell University Press.

Whalen, C. K., & Henker, B. (1992). The social profile of attention-deficit hyperactivity disorder: Five fundamental facets. In G. Weiss (Ed.), *Child and adolescent psychiatric clinics of North America: Attention-deficit hyperactivity disorder* (pp. 395–410). Philadelphia: Saunders.

Whalen, C. K., & Henker, B. (1999). The child with attention-deficit/hyperactivity disorder in family contexts. In H. C. Quay & A. E. Hogan (Eds.), *Handbook of disruptive behavior disorders* (pp. 139–155). New York: Kluwer, Academic/Plenum.

Whaley, S. E., Pinto, A., & Sigman, M. (1999). Characterizing interactions between anxious mothers and their children. *Journal of Consulting and Clinical Psychology, 67,* 826–836.

White, H. R., Loeber, R., Stouthamer-Loeber, M., & Farrington, D. P. (1999). Developmental associations between substance use and violence. *Development and Psychopathology, 11,* 785–803.

White, H. R., & Widom, C. S. (2003). Intimate partner violence among abused and neglected children in young adulthood: The mediating effects of early aggression, antisocial personality, hostility and alcohol problems. *Aggressive Behavior, 29,* 332–345.

White, J. L., Moffitt, T. E., Caspi, A., Bartusch, D. J., Needles, D. J., & Stouthamer-Loeber, M. (1994). Measuring impulsivity and examining its relationship to delinquency. *Journal of Abnormal Psychology, 103,* 192–205.

Whitehurst, G. J., Fischel, J. E., Arnold, D. S., & Lonigan, C. J. (1992). Evaluating outcomes with children with expressive language delay. In S. F. Warren & J. Reichle (Eds.), *Causes and effects in communication and language intervention* (pp. 277–313). Baltimore: Brookes.

Whitehurst, G. J., Fischel, J. E., Lonigan, C. J., Valdez-Manchaca, M. C., Debaryshe, B. D., & Caulfield, M. B. (1988). Verbal interaction in families of normal and expressive-language-delayed children. *Developmental Psychology, 24,* 690–699.

Whitman, T. L., Scherzinger, M. F., & Sommer, K. S. (1991). Cognitive instruction and mental retardation. In P. C. Kendall (Ed.), *Child and adolescent therapy: Cognitive-behavioral procedures* (pp. 276–315). New York: Guilford Press.

Wickramaratne, P. J., Greenwald, S., & Weisman, M. M. (2000). Psychiatric disorders in the relatives of probands with prepubertal-onset or adolescent-onset major depression. *Journal of the American Academy of Child and Adolescent Psychiatry, 39,* 1396–1405.

Widiger, T. A. (1993). The DSM-III-R categorical personality disorder diagnoses: A critique and an alternative. *Psychological Inquiry, 4,* 75–90.

Widom, C. S. (1989a). Does violence beget violence? A critical examination of the literature. *Psychological Bulletin, 106,* 3–28.

Widom, C. S. (1989b). The cycle of violence. *Science, 244,* 160–165.

Widom, C. S. (1996, May/June). Childhood sexual abuse and its criminal consequences. *Society,* pp. 47–53.

Widom, C. S. (1999). Posttraumatic stress disorder in abused and neglected children grown up. *American Journal of Psychiatry, 156,* 1223–1229.

Wilens, T. E., Beiderman, J., Millstein, R. B., Wozniak, J., Hahesy, A. L., & Spencer, T. J. (1999). Risk for substance use disorders in youths with child- and adolescent-onset bipolar disorders. *Journal of the American Academy of Child and Adolescent Psychiatry, 38,* 680–685.

Wilens, T. E., Faraone, S. V., Biederman, J., & Gunawardene, S. (2003). Does stimulant therapy of attention-deficit/hyperactivity disorder beget later substance abuse? A meta-analytic review of the literature. *Pediatrics, 111,* 179–185.

Wilkerson, D. S., Volpe, A. G., Dean, R. S., & Titus, J. B. (2002). Perinatal complication as predictors of infantile autism. *International Journal of Neuroscience, 112,* 1085–1098.

Willcutt, E. G., Pennington, B. F., & DeFries, J. C. (2000). Etiology of inattention and hyperactivity/impulsivity in a community sample of twins with learning difficulties. *Journal of Abnormal Child Psychology, 28,* 149–159.

Williams, A. L., Singh, K. D., & Smith, A. T. (2003). Surround modulation measured with functional MRI in the human visual cortex. *Journal of Neurophysiology, 89 (1),* 525–533.

Williams, L. M. (2003). Understanding child abuse and violence against women: A life course perspective. *Journal of Interpersonal Violence Special Issue: Children and domestic violence, 18,* 441–451.

Williams, P. G., Holmbeck, G. N., & Greenley, R. N. (2002). Adolescent health psychology. *Journal of Consulting and Clinical Psychology, 70,* 828–842.

Williams, R. J., & Chang, S. Y. (2000). A comprehensive and comparative review of adolescent substance abuse treatment outcome. *Clinical Psychology: Science and Practice, 7,* 138–166.

Willis, D. J. (2002). Introduction to the Special Issue: Economic, health, and mental health disparities among ethnic minority children and families. *Journal of Pediatric Psychology, 27,* 309–314.

Willoughby, M. T. (2003). Developmental course of ADHD symptomatology during the transition from childhood to adolescence: A review with recommendations. *Journal of Child Psychology and Psychiatry, 44,* 88–106.

Willoughby, M. T., Curran, P. J., Costello, E. J., & Angold, A. (2000). Implications of early versus late onset of attention-deficit/hyperactivity disorder symptoms. *Journal of the American Academy of Child and Adolescent Psychiatry, 39,* 1512–1519.

Wills, T. A., & Dishion, T. J. (2004). Temperament and adolescent substance use: A transactional analysis of emerging self-control. *Journal of Clinical Child and Adolescent Psychology, 33,* 69–81.

Wilson, G. T. (1995). Behavior therapy. In R. J. Corsini & D. Wedding (Eds.), *Current psychotherapies* (5th ed., pp. 197–228). Itasca, IL: F. E. Peacock.

Wilson, G. T. (1999). Eating disorders and addiction. *Drugs and Society, 15,* 87–101.

Wilson, G. T., Becker, C. B., & Heffernan, K. (2002). Eating disorders. In E. J. Mash & R.A. Barkley (Eds.), *Child psychopathology* (2nd ed., pp. 687–715). New York: Guilford Press.

Wilson, K. K., & Melton, G. B. (2002). Exemplary neighborhood-based programs for child protection. In G.B. Melton, R. A. Thompson, & M. A. Small (Eds.), *Toward a child-centered, neighborhood-based child protection system: A report of the consortium on children, families, and the law* (pp. 197–213). Westport, CT: Praeger Publishers/Greenwood Publishing Group.

Wilson, K., Mills, E., Ross, C., McGowan, J., & Jadad, A. (2003). Association of autistic spectrum disorder and the measles, mumps, and rubella vaccine: A systematic review of current epidemiological evidence. *Archives of Pediatric and Adolescent Medicine, 157,* 628–634.

Wing, L., & Potter, D. (2002). The epidemiology of autistic spectrum disorders: Is the prevalence rising? *Mental Retardation and Developmental Disabilities Research Reviews, 8,* 151–161.

Winsler, A., Diaz, R. M., McCarthy, E. M., Atencio, D. J., & Chabay, L. A. (1999). Mother-child interaction, private speech, and task performance in preschool children with behavior problems. *Journal of Child Psychology and Psychiatry, 40,* 891–904.

Witkin, H. A., Oltman, P. K., Raskin, E., & Karp, S. (1971). *A manual for the embedded figures tests.* Palo Alto, CA: Consulting Psychologists Press.

Witt, W. P., Riley, A. W., & Coiro, M. J. (2003). Childhood functional status, family stressors, and psychological adjustment among school-aged children with disabilities in the United States. *Archives of Pediatric and Adolescent Medicine, 157,* 687–695.

Wittchen, H., Stein, M., & Kessler, R. (1999). Social fears and social phobias in a community sample of adolescents and young adults: Prevalence, risk factors, and comorbidity. *Psychological Medicine, 29,* 309–323.

Wolfe, D. A. (1991). *Preventing physical and emotional abuse of children.* New York: Guilford Press.

Wolfe, D. A. (1999). *Child abuse: Implications for child development and psychopathology.* Thousand Oaks, CA: Sage.

Wolfe, D. A., Crooks, C. V., Lee, V., McIntyre-Smith, A., & Jaffe, P. G. (2003). The effects of exposure to domestic violence on children: A meta-analysis and critique. *Clinical Child and Family Psychology Review, 6,* 171–187.

Wolfe, D. A., & Jaffe, P. (2001). Prevention of domestic violence: Emerging initiatives. In S. A. Graham-Bermann & J. L. Edleson (Eds.), *Domestic violence in the lives of children: The future of research, intervention and social policy* (pp. 283–298). Washington DC: American Psychological Association.

Wolfe, D. A., Jaffe, P., & Crooks, C. (in press). *Beyond risk reduction: Promoting healthy relationships in adolescents.* New Haven: Yale University Press.

Wolfe, D. A., Jaffe, P., Jette, J., & Poisson, S. (2003). The impact of child abuse in community institutions and organizations: Advancing professional and scientific understanding. *Clinical Psychology: Science and Practice, 10,* 179–191.

Wolfe, D. A., & Mash, E. J. (Eds.) (in press). *Behavioral and emotional disorders in adolescents: Nature, assessment, and treatment.* New York: Guilford Press.

Wolfe, D. A., & Mosk, M. D. (1983). Behavioral comparisons of children from abusive and distressed families. *Journal of Consulting and Clinical Psychology, 51,* 702–708.

Wolfe, D. A. & Nayak., M. B. (2003). Child abuse in peacetime. In B. L. Green, M. J. Friedman, J. de Jong, S. D. Solomon, T. M. Keane, J. A. Fairbank, B. Donelan, & E. Frey-Wouters (Eds.), *Trauma interventions in war and peace: Prevention, practice, and policy* (pp. 75–104). Kluwer Academic/Plenum.

Wolfe, D. A., Sas, L., & Wekerle, C. (1994). Factors associated with the development of posttraumatic stress disorder among child victims of sexual abuse. *Child Abuse and Neglect, 18,* 37–50.

Wolfe, D. A., Scott, K., Wekerle, C., & Pittman, A. (2001). Child maltreatment: Risk of adjustment problems and dating violence in adolescence. *Journal of the American Academy of Child and Adolescent Psychiatry, 40,* 282–298.

Wolfe, D. A., & St. Pierre, J. (1989). Child abuse and neglect. In T. H. Ollendick & M. Hersen (Eds.), *Handbook of child psychopathology* (2nd ed., pp. 377–398). New York: Plenum.

Wolfe, D. A., & Wekerle, C. (1993). Treatment strategies for child physical abuse and neglect: A critical progress report. *Clinical Psychology Review, 13,* 473–500.

Wolfe, D. A., Wekerle, C., Scott, K., Straatman, A., & Grasley, C. (in press). Predicting abuse in adolescent dating relationships over one year: The role of child maltreatment and trauma. *Journal of Abnormal Psychology.*

Wolfe, V. V., & Finch, A. J. (1987). Negative affectivity in children: A multitrait-multimethod investigation. *Journal of Consulting and Clinical Psychology, 55,* 245–250.

Wolfson, A. R., & Carskadon, M. A. (1998). Sleep schedules and daytime functioning in adolescents. *Child Development, 69,* 875–887.

Wolke, D., Rizzo, P., & Woods, S. (2002). Persistent infant crying and hyperactivity problems in middle childhood. *Pediatrics, 109,* 154–160.

Wolraich, M. L. (2003). The use of psychotropic medications in children: an American perspective. *Journal of Child Psychology and Psychiatry, 44,* 159–168.

Wonderlich, S. A., Crosby, R. D., Mitchell, J. E., Roberts, J. A., Haseltine, B., DeMuth, G., & Thompson, K. M. (2000). Relationship of childhood sexual abuse and eating disturbance in children. *Journal of the American Academy of Child and Adolescent Psychiatry, 39,* 1277–1283.

Wood, F. B., Felton, R. H., Flowers, L., & Naylor, C. (1991). Neurobehavioral definition of dyslexia. In D. D. Duane & D. B. Gray (Eds.), *The reading brain: The biological basis of dyslexia* (pp. 1–26). Parkton, MD: York Press.

Wood, J. J., McLeod, B. D., Sigman, M., Hwang, W., & Chu, B. C. (2003). Parenting and childhood anxiety: Theory, empirical findings, and future directions. *Journal of Child Psychology and Psychiatry, 44,* 134–151.

Wood, J. M., Lilienfeld, S. O., Garb, H. N., Nezworski, M. T. (2000). "The Rorschach test in clinical diagnosis": A critical review, with a backward look at Garfield (1947). *Journal of Clinical Psychology* Vol 56 (Mar 2000): 395–430.

Woodhouse, W., Bailey, A., Rutter, M., Bolton, P., Baird, G., & Le Couteur, A. (1996). Head circumference in autism and other pervasive developmental disorders. *Journal of Child Psychology and Psychiatry, 37,* 665–671.

Woodward, L. J., & Fergusson, D. M. (1999). Early conduct problems and later risk of teenage pregnancy in girls. *Development and Psychopathology, 11,* 127–141.

Woodward, L. J., & Fergusson, D. M. (2001). Life course outcomes of young people with anxiety disorders in adolescence. *Journal of the American Academy of Child and Adolescent Psychiatry, 40,* 1086–1093.

Woolston, J. L. (1991). *Eating and growth disorders in infants and children.* Newbury Park, CA: Sage.

Wootton, J. M., Frick, P. J., Shelton, K. K., & Silverthorn, P. (1997). Ineffective parenting and childhood conduct problems: The moderating role of callous-unemotional traits. *Journal of Consulting and Clinical Psychology, 65,* 292–300.

World Health Organization (1999, March). *Report of the consultation on child abuse prevention.* WHO, Geneva: Author.

Wright, J., & Jacobs, B. (2003). Teaching phonological awareness and metacognitive strategies to children with reading difficulties: A comparison of the two instructional methods. *Educational Psychology, 23,* 17–45.

Wu, P., Hoven, C. W., Bird, H. R., Moore, R. E., Cohen, P., Alegria, M., et al. (1999). Depressive and disruptive disorders and mental health service utilization in children and adolescents. *Journal of the American Academy of Child and Adolescent Psychiatry, 38,* 1081–1090.

Wunderlich, S. A., Crosby, R. D., Mitchell, J. E., Roberts, J. A., Haseltine, B., DeMuth, G., Thompson, K. M. (2001). Relationship of child sexual abuse and eating disturbance in children. *Journal of the American Academy of Child and Adolescent Psychiatry, 39,* 1277–1283.

Wyman, P.A., Sandler, I., Wolchik, S., & Nelson, K. (2000). Resilience as cumulative competence promotion and stress protection: Theory and intervention. In D. Cicchetti, J. Rappaport, I. Sandler, & R. P. Weissberg (Eds.), *The promotion of wellness in children and adolescents* (pp. 133–184). Washington, DC: Child Welfare League of America, Inc.

Wysocki, T., Harris, M. A., Greco, P., Bubb, J., Danda, C. E., Harvey, L. M., et al. (2000). Randomized, controlled trial behavior therapy for families of adolescents with insulin-dependent diabetes mellitus. *Journal of Pediatric Psychology, 25,* 23–33.

Yang, Q., Rasmussen, S. A., & Friedman, J. M. (2002). Mortality associated with Down's syndrome in the USA from 1983 to 1997: A population-based study. *Lancet, 359,* 1019–1025.

Yates, A. (1989). Current perspectives on the eating disorders: I. History, psychological, and biological aspects. *Journal of Child and Adolescent Psychiatry, 28,* 813–828.

Yeargin-Allsopp, M., Rice, C., Karapurkar, T., Doernberg, N., Boyle, C., & Murphy, C. (2003). Prevalence of autism in a US metropolitan area. *Journal of the American Medical Association, 289,* 87–89.

Yeganeh, R., Beidel, D. C., Turner, S. M., Pina, A. A., & Silverman, W. K. (2003). Clinical distinctions between selective mutism and social phobia: An investigation of childhood psychopathology. *Journal of the American Academy of Child and Adolescent Psychiatry, 42,* 1070–1075.

Yonan, A. L., Alarcon, M., Cheng, R., Magnusson, P. J., Spence, S. J., Palmer, A. A., et al. (2003). A genomewide screen of 345 families for autism-susceptibility loci. *American Journal of Human Genetics, 73,* 886–897.

Yoritomo-Tashi. (1916). *Timidity: How to overcome it.* (M. W. Artois, Trans.). New York: Funk & Wagnalls.

Young, A. R., Beitchman, J. H., Johnson, C., Douglas, L., Atkinson, L., Escobar, M. et al. (2002). Young adult academic outcomes in a longitudinal sample of early identified language impaired and control children. *Journal of Child Psychology & Psychiatry & Allied Disciplines, 43,* 635–645.

Young, A. R. (in press). Learning disorders in girls. In D. Bell, S. Foster, & E. J. Mash (Eds.), *Handbook of emotional and behavioral problems in girls.* New York: Kluwer Academic.

Young, L. (2003). Residential and lifestyle changes for adults with an intellectual disability in Queensland 1960–2001. *International Journal of Disability, Development, & Education, 50,* 93–106.

Youngstrom, E. A., Findling, R. L., & Calabrese, J. R. (in press). Towards an evidence-based assessment of pediatric bipolar disorder. *Journal of Clinical Child and Adolescent Psychology.*

Zahn-Waxler, C., Klimes-Dougan, B., & Slattery, M. J. (2000). Internalizing problems of childhood and adolescence: Prospects, pitfalls, and progress in understanding the development of anxiety and depression. *Development and Psychopathology, 12,* 443–466.

Zahn-Waxler, C., Race, E., & Duggal, S. (in press). In D. Bell, S. L. Foster, & E. J. Mash (Eds.), *Behavioral and emotional problems in girls.* New York: Kluwer Academic/Plenum Publishing.

Zaider, T., Johnson, J., & Cockell, S. (2000). Psychiatric comorbidity associated with eating disorder symptomatology among adolescents in the community. *International Journal of Eating Disorders, 28,* 58–67.

Zametkin, A. J., Ernst, M., & Silver, R. (1998). Laboratory and diagnostic testing in child and adolescent psychiatry: A review of the past 10 years. *Journal of the American Academy of Child and Adolescent Psychiatry, 37,* 464–472.

Zeanah, C. H., Jr. (Ed.). (2000). *Handbook of infant mental health (2nd ed.).* New York: Guilford.

Zelazo, P. D., & Mueller, U. (2002). Executive function in typical and atypical development. In U. Goswami (Ed.), *Handbook of childhood cognitive development* (pp. 445–469). Oxford: Blackwell.

Zelizer, V. A. (1994). *Pricing the priceless child: The changing social value of children.* Princeton: Princeton University Press.

Zentall, S. S. (1985). A context for hyperactivity. In K. Gadow & I. Bialer (Eds.), *Advances in learning and behavioral disabilities* (Vol. 4, pp. 273–343). Greenwich, CT: JAI Press.

Zigler, E. (1967). Familial mental retardation: A continuing dilemma. *Science, 155,* 292–298.

Zigler, E., & Hodapp, R. (1986). *Understanding mental retardation.* New York: Cambridge University Press.

Zilbovicius, M., Garreau, B., Samson, Y., Remy, P., Barthelemy, C., Syrota, A., & Lelord, G. (1995). Delayed maturation of the frontal cortex in childhood autism. *American Journal of Psychiatry, 152,* 248–252.

Zimmerman, M. A., & Arunkumar, R. (1994). Resiliency research: Implications for schools and policy. *Social Policy Report, 8(4),* 1–17.

Zito, J., Safer, D., dosReis, S., Gardner, J., Magder, L., Soeken, K., Boles, M., Lynch, F., & Riddle M. A. (2003). Psychotropic practice patterns for youth: A 10-year perspective. *Archives of Pediatric and Adolescent Medicine, 157,* 17–25.

Zoccolillo, M. (1992). Co-occurrence of conduct disorder and its adult outcomes with depressive and anxiety disorders: A review. *Journal of the American Academy of Child and Adolescent Psychiatry, 31,* 547–556.

Zoccolillo, M. (1993). Gender and the development of conduct disorder. *Development and Psychopathology, 5,* 65–78.

Zoccolillo, M., Pickles, A., Quinton, D., & Rutter, M. (1992). The outcome of conduct disorder: Implications for defining adult personality disorder and conduct disorder. *Psychological Medicine, 22,* 971–986.

Zoccolillo, M., & Rogers, K. (1991). Characteristics and outcome of hospitalized adolescent girls with conduct disorder. *Journal of the American Academy of Child and Adolescent Psychiatry, 30,* 973–981.

Zoccolillo, M., & Rogers, K. (1992). Characteristics and outcome of hospitalized adolescent girls with conduct disorder: Erratum. *Journal of the American Academy of Child and Adolescent Psychiatry, 31,* 561.

Zoglin, R. (1996, February 19). Chips ahoy. *Time,* pp. 46–49.

Photo Credits

Name Index

Brambilla, F., 395
Brambilla, P., 302
Bramble, D., 136
Brame, B., 163
Brandeis, D., 117
Bratton, S., 102
Breaux, A. M., 268
Brechman-Toussaint, M., 104
Breen, C. G., 280
Breggin, P., 128
Brehaut, J. C., 120
Breiger, D., 312
Bremmer, J. D., 416
Bremner, R., 281
Brendgen, M., 155
Brener, N. D., 143
Brennan, P. A., 154, 241, 242
Brent, D. A., 158, 227, 235, 242, 243, 244
Breslau, N., 348
Brestan, E. V., 174, 175
Bretherton, I., 42, 47
Breton, J., 124
Bridge, J., 158, 243
Bridges, D., 152
Bridges, M., 56
Briere, J., 421
Briggs-Gowan, M. J., 124
Bright, P., 325
Brinch, M., 381
Brinkmeyer, M. Y., 175
Broadhurst, D. D., 409, 410, 411, 412, 413–414
Brocque, R. L., 242
Brody, G. H., 20
Brody, L., 211
Broidy, L. M., 145, 148, 159
Bromet, E. J., 314
Bromfield, R., 96, 265
Bromley, E., 95
Brondino, M., 176
Brondino, M. J., 375
Bronfenbrenner, U., 4
Bronik, M.D., 245
Brook, J. S., 120, 157–158, 158, 169, 172, 205, 211, 226
Brooks-Gunn, J., 15, 18, 171, 259, 264, 378, 382, 387, 388, 396
Brown, E., 288
Brown, J., 419, 420
Brown, K., 223, 240
Brown, L. K., 360
Brown, L. M., 396
Brown, N. M., 165
Brown, R. L., 325
Brown, R. T., 157, 357, 364, 366
Brown, S. A., 370, 371, 372, 373, 374, 375
Brown, T., 118
Brown, T. E., 118
Brown, W. L., 219
Brown, W. S., 315
Browne, A., 417, 421
Browne, K., 429
Brownell, K. D., 377, 379, 386, 396
Bruce, J., 417

Bruch, H., 398
Bruck, M., 335
Bruer, J. T., 33
Bruitelaar, J. K., 240
Brumberg, J. J., 388
Bruni, G., 102
Bryant, R. A., 202
Bryant-Waugh, R., 393, 400, 401
Bryson, S. E., 297, 298, 299, 300, 305
Bucholz, K. K., 225
Buckley, M. E., 250
Budd, K. S., 382–383
Buican, B., 268
Buka, S. L., 19, 242
Bukowski, W. M., 364
Bulik, C. M., 379, 395, 402
Bullock, B. M., 155, 157
Bumbarger, B., 375
Bunk, D., 316
Burack, J. A., 34
Burbach, D. J., 365
Burcusa, S. L., 239
Burd, L., 120
Burg, S. J., 375
Burge, D., 236, 243
Burgess, K. B., 169, 209
Burke, J. D., 120, 145, 162, 226
Burke, K. C., 226
Burke, L., 382
Burley, S. K., 386
Burns, B. J., 107, 207
Burns, G. L., 112, 117, 123, 147
Burns, J., 247
Burr, J., 395
Burt, S. A., 123
Burton, E. M., 399
Burton, L. M., 47
Burwell, R. A., 385
Burwinkle, T. M., 383
Bush, L., 83
Bush, M., 266–267
Bushman, B. J., 155, 172
Bussing, R., 121
Butcher, C., 328
Butcher, J. N., 90
Butler, J. V., 273
Butler, L., 271
Buysse, A., 129
Byely, L., 378
Bynum, M. S., 20
Byrd, D. A., 224

C
Cabrara, N. J., 47
Cadman, D., 362
Cairney, J., 228
Calabrese, J. R., 248
Calder, J., 3
Calkins, S. D., 37
Callahan, S. Λ., 205
Calvert, S., 264
Cameron, R., 379
Camic, P. M., 68–69
Campbell, F. A., 258, 271, 278
Campbell, S. B., 27, 30, 100, 126, 133, 139, 162

Campbell, S. M., 384
Campbell, T. F., 325
Campbell, V. A., 102
Campbell, V. L., 88
Campbell, W. K., 155
Canino, I. A., 76
Canivez, G. L., 258
Cannon, T. D., 34, 35
Cantwell, D. P., 118, 123, 139, 223, 227–228, 298
Capage, L. C., 99
Capaldi, D. M., 157, 170
Caplan, R., 312, 313
Capps, L., 210, 289
Capron, C., 271
Cardinal, D. N., 52
Carlson, C. L., 116, 125, 129, 156
Carlson, E. A., 48, 414, 416, 421
Carlson, G. A., 225, 248, 250, 251, 252
Carlson, S. M., 297
Carosella, N., 315
Carpentieri, S., 365
Carper, R., 298
Carper, R. A., 302
Carr, A., 213, 431
Carr, E. G., 298, 305
Carroll, M. D., 384
Carskadon, M. A., 349
Carson, J., 368
Cart, C. U., 375
Carter, A. S., 185, 198, 237
Carter, M., 267
Carter, R. C., 384
Carver, L. J., 307
Casanova, M. F., 315
Cash, T. F., 392
Casper, R., 398
Caspi, A., 18, 19, 30, 43, 44, 75, 145, 154, 159, 161, 162, 163, 164–165, 166, 167, 168, 170, 171, 239
Cass, L. K., 94
Cassidy, J., 47
Castellanos, F. X., 132
Catron, T., 18, 57, 107
Ceci, S. J., 258
Chabay, L. A., 157
Chaiyasit, W., 21, 125, 126, 207
Challman, T. D., 297
Chambers, M. J., 346
Champion, K., 416
Chan, A. S., 322
Chan, E., 120
Chandler, L. A., 87
Chandler, M., 45
Chandra, R. K., 382
Chang, S. Y., 374
Chansky, T. E., 205
Charcot, J. M., 347
Charman, T., 298
Charmin, T., 289
Charney, D., 240
Charney, D. S., 248
Chase, C., 302
Chassin, L., 370, 371, 372, 373
Chen, E., 363
Chen, H., 362

Rumsey, J. M., 302
Rush, B., 4
Rushton, J. L., 229
Russell, A. T., 312, 313
Russell, J., 296
Rutherford, M. D., 295
Rutter, M., 16, 19, 25, 28, 29, 30, 32–
    33, 35, 36, 37, 47, 48, 75, 154, 157,
    158, 159, 160, 164, 165, 171, 172,
    178, 205, 209, 222, 223, 258, 268,
    285, 294, 297, 298, 300, 301, 311,
    413
Ruzicka, D. L., 348
Ryan, B. P., 328
Ryan, N. D., 235, 240, 244
Ryan, N. E., 243
Ryan, R. M., 418
Ryan, S., 421
Ryan, S. M., 211
Rydell, A. M., 377

S
Sabaratnam, M., 271
Sachdev, S., 427
Sadeh, A., 120, 348, 352
Saelens, B., 386
Safer, D. J., 136
Safford, S. M., 187
Sagun, J., 268
Sallee, R., 210
Salmond, C. H., 302
Salter, D., 421
Saltzman, H., 10, 21, 238
Salzinger, S., 420
Samaan, R. A., 20
Sameroff, A. J., 14, 29, 31, 33, 35, 47,
    48
Sammons, C., 313
Samoilina, T. G., 337
Sampson, P. D., 274
Sampson, R. J., 170, 171
Sander, J. B., 245
Sanders, M. R., 60, 177
Sanders, S. A., 258
Sandler, I., 15
Sandler, J., 406
Sandoval, J., 124
Sands, R., 377, 378
Sandy, J. M., 126
Sanson, A., 165, 209
Santangelo, S. L., 124
Santos, A. B., 174
Sapolsky, R., 37
Sappenfield, W., 359
Sargent, R. G., 378, 379
Sarigiani, P. A., 233
Sas, L., 404, 417, 418
Sasso, G. M., 65
Sassone, D., 124
Sattler, J. M., 58, 74, 80, 82, 86, 89,
    258, 322
Saunders, B., 373
Saunders, B. E., 431, 433
Saunders, G., 342
Sawyer, M. G., 364
Saxe, J. G., 60

Sayer, J., 131
Saywitz, K. J., 433, 434
Scanlan, S. W., 119, 154
Scanlon, D. M., 322
Scarr, S., 407
Schachar, R., 112, 119
Schaefer, C. E., 181
Schalock, R. L., 263
Schanberg, L. E., 366
Schectman, R. M., 229
Scherzinger, M. F., 280
Schewel, R., 335
Schmidt, C. W., Jr., 423
Schmidt, K. L., 237
Schmidt, M. H., 59
Schmidt, N. B., 399
Schmidt, S., 227
Schmidt, U., 400
Schniering, C. A., 237
Schoenwald, S. K., 174, 176
Schooler, N. R., 71
Schouten, E., 205
Schraedley, P. K., 228, 229, 247
Schreier, H. A., 424
Schroeder, C. S., 74, 355–356
Schroeder, M. L., 399
Schroeder, S. R., 276
Schuengel, C., 48
Schulenberg, J. E., 372
Schultz, L. H., 166
Schultz, R., 288
Schultz, R. T., 284
Schulz, C., 232
Schulz, E., 314
Schwab-Stone, M., 99, 202, 230
Schwab-Stone, M. E., 124
Schwartz, A. A., 52, 303
Schwartz, C. E., 209, 210
Schwartzman, A. E., 159
Schwimmer, J. B., 383
Schwoeri, L. D., 99
Sclar, D. A., 75
Scott, C. V., 103
Scott, K., 422
Scott, K. L., 35, 421
Scotti, J. R., 92
Scourfield, J., 131, 239
Scullin, M. H., 258
Searight, H. R., 393
Sears, M. R., 133
Secher, S. M., 233
Secord-Gilbert, M., 281
Sedgwick, P., 379
Sedlak, A. J., 409, 410, 411, 412, 413–
    414
Seeley, J., 399
Seeley, J. R., 206, 222, 225, 226, 227,
    230, 231, 232, 239, 242, 250, 373
Sefa-Dedeh, A., 396
Seidell, J., 393
Seiden, J. A., 132
Seifer, R., 267
Seitz, P., 88
Selemon, L. D., 315
Selfe, L., 294
Seligman, L. D., 205, 224, 226

Seligman, M. E., 236, 244
Seligman, M. E. P., 192, 232
Selman, R. L., 166
Semenak, S., 298, 304
Semrud-Clikeman, M., 119, 132
Sena, R., 210
Serbin, L. A., 159
Sergeant, J., 128
Sergeant, J. A., 115
Serketich, W. J., 175
Seroczynski, A. D., 233, 237
Sexton, J., 404
Shadish, W. R., 107
Shaffer, D., 221, 230, 235, 247, 311
Shafron, R., 218
Shah, B., 258, 268, 273
Shalala, D. E., 145
Shalev, R. S., 332, 337
Shankweiler, D., 322
Shanley, N., 237
Shapiro, T., 300, 319, 325
Sharp, R. N., 238
Sharpe, D., 364
Shatte, A. J., 247
Shaver, P. R., 47
Shaw, D., 75, 159, 160
Shaw, D. S., 27, 28, 126, 162, 169, 170
Shaw, H., 399
Shaywitz, B. A., 325, 331, 336, 337
Shaywitz, S. E., 325, 331, 332, 336,
    337, 341
Shea, S. E., 97
Sheddon, H., 383
Sheeber, L., 241, 242–243
Sheeran, T., 363
Sheffield, J. K., 247
Shelley-Tremblay, J. F., 128
Shelton, K. K., 169
Shelton, T. L., 118
Shema, S., 365
Shepard, C., 17
Shepherd, J., 241
Sherak, D. L., 227–228
Sherick, R. B., 232
Sherman, B. J., 386
Sherman, G. F., 337
Shields, A., 418
Shields, S. A., 4
Shifflett, H., 210
Shih, J., 242
Shillington, E. R., 19
Shilton, P., 429–430
Shin, L. M., 209
Shindledecker, R., 18
Shiner, R., 43
Shipman, K., 416
Shisslak, C. M., 393
Sholevar, G. P., 99
Shores, R. E., 280
Shortt, A. L., 205, 217
Shortt, L., 373
Shriberg, L. D., 324, 325
Sickmund, M., 143, 146, 147, 157
Siegel, J., 320–321, 328
Siegel, J. A., 420, 422
Siegel, L. J., 202, 334, 347

Stromswold, K., 325
Stuber, M., 363
Studer, D., 411
Sturm, R., 17
Sugarman, A., 205
Sullivan, P. F., 314, 394, 395
Sullivan, P. M., 426
Sund, A. M., 228
Sundelin, C., 377
Sussman, S., 146
Sutker, P. B., 152
Sutphen, J., 355
Sutphen, J. L., 356
Sutton, A., 277
Suwanlert, S., 21, 125, 126, 207
Suzuki, D., 420
Swackhamer, K., 285, 303
Swales, T., 366
Swan, S., 368
Swank, P. R., 410
Swanson, D. P., 55
Swanson, H. L., 335
Swanson, J., 132
Swanson, J. M., 136, 139
Swearer, S., 245
Swedo, S. E., 198
Swenson, C. C., 107
Swinson, R. P., 211
Systema, S., 357–358
Szabo, M., 247
Szapocznik, J., 103
Szasz, T. S., 6
Szatmari, P., 125, 210, 298, 362
Szumoski, E., 127
Szumoski, E. K., 133
Szymanski, L., 263

T

Tager-Flusberg, H., 292, 295
Tallal, P., 318–319, 322, 324, 325, 326,
    331, 332, 334, 335, 336, 337, 341,
    342, 343
Tamis-LeMonda, C. S., 47
Tamm, L., 129, 156
Tamplin, A., 233
Tanaka, J., 288, 289
Tanaka-Matsumi, J., 76
Tang, B., 313
Tanguay, P., 303
Tanguay, P. E., 299
Tannenbaum, L., 149
Tannock, R., 115, 118, 119, 120, 123,
    125, 130, 348
Tanofsky-Kraff, M., 385
Tapert, S. F., 373
Tapscott, M., 170
Target, M., 7
Tarver-Behring, S., 121
Taska, L., 417
Tate, D. C., 174
Taylor, A., 18, 168
Taylor, C. B., 379
Taylor, E., 113, 129, 133
Taylor, H. G., 91, 332, 339
Taylor, J., 165
Taylor, S. J., 254, 260, 266, 267

Taylor-Ferreira, J. C., 189
Teasdale, J. D., 236
Teegarden, L. A., 112
Teicher, M. H., 36, 114
Temple, E., 341, 343
Tennebaum, A., 280
Terdal, L. G., 58, 74, 83, 84, 92, 94, 96,
    110, 182, 332, 339, 342
Terr, L. C., 203–204, 421
Thapar, A. J., 130, 239
Thatcher, J. E., 416
Thatcher, R. W., 35–36
Thede, L. L., 123
Thomas, A., 43, 133
Thomas, C., 148
Thomas, C. B., 94
Thompson, A. H., 10
Thompson, K. M., 364
Thompson, L. A., 165
Thompson, M., 121
Thompson, M. P., 243
Thompson, P., 314
Thompson, P. M., 39
Thompson, R. A., 33, 243, 429
Thompson, R. J., Jr., 359, 360, 361,
    364, 365, 366, 368
Thompson, S., 355
Thompson, S. H., 378, 379
Thompson, T., 276
Thomsen, A. H., 238
Thomsen, C. J., 421
Thomsen, P. H., 125
Thornberry, T. P., 170
Tinney, L., 189
Titus, J. B., 300
Tizard, J., 223, 268
Tobin, M. J., 166
Toch, T., 143
Toga, A. W., 315
Tolan, P. H., 171, 174, 177
Tolley-Schell, S. A., 416
Tolstrup, K., 381
Tomblin, J. B., 324
Tompson, M., 315
Tompson, M. C., 311
Tonge, B. J., 188
Toogood, I., 364
Toppelberg, C. O., 319, 325
Torgesen, J., 341
Toth, S., 266–267
Toth, S. L., 236, 247, 409, 414, 417,
    421, 429
Toupin, J., 154
Towbin, K. E., 248
Townsend, J. P., 302
Toyer, E. A., 382
Tran, Y., 327
Trane, S. T., 421
Treadwell, K. H., 207
Treasure, J., 400
Treboux, D., 35
Treffers, P. D. A., 181, 207
Tremblay, M. S., 384
Tremblay, R., 19, 154
Tremblay, R. E., 30, 145, 155, 162, 163,
    164, 169

Tressoldi, P. E., 338
Treuting, J. J., 119
Trickett, P. K., 414, 419, 421
Trim, R. S., 370
Trocmé, N., 21, 412, 413–414
Troiano, R. P., 384
Trott, G., 314
Trottier, G., 300
Truglio, R., 205, 231
Truman, H. S., 97
Tsatsanis, K. D., 299
Tsuang, M., 314
Tsuang, M. T., 124, 170
Tucker, C. L., 368
Tumuluru, R., 276
Turk, J., 301
Turkheimer, E., 259
Turner, B. G., 189
Turner, G., 272
Turner, H., 393
Turner, M., 292, 293
Turner, M. W., 189
Turner, S., 275
Turner, S. M., 194, 195, 204, 207, 209,
    210, 211, 216
Twain, M., 1, 53, 154
Twigg, D. A., 428
Tyc, V. L., 368
Tyler, K. A., 421
Tyler, L., 152
Tyree, A., 422
Tyrka, A. R., 379, 388

U

Uhde, T. W., 195
Ullman, J. B., 241
Ulman, A., 419
Underwood, M. K., 160
Unis, A. S., 232
Usher, B., 152

V

Valente, E., 167–168
Valenti-Hein, D., 280
Valeri, S. M., 244
Vallance, D. D., 335
Van Acker, R., 155
Van Acker, R. P., 155
Van Ameringen, M., 204
van Ameringen, M., 210
van den Oord, E. J. C. G., 37
van der Ende, J., 19, 20, 181, 206
van der Molen, M., 128
van Dulmen, M., 419
Van Hasselt, V. B., 74, 81, 82, 106, 384
van Hoeken, D., 393
Van Horn, Y., 149
Van Houten, R., 279
van Ijzendoorn, M. H., 48
Van Oost, P., 129
Van Slyke, D. A., 357–358
VanBrakle, J., 121
Vance, Y. H., 362–363
Vande Kemp, H., 421
Vardill, R., 264
Vargha-Khadem, F., 302

Subject Index

Note to the reader: Numerals followed by "f" refer to figures and illustrations; numerals followed by "t" refer to tables; numerals followed by "b" refer to boxed information.

race and ethnicity, 20
  sexual exploitation and, 412
Prader-Willi syndrome, 273
Pragmatics, 292
Predominantly hyperactive-impulsive
  type (ADHD-HI), 116
Predominantly inattentive type
  (ADHD-PI), 116, 123
Pregnancy. *See* Development, fetal
Preservation of sameness, 284
Prevalence rates, 54
Prevention, defined, 98, 99f
Primary and Secondary Control En-
  hancement Training (PASCET), 245
Proactive-aggressive children, 156
Problem-solving skills training (PSST),
  174t, 175–176, 176b
Prognosis, defined, 78
Projective tests, 87–89, 90
Pronoun reversals, 291
Prostitution, 412
Protective factors, 16, 56
Protodeclarative gestures, 290
Protodyssomnia, 351t
Protoimperative gestures, 290
Prozac, 246
Psychoanalytic theory, 7–8, 208, 220
Psychodynamic theory of depression,
  235t, 236
Psychodynamic treatments, 102
Psychological disorders, defining, 11–12
Psychological factors affecting physical
  condition, 358
Psychological testing, 85–91
Psychophysiological disorders, 347
Psychophysiological methods, 59–60
Psychosocial functioning. *See* Social
  interaction
Psychosomatic disorders, 347
Psychotic symptoms, 313, 316
Puberty, 36, 39, 228
Public health approach, 148
Punishment
  conduct problems and, 166
  corporal, 430, 430b
  operant conditioning and, 44
Purging, 379, 389, 399
Purging type (bulimia), 391t

Qualitative research, 68–69, 69b, 69t
Questionnaires, 59t

Race and ethnicity. *See also* Culture
  access to treatment, 20
  anxiety disorders and, 207
  child abuse and, 429
  chronic illness, 360
  conduct problems and, 173
  depression and, 228–229
  eating disorders, 393, 396
  learning disorders and, 333–334
  obesity and, 385
  rate of disorders and, 21
  reports on mental health, 22b
  substance use/abuse, 372, 374
Random assignment, 62, 63

Rating scales, 84
Reactive-aggressive children, 155–156
Reading comprehension, 321–322, 324,
  337, 341
Reading disorder, 330–331, 333, 337,
  339, 341
Reading programs, 343b
Real-time prospective designs, 64
Reciprocal influence, 168
Referral biases, 75
Regular education initiative (REI), 340
Reinforcement, 44, 183, 208, 215
Reinforcement trap, 169
Relational disorders, 423
Relationships, social. *See* Peers; Social
  interaction
Relaxation, 215
Reliability, 58f, 58
Religion, 4, 6b, 255, 428b
Repetitive behavior, 185, 292–293
Reports on mental health issues, 22b
Representational models, 417
Research, 50–72
  ethics and pragmatic issues, 53, 65,
    70–71
  issues addressed by, 2–3
  methods of, 57–61, 58f, 59t
  process of, 53–57, 53f
  scientific approach to, 50–53
  strategies/designs, 55, 61–70, 65f,
    66f, 68b, 69t
Research therapy *vs.* clinic therapy, 107
Residential care, 281
Resilience
  adaptation and, 15
  characteristics of, 16f
  child abuse and, 415–416
  gender and, 19
  learning disorders and, 336b
Resilience factors, 15–16
Response-cost procedures, 138
Response inhibition deficits in ADHD,
  129b
Response prevention, 215
Restricting type (anorexia nervosa),
  389
Retrospective designs, 63–64
Rett's disorder, 309–310
Rewards, 137, 166
Rights
  abuse and, 405–406
  of children, 4, 9, 101
  mental retardation and, 279
Risk factors
  overview, 14–16, 18–21, 23
  "causes" as, 28, 56
  for eating disorders, 378, 379, 384–
    385, 397–398, 399–400, 400f
  for substance abuse, 157, 372, 373–
    374, 420
  temperament and, 43
Risk-taking behavior, 120, 250, 373–
  374
Ritalin, 135–136, 276
Rituals, 185, 197
Role-play simulation, 85, 106f

Samples, research, standards for, 61–62
Samples of convenience, 62
Savants, 286, 294, 294f
Schizophrenia, childhood-onset (COS),
  311–316
Schizotypal personality disorder (SPD),
  315
School refusal behavior, 10, 105, 187,
  188
School-based programs, 105b
Schools. *See also* Education
  conduct problems and, 165t, 171
  disabilities: inclusion movement, 281,
    325, 340–341
  dropouts, cost of, 147t
  eating habits and, 387
  inclusion, 281, 325
Science. *See* Research
Screening, 86
Selective attention, 113
Selective mutism, 195
Self-control theories of depression, 238
Self-esteem
  ADHD and, 119, 124
  bipolar disorder and, 248
  bowel/bladder problems and, 353,
    354
  child abuse and, 417–418, 421
  communication disorders and, 329
  conduct problems and, 155
  depression and, 228, 232–233, 237
  eating disorders and, 392, 396
  interventions and, 103
  learning disorders and, 334, 335
  obesity and, 384
Self-identity and abuse, 417–418
Self-injurious behavior (SIB), 65–66,
  65f, 66f, 268, 298, 416
Self-instructural training, 280
Self-regulation, 43, 129b, 242–243
Self-stimulatory behaviors, 293f, 293
Sensory impairments in autism, 294–
  295
Separation anxiety disorder (SAD), 181,
  186–189, 186b, 187t
Serotonin, 41t, 210, 239, 302, 395–396
Set point (body weight), 380, 383
Sex roles, 396, 429
Sexual abuse
  causes of, 423, 427–429, 428f
  defined, 410–411
  development and, 419t
  eating disorders and, 204, 397–398
  exploitation of children, 412
  gender and, 413
  outcomes, 419–420, 421, 422b, 428–
    429, 434
  perpetrators of, 414
  prevalence of, 412, 413
  PSTD and, 204
  self-esteem and, 417
  treatments for, 433–434
Sexual adjustment, 421
Sign language training, 307
Similar sequence hypothesis, 265
Similar structure hypothesis, 265

TO THE OWNER OF THIS BOOK:

I hope that you have found *Abnormal Child Psychology*, Third Edition, useful. So that this book can be improved in a future edition, would you take the time to complete this sheet and return it? Thank you.

School and address: _____

_____

Department: _____

Instructor's name: _____

1. What I like most about this book is:_____

_____

_____

2. What I like least about this book is: _____

_____

_____

3. My general reaction to this book is: _____

_____

_____

4. The name of the course in which I used this book is: _____

_____

5. Were all of the chapters of the book assigned for you to read? _____

   If not, which ones weren't? _____

6. In the space below, or on a separate sheet of paper, please write specific suggestions for improving this book and anything else you'd care to share about your experience in using this book.

_____

_____

_____

_____

_____

_____

BUSINESS REPLY MAIL
FIRST-CLASS MAIL   PERMIT NO. 102   MONTEREY CA

POSTAGE WILL BE PAID BY ADDRESSEE

Attn: Marianne Taflinger, Psychology Editor

BrooksCole/Thomson Learning
60 Garden Ct Ste 205
Monterey CA 93940-9967

OPTIONAL:

Your name: _____ Date: _____

May we quote you, either in promotion for *Abnormal Child Psychology,* Third Edition, or
in future publishing ventures?

Yes: _____   No: _____

Sincerely yours,

Eric J. Mash, David A. Wolfe